the Morley-Michelson measurements of light, the movements of the planet Mercury, the unexplained aberrancies of the moon from its predicted place. Einstein went back to facts or told others where they should go to confirm or to reject his theory—by observation of stellar positions during a total eclipse. . . .

. . . It is not necessary, of course, for the verification of a new theory to be done personally by its propounder. Theoretical reasoning from facts is as essential a part of economic science as of other sciences, and in a wise division of labour there is room, in economics, as elsewhere, for the theoretician pure and simple, for one who leaves the technical business of verification to those who have acquired a special technique of observation. No one demanded of Einstein that he should visit the South Seas in person, and look through a telescope; but he told others what he expected them to see, if they looked, and he was prepared to stand or fall by the result. It is the duty of the propounder of every new theory, if he has not himself the equipment for observation, to indicate where verification of his theory is to be sought in facts—what may be expected to happen or to have happened if his theory is true, what will not happen if it is false.

[Now consider by way of contrast the behaviour of the participants in a current controversy in economics.] . . . None of them takes the point that the truth or falsehood of . . . [a] theory cannot be established except by appeal to facts; none of them tests it by facts himself. The distinguishing mark of economic science, as illustrated by this debate, is that it is a science in which verification of generalisations by reference to facts is neglected as irrelevant.

. . . I do not see how . . . [members of the public who survey the controversy] can avoid the conclusion that economics is not a science concerned with phenomena, but a survival of medieval logic, and that economists are persons who earn their livings by taking in one another's definitions for mangling. . . .

I know that in speaking thus I make enemies. I challenge a tradition of a hundred years of political economy, in which facts have been treated,

(Continued on back endpapers)

Economics

HARPER & ROW, PUBLISHERS, New York
Cambridge, Hagerstown, Philadelphia, San Francisco,
London, Mexico City, São Paulo, Sydney

Economics

SIXTH EDITION

Richard G. Lipsey
Queen's University

Peter O. Steiner
The University of Michigan

SPONSORING EDITOR: John Greenman
SPECIAL PROJECTS EDITOR: Mary Lou Mosher
PROJECT EDITOR: Robert Ginsberg
DESIGNER: Emily Harste
SENIOR PRODUCTION MANAGER: Kewal K. Sharma
COMPOSITOR: Ruttle, Shaw & Wetherill
PRINTER AND BINDER: Kingsport Press
ART STUDIO: Danmark and Michaels Inc.

ECONOMICS, Sixth Edition

Library of Congress Cataloging in Publication Data

Lipsey, Richard G   1928–
   Economics.

   "Portions of this work were first published in the United Kingdom as An introduction to positive economics, © 1963 by Richard G. Lipsey."
   Includes index.
   1. Economics. I. Steiner, Peter Otto, 1922–joint author. II. Title.
HB171.5.L733 1981   330   80-26594
ISBN 0-06-043969-1

Brief Contents

Contents

Preface

Our basic motivation in writing *Economics* always has been, and in this sixth edition still is, to provide a book that reflects the enormous changes in economics over the last 40 years. Economics is always changing, but in the years since World War II there has been a change of such importance that we do ourselves and our students a great disservice if we neglect it. During this period economics has moved very rapidly toward becoming a genuine science. We apply the term *science* neither to praise nor to castigate economics, but to describe its movement toward the characteristic that distinguishes any science: the systematic confrontation of theory with observation.

The quotation from Lord William Beveridge on the endpapers of this book is our text — in the preacher's sense of that word. Beveridge was scolding the profession in 1937, but things since then have clearly changed for the better. Today we all agree that economics is not a stage on which we parade our pet theories and ask to have them admired solely for their elegance or their conclusions, nor is it a container in which we collect quantities of unrelated institutional and statistical material about the economy. Economists are making a serious attempt to push back the frontiers of ignorance about the economic environment in order both to understand it and to control it. As we repeatedly discover, new problems and new phenomena challenge our existing knowledge. Economists must therefore continually be concerned with the relations among theory, institutions, and facts and must regard every theory as subject to empirical challenge.

A second major theme of this book concerns the relations between economic theory and economic policy. An appreciation of these relations is not new to economics. Indeed, many nineteenth-century economists expressed the modern view that although economic theory can show us some of the consequences of our actions, it can never show us what we ought to do. What is new today is the realization of how little can be said about policy on the basis of the purely qualitative theories, and the resulting successful application of the quantitative revolution of the last 40 years to matters of policy. Four decades of systematic observations have provided us with a much better idea of how things are related to one another quantitatively, and this knowledge has greatly increased the economist's power to say sensible and relevant things about public policy. This is not to deny that there are still great areas where economists' knowledge is painfully sparse, as the current debates about how to cope with the twin problems of unemployment and inflation, and on the relative efficacy of monetary and fiscal policy, remind us.

The third major feature of the book relates to the way we view modern students. We have tried in several different ways to be as honest with them as is possible within the confines of an introductory textbook. No subject worth studying is always easy, and we have not glossed over hard points just because they are hard. We have tried to follow Einstein's advice: make things as simple as possible, but not simpler. We do not approve of slipping particularly hard bits of analysis past students without letting them see what is happening and what has been assumed, nor do we approve of teaching them things they will have to unlearn if they go on in economics (a practice sometimes justified on the grounds that it is important to get to the big issues quickly).

Every student who continues in economics soon learns that, although economics has many triumphs to its credit, there are areas where present knowledge is woefully inadequate. It is sometimes argued that in an elementary course such inadequacies should be played down or altogether suppressed so that beginning students will not lose faith in their subject. We reject this view. Both the students' education and our subject depend upon careful criticism. We have devoted some space to examining both sensible and foolish criticisms of economic theories. In doing this, we hope to give students some inkling of how it is possible to criticize effectively, and hence to improve, the existing body of economic theory.

Effective criticism of existing ideas is the springboard to progress in science, and we believe that an introduction to economics should also introduce students to methods for testing, criticizing, and evaluating the present state of the subject. We do not accept the notion that if you suggest the possibility of criticism to students, they will make hasty and confused criticisms. Students will always make criticisms and evaluations of their courses, and their criticisms are much more likely to be informed and relevant if they are given both practice and instruction in how to go about challenging in an effective, constructive manner what they have been taught rather than reverting to mere dogmatic assertion of error or irrelevance.

MAJOR REVISIONS IN THIS EDITION

This revision is the most comprehensive we have undertaken since the second edition. Users of the fifth edition will want to check the details of the new table of contents carefully. The most basic change is the revision of the core of macroeconomic theory and policy, as described in detail below. But other major changes have been made throughout the book. We believe our treatment is now more up-to-date, more relevant to contemporary issues, and easier for students. Only time—and your letters—will tell us if we are right.

Changes in Microeconomics

We have expanded Supply and Demand in Action to two chapters in order to add full discussions of the economics of the draft and of rent control, and to add a summary section on General Lessons About Resource Allocation. The discussion of cost in Part Four has been reorganized, combining the long run and the very long run (formerly two chapters) into a single chapter and deferring the discussion of social cost to a greatly expanded Chapter 24, Benefits and Costs of Government Intervention in the Market Economy.

In this revision we have expanded the discussion of just when and how markets prove to be efficient and inefficient. This affects Chapters 14, 15, 18, and 24. We have also added a parallel discussion of government success and government failure (see especially the final half of Chapter 24).

Among the new applications of economics to current microeconomic problems is an extended discussion of OPEC and the price of gasoline (Chapter 17), and the proposal for a greatly expanded program of federally subsidized medical care (Chapter 25).

To make room for these and other additions, some of the fifth edition coverage of isoquants, long-run equilibrium, and monopolistic competition has been placed in appendixes, where these topics remain available to those who wish to assign them but can be readily omitted.

Changes in Basic Macroeconomics

Parts Eight, Nine, and Eleven of the fifth edition (Parts Eight, Nine, and Ten of this edition) have been totally rewritten to let aggregate demand and aggregate supply curves bear much of the weight of the analysis. This has a number of substantial advantages for teaching economics in the 1980s. First, the price level can be allowed to vary from the outset. Our experience is that contemporary students become increasingly restive with a treatment that holds the price level constant while most of national income theory is being covered. Second, it is much easier to deal with supply shocks and to explain stagflation. Third, the treatment of the definition and determination of national income can be greatly simplified. The present Chapter 27 is very much

simpler than its fifth edition counterpart, Chapter 26. Gone are the four increasingly complex economies (spendthrift, frugal, governed, and open) with which we formerly built the analysis. Gone too is the withdrawals-injections explanation of equilibrium. (These concepts, in the Swedish process-analysis tradition, have much to commend them, but many students find them harder than the more static approach embodied in aggregate demand and supply diagrams.)

No approach is without its own difficulties. The major difficulty with aggregate demand-supply lies in the instability of the aggregate supply curve. Although the economy can move up and down a given aggregate demand curve in response to shifts in aggregate supply, the reverse is not true. The aggregate supply curve will itself shift in response to some aggregate demand curve shifts, owing partly to the downward rigidity of prices. The complications inherent in this instability of the aggregate supply curve can often be sidetracked, where they are unimportant, by using a kinked aggregate supply curve (that suppresses the intermediate gradually rising portion) and this we do where we can. A second difficulty is that the downward slope of the aggregate demand curve cannot be fully explained until after money is introduced. The full explanation does not come, therefore, until Chapter 34. One important pedagogical payoff to our current approach is the overview of recent economic events that can be provided at the very outset, in Chapter 26, and in detail in Chapter 37.

The shift to an aggregate demand-aggregate supply approach pervades Part Eight (National Income and Fiscal Policy), Part Nine (Money, Banking, and Monetary Policy), and Part Ten (Macroeconomic Policy in Action: The Control of Inflation and Unemployment). The essential unity of these three parts had led us to put all three before the discussion of International Trade and Finance (Part Eleven).

In addition to this major change in approach, a number of other significant changes have been made in these parts. The chapter on fiscal policy has been heavily revised to eliminate policy debates from previous decades in favor of such current debates as "Can and should the budget be balanced?" and "How can the stance of fiscal policy be judged?" The Role of Money in Macroeconomics (Chapter 34) has been completely rewritten. The explanation of the demand for money now is rooted in the analysis of Tobin rather than Keynes. The chapter includes the full explanation of the shape of the aggregate demand curve as well as an explanation of why continuous inflations require monetary validation. The Classical Quantity Theory of Money has been placed in an appendix. Chapter 36 provides an expanded discussion of employment, inflation, and the possible relation between the two. It is not analytically demanding. The rather difficult analysis of the Phelps-Friedman theory of expectational inflation and stagflation is now given in the appendix to Chapter 36.

Many students have read or heard that economists cannot understand the inflation-unemployment experience of the last decade. They will be pleasantly surprised in reading the wholly new Chapter 37, Macroeconomic Experience, to learn that economics can yield a good explanation of the decade-by-decade experience of the economy over the last half century.

The discussion of current policy issues in macroeconomics has been updated and expanded. Among the topics receiving expanded attention are wage and price controls, rational expectations, and the so-called natural rate of unemployment.

Changes in International Trade and Finance

This part was overdue for a major revision to reflect two major events. The first is the replacement of fixed exchange rates by managed, floating rates. The second is the rising importance of nontariff barriers to trade, which threaten a reversal of the long-term trend away from economic protectionism.

In this edition we have both updated and reorganized the trade material. We begin with the two "real" chapters: The Gains from Trade (Chapter 39) and Barriers to Free Trade (Chapter 40). The first is little changed, the second is both expanded and modernized. The two monetary trade chapters are much changed. Chapter 41 shifts the emphasis from the balance of payments (important in a world of fixed exchange rates) to the theory and management of flexible exchange rates. Chapter 42 is an updated discussion of international monetary systems.

TEACHING AIDS

Tag lines and captions for figures and tables. The boldface tag line below the figure or table indicates succinctly the central conclusion intended by the illustration; the lightface caption provides information needed to reach that conclusion. Titles, tag lines, and captions are, with the figure or table, a self-contained set, and many students find them a useful device for reviewing a chapter.

Boxes. The material in green "boxes" contains examples or materials that are relevant extensions of the text narrative but need not be read in sequence.

End-of-chapter material. Each chapter contains a Summary, a list of Topics for Review, and a set of Discussion Questions. The questions are particularly useful for class discussion or for "quiz sections." They are answered in the Instructor's Manual.

Mathematical notes. Mathematical notes to the body of the text are collected in a self-contained section at the end of the book. Since mathematical notation and derivation is not required to understand the principles of economics, but is helpful in more advanced work, this seems to us to be a sensible arrangement. It provides clues to the uses of mathematics for the increasing numbers of students who come to beginning economics with some background in math, without encumbering the text with notes that may appear formidable to those who find mathematics arcane or frightening. Students with a mathematical background have many times told us they find the notes helpful.

Glossary. The glossary covers widely used definitions of economic terms. Because some users treat micro- and macroeconomics in that order, and others in reverse order, words in the glossary are printed in boldface type when they are first mentioned in *either half* of the text.

Endpapers. Inside the front cover is a list of the most commonly used abbreviations in the text. Inside the back cover is a set of useful data about the U.S. economy.

Supplements

Our book is accompanied by a workbook, *Study Guide and Problems,* prepared by Professor Dascomb R. Forbush and Professor Frederic C. Menz. The workbook is designed to be used either in the classroom or by the students working on their own.

An *Instructor's Manual,* prepared by us, and a *Test Bank,* prepared under our supervision, are available to instructors adopting the book. The Test Bank is also available in a computerized form known as ACCESS; contact the publisher for details.

USING THE BOOK

This textbook reflects to some extent the way its authors would teach their own courses. Needs of students differ; some want to have material that goes beyond the average class level, but others have gaps in their backgrounds. To accommodate the former, we have included more material than we would assign to every student. Also, because there are many different kinds of first-year economics courses in colleges and universities, we have included more material than normally would be included in any single course. Requests and suggestions from users of previous editions have prompted us to include some additional alternative material.

Although teachers can best design their own courses, it may be helpful if we indicate certain views of our own as to how this book *might* be adapted to different courses.

Sequence

Because the choice of order between macro and micro is partly a personal one, it cannot be decided solely by objective criteria. We believe that in the 1980s there are good reasons for preferring the micro-macro order. Whereas in the immediate post-World War II years, the major emphasis was on the development of both the theory and the policy implications of Keynesian economics, the thrust over the last 20 years has been to examine the micro underpinnings of macro functions and to erect macroeconomics on a firmer base of micro behavioral relations. Changes have occurred not only in economic theory but in the problems that excite students. Although macroeconomic problems such as inflation and unemployment are still of great concern, many of the problems that students find most challenging today—the plight of the cities, poverty, pollution, and managing wage and price controls—are microeconomic in character. The micro-macro order, moreover, reflects the historical evolution of the subject. A century of classical and neoclassical development of microeconomics preceded the Keynesian development of macroeconomics.

For those who prefer the macro-micro order and who wish to reverse the order of our book, we have attempted to make reversibility virtually painless. The overview chapter that ends Part One has been built up to provide an improved base on which to build either the microeconomics of Part Two or the macroeconomics of Part Eight. Chapter 5 is worth assigning after Chapter 4, even in macro-first courses. Where further microeconomic concepts are required—as in the macro investment chapter—we have added brief sections to make the treatment self-contained, while providing review material for those who have been through the microeconomic section.

One-Semester Courses

Thorough coverage of the bulk of the book supposes a two-semester course in economics. A great many first courses in economics are only one semester (or equivalent) in length and our book can be easily adapted to such courses. Suggestions for use of this book for such courses are given on pages xxv–xxvi. We recognize that for any one-semester course a choice must be made among emphases. Most one-semester survey courses necessarily give some coverage to theory and to policy, to micro- and to macroeconomics, but the relative weights vary. Instructors will wish to choose the topics to be included or excluded and to vary the order to suit their own preferences.

ACKNOWLEDGMENTS

So many teachers, colleagues, students, and friends contributed to the original book and to its continuing revision that it is impossible for us to acknowledge our debts to all of them individually. Hundreds of users, both teachers and students, have written to us with specific suggested improvements, and much of the credit for the fact that the book does become more and more teachable belongs to them. We can no longer list them individually but we thank them all, most sincerely. A few individuals provided reviews of the fifth edition that were most helpful in preparing the present edition. These are Charles Brown, Stephen F. Austin State University; Eric Gustafson, University of California at Davis; Rodney H. Mabry, Northeast Louisiana University; James R. Marsden, University of Kentucky; Felipe Montt, University of Minnesota; Stephen Nord, Northern Illinois University; Gerard T. O'Boyle, St. John's University; Stephen E. Reynolds, University of Utah; William J. Swift, Pace University; and Josephine K. Tan, University of Central Arkansas. In addition, the following reviewed draft manuscript of Chapters 26–31: Robert M. Aduddell, Loyola University of Chicago; David Terkla, Boston University; Stanislaw Wasowski, Georgetown University; and William C. Wood, University of Virginia.

Patricia O. Steiner contributed greatly to the updating of the illustrative examples and to the end-of-chapter questions. Judith Roberts, Mark Meyer, and Cappy Hill provided significant research assistance. Frederick Menz, Dascomb Forbush, Douglas Auld, and Kenneth Grant, who contributed to the supplements, have all contributed to this edition as well.

We owe special thanks to Carolyn Shaw Bell, Richard C. Porter, and Douglas Purvis for detailed suggestions for revision of particular chapters in their areas of specialty.

Dorothy O'Reilly and Marlene Rego coped with mountains of manuscript with extraordinary skill and patience under difficult circumstances. Weidenfeld and Nicholson generously gave permission to use material first prepared for the fifth edition of *An Introduction to Positive Economics* by R. G. Lipsey.

Finally it is with great sadness we report the death of our long-time collaborator and friend, Dorothy Fitts Forbush, and we dedicate this sixth edition to her memory.

Richard G. Lipsey
Peter O. Steiner

Suggested Outline
for a One-semester
Course[1]

Basic core chapters for courses
covering both micro and macro

[1] A full semester course can cover not more than 25 full chapters. The core consists of about 18 chapters. Selections from other chapters, as listed below or according to the instructor's own preferences, can produce courses with various emphases.

Chapters that can be added to give different emphases to different courses[2]

[2] Chapters shown with an * are particularly appropriate for courses with a heavy policy orientation. Chapters not listed here or in the core seem to us to be of lower priority in a one-semester course.

To the Student

A good course in economics will give you some real insight into how an economy functions and into some of the policy issues that are currently the subject of serious debate. Like all rewarding subjects, economics will not be mastered without effort. A book on economics must be worked at. It cannot be read like a novel.

Each student must develop an individual technique for studying, but the following suggestions may prove helpful. It is usually a good idea to read a chapter quickly in order to get the general run of the argument. At this first reading you may want to skip the "boxes" of text material and any footnotes. Then, after reading the Topics for Review and the Discussion Questions, reread the chapter more slowly, making sure that you understand each step of the argument. With respect to the figures and tables, be sure you understand how the conclusions stated in the brief tag lines below each table or figure have been reached. You should be prepared to spend time on difficult sections; occasionally, you may spend an hour on only a few pages. Paper and a pencil are indispensable equipment in your reading. It is best to follow a difficult argument by building your own diagram while the argument unfolds rather than by relying on the finished diagram as it appears in the book. It is often helpful to invent numerical examples to illustrate general propositions. The end-of-chapter questions require you to apply what you have studied. We advise you to outline answers to some of the questions. In short, you must seek to understand economics, not to memorize it.

After you have read each part in detail, reread

it quickly from beginning to end. It is often difficult to understand why certain things are done when they are viewed as isolated points, but when you reread a whole part, much that did not seem relevant or entirely comprehensible will fall into place in the analysis.

We call your attention to the glossary at the end of the book. Any time you run into a concept that seems vaguely familiar but is not clear to you, check the glossary. The chances are that it will be there, and its definition will remind you of what you once understood. If you are still in doubt, check the index entry to find where the concept is discussed more fully. Incidentally, the glossary, along with the captions under figures and tables and the end-of-chapter summaries, may prove very helpful when reviewing for examinations.

The bracketed green numbers in the text itself refer to a series of nearly 50 mathematical notes that are found starting on page 930. For those of you who like mathematics or prefer mathematical argument to verbal or geometric exposition, these may prove useful. Others may ignore them.

We hope that you will find the book rewarding and stimulating. Students who used earlier editions made some of the most helpful suggestions for revision, and we hope you will carry on the tradition. If you are moved to write to us, please do.

Economics

Part One

The Nature
of Economics

The Economic Problem

1

Many of the world's most compelling problems are economic. The dominant problem of the 1930s was the massive unemployment of workers and resources known as the Great Depression. The wartime economy of the 1940s solved that problem but created new ones, especially the question of how quickly to reallocate scarce resources between military and civilian needs. By the 1950s inflation was appearing as a major problem in many countries. It is still with us. Much attention in the 1960s was devoted to trying to understand and to combat a slowdown in the pace of economic growth. The central problems of the 1970s were the rising cost of energy—oil prices increased tenfold over the decade—and the emergence of the disturbing combination of high unemployment *and* high rates of inflation. Problems change from decade to decade, yet there are always problems.

Of course, not all of the world's serious problems are primarily economic. Political, biological, social, cultural, and philosophic issues often predominate. But no matter how "noneconomic" a particular problem may seem, it will almost always have a significant economic dimension.

The crises that lead to wars often have economic roots. Nations fight for oil and rice and land to live on, although the rhetoric of their leaders evokes God and Glory and the Fatherland. Arabs and Israelis fight for a homeland, to be sure, but also for pastures and farms and water and transportation routes.

A population explosion threatens to overrun the globe as a result of humanity's spectacular ability to reduce mortality rates much faster than birth rates. The current rate of world population growth is 2.2 persons a second, or about 70 million per year. The causes are mainly biological, medical, and cultural, but the economic consequences are steady pressures against the available supplies of natural resources and agricultural land. Unless the human race can find ways to increase its food supply as fast as its numbers, increasing millions face starvation.

Race is not primarily an economic phenomenon, but the problem of racial discrimination has important economic effects on individuals and on the economy. It means untapped human talent. It means a waste of social resources. It means children growing up undernourished, undereducated, unqualified for good jobs, and hostile to an alien world.

Economic Problems of the Eighties

UNEMPLOYMENT AND INFLATION

Congress in 1978 enacted the Humphrey-Hawkins Full Employment and Balanced Growth Act, which officially established full employment and stable prices as twin goals of economic policy. Reasonable as that may sound as a goal of policy, the fact is that we have seldom had both full employment and completely stable prices at the same time, and as the eighties began we had neither. At the start of the decade, unemployment stood at 6 percent of the labor force and prices were rising at an annual rate of 18 percent. The Humphrey-Hawkins bill specified 4 percent unemployment and 3 percent inflation by 1983 as attainable medium-term goals. Most economists believe that achieving them will be all but impossible in our economic and political system.

How did the unprecedented persistence of both "too high" unemployment and "too high" inflation arise, and how may it be avoided? Are zero unemployment and zero inflation reason-

able *long-run* goals? What is an acceptable level of unemployment? Can we be sure we will never again experience the trauma of the 1930s, when up to a quarter of all those who sought work were unable to find it?

What is an acceptable amount of inflation? Will not any inflation ultimately get out of hand and wipe out the value of money and savings? Why do prices in some countries rise 30 percent or 40 percent a year while in others they rise at a rate of 5 or 6 percent? Why did inflation accelerate dramatically over most of the world in the early 1970s? Why did consumer prices in the United States rise by only 26 percent between 1960 and 1970 but by more than 100 percent between 1970 and 1980? Can a country control inflation?

These questions concern the stability of the economy and the causes and consequences of depression and inflation. They also concern the ability of people, individually or through governments, to control and change their economic environment.

ENERGY

Energy is vital to an industrial economy. Over the last 200 years American output has grown, and with it America's demand for the earth's limited fossil fuels. The amount of energy used in the United States doubled between 1950 and 1970, and it is expected to have doubled again by 1985.

Throughout most of American history the increase in energy consumption caused no serious problems because new supplies were discovered as rapidly as old ones were exhausted. Around the middle of the 1960s, however, a dramatic change occurred. Although historically energy consumption had grown at a slightly *less* rapid rate than domestic production, since 1965 output has increased at about 3 percent per year while energy consumption has risen by 5 percent per year. This rapidly increasing demand for energy has not been matched by a corresponding increase in the rate of discovery of new reserves.

Even before the formation of the OPEC cartel, which raised prices and limited production, proven reserves were falling. Today we take the high cost of energy as an unpleasant fact of life. Can we adjust to it? Can we discover a new, abundant, cheap source of energy?

The United States, with one-twentieth of the world's population, uses a third of the world's energy. To what extent are the *world's* supplies of oil and gas (e.g., in Alaska, in the USSR, in Saudi Arabia, and under the oceans) adequate to the world's demands for energy? If they are adequate, is the U.S. shortage only a problem in trade, transportation, or foreign policy? To what extent can nuclear or solar energy render coal and oil and gas as unnecessary as oil and gas rendered whale oil?

Does the energy crisis portend an inevitable exhaustion of our energy resources and thus a limit to the future growth of our standard of living, or is it a temporary and transitory phenomenon? A great debate has developed concerning the appropriate response to the skyrocketing price of energy. Some have argued that if the government does not force us to make major changes now in how we use fuel, we will face disaster before the end of the century. In this view the energy crisis is the equivalent of a war of survival. Others, less alarmed, have argued that the price rises now occurring will lead to an automatic correction of the problem by decreasing the amount of energy we consume and at the same time making it profitable to discover or develop new sources of energy. They believe that the problems are transitory, that they will exist only for the next 10 or 20 years and then be solved. Which group is closer to the truth?

These questions concern our ability to discover and bring to market the basic resources we need, our ability to make more resources available by trade with other countries, our ability to find new substitutes for depleted resources, and our ability to adapt to scarcities by changing our techniques of production. The questions also concern the roles of the free price system and of government intervention in the workings of our market economy.

PRODUCTIVITY AND GROWTH

Americans not very long ago prided themselves on having the highest standard of living in the world and a rate of growth in the output of goods and services per person that resulted in living standards that doubled every generation. This happened most recently between 1946 and 1970. Between 1970 and 1975 the annual rate of growth dropped to half of that of the 1946–1970 period, and from 1975 to 1980 it dropped to a third. At the rate achieved in the second half of the 1970s, it will take 70 or 80 years to achieve the gains in living standards that we were realizing every 20 or 25 years before 1975. During 1979 there was no growth at all. As a result of these trends America is no longer the world's richest country, having been passed by a handful of others. Few Americans a generation ago would have believed this possible.

What caused this loss of momentum in the economy? The statistics show a decreasing share of the nation's output going into new machines, equipment, and factories as well as a falloff in the rate of invention and innovation. But what *causes* these things? Is it the unstable and uncertain state of today's economy? Is it the burden of high taxes on people and businesses? Is it the heavy drain imposed on the economy by government regulating business in more and more ways in order to provide cleaner, safer working conditions, bigger unemployment benefits, and more generous pensions and medical care?

Can we find ways to reverse the slowdown in our nation's growth? Will it require more government involvement with the market — or less?

GROWTH AND POLLUTION

Do we *want* another century of rapid growth and industrialization? Without the automobile, the airplane, and electricity, ours would be a different and less comfortable world. But because of them air pollution has become a major problem. Without steel and cement and factories and tractors, the industrial development of the past century would have been impossible; with them, the volume of wastes discharged into water and air has grown to alarming proportions. Insecticides have increased agricultural production manyfold and virtually eliminated malaria and cholera, but they have all but extinguished the peregrine falcon, endangered other species, including *Homo sapiens,* in ways not yet fully known, and biologically destroyed many lakes and streams. Is large-scale pollution the inevitable companion of economic growth? If it is, how much growth do we really want? If it is not, how can we ensure growth with less pollution?

These questions concern the use, and abuse, of society's resources. They are among the basic economic questions, and they involve understanding why markets sometimes fail to work satisfactorily and how to deal with such failures. They also involve understanding why government intervention sometimes works and sometimes fails.

POVERTY, MEDICAL CARE, AND GOVERNMENT POLICIES

Poverty is still a major problem in America despite the fact that the average American continues to be among the richest individuals in the world. How can poverty survive in the midst of relative plenty? Who are the poor, and what makes them so? Does poverty take care of itself as average income rises? Can poverty ever be eliminated in the United States? In the world? Is equality of income a desirable or attainable national goal?

These questions involve two basic economic issues: what determines the level of income and what determines the distribution of that income.

Medical science has greatly improved what can be done for victims of accident or disease. But costs have risen to the point where a major operation or illness is far beyond the capacity of an average family to afford out of its earnings or savings. Should the government provide medical and hospital care to all who need it, as a matter of giving every man, woman, and child an equal right to life and health?

This question concerns what things the gov-

ernment should do and what things it should leave to private decision makers. Do we, as John Kenneth Galbraith charges, allocate too little to government expenditure on such valuable things as health and education, while growing sated with privately produced goods such as big cars and electric can openers? Do we instead, as Milton Friedman charges, have the government do badly many things private groups could do well? Or do we do both?

What Is Economics?

We have listed a few issues that are important today and on which economic analysis is supposed to shed light. One way to define the scope of economics is to say that it is the social science that deals with such problems. Fifty years ago such all-embracing definitions were popular. Perhaps the best known was Alfred Marshall's: "Economics is a study of mankind in the ordinary business of life." Because economic problems have certain common features, one may, by looking at them, arrive at a more penetrating definition.

The problems of economics arise out of the use of scarce resources to satisfy unlimited human wants. Scarcity is inevitable and is central to economic problems.

What are society's resources? Why is scarcity inevitable? What are the consequences of scarcity?

RESOURCES AND COMMODITIES

A society's resources consist of the free gifts of nature, such as land, forests, and minerals; human resources, both mental and physical; and all sorts of man-made aids to further production, such as tools, machinery, and buildings. Economists call such resources **factors of production**[1] because they are used to *produce* those things

---

[1] The definitions of the terms in **boldface** type are gathered together in the glossary at the end of the book.

that people desire. The things produced are called **commodities.** Commodities may be divided into goods and services. **Goods** are tangible (e.g., cars or shoes), and **services** are intangible (e.g., haircuts or education). Notice the implication of positive value contained in the terms "goods" and "services." (Compare the terms "bads" and "disservices.")

Goods and services are the means by which people seek to satisfy some of their wants. The act of making goods and services is called **production,** and the act of using them to satisfy wants is called **consumption.** For most people in most societies goods are not regarded as desirable in themselves; few people want to pile them up endlessly in warehouses, never to be consumed. They are valued because people want the services they provide. An automobile, for example, helps to satisfy its owner's desires for transportation, mobility, and possibly status.

SCARCITY

For all practical purposes, human wants may be regarded as limitless. An occasional individual may "have everything," but human capacity to generate new wants as fast as old ones are satisfied is well known to psychologists. For the overwhelming preponderance of the world's 4 billion human beings, *scarcity* is real and ever present. In relation to the desires of individuals (for more and better food, clothing, housing, schooling, vacations, entertainment, etc.), the existing supply of resources is woefully inadequate; there are enough to produce only a small fraction of the goods and services that people desire.

Is not America rich enough that scarcity is nearly banished? After all, we have been characterized as the affluent society. Whatever affluence may mean, it does not end the problem of scarcity. Most households that spend $50,000 a year (a princely amount by worldwide standards) have no trouble spending it on things that seem useful to them. Yet it would take many times the present output of the American economy to produce enough to allow all American households to consume that amount.

CHOICE

Because resources are scarce, all societies face the problem of deciding what to produce and how to divide it among their members. Societies differ in who makes the choices and how they are made, but the need to choose is common to all.

Just as scarcity implies the need for choice, so choice implies the existence of cost.

Opportunity Cost

A decision to have more of one thing requires a decision to have less of something else. It is this fact that makes the first decision costly. We offer first a trivial example and then one that vitally affects all of us; both examples involve precisely the same fundamental principles.

Consider the choice that must be made by a small boy who has 10¢ to spend and who is determined to spend it all on candy. For him there are only two kinds of candy in the world: gumdrops, which sell for 1¢ each, and chocolates, which sell for 2¢. The boy would like to buy 10 gumdrops and 10 chocolates, but he knows (or will soon discover) that this is not possible. (In technical language, it is not an *attainable combination* given his scarce resources.) There are, however, several attainable combinations that he might buy: 8 gumdrops and 1 chocolate, 4 gumdrops and 3 chocolates, 2 gumdrops and 1 chocolate, and so on. Some of these combinations leave him with money unspent, and he is not interested in them. Only six combinations (as shown in Figure 1-1) are both attainable and use all his money.

After careful thought, the boy has almost decided to buy 6 gumdrops and 2 chocolates, but at the last moment he decides that he simply must have 3 chocolates. What will it cost him to get this extra chocolate? One answer to this question is 2 gumdrops. In order to get the extra chocolate he must sacrifice 2 gumdrops, as is seen in Figure 1-1. Economists say that the opportunity cost of

FIGURE 1–1

A Choice Between Gumdrops and Chocolates

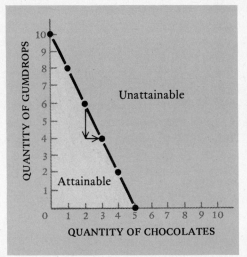

A limited amount of money forces a choice among alternatives. Six combinations of gumdrops and chocolates are attainable and use all of the boy's money. The downward-sloping line provides a boundary between attainable and unattainable combinations. The arrows show that the opportunity cost of 1 more chocolate is 2 gumdrops. In this example, the opportunity cost is constant and therefore the boundary is a straight line.

the third chocolate is what he must sacrifice in order to get it, which in this case is 2 gumdrops.

Another answer is that the cost of the third chocolate is 2¢, but given the boy's budget and his intentions, this answer is less revealing than the first one. Where the real choice is between more of this and more of that, the cost of "this" is fruitfully looked at as what you must sacrifice of "that." The idea of **opportunity cost** is one of the central insights of economics.

Every time one is forced by scarcity to make a choice, one is incurring opportunity costs. These costs are measured in terms of forgone alternatives.

Production Possibilities

Although the previous example concerned a minor consumption decision, the essential nature of the decision is the same whatever the choice being considered.

Exactly the same problems arise, for example, in the important social choice between military and nonmilitary goods—between swords and plowshares. Throughout the 1960s and 1970s, about 10 percent of the American gross national product was spent for defense. The American government made a choice as to the relative amounts of the production of goods for civilian consumption and the production of arms. Such a choice is similar in form to the one facing the boy deciding what candies to buy with his dime. It is not possible to produce an unlimited quantity of both arms and civilian goods. If we have full employment of resources and we wish to produce more arms, then we must produce less of all other goods, thereby reducing the quantity of goods available to satisfy civilian wants. The opportunity cost of more arms is forgone civilian goods, and somehow a choice must be made.

The choice is illustrated in Figure 1-2. Because resources are limited, some combinations—those that would require more than the total available supply of resources for their production—cannot be obtained. The downward-sloping curve on the graph divides the combinations that can be obtained from those that cannot be obtained. Points to the right of this curve cannot be obtained because there are not enough resources; points to the left of the curve can be obtained without using all of the available resources; and points on the curve can just be obtained if all the available resources are used. The curve is called the **production possibility boundary.** It slopes downward because, when all resources are being used, to get more of one kind of goods, some of the other kind must be sacrificed.

A downward-sloping production possibility boundary illustrates three concepts: scarcity, choice, and opportunity cost.[2] Scarcity is implied

[2] The importance of scarcity, choice, and opportunity cost has led many to define economics as the problem of allocating scarce resources between alternative and competing ends. The issues emphasized by this definition are very important, but, as will be seen in the next section, there are other, equally important issues in economics that the definition does not stress.

FIGURE 1–2
A Production Possibility Boundary

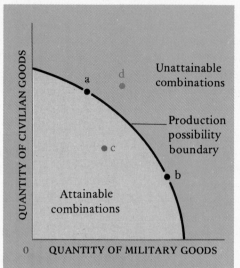

The downward-sloping boundary shows the combinations that are just attainable when all of the society's resources are efficiently employed. The quantity of military goods produced is measured along the horizontal axis, the quantity of civilian goods along the vertical axis. Thus any point on the diagram indicates some amount of each kind of good produced. The production possibility boundary separates the attainable combinations of goods such as *a, b,* and *c* and unattainable combinations such as *d.* It slopes downward because resources are scarce: more of one good can be produced only if resources are freed by producing less of the other good. Points *a* and *b* represent efficient combinations that use all of society's resources. Point *c* represents either inefficient use of resources or failure to use all the available resources.

by the unattainable combinations above the boundary; choice, by the need to choose among the attainable points; opportunity cost, by the downward slope of the boundary.

The production possibility boundary in Figure 1-2 is drawn *concave* downward, which means that more and more civilian goods must be given up to achieve equal successive increases in military goods. This shape implies that the opportunity cost grows larger and larger as we increase the amount of arms produced. (Drawn as a straight line, as in Figure 1-1, the curve implies that the opportunity cost of each good stays constant, no matter how much of it is produced.) As we shall see, there are reasons to believe that the rising opportunity cost case applies to many important choices.

A CLASSIFICATION OF ECONOMIC PROBLEMS

Modern economies involve thousands of complex production and consumption activities. While the complexity is important, many basic decisions that must be made are not very different from those made in a primitive economy in which people work with few tools and barter with their neighbors. Nor do capitalist, socialist, and communist economies differ in their need to solve the same basic problems, though they do differ, of course, in how they solve the problems. Most problems studied by economists fall within six areas.

1. What Goods and Services Are Being Produced and in What Quantities?

This question concerns the allocation of scarce resources among alternative uses, called **resource allocation.** Any economy must have some mechanism for making decisions on the problem of resource allocation.

How are choices made between points such as *a* and *b* in Figure 1-2? In free-market economies, most decisions about the allocation of resources are made through the price system. In other systems, more of the decisions are made by central planners. Economists are interested in the consequences of different kinds of decision making on resource allocation.

2. By What Methods Are Goods and Services Produced?

Generally, there is more than one technically possible way in which a commodity can be made. Agricultural commodities, for example, can be produced by taking a small quantity of land and applying to it large quantities of fertilizer, labor, and machinery or by using a large quantity of land and applying only small quantities of fertilizer, labor, and machinery. Either method can be used to produce the same quantity of some crop.

Which alternative method should be adopted? A common criterion is the avoidance of inefficient methods. Any scheme of production that uses all of society's resources but produces inefficiently leads to an output combination that falls *inside* the production possibility boundary (at a point such as *c* in Figure 1-2). It would be possible to get more of either (or both) goods by using more efficient methods of production. Because resources are scarce, efficient methods of production are desirable. Economists are interested in distinguishing between efficient and inefficient methods, in determining how the choice of efficient methods can be assured, and in learning why inefficient methods are sometimes chosen.

3. How Is the Supply of Goods Allocated Among the Members of the Society?

Economists want to know what determines how a nation's total income is distributed among the population. Everyone knows it is not distributed equally. What determines the distribution of income among such groups as landowners, laborers, and capitalists? Or among other groups such as farmers, union members, blacks, and the poor? Economists are interested also in the consequences of government policies designed to change the distribution of income by using devices such as progressive income taxes, farm price supports, and programs of social insurance.

These first three questions fall within **microeconomics,** which concerns the allocation of resources and the distribution of income as they are affected by the workings of the price system and by some government policies.

4. Are the Country's Resources Being Fully Utilized, or Are Some Lying Idle and Thus Going to Waste?

It may seem strange that this question needs to be asked at all. Surely, if resources are so scarce that there are not enough of them to produce all urgently required goods, then available resources will not be left idle. Yet one of the most disturbing characteristics of free-market economies is that such waste sometimes occurs. Unemployed workers would like to have jobs, the factories in which they could work are available, the managers and owners would like to be able to operate their factories, raw materials are available in abundance, and the goods that could be produced by these resources are needed by individuals in the community. But for some reason nothing happens.

Massive unemployment occurred in the Great Depression of the 1930s. Although that disastrous experience—25 percent unemployment—has not been repeated, the problem is still with us in significant though lesser degree. In 1975, for example, unemployment reached 8.5 percent. Unemployment forces the economy *inside* its production possibility boundary, at a point such as *c* in Figure 1-2.

Unemployment of resources is thus similar to an inefficient use of them (discussed above under question 2) in that both lead to production inside the full-employment production possibility boundary. They are not the same problem, however, and the remedies are very different.

5. Is the Purchasing Power of Money and Savings Constant, or Is It Being Eroded Because of Inflation?

The world's economies have often experienced periods of prolonged and rapid changes in price levels. Over the long swing of history, price levels have sometimes risen and sometimes fallen. In recent decades, however, the course of prices has almost always been upward. The seventies saw a period of accelerating inflation in the United States and in most of the world.

Inflation reduces the purchasing power of money and savings. It is closely related to the amount of money in the economy. Money is the invention of human beings, not of nature, and the amount in existence can be controlled by them. Economists ask many questions about the causes and consequences of changes in the quantity of money and the effects of such changes on the price level. They also ask about other causes of inflation.

6. Is the Economy's Capacity to Produce Goods Growing or Remaining the Same over Time?

Productive capacity grows rapidly in some countries and slowly in others, and in some countries it actually declines. Generally the most rapid growth in productive capacity has occurred in those countries that already have relatively high standards of living. As a result, living standards diverge more and more between the "have" and the "have not" countries. Growth in productive capacity can be represented in a production possibility diagram as a pushing outward of the boundary, as shown in Figure 1-3. If the economy's capacity to produce goods and services is growing, combinations that are unattainable today will become attainable tomorrow. Clearly, in an economy in which not nearly enough can be produced to satisfy all wants, growth will be important because growth makes it possible to have more of all goods. But growth is not free. What are the ways in which growth occurs and what are its costs?

Questions 4 to 6 fall within **macroeconomics,** the study of the determination of economic aggregates such as total output, total employment, the price level, and the rate of economic growth.

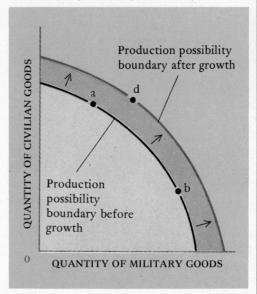

FIGURE 1–3
The Effect of Economic Growth on the Production Possibility Boundary

Economic growth shifts the boundary outward and makes it possible to have more of all commodities. Before growth in productive capacity, points a and b were on the production possibility boundary and point d was an unattainable combination. After growth, point d and many other previously unattainable combinations are attainable, as shown by the dark shaded band.

ECONOMICS: A WORKING DEFINITION

The six-way classification just discussed does not embrace all the things that interest economists. Additional topics such as the problems of international trade or comparative economic systems might be included in one or more of those categories, or they might be treated separately. Similarly, the theory of economic policy might be regarded as affecting all of the problem areas mentioned, or it might be treated separately.

Our purpose in listing these problem areas is to outline the scope of economics more fully than can be done with short definitions. Economics today is regarded much more broadly than it was even half a century ago. Earlier definitions stressed the alternative and competing uses of resources. Such definitions focused on choices between alternative points on a stationary production possibility boundary. Important additional economic problems concern failure to achieve the boundary (problems of inefficiency or underemployment of resources) and the outward movement of the boundary over time (problems of growth and development).

Economics, broadly defined, concerns:

1. **The ways in which a society uses its resources and distributes the fruits of production to individuals and groups in the society.**
2. **The ways in which production and distribution change over time.**
3. **The efficiencies of economic systems.**

Economic Analysis and Economic Policy

Economics helps in understanding and predicting some aspects of human behavior. People, by nature curious about their environment, want to predict this behavior in order that they may control their environment and adapt it to their needs.

THE PERVASIVENESS OF POLICY DECISIONS

Governments derive their authority to form and carry out policy from their police power—indeed, the words "policy" and "police" come from the Greek word for state, *politeia.*

Some governments lean toward a policy of laissez faire, or non-interference; others toward a policy of attempting strict control over every facet of the economy.

All governments have economic policies. Even the decision not to act but to let nature take its course is a policy decision.

Whether to rely on marketplace decision making or to replace it is as much a policy decision as is a government's decision to tax cigarettes.

Every year thousands of economic policy decisions are made by local, state, and federal governments. Most of them are never seriously debated. Nor is every facet of existing policy debated anew each year; indeed, many policy decisions now in force (such as giving unions the right to organize) were made decades ago. Only a few policy issues attract attention and become the subject of earnest and heated argument in a particular year.

THE ROLES OF THE ECONOMIST IN ECONOMIC POLICY

Any policy action has two aspects: the goals (or ends) that the decision makers are attempting to achieve and the means by which the desired ends are to be achieved. The United States government simultaneously pursues many broad policy goals such as efficient use of resources, growth, justice, national security, and economic stability. Economists do not establish goals, but they are often involved in helping to resolve conflicts among competing goals, in forging the links between goals and the means available to achieve them, and in evaluating policy proposals.

Defining Conflicts of Policy

Governments have many goals. A particular policy that serves one goal may hinder another and have no effect on yet a third. Unemployment compensation, for example, may promote justice by protecting unemployed families from debilitating hardships; at the same time it may hinder the quickness with which labor moves from labor-surplus to labor-scarce occupations, thereby decreasing efficient use of resources. Moreover, it will have no effect one way or the other on air pollution.

Economics has a large role to play in defining goal conflicts by identifying the effects, indirect as well as direct, of a proposed policy. Raising the minimum wage may seem extremely desirable to people who believe that the lowest-paid workers are not getting enough income to live at a decent standard of living. But if that policy results in some workers being laid off and becoming unemployed, the benefits to those who get higher wages must be balanced by the costs of the extra unemployment.

Proposing Policies

It is frequently the role of the economist to suggest policies. Given a statement of objectives, economic analysis can be used to invent or publicize proposed policies that will achieve the objectives. Economists in and out of government have had a major impact on policy.

The Employment Act of 1946 created a Council of Economic Advisers to advise the president on the state of the economy and on how the goal of full employment could best be achieved. The Humphrey-Hawkins Act expanded the responsibility of the Council to formulate policies for achieving reasonable price stability along with increased employment, decreased unemployment, and more rapid growth. By 1980 three dozen professional economists had served as members of the three-person Council, and hundreds had served on the professional staff. (A list of past and present Council members is always contained in the Council's annual report.) The present chairman is Charles Schultze; his distinguished predecessors include Arthur Burns, Walter Heller, Paul McCracken, Gardner Ackley, Alan Greenspan, and the late Arthur Okun.

Other economists play major policy roles in the cabinet, on regulatory commissions and boards, and in many executive departments and administrative agencies. Congress, too, utilizes economic advisers such as Alice Rivlin, director of the influential Congressional Budget Office.

Nor is it necessary to be in government to affect government policy. Dozens of economists have had significant influence on economic policy from the sidelines. Milton Friedman, Paul Samuelson, James Tobin, Otto Eckstein, and Lawrence Klein are prominent among those whose widely reported statements influence policy decisions. John Kenneth Galbraith has had

an enormous effect on public opinion about economic matters with his best-selling books, and Leonard Silk writes an influential column for the *New York Times*.

Forming and Evaluating Policies

Economists must frequently determine whether a particular policy proposal—which may or may not have originated with them—is the best way to meet a particular problem. While each issue has its own special characteristics, there are also common concerns. Five main questions need to be asked in every case: (1) What are the policy goals? (2) Do the proposed means achieve those goals? (3) What costs are directly imposed? (4) Do the proposed means have adverse side effects? (5) Are there better alternative means?

Consider an example. A team of economists is asked to evaluate a proposal that the federal government institute rationing of gasoline by issuing coupons to every registered automobile owner. Each dated coupon permits the holder to purchase a specific number of gallons of gasoline during a specific week. How might the economists go about evaluating this proposal?

The economists would start by asking what goals gasoline rationing is meant to achieve. They might find that its purpose is, first, to limit total purchases of gasoline to a specific number of gallons per week and, second, to do so in a way that shares the reduction in gasoline supply equitably among all drivers.

Given these goals, the economists would next ask how well the proposal meets them. If the authorities can effectively enforce the rule that gasoline not be sold without coupons, the quantity of coupons will assure that no more than that number of gallons will be sold. This amount will be an upper limit, not the actual quantity, because it takes *both* money and coupons to get gasoline. Some users will not want to buy their full allotment of gasoline; others will want to buy more than they are allowed.

The number of coupons issued that will actually be used may be hard to predict. It will certainly be less than the total number issued if there is no legal way to transfer surplus coupons from those who would not use them to those who want extra coupons. While the coupons are not transferable, there may nevertheless be an illegal trade in the coupons unless the government takes severe measures to prevent it.

The economists may well conclude that the proposal can achieve its first objective, to control the quantity of gasoline actually sold. Examining the second objective, however, they may find that issuing coupons to *owners* does not achieve equal treatment of *drivers*. Some persons own two or more cars; others own no car and depend on borrowed or rented cars. Moreover, some persons must drive long distances to and from work, while others need not. The rationing plan tends to impose equal mileage, not equal sacrifice of mileage, on coupon receivers. Thus it imposes a greater sacrifice on people who need to drive above average distances and a lesser sacrifice on people who drive below average distances. The same allotment of gallons per week may seem generous to a retired couple living in Rhode Island and ridiculously small to a ranching couple in Wyoming.

On the basis of this much analysis, the economists are likely to report that the plan does *not* meet its second objective. They will urge rejection or modification of the proposal. They will also point out that a revised allocation plan, based on demonstrated needs plus a small free-driving allowance, would correct the deficiency. Yet there are many other difficulties. Let us suppose that a number of modifications in the plan have been made and that the economists have concluded it will fulfill its basic purposes.

The economists will now ask how costly the plan would be to put into effect and enforce. They would estimate the direct costs of printing and distributing the coupons, of developing and running an allocation system, of establishing a means to hear the inevitable appeals from outraged citizens, of policing the use of coupons, and of enforcing the nontransferability of coupons. The total estimated costs would be reported to the policymakers. If the costs seemed too large relative to the benefits, the entire plan

might be dropped right there. But suppose the costs, although large, seem to be small enough to be offset by the benefits of the gasoline rationing scheme.

Next the economists might search for ways in which this policy serves or conflicts with other goals. Does it serve the public interest by encouraging production of more efficient cars? Does it work against the public interest by encouraging crime in the form of the counterfeiting or theft of ration coupons or the bribing of officials who allocate coupons? Does it fail to prevent some people from using gasoline frivolously while it forces others to curtail vital activities? There are a host of similar questions to be asked.

Ideally, the existence and importance of each side effect must be estimated. When a policy action helps to achieve one goal but hinders the attainment of others, it is necessary to establish trade-offs among them. Usually there will be some rate at which people will be willing to trade a loss in one direction for a gain in another. Let us suppose that if this were the end of the matter, the economists and policymakers would conclude that, all things considered, the gasoline rationing plan is better than nothing and deserves further study.

The final step for the economists is to consider whether modifications of the plan, or alternatives to it, will achieve the goals equally well but at lower cost or less sacrifice in terms of setbacks to other policy objectives. They may well consider, for example, whether allowing the coupons to be sold will lead to fairer, more efficient gasoline usage, less crime, and smaller enforcement costs. Another proposal they may consider is to discourage gas consumption by a 50¢ per gallon gasoline tax, combined with a series of money grants to poorer people who must drive as part of their work.

This final step is very important. It compares a particular feasible proposal, not only against "do nothing," but against other feasible proposals.

At any stage of their investigation, the economists may conclude that gasoline rationing is not a very effective means of achieving the policymakers' objectives. (In fact many economists have reached that conclusion.) But suppose that the team of economists concludes that gasoline rationing *does* achieve the desired goals, that the direct costs and undesirable effects in other directions are judged (by the policymakers) to be less important than the desirable effects in achieving the stated policy goals, and that there are no other practicable measures that would better achieve the goals? The team will then conclude that there is a strong case in favor of the proposal.

Do the views—and prejudices—of the investigators have a great deal to do with the outcome of their investigation? A particular group of economists may have strong views on the specific measure it is attempting to assess. If the economists do not like the measure, they are likely to be relentless in identifying costs and searching out possible unwanted effects and somewhat less than thorough in discovering effects that help to achieve the desired goals. It is important though difficult to guard against an unconscious bias of this sort. Fortunately there are likely to be others with different biases. One advantage of publishing evaluations and submitting them to review and discussion is that it provides opportunities for those with different biases to discover arguments and evidence originally overlooked.

ECONOMIC AND POLITICAL OBJECTIVES

Actual policy making is more complicated than the previous discussion suggests, and a few of the many reasons policy issues get settled in a less systematic fashion deserve mention.

Decisions on interrelated issues of policy are made by many different bodies. Congress passes laws, the Supreme Court interprets laws, the administration decides which laws to enforce with vigor and which to soft-pedal. The Treasury and the Federal Reserve System influence monetary factors, and a host of other agencies and semi-autonomous bodies determine actions in re-

spect to different aspects of policy goals. Because of the multiplicity of decision makers, it would be truly amazing if fully consistent behavior resulted. The majority of Americans believe that there are advantages to this separation of responsibilities, but one of its consequences is that inconsistent decisions will be made.

Furthermore, in a system such as ours, inconsistent decisions may result from political compromises between two or more interested groups, factions, or agencies. Such compromises are common in Congress, between Congress and the executive, and among executive departments.

Another problem arises from the fact that legislators in a democracy have their own and their party's reelection as one of their important goals. This means, for example, that any measure that imposes large costs and few benefits obvious to the electorate over the next few years is unlikely to find favor, no matter how large the long-term benefits are. There is a strong bias toward myopia in an elective system. Although much of this bias stems from shortsightedness and selfishness, another part reflects genuine uncertainty about the future. The further into the future the economist calculates, the wider the margin of possible error. It is not surprising that politicians who must worry about the next election often tend to worry less about the long-term effects of their actions. "After all," they may argue, "who can tell what will happen 20 years hence?"

These problems of political decision making are what George Bernard Shaw had in mind when he said that the only strong argument in favor of democracy is that all of its alternatives are even worse.

Summary

1. Economic problems are among the important concerns of every generation. A common feature of such problems is that they concern the use of limited resources to satisfy virtually unlimited human wants.

2. Scarcity is a fundamental problem faced by all economies. Not enough resources are available to produce all the goods and services that people would like to consume. Scarcity makes it necessary to choose. All societies must have a mechanism for deciding what commodities will be produced and in what quantities.

3. The concept of opportunity cost emphasizes the problem of scarcity and choice by measuring the cost of obtaining a unit of one commodity in terms of the number of units of other commodities that could have been obtained instead.

4. Six basic questions faced by all economies are: What commodities are being produced and in what quantities? By what methods are the commodities produced, and are those methods efficient? Who gets the commodities that are produced and in what quantities? Are the society's resources being fully utilized? What is happening to the purchasing power of money and savings? Is the economy's capacity to produce growing over time or remaining static?

5. Not all economies resolve these questions in the same ways or equally satisfactorily. Economists study how these questions are answered in various societies and the consequences of using one method rather than another to provide answers.

6. Governments, in varying degree, choose to intervene in the functioning of the economy. In so doing, they pursue economic policies.

7. It is necessary to distinguish between certain ends that are being sought and the means by which they will be achieved. Economics does not allow a "scientific" choice between alternative ends: It does not tell which of competing goals should be adopted. Economic analysis can help to determine whether a particular measure contributes to stated goals and at what cost.

8. One of the main reasons particular policies will always be subject to debate and disagreement is that most policies that are effective in bringing us closer to some goals take us further

away from others. This leads to policy conflicts, and it is necessary to judge how much of one objective is to be sacrificed in order to get more of another.

Topics for Review

Scarcity and the need for choice
Choice and opportunity cost
Production possibility boundary
Resource allocation
Unemployed resources
Growth in productive capacity
Steps in evaluating economic policies
Conflicts of policies

Discussion Questions

1. What does each of the following quotations tell you about the policy conflicts perceived by the person making the statement and about how he or she has resolved them?
   a. President Carter, January 1977: "We've got so many people out of work, and we've got so much unused industrial capacity, that I think if we carefully target employment opportunities around the country, we can decrease unemployment substantially before we start becoming equally concerned about inflation."
   b. Russell Baker, commenting on the decision of Nantucket Island residents to approve a Holiday Inn to cater to oil drillers: "Economics compels us all to turn things into slums. Although it will be too bad, it will be absolutely justifiable. An economic necessity. Another step down the ladder to paradise."
   c. *Time* magazine: "Considering our limited energy resources and the growing demand for electricity, the United States really has no choice but to use all of its possible domestic energy sources, including nuclear energy. Despite possible environmental and safety hazards, nuclear power is a necessity."
   d. King Khalid of Saudi Arabia: "Increasing oil production in order to lower oil prices would be the most damaging thing that could happen to humanity. Experts say that if oil consumption continues to increase as it has, oil reserves will dry up by the end of this century."
2. When candidate Jimmy Carter was campaigning in October 1976, he said: "If I am elected I will take quick

steps to make our postal service efficient and dependable again." To do so, the postal service estimates, would require an annual subsidy of $5 billion per year for five years. Are there opportunity costs to doing this? If so, what might they be? What alternatives to a subsidy might be used to achieve President Carter's objectives?

3. Consider the right to free speech in political campaigns. Suppose that the Flat Earth Society, the Socialist party, and the Republican party all demand equal time on network television in a presidential election. What economic questions are involved? Can there be freedom of speech without free access to the scarce resources needed to make one's speech heard?

4. The United States entered World War II with substantial unemployment of resources and gradually moved to full employment of available resources. Contrast the opportunity costs of fighting the war under these circumstances with the opportunity costs for an economy already at full employment.

5. Evidence accumulates that the use of chemical fertilizers, which increases agricultural production greatly, causes damage to water quality. Show the choice involved between more food and cleaner water in using such fertilizers. Use a production possibility curve with agricultural output on the vertical axis and water quality on the horizontal axis. In what ways does this production possibility curve reflect scarcity, choice, and opportunity cost? How would an improved fertilizer that increased agricultural output without further worsening water quality affect the curve? Suppose a pollution-free fertilizer were developed; would this mean there would no longer be any opportunity cost of using it?

6. What is the difference between scarcity and poverty? If everyone in the world had enough to eat, could we say that food was no longer scarce?

7. Does the United States government have a policy on old-age pensions? Did it have one before the Social Security Act was passed in 1935? Is there any defined issue on which the government can be said not to have a policy? Why or why not?

8. What goals might lead people to prefer allocating gas by coupon rather than letting price rise? What goals might lead to a preference for having such coupons salable rather than nontransferable? What factual questions might bear on each decision?

Economics as a Social Science

2

Economics is generally regarded as a social science. What exactly does it mean to be scientific? Can economics ever hope to be "scientific" in its study of those aspects of human behavior with which it is concerned? The first step in answering these questions is to be able to distinguish between positive and normative statements. The ability to make this distinction has been one of the reasons for the success of science in the last 300 years.

THE DISTINCTION BETWEEN POSITIVE AND NORMATIVE

Positive statements concern what is, was, or will be. **Normative statements** concern what ought to be.

Positive statements, assertions, or theories may be simple or complex, but they are basically about matters of fact.

Disagreements over positive statements are appropriately settled by an appeal to the facts.

Normative statements, because they concern what ought to be, are inextricably bound up with philosophical, cultural, and religious systems. A normative statement is one that makes, or is based on, a value judgment—a judgment about what is good and what is bad.

Disagreements over normative statements cannot be settled merely by an appeal to facts.

The Distinction Illustrated

The statement "It is impossible to break up atoms" is a positive statement that can quite definitely be (and of course has been) refuted by empirical observations, while the statement "Scientists ought not to break up atoms" is a normative statement that involves ethical judgments. The questions "What government policies will reduce unemployment?" and "What policies will prevent inflation?" are positive ones, while the question "Ought we to be more concerned about unemployment than about inflation?" is a normative one. The statement "A government deficit will reduce unemployment and cause an increase in prices" is a very simple hypothesis in positive economics, a hypothesis that can be tested by an appeal to empirical observation, while the statement "Because unemployment ought to matter more than inflation, a government deficit is sound policy" is a normative hypothesis that cannot be settled solely by an appeal to observation.

Having grasped this distinction, be careful not to turn it into an inquiry-stopping, dogmatic rule. From the fact that positive economics does not include normative questions (because its tools are inappropriate to them) it does *not* follow that the student of positive economics must stop her or his inquiry as soon as someone says the word "ought." Consider the statement "It is my value judgment that we *ought to have* rent control because controls are *good*." It is quite in order for a practitioner of positive economics to ask "Why?" It may then be argued that controls have certain consequences and it is these consequences that are judged to be good. But the statements about the consequences of rent control will be positive, testable statements.

Thus the pursuit of what appears to be a normative statement will often turn up positive hypotheses on which the *ought* conclusion depends. For example, there are probably relatively few people who believe that government control of industry is in itself good or bad. Their advocacy or opposition will be based on certain beliefs about relations that can be stated as positive rather than normative hypotheses. For example: "Government control reduces (increases) efficiency, changes (does not change) the distribution of income, leads (does not lead)

to an increase of state control in other spheres." A careful study of this emotive subject would reveal enough positive economic questions to keep a research team of economists occupied for many years.

The Importance of the Distinction

If we think something ought to be done, we can deduce other things that, if we wish to be consistent, ought to be done; but we can deduce nothing about what is done (i.e., is true). Similarly, if we know that two things are true, we can deduce other things that must be true, but we can deduce nothing about what is desirable (i.e., *ought* to be).

The distinction between positive and normative statements is critical because it is logically impossible to deduce normative statements from positive statements and vice versa.

First, consider an example involving both normative and positive statements. Suppose I believe that (1) as a moral principle I ought to be charitable to all human beings. Then if I am told that (2) the inhabitants of China are not Christians but are human beings, it follows that (3) therefore I ought to be charitable toward Chinese. From (1) and (2) a normative rule has been deduced about how I ought to behave in a particular case. However, no positive statement about how I *do* behave can be deduced from (1) and (2).

Now suppose someone else comes along and says, "You ought not to be charitable toward the Chinese because my moral principles dictate that you should be charitable only toward Christians." If an argument arises about whether to be charitable toward the Chinese, this argument will turn on value judgments about how we ought to behave. These are questions on which reasonable people sometimes have to agree to disagree. If both sides insist on holding to their views on charity, even if both are perfectly reasonable, there is no civilized way of forcing either to admit error.

Second, consider an example involving only

positive statements. Assume I say that (1) capital punishment is a strong disincentive to murder and that (2) the Chinese abolished capital punishment after the Revolution, so that (3) therefore the number of murders must have risen in China since the Revolution. The two factual statements, (1) and (2), and the deduction that follows from them are all positive statements. Nothing can be deduced about the moral desirability of abolishing capital punishment from statements (1) and (2), even if they are factually correct.

Now suppose you say, "The number of murders has not risen in China since the Revolution; in fact, the number has fallen." If you hold to this view, you must deny one or the other of the first two positive statements. You could deny statement (1) by saying, for example, that capital punishment is actually an incentive to commit murder. You could deny statement (2) by saying, for example, that, although the Chinese pretended to abolish capital punishment as a propaganda move, they in fact retained it after the Revolution. In both cases the disagreement is over factual statements. If enough facts were gathered, and if both parties were reasonable, one party could be forced to admit being wrong.

The distinction between positive and normative allows us to keep our views on how we would like the world to work separate from our views on how the world actually does work. We may be interested in both. It can only obscure the truth, however, if we let our views on what we would like to be bias our investigations of what actually is. It is for this reason that the separation of the positive from the normative is one of the foundation stones of science and that scientific inquiry, as it is normally understood, is usually confined to positive questions.

Positive and Normative Statements in Economics

Economics, like other sciences, is concerned with questions, statements, and hypotheses that could conceivably be shown to be wrong (that is, false) by actual observations of the world. It is not necessary to show them to be either consistent or inconsistent with the facts tomorrow or the next day; it is only necessary to be able to imagine evidence that could show them to be wrong. *Thus an appeal to the facts is an appropriate way in which to deal with them.* Other questions, including normative ones, cannot be settled by a mere appeal to empirical observation. This does not, of course, mean that they are unimportant. Such questions as "Should we subsidize higher education?" and "Should we send food to Iran?" must be decided by means other than a simple appeal to facts. In democratic practice, such questions are usually settled by voting on them.

THE SCIENTIFIC APPROACH

Very roughly, the scientific approach, or the scientific method as it is sometimes called, consists of relating questions to evidence. When presented with a controversial issue, scientists will ask what the evidence is both for and against it. They may then take a stand on the issue, with more or less conviction depending on the weight of the evidence. If there is little or no evidence, scientists will say that at present it is impossible to take a stand. They will then set about searching for relevant evidence. If they find that the issue is framed in terms that make it impossible to gather evidence for or against it, they will then usually try to recast the question so that it can be answered by an appeal to the evidence. This approach to a problem is what sets scientific inquiries off from other inquiries.

In some fields, the scientist, having reframed the question, is able to generate observations that will provide evidence for or against the hypothesis. Experimental sciences such as chemistry and some branches of psychology have an advantage because it is possible for them to produce relevant evidence through controlled laboratory experiments. Other sciences such as astronomy and economics cannot do this. They must wait for natural events to produce observations that may be used as evidence in testing their theories, or they must rely on nonlaboratory experiments that are not fully controlled. An example of the latter is the space probe programs of recent years, which have added greatly to astronomers' knowledge about the universe.

The ease or difficulty with which one can collect evidence does not determine whether a subject is scientific or nonscientific.

How scientific inquiry proceeds and the ease with which it can be pursued do, however, differ substantially between fields in which laboratory experiment is possible and those in which it is not. Some of these differences will be discussed in Chapter 3. Until then we shall consider general problems more or less common to all sciences.

IS HUMAN BEHAVIOR PREDICTABLE?

Natural versus social sciences. Is it possible to conduct a scientific study in the field of human behavior? When considering whether it is possible to make a scientific study of such subjects as the causes of unemployment and the consequences of a large national debt, it is sometimes argued that natural sciences deal with inanimate matter that is subject to natural "laws" while the social sciences deal with human beings who have free will and therefore cannot be made the subject of natural laws.

This view implies that inanimate matter will show stable responses to certain stimuli, but animate matter will not. For example, if you put a match to a dry piece of paper, the paper will burn, whereas if you subject human beings to torture, some will break down and do what you want them to do and others will not. Even more confusing, the same individual may react differently to torture at different times.

Does human behavior show sufficiently stable responses to factors influencing it to be predictable within an acceptable margin of error? This is a positive question that can be settled only by an appeal to evidence and not by *a priori* speculation. (*A priori* may be defined as the use of knowledge that is prior to actual experience.) The question itself might concern either the behavior of groups or that of isolated individuals.

Group versus individual behavior. It is a matter of simple observation that when a group of individuals is considered, they do not behave capriciously but instead display stable responses to various forces that act on them. The warmer the weather, for example, the more people visit the beach and the higher the sales of ice cream and Coca-Cola. It may be hard to say when or why one individual will buy an ice cream cone or a Coke, but a stable response pattern from a large group of individuals can be seen: the higher the temperature, the greater the sales of these two products at the beach.

There are many situations in which group behavior can be predicted accurately without certain knowledge of individual behavior. No social scientist can predict, for example, when an apparently healthy individual is going to die, but death rates for large groups are stable enough to make life insurance a profitable business. This would not be so if group behavior were capricious. Although social scientists cannot predict what particular individuals will be killed in auto accidents in the next holiday weekend, they can come very close to knowing the total number who will die. The more objectively measurable data they have (for example, the state of the weather on the days in question and the change in auto sales over the previous year), the more closely they will be able to predict total deaths.

The well-known fact that pollsters do a good job of predicting elections on the basis of sample surveys provides evidence that human attitudes do not change capriciously. If group behavior were truly capricious, there would be no point in trying to predict anything on the basis of sample surveys. The fact that 80 percent of the voters sampled said they intended to vote for a certain candidate would give no information about the probable outcome of the election. Today's information would commonly be reversed tomorrow.

The difference between predicting individual and group behavior is illustrated by the fact that economists can predict with fair accuracy what households as a group will do when their take-home pay is increased. Some individuals may do surprising and unpredictable things, but the total response of all households to a permanent change in tax rates that leaves more money in their hands is predictable within quite a narrow margin of error. This stability in the response of households' spending to a change in their available income is the basis of economists' ability to predict successfully the outcome of major revisions in the tax laws.

This does not mean that people never change their minds or that future events can be foretold by a casual study of the past. People sometimes think in terms of a simple dichotomy: Either there are historical laws apparent to the casual observer or there is random behavior. They observe a prophet predicting that some change will take place in the future merely because it took place in the past. Upon seeing the prophet make an utterly mistaken prophecy, they conclude that, because the prophet cannot prophesy, human behavior is random and thus unamenable to scientific study. The stability discussed here is a stable response to causal factors (e.g., next time it gets warm, ice cream sales will rise) and not merely inertia (e.g., ice cream sales will go on rising in the future because they have risen in the past).

The "Law" of Large Numbers

Successful predictions about the behavior of large groups are made possible by the statistical "law" of large numbers. Broadly speaking, this law asserts that random movements of many individual items tend to offset one another. This law is based on one of the most beautiful constants of behavior in the whole of science, natural and social, and yet it can be derived from the fact that human beings make errors! The law is based on the *normal curve of error,* which is encountered in elementary statistics.

What is implied by this law? Ask any one person to measure the length of a room and it will be almost impossible to predict in advance what sort of error of measurement he or she will make. Dozens of things will affect the accuracy of the measurement and, furthermore, the person may make one error today and quite a different one tomorrow. But ask a thousand people to measure the length of the same room, and it can be predicted within a very small margin just how this *group* will make its errors. It can be asserted with confidence that more people will make small errors than will make large errors, that the larger the error, the fewer will be the number making it, that roughly the same number of people will overestimate as will underestimate the distance, and that the average error of all individuals will be zero.

If a common cause should act on each member of the group, it is possible to predict the average behavior of the group even though any one member may act in a surprising fashion. If, for example, each of the thousand individuals is given a tape measure that understates "actual" distances, it can be expected that, on the average, the group will underestimate the length of the room. It is, of course, quite possible that one member, who had in the past been consistently undermeasuring distance because of psychological depression, will now overestimate the distance because the state of his health has changed. But some other event may happen to another individual that will turn her from an overmeasurer into an undermeasurer. Individuals may act strangely for inexplicable reasons. But the group's behavior, when the inaccurate tape is substituted for the accurate one, will be predictable precisely because the odd things that one individual does will tend to cancel out the odd things some other individual does.

Irregularities in individual behavior tend to cancel one another out, and the regularities tend to show up in repeated observations.

THE NATURE OF SCIENTIFIC THEORIES

There is abundant evidence of stable response patterns in human behavior. Some regularity between two or more things is observed, and we ask why this should be so. A *theory* attempts to explain why. Once we have a theory it enables us to predict as yet unobserved events. For example, national income theory predicts that an increase in the government's budget deficit will reduce the amount of unemployment. The simple theory of market behavior predicts that, under specified conditions, the introduction of a sales tax will be accompanied by an increase in the price of the commodity concerned and that the price increase will be less than the amount of the tax. It also lets us predict that if there is a partial failure of the potato crop, the total receipts earned by potato farmers will rise!

Theories are used in explaining observed phenomena. A successful theory enables us to predict the consequences of various occurrences.

The Pervasiveness of Theories

Observations concern sequences of events. Any explanation whatsoever of how these events are linked together is a theoretical construction. Theories are what are used to impose order on observations, to explain how what is seen is linked together. Without theories there would be only a shapeless mass of meaningless observations.

The choice is not between theory and observation but between better or worse theories to explain observations.

In a particular case we might see an increase in interest rates followed by a reduction in borrowing by corporations. The practical person may think the link is obvious, and indeed in some sense it may be, but nonetheless it requires a theoretical construction. Before these two events can be linked together, it is necessary to have a theory of what the corporate managers are trying to do and how they try to do it, plus the assump-

tion that the managers know what behavior will achieve their goals.

True in Theory but Not in Practice

Misunderstanding about the place of theories in scientific explanation gives rise to many misconceptions. One of these is illustrated by the phrase "True in theory but not in practice." The next time you hear someone say this (or, indeed, the next time you say it yourself) you should immediately reply, "All right then, tell me what does happen in practice." Usually you will not be told mere facts, but you will be given an alternative theory — a different explanation of the facts. The speaker should have said, "The theory in question provides a poor explanation of the facts" (that is, it is contradicted by some factual observations); "I have a different theory that does a much better job."

WHAT IS A THEORY AND HOW IS IT TESTED?

A theory consists of (1) a set of definitions that clearly define the *variables* to be used, (2) a set of *assumptions* that outline the conditions under which the theory is to apply, (3) one or more *hypotheses* about the relationships of variables, and (4) *predictions* that are deduced from the assumptions of the theory and can be tested against actual empirical observations.

Variables

Theories are concerned with how various things are related to each other. If we know how two things are related, then we know how one of them will change as the other changes. The things that we relate to each other are called variables. A **variable** is some magnitude that can take on different possible values. Variables are the basic elements of theories, and each one needs to be carefully defined.

Kinds of Variables

Endogenous and Exogenous Variables

Endogenous variables are those that are explained within a theory. **Exogenous variables** are those that influence the endogenous variables but are themselves determined by considerations outside of the theory. Consider the theory that the price of apples in Seattle on a particular day is a function of several things, one of which was the weather in Wenatchee, Washington, during the previous apple-growing season. We can safely assume that the state of the weather is not determined by economic conditions. The price of apples in this case is an endogenous variable—something determined within the framework of the theory. The state of the weather in Wenatchee is an exogenous variable; changes in it influence prices because they affect the supply of apples, but the weather is uninfluenced by these prices.

Other words are sometimes used for the same distinction. One frequently used pair is *induced,* for endogenous and *autonomous,* for exogenous.

Stock and Flow Variables

A distinction between variables that is important in economics is that between stocks and flows. A flow variable has a time dimension; it is so much per unit of time. The quantity of grade A large eggs purchased in Cleveland is a flow variable. No useful information is conveyed if we are told that purchases were 2,000 dozen eggs unless we are also told over what period of time these purchases occurred. Two thousand dozen per hour would indicate an active market in eggs, while 2,000 dozen per week would indicate a sluggish market. A stock variable has no time dimension; it is just so much. Thus, if the egg producers' cooperative has 2 million dozen eggs in warehouses around the country, the quantity is a stock. All those eggs are there at one time. The stock variable is just a number, not a rate of flow of so much *per day* or *per month*.

Economic theories use both stock variables and flow variables, and it takes a little practice to keep them straight. The amount of income earned is a flow; there is so much per year or per month or per hour. The amount of a household's expenditure is also a flow—so much spent per week or per month. The amount of money in a bank account or a miser's hoard (earned, perhaps, in the past, but unspent) is a stock—just so many thousands of dollars. What of the interest earned by the miser who puts money into a savings bank? It is a flow. The key test is always whether a time dimension is required to give the variable significant meaning.

Price is an example of an important economic variable. The price of a commodity is the amount of money that must be given up to purchase one unit of that commodity. To define a price we must first define the commodity to which it attaches. Such a commodity might be one dozen grade A large eggs. We could then inquire into the price of such eggs sold in, say, supermarkets in Fargo, North Dakota. This would define the variable. The particular values taken on by the variable might be 98¢ on July 1, 1980, $1.02 on July 8, 1980, and 99¢ on July 15, 1980. A series of observations on the values of a variable at different points in time, such as these on egg prices, is called a **time series.**

There are many distinctions between kinds of variables; two of the most important are discussed in the box above.

Assumptions

Assumptions play a vital role in theorizing. Students are often greatly concerned about the justification of assumptions, particularly if they seem unrealistic. Suppose an economic theory starts out: "Assume that there is no government." Surely, says the reader, this assumption is totally unrealistic, and I cannot therefore take seriously anything that comes out of the theory. But this assumption may merely be the economist's way of saying that, whatever the government does, even whether it exists, *is irrelevant for the purposes of this particular theory.*

Now, put this way, the statement becomes an empirical assertion. The only way to test it is to see if the predictions that follow from the theory do or do not fit the facts that the theory is trying to explain. If they do, then the theorist was correct in the assumption that the government could be ignored for the particular purposes at hand. In this case the criticism that the theory is unrealistic because there really is a government is completely beside the point.

Another important use of an apparently unrealistic assumption may be to outline the set of conditions under which a theory is meant to hold. Consider a theory that assumes the government has a balanced budget. This may mean that the theorist intends that theory to apply only when there is a balanced budget; it may *not* mean that the size of the government's budget surplus or deficit is irrelevant to the theory.[1]

Usually it is not appropriate to criticize the simplifying assumptions of a theory only on the grounds that they are unrealistic. All theory is an abstraction from reality. If it were not, it would merely duplicate the world and would add nothing to the understanding of it. A good theory abstracts in a useful and significant way; a poor theory does not. If we believe that the theorist has assumed away something important for the problem at hand, then we must believe, and try to show, that the conclusions of the theory are contradicted by the facts.

Hypotheses

Relations among variables. The critical step in theorizing is formulating hypotheses. A hypothesis is a statement about how two or more variables relate to each other. For example, it is a basic hypothesis of economics that the quantity produced of any commodity depends, among other things, on its price. Thus the two variables, the price of eggs and the quantity of eggs produced, are related to each other according to an economic hypothesis.

Functional relations. A **function,** or a functional relation, is a formal expression of a relation among variables.

The particular hypothesis that the quantity of eggs produced is related to the price of eggs is an example of a functional relation in economics. In its most general form, it merely says that quantity produced is related to price. More specifically, however, the hypothesis may be that as the price of eggs falls, the quantity produced will also fall. In other words, in this hypothesis price and quantity vary *directly* with each other. In the case of many hypotheses of this kind economists can be even more specific about the nature of the functional relation. On the basis of detailed factual studies, economists often have a pretty good idea of by *how much* quantity produced will change as a result of specified changes in price—that is, about magnitude as well as direction.[2]

---

[1] As the text illustrates, an assumption may mean many different things. When you encounter an assumption in economic theory, ask yourself whether it is being used to convey the idea that (1) the world actually behaves as assumed, (2) the factor under consideration is irrelevant to the theory, (3) the theory only holds when the condition specified in the assumption actually holds, or (4) a convenient fiction is being introduced to simplify some quite complex piece of behavior.

[2] The appendixes for each chapter appear starting on page 867. The appendix to this chapter (page 869) gives a more detailed discussion of functional relations.

Predictions

A scientific prediction is not the same thing as a prophecy.

A scientific prediction is a conditional statement that takes the form: *If* **you do this,** *then* **such and such will follow.**

If hydrogen and oxygen are mixed under specified conditions, *then* water will be the result. *If* the government has a large budget deficit, *then* the amount of employment will be increased. It is most important to realize that this prediction is very different from the statement: "I prophesy that in two years' time there will be a large increase in employment because I believe the government will decide to have a large budget deficit." The government's decision to have a budget deficit or surplus in two years' time will be the outcome of many complex factors, emotions, objective circumstances, chance occurrences, and so on, few of which can be predicted by the economist. If the economist's prophecy about the level of employment turns out to be wrong because in two years' time the government does not have a large deficit, then all that has been learned is that the economist is not a good guesser about the behavior of the government. However, *if* the government does have a large deficit (in two years' time or at any other time) and *then* the amount of employment does not rise, a conditional scientific prediction in economic theory has been contradicted.

Testing Theories

A theory is tested by confronting its predictions with evidence. It is necessary to discover if certain events are followed by the consequences predicted by the theory. For example, is an increase in the government's budget deficit followed by a reduction in unemployment? Testing is never easily accomplished (some of the problems involved are discussed in Chapter 3).

As a generalization, it can be said that theories tend to be abandoned when they are no longer useful. And theories cease to be useful when they cannot predict the consequences of actions in which one is interested better than the next best alternative. When a theory consistently fails to predict better than the available alternatives, it is either modified or replaced. Figure 2-1 summarizes the discussion of theories.

ECONOMICS AS A DEVELOPING SCIENCE

Economics is like other sciences in at least two respects. First, there are many observations of the world for which there are, at the moment, no fully satisfactory theoretical explanations. Second, there are many predictions that no one has yet satisfactorily tested. Serious students of economics must not expect to find a set of answers to all their questions as they progress in their study. Very often they must expect to encounter nothing more than a set of problems that provides an agenda for further research. Even when they do find answers to problems, they should accept these answers as tentative and ask even of the most time-honored theory, "What observations would be in conflict with this theory?"

Economics is still a young science. On the one hand, economists know a good deal about the behavior of the economy. On the other hand, many problems are almost untouched. Students who decide to specialize in economics may find themselves, only a few years from now, publishing a theory to account for some of the problems mentioned in this book; or they may end up making a set of observations that will refute some venerable theory described in these pages.

A final word of warning: Having counseled a constructive disrespect for the authority of accepted theory, it is necessary to warn against adopting an approach that is too cavalier. No respect attaches to the person who says, "This theory is for the birds, it is *obviously* wrong."

This is too cheap. To criticize a theory effectively on empirical grounds, one must demonstrate, by a carefully made set of observations, that some aspect of the theory is contradicted by the facts. This is a task worth attempting, but it is seldom easily accomplished.

FIGURE 2–1
The Interaction of Deduction and Measurement in Theorizing

Definitions, assumptions, and hypotheses about behavior

The existing theory is amended or a new theory is proposed in light of the newly acquired empirical knowledge

a process of logical deduction

Predictions (often called implications)

a process of empirical observation

Conclusion: The theory does or does not provide a better explanation of the facts than alternative competing theories

If the theory is in conflict with the evidence

either

or

If the theory passes the test, no consequent action is necessary, although, of course, the theory should be subjected to continued scrutiny

The theory is discarded in favor of a superior competing theory

Theory and observation are in continuous interaction. Starting (at the top left) with the definitions of terms and the assumptions of a theory, the theorist deduces by logical analysis everything that is implied by the assumptions. These implications are the predictions of the theory. The theory is then tested by confronting its predictions with evidence. If the theory is in conflict with facts, it will usually be amended to make it consistent with those facts (thereby making it a better theory); in extreme cases it will be discarded, to be replaced by a superior alternative. The process then begins again: the new or amended theory is subjected first to logical analysis and then to empirical testing.

Summary

1. It is possible, and fruitful, to distinguish between positive and normative statements. Positive statements concern what is, was, or will be, while normative statements concern what ought to be. Disagreements over positive statements are appropriately settled by an appeal to the facts. Disagreements over normative statements can never be settled by a mere appeal to factual evidence.

2. The success of scientific inquiry depends on separating positive questions about the way the world works from normative questions about how one would like the world to work. The scientific approach involves formulating positive questions precisely enough so that they can be settled by an appeal to evidence and then finding means of gathering or producing the necessary evidence.

3. Some people feel that although natural phenomena can be subject to scientific inquiry and "laws" of behavior, human phenomena cannot. The evidence, however, is otherwise. Social scientists have observed many regular and stable human behavior patterns, and these form the basis for successful predictions of how people will behave under certain conditions.

4. The fact that people sometimes act strangely, even capriciously, does not destroy the possibility of a scientific study of group behavior. Indeed, the odd and inexplicable things that one person does will tend to cancel out the odd and inexplicable things that another person does. Observation of group behavior often discloses fairly stable and predictable responses to things that exert a significant influence on the members of the group.

5. Observations reveal only sequences of events. Theories are designed to give meaning and coherence to these events. Theories thus pervade all attempts to explain events. A theory consists of a set of definitions of the variables to be employed, a set of assumptions giving the conditions under which the theory is meant to apply, and a set of hypotheses about how things behave. Any theory has certain logical implications that must be true if the theory is true.

6. A theory provides predictions of the type *"if* one event occurs, *then* another event will also occur." An important method of testing theories is to confront their predictions with evidence. When theories fail to predict better than the available alternatives, theories tend to be rejected. The progress of any science lies in finding better explanations of events than are now available. Thus, in any developing science, one must expect to discard present theories and replace them with demonstrably superior alternatives. Such a process improves the quality of the explanations.

7. The important concept of a functional relation is discussed in more detail in the appendix to this chapter, which begins on page 869.

Topics for Review

Positive and normative statements
The law of large numbers and the predictability of human behavior
The roles of variables, assumptions, and predictions in theorizing
Endogenous and exogenous variables
Stock and flow variables
Functional relations
Prediction versus prophecy
The scientific approach

Discussion Questions

1. A baby doesn't "know" of the theory of gravity, yet in walking and eating the child soons learns to use its principles. Distinguish between behavior and prediction of behavior. Does a business executive or a farmer have to understand economic theory to behave in a pattern consistent with economic theory?
2. "If human behavior were completely capricious and unpredictable, life insurance could not be a profitable business." Explain. Can you think of any businesses that do *not* depend on predictable human behavior?

3. Write five statements about inflation. (It does not matter whether the statements are correct, but you should confine yourself to those you think might be correct.) Classify each statement as positive or normative. If your list contains only one type of statement, try to add a sixth statement of the other type. Check the validity of your positive statements as well as you can against the data given in this text (see *Inflation* in the index). If this does not satisfy you about their validity, outline how you would go about completing the test of your statements.

4. Each of the following unrealistic assumptions is sometimes made. See if you can visualize situations in which each of them might be useful.
   a. The earth is a plane.
   b. There are no differences between men and women.
   c. There is no tomorrow.
   d. A bond will pay $100 interest a year forever.

5. "The following theory of wage determination proceeds on the assumption that labor unions do not exist." Of what use can such a theory be in the United States today?

6. Emotional statements can often be reworded so as to be tested by an appeal to evidence. How might you do that with respect to each of the following assertions?
   a. The American economic system is the best in the world.
   b. The provision of free medical care for more and more people will inevitably end in socialized medicine for all, and socialized medicine will destroy our standards of medical practice by destroying the doctor's incentive to do his or her job well.
   c. The periodic gasoline shortages result from a plot by the oil producers to exploit the public by restricting output to gain profits.
   d. Inflation is ruining the standard of living of the American worker and destroying the integrity of the family.

The Role of Statistical Analysis

3

In this chapter we look at two very different problems in statistics. We study first the important statistical tool of index numbers, which are used throughout economics and occur constantly in this book. You cannot read far in a newspaper or a news magazine without encountering important index numbers such as the Consumer Price Index, measures of productivity growth, and indexes of industrial output. Then we discuss some very general questions concerning the use of theory to measure and test economic relationships.

Index Numbers

Economists frequently seek simple answers to questions such as "How much have prices risen this year?" or "Has the quantity of industrial production increased this year, and, if so, by how much?" There is no perfectly satisfactory answer to the first question because all prices do not move together, nor to the second because one cannot simply add up tons of steel, pieces of furniture, and gallons of gasoline to get a meaningful total. Yet these are not foolish questions. There *are* trends in prices and production, and thus there are real phenomena to describe. It is of no help to someone who asks about price changes over some period to be given a list of 4,682 individual prices and told, "See for yourself, they varied."

Index numbers are statistical measures that are used to give a concise summary answer to the inherently complex questions of the kind just suggested. An **index number** measures the percentage change in some broad average since some base period. As such it points to overall tendencies or general drifts, not to specific single facts. The two most important kinds of index numbers are price indexes and production indexes.

INDEX NUMBERS OF PRICES

A **price index** shows the average percentage change that has occurred in some group of prices over some period of time. The point in time from which the change is measured is called the **base period** (or base year), while the point in time to which the change is measured is called the **given period** (or given year). There are several elements in the definition of index numbers.

First, what group of prices should be used? This depends on the index. The **Consumer Price Index,** known affectionately as the **CPI,** covers prices of commodities commonly bought by households. Changes in the CPI are meant to measure changes in the typical household's "cost of living." The Producer Price Index (formerly the wholesale price index) measures a different group of commodities commonly bought and sold by wholesalers. The "national income deflator" is a price index that covers virtually all of the goods and services produced in the economy; it includes not only the prices of consumer goods and services bought by households but the prices of capital goods such as plant and machinery bought by firms.

Second, what kind of average should be used? If all prices were to change in the same proportion, this would not be an important question. A 10 percent rise in each and every price covered means an average rise of 10 percent no matter how much importance we give to each price change when calculating the average. But what if—as is almost always the case—different prices change differently? Now it does matter how much importance we give to each price change. A rise of 50 percent in the price of caviar is surely much less important to the average consumer than a rise of 40 percent in the price of bread. And this in turn is surely less important than a rise of 30 percent in the cost of housing. Why? The reason is that the typical household spends less on caviar than on bread and less on bread than on housing.

In calculating any price index, statisticians seek to weight each price according to its importance. Let us see how this is done for the CPI. Government statisticians survey periodically a group of households to discover how they spend their incomes. The average bundle of goods bought is calculated, and the quantities in this bundle become the weights attached to the prices. In this way the average price change heavily weights commodities on which consumers spend a lot and and lightly weights commodities on which consumers spend only a little. The procedure is illustrated in Table 3-1.

Finally, how is the average change calculated? This is done by comparing the costs of purchasing the typical bundle of commodities in the base period and in the given year. The given year cost is expressed as a percentage of the base period cost, and this figure is the index number of the new period. Thus, for example, a CPI of 110 means that the cost of purchasing the "representative" bundle of goods is 110 percent of what it was in the base period.

A price index number of a given year tells the ratio of the cost of purchasing a bundle of commodities in that year to the cost of purchasing the same bundle in the base year multiplied by 100 [1][1]

The percentage *change* in the cost of purchasing the bundle is thus the index number minus 100. An index number of 110 indicates a percentage increase in prices of 10 percent over those ruling in the base year.

Some Difficulties

An index number is meant to reflect the broad trend in prices rather than the details. This means that although the information it gives may be extremely valuable, it must be interpreted

[1] Notes giving mathematical demonstrations of the concepts presented in the text are designated by colored reference numbers. These notes can be found beginning on page 930.

TABLE 3–1
The Calculation of a Price Index Covering Three Commodities

Commodity	Quantity in fixed bundle	Base year 1980		Given year 1981	
		Price in 1980	Value in 1980	Price in 1981	Value in 1981
A	500 units	$1.00	$ 500	$2.00	$1,000
B	200 units	5.00	1,000	7.00	1,400
C	50 units	2.00	100	9.60	480
			1,600		2,880

$$\text{Index value 1980} = \frac{1600}{1600} \times 100 = 100$$

$$\text{Index value 1981} = \frac{2880}{1600} \times 100 = 180$$

A price index shows the ratio of the costs of purchasing a fixed bundle of goods between two years (multiplied by 100). The cost of purchasing the fixed bundle is calculated at the prices ruling in each year. The index for year 1981 is the cost of purchasing that bundle in 1981 expressed as a percentage of the cost of purchasing the same bundle in the base year (which is 1980 in this example). The price index is thus always 100 in the base year. The index of 180 means that prices have risen on average by 80 percent between the base year and the year in question. This average weights price changes by their *importance* in the average household's budget in the base year.

with care. Here are three of the many reasons why care is required.

First, the weights in the index refer to an average bundle of goods. This average, although "typical" of what is consumed in the nation, will not be typical of what each household does. The rich, the poor, the young, the old, the single, the married, the urban, and the rural households typically consume bundles that differ from one another. An increase in air fares, for example, will raise the cost of living of a middle-income traveler while leaving that of a poor stay-at-home unaffected. In the example of Table 3-1, the cost of living would have risen by 100 percent, 40 percent, and 380 percent respectively for three different families one of whom consumed only commodity A, one only commodity B, and one only commodity C. The index in the table shows, however, that the cost of living went up by 80 percent for a family that consumed all three goods in the relative quantities indicated.

The more an individual household's consumption pattern diverges from that of the typical pattern used to weight prices in the price index, the less well the price index will reflect the average change in prices relevant to that household.

To assess the importance of this problem, separate indexes are calculated for different subgroups. For example, since January 1980, there has been both an "all-urban" CPI and a separate index for "urban wage and clerical workers." These indexes differ because the typical consumption pattern of wage and clerical workers differs from that of other urban dwellers.

Second, households usually alter their consumption patterns in response to price changes. A price index that shows changes in the cost of purchasing a fixed bundle of goods does not allow for this. For example, a typical cost of living index for middle-income families at the turn of the century would have given heavy weight to the cost of maids and children's nurses. A doubling of servants' wages in 1900 would have greatly increased the middle-class cost of living. Today it would have little effect, for the rising cost of labor has long since caused middle-income families to cease to employ full-time servants. A household that has dispensed altogether with a commodity whose price is rising rapidly does not have its cost of living rise as fast as a household that continues to consume that commodity in an undiminished quantity.

A fixed-weight price index tends to overstate cost of living changes because it does not allow for changes in consumption patterns that shift expenditure away from commodities whose prices rise most and toward those whose prices rise least.

Third, as time goes by, new commodities enter the typical consumption bundle and old ones leave. A cost of living index in 1890 would have had a large item for horse-drawn carriages but no allowance at all for automobiles and gasoline.

A fixed-weight index makes no allowance for the rise of new products nor for the declining importance of old ones in the typical household's consumption bundle.

The longer the period of time that passes, the less some fixed consumption bundle will be typical of current consumption patterns. For this reason the Bureau of Labor Statistics (BLS), the government body responsible for the CPI, makes a new survey of household expenditure patterns about once every 10 years and revises the weights. The base period is then usually changed to conform to the year in which the new set of commodity weights was calculated. At the beginning of the 1980s the CPI stood at 230 (base 1967). This meant that the cost of purchasing the bundle of goods bought by a typical household in 1967 had risen 130 percent in the intervening 13 years. (Thirteen years is a long time for a fixed-weight price index to be used, and at the turn of the decade the BLS was busy estimating a new set of weights preparatory to shifting the base year of the CPI to some year in the early 1980s.)

INDEX NUMBERS OF PHYSICAL OUTPUTS

There are many output indexes, and the Federal Reserve Board's Index of Industrial Production is one of the leading economic indicators. This index stood at 125.8 in June 1974 but had fallen to 110.0 in March 1975. By January 1980 it had reached 152.2. In each case, 1967 was the base period (for which the index was 100). This means that whatever the index measured was 25.8 percent higher in June 1974 than in the base period, but fell 15.8 points (approximately 13 percent) in the next three months. By the end of the decade it was 52 percent above its value in the 1967 base period. To the extent that the index is meaningful it measures both the growth of the American economy in the period 1967–1980 and a recession between mid-1974 and early 1975. But what exactly does the index measure?

Like the price indexes discussed above, it is an average of the changes in thousands of individual items. It is not hard to measure the change in production of tons of steel from month to month or year to year, nor that of tires or television sets. It is somewhat harder to measure the quantity of printing, of furniture, and of aircraft because the unit of output is less well defined; but these too can be approximated.

The compilers of the Index of Industrial Production first compute indexes of the change in quantity of output for individual industries and then combine them into an overall index by using the value of output in each industry as a weighting device. Table 3-2 illustrates in simplified form the kind of computation for a two-industry world. The final computation says the index has increased by 29.2 percent between year zero and year 1. This is the weighted average of the 25 percent increase in production of industry A and the 50 percent increase in industry B. Nothing tangible increased by 29.2 percent. Yet this average reflects the fact that both industries expanded output and that industry A was in the aggregate five times as important as industry B. The procedure used in Table 3-2 can be extended to include thousands of commodities, and this leads to an overall index of physical production. Compilers of index numbers of physical output face many practical problems—which products to include, how to adjust for changes in quality of product, and which values to use as weights.

TABLE 3–2
The Calculation of a Quantity Index

	Output		Quantity relative	Value of output (billions of dollars)	
	Year 0 (Q_0)	Year 1 (Q_1)	Q_1/Q_0	V_0	$\frac{Q_1}{Q_0} \times V_0$
Industry A	40,000 tons	50,000 tons	1.25	$10	$12.5
Industry B	200,000 yards	300,000 yards	1.50	2	3.0
Total				$12	$15.5
Index value (year 0 = 100)				100	129.2

This quantity index weights quantity changes by the relative importance of the quantities in the base year. The increase in quantity in each industry is shown in the "quantity relative" column, Q_1/Q_0. Industry A is more important than industry B, as is shown by V_0, the values of outputs in year zero. Thus industry A gets greater weight in computing the price index. The total value of output in year 0 was $12 billion. The last column shows the increase in value of output caused by the increase in quantity, assuming that prices and relative importance of the two commodities did not change. This computed value is $15.5 billion for year 1. The index for year 1 is

$$\frac{15.5}{12.0} \times 100 = 129.2.$$

THE ACCURACY AND SIGNIFICANCE OF INDEX NUMBERS

Index numbers of either price or output are by their very nature crude approximations. Given the changing nature of goods and products over time (a 1967 car is different from a 1981 car) and the changing relative importance of different commodities (the declining role of food in consumers' total budgets and the rising role of services), any fixed bundle of commodities becomes out of date very quickly. But if an important trend of prices or production is under way, there is need to measure it approximately.

It would be foolish to make very much of the fact that the Consumer Price Index rose from 202.0 to 202.9 (1967 = 100) between November and December 1978, for an index number is the average of many changes. Some prices rose and others fell; some rose a lot, others very little, and so on. When the net change is so small, it may not mean very much by itself. This result, however, taken in conjunction with similar monthly increases throughout that year and the next, revealed a strong inflationary trend.

Index numbers are useful, then, as general indicators. Yet people often become mesmerized by them and treat them as though they had an accuracy that their compilers do not claim for them. Being aware of their limitations should not lead one to neglect index numbers for the useful information they do show: average changes over time.

Measurement and Testing of Economic Relations

It is one thing for economists to theorize that two variables are related to each other; it is quite another for them to be able to say *how* these variables are related. Economists might generalize on the basis of a casual observation that when households receive more income, they are likely to buy more of most commodities. But precisely how much will the consumption of a particular commodity rise as household incomes rise? Are there exceptions to the rule that the purchase of a commodity rises as income rises? For estimating precise magnitudes and for testing general rules or hypotheses, common sense, intuition, and casual observation do not take us very far. More systematic statistical analysis is required.

Statistical analysis is used to test the hypothesis that two things are related and, when they are, to estimate the numerical values of the function that describes the relation.

In practice, the same data can be used simultaneously to test whether a relationship exists and, when it does exist, to provide a measure of it.

TECHNIQUES FOR TESTING THEORIES

The techniques used to test theories differ considerably between those disciplines that can use laboratory methods and those that cannot.

Laboratory Sciences

In some sciences all the observations required for testing theories can be obtained from controlled experiments made under laboratory conditions. In these experiments all the factors that are thought to affect the outcome of the process being studied are held constant. These factors are then varied one by one and the influence of each variation observed.

Suppose chemists have a theory predicting that the rate at which a substance burns is a function of (1) the rate at which oxygen is made available during the process of combustion and (2) the chemical properties of the substance. To test this theory they may take many identical pieces of a substance and burn them, varying the amount of available oxygen in each case. This procedure will show how combustion varies with the quantity of oxygen supplied. They may then take a number of substances with different chemical compositions and burn them, using identical amounts of oxygen in each case. This procedure will show how combustion varies with chemical composition.

Being able to conduct such experiments, scientists are never forced to use data in which both chemical composition and the quantity of oxygen vary at once. Laboratory conditions serve to hold other factors constant and to produce data for situations in which factors can be varied one at a time.

Nonlaboratory Sciences

In many sciences factors cannot be isolated individually in laboratory experiments. In these sciences observations can be used to establish relationships and to test theories, even though they show what happens when several causes operate at the same time.

Consider the hypothesis that the health of an adult depends on that adult's diet as a child. Clearly, hundreds of factors affect the health of adults: heredity, conditions of childhood other than nutrition, and various aspects of adult environment. There is no acceptable way to examine this hypothesis as a controlled experiment, for scientists cannot subject a group of children to varying diets and then ensure that all other influences are the same as each person grows into an adult.

Are we then to conclude that the hypothesis cannot be tested because other factors cannot be held constant? No, because to do so would be to deny many advances in medicine, biology, and other life sciences made during the last 100 years. Testing is more difficult where laboratory methods cannot be used, but not only is it possible, it is frequently done.

In a situation in which many influences vary at once, data must be used carefully. If only two men are studied and it is found that the one with the better nutritional standards during youth has the poorer adult health record, this finding would not disprove the hypothesis that a good diet contributes to better health. It might well be that some other factor has exerted an overwhelming influence. The less healthy man may have lived most of his adult life in a disease-ridden area, while the healthier man may have lived in a relatively healthy place. A single exception does not disprove the hypothesis that two variables are related as long as we admit that other variables can also influence the outcome. But if thousands of people are studied with respect to childhood diet and adult health record, individual irregularities may be expected to cancel out and an underlying regularity to show up.

Contrast this strategy of basing decisions on a

large number of observations with the practice in much ordinary conversation of acting as though a single contrary case disproved a theory. Notice how often one person advances a possible relation (e.g., between legal education and some facet of character) and someone else "refutes" this theory by citing a single counterexample (e.g., "Ralph Nader went to law school and did not turn out like that").

THE STATISTICAL TESTING OF ECONOMIC THEORIES: AN EXAMPLE

Economics is a nonlaboratory science. It is rarely possible to conduct controlled experiments with the economy. However, millions of *uncontrolled experiments* are going on every day. Households are deciding what to purchase in the face of changing prices and incomes; firms are deciding what to produce and how to produce it; and government is intervening with taxes, subsidies, and controls.

Because all these acts can be observed and recorded, a mass of data is produced continually by the economy. Most items in which economists are interested, such as the volume of unemployment, the level of prices, and the distribution of income, are influenced by a large number of factors, all of which vary simultaneously. If economists are to test their theories about relations in the economy, they must use statistical techniques designed for situations in which other things could not be held constant.

Consider testing the hypothesis that the quantity of beef purchased by low-income and middle-income American households increases as their incomes increase. To begin with, observations should be made of household income and beef purchases. It is impossible to list all the households involved, so a small number (called a **sample**) must be observed on the assumption that they are typical of the entire group.

The Sample

We start by observing a sample of three households. The data listed in Table 3-3 may lead us to

TABLE 3–3

Three Observations on Beef Purchases and Income

Household	Household income	Beef purchases, pounds per week
1	$9,000	5.10
2	11,000	5.05
3	13,000	4.93

These three observations suggest that beef purchases go down as income rises, but a sample of three is too small to be reliable.

wonder whether the hypothesis is wrong, but before we jump to that conclusion we note that "by chance" the three households selected may not be typical of all the households in the country. Expenditure on food, for example, is influenced by factors other than income. Possibly these other factors just happen to be the dominant forces in the three cases.

Increasing the number of households in the sample may reduce the chances of consistently picking untypical households. Suppose the next sample checked is larger: it consists of 100 households selected from among friends and acquaintances. A statistician points out, however, that the new group is a *biased* sample, for it contains households from only a limited geographical area, probably with only a limited occupational range, and possibly with incomes very similar to one another. (Since the way in which purchases of beef vary as income varies is of special interest, this last point is likely to have serious consequences.) As a result of these limitations, it is unlikely that this sample of households will be representative of all low-income and middle-income households in the United States, the group in which we are interested.

The statistician suggests that a random sample of households be taken. A **random sample** is one chosen according to a rigidly defined set of conditions that guarantees, among other things, that every household in which we are interested has an equal chance of being selected. Choosing the sample in a random fashion has two important consequences.

First, it becomes more unlikely that the sample will be unrepresentative of all households. Second, and more important, it allows us to calculate just how likely it is that the sample is unrepresentative in any given aspect by any stated amount. This second result is important because it allows us to make statements about the probability that the behavior of all households in the United States will differ by any quantitative amount from that of households in the sample. The reason this can be done is that the sample was chosen by chance and chance events are predictable.

That chance events are predictable may sound paradoxical. But if you pick a card from a deck of ordinary playing cards, how likely is it that you will pick a heart? an ace? an ace of hearts? You play a game in which you pick a card and win if it is a heart and lose if it is anything else; a friend offers you $5 if you win against $1 if you lose. Who will make money if the game is played a large number of times? The same game is played again, but now you get $3 if you win and pay $1 if you lose. Who will make money over a large number of draws? If you know the answers to these questions (we will bet that most of you do), you must believe that chance events are in some sense predictable.

Suppose that a random sample of 4,827 households has been chosen. (How representative the sample is of all relevant households can be checked by comparing some characteristic of the households in it with a result that is known to hold for all American households, e.g., how many have two cars or incomes over $8,000?) Once the sample is chosen and checked for representativeness, the information required from it is collected. In this case, the information desired is the income of each household and its weekly purchases of beef.

Analysis of the Data

There are several ways in which the data may be used to evaluate the hypothesis. One is the scat-

FIGURE 3–1

A Scatter Diagram Relating Beef Purchases to Income

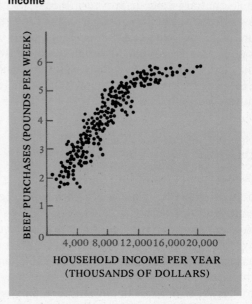

The scatter pattern shows a clear tendency for beef consumption to rise with income. Household income is measured along the horizontal axis and purchases of beef along the vertical axis. Each dot represents the beef purchases of one household. The dots fall within a narrow, rising band, suggesting the existence of a systematic relationship. (There are 4,827 observations in the original sample, but only a sample of these is shown in the figure because a scatter diagram with 4,827 points would be unintelligible.)

ter diagram.[2] Figure 3-1 is a scatter diagram that relates household income to purchases of beef. The pattern of the dots suggests that there is a strong tendency for purchases of beef to be higher, the higher is household income. It thus supports the hypothesis.

There is some scattering of the dots because the relationship is "not perfect"; in other words, there is some variation in food purchases that

[2] The appendix to this chapter outlines the elements of graphs and the graphical analysis of economic data and of functional relations between economic variables. If you find graphical analysis baffling, you might read this appendix now.

cannot be associated with variations in household income. These "unexplained variations" in beef purchases occur for two main reasons. First, factors other than income influence beef purchases, and some of these other factors will undoubtedly have varied between the households in the sample. Second, there will inevitably be some errors in measurement. For example, a household might incorrectly report its beef purchases.

Another way to examine the hypothesis that beef purchases vary directly with income is with a cross-classification table. Table 3-4 cross-classifies households by their income and their average beef purchases. At the loss of considerable detail, the table makes clear the general tendency for beef purchases to rise as income rises.

While both the scatter diagram and the cross-classification table reflect the general relationship between beef purchases and household income, neither concisely characterizes the specific rela-

tionship. **Regression analysis,** a widely used technique, provides quantitative measures of what the relationship is and how closely it holds. Regression analysis may be used if certain conditions are fulfilled.[3] A **regression equation** represents the best estimate of the *average* relationship between household income and beef purchases. Such an equation for our example will describe the tendency for higher household income to be associated with higher consumption of beef.[4]

A measure of how closely the relationship holds can be obtained by calculating the percentage of the variance in household expenditure on beef that can be accounted for by variations in household income.[5] This measure is called the **coefficient of determination (r^2).** It indicates, specifically in this case, the proportion of the variance in beef purchases that can be "explained" by associating it with variations in household incomes.

A "significance test" can be applied to determine the odds that the relation discovered in the sample does not exist for the whole population but has arisen by chance because the households selected happen not to be representative of the American households in which we were interested. It turns out, in this example, that there is less than one chance in 1 million that the rising pattern of dots shown in Figure 3-1 would have been observed if there were no increasing relation between income and beef purchases for U.S. households. Since this chance is very small, we believe the hypothesis that these two variables— beef purchases and household income—are in fact positively related in the United States. Sta-

TABLE 3–4
Income Class and Average Beef Purchases

Annual household income	Average weekly beef purchases in pounds	Number of households
$0– 1,999	2.13	532
2,000– 3,999	2.82	647
4,000– 5,999	3.70	692
6,000– 7,999	4.25	867
8,000– 9,999	4.86	865
10,000–11,999	5.16	513
12,000–13,999	5.20	371
14,000–15,999	5.30	159
16,000–17,999	5.52	121
18,000–19,999	5.90	60

Average beef purchases rise steadily as income rises. This sample of 4,827 U.S. households has been cross-classified according to income and average beef purchases. Thus, in the first row, the 532 households with incomes below $2,000 per year are grouped together and their average beef purchases calculated. In the second row, all households with incomes between $2,000 and $3,999 have been grouped together. This method reduces a mass of 4,827 pairs of observations to a mere 10.

[3] The detailed discussion of techniques and conditions is left to courses in statistics and econometrics.

[4] The equation of a straight line fitted to the data shown in Figure 3-1 is $B = 2.35 + 0.24Y$, where B is purchases of beef in pounds and Y is income in thousands of dollars per year. The equation shows that for every increase of $1,000 in household income, beef consumption tends to increase by about a quarter of a pound per week. The straight line is only an approximation to the true relation, which the scatter diagram suggests has a slight curvature.

[5] *Variance* is a precise statistical measure of the amount of variability (dispersion) in a set of data.

TABLE 3–5

Average Weekly Beef Purchases (in Pounds) Cross-Classified by Income and Price

Annual household income	Average price of beef per pound			
	$1.60–1.99	$2.00–2.39	$2.40–2.79	$2.80–3.19
$0– 3,999	2.65	2.59	2.51	2.43
4,000– 7,999	4.14	4.05	3.94	3.88
8,000–11,999	5.11	5.00	4.97	4.84
12,000–15,999	5.35	5.29	5.19	5.07
16,000–19,999	5.79	5.77	5.60	5.53

Beef purchases vary directly with income and inversely with price. Each row in the table shows the effect of price on the purchases of beef for a given level of income. For example, reading across the second row, households with incomes between $4,000 and $7,999 bought an average of 4.14 pounds of beef when the price was between $1.60 and $1.99, 4.05 pounds when the price was between $2.00 and $2.39, and so on. The declining numbers across each row suggest that beef purchases decline as prices rise, for particular income groups. Each column of the table shows the effect of income on purchases of beef for a given price of beef.

tistically the relationship is said to be "significant."

Extending the Analysis

The scatter diagram shows that *all* the variation in households' purchases of beef cannot be accounted for by observed variations in household income. If it could, all the dots would lie on a line. Since they do not, some other factors must influence food expenditure. What could make one household with an income of $12,000 buy 20 percent more beef than another household with the same income?

One possible reason is that households in different parts of the country may have been faced with different prices of beef. (There will be other reasons, such as family size and religion, but price is an important second reason.) Assume that the survey also collected data on the prices of various cuts of beef in each city or town from which a household in the sample bought its meat. These data were then used to calculate the average price of beef facing each household.

There are now *three* observations for each of the 4,827 households: annual income, weekly purchases of beef, and average price of beef facing it. How should these data be handled? Unfortunately, the scatter diagram technique is not available because the relation between three data cannot easily be shown on a two-dimensional graph.

Instead the data may once again be grouped. This time there are two variables that are thought to influence beef consumption, and the data have to be cross-classified in a more complicated manner, as shown in Table 3-5. (To prevent the table from becoming too large, households have been lumped into income groups of $4,000. This is only a matter of convenience; the classification can be made as detailed as required.)

The device of cross-classification shown in Table 3-5 demonstrates clearly the way in which we hold one variable constant while allowing another to vary. Reading across any row, income is held constant within a specified range and price is being varied; reading down any column, price is held constant within a specified range and income is being varied.

To estimate a numerical relation between household income, average price, and beef purchases, **multiple regression analysis** may be used.[6] It allows estimation of both the separate and joint effects on beef purchases of variations

---

[6] Where three or more variables are involved, "multiple" rather than "simple" regression is used. The symbol R^2 (instead of r^2) is used for the coefficient of determination in a multiple regression analysis.

in the price of beef and variations in household income by fitting to the data an equation that "best" describes them. It also permits measurement of the proportion of the total variation in beef purchases that can be explained by associating it with variations both in income and in price. Finally, it permits use of significance tests to determine how likely it is that the relations found in the sample are the result of chance rather than an underlying relationship for all U.S. households. Chance enters because, by bad luck, an unrepresentative sample of households might have been chosen.

EVALUATING THE EVIDENCE

Statistical techniques can help to measure the nature and strength of economic relationships and show how probable it is that a certain result has occurred by chance. What they cannot do is prove that a hypothesis is either true or false. Nor can they tell us when the hypothesis should be accepted or rejected.

Can a Hypothesis Be Proven True or False?

Most hypotheses in economics are universal hypotheses. They say that whenever certain specified conditions are fulfilled, cause X will always produce effect Y. Such universal hypotheses cannot be proven correct with 100 percent certainty. No matter how many observations are collected that agree with the hypothesis, there is always some chance that a long series of untypical observations has been made or that there have been systematic errors of observation. After all, the mass of well-documented evidence accumulated several centuries ago on the existence of the power of witches is no longer accepted, even though it fully satisfied most contemporary observers. The existence of observational errors — even on a vast scale — has been shown to be possible, although (one fervently hopes) it is not very frequent. Observations that disagree with the theory may begin to accumulate, and after

some time a theory that looked nearly certain may begin to look rather shaky.

By the same token a universal hypothesis can never be proven false with 100 percent certainty. Even when current observations consistently conflict with the theory, there are the same possibilities of the selection of a large number of untypical cases or systematic errors of observation. For instance, evidence was once gathered "disproving" the hypothesis that high income taxes tend to discourage work. More recent research suggests that economists may have been wrong to reject the theory that high taxes tend to discourage work. As a result of measurement errors and bad experimental design, the conflicting evidence may not have been as decisive as was once thought.

There is no absolute certainty in any knowledge. No doubt some of the things we now think true will eventually turn out to be false, and some of the things we currently think false will eventually turn out to be true. Yet while we can never be certain, we can assess the balance of evidence.

Some hypotheses are so unlikely to be true, given current evidence, that for all practical purposes we may regard them as false. Other hypotheses are so unlikely to be false, given current evidence, that for all practical purposes we may regard them as true.

This kind of practical decision must always be regarded as tentative. Every once in a while we will discover that we have to change our mind: something that looked right will begin to look doubtful, or something that looked wrong will begin to look possible.

The Decision to Reject or Accept

In general, a hypothesis can never be proved or refuted conclusively, no matter how many observations are made. Nonetheless, since decisions have to be made, it is necessary to accept some hypotheses (to act as if they were proven) and reject some hypotheses (to act as if they were refuted). Just as a jury can make two kinds of errors (finding an innocent person guilty or letting a guilty person go free) so can statistical decision makers make two kinds of errors. They can reject hypotheses that are true, and they can accept hypotheses that are false. Luckily, like a jury, they can also make correct decisions—and indeed they expect to do so most of the time.

Although the possibility of error cannot be eliminated in statistics, it can be controlled.

The method of control is to decide in advance how large a risk to take of rejecting a hypothesis if it is in fact correct.[7] Conventionally in statistics this risk is often set at 5 percent or 1 percent. When the 5 percent cutoff point is used, we will reject the hypothesis if the results that appear to contradict it could have happened by chance no more than one time in 20. Using the 1 percent decision rule gives the hypothesis a greater measure of reasonable doubt. A hypothesis is rejected only if the results that appear to contradict it could have happened by chance no more than one time in 100.

When action must be taken, some rule of thumb is necessary. But it is important to understand, first, that no one can ever be *certain* about being right in rejecting any hypothesis and, second, that there is nothing magical about arbitrary cutoff points. Some cutoff point must be used whenever decisions have to be made.

Finally, recall that the rejection of a hypothesis is seldom the end of inquiry. Decisions can be reversed should new evidence come to light. Often the result of a statistical test of a theory is to suggest a new hypothesis that "fits the facts" better than the old one. Indeed, in some cases just looking at a scatter diagram or making a regression analysis uncovers apparent relations that no one anticipated and leads economists to formulate a new hypothesis.

---

[7] Return to the jury analogy: Our notion of a person being innocent unless the jury is persuaded of guilt "beyond a reasonable doubt" rests on our wishing to take only a small risk of rejecting the hypothesis of innocence if the person being tried is in fact innocent.

Summary

1. Index numbers are summary measures that give the average percentage change in a set of related items between a "base" year and another "given" year.

2. The Consumer Price Index (CPI) measures the percentage change in the cost of purchasing a typical bundle of commodities since the base year. It is thus a measure of the average change in prices in which each price is "weighted" by the importance of that commodity in the typical consumption bundle.

3. Some problems with index numbers are: (1) the weights on which they are based are broad averages that do not reflect each individual's expenditure pattern, (2) the fixed weights make no allowance for changes in consumption patterns that occur in response to price changes, and (3) the fixed weights cannot allow for important new products, the decline of old ones, and changes in the quality of commodities that continue to be bought. For these and other reasons the weights are revised periodically.

4. Quantity indexes measure average changes in quantities of commodities where each quantity is weighted by its value in the base year.

5. Index numbers measure broad trends, and therefore not too much importance should be given to small changes. However, they provide very valuable information—provided it is understood that they are only meant to reflect major changes.

6. Theories are tested by checking their predictions against actual evidence. In some sciences, these tests can be conducted under laboratory conditions where only one thing changes at a time. In other sciences, testing must be done using the data produced by the world of ordinary events, where many factors are changing all at once. Modern statistical analysis is designed to test hypotheses where many variables are changing at once.

7. Sample data are often used in testing economic hypotheses. If the sample is random, the probability of the measured characteristics of the sample being misleading (because of the unlucky choice of a nonrepresentative sample) can be calculated.

8. Scatter diagrams are relatively simple devices for exploring the presence of systematic relationships between two variables. Regression analysis permits more specific measures of the relationship: what it is, how closely it holds, and whether or not it is "significant."

9. Hypotheses involving several variables require more sophisticated statistical techniques such as use of complex cross-classification tables and multiple regression analysis, each of which attempts to identify the separate and joint effects of several variables on one another.

10. While statistical tests allow us to assess the probability that what we observe is consistent with a particular hypothesis, they never allow determination of the truth or falsity of a hypothesis beyond any doubt. Because it is often necessary to act as though certain hypotheses are true and others false, decision rules may be required. Two frequently used cutoff points are 5 percent and 1 percent.

11. Methods of graphing economic observations and functional relations are further discussed in the appendix to this chapter.

Topics for Review

Price indexes and quantity indexes
Base years and given years
Quantity weights in price indexes
Value weights in quantity indexes
Problems with fixed-weight indexes calculated over long time periods
The twofold role of statistical analysis: measurement and testing
Cross-classification tables

The difference between proving a hypothesis true and accepting the hypothesis
The difference between proving a hypothesis false and rejecting the hypothesis

Discussion Questions

1. According to a senior vice-president of Mellon Bank: "When it comes to forecasting the economy, the stock market has as good a record—if not better—than most economists." Can this hypothesis be tested? If so, how? If not, why not?

2. In the seventies the cost of automobile insurance rose sharply. The American Automobile Association said its increase was due not (as some charged) to the passage by many states of no-fault insurance laws but to the inflation in the cost of parts used in repairing cars. How might the AAA's hypothesis be tested?

3. "The simplest way to see that capital punishment is a strong deterrent to murder is to ask yourself whether you might be more inclined to commit murder if you knew in advance that you ran no risk of ending in the electric chair, the gas chamber, or on the gallows." Comment on the methodology of social investigation implied in this statement. What alternative approach would you suggest?

4. There are hundreds of eyewitnesses to the existence of flying saucers and other UFOs. There are films and eyewitness accounts of Nessie, the Loch Ness monster. Are you persuaded of their existence? If not, what would it take to persuade you? If so, what would it take to make you change your mind?

5. What is the role of the law of large numbers in making economic statements testable? Does not the fact that it depends on errors mean that any science that relies on it will be inviting errors?

6. A classic example of biased sampling was the attempt made by the *Literary Digest* in 1936 to predict the result of the presidential election. The magazine forecast a substantial Republican victory, and its subsequent demise has been attributed to this error. (Franklin D. Roosevelt won every state but Maine and Vermont from Republican Alfred Landon, and the political platitude "As Maine goes, so goes the nation" was reworded to "As Maine goes, so goes Vermont.") The Literary Digest poll was based on a random sample of names in telephone directories. Can you spot a potential flaw in this sample? Remember that this happened in 1936. Would the same bias have existed if the survey

had been made in 1976? By 1948 the selection of the sample was much more sophisticated, but the Roper polls predicted Dewey over Truman by such a substantial margin that polling was discontinued after September 30. Truman, of course, won the election. What was the nature of the sampling error this time?

7. Look up in the *Economic Report of the President* the behavior of the major categories of the CPI over the last two years. Compare the rise in the costs of living of someone who spent most of his income on food and someone who spent her income in proportion to the overall CPI weights. What commodity groups would have heavy weights in the budget of a person whose cost of living had risen much less than the average? What about the budget of a person whose cost of living had risen much more than the average?

8. Look up the CPIs for ''all urban'' and for ''urban wage and clerical workers.'' How much have they diverged since January 1980? How much difference would it have made if individuals in each group had their money wages tied to their own CPI rather than to the overall CPI?

An Overview of the Economy

The Evolution of Market Economies

The great seventeenth century British political philosopher Thomas Hobbes described life in a state of nature as "nasty, brutish and short." Modern study of the several surviving food-gathering societies suggests that Hobbes' ideas were wide of the mark. In fact societies in the pre-agricultural stage are characterized by a

relative simplicity of the material culture (only 94 items exist among Kung bushmen); the lack of accumulation of individual wealth [and mobility]. . . . Subsistence requirements are satisfied by only a modest effort—perhaps two or three days work a week by each adult; they do not have to struggle over food resources; the attitudes toward ownership are flexible and their living groups open. Such features set hunters and gatherers apart from more technologically developed societies whose very survival depends upon their ability to maintain order and to control property.[1]

Most of the characteristic problems of economics do not arise in these primitive societies. Indeed the economic problem as we know it today has been with us a mere eight or ten thousand years, or relatively little more than an instant of the millions of years in which humanoid creatures have been on earth. It began with the original agricultural revolution, when human beings first found it possible to stay in one place and survive. Gradually abandoning their nomadic life of hunting and food gathering, people settled down to tend crops that they had learned

[1] *The Times Atlas of World History* (Maplewood, N.J.: Hammond, 1979), page 39.

to plant and animals that they had learned to domesticate. All societies since that time have faced the problem of choice under conditions of scarcity.

SURPLUS, SPECIALIZATION, AND TRADE

Along with permanent settlement, the agricultural revolution brought surplus production: farmers could produce substantially more than they needed to survive. The agricultural surplus allowed the creation of new occupations and thus new economic and social classes such as artisans, soldiers, priests, and government officials. Freed from having to grow their own food, these new classes turned their talents to performing specialized services and producing goods other than food. They also produced more than they themselves needed, so they traded the excess to obtain whatever they required.

Economists called this allocation of different jobs to different people **specialization of labor.** Specialization has proven extraordinarily efficient compared to universal self-sufficiency for at least two reasons. First, individual talents and abilities differ, and specialization allows each person to do the job he or she can do relatively best, while leaving everything else to be done by others. People not only do their thing; they do their own best thing. Second, a person who concentrates on one activity becomes better at it than could a jack-of-all-trades.

The exchange of goods and services in early societies commonly took place by simple mutual agreement among neighbors. In the course of time, however, trading became centered in particular gathering places called markets. Today we use the term **market economy** to refer to a society in which people specialize in productive activities and meet most of their material wants through exchanges voluntarily agreed upon by the contracting parties.

Specialization must be accompanied by trade. People who produce only one thing must trade most of it to obtain all the other things they require.

The earliest market economies depended on **barter,** the trading of goods directly for other goods. But barter can be a very costly process in terms of time spent searching out satisfactory exchanges. *Money* evolved to make trade easier. It eliminates the inconvenience of barter by allowing the two sides of the barter transaction to be separated. If a farmer has wheat and wants a hammer, he does not have to search for an individual who has a hammer and wants wheat. He merely has to find someone who wants wheat. The farmer takes money in exchange, then finds another person who wishes to trade a hammer and swaps the money for the hammer.

By eliminating the need for barter, money greatly facilitates trade and specialization.

FACTOR SERVICES AND DIVISION OF LABOR

Market transactions in early economies mainly involved goods and services for consumption. Producers specialized in making a commodity and then traded it for the other products they needed. The labor services required to make the product would usually be provided by the makers themselves, by apprentices learning to be craftsmen, or by slaves. Over the last several hundred years many technical advances in methods of production have made it efficient to organize agriculture and industry on a very large scale. These technical developments have made use of what is called the **division of labor.** This term refers to specialization within the production process of a particular commodity. The labor involved is divided into a series of repetitive tasks, and each individual does a single task that may be just one of hundreds of tasks necessary to produce the commodity. Today it is possible for an individual to work on a production line without knowing what commodity emerges at the end of that line!

To gain the advantages of the division of labor it became necessary to organize production in large and expensive factories. With this development workers lost their status as craftsmen (or peasants) and became members of the working class, wholly dependent on their ability to sell their labor to factory (or farm) owners and lacking a plot of land to fall back on for subsistence in times of need. The day of small craftsmen who made and sold their own goods was over. Today's typical workers do not earn their incomes by selling commodities they personally have produced; rather they sell their labor services to firms and receive money wages in return. They have increasingly become cogs in a machine that they do not fully understand or control.

SCARCITY AND THE ALLOCATION OF RESOURCES

The term **allocation of resources** refers to the way in which the available factors of production are distributed among the various uses to which they might be put. All economies that have existed since the original agricultural revolution have been faced with the problem of scarcity. There are not enough resources to produce all of the goods and services that could be consumed. It is therefore necessary to allocate the available resources among their various possible uses and in so doing to choose what to produce and what not to produce. In a market economy, millions of consumers decide what commodities to buy and in what quantities; a vast number of firms produce these commodities and buy the factor services that are needed to make them; and millions of factor owners decide to whom they will sell these services. These individual decisions collectively determine the economy's allocation of resources.

In a market economy, the allocation of resources is the outcome of countless independent decisions made by consumers and producers, all acting through the medium of markets.

Our main objective in this chapter is to provide an overview of this market mechanism.

The Decision Makers

Economics is about the behavior of people. Much that we observe in the world, and that

economists assume in their theories, can be traced back to decisions made by individuals. There are millions of individuals in most economies. To make a systematic study of their behavior more manageable, we categorize them into three important groups: households, firms, and central authorities. These groups are economic theory's cast of characters, and the stage on which their play is enacted is the market.

HOUSEHOLDS

A **household** is defined as all the people who live under one roof and who make, or are subject to others making for them, joint financial decisions. Economic theory gives households a number of attributes.

First, it assumes that each household makes consistent decisions, as though it were composed of a single individual. Thus economists ignore many interesting problems of how the household reaches its decisions. Intrafamily conflicts and the moral and legal problems concerning parental control over minors are dealt with by other social sciences.[2] These problems are avoided in economics by the assumption that the household is the basic decision-making atom of consumption behavior.

Second, we assume that each household is consistently attempting to achieve some goal when it makes choices. In demand theory we assume that the goal of the household is the maximization of its *satisfaction* or *well-being* or *utility,* as the concept is variously called. The household tries to do this within the limitations of its available resources.

Third, we assume that households are the principal owners of factors of production. They sell the services of these factors to firms and receive their incomes in return.

Is it correct to assume that factors of production are principally owned by households? It is

---

[2] In academic work, as elsewhere, a division of labor is useful. However, it is important to remember that when economists speak of *the* consumer or *the* individual, they are in fact referring to the group of individuals composing the household. Thus, for example, the commonly heard phrase *consumer sovereignty* really means *household sovereignty.*

The Division of Labor

Adam Smith began his famous treatise on *The Wealth of Nations* with a long study of the division of labor. Among other things, he had this to say.

The greatest improvements in the productive powers of labour ... have been the effects of the division of labour.

To take an example ... the trade of the pinmaker; a workman not educated to this business (which the division of labour has rendered a distinct trade), nor acquainted with the use of the machinery employed in it could scarce, perhaps, with his utmost industry, make one pin in a day, and certainly could not make twenty. But in the way in which this business is now carried on ... it is divided into a number of branches. ... One man draws out the wire, another straightens it, a third cuts it, a fourth points it, a fifth grinds it at the top for receiving the head; to make the head requires two or three distinct operations; to put it on, is a peculiar business, to whiten the pins is another; it is even a trade by itself to put them into the paper; and the important business of making a pin is, in this manner, divided into about eighteen distinct operations, which, in some manufactories, are all performed by distinct hands, though in others the same man will sometimes perform two or three of them.

Smith observes that even in smallish factories, where the division of labor is exploited only in part, output is as high as 4,800 pins per person per day!

Later Smith discusses the general importance of the division of labor and the forces that limit its application.

Each animal is still obliged to support and defend itself, separately and independently, and derives no sort of advantage from that variety of talents with which nature has distinguished its fellows. Among men, on the contrary, the most dissimilar geniuses are of use to one another; the different produces of their respective talents, by the general disposition to truck, barter, and exchange, being brought, as it were, into a common stock, where every man may purchase whatever part of the produce of other men's talents he has occasion for.

As it is the power of exchanging that gives occasion to the division of labour, so the extent of this division must always be limited by the extent of that power, or, in other words, by the extent of the market. When the market is very small, no person can have any encouragement to dedicate himself entirely to one employment for want [i.e., lack] of the power to exchange all that surplus part of the produce of his own labour, which is over and above his own consumption, for such parts of the produce of other men's labour as he has occasion for.

Smith notes that there is no point in specializing to produce a large quantity of pins, or anything else, unless there are enough persons making other commodities to provide a market for all the pins that are produced. Thus the larger the market, the greater the scope for the division of labor and the higher the resulting opportunities for efficient production.

---

obvious that labor is "owned" by those individuals who sell their labor and receive wages and salaries in return. Most capital equipment is owned by firms; but firms are in turn owned by households. Corporations, for example, are owned by the households that hold those companies' stocks. These households provide firms with the money needed to carry on business, and they receive the firms' profits as their income. Land is owned by households and firms — which are in turn owned by households. A household may use its land itself, or it may make the land available to some other user in return for rent, which becomes the household's income.[3]

Again, we assume that in making these decisions on how much to sell and to whom to sell it, each household seeks to maximize its utility.

[3] The main group that owns capital and land without itself being a household, or being owned by a household, is the government.

FIRMS

A **firm** is defined as the unit that employs factors of production to produce commodities that it sells to other firms, to households, or to the central authorities (defined below). For obvious reasons a firm is often called a *producer*. Economic theory gives firms several attributes.

First, economists assume that each firm makes consistent decisions, as though it were composed of a single individual. Thus economic theory ignores the internal problems of who reaches particular decisions and how they are reached. In doing this, economists assume that the firm's internal organization is irrelevant to its decisions. This allows them to treat the firm as the atom of behavior on the production or supply side of commodity markets, just as the household is treated as the atom of behavior on the consumption or demand side.

Second, economists assume that most firms make their decisions with a single goal in mind: to make as much profit as possible.[4] This goal of *profit maximization* is analogous to the household's goal of utility maximization. There is a difference, however; although household satisfaction cannot be directly measured, a firm's profits can be. (The assumption of profit maximization has come under serious criticism, and currently there are several competing theories of the motivation of firms. Alternative theories of firm behavior are treated later in the micro part of this book. Meanwhile, we can go far using the simple assumption of profit maximization.)

Third, economists assume that firms in their role as producers are the principal users of the services of factors of production. In markets where factor services are bought and sold, the roles of firms and households are thus reversed from what they are in commodity markets: in factor markets firms do the buying and households do the selling.

[4] There is a second class of firms: nonprofit organizations such as hospitals and private universities. They employ factors of production to produce a commodity that they sell on the market. But they are in business as a public service, not to make profits.

CENTRAL AUTHORITIES

The **central authorities,** often called "the government," are defined to be public agencies, government bodies, and other organizations belonging to or under the direct control of governments. State and local governments, as well as the federal government, are included. In the United States, the term "central authorities" includes the president, the Federal Reserve System, the city council, commissions and regulatory bodies, the legislature, the police force, and all other government bodies that exercise control over the behavior of firms and households. It is not important to draw up a comprehensive list of all central authorities, but one should have in mind a general idea of the organizations that have legal and political power to exert control over individual decision makers and over markets.

It is *not* a basic assumption of economics that the central authorities always act in a consistent fashion or as though they were a single individual. Three important reasons for this may be mentioned here. First, the mayor of Los Angeles, a Utah state legislator and a United States senator from Maine represent different constituencies, and therefore they may express different and conflicting views and objectives.

Second, individual public servants, whether elected or appointed, have personal objectives (such as staying in office, achieving higher office, power, prestige, and personal aggrandizement) as well as public service objectives. Although the balance of importance given to the two types of objectives will vary among persons and among types of office, both will almost always have some importance. It would be a rare senator, for example, who would vote against a measure that slightly reduced the "public good" if this vote almost guaranteed his defeat at the next election. ("After all," he could reason, "if I am defeated, I won't be around to vote against *really* bad measures.")

Third, the whole system of checks and balances is designed to set one part of the government against another part, thereby producing the characteristic American pluralism in government. (Here American practice differs sharply from that of most of the rest of the English-speaking world, whose governments are based on the British parliamentary system that was not designed to produce pluralism.) For all of these reasons in America, and for most of them in other countries, conflict between different central bodies is the subject of much of the theory about the control of the economy.

OTHER DECISION MAKERS

Although in basic economic theory we can get away with three sets of decision makers, it is worth noting that there are others. Probably the most important are charities such as the American Cancer Society and funding organizations such as the Ford Foundation. These bodies are responsible for allocating some of the economy's resources. They ensure, for example, that resources are channeled to medical and academic research. In most cases, however, these organizations do not directly produce goods.

Markets and Economies

We have seen that firms, households, and central authorities are the main actors in the economic drama. Their action takes place in individual markets.

MARKETS

The word "market" originally designated a place where goods were traded. The Fulton Fish Market in New York is a world-famous modern example of markets in the everyday sense, and most cities have produce markets where fresh produce is brought early in the morning and promptly sold. Much early economic theory attempted to explain price behavior in just such markets. Why, for example, can you sometimes obtain tremendous bargains at the end of the day and at other times get what you want only at prices that appear exorbitant in relation to prices quoted only a few hours before?

As theories of market behavior were devel-

oped, they were extended to cover commodities such as wheat. Wheat produced anywhere in the world can be purchased almost anywhere else in the world, and the price of a given grade of wheat tends to be nearly uniform the world over. When we talk about the wheat market, the concept of a market has been extended well beyond the idea of a single place to which the producer, the store-keeper, and the homemaker go to sell and to buy.

For present purposes, a **market** is satisfactorily defined as an area over which buyers and sellers negotiate the exchange of a well-defined commodity. Economists distinguish two broad types of markets: **product markets,** in which firms sell their outputs of goods and services, and **factor markets,** in which households sell the services of the factors of production they control.

ECONOMIES

An **economy** is rather loosely defined as a set of interrelated production and consumption activities. It may refer to this activity in a region of one country (*the economy of New England*); it may refer to this activity in a country (*the American economy*); or it may refer to this activity in a group of countries (*the economy of Western Europe*). In any economy the allocation of resources is determined by the production, sales, and purchase decisions made by firms, households, and central authorities.

A **free-market economy** is an economy in which the decisions of individual households and firms (as distinct from the central authorities) exert the major influence over the allocation of resources.[5]

The opposite of a free-market economy is a **command economy,** in which the major decisions

[5] Free-market economies are sometimes called capitalist economies; in fact, the term "capitalist" is often used as a synonym for "free market." In Marxist literature "capitalist" refers to the private ownership of the factor of production, capital. But it is possible to be capitalist in Marx's sense of the word and yet have overwhelming public intervention into markets. Thus "capitalist" (private ownership of capital) does not mean the same as "free (uncontrolled) market." For most purposes of modern economics, it is who controls the markets rather than who owns the capital that is the important matter.

about the allocation of resources are made by the central authorities and in which firms and households produce and consume only as they are ordered.

The terms *free market* and *command economy* are used to describe tendencies that are apparent, even though no real economies rely solely either on free markets or on commands. Thus in practice all economies are **mixed economies** in the sense that some decisions are made by firms and households and some by central authorities.

SECTORS OF AN ECONOMY

Parts of an economy are usually referred to as **sectors** of that economy. For example, the agricultural sector is the part of the economy that produces agricultural commodities.

Market and Nonmarket Sectors

Producers make commodities. Consumers use them. There are two basic ways in which commodities may pass from one group to the other: they may be sold by producers and bought by consumers through markets; or they may be given away.

When commodities are bought and sold, producers must cover their costs with the revenue they obtain from selling the product. We call this production *marketed production,* and we refer to this part of the country's activity as belonging to the **market sector.**

When the product is given away, the costs of production must be covered from some source other than sales revenue. We call this production *nonmarketed production,* and we refer to this part of the country's activity as belonging to the **nonmarket sector.** In the case of private charities, the money required to pay for factor services may be raised from the public by voluntary contributions. In the case of production by governments—which accounts for the bulk of nonmarketed production—the money is provided from government revenue, which in turn comes mainly from taxes.

Whenever a government enterprise *sells* its output, its production is in the market sector. But much state output is in the nonmarket sector by the very nature of the product provided. For example, one could hardly expect the criminal to pay the judge for providing the service of criminal justice. Other products are in the nonmarket sector because governments have decided that there are advantages to removing them from the market sector. This is the case, for example, with most of American education. Public policy places it in the nonmarket sector even though much of it could be provided by the market sector.

All of a country's national product can be assigned to either the market sector or the nonmarket sector of the economy.[6]

The Public and Private Sectors

The productive activity of a country is often divided in a different way than between market and nonmarket sectors. In this alternative division, the **private sector** refers to all production that is in private hands and the **public sector** refers to all production that is in public hands. The distinction between the two sectors depends on the legal distinction of ownership. In the private sector, the organization that does the producing is owned by households or other firms; in the public sector, it is owned by the state. The public sector includes all production of goods and services by central authorities plus all production by nationalized industries that is sold to consumers through ordinary markets.

The distinction between market and nonmarket sectors is economic: it depends on whether or not the costs of producing commodities are recovered by selling them to their users. The distinction between the private and the public sectors is legal: it depends on whether the producing organizations are privately or publicly owned.

---

[6] The assignment is obvious when the product is sold for a price that covers its full costs or is given at a zero price. But what of products that are sold for a price that does not cover full costs? In these cases production falls partly into one sector and partly into the other. If, for example, 10 percent of costs is covered by small charges made to users and 90 percent by the government, then the production is 10 percent in the market sector and 90 percent in the nonmarket sector.

HOW INDIVIDUAL MARKETS WORK: AN OVERVIEW OF MICROECONOMICS

Early economists observed the market economy with wonder. They saw that most commodities were made by a large number of independent producers and yet in approximately the quantities that people wanted to purchase them. Natural disasters aside, there were neither vast surpluses nor severe shortages of products. They also saw that in spite of the ever-changing requirements in terms of geographical, industrial, and occupational patterns, most laborers were able to sell their services to employers most of the time.

How does the market produce this order in the absence of conscious coordination by the central authorities? It is one thing to have the same good produced year in and year out when people's wants and incomes do not change; it is quite another thing to have production adjusting continually to changing wants, incomes, and techniques of production. Yet this *relatively* smooth adjustment is accomplished by the market—albeit with occasional, and sometimes serious, interruptions.

The great discovery of eighteenth century economists was that the price system is a social control mechanism.

Adam Smith, in his classic *The Wealth of Nations,* published in 1776, spoke of the price system as "the invisible hand." It allows decision making to be decentralized under the control of millions of individual producers and consumers but nonetheless to be coordinated. Two examples may help to illustrate how this coordination occurs.

A Change in Demand

For the first example, assume that households wish to purchase more of some commodity than previously. To see the market's reaction to such a change, imagine a situation in which farmers find it equally profitable to produce either of two crops, carrots or brussels sprouts, and so are willing to produce some of both commodities, thereby satisfying the demands of households who wish to consume both. Now imagine that consumers develop a greatly increased desire for brussels sprouts and a diminished desire for carrots. This change might have occurred because of the discovery of hitherto unsuspected nutritive or curative powers of brussels sprouts, or it might have been the result of a successful advertising campaign on the part of the association of brussels sprout producers: "Eat brussels sprouts; they're grown *above* ground." Whatever the reason, there has been a major shift toward sprouts and away from carrots.

What will be the effects of this shift? When consumers buy more brussels sprouts and fewer carrots, a shortage of brussels sprouts and a glut of carrots develop. In order to unload their surplus stocks of carrots, merchants reduce the price of carrots—in the belief that it is better to sell them at a reduced price than not to sell them at all. Sellers of brussels sprouts, however, find that they are unable to satisfy all their customers' demands for that product. Sprouts have become a scarce commodity, so the merchants charge more for them. As the price rises, fewer people are willing and able to purchase sprouts. Thus making them more expensive limits the demand for them to the available supply.

Farmers see a rise in the price of brussels sprouts and a fall in the price of carrots. Brussels sprout production has become more profitable than in the past: the costs of producing sprouts remain unchanged at the same time that their market price has risen. Similarly, carrot production will be less profitable than in the past because costs are unchanged but the price has fallen. Attracted by high profits in brussels sprouts and deterred by low profits or potential losses in carrots, farmers expand the production of sprouts and curtail the production of carrots. Thus the change in consumers' tastes, working through the price system, causes a reallocation of resources—land and labor—out of carrot production and into brussels sprout production.

As the production of carrots declines, the glut

of carrots on the market diminishes and their price begins to rise. On the other hand, the expansion in brussels sprout production reduces the shortage and the price begins to fall. These price movements will continue until it no longer pays farmers to contract carrot production and to expand brussels sprout production. When the dust settles, the price of sprouts is higher than it was originally but lower than it was when the shortage sent the price soaring before output could be adjusted; and the price of carrots is lower than it was originally but higher than when the initial glut sent the price tumbling before output could be adjusted.

The reaction of the market to a change in demand leads to a transfer of resources. Carrot producers reduce their production; they will therefore be laying off workers and generally demanding fewer factors of production. Brussels sprout producers expand production; they will therefore be hiring workers and generally increasing their demand for factors of production.

Labor can probably switch from carrot to sprout production without much difficulty. Certain types of land, however, may be better suited for growing one crop rather than the other. When farmers increase their sprout production, their demands for those factors especially suited to sprout production also increase—and this creates a shortage of these resources and a consequent rise in their prices. Meanwhile, with carrot production falling, the demand for land and other factors of production especially suited to carrot growing is reduced. A surplus results, and the prices of these factors are forced down.

Thus factors particularly suited to sprout production will earn more and will obtain a higher share of total national income than before. Factors particularly suited to carrot production, however, will earn less and will obtain a smaller share of the total national income than before.

Changes of this kind will be studied more fully later; the important thing to notice now is how a change in demand initiated by a change in consumers' tastes causes a reallocation of resources in the direction required to cater to the new set of tastes.

A Change in Supply

For a second example, consider a change originating with producers. Begin as before by imagining a situation in which farmers find it equally profitable to produce either sprouts or carrots and in which consumers are willing to buy, at prevailing market prices, the quantities of these two commodities that are being produced. Now imagine that, at existing prices, farmers become more willing to produce sprouts than in the past and less willing to produce carrots. This shift might be caused, for example, by a change in the costs of producing the two goods—a rise in carrot costs and a fall in sprout costs that would raise the profitability of sprout production and lower that of carrot production.

What will happen now? For a short time, nothing at all; the existing supply of sprouts and carrots on the market is the result of decisions made by farmers at some time in the past. But farmers now begin to plant fewer carrots and more sprouts, and soon the quantities on the market begin to change. The quantity of sprouts available for sale rises, and the quantity of carrots falls. A shortage of carrots and a glut of sprouts results. The price of carrots consequently rises, and the price of sprouts falls. This provides the incentive for two types of adjustments. First, households will buy fewer carrots and more sprouts. Second, farmers will move back into carrot production and out of sprout production.

This example began with a situation in which there was a shortage of carrots that caused the price of carrots to rise. The rise in the price of carrots removed the shortage in two ways: it reduced the quantity of carrots demanded and it increased the quantity offered for sale (in response to the rise in the profitability of carrot production). Remember that there was also a surplus of brussels sprouts that caused the price to fall. The fall in price removed the surplus in two ways: it encouraged the consumers to buy more of this commodity and it reduced the quantity of sprouts produced and offered for sale (in response to a fall in the profitability of sprout production).

These examples illustrate a general point:

The price system is a mechanism that coordinates individual, decentralized decisions.

The existence of such a control mechanism is beyond dispute. How well it works in comparison with alternative coordinating systems has been in serious dispute for over a hundred years. It remains today a major unsettled social question.

The Circular Flow: From Microeconomics to Macroeconomics

Figure 4-1 illustrates the two sets of markets, factor markets and product markets, through which the decisions of firms and households are coordinated. Consider households first. The members of households want commodities to keep them fed, clothed, housed, entertained, healthy, and secure; they also want them to educate, edify, beautify, stupefy, and otherwise amuse themselves. Households have, in varying amounts, resources with which to attempt to satisfy these wants. But all of them cannot be satisfied with the resources available. Households are forced, therefore, to make choices as to what goods and services to buy in product markets that offer them myriad ways to spend their incomes.

The signals to which households respond are product-market prices; for each given set of prices, households make a set of choices. In so doing they also, in the aggregate, affect those prices. The prices also serve as signals to firms of what goods *they* may profitably provide. Given technology and the cost of factors, firms must choose among the products they might produce and sell, among the ways of producing them, and among the various quantities (and qualities) they can supply. By so doing, the firms too affect prices.

Firms must buy factors of production. The quantities demanded depend on the firms' production decisions, which in turn depend on consumers' demands. The demands for factors will in turn affect the prices of labor, managerial skill, raw materials, buildings, machinery, use of

capital, land, and all other factors. The households who are owners of factors (or who possess the skills that can provide the factor services) respond to factor prices and make *their* choices about where to offer their services. These choices determine factor supplies and affect factor prices. Payments by firms to factor owners provide the owners of the factors with incomes. The recipients of these incomes are households whose members want commodities to keep them fed, clothed, housed, entertained. We have now come full circle!

The action of the drama involves firms and households inextricably bound up with each other. Payments flow from households to firms and back to households again.

AN OVERVIEW OF MACROECONOMICS

The idea of payments and incomes flowing in a closed circuit, suggested in Figure 4-1, is basic to macroeconomics. The figure shows flows in two directions. The counterclockwise flows are those of factor services from households to firms and of commodities from firms to households. These are called **real flows.** The clockwise flows are those of money from firms to households (to pay for factor services bought by firms) and from households to firms (to pay for the commodities bought by households). These are called **money flows.** The money spent to purchase factor services becomes income to the households who sell the factor services, and the money spent by households to buy the goods produced by firms becomes the income of the firms. If households spent all the income they received on buying goods and services produced by firms, and if firms distributed all the income they received to households either by purchasing factor services or by distributing profits to their owners, then the circular flow would be very simple indeed. Everything that households received would be passed on to firms, and everything that firms received would be passed on to households. The circular flow would be a completely closed system.

There are two main reasons why the circular flow is not a completely closed system. First, nei-

FIGURE 4–1
The Circular Flows of Goods and Services and Money Payments Between Firms and Households

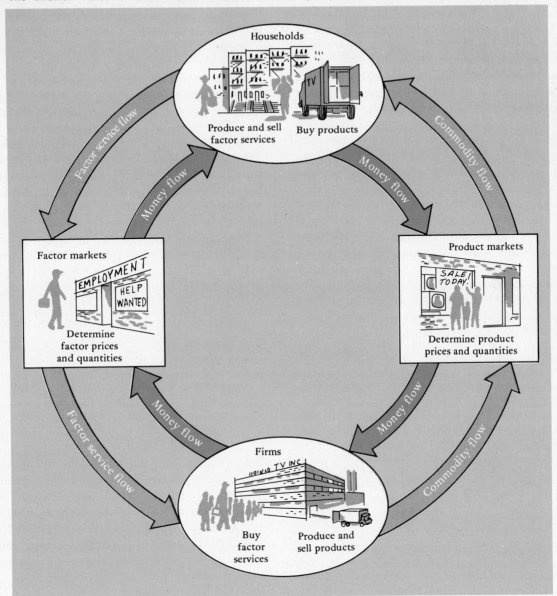

The interaction of firms and households in factor and product markets generates both real and money flows. Factor services are sold through factor markets. The real flow is of factor services from households to firms and the money flow is of income from firms to households. Goods and services for consumption are sold through product markets. The real flow is of goods and services from firms to households and the money flow is of payments from households to firms.

ther households nor firms spend all of the income they receive on purchasing goods and services from the other. Households, for example, have to pay income taxes, and some of their after-tax income is saved. Some of the money that households do spend on purchasing goods and services goes to governments rather than firms because of sales taxes; only what is left becomes the receipts of firms. Furthermore, not all of the income received by firms is paid out to factors; some is paid to governments in the form of business taxes, and some is saved by the firms.

The second reason why the circular flow of income is not a completely closed system is that firms receive income that does not arise from the spending of households and households receive income that does not arise from the spending of firms. When governments spend money on goods and services that are produced by firms, for example, this creates income for the firms that does not arise directly out of the expenditure of private households. When governments hire the services of civil servants, mine inspectors, road builders, and other workers, they create income for households that does not arise directly out of the spending of firms. Similarly, if some firms purchase machines and equipment (say, out of funds borrowed from banks), this creates income for the other firms that manufacture the equipment (and for the households that supply the required factor services); but such income does not arise directly out of household spending.

There is a basic element of circularity in the economy because much income received by households is passed on to firms and much income received by firms is passed on to households. But there are also incomes received by one group and not passed on to the other and incomes received by one group that do not arise out of the spending of the other.

It should be intuitively clear from this discussion that the size of the total incomes received by households and firms depends not only on their total purchases from one another but also on what they receive from other sources of spending. Macroeconomics studies the determinants of all these flows of spending. Why are they the size they are, and why do they change? These are important questions since the flows themselves determine the total output produced, the total income earned, and the total amount of employment available.

MICRO- AND MACROECONOMICS COMPARED

Microeconomics deals with the determination of prices and quantities in individual markets and with the relations among these markets. Micro-

economics thus looks at the details of the market economy. In contrast, macroeconomics suppresses much detail and paints the economy with a very broad brush. Macroeconomics deals with such aggregates as the total flow of payments from households to firms and the total flow of factor income from firms to households.

Microeconomics and macroeconomics look at different aspects of the circular flow of income. Both deal with important questions concerning the functioning of the economy. Whichever is studied first, it is important to remember that they are complementary, not competing, theories and that both are needed for a full understanding of the functioning of a modern economy.

Summary

1. This chapter provides an overview of the workings of the market economy. All modern economies are based on specialization and division of labor, which necessitate the exchange of goods and services. Exchange takes place in markets and is facilitated by the use of money. Much of economics is devoted to a study of how free markets work to coordinate millions of individual, decentralized decisions.

2. In economic theory, three kinds of decision makers—households, firms, and central authorities—interact in markets. It is assumed that households seek to maximize their satisfaction (to the best of their ability) and that firms seek to maximize their profits, but that central authorities may have multiple objectives.

3. A market is defined, for the present, as an area over which buyers and sellers negotiate the exchange of a well-defined commodity. A free-market economy is one in which the allocation of resources is determined by the production, sales, and purchase decisions made by firms and households acting in response to such market signals as prices and profits.

4. Subdivisions of an economy are called sectors. Two common divisions of an economy are into market and nonmarket sectors, and into public and private sectors. These divisions cut across each other; the first is based on the economic distinction of how costs are covered, and the second is based on a legal distinction of ownership.

5. The price system provides a set of signals that reflects changes in demand and supply and to which producers and consumers can react individually but in a nonetheless coordinated manner.

6. The interactions between households and firms through markets are illustrated in a circular-flow diagram that traces both goods and money flows between households and firms. The real flows of goods and services from households to firms and from firms to households play a major role in generating the circular flow of income. This is the key concept of macroeconomics.

7. Not all income received by households is spent for the output of firms and some income received by firms is not paid out to households. Also some payments to firms do not result from the spending of households and some payments to households do not result from the spending of firms. The flows of expenditure in the economy determine total output, total income, and total employment.

8. Macroeconomics is largely concerned with what determines the size of the expenditure flows in the economy as a whole. Microeconomics is concerned with behavior in individual markets and the interrelations among markets. Microeconomics and macroeconomics are complementary parts of economic theory. They study different aspects of a single economic system, and both are needed for an understanding of the whole.

Topics for Review

Specialization and the division of labor
Economic decision makers
Markets and market economies
The private sector and the public sector
Market and nonmarket sectors
The price system as a social control mechanism
Linkages between firms and households
The circular flow of income
Real flows and money flows
The relation between microeconomics and macroeconomics

Discussion Questions

1. Suggest some examples of specialization and division of labor among people you know.
2. There is a greater variety of specialists and specialty stores in large cities than in small cities having the same average income of the population. Explain this in economic terms.
3. Define the household of which you are a member. Consider your household's income last year. What proportion of it came from the sale of factor services to firms? Identify the other sources of income. Approximately what proportion of the expenditures by your household became income for firms?
4. "It is not from the benevolence of the butcher, the brewer, or the baker that we expect our dinner, but from their regard to their self-interest. We address ourselves, not to their humanity, but to their self-love, and never talk to them of our necessities, but of their advantages." Do you agree with this quotation from *The Wealth of Nations?* How are "their self-love" and "our dinner" related to the price system? What are assumed to be the motives of firms and of households?
5. Trace the effect of a sharp change in consumer demand away from cigarettes and toward chewing gum as a result of continuing reports linking smoking with lung cancer and heart disease. Can producers of cigarettes do anything to prevent their loss of profits?
6. Make a list of decision makers in the U.S. economy today that do not fit into the categories of firm, household, and central authority. Are you sure that the concept of a firm will not stretch sufficiently to cover some of the items on your list?
7. Consider a major baby boom such as occurred following World War II. Trace out some significant microeconomic and macroeconomic effects of such a boom. Is there a clear line between them in every case?
8. Can you visualize one $20 bill being used in transactions that create $200 of income in one month? If so, how? If not, why not? Can you visualize it not being used in any transactions that create income in one month? If so, how? If not, why not? Do your answers imply that money and income are not related to one another?

Part Two

A General View
of the Price System

Demand, Supply, and Price

5

Some people believe that economics begins and ends with the "law" of supply and demand. It is, of course, too much to hope for "economics in one lesson." (An unkind critic of a book with that title remarked that the author needed a second lesson.) The so-called laws of supply and demand are an important beginning in the attempt to answer vital questions about the workings of a market system.

A first step is to understand what determines the demands for commodities and the supplies of them. Then we can see how supply and demand operate together to determine price and how the price system as a whole allows the economy to reallocate resources in response to changes in demand and in supply. Supply and demand prove to be helpful concepts in discussing both the price system's successes and its failures. They also can be used to discuss the consequences of particular forms of government intervention such as price controls, minimum-wage laws, and sales taxes.

The Basic Theory of Demand

The American consumer spent about $1.5 trillion on goods and services in 1979. What was it spent on, and why? Table 5-1 shows the composition of this expenditure and how it has changed over nearly 30 years. Economists ask many questions about the pattern of consumer expenditure: Why is it what it is at any moment of time? Why does it change in the way it does? Why did the fraction of total consumer expenditure for food decline from more than one-third in 1910 to only one-fifth by 1979? Why did U.S. consumers allocate a negligible percentage of

TABLE 5-1
Composition of Personal Consumption Expenditures, 1955 and 1979 (Percentages)

	1955		1979	
Durable goods		15.2		14.4
Motor vehicles and parts	7.0		6.3	
Furniture and household equipment	6.4		5.7	
Other	1.8		2.4	
Nondurable goods		48.5		39.4
Food	26.5		20.0	
Clothing and shoes	9.1		6.7	
Gasoline and oil	3.4		4.1	
Other	9.5		8.6	
Services		36.3		46.2
Housing and household operation	19.0		22.6	
Other	17.3		23.6	
Total		100.0		100.0

Source: Economic Report of the President, 1980

The declining relative importance of food and clothing and the rising importance of gasoline and oil and services of all kinds stand out.

their total expenditure to automobiles in 1920, 4 percent in 1929, only 2 percent in 1932, 7 percent in 1972, 5 percent in 1975, and 6 percent in 1979? Why do Americans now heat their homes with electricity, oil, and natural gas when 30 years ago they used coal? How will they react to the large changes in fuel prices that are coming in the 1980s? Why do people who build houses in Norway and the American West rarely use brick while it is commonly used in England and the eastern United States? Why have the maid and the washerwoman been increasingly replaced by the vacuum cleaner and the washing machine?

The Nature of Quantity Demanded

The total amount of a commodity that all households wish to purchase is called called the **quantity demanded** of that commodity.[1] It is important to notice three things about this concept. First, quantity demanded is a *desired* quantity. It is how much households are willing to purchase, given the price of the commodity, other prices, their incomes, tastes, and so on. This may be a

different amount than households actually succeed in purchasing. If sufficient quantities are not available, the amount households wish to purchase may exceed the amount they actually do purchase. To distinguish these two concepts, the term *quantity demanded* is used to refer to desired purchases, and phrases such as **quantity actually bought,** or **quantity exchanged** are used to refer to actual purchases.

Second, *desired* does not refer to idle dreams or future possibilities but to effective demands—that is, to the amounts people are willing to *buy* given the price they must pay for the commodity. For persons intending to spend $100 this year on a commodity whose price is $20, the quantity demanded is 5 units even though they would prefer to consume much more if only they did not have to pay for it.

Third, quantity demanded refers to a continuous *flow* of purchases. It must therefore be expressed as so much per period of time: 1 million oranges *per day,* 7 million *per week,* or 365 million *per year.* If you were told, for example, that the quantity of new television sets demanded (at current prices) in the United States was 500,000, this would mean nothing until you were also told the period of time involved. Five hundred thousand television sets demanded *per day* would be an enormous rate of demand; 500,000 *per year* would be a very small rate.

[1] In this chapter we concentrate on the demand of *all* households for commodities. Of course, what all households do is only the sum of what each individual household does, and in Part Three we shall study the behavior of individual households in greater detail.

(The important distinction between stocks and flows was discussed in the box on page 23.)

WHAT DETERMINES QUANTITY DEMANDED?

How much of some commodity will all households be willing to buy per month? This amount will be influenced by a number of variables. The following are the most important. [2]

1. The commodity's own price.
2. The prices of related commodities.
3. Average household income.
4. Tastes.
5. The distribution of income among households.
6. The size of the population.

This list of variables that influence the quantity of a commodity demanded is even longer than it looks, for *many* prices are covered under the second point. We can neither develop a simple theory nor understand the separate influence of each variable if we start by trying to consider what happens when everything changes at once.

Fortunately, there is an easier way: We can consider the influence of the variables one at a time. To do this, we hold all but one of them constant. Then we let that one selected variable vary and study how it affects quantity demanded. We can do the same for each of the other variables in turn, and in this way we can come to understand the importance of each.[2] Once this is done, we can aggregate the separate influences of two or more variables to discover what would happen if several things changed at the same time—as they often do in practice.

Holding all other influencing variables constant is often described by the words "other things being equal" or by the equivalent Latin phrase, *ceteris paribus.* When economists speak

[2] A relation in which many variables—in this case average income, population, tastes, and many prices—influence a single variable—in this case quantity demanded—is called a *multivariate* relation. The technique of studying the effect of each of the influencing variables one at a time, while holding the other variables constant, is common in science and mathematics. Indeed it is such a common procedure that there is a mathematical concept, the partial derivative, explicitly designed to accomplish this task.

of the influence of the price of wheat on the quantity of wheat demanded *ceteris paribus*, they refer to what a change in the price of wheat would do to the quantity demanded if all other factors that influence the demand for wheat did not change.

DEMAND AND PRICE

We are interested in developing a theory of how commodities get priced. Thus we are necessarily interested in the influence on quantity demanded of each commodity's own price. We begin by holding all other influences constant and asking: How do we expect the quantity of a commodity demanded to vary as its own price varies?

A basic economic hypothesis is that the lower the price of a commodity, the larger the quantity that will be demanded, other things being equal.

Why might this be so? Commodities are used to satisfy desires and needs, and there is almost always more than one commodity that will satisfy any given desire or need. Such commodities compete with one another for the purchasers' attention. Hunger may be satisfied by meat or vegetables, a desire for green vegetables by broccoli or spinach. The need to keep warm at night may be satisfied by several woollen blankets or one electric blanket, or for that matter by a sheet and a lot of oil burned in the furnace. The desire for a vacation may be satisfied by a trip to the seashore or to the mountains, the need to get there by different airlines, a bus, a car, even a train. And so it goes: Name any general desire or need, and there will be at least two and often dozens of different commodities that will satisfy it. Even something so basic as the body's need for fluid may be satisfied by drinking water, tea, coffee, Coke, Dr. Pepper, lemonade, beer, and so on.

We can now see what happens if we hold income, tastes, population, and the prices of all other commodities constant and vary only the price of one commodity. As that price goes up, the commodity becomes an increasingly expensive way to satisfy a want. Some households will stop buying it altogether; others will buy smaller amounts; still others will continue to buy the same quantity. Because many households will switch wholly or partially to other commodities to satisfy the same want, it follows that less will be bought of any commodity whose price has risen. As meat becomes more expensive, for example, households may switch to some extent to meat substitutes; they may also forgo meat at some meals and eat less meat at others. As carrots get increasingly expensive, people may switch to brussels sprouts or broccoli to satisfy their desire for vegetables.

Alternatively, a fall in a commodity's price makes it a cheaper method of satisfying a want. Purchasers as a whole will buy more of it. Consequently they will buy less of similar commodities whose prices have not fallen and which as a result have become expensive *relative to* the commodity in question. As pocket calculators have fallen in price over the last 10 or 15 years, more and more of them have been purchased. When a bumper tomato harvest drives prices down, shoppers switch to tomatoes and cut their purchases of many other vegetables that now look relatively more expensive.

THE DEMAND SCHEDULE AND THE DEMAND CURVE

How can the relationship between quantity demanded and price be portrayed? One method is to use a **demand schedule.** This is a numerical tabulation showing the quantity that is demanded at selected prices.

Table 5-2 is a hypothetical demand schedule for carrots. It lists the quantity of carrots that would be demanded at various prices on the assumption that average household income is fixed at $20,000 (and that tastes and all other prices do not change.) The table gives the quantities demanded for six selected prices, but actually there is a separate quantity that would be demanded at each possible price from one cent to several hundreds of dollars.

A second method of showing the relation between quantity demanded and price is to draw a graph. The six price-quantity combinations shown in Table 5-2 are plotted on the graph shown in Figure 5-1, which has price on the vertical axis

TABLE 5–2
A Demand Schedule for Carrots

	Price per ton p	Quantity demanded when average household income is $20,000 per year (thousands of tons per months) D
U	$ 20	110.0
V	40	90.0
W	60	77.5
X	80	67.5
Y	100	62.5
Z	120	60.0

The table shows the quantity of carrots that would be demanded at various prices, *ceteris paribus.* **Row W indicates that if the price of carrots were $60 per ton, consumers would desire to purchase 77,500 tons of carrots per month, given the values of other variables that may affect quantity demanded (such as average household income).**

FIGURE 5–1
A Demand Curve for Carrots

This demand curve relates quantity demanded to the price of carrots; its downward slope indicates that quantity demanded increases as price falls. There are six points corresponding to the price-quantity combinations shown in Table 5-2. Each row in the table defines a point on the demand curve. The smooth curve drawn through all of the points and labeled *D* is the demand curve.

and quantity on the horizontal axis. The smooth curve drawn through these points is called a **demand curve.** It shows the quantity of carrots that purchasers would like to buy at each price. The curve slopes downward to the right; this indicates that the quantity demanded increases as the price falls.

A single point on the demand curve indicates a single price-quantity combination. Notice that while any point on the demand curve represents a specific quantity demanded, the demand curve as a whole shows more.

The whole demand curve represents the complete relation between quantity demanded and price, other things being equal.

When economists speak of the conditions of demand in a particular market as being given or known, they are referring not just to the particular quantity being demanded at the moment (i.e., not just to a particular point on the demand curve) but to the entire demand curve — to the complete functional relation whereby desired purchases are related to all the possible alternative prices of the commodity.

Thus the term **demand** refers to the entire relation between price and quantity (as shown, for example, by the schedule in Table 5-2 or the curve in Figure 5-1). In contrast, a single point on a demand schedule or curve is the *quantity demanded* at that point (for example, at point W in Figure 5-1, 77,500 tons of carrots a month are demanded at a price of $60 a ton).

Shifts in the Demand Curve

The demand schedule is drawn up, and the demand curve plotted, on the assumption of *ceteris paribus*. But what if other things change, as surely they must? What, for example, if households find themselves with more income? If households spend their extra income, they will buy additional quantities of commodities *even though prices have not changed.*

But if households increase their purchases of any one commodity whose price has not changed, the purchases cannot be represented on

the original demand curve. When they are represented on a new demand curve, the new curve must be to the right of the old curve. Thus the rise in household income has shifted the demand curve to the right. This illustrates the operation of an important general rule.

A demand curve is drawn on the assumption that everything except the commodity's own price is held constant. A change in any of the variables previously held constant will shift the demand curve to a new position.

A demand curve can shift in many ways; two of them are particularly important. If more is bought at *each* price, the demand curve shifts right so that each price corresponds to a higher quantity than it did before. If less is bought at *each* price, the demand curve shifts left so that each price corresponds to a lower quantity than it did before.

The influence of changes in variables other

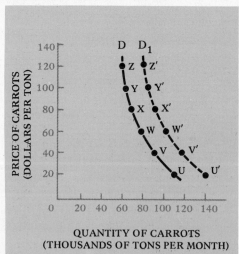

FIGURE 5–2
Two Demand Curves for Carrots

The rightward shift in the demand curve from *D* to *D*₁ indicates an increase in the quantity demanded at each price. The lettered points correspond to those in Table 5-3. A rightward shift in the demand curve indicates an increase in demand in the sense that more is demanded at each price and that a higher price would be paid for each quantity.

TABLE 5-3
Two Alternative Demand Schedules for Carrots

	Price per ton p	Quantity demanded when average household income is $20,000 per year (thousands of tons per month) D	Quantity demanded when average income is $24,000 per year (thousands of tons per months) D_1	
U	$20	110.0	140.0	U'
V	40	90.0	116.0	V'
W	60	77.5	100.8	W'
X	80	67.5	87.5	X'
Y	100	62.5	81.3	Y'
Z	120	60.0	78.0	Z'

An increase in average income increases the quantity demanded at each price. When average income rises from $20,000 to $24,000 per year, quantity demanded at a price of $60 per ton rises from 77,500 tons per month to 100,800 tons per month. A similar rise occurs at every other price. Thus the demand schedule relating columns p and D is replaced by one relating columns p and D_1. The graphical representations of these two functions are labeled D and D_1 in Figure 5-2.

than price may now be studied by determining how changes in each variable shift the demand curve. Any change will shift the demand curve to the right if it increases the amount people wish to buy, other things remaining equal, and to the left if it decreases the amount households wish to buy, other things remaining equal.

Average household income. If the income of the average household increases, households can be expected to purchase more of most commodities even though commodity prices remain the same. Considering all households, we expect that no matter what price we pick, more of any commodity will be demanded than was previously demanded at the same price. This shift is illustrated in Table 5-3 and Figure 5-2.

A rise in average household income shifts the demand curve for most commodities to the right. This indicates that more will be demanded at each possible price.

Other prices. We saw that the downward slope of a commodity's demand curve occurs because the lower its price, the cheaper the commodity is, relative to other commodities that can satisfy the same needs or desires. Those other commodities are called **substitutes.** Another way to accomplish the same change in relative cheapness is for the price of the substitute commodity to rise. For example, carrots can be made cheap relative to cabbage either by lowering the price of carrots or by raising the price of cabbage. Either change will tend to increase the amount of carrots households are prepared to buy.

A rise in the price of a substitute for a commodity shifts the demand curve for the commodity to the right. More will be purchased at each price.

For example, a rise in the price of a substitute for carrots could shift the demand curve for carrots from D to D_1 in Figure 5-2.

Another class of commodities is called **complements.** These are commodities that tend to be used jointly with each other. Cars and gasoline are complements; so are golf clubs and golf balls, electric stoves and electricity, an airplane trip to Vail and lift tickets on the mountain. Since complements tend to be consumed together, a fall in the price of either will increase the demand for both.

A fall in the price of a complementary commodity will shift a commodity's demand curve to the right. More will be purchased at each price.

For example, a fall in the price of airplane trips to Vail will lead to a rise in the demand for lift tickets at Vail even though their price is unchanged.

Tastes. Tastes have a large effect on people's desired purchases. A change in tastes may be long lasting, such as the shift from fountain pens to ball-point pens or from slide rules to pocket calculators. Or it may be a short-lived fad such as the craze for hula hoops or pet rocks. In either case a change in tastes in favor of a commodity shifts the demand curve to the right. More will be bought at each price.

Distribution of income. If a constant total of income is redistributed among the population, demands may change. If, for example, the government increases the deductions for children on the income tax and compensates by raising basic tax rates, income will be transferred from childless persons to heads of large families. The type of commodity more heavily bought by the childless will decline in demand, while that bought by those with large families will increase in demand.

A change in the distribution of income will shift to the right the demand curves for commodities bought most by those gaining income. On the other hand, it will shift to the left the demand curves for commodities bought most by people losing income.

Population. Population growth does not by itself create new demand. The additional people must have purchasing power before demand is changed. Extra people of working age, however, usually means extra output, and if they produce, they will earn income. When this happens, the demand for all the commodities purchased by the new income earners will rise. Thus it is usually (although not always) true that:

A rise in population will shift the demand curves for commodities to the right, indicating that more will be bought at each price.

These shifts are summarized in Figure 5-3 and its caption.

Movements Along the Demand Curve Versus Shifts of the Whole Curve

Suppose you read in today's newspaper that the rising price of housing has caused a declining demand as people have found ways of economiz-

FIGURE 5–3
Shifts in the Demand Curve

A shift in the demand curve from *D* to *D₁* indicates an increase in demand; a shift from *D* to *D₂* indicates a decrease in demand. An increase in demand means more is demanded at each price. Such a rightward shift can be caused by a rise in income, a rise in the price of a substitute, a fall in the price of a complement, a change in tastes in favor of the commodity, an increase in population, and a redistribution of income toward groups who favor the commodity.

A decrease in demand means less is demanded at each price. Such a leftward shift can be caused by a fall in income, a fall in the price of a substitute, a rise in the price of a complement, a change in tastes against the commodity, a decrease in population, and a redistribution of income away from groups who favor the commodity.

ing on their use of housing. Then tomorrow you read that the rising price of housing has been caused by a rising demand for housing. The two statements appear to contradict each other. The first associates a rising price with a declining demand, the second associates a rising price with a rising demand. How can both statements be true? The answer is that they refer to different things. The first describes a movement along a demand curve in response to a change in price; the second describes a shift in the whole demand curve. Using the words "rising demand" or "declining demand" in each case can only cause confusion.

Consider first the statement that less is being bought because it has become more expensive. This refers to a movement along a given demand curve, to a change between two specific quantities being bought, one before the price rose and one afterward. Any one point on a demand curve represents a specific amount being bought at a specified price. It represents, therefore, a particular quantity demanded. A movement along a demand curve is referred to as a change in the quantity demanded. [3]

A movement down a demand curve is called an increase (or a rise) in the quantity demanded; a movement up the demand curve is called a decrease (or a fall) in the quantity demanded.

Now consider the shift in demand. We have seen that *demand* refers to the whole demand curve. Economists reserve the term **change in demand** to describe a shift in the whole curve— that is, a change in the amount that will be bought at *every* price.

An *increase in demand* means that the whole demand curve has shifted to the right; a *fall in demand* means that the whole demand curve has shifted to the left.

To illustrate this terminology, look again at Table 5-3. When average income is $20,000, an increase in price from $60 to $80 decreases the *quantity demanded* from 77.5 to 67.5 thousand tons a month. An increase in average income from $20,000 to $24,000 increases *demand* from D to D_1.

The Basic Theory of Supply

America's private sector produced goods and services worth nearly $2 trillion in 1979. A broad classification of *what* was produced is given in Table 5-4. Economists have as many questions to ask about production and its changing com-

TABLE 5–4

Composition of National Product by Industry of Origin, 1955 and 1979 (Percentages)

Industry group[a]	1955	1979
Manufacturing	36.6	30.5
Mining and construction	7.7	7.7
Agriculture, forestry, fisheries	5.4	3.7
Transport, communications, utilities	9.4	9.4
Wholesale and retail trade	17.7	17.2
Finance, insurance, real estate	12.0	13.9
Other services	10.5	16.2
Other	0.7	1.4
	100.0	100.0

Source: Survey of Current Business, 1980.
[a] Excluding government and government enterprises.

Over a generation manufacturing, agriculture, forestry, and fisheries have all declined in relative importance while services of all kinds have become more important.

position as they do about consumption. The percentages shown in Table 5-4 reflect some of the changes in 24 years. Even more dramatic changes are visible in more detailed data.

For example, the increase in output of the chemical industries was almost sixteen times that of the primary metals industries, seven times that of mining industries, and three times that of the petroleum industry in the quarter century since 1955. Economists want to know why. Why did the aluminum industry grow faster than the steel industry? Why, even within a single industry, did some firms prosper and grow, others hold their own, and still others decline and fail? Why and how do firms and industries come into being? All these questions and many others are aspects of a single question: *What determines the quantities of commodities that firms will produce and offer for sale?*

Full discussion of these questions of supply will come later (in Part Five). For now it is enough (1) to develop the basic relation between the price of a commodity and the quantity that will be produced and offered for sale by firms and (2) to understand what forces lead to shifts in this relationship.

Much of what needs to be said about supply parallels what we have said about demand.

THE NATURE OF QUANTITY SUPPLIED

The amount of a commodity that firms wish to sell is the **quantity supplied** of that commodity. This is the amount that firms are willing to offer for sale; it is not necessarily the amount they succeed in selling. The term **quantity actually sold** or **quantity exchanged** indicates what they actually succeed in selling. Quantity supplied is a flow: it is so much per unit of time, per day, per week, or per year.

Notice that while we use different terms (quantity demanded and quantity supplied) to distinguish desired purchases from desired sales, we use the same term, *quantity exchanged,* to describe actual purchases and actual sales. This reflects an important fact of life: although households may desire to purchase an amount that differs from what sellers desire to sell, they cannot succeed in buying what someone else does not sell. A purchase and a sale are merely two sides of the same transaction. Looked at from the buyer's side, there is a purchase; looked at from the seller's side, there is a sale.

Since desired purchases do not have to equal desired sales, different terms are needed to describe the two separate amounts. But because the quantity actually purchased must be the same amount as the quantity actually sold, both can be described by a single term, quantity exchanged.

WHAT DETERMINES QUANTITY SUPPLIED?

How much of a commodity will firms be willing to produce and offer for sale? The amount will be influenced by a number of variables. The following are the most important: [4]

1. The commodity's own price.
2. The prices of other commodities.
3. The costs of factors of production.
4. The goals of the firm.
5. The state of technology.

The situation is the same here as it is on the demand side. The list of influencing variables is long, and we will not get far if we try to discover what happens when they all change at the same time. So again we use the very convenient *ceteris paribus* technique to study the influence of the variables one at a time.

SUPPLY AND PRICE

Since we want to develop a theory of how commodities get priced, we are necessarily interested in the influence on quantity supplied of a commodity's own price. We start by holding all other influences constant and asking: How do we expect the quantity of a commodity supplied to vary with its own price?

A basic economic hypothesis is that for many commodities the higher their price, the larger the quantity that will be supplied, other things being equal.

Why might this be so? It is because the profits that can be earned from producing a commodity are almost certain to increase if the price of that commodity rises while the costs of factors used to produce it remain unchanged. Furthermore, if the prices of other commodities remain unchanged, the profits that can be earned by producing them will be unchanged, and as a result there will be a rise in *relative* profitability of producing the commodity whose price has risen. This will make firms, which are in business to earn profits, wish to produce more of the commodity whose price has risen and less of other commodities.

Notice, however, the qualifying word "many" in the hypothesis stated above. "Many" is used because, as we shall see in Part Five, there are exceptions to this rule. Although the rule states the usual case, a rise in price (*ceteris paribus*) is not always necessary to call forth an increase in quantity in the case of all commodities.

THE SUPPLY SCHEDULE AND THE SUPPLY CURVE

The general relationship just discussed can be illustrated by a supply schedule that shows the quantities that producers would wish to sell at alternative prices of the commodity. A **supply schedule** is analogous to a demand schedule: the former shows what producers would be willing to sell, while the latter shows what households would be willing to buy at alternative prices of the commodity. Table 5-5 presents a hypothetical supply schedule for carrots.

A **supply curve,** the graphic representation of the supply schedule, is illustrated in Figure 5-4. Once again, while each point on the supply curve represents a specific price-quantity combination, the whole curve shows more.

The whole supply curve represents the complete relation between quantity supplied and price, other things being equal.

When economists speak of the conditions of supply as being given or known, they refer not just to the particular quantity being supplied at the moment (that is, not to just a particular point on the supply curve) but to the entire supply curve, to the complete functional relation by which desired sales are related to all possible alternative prices of the commodity.

Supply refers to the entire relation between supply and price. A single point on the supply schedule or curve refers to the *quantity supplied* at that price.

Shifts in the Supply Curve

A shift in the supply curve means that at each price a different quantity will be supplied than previously. An increase in the quantity supplied at each price is shown in Table 5-6 and graphed in Figure 5-5. This change appears as a rightward shift in the supply curve. In contrast, a decrease in the quantity supplied at each price would appear as a leftward shift. A shift in the supply curve must be the result of a change in one of the

TABLE 5–5
A Supply Schedule for Carrots

	Price per ton p	Quantity supplied (thousands of tons per month) S
u	$ 20	5.0
v	40	46.0
w	60	77.5
x	80	100.0
y	100	115.0
z	120	122.5

The table shows the quantities that producers wish to sell at various prices, *certeris paribus.* For example, row y indicates that if the price were $100 per ton, producers would wish to sell 115,000 tons of carrots per month.

FIGURE 5–4
A Supply Curve for Carrots

This supply curve relates quantity supplied to the price of carrots; its upward slope indicates that quantity supplied increases as price increases. There are six points corresponding to the price-quantity combinations shown in Table 5-5. Each row in the table defines a point on the supply curve. The smooth curve drawn through all of the points and labeled *S* is the supply curve.

TABLE 5–6
Two Alternative Supply Schedules for Carrots

	Price per ton p	Quantity supplied before cost-saving innovation (thousands of tons per month) S	Quantity supplied after the innovation (thousands of tons per month) S_1	
u	$ 20	5.0	28.0	u'
v	40	46.0	76.0	v'
w	60	77.5	102.0	w'
x	80	100.0	120.0	x'
y	100	115.0	132.0	y'
z	120	122.5	140.0	z'

A cost-saving innovation increases the quantity supplied at each price. As a result of the cost-saving innovation, quantity supplied at $100 per ton rises from 115,000 to 132,000 tons per month. A similar rise occurs at every price. Thus the supply schedule relating p and S is replaced by one relating p and S_1.

factors that influence the quantity supplied other than the commodity's own price. The major possible causes of such shifts are summarized in the caption of Figure 5-6 and are considered briefly below.

For supply, as for demand, there is an important general rule.

A change in any of the variables (other than the commodity's own price) that affect the amount of a commodity that firms are willing to produce and offer for sale will shift the whole supply curve for that commodity.

Other prices. Commodities may be substitutes or complements in production as well as in consumption. Land that grows wheat can also grow corn, or it can be used to raise hogs. Suppose the price of corn falls and as a result corn is less profitable to produce. Some farmers will shift from corn to wheat production. Thus a fall in the price of corn may shift the supply curve of wheat to the right, indicating that at each price of wheat more will be supplied than before.

Since commodities are alternative outputs for producers, a fall in the price of one commodity may shift the supply curve of another to the right.

Prices of factors of production. The price paid for a factor of production is a cost to a firm that uses it. A change in factor prices changes the quantity that producers will be willing to offer for sale because it changes costs and hence profits.

FIGURE 5–5
Two Supply Curves for Carrots

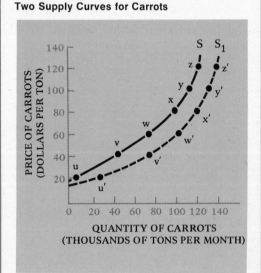

The rightward shift in the supply curve from S to S_1 indicates an increase in the quantity supplied at each price. The lettered points correspond to those in Table 5-6. A rightward shift in the supply curve indicates an increase in supply in the sense that more carrots are supplied at each price.

FIGURE 5–6
Shifts in the Supply Curve

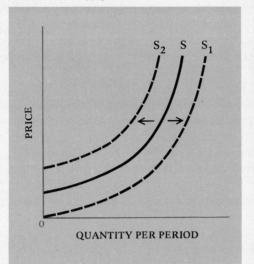

FIGURE 5–6
Shifts in the Supply Curve

S_2 S S_1

PRICE

0   QUANTITY PER PERIOD

A shift in the supply curve from S to S_1 indicates an increase in supply; a shift from S to S_2 indicates a decrease in supply. An increase in supply means more is supplied at each price. Such a rightward shift can be caused by some kinds of changes in producers' goals, improvements in technology, decreases in the prices of other commodities, and decreases in the prices of factors of production that are important in producing the commodity.

A decrease in supply means less is supplied at each price. Such a leftward shift can be caused by some kinds of changes in producers' goals, increases in the prices of other commodities, and increases in the prices of factors of production that are important in producing the commodity.

The goals of the firm. In elementary economic theory, the firm is assumed to have the single goal of profit maximization. Firms might, however, have other goals either in addition to or as substitutes for profit maximization. If the firm worries about risk, it will pursue safer lines of activity even though they promise lower probable profits. If the firm values size, it may produce and sell more than the profit-maximizing quantities. If it worries about its image in society, it may forsake highly profitable activities (such as the production of napalm) when there is major public disapproval. However, as long as the firm prefers more profits to less, it will respond to changes in the profitabilities of alternative lines of action, and supply curves will slope upward.

A change in the importance that firms give to other goals will shift the supply curve one way or the other, indicating a changed willingness to supply the quantity at any given price and hence a changed level of profitability.

Technology. At any time, what is produced and how it is produced depends on what is known. Over time knowledge changes; so do the quantities of individual commodities supplied. The enormous increase in production per worker that has been going on in industrial societies for about 200 years is largely due to improved methods of production. Yet the Industrial Revolution is more than a historical event; it is a present reality. Discoveries in chemistry have led to lower costs of production of well-established products, such as paints, and to a large variety of new products made of plastics and synthetic fibers. The invention of transistors and silicon chips has revolutionized production in television, high-fidelity equipment, computers, and guidance-control systems.

Any technological change that decreases production costs will increase the profits that can be earned at any given price of the commodity. Since increased profitability tends to lead to increased production, this change will shift the supply curve to the right, indicating an increased willingness to produce the commodity and offer it for sale at each possible price.

Just as profits are increased by an *increase* in the commodity's price, factor costs remaining constant, so are they increased by a fall in factor prices, the price of the commodity remaining constant. A rise in factor prices reduces the profitability of a commodity at any given price of that commodity. The initial profitability can be restored only if the price of the commodity rises.

A rise in the costs of factors of production shifts to the left the supply curve of a commodity that uses that factor, indicating that less will be supplied at any given price.

Movements Along the Supply Curve Versus Shifts of the Whole Curve

As with demand, it is important to distinguish movements along supply curves from shifts of the whole curve. The term **change in supply** is reserved for a shift of the whole supply curve. This means a change in the quantity supplied at each price of the commodity. A movement along the supply curve indicates a *change in the quantity supplied* in response to a change in the price of the commodity. Thus an *increase in supply* means that the whole supply curve has shifted to the right; an *increase in the quantity supplied* means a movement upward to the right along a given supply curve.

The Determination of Price by Demand and Supply

So far demand and supply have been considered separately. The next question is: How do the two forces interact to determine price in a competitive market? The theory that answers this question is called **price theory.** (In developing this theory we shall continue, until the final section of this chapter, with the simplifying assumption that all forces that might influence demand or supply,

other than the commodity's own price, are held constant.)

Table 5-7 brings together the demand and supply schedules from Tables 5-2 and 5-5. The quantities of carrots demanded and supplied at each price may now be compared (see column 4 of Table 5-7).

There is only one price, $60 a ton, at which the quantity of carrots demanded equals the quantity supplied. At prices of less than $60 a ton there is a shortage of carrots because the quantity demanded exceeds the quantity supplied. This is often called a situation of **excess demand** or, what is the same thing, one of deficient supply. At prices greater than $60 a ton there is a surplus of carrots because the quantity supplied exceeds the quantity demanded. This is called a situation of **excess supply** or one of deficient demand.

In order to discuss the determination of market price, suppose first that the price is $100 a ton. At this price, 115,000 tons would be offered for sale but only 62,500 tons would be demanded. There would be excess supply of 52,500 tons a month. We assume that sellers will then cut their prices in order to get rid of this surplus and that purchasers, observing the stock of unsold carrots, will offer less for what they are prepared to buy.

TABLE 5–7
Demand and Supply Schedules for Carrots and Equilibrium Price

(1) Price per ton p	(2) Quantity demanded (thousands of tons per month) D	(3) Quantity supplied (thousands of tons per month) S	(4) Excess demand (+) Excess supply (−) (thousands of tons per month) D − S
$ 20	110.0	5.0	+105.0
40	90.0	46.0	+ 44.0
60	77.5	77.5	0.0
80	67.5	100.0	− 32.5
100	62.5	115.0	− 52.5
120	60.0	122.5	− 62.5

Equilibrium occurs where quantity demanded equals quantity supplied—where there is neither excess demand nor excess supply. These schedules are those of Tables 5–2 and 5–5. The equilibrium price is $60. For lower prices there is excess demand; for higher prices there is excess supply.

The tendency for buyers to offer, and sellers to ask for, lower prices when there is excess supply implies a downward pressure on price.

Next consider the price of $20 a ton. At this price, there is excess demand. The 5,000 tons produced each month are snapped up very quickly, and 105,000 tons of desired purchases cannot be made. Rivalry between would-be purchasers may lead to their offering more than the prevailing price in order to outbid other purchasers. Also, perceiving that they could have sold their available supplies many times over, sellers may begin to ask a higher price for the quantities that they do have to sell.

The tendency for buyers to offer, and sellers to ask for, higher prices when there is excess demand implies an upward pressure on price.

Finally, consider a price of $60. At this price, producers wish to sell 77,500 tons a month and purchasers wish to buy that quantity. There is neither a shortage nor a surplus of carrots. There are no unsatisfied buyers to bid the price up, nor are there unsatisfied sellers to force the price down. Once the price of $60 has been reached, therefore, there will be no tendency for it to change.

An equilibrium implies a state of rest, or balance, between opposing forces. The **equilibrium price** is the one toward which the actual market

Supply and Demand: What Really Happens

"The theory of supply and demand is neat enough," said the skeptic, "but tell me what really happens."

"What really happens," said the economist, "is that first, demand curves slope downward; second, supply curves slope upward; third, prices rise in response to excess demand; and fourth, prices fall in response to excess supply."

"But that's theory," insists the skeptic. "What about reality?"

"That is reality as well," said the economist.

"Show me," said the skeptic.

The economist produced the following passages from recent articles in the *New York Times*.

Increased demand for macadamia nuts causes price to rise above competing nuts. Major producer now plans to double the size of its orchards during the next five years.

* *

The ghost town of de Lamar, Idaho, is a mute witness to the recent unprofitability of silver min-ing. But now silver is stirring again. Prices rose between 1970 and 1979 from $1.30 an ounce to about $50.00, making it economical to begin mining again. De Lamar is now coming back in production at a rate that is expected soon to make it the third largest silver producer in the U.S.

* *

The average price of cocoa beans has dropped about 50 cents a pound since last November because of increases in supplies.

* *

The effects of [the first year of] deregulation of the nation's airlines have been spectacular: cuts in air fares of up to 70 percent in some cases, record passenger jam-ups at the airports, and a spectacular increase in the average load factor [the proportion of occupied seats on the average commercial flight]. (In the second year of airline deregulation airline prices have risen substantially as airlines passed on the rising cost of aviation fuel.)

The skeptic's response is not recorded, but you will have no trouble telling which clippings illustrate which of the economist's four statements about "what really happens."

price will tend. It will persist once established, unless it is disturbed by some change in market conditions.

The price at which the quantity demanded equals the quantity supplied is called the equilibrium price.

Any other price is called a **disequilibrium price:** quantity demanded does not equal quantity supplied, and price will be changing. A market that exhibits excess demand or excess supply is said to be in a state of **disequilibrium.**

When the market is in equilibrium, quantity demanded equals quantity supplied. Anything that must be true if equilibrium is to be obtained is called an **equilibrium condition.** In the competitive market, the equality of quantity demanded and quantity supplied is an equilibrium condition. [5]

This same story is told in graphic terms in Figure 5-7. The price of $60 is the equilibrium price because there is neither excess supply nor excess demand. All other prices are disequilibrium prices, and if they occur, the market will not be in a state of rest. At prices below the equilibrium, there will be shortages and rising prices; at prices above the equilibrium, there will be surpluses and falling prices.

The quantities demanded and supplied at any price can be read off the two curves, while the magnitude of the shortage or surplus is shown by the horizontal distance between the curves at each price. The figure makes it clear that the equilibrium price occurs where the demand and supply curves intersect. Below that price there will be a shortage and hence an upward pressure on the existing price. Above it there will be a surplus and hence a downward pressure on price. These pressures are represented by the vertical arrows in the figure.

THE "LAWS" OF SUPPLY AND DEMAND

Changes in any of the variables other than price that influence quantity demanded or supplied will cause a shift in either the supply curve or the

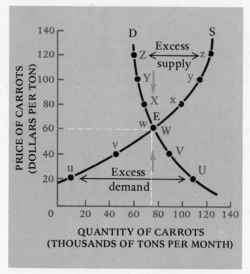

FIGURE 5–7

The Determination of the Equilibrium Price of Carrots

The equilibrium price corresponds to the point where demand and supply curves intersect. Point *E* indicates the equilibrium. At a price of $60, quantity demanded equals quantity supplied. At prices above the equilibrium, there is excess supply and downward pressure on price. At prices below equilibrium, there is excess demand and upward pressure on price.

demand curve (or both). There are four possible shifts: (1) a rise in demand (a rightward shift in the demand curve); (2) a fall in demand (a leftward shift in the demand curve); (3) a rise in supply (a rightward shift in the supply curve); and (4) a fall in supply (a leftward shift in the supply curve).

To analyze the effects of any of these shifts we use the method known as **comparative statics.** We start from a position of equilibrium and then introduce the change to be studied. The new equilibrium position is determined and compared with the original one. The differences between the two positions of equilibrium must be due to the changes in the data that were introduced—for everything else has been held constant. The term is *comparative statics* because the method of an-

FIGURE 5-8
The "Laws" of Supply and Demand

(i) The effect of shifts in the demand curve

(ii) The effect of shifts in the supply curve

The effects on equilibrium price and quantity of shifts in either demand or supply are called the laws of supply and demand.

A rise in demand. In (i) if demand rises from D to D_1, excess demand of q-q_2 develops at price p. Price and quantity both rise to their new equilibrium values at p_1 and q_1.

A fall in demand. In (i) if demand falls from D_1 to D, an excess supply develops at p_1. Price and quantity both fall to their new equilibrium values at p and q.

A rise in supply. In (ii) if supply rises from S to S_1, an excess supply of q-q_2 develops at p. Price falls and quantity rises to their new equilibrium values at p_1 and q_1.

A fall in supply. In (ii) if supply falls from S_1 to S, an excess demand develops at p_1. Price rises and quantity falls to their new equilibrium values at p and q.

alysis is to compare two positions of static equilibrium.

Figure 5-8 shows the effects of these four shifts, which are the four so-called laws of supply and demand.[3]

1. **A rise in demand causes an increase in both the equilibrium price and the equilibrium quantity exchanged.**
2. **A fall in demand causes a decrease in both the equilibrium price and the equilibrium quantity exchanged.**
3. **A rise in supply causes a decrease in the equilibrium price and an increase in the equilibrium quantity exchanged.**
4. **A fall in supply causes an increase in the equilibrium price and a decrease in the equilibrium quantity exchanged.**

In this chapter we have studied many forces that can cause demand or supply curves to shift. These were summarized in Figures 5-3 and 5-6. By combining this analysis with the four "laws" of supply and demand, we can take many real-world events that cause demand or supply curves to shift and link them to resulting changes in market prices and quantities. To take one example, a large rise in the price of beef will lead to an increase in both the price and the quantity exchanged of both chicken and pork (because a rise in the price of one commodity causes a rightward shift in the demand curves for its substitutes).

The theory of the determination of price by demand and supply is beautiful in its simplicity yet, as we shall see, powerful in its wide range of applications.

[3] The detailed argument in each case follows that of pages 70–71 and Figure 5-7 as to what happens when supply does not equal demand. Be sure you understand the market *behavior* that gives rise to each of the four "laws" summarized here.

Laws, Predictions, Hypotheses

In what sense can the four propositions developed for supply and demand be called laws? They are not like acts passed by Congress, interpreted by courts, and enforced by the police; they cannot be repealed if people do not like their effects. Nor are they like the laws of Moses, revealed to man by the voice of God. Are they "natural laws" similar to Newton's law of gravity? It was clearly this last sense that classical economists had in mind when they labeled them as laws, and it was Newton's laws that they had in mind as analogies.

The term *law* is used in science to describe a theory that has stood up to substantial testing. A law of this kind is not something that has been proven to be true for all times and all circumstances, nor is it regarded as immutable. As observations accumulate, laws may often be modified or the range of phenomena to which they apply may be restricted or redefined. Einstein's theory of relativity, for one example, forced such amendments and restrictions on Newton's laws.

The "laws" of supply and demand have stood up well to many empirical tests, but no one believes that they explain all market behavior. Indeed the range of markets over which they seem to meet the test of providing accurate predictions is now much smaller than it was 80 years ago. It is possible—though most economists would think it unlikely—that at some future time they would no longer apply to any real markets. They are thus laws in the sense that they predict certain kinds of behavior in certain situations and the predicted behavior occurs sufficiently often to lead people to continue to have confidence in the predictions of the theory. They are not laws—any more than are the laws of natural science—that are beyond being challenged by present or future observations that may cast their predictions in doubt. Nor is it a heresy to question their applicability to any particular situation.

Laws, then, are hypotheses that have led to predictions that seem to account for observed behavior. They are theories that seem—in some circumstances at least—to have survived attempts to refute them and have proven useful. It is possible, in economics as in natural sciences, to be impressed both with the "laws" we do have and with their limitations: to be impressed, that is, both with the power of what we know and with the magnitude of what we have yet to understand.

THE THEORY OF PRICE IN AN INFLATIONARY WORLD

Up to now we have developed the theory of the prices of individual commodities under the assumption that all other prices remained constant. Does this mean that the theory is inapplicable to an inflationary world when virtually all prices are rising? Fortunately the answer is no.

The key lies in what are called relative prices. We have mentioned several times that what mattered for demand and supply was the price of the commodity in question relative to the prices of other commodities. A **relative price** measures the price of the specific commodity relative to other prices.

In an inflationary world we are often interested in the price of a given commodity as it relates to the average price of all other commodities. If, during a period when the general price level rose by 40 percent, the price of oranges rose by 60 percent, then the price of oranges rose relative to the price level as a whole. Oranges became *relatively* expensive. However, if oranges had risen in price by only 30 percent when the general price level rose by 40 percent, then the relative price of oranges would have fallen. Although the money price of oranges rose substantially, oranges became *relatively* cheap.

In Lewis Carroll's famous story *Through the Looking Glass,* Alice finds a country where you have to run in order to stay still. So it is with inflation. A commodity's price must rise as fast as the general level of prices just to keep its relative price constant.

It has been convenient in this chapter to analyze a change in a particular price in the context of a constant price level. The analysis is easily extended to an inflationary period by remembering that any force that raises the price of one commodity when other prices remain constant will, given general inflation, raise the price of that commodity faster than the price level is rising. For example, a change in tastes in favor of carrots that would raise their price by 20 percent when other prices were constant, would raise their price by 32 percent if at the same time the general price level goes up by 10 percent.[4] In each case the price of carrots rises 20 percent *relative to the average of all prices.*

In price theory, whenever we talk of a change in the price of one commodity we mean a change relative to all other prices.

If the price level is constant, this change requires only that the money price of the commodity in question should rise. If the price level is itself rising, this change requires that the money price of the commodity in question should rise faster than the price level.

Summary

1. The amount of a commodity that households wish to purchase is called the quantity demanded. It is a flow expressed as so much per period of time. This quantity is determined by the commodity's own price, the prices of related commodities, average household income, tastes, the

distribution of income among households, and the size of the population.

2. Quantity demanded is assumed to increase as the price of the commodity falls, *ceteris paribus.* The relationship between quantity demanded and price is represented graphically by a demand curve that shows how much will be demanded at each market price. A movement along a demand curve indicates a change in the quantity demanded in response to a change in the price of the commodity.

3. The demand curve shifts to the right (an increase in demand) if average income rises, if the price of a substitute rises, if the price of a complement falls, if population rises, or if there is a change in tastes in favor of the product. The opposite changes shift the demand curve to the left (a decrease in demand). A shift of a demand curve represents a change in the quantity demanded at each price and is referred to as a change in demand.

4. The amount of a commodity that firms wish to sell is called the quantity supplied. It is a flow expressed as so much per period of time. This quantity depends on the commodity's own price, the prices of other commodities, the costs of factors of production, the goals of the firm, and the state of technology.

5. Quantity supplied is assumed to increase as the price of the commodity increases, *ceteris paribus.* A movement along a supply curve indicates a change in the quantity supplied in response to a change in price.

6. The supply curve shifts to the right (an increase in supply) if the prices of other commodities fall, if the costs of producing the commodity fall, or if, for any reason, producers become more willing to produce the commodity. The opposite changes shift the supply curve to the left (a decrease in supply). A shift in the supply curve indicates a change in the quantity supplied at each price and is referred to as a change in supply.

7. The equilibrium price is the one at which the

---

[4] In the first case the price level is 100 and an index of carrot prices rises from 100 to 120 ($100 \times 1.2 = 120$). In the second case the index of the price level becomes 110 and the index of carrot prices must rise to 132 ($110 \times 1.2 = 132$).

quantity demanded equals the quantity supplied. At any price below the equilibrium there will be excess demand, while at any price above the equilibrium there will be excess supply. Graphically, equilibrium occurs where demand and supply curves intersect.

8. Price is assumed to rise when there is a shortage and to fall when there is a surplus. Thus the actual market price will be pushed toward the equilibrium price, and when it is reached, there will be neither shortage nor surplus and price will not change until either the supply curve or the demand curve shifts.

9. Using the method of comparative statics, the effects of a shift in either demand or supply can be determined. A rise in demand raises both equilibrium price and quantity; a fall in demand lowers both. A rise in supply raises equilibrium quantity but lowers equilibrium price; a fall in supply lowers equilibrium quantity but raises equilibrium price. These are the so-called laws of supply and demand.

10. Price theory is most simply explained against a backdrop of a constant price level. Price changes discussed in the theory are changes *relative to* the average level of all prices. In an inflationary period, a rise in the relative price of one commodity means that its price rises more than does the price level; a fall in its relative price means that its price rises by less than does the price level.

Topics for Review

Quantity demanded and quantity exchanged
Demand schedules and demand curves
Quantity supplied and quantity exchanged
Supply schedules and supply curves
Movements along a curve and shifts in the curve
Changes in quantity demanded and changes in demand
Changes in quantity supplied and changes in supply
Equilibrium, equilibrium price, and disequilibrium
The determination of equilibrium
Comparative static analysis
The "laws" of supply and demand
Relative price

Discussion Questions

1. What shifts in demand or supply curves would produce the following results? (Assume that only one of the two curves has shifted.)
    a. The price of pocket calculators has fallen over the last few years and the quantity exchanged has risen greatly.
    b. As the American standard of living rose over the past three decades, both the prices and the consumption of prime cuts of beef rose steadily.
    c. During the recession of 1974–1975 the prices *and* quantities exchanged of lead, copper, and tin fell substantially.
    d. Because federal safety and antipollution regulations have led to large increases in the cost of producing automobiles, it has been suggested that if strong regulations continue, the prices of cars will rise and the sales of cars will fall.

2. Recently the Department of Agriculture predicted bumper crops of corn and wheat. But its chief economist, Don Paarlberg, warned consumers not to expect prices to decrease since the costs of production were rising and foreign demand for American crops was increasing. "The classic pattern of supply and demand won't work this time," Mr. Paarlberg said. Discuss his observation.

3. Explain each of the following in terms of changes in supply and demand.
    a. DuPont increased the price of synthetic fibers, although it acknowledged demand was weak.
    b. Some of the first $10 Canadian Olympic coins were imperfectly stamped. Dealers and collectors are paying as much as $500 for these flawed pieces.
    c. "Master Charge has replaced sugar-daddy," a Beverly Hills furrier said, explaining the rise in sales of mink coats.
    d. The Edsel was a lemon when produced in 1958–1960 but is now a best seller among cars of its vintage.
    e. When a frost hit the Florida citrus industry, a spokesperson for the Israel citrus marketing board said Mediterranean producers would receive better prices for their crops everywhere in the world.

4. Suppose that tape recorder producers find that they are selling more tape recorders at the same price than they did two years ago. Is this a shift of the demand curve or a movement along the curve? Suggest at least four reasons why this rise in sales at an unchanged price might occur.

5. What would be the effect on the equilibrium price and quantity of marijuana if its sale were legalized? What would be the effect on the equilibrium prices of gold and paper if all the world's banks sold off their gold supplies and replaced them with paper certificates that were officially accepted as reserves?

6. The relative price of a color television set has dropped drastically over time. Would you explain this falling price in terms of demand or supply changes? What factors are likely to have caused the demand or supply shifts that did occur?

7. Classify the effect of each of the following as (a) a decrease in the demand for fish, (b) a decrease in the quantity of fish demanded, or (c) other. Illustrate each diagrammatically.

   a. The government of Iceland bars fishermen of other nations from its waters.

   b. People buy less fish because of a rise in fish prices.

   c. The Roman Catholic Church relaxes its ban on eating meat on Fridays.

   d. The price of beef falls and as a result households buy more beef and less fish.

   e. In the interests of training marine personnel for national defense, the U.S. government decides to subsidize the American fishing industry.

   f. It is discovered that eating fish is better for one's health than eating meat.

8. "The effect of price changes often eludes analysis. For example, two of the food groups that have shown absolute decreases in consumption per capita—flour and potatoes—have also shown decreases in price relative to the prices of all goods. Consumption of meat per capita has been rising in the face of an increase in relative prices." Do the changes elude your analysis? How would you reword this statement to make clear what you think did happen?

Elasticity of Demand and Supply

When flood damage led to major destruction of the onion crop, onion prices rose generally. In Hartford, Connecticut, they rose 42 percent in one week. Not surprisingly consumption fell. Very often it is not enough to know merely whether quantity rises or falls in response to a change in price; it is also important to know by how much. In this case, the press reported that the effect was to cause many consumers to stop using onions altogether and to substitute onion salt, sauerkraut, cabbage, and other products. Other consumers still bought onions but in reduced quantities. Overall consumption was down sharply. Were aggregate dollar sales of onions (price *times* quantity) higher or lower? The data above do not tell, but this is the sort of information that may matter a good deal. A government concerned with the effect of a partial crop failure on farm income will not be satisfied with being told that food prices will rise and quantities consumed will fall; it will need to know by approximately how much they will rise and fall if it is to assess the effects on farmers.

Demand Elasticity

Suppose there is a fall in the supply of a farm crop. The two parts of Figure 6-1 show the same leftward shift in the supply curve. Because the demand curves are different, the effects on equilibrium price and quantity are different. In the first case, the quantity demanded varies greatly with price. A small rise in price restores equilibrium by removing the excess demand. In the sec-

FIGURE 6–1

The Effect of the Shape of the Demand Curve

(i)

(ii)

The flatter the demand curve, the less is the change in price and the greater is the change in quantity. Both parts of the figure show the same leftward shift in the supply curve. In each part, initial equilibrium is at price p and output q and the new equilibrium is at p_1

and q_1. In (i) the effect of the shift in supply from S to S_1 is a slight rise in the price and a large decrease in quantity. In (ii) the effect of the identical shift in the supply curve from S to S_1 is a large increase in the price and a relatively small decrease in quantity.

ond case, the quantity demanded is very insensitive to price changes and equilibrium is restored only when a large price rise has called forth the extra quantity necessary to satisfy the almost unchanged quantity demanded.

The difference may have great policy significance. Consider what would happen if the government persuaded farmers to produce more of a certain crop. (It might, for example, pay a subsidy to farmers for growing this crop.) If the government is successful, then at every possible price of the product there will be an increase in the quantity that farmers would be willing to produce. Thus the whole supply curve of the product would shift to the right. This may be visualized in both parts of Figure 6-1 by assuming that the supply curve shifts from S_1 to S.

Figure 6-1(i) illustrates a case in which the quantity that consumers demand is very sensi-

tive to price changes. The extra production brings down price, but because the quantity demanded is very responsive, only a small change in price is necessary in order to restore equilibrium. The effect of the government's policy, therefore, is to achieve a large increase in the production and sales of this commodity and only a small decrease in price.

Figure 6-1(ii) shows a case in which the quantity demanded is quite unresponsive to price changes. As before, the increase in supply at the original price causes a surplus that brings the price down. But this time the quantity demanded by consumers does not increase very much in response to the fall in price. Thus the price continues to drop until, discouraged by lower and lower prices, farmers reduce the quantity supplied very nearly to the level attained before they received the increased incentive to produce. The effect of the government's policy is to bring about a large fall in the price and only a small increase in the quantity produced and sold.

In comparing the cases diagrammed in Figure 6-1, it can be seen that the government's policy has exactly the same effectiveness as far as farmers' willingness to supply the commodity is concerned (the supply curve shifts are identical). But the effects on the equilibrium price and quantity are very different because of the different degrees to which the quantity demanded by consumers responds to price changes. If the purpose of the policy is to increase the quantity of this commodity produced and consumed, then the policy will be a great success when the demand curve is similar to the one shown in Figure 6-1(i), but it will be a failure when the demand curve is similar to the one shown in Figure 6-1(ii). If, however, the main purpose of the policy is to achieve a large reduction in the price of the commodity, the policy will be a failure when demand is as shown in (i) but it will be a great success when demand is as shown in (ii).

A shift in supply can have very different effects, depending on the shape of the demand curve.

PRICE ELASTICITY: A MEASURE OF THE RESPONSIVENESS OF QUANTITY DEMANDED TO PRICE CHANGES

When considering the responsiveness of the quantity demanded to changes in price, we may wish to make statements such as "The demand for carrots was more responsive to price changes ten years ago than it is today" or "The demand for meat responds more to price changes than does the demand for green vegetables." In order to make such comparisons, a measure of the degree to which quantity demanded responds to changes in price is required.

In the previous examples it was possible to make comparisons between the two demand curves in Figure 6-1 on the basis of their geometrical steepness, because the curves were both drawn on the same scale. Thus, for any given price change, the quantity changes more on the flatter curve than it does on the steeper one. However, it can be very misleading to inspect a *single* curve and to conclude from its general appearance something about the degree of responsiveness of quantity demanded to price changes. You can make a curve appear as steep or as flat as you like by changing the scales. For example, a curve that looks steep when the horizontal scale is 1 inch = 100 units will look much flatter when 1 inch = 1 unit if the same vertical scale is used in each case.

Instead of gaining a vague general impression from the shape of demand curves, one could note the actual change in quantity demanded in response to a certain price change. But it would still be impossible to compare degrees of responsiveness for different commodities.

Assume that we have the information shown in Table 6-1. Should we conclude that the demand for radios is not so responsive to price changes as the demand for beef? After all, price cuts of 20¢ cause quite a large increase in the quantity of beef demanded but only a small increase in radios.

There are two problems here. First, a reduction in price of 20¢ will be a large price cut for a low-priced commodity and an insignificant price cut for a high-priced commodity. The price reductions listed in Table 6-1 represent very different fractions of the total prices. Actually it is more revealing to know the percentage change in the prices of the various commodities. Second,

TABLE 6-1
Price Reductions and Corresponding Increases in Quantity Demanded

Commodity	Reduction in price	Increase in quantity demanded
Beef	$.20 per pound	7,500 pounds
Men's shirts	.20 per shirt	5,000 shirts
Radios	.20 per radio	100 radios

TABLE 6–2
Price and Quantity Information Underlying Data of Table 6–1

Commodity	Unit	Original price	New price	Average price	Original quantity	New quantity	Average quantity
Beef	per pound	$ 1.70	$ 1.50	$ 1.60	116,250	123,750	120,000
Men's shirts	per shirt	8.10	7.90	8.00	197,500	202,500	200,000
Radios	per radio	40.10	39.90	40.00	9,950	10,050	10,000

These data provide the appropriate context of the data given in Table 6–1. The table relates the $.20 per unit price reduction of each commodity to the actual prices and quantities demanded.

by an analogous argument, knowing the quantity by which demand changes is not very revealing unless the level of demand is also known. An increase of 7,500 tons is quite a significant reaction of demand if the quantity formerly bought was 15,000 tons, but it is only a drop in the bucket if the quantity formerly demanded was 10 million tons.

Table 6-2 shows the original and new levels of price and quantity. Changes in price and quantity expressed as percentages of the average prices and quantities are shown in the first two columns of Table 6-3.[1] **Elasticity of demand,** the measure of responsiveness of quantity demanded to price changes, is defined as [6]

percentage change in quantity demanded
percentage change in price

When it is necessary to distinguish this measure of elasticity from other related concepts, it is sometimes called "price elasticity of demand," since the variable causing the change in quantity demanded is the commodity's own price.

[1] The use of averages is designed to avoid the ambiguity caused by the fact that, for example, the $.20 change in the price of beefsteak is a different percentage (1·1.8) of the original price, $1.70, than it is (13.3) of the new price, $1.50. We want the elasticity of demand between any two points (A and B) to be independent of whether we move from A to B or from B to A; as a result, using either "original" prices and quantities or "new" prices and quantities would be less satisfactory than using averages. In this illustration, $.20 is unambiguously 12.5 percent of $1.60 and applies to a price increase from $1.50 to $1.70, as well as to the decrease discussed in the text.

Interpreting Numerical Values of Elasticity of Demand

Because demand curves slope downward an *increase* in price is associated with a *decrease* in quantity demanded and vice versa. Since the percentage changes in price and quantity have opposite signs, demand elasticity is a negative number. We shall follow the usual practice of ignoring the negative sign and speak of the measure as a positive number, as we have done in Table 6-3. Thus, the more responsive the quantity demanded (radios relative to beef in the example), the greater the elasticity of demand and the higher the measure (2.0 compared to 0.5).

The numerical value of elasticity can vary from zero to infinity. Elasticity is zero if there is

TABLE 6–3
The Calculation of Demand Elasticities

Commodity	(1) Percentage decrease in price	(2) Percentage increase in quantity	(3) Elasticity of demand (2) ÷ (1)
Beef	12.5	6.25	0.5
Men's shirts	2.5	2.5	1.0
Radios	0.5	1.0	2.0

Elasticity is the percentage change in quantity divided by the percentage change in price. The percentage changes are based on average prices and quantities shown in Table 6–2. For example, the $.20 per pound decrease in the price of beef is 12.5 percent of $1.60. A $.20 change in the price of radios is only 0.5 percent of the average price per radio of $40.

FIGURE 6–2

Elasticity Along a Straight-Line Demand Curve

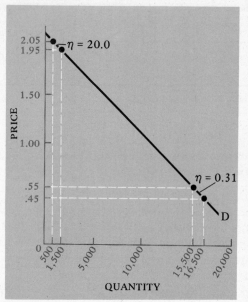

Moving down a straight-line demand curve, elasticity falls continuously. On this straight line, reduction in price of 10¢ always leads to the same increase (1,000 units) in quantity. Near the upper end of the curve, however, where price is $2 and quantity is 1,000 units, a reduction in price of 10¢ (from $2.05 to $1.95) is only a 5 percent reduction, but the 1,000-unit increase in quantity is a 100 percent increase. Elasticity, which is often symbolized by the Greek letter eta (η), is 20. At the price of 50¢ and quantity of 16,000 units, a price reduction of 10¢ (from 55¢ to 45¢) leads to the same 1,000-unit increase in demand. A 20 percent price decrease combines with a 6.25 percent quantity increase to give an elasticity of 0.31.

no change at all in quantity demanded when price changes, that is, when quantity demanded does not respond to a price change. The larger the elasticity, the larger is the percentage change in quantity for a given percentage change in price. As long as the elasticity of demand has a value of less than one, however, the percentage change in quantity is less than the percentage change in price. When elasticity is equal to one, then the

two percentage changes are equal to each other. When the percentage change in quantity exceeds the percentage change in price, the value for the elasticity of demand is greater than one.

When the percentage change in quantity is less than the percentage change in price (elasticity less than one), the demand is said to be **inelastic.** When the percentage change in quantity is greater than the percentage change in price (elasticity greater than one), the demand is said to be **elastic.** This terminology is important, and you should become familiar with it.

A demand curve need not—and usually does not—have the same elasticity over every part of the curve. Figure 6-2 shows that a downward-sloping, straight-line demand curve does not have a constant elasticity. The only two cases in which a straight line has constant elasticity are when it is vertical and when it is horizontal. Figure 6-3 illustrates three special demand curves with constant elasticities.

Elasticity of Demand and Changes in Total Expenditure and Total Revenue

Money spent in purchasing a commodity is received by the sellers of the commodity. The total amount spent by purchasers is thus the gross revenue of the sellers. How does total expenditure made by purchasers of a commodity or total gross revenue received by sellers of a commodity (the same thing) react when the price of a product is changed? The simplest example will show that total revenue may rise or fall in response to a decrease in price. Suppose 100 units of a commodity are being sold at a unit price of $1. The price is then cut to 90¢. If the quantity sold rises to 110, the total revenue of the sellers falls from $100 to $99; but if quantity sold rises to 120, total revenue rises from $100 to $108.

Generally what happens to total revenue depends on the price elasticity of demand. If this is less than unity (that is, less than one), the percentage change in price will exceed the percentage change in quantity. The price change will then dominate so that total revenue will change in the same direction as the price changes. If,

FIGURE 6–3

Three Demand Curves

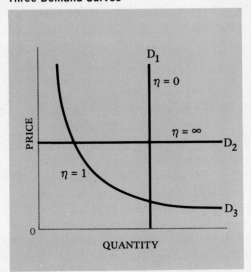

Each of these demand curves has constant elasticity. D_1 has *zero elasticity:* the quantity demanded does not change at all when price changes. D_2 has *infinite elasticity:* there exists a small price increase that decreases quantity demanded from an indefinitely large amount to zero. D_3 has *unit elasticity:* a given percentage increase in price brings an equal percentage decrease in quantity at all points on the curve.

same direction as quantity changes (that is, in the opposite direction to the change in price).

Notice what happened to total revenue when price fell in the example of radios, shirts, and beef. (The calculations are shown in Table 6-4.) In the case of beef, the demand is inelastic and a cut in price lowered the revenue of sellers; in the case of radios, the demand is elastic and a cut in price raised the revenue earned by sellers. The borderline case is men's shirts; here the demand elasticity is unity and the cut in price leaves total revenue unchanged.

These examples illustrate more general relationships:

1. If demand is elastic, a fall in price increases total expenditure and a rise in price reduces it.
2. If demand is inelastic, a fall in price reduces total expenditure and a rise in price increases it.
3. If elasticity of demand is unity, a rise or a fall in price leaves total expenditure unaffected. [7]

Consider two real examples. When a bumper potato crop in the United States sent prices down 50 percent, quantity sold increased only 15 percent and potato farmers found their revenues falling sharply. Demand was clearly inelastic. When in the 1970s Salt Lake County's Utah Transit Authority cut its bus fares from 25 cents to 15 cents for the average journey, the volume of passenger traffic increased from 4.4 million to 14 million journeys within two years and revenues rose sharply. Demand was clearly elastic.

however, elasticity exceeds unity, the percentage change in quantity will exceed the percentage change in price. The quantity change will then dominate so that total revenue will change in the

TABLE 6–4

The Changes in Total Revenue (Total Expenditure) for the Example of Table 6–2

Commodity	Price × quantity (original prices and quantities)	Price × quantity (new prices and quantities)	Change in revenue (expenditure)	Elasticity of demand from Table 6–3
Beef	$ 197,625	$ 185,625	−$12,000	0.5
Men's shirts	1,599,750	1,599,750	0	1.0
Radios	398,995	400,995	+ 2,000	2.0

Whether revenue increases or decreases in response to a price cut depends on whether demand is elastic or inelastic. The $197,625 figure is the product of the original price of beef ($1.70) and the original quantity (116,250 pounds). The $185,625 is the product of the new price ($1.50) and quantity (123,750), and so on.

What Determines Elasticity of Demand?

A great deal of work has been put into the measurement of demand elasticity, and in Chapter 10 we summarize some actual measurements. One of the most important determinants of elasticity is undoubtedly the degree of availability of close substitutes. Some commodities, such as margarine, cabbage, pork, and Fords, have quite close substitutes — butter, other green vegetables, beef, and similar makes of cars. A change in the price of these commodities, *the prices of the substitutes remaining constant,* can be expected to cause much substitution — a fall in price leading consumers to buy more of the commodity in question and a rise in price leading consumers to buy more of the substitute. Other commodities, such as salt, housing, and all vegetables as a group, have few if any satisfactory substitutes, and a rise in their price can be expected to cause a smaller fall in quantity demanded than would be the case if close substitutes were available.

To a great extent, elasticity depends on how widely or narrowly a commodity is defined.

Food and shelter are necessities in the sense that life cannot go on without some minimum quantity of them. It is a fact that food as a whole has an inelastic demand over a large price range. It does not follow, however, that any one food, such as white bread or cornflakes, is a necessity in the same sense. There is every reason to believe that the quantity demanded for any one food can and will fall greatly as a result of a rise in its price.

OTHER DEMAND ELASTICITIES

The purpose of measuring demand elasticity is to discover the degree to which the quantity demanded responds to a change in one of the factors that influence it. So far the response of the quantity of a commodity demanded to changes in the commodity's own price has been considered. It is also important to know how demand responds to changes in incomes and the prices of other goods.

Income Elasticity of Demand

The responsiveness of demand to changes in income is termed **income elasticity of demand,** and it is defined as

$$\frac{\text{percentage change in quantity demanded}}{\text{percentage change in income}}$$

For most goods, increases in income lead to increases in demand and income elasticity will be positive. These are called **normal goods.** Goods for which consumption decreases in response to a rise in income have negative income elasticities and are called **inferior goods.**

The income elasticity of normal goods may be less than unity (inelastic) or greater than unity (elastic), depending on whether (say) a 10 percent increase in income leads to less than or more than a 10 percent increase in the quantity demanded. Not surprisingly, different commodities have different income elasticities (as the studies examined in Chapter 10 show). Goods that consumers at a given level of income regard as necessities tend to have lower income elasticities than do luxuries, for the obvious reason that as incomes rise it becomes possible for households to devote a smaller proportion of their income to meeting basic needs and a larger proportion to buying things they have always wanted but could not afford.

The reaction of demand to changes in income is extremely important. In most Western economies we know that economic growth has caused the level of income to double every 20 to 30 years over a sustained period of at least a century. This rise in income is shared to some extent by most of the households in the country. As they find their incomes increasing, they increase their demands for most commodities. But the demands for some commodities such as food and basic clothing will not increase very much as incomes rise while the demands for other commodities increase rapidly as incomes rise. In developing countries such as Ireland and Mexico the

Terminology of Elasticity

TERMINOLOGY	NUMERICAL MEASURE OF ELASTICITY	VERBAL DESCRIPTION
A. Price elasticity of demand [supply]		
Perfectly or completely inelastic	Zero	Quantity demanded [supplied] does not change as price changes
Inelastic	Greater than zero, but less than one	Quantity demanded [supplied] changes by a smaller percentage than does price
Unit elasticity	One	Quantity demanded [supplied] changes by exactly the same percentage as does price
Elastic	Greater than one, but less than infinity	Quantity demanded [supplied] changes by a larger percentage than does price
Perfectly, completely, or infinitely elastic	Infinity	Purchasers [sellers] are prepared to buy [sell] all they can at some price and none at all at an even slightly higher [lower] price
B. Income elasticity of demand		
Inferior good	Negative	Quantity demanded decreases as income increases
Normal good	Positive	Quantity demanded increases as income increases:
Income inelastic	Greater than zero, less than one	less than in proportion to income increase
Income elastic	Greater than one	more than in proportion to income increase
C. Cross elasticity of demand		
Substitute	Positive	Price increase of a substitute leads to an increase in quantity demanded of this good (and less of the substitute)
Complement	Negative	Price increase of a complement leads to a decrease in quantity demanded of this good (and less of the complement)

demand for durable goods is increasing most rapidly as household incomes rise, while in the United States it is the demand for services that is rising most rapidly. The uneven impact of the growth of income on the demands for different commodities has very important effects on the economy and groups in it, and these will be studied at several different points in this book.

The income elasticity of a particular good is expected to be different at widely different income levels. Consider how a family's diet may change as its income level rises. When incomes are very low, households may eat virtually no meat and consume lots of starchy foods such as bread and potatoes; at higher levels, they may eat the cheaper cuts of meat and more green vegetables along with their bread and potatoes; at yet higher levels they are likely to eat more (and more expensive) meat, to substitute frozen for canned vegetables, and to eat a greater variety of foods. In this sequence the income elasticity of hamburger may be high at low levels of income but decrease as income rises and steak replaces hamburger. Different commodities will show different patterns. Potatoes are likely to exhibit low income elasticity while steak proves to be income-elastic over a wide range of income.[2] Figure 6-4 shows one particular pattern of income elasticity varying with income.[3]

[2] It is common to use the terms *income-elastic* and *income-inelastic* to refer to income elasticities of greater or less than unity. See the box on page 85.

[3] The curve in Figure 6-4, like the demand curve studied in Chapter 5, shows the relation of quantity demanded to *one* variable, *ceteris paribus*. This time the variable is income instead of price. (An increase in price of the commodity, incomes remaining constant, would shift downward the curve shown in Figure 6-4).

In this chart, in contrast to the ordinary demand curve, quantity demanded is on the vertical axis. This follows the usual practice of putting the to-be-explained variable (called the dependent variable) on the vertical axis and the explanatory variable (called the independent variable) on the horizontal axis. It is the ordinary demand curve that has the axes "backwards." This practice dates to Alfred Marshall's *Principles of Economics* (1890), the classic that is one of the foundation stones of modern price theory. [8] For better or worse, Marshall's scheme is now used by everybody—although mathematicians never fail to wonder at this further example of the odd ways of economists.

Cross Elasticity

The responsiveness of demand to changes in the prices of other commodities is called **cross elasticity of demand.** It is defined as

$$\frac{\text{percentage change in quantity demanded of one good, } X}{\text{percentage change in price of another good, } Y}$$

Cross elasticity can vary from minus infinity to plus infinity. Complementary commodities will have negative cross elasticities. Cars and gasoline, for example, are complements. A large rise in the price of gasoline will lead (as it has in America) to a decline in the demand for cars as some people decide to do without a car and others decide not to buy a second (or a third) car. Substitute commodities have positive cross elasticities. Cars and public transport are substitutes. A large rise in the price of cars (relative to public transport) would lead to a rise in the demand for public transport as some people shifted from cars to public transport.

Measures of cross elasticity sometimes prove helpful in defining whether producers of similar products are in competition with each other. Glass bottles and tin cans have a high cross elasticity of demand. The producer of bottles is thus in competition with the producer of cans. If the bottle company raises its price, it will lose substantial sales to the can producer. Men's shoes and women's shoes have a low cross elasticity. Thus a producer of men's shoes is not in close competition with a producer of women's shoes. If the former raises its price, it will not lose many sales to the latter. This kind of knowledge has been extremely important in antitrust cases where the issue was whether a firm in one industry was or was not in active competition with firms in another industry.

SUPPLY ELASTICITY

The concept of elasticity relates to supply as well as to demand. Just as elasticity of demand measures the response of quantity demanded to changes in any of the forces that influence it, so

FIGURE 6–4

An Income-Consumption Curve Relating Quantity Demanded to Level of Income

Different shapes of the curve relating quantity demanded to income correspond to different ranges of income elasticity. The product whose income-consumption curve is shown by the heavy curve is a normal good for incomes up to I_3 and an inferior good above I_4. Whenever the curve is horizontal (from 0 to I_1 and from I_3 to I_4) income elasticity is zero. Between I_1 and I_2 quantity demanded is rising proportionally more rapidly than income (income elasticity greater than plus unity); between I_2 and I_3 quantity demanded is rising but less than proportionally (income elasticity greater than zero, less than unity). Different commodities will have different patterns: For example, if the income-consumption curve for some commodity was the heavy curve to I_3 and the screened curve thereafter, that commodity would not be an inferior good at any level of income.

elasticity of supply measures the response of quantity supplied to changes in any of the forces that influence it. We will focus on the commodity's own price as a factor influencing supply.

Elasticity of supply measures the responsiveness of the quantity supplied to a change in the commodity's own price. It is defined as

$$\frac{\text{percentage change in quantity supplied}}{\text{percentage change in price}}$$

The supply curves considered in this chapter all have positive slopes: an increase in price causes an increase in quantity sold. Such supply curves all have positive elasticities.

There are important special cases. If the supply curve is vertical—the quantity supplied does not change as price changes—elasticity of supply is zero. This would be the case, for example, if suppliers produced a given quantity and dumped it on the market for whatever it would bring. A horizontal supply curve has an infinitely high elasticity of supply: A small drop in price would reduce the quantity producers are willing to supply from an indefinitely large amount to zero. Between these two extremes elasticity of supply will vary with the shape of the supply curve.[4]

What Determines Elasticity of Supply?

Supply elasticities are very important for many problems in economics. The brevity of this discussion reflects two main facts. First, much of the treatment of demand elasticity carries over to the case of supply and does not need repeating. Second, there will be more about the determinants of supply elasticity in Part Four.

In the meantime it should be noted that supply elasticity depends to a great extent on how costs behave as output is varied. If costs of production rise rapidly as output rises, then the stimulus to expand production in response to a price rise will quickly be choked off by increases in costs. In this case supply will tend to be rather inelastic. If, however, costs rise only slowly as production increases, a rise in price that raises profits will call forth a large increase in quantity supplied before the rise in costs puts a halt to the expansion in output. In this case supply will tend to be rather elastic.

Summary

1. Elasticity of demand (also called *price elasticity*) is a measure of the extent to which the quantity demanded of a commodity responds to a change in its price. We define it as the percentage change in quantity divided by the percentage change in price that brought it about. Elasticity is here defined to be a positive number that varies from zero to infinity.

---

[4] Steepness, which relates to absolute rather than percentage changes, is *not* always a reliable guide. As is proven in the appendix to this chapter, any upward-sloping straight line through the origin has an elasticity of $+1.0$ over its entire range.

2. When the numerical measure of elasticity is less than one, demand is *inelastic*. This means that the percentage change in quantity is less than the percentage change in price that brought it about. When the numerical measure exceeds unity, demand is *elastic*. This means that the percentage change in quantity is greater than the percentage change in price that brought it about.

3. Elasticity and total revenue of sellers are related in this way: If elasticity is less than unity, a fall in price lowers total revenue; if elasticity is greater than unity, a fall in price raises total revenue; and if elasticity is unity, total revenue does not change as price changes.

4. The main determinant of the price elasticity of demand is the availability of substitutes for the commodity. The more and better the substitutes, the higher the elasticity.

5. Income elasticity is the percentage change in quantity demanded divided by the percentage change in income that brought it about. The income elasticity of demand for a commodity may well change as income varies. For example, a commodity that has a high income elasticity at a low income (because increases in income bring it within reach of the typical household) may have a low or negative income elasticity at higher incomes (because with further rises in incomes it can be replaced by a superior substitute).

6. Cross elasticity is the percentage change in quantity demanded divided by the percentage change in the price of some other commodity that brought it about.

7. Elasticity of supply is an important concept in economics. It measures the ratio of the percentage change in the quantity supplied of a commodity to the percentage change in its price. It is the analogue on the supply side to the elasticity of demand.

8. An appendix to this chapter, for students with some mathematical background, extends the analysis.

Topics for Review

Elasticity of demand
Significance of elastic and inelastic demands
The relation between demand elasticity and total
  expenditure
Income elasticity of demand
Normal goods and inferior goods
Cross elasticity of demand
Elasticity of supply

Discussion Questions

1. What, if anything, does each of the following newspaper quotations tell you about elasticity of demand?
   a. "Ridership always went up when bus fares came down, but the increased patronage never was enough to prevent a decrease in overall revenue."
   b. "When the Cincinatti Telephone Company started charging for directory assistance calls, the number of [such] calls dropped 80 percent."
   c. "The increase in postal rates has led us [The Narrangansett Electric Co.] to have 60 percent of our bills hand delivered instead of mailed."
   d. "Coffee to me is an essential—you've gotta have it."
2. It is being proposed to the Securities and Exchange Commission that brokerage commissions charged to investors be changed in order to help brokerage houses increase their revenues and thereby help avoid bankruptcy. In which direction should they be changed to meet the objective?
3. What would you predict about the relative price elasticity of demand of (a) food, (b) meat, (c) beef, (d) chuck roast, (e) Safeway chuck roast? What would you predict about their relative income elasticities?

4. The price of gasoline has quadrupled over the last decade.
   a. How would you have expected demand to respond the first year or two after the price increases began?
   b. How would you expect demand to have responded after a decade of price rises?
5. If the elasticity of demand for railroad passenger travel is unity in the neighborhood of present prices and the railroads are losing money on their passenger traffic, how (if at all) can they make their passenger service profitable?
6. Consider the demand for margarine expressed in this quotation: "We always buy Fleischmann's now—I don't even have butter in the house. In the beginning it was the price, now I don't even consider that. We're very cholesterol conscious in our family." Interpret this in terms of elasticity of demand for butter and for margarine.
7. What elasticity measure or measures would be useful in answering the following questions?
   a. Will cheaper transport into the central city help keep downtown shopping centers profitable?
   b. Will raising the bulk-rate postage rate increase or decrease the postal deficit?
   c. Are producers of toothpaste and mouthwash in competition with each other?
   d. Would an increase in gas field prices solve the natural gas shortage within a decade?
   e. Would raising U.S. oil prices to the world price level help to reduce U.S. oil imports by a significant amount?
   f. In the mid 1970s there was considerable new planting of cocoa trees. Why, when the additional output began to come on the market in 1979, did the price of cocoa fall drastically even though the increase in supply was as yet very modest?

Supply and Demand in Action I: Agriculture and the Volunteer Army

7

The laws of supply and demand and the concepts of elasticity of demand and supply have immediate application to many real-world problems. In this chapter and the next we apply these basic concepts and the method of comparative statics, first encountered on page 72. The method, you will recall, is to start from a position of equilibrium in the market and then introduce the change to be studied—for example, a shift to the left of the supply curve. Then we determine the new equilibrium position and compare it with the original one. The differences between the two positions of equilibrium (higher price, lower quantities actually exchanged) can be attributed to the change introduced, for that is the only change that has been allowed to occur.

Agriculture and the Farm Problem

The spring of 1973 was one of the wettest in American history; excess rainfall and flooding diminished many crop yields. The destruction of most of the California lettuce crop forced lettuce prices up from about 39¢ a head to 69¢ in two weeks. As a result, the quantity demanded was reduced to the available supply. Shoppers spent more on tomatoes and cottage cheese and refused to buy lettuce. Lettuce seed sales spurted as many families planted lettuce in their backyards.

The winter and spring of 1976 were mild and warm, and the good weather generated bumper fruit crops in California, where more than half of America's fruit—and virtually the entire crop for canning—is grown. At prevailing prices the state director of food and agriculture predicted 100,000 tons of unsold peaches, 50,000 tons of unsold pears, and large surpluses of apricots, cherries, and nectarines. California's canneries would take the surplus but only at sharply reduced prices, prices that meant lower incomes for fruit growers. While growers cursed a bountiful nature, consumers stood to benefit.

These examples suggest why even the simple theory of supply and demand is so useful. Fluctuations in the supply of these products had just the effects that economic theory predicts for products with inelastic demands.

The theory of supply and demand can also explain more indirect and complex chains of effects. When bad weather destroyed 80 percent of the U.S. soybean crop in a year when most other grains were also in short supply, a series of indirect but predictable results occurred. Soybeans are a primary ingredient of chicken feed for the mass-production broiler chicken industry. The decrease in supply of soybeans (a leftward shift of the supply curve) caused the price of soybeans to triple in two months. Chicken farmers found the cost of soybeans rising so fast that it did not pay to continue feeding baby chicks. Millions were simply killed, and many more millions were not allowed to hatch. This led to a decrease in the supply of chickens (a leftward shift in the supply curve of chickens) and a rise in the price of chickens to households.

In an attempt to increase the supply of soybeans available for chicken feed and thereby stem the rise in chicken prices, the U.S. government restricted exports of soybeans to Japan and other countries. This helped some—in the United States. In Japan, where imported soybeans are a staple of the human diet, a food shortage loomed and prices of soybeans soared. For many Japanese an already marginal diet became inadequate until alternative food supplies were secured. The failure of the U.S. soybean crop can be charted in the Japanese demographic statistics: a higher death rate and a lower marriage rate in the year of the failure and in the subsequent year.

THE NATURE OF THE FARM PROBLEM

For the last half century the "farm problem" has challenged and troubled U.S. policymakers. The problem has traditionally been one of large fluctuations in farm income around an average level that is below the level of incomes earned in most other sectors of the economy.

As a whole the agricultural sector has had a level of prosperity below the U.S. average. Less than 8 million people—3.7 percent of the population—lived on farms in 1979, and they earned 3.2 percent of all personal income. Of this income, only 47 percent was from farm sources. Farm employment was 4 percent of national employment, but income earned by farmers from farming was only about 1.5 percent of personal income.

While farmers, farm operators, and farm workers today lag behind the rest of the population in earning power, a revolution in agricultural methods is occurring that may one day close the gap. Farming is increasingly a vast, capital-intensive, corporate activity. Mechanization, large-scale production, and computerized analysis of day-to-day decisions are common. Many a modern American farmer has a college degree, even a postgraduate degree in business administration, and spends more time in the office analyzing computer printouts than in the fields. In some ways large-scale modern farming resembles an automobile assembly line more than it does the traditional small and often poor family farm. The "farm problem" today is really two different problems: the problem of *relatively* poor, small, or medium-size farms and the problem of large, mechanized, "mass-production" farms.

Ninety-eight percent of all farms in 1980 were family farms with an average size of 450 acres; the other 2 percent were corporate farms, some with more than 100,000 acres in cultivation. That 2 percent accounted for over one-third of all farm output in 1980, and the percentage of acreage in corporate farming is increasing year by year.

Despite the growing role of the corporate farm, small family farmers remain the major political force in many states. They wield political influence, especially in the U.S. Senate, that is disproportionate to their numbers, and farmers' problems have led Congress to employ a wide variety of farm policies over the last 50 years. Consequently, "parity," "production controls," "crop insurance," and "price supports" are terms regularly seen in the press.

American farm problems are important not only because of the importance of farmers in American life but also because American agriculture is critical to the world's food supply. Although traditionally regarded as a manufacturing nation, the United States now provides two-thirds of all grain and soybeans exported in world trade. American agriculture is the regular supplier to hundreds of millions of people outside the United States and the buffer against crop failure for more than 3 billion others. People around the globe depend for their very survival on America's remaining one of the world's greatest granaries.

FLUCTUATIONS AND TRENDS IN PRICES AND INCOMES

The farm problem that is common to all types of agriculture has three main sources: short-term fluctuations due to uncontrollable variations in supply; cyclical fluctuations due to variations in demand as the economy expands and contracts; and long-term trends in both demand and supply due to economic growth.

Short-term Fluctuations

Short-term volatility of prices is typical of many agricultural markets. Why do such fluctuations occur?

Farm crops are subject to variations in output because of many factors that are completely beyond farmers' control. Some variation is simply a matter of season, but pests, floods, and lack of rain can drastically reduce farm output, and exceptionally favorable conditions can cause production greatly to exceed expectations. By now you should not be surprised to hear that such unplanned fluctuations in output cause fluctuations in farm prices. Not only does price theory predict this obvious consequence, it also predicts other, less obvious ones that help us to understand some of the farmer's problems.

The basic behavior is illustrated in Figure 7-1. Because demand curves slope downward, variations in farm output placed on the market cause price fluctuations in the opposite direction to crop sizes. A bumper crop sends prices down, a small crop sends them up. The price change will be larger, the less elastic the demand curve.

Because many agricultural products have inelastic demands, fluctuations in their prices tend to be large in response to unplanned changes in production.

What are the effects on the receipts of farmers? If the commodity in question has an elasticity of demand greater than unity, farmers' receipts will vary directly with quantity supplied. If the demand is inelastic, farmers' receipts will vary inversely with quantity supplied.

If demands are inelastic, good harvests will bring reductions in total farm receipts and bad harvests will bring increases.

Because most farm products have inelastic demands, farm receipts tend to vary inversely with crop size. When nature is bountiful and produces a bumper crop, farmers' receipts dwindle; when nature is moderately unkind and output falls unexpectedly, their receipts rise. The interests of the farmer and the consumer are exactly opposed in such cases. This conflict is dramatically illustrated every time a partial crop failure sends food prices soaring but raises farm incomes, and whenever a bumper crop that brings relief to consumers nevertheless evokes a cry for help from the farm belt, where incomes are shrinking.

Cyclical Fluctuations in Prices and Incomes

As the tide of national prosperity ebbs and flows, demand curves for all commodities rise and fall.

FIGURE 7–1
The Effect on Price of Unplanned Variations in Output Depends on Elasticity of Demand

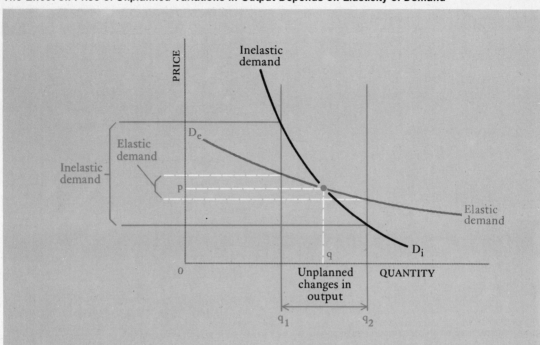

An unplanned fluctuation in output of a given size leads to a much sharper fluctuation in price if the demand curve is inelastic than if it is elastic. Suppose the expected price is p and the planned output q. The two curves D_i and D_e are *alternative* demand curves. If actual production always equaled planned production, the equilibrium price and quantity would be p and q with either demand curve. Unplanned variations in output, however, cause quantity to fluctuate year by year between q_1 (a bad harvest) and q_2 (a good harvest). When demand is inelastic (shown by the heavy curve), prices will show large fluctuations. When demand is elastic (shown by the screened curve), price fluctuations will be much smaller.

The effects on prices and outputs depend on the elasticity of *supply*. Industrial products typically have rather elastic supply curves, so shifts in demand cause fairly large changes in outputs but only small changes in prices. Agricultural commodities typically have rather inelastic supply curves.

The very different patterns of response in the agricultural and manufacturing sectors of the economy are explained in Figure 7-2. These patterns of unregulated markets have been observed and accepted as part of the nature of things in most depressed periods of American economic history. They occurred once more in the early 1930s when America, along with the rest of the world, suffered the greatest depression ever. But in the 1930s the government attempted to intervene, and since then farm policy has been continuous and active.

To the public (and to many in Congress) the economic plight of farmers during the Great Depression seemed to be caused by the great fall in prices, which was caused by the fall in demand for commodities with an inelastic supply curve. The notion of **price parity**, the ratio of the prices farmers received for things they sold to the

FIGURE 7–2
The Effect on Receipts of a Decrease in Demand

(i) Inelastic supply

(ii) Elastic supply

Either an inelastic or an elastic supply curve can lead to a sharp decrease in receipts, but the effect on prices is very different in the two cases. In each part of the diagram, when demand decreases from D to D_1, price and quantity decrease to p_1 and q_1 and total receipts decline by the shaded area. In (i) the cause is mainly the sharp decrease in price. Output and employment remain high, but the drastic fall in price will reduce or eliminate profits and put downward pressure on wages. In (ii) the cause is primarily the sharp decrease in quantity. Employment and total profits earned fall drastically, though wage rates and profit margins on what is produced may remain close to their former level.

prices they paid for things they bought, was invoked to measure their hardship. As a result programs were proposed to restore price parity to farmers.

But this appealing diagnosis is incomplete. It is income received, not prices, that determines how much people have to spend. As Figure 7-2(ii) shows, a very elastic supply can be as much a curse as a very inelastic one in the face of a decrease in demand! The loss in receipts in this case is primarily due to a decline in *quantity* sold rather than to a decline in *price*, but that does not make it less painful.

From 1929 to 1932 agricultural output fell by 1 percent while prices fell by 56 percent. Manufacturing output was nearly halved, but manufacturing prices fell only moderately. In fact, over that period, total revenues earned actually fell by more in manufacturing than in agriculture.

Agriculture and industry both suffered in the Great Depression but with different symptoms: farmers via low prices, industry via low production and high unemployment of workers and resources. While farmers clamored for the government to do something about prices, industry and industrial workers clamored for the government to act to overcome unemployment of people and underemployment of factories.

Long-term Trends

Paradoxically, it has been steady growth over time in the productive capacity and wealth of the American economy that has caused many long-term problems for American agriculture. Pressure has come from both the demand and the supply sides of agricultural markets.

Demand. Workers can produce more per worker than they previously did. In this century output per worker has increased more than fivefold in the United States. Such increases in production lead to increases in the income of the population. How do households wish to consume their extra income? The relevant measure is income elasticity of demand, which measures the effect of increases in income on the demands for various goods. Income elasticities vary considerably among goods. At the levels of income existing in the United States and other advanced industrial nations, most foodstuffs have low income elasticities because most people are already well fed. When these people get extra income, they tend to spend much of it on consumers' durables, entertainment, and travel. Thus, as incomes grow, the demand for agricultural goods tends to increase relatively slowly (if population remains relatively stable).

If productivity is expanding uniformly among industries, the demands for goods with low income elasticities will be expanding more slowly than output. In such industries excess supplies will develop, prices and profits will be depressed, and resources will be induced to move elsewhere. Exactly the reverse will happen for industries producing goods with high income elasticities. Demands will expand faster than supplies, prices and profits will tend to rise, and resources will move into the industries producing these goods.

Supply. The need to transfer resources out of agricultural industries is even greater than would be required by their low income elasticities. The reason is that growth in agricultural productivity has been well *above* the average for the economy. Encouraged by government-financed research, by subsidies, and by a government-assured demand for farm output at a stable price, agricultural productivity has increased enormously in this century. American farm output per agricultural worker has grown at the rate of about 5 percent per year since 1930, faster than the rate of growth of output per nonagricultural worker.

These productivity increases tend to shift the supply curves of agricultural goods to the right, indicating a greatly increased ability and willingness to produce at each price. In 1929 there were 12.8 million people employed on farms. The output they produced in 1929 could be produced today by 1.7 million people! If resources had not been reallocated out of farming, there would have been enormous increases in output which could hardly have been sold within the United States at any price. Fortunately, resources did move: actual employment on farms in 1979 was 3.9 million.

The movement out of farming has not, however, been quite as fast as required. Adjusting for both productivity increases and population increases, about 3 million farmers in 1979 could have supplied every American with the same output of agricultural goods as each American consumed in 1929. This number is almost 1 million fewer farmers than we had in 1979. Since per capita consumption of all agricultural products had not risen sharply, there were necessarily excess supplies of farm products. This process is further illustrated in the box on page 96.

The process just described is painful—indeed, pain is the spur to those who live and work on farms, especially when resources move slowly in response to depressed incomes. It may be easy for the farmer's son or daughter to move to the city; it may be quite difficult for the farmer and the farmer's parents, who are set in their ways. Because farmers are people—and voters—governments tend to respond to their cries for help in overcoming the depressed conditions in agriculture that free markets often produce.

Notice that the same problem exists for any industry where growth in demand is low while productivity growth is high. It is quite possible that in the future a similarly gradual but continuing decline will affect durable consumer goods industries such as automobiles and refrigerators.

Export markets. Recent changes in export markets have altered the problems faced by agricultural products, such as wheat, that are sold internationally. World demand for agricultural goods has expanded faster than world supply since the early 1970s. This has meant an upward trend in some major agricultural prices. As a result, the long-term tendency toward depressed prices and

---

How Agricultural Surpluses May Become Chronic, and Agriculture a Depressed Sector

Imagine a simplified economy that has only two sectors, "agriculture" and "manufacturing," each of which grows at 6 percent per year. The income elasticity of demand is assumed to be 0.5 in agriculture and 1.5 in manufacturing. Assume that production is 50 units in each sector in "year zero." Supposing first that there is no movement of resources between the two sectors, the growth rate assures that output in each sector will double in 12 years, and thus that national income will double. Thus, based on income elasticities of demand, we know that demand for agricultural goods increases by 50 percent, while demand for manufacturing goods increases by 150 percent. The table below shows how, within the short space of 12 years, massive surpluses will appear in agriculture and shortages will occur in manufacturing.

Clearly, in such a case, resources need to be shifted out of agriculture and into manufacturing. Further, if the productivity increases are going on continuously, there will be a continual tendency toward excess supply of agricultural goods and excess demand for manufactured goods and a continuing need for resource reallocation.

But we have neglected prices and incomes so far. Because output is expanding faster than demand in the agricultural sector, prices will fall and incomes of producers will fall. In response to falling farm prices, there will be a decline in the demand for farm labor and the other factors of production used in agriculture, and the earnings of these factors will decline. At the same time, exactly the opposite tendencies will be observed in manufacturing. Here demand is expanding faster than output; prices will rise, incomes and profits of producers will be rising, and there will be a large demand for the factors of production used in manufacturing industries. So the price of these factors, and consequently the incomes that they earn, will be bid upward. In short, manufacturing will be a buoyant sector and agriculture a depressed sector. Now if resources move freely, there will be a continuing flow of labor (and land and other factors of production) from agriculture to manufacturing. But if resources move too slowly, there will be a continuing depression in agriculture and chronic surpluses, while manufacturing will be buoyant with chronic scarcities.

	Agriculture	Manufacturing
Production in year zero	50	50
Production in year 12	100	100
Assumed income elasticity of demand	.50	1.50
Quantity demanded in year 12, at year zero prices	75	125
Therefore production in year 12 leads to a shortage or surplus of	25 (surplus)	25 (shortage)

incomes seems to have been eased in much of American agriculture. Short-term and cyclical fluctuations are still serious problems, but those sectors that have shared in the export boom have found that average incomes, around which fluctuations occurred, are no longer depressed well below incomes earned elsewhere in the economy.

AGRICULTURAL STABILIZATION AND SUPPORT

Governments throughout the world intervene in agricultural markets in attempts to deal with the problems just studied. They try to stabilize agricultural prices and incomes in the face of short-term and uncontrollable fluctuations in supply and cyclical fluctuations in demand. They also seek to support agricultural prices and incomes at levels sufficient to guarantee farmers what is regarded as reasonable or decent living standards. In so doing they often weaken the incentives for resources to leave farming. This makes the long-run problem of excess resources worse.

Because income stabilization and price stabilization are not the same, there has been confusion about what is intended by programs designed to achieve "orderly agricultural marketing" or "farm parity"—phrases used in American legislation. We shall consider several plans.

Suppose the supply curve in each case refers to planned (or average) production per year, but actual production fluctuates around that level. In a free market, as we have seen, this causes both prices and farmers' receipts to fluctuate widely from year to year.

The Ever-normal Granary

One method of preventing fluctuations in prices and gross receipts is for individual farmers to form a producers' association that tries to stabilize—to keep "ever normal"—the supply *actually coming onto the market,* in spite of variations in production. It does this by storing a crop, say grain, in years of above-average production and

selling out of its storage elevators in years of below-average production.

Since one farmer's production is an insignificant part of total production, there is no point in an individual farmer's holding some production off the market in an effort to prevent a fall in price in a year of bumper crops. But if all farmers get together and agree to vary the supply coming onto the market, then, collectively, they can have a major effect on price. The appropriate policy is shown in Figure 7-3.

Since revenues accrue to the producers when the goods are actually sold on the market, total revenues can be stabilized by keeping sales constant at the equilibrium output even though pro-

FIGURE 7–3

Stabilizing Sales Despite Variable Production: The Ever-normal Granary

The ever-normal granary scheme sells the equilibrium quantity each year even though actual production varies. The planned supply curve is S; p and q are the equilibrium price and quantity. Actual production varies between q_1 and q_2. When production is q_2 the producers' association sells q and stores qq_2. When production is q_1 it still sells q, supplementing the current production by selling q_1q from its stored crops. Producers' revenue is stabilized at $p \cdot q$ (the shaded area) every year.

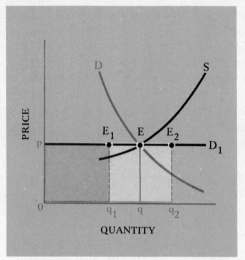

FIGURE 7–4
Government Price Supports at the Equilibrium Price

Government price supports at the equilibrium price stabilize prices and do not accumulate surpluses but cause revenues to vary directly with production. Actual production varies around the equilibrium level of q. When production is q_2 the government buys qq_2 and stores it. When production is q_1 the government sells q_1q from storage. The quantity sold to the public is always q, and this stabilizes price at p. The government policy converts the demand curve to D_1. If q is average production, there is no trend toward accumulation of storage crops.

Farmers' revenue varies from pq_1 (the darker shaded area) when production is q_1, to pq_2 (the entire shaded area) when production is q_2.

find itself with ever-increasing stockpiles of the crop.

Government Price Supports at the Equilibrium Price

Because there are many difficulties in organizing and administering private stabilization programs such as the ever-normal granary, why cannot the government do the same thing and do it more efficiently?

Suppose the government, instead of the producers' association, enters the market, buying in the market and adding to its own stocks when there is a surplus and selling in the market—thereby reducing its stocks—when there is a shortage. If it had enough grain elevators and warehouses, and if its support price were set at a realistic level, the government could stabilize prices indefinitely. But, as Figure 7-4 illustrates, it would not succeed in stabilizing farmers' revenues and incomes, for farmers would find their revenues high with a bumper crop and low with a poor crop.

Government price supports at the equilibrium price would not stabilize revenues. They would however reverse the pattern of revenue fluctuation of a crop with inelastic demand and a fluctuating supply.

In effect, the government policy imposes a demand curve that is perfectly elastic at the support price. This stabilizes price, but it does not stabilize receipts to producers.

duction varies. This can be accomplished by adding to or subtracting from inventories the excesses or shortages of production.

The fully successful every-normal granary stabilizes both prices and revenues of producers.

The costs of this plan are those of providing storage and organizing and administering the program. A potential danger is that the producers' association will sell on average less than is produced (in order to get higher prices) and will

Government Stabilization of Farmers' Revenues by Open Market Purchases and Sales

Obviously there must be a government buying and selling policy that will stabilize farmers' receipts. What are its characteristics? As has been seen, too much price stability causes receipts to vary directly with production and too little price stability causes receipts to vary inversely with production. It appears that the government should aim at some intermediate degree of price stability. If the government allows prices to vary in inverse proportion to variations in production, then receipts will be stabilized. A 10 percent rise in production should be met by a 10 percent fall in price, and a 10 percent fall in production by a 10 percent rise in price.

To stabilize farmers' receipts, the government must make the demand curve facing the farmers one of unit elasticity. It must buy in periods of high output and sell in periods of low output, but only enough to let prices change in inverse proportion to farmers' output.

Government Price Supports Above the Free-market Equilibrium Level

To avoid long-term problems, the government policy just described should allow prices to fluctuate around the free-market level. In practice, however, stabilization plans involving price supports usually set prices above the average free-market equilibrium level. Partly this is due to the fact that stabilization is not the only goal, and there is a desire to assure farmers a standard of living comparable with that of city dwellers. This involves attempting to *raise* farm incomes in addition to stabilizing them.

Here too the government buys in periods of high output and sells in periods of low output, but on average it buys much more than it sells. This is illustrated in Figure 7-5.

Stabilization of prices above the free-market equilibrium level is an example of what is more generally known as establishing a minimum price, or **price floor,** below which the commodity cannot be sold. Whenever price is maintained above the free-market level, the quantity that suppliers wish to sell will exceed the quantity demanded. Either an unsold surplus will exist or someone—in this case, the government—must step in and buy the excess production. In the average year there is a surplus, and this results in a situation in which over time the stabilizing authority buys more than it sells, so unsold surpluses accumulate. The cost to the taxpayers

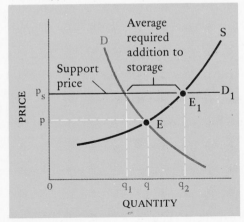

FIGURE 7–5
Price Supports Above the Equilibrium Price

The support price becomes a price floor, and the government must purchase the excess supply at that price. Average annual demand and supply are *D* and *S*. The free-market equilibrium is at *E*. If the government will buy any quantity at p_s, the demand curve becomes the black curve D_1 and equilibrium shifts to E_1. The average addition to storage is the quantity q_1q_2. The government purchases add to farmers' receipts and to government expenditures.

includes any part of the outlay not ultimately recovered by sale of the crop, plus costs of storage, handling, and administration.

PROBLEMS WITH AGRICULTURAL STABILIZATION AND SUPPORT PLANS

A first difficulty of plans that seek to raise farm income by raising prices above free-market levels is the tendency to accumulate surpluses. Eventually, if agricultural surpluses persist, the stored crops will have to be destroyed, dumped on the market for what they will bring, or otherwise disposed of at a fraction of their cost. If the crops are thrown on the market and allowed to depress the price, then the original purposes for which the crops were purchased—price stabilization and raising of farm incomes—are defeated. If the crops are destroyed or allowed to rot, the efforts of a large quantity of the country's scarce factors of production (the land, labor, and capital that went into producing the stored goods) will have been completely wasted.

Destroying crops is a vexing moral problem when millions are starving, but if the stored crops are not to depress the price, they must be kept off the market. Giving crops away to those who would not otherwise buy them is sometimes attempted but is hard to achieve. Selling grain at cut-rate prices for conversion to gasohol has recently been proposed.

Any of these "solutions" will mean that the agricultural support program will show a deficit, for goods will have been purchased that cannot be sold except at a large loss. This deficit means that taxpayers generally will be paying farmers for producing goods that no one in the nation is willing to purchase at prices that come near to covering costs.

When support schemes begin to produce ever-larger surpluses, the next step is often to try to limit each farmer's production. Quotas may be assigned to individual farmers and penalties imposed for exceeding the quotas. Or, as has been done in the past, bonuses may be paid for leaving the land idle and for plowing crops under. Such measures waste resources because the desired output could be produced with fewer resources and the remaining resources used to produce other goods. All they dispense with is the visible symbol of trouble, the accumulating surpluses.

A second difficulty arises because the long-term need to reallocate resources out of agriculture (a result of the low income elasticity of demand) will conflict with plans designed to stabilize farm incomes at a high level. A program that succeeds in giving the rural sector a high level of income will partially frustrate the market mechanism for inducing excess resources to move out of agriculture. Indeed it may make matters worse. If the artificially profitable and stable market provides a stimulus for research and development that greatly increases productivity in the farm sector, it will shift the supply curve to the right, creating a further excess of quantity supplied over quantity demanded at the stabilized price.

AMERICAN FARM POLICY SINCE 1929

The American experience in trying to help the large, often poor, and always politically influential farm population illustrates the theory just developed. In particular, the twin difficulties of surplus production and insufficiently rapid shifting of resources out of agricultural production have occurred.

Before World War II

The first serious government intervention in agricultural markets was in 1929, when the Federal Farm Board was set up to buy and sell farm produce in order to promote "orderly agricultural marketing." The Board's operations failed when its attempt to support prices led to the accumulations of large stocks and a rapid exhaustion of available funds.

The Roosevelt administration (1933–1945) had learned the lesson that unless output can be restricted, holding prices above the market level requires unending injections of federal money to buy crops that can never be sold. It could not, however, politically or morally abandon the farmers, who were among the earliest victims of the Great Depression. The primary objective of New Deal farm policy was to achieve some form of parity between farmers' incomes and other incomes in the nation. It was hoped (naively, perhaps) that income parity could be achieved by legislating for price parity. The relative prices of the agricultural crops farmers sold and the manufactured goods farmers bought were to be restored to what they were in the period just before World War I, 25 years earlier. Since farm prices had fallen relative to the prices of manufactured goods, this meant that they were to be supported by the government at levels well above the free-market equilibrium levels.

A prominent feature of the New Deal program was designed to prevent the buildup of surplus output by paying farmers *not to produce* as well as paying them for what they did produce. The farm program also imposed acreage restrictions and marketing quotas on individual farmers.

But supported prices and guaranteed sales, government-financed research, and government loans for farm improvements were an enormous incentive to productivity, and output per acre and output per worker soared. Thus total output was not held down in spite of acreage limitations, and the federal costs for buying the resulting surplus crops or storing and eventually destroying them, or selling them abroad at low prices, remained at a very high level.

From the Mid 1940s to the 1970s

After World War II farm policy was modified but not basically changed. In the 1950s the notion of parity with pre-World War I relative prices was finally dropped, and the base for parity was made the average of prices ruling during the previous 10 years. Moreover actual prices were allowed to fall to a certain fraction of parity prices before the full price support was given. While this modification allowed a decline in relative prices over time, the permitted decline could occur only slowly, and at the same time the effects of even these small price changes were weakened by additional measures that gave further assistance to farmers. The details are unimportant; what matters is that by subsidizing farmers, government reduced the incentive to shift resources out of farming and encouraged further research and development.

Meanwhile, the so-called soil bank and other programs continued to pay farmers not to produce commodities that consumers would not buy at the prevailing prices. By the end of the decade of the sixties, the federal government was paying about $3 billion per year to farmers for leaving 233 million acres unplanted. This acreage could have been used to increase grain output (say) by roughly 20 to 25 percent. But that would have either depressed prices or added to the 100 million tons already in storage.

The Past Decade

1970 to 1974. Quite unexpectedly, dramatic shifts on the demand side changed the entire farm outlook during the first half of the 1970s. Rising world population, growing world income, and some massive crop failures around the world created the specter of a worldwide food shortage and hunger and starvation. Decreases in the value of the dollar relative to many other currencies, along with productivity gains, made American farm products cheaper abroad. The increasing demand for wheat, cotton, soybeans, and livestock depleted stored reserves and in some cases led to shortages.

World reserves of wheat and feed grains, for example, which were over 140 million tons in 1964 (90 percent of which were held in North America), were all but depleted by 1975. Predictably, market prices rose. An index of prices received by farmers (1967 = 100) that stood at 113 in 1971 was at 192 by 1974.

Rising demand caused farm income as well as farm prices to rise. In 1973–1974 income reached unprecedented heights, and the ongoing changes on the supply side were accelerated. Farm size grew, labor-saving equipment was purchased at a more rapid rate, computer analysis became common. Crop quality and acreage yields increased. Such was the growth in scale and capitalization that it was possible for a farm owner with half a million dollars worth of farm machinery to be described in the press as a typical modern farmer.

This period of prosperity gave the federal government a chance to change some agricultural support programs that had proved so troublesome in the past. Schemes under which the government purchased and stored farm crops were dropped and replaced by two major provisions, which continue in effect.

First, the government makes direct cash payments to farmers only when market prices fall below government-set "target prices" that are designed to cover most but not all production costs. These payments do not guarantee farmers a "reasonable" profit, as did many earlier schemes, but they do shield them from large losses. And they leave the crops in the farmers' hands, to be sold when the farmers wish. Second, the government makes low-interest loans to allow farmers to purchase their own storage facilities. Thus modern farmers have had to become expert in marketing as well as production. They must decide from month to month how much of a crop to hold in storage and how much to sell at current market prices.

1974 to 1979. The cyclical peak of farm prosperity was reached in 1973–1974. Then in 1974 the world entered the most serious economic recession since the 1930s. Hard times hit every sector of the economy. Buoyant international demand and declining export surpluses elsewhere in the world, however, shielded U.S. agriculture from a repetition of the 1930s. But for farmers who had incurred a heavy debt to expand and mechanize rapidly during the early 1970s, even a mild decline threatened disaster. Between 1974 and 1978, prices *paid* by farmers rose by 31 percent but prices received by them rose only 9 percent. When the market ceased to expand as fast as expected, farmers facing rising costs found it difficult to keep up the payments on their loans.

This experience shows that large-scale agriculture is still subject to the old cyclical problems even though the underlying trend seems to point in the direction of greater average prosperity. That farmers do not think the farm problem is solved is clear. The period of decline culminated in protest marches and threatened "strikes" in 1978 and 1979. In 1978 farmers marched for higher government support prices to protect their investments. The protests of 1978 were soon stilled, however, by the prosperity that followed the general world economic recovery and the heavy demand for U.S. agricultural exports.

In the spring of 1979 a second protest march occurred, supported by a significant but by no means overwhelming fraction of farmers. They drove tractors to Washington to demand 90 per-

cent parity. The protest did millions of dollars of damage to the streets of Washington, but it fell largely on deaf ears for at least two reasons. One was the striking contrast between protesting farmers driving new $50,000 tractors and the stereotype of the poor family farmer; the second was the all but incredible demand for 90 percent parity. That would have restored the relative price of farm and manufactured products to nearly what it was 55 years earlier, in the period before World War I, despite enormous increases in the relative productivity of agriculture.

From an economic point of view, the notion of parity over long periods of time is not appealing.

To freeze relative prices at levels existing at any one time prevents the price system from allocating resources in response to changes in tastes and incomes on the demand side and to costs and availabilities on the supply side.

Parity in effect freezes relative prices; it is a very inefficient way of achieving a redistribution of income.

The dilemma of the farmer unable to pay the continuing costs of new machinery may seem to the average student to be a new type of problem, possibly a crisis typical of the declining phases of capitalism. This is not so. Throughout history new products and new techniques have led to investment resulting from the need to install new productive capacity. Investment booms often tended to go too far as investors rushed to get rich quick. In the period of consolidation following such a boom, some investments would prove unprofitable, some firms would go bankrupt, and many investors would lose their money. After this "shakeout" the remaining investment would be "here to stay."

In the late 1970s, then, farmers were suffering from an age-old problem: too much investment in new technologies during boom times. Only their reaction to it was novel. Present-day farmers expected the government to protect their investment from the losses they saw looming. In the past the suffering that hit individuals who lost their money—often their entire life savings—

through overly optimistic investments was thought to be the personal problem of those involved. Farmers are not alone in this change in attitude, which Gardner Ackley of the University of Michigan has labeled the "politics of redress." Today, for better or for worse, such investment losses are often considered social problems to be dealt with by the government when the losses affect any large and politically influential segment of the society.

PROSPECTS FOR AGRICULTURE IN THE 1980s

What does the future hold for agriculture? Is the farm problem solved? Will it remain with us forever? Will past policy failures be repeated? Will future policies be paragons of economic sense? As might be expected, the questions probably cannot be answered with a simple yes or no.

Support Programs

The new support programs of the 1970s were designed to avoid some of the excesses of earlier programs. Certainly current policies are less likely than past ones to produce an endless accumulation of unsold and unsalable surpluses in government warehouses. However, pressure groups are still with us, and on some occasions they will succeed in getting supports at above free-market levels. Whenever Congress gives in to their demands, the problem of government surpluses can reemerge virtually overnight.

A recent example occurred with sugar. In 1977 Congress passed, over the president's opposition, a sugar support bill that allowed growers to borrow money from the government and turn over their crop as security. (Nearly 15¢ a pound could be borrowed at a time when the world price was less than 10¢.) The growers could later repay the loan and reclaim the sugar, or they could forfeit the crop and keep the loan proceeds. In effect this provided a guaranteed price to growers of not less than 15¢ per pound.

Under this kind of support, the grower gets all the profit if the market price rises above the support price, but the taxpayer takes the entire loss if the market price remains below it. The taxpayer is worse off than when the government simply bought the crop at the support price, for then the government would realize any gains if the price rose.

With this alternative available, no grower would sell a crop on the open market for less than the loan price. Since the world price was below this level, many domestic producers availed themselves of the "loan" scheme and forfeited their crops to the government — which accumulated vast amounts of sugar. The sugar piled up in makeshift warehouses and threatened to spoil long before it could be sold at a price that would cover the government's costs. (In 1979 Congress rejected a bid by sugar producers to raise the support price to 17¢ with the world price less than 13¢ per pound.)

Cyclical and Random Fluctuations

Nothing in modern agriculture makes it immune to the two traditional problems of fluctuations: those due to such random factors as the weather and those due to the business cycle. Indeed, as the events of 1974–1979 show, the modern high-technology sector may be increasingly vulnerable. Even minor fluctuations leave it unable to meet interest payments on the debt required to finance any highly mechanized form of modern production. Apparently all sectors of American agriculture will continue to suffer from short-term and cyclical fluctuations in prices and incomes.

Two Agricultural Worlds

The dynamic, large-scale, highly mechanized modern farm promises to become increasingly important and to hasten the end of small-scale family farming in most mainline agricultural crops. Heavy foreign demand and continued cost-saving innovations hold out the prospect that the large-scale sector may be profitable on average for a long time.

Yet small-scale, low-income, poorly capitalized farms will continue to exist in some areas and for some crops. For them the traditional problem of fluctuations around a low average level of income will still be an ever-present reality.

Productivity Growth

American agriculture remains one of the most rapidly innovative of the world's industries. New seeds, new crops, new mechanical methods, cloning (yes, strawberries are now literally cloned rather than grown from fertilized seeds), computerization, and a host of other new methods give continued promise of rising productivity.

Already the results are spectacular. Rough estimates of the number of people who can be fed per worker employed on the land are 59 in the United States, 19 in Western Europe, 14 in Japan, and 10 in the Soviet Union, with all other countries bringing the world average down to just over 5!

This productivity growth means that American agricultural output is growing faster than that of any other large producing nation. Does not this, combined with an ever-increasing world demand for food, spell the beginning of a new era of prosperity for American farmers? The prospects for major U.S. crops look better than at any time since the late 1940s. Whether high demand will translate this increase in supply into prosperity for farmers depends in part on American costs remaining competitive (the recent devaluations of the dollar help in this respect) and in part on the rest of the world being able to earn the purchasing power to turn its *need* for agricultural goods into an effective *demand* for them.

Can American agriculture, with its high wages and high expectations for farmers' incomes (based on American standards of income), compete successfully in world markets without government subsidy? U.S. households are finding American food prices "out of sight," yet American food prices look vastly higher in New Delhi.

If the answer to this question is yes, all may be well; if it is no, the farm problem may soon be severe again.

The Volunteer Army Versus the Draft

From 1940 to 1973, the United States relied heavily on "selective service" to provide enough recruits to supplement volunteers and to fill the requirements of the American armed services. The "draft" was never popular with those who might be called, but it was not until the end of American ground participation in the Vietnam War that the draft was ended and the armed forces became composed entirely of volunteers.

With rising tension in the Middle East as a result of events in Iran and Afghanistan, President Carter in 1980 called for a resumption of registration of persons of military age. A reinstitution of the draft is again being discussed in Congress and on the nation's campuses.

What difference does it make? The simple theory of supply and demand sheds a good deal of light on this question.

A volunteer army enlists only those who choose voluntarily to be soldiers. But, as with any civilian occupation, the main method of adjusting quantity supplied to quantity demanded is by altering the market price. Thus the volunteer army is a price-system army—one in which soldiers' pay, and their nonmonetary rewards, are adjusted until the required size army is obtained. In contrast, the **draft** uses legal compulsion to raise the requisite size army. By various means, certain individuals are chosen for service, and the legal power of the state is used to force service from all who are not willing to face the penalties for refusing to serve.

The two most important kinds of drafts are the **lottery draft,** in which chance selects from the eligible pool of potential draftees, and the **exemption draft,** in which the central authorities grant exemptions on the basis of such attributes as age, health, occupation, and family status.

EFFECTS OF ALTERNATIVE METHODS

Some people enjoy the military life, possibly because they have martial temperaments or because they are otherwise suited to the autocratic structure and discipline of the military organization. Thus, if wages for military service were exactly equal to wages for civilian occupations requiring similar amounts of education, training, and physical condition, some persons would choose military careers. For others, a preference for civilian occupations might be overcome by various premiums in military pay; for yet others, abhorrence of the army and of wars might mean that no level of pay would induce them to serve voluntarily. For these reasons, the supply curve for military service can be expected to be rising, as shown in Figure 7-6.

Suppose that at any moment the nation's military requirements can be represented by a wholly inelastic demand curve. This reflects the assumption that the size of the required army is set by Congress on the basis of considerations other than the level of military pay. If at the going wage rate the military cannot enlist enough recruits, it will have to induce extra men and women to serve by raising military pay or compel them to serve by law. This is true in both peacetime and wartime, and thus the theory is the same. As a practical matter, however, the problems are likely to be much more severe in war because the size of the extra group of recruits required is usually very large and the supply curve is likely to be quite inelastic for a large army. No major war has been fought in modern times with an all-volunteer army.

Who Serves?

In the volunteer army, those who serve will be those who are the least reluctant to do so. Unless there is a great wave of patriotic enlistment, it is unlikely that many nuclear physicists or successful lawyers will volunteer, or that many others with high-paying civilian jobs will do so. It is also unlikely that many rich people or their children

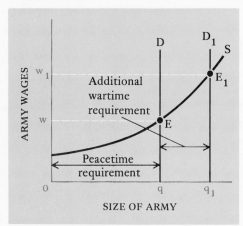

FIGURE 7–6
Supply and Demand for Soldiers

Increases in army wage rates and the draft are alternative means of raising an army of a given size. Suppose the going army wage rate is w and D and S are the demand for and supply of soldiers. A volunteer army of size q will be recruited. Now let demand shift to D_1 because of the outbreak of war. We assume the supply curve does not change. To induce an additional qq_1 soldiers to serve, the wage rate must rise to w_1 or qq_1 soldiers must be drafted, with the wage rate held at w.

will choose to enlist. One might reasonably expect the army to be recruited mainly from the poor, the undereducated, and the unemployed. These are the people with the lowest opportunity costs, so they are the most likely to be attracted by the steady pay, educational potential, and job security that goes with the army. This has been the experience of volunteer armies in the past, and it is the experience today. The only exceptions are major, "popular" wars where patriotic fervor assures a large representative group of volunteers.

The lottery draft (if it is a true lottery) will select a random cross section of people with respect to such attributes as education, occupation, and wealth. The pianist, the plumber, the plutocrat, and the physicist all have an equal chance of service. This system provides equal treatment that is readily understood by everyone, but it has other consequences. It will cause a much greater reduction in the value of civilian output than other methods. Moreover, it does not allow the government to establish its own priorities and to designate certain groups of individuals as too valuable in the civilian economy to be released into the army.

The exemption draft permits the government to establish exemptions based on some criteria of value to the civilian economy. To minimize the loss in civilian production, the authorities might exempt people with the highest earnings and draft only those with the lowest earnings. Most people would reject such an income-based exemption system on grounds of equity, but it is interesting to observe that it would produce broadly the same sort of army as would the volunteer system. An exemption draft more usually exempts on some criteria of social desirability, or the value to the nation of an individual's occupation, rather than on the basis of income. A physicist may be exempted because his services are regarded as essential to the war effort or to the general national interest; a baseball superstar may not be exempted even though the money value of his civilian services is very high, vastly higher than the physicist's.

When the required army is so large that the number of allowable exemptions must be small — for example, in a war such as World War II — general agreement on who should be exempted is probably easily reached. When the required army is smaller — for example, in the Vietnam War — and many more exemptions are possible, there is room for considerable conflict. Should women be drafted? Should graduate students in physics, economics, and German literature receive exemptions? Because their protests are thought by the authorities to be of negative social value, should the social revolutionary and the antiwar demonstrator lose the exemptions to which they would otherwise be entitled?

There is plenty of room for genuine disagreement over which social values should be used, as well as for actual abuse when exemptions are denied or removed as a punishment levied

without normal legal processes and against which there is little chance of appeal. Generally, the difficulties of the exemption draft can be expected to increase, the greater the range of exemptions allowed and the greater the disagreement in society over the use of the armed forces.

A volunteer army will be much less representative of the population as a whole than an army raised by a lottery draft. An exemption draft will be intermediate between them.

Who Pays?

The various systems affect the total bill and who must pay it, as is analyzed in Figure 7-7.

In the volunteer army the extra soldiers are at-

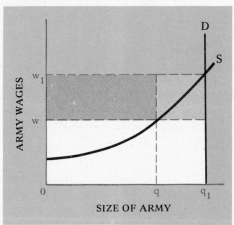

FIGURE 7–7
Who Pays the Army Wage Bill?

Taxpayers lose and willing soldiers gain from the volunteer army; draftees lose and taxpayers gain from the draft. With wage rate w, if the army is increased in size from q to q_1 using the draft, the total wage payments are the white area. A volunteer army can be recruited by offering the wage rate w_1. The total wage bill rises by the entire shaded area. Of this, the light shaded area represents payments to the new recruits in excess of the amount that would have been paid to draftees. The dark shaded area represents a windfall to soldiers already in the army. They receive a wage increase not needed to cause them to serve.

tracted by an increase in pay. The total wage bill rises, and the taxpayer pays the cost. Much of the extra pay goes to new recruits, but some of it goes to people who would have served in any case. They benefit from the reluctance of their fellow citizens to serve. Thus the total extra cost is borne by taxpayers, but only part of it is received by the new volunteers.

In the draft all soldiers are paid the basic army wage. The taxpayer pays much less, but (by compulsion) an army of the same size is raised. The difference in cost is paid by the draftees in the form of lost civilian opportunities and lost freedom of choice. Depending on who the draftees are, how they react to army life, and what their alternatives for employment may be, the cost may be very small or very large.

A volunteer army benefits financially those who would have volunteered even with a draft; it also benefits all who would have been forced to serve against their will. But it is more expensive to taxpayers.

EVALUATION OF ALTERNATIVES

More than economics is involved in evaluating alternative plans; there are, especially in wartime, issues of equity, of equal exposure to risk, and of patriotism. But economic differences in terms of who serves, who pays, and who ends up doing something he or she would prefer not to do are also important. The predictions we have reached can help in understanding the economic issues even though they cannot settle the debate on which system is best.

Who Should Pay?

What affects who should pay? In the volunteer army it is the general taxpayer who pays the full cost. Because the services of the army are supposed to be for the public good, some regard this as wholly appropriate. But others ask why a relatively low-income taxpayer should have to pay the cost of raising soldiers' wages because the children of the wealthy do not choose to serve.

In either the lottery or the exemption draft of young men, the unwilling draftee bears a good part of the cost of his service by virtue of being unlucky enough to be drafted or to lack the skills that would have led to exemption. (Note that these skills may themselves be related to wealth or economic status: the son of wealthy white parents is more likely to be a doctor, a student, or a scientist than is the son of poor blacks.) Because there are poor and rich among draftees, among taxpayers, and to a lesser extent among volunteers, the purely distributional issues of how to raise an army are complex. Who is the primary beneficiary of an exemption from service? When an individual serves in the army against his will, he may be regarded as discharging a personal obligation to his country or providing a public service—or both. When a congressman or a concert pianist is allowed to avoid military service, who is the big gainer? If he is the gainer, perhaps he should pay; if you are, perhaps you should pay. People differ in their views as to who really benefits and on whether this should affect who should pay.

The issues are clearly dependent on competing values: on equity of treatment, on the desired composition of a citizen army, on the efficient use of human resources, and on the justice of alternative ways of paying the cost. Economic analysis can sharpen the debate by making clear which schemes have which effects. It can also identify important quantitative magnitudes. One example is whether or not the volunteer army involves a large cost to the taxpayer and a large premium to the already willing soldier; the amounts depend on the *slope* of the supply curve (such as that shown in Figure 7-7). If the supply curve is very steep. it will take a large increase in wages to induce volunteers, and the shaded areas will loom large. If the supply curve is very flat, a small wage increase will suffice, and the extra costs will be small.

The evidence of the recent peacetime volunteer army has not shed much light on the shape of the supply curve. Both the number of recruits and military pay relative to civilian pay fell gradually between 1973 and 1979, but the variations are too small to be useful for predicting what increase in pay would be necessary for an increase of, say, 25 percent in the size of the armed forces. Despite the lack of concrete evidence, most of those in the military believe the supply curve is quite steep for increases from present levels.

Who Should Serve?

One of the hot issues of a renewed draft will surely be whether women should be included. However that issue is decided, a person who feels strongly that military service should be an overriding and equal obligation of all, independent of taste, wealth, talent, or temperament, will probably prefer the lottery draft. Similarly, if one wants the army to represent as wide a cross section of the society as possible so that the places and the manner in which the army is used are a subject of serious concern to all groups in the nation, the lottery draft is most likely to be satisfactory. This does not change the fact that the lottery draft involves both compulsion and a higher loss in the value of civilian output than any other system. The exemption draft provides less equal treatment of individuals and a less representative army than the lottery draft, but it allows scope to exempt from service those whose civilian talents are regarded by the government as especially important. Thus it may avoid certain inefficiencies in the use of personnel, but those with no special merit (in the eyes of the authorities) cannot avoid service by reason of mere wealth.

If efficiency and lack of compulsion are given great weight as goals, the volunteer army becomes attractive. It does not use people of high earning power, and thus it avoids certain evident inefficiencies. It provides less compulsion than other schemes. The volunteer army compels only by economic pressures. It leads, however, to an unrepresentative military, with a predominance of poorer, relatively uneducated people in it. It is racially different too, with a larger per-

centage of blacks and other minority groups. For those who believe the army will be more responsive to civilian influences if it is a cross section of the population, this unrepresentativeness is a major disadvantage.

Summary

1. The elementary theory of supply, demand, and price provides powerful tools for analyzing and understanding some real-world problems and policies. The chapter illustrates this with respect to agricultural policies and the volunteer army.

2. Agricultural commodities are subject to wide fluctuations in market prices, and these often lead to fluctuations of producers' incomes. This is because of year-to-year unplanned fluctuations in supplies combined with inelastic demands, and because of cyclical fluctuations in demands combined with inelastic supplies. Where demand is inelastic, large crops tend to be associated with low total receipts and small crops with high total receipts.

3. Fluctuations in farmers' gross receipts can be reduced by a producer's association that stores crops unsold when output is high and sells from inventories when output is low, or by appropriate government purchases and sales in the open market.

4. Price stabilization schemes historically tend to involve stabilization above average free-market equilibrium levels. The result is a buildup of surpluses. To avoid these surpluses, attempts to stabilize prices at levels above the free-market equilibrium prices have tended to become associated with plans to restrict farmers' output. The tendency toward the buildup of large unsold surpluses as well as later attempts to restrict output were both features of U.S. agricultural policy from 1930 to 1970.

5. The long-term problems of agriculture arise from a high rate of productivity growth on the supply side and a low income elasticity on the demand side. This means that, unless many resources are being transferred out of agriculture, quantity supplied will increase faster than quantity demanded year after year. If existing prices are maintained, and if farmers are guaranteed a market for all of their output at these prices, the yearly farm surplus will tend to increase.

6. A long-term solution to persistent surpluses requires a transfer of resources out of agriculture and into sectors where demand is growing faster than supply. In a free market, the incentive for this transfer would be provided by a continuing tendency for agricultural prices and incomes to be depressed. The political and social consequences of the hardships this would impose are not likely to appeal to any American political party.

7. Equitable and compassionate treatment of farmers is also part of farm policy. But the efforts of the government to maintain farm income at a level that compares favorably with incomes earned elsewhere tends to inhibit the reallocation mechanism and thus to increase farm surpluses above what they would otherwise be.

8. Whether the boom in American agriculture experienced during the 1970s reflects a reversal of the need to transfer resources out of agriculture or a mere pause in the long-term trend is not clear as the 1980s begin.

9. The volunteer army, the lottery draft, and the exemption draft are alternative ways to raise an army of given size. In a volunteer army, the wage paid is raised until an army of the required size is met by voluntary enlistment. In a lottery draft, those selected are chosen by lot, and every eligible person has an equal chance of being selected. In an exemption draft, the authorities grant exemptions to classes of persons on the basis of criteria established by the government.

10. Several differences among these systems can be analyzed using the tools of demand and sup-

ply. Who will serve? The volunteer army will produce an army of persons with the lowest opportunity cost in civilian life. This will tend to weight the army heavily with the poor, the undereducated, and the unemployed. The exemption draft excludes the groups the authorities wish to exclude and produces a cross section of the rest. The strict lottery draft selects a cross section of the whole population and is likely to have soldiers with a higher average civilian opportunity cost than any of the other systems.

11. Who will pay? The cost to the taxpayer is highest in the volunteer army. In the lottery or exemption drafts, draftees pay much of the cost in lost civilian opportunities. With the volunteer army, those who were willing to serve in any event are paid more than is necessary to have them serve; they benefit from the reluctance of others to serve.

12. Economics does not answer the question of which method of raising an army is best, but it does clarify the issues, both by identifying the competing values and by showing on what the actual costs to different groups will depend.

Topics for Review

Comparative statics
Price supports at and above the level of free-market equilibrium
Price stabilization versus income stabilization
Parity
Income elasticity and long-term resource reallocation
Benefits and costs of a volunteer army

Discussion Questions

1. "If you are a farmer, the weather is always bad." Discuss the sense in which this statement might be true.
2. "This ought to be a time of rejoicing in the vineyards of California. The crop of wine grapes has rarely been richer, the harvest is nearly complete, and Americans are drinking more California wine than ever before." Why then were there falling profits and a record number of bankruptcies in the industry?

3. The Kenya Meat Commission (KMC) decided it was un-democratic to allow meat prices to be out of the reach of the ordinary citizen. It decided to freeze meat prices. Six months later, in a press interview, the managing commissioner of the KMC made each of the following statements.

   a. "The price of almost everything in Kenya has gone up, but we have not increased the price of meat. The price of meat in this country is still the lowest in the world."

   b. "Cattle are scarce in the country, but I do not know why."

   c. "People are eating too much beef, and unless they diversify their eating habits and eat other foodstuffs the shortage of beef will continue."

   Do the facts alleged make sense, given KMC's policy?

4. "If a farmer borrows money to buy a mechanical picker that replaces 100 hand pickers, this may make his operations more profitable in an average year while si-multaneously leaving him more vulnerable to even minor cyclical downturns." Explain.

5. In the case of each of the following alternative major objectives, what method to increase the size of the army might be favored?

   a. to minimize the cost to the taxpayer

   b. to have an army that is broadly representative of the whole society

   c. to minimize the loss in value of civilian output

   d. to give the individual maximum freedom of choice as to whether to serve

   e. to use service in the army as a sanction against behavior disapproved of by the authorities

6. How might each of the following affect the willingness of Congress to utilize the volunteer army?

   a. the size of the armed forces required

   b. the state of patriotism among the nation's youth

   c. the level of unemployment in the economy

   d. evidence of a taxpayers' revolt

Supply and Demand in Action II: Price and Rent Ceilings

8

It is common in wartime, and increasingly frequent in peacetime, for governments to fix the maximum prices at which certain goods and services may be sold. A growing number of American cities are controlling the prices at which apartments can be rented, and during much of the 1970s the prices of many petroleum products in the United States were fixed well below world prices. Indeed, in the face of continuing inflation there is an increasing call for price controls in America in order to prevent the hardships imposed on consumers by continuing rises in the prices of commodities such as food, housing, gasoline, and medical care. What would the consequences be if such price controls were adopted? In this chapter we look at price controls in general and then examine more closely the experience with rent controls.

The Theory of Price Ceilings

In a free market, price tends to move toward its equilibrium value, where the quantities demanded and supplied are equal. Government price controls are designed to hold the market price below equilibrium. In so doing they cause quantity demanded to exceed quantity supplied at the controlled price. This in turn leads to further consequences.

QUANTITY EXCHANGED AT NON-EQUILIBRIUM PRICES

In competitive markets, price tends to change whenever quantity supplied does not equal quan-

FIGURE 8–1

The Determination of Quantity Exchanged in Disequilibrium

In disequilibrium, quantity exchanged is determined by the *lesser* of quantity demanded or quantity supplied. At p the market is in equilibrium with quantity demanded equal to quantity supplied at q. For prices below p, such as p_1, the quantity exchanged will be determined by the supply curve. For example, the quantity q_1 will be exchanged at the disequilibrium price p_1 in spite of the excess demand of q_1q_2. For prices above p, such as p_2, the quantity exchanged will be given by the demand curve. For example, the quantity exchanged will be only q_1 at the price p_2 in spite of the excess supply of q_1q_3. Thus the heavy black line shows the whole set of actual quantities exchanged, at different prices.

tity demanded. Thus price will move toward its equilibrium value, where there are neither unsatisfied suppliers nor unsatisfied demanders. However, price controls create the possibility that price may be held indefinitely at a disequilibrium value. When this happens, what determines the quantity actually traded on the market? A moment's thought will show that any voluntary market transaction requires both a willing buyer and a willing seller. This means that if quantity demanded is less than quantity supplied, the former will determine the amount actually exchanged and the rest of the quantity supplied will remain in the hands of the unsuccessful sellers. On the other hand, if quantity demanded

exceeds quantity supplied, the latter will determine the amount actually traded and the rest of the quantity demanded will represent desired purchases of unsuccessful buyers.

At any disequilibrium price, quantity exchanged is determined by the *lesser* of quantity demanded or quantity supplied.

This is shown graphically in Figure 8-1. Quantity exchanged at any price is determined by the curve *on the left* at that price—that is, the demand curve above, and the supply curve below, the equilibrium price.

EFFECTIVE CEILING PRICES

Although frequently referred to as fixed or "frozen" prices, most price controls specify the highest permissible price, often called the **ceiling price,** that producers may legally charge. If the ceiling price is set at or above the equilibrium price, it will have no effect because equilibrium will still be attainable and will not be inconsistent with the ceiling price required by law. If, however, the ceiling price is set below equilibrium, it is binding.[1] This means that the free-market price must be reduced. The forced reduction will cause a fall in the quantity supplied, an increase in the quantity demanded, and a shortage of the commodity (see Figure 8-2). A first prediction of the effect of price control in a competitive market is:

Binding ceiling prices lead to excess demand for the commodity, and the quantity exchanged will fall below its equilibrium amount.

In inflationary situations, price controls often take the form of "freezing" prices at current free-market levels. At the moment of imposition the price control is not effective, but as inflation occurs the free-market price would rise, and thus the controlled price becomes an effective ceiling price.

[1] Binding price ceilings are sometimes said to be "effective"; this is a very special meaning of the word effective.

FIGURE 8-2
A Price Ceiling and Black Market Pricing

A ceiling price below the equilibrium price causes excess demand and invites a black market. Equilibrium price is at p. If a price ceiling is set at p_1, the quantity demanded will rise to q_1 and the quantity supplied will fall to q_2. Quantity actually exchanged will be q_2. Although excess demand is q_2q_1, price may not legally rise to restore equilibrium. If all the available supply of q_2 were sold on a black market, price to consumers would rise to p_2, with black marketeers earning receipts shown by the shaded areas. The dark shaded area is the profit of those who buy at the ceiling price and sell at the black market price.

ALLOCATING A COMMODITY IN SHORT SUPPLY

What happens to the excess demand that is always produced by binding price ceilings? The free-market way of eliminating excess demand is to allow price to rise so as to allocate the available supply among would-be purchasers. Since this does not happen, some other method of allocation must be adopted. Experience shows that certain alternatives are likely.

If stores sell their available supplies on a first-come, first-served basis, people will rush to those stores that are said to have stocks of any commodity in short supply. In Europe during World War II, the word—even the rumor—that a shop was selling supplies of a scarce commodity could cause a local stampede. Buyers often spent hours in line, waiting to get into the shop, and supplies were usually exhausted long before all were served. Standing in lines is a way of life in many command economies today.

A different system will develop if storekeepers individually decide who will get the scarce commodities. Goods may be kept "under the counter" and sold only to regular customers. This happened in 1978, during periods of gasoline shortages, as some gas station operators sold only to their regular customers. When sellers decide to whom they will (and will not) sell scarce supplies, allocation is by **sellers' preferences.**

If the government dislikes the distribution that results from sellers' preferences, it can do at least two things.

First, it can pass laws requiring suppliers to sell on a first-come, first-served basis. Some non-discriminatory legislation exists in the United States, and to the extent that it is effective it leads to allocation according to willingness to stand in line. These laws are not easily enforceable, however, and there is little doubt that some available supplies are sold to favored customers according to sellers' preferences.

Second, a more drastic measure, the government can ration the commodity. To do so, it prints only enough coupons to match the available supplies and then distributes the coupons to purchasers, who will need both money and ration coupons to buy the commodity. The coupons may be distributed equally among the population or on the basis of age, family status, occupation, or any other criterion.

Rationing substitutes the central authorities' preferences for the seller's preferences in allocating a price-controlled commodity.

Coupon rationing appeals to many people because other schemes, such as first-come, first-served or allocation by sellers' preferences, may appear arbitrary or capricious—and thus unfair.

Black Markets

Ceiling prices, with or without rationing, usually give rise to black markets. A **black market** is one in which goods are sold (illegally) at prices above the legal maximum price. For most products there are many retailers, and although it may be easy to police the producers, it is often impossible to control effectively the price at which retailers sell to the general public.

Suppose the government can control producers but not retailers. Production remains unchanged because the producers would continue to receive the controlled price for their product. At the retail level, however, the opportunity for a black market arises because purchasers are willing to pay more than the ceiling price for the limited amounts of the commodity that are available. The theory of supply and demand leads to this prediction:

The potential for a black market always exists when binding price ceilings are imposed because it will pay someone to buy at the controlled price and sell at the black market price.

Figure 8-2 illustrates the limiting case in which all the available supply is sold on a black market. The development of such a market depends on there being a few people willing to risk heavy penalties by running a black market supply organization and a reasonably large number of persons prepared to purchase goods illegally on such a market. This case is extreme because there are honest people in every society and because governments ordinarily have considerable power to enforce their price laws. Usually some, not all, of a price-controlled commodity is sold at a black market price. (It is a revealing comment on human nature that there are few known cases in which binding price ceilings were not accompanied by the growth of a black market.)

Does the existence of a black market mean that the goals sought by imposing a price ceiling have been thwarted? This question can be answered only when we know what the government hopes to achieve with its ceiling price.

Governments may be interested mainly in (1) restricting production (in order perhaps to release resources for war production), (2) keeping prices down, or (3) satisfying notions of equity in the consumption of a commodity that is temporarily unusually scarce. Ceiling prices with a black market achieve the first but not the second and third objectives. The second objective is frustrated to the extent that goods find their way onto the black market. If equity is the goal, an effective price ceiling on manufacturers plus an extensive black market at the retail level will produce the worst possible results. There will be less to go around than if there were no controls, and the available quantities will tend to go to those with the most money and the least social conscience.

THE EXPERIENCE WITH CEILING PRICES

There is evidence to confirm all these predictions about ceiling prices. Practically all belligerent countries in World War I and World War II put ceilings on prices of certain key items made exceptionally scarce by wartime requirements. These ceilings were always followed first by shortages, second by either the introduction of rationing or the growth of some alternative method of allocation such as sellers' preferences, and third by the rise of a black market. Price ceilings were more effective in limiting consumption than in controlling prices, although they did restrain price increases because the patriotic response of many people to wartime controls led them to do without rather than to patronize the black market.

A more comprehensive kind of ceiling price control is sometimes attempted in peacetime, in an effort to curb inflation. A freeze is put on virtually all prices. But if there is general excess demand, this kind of policy is sure to fail unless something is done to attack the causes of the excess of demand over supply. Price freezes sometimes work for a while, but eventually the backlog of purchasing power bursts out somewhere, and black markets follow. Pressure builds up on the government to remove the controls. Only after prices rise do supplies increase. This happened in the United States after the Nixon administration imposed a price freeze in 1971, and it has happened throughout the world whenever general ceiling prices have been imposed.

Rent Controls

A widespread, growing use of ceiling prices in America today relates to the rental of houses and apartments for private occupancy. Rent controls have been used in many places the world over, and the consequences have almost always been the same: the creation of a severe housing shortage.

Controls have existed in New York City since World War II. More recently they have been introduced or seriously advocated in many other American cities. In Sweden and Britain, where rent control on unfurnished apartments has existed for decades, housing shortages are endemic except in neighborhoods where population is declining. Whole areas of London are full of abandoned, rotting houses that would have lasted for centuries but which, at controlled rentals, did not even pay the owner the cost of upkeep. When British controls were extended to furnished apartments in 1973, the supply of such accommodations dried up, at least until loopholes were found in the law. When rent controls were initiated in Rome in 1978, a housing shortage developed virtually overnight. This kind of rent control-induced shortage led University of Chicago Professors George Stigler and Milton Friedman to point to the conflict between "ceilings" and "roofs."

Rent controls are spreading in the United States, yet many advocates of such controls seem to have little appreciation of their consequences. Economic theory makes a number of predictions that are useful in understanding the current American experience with rent controls and in predicting the consequences.

THE THEORY OF CEILING PRICES APPLIED TO RENT CONTROLS

Rent controls are just a special case of ceiling prices. Controls are usually imposed to freeze rents at their current level at a time when equilibrium rents are rising either because demand is shifting rightward (due to forces such as rising population and income) or because supply is shifting leftward (due to forces such as rising costs). The result is that soon rents are being held below the free-market equilibrium level and excess demand appears. Figure 8-2 can be applied to rent controls. The following predictions about rent controls are simply applications to housing of results that apply to any commodity subject to binding ceiling prices.

1. There will be a housing shortage in the sense that quantity demanded will exceed quantity supplied.
2. The actual quantity of accommodation will be less than if free market rents had been charged.
3. The shortage will lead to alternative allocation schemes. Landlords may allocate by sellers' preferences, or the government may intervene. In the housing market, government intervention usually takes the form of security-of-tenure laws, which protect the tenant from eviction and thus give existing tenants priority over potential new tenants.
4. Black markets will appear. Landlords may require large lump-sum entrance fees from new tenants. In general, the larger the housing shortage, the bigger the sum required. In the absence of security-of-tenure laws, landlords may force tenants out when their leases expire, and they may even try to evict them in order to extract a large entrance fee from new tenants.

SPECIAL ASPECTS OF THE HOUSING MARKET

Housing has unusual attributes that make the analysis of rent controls somewhat special. The most important is the nature of the commodity it-

Rent Control in Paris*

A dollar a month will pay a wage earner's rent in Paris.† Such cheapness is amazing. Rent is reckoned as equal in cost to transport to and from work. To put it another way, a month's rent for a large family of six costs as much as eleven packets of cigarettes. Parisians spend on entertainment every month far more than they pay for three months' rent.

Even in a very modest budget such an expenditure absorbs but a small part of income. On average, rent makes up 1.4 percent of a wage earner's expenditures. Such low rents are not a privilege confined to wage earners. Rent seldom rises above 4 percent of any income; frequently it is less than 1 percent.

This may seem a very desirable state of affairs. It has its drawbacks. While you pay no more than these quite ridiculous prices if you are lucky enough to be in possession of a flat, if you are searching for lodgings you cannot find them at any price. *There are no vacant lodgings,* nor is anyone going to vacate lodgings which cost so little, nor can the owners expel anyone. Deaths are the only opportunity.

*This account is excerpted from a paper, "No Vacancies," first published in the United States in 1948 and reprinted in F. A. Hayek et al., *Rent Control—A Popular Paradox* (Vancouver B. C.: The Fraser Institute, 1976), pp. 105–112. The author, Bertrand de Jouvenal, is a noted French journalist. The general situation described here still exists today.

† All prices are in terms of 1946 dollars. To think of them in 1980 terms, multiply by four.

Young couples must live with in-laws, watching out for deaths. Tottering old people out to sun themselves will be shadowed back to their flat by an eager young wife who will strike a bargain with the *concierge,* so as to be first warned when the demise occurs. Other apartment chasers have an understanding with the undertakers.

There are two ways of obtaining an apartment which death has made available. Legally, you may obtain from a public authority a requisition order: you will usually find that the same order for the same apartment has been given to other candidates. The illegal method is the surest: deal with the heir, and with his complicity immediately carry in some pieces of your furniture. As soon as you are in, you are king of the castle.

Buying one's way into an apartment will cost anything from $500 to $1,500 per room. At such prices wage earners may as well give up hope of setting up house; they will have to stay with their families.

In short, rents are very low but there are no lodgings available. Nor are any being built—practically none have been built for the last 12 years.

There are some 84,000 buildings for habitation in Paris: 23,000 were built before 1850; 48,000 before 1880; 75,000 were built before World War I.

self. So far in this book we have mainly considered markets for commodities that are consumed soon after they are purchased. But housing is an example of a **durable good,** a good that yields its services only gradually over an extended period of time. Once built, an apartment lasts for decades or even centuries, yielding its valuable ser- vices continuously over that time. Thus the supply of rental accommodation depends on the *stock* of rental housing available, and in any year it is composed mainly of buildings built in prior years. The stock is added to by conversions of housing from other uses and construction of new buildings, and it is diminished by conversions to

Sixteen thousand buildings are in such a state of disrepair that there is nothing that can be done but pull them down. Nor are the remainder altogether satisfactory. To go into sordid details, 82 percent of Parisians have no bath or shower, more than half must go out of their lodgings to find a lavatory, and a fifth do not even have running water. Little more than one in six of existing buildings is pronounced in good condition by the public inspectors. Lack of repair is ruining even these.

Owners can hardly be blamed. They are not in a financial position to keep up their buildings, let alone improve them. To take an example, here is a lady who owns three buildings containing 34 apartments, all inhabited by middle-class families. Her net loss from the apartments, after taxes and repairs, is $80 a year. Not only must her son put her up and take care of her, but he must also pay out the $80. She cannot sell; there are no buyers.

When the owner tries to cut down the repairs, he runs great risks. One postponed repairs on his roofs, and rain filtering into an apartment spoiled a couple of armchairs. He was sued for damages and condemned to pay a sum amounting to three years of the tenant's paltry rent.

The miserable condition of owners is easily explained. While rents since 1914 have multiplied 6.8 times, taxes have grown 13.2 times and the cost of repairs has increased from 120 to 150 times the 1914 price!

A "right" has developed, the "right" to dig in. The French now have struck roots in their rented lodgings. One cannot allow the owner to dispossess tenants, because in that case he might so easily make an agreement secretly with a new tenant: rent control implied necessarily the denial of the owner's right to evict. The tenant's right to retain possession has been confirmed, and the rent is raised slightly from time to time.

If a builder were now to put up flats similar to those in existence, these new apartments would have to be let for prices representing 10 times present rent ceilings, in order to reward the costs of construction and the capital invested. As long as the rents of existing buildings are held down artificially far below costs, it will be psychologically impossible to find customers at prices 10 times higher, and hence construction will not be undertaken.

Such is the differential between the legal and the economic price of lodgings that even the most fervent advocates of freedom are scared at the prospect of a return to it. They feel that if the right to dismiss tenants and the right to bargain and contract with them were restored, evictions could not be executed, the whole nation of tenants sitting down to nullify the decision. The thing, they say, has now gone too far, the price of rent is too far removed from the cost.

other uses and demolition or abandonment of existing buildings whose economic life is over. The stock usually changes slowly from year to year.

These considerations mean we can draw more than one supply curve for rental accommodation, depending on how much time is allowed for reactions to occur to any given level of rents. We shall distinguish just two such curves. The *long-run supply curve* relates rents to the quantity of rental accommodation that will be supplied after sufficient time has passed for all adjustments to be made. The *short-run supply curve* relates rents to quantity supplied when only a short time —say, a few months—is allowed for adjustments to be made in response to a change in rents. We shall assume that in the short run very few new conversions and very little new construction can occur.

The Long-run Supply Curve

Among the many suppliers of rental accommodation are large investment companies and individuals with modest savings invested in one or two small apartments. There is a large potential source of supply, for it is relatively easy to build a new apartment or to convert an existing house and offer its units for rent. If the expected return from investing in new apartments rises significantly above the return on comparable other investments, there will be a flow of investment funds into the building of new apartments. However, if the return from apartments falls significantly below that obtainable on comparable investments, funds will go elsewhere. The construction of new apartments will fall off and possibly stop altogether. Old apartments will not be replaced as they wear out, so the quantity available will fall drastically. Therefore the long-run supply curve of apartments is highly *elastic*.

The Short-run Supply Curve

Now consider the supply response over a few months. What if rents rise? Even though it immediately becomes profitable to invest in new apartments, it may well take years for land to be obtained, plans drawn up, and construction completed. Thus a long time may pass between the decision to create more apartments and the occupancy by tenants of the new apartments built in response to market signals. Of course some existing housing can be more quickly converted to rental uses, but in many cases even this is likely to take more than a few months.

What if rents fall? New construction will fall off, and this will surely decrease the supply at some time in the future. It will, however, pay the owners of existing apartments with no attractive alternative use of their rental units to rent them for whatever they will earn, providing that the rentals at least cover current out-of-pocket costs such as taxes and heating. Some rental housing can be abandoned or converted to other uses, but, again, this will not usually happen very quickly.

Thus the short-run supply curve that relates rentals to the quantity supplied tends to be quite *inelastic* at the level of the quantity currently supplied. The longer the time horizon, the less inelastic it will be. For the very short run, however, it is likely to be almost completely inelastic.

SUPPLY RESPONSE TO CHANGES IN RENTS

If rents rise, what will the supply response be? In the short run, the quantity will remain more or less the same because the short-run supply curve is inelastic. For a while existing landlords will make **windfall profits,** profits that bear no relation to current or historical costs. Yet these profits are the spur to the long-run allocation of resources. In a rush to gain some of the profits, new construction will begin. After a year or two new rental units will begin to come onto the market. The quantity will continue to expand until the housing stock is fully adjusted to the new, higher rents. At that time, a new point on the long-run supply curve will have been attained.

If rents decrease, the quantity supplied will remain more or less unchanged because of the inelastic short-run supply curve. But the profitability of supplying rental accommodations will fall, and new construction will be curtailed as a result. How long it will be before the current stock of old housing shrinks to its new, lower equilibrium level—to its new point on the long-run supply curve—depends on the type of adjustment that leads to the long-run shrinkage in the quantity supplied. Because houses are durable, they will not quickly disappear. But owners of rental properties can speed the shrinkage in various ways.

Many apartments have alternative uses. Some can be withdrawn from the rental market and sold to owner-occupiers more or less on an "as is" basis. Others can be converted into cooperatives or condominiums, each of which involves occupant ownership, with a centralized management providing janitorial and other services. As soon as leases on rental units expire, conversions of this sort can begin. Even small reductions in rents may be sufficient to cause a withdrawal from the market of those apartments that are suitable for conversion to condominiums. Other apartments occupy land with valuable alternative uses. If rents fall far enough, it will pay to demolish those apartments and use the land for something else, but it requires a substantial and long-lasting fall in rents before demolition costs are worth incurring.

Many existing apartment buildings and other rental accommodations have no real alternative uses and will continue to serve as apartments until they are abandoned as useless. Yet the useful life of an apartment depends on how well it is maintained. In general, the less spent on maintenance and repairs, the shorter the structure's effective life. If nothing is spent, the building will deteriorate rapidly and may become uninhabitable in a very few years. How much it pays landlords to spend on maintenance and repairs depends on the level of rents. The lower the rents, the less will it pay to spend on upkeep and thus the faster will the apartment "wear out."

If rental revenues fall below the minimum costs of operation (which include taxes and heating), the owner may simply abandon the apartment. Apartments once abandoned fall quickly into total disrepair. Although this may sound extreme, it has happened repeatedly in both America and Europe. When it happens, a stock of housing that might have lasted decades or even centuries is dissipated within a few years.

The special features of the housing market lead to an important additional prediction about rent controls.

Because the long-run supply curve of rental housing is highly elastic, rent controls that hold rents below their free-market levels for an extended period will inevitably lead to a large reduction in the quantity of rental housing available.

FIGURE 8–3

Effects of Rent Control in the Short and Long Run

Rent controls cause housing shortages that worsen as time passes. The controlled rent, r_c, is below the equilibrium rent, r. The short-run supply of housing is the inelastic curve S_s. Thus quantity supplied remains at q_1 in the short run, and the housing shortage is q_2q_1. Over time the quantity supplied shrinks as shown by the long-run supply curve S_L. In long-run equilibrium there are only q_3 units of rental accommodation, far fewer than when controls were instituted. Since the long-run supply is quite elastic, the housing shortage of q_3q_2 that occurs after supply has fully adjusted ends up being much larger than the initial shortage of q_2q_1.

This prediction is illustrated in Figure 8-3. The speed with which the reduction occurs will depend on the extent to which controlled rents depart from their free-market levels: the greater the discrepancy, the faster the rental housing stock will shrink.

THE DEMAND FOR RENTAL HOUSING

There are many reasons to expect the demand for apartments and other forms of rental housing to be quite elastic. As the price of rental accommodation in an area rises, each of the following will occur:

1. Some people will stop renting and buy instead.

2. Some will move to where rental housing is cheaper.
3. Some will economize on the amount of housing they consume by renting smaller, cheaper accommodations (or renting out a room or two in their present accommodations).
4. Some will double up and others will not "undouble" (for example, young adults will not move out of parental homes as quickly as they might otherwise do).

Such occurrences contribute to a substantial elasticity of the demand for rental housing: Increases in rents will sharply decrease the quantity demanded.

The effect of rent controls is to prevent such increases in rents from occurring. Thus, even while the supply of rental housing is shrinking for the reasons discussed above, the signal to economize on rental accommodation is *not* given through rising rentals. The housing shortage grows as the stock of rental accommodation shrinks while nothing decreases the demand for it. This too is illustrated in Figure 8-3.

WHEN RENT CONTROLS WORK: SHORT-TERM SHORTAGES

Pressure for rent controls seems to arise in response to rapidly rising rents for housing. The case for controlling rising rentals is strongest when the shortages causing the increasing rents are temporary.

Temporary Ban on Building

If the quantity of housing cannot expand in response to a rise in rentals, then one major function of price signals is defeated. During major wars, such as World War II, governments allocate as many resources as possible to producing war materials, and this has two consequences. First, the movement of labor into the areas that produce war goods creates severe local housing shortages. Second, the government is typically unwilling to allow substantial resources to move

into new apartment construction. In a free market, rents would rise greatly. There would be a large transfer of income from tenants to landlords but few induced supply responses because resources are not made available to the construction industry. The government may then feel that rent control (and some alternative allocation scheme) is required for fairness.

After the war, if the extra population moves away, demand will decrease and free-market rents will return to the controlled level. Controls can then be removed with few adverse effects. If much of the extra population stays (as it did on the West Coast after World War II), rents will rise after controls are removed. With the cessation of war production, however, resources will again be available to the construction industry. The high rents will induce new construction that will ease the housing shortage and bring rents to a long-run equilibrium level. Temporary rent controls in response to such wartime pressures achieve a degree of fairness without long-run adverse effects. Many programs of rent control originated in such wartime situations.

Temporary Increases in Demand

Sometimes, in peacetime, there is a temporary influx of population into an area. Possibly a pipeline or a power complex is being built, and many workers are required for the construction even though few will remain behind to run the automated equipment. When the construction workers flood in, market rents will rise. New construction of apartments will not occur, however, because investors recognize the rise in demand and rentals as temporary. In this case, rent control may stop existing owners from gaining windfall profits, with few harmful supply effects since a long-run supply response is not expected in any case. After the boom is over, demand will fall and free-market rents will return to the controlled level (their original level). Controls may then be removed with little further effect. This is illustrated in Figure 8-4.

Even in cases where rent controls have no

FIGURE 8-4

Rent Controls in Response to Increasing Demand

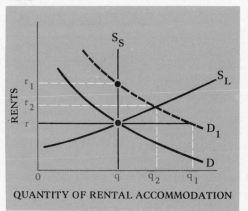

QUANTITY OF RENTAL ACCOMMODATION

Rent controls prevent a temporary skyrocketing of rents when demand rises, but they also prevent the long-term supply adjustment to demand increases.

Temporary demand fluctuations. The short-run supply curve S_S applies. In the free market a temporary rise in demand from D to D_1 and then back to D will change rents from r to r_1 and then back to r. Rent control would hold rents at r throughout; it would create a housing shortage due to excess demand of qq_1 as long as demand was D_1, but it would not affect the quantity of housing available.

Permanent changes in demand. The long-run supply curve S_L applies. A permanent rise in demand from D to D_1 will cause free-market rents to rise from r to r_1 and then to fall to r_2 as the quantity of accommodation supplied grows from q to q_2. Controlling the rent at r, in order to prevent windfall profits, produces a permanent housing shortage of qq_1.

porary accommodation (mobile homes, for example) will increase. Such reactions are induced by the signal of rising rents but inhibited by controls.

WHEN RENT CONTROLS FAIL: LONG-TERM SHORTAGES

Long-run Increases in Demand

What if the rise in demand for rental accommodation is not temporary, and the ability to expand supply is not limited arbitrarily by government decree? An example is provided by the sun belt states, where in-migration is increasing the population rapidly, creating severe local housing shortages and forcing up rents. Such increases in rentals give the signal that apartments are very profitable investments. A consequent building boom will lead to increases in the quantity supplied, and it will continue as long as large profits can be earned.

If rent controls are imposed in the face of such long-term increases in demand, they will prevent short-run windfalls, but they will also prevent the needed long-run construction boom from occurring. Thus controls will convert a temporary shortage into a permanent one. This too is illustrated in Figure 8-4.

Inflation in Housing Costs

A second situation in which rent controls fail comes about when they are introduced to protect tenants from rent increases in an inflationary world. Inflation raises both the costs of construction of new housing and the costs of operating and maintaining existing housing. As we saw in Chapter 5, a rise in costs shifts the supply curve upward and to the left.

Fixed rent controls in an economy that is experiencing a steady inflation will produce a housing shortage that grows over time. If inflation is combined with growth in demand, the growth in the housing shortage becomes very large (see Figure 8-5).

long-run adverse effect, there will be some disadvantages. At controlled rents there will be a severe housing shortage but no incentive to existing tenants to economize on housing and no incentive for potential suppliers to improvise by finding ways of providing extra short-run accommodation. If rents rise on the free market, existing tenants will economize and some tenants and owners will find it profitable to rent out rooms. Even though the supply of permanent apartments does not change, the supply of casual tem-

FIGURE 8–5
FIGURE 8–5
An Ever-growing Housing Shortage

QUANTITY OF RENTAL ACCOMMODATION

In a growing, inflation-prone economy, rent controls will cause the housing shortage to worsen year by year. In a growing economy the demand curve is continually shifting rightward as more people with higher real incomes demand more housing. In an inflationary economy the supply curve is continually shifting leftward because construction, maintenance, and operating costs are rising. Such shifts when combined with rent controls cause the housing shortage to grow over time. For example, when the curves are D and S, rent control at r is accompanied by a housing shortage of q_1q_2. When the curves have shifted to D_1 and S_1, however, the same controlled rent causes an overall housing shortage of q_3q_4.

Of course the housing shortage does not need to grow if the controlled rent is allowed to rise as fast as the equilibrium rent. But the usual *purpose* of controls is to hold rents down in the face of rapid increases in costs and demand. As a result, controlled rents have been allowed to rise over the years much less fast than the rate of inflation. Thus the housing shortage in fact grows over the years, although not as fast as it would if controlled rents were *never* changed.

RENT CONTROLS IN THE UNITED STATES TODAY

American rent controls are of two sorts: controls that were imposed "temporarily" in World War

II but have never been removed and new controls that are a response to the rapidly changing housing markets of the 1970s and 1980s.

During World War II, many cities imposed rent controls for reasons related to the temporary shortages. Most cities removed controls after the war to allow the housing supply to expand when factors of production were again available for construction. A few cities, such as New York, kept the controls. While not extending controls to new buildings, New York maintains them on the large stock of existing buildings as long as the apartments are occupied by the existing tenants. In many cases it has not paid landlords to maintain buildings well, and thus the rate of decay has accelerated. Over time, inflationary cost increases have outstripped increases in controlled rents. Consequently more and more landlords, finding their rental revenues falling short of minimum unavoidable costs, have abandoned their buildings. Title then reverts to the city on account of unpaid taxes. Large areas in the Bronx and Brooklyn have suffered this fate.

Faced with the serious plight of tenants in abandoned buildings, the city government is forced to become a "slumlord." By 1980 New York City owned 75,000 occupied apartments and many unoccupied apartments, most of them taken over when abandoned by landlords. To fix up these apartments and operate them at the controlled rents has been a significant drain on the city's already strained finances.

The recent renewed interest in rent control around the country is not the legacy of World War II. The new rent controls are meant to protect the average tenant against both "profiteering" by landlords in the face of severe local shortages and the steadily rising cost of housing, the result of inflation and economic growth. From Cambridge, Massachusetts, to Santa Monica, California, many cities have adopted rent controls, and others are considering them.

The new controls have not existed long enough for all of the predicted consequences to be seen as yet. The predicted permanent, major housing crisis in controlled areas may lie as much as 10 or 20 years in the future. But some predicted short-term consequences have occurred. Many apartments have been converted to condominiums. During the first three years of the Cambridge rent control law, over 2,000 tenants were dispossessed as apartments were converted to condominiums. Pressure for security-of-tenure laws is already building. Some communities prohibit landlords from refusing to renew leases of existing tenants because of condominium conversion, or require approval of conversion by a majority of the existing tenants.

The Clamor for Rent Control

In the face of these predicted and observed consequences, why does rent control persist and even grow? The answer is largely that the primary victims of rent control do not identify themselves as such, while the primary beneficiaries do. Furthermore, the beneficiaries are a large, identifiable, and often sympathetic group with strong political power and support.

Because housing costs consume a large part of the average household's income, the desire to seek protection from forces that raise housing expenditures is understandable. Having the government hold down the rent gives future protection to tenants who either have long-term leases or hope to be protected in their occupancy by security-of-tenure laws.

Whatever the overall effects of rent control, existing tenants who can stay in their present locations will benefit from it.

Existing tenants know that rent controls hold down the cost of housing. (The only risk to them comes if landlords neglect maintenance and allow their apartment buildings to deteriorate.) And existing tenants constitute an important political constituency for rent controls in cities in which large fractions of the population live in rental units.

Not only are renters a large group, they include many people who are regarded as needing help. Many renting families live on incomes that are small, fixed, and being eroded steadily by inflation. Renters include a disproportionate fraction of the aged, the unemployed, welfare recipients, and members of minority groups living in urban ghettos. They also include many students. A high percentage of these groups are now paying at least half their money incomes to a landlord (who seems never to be in view except to collect the rent), and these groups are truly being squeezed by the rising costs of everything. (Of course not all existing renters are poor, nor landlords rich. New York's rent control, for example, benefits many apartment dwellers who are above average in income and wealth and some who are extremely wealthy; and it squeezes many small investors whose modest incomes depend on rental income.)

If the beneficiaries of rent control are existing tenants who can and want to stay in their present housing, who are the victims? The housing shortage hurts those who will want rental housing that will not be there in the future. The elderly couple who fight to keep rent control on the apartment they occupy are behaving wholly in their own best interest. But they are making life more difficult for the next generation of aged couples, many of whom will not find housing of the same quality if rent controls are kept. The welfare family protected today will have a hard time finding housing if it moves to a new city, or to a new area of the same city, when the opportunity for a job arises or when its present apartment house is abandoned. Minority groups generally will find that their members are hurt in the long run by the steadily shrinking quantity and quality of available rental housing.

One group often identified among the most active advocates of rent controls is made up of college students and other young adults, many of whom are not yet permanently established. Why should they favor rent controls when control-induced shortages will make it more difficult for them to find a suitable apartment? The answer, when it is not an ideological dislike of landlords, seems to be that they do not recognize the link between the lower rents they will pay—if they are lucky enough to find a rent controlled apartment where they want it—and the *decreased chance* of finding such an apartment. "After all," you hear one couple say, "David and Susan Murphy found a great place last week, at only $230 a month. We'll just keep looking." If this couple knew they would have to wait four years, living with mother in the meantime, they might prefer to pay the free-market rent. But they do not know this—and once "in," they will be protected by rent controls until the next time they have to move. Indeed, the existence of shortages may make those living in controlled apartments reluctant to move, even though it would be sensible for them to do so were it not for the housing shortage.

Thus the call for rent control comes both from existing tenants, who gain at the expense of those who do not have secured leases in rental housing, and from potential tenants, who underestimate the adverse effects on *them* of the rent control-induced housing shortage. In contrast, the *articulate* opposition is the much smaller (and less sympathetic) group of landlords. The silent victims, who are the future unsuccessful searchers for rental units, may never realize the causal link between rent controls and the housing shortage from which they suffer.

The Politics of Rent Control

That many individuals are either selfish or myopic in calling for rent control is understandable. That their leaders and public representatives do not appreciate and weigh the long-term consequences is less comprehensible except in very political terms. Worldwide experience as well as economic theory demonstrates that rent controls create shortages, that shortages do not benefit the population as a whole, that the real costs of providing housing do not diminish when controls are imposed, and that when the private market does not provide housing, either tenants will bear the cost by doubling up or doing without or public taxes will have to be raised to provide public housing. Perhaps the politicians are myopic too, judging next month's election (and hence today's constituency) to be more important than adverse, long-run, future effects.

WHAT ARE THE ALTERNATIVES?

Advocates of continuing rent controls often say that construction costs are now too high to erect buildings that offer apartments at rents that middle-class people can afford. What are the alternatives? One possibility is to let rents rise on the free market sufficiently to cover costs. If "middle-class people" (and others) really decide they cannot afford these apartments and will not rent them, then the building of apartments will cease. It is more likely, however, in light of past consumer behavior, that agonizing choices will be made to spend a higher proportion of total income on housing and/or to economize on housing.

A second possibility is to control rents below the cost of new building, with the inevitable consequence of a shortage of rental housing that grows as the stock of rental accommodation wears out and is not replaced. A further alternative is for government to step in with public housing and fill the gap between total demand and private supply. Subsidized public housing will then be financed at the taxpayer's expense (since the high costs of housing must be paid by someone).

The costs of providing additional housing cannot be voted out of existence; they can only be transferred from one set of persons to another.

Some European countries, notably Great Britain and Sweden, have been through the whole process of imposing rent controls to protect tenants and ending up with excess demand and an increasingly expensive program of subsidized public housing. In the face of other public needs, they are trying to give more scope to private markets for housing, but policies of rent controls are always politically popular. Only time will tell how far the United States is to travel the same path. Economics cannot tell society which hard choice to make, but it can show what the choices are. The greatest danger is that the long-run costs will be neglected in making the choice.

Four General Lessons About Resource Allocation

In Chapters 7 and 8 we have examined several examples of government intervention in markets that might have been left unregulated. Public debate about the desirability of more or less intervention is lively today, both with respect to deregulation in areas of existing regulation and with respect to imposing wage and price controls to cope with the ever-rising prices in our inflationary economy. Our discussion suggests four widely applicable lessons.

1. COSTS MAY BE SHIFTED, BUT THEY CANNOT BE AVOIDED

Production, whether in response to free-market signals or to government controls, uses resources; thus it involves costs to members of society. If it takes 5 percent of the nation's resources to provide housing to some stated average standard, then those resources will not be available to produce other commodities. For society there is no such thing as free housing. The average standard of living depends on the amounts of resources available to the economy and the efficiency with which these resources are used. *It follows that costs are real* and are incurred no matter who provides the goods. Rent controls, housing subsidies, or public provision of housing can change the share of the costs of housing paid by particular individuals or groups — lowering the share for some, raising the share for others — but they cannot make the costs go away.

Different ways of *allocating* the costs may also affect the total amount of resources used, and thus the amount of costs incurred. Controls that keep prices and profits of some commodity below free-market levels will lead to increased quantities demanded and decreased quantities supplied. Unless government steps in to provide additional supplies, fewer resources will be allocated to producing the commodity. If government chooses to supply all the demand at the controlled prices, more resources will be allocated to it, which means fewer resources will be devoted to other kinds of goods and services. The opportunity cost of more housing is less of something else.

2. FREE-MARKET PRICES AND PROFITS ENCOURAGE ECONOMICAL USE OF RESOURCES

Prices and profits in a market economy provide signals to both demanders and suppliers. Prices that are high and rising (relative to other prices) provide an incentive to purchasers to economize on the commodity. They may choose to satisfy the want in question with substitutes whose prices have not risen so much (because they are less costly to provide) or to satisfy less of that want by shifting expenditure to the satisfaction of other wants. There is substantial scope for such economizing reactions even for commodities as "necessary" as housing: *some* housing is necessary, but a particular quantity is not.

On the supply side, rising prices tend to produce rising profits. High profits attract further resources into production. Short-term windfall profits that bear no relation to current costs repeatedly occur in market economies; they cause resources to move into those industries with profits until profits fall to levels that can be earned elsewhere in the economy.

Falling prices and falling profits provide the opposite motivations. Purchasers are inclined to buy more; sellers are inclined to produce less and to move resources out of the industry and into more profitable undertakings.

The pattern we have described may be summarized:

Free-market prices and profits are signals to producers and consumers. Changing relative prices and profits signal a need for change to which consumers and producers respond.

3. CONTROLS INHIBIT THE ALLOCATIVE MECHANISM

Some controls prevent prices from rising (in response, say, to an increase in demand). If the price is held down, the signal is never given to consumers to economize on a commodity that is in short supply. On the supply side, when prices and profits are prevented from rising (on the grounds, for example, that no more than a "fair" return should be earned at all times), the profit signals that would attract new resources into the industry are never given. The shortage continues, and the movements of demand and supply that would resolve it are not set in motion.

In the opposite case, where there is excess supply, an appropriate response would be some increase in quantity purchased and some decrease in production accompanied by a shift of resources to production of other, more valued commodities. Falling prices and profits would motivate such shifts. When prices are prevented from falling in the face of temporary surpluses (on the grounds, for example, that producers of an essential product must have a fair return guaranteed to them), the signals that would increase purchases or push resources out of an industry are never given.

The results tend to be the same no matter what the motives for intervention. For rent controls and other maximum prices, public policy rests on the view that consumers need protection from producers. Landlords who provide rental accommodations are left to bear any windfall losses themselves yet are prevented from earning windfall gains. In agriculture, however, public policy since the 1930s has often taken the opposite view: to protect farmers at the expense of consumers or taxpayers. In the case of the draft, the use of controls is based at least in part on the assumption of the need to protect taxpayers against the wage demands of reluctant recruits into the armed services.

The underlying reasons for these views are complex. One may start with stereotypes of rich landlords, poor tenants, struggling family farmers, beleaguered taxpayers, and selfish youth unwilling to do their share in defense of the country. Yet even superficial analysis shows that these are only stereotypes, that there are lots of struggling landlords, rich tenants, corporate farms, and unemployed minority members among the recruits for military service.

4. CONTROLS REQUIRE ALTERNATIVE ALLOCATIVE MECHANISMS

If the price system with its profit incentives is not used to allocate resources, alternative methods will necessarily appear. Temporary fluctuations in demand and supply will give rise to severe shortages and surpluses. During times of shortages, allocation will be by sellers' preferences unless the state imposes rationing. During periods of surplus, there will be unsold supplies or illegal price cutting unless the state buys and stores the surpluses. Long-run changes in demand and costs will not induce resource reallocations through private decisions. As a result, the state will be put under strong, long-run pressure to step in. It will have to force or order resources out of industries where prices are held too high—as it tried to do in agriculture in the 1950s and 1960s. It will also have to force or order resources into industries where prices are held too low—as it can do, for example, by providing public housing or using its power to draft young people for military service.

Whenever a specific alternative scheme of allocation is imposed, it is costly in a number of additional ways. First, the allocation itself usually requires the use of resources for administering and enforcing the rules. Second, the use of the state's power takes the mixed economy one step further away from the free enterprise economy and toward a command economy. Third, the freedom of some individuals to act in what they consider their own best interest is limited. Sometimes the benefits of the policies will justify the costs, sometimes they will not. Justified or not, the costs are always present and are often large.

Summary

1. This chapter continues the application of the elementary theory of supply, demand, and price to real-world problems.

2. Price ceilings are binding ("effective") whenever they hold price below the free-market equilibrium price. Binding ceiling prices cause shortages to appear, lead to allocation by sellers' or government's preferences, and provide a strong incentive for black marketeers to buy at the controlled price and sell at the higher free-market price.

3. Rent controls are a persistent and spreading form of price ceiling. The major effect of rent control is a shortage of rental accommodation that gets worse due to a slow but inexorable decline in the quantity of rental housing.

4. Rent controls can be an effective response to temporary situations in which there is a ban on building or a transitory increase in demand. They will almost surely fail when they are introduced as a response to a long-run increase in demand or to inflation in the costs of providing rental housing.

5. The popularity of rent controls, despite their long-run adverse effects, is due to the fact that existing tenants, the constituency which benefits most, are a large, identifiable, and often sympathetic group, while the people who will suffer most from the future shortage of housing are not identified.

6. Four general lessons about resource allocation are: (1) costs may be shifted, but they cannot be avoided, (2) free-market prices and profits encourage economical use of resources, (3) controls inhibit the allocative mechanism, and (4) controls require alternative allocative mechanisms.

Topics for Review

Ceiling prices
Black markets
Allocative function of windfall profits
The effect of controls on allocation
Alternative allocative mechanisms

Discussion Questions

1. "When a controlled item is vital to everyone, it is easier to start controlling the price than to stop controlling it. Such controls are popular with consumers, regardless of their uneconomic consequences. In this respect oil price controls resemble rent controls." Explain why it may be uneconomic to have such controls, why they may be popular, and why, if they are popular, the government might nevertheless choose to decontrol prices.

2. Journalist William Safire calls the energy crisis in natural gas "the unnatural shortage of natural gas." He writes: "Be angry at the real villains: the Washington-knows-best Congressmen, the self-anointed consumer 'protectors' and the regulatory bureaucracy. They thought they could protect the consumer by breaking the laws of supply and demand, and as a result have made a classic case against government intervention." From these remarks what do you judge the policy to have been? Could *producers* have created the shortage of natural gas? If so, how? How would you define a "shortage"? Is there a valid distinction between a "natural shortage" and an "unnatural shortage"?

3. Medical and hospital care in Britain is provided free to individuals by the National Health Service, with the costs paid by taxation. Some British doctors complain that patients want "too much" medical care; patients complain that they have to wait "too long" in doctors' offices for the care they get and months or years for needed operations. Use the theory of supply and demand to discuss these complaints. Would you expect a private (pay) medical market to grow up alongside the National Health Service? Would you expect the government to welcome or discourage such a second service?

4. The Yarvard Law School, in Princetown, has 1,000 qualified applicants for 200 places in the first-year class. It is debating a number of alternative admission criteria: (a) a lottery, (b) date of initial application, (c) LSAT score, (d) recommendations from alumni, (e) place of residence of applicant. An economist on the faculty determined that if the tuition level is doubled, the excess demand will disappear. Argue for (or against) using the tuition rate to replace each of the other suggested criteria.

5. The demand for housing (rented or owned) is downward sloping. List some of the reasons why a rise in the price of all forms of housing (due to, say, a rise in construction costs) would lead to a reduction in the quantity of housing demanded. Do some of the reasons apply particularly to rental housing? To owner-occupied housing?

6. It is sometimes asserted that the rising costs of construction are putting housing out of the reach of ordinary citizens. Determine who bears the cost when rentals are kept down by (a) rent controls, (b) a subsidy to tenants equal to some fraction of their rent payments, and (c) low-cost public housing.

7. In England rents are set by public bodies that are instructed to fix fair rents without regard for local conditions of demand and supply. What might this mean? Analyze some of the effects of this policy on the workings of local housing markets.

8. If landlords always charged rents directly related to their costs and never "profiteered" from local scarcities or cut rents below costs, what effect would this have on the working of local housing markets?

Part Three

Demand

Household Consumption Behavior

9

Early economists, struggling with the problem of what determines the relative prices of commodities, encountered what they came to call the **paradox of value:** necessary commodities such as water have prices that are low compared to the prices of luxury commodities such as diamonds. Water is necessary to our existence, these economists of some 200 years ago argued, while diamonds are frivolous and could disappear from the face of the earth tomorrow without causing any real upset. Does it not seem odd, then, that water is so cheap and diamonds are so expensive? It took a long time for economists to resolve this apparent paradox, so it is not surprising that even today the confusion persists in many quarters and clouds some current policy discussions.

We have already met one answer: It is supply and demand, not "necessity" or "luxury," that determine price in any competitive market. The equilibrium price that equates supply and demand is relatively low for water and relatively high for diamonds. But why is the demand for a necessity not enough to assure that its price will be high? After all, water is essential to life itself.

To address this more fundamental question we must go behind the market demand curve, which is the aggregate of all households' desired purchases at each possible price, and consider the behavior and motivation of individual households. This involves looking first at the relation between the market demand curve and the demand curves of individual households, then at individual behavior.

THE RELATION BETWEEN MARKET AND HOUSEHOLD DEMAND CURVES

Market demand curves tell how much is demanded by all purchasers. For example, in Figure 5-1 (see page 61) the market demand for carrots was 90,000 tons when the price was $40 per ton. This 90,000 tons is the sum of the quantities demanded by millions of different households. It may be made up of 4 pounds for the McDaniels, 7 pounds for the Gonzaleses, 1.5 pounds for the Wilsons, and so on. The demand curve for carrots also tells us that when the price rises to $60, aggregate quantity demanded falls to 77,500 tons per month. This quantity too can be traced back to individual households. The McDaniels might buy only 3 pounds, the Gonzaleses 6.5 pounds, and the Wilsons perhaps none at all. Notice that we have now described two points, not only on the market demand curve but on the demand curves of each of these households.

Aggregate behavior is merely the sum of the behavior of individual households. The market demand is the horizontal sum of the demand curves of the individual households.

It is the *horizontal* sum because we wish to add quantities demanded at a given price, and quantities are measured in the horizontal direction on a conventional demand curve graph. This process is illustrated in Figure 9-1.

The Marginal Utility Theory of Household Behavior

MARGINAL AND TOTAL UTILITY

The satisfaction someone receives from consuming commodities is called his or her **utility.** The total utility obtained from consuming some commodity can be distinguished from the marginal utility of consuming one unit more or one unit less of it.

FIGURE 9–1
The Relation Between Household and Market Demand Curves

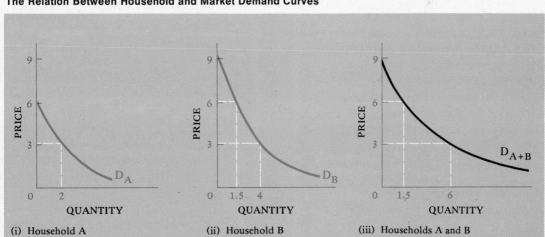

(i) Household A   (ii) Household B   (iii) Households A and B

An aggregate demand curve is the horizontal sum of the individual demand curves of all households in the market. The figure illustrates aggregation over only two households. At a price of $3, household A purchases 2 units and household B purchases 4 units; thus together they purchase 6 units. No matter how many households are involved the process is the same.

Total utility refers to the total satisfaction from consuming some commodity. **Marginal utility** refers to the change in satisfaction resulting from consuming a little more or a little less of the commodity. Thus, for example, the total utility of consuming ten units of any commodity is the total satisfaction that those ten units provide. The marginal utility of the tenth unit consumed is the satisfaction added by the consumption of that unit—or, in other words, the difference in total utility between consuming nine units and consuming ten units.[1]

The significance of this distinction can be seen by considering two questions: (1) If you had to give up consuming one of the following commodities completely, which would you choose: water or the movies? (2) If you had to choose between one of the following, which would you pick: increasing your water consumption by 35 gallons a month (the amount required for an average bath) or attending one more movie a month?

In (1) you are comparing the value you place on your total consumption of water with the value you place on all your attendances at the movies. You are comparing the *total utility* of your water consumption with the *total utility* of your movie attendances. There is little doubt that everyone would answer (1) in the same way, revealing that the total utility derived from consuming water exceeds the total utility derived from attending the movies.

In (2) you are comparing the value you place on a small addition to your water consumption with the value you place on a small addition to your movie attendances. You are comparing your *marginal utility* of water with your *marginal utility* of movies. The response to choice (2) is far less predictable than the response to choice (1). Some might select the extra movie; others

might decide they have seen all the movies they can stand (marginal utility of another visit to the movies, *zero*) and would select the extra water. Furthermore, their choice would depend on whether it was made at a time when water was plentiful, so that they had more or less all the water they wanted (marginal utility of a little more water, *low*), or when water was scarce, so that they might put quite a high value on obtaining a little more water (marginal utility of a little more water, *high*).

Choices of type (1) are encountered much less commonly than are choices of type (2). If our income rises a little, we have to decide to have some more of one thing or another. When we find that we are overspending, or when our income falls, we have to decide what to cut down on, to have a little less of this or a little less of that.

Real choices are rarely conditioned by total utilities; it is marginal utilities that are relevant to choices concerning a little more or a little less.

The Hypothesis of Diminishing Marginal Utility

The basic hypothesis of utility theory, sometimes called the law of diminishing marginal utility, is:

The utility that any household derives from successive units of a particular commodity will diminish as total consumption of the commodity increases, the consumption of all other commodities being held constant.

Consider further the case of water. Some minimum quantity is essential to sustain life, and a person would, if necessary, give up all his or her income to obtain that quantity of water. Thus the marginal utility of that much water is extremely high. More than this bare minimum will be drunk, but the marginal utility of successive glasses of water drunk over a period will decline steadily.

Evidence for this hypothesis will be considered later, but you can convince yourself that it is at least reasonable by asking yourself a few questions. How much money would induce you to cut

---

[1] Here and elsewhere in elementary economics it is common to use interchangeably two concepts that mathematicians distinguish between. Technically, *incremental* utility is measured over a discrete interval, such as from nine to ten, while marginal utility is a rate of change measured over an infinitesimal interval. But common usage applies the word *marginal* when the last unit is involved, even if a one-unit change is not infinitesimal. [9]

your consumption of water by one glass per week? The answer is, very little. How much would induce you to cut it by a second glass? By a third glass? To only one glass consumed per week? The answer to the last question is, quite a bit. The fewer glasses you are consuming already, the higher the marginal utility of one more or one less glass of water.

But water has many uses other than for drinking. A fairly high marginal utility will be attached to some minimum quantity for bathing, but much more than this minimum will only be used for more frequent baths and for having a water level in the tub higher than is absolutely necessary. The last weekly gallon used for bathing is likely to have quite a low marginal utility. Again, some small quantity of water is necessary for tooth brushing, but many people leave the water running while they brush. They can hardly pretend that the water going down the drain between wetting and rinsing the brush has a high utility. When all the extravagant uses of water by the modern consumer are considered, it is certain that the marginal utility of the last, say, 30 percent of all units consumed is very low, even though the total utility of *all* the units consumed is extremely high.

Utility Schedules and Graphs

Assuming that utility can be measured, it is possible to illustrate the hypothesis. The schedule in Table 9-1 is hypothetical. It merely illustrates the assumptions that have been made about utility. The table shows that total utility rises as the number of movies attended each month rises. Everything else being equal, the household gets more satisfaction, the more movies it consumes each month—at least over the range shown in the table. But the marginal utility of each additional movie per month is less than that of the previous one (even though each movie adds something to the household's satisfaction). The marginal utility schedule declines as quantity consumed rises. The same data are shown graphically in the two parts of Figure 9-2. [10]

TABLE 9–1
Total and Marginal Utility Schedules

Number of movies attended (per month)	Total utility	Marginal utility
0	0	
		30
1	30	
		20
2	50	
		15
3	65	
		10
4	75	
		8
5	83	
		6
6	89	
		4
7	93	
		3
8	96	
		2
9	98	
		1
10	99	

Total utility rises but marginal utility declines as the consumption of this household increases. The marginal utility of 20, shown as the second entry in the last column, arises because total utility increased from 30 to 50—a difference of 20—with attendance at the second movie. Technically this is "incremental utility" over the interval from 1 to 2 units. To indicate that the marginal utility is associated with the change from one rate of movie attendances to another, the figures are recorded between the rows. When plotting marginal utility on a graph, it is plotted at the midpoint of the interval over which it is computed.

Can marginal utility reach zero? With many commodities there is some maximum consumption after which additional units give no additional utility. If the individual were forced to consume more, the additional units would actually reduce his or her total utility.

Cigarettes are an obvious example. There is a maximum number of cigarettes that most people would smoke per day, even if they did not have to worry about cost. For nonsmokers that number is zero. Few smokers would want to go to the point of chain-smoking from the second they awoke until the moment they fell asleep. Long before consumption reached this point, additional cigarettes smoked would cease to add to utility and would begin to subtract from it; that is, additional cigarettes would have a negative

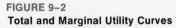

FIGURE 9–2
Total and Marginal Utility Curves

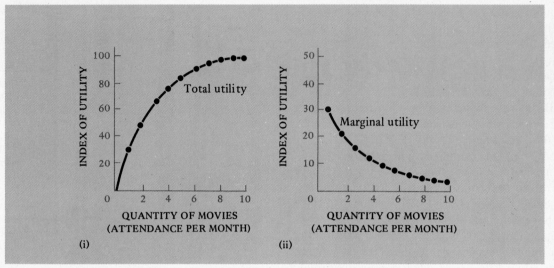

(i)   (ii)

The total utility curve rises but the marginal utility curve falls as the quantity consumed rises. The dots reflect the points listed in Table 9-1; smooth curves have been drawn through them.

marginal utility or, as it is sometimes called, a marginal *disutility*. The same is true of many other commodities such as food, alcoholic beverages, and most recreation. (Although a few fanatics might be happy to play golf from sunup to sunset seven days a week for the rest of their lives, most people would not.)

MAXIMIZING UTILITY

A basic assumption of the economic theory of household behavior is that households consistently follow a particular rule.

The members of a household are assumed to maximize their total utility.

This is one way of saying that the members of households try to make themselves as well off as they possibly can in the circumstances in which they find themselves. Sometimes this assumption is taken to mean that households are narrowly selfish and have no charitable motives. Not so; if,

for example, the household derives utility from giving its money away to others, this can be incorporated into the analysis. The marginal utility it gets from a dollar given away can be compared with the marginal utility it gets from a dollar spent on itself.

The Equilibrium of a Household

How can a household adjust its expenditure so as to maximize the total utility of its members? Should it go to the point at which the marginal utility of each commodity is the same, that is, the point at which it would value equally the last unit of each commodity consumed? This would make sense only if each commodity had the same price per unit. But if a household must spend $3 to buy an additional unit of one commodity and only $1 for a unit of another, the first commodity would represent a poor use of its money if the marginal utility of each were equal: It would be spending $3 to get satisfaction that it could have acquired for only $1.

The household maximizing its utility will allocate its expenditure among commodities so that the utility of the last dollar spent on each is equal.

Imagine that the household is in a position in which the utility of the last dollar spent on carrots yields three times the utility of the last dollar spent on brussels sprouts. In this case total utility can be increased by switching a dollar of expenditure from sprouts to carrots and gaining the difference between the utilities of a dollar spent on each.

The utility-maximizing household will continue to switch its expenditure from sprouts to carrots as long as a dollar spent on carrots yields more utility than a dollar spent on sprouts. But this switching reduces the quantity of sprouts consumed and, given the law of diminishing marginal utility, raises the marginal utility of sprouts; at the same time, it increases the quantity of carrots consumed and thereby lowers the marginal utility of carrots. Eventually the marginal utilities will have changed enough so that the utility of a dollar spent on carrots is just equal to the utility of a dollar spent on sprouts.

At this point there is nothing to be gained by a further switch of expenditure from sprouts to carrots. If the household persisted in reallocating its expenditure, it would further reduce the marginal utility of carrots (by consuming more of them) and raise the marginal utility of sprouts (by consuming less of them). Total utility would then be lower because the utility of a dollar spent on sprouts would now exceed the utility of a dollar spent on carrots.

Let us now leave carrots and sprouts and deal with commodities in general. Denote the marginal utility of the last unit of X by MU_x and its price by p_x. Let MU_y and p_y refer to a second commodity. The marginal utility per dollar of X will be MU_x/p_x. For example, if the last unit adds 30 units to utility and costs \$2, then its marginal utility per dollar is $30/2 = 15$.

The condition required for a household to maximize its utility is, for any pair of commodities,

$$\frac{MU_x}{p_x} = \frac{MU_y}{p_y} \qquad [1]$$

This says that the household will allocate its expenditure so that the utility gained from the last dollar spent on each commodity is equal.

This is the fundamental equation of the utility theory of demand. Each household demands each good (for example, movie attendance) up to the point at which the marginal utility per dollar spent on it is the same as the marginal utility of a dollar spent on another good (for example, water). When this condition is met, the household cannot shift a dollar of expenditure from one commodity to another and increase its utility.

An Alternative Interpretation of Household Equilibrium

It is possible to rearrange the terms in equation [1] to gain an additional insight into household behavior.

$$\frac{MU_x}{MU_y} = \frac{p_x}{p_y} \qquad [2]$$

The right-hand side of this equation is given to the household by the market; it states the *relative* price of the two goods. It is determined by the market and is outside the control of the individual household, which reacts to these market prices but is powerless to change them. The left-hand side concerns the ability of the goods to add to the household's satisfaction; it is within the control of the household. In determining the quantities of different goods it buys, the household determines also their marginal utilities. (If you have difficulty seeing why, look again at Figure 9-2(ii).)

If the two sides of equation [2] are not equal, the household can increase its total satisfaction by rearranging its purchases. Assume, for example, that the price of a unit of X is twice the price of a unit of Y, $(p_x/p_y = 2)$, while the marginal utility of a unit of X is three times that of a unit of Y, $(MU_x/MU_y = 3)$. It will now pay the household to buy more X and less Y. If, for example, it reduces its purchases of Y by two units, it will free enough purchasing power to buy a unit of X. Since one new unit of X bought yields 1.5 times the satisfaction of two units of Y forgone, this switch is worth making. What about a further switch of X for Y? As the household buys more X and less Y, the marginal utility of X will fall and the marginal utility of Y will rise. The household will go on rearranging its purchases—reducing Y consumption and increasing X consumption—until, in this example, the marginal utility of X is only twice that of Y. At this point there is no further room to increase total satisfaction by rearranging purchases between the two commodities.

Now consider what the household is doing. It is faced with a set of prices that it cannot change. The household responds to these prices, and maximizes its satisfaction, by adjusting the things it can change—the quantities of the various goods it purchases—until equation [2] is satisfied for all pairs of commodities.

This sort of equation—one side representing the choices the outside world gives decision makers and the other side representing the effect of those choices on their welfare—recurs in economics again and again. It reflects the equilibrium position reached when decision makers have made the best adjustment they can to the external forces that limit their choices.

When all households are fully adjusted to a given set of market prices, each and every household will have identical ratios of its marginal utilities for each pair of goods. This is because each household faces the same set of market prices. Of course a rich household may consume more of each commodity than will a poor household. The rich and the poor households (and every other household) will, however, adjust their *relative* purchases of each commodity so that the relative marginal utilities are the same for each household. Thus, if the price of X is twice the price of Y, each household will purchase X and Y to the point at which the household's marginal utility of X is twice its marginal utility of Y.

The Derivation of the Household's Demand Curve[2]

To derive the household's demand curve for a commodity, it is only necessary to ask what happens when there is a change in the price of that commodity. To do this for candy, take equation [2] and let X stand for candy and Y for all other commodities. Assume that candy involves such a small proportion of the consumer's total expenditure that the marginal utilities of all other goods are unaffected when the household spends a little more or a little less on candy. If total expenditure on candy rises from $1 a month to $2 in response to a 10 percent fall in the price of candy, this represents a large increase in candy consumption, and the marginal utility of candy must fall. But the extra dollar spent on candy may mean only 1¢ less spent on each of a hundred different commodities, and this reduction in the consumption of each of them is so small that it will have a negligible effect on their marginal utilities.

What will happen if, with all other prices constant, the price of candy rises? The household that started from a position of equilibrium will now find itself in a position in which[3]

$$\frac{MU \text{ of candy}}{MU \text{ of } Y} < \frac{\text{price of candy}}{\text{price of } Y} \qquad [3]$$

To restore equilibrium, it must buy less candy, thereby raising its marginal utility until once again equation [2] is satisfied (where X is candy). The common sense of this is that the marginal utility of candy *per dollar* falls when its price rises. The household began with the utility of the last dollar spent on candy equal to the utility of the last dollar spent on all other goods, but the rise in candy prices changes this. The household buys less candy (and more of other goods) until the marginal utility of candy rises enough to make the utility of a dollar spent on candy the

[2] This section, which derives from utility theory the prediction that demand curves slope downward, may be omitted without loss of continuity.

[3] The inequality sign (<) always points to the smaller of two magnitudes. When the price of candy rises, the right-hand side of equation [2] increases. Until the household adjusts its consumption patterns, the left-hand side will stay the same. Thus equation [2] is replaced by inequality [3].

same as it was originally. Thus, if candy prices have doubled, the quantity purchased must be reduced until the marginal utility of candy has doubled.

This analysis leads to the basic prediction of demand theory.

A rise in the price of a commodity (with income and the prices of all other commodities held constant) will lead to a decrease in the quantity of the commodity demanded by each household.

If this prediction is valid for each household, it is also true for all households taken together. Thus the theory predicts a downward-sloping market demand curve.

APPLYING THE DISTINCTION BETWEEN MARGINAL AND TOTAL UTILITY

The Paradox of Value Revisited

We saw at the beginning of this chapter that early economists found it paradoxical that the market often valued necessary commodities such as water much lower than it valued such luxuries as diamonds. To state the "paradox" they distinguished a commodity's *value in use* (its total utility) and its *value in exchange* (its total market value, that is, price *times* quantity).[4] It seemed reasonable to them that commodities with high use values should have high market values. A precise statement of what they expected is: For any two commodities, the ratio of their values in exchange should conform to the ratio of their values in use. In the case of water and diamonds this led to the *incorrect* prediction that

$$\frac{p \times q \text{ of diamonds}}{p \times q \text{ of water}} = \frac{\text{total utility of diamonds}}{\text{total utility of water}} \quad [4]$$

The paradox of value was resolved when later economists discovered that equation [4] was inconsistent with the assumption that households

---

[4] The total utilities of two commodities cannot be simply related to their relative market *prices*, since the latter can be made anything we want by choosing the units appropriately. For example, one barrel of diamonds is expensive relative to one barrel of water, but a one-carat diamond is cheap relative to one reservoir full of water.

are utility maximizers. The reason is that utility-maximizing behavior relates *marginal* utilities to prices (as shown in equation [2]), not total utilities to total values purchased (as hypothesized in equation [4]).

Thus, for example, the fact that air is free means that people will use it until its marginal utility is zero. However, its zero value in exchange does not preclude its having a high value in use (total utility). To understand the case of water and diamonds, remember that water is cheap because there is enough of it that people consume it to the point at which its *marginal* utility is very low; they are not prepared to pay a high price to obtain a little more of it. Diamonds are expensive because they are scarce (the owners of diamond mines keep diamonds scarce by limiting output), and those who buy them have to stop at a point where marginal utility is still high; they are prepared to pay a high price for an additional diamond.

Elasticity of Demand, Necessities and Luxuries

Closely related to the paradox of value is the idea of relating elasticities to total utilities. It is possible to define necessities and luxuries in terms of total utilities. Certain commodities, called luxuries, have low total utilities; they can be dispensed with altogether if circumstances require. Other commodities, called necessities, are essential to life; they have high total utilities because certain minimum quantities of them are essential indeed.

So far so good. Error often creeps in, however, when people try to use commonsense knowledge about luxuries and necessities to predict demand elasticities and to dispense with the need for measurement. They argue that since luxuries can easily be given up, they will have highly elastic demands because when their prices rise, households can stop purchasing them. On the other hand, necessities have almost completely inelastic demands because when prices rise, households have no choice but to continue to buy them.

If it worked, this approach would save us time; we would have to determine only whether a particular commodity was a necessity or a luxury to be able to predict its elasticity of demand. But

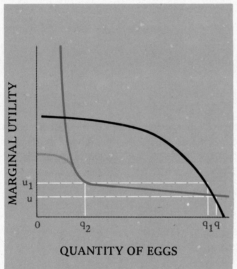

FIGURE 9–3

The Relation of Elasticity of Demand to Utility

Elasticity of demand is determined by marginal utilities in the relevant range, not total utilities. The household originally consumes q dozen eggs per month, and the last egg consumed has a marginal utility of u. The price of eggs now doubles. To achieve a new equilibrium the household must cut its egg consumption until the marginal utility of eggs doubles, rising from u to u_1. If the black line is the household marginal utility curve, consumption only falls to q_1 and the household will have a very inelastic demand curve for eggs. If, however, the colored line is the household's marginal utility curve, consumption falls to q_2 and the household will have a very elastic demand curve. While the shape of the marginal utility curve in the relevant range is thus important, its shape outside of this range is irrelevant. To see this, let the colored curve have two alternative shapes in the range above u_1. The dark curve indicates a much higher total utility of the first units consumed than does the light curve, yet these alternative shapes have no influence on the household's behavior when it seeks to raise the marginal utility of eggs from u to u_1.

elasticity of demand depends on marginal utilities, not total utilities.

Demand theory leads to the prediction that when the price of a commodity — say, eggs — rises, the household will reduce its purchase of eggs enough to increase their *marginal* utility to the point where the marginal utility per dollar spent on eggs is the same as for other commodities whose prices did not rise. But will the reduction in quantity required to raise the marginal utility be a little or a lot? This depends on the shape of the marginal utility curve in the range that is relevant. If the marginal utility curve is flat, a large change in quantity is required and demand will be elastic. If the curve is steep, a small change will suffice and demand will be inelastic. Figure 9-3 considers several possibilities in response to a doubling in the price of eggs. It leads to these important conclusions:

The response of quantity demanded to a change in price (i.e., the elasticity of demand) depends on the marginal utility over the relevant range and has no necessary relation to the total utility of the good.

"Just" Prices

The emotional reaction to goods is often a response to their total utilities rather than to their marginal utilities. We often hear an argument such as this: Water is a necessity of life of critical importance to rich and poor; it is wrong, therefore, to make people pay for so necessary a commodity.

Such views often produce curious results. If, for example, water is provided free instead of at a modest cost, the extra consumption that will occur will be for many uses that yield a relatively low utility (such as letting the water run while brushing teeth). The relevant question when deciding between a zero price and a modest price for water is not "Is water so necessary that we do not want to deprive anyone of *all* of it?" but rather "Are the marginal uses of water such that we do not want to discourage anyone from using water for these purposes?" Clearly, the two questions can be given different answers.

What Do Attitude Surveys Measure?

Consider a type of survey that is popular both in the daily newspapers and in sociology and political science. These surveys take the form of asking such questions as:

Do you like the Republicans more than the Democrats?

In deciding to live in area A rather than B, what factors influenced your choice? List the following in order of importance: neighbors, schools, closeness to swimming area, price and quality of housing available, play areas for children, general amenities.

In choosing a university, what factors were important to you? List in order of importance: environment, academic excellence, residential facilities, parents' opinion, school opinion, athletic facilities, tuition.

You should be able to add other examples to this list (which was drawn from real cases). *All of the above survey questions, and most of those you will be able to add, attempt to measure total rather than marginal utilities.* There is of course nothing illegal or immoral about this. People are free to measure anything that interests them, and in some cases knowledge of total utilities may be of practical value. But in many cases actual behavior will be determined by marginal utilities, and anyone who attempts to predict such behavior from a (correct) knowledge of total utilities will be hopelessly in error.

Where the behavior being predicted involves an either-or decision, such as a vote for the Democratic or the Republican candidate, the total utility that is attached to each choice will indeed be what matters because the voters are choosing one or the other. But where the decision is marginal, between a little more and a little less, total utility is not what will determine behavior.

A recent newspaper poll in a large midwestern city showed that two-thirds of the city's voters rated its excellent school system as one of its important assets. Yet in a subsequent election the voters turned down a school bond issue. Is this irrational behavior, as the newspaper editorials charged? Does it show a biased sample in the poll? It demonstrates neither. The poll measured the people's assessment of the total utility derived from the school system, while the bond issue vote depended on the people's assessment of the marginal utility of a little more money spent on the school system. There is nothing contradictory in anyone's feeling that the total utility of the city's fine school system is very large but that the city has other needs that have a higher marginal utility than further money spent on school construction.

A recent survey showed—paradoxically, it claimed—that many Americans are getting more pleasure from their families just at the time that they are electing to have smaller families. There is nothing paradoxical about a shift in tastes that increases the marginal utility of the first two or three children and reduces the marginal utility of each further child. Nor is there any paradox in a parent's getting a high total utility from the total time spent with the children but assigning a low marginal utility to the prospect of spending a little additional time with them each evening.

Evidence about the consumption of water at various prices suggests that the marginal utility curve for water is shaped like the curve in Figure 9-4. The difference between providing water free and charging a modest price for it may mean a great deal in the quantity of water consumed. The additional water is costly to provide, and its provision requires scarce resources that could have been used to produce other things. If the utility of the commodities forgone is higher than the utility of the extra water consumed, then people are worse off as a result of receiving water free. A charge for water would release resources from water production to produce goods that yield a higher utility. Of course some minimum quantity of water could be provided free to every household, but the effects of this would be very different from those of making water generally free.

FIGURE 9–4
A Hypothetical Marginal Utility Curve for Water

The imposition of a modest price may greatly reduce the quantity of water consumed without causing a large total sacrifice in the utility derived from water consumption. If water is priced at p, consumers will consume q units per month. Lowering the price to zero would increase the consumption to q_1. Much of the water that a household would consume at a zero price has a very low marginal utility.

Similar considerations apply to food, medical services, and a host of other commodities that are necessities of life but that have numerous extravagant uses which yield low utility and which will only be indulged if the commodity is very cheap or free.

Free Goods and Scarce Goods

A **free good** is one for which no price needs to be paid. Since a household's total utility can always be increased by consuming more of any good having a positive marginal utility, it follows that free goods will be consumed up to the point where their marginal utilities are zero.

Free goods may arise naturally or through government policy. When a good is naturally free, the amount supplied by nature is so plentiful that every household can consume it to the point of zero marginal utility without exhausting the available supply. When a good that is not naturally free is provided free to consumers by an appropriate government policy, households will once again consume it to the point of zero marginal utility even though the last unit is costly to produce.

A **scarce good** is one that commands a positive price. It follows that scarce goods will have positive marginal utilities. Most goods are scarce. Not enough can be produced to satisfy demand at a zero price.

The meaning of the scarcity principle first discussed in Chapter 1 may now be reinterpreted. If all goods had zero prices, the total amounts that people would want to consume would greatly exceed the amounts that could be produced by all of the economy's resources. Thus goods are scarce in relation to households' potential demands, and resources are scarce in relation to households' desires for the goods they can produce.

Consumers' Surplus

Assume that you would be willing to pay as much as $100 a month for the amount of a commodity you consume rather than do without it. Further, assume that you actually buy the commodity for $60 instead of $100. What a bargain! You have paid $40 less than the top figure you were willing to pay. Yet this sort of bargain is not rare; it occurs every day in any economy where prices do the rationing. Indeed it is so common that the $40 "saved" in this example has a name: *consumers' surplus*. A precise definition will come later; in the meantime, let us see how this surplus arises.

Consumers' surplus is a direct consequence of diminishing marginal utility. To illustrate the connection, suppose we have collected the information shown in Table 9-2 on the basis of an interview with Mrs. Schwartz. Our first question is, If you were getting no milk at all, how much would you be willing to pay for one glass per

week? With no hesitation, she replies, $3. We then ask, If you had already consumed that one glass, how much would you pay for a second glass per week? After a bit of thought she answers, $1.50. Adding one glass per week with each question, we discover that she would be willing to pay $1 to get a third glass per week and 80¢, 60¢, 50¢, 40¢, 30¢, 25¢, and 20¢ for successive glasses from the fourth to the tenth glasses per week. The information shows that she puts progressively lower valuations on each additional glass of milk, and this illustrates the general concept of diminishing marginal utility.

But Mrs. Schwartz does not have to pay a different price for each glass of milk she consumes each week. Instead she finds that she can buy all the milk she wants at the prevailing market price. Suppose the price is 30¢. She will buy eight glasses per week (one each weekday and two on Sunday) because she values the eighth glass just at the market price while valuing all earlier glasses at higher amounts. Because she values the first glass at $3 but gets it for 30¢, she makes a "profit" of $2.70 on that glass. Between her $1.50 valuation of the second glass and what she has to pay for it she clears a "profit" of $1.20. She clears 70¢ on the third glass, and so on. These "profit" amounts are called her consumers' surpluses on each glass. They are shown in column 3 of the table; the total surplus is $5.70 per week.[5]

While other consumers would put different numerical values into Table 9-2, diminishing marginal utility implies that the figures in column 2 would be declining for each consumer. Since a consumer will go on buying further units until the value he or she places on the last unit equals the market price, it follows that there will be a consumers' surplus on every unit consumed except the last one.

TABLE 9-2
Consumers' Surplus on Milk Consumption by One Consumer

(1) Glasses of milk consumed per week	(2) Amount the consumer would pay to get this glass	(3) Consumers' surplus if milk costs 30¢ per glass
First	$3.00	$2.70
Second	1.50	1.20
Third	1.00	0.70
Fourth	0.80	0.50
Fifth	0.60	0.30
Sixth	0.50	0.20
Seventh	0.40	0.10
Eighth	0.30	0.00
Ninth	0.25	——
Tenth	0.20	——

Consumers' surplus on each unit consumed is the difference between the market price and the maximum price the consumer would pay to obtain that unit. The table shows the value that a single consumer, Mrs. Schwartz, puts on successive glasses of milk consumed each week. Because marginal utility declines, she would pay successively lower amounts for each additional unit consumed. As long as she would be willing to pay more than the market price for any unit, she will buy that unit and obtain a consumers' surplus on it. The marginal unit is the one valued just at the market price and on which no consumers' surplus is earned.

[5] Instead of summing her consumers' surplus on each glass, we could arrive at the same total in a different way. First, add up the valuation she places on each of the eight glasses. This total value is $8.10. Then determine what she actually paid: 8 × .30 = $2.40. Subtract $2.40 from $8.10, and the consumers' surplus is $5.70.

FIGURE 9–5
Consumers' Surplus for an Individual

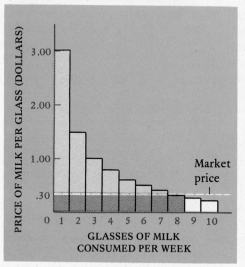

Consumers' surplus is the sum of the extra valuations placed on each unit over and above the market price paid for each. This figure is based on the data in Table 9-2. Mrs. Schwartz will pay the dark shaded area for the eight glasses of milk she will consume per week when the market price is 30¢ a glass. The total value she places on these eight glasses is the entire shaded area. Hence her consumers' surplus is the light shaded area.

In general, **consumers' surplus** is the difference between the total value consumers place on all the units consumed of some commodity and the payment they must make to purchase the same amount of that commodity. The total value placed by each consumer on the total consumption of some commodity can be estimated in at least two ways: The valuation that the consumer places on each successive unit may be summed; or the consumer may be asked how much he or she would pay to consume the amount in question if the alternative were to have none of the commodity.[6]

FIGURE 9-6
Consumers' Surplus for the Market

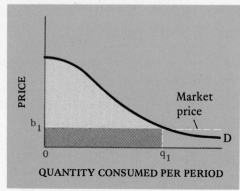

Total consumers' surplus is the area under the demand curve and above the price line. The demand curve shows the amount consumers would pay for each unit of the commodity if they had to buy their units one at a time. The area under the demand curve shows the total valuation consumers place on all units consumed. For example, the total value that consumers place on q_1 units is the entire shaded area under the demand curve up to q_1. At a market price of p_1 the amount paid for q_1 units is the dark shaded area. Hence consumers' surplus is the light shaded area.

The data in Columns 1 and 2 of Table 9-2 give Mrs. Schwartz's demand curve for milk. It is her demand curve because she will go on buying glasses of milk as long as she values each glass at least as much as the market price she must pay for it. When the market price is $3 per glass, she will buy only one glass; when it is $1.50, she will buy two glasses—and so on. The total valuation is the area below her demand curve, and consumers' surplus is that part of the area that lies above the price line. This is shown in Figure 9-5. Figure 9-6 shows that the same relation holds for the smooth market demand curve that indicates the total amount all consumers would buy at each price.

---

[6] This is only an approximation, but it is good enough for our purposes. More advanced theory shows that the calculations presented here ignore an "income effect." As a result they slightly overestimate consumers' surplus. Although it is sometimes necessary to correct for this bias, no amount of re-

finement upsets the general result that we establish here: When consumers can buy all units they require at a single market price, they pay for the quantity consumed much less than they would be willing to pay if faced with the choice between that amount and nothing.

Household Choice: An Alternative Analysis

The marginal utility approach to household behavior came first historically, and it is still valued because of the great insights that the concept of marginal utility opened up. With the publication in 1939 of Sir John R. Hicks' classic *Value and Capital,* an alternative approach often called indifference curve analysis became popular in English-language economics.[7] This is not a competing theory but a slightly different way of looking at choices by households. Its major innovation was to dispense with the notion of a *measurable* concept of utility that is required by marginal utility theory.

THE BUDGET LINE

Consider a household faced with the choice between only two goods, food (*F*) and clothing (*C*). (Such choices between two goods reveal everything necessary for elementary theory.) Assume that the household has a certain money income, say $120 a week, and that the prices for food and clothing are fixed—at the outset at $4 a unit for food and $2 a unit for clothing. The household does not save; its only choice is in deciding how much of its $120 to spend on food and how much to spend on clothing.

The household's problem is illustrated by the line *ab* in Figure 9-7, which shows the combina-

---

[7] Hicks, whose career has been spent mainly at Oxford, was the first British recipient of the Nobel prize in economics, for the contributions to economics that he made in *Value and Capital* and elsewhere. He did not invent indifference curve analysis; he took over, popularized, and extended the use of a concept developed by the great Italian economist Vilfredo Pareto in the first decade of this century. As is so often true in science, it is not the discoverer or the inventor, but the one who makes the timely and insightful application, who has the major impact. Thus it was Hicks, not Pareto, who led to the almost universal use of indifference analysis by economists in the 1940s and 1950s. Pareto in his time was following "hints" given in 1896 by the American economist Irving Fisher and in a slim volume published in 1886 by the Italian engineer Giovanni Antonelli. Such is the history of ideas.

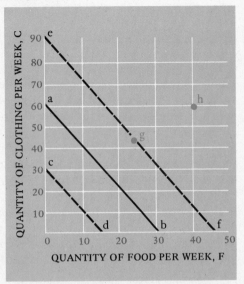

FIGURE 9-7
Budget Lines

The budget line shows the quantities of goods available to a household given its money income and the prices of the goods it buys. Any point indicates a combination (or *bundle*) of so much food and so much clothing. Point *h*, for example, indicates 60 units of clothing and 40 units of food per week. With an income of $120 a week and prices of $4 for food and $2 for clothing, the household's budget line is *ab*. This line shows all the combinations of *F* and *C* available to a household spending that income at those prices.

An increase in money income from $120 to $180, with money prices of *F* and *C* constant, shifts the budget line outward, parallel to itself, to *ef*. A decrease in money income to $60 shifts the budget line to *cd*.

---

tions of food and clothing available to it. The household could spend all its income on clothing and obtain 60*C* and no *F* per week. Or it could decide to have 1*F* each week, at a cost of $4, and only 58*C*. It could also go to the other extreme and purchase only food, buying 30*F* and no *C*.

When all the points indicating combinations that are available to the household if it spends all its income are joined, the result is called the household's **budget line.** (It is also sometimes called an "isocost" line since all points on the line represent bundles of goods with the same total cost of purchase.)

Among the important properties of the budget line are the following. (You should check enough examples against Figure 9-7 to satisfy yourself that they are true.)

1. Points on the budget line represent bundles of commodities that exactly use up the household's income. (Try, for example, the point 20*C* and 20*F*.)
2. Points between the budget line and the origin represent bundles of commodities that use up less than the household's income. (Try, for example, the point 20*C* and 10*F*.)
3. Points above the budget line represent combinations of commodities costing more to purchase than the household's present income. (Try, for example, the point 30*C* and 40*F*.)

The budget line shows all combinations of commodities that are available to the household given its money income and the prices of the goods that it purchases, if it spends all its income on them.

Changes in Money Income

What happens to the budget line when money income changes? If the household's money income is halved from $120 to $60 per week, prices being unchanged, then the amount of goods it can buy will also be halved. If it spends all its income on clothing, it will now get 30*C* and no *F* (point *c* in Figure 9-7); if it spends all its income on food, it will get 15*F* and no *C* (point *d*). All possible combinations now open to the household appear on budget line *cd*, which is closer to the origin than the original budget line.

If the household's income rises to $180, it will be able to buy more of both commodities than it could previously. The budget line shifts outward. If the household buys only clothing, it can have 90*C*; if it buys only food, it can have 45*F*; if it divides its income equally between the two goods, it can have 45*C* and 22.5*F*.

Variations in the household's money income, with prices constant, shift the budget line parallel to itself.

Proportional Changes in Prices of Both Goods

Changing both prices in the same proportion shifts the budget line parallel to itself in the same way that a money income change shifted it. Doubling both prices with money income constant halves the amount of goods that can be purchased and thus has exactly the same effect on the household's budget line as halving money income with money prices constant. In both cases the household's original budget line is shifted inward.

It is now apparent that it is possible to have exactly offsetting changes in prices and money incomes. A change in money income and a *proportional* change of the same amount in all money prices leaves the position of the budget line—and hence the real choices available to the household—unchanged.

The **indexing** of money values is an arrangement that automatically increases them as the average level of all prices rises during an inflation. For example, when money wages are indexed, they are increased in proportion to increases in the price level. The purpose of indexing is to accomplish the offsetting changes analyzed in the preceding paragraph. Prices rise, shifting inward the budget line for a constant money income. Indexing then raises incomes in proportion to the price rise. This shifts the budget line back to its original position and leaves the purchasing power of wages unaffected by the inflation.

Changes in Relative Prices

Absolute price or *money price* or merely *price* of a commodity means the amount of money that must be spent to acquire 1 unit of the commodity. A **relative price** is the ratio of two absolute prices. The statement "the price of *F* is $2" refers to an absolute price; "the price of *F* is twice the price of *C*" refers to a relative price.

A change in a relative price can be accomplished either by changing both of the money

FIGURE 9-8

The Effect on the Budget Line of Changes in the Price of Food

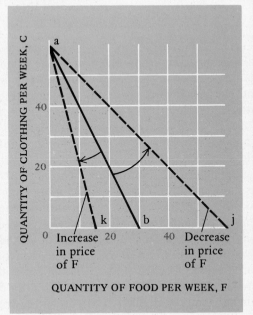

A change in the price of one commodity changes relative prices and thus changes the slope of the budget line. The original budget line *ab* arose from a money income of $120, with units of *C* priced at $2 and units of *F* at $4. A fall in the price of *F* to $2 doubles the quantity of *F* obtainable for any given quantity of *C* purchased and pivots the budget line outward to *aj*. A rise in the price of *F* to $8 reduces the quantity of *F* obtainable and pivots the budget line inward to *ak*.

prices in different proportions or by holding one price constant and changing the other. It is useful for our purposes to do the latter. The effects of such a change are shown in Figure 9-8. The basic conclusion that emerges is this:

A change in relative prices—such as occurs when one price changes while the other price remains constant—changes the slope of the budget line.

The economic significance of the slope of the budget line for food and clothing (which we have just seen to be related to the relative prices of the two commodities) is that it reflects the opportunity cost of food in terms of clothing. To increase food consumption with expenditure constant, one must move along the budget line, consuming less clothing. Suppose the price of food (p_F) is $2 and the price of clothing (p_C) is $1. With income fixed, it is necessary to forgo the purchase of 2 units of clothing to acquire 1 unit extra of food. The opportunity cost of food in terms of clothing is thus 2 units of clothing. But it can also be stated as p_F/p_C, which is the relative price. Notice that this relative price ($p_F = 2p_C$) is consistent with an infinite number of absolute prices. If $p_F = \$40$ and $p_C = \$20$, it still takes the sacrifice of 2 units of clothing to acquire 1 unit of food. This shows that it is relative, not absolute, prices that determine opportunity cost. The general conclusion is that the opportunity cost of *F* in terms of *C* is measured by the slope of the budget line or (the equivalent) by the relative price ratio. [11]

The Basic Conclusions Restated

It may be helpful to restate the earlier conclusions in terms of absolute and relative prices. (You should reread what has gone before if you cannot prove them yourself.)

1. A change in money income, with absolute prices constant, shifts the budget line parallel to itself—inward toward the origin when income falls and outward away from the origin when income rises.
2. An equal proportional change in all absolute prices leaves relative prices unchanged. Multiplying all money prices by the same constant, with money income constant, has exactly the same effect on the budget line as dividing money income by the same constant with money prices constant.
3. An equal percentage change in all absolute prices and money income leaves the budget line exactly where it was before the changes occurred.
4. A change in relative prices causes the budget line to change its slope.

Real and Money Income

A household's **money income** is its income measured in money units, so many dollars and cents per month or per year. A household's **real income** is the purchasing power of its money income, that is, the quantity of goods and services that can be purchased with its money income.

If money prices remain constant, any change in money income will cause a corresponding change in real income. If the household's money income rises by 10 percent (say from $10,000 to $11,000), the household can if it wishes buy 10 percent more of all commodities—its real income has also risen by 10 percent.

If prices change, however, real and money incomes will not change in the same proportion—indeed, they can easily change in opposite directions. Consider a situation in which all money prices rise by 10 percent. If money income falls, or rises by any amount less than 10 percent, real income falls. If money income also rises by 10 percent, real income will be unchanged. Only if money income rises by more than 10 percent will real income also rise.

Changes in real income are shown graphically by shifts in the budget line. When the budget line in Figure 9-7 shifts outward, away from the origin, real income rises. When the line shifts inward, toward the origin, real income falls.

If we are interested in the household's potential standard of living, we are interested in its ability to purchase goods and services; this is appropriately measured by real income, not by money income.

INDIFFERENCE CURVE ANALYSIS[8]

What the household does is determined by both what it can do and what it would like to do. The budget line shows what the household *can do;* the choices that it can make given its money in-

come and the prices of the commodities that it buys. What the household *wants to do* is determined by its tastes.

An Indifference Curve

Take an imaginary household and give it some quantity of each of the two goods, say 18 units of clothing and 10 units of food. (A consumption pattern for a household that contains quantities of two or more distinct goods is called a *bundle* or a *combination* of goods.) Now offer the household an alternative bundle of goods, say 13 units of clothing and 15 units of food. This alternative has 5 fewer units of clothing and 5 more units of food than the first one. Whether the household prefers this bundle depends on the relative valuation that it places on 5 more units of food and 5 fewer units of clothing. If it values the extra food more than the forgone clothing, it will prefer the new bundle to the original one. If it values the food less than the clothing, it will prefer the original bundle.

There is a third alternative: If the household values the extra food the same as it values the forgone clothing, it would gain equal satisfaction from the two alternative bundles of food and clothing. In this case the household is said to be *indifferent* between the two bundles.

Assume that after much trial and error a number of bundles have been identified, each of which gives equal satisfaction. These are shown in Table 9-3.

There will of course be combinations of the two commodities other than those enumerated in the table that will give the same level of satisfaction to the household. All of these combinations are shown in Figure 9-9 by the smooth curve that passes through the points plotted from the table. This curve is an indifference curve. In general, an **indifference curve** shows all combinations of goods that yield the same satisfaction to the household. A household is *indifferent* between the combinations indicated by any two points on one indifference curve.

Any points above and to the right of the curve

---

[8] The remainder of this chapter may be omitted without loss of continuity.

show combinations of food and clothing that the household would prefer to combinations indicated by points on the curve. Consider, for example, the combination of 20 food and 18 clothing, which is represented by point g in the figure. Although it might not be obvious that this bundle must be preferred to bundle a (which has more clothing but less food), it is obvious that it will be preferred to bundle c, because there is both less clothing and less food represented at c than at g. Inspection of the graph shows that *any* point

TABLE 9–3
Alternative Bundles Giving a Household Equal Satisfaction

Bundle	Clothing	Food
a	30	5
b	18	10
c	13	15
d	10	20
e	8	25
f	7	30

These bundles all lie on a single indifference curve. Since all of these bundles of food and clothing give equal satisfaction, the household is "indifferent" among them.

FIGURE 9–9
An Indifference Curve

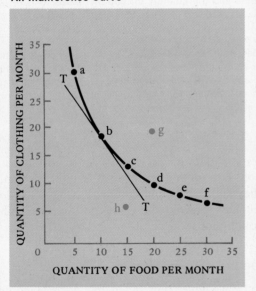

An indifference curve shows combinations of food and clothing that yield equal satisfaction and among which the household is indifferent. Points a to f are plotted from Table 9-3. The smooth curve through them is an indifference curve; each combination on it gives equal satisfaction to the household. Point g above the line is a preferred combination to any point on the line; point h below the line is an inferior combination to any point on the line. The slope of the line T-T gives the marginal rate of substitution at point b. Moving down the curve from b to f the slope flattens. This shows that the more food and the less clothing the household has, the less willing it will be to sacrifice further clothing to get more food.

above the curve will be obviously superior to *some* points on the curve in the sense that it will contain both more food and more clothing than those points on the curve. But since all points on the curve are equal in the household's eyes, the point above the curve must be superior to *all* points on the curve. By a similar argument, points below and to the left of the curve represent bundles of goods that are inferior to bundles represented by points on the curve.

The Marginal Rate of Substitution

How much clothing would the household be prepared to give up to get one more unit of food? The answer to this question measures what is called the marginal rate of substitution of clothing for food. The **marginal rate of substitution (MRS)** is the amount of one commodity a consumer would be prepared to give up to get one more unit of another commodity. The first basic assumption of indifference theory is that the algebraic value of the MRS is always negative. This means that to gain a positive change in its consumption of one commodity, the household is prepared to incur a negative change in its consumption of a second.

Graphically the negative marginal rate of substitution is shown by the downward slope of all indifference curves. (See for example the curve in Figure 9-9.)

The Hypothesis of Diminishing Marginal Rate of Substitution

The second basic assumption of indifference theory is that the marginal rate of substitution between any two commodities depends on the amounts of the commodities currently being consumed by the household. Consider a case where the household has a lot of clothing and only a little food: Common sense suggests that the household might be willing to give up quite a bit of its plentiful clothing in order to get one unit more of very scarce food. Now consider a case where the household has only a little clothing and quite a lot of food: Common sense suggests that the household would be willing to give up only a small amount of its scarce clothing in order to get one more unit of already plentiful food.

This example illustrates the hypothesis of the **diminishing marginal rate of substitution.** In terms of our clothing-food example, the hypothesis states that the less clothing and the more food the household has already, the smaller will be the amount of clothing it will be willing to give up to get one further unit of food.

The hypothesis says that the marginal rate of substitution changes systematically as the amounts of two commodities presently consumed vary. Take any two commodities, A and B. The more A and the less B the household currently has, the less B will it be willing to give up to get a further unit of A. The graphical expression of this hypothesis is that the slope of any indifference curve becomes flatter as the household moves downward to the right along the curve. [12] In Figure 9-9 a movement downward to the right means less clothing and more food is being consumed. The decreasing steepness of the curve means that less and less clothing will be sacrificed to get one further unit of food.

The hypothesis is illustrated in Table 9-4, which is based on the example of food and clothing in Table 9-3. The last column of the table shows the rate at which the household is prepared to sacrifice units of clothing per unit of food obtained. At first the household will sacri-

TABLE 9–4
The Marginal Rate of Substitution Between Clothing and Food

Movement	(1) Change in clothing	(2) Change in food	(3) Marginal rate of substitution (1) ÷ (2)
From a to b	−12	5	−2.4
From b to c	− 5	5	−1.0
From c to d	− 3	5	− .6
From d to e	− 2	5	− .4
From e to f	− 1	5	− .2

The marginal rate of substitution of clothing for food declines as the quantity of clothing in the bundle declines and the quantity of food increases. This table is based on Table 9–3. When the household moves from a to b, it gives up 12 units of clothing and gains 5 units of food; it remains at the same level of overall satisfaction. The household at point a was prepared to sacrifice 12 clothing for 5 food (i.e., $^{12}/_5$ = 2.4 units of clothing per unit of food obtained). When the household moves from b to c, it sacrifices 5 clothing for 5 food (a rate of substitution of 1 unit of clothing for each unit of food).

fice 2.4 units of clothing to get 1 unit more of food, but as its consumption of clothing diminishes and that of food increases, the household becomes less and less willing to sacrifice further clothing for more food.[9]

The Indifference Map

So far we have constructed only a single indifference curve. However, there must be a similar curve through other points in Figure 9-9. Starting at any point, such as g, there will be other combi-

[9] Movements between widely separated points on the indifference curve have been examined. In terms of a very small movement from any of the points on the curve, the rate at which the household will give up clothing to get food is shown by the slope of the tangent to the curve at that point. The slope of the line T which is a tangent to the curve at point b in Figure 9-9 may thus be thought of as the slope of the curve at that precise point. It tells us the rate at which the household will sacrifice clothing per unit of food obtained when it is currently consuming 18 clothing and 10 food (the coordinates of point b).

nations that will yield equal satisfaction to the household and, if the points indicating all of these combinations are connected, they will form another indifference curve. This exercise can be repeated as many times as we wish, and as many indifference curves as we wish can be generated. The farther any indifference curve is from the origin, the higher will be the level of satisfaction given by any of the combinations of goods indicated by points on the curve.

A set of indifference curves is called an **indifference map,** an example of which is shown in Figure 9-10. It specifies the household's tastes by showing its rate of substitution between the two commodities for every level of current consumption of these commodities. When economists say that a household's tastes are *given,* they do not mean that the household's current consumption pattern is given; rather, they mean that the household's entire indifference map is given.

The Equilibrium of the Household

Indifference maps describe the preferences of households. Budget lines describe the possibilities open to the household. To predict what households will actually do, both of these sets of information must be put together. This is done in Figure 9-11. The household's budget line is shown in the figure by the straight line, while its tastes are shown by its indifference map (a few of whose curves are shown in the figure). Any point on the budget line is attainable. But which point will actually be chosen by the household that is interested in maximizing its satisfactions?

Since the household wishes to maximize its satisfactions, it wishes to reach its highest attainable indifference curve. Inspection of the figure shows that if the household purchases any bundle on its budget line where an indifference curve cuts the budget line, a higher indifference curve can be reached. Only when the bundle purchased is one where an indifference curve is tangent to the budget line is it impossible for the household to alter its purchases and reach a higher curve.

The household's satisfaction is maximized at the point at which an indifference curve is tangent to its budget line.

At such a tangency position, the slope of the indifference curve (the marginal rate of substitution of the goods in the household's preferences) is the same as the slope of the budget line (the relative prices of the goods in the market). The common sense of this result is that if the household values goods at a different rate than the market does, there is room for profitable exchange. The household can give up some of the good it values relatively less than the market and take in return some more of the good it values relatively higher than the market does. When the household is prepared to swap goods at the same rate as they can be traded on the market, there is

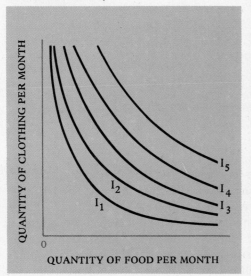

FIGURE 9–10
An Indifference Map

QUANTITY OF CLOTHING PER MONTH

I_1 I_2 I_3 I_4 I_5

0

QUANTITY OF FOOD PER MONTH

An indifference map consists of a set of indifference curves. All points on a particular curve indicate alternative combinations of food and clothing that give the household equal satisfaction. The further the curve from the origin, the higher the level of satisfaction it represents. Thus I_5 is a higher indifference curve than I_4 and represents a higher level of satisfaction.

FIGURE 9–11
The Equilibrium of a Household

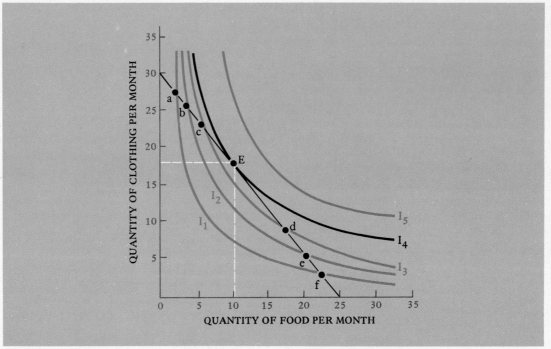

Equilibrium occurs at E where an indifference curve is tangent to the budget line. The household has an income of $750 a month and faces prices of $25 a unit for clothing and $30 a unit for food. A combination of C and F indicated by point a is attainable, but by moving along the budget line higher indifference curves can be reached. The same is true at b and c. At E, however, where an indifference curve is tangent to the budget line, it is impossible to reach a higher curve by moving along the budget line. If the household did alter its consumption bundle by moving from E to c or d, for example, it would move to lower indifference curves and thus to lower levels of satisfaction.

no further opportunity for it to raise its satisfaction by substituting one commodity for the other.

The household is presented with market information (prices) that it cannot itself change. It adjusts to these prices by choosing a bundle of goods such that, at the margin, its own subjective evaluation of the goods conforms with the evaluations given by market prices.

The Reaction of the Household to a Change in Income

We have seen that a change in income leads to parallel shifts of the budget line—inward toward the origin when income falls and outward away from the origin when income rises. For each level of income there will be an equilibrium position at which an indifference curve is tangent to the relevant budget line. Each such equilibrium position means that the household is doing as well as it possibly can for that level of income. If we move the budget line through all possible levels of income, and if we join up all the points of equilibrium, we will trace out what is called an **income-consumption line,** an example of which is shown in Figure 9-12. This line shows how consumption bundles change as income changes, with relative prices held constant.

FIGURE 9–12
The Income-Consumption Line

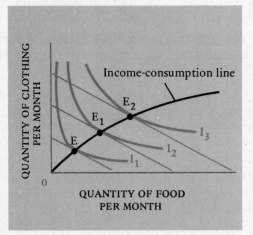

The **income-consumption line** shows how the household's purchases react to a change in income with relative prices held constant. Increases in income shift the budget line out parallel to itself, moving the equilibrium from E to E_1 to E_2. By joining up all the points of equilibrium, an income-consumption line is traced out.

FIGURE 9–13
The Price-Consumption Line

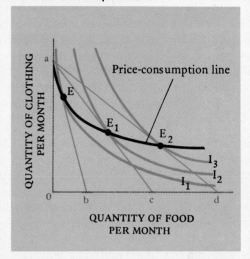

The **price-consumption line** shows how the household's purchases react to a change in one price with money income and other prices held constant. Decreases in the price of food (with money income and the price of clothing constant) pivot the budget line from ab to ac to ad. The equilibrium position moves from E to E_1 to E_2. By joining up all the points of equilibrium, a price-consumption line is traced out.

The Reaction of a Household to a Change in Price

We already know that a change in the relative price of the two goods changes the slope of the budget line. If the price of food is varied continuously, there will be an equilibrium position for each price. Connecting these traces out a **price-consumption line,** as in Figure 9-13. Notice that as the relative price of food and clothing changes, the relative quantities of food and clothing purchased also change. In particular, as the price of food falls the household buys more food.[10]

We are now very close to deriving a demand curve for food. Figure 9-13 shows how the quantity of food consumed varies as the price of food varies. This gives us the information needed to plot a demand curve. All we need to do is to transfer this information to a new diagram with the price of food on one axis and the quantity of food consumed on the other.[11]

Summary

1. Marginal utility theory distinguishes between the total utility gained from the consumption of all units of some commodity and the marginal utility resulting from the consumption of one more unit of the commodity. The basic assumption about a household's tastes made in utility theory is that the utility the household derives from the consumption of successive units of a

---

[10] There is a rarely encountered but theoretically possible exception to this rule, a Giffen good, that is described in the appendix to this chapter.

[11] The derivation of demand curves from indifference curves is further explored in the appendix to this chapter.

commodity per period of time will diminish as the consumption of that commodity increases.

2. The household maximizes its utility and thus reaches equilibrium when the utility derived from the last dollar spent on each commodity is equal. Another way of putting this is that the marginal utilities derived from the last unit of each commodity consumed will be proportional to their prices.

3. It is vital to distinguish between total and marginal utilities because most choices are related to marginal utilities and cannot be predicted from a knowledge of total utilities. The paradox of value involved a confusion between total and marginal utilities. Whether goods are "necessities" or "luxuries," while perhaps determining the total utilities they produce, tells nothing about marginal utilities. But it is marginal utilities that are required for defining elasticity and understanding market behavior.

4. Indifference curves and indifference theory provide an alternative way of studying household consumption behavior. The basic constructs of indifference curve analysis are the budget line and the indifference map.

5. Consumers' surplus arises when a household can purchase every unit of a commodity at a price equal to the value that it places on the last unit purchased. Diminishing marginal utility implies that the household places a higher value on all other units purchased and hence that all but the last unit purchased will yield a consumers' surplus.

6. While the budget line describes what the household *can* purchase, indifference curves describe the household's tastes and, therefore, refer to what it would *like* to do. A single indifference curve joins combinations of commodities that give the household equal satisfaction and among which it is therefore indifferent.

7. The basic hypothesis about tastes is that of diminishing marginal rate of substitution. This hypothesis states that the less of one good and the more of another that the household has, the less willing it will be to give up some of the first good to get a further unit of the second.

8. The household maximizes its satisfactions, given its budget line, at the point at which an indifference curve is tangent to its budget line.

9. The income-consumption line shows how quantity consumed changes as income changes. The price-consumption line shows how quantity consumed changes as relative prices change. When prices change, the household will consume relatively more of the commodity whose relative price falls and relatively less of the commodity whose relative price rises.

10. The appendix to this chapter carries further the derivation of downward-sloping demand curves using indifference theory. It also considers the theoretical possibility that a demand curve could slope upwards.

Topics for Review

Market demand and individual household demand curves
The hypothesis of diminishing marginal utility
Conditions for maximizing utility
The interpretation of $MU_x/MU_y = p_x/p_y$
The paradox of value
Consumers' surplus
The budget line
Real income and money income
Indifference curves and indifference maps
The marginal rate of substitution
The tangency of the budget line and an indifference curve
The price-consumption and income-consumption lines

Discussion Questions

1. Why is market demand the *horizontal* sum of individual demand curves? Is the vertical sum different? What would a vertical sum of individual demand curves show? Can you imagine any use of vertical summation of demand curves?
2. Which of the choices implied below involve a consideration of marginal utilities and which total utilities?
   a. The State Legislature debates whether 17-year-olds should be given the vote.

b. A diet calls for precisely 1,200 calories per day.

c. My doctor says I must give up smoking and drinking or else accept an increased chance of heart attack.

d. In 1976 Armand Hammer decided to buy the Rembrandt painting *Juno* for a record $3.25 million and called it the "crown jewel of my collection."

e. I enjoyed my golf game today, but I was so tired that I decided to stop at the 17th hole.

3. Are the transactions described in the following quotations consistent with the utility of the commodity? Interpret "worthless" and "priceless" as used here.

a. "Bob Koppang has made a business of selling jars of shredded U.S. currency. The money is worthless, and yet he's sold 53,000 jars already and has orders for 40,000 more—at $5.00 a jar. Each jar contains about $10,000 in shredded bills."

b. "Leonardo da Vinci's priceless painting *Genevra de' Benci* was sold to the National Gallery of Art for $5 million."

4. The *New York Times* called it the great liver crisis. Chopped liver is a delicacy on the table, particularly the kosher table, but in the late 1970s it was a glut on the market. Prices had sunk to a 20-year low as supplies had risen to an all-time high due to a very high cattle slaughter. What do the following quotations from the *Times'* story tell you about the marginal and total utility of liver?

a. "Grade A-1 liver is being used for cats and dogs instead of people. It's unheard of, it's a waste," says the manager of Kosher King Meat Products. "Even Israel is drowning in chopped liver."

b. "They're falling all over their feet to sell to me," said the president of Mrs. Weinberg's Kosher Chopped Liver Co., which uses 3,500 pounds of liver daily.

"I've been offered prices so low I can't believe them."

c. "The nature of people being what they are, even though they like a good bargain, they're not going to eat something that doesn't agree with their taste."

5. John Ehrlichman, after leaving government service but before serving a prison sentence, was quoted as saying: "When I get to be king of the world, everybody is going to have four or five hours every day just for themselves, and the world will be a better place." What does this tell you about Mr. Ehrlichman's utility schedule? Under what circumstances would the world be a better place if someone made it obligatory for everyone to have several hours "just for themselves"?

6. Is a household relatively better off if its money income is decreased by 10 percent or if the prices of all the goods it buys are increased by 10 percent? Does it matter in answering this question whether the household spends all its income?

7. Some people do not care about the difference between two similar products. To see what effect this would have on their behavior, draw a typical indifference curve of a man who values white and whole wheat bread identically. Show his consumption equilibrium position when the price of white bread is held constant at $1 a loaf while that of whole wheat changes from 80¢ to $1 to $1.20. How does this behavior differ from that of a household that likes both kinds of bread but values them differently?

8. Between 1977 and 1978 the after-tax money incomes of American households rose by 11.7 percent while the CPI rose by 7.7 percent. What happened to real incomes?

Demand Theory in Action

10

Students of economics, along with many critics of the subject, often find demand theory excessively abstract. How can so unrealistic a theory, they ask, have any application to the real world?

Yet applied economists use the result of demand theory, abstract or not, in their everyday work. Indeed much of what economists do to earn a living involves demand measurements. Economists are asked by electric utility companies to draw up long-term investment plans based on the projected future demand for electric power. The National Park Service calls on economists to review its systems for selling grazing rights and timber stands to private firms. Whether—and to what extent—raising tolls will help ease the deficits of the New York City transit system and the Indiana Turnpike are questions that cannot be answered correctly without a knowledge of price elasticity of demand. When the FAO (the United Nations Food and Agricultural Organization) or a producers co-op wants to make agricultural demand projections by crops and areas, it needs to know income elasticities of demand. Many industries need to know the cross elasticities of demand for their products with oil and gas in order to estimate the effects on them of the sharply rising prices of oil and gas.

To deal effectively with many substantive issues, knowledge of relevant demand conditions is essential. Fortunately a great deal of the demand information that the economist requires is available. In this chapter we look at some of the empirical knowledge that has been collected over the last few decades.

Even where information is not already available, it is often possible to obtain it without great cost or difficulty. The appropriate methods have been carefully worked out. Solutions to two of the most troubling measurement problems are discussed at the end of the first part of the chapter.

Critics of demand theory do not quarrel with the *need* for demand information, or even with the usefulness of applied economics, but they have often suggested that the theory is only an elaborate way of saying that anything can happen. Others have suggested that it is based on totally unrealistic assumptions about how households actually behave. Thoughtful students are often worried by such doubts. In the second part of this chapter we consider such criticisms and show that they do not point to fatal flaws in demand theory.

Measurement of Demand

MODERN MEASURES OF DEMAND

Many statistical problems associated with demand measurement were solved earlier in this century. Since that time large quantities of data on demand elasticities have been accumulated. The value of these data to the applied economist is the ultimate proof of the usefulness of demand theory.

Price Elasticities

Table 10-1 shows a few estimated price elasticities of demand, covering agricultural and nonagricultural commodities. Much pioneering work on demand measurement concerned the price elasticity of demand of agricultural products. This attention was due in part to the large price variations (caused by fluctuating crop yields and competitive market conditions) in those commodities; such price variations provided the empirical evidence needed to measure demand elasticities. It was due also to concern about the level of farm incomes and the relation of farmers' welfare to fluctuating crops. Professors Henry

TABLE 10–1

Estimated Price Elasticities of Demand in the United States[a] (Selected Commodities)

Inelastic demand (less than unity)	
Potatoes	0.3
Sugar	0.3
Public transportation	0.4
All foods	0.4
Cigarettes	0.5
Gasoline	0.6
All clothing	0.6
Consumer durables	0.8
Demand of approximately unit elasticity[b]	
Beef	
Beer	
Marijuana	
Elastic demand (greater than unity)	
Furniture	1.2
Electricity	1.3
Lamb and mutton (U.K.)	1.5
Automobiles	2.1
Millinery	3.0

[a] For the United States except where noted.
[b] Greater than 0.9 and less than 1.1.

The wide range of price elasticities is illustrated by these selected measures. These elasticities, from various studies, are representative of literally hundreds of existing estimates. Explanations of some of the differences are discussed in the text.

Schultz in the United States and Richard Stone in the United Kingdom were prominent in these efforts. Many agricultural research centers (such as the Giannini Foundation of the University of California) extended this work and even today produce estimates of price elasticities of foodstuffs. These data mostly confirm the general belief in low price elasticities for individual crops and for food products as a whole.

The policy payoff of this knowledge in terms of understanding the farm problem was enormous; it represents an early triumph of empirical work in economics. (See the discussion in Chapter 7.)

Although agricultural commodities often have inelastic demands, notice in Table 10-1 that some commodities, such as beef in the United States and domestically produced lamb and mutton in the United Kingdom, have been found to be elastic. The reason for this is that they have close substitutes.

For example, British households can choose between locally produced lamb and mutton and imported lamb and mutton (which typically has a somewhat lower quality and price than the domestic product). Similarly, American households can and do choose between beef, pork, and chicken on the basis of price. The broader the category of related products, the lower the observed price elasticity of demand.

Although the importance of the agricultural problem led early investigators to concentrate on the demand for foodstuffs, modern studies have expanded to include virtually the whole range of commodities on which the household spends its income.

How then can we explain the relatively low (0.8) price elasticity for durables shown in Table 10-1? Again, the answer lies in the broadness of the category. Durables as a whole are less elastic than individual kinds of durable goods. For example, when the price of television sets rises, many households may replace their lawnmower or their vacuum cleaner instead of buying that extra television set. Thus, while their purchases of television sets fall, their total purchases of durables do not.

Because most specific manufactured goods have close substitutes, studies show they tend to have price-elastic demand. Millinery, for example, has been estimated to have an elasticity of 3.0. In contrast, "all clothing" tends to be inelastic.

The accumulated data on price elasticity confirm this generalization:

Any one of a group of close substitutes will tend to have an elastic demand, even though the demand for the group as a whole may be inelastic.

Income Elasticities

Table 10-2 provides a sample of the data on income elasticities. Because the demand over time for particular basic commodities is so greatly affected by income elasticities, the FAO has es-

timated income elasticities for dozens of products, country by country.

These data tend to show that the more basic or staple a commodity, the lower is its income elasticity: food as a whole has an income elasticity of 0.2, durables of 1.8. In the United States pork and such starchy roots as potatoes are inferior goods; their quantity consumed falls as income rises.

Does the distinction between luxuries and necessities explain differences in income elasticities? The table suggests that it does. The case of meals eaten away from home is one example; such meals are almost always more expensive, calorie for calorie, than meals prepared at home. It would thus be expected that at lower ranges of

TABLE 10–2

Estimated Income Elasticities of Demand[a] **(Selected Commodities)**

Inferior goods (negative income elasticities)	
Whole milk	−0.5
Pig products	−0.2
Starchy roots	−0.2
Inelastic normal goods (0.0 to 1.0)	
Coffee	0.0
Wine (France)	0.1
All food	0.2
Poultry	0.3
Cheese	0.4
Beef	0.5
Housing	0.6
Cigarettes	0.8
Elastic normal goods (greater than 1.0)	
Gasoline	1.1
Wine	1.4
Cream (U.K.)	1.7
Wine (Canada)	1.8
Consumer durables	1.8
Poultry (Ceylon)	2.0
Restaurant meals (U.K.)	2.4

[a] For the United States except where noted.

Income elasticities vary widely across commodities and sometimes across countries. The basic source of food estimates by country is the FAO, but many individual studies have been made. Explanations of some of the differences are discussed in the text.

"Affordable Housing" and the Theory of Demand

By 1976 the residential home building industry was in the midst of a switch from big, expensive, fancy houses to smaller, cheaper, no-frills houses. While this might have reflected a change in taste for houses, the evidence suggests it was an economic response to economic events. The theory of demand predicts that housing demand will be responsive to changes in household income, to changes in the price of housing relative to other goods households buy, and to the prices of substitute and complementary commodities.

The central fact is that by the end of 1975 the American house building industry was in a massive slump: between 1972 and 1975, housing starts fell from 2.4 to 1.2 million units. What were the causes? Because of the economic recession of 1973–1975, real disposable income was well below its usual growth rate. Demand theory predicts that this would lead to a decrease in quantity of housing demanded. The price of new residential housing was up relative to the cost of renting and of nonshelter items. Demand theory predicts that such changes in relative prices would lead to decreases in quantity demanded, as consumers spent more of their incomes on substitute (rental) housing and on other goods. When buying a house, one cannot avoid "buying" a complementary package of municipal services (whose "price" is property taxes); most home buyers also "buy" a mortgage (and pay interest). The "prices" of these complementary goods—property taxes and mortgage interest rates—rose sharply over the period. This too is predicted to lead to a decrease in quantity of housing demanded. Thus economists were not surprised by the slump.

Builders must take some of the blame. As one of them said recently, "We just didn't pay much attention to costs; if something cost $500 more, we said, 'Fine. We'll just get an extra thou' for it.'" Not surprisingly, they sold fewer houses: The elasticity of demand turned out to be higher than the builders thought it was.

Home builders began to realize that perhaps they might do more than wait for the recession to end and interest rates to fall. Because their profits were already low, they could cut prices only if they cut costs. One way of doing so was described by Bill Levitt (who a generation ago had made Levittown a household word):

Panelization is a method of building standardized modules . . . that are already painted and have the wiring, plumbing, insulation and so forth installed in the factory. . . . The bulk of the work can be done by machinery and by people who work on assembly lines like automobile workers. You won't have to pay $15 an hour to construction workers—only what General Motors pays for its assembly line workers, $4 or $4.50 an hour.

The builders were doing what the theory of demand predicts. They were buying more of a relatively inexpensive substitute (factory workers' labor) in response to a rise in the price of construction workers' labor. Other ways of cutting costs included using plans that called for standard lengths of wood (saving carpenters' time), using standardized rather than custom-built plumbing and heating systems (saving plumbers' wages), and eliminating carpeting, fireplaces, and unneeded walls and partitions. Builders in many areas have brought back the basic $20,000–35,000 three-bedroom house in place of the $35,000–50,000 houses that were unaffordable by many potential home buyers. Buyers are responding in what builders hope will prove to be a flood.

Carla A. Hills, when secretary of housing and urban development in the Ford administration, described the response of the house builders as an example of "the genius of the free enterprise system." Whether or not it is that, it is surely evidence that markets work in the manner predicted by the theory of demand.

income restaurant meals would be regarded as an expensive luxury, but the demand for them would expand substantially as households became richer. This is in fact what happens.

Does this mean that the market demand for the foodstuffs that appear on restaurant menus will also have high income elasticities? Generally the answer is no; when a household eats out rather than preparing meals at home, the main change is not in what is eaten but in who prepares it. The additional expenditure on "food" goes mainly to pay the wages of cooks and waiters and to yield a return on the restaurateur's capital. Thus, when a household expands its expenditure on restaurant food by 2.4 percent in response to a 1 percent rise in its income, most of the extra expenditure on "food" goes to workers in the service industry; little, if any, finds its way into the pockets of farmers. Here is a striking example of the general tendency for households to spend a higher proportion of their incomes on services as their incomes rise.

The revealing relationship shown in the table between whole milk, cheese, and cream suggests that as incomes rise people tend to change the form of the milk products they consume — less whole milk, more cheese, and more cream. (Ice cream, not included in the FAO data, had a high income elasticity for American consumers in measurements of three or four decades ago. Today the income elasticity is lower. To an earlier generation ice cream was a special treat; at current American income levels and prices, ice cream has become a staple.)

Empirical studies tend to confirm that, as income rises, household expenditures follow broadly similar paths in different countries. Summarizing recent studies, Robert Ferber wrote that they "tend to bear out earlier findings on income elasticity yielding low elasticities for food and housing, elasticities close to unity for clothing and education, and higher elasticities for various types of recreation, personal care, home operation and other services."

The accumulated data on income elasticity confirm this generalization:

The more basic an item in the consumption pattern of households, the lower its income elasticity.

Cross Elasticities of Demand

Many of the most interesting studies of cross elasticity have been made to determine whether specific products are substitutes as part of antitrust inquiries (see Chapter 18, page 303). Whether cellophane and Saran Wrap, or aluminum cable and copper cable, are or are not substitutes may determine questions of monopoly under the law. As we have seen, the positive or negative sign and the size of cross elasticities sheds light on whether or not goods are substitutes.

Other Variables

Modern studies show that demand is influenced by many socioeconomic factors — family size, age, geographical location, type of employment, wealth, and income expectations — not included in traditional demand theory. Although significant, the total contribution of all these factors to changes in demand is small. Typically, less than 30 percent of the variations in demand are accounted for by these "novel" factors, with a much higher proportion governed by the traditional variables of prices and current incomes.

PROBLEMS OF MEASUREMENT

The knowledge of demand elasticities that we have just surveyed could not be developed until econometricians overcame major problems in measuring demand relationships. One particular aspect of such measurement is troubling to many students: Since in a market economy all kinds of things are happening at once, how can they be sorted into neat theoretical categories? When market demand changes over time, invariably the influences that affect demand will all be changing. What, for example, is to be made of the observation that the quantity of butter consumed per capita rose by 10 percent over a period in

The Identification Problem

The three-part diagram below illustrates the so-called identification problem. If, as in (i), the demand curve stays put while the supply curve moves up and down—perhaps because of crop variations in some agricultural commodity—then market observations in prices and quantities (shown by the black dots) trace out the demand curve. If, as in (ii), the supply curve stays put while the demand curve moves about—owing perhaps to changes in the number of consumers or their incomes—then market observations trace out the supply curve.

So far so good. But what if both curves shift randomly back and forth between the four positions shown in (iii)? In such a situation a series of market observations will be obtained that will not trace out either the demand or the supply curves that generated them. A few such points are shown in the panel. Points E_1, E_2, E_3, and E_4—market observations of quantities and prices at different times—do not *identify* either the demand curve or the supply curve.

The identification problem is surmountable. The key to identifying the demand and supply curves separately is to bring in other variables than price and then to relate demand to one (or more) of them and supply to *some other* variables. For example, supply of the commodity might be related not only to the price of the commodity but also to its costs of production; demand might be related not only to the price of the commodity but also to consumers' incomes. Provided that both of these other factors, cost of production and income, vary sufficiently, it is possible to determine the relation between quantity supplied and price as well as the relation between quantity demanded and price.

Neglect of the identification problem can cause serious errors in interpreting economic data. Consider this analysis: "Last year the price of scotch whisky rose by 10 percent and scotch imports hardly fell at all, so we know that the market for scotch in the United States must have a low elasticity of demand." Has the analysis really identified the demand curve? It may have if the rise in price reflects a shift of the supply curve. But if the rise in price was due mainly to a rise in demand for scotch, the analysis may actually have discovered that the short-run supply curve of scotch is very inelastic (because scotch takes several years to manufacture). The general rule to keep in mind is that, unless there is additional information that provides clues to how much each curve shifted, nothing can be told about the shape of either the demand or the supply curve from price and quantity data alone.

(i) Supply curve shifts

(ii) Demand curve shifts

(iii) Both supply and demand curves shift

which average household income rose by 5 percent, the price of butter fell by 3 percent, and the price of margarine rose by 4 percent?

A first set of questions concerns how much of the change is due to income elasticity of demand, how much to price elasticity, and how much to the cross elasticity between butter and margarine. If there is only one observation, the question cannot be answered. If, however, there is a large number of observations showing, say, quantity demanded, income, price of butter, and price of margarine every month for four or five years, it is possible, as we saw in Chapter 3, to discover the separate influence of each of the variables. The most frequently used technique for estimating the separate effect of each variable on demand is called multiple regression analysis, which can be used directly to estimate each of the elasticities mentioned.

A second set of questions concerns using data on quantity actually *consumed* to estimate quantity *demanded*. The problem arises because both demand shifts and supply shifts can change the quantity actually consumed, and thus the shape of the demand curve may not be definitively established from data on prices and quantities alone. This **identification problem,** too, can yield to statistical solution, as suggested in the box.

Criticisms of Demand Theory

Some critics dismiss demand theory, saying that it is based on the ridiculous assumption that all households make decisions using careful marginal calculations about the effects of minor adjustments in expenditure patterns. They argue that this assumption might describe the behavior of a few record-keeping middle-class groups but not that of most households.

Other critics maintain that demand theory has little real content. According to them, the theory is a complex theoretical apparatus that offers little more than the proposition that most demand curves slope downward most of the time. If this is all we get from the elaborate theory, then

demand theory really is a lot of sound and fury signifying (almost) nothing. What about these criticisms?

DOES DEMAND THEORY MAKE UNREASONABLE ASSUMPTIONS ABOUT RATIONAL HOUSEHOLD DECISION MAKING?

In developing the theory of household behavior in Chapter 9, we deduced that if households wished to maximize their utility or satisfaction, they would vary their consumption patterns so that relative marginal utilities would be exactly proportional to relative market prices (marginal utility theory) or marginal rates of substitution would be exactly equal to relative market prices (indifference theory). It is tempting to dismiss these theories out of hand with the objection that it is unrealistic to pretend that households always act with the mechanical consistency that such theories apparently assume. After all, most of us know people who occasionally buy strawberries in spite of, or even because of, a rise in their price, or who spend a week's pay on a binge or a frivolous purchase.

To see what to make of such conflicting observations, it is helpful to distinguish three possible uses of demand theory. The first use is to study the aggregate behavior of all households—as illustrated, for example, by the market demand curve for a product. The second use is to make statements about an individual household's probable actions. The third use is to make statements about what each household will certainly do.

Now consider an automobile firm that is wondering about the effect on its sales of a price increase. Clearly the first use of demand theory is what interests the automobile firm. It does not care what every last household will do, nor, really, does it care what *you* will do; it wants to know whether in the aggregate, and by how much, its sales will decrease if it raises prices.

This aggregate use of demand theory is the most common one in economics. The analysis of Chapters 7 and 8, you will recall, depended on having knowledge of the shapes of relevant market demand curves. It did not, however, require that we know the behavior of each individual household. The second use of demand theory, though much less common than the first, is occasionally important; it is sometimes desirable to be able to say what a single household (or a group of households) will probably do. The third use is by far the least important, for it is rarely necessary, possible, or even interesting to try to state categorically what each household will always do.

The criticisms cited at the beginning of this section apply only to the third use of demand theory. The observations referred to earlier refute only the prediction that *all* households *always* behave as assumed by the theory. In order to predict the existence of a relatively stable downward-sloping market demand curve (the first use), or to predict what an individual household will probably do (the second use), we do not require that *all* households behave as is assumed by the theory all of the time. Consider two illustrations.

First, some households may always behave in a manner not assumed by the theory. Households whose members are mental defectives or have serious emotional disturbances are obvious possibilities. The inconsistent or erratic behavior of such households will not cause market demand curves to depart from their downward slope, provided these households account for a minority of total purchasers of any product. Their erratic behavior will be swamped by the normal behavior of the majority of households.

Second, an occasional irrationality or inconsistency on the part of every household will not upset the downward slope of the market demand curve so long as these isolated inconsistencies do not occur at the same time in all households. As long as such inconsistencies are unrelated across households, occurring now in one and now in another, their effect will be offset by the normal behavior of the majority of households.[1]

[1] See the discussion in Chapter 2, pages 20–21.

The downward slope of the demand curve requires only that at any moment of time most households are behaving as assumed by the theory. This is compatible with inconsistent behavior on the part of some households all of the time and on the part of all households some of the time.

IS DEMAND THEORY ONLY AN ELABORATE WAY OF SAYING THAT ANYTHING CAN HAPPEN?

Demand theory predicts that the quantity of a good demanded varies with its own price, the prices of other goods, income, and tastes. Critics argue that because quantity demanded may rise, fall, or stay unchanged as any one of these influencing factors changes, the theory is merely an elaborate way of saying anything can happen.

While it is true that anything can happen, this does not mean that every possible outcome is equally likely. Because theory and empirical work tell us when one outcome is more likely than another, the theory is useful.

To discuss this issue, it is necessary to consider the relation between quantity demanded and each of the variables that influence it. We shall ask in each case whether the theory offers interesting or useful predictions about the behavior of demand and then whether there is evidence confirming these predictions.

Quantity Demanded and the Commodity's Own Price

Early demand theory predicted that all demand curves must always slope downward. This prediction was known for a long time as the law of demand: The price of a product and the quantity demanded vary inversely with each other. Criticisms of the law of demand have taken various forms, focusing on the Giffen good, the conspicuous consumption good, and (by far the most important) the good whose demand is perfectly inelastic.

The Giffen good. Great interest was attached to an apparent refutation of the law of demand by the Victorian economist Sir Robert Giffen. Giffen is supposed to have observed that during the nineteenth century a rise in the price of imported wheat led to an increase in the price of bread, but that the consumption of bread by the British working class increased. If this observation is correct (i.e., if Giffen really made it—which now appears to be in doubt—and if his measurements were correct), it would refute the prediction that *all* demand curves *always* slope downward. It would not be inconsistent with the theory because this is precisely the sort of exception envisaged by modern theory and mentioned in the appendix to Chapter 9. This kind of exception is, in any case, extraordinarily limited in theory and is all but unknown in actuality.[2]

Conspicuous consumption goods. Thorstein Veblen in *The Theory of the Leisure Class* (1899) suggested that some commodities were consumed not for their intrinsic qualities but because they carried a snob appeal. The more expensive such a commodity became, the *greater* might be its ability to confer status on its purchaser.

This is, of course, possible. Elizabeth Taylor and Joe Namath may buy diamonds, not because they particularly like diamonds per se but because they wish to show off their wealth in an ostentatious but socially acceptable way. They are assumed to value diamonds precisely because they are expensive; thus a fall in price might lead them to stop buying diamonds and to switch to a more satisfactory object of conspicuous consump-

tion. People of this sort will have upward-sloping *individual* demand curves for diamonds. They may also behave in the same way with respect to luxury cars: they may buy them *because* they are expensive.

However, no one has ever observed statistically an upward-sloping *market* demand curve for commodities such as diamonds or luxury cars. The reason for this, notwithstanding the snob appeal of certain goods, is easy to discover. Consideration of the countless lower-income consumers who would be glad to buy diamonds or Cadillacs if only they were sufficiently inexpensive suggests that upward-sloping demand curves for a few individual wealthy households are much more likely than is an upward-sloping market demand curve for the same commodity. Recall the discussion (page 161) about the ability of the theory of the downward-sloping demand curve to accommodate odd behavior on the part of a small group of households. In this case the "odd" group is the group of the rich rather than that of the mentally defective or the emotionally disturbed.

Perfectly inelastic demand curves. Even if demand curves do not slope *upward to the right* as the previous cases have suggested, the substantial insight provided by the law of demand would be diminished if there were many important commodities for which changes in price had virtually no effect on quantity demanded.

It is surprising how often the assumption of a vertical demand curve is implicit. A common response of urban bus or subway systems to financial difficulties is to propose a percentage fare increase equal to the percentage their deficit is of their revenues. Even professors are not immune: At a recent meeting of the American Association of University Professors, a motion was introduced "to raise annual dues by 20 percent, in order to raise revenues by 20 percent"—in spite of the empirical evidence that a previous increase in dues had led (as the theory would predict) to a significant drop in membership.

It was once widely argued that the demand for

---

[2] The commodity must be a good with a large negative income effect (an inferior good) *and* play so large a part in most households' budgets that an increase in its price leads to a large decrease in households' real incomes. An example might be bread in a very poor economy where it is the diet staple. Suppose, in such an economy, that the price of bread rises sharply. This may be expected to lead to larger expenditures on bread, which will further impoverish many households to the point where they are forced to substitute bread (even though it is more expensive) for other more luxurious forms of nourishment.

gasoline was virtually perfectly inelastic — on the ground that people who had paid thousands of dollars for cars would never balk at a few pennies extra for gas. The events of recent years have proven how wrong that argument was: Higher gas prices have led to smaller cars, to more car pools, to more economical driving speeds, and to less pleasure driving.

As we have seen, a mass of accumulated evidence suggests that most demand curves do in fact slope downward to an appreciable degree.

For practical purposes, the hypothesis of the downward-sloping demand curve can be regarded as conforming with the evidence.

Most firms have an intuitive idea of the elasticities they face, although they seldom use the economist's language in referring to them. There is also evidence that even sophisticated business executives may underestimate price elasticities and thus overprice their commodities. For example, the transatlantic airlines bitterly resisted the efforts of English entrepreneur Sir Freddie Laker to introduce his cut-price "skytrain" between London and New York. When the service was finally introduced in the mid 1970s, the other carriers slashed prices on standby tickets in self-defense. And they were surprised at the overwhelming increase in demand as the low fares attracted a new type of traveler. Demand rose and the number of empty seats fell. Soon it was clear that the lower fares were increasing revenues and profits.[3] Cases in which companies have raised prices and been surprised at the resulting drop in sales have also been documented.

Quantity Demanded and Household Income

Demand theories give no single prediction about how quantity demanded changes as income changes. They say that a rise in income may

[3] Although air fares have since risen as a result of rising fuel costs, the standby fares introduced to compete with Laker's low skytrain fares remain *relatively* cheap ways of crossing the Atlantic.

cause the quantity demanded to rise, to fall, or to remain unchanged. This states only that anything can happen; hence it makes no useful prediction about what could be expected to happen to demand when income changes. But "anything can happen" does not mean that the theory is empty; various kinds of empirical observations help to make it meaningful.

The approximate income elasticity of demand often tends to be identifiable from the technical data about commodities. An inferior good is typically the cheaper and less satisfactory of a number of commodities, all of which satisfy more or less the same need. Consider transport. When people are very poor, they walk. At a slightly higher level of income, they can acquire a bicycle; cycling was the dominant form of transport for industrial workers in Europe as recently as the 1950s. At higher levels of income, motorized bicycles, motor scooters, and motorcycles can be substituted for bicycles; Italy was once overrun with motor scooters, and enormous numbers of them are still used by workers in Portugal. Finally, a level of income is reached, as it was in the more advanced industrial countries of Western Europe during the 1950s and 1960s, at which ordinary workers feel they can get rid of their two-wheeled conveyances and buy an automobile. For each of these modes of transportation there is a range of income over which the income elasticity of demand is high, and then a higher range over which the income elasticity falls and eventually becomes negative.

Another important set of empirical observations shows clearly that income elasticities change only gradually over time. Over the last 40 years, many service industries have encountered income elasticities that are well in excess of unity and rising over time. These elasticities are not expected to drop suddenly to very low levels, and thus it is possible to predict that, unless service industries achieve rates of productivity growth very much higher than the national average, there will be a continuing pressure coming from the price system for more resources to move into the service industries. The fact that income elasticities are known not to change rapidly or capriciously permits predictions about the near future on the basis of present knowledge.

A third set of observations reveals that with respect to broad categories of consumption expenditure, households in any one Western country behave in a fashion roughly similar to those in other Western countries. (Indeed, it is not even clear that the qualification *Western* is necessary if income levels are approximately the same.) At low income levels, food tends to have a fairly high income elasticity of demand, but as the level of income rises, the income elasticity of demand for food tends to fall well below unity, so that only a small amount of any additional income gets spent on food. This phenomenon has been observed in every growing country that has approached the levels of income currently enjoyed by America and Western Europe. Thus it can be predicted that as long as productivity growth continues in agriculture, the long-run drift from the land will continue in Western countries, and that when other countries of the world succeed in achieving sustained rates of growth, they will encounter within a predictable time period the problem of a declining agricultural sector.

Similarly, a significant phenomenon of the past two decades in the United States and the most highly developed countries of Western Europe is that the income elasticity of demand for consumer durables has been declining, while that for many services has been rising. Other countries can look forward to similar pressures on the pattern of resource allocation within a generation.

The real incomes of most Western countries are doubling every 30 years or so. Thus, over such a period of time, changes in income exert a major influence on changes in demand.

A knowledge of what income elasticities are and are likely to be is one of the most potent tools at the economist's command for predicting the future needs of the economy in many different aspects.

Quantity Demanded and the Prices of Other Commodities

The theory of demand predicts that the quantity demanded of one commodity may be affected by the changing prices of other commodities: It will tend to increase as the price of a complementary good declines (because they are used jointly), and it will tend to decrease as the price of a substitute good declines (because its users shift to the now relatively cheaper substitute). Of course there are also many pairs of commodities which are sufficiently unrelated that the price of one has no appreciable effect on the quantity demanded of the other. These three reactions—quantity demanded rising, falling, or remaining unchanged—cover all conceivable possibilities. The basic theory does not rule out any possibility, so by itself it is of no more use in predicting the reactions to changes in the prices of other goods than it is in predicting reactions to changes in income.

Just as with income, however, this is not the end of the story. It is often possible to tell from the technical nature of the goods alone which will be substitutes and which complements. Although the demand for factors of production will not be considered fully until Part Six, it is worth noting here just how often technical data tell where to expect complementarity and where substitutability. Steel plates, electric welders, and welder operators are complementary, so it can be predicted that a fall in the price of any one will lead to an increase in the demand for all three. Cranes and crane operators, steam shovels and trucks, trains and rails, roads and signs, any piece of equipment and its human operator—all are examples of pairs of goods that are complements for each other. For each set of complementary goods, it can be expected that a fall in the price of one good will lead to a rise in demand for the others.

A similar list of inputs that are substitutes might include such items as wood, bricks, and concrete in construction; manure and artificial fertilizers; a roomful of statistical clerks with desk calculators and a small electronic digital computer. With these pairs of substitute goods, it can be expected that a fall in the price of one of them will lead to a fall in the demand for the other.

There are also consumers' goods for which complementarity or substitutability can be predicted in advance. Complementarity exists, for example, between razors, razor blades, and shaving cream; golf clubs and golf balls; grass seed and lawn mowers; electric stoves and electricity; houses and mortgages; wedding rings and the services of obstetricians, marriage guidance counselors, and divorce court judges. The list of substitute goods might include such obvious examples as cabbage and spinach, beef and pork, private cars and public transport, gas stoves and electric stoves, and vacations in Arizona and on the Italian Riviera. It could be extended indefinitely. If the technical data tell which goods are substitutes and which are complements, then the effect of a change in the price of one good on the demand for the other can be predicted.

Quantity Demanded and Tastes

Changes in demand that are due to changes in taste cannot be identified because taste changes cannot be measured. This usually causes trouble when the relation between demand and other factors is considered. Whenever something happens that does not agree with theory, it is always possible that a change in tastes accounted for what was seen. Say, for example, incomes and other prices were known to be constant, while the price of some commodity rose and, at the same time, more was bought. This could mean an upward-sloping demand curve or a shift in the demand curve caused by a change in tastes.

If there are only two observations, it will be impossible to distinguish between the two possibilities because there is no independent way of telling whether tastes changed. But if there are many such observations, it is possible to get some idea of where the balance of probabilities lies between the two situations. Assume, for ex-

ample, that we have 26 observations on prices and quantities of some commodity whose price has changed once a week over a six-month period. Assume further that *after removing the effects estimated to be due to changes in income,*[4] price and quantity changed in the same direction each week. Now it will be hard to avoid the conclusion that the evidence conflicts with the hypothesis of a downward-sloping demand curve.

Of course, this conflict can be explained away by saying that tastes must have changed in favor of this commodity each time that its price rose and against the commodity each time that its price fell. This "alibi" can be used with effect to explain away a single conflicting observation, but it would be uncomfortable to use the same alibi 26 times in six months—"uncomfortable" because the situation is extremely improbable. [13] Instead one would suspect a fault in the hypothesis that quantity demanded and price vary inversely with each other in the case of this commodity.

This is now a problem in statistical testing. Economists will not usually abandon a theory as a result of only one conflicting observation, but they are prepared to abandon it as soon as the accumulating evidence makes it seem very unlikely that the theory is correct. Thus, statistically, the theory is testable.

Summary

1. Knowledge of demand elasticities is of major importance in applied economics. Modern work on the measurement of demand has provided a great deal of evidence on the size of the reaction of quantity demanded to prices, incomes, and other socioeconomic data.

2. The price elasticity of a commodity group tends to be higher the more narrowly it is defined

---

[4] This can be done through multiple regression analysis or other sophisticated statistical techniques. (See Chapter 3.)

and the more adequate are its substitutes. Any one of a group of close substitutes will tend to have an elastic demand even though the group as a whole has a highly inelastic demand.

3. Income elasticity tends to be lower the more basic, or staple, is the commodity. Thus luxuries tend to have higher income elasticities than necessities. The patterns of measured income elasticity are remarkably similar across countries.

4. Economists concerned with the measurement of demand have faced and surmounted a number of serious technical problems. Regression analysis has proved useful in dealing with situations where many things vary at once.

5. Demand theory does not, as some critics assert, assume that all households act with perfect rationality all of the time. The predictions of demand theory about the market demand function require only that at any one time most of the households in the market are behaving as assumed by the theory.

6. The fact that anything can happen in modern demand theory does not mean the theory is useless, for economists can specify the conditions under which different outcomes are to be expected. The so-called law of demand leads to the prediction that the market demand curve for a commodity will slope downward and to the right except in very special circumstances. Possible exceptions to the general prediction of demand have been suggested but have received no empirical support. A great accumulation of empirical evidence supports the law of demand.

7. While demand theory makes no single prediction about the effect of a change in income on quantity demanded, useful predictions can be made about the relationship because (a) it is often possible to identify approximate income elasticities from technical data; (b) income elasticities change gradually rather than erratically from year to year; (c) income elasticities tend to be similar at similar levels of income in different countries, so that knowledge of what happened at a certain level of income in country A helps to predict what will happen when country B reaches that same level of income.

8. While demand theory makes no single prediction about the effect on the quantity demanded of a change in the price of another commodity, the theory is nevertheless useful because it is often possible to tell from technical data alone whether goods are complements or substitutes.

9. Changes in tastes are an ever-present possible alibi to explain away any observations that appear to conflict with the theory. If prices are cut and less is sold, one can always say that the price cut just happened to be accompanied by a change in tastes away from the commodity. However, when there is a large number of observations of changing prices and quantities, it is possible to calculate the probability that taste changes account for what was seen. If, to save a hypothesis, highly improbable circumstances are needed, it is preferable to reject the hypothesis.

Topics for Review

The role of statistical measurement of demand

The difference between price and income elasticities and what such elasticities show

The difference between an inferior good and a Giffen good

The difference between a luxury and a conspicuous consumption good

The difference between inelastic and perfectly inelastic demand curves

Discussion Questions

1. When no-frills houses came on the market, they were regarded as a response to high prices. But they have captured more of the market than expected. Some builders estimate they may ultimately constitute 80 percent of all houses sold. Suggest alternative explanations of this unexpected success. A leading builder says, "It's just like people driving smaller cars and drinking beer instead of Scotch." Is it also like students wearing long hair instead of short, or today's parents having fewer children than their parents did?

Which of these things represent changes in taste, and which represent responses to changes in prices or incomes? If you don't know, what economic data would be useful in answering the question?

2. "A survey shows that most people prefer butter to margarine." What exactly might this mean? Supposing it to be true, can you account for the facts that many people buy some of both butter and margarine each month and that in total more pounds of margarine are sold than pounds of butter?

3. In the early empirical studies of demand theory, agricultural products were studied extensively. Can you think of a reason why these early studies were able to identify many demand curves without great difficulty?

4. A reliable newspaper reports that synthetic motor oil is gaining in sales despite its high price relative to natural oil. What can account for a synthetic oil's selling at $3.95 a quart when the best conventional oils were readily available at about $1.00?

5. Predict the effect on the demand for owner-occupied housing of (a) a rise in mortgage interest rates, (b) a decline in the price of rental housing. If over the period in which both (a) and (b) occurred the quantity of new housing sold increased, what would you conclude about the theory of demand?

6. It has been observed recently that obesity is a more frequent medical problem for the relatively poor than for the middle-income classes. Can you use the theory of demand to shed light on this observation?

7. At an auction in New Orleans, a Los Angeles oilman bid against the owner of Brennan's Restaurant and ended up paying $14,200 for a 1806 bottle of Chateau Lafite-Rothschild. Wine authorities say it may not even be drinkable. But the bottle may be the last of its kind, and the buyer said he wanted it for his collection. Does this behavior suggest an upward-sloping demand curve for luxuries? If the wine is undrinkable, will the price paid for the bottle prove to have been unwisely high?

8. Suggest commodities that you think might have the following patterns of elasticity of demand.
    a. High income elasticity, high price elasticity
    b. High income elasticity, low price elasticity
    c. Low income elasticity, low price elasticity
    d. Low income elasticity, high price elasticity

9. Look at Table 10-1. Can you suggest why cigarettes and gasoline are inelastic but electricity is elastic? Why is furniture more elastic than all consumer goods taken together?

10. Look at Table 10-2. Can you suggest why gasoline is more income elastic than cigarettes or housing? Or why coffee is more income elastic than beef?

Part Four

Production and Cost

The Firm, Production, and Cost

11

Ask almost anyone you know to name ten American business firms. The odds are overwhelming that the list will include some of these firms: General Motors Corporation, U.S. Steel, General Electric, American Telephone & Telegraph, Dow Chemical, Standard Oil, Du Pont, the Bank of America, United Airlines, the Prudential Insurance Company, and the National Broadcasting Company. Drive around Ypsilanti, Michigan, and note at random ten firms that come into view. They will likely include an A & P supermarket, Richardson's Pharmacy, a Shell service station, Schaeffer's Hardware Store, Haabs, and the First National Bank of Ypsilanti. Drive through Iowa or Nebraska and look around you: Every farm is a business firm as well as a home.

Firms develop and survive because they are efficient institutions for organizing resources to produce goods and services and for organizing their sale and distribution. While General Motors, Haabs, and the Iowa farm are all *firms*, what do they have in common? It is not hard to count ways in which they are different. But there may also be insight to be gained in treating them all under a single heading. This is what economic theory does. Economists usually assume that the firm's behavior can be understood in terms of a common motivation. Whether the firm is Ma and Pa's Bar and Grill or the Ford Motor Company and whether a particular decision is made by the board of directors, the third vice-president in charge of advertising, or the owner-manager is regarded as irrelevant to predicting what decisions are made.

Before studying how the firm is treated in economic theory, we shall examine more closely the firm in America today, to see from what we are abstracting. Criticisms that the theory neglects differences among firms will be considered in Chapter 19.

The Organization of Production

PROPRIETORSHIPS, PARTNERSHIPS, AND CORPORATIONS

There are three major forms of business organization: the single proprietorship, the partnership, and the corporation. In the **single proprietorship,** a single owner makes all decisions and is personally responsible for everything done by the business. In the **partnership,** there are two or more joint owners. Either may make binding decisions, and each partner is personally responsible for everything done by the business. In the **corporation,** the firm legally has an entity of its own. The owners (the stockholders) are not each personally responsible for everything that is done by the business. Owners elect a board of directors who hire managers to run the firm under the board's supervision.

In the United States today, there are about seven million single proprietorships (not counting farms), one million partnerships, and nearly two million corporations.

Corporations account for more than two-thirds of the nation's privately produced income.

In manufacturing, transportation, public utilities, and finance, corporations do almost all of the nation's business. In trade and construction, they do about half the total business. Only in agriculture and in services (such as hair styling, medicine, and accounting) is the corporation relatively unimportant, yet even here its share of the business is steadily rising.

The Proprietorship and the Partnership: Advantages and Disadvantages

The major advantage of the single proprietorship is that the owner can readily maintain full control over the firm. The owner is the Boss. The disadvantages are, first, that the size of the firm is limited by the capital the owner can personally raise and, second, that the owner is personally responsible in law for all debts of the firm.

The ordinary (or general) partnership overcomes to some extent the first disadvantage of the proprietorship but not the second. Ten partners may be able to finance a much bigger enterprise than could one owner, but they are still subject to unlimited liability. Each partner is fully liable for all the debts of the firm. This liability is independent of the amount of money a particular partner may have invested in the firm. If a tenth partner makes $1,000 available (or $100, or nothing, for that matter) when joining a firm that subsequently goes bankrupt with debts of $100,000, this individual, and each of the other nine partners, is fully liable for the $100,000. If none of the other partners has salable personal assets, while the tenth partner has a house, a car, furniture, and some investments, he or she may lose all personal possessions so that the debts of the partnership can be cleared.

Obviously, people with substantial personal assets will be unwilling to enter a partnership unless they have complete trust in the other partners and a full knowledge of all the obligations of the firm. This need for trust is compounded because each partner usually has full power to sign contracts that bind the firm in its ordinary lines of business. One partner's fortune is at the mercy of every other partner's judgment. As a direct consequence of this authority and of the fact of unlimited liability, it is difficult to raise money through a partnership from persons who wish to invest but not be active in the business. Investors may be willing to put up $1,000 but unwilling to jeopardize their entire fortune; if, however, a person joins a partnership in order to do the former, he or she may also do the latter.

A further disadvantage of an ordinary partnership is that any time a partner dies or resigns the partnership agreement must be redrawn. This may make it difficult to have as a partner someone who is not genuinely interested and involved in the business but who wants to invest in it. For such a partner may decide at any time to liquidate his or her interest and so dissolve the partnership.

The **limited partnership** is designed to avoid some of these difficulties. General partners continue to have unlimited authority and unlimited liability, but there will also be limited partners. The limited partner's liability is restricted to the amount that he or she has invested in the firm. Such partners do not participate in the management of the firm or engage in agreements on behalf of the partnership. In effect, the limited partnership permits some division of the functions of decision making, provision of capital, and risk taking.

In most respects, this division of responsibility is more effectively achieved through the corporation. But there are certain professions in which general partnership is traditional. These include law, medicine, and (until very recently) brokerage. Partnerships survive in these fields partly because each depends heavily on a relationship of trust with its clients, and the partners' unlimited liability for one another's actions is thought to enhance public confidence in the firm.

The Corporation: Advantages and Disadvantages

The corporation is regarded in law as an entity separate from the individuals who own it. It can enter into contracts, it can sue and be sued, it can own property, it can contract debts, and it can generally incur obligations that are the legal obligations of the corporation *but not of its owners.* This means that the corporation can enter into contracts in its own right and that its liability to adhere to such contracts can be en-

forced only by suing the corporation, not by suing the owners. The right to be sued may not seem to be an advantage, but it is, because it makes it possible for others to enter into enforceable contracts with the corporation.

Although some corporations are very small or are owned by just a few stockholders who also manage the business, the most important type of corporation is one that sells shares to the general public. The company raises the funds it needs for the business by the sale of stock, and the shareholders become the company's owners. They are entitled to share in corporate profits. Profits, when paid out, are called **dividends. Undistributed profits** also belong to the owners, but they are usually reinvested in the firm's operations. If the corporation is liquidated, shareholders split up any assets that remain after all debts are paid.

Diffuse ownership of corporate shares usually means that the owners cannot all be managers. Stockholders, who are entitled to one vote for each share they own, elect a board of directors. The board defines general policy and hires senior managers who are supposed to translate this general policy into detailed decisions.

Should the company go bankrupt, the personal liability of any one shareholder is limited to whatever money that shareholder has actually invested in the firm. This is called **limited liability.**

From a shareholder's viewpoint, the most important aspect of the corporation is limited liability.

The corporation's advantage is that it can raise capital from a large number of individuals, each of whom shares in the firm's profits but has no liability for corporate action beyond risking the loss of the amount invested. Thus investors know their exact maximum risk and may simply collect dividends without needing to know anything about the policy or operation of the firm that they own collectively. Because shares are easily transferred from one person to another, a corporation has a continuity of life unaffected by frequent changes in the identity of its owners.

From the individual owner's point of view,

there are disadvantages in investing in a corporation. First, the owner may have little to say about the management of the firm. For example, if those who hold a majority of the shares decide that the corporation should not pay dividends, an individual investor cannot compel the payment of "his" share of the earnings. Second, the income of the corporation is taxed twice. The corporation is taxed on its income at a rate of nearly 50 percent before dividends are paid. Dividends are paid out of the after-tax income. Then individual stockholders are also taxed on any dividends paid to them. This "double taxation" of corporate income is viewed by some as clearly unfair and discriminatory; others see it as the price to be paid for the advantage of incorporation. Judging from the continuing importance of the corporation in the United States, despite a corporate income tax rate of about 50 percent, the price has not been prohibitive.

THE RISE OF THE MODERN CORPORATION

The corporate form of organization is employed today wherever large enterprises are found. The principal reason is that it has decisive advantages over any other form in raising the vast sums of capital required for major enterprises. Historically, wherever and whenever large accumulations of capital in a single firm were required, the limited liability company developed. The corporate form has spread even to the service industries and agriculture, as firms in these industries grew to the point where they needed a lot of capital to function effectively.

Although historians have found roots of the corporation in Roman law and in the medieval guild system, the direct predecessor of the modern corporation was the English chartered company of the sixteenth century. The Muscovy Company, granted a charter in 1555, the East India Company, first chartered in 1600, and the Hudson's Bay Company, chartered in 1609 and still going strong in Canada 370 years later, are famous early examples of joint-stock ventures

with limited liability. These companies were granted charters by the Crown so that English merchants could trade with particular regions. The special needs for many investors to finance a ship that would not return with its cargo for years —if it returned at all—made this *exceptional* form of organization seem desirable.

In the next three centuries, the trading company's critical attributes (e.g., large capital requirements and need to diversify risk) were seen to exist in other fields, and charters were granted in the fields of insurance, turnpikes and canals, and banking, as well as foreign trade. The Industrial Revolution, which made the large firm efficient, extended the needs for large amounts of capital committed over long periods of time to many more fields, and, during the nineteenth century, the demand for a general rather than a special privilege of incorporation became strong. General laws permitting incorporation with limited liability, *as a matter of right rather than special grant of privilege,* became common in England and in the United States during the late nineteenth century.

Today incorporation is relatively routine, although it is subject to a variety of state laws. Moderate fees are charged for the privilege of incorporation, and competition among the states for the incorporation fees has served to liberalize the conditions for incorporation throughout the country. Delaware is an example of a small state that at one time had a highly disproportionate share of incorporations because of its permissive laws. In insurance, Connecticut took the lead; most insurance companies founded before 1930 have Connecticut charters.

THE FIRM IN ECONOMIC THEORY

General Motors and Alice's Restaurant certainly make decisions in different ways. Indeed, within a single large corporation not all decisions are made by the same people or in the same way. Nor are all decisions equally important. To take an example, someone at General Motors decided to introduce a new model car in 1975. Someone

Different Kinds of Firms

In economic theory the firm is defined as the unit that makes decisions with respect to the production and sale of commodities. This single definition covers a variety of business organizations from the single proprietorship to the corporation, and a variety of business sizes from the unshaven inventor operating in his garage and financed by whatever he can extract from a reluctant bank manager to vast undertakings with tens of thousands of shareholders and creditors. We know that in large firms, decisions are actually made by many different individuals. We can, nonetheless, regard the firm as a single consistent decision-making unit because of the assumption that all decisions are made in order to achieve the common goal of maximizing the firm's profits.

Whether a decision is made by a small independent proprietor, a plant manager, or a board of directors, that person or group is the firm for the purpose of that decision. This is a truly heroic assumption; it amounts to saying that for purposes of predicting those aspects of their behavior that interest us, we can treat a farm, a corner grocery, a department store, a small law partnership, General Motors, and a giant multinational corporation, all under the umbrella of a single theory of the behavior of the firm. If this turns out to be even partially correct, it will prove enormously valuable in revealing some unity of behavior where to the casual observer there is only bewildering diversity.

You should not be surprised, therefore, if at first encounter the theory appears rather abstract and out of touch with reality. In order to generalize over such a wide variety of behavior, the theory must ignore many features with which we are most familiar and which distinguish the farmer from the grocer and each of them from the Exxon Corporation. Any theory that generalizes over a wide variety of apparently diverse behavior necessarily has this characteristic because it ignores those factors that are most obvious to us and which create in our minds the appearance of diversity. If it were not possible to do this, it would be necessary to have dozens of different theories, one for each type of firm. The task of learning economics would then be much more complex than it now is!

else decided to call it the Chevette. Someone else decided how and where to produce it. Someone else decided its price. Someone else decided how to promote its sales. The common aspect of these decisions is that all were in pursuit of the same goal—the manufacture and sale of successful automobiles and other products to earn profits for the owners of General Motors.

Economic theory assumes that the same principles underlie each decision made within a firm and that the decision is uninfluenced by who makes it. Thus the firm can be regarded as a decision-making unit with objectives that makes decisions designed to achieve these objectives.

Motivation: Profit Maximization

It is assumed that the firm makes decisions in such a way that its profits will be as large as possible. In technical language, it is assumed that the firm *maximizes its profits*. The concept of profits requires careful definition, which will be given later in this chapter. For now we may treat it in the everyday sense of the difference between the value of the firm's sales and the costs to the firm of producing what is sold.

The assumption of profit maximization provides a principle by which a firm's decisions can be predicted.

Economists predict the firm's behavior in regard to the choices open to it by studying the effect that making each of the choices would have on the firm's profits. They then predict that from these alternatives the firm will select the one that produces the largest profits.

At this point you may well ask if it is sensible to build an elaborate theory on such a simple assumption about the motives of business people. Of course some business people are inspired by motives other than an overwhelming desire to make as much money as possible. Cases in which they use their positions to seek political influence or pursue charitable objectives are not difficult to document.

This theory does not say, however, that profit is the *only* factor that influences business people. It says only that profits are so important that a theory that assumes profit maximization to be the business firm's sole motive will produce predictions that are substantially correct. It follows that to point out that business people are *sometimes* motivated by considerations other than profits does not refute the theory. It is always possible that the profit-maximizing assumption could be substantially wrong. If so, the way to demonstrate this is to show that the predictions following from the theory are inconsistent with the facts.

Why is this assumption made? First, it is necessary to make *some* assumption about what motivates decision makers if the theory is to predict how they will act. Second, a great many of the predictions of theories based on this assumption have been confirmed by observation. Third, there is no general agreement that an alternative assumption has yet been shown to yield substantially better results. However, the assumption has been criticized, and alternatives have been suggested (see Chapter 19).

Factors of Production

The firm is in business to make profits. It does this by producing and selling one or more commodities. Production is roughly like a sausage

machine. Certain elements, such as raw materials and the services of capital and labor, are fed in at one end, and a product emerges at the other. The materials and factor services used in the production process are called **inputs,** and the products that emerge are called **outputs.** One way of looking at the process is to regard the inputs as being combined to produce the output. Another equally useful way is to regard the inputs as being used up, or sacrificed, in order to gain the output.

Each distinct input into the production process can be regarded as a factor of production. Literally hundreds of inputs enter into the output of a specific good. Among the inputs entering into automobile production are, to name only a few, sheet steel, rubber, spark plugs, electricity, machinists, cost accountants, fork-lift operators, managers, and painters. These inputs can be grouped into four broad classes: (1) those that are inputs to the automobile manufacturer but outputs to some other manufacturer, such as spark plugs, electricity, and sheet steel; (2) those that are provided directly by nature, such as land; (3) those that are provided directly by households, such as labor; and (4) those that are provided by the machines used for manufacturing automobiles.

The first class of inputs is made up of goods produced by other firms. These products appear as inputs only because the stages of production are broken up between different firms so that, at any one stage, a firm is using as inputs goods produced by other firms. If these products are traced back to the firms that provided them, it will be found that they were produced with the same four types of inputs.

Eventually, however, if these products are traced back to their sources, all production can be accounted for by the services of only three kinds of inputs, which are often called the basic factors of production. All the gifts of nature, such as land and raw materials, the economist calls **land.** All physical and mental efforts provided by people are called **labor** services. All machines and other production equipment are grouped in a

Technological Versus Economic Efficiency: An Example

Suppose, given the state of technology, there are only four known ways to produce 100 widgits per month:

	Quantity of inputs received	
	Capital	Labor
Method A	6	200
Method B	10	250
Method C	10	150
Method D	40	50

Method B is technologically inefficient because it uses more of both inputs than does method A. It thus wastes 4 units of capital and 50 units of labor. Among the other three methods, method A uses the least capital, but it is the most labor-using.* Method D conserves labor but uses much more capital. Method C is intermediate between them. (If you are tempted to consider method D tech-

nologically most efficient because it uses only 90 units of all resources, think again.)

Methods A, C, and D are all technologically efficient because no one of them uses more of both resources than either of the others.

Which one is the least costly—that is, is economically efficient? We cannot tell without knowing the costs of capital and of labor. Economic efficiency depends on factor prices. Consider the three cases shown in the table below. As we move from Case I to II to III, a unit of labor becomes increasingly expensive *relative to* a unit of capital.

Method A is economically efficient when labor is cheap relative to capital. Method C becomes efficient when labor gets somewhat more expensive relative to capital. Finally, when labor gets very expensive relative to capital, Method D, which uses least labor per unit of capital, becomes economically efficient.

To test your understanding, answer these questions:

1. Can a technologically *inefficient* method ever be economically efficient?
2. Is there a set of factor prices for which *both* method C and method D will be economically efficient?

* This is yet a third concept of efficiency, "engineering efficiency," in which least use of a particular factor is involved. When engineers speak of the efficiency of an engine, they may mean how much of the fuel it turns into power. Similarly, a maker of labor-saving machines might consider method D the most efficient because it uses the least amount of labor.

	Factor prices per unit		Total cost of factors		
	Capital	Labor	Method A	Method C	Method D
Case I	$50	$3	$ 900	$950	$2,150
Case II	20	5	1,120	950	1,050
Case III	15	5	1,090	900	850

category called **capital,** defined as man-made aids to further production.

Extensive use of capital—the services of machines and other capital goods—is one distinguishing feature of modern as opposed to primitive production. Instead of making consumer goods directly with only the aid of simple natural tools, productive effort goes into the manufacture of tools, machines, and other goods that are desired not in themselves but as aids to making further goods. The use of capital goods renders the production processes *roundabout*. Instead of making what is wanted directly, a roundabout process first makes tools that will subsequently be used to make what is finally wanted.

Economic Efficiency

Firms must decide not only what and how much to produce but by what method goods will be produced. In general, there is more than one way to produce a given product. Indeed, if this were not the case, there would be no need for firms to face the decision of *how* to produce. It is possible to produce agricultural commodities by farming a small quantity of land, combining a great deal of labor and capital with each acre of land, as is done in Belgium; it is also possible to produce the same commodities by farming a great deal of land, using only a small amount of labor and capital per acre of land, as is done in Australia.

What does it mean to ask which process is best? One meaning of "best" is that, if the output is the same, the best process is the one that uses the fewest inputs or, in other words, the one that is technically most efficient. **Technological efficiency** measures use of inputs in physical terms; **economic efficiency** measures use in terms of costs.

The economically most efficient method is the one that *costs* the least. Economic efficiency depends on factor prices *and* on technological efficiency.

Cost and Profit to the Firm

THE MEANING AND MEASUREMENT OF COST

Economic efficiency has been defined in terms of cost. But what is cost? **Cost,** to the producing firm, is the *value* of the factors of production used in producing its output.

Notice the use of the word "value" in the definition. A given output produced by a given technique, say 6,000 cars produced each week by American Motors with its present production methods, will have a given set of inputs associated with it—so many working hours of various types of laborers, supervisors, managers, and technicians, so many tons of steel, glass, and aluminum, so much electric light and other services, and so many hours of the time of various machines. To know the cost of this diverse set of factor inputs, the value of each in money terms must be calculated. The sum of these separate costs is the total cost to American Motors of producing 6,000 cars per week. "Costing" may be very easy or very difficult.

Purpose in Assigning Costs

Economists' interest in costs is a direct consequence of the notion that factor services are scarce and, as a result, valuable. Thus, in using them up to produce outputs, the firm uses things that have value. From the point of view of a profit-maximizing firm, the profit from production consists of the difference between the value of the outputs and the value of the inputs. Knowing costs, then, is a precondition to knowing profits, and knowing profits is necessary to understanding behavior. An economist might discuss this behavior for several reasons: (1) to *describe* actual behavior of a firm, (2) to *predict* how the firm's behavior will respond to specified changes in the conditions it faces, (3) to *help* the firm make the best decisions it can in achieving its goals, and (4) to *evaluate* how well firms use scarce resources.

The same measure of cost need not be correct for all of these purposes. For example, if the firm happens to be misinformed about the value of some resource, it will behave according to that misinformation. In describing or predicting the firm's behavior, economists should use the information the firm actually uses, even if the economist knows it is incorrect. But in helping the firm to achieve its goals, economists should substitute the correct information.

Economists use a well-established definition of costs in solving problems of the kind cited in items 3 and 4 of the above list. If business people use the same definition and have the same information, the economist's definition will be appropriate for problems of types 1 and 2 as well. This will be assumed for the moment.

Opportunity Cost

Although the details of economic costing vary, they are governed by a common principle that is sometimes called user cost but is more commonly called **opportunity cost.**

The cost of using something in a particular venture is the benefit forgone (or opportunity lost) by not using it in its best alternative use.

An old Chinese merchants' proverb says: "Where there is no gain, the loss is obvious." The economic sense of this proverb is that the merchant who shows no gain has wasted time — time that could have been used in some other venture. The merchant has neglected the opportunity cost of his time.

What is given up *is* the cost of the indicated action. One of the problems in evaluating costs is that different people (or groups) may see or care about different alternatives. Jones sees the alternative to watching television on a Saturday afternoon as playing golf; his wife regards the alternative as a family outing. For the present, analysis will be limited to cost as seen by the firm. In Chapter 24 other points of view will be considered.

THE MEASUREMENT OF OPPORTUNITY COST BY THE FIRM

In principle, measuring opportunity cost is easy. The firm must assign to each factor of production it has used a monetary value equal to what it has sacrificed in order to use the factor. Applying this principle to specific cases, however, reveals some tough problems.

Purchased and Hired Factors

Assigning costs is a straightforward process when factors purchased in one period are used up in the same period and where the price the firm pays is set on a competitive market by the forces of supply and demand. Many raw material and intermediate-product purchases fall into this category. From the point of view of the firm purchasing in a competitive market, if it pays $25 per ton for coal delivered to its factory, it has sacrificed its claims to whatever else $25 can buy, and thus the purchase price is a reasonable measure of the opportunity cost to it of using one ton of coal.

For hired factors of production, where the rental price is the full price, the situation is identical. Borrowed money is paid for by payment of **interest.** An **interest rate** is the money price paid to use $1 for one year. Interest payments measure the opportunity cost of borrowed funds. Most labor services are hired, but typically the cost is more than the wages paid because employers usually must contribute to social security, to pension funds, to unemployment and disability insurance, and to other fringe benefits. The cost of these benefits must be added to the direct wage in determining the opportunity cost of labor services used.

Imputed Costs

The cost must also be assessed for factors of production that the firm uses but neither purchases nor hires for current use. Since no payment is made to anyone outside the firm, these costs are not so obvious. They are called **imputed**

Opportunity Cost More Generally

Opportunity cost plays a vital role in the economic analysis, but it is a fundamental principle that applies to a wide range of situations. It is one of the great insights of economics. Consider some examples:

■ George Bernard Shaw, on reaching his 90th birthday, was asked how he liked being 90. He is reputed to have said, "It's fine, when you consider the alternative."

■ Llewelyn Formed likes to hear both Dan Rather and John Chancellor. If he finally settles on Chancellor, what is the opportunity cost of this decision?

■ Link Hearttrob, a 31-year-old bachelor, is thinking about marrying at last. But, although he thinks Miss Piggy is a lovely girl, he figures that if he marries her, he will give up the chance of wedded bliss with another girl he may meet next year. So he decides to wait a while. What additional information do you require to determine the opportunity cost of the decision?

■ Serge Ginn, M.D., complains that now that he is earning large fees he can no longer afford to take the time for a vacation trip to Europe. In what way does it make sense to say that the opportunity cost of his vacation depends upon his fees?

■ Retired General William Russ, who is married to a very wealthy woman, has decided to contribute $5,000 to a political candidate he likes very much. His lawyer points out to him that since he is in the 50 percent tax bracket, and since political contributions are not deductible from his income, the real cost of his contribution is the same as giving an extra $10,000 to his favorite charity, the Gen. Russ Foundation. Is the opportunity cost of the political contribution $5,000 or $10,000?

■ Hard-Luck Harry loses $100 a week in a dice game. He knows the game is crooked but plays anyway because, as he says, "it's the only game in town." A reform mayor is elected and shuts down all gambling establishments. What is the opportunity cost to Harry?

costs. If the most profitable lines of production are to be discovered, the opportunity cost of these factors should be reckoned at values that reflect what the firm might earn from the factors if it shifted them to their next best use. Some important imputed costs arise because of the use of owners' money, the depreciation of capital equipment, the need to compensate risk taking, and the need to value any special advantages (such as franchises or patents) that the firm may possess.

The cost of money. Consider a firm that uses $100,000 of its own money that it could instead have loaned out at interest at a rate of 10 percent per year.

Thus $10,000 (at least) should be deducted from the firm's revenue as the cost of funds used in production. If, to continue the example, the firm makes only $6,000 over all other costs, then one should say not that the firm made a profit of $6,000 by producing but that it lost $4,000. For if it had closed down completely and merely loaned out its money to someone else, it could have earned $10,000.

The cost of money may be higher than this if the best alternative use of the money could yield more than the market interest rate. Many firms cannot obtain nearly as much money as they would wish by borrowing. If a firm is rationed in the amount of funds it can borrow, it will place a high value on the funds that it does have. In these circumstances, the firm must look at the other ventures it might have undertaken in order to assign opportunity cost because its inability to raise all the capital it wants means that it will be unable to do all the things it wants. Many business firms operate with "cut-off rates of return" that approximate the opportunity cost of money to the firm. They are chosen to approximate the return on projects that the firm cannot undertake because it lacks sufficient funds.[1]

Depreciation. The costs of using assets owned by the firm, such as buildings, equipment, and machinery, consist of the cost of the money tied up in them and a charge, called **depreciation**, for the loss in value of the asset because of its use in production. Depreciation includes both the loss in value due to physical wear and tear and that due to obsolescence. The economic cost of using an asset for a year is the loss in value of the asset during the year.

Accountants use several conventional methods of depreciation based on the price originally paid for the asset. One of the most common is *straight-line depreciation,* in which the same amount of historical cost is deducted in every year of useful life of the asset. While historical costs are often useful approximations, they may in some cases differ seriously from the depreciation required by the opportunity cost principle. Consider two examples of the possible error involved.

Example 1. A woman buys a $6,000 automobile that she intends to use for six years. She may think that, using straight-line depreciation, this will cost her $1,000 per year. But if after one year the value of her car on the used-car market is $4,000, it has cost her $2,000 to use the car during the first year. Why should she

charge herself $2,000 depreciation during the first year? After all, *she* does not intend to sell the car for six years. The answer is that one of the purchaser's alternatives was to buy a one-year-old car and operate it for five years. Indeed, that is the very position she is in after the first year. Whether she likes it or not, she has paid $2,000 for the use of the car during the first year of its life. If the market had valued her car at $5,500 after one year (instead of $4,000), the depreciation would have been only $500.

Example 2. In the previous example an active used-asset market was considered. At the other extreme, consider an asset that has no alternative use. This is sometimes described as the case of "sunk" costs. Assume that a firm has a set of machines it purchased some time ago for $100,000. These machines should last ten years, and the firm's accountant calculates the depreciation costs of these machines by the straight-line method at $10,000 per year. Assume also that the machines can be used to make one product and nothing else. Since they are installed in the firm's plant, they cannot be leased to any other firm, and their scrap value is negligible. In other words, the machines have no value, except to this firm in its current operation. Assume that if the machines are used to produce this product, the cost of all other factors utilized will amount to $25,000, while the goods produced can be sold for $29,000.

Now, if the acccountant's depreciation "costs" of running the machines are added in, the total cost of operation comes to $35,000; with revenues at $29,000, this makes an annual loss of $6,000 per year. It appears that the goods should not be made!

The fallacy in this argument lies in adding in a charge based on the historical cost of the machines as one of the costs of current operation. The machines have no alternative uses whatsoever. Clearly their opportunity cost is zero. The total costs of producing this line of goods is thus only $25,000 per year (assuming all other costs have been correctly assessed), and the line of production shows an annual profit of $4,000, not a loss of $6,000.

[1] Empirical studies of certain American manufacturing industries suggest that the opportunity cost of money is substantially higher than the rate of interest on bonds and long-term loans. An accurate figure may well be as high as 35 percent. The fact that it is so high helps explain why many firms are anxious to retain a major portion of their profits and why many stockholders (who do not have similar personal investment opportunities) are willing to have corporations pay dividends that are substantially less than earnings and reinvest the remainder to earn their internal rate of return.

To see why the second calculation leads to the correct decision, notice that if the firm decides this line of production is unprofitable and does not continue it, it will have no money to pay out and no revenue received on this account. If the firm takes the economist's advice and pursues the line of production, it will pay out $25,000 and receive $29,000, thus making it $4,000 per year richer than if it had not done so. Clearly, production is worth undertaking. The amount the firm happened to have paid out for the machines in the past has no bearing whatever on deciding the correct use of the machines once they are installed on the premises.

Bygones are bygones; they should have no influence on deciding what is currently the most profitable thing to do.

The "bygones are bygones" principle extends well beyond economics and is often ignored in poker, in war, and perhaps in love. Because you have invested heavily in a poker hand, a battle, or a courtship does not mean you should stick with it if the prospects of winning become very small. At every moment of decision, you should be concerned with how benefits from this time forward compare with current and future costs.

Risk taking. One difficult problem in imputing costs concerns the evaluation of the service of risk taking. Business enterprise is often a risky affair. The risk is borne by the owners of the firm who, if the enterprise fails, may lose the money they have invested in the firm. The owners will not take these risks unless they receive a remuneration in return. They expect a return that exceeds what they could have obtained by investing their money in a virtually riskless manner, say, by buying a government bond.

In the sense in which the term is used here, risk taking is a factor of production and thus has a cost. It is a service that must be provided if the firm is to carry on production, and it must be paid for by the firm. If a firm does not yield a return sufficient to compensate for the risks involved, the firm will not be able to persuade people to contribute money to it in return for a part ownership in the firm.

Investors demand a higher return on a risky venture than on a sure one because, in addition to having their capital used, they take the chance of never getting it back. In order to earn the required return on their total investments—the successful and the unsuccessful—investors require a greater return on the successful investments.

Suppose, in investing $100,000 in a class of risky ventures, a businesswoman expects that most of the ventures will be successful but some will fail. In fact she expects about $10,000 worth to be a total loss. (She does not know which specific projects will be the losers, of course.) Suppose further that she requires a 20 percent return on her total investment. In order to earn $20,000 profit and recover the $10,000 expected loss, she needs to earn $30,000 profit on the $90,000 of successful investment. This is a rate of return of $33\frac{1}{3}$ percent. She charges 20 percent for the use of the capital, $13\frac{1}{3}$ percent for the risk she takes.

Special advantages. Suppose a firm owns a valuable patent or a highly desirable location, or produces a popular brand-name product such as Coca-Cola, Chevrolet, or Marlboro. Each of these involves an opportunity cost to the firm in production (even if it was acquired free) because if the firm does not choose to *use* the special advantage itself, it could sell or lease it to others. Typically, the value of these advantages will differ from their historical cost.

PROFITS: THEIR MEANING AND SIGNIFICANCE

Profits, although often defined loosely in everyday usage, may be given a series of more precise definitions. **Economic profits** on goods sold are defined as the difference between revenues received from the sale and the opportunity cost of the resources used to make them. (If costs are greater than revenues, such "negative profits" are called *losses*.)

This definition includes in costs (and thus excludes from profits) the imputed returns to capital and to risk taking. This use of the words

TABLE 11-1

The Calculation of Economic Profits: An Example

Gross revenue from sales	$1,000
Less: direct costs of goods sold (materials, labor, electricity, etc.)	650
"Gross profits" (or "contributions to overhead")	350
Less: indirect costs (depreciation, overhead, management salaries, etc.)	140
"Net profits" before income taxes	210
Less: imputed charges for own capital used and for risk taking $\Big\} =$ "normal profits"	100
Economic profits before income taxes	110
Less: income taxes payable	100
Economic profits after income taxes	$ 10

The main difference between "economic profits" and the usual everyday definition of profits is the subtraction of imputed charges for use of capital owned by the firm and for risk taking. Income tax is levied on whatever definition of profits the taxing authorities choose, usually closely related to "net profits."

"profit" and "loss" gives specialized definitions to words that are in everyday use. They are, therefore, a potential source of confusion to the student who runs into other uses of the same words. Table 11-1 may help clarify the definition.

Some economists, while following substantially the same definitions, label as **normal profits** the imputed returns to capital and risk taking just necessary to prevent the owners from withdrawing from the industry. These normal profits are, of course, what has been defined as the opportunity costs of risk taking and capital. Whatever they are called, they are costs that have to be covered if the firm is to stay in operation in the long run.

Other Definitions of Profits

Business firms define profits as the excess of revenues over the costs with which accountants provide them. We will explore in the appendix to this chapter some of the differences between accountants' and economists' views of business transactions. Some of these differences affect the meaning of profits. Accountants do not include as costs charges for risk taking and use of owners' own capital, and thus these items are recorded by businesses as part of their profits. When a businessman says he *needs* profits of such and such an amount in order to stay in business, he is making sense within his definition, for his "profits" must be large enough to pay for those factors of production that he uses but that the accounting profession does not include as costs.

The economist would express the same notion by saying that the business needs to cover *all* its costs, including those not accepted by accounting conventions. If the firm is covering all its costs (in the sense that we have defined costs), then it could not do better by using its resources in any other line of activity than the one currently being followed. Indeed, it would probably do worse in most other lines of activity.

A situation in which revenues equal costs (economic profits of zero) is a satisfactory one—because all factors, hidden as well as visible, are being rewarded at least as well as in their *best* alternative uses.

With zero profits then, in the economist's sense of that concept, you can do no better, although you might do worse. To reverse the Chinese proverb cited earlier, "Where there is no loss compared to the best alternative use of every factor, the gain is obvious."

The income tax authorities have yet another definition of profits, which is implicit in the thousands of rules as to what may and may not be included as a deduction from revenue in arriving at taxable income. In some cases, the taxing authorities allow more for cost than the accountant recommends; in other cases, they allow less.

It is important to be clear about different meanings of the term "profits," not only to avoid fruitless semantic arguments, but because a theory that predicts that certain behavior is a function of profits defined in one way will not necessarily predict behavior accurately, given some other definition. For example, if economists predict that new firms will seek to enter an industry whenever profits are earned, this prediction will frequently be wrong if the accountants' definition is used to determine profits. The definition of profits as an excess over all opportunity costs is for many purposes the most useful, but in order to apply it to business behavior or to tax policy, appropriate adjustments must be made. And in order to apply accounting or tax data to particular theories, the data must be rectified.

Profits and Resource Allocation

When resources are valued by the opportunity cost principle, their costs show how much these resources would earn if used in their best alternative uses. If there is an industry in which all firms' revenues exceed opportunity costs, all the firms in that industry will be earning profits. Thus the owners of factors of production will want to move resources into this industry because the earnings potentially available to them are greater there than in alternative uses of the resources. If in some other industry firms are incurring losses, some or all of this industry's resources are more highly valued in other uses, and owners of the resources will want to move them to those other uses.

Economic profits and losses play a crucial signaling role in the workings of a free-market system.

Profits in an industry are the signal that resources can profitably be moved into the industry. Losses are the signal that the resources can profitably be moved elsewhere. Only if there are zero economic profits is there no incentive for resources to move into or out of an industry.

Summary

1. The firm is the economic unit that produces and sells commodities. The economist's definition of the firm abstracts from real-life differences in size and form of organization of firms.

2. The single proprietorship, the partnership, and the corporation are the major forms of business organization in the United States today. The corporation is by far the most common business wherever large-scale production is required. The corporation is recognized as a legal entity; its owners, or shareholders, have a liability that is limited to the amount of money they have actually invested in the organization. Corporate ownership is readily transferred by sale of shares in organized securities markets.

3. Economic theory assumes that the same principles underlie each decision made within the firm and that the actual decision is uninfluenced by who makes it. The key behavioral assumption is that the firm seeks to maximize its profit.

4. Production consists of transforming inputs (or factors of production) into outputs (or goods and services). It is often convenient to divide factors of production into categories. One common classification is land, labor, and capital. Land includes all primary products, labor means all human services, and capital denotes all man-made aids to further production. An outstanding feature of modern production is the use of capital goods and roundabout methods of production.

5. Because there is more than one way to engage in production, the firm must decide *how* to produce. Efficiency is a measure of the relative amount of input necessary to produce a given output. Technological efficiency evaluates units of input in physical terms. Economic efficiency evaluates them in terms of costs.

6. The opportunity cost of using a resource is the value of that resource in its best alternative use. If the opportunity cost of using a resource in one way is less than or equal to the gain from using the resource in this way, there is no superior way of using it.

7. Measuring opportunity cost to the firm requires some difficult imputations in cases involving resources not purchased or hired for current use. Among these imputed costs are those for use of owners' money, depreciation, risk taking, and any special advantages that the firm may possess.

8. A firm maximizing profits, defined as the difference between revenue and opportunity cost, is making the best allocation of the resources under its control, according to the firm's evaluation of its alternatives.

9. Profits and losses provide important signals concerning the reallocation of resources. Profits earned in an industry provide a signal that more resources can profitably move into the industry. Losses show that some resources have more profitable uses elsewhere and serve as a signal for them to move out of that industry.

10. The appendix to this chapter introduces balance sheets and profit and loss statements and uses them to discuss some of the differences between the concepts of profits used by accountants and economists.

Topics for Review

The firm in theory and in the U.S. economy
The role of profit maximization
Single proprietorship, partnership, and corporation
Advantages of the corporation
Factors of production
Economic efficiency
Opportunity costs
Economic and other definitions of profits
Profits and resource allocation

Discussion Questions

1. Many modern firms go through stages of being in turn a single proprietorship, a partnership, and a corporation. Can you suggest why such an evolution might be sensible? If you were to start a business, which form would you choose? Why?

2. Can the economic theory of the firm be of any help in analyzing the productive decisions of such nonprofit organizations as governments, churches, and colleges? What, if any, role does the notion of opportunity cost play for them?

3. In *The Engineers and the Price System* Thorstein Veblen argued that businessmen who made decisions about financing, pricing, and the like were largely superfluous to the operation of a business. In his view, knowledge of the technology would be sufficient to ensure efficient operation of firms. Discuss Veblen's contention.

4. "There is no such thing as a free lunch." Can anything be costless? Gas stations have traditionally provided free services, including windshield cleaning, air pumps for tire inflation, and road maps. Now, many sell road maps and have discontinued free services. Indeed, self-service stations are becoming increasingly popular with motorists who like the lower gas prices of those stations. Under what conditions will profit-maximizing behavior lead to the coexistence of full-service and self-service gas stations? What would determine the proportions in which each occurred?

5. What is the opportunity cost of:
   a. a politician being fined $10,000 and sent to prison for one year
   b. lending $500 to a friend
   c. not permitting a $116 million electric power dam to be built because it would destroy the snail darter, a rare 3-inch long fish found only in that particular river
   d. towing icebergs to Saudi Arabia to provide drinking water at the cost of 50¢ per cubic meter

6. Is straight-line depreciation an appropriate method of assessing the annual cost to the typical American household of using a passenger automobile? Some firms that use trucks allocate the cost on a per-mile basis. Why might this method be more nearly appropriate for trucks than for automobiles owned by households?

7. Having bought a used car from Smiling Sam for $900, you drive it two days and it stops. You now find that it requires an extra $500 before it will run. Assuming that the car is not worth $1,400 fixed, should you make the repairs?

8. "The higher the opportunity cost, the poorer the investment." Do you agree with this statement? If you do not, how could you formulate the maxim so that you did agree?

9. Which concept of profits is implied in the following quotations:
   a. "Profits are necessary if firms are to stay in business."
   b. "Profits are signals for firms to expand production and investment."
   c. "Increased depreciation lowers profits and thus benefits the company's owners."

Production and Cost in the Short Run

12

The American automobile industry in 1979 consisted of four firms who together produced and sold 8.1 million new cars (not included in this total are 167,000 Volkswagons produced in the United States). However, their individual shares of the market were not anything like equal. General Motors sold 60 percent, Ford sold 26 percent, Chrysler sold 12 percent, and American Motors sold 2 percent. The prices charged for comparable models were approximately the same, but the profits *per automobile* made and sold were very different for the companies not only in 1979 but on the average over many years. General Motors has consistently shown the highest profit per unit; Ford has been next most profitable, while Chrysler and American Motors each earned much lower profits per car than the other two. In 1979 Chrysler's losses of about $1 billion threatened the ability of that company to continue in business and led to a massive federal loan guarantee of $1.5 billion. Ford, too, lost money on its North American operations, but foreign operations kept it in the black overall.

One reason for the differences in profitability lies in the *cost* of making and selling a car, which tends to be lower the more cars are produced. Over the past 40 years several once-profitable smaller producers, among them Packard, Crosley, Studebaker, and Kaiser-Frazer, were unable to increase their volume and found that costs had become greater than revenues. They left the industry after suffering heavy losses. This experience illustrates one aspect of the theory of cost of production: cost of production per unit may be very different for different levels of output.

A different aspect of the theory of costs relates to factor prices. When rising chicken feed prices reached the point where it cost more to feed chickens as they grew than they sold for when fully grown, chicken farmers shut down temporarily. Similarly, when meat packers were squeezed between the legal maximum price at which they could sell and the rising cost of the livestock they bought, some of them suspended production.

In order to understand firms' behavior, we need to know what determines their costs of production and how those costs vary as output varies. The principle of opportunity cost shows how to put a money value on the factor services that are used up in the process of production. These money values for all the factor services used to produce a certain output are added up to get the total cost of producing that output. But how are these costs related to output?

Real Choices Open to the Firm

Consider a firm producing a single product in a number of different plants. If its rate of sales has fallen off, should production be reduced correspondingly? Or should production be held at the old rate and the unsold amounts stored up against an anticipated future rise in sales? If production is to be reduced, should a single plant be closed or should all plants be operated fewer hours per week? If demand increases sharply and unexpectedly, how can more production be squeezed out of the existing facilities?

All these matters concern how best to use *existing* plant and equipment. They also involve time periods too short to build new plants or to install more equipment. The decisions made will be implemented quickly: A plant can be shut down on a week's notice, overtime can be increased tomorrow, and new production workers can be added as soon as they can be hired and trained.

More weighty decisions must be made when managers do long-range planning. Should the firm adopt a highly automated process that will greatly reduce its wage bill, even though it must borrow large sums of money to buy the equipment? Or should it continue to build new plants that use the same techniques it is now using? Should it build new plants in an area where labor is plentiful, but that is distant from its sources of raw materials? These matters concern what a firm should do when it is changing or replacing its plant and equipment. Such decisions may take a long time to put into effect.

In the above examples, managers make decisions from known possibilities. Large firms also have research and development staffs whose job it is to discover new methods of production. But the firm must decide how much money to devote to this function and in what areas the payoff for new development will be largest. If, for example, a shortage of a particular labor skill or raw material is anticipated, the research staff can be told to try to find ways to economize on that input or even eliminate it from the production process.

TIME HORIZONS FOR DECISION MAKING

In order to reduce to manageable proportions the decisions firms are constantly making, economists organize the decisions into three theoretical groups: (1) How best to employ existing plant and equipment (the "short run"). (2) What new plant and equipment and production processes to select, given the framework of known technical possibilities (the "long run"). (3) What to do about encouraging the invention of new techniques (the "very long run"). In using these periods economists abstract from the more complicated nature of real decisions and focus on the key factors that restrict the range of choice in each set of decisions.

The Short Run

Short-run decisions are those made when the quantity of some inputs cannot be varied. The firm cannot get more of the **fixed factors** than it has on hand, and it is committed to make any money payments that are associated with these fixed factors.[1] Factors that can be varied in the short run are called **variable factors.**

In the short run, what matters is that at least one significant factor is fixed. The factor is fixed in the sense that while the firm may or may not use all that it has, it cannot get more for the duration of the short run. The fixed factor is usually an element of capital (such as plant and equipment), but it might be land, the services of management, or even the supply of skilled labor.

The short run does not correspond to a definite number of months or years. In some industries it may extend over many years; in others it may be only a matter of months or even weeks. Furthermore, it may last a different period of time in an expanding phase of an industry than in a contracting one.

In the electric power industry, for example, it takes three or more years to acquire and install a steam-turbine generator. An unforeseen increase in demand will involve a long period during which the extra demand must be met as best it can with the existing capital equipment. Once installed, this equipment has a very long life, and a decrease in demand leaves the firm committed, possibly for decades, to all the costs of this equipment that do not vary with output.

In contrast, a machine shop can acquire new equipment or sell existing equipment in a very few weeks, so the short run is correspondingly short. An increase in demand will have to be met with the existing stock of capital for only a brief time, after which it will be possible to adjust the stock of equipment to the level made desirable by the higher demand.

The Long Run

Long-run decisions are those made when the inputs of all factors of production may be varied but the basic technology of production is unchanged. Again, the long run does not correspond to a specific period of time.

The special importance of the long run in production theory is that it corresponds to the situation facing the firm when it is planning to go into business, to expand the scale of its operations, to branch out into new products or new areas, or to modernize, replace, or reorganize its method of production.

The firm's *planning decisions* characteristically are made with fixed technical possibilities but with freedom to choose from a variety of production processes that will use factor inputs in different proportions.

The Very Long Run

Unlike the short and the long run, the **very long run** concerns the opportunities arising from changing technology. A central characteristic of modern industrial society has been the continuously changing technology that leads to new and improved products and new and improved production methods. Some of these technological advances arise from within the firm as part of its own research and development efforts. For example, much of the innovation in cameras and films has been due to the efforts of the Kodak and Polaroid companies. Or firms may merely adopt technological changes made by other firms. For example, the transistor and the electronic chip have revolutionized dozens of industries that had nothing to do with developing them in the first place. In either case, decisions are required on the part of the firm as to how much to spend in its efforts to change the firm's technology either by developing new techniques or adapting techniques developed by others.

---

[1] Sometimes it is physically impossible to increase the quantity of a fixed factor in a short time. For instance, there is no way to build a hydroelectric dam or a nuclear power plant in a few months. Other times it might be physically possible, but prohibitively expensive, to increase the quantity. For example, a suit-manufacturing firm could conceivably rent a building, buy and install new sewing machines, and hire a trained labor force in a few days if money were no consideration. Economists regard prohibitive cost along with physical impossibility as a source of fixed factors.

CONNECTING THE RUNS: THE PRODUCTION FUNCTION

Although it is convenient to treat production decisions in several stages—or in separate compartments—they are thoroughly interrelated. The plant built today (a long-run decision) affects tomorrow's short-run decisions. Similarly, an alternative to coping with a plant of inadequate size by running overtime shifts (a short-run expedient) is constructing a new wing (a long-run decision) or an entirely new plant (another long-run decision) or searching for a new technique of production (a very-long-run decision).

The various "runs" are simply different aspects of the same basic problem: getting output from inputs efficiently. They differ in terms of what the firm is able to change.

The relation between factor services used as inputs into the production process and the quantity of output obtained is called the **production function.** A simplified production function in which there are only two factors of production, labor and capital, will be considered here, but the conclusions apply equally when there are many factors. The variation of output and cost under the assumption that one of the two factors is fixed is examined in this chapter. (Capital is taken to be the fixed factor and labor the variable one.) The long-run situation in which both factors can be varied is covered in the next chapter.

Short-run Choices

TOTAL, AVERAGE, AND MARGINAL PRODUCTS

Assume that a firm starts with a fixed amount of capital (say, 4 units) and contemplates applying various amounts of labor to it. Table 12-1 shows three different ways of looking at how output varies with the quantity of the variable factor. As a first step, some terms need to be defined.

1. **Total product** (*TP*) means the total amount produced during a given period of time by all the

TABLE 12-1

The Variation of Output with Capital Fixed and Labor Variable

(1) Quantity of labor (L)	(2) Total product (TP)	(3) Average product (AP)	(4) Marginal product (MP)
0	0	—	
			15
1	15	15.0	
			19
2	34	17.0	
			14
3	48	16.0	
			12
4	60	15.0	
			2
5	62	12.4	

The relation of output to changes in the quantity of labor can be looked at in three different ways. Capital is assumed to be fixed at 4 units. As the quantity of labor increases, the rate of output (the total product) increases. Average product increases at first and then declines. The same is true of marginal product.

Marginal product is shown between the lines because it refers to the *change* in output from one level of labor input to another. When graphing the schedule, *MPs* of this kind should be plotted at the midpoint of the interval. Thus, graphically, the marginal product of 12 would be plotted to correspond to quantity of labor of 3.5.

factors of production employed. If the inputs of all but one factor are held constant, total product will change as more or less of the variable factor is used. This variation is shown in columns (1) and (2) of Table 12-1, which gives a total product schedule. Figure 12-1(i) shows such a schedule graphically. (The shape of the curve will be discussed shortly.)

2. **Average product** (*AP*) is merely the total product per unit of the variable factor, labor. The number of units of labor will be denoted by *L*.

$$AP = \frac{TP}{L}$$

It is shown in column (3) of Table 12-1. Notice that as more of the variable factor is used, average product first rises and then falls. The level of output (34 units in the example) where average product reaches a maximum is called the **point of diminishing average productivity.**

3. **Marginal product** (*MP*), sometimes called

FIGURE 12–1

Total, Average, and Marginal Product Curves

(i) Total product curve

(ii) Average and marginal product curves

TP, AP, **and** *MP* **curves often have the shapes shown here.** (i) The total product curve shows total product steadily rising, first at an increasing rate, then at a decreasing rate. This leads both average and marginal product curves in (ii) to rise at first and then decline. The point of maximum average product (also called the point of diminishing average productivity) is q_1. At this point $MP = AP$.

incremental product, is the change in total product resulting from the use of 1 unit more of the variable factor.[2] **[14]**

$$MP = \frac{\Delta TP}{\Delta L}$$

Computed values of marginal product are shown in column (4) of Table 12-1. The figures in this column are placed between the other lines of the table to stress that the concept refers to the *change* in output caused by the *change* in quantity of the variable factor. For example, the increase in labor from 3 to 4 units ($\Delta L = 1$) raises output by 12 from 48 to 60 ($\Delta TP = 12$). Thus the *MP* equals 12, and it is recorded between 3 and 4 units of labor. Note that the *MP* in the example rises and then falls. The level of output where marginal product reaches a maximum is called the **point of diminishing marginal productivity.**

Figure 12-1(ii) plots average product and marginal product curves. Although three different schedules are shown in Table 12-1 and three different curves are shown in Figure 12-1, they are all aspects of the same single relationship that is described by the production function. As we vary the quantity of labor, with capital fixed, output changes. Sometimes it is interesting to look at the total increase in output, sometimes at the average increase, and sometimes at the marginal increase.

Finally, bear in mind that the schedules of Table 12-1 and the curves of Figure 12-1 all assume a specified quantity of the fixed factor. If the quantity of capital had been, say, 6 or 10 instead of the 4 units that were assumed, there would be a different set of total product, average product, and marginal product curves. The reason for this is that if any specified amount of labor has more capital to work with, it can produce more output—that is, its total product will be greater.

[2] The Greek delta (Δ) is a standard symbol meaning "the change in." Thus ΔL is read "a change in the quantity of labor." For the definition of marginal product we want a 1-unit change in labor, that is, $\Delta L = 1$.

Diminishing Returns

The phenomenon of eventually diminishing returns when more of a variable factor is applied to one or more fixed factors is illustrated by the following examples. In each case you should be able to identify the variable factor and the fixed factor or factors, as well as the "product" that is subject to diminishing returns.

■ When Southern California Edison was required by the State of California to modify its Mojave power plant to reduce the amount of fly ash emitted into the atmosphere, it discovered that a series of filters applied to the smokestacks could do the job. A single filter eliminated half the discharge. Five filters in series reduced the fly ash discharge to the three percent allowed by law. When a state senator proposed a new standard that would permit no more than one percent fly ash emission, the company brought in experts who testified that such a requirement (if it could be met) would require at least 15 filters per stack and would triple the cost.

■ Experimenters with chemical fertilizers at the Rothampsted Experimental Station, an agricultural research institute in Hertfordshire, England, in 1921 applied different amounts of a particular fertilizer to ten apparently identical quarter-acre plots of land. For one such test, using identical seed grain, the results were:

Plot	Fertilizer dose	Yield index*
1	15	104.2
2	30	110.4
3	45	118.0
4	60	125.3
5	75	130.2
6	90	132.4
7	105	131.9
8	120	132.3
9	135	132.5
10	150	132.8

*Yield without fertilizer = 100

You may find it useful to compute the average and marginal product of fertilizer and identify the (approximate) points of diminishing average and marginal productivity.

■ Idaho's Salmon River, a noted sport fishing river, has become the center of a thriving, well-promoted tourist trade. As the fishing pressure in the Salmon River has increased, the total number of fish caught has steadily increased; but the number of fish per person

THE SHAPE OF THE MARGINAL AND AVERAGE PRODUCT CURVES

The Law (Hypothesis) of Diminishing Returns

The variations in output that result from applying more or less of a variable factor to a given quantity of a fixed factor are the subject of a famous economic hypothesis. Usually it is called the **law of diminishing returns.**

The hypothesis states that if increasing amounts of a variable factor are applied to a given amount of a fixed factor, eventually a situation will be reached in which each additional unit of the variable factor adds less to total product than did the previous unit.

The common sense of diminishing marginal product is that the fixed factor limits the amount of additional output that can be realized by adding more of the variable factor. The hypothesis of diminishing returns predicts only that sooner or later the *MP* curve will decline. It is conceivable that marginal returns might diminish from fishing has decreased, and the average hours fished for each fish caught has increased. The average weight of the fish caught has remained the same.

■ Gallup, Roper, and all other pollsters, as well as all students of statistics, know that you can use a sample to estimate characteristics of a very large population. Even a relatively small sample can provide a useful estimate — at a tiny fraction of the cost of a complete enumeration of the population. However, sample estimates are subject to *sampling error*. If, for example, 38 percent of a sample approves of a certain policy, the percentage of the population that approves of it is likely to be close to 38 percent, but it might well be anywhere from 36 to 40 percent. The theory of statistics shows that the size of the expected sampling error can always be reduced by increasing the sample size. The four percent interval (in the example above) could be cut in half — to two percent — by *quadrupling* the sample size. That is, if the original sample had been 400, a new sample of 1,600 would halve the expected error. To reduce the interval to one percent, the new sample would have to be quadrupled again — to 6,400. In other words, there are diminishing marginal returns to sample size.

■ During World War II decisions had to be made repeatedly concerning how many bombs to drop on a particular military target. Given the scarcity of bombs and bombers, an over-bombing of one site would have an opportunity cost: it would leave other targets untouched. Consider the bombing of a German steel mill. The first bomb, even if it were a direct hit, could not knock out the factory; thus, if the goal was to stop steel production, the amount of effective damage would be expected to increase with further bombs. Eventually, when the operation of the steel plant had been crippled, additional bombs, while adding to the problems of resuming production, would surely have less marginal effect than earlier ones because much of their force would only redistribute the rubble from earlier hits.

■ An oldtime Texas rancher interviewed in a television documentary, *The New Dust Bowl?*, denied vehemently that there was a serious water problem in his state. "The water's there, just like it's always been," he said. "Get yourself a rig and start drilling. Either you'll hit oil, in which case you'll forget about water, or you'll find water. I've been doing it for 30 years. Used to hit water at 12 to 18 feet; now it's more like 70 to 80 feet, but it's there just the same."

the outset, so that the first unit of labor contributes most to total production and each successive unit contributes less than the previous unit. (This is the case in what is known as the Cobb-Douglas production function.) It is also possible for the marginal product to rise at first and decline later.[3] The reason is clear when seen in the context of the organization of production.

Consider the use of a variable number of workers in a manufacturing operation. If there is only one worker, that worker must do all the tasks, shifting from one to another and becoming competent in each. As a second, third, and subsequent workers are added it is often possible to break the tasks into a large number of separate jobs, with each laborer specializing in one job and becoming expert at it. This process is called the *division of labor*. If additional workers permit more and more efficient divisions of labor, marginal product will be rising. This may go on for some time, but (according to the hypothesis

---

[3] Thus what is called the law of diminishing marginal returns might more accurately be described as the law of eventually diminishing returns.

of diminishing returns) the scope for such economies must eventually disappear and sooner or later the marginal products of additional workers must decline. When this happens each additional worker will increase total output by less than the previous worker increased it. This sort of case is the one illustrated in Figure 12-1, where marginal product rises at first and then declines. Eventually marginal product may reach zero and even decline. It is not hard to see why, when you consider the extreme case where there are so many workers in a limited space that additional workers simply get in the way.

The hypothesis is usually described in terms of diminishing marginal returns, but it can equally well be stated in terms of diminishing average returns. The law of diminishing *average* returns states that if increasing quantities of a variable factor are applied to a given quantity of fixed factors, the average product of the variable factor will eventually decrease. [15]

The Significance of the Law of Diminishing Returns

There is a great deal of empirical confirmation of both diminishing marginal and diminishing average returns. Some examples are reflected in the box. One might, however, wish that it were not so. The consequence of diminishing returns is easily seen in a single example. If the hypothesis were not true, there would be no reason to fear that the world population explosion will bring with it a food crisis. If the marginal product of additional workers applied to a fixed quantity of land were constant, then world food production could be expanded in proportion to the population merely by keeping a constant fraction of the population on farms. But with fixed techniques, the hypothesis of diminishing returns predicts an inexorable decline in the marginal product of each additional laborer because an expanding population has a fixed world supply of agricultural land. Thus, unless there is a continual improvement in the techniques of production, continuous population growth will bring with it,

according to the hypothesis of diminishing returns, declining average living standards and eventually widespread famine.

This was the gloomy prediction of the early nineteenth-century English economist Thomas Malthus. No wonder economics was popularly known at the time as the dismal science!

The Relation Between Marginal and Average Curves

Notice that in Figure 12-1(ii) the *MP* curve cuts the *AP* curve at the latter's maximum point. Although the relation between marginal and average curves is a mathematical one and not a matter of economics, it is important to understand how these curves are related. [16]

The average product curve slopes upward as long as the marginal product curve is above it; it makes no difference whether the marginal curve is itself sloping upward or downward. The common sense of this relation is that if an additional worker is to raise the average product of all workers, his or her output must be greater than the average output of all other workers. It is immaterial whether the new worker's contribution to output is greater or less than the contribution of the worker hired immediately before; all that matters is that his or her contribution to output exceeds the average output of *all* workers hired previously. (The relation between marginal and average measures is further illustrated in the box about Ted Williams.)

SHORT-RUN VARIATIONS IN COST

We now shift our attention from the firm's production function to its costs. We consider firms that are not in a position to influence the prices of the factors of production they employ. These firms must pay the going market price for all factors.[4] Given the prices paid for factors and the

---

[4] The important problems that arise when the firm is in a position to influence the prices it pays for its factors of production are considered in Chapter 21.

The Batting Average of Ted Williams: Marginal and Lifetime

The relationship between "marginal" and "average" concepts is very general. An illuminating example comes from the *Baseball Encyclopedia*. The table gives the batting average (number of hits—output—divided by official times at bat—input) of Ted Williams over his illustrious career with the Boston Red Sox. For each year, column (2) gives his batting average for his whole major-league career before that year. It is his lifetime average on opening day. Column (3) gives his average during the current, or "marginal," year.

Whenever his current year average is above the lifetime-to-date average, the latter rises. See, for example, 1941, 1948, and 1957. Whenever his current year is below the lifetime, the latter falls. See, for example, 1946, 1950, and 1959. This is true whether the marginal itself is rising or falling. For example, both 1950 and 1951 were below-average years for Williams and lowered his average, even though 1951 was better than the previous year had been (marginal rising) and 1950 was worse than the previous year had been (marginal falling). *If the average is to fall, all* *that matters is that the marginal is below the average.*

Year	(1) Games played	(2) Lifetime batting average on opening day	(3) Batting average during year
1939	149	.000	.327
1940	144	.327	.344
1941	143	.335	.406
1942	150	.359	.356
1943–45*	0	.358	—
1946	150	.358	.342
1947	156	.355	.343
1948	137	.353	.369
1949	155	.355	.343
1950	89	.354	.317
1951	148	.351	.318
1952–53*	43	.348	.406
1954	117	.350	.345
1955	98	.349	.356
1956	136	.350	.345
1957	132	.349	.388
1958	129	.352	.328
1959	103	.351	.254
1960	113	.346	.316
Lifetime	2292	.344	

*Military service

physical returns summarized by the product curves, the costs of different levels of output can be calculated.

Cost Concepts Defined

The following brief definitions of several cost concepts are closely related to the product concepts just introduced.

1. **Total cost** (*TC*) means the total cost of producing any given level of output. Total cost is divided into two parts, total fixed costs (*TFC*) and total variable costs (*TVC*). **Fixed costs** are those that do not vary with output; they will be the same if output is 1 unit or 1 million units. These costs are also often referred to as "overhead costs" or "unavoidable costs." All costs that vary directly with output, rising as more is produced and falling as less is produced, are called **variable costs**. In the example of Table 12-1, since labor was the variable factor of production, the wage bill would be a variable cost. Variable costs are often referred to as "direct costs" or "avoidable costs."

2. **Average total cost** (*ATC*), also called **average cost** (*AC*), is the total cost of producing any given output divided by the number of units produced, or the cost per unit. *ATC* may be

TABLE 12–2
The Variation of Costs with Capital Fixed and Labor Variable

Labor (L)	Output (q)	Total cost ($)			Average cost ($ per unit)			Marginal cost (MC)
		Fixed (TFC)	Variable (TVC)	Total (TC)	Fixed (AFC)	Variable (AVC)	Total (ATC)	
0	0	100	0	100	—	—	—	
1	15	100	10	110	6.67	0.67	7.33	0.67
2	34	100	20	120	2.94	0.59	3.53	0.53
3	48	100	30	130	2.08	0.62	2.71	0.71
4	60	100	40	140	1.67	0.67	2.33	0.83
5	62	100	50	150	1.61	0.81	2.42	5.00

The relation of cost to level of output can be looked at in several different ways. These cost curves are computed from the product curves of Table 12–1, given the price of capital of $25 per unit and the price of labor of $10 per unit. Notice that the average curves are cost per unit of output. Thus, for example, the ATC of $3.53 arises because 34 units of output cost a total of $120. The marginal cost of $.71

shown in the next line is the increase in total cost of $10 associated with hiring one more laborer *divided by* the increase in output of 14 caused by employing one more laborer (output rises from 34 to 48). For graphical purposes, marginal costs should be plotted midway in the interval over which they are computed. The MC of $.71 would be plotted at output 41.

divided into **average fixed costs** (*AFC*) and **average variable costs** (*AVC*) in the same way that total costs were divided.

Although average *variable* costs may rise or fall as production is increased (depending on whether output rises more rapidly or more slowly than total variable costs), it is clear that average fixed costs decline continuously as output increases. A doubling of output always leads to a halving of fixed costs per unit of output. This is a process popularly known as "spreading one's overhead."

3. **Marginal cost** (*MC*), sometimes called **incremental cost,** is the increase in total cost resulting from raising the rate of production by 1 unit. Because fixed costs do not vary with output, marginal fixed costs are always zero. Therefore marginal costs are necessarily marginal variable costs, and a change in fixed costs will leave marginal costs unaffected. For example, the marginal cost of producing a few more potatoes by farming a given amount of land more intensively is the same, whatever the rent paid for the fixed amount of land. [17]

These three measures of cost are simply different ways of looking at a single phenomenon. They are mathematically interrelated.

Short-run Cost Curves

Take the production relationships in Table 12-1. Assume that the price of labor is $10 per unit and the price of capital is $25 per unit. The cost schedules computed for these values are shown in Table 12-2.[5]

Figure 12-2 plots cost curves that are similar in shape to those arising from the data in Table 12-2. Notice that the marginal cost curve cuts the *ATC* and *AVC* curves at their lowest points. This is another example of the relation (discussed above) between a marginal and an average curve. The *ATC* curve, for example, slopes downward as long as the marginal cost curve is below it; it makes no difference whether the marginal cost curve is itself sloping upward or downward.

In Figure 12-2 the average variable cost curve reaches a minimum and then rises. With fixed factor prices, when average product per worker is a maximum, average variable cost is a minimum. [18] The common sense of this proposition is that each additional worker adds the same

[5] If you do not see where any of the numbers come from, review Table 12-1 and the definitions of cost just given.

amount to cost but a different amount to output, and when output per worker is rising, the cost per unit of output must be falling—and vice versa.

The hypothesis of eventually diminishing average productivity implies eventually increasing average variable costs.

Short-run *ATC* curves are often drawn U-shaped. This reflects the assumptions that (1) average productivity is increasing when output is low but (2) at some level of output average productivity begins to fall fast enough to cause average variable costs to increase faster than average fixed costs fall. When this happens, *ATC* increases.

The Definition of Capacity

The output that corresponds to the minimum short-run average total cost is often called by economists and business people the **capacity** of the firm. Capacity, in this sense, is not an upper limit on what can be produced. Instead it is the largest output that can be produced without encountering rising average costs per unit. In the example of Figure 12-2(ii) capacity output is q_c units, but higher outputs can be achieved, provided the firm is willing to accept the higher per-unit costs that accompany output "above capacity." A firm producing with **excess capacity** is producing at an output smaller than the point of minimum average total cost.

FIGURE 12–2
Total, Average, and Marginal Cost Curves

(i) Total cost curves

(ii) Marginal and average cost curves

TC, AC, and *MC* **curves often have the shapes shown here.** (i) Total fixed cost does not vary with output. Total variable cost and the total of all costs *(TC = TVC + TFC)* rise with output, first at a decreasing rate, then at an increasing rate. The total cost curves in (i) give rise to the average and marginal curves in (ii). *AFC* declines as output increases. *AVC* and *ATC* fall and then rise as output increases. *MC* does the same and intersects *ATC* and *AVC* at their minimum points. Capacity output is q_c, the minimum point on the *ATC* curve.

The technical definition gives the word "capacity" a meaning different from that in everyday speech, but the concept proves useful, and in any case it is widely used in economic and business discussions.

A Family of Short-run Cost Curves

A short-run cost curve shows how costs vary with output for a given quantity of the fixed factor—say a given size of plant.

There is a different short-run cost curve for each given quantity of the fixed factor.

A small plant for manufacturing nuts and bolts will have its own short-run cost curve. A medium-size plant and a very large plant will each have its own short-run cost curve. If a firm expands and replaces its small plant with a medium-size plant, it will move from one short-run cost curve to another. This change from one plant size to another is a long-run change. How short-run cost curves of plants of different size are related to each other is studied in the next chapter.

Summary

1. The firm's production decisions can be classified into three groups: (a) how best to employ existing plant and equipment (the short run); (b) what new plant and equipment and production processes to select, given the framework of known technical possibilities (the long run); and (c) what to do about encouraging, or merely adapting to, the invention of new techniques (the very long run).

2. The short run involves decisions in which one or more factors of production are fixed. The long run involves decisions in which all factors are variable, but in which technology is unchanged. In the very long run, technology can change.

3. The production function describes the ways in which different inputs may be combined to produce different quantities of output. Short-run and long-run situations can be interpreted as implying different kinds of constraints on the production function. In the short run, the firm is constrained to use no more than a given quantity of some fixed factor; in the long run, it is constrained only by the available techniques of production.

4. The theory of short-run cost behavior depends on the productivity of variable factors when applied to fixed factors. The concepts of total, average, and marginal product represent alternative ways of looking at the relation between output and the quantity of the variable factor of production.

5. The hypothesis, or "law," of eventually diminishing returns asserts that if increasing quantities of a variable factor are applied to a given quantity of fixed factors, the marginal and the average product of the variable factor will eventually decrease. This hypothesis leads directly to implications of rising marginal and average costs.

6. Given physical productivity schedules and the costs per unit of factors, it is a simple matter of arithmetic to develop the whole family of short-run cost curves.

7. Short-run average total cost curves are drawn as U-shaped to reflect the expectation that average productivity increases for small outputs but eventually declines sufficiently rapidly to offset advantages of spreading overheads. The output corresponding to the minimum point of a short-run average total cost curve is called the plant's capacity.

8. There is a whole family of short-run cost curves, one for each quantity of the fixed factor.

Topics for Review

Short run, long run, and very long run
Marginal and average productivity
The hypothesis of diminishing returns
The relation between marginal and average curves
The relation between productivity and cost

Marginal cost and average cost
Capacity and excess capacity

Discussion Questions

1. Is the short run the same number of months for increasing output as for decreasing it? Must the short run in industry A be the same length for all firms in the industry? Under what circumstances might the short run actually involve a longer time span than even the very long run?

2. How would the following factors increase or reduce the relative importance of short-run decisions for management?
   a. a guaranteed annual employment contract of at least 48 40-hour weeks of work for all employees.
   b. a major economic depression during which there is substantial unemployment of labor and in which equipment is being used at well below capacity levels of production
   c. a speeding up of delivery dates for new easy-to-install equipment

3. Indicate whether each of the following conforms to the hypothesis of diminishing returns; and, if so, whether it refers to marginal or average returns, or both.
   a. "The bigger they are, the harder they fall."
   b. As more and more of the population receive smallpox vaccinations, the reductions in the smallpox disease rate for each additional 100,000 vaccinations become smaller.

   c. For the seventh year in a row, the average depth of drilling required to hit oil in Texas increased.
   d. Five workers produce twice as much today as ten workers did 40 years ago.

4. Consider the education of a human being as a process of production. Regard years of schooling as one variable factor of production. What are the other factors? What factors are fixed? At what point would you expect diminishing productivity to set in? For an Einstein would it set in during his lifetime?

5. Suppose that each of the following news items is correct. Discuss each in terms of its effects on the level of average total cost.
   a. The U.S. Office of Education reports that the increasing level of education of our youth has led both to higher productivity and to increases in the general level of wages.
   b. During the winter of 1977 many factories were forced by fuel shortages to reduce production and to operate at levels of production far below capacity.
   c. For the third year in a row, the Post Office's production exceeded its capacity.
   d. NASA reports that the space program has led to development of electronic devices that have brought innovations to many industries.

6. "Because overhead costs are fixed, increasing production lowers costs. Thus small business is sure to be inefficient. This is a dilemma of modern society which values both smallness *and* efficiency." Discuss.

Production, Substitution, and Productivity Increases: Cost in the Long and Very Long Run

13

While an analysis of the short-run behavior of the firm is important to an understanding of how markets work to allocate resources, it neglects the major sources that have led to high and rising standards of living for much of the world's population. In this chapter we turn to the firm's long-run behavior, when it is free to vary all factors of production. Should the firm adopt a technique that uses a great deal of capital and only a small amount of labor? Or should it adopt a technique that uses less capital and more labor? What implications will these decisions have for the firm's costs?

In the second part of the chapter we examine the improvements in techniques and productivity that so dramatically increased output and incomes in the United States for more than 100 years but more recently have shown signs of a slowdown. The causes of the rapid growth and the present slowdown are subject to some debate; we shall discuss briefly what is known about them.

The Long Run: No Fixed Factors

The long run is a situation in which all factors can be varied. When this is the case, there are alternative ways of achieving the same total output, and it is necessary to choose among them. The long run is concerned with firms' planning how to design their plant and equipment for maximum profits.

The hypothesis of profit maximization provides a simple rule for doing this: Any firm that is trying to maximize its profits should select the method that produces its output at the lowest possible cost. This implication of the hypothesis of profit maximization is called the implication of **cost minimization.**

From the alternatives open to it, the firm chooses the least costly ways of achieving any specific output.

If there is a stable, required output rate, and if the costs of factors are known, that is all there is to it. In other words, the firm selects the economically efficient way of producing any level of output.

These long-run planning decisions are important because today's variable factors are tomorrow's fixed factors. A firm deciding on a new plant and the machinery to go into it will choose among many alternatives. But once installed, the new equipment is fixed for a long time. If the firm errs now, its survival may be threatened; if it estimates shrewdly and its rivals do not, it may reward both its owners and its foresighted managers with large profits and bonuses.

These decisions are among the most difficult and important the firm makes. They are difficult because the firm must anticipate what methods of production will be efficient not only today but in the years ahead, when costs of labor and raw materials may have changed. The decisions are difficult, too, because the firm must estimate how much output it will want to be producing. Is the industry of which it is a member growing or declining? Is it going to increase or decrease its share of the market? Will new products emerge to render its buggy whips less useful than an extrapolation of past sales suggests?

CONDITIONS FOR COST MINIMIZATION

What should the firm do to make its costs as low as possible? The firm does not have the least costly method of production if it is possible to substitute one factor for another so as to keep its output constant while reducing its total cost.

This idea can be stated more formally: The firm should substitute one factor (for example, capital) for another factor (for example, labor) as long as the marginal product of the one factor *per dollar expended on it* is greater than the marginal product of the other factor *per dollar expended on it*. The firm cannot have minimized its costs as long as these two magnitudes are unequal. Using K to represent capital, L labor, and p the price of a unit of the factor, the necessary condition of cost minimization may be stated:

$$\frac{MP_K}{p_K} = \frac{MP_L}{p_L} \qquad [1]$$

This equation is analogous to the condition for the utility-maximizing household, given on page 135, in which the household equated the marginal utility per dollar of two goods.[1]

To see why this equation needs to be satisfied if costs of production are really minimized, suppose that the left-hand side of [1] is equal to 10, showing that the last dollar spent on capital produced 10 units of output, while the right-hand side is equal to 4, showing that the last dollar spent on labor added only 4 units to output. In such a case, the firm, by using $2.50 less of labor, would reduce output by 10 units. But it could regain that lost output by spending $1 more on capital.[2] Making such a substitution of capital for labor would leave output unchanged and reduce cost by $1.50. Thus the original position was not the cost-minimizing one. Whenever the two sides of [1] are not equal, there are factor substitutions that will reduce costs.

By rearranging the terms in [1] we can look at the cost-minimizing condition a bit differently.

$$\frac{MP_K}{MP_L} = \frac{p_K}{p_L} \qquad [2]$$

The ratio of the marginal products on the left-

---

[1] In the appendix to this chapter the condition is given a graphic analysis similar to that given household behavior in the second half of Chapter 9.

[2] The argument in the previous two sentences assumes that the marginal products do not change when expenditure is changed by a few dollars.

hand side compares the contribution to output of the last unit of capital and the last unit of labor. If the ratio is 4, this means 1 unit more of capital will add 4 times as much to output as one unit more of labor. The right-hand side shows how the cost of 1 unit more of capital compares to the cost of 1 unit more of labor. If it is also 4, it does not pay the firm to substitute capital for labor or vice versa. But suppose the right-hand side is 2. Capital, although twice as expensive, is 4 times as productive. It will pay the firm to switch to a method of production that uses more capital and less labor. If, however, the right-hand side is 6 (or *any* number more than 4), it will pay to substitute labor for capital.

This formulation shows how the firm can adjust the elements over which it has control (the quantities of factors used, and thus the marginal products of the factors) to the prices or opportunity costs of the factors given to it by the market. A precisely analogous adjustment process is involved when households adjust their consumption of goods to the market prices of those goods (see page 135).

THE PRINCIPLE OF SUBSTITUTION

Suppose that a firm is producing where the cost-minimizing conditions shown in [1] or [2] are met but that the cost of labor increases while the cost of capital remains unchanged. As we have just seen, the least-cost method of producing any output will now use less labor and more capital than was required to produce the same output before the factor prices changed. The prediction called the **principle of substitution** follows from the assumption that firms try to minimize their costs.

Methods of production will change if the relative prices of factors change. Relatively more of the cheaper factor will be used and relatively less of the more expensive one.

This prediction plays a central role in the way the market system allocates resources because it relates to the way the individual firm will respond to changes in relative factor prices. Such changes in relative factor prices are caused by the changing relative scarcity of factors to the economy as a whole. The individual firm is thus motivated to use less of factors that have become scarcer to the economy.[3]

The Significance of the Principle of Substitution to the Economy as a Whole

The relative prices of factors of production will tend to reflect their relative scarcities. One country has a great deal of land and a small population. Here the price of land will be low while, because labor is in short supply, the wage rate will be high. Producers of agricultural goods will tend to make lavish use of the cheap land while economizing on expensive labor; thus a production process will be adopted that utilizes a low ratio of labor to land.

A second country is small in area and has a large population. Here the demand for land will be high relative to its supply, and land will be relatively expensive while labor will be relatively cheap. Firms producing agricultural goods will tend to economize on land by using a great deal of labor per unit of land; thus a productive process will be adopted that uses a high ratio of labor to land.

Similar decisions will be made with respect to the relative scarcity of any factor. If capital is scarce relative to other factors, it will be expensive; firms following their own self-interest will use it sparingly. If capital is plentiful relative to other factors, it will be cheap and firms will adopt production processes that make lavish use of capital.

Thus relative factor prices will reflect the relative scarcities (in relation to demand) of different factors of production: abundant factors will have prices that are low relative to the prices of factors that are scarce. Firms seeking their own

---

[3] A numerical example of the principle of substitution is shown on page 176. As labor became relatively more expensive, moving from Case I to Case III, the firm shifted from method A, using much labor, to method D, using less labor.

private profit will be led to use large amounts of the factors that are plentiful in the country and to economize on factors that are scarce.

Once again we see that the price system is an automatic control system. No single firm needs to be aware of national factor surpluses and scarcities. Prices determined in the competitive market tend to reflect them, and individual firms that never look beyond their own private profit are nonetheless led to economize on factors that are scarce to the nation as a whole. Thus the price system leads profit-maximizing firms to take account of the nation's relative factor scarcities when deciding which of the possible methods of production to adopt.

This discussion suggests why methods of producing the same commodity differ among countries. In the United States, where labor is highly skilled and very expensive, a steel company may use elaborate machinery to economize on labor. In China, where labor is abundant and capital scarce, a much less mechanized method of production is appropriate. The Western engineer who believes that the Chinese lag behind Westerners because they are using methods long dismissed in the West as inefficient may be missing the truth about economic efficiency in use of resources. The frequent suggestion that to aid underdeveloped countries we only have to export Western "know-how" is incomplete.

COST CURVES IN THE LONG RUN

There is a best (least-cost) method of producing each level of output when all factors are free to be varied. In general this method will not be the same for different levels of output. If factor prices are given, a minimum cost can be found for each possible level of output and, if this minimum achievable cost is expressed as an amount per unit of output, we can obtain the long-run average cost of producing each level of output. When this information is plotted on a graph, the result is called a **long-run average cost curve** (*LRAC*). Figure 13-1 shows such a curve.

This long-run average cost curve is determined by the technology of the industry (which is assumed to be fixed) and by the prices of the factors of production. It is a "boundary" in the sense that points below the curve are unattainable, points on the curve are attainable if sufficient time elapses for all factors to be adjusted, and points above the curve are also attainable. Indeed, points above the *LRAC* curve may represent the best that can be done in the short run when all factors are not freely variable.

The *LRAC* curve divides the cost levels that are attainable with known technology and given factor prices from those that are unattainable.

The Shape of the Long-run Average Cost Curve

The long-run average cost curve shown in Figure 13-1 falls at first and then rises. This curve is often described as U-shaped, although "saucer-shaped" might be more descriptive.

Decreasing costs. Over the range of output from zero to q_m the firm has falling long-run average costs. An expansion of output results in a reduction of costs per unit of output once enough time has elapsed to allow adjustments in the techniques of production. Since the prices of factors are assumed to be constant, the reason for the decline in costs per unit must be that output increases faster than inputs as the scale of the firm's production expands. Over this range of output the firm is often said to enjoy long-run **increasing returns.**[4] Increasing returns may arise as a result of increased opportunities for specialization of tasks made possible by the division of labor even with no substitution of one factor of production for another. Or they may arise because of factor substitution. Even the most casual observation of the differences in production

---

[4] Economists shift back and forth between speaking in physical terms (i.e., increasing *returns* to production) and cost terms (i.e., decreasing *costs* of production). Thus the same firm may be spoken of as having decreasing costs or enjoying increasing returns.

FIGURE 13–1

A Long-run Average Cost Curve

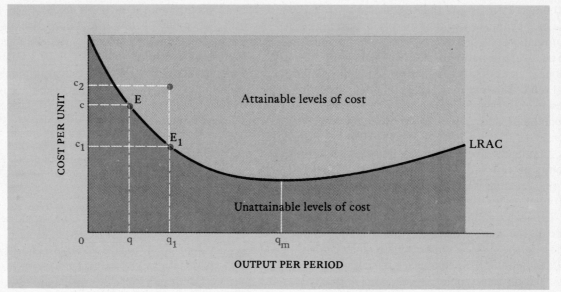

The long-run average cost curve provides a boundary between attainable and unattainable levels of cost. If the firm wishes to produce output q, the lowest attainable cost level is c per unit. Thus point E is on the LRAC curve. E_1 represents the least-cost method of producing q_1. Suppose a firm is producing at E and desires to increase output to q_1. In the short run it will not be able to vary all factors, and thus costs above c_1, say c_2, must be accepted. In the long run a plant optimal for output q_1 can be built and cost of c_1 can be attained. Output q_m is that at which the firm attains its lowest possible per unit cost of production for the given technology and factor prices.

technique used in large-size and small-size plants shows the differences in factor proportions. These differences arise because large, specialized equipment is useful only when the volume of output that the firm can sell justifies its employment.

For example, assembly line techniques, body-stamping machinery, and multiple-boring engine-block machines in automobile production are economically efficient only when individual operations are repeated thousands of times. Using elaborate harvesting equipment (which combines many individual tasks that would otherwise be done by hand and by tractor) provides the least-cost method of production on a big farm but not on a few acres.

Typically, as the level of planned output increases, capital is substituted for labor and complex machines for simpler machines. Automation is a contemporary example. Electronic devices can handle huge volumes of operations very quickly, but unless the level of production requires very large numbers of operations, it does not make sense to use automation.

Increasing costs. Over the range of outputs greater than q_m the firm encounters rising costs. An expansion in production, even after sufficient time has elapsed for all adjustments to be made, will be accompanied by a rise in average costs per unit of output. If costs per unit of input are constant, this rise in costs must be the result of an expansion in output less than in proportion to the expansion in inputs. Such a firm is said to suffer long-run **decreasing returns.**[5] Decreasing returns imply that the firm suffers some diseconomy of scale. As its scale of operations increases, diseconomies—of management or otherwise—are encountered that increase its per unit costs of production.

Lowest LRAC. At output q_m in Figure 13-1 the firm has reached its lowest possible long-run costs per unit of output. While every point on the *LRAC* is efficient in the sense that *that output* is not attainable at a lower cost per unit (given current technology and factor prices), the output q_m is efficient in a second sense: no other output can be produced at so low a cost. Under certain conditions, called those of perfect competition, each firm in equilibrium will produce at the minimum point on its *LRAC*. (See Chapter 14 and its appendix for a full discussion of this proposition.)

Constant returns. In Figure 13-1 the firm's long-run average costs fall to output q_m and rise thereafter. Another possibility should be noted: The firm's *LRAC* might have a flat portion over a range of output around q_m. With such a flat portion, the firm would be encountering constant costs over the relevant range of output. This would mean that the firm's average costs per unit of output were not changing as its output changed. Since factor prices are assumed to be fixed, this must mean that the firm's output is increasing exactly as fast as its inputs are increasing. Such a firm is said to be encountering **constant returns.**

THE RELATION BETWEEN LONG-RUN AND SHORT-RUN COSTS

The various short-run cost curves mentioned at the conclusion of Chapter 12 and the long-run

curve studied in this chapter are all derived from the same production function. Each assumes given prices for all factor inputs. In the long run, all factors can be varied; in the short run, some must remain fixed. The long-run average cost curve (*LRAC*) shows the lowest cost of producing any output when all factors are variable. The short-run average cost curve (*SRAC*) shows the lowest cost of producing any output when one or more factors is not free to vary.

The short-run cost curve cannot fall below the long-run curve because the *LRAC* curve represents the *lowest* attainable costs for every output. It might be the same curve if precisely the same-size plant was the best for any level of output. But that is not likely. The usual situation is that as the level of output is increased, a larger plant makes it possible to lower unit costs. Thus a larger plant is required to achieve the lowest attainable costs. This is shown in Figure 13-2.

FIGURE 13–2
Long-run and Short-run Average Cost Curves

The short-run average cost curve is tangent to the long-run curve at the output for which the quantity of the fixed factors is optimal. If output is varied around q units with plant and equipment fixed at the optimal level for producing q, costs will follow the short-run cost curve. While *SRAC* and *LRAC* are at the same level for output q, since the fixed plant is optimal for that level, for all other outputs there is too little or too much of the fixed factor and *SRAC* lies above *LRAC*. If some output other than q is to be sustained, costs can be reduced to the level of the long-run curve when sufficient time has elapsed to adjust all factor inputs.

---

[5] Long-run decreasing returns differ from the short-run diminishing returns that we encountered earlier. In the short run at least one factor is fixed and the law of diminishing returns ensures that returns to the variable factor will eventually diminish. In the long run all factors are variable and it is possible that physically diminishing returns would never be encountered—at least as long as it was genuinely possible to increase inputs of all factors.

Jacob Viner's Famous Error

The relationship of *SRAC* and *LRAC* is such that the short-run curve touches the long-run curve at one point and lies above it everywhere else. This leads to an important, though subtle, consequence. Two curves that are tangent at a point have the same slope at that point. If *LRAC* is decreasing where it is tangent to *SRAC*, then *SRAC* must also be decreasing. Thus, unless *LRAC* is horizontal at the point of tangency, it will not be tangent at the minimum point of *SRAC*.

The economic sense of the fact that tangency is *not* at the minimum points of *SRAC* rests on the subtle distinction between the most efficient way to utilize a given plant and the most efficient way to produce the amount of output required. It is the second point that interests us as economists. If bigger plants can achieve lower costs per unit, there will be a gain in building a bigger plant and underutilizing it whenever the gains from using the bigger plant are enough to offset the costs of being inefficient in the use of the plant. If there are some gains from building bigger plants (if *LRAC* is declining), there is always some underutilization that is justified.

The student who finds the relationship between *SRAC* and *LRAC* hard to understand may take some comfort from the fact that when these relations were first being worked out by economists, one of the world's leading economic theorists, the late Jacob Viner of Princeton University, instructed his draftsman to draw the *LRAC* through the minimum points of the *SRAC* but "so as never to lie above" the *SRAC*. He reports of his draftsman, "He is a mathematician, however, not an economist, and he saw some mathematical objection to this procedure which I could not succeed in understanding. I could not persuade him to disregard his scruples as a craftsman and to follow my instructions, absurd though they might be."

Viner's article was published in 1931. Since that time generations of students have experienced great satisfaction when they finally figured it out. Professor Viner's article, justly a famous one despite the error, was often reprinted, but he always rejected suggestions that he correct the error because he did not wish to deprive other students of the pleasure of feeling one-up on him.

We saw at the end of Chapter 12 that a *SRAC* curve such as that in Figure 13-2 is one of many such curves. Each curve shows how costs vary as output is varied from a base output, holding some factors fixed at the quantities most appropriate to the base output (see Figure 13-3). The long-run curve is sometimes called an **envelope curve** because it encloses the whole family of short-run curves. Each short-run cost curve is tangent to (touches) the long-run curve at the level of output for which the quantity of the fixed factor is optimal and lies above it for all other levels of output.

SHIFTS IN COST CURVES

The cost curves derived so far show how cost varies with output, given constant factor prices and fixed technology. Changes in either technological knowledge or factor prices will cause the entire family of short-run and long-run cost curves to shift. Loss of existing technological knowledge is rare, so technological change normally works in only one direction, to shift cost curves downward. Improved ways of making existing commodities will mean that lower cost methods of production become available. Tech-

FIGURE 13–3

The Envelope Relation Between the Long-Run Average Cost Curve and All the Short-Run Average Cost Curves

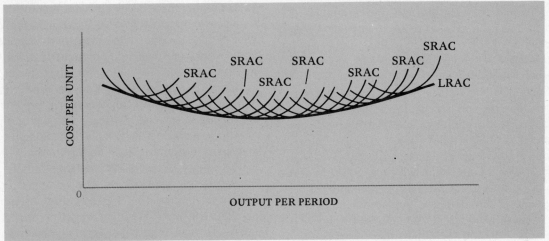

To every point on the long-run cost curve there is an associated short-run curve tangent at that point. Each short-run curve shows how costs vary if output varies, with the fixed factor held constant at the level that is optimal for the output at the point of tangency.

nological change is discussed in the next section of this chapter.

Factor price changes can exert an influence in either direction. If a firm has to pay more for any factor that it uses, the cost of producing each level of output will rise; if the firm has to pay less, costs will fall.

A rise in factor prices shifts the family of short-run and long-run cost curves upward. A fall in factor prices or a technological advance shifts the entire family of cost curves downward.

Although factor prices usually change gradually, they sometimes rise suddenly and drastically. This was the case in the seventies. One reason was the sharp general inflation that beset the American economy; a second reason was the sudden and dramatic increase in energy prices that was triggered by the rise in the price of oil following the formation of OPEC.

Oil prices quadrupled within a year and had increased tenfold by the end of the decade. The effect of this was to shift upward the cost curves of all users. The size of the shift varied from product to product, depending on how important particular inputs were to total production. Oil price increases had some effects on almost all industries, and they had a major effect on such industries as synthetic rubber, plastics, and airlines.

The Very Long Run: Progress and Productivity

Three sets of changes in the very long run tend to dominate the production function. All are related to technology, broadly defined. The first is the change in the techniques available for producing existing products. Over an average person's lifetime, these changes often can be dramatic. Seventy years ago roads and railways were built by gangs of workers using buckets, spades, and draft horses; today bulldozers, steam shovels, giant trucks, and other specialized equipment have completely banished the workhorse from construction sites and to a great extent have displaced the worker with his shovel. Indeed, the pace of general mechanization has been so fast that within the space of one lifetime, humanity's more than 4,000-year partnership with the horse in war and peace all but came to an end. About the same amount of coal is produced today as 50 years ago, but the number of coal miners is less than one-tenth of what it was then.

Second is the change in new goods and services that become available. Television, polio vaccine, nylon clothing, and many other consumer products of today did not exist two generations ago. Other products are so changed that their nominal connection with the "same" commodity produced in the past is meaningless. A 1981 Ford automobile is very different from a 1931 Ford. Modern jets such as the jumbo 747, the new 787, and the supersonic Concorde are each revolutionary compared with the DC-3, which itself barely resembled the *Spirit of St. Louis*. In their first year of operation, 100 Boeing 747s logged passenger miles that would have required a fleet of 23,000 DC-3s.

Third, improvements in such things as health and education improve the quality of labor services. Today's managers and workers are in better health and are better clothed and better housed than their counterparts in their grandparents' generation. On the average they are better educated. Even unskilled workers today tend to be literate and competent in arithmetic, and their managers are apt to be trained in modern scientific methods of business control.

These kinds of technological change have been vital features of the so-called developed (or industrialized) countries. Recently there has been evidence of a slowdown in the rate of technological change. To understand either the historical growth or the recent slowdown, it is necessary to understand the forces that affect technological change. Is it influenced significantly by the decisions of firms? Is it encouraged or discouraged significantly by government policies and external events? Answers to these questions are vital to an understanding of the long-run story of production and cost.

THE NATURE AND SIGNIFICANCE OF PRODUCTIVITY

In discussing these issues, it is not helpful simply to discuss the cost of a well-defined unit of a well-defined product. Measuring output and cost in a world of changing products is hard and involves a serious index number problem.[6] Economists utilize the notion of **productivity**, defined as a measure of output per unit of resource input, instead of simply the cost of a unit of output. This does not resolve the difficulties of measuring output, but it shifts the attention to society's ability to get more and better output out of the basic resources of the economy. One widely used measure of productivity is output per hour of labor.[7] Labor is taken as representative of the economy's basic resources because we are a society of people and we value our leisure. There is enough year-to-year stability in the nature of products produced that rates of increase in productivity year by year provide useful measures of progress caused by technical change.

Productivity increases are a potent force for increasing living standards. In the United States there is no doubt that over the last 100, 50, or even 20 years, the material standard of living of the typical American family has increased enormously. Indeed, our great-grandparents would have regarded today's standard of living in most industrialized countries as unattainable (if not incomprehensible).

Figure 13-4 shows the average increases in productivity in the United States over the recent past. The apparently modest rate of increase of output per hour of labor of 2 percent per year leads to a doubling of output per hour of labor every 35 years. Productivity in the United States increased at more than this rate in every decade of this century up to 1970. On average, since World War II productivity growth in the United

---

[6] See pages 29–33 for a discussion of index numbers.

[7] It is the measure we shall use. Other possible measures include output per worker and output per person.

The Recent Trend of Productivity Growth in the United States

The historical rate of growth of productivity of about 3 percent per year has declined sharply since 1967. Each bar shows the average annual rate of increase in output per hour worked for a five-year period. Until 1967 such productivity increases were usually between 2.5 and 3.5 percent. They fell to just over 2 percent from 1967 to 1972, and to 1.3 percent from 1972 to 1977. During the last two years of the decade productivity growth was virtually zero. (See the latest *Economic Report of the President* for more recent data.)

States has been nearly 3 percent per year, a rate that doubles output every 23 years.

In other countries the rate of growth has been higher. In Germany productivity increased at 5 percent per year, doubling output every 14 years, and in Japan it has increased at more than 9 percent per year—a rate that doubles output per hour of labor approximately every 8 years! In many countries, including the United States, productivity growth at a stable rate came to be taken for granted, to be expected. Productivity growth was not something to be worried about but to be counted on.

When productivity growth in the United States dropped sharply after 1972, it caused surprise

and some alarm. During 1978 and 1979 productivity did not increase appreciably, and that did nothing to alleviate fears that the days of substantial automatic increases in productivity were past.

Why do we care about productivity growth? If there is less productivity growth with the same level of employment, the rate of increase of real output declines. Combined with declining employment, it may actually contribute to declining output per person. Decreases in rates of productivity growth can also add to inflationary pressures. In recent decades Americans have come to expect to receive the gains in productivity in the form of wage and profit increases. If productivity increases at 4 percent per year, factor prices can increase 4 percent per year on average without leading to price increases. But the same factor price increases become inflationary once productivity growth falls below that level.

MAJOR SOURCES OF INCREASING PRODUCTIVITY

The decline in the historical rate of productivity growth has led to a good deal of research into the causes of productivity changes.

Productivity is defined as output per hour worked. Thus anything that increases output while keeping hours worked the same, or that decreases the hours required to attain the same output, increases productivity. Several major historical sources of productivity increase have been identified.

Energy Substitution

One principal means has been the increasing reliance on inanimate energy for production. Energy to plow fields, to turn machines, to move goods, to provide heat, and to transform natural resources is a major determinant of the productive power of an economy. In 1900 more than half of all energy requirements in the United States was supplied by human beings, horses, mules, and

FIGURE 13–5

The Production of Inanimate Energy, United States, 1900–1978

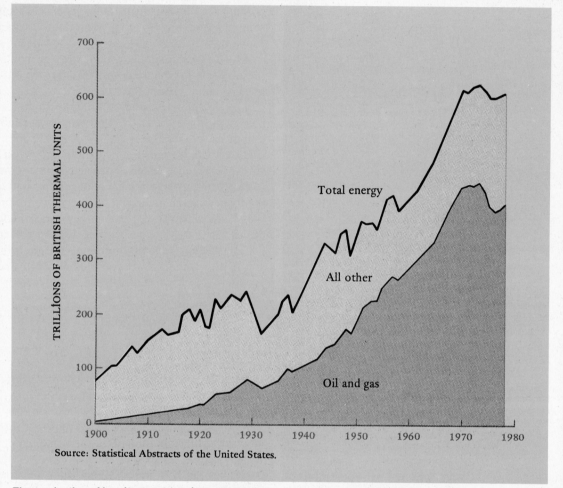

Source: Statistical Abstracts of the United States.

The production of inanimate energy has grown enormously in this century and has increasingly replaced animal and human power. The explosive growth in production of energy has occurred through the use of oil and gas. Whether the rising costs of oil and gas will lead to a permanent reversal of these trends is a major unknown of the next decades. Much of the answer depends on the development of technology with respect to nuclear and solar energy and the gasification of coal.

oxen. By 1980 animal and human power provided less than 10 percent of all energy; it has been increasingly replaced by such inanimate sources of power as coal, oil, gas, and water power. The overall growth in inanimate fuels is shown in Figure 13-5. Total energy from these fuels increased fivefold over the first seven dec-

ades of this century—an increase more than twice as large as the increase in population. This reflected the development of new methods for substituting relatively cheap energy for relatively expensive labor.

This source of the historical trend toward ever-increasing energy substitution cannot be expected to continue as energy becomes relatively scarce and therefore relatively more expensive. Just as falling energy costs led to rapidly rising productivity, rising energy costs may be expected to slow the productivity increase. Much of the future of energy substitution will depend on the effectiveness of policies designed to discover new and cheaper sources of fuel.

Substitution of Capital for Labor

A major means of increasing productivity has been the substitution of machinery and equipment for labor. In manufacturing, transportation, communications, and mining, the process of substitution of capital for labor is so obvious that we need only mention it. It has been large also in agriculture and in some services. This substitution can be measured by changes in the amount of capital per worker, which has steadily increased over the last 100 years and has been accompanied by increasing productivity.

Three motives for this substitution can be identified. The first is the rising price of labor relative to capital goods. The second is the development of new, improved (i.e., more productive) machines to replace older ones. The third is the opportunity provided by population growth, and by growth in demand, to utilize more capital to take advantage of economies of the larger scale that growth fosters.

As industrialization proceeds, the opportunities for the substitution of capital for labor naturally decline somewhat simply because there is less and less labor left to substitute for. At the extreme, once a process is fully automated, no further substitution is possible.

Improved Characteristics of Labor

While an "hour of work" is a readily measurable unit of human labor effort and is thus a convenient yardstick for measuring productivity, the things a human being can do in one hour vary greatly. One individual's contribution to the level of output in a single hour will depend on his or her health, education, and training. Over the last 100 years the level of these things in the population (and therefore in the work force) has steadily increased and has led to continuing increases in the productivity of labor. Because of their beneficial effects on production, expenditures on health, education, and training are sometimes spoken of as investments in human capital.

The effective use of an individual's labor skills requires that they be available in the right place at the right time. A skilled mechanic may be needed in Seattle, but if he or she is trapped by education, ill health, or poverty in Birmingham, neither the individual nor the national product will benefit. Education and health are now known to increase the adaptability and mobility of labor between jobs, occupations, and places— and thus to contribute indirectly as well as directly to rising productivity.

Other Sources of Productivity Increase

While the three sources just described have all been major contributors to productivity increases in virtually every industrializing society, there are dozens of other, individually smaller yet cumulatively large sources of increasing productivity. Let us name two.

One is the increase in the quality of many nonlabor inputs into production. For example, the kind and quality of metals has changed: steel replaces iron and aluminum substitutes for steel in a process of change that makes a statistical category such as "primary metals" seem unsatisfactory and obsolete. Even for a given category, such as "steel," today's product is lighter, stronger, and more flexible than the product manufactured only 15 years ago.

Another secondary source of productivity increases may be described as managerial. Better organization of production will in itself account for increases in productivity. New ideas raise efficiency when they are applied to new products or new processes. Imagination can design a more efficient assembly line with no change in the quantity, quality, or proportions of factors.

INVENTION

Invention is the discovery of something new, such as a new production technique or a new product. **Innovation** is the introduction of an invention into use. Invention is a necessary precondition to innovation.

Invention is cumulative; a useful invention is used, a useless one is discarded. Except where whole societies disappear, knowledge is seldom lost, and the state of technical knowledge improves or stays the same. For this reason, the cumulative impact of many small inventions may be fully as large as or larger than that of the occasional dramatic invention such as the steam engine, the cotton gin, or the sewing machine. Indeed, none of these famous inventions burst into full bloom as a result of a single act of creative inspiration; each depended on the contributions of prior inventors. The backlog of past inventions constitutes society's technical knowledge, and in turn it conditions innovation.

To understand innovation and productivity increases, then, we must first understand what creates the pool of inventions from which innovation will occur. While there are many motives that spur invention, there is no longer any doubt that major changes in the store of technical knowledge are the result of expenditures on research and development (R&D) by private firms, by the government, and by scholars and scientists in universities and other nonprofit and nongovernmental research institutions.

Money can buy invention. In the United States in 1980, about $50 billion was devoted to R&D expenditures, of which roughly 40 percent was expended by the federal government, 40 percent in private industry, and the rest in universities and other places. Among the corporate research centers are such giants as AT&T's Bell Labs (with 17,000 employees) and the research centers of IBM and General Electric in New York and Texas Instruments in Texas. Most major industrial companies have research and development centers or divisions, and hundreds of small, private R&D firms do contract research.

Approximately 2 percent of the gross business revenue from sales in 1979 went to R&D; in some years the figure has been over 3 percent.

R&D by businesses is sometimes very applied (to develop a new carburetor, for example), but company-financed basic research has led to major breakthroughs. The transistor and the silicon chip, for example, are revolutionizing data processing, communications, and many other fields. The results of federal government research efforts were most visible in the crash programs that led to the atomic bomb in World War II and the exploration of space in the 1960s. Out of those efforts have come a host of products and processes that have proven useful in the production of goods and services for consumption and have led to productivity increases. And government R&D efforts did not end with the moon landing. At the Lawrence Livermore Laboratory at the University of California, basic laser research is now under way, financed by the Department of Energy. Solar energy is another new area of expanded federal research. Scientific and medical R&D efforts in the universities and in hospitals, often financed by private foundations or public appeals for funds, have transformed the world we live in.

Because R&D expenditures increase the potential for technological innovation, decreases in relative spending for R&D may be expected to have a dampening effect on productivity growth. When R&D expenditure declines as sharply as it did—from about 3 percent of GNP in the 1960s to about 2 percent in the 1970s—it tends to shift the emphasis to more immediate, less "basic" research. This may lead to greater benefits in the short run, but it will result in fewer breakthroughs.

Another shift alleged to contribute to declines in productivity growth has been the deflection of many corporate R&D dollars from "offensive" attempts to increase output and reduce cost to "defensive" changes such as meeting newly imposed government requirements for reduced pollution and increased safety. If "cleaner air" does not count as national output, productivity does not increase when cleaner air is produced.

Some critics of programs to encourage more R&D expenditures have argued that the important kinds of invention, the kinds that really affect productivity, would occur with or without such expenditures. Much of what is called R&D, they say, is merely cosmetic — designed to sell the "new improved" brand of soap, cereal, or clothing — rather than material change. A great deal of evidence now contradicts this view and shows that productivity growth is to a significant degree a response to expenditures on R&D. Those countries (particularly Germany and Japan) that have stepped up their R&D expenditures have experienced much higher levels of productivity growth than have countries (the United States, Canada, and the United Kingdom) that have let such expenditures lag. Similarly, industries that are major R&D spenders (chemicals, electrical equipment, air transport) have maintained productivity growth much better than others that engage in very little R&D (steel, leather, construction). Of course some sectors that do little R&D, such as coal mining and farming, may buy their equipment from industries that do a great deal, and thus they achieve gains in productivity. Such an industry is buying R&D in the price it pays for its equipment.

INCENTIVES AND DISINCENTIVES FOR INNOVATION

Innovation requires both the availability of technical knowledge and its introduction into use. New methods, machines, materials, and products are introduced not "because they are there" but because (and when) it appears *profitable* to introduce them. Productivity growth may decline because the profit incentives to innovate are weak or nonexistent. Profit incentives in turn are affected by many aspects of the economic climate. Many contemporary scholars see changes in the latter as the main reason for the lagging productivity growth of the U.S. economy.

The Growth Rate of the Economy

The opportunities for the profitable introduction of innovations are much greater in a growing economy than in a stagnant one. New machines and new methods are more easily introduced when new needs arise because the extra demand must be met by additional machines rather than by the continued use of existing but less advanced machines that may still have productive life. The durability of existing equipment slows innovation in an industry that is not growing. An electric utility faced with an increase in demand will introduce the latest kind of steam turbine generator and use it alongside older vintages of turbine generators until they wear out. A utility that is not growing will postpone its modernization, perhaps for decades. A growing industry often has profitable opportunities for investment in additional machines as well as machines geared to larger scale of output. It may also have incentives to introduce new products. Every time it seeks new investment it is likely to look at the latest, most modern technology available. The introduction of that technology leads to productivity increases.

A growing economy can also adapt more easily to the changing skills requirements of its labor force. It is often as hard to retrain existing workers as it is to retool existing machines; it is relatively easy to educate and train new entrants into the labor force with the new skills they will need. Moreover, the presence of job and promotion opportunities in new occupations where there is no long seniority problem to overcome tends to motivate young people preparing for entry into the labor force to acquire the requisite skills.

One of the sources of the slowdown of productivity growth in the United States in the 1970s was the slowdown in the rate of growth of output of the economy. That slowdown was in good part a deliberate reponse by government, which sought to restrain the inflationary pressures of the 1970s by reducing total demand. As a result fewer industries and firms were expanding and less investment was taking place. When investment is not rapid, the capital stock is neither growing nor improving very rapidly.

When investment fell during the 1970s, not only did productivity growth slow on that account, but the number of new job opportunities also fell, and this had a secondary dampening effect on productivity.

Stagnation in growth of output leads to less investment, less innovation, fewer jobs, and fewer incentives to acquire special skills. Thus it tends to retard productivity increases.

The Level of Capacity Utilization

There are several reasons why an economy with substantial economic slack (in capacity utilization or in labor utilization) may find its productivity growth slowing. One of the most important is that in such a period new investment is likely to fall sharply as expansion is postponed. Firms with excess capacity not only delay expansion, they postpone replacing existing equipment as it wears out. Since new investment is a main source of introducing innovations, the postponement of investment is directly harmful to productivity growth.

Second, bottlenecks in production are infrequent when there is general slack in the economy. Bottlenecks trigger both the substitution of one input for another and the invention of substitutes for scarce items. With excess capacity, firms' activities are likely to shift to attempts to increase demand rather than to reduce costs.

The failure of the U.S. economy to achieve anything like full utilization of its capacity during the period 1973–1980 added a cyclical damper to productivity growth that accentuated the effects of the slowdown in economic growth.

Shifts in Demand and the Composition of Output

Industries, and sectors of the economy, differ greatly from one another in what is called their technological base, that is, in their opportunities for increasing productivity. It is much harder for social workers to increase their output (cases handled per year) than it is for airline pilots to increase their output (passenger miles flown per year). This has nothing to do with the skill or the dedication of the social worker and the pilot; it concerns the nature of their tasks and the tools at their disposal. The bigger, faster plane that increases the pilot's productivity has no counterpart for the social worker.

The overall productivity level of the economy is the weighted average of the level of productivity of its sectors. If production shifts from high productivity sectors to low productivity sectors, aggregate productivity falls even though the level of productivity in each individual sector remains unchanged. The same is true of growth in productivity. Suppose, for example, there are only two sectors. In "manufacturing" productivity grows at 5 percent per year; in "services" productivity grows by 1 percent per year. If each sector produces one-half of total output, total productivity growth will be 3 percent per year. But if services becomes 75 percent of the total and manufacturing 25 percent, the aggregate productivity increase will fall to 2 percent.[8]

In the early stages of industrial development, factors of production tend to be shifting from sectors where productivity is both low and only slowly increasing (such as subsistence agriculture) to sectors where it is higher and more rapidly growing. This leads to sharp rises in productivity levels and rates of productivity growth. As economies become more fully industrialized, one kind of slowdown is that the opportunities for shifting resources out of low productivity sectors decrease: the smaller the sectors become, the less possible is further shrinkage.

A second kind of shift also occurs because the nature of goods and services that the population wants may change. Many commodities with high income elasticities of demand have relatively low

---

[8] In the first case productivity growth is $\frac{1}{2} \times 5 + \frac{1}{2} \times 1 = 3$ percent. In the second case productivity growth is $\frac{1}{4} \times 5 + \frac{3}{4} \times 1 = 2$ percent.

A Conservative's View of the Difficulty of Innovation

TAKING A PRODUCT FROM LAB TO MARKET

It takes more than ingenuity to produce a technological innovation. Unforeseen delays occur, and R&D costs often rise. No two histories are the same, but this hypothetical scenario shows what can happen as a company tries to bring an idea from lab to market.

. . . Scientist I. M. Genius of Chemtrust Industries comes up with a formula for an additive that will increase gasoline mileage by 75 percent. He and his boss decide to ask top management for a financial commitment to develop the product.

. . . After viewing the scientist's demonstrations of how the additive works, Chemtrust chairman Balthazar Bottomline recommends that development proceed. His board earmarks $1 million for research and development—and demands results within two years so Chemtrust can beat potential competitors.

. . . Eighteen months later, Chemtrust researchers learn that a Japanese company is working on a similar project. They quickly file a patent, even though they are not sure whether X-7 is commercially feasible.

. . . Chemtrust notifies several federal regulators, including Ralph Riskless of the Environmental Protection Agency, that it is working on the new product and submits its test data.

. . . By now delays and inflation have ratcheted up the cost of R&D to $3 million. EPA's Riskless demands further testing to make sure that the new chemical is not environmentally harmful. That in turn requires two more years and another $2 million in R&D.

. . . Chemtrust commits $20 million to a new plant, promising that the new product will be on the market in two years. But the community chosen as the plant site balks. Litigation pushes the construction cost to $30 million before approval is granted.

. . . No sooner is ground broken, however, than local construction workers walk off the job for six months. It takes three years to finish the new plant —at a total cost of $35 million. Meanwhile, the company has spent $10 million to train employees to make the new product and to launch an ambitious advertising campaign.

. . . Nearly a decade and $50 million later, X-7 hits the market. But so does the additive from Japan. Because it has been partly underwritten by its government, the Japanese product undercuts Chemtrust's price.

productivity and a low technological base. This is true, for example, of services designed to provide amenities of various kinds, including civic services such as garbage collection, parks, police protection, and libraries. Demands for medical and hospital care increase relative to demands for copper, manufactured goods, and transportation. Similarly, such things as clean air and safer consumer products may be desired even though they add to the costs of the goods produced.

There is little doubt that some of the decrease in productivity growth in the United States in the 1970s reflected these kinds of shifts in the demands for various goods.

The Institutional Climate

The profits from innovation depend largely on such things as the tax laws and regulatory requirements. If innovators are allowed to reap large gains from successful innovations, they will be more likely to take the risks of innovation. Innovation can be encouraged by investment credits, patent laws, low tax rates, government subsidies, and government-assisted R&D. It can be discouraged by regulatory burdens involving environmental impact statements, safety regulation, and the hassles and delays involved in meeting government requirements. The antitrust laws restrict what firms can do, and many regulatory commissions limit entry into fields in which an innovative firm might see profit opportunities.

A different aspect of the institutional climate is the ability and desire of the members of a relatively rich country to protect individuals and firms from the harsh forces of economic competition. The rigors of the marketplace may compel improving productivity because it is essential to survival; protecting people may remove the incentives. Foreign competition that threatens domestic firms may spur them to adopt more efficient techniques; restrictions on that competition may remove the need and the incentive for such innovations. Similarly, the protection of unemployed labor by various welfare schemes, while ameliorating the distress of workers, decreases their geographic and occupational mobility.

Many believe that the institutional climate in the United States has become increasingly hostile to private innovation in recent decades and that high taxes, government regulation, and economic protection have all added to the forces that inhibit innovation and growth.

HOW MUCH PRODUCTIVITY GROWTH DO WE WANT?

Decreases in cost levels that are possible by choosing among known techniques and among alternative levels of output are limited in scope. We can never do better than a 100 percent utilization of what is currently known. Yet improvements by invention are potentially limitless. For this reason, the long-term struggle to

get more from the world's limited resources is critically linked to discovery.

Economics used to be known as the dismal science because some of its predictions were dismal. The classical economists' basic prediction about the long run was that world population would continue to expand and the pressure of more and more persons on the world's limited resources would cause a decline in output per person. Human history would be one of more and more people living less and less well, with the surplus of persons that could not be supported at all dying off in plague, famine, and pestilence. This prediction has been dramatically correct in some of the countries now called underdeveloped. It has, however, been wrong for the industrial countries for several reasons. First, because of voluntary restriction on population growth, the population did not expand as rapidly as was foreseen by economists writing before the wide availability of birth control techniques. Second, pure knowledge and its applied techniques have expanded so rapidly during the last 150 years that our ability to squeeze more out of limited resources has expanded faster than the population has expanded.

Even in the industrial nations the race between consumption and production is a close one, and if the rate at which the frontiers of knowledge are being expanded should again fall below the rate of population increase, economics may once again become a dismal science.

Undesired Restraints

Some of the sources of decreasing rates of productivity growth are plainly undesired. These include a sluggish economy and the failure of firms and households to fully adapt to higher energy prices.

Government policies (considered in full in the macroeconomic half of this book) are designed to avoid economic slack and to stimulate innovation. Similarly, energy policies may reduce the impact of the oil price increases.

Quite apart from government actions, the market mechanism, if allowed to work, will tend to lessen the force of these inhibitions to growth in productivity. Consider, for example, the slowdown in growth of productivity due to increases in oil prices. One may expect the higher price of oil and the products that use it to have several effects that mitigate the energy shortage. One effect is to stimulate the search for new methods of finding oil. A second is to lead people to economize on oil consumption by discovering oil-saving techniques. A third is to encourage the development of new sources of fuel that will substitute for oil. The most publicized alternatives are nuclear and solar energy. But inventors also consider what others regard as fanciful. Two companies in the Southwest have already signed agreements to provide 1.2 billion cubic feet of "bio-gas" made from cow manure. Its proponents claim that it is in every way as good as natural gas and that it could supply up to 15 percent of total American energy requirements if we utilized all the available cow manure.

It is worth noticing that these adaptations *will result from* the price rise. There are those who urge the government to hold down the price of oil during this period of shortage for political reasons or to save households and firms from the hardships that a rising price of oil imposes on them. But such a policy, if it occurs, will inhibit the long-run process that promises to free us from such a heavy dependence on foreign oil.

Desired Restraints on Productivity?

Other aspects of the slowdown in productivity growth may not be remedied—not because we do not understand them, but because they are the by-products of desired changes. The shift to production of commodities with high income elasticities but low productivity levels is the most obvious example. The population evidently does not want more goods if it means less police protection, or more food at the cost of less recreation even though such shifts would increase productivity growth.

Growth in productivity has often been accompanied by increased pollution and more industrial accidents. Whether cleaner air and more safety are demanded by the public or are instead part of the bureaucratic burden imposed on an unwilling populace is a matter of debate. To many in the business community, big government is guilty of slowing productivity growth by its policies.

Mobil Oil chairman Rawleigh Warner, Jr., has said, "Our government has adopted a gratuitously hostile attitude. Industry has been compelled to spend more and more of its research dollars to comply with environmental, health and safety regulations—and to move away from longer-term efforts aimed at major scientific advance." To others, such efforts are desirable. They argue that a cleaner environment, safer working conditions and products, and better health are also forms of output—output that people have indicated they prefer to faster cars and more lethal pesticides.

"Progress," as measured by productivity growth, is thus no longer an unquestioned overriding goal of society. Progress has come to mean growth, and growth has long meant industrialization. Applied to the economy as a whole, industrialization and its accompanying changes in productivity clearly have vastly increased our material well-being and permitted more and more people to escape the ravages of hunger and the relentless struggle to subsist.

But nothing is without its cost, and in the case of growth this is increasingly being recognized. The gasoline engine, the steel mill, the jet airplane, DDT, plastics, and the skyscraper with its hundreds of thousands of electric lights are the artifacts of our progress over the last century. Have they lowered the quality of life, while raising the standard of living?

Just as humankind can benefit (at some stage in its development) from more production of luxuries and less of basic necessities, so too may it benefit from more amenities and lower productivity growth. To the extent that it can, a slower rate of productivity growth may reflect a better life, not a worsening one.

Summary

1. There are no fixed factors in the long run. The profit-maximizing firm chooses, from the alternatives open to it, the least costly way of achieving any specific output. A long-run cost curve represents the boundary between attainable and unattainable levels of cost for the given technology.

2. The principle of substitution says that efficient production will substitute cheaper factors for more expensive ones. If the relative prices of factors change, relatively more of cheaper factors and relatively less of more expensive ones will be used. An alternative development of production in the long run, using isoquants, appears in the appendix to this chapter.

3. The shape of the long-run cost curve depends on the relationship of inputs to outputs as the whole scale of a firm's operations changes. Increasing, constant, and decreasing returns lead to decreasing, constant, and increasing long-run average costs.

4. The relation between long-run and short-run cost curves is shown in Figures 13-2 and 13-3. Every "long-run" cost corresponds to *some* quantity of each factor and is thus on some short-run cost curve. The short-run cost curve shows how costs vary when that particular quantity of a fixed factor is used to produce outputs greater than or less than those for which it is optimal.

5. Cost curves shift upward or downward in response to changes in the prices of factors or the introduction of changed technology. Increases in factor prices shift the cost curves upward. Decreases in factor prices or technological advances that make it possible to produce the same amount of output with lower quantities of all inputs shift cost curves downward.

6. Over extended periods, the most important influence on costs of production and the standard of living has been the increases in output made possible by new technology and reflected in increasing productivity. The relatively modest rate of productivity increase of 3 percent per year leads to a doubling of output per labor hour every 23 years.

7. Major sources of productivity growth in industrializing countries have been the increased use of inanimate energy, the substitution of capital for labor, improved health, the education and training of labor, improved materials, and better organization of production.

8. Behind improvements in productivity lie invention and innovation. Invention—the discovery of new methods—occurs in many ways, but research and development expenditures play a major role. Changes in the level and type of R&D can be traced in an economy's productivity record.

9. Innovation requires invention and also profitable opportunities for the introduction of available knowledge. The economic climate (its growth and its level of capacity utilization), the institutional climate, and the differences in technological possibilities in sectors where demand is growing and declining all affect the opportunities for innovation.

10. The slowdown in productivity growth in the United States during the 1970s, with its consequent reduction in the average growth rate of living standards, has been due to a combination of circumstances: lower growth in national output, economic slack, increased regulatory burdens, and a shift in demand from high productivity to lower productivity activities.

11. Not all of the slowdown in measured productivity growth represents a worsening of the quality of life. Material progress leads both to more goods and services per person and to opportunities for better living. Yet progress of this kind is not an unmixed blessing; pollution of the environment accompanies growth, and an increased number of injuries and accidents occur. Whether the current level of government regulation of health and safety has gone too far is an issue highly debated today.

Topics for Review

The implication of cost minimization
The interpretation of $MP_K/MP_L = p_K/p_L$
The principle of substitution
Increasing, decreasing, and constant returns
The envelope curve
The distinction between production and productivity
The level of productivity and the rate of growth of productivity
Sources of increasing productivity
Invention and innovation
Research and development (R&D)
Determinants of innovation

Discussion Questions

1. Why does the profit-maximizing firm choose the least costly way of producing any given output? Might a nonprofit-maximizing organization such as a university or a church or a government intentionally choose a method of production other than the least costly one? Might an ordinary business corporation do so intentionally?

2. In Dacca, Bangladesh, where gasoline costs $3 a gallon and labor is typically paid less than 20¢ an hour, Abdul Khan pedals a bicycle-ricksha (pedicab) for his living. It's exhausting work that is coming under increasing attack by those who feel it is an inhumane practice. "We really want to get rid of them and move to motorized taxis, but I'm afraid it will take a long, long time," says the Bangladesh information officer. Ricksha drivers earn $2 a day, which is more than a skilled worker gets in Dacca. Explain the use of pedicabs in Dacca but not in New York or Tokyo. Comment on the information officer's statement.

3. Use the principle of substitution to predict the effect of each of the following:
   a. During the 1960s salaries of professors rose much more rapidly than those of teaching assistants. During the 1970s salaries of teaching assistants rose more than those of professors.
   b. The cost of land in big cities increases more than the cost of high-rise construction.
   c. Gold leaf is produced by pounding gold with a hammer. The thinner it is, the more valuable. The price of gold is set on a world market, but the price of labor varies among countries. Gold leaf is thinner in some countries than in others.
   d. OPEC keeps oil prices increasing faster than prices of most other raw materials.
   e. Wages of textile workers and shoe machinery operators rise more in New England than in South Carolina.

4. The long-run average cost curve can be thought of as consisting of points from each of a number of short-run average cost curves. Explain in what sense any point on the long-run curve is also on some short-run curve. What is the meaning of a move from one point on a long-run cost curve to another point on the same curve? Contrast this with a movement along a short-run curve.

5. The director of federal energy programs urged the American people to make necessary "long-run adjustments to the energy shortage by reducing energy input per unit of output." How exactly might this be done? Is this use of "long-run" the economists' use of that concept?

6. Israel, a small country, imports the "insides" of its automobiles but manufactures the bodies. If this makes economic sense, what does it tell us about cost conditions of automobile manufacture?

7. Name five important modern products that were not available when you were in grade school. Make a list of major products that you think have increased their sales at least tenfold in the last 30 years. Check your judgment by consulting the *Statistical Abstract of the United States, Business Statistics* (biennial of the U.S. Department of Commerce) or similar sources. Consider to what extent the growth in each series may reflect product or process innovation.

8. By 1980 thousands of firms had switched from an eight-hour day, five-day week, to a four-day week, with each day ten hours long. Output per week appears to have increased significantly. Is this an increase in productivity? Is it an innovation? Would you predict that this success will lead to a general substitution of the four-day week for the five-day week wherever the latter is now standard?

9. What do you believe to have been the primary spur for each of the following inventions and innovations: color television, the cotton gin, nuclear power, peni-

cillin, the assembly line, radar, the smashing of the atom, the nuclear bomb, the Frisbee, synthetic rubber, polio vaccine, the airplane, motion pictures, and the wheel? Are any of these attributable to more than one source?

10. Each of the following is a means of increasing productivity. Discuss which groups within the society might oppose each one.

a. A labor-saving invention that permits all goods to be manufactured with less labor than before.
b. A rapidly increasing growth of population in the economy.
c. Removal of all government production safety rules.
d. A reduction in corporate income taxes.
e. Discovery of a new, cheap substitute for oil.

Part Five

Markets and Pricing

Pricing in Competitive Markets

14

Is Goodyear in competition with Goodrich? Does Macy's compete with Gimbels? Is the farmer from Wheatland, Iowa, in competition with a wheat farmer from North Platte, Nebraska? In the ordinary meaning of the noun "competition" and the verb "compete," the answers to the first two of these questions are plainly yes, and the answer to the third question is probably no.

Goodyear and Goodrich both advertise extensively to persuade tire buyers to buy *their* product. Goodrich has even been known to confuse the issue: "See that blimp up there? It's theirs, not ours. If you want Goodrich tires you'll just have to remember Goodrich." Everyone knows that Macy's and Gimbels watch each other like hawks and that swarms of comparison shoppers check their respective prices and qualities every day. But there is nothing that the Iowa farmer can do that will affect the sales or the profits of the Nebraska farmer.

Firm Behavior and Market Structure

To sort out the questions of who is competing with whom and in what sense do they compete, it is necessary to distinguish between the behavior of individual firms and the type of market in which the firms operate. Economists use the term *market structure* to refer to the latter concept. The concept of competitive behavior is quite distinct from the concept of competitive market structure. The degree of *competitive behavior* refers to the degree to which individual firms actively compete with one another. The degree of *competitiveness of the market structure* refers to the extent to which individual firms have power over that market—power to influence the price or other terms on which their product is sold. In everyday use "competition" usually refers only to competitive behavior; economists, however, are interested both in the behavior of individual firms and in market structures.

Goodrich and Goodyear certainly engage in competitive (i.e., rivalrous) behavior. It is also true that both individually and together they have some power over the market. Either firm could raise its prices and still continue to sell tires; each has the power to decide—within limits set by buyers' tastes and the prices of competing tires—what price consumers will pay for its own product.

The Iowa and the Nebraska wheat farmers do not engage in active competitive behavior with each other. They operate, however, in a market over which they have no power. Neither has significant power to change the market price for its wheat by altering its behavior.

At one extreme of competitive market structures, economists use a theory in which no single firm has any market power. There are so many firms that each must accept the price set by the forces of market demand and supply. In this theory of the perfectly competitive market structure there is no need for individual firms to behave competitively with respect to one another since none has any power over the market. One firm's ability to sell its product is uninfluenced by the behavior of any other firm. The apparent paradox that interfirm competition does not occur in perfectly competitive markets is resolved when we recognize the distinction between interfirm competitive *behavior* and the competitive *structure* of the market in which the firm operates.

The theory of the perfectly competitive market

structure applies directly to a number of real-world markets. It also provides a benchmark for comparison with other market structures in which there are so few firms that each has some significant market power.

THE SIGNIFICANCE OF MARKET STRUCTURE

Although market demand curves and cost curves of individual firms are the basic elements of the theory of product pricing, they are not themselves sufficient to provide a theory of price. Hypotheses are needed that tell how these elements interact and finally come together in the market. At the outset we need to define two basic concepts, the market and the industry.

From the point of view of a household, the **market** consists of those firms from which it can buy a well-defined product; from the point of view of a firm, the market consists of those buyers to whom it can sell a well-defined product. A group of firms that sells a well-defined product, or closely related set of products, is said to constitute an **industry.** The market demand curve is the demand curve for an industry's product. An industry may sell in many different markets.

Consider a firm that produces a specific product for sale in a particular market and competes for customers with other firms in the same industry. If a profit-maximizing firm knows precisely the demand curve it faces, it knows the price it could charge for each rate of sales and thus knows its potential revenues. If it also knows its costs, the firm can readily discover the profits that would be associated with any rate of output and can choose the rate that maximizes its profits. But what if the firm knows its costs and only the *market* demand curve for its product? It does not know what its own sales would be. In other words, the firm does not know its *own* demand curve. In order to determine what fraction of the total market demand will be met by other sellers, it needs to know how other firms will respond to its change in price. If it reduces its price by 10 percent, will other sellers leave their prices unchanged or will they also reduce them? If they reduce their prices, will they do so by less than 10 percent, by exactly 10 percent, or by more than 10 percent? Obviously, each possible outcome will have a different effect on the firm's sales and thus on its revenues and profits.

The answers to questions about the relation of a firm's demand curve to the market demand curve depend on such variables as the number of sellers in the market and the similarity of their products. These are aspects of **market structure,** which is defined as the characteristics of market organization that are likely to affect a firm's behavior and performance.

For example, if there are only two large firms in an industry, each may be expected to meet most price cuts that the other makes; but if there are 5,000 small firms, a price cut by one may go unmatched. If two firms are producing identical products, they may be expected to behave differently with respect to each other than if they were producing similar but not identical products.

The central hypothesis of industrial organization economics is that firm behavior will be affected by market structure.

There are many other aspects of market structure that may affect firm behavior, such as the ease of entering the industry, the nature and size of the purchasers of the firm's products, and the firm's ability to influence demand by advertising. To reduce these aspects to manageable proportions, economists have focused on a few theoretical market structures that they believe represent a high proportion of the cases actually encountered in market societies. In this chapter and the next two, we shall look at four market structures: perfect competition, monopoly, monopolistic competition, and oligopoly.

Before considering any of these market structures, it is useful to deal with the rules of behavior common to all firms that seek to maximize their profits.

BEHAVIORAL RULES FOR THE PROFIT-MAXIMIZING FIRM[1]

A firm should produce only if it will do better than it could by not producing. The firm always has the option of producing nothing. If it produces nothing, it will have an operating loss equal to its fixed costs. If it decides to produce, it will add the variable cost of production to its fixed costs and the receipts from the sale of its products to its revenue. If revenue exceeds variable cost, it will pay the firm to produce; if revenue is less than variable cost, the firm will actually lose less by not producing than by producing. This leads to the first rule for profit maximizing:

Rule 1. A firm should not produce at all if the average revenue from its product does not equal or exceed its average variable costs. [19]

If a firm decides that, according to rule 1, production is worth undertaking, it must decide how much to produce. Common sense dictates that on a unit-by-unit basis, if any unit of production adds more to revenue than it does to cost, that unit will increase profits; if it adds more to cost than to revenue, it will decrease profits. If the firm is in a position where a further unit of production will increase profits, it should expand output; if it is in a position where the last unit of production decreased profits, it should contract output. The notion of the change in cost brought about by an additional unit is, of course, marginal cost (MC). A parallel concept, **marginal revenue** (MR), may be defined as the change in total revenue resulting from the sale of one additional unit.

A second rule may now be stated formally:

Rule 2. Assuming that it pays the firm to produce at all, it will be profitable for the firm to expand output whenever marginal revenue is greater than marginal cost; expansion should thus continue until marginal revenue equals marginal cost. [20]

[1] Formal proofs of the propositions discussed in the text are given in the Mathematical Notes.

These two rules can be restated as three necessary conditions for a firm to be maximizing its profits. It must be producing an output where (a) price is at least as great as average variable cost, (b) marginal revenue equals marginal cost, and (c) the marginal cost curve cuts the marginal revenue curve from below.[2] [21]

These rules apply to all profit-maximizing firms whatever the market structure in which they operate. The rules refer to the firm's costs and its revenues. Before we can apply the rules we need to consider particular market structures in order to provide links between the demand curve for an industry's product and the demand curves—and thus the revenue curves—facing individual firms.

The Elements of the Theory of Perfect Competition

THE ASSUMPTIONS OF PERFECT COMPETITION

The theory of **perfect competition** is built on two critical assumptions, one about the behavior of the individual firm and one about the nature of the industry in which it operates.

The *firm* is assumed to be a **price taker;** that is, the firm is assumed to act as though it can alter its rate of production and sales within any feasible range without such action having a significant effect on the price of the product it sells. Thus the firm must passively accept whatever price happens to be ruling on the market.

The *industry* is characterized by **freedom of entry and exit;** that is, any new firm is free to set up production if it so wishes, and any existing firm is free to cease production and leave the industry. Existing firms cannot bar the entry of new firms, and there are no legal prohibitions on entry or exit.

The ultimate test of the theory based on these assumptions will be the usefulness of its predictions, but because students are often bothered by the first assumption, it is worth examining whether it is in any way reasonable. To see what is involved in the assumption of price taking, contrast the demands for the products of an automobile manufacturer and a wheat farmer.

An automobile manufacturer. General Motors is aware that it has market power. If it substantially increases its prices, sales will fall off; if it lowers prices substantially, it will sell more of its products. If GM decides on a large increase in production that is not a response to a known or anticipated rise in demand, it will have to reduce prices in order to sell the extra output. The automobile manufacturing firm is *not* a price taker. The quantity that it is able to sell will depend on the price it charges, but it does not have to accept passively whatever price is set by the market. In other words, the firm manufacturing automobiles is faced with a downward-sloping demand curve for its product. It may select any price-quantity combination consistent with that demand curve.

A wheat farmer. In contrast, an individual firm producing wheat is just one of a very large number of firms all growing the same product; one firm's contribution to the total production of wheat will be a tiny drop in an extremely large bucket. Ordinarily the firm will assume that it has no effect on price and will think of its own demand curve as being horizontal. Of course the firm can have *some* effect on price, but a straightforward calculation will show that the effect is small enough that the firm can justifiably neglect it.

The market elasticity of demand for wheat is approximately 0.25. This means that if the quantity of wheat supplied in the world increased by 1

---

[2] The third condition is designed to distinguish between profit-maximizing and profit-minimizing positions. Consider a situation in which *MC* cuts *MR* from above: For outputs to the left of the intersection marginal cost exceeds marginal revenue, which indicates that these units reduce profits and thus that profits could be increased by *reducing* output. For outputs to the right of the intersection marginal revenue exceeds marginal cost, which indicates that these units increase profits and thus that profits could be increased by *increasing* output. The intersection must thus represent minimum profits.

TABLE 14-1
The Calculation of a Firm's Elasticity of Demand (η_F) from Market Elasticity of Demand (η_M)

Given
$\eta_M = 0.25$
World output = 200 million tons
Firm's output increases from 40,000 to 60,000 tons, a 40% increase over the average quantity of 50,000 tons

Step 1. Find the percentage change in world price

$$\eta_M = -\frac{\text{percentage change in world output}}{\text{percentage change in world price}}$$

$$\text{Percentage change in world price} = -\frac{\text{percentage change in world output}}{\eta_M}$$

$$= -\frac{\frac{1}{100} \text{ of } 1\%}{0.25}$$

$$= -\frac{4}{100} \text{ of } 1\%$$

Step 2. Compute the firm's elasticity of demand:

$$\eta_F = -\frac{\text{percentage change in firm's output}}{\text{percentage change in world price}}$$

$$= -\frac{+40\%}{-\frac{4}{100} \text{ of } 1\%} = +1000$$

Because even a large change in output to the firm is a minute change in world wheat production, the effect on world price is very small. Thus the firm's elasticity of demand is high. This table relies on the concept of elasticity of demand developed in Chapter 6. Step 1 shows that a 40 percent increase in the firm's output leads to only a tiny decrease in the world's price. Thus, as step 2 shows, the firm's elasticity of demand is very high: 1000

The arithmetic is not important, but understanding why the wheat farm will be a price taker in these circumstances is vital.

---

percent, the price would have to fall by 4 percent to induce the world's wheat buyers to purchase the whole crop. Even huge farms produce a very small fraction of the total crop. In a recent year an extremely large Canadian wheat farm produced about 50,000 tons, only about 1/4,000 of the world production of 200 million tons. Suppose a large wheat farm increased its production by 20,000 tons, say from 40,000 to 60,000 tons. This would be a big percentage increase in its own production but an increase of only 1/100 of 1 percent in world production. Table 14-1 shows that this increase would lead to a decrease in the world price of 4/100 of 1 percent (4¢ in $100) and give the firm an elasticity of demand of 1,000! This is a very high elasticity of demand; the farm would have to increase its output 1,000

percent to bring about a 1 percent decrease in the price of wheat. Because the farm's output cannot be varied this much, it is not surprising that the firm regards the price of wheat to be unaffected by any change in output that it could conceivably make.

It is only a slight simplification to say that the firm is unable to influence the world price of wheat and that it is able to sell all that it can produce at the going world price. In other words, the firm is faced with a perfectly elastic demand curve for its product—it is a price taker.

The difference between firms producing wheat and firms producing automobiles is one of degree of market power. The wheat firm, as an insignificant part of the whole market, has no power to influence the world price of wheat. But the automobile firm does have power to influence the price of automobiles because its own production represents a significant part of the total supply of automobiles.

DEMAND AND REVENUE CURVES FOR THE PERFECTLY COMPETITIVE FIRM

Students sometimes confuse the individual firm's demand curve under perfect competition with the market demand curve for the product. The market demand curve is downward-sloping for the reasons discussed at length in Part Three. A consequence, as we saw, is that a rightward shift of the supply curve will lead to a fall in market price, other things being equal.

The demand curve facing a single firm in perfect competition is infinitely elastic because variations in its production *over the range that we need to consider for all practical purposes* will have such a small effect on price that the effect can safely be assumed to be zero. Of course, if

the single firm increased its production by a vast amount, a thousandfold say, this would cause a significant increase in supply and the firm would be unable to sell all it produced at the going price. The perfectly elastic demand curve does not mean that the firm could actually sell an infinite amount at the going price; rather, that the variations in production *that it will normally be practicable for the firm to make* will leave price virtually unaffected. This is shown in Figure 14-1.

Total, Average, and Marginal Revenue Curves

The notions of total, average, and marginal revenue are the demand counterparts of the notions of total, average, and marginal cost that we considered in Chapter 12. We focus now on the receipts to a seller from the sale of a product.

Total revenue (TR) is the total amount received by the seller. If q units are sold at p dollars each, $TR = p \cdot q$. (The dot between p and

FIGURE 14-1
Three Demand Curves of Differing Elasticity

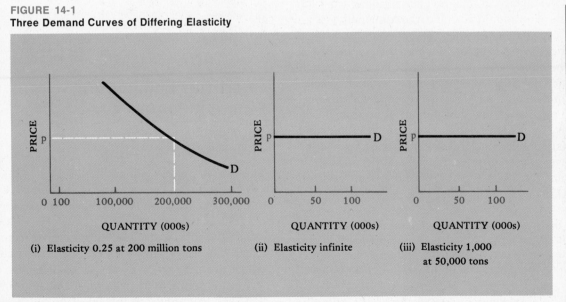

(i) Elasticity 0.25 at 200 million tons

(ii) Elasticity infinite

(iii) Elasticity 1,000 at 50,000 tons

For practical purposes, the demand curves in (ii) and (iii) are indistinguishable from each other. The firm's demand curve in (iii) appears horizontal because of the change in the quantity scale compared to (i). If the quantity scale in (i) were stretched to 1,000 times its present size, that demand curve, too, would appear horizontal.

TABLE 14-2
Revenue Concepts for a Price-taking Firm

Price p	Quantity q	$TR =$ $p \times q$	$AR =$ TR/q	$MR =$ $\Delta TR/\Delta q$
$3.00	10	$30.00	$3.00	
3.00	11	33.00	3.00	$3.00
3.00	12	36.00	3.00	3.00
3.00	13	39.00	3.00	3.00

When price is fixed, $AR = MR = p$. Marginal revenue is shown between the lines because it represents the change in total revenue (e.g., from $33 to $36) in response to a change in quantity (from 11 to 12 units),

$$MR = \frac{36-33}{12-11} = \$3 \text{ per unit.}$$

q is a "times" sign, frequently used instead of $p \times q$, to avoid confusion with variables labeled x.)

Average revenue (AR) is the amount of revenue *per unit* sold. This is the price of the product.

Marginal revenue (MR), sometimes called incremental revenue, has already been defined. It is the change in total revenue resulting from the sale of an additional unit of the commodity. [22]

Calculations of these revenue concepts for a price-taking firm are illustrated in Table 14-2. The table shows that as long as the firm's output does not affect the price of the product it sells, both average and marginal revenue will be equal to price at all levels of output. Thus, graphically (as in Figure 14-2), average revenue and marginal revenue are both horizontal lines at the level of market price. Since the firm can sell any quantity it wishes at this price, the same horizontal line is also the *firm's* demand curve.

If the market price is unaffected by variations in the firm's output, then the firm's demand curve, the average revenue curve, and the marginal revenue curve coincide in the same horizontal line.

Total revenue, of course, does vary with output; since price is constant, it follows that total revenue rises in direct proportion to output.

FIGURE 14-2
Revenue Curves for a Price-taking Firm

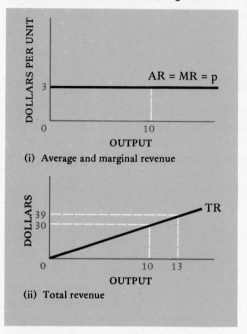

(i) Average and marginal revenue

(ii) Total revenue

This is a graphic representation of the revenue concepts of Table 14-2. Because price does not change, neither marginal nor average revenue varies with output. When price is constant, total revenue is a rising straight line from the origin.

Short-run Equilibrium: Firm and Industry

EQUILIBRIUM OUTPUT OF A FIRM IN PERFECT COMPETITION

The firm in perfect competition is a price taker and can adjust to varying market conditions only by changing the quantity it produces. In the short run it has fixed factors, and the only way to vary its output is by using more or less of those factors that it can vary. Thus the firm's short-run cost curves are relevant to its output decision.

We saw earlier that any profit-maximizing firm will seek to produce at a level of output where marginal cost equals marginal revenue. In the immediately preceding section we saw that a perfectly competitive firm's demand and marginal revenue curves coincide in the same horizontal line whose height represents the price of the product. Thus price equals marginal revenue. It follows immediately that a perfectly competitive firm will equate its marginal cost of production to the market price of its product (as long as price exceeds average variable cost).

The market determines the highest price at which the firm can sell its product. The firm picks the quantity of output that maximizes its profits. This is the output for which $p = MC$. When the firm is maximizing profits, it has no incentive to change its output. Therefore, unless prices or costs change, the firm will continue producing this output because it is doing as well as it can do, given the situation. The firm is said to be in **short-run equilibrium,** which is illustrated in Figure 14-3.

The perfectly competitive firm is a mere quantity adjuster. It pursues its goal of profit maximization by increasing or decreasing quantity until it equates its short-run marginal cost with the prevailing price of its product — a price that is given to it by the market.

The market price to which the perfectly competitive firm responds is itself set by the forces of demand and supply. The individual firm, by adjusting quantity produced to whatever price is ruling on the market, helps to determine market supply. The link between the behavior of the firm and the behavior of the competitive market is provided by the market supply curve.

SHORT-RUN SUPPLY CURVES

The supply curve shows the relation between the quantity supplied and price. For any given price we need to ask what quantity will be supplied. This question may be answered by supposing that a price is specified and then determining how much each firm will choose to supply. Then a different price is supposed and quantity supplied again determined — and so on, until all possible prices have been considered.

The Supply Curve of One Firm

Figure 14-4(i) shows a firm's marginal cost curve with four alternative demand curves. The firm's marginal cost curve gives the marginal cost corresponding to each level of output. A supply curve is needed that gives the quantity the firm will supply at every price. For prices below AVC, the firm will supply zero units (rule 1). For prices above AVC, the firm will equate price and marginal cost (rule 2 modified by the proposition that $MR = p$ in perfect competition). From this it follows that:

In perfect competition the firm's supply curve has the identical shape as the firm's marginal cost curve above AVC.

FIGURE 14-3
The Equilibrium of a Competitive Firm

The firm chooses the output for which $p = MC$ above the level of AVC. When $p = MC$ as at q_E, the firm would decrease its profits if it either increased or decreased its output. At any point left of q_E, say q, price is greater than the marginal cost, and it pays to increase output (as indicated by the left-hand arrow). At any point to the right of q_E, say q_1, price is less than the marginal cost, and it pays to reduce output (as indicated by the right-hand arrow). The equilibrium output for the firm is q_E.

FIGURE 14-4
Deriving the Supply Curve for a Price-taking Firm

(i) MC and AVC curves

(ii) The supply curve

For a price-taking firm, the supply curve has the same shape as its *MC* curve above the level of *AVC.* As prices rise from $2 to $3 to $4 to $5, the firm wishes to increase its production from q to q_1 to q_2 to q_3. For prices below $2, output would be zero because the firm is better off if it shuts down. The point *E,* where price equals *AVC,* is called the shutdown point. The firm's supply curve is shown in (ii).

The Supply Curve of an Industry

Figure 14-5 illustrates the derivation of an industry supply curve for an example of only two firms. The general result is that:

In perfect competition the industry supply curve is the horizontal sum of the marginal cost curves (above the level of average variable cost) of all firms in the industry.

The reason for this is that each firm's marginal cost curve tells us how much that firm will supply at any given market price, and the industry supply curve is the sum of what each firm will supply at each market price.

This supply curve, based on the short-run marginal cost curves of the firms in the industry, is the industry's **short-run supply curve.**

THE DETERMINATION OF SHORT-RUN EQUILIBRIUM PRICE

The short-run supply curve and the demand curve for the industry's product together determine the market price. (This happens in the manner analyzed in Chapter 5.) Although no one firm can influence market price significantly, the collective actions of all firms in the industry (as shown by the industry supply curve) and the collective actions of households (as shown by the industry's demand curve) together determine market price at the point where the demand and supply curves intersect.

At the equilibrium market price each firm is producing and selling a quantity for which its marginal cost equals the market price. No firm is motivated to change its output in the short run. Since total quantity demanded equals total quan-

FIGURE 14-5

The Derivation of an Industry Supply Curve

(i) Firm A   (ii) Firm B   (iii) Firms A and B

The industry supply curve is the horizontal sum of the supply curves of each of the firms in the industry. At a price of $3 firm A would supply 4 units and firm B would supply 3 units. Together, as shown in (iii), they would supply 7 units. If there are hundreds of firms, the process is the same: Each firm's supply curve (which is derived in the manner shown in Figure 14-4) shows what the firm will produce at any given price p. The industry supply curve relates the price to the sum of the quantities produced by each firm. In this example, because firm B does not enter the market at prices below $2, the supply curve S_{A+B} is identical with S_A up to price $2 and is the sum of $S_A + S_B$ above $2.

tity supplied, there is no reason for market price to change in the short run; the market and all the firms in the industry are in short-run equilibrium.

SHORT-RUN PROFITABILITY OF THE FIRM

Although we know that when the industry is in short-run equilibrium, the competitive firm is maximizing its profits, we do not know *how large* these profits are. It is one thing to know that a firm is doing as well as it can in particular circumstances; it is another to know how well it is doing.

Figure 14-6 shows three possible positions for a firm in short-run equilibrium. In all cases, the firm is maximizing its profits by producing where $p = MC$, but in (i) the firm is making losses, in (ii) it is just covering all costs, and in (iii) it is making profits in excess of all costs. In (i) it might be better to say that the firm is minimizing its losses rather than maximizing its profits, but both state-

ments mean the same thing. The firm is doing as well as it can, given its costs and prices.

Long-run Equilibrium

While Figure 14-6 shows three possible short-run equilibrium positions for the profit-maximizing firm in perfect competition, not all of them are possible equilibrium positions in the long run.

THE EFFECT OF ENTRY AND EXIT

The key to long-run equilibrium under perfect competition is entry and exit. We have seen that when firms are in *short-run* equilibrium, they may be making profits or losses or just breaking even. Since costs include the opportunity cost of capital, firms that are just breaking even are doing as well as they could if they invested their capital elsewhere. Thus there will be no incentive for existing firms to leave the industry; neither will there be an incentive for new firms to

FIGURE 14-6

Alternative Short-run Equilibrium Positions of a Competitive Firm

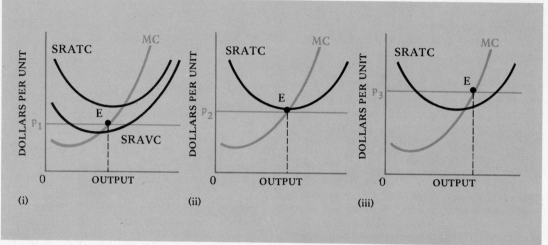

When it is in short-run equilibrium, a competitive firm may be suffering losses, breaking even, or making profits. The diagrams show a firm with given costs faced with three alternative prices p_1, p_2, and p_3. In each part of the diagram E is the point at which $MC = MR = $ price. Since in all three cases price exceeds AVC the firm is in short-run equilibrium.

In (i) price is p_1 and the firm is suffering losses because price is below average total cost. Since price

exceeds average variable cost, it pays the firm to keep producing, but it does *not* pay it to replace its capital equipment as the capital wears out.

In (ii) price is p_2 and the firm is just covering its total costs. It does pay the firm to replace its capital as it wears out since it is covering full opportunity cost of its capital.

In (iii) price is p_3 and the firm is earning profits in excess of all its costs.

enter the industry, for capital can earn the same return elsewhere in the economy. If, however, existing firms are earning profits over all costs, including the opportunity cost of capital, new capital will enter the industry to share in these profits. If existing firms are making losses, capital will leave the industry because a better return can be obtained elsewhere in the economy. Let us consider the process in a little more detail.

If all firms in the competitive industry are in the position of the firm in Figure 14-6(iii), new firms will enter the industry, attracted by the profits being earned by existing firms. Suppose that in response to high profits for 100 existing firms, 20 new firms enter. The market supply curve that formerly added up the outputs of 100 firms now must add up the outputs of 120 firms. At any price, more will be supplied because there are more suppliers.

This shift in the short-run supply curve, with an unchanged market demand curve, means that the previous equilibrium price will no longer prevail. The shift in supply will cause the equilibrium price to fall, and both new and old firms will have to adjust their output to this new price. This is illustrated in Figure 14-7. New firms will continue to enter and price will continue to fall until all firms in the industry are just covering their total costs. Firms will then be in the position of the firm in Figure 14-6(ii), which is called a *zero-profit equilibrium*.

Profits in a competitive industry are a signal for the entry of new capital; the industry will expand, forcing price down until the profits fall to zero.

If the firms in the industry are in the position of the firm in Figure 14-6(i), they are suffering losses. They are covering their variable costs, but the return on their capital is less than the opportunity cost of this capital; the firms are not covering their total costs. This is a signal for the exit of firms. As plant and equipment are discarded they will not be replaced. As a result, the industry's short-run supply curve shifts left and market price rises. Firms will continue to exit and price will continue to rise until the remaining firms can cover their total costs—that is, until they are all in the zero-profit equilibrium illustrated in Figure 14-6(ii). Exit then ceases.

Losses in a competitive industry are a signal for the exit of capital; the industry will contract, driving price up until the remaining firms are covering their total costs.

In all of this we see profits serving their function of allocating resources among the industries of the economy.

THE LEVEL OF COST AT EQUILIBRIUM

An industry is nothing more than a collection of firms; for an industry to be in long-run equilibrium each firm must be in long-run equilibrium. It follows that when a perfectly competitive industry is in long-run equilibrium, all firms in the industry will be selling at a price equal to minimum average total cost—that is, they must be in zero-profit equilibrium, as in Figure 14-6(ii). This result plays an important role in the appeal that perfect competition has had to economists, as we shall see. (Further discussion of the level of cost in long-run equilibrium will be found in the appendix to this chapter.)

Let us now apply this theory to two commonly observed situations.

THE LONG-RUN RESPONSE OF A PERFECTLY COMPETITIVE INDUSTRY TO A CHANGE IN TECHNOLOGY

Consider an industry in long-run equilibrium. Since the industry is in equilibrium, each firm must be in zero-profit equilibrium. Now assume that some technological development lowers the cost curves of newly built plants. Since price is just equal to the average total cost for the old plants, new plants will now be able to earn profits, and more of them will now be built. But this expansion in capacity shifts the short-run supply curve to the right and drives price down. The expansion in capacity and the fall in price will continue until price is equal to the *ATC* of the *new* plants. At this price old plants will not be covering their long-run costs. As long as price exceeds their average variable cost, however, such plants will continue in production. As the outmoded plants wear out they will gradually disappear. Eventually a new long-run equilibrium will be established in which all plants use the new technology.

What happens in a competitive industry in which technological change occurs not as a single isolated event but more or less continuously?

FIGURE 14-7
The Effect of New Entrants on the Supply Curve

New entrants shift the supply curve to the right and lower the equilibrium price. Initial equilibrium is at *E*. If the supply curve shifts to S_1 by virtue of entry, the equilibrium price must fall to p_1 while output rises to q_1. At this price before entry, only *q* would have been produced. The extra output is supplied by the new productive capacity.

FIGURE 14-8

Plants of Different Vintages in an Industry with Continuing Technical Progress

(i) Plant 1   (ii) Plant 2   (iii) Plant 3

Entry of progressively lower-cost firms forces price down, but older plants with higher costs remain in the industry as long as price covers average variable cost. Plant 3 is the newest plant with the lowest costs. Price will be determined by the average total costs of plants of this type since entry will continue as long as the owners of the newest plants expect to earn profits from them. Plant 1 is the oldest plant in operation; it is just covering its *AVC*, and if the price falls any further it will be closed down. Plant 2 is a plant of intermediate age. It is covering its variable costs and earning some return on its capital. The return will shrink over time as entry of new plants with lower and lower costs drives price lower and lower.

Plants built in any one year will tend to have lower costs than plants built in any previous year. This is a common occurrence in the real world; it is illustrated in Figure 14-8. Such industries have a number of interesting characteristics.

One is that plants of different ages and different levels of efficiency will exist side by side. This characteristic is dramatically illustrated by the variety of vintages of steam turbine generators found in any long-established electric utility. Critics who observe the continued use of older, less efficient plants and urge that "something be done to eliminate these wasteful practices" miss the point of economic efficiency. If the plant is already there, the plant can be profitably operated as long as it can do anything more than cover its variable costs. As long as a plant can produce goods that are valued by consumers at an amount above the value of the resources currently used up for their production (variable costs), the value

of society's total output is increased by using that plant to produce goods.

A second characteristic of such an industry is that price will be governed by *the minimum ATC of the most efficient plants*. Entry will continue until plants of the latest vintage are just expected to earn normal profits over their lifetimes. The benefits of the new technology are passed on to consumers because all units of the commodity, whether produced by new or old plants, are sold at a price that is related solely to the *ATC* of the new plants. Owners of older plants find their returns over variable costs falling steadily as more and more efficient plants drive the price of the product down.

A third characteristic is that old plants will be discarded (or "mothballed") when the price falls below their *AVC*. This may occur well before the plants are physically worn out. In industries with continuous technical progress, capital is usually discarded because it is economically obsolete, not because it has physically worn out. This illustrates the economic meaning of obsolete:

Old capital is obsolete when its average variable cost exceeds the average total cost of new capital.

INDUSTRIES THAT ARE DECLINING DUE TO A STEADY DECREASE IN DEMAND

What happens when a competitive industry in long-run equilibrium begins to suffer losses due to a permanent and continuing decrease in the demand for its products? As demand declines, price falls and firms that were previously covering *ATC* are not now able to do so. They find themselves in the position shown in Figure 14-8(ii). Firms earn losses instead of breaking even, and the signal for exit of capital is given. But exit takes time. The economically correct response to a steadily declining demand is not to replace old equipment but to continue to operate with existing equipment as long as the firm can cover its variable costs of production.

Gradually equipment will break down and not be repaired or replaced. The capacity of the industry will shrink, slowly at first. If demand keeps declining, capacity must keep shrinking.

Declining industries typically present a sorry sight to the observer. Revenues are below long-run total costs, and as a result new equipment is not brought in to replace old equipment as it wears out. The average age of equipment in use thus rises steadily. The untrained observer seeing the industry's very real plight is likely to blame it on the antiquated equipment in use.

The antiquated equipment in a declining industry is the effect rather than the cause of the industry's decline.

It would not usually make sense for firms to modernize in the face of steadily falling demand even when new, improved equipment is available. To do so would increase the industry's capacity and its output, thereby making its overall plight still worse. Price would fall even more rapidly, adding further to the losses of existing firms.

A striking example of the confusion of cause and effect in a declining industry occurred during the debate over the nationalization of the coal industry in Great Britain in the period between the two world wars.

The view that public control was needed to save an industry from the dead hand of third-rate, unenterprising private owners was commonly held about the British coal industry and was undoubtedly a factor leading to its nationalization in 1946. This view was held by the commission which reported in 1926 on the state of the coal industry: "It would be possible to say without exaggeration of the miners' leaders that they were the stupidest men in England, if we had not had frequent occasion to meet the owners."

The late Sir Roy Harrod, a leading British economist from the 1920s to the 1960s, shocked many by taking the opposite view, arguing that the rundown state of the coal industry in South Wales and Yorkshire represented the correct response of the owners to the signals of the market.

Economic efficiency does not consist in always introducing the most up-to-date equipment that an engineer can think of but rather in the correct adaptation of the amount of new capital sunk to the earning capacity of the old asset. In not introducing new equipment, the managements may have been wise, not only from the point of view of their own interest, but from that of national interest, which requires the most profitable application of available capital . . . it is right that as much should be extracted from the inferior mines as can be done by old-fashioned methods [i.e., with equipment already installed], and that they should gradually go out of action.[3]

The general point that Professor Harrod makes is extremely important. It is in the public and the private interest that what appear to be antiquated methods be employed in declining industries. Capital resources are scarce; to install new plant and equipment in a genuinely declining

[3] Roy Harrod, *The British Economy* (New York: McGraw-Hill, 1963), page 54.

industry is to use the nation's scarce resources of new capital where they will not lead to the largest possible increases in the value of output.

The Appeal of Perfect Competition

The theory of perfect competition shows that profit-maximizing price-taking firms, responding to prices set by the impersonal forces of supply and demand, will be motivated to provide all commodities for which total revenues are equal to or greater than total costs. They will be motivated to produce every unit for which price is greater than marginal cost, and they will thus expand production up to the point where price equals marginal cost. The entry and exit of firms will, in long-run equilibrium, push prices to the level of minimum average total costs—that is, to the lowest level attainable for the given technology and factor prices.

Consider an economy in which every industry operates as a perfectly competitive industry. For the nineteenth century liberal economists, such a world was more than a theoretical model, it was a most attractive ideal. One of them, Bascom, glowingly characterized such an economic system as "more provocative of virtue than virtue herself." The appeal of a competitive economy has both noneconomic and economic aspects.

THE NONECONOMIC APPEAL OF COMPETITION

In a perfectly competitive economy there are many firms and many households. Each is a price taker, responding as it sees fit, freely and without coercion, to signals sent to it by the market. For one who believes in the freedom of individuals to make decisions, and who distrusts all power groups, the perfectly competitive model is almost too good to be true. No single firm and no single consumer has any power over the market. Individual consumers and producers are passive quantity adjusters who respond to market signals.

Yet the impersonal force of the market produces an appropriate response to all changes. If tastes change, for example, prices will change, and the allocation of resources will change in the appropriate direction. Throughout the entire process, no one will have any power over anyone else. Dozens of firms will react to the same price changes, and if one firm refuses to react, there will be countless other profit-maximizing firms eager to make the appropriate changes.

Because the market mechanism works, it is not necessary for the government to intervene. Market reactions, not public policies, will eliminate shortages or surpluses. There is no need for government regulatory agencies or bureaucrats to make arbitrary decisions about who may produce what, or how to produce it, or how much it is permissible to charge for the product. If there are no government officials to make such decisions, there will be no one to bribe to make one decision rather than another.

In the impersonal decision-making world of perfect competition, neither private firms nor public officials wield economic power. The market mechanism, like an invisible hand, determines the allocation of resources among competing uses.

THE ECONOMIC APPEAL OF PERFECT COMPETITION: EFFICIENCY

Resources are scarce relative to the wants of society's members, so it is desirable not to waste the resources we have. The most obvious way to waste resources is not to use them at all. When labor is unemployed and factories lie idle (as occurs in serious depressions), their potential current output is lost. If these resources could be reemployed, total output would be increased and hence everyone could be made better off.

But full employment of resources by itself is not enough to prevent the waste of resources. Even when resources are being fully used, they may be used inefficiently.

Let us look at three possible sources of inefficiency in resource use.

1. If firms do not use the least costly method of producing their chosen outputs, they will waste resources. By adopting the least costly method they would free resources to be used to make other commodities. In a firm that achieves its monthly production of 30,000 pairs of shoes at a resource cost of $400,000 when it could be done at a cost of only $350,000, resources are being used inefficiently. If the lower cost method were used, $50,000 worth of other commodities could be produced each month by transferring the resources saved to their best alternative use.

2. If some firms are too large and others too small, each will not be producing at the lowest point on its long-run average cost curve. Thus any given level of the industry's production will use more resources than is necessary.

3. If too much of one product and too little of another is produced, resources are also being used inefficiently. To take an extreme example, say that so many shoes were produced that their *marginal* utility was zero while the marginal utility of coats remained high at the current level of output. Since no one places any value on the last pair of shoes produced, while everyone places a high value on an additional coat, no one will be made worse off by reducing the output of shoes, yet someone will be made better off by using the resources to increase the production of coats.

These examples suggest that we must refine our ideas of the waste of resources beyond the simple notion of ensuring that all resources are used. Economists define rather precisely what is meant by efficiency and inefficiency in resource use.

Resources are said to be used *inefficiently* when it would be *possible* by using them differently to make at least one household better off without making any household worse off. Conversely, resources are said to be used *efficiently* when it is *impossible* by using them differently to make any one household better off without making at least one other household worse off.

Inefficiency implies that we can help someone without hurting someone else. Efficiency implies that we cannot. When resources are already being used efficiently, we can only make one household better off at the cost of making another household worse off.

Efficiency in the use of resources is often called **Pareto-efficiency** or **Pareto-optimality** in honor of the great Italian economist Vilfredo Pareto (1848–1923), who pioneered in the study of efficiency.

So much for the meaning of efficiency; now how do we achieve it? The three sources of inefficiency numbered above suggest important conditions that must be fulfilled if economic efficiency is to be attained.

Productive Efficiency

The first condition of economic efficiency is that whatever output the *firm* selects must be produced at the lowest possible cost of producing that level of output. Otherwise more resources will be used for this output than are necessary. This condition will be fulfilled by any profit-maximizing firm. A firm is obviously not maximizing its profits when it produces its desired output at a higher cost than is necessary.

The second condition is that the costs of producing the *industry* output should be as low as possible. This condition is fulfilled under perfect competition. We saw on page 231 that when a perfectly competitive industry is in long-run equilibrium, every firm is producing at the minimum point on its long-run average total cost curve.

These two conditions concern what is called **productive efficiency.** The first guarantees that firms produce on, rather than above, their long-run average total cost curves. The second guarantees that firms produce at the point of *lowest* long-run average total cost. Together they ensure that each product is produced as cheaply as possible.

Allocative Efficiency

The third condition concerns the appropriate mix of products. Resources are not being used efficiently when they are being used to produce products that no one wants. **Allocative efficiency** refers to the allocation of resources among the economy's various industries; it obtains when it is impossible to change that allocation in such a way as to make someone better off without making someone else worse off.

What is the right mix? How many shoes and how many coats should be produced for allocative efficiency? The answer is that (under certain conditions that we shall specify later) the allocation of resources to any one commodity is efficient when its price is equal to its marginal cost of production, that is, $p = MC$.

This rather subtle condition has been one of the most influential ideas in the whole of economics. To understand it, we need to remind ourselves of two points established earlier: first, the price of any commodity indicates the value that each household places on the last unit of the commodity that it consumes (per period); second, marginal cost indicates the value that the resources used to produce the marginal unit of output would have in their best alternative uses.

The first proposition follows directly from marginal utility theory (see page 141). A household will go on increasing its rate of consumption of a commodity until the *marginal* valuation that it puts on the commodity is equal to its price. The household gets a consumers' surplus on all but the marginal unit because it values them more than the price it has to pay. On the marginal unit, however, it only "breaks even" because the valuation placed on it is just equal to its price.

The second proposition follows from the nature of opportunity cost (see page 178). The marginal cost of producing some commodity is the opportunity cost of the resources used. Opportunity cost means the value of the resources in their best alternative uses.

To see how these propositions fit together, assume that shoes sell for $30 a pair but have a marginal production cost of $40. If one less pair of shoes were produced, the value that households place on the pair of shoes not produced would be $30. But by the meaning of opportunity cost, the resources that would have been used to produce that pair of shoes could instead produce other goods (say a coat) valued at $40. If society can give up something its members value at $30 and get in return something its members value at $40, the original allocation of resources is inefficient. Someone can be made better off, and no one need be worse off. This is easy to see when the same household gives up the shoes and gets the coat. But it follows even when different households are involved, for the gaining household can compensate the losing household and still come out ahead.

Assume next that shoe production is cut back until the price of a pair of shoes rises from $30 to $35 while its marginal cost falls from $40 to $35. The efficiency condition is now fulfilled in shoe production because $p = MC = \$35$. Now if one less pair of shoes were produced, $35 worth of shoes would be sacrificed while at most $35 worth of other commodities could be produced with the freed resources. In this situation the allocation of resources to shoe production is efficient because it is not possible to change it and make someone better off without making someone else worse off. If one household were to sacrifice the pair of shoes, it would give up goods worth $35 and would then have to get all of the new production of the alternative commodity produced just to break even. It cannot gain without making another household worse off. The same argument can be repeated for every commodity, and it leads to this conclusion:

The allocation of resources among commodities is efficient when for each commodity price equals marginal cost.

Allocative efficiency is thus satisfied when $p = MC$ in all industries. For every industry in perfect competition, $p = MC$ in equilibrium. Thus:

Universal perfect competition fulfills the condition for allocative efficiency by ensuring that price equals marginal cost in every industry.

A Graphic Interpretation of Allocative Efficiency

Consider a competitive industry where forces of demand and supply establish a competitive price. Because the industry supply curve represents the sum of the marginal cost curves of the firms in the industry, the market clearing price is one at which $p = MC$. In the figure, such a price is shown as $p\star$, and the corresponding output is $q\star$. For every unit produced up to this output, the value consumers would be willing to pay (as shown by the demand curve) is greater than the opportunity cost of the resources used to produce it (as shown by the $S = MC$ curve).

The shaded areas represent the excess of consumer valuation over opportunity cost. It is customary to divide the total shaded area into two parts: that above the price line (dark shade) is called *consumers' surplus* (encountered in Chapter 9); that below the price line (light shade) is an analogous quantity called *producers' surplus* — because producers would have been willing to provide each unit at its marginal cost but are actually paid $p\star$ (which is greater than marginal cost for all but the last unit). The two shaded areas together represent the *sum* of consumers' surplus and producers' surplus.

Allocative efficiency is achieved when the sum of the surpluses is maximized. This occurs at the output $q\star$, where $p = MC$. For any output less than $q\star$, such as q_1, there is a price (e.g., $p\star$) such that there is an addition to both consumers' and producers' surplus if more is produced. For any output greater than $q\star$, such as q_2, this is not the case. For every unit beyond $q\star$ the demand curve (what consumers would pay) is below the supply curve (what producers must be paid). Thus there is no price that would satisfy both consumers and producers. At the price $p\star$, extra units beyond $q\star$ would subtract from both producers' and consumers' surpluses.

Thus producers' plus consumers' surplus is maximized *only* at output $q\star$. If some invisible authority were to instruct producers to "maximize the sum of producers' and consumers' surplus," producers would produce every unit up to $q\star$. The perfectly competitive market price, $p\star$, provides exactly that signal!

SOME WORDS OF WARNING ABOUT THE EFFICIENCY OF PERFECT COMPETITION

An economy that consisted of perfectly competitive industries would in equilibrium achieve allocative efficiency. Further, if the costs for each such industry were the lowest costs attainable, the economy would also achieve productive efficiency in the production of every commodity. This is because the forces of competition push equilibrium price to the level where $p = MC = ATC$.

Before jumping to the conclusion that perfect competition is the best of all possible worlds and that government policy ought to do everything possible to achieve it, we must consider certain qualifications. Four will be mentioned here, to be developed in later chapters.

Costs may be higher under perfect competition than under alternative market structures. In a competitive industry, production occurs at the lowest level of cost attainable by the competitive firm. But, as we shall see, it is possible that the existence of unexploited economies of large-scale production can render an industry made up of competitive firms less productively efficient than (say) a monopoly. It is also possible that firms in a perfectly competitive industry may not innovate as rapidly as firms in another industry structure, and thus the cost of producing the competitive output will not be as low as it might be.

These matters are discussed more fully in Chapters 15, 16, and 18.

Perfect competition may not pertain simultaneously everywhere in the economy. Our argument about allocative efficiency rested on $p = MC$ everywhere in the economy. But there may be some industries where price does not and cannot equal marginal cost. (The reasons will be explored in Chapter 18). In such a world there is no general presumption of what the effect will be of prices equaling marginal costs *somewhere* in the economy. Thus, if price does not equal marginal cost in industry A, the fact that $p = MC$ in industry B may not lead to allocative efficiency.

This proposition illustrates what is known as the "theory of the second best": We may know how to identify the best of all possible worlds (from the limited point of view of the optimum we are discussing), but we may have a harder task when attempting to rank order two situations in the very imperfect world in which we live.

Private costs may be poor measures of society's costs. Producing a good up to the point at which the price just equals the *firm's* marginal cost is efficient from society's point of view only if the firm's private costs reflect the opportunity costs to society of using the resources elsewhere. As we shall see in Chapter 24, this is often not the case because of what are called externalities. For example, if the competitive firm uses resources it does not pay for (such as the clean air around its factories), it may produce too much output and too much pollution to be efficient. It does so because *its* own marginal costs fail to include the value that members of society place on some of the resources (clean air) it uses up.

Efficiency is not the only goal. A competitive economy distributes output as well as produces it. A freely functioning competitive economy might produce a distribution of income consisting of one millionaire and 999 paupers. Such an economy can be just as efficient, even more efficient, than an economy with 1,000 persons of roughly equal income. Before one can speak of a competitive economy as being "virtuous," one must consider goals other than efficiency. This matter is discussed further in Chapter 24.

Summary

1. Competitive behavior is concerned with how individual firms compete against each other; competitive market structure is concerned with the degree of power that individual firms have to influence such market variables as the price of the product. Under perfect competition individual firms are powerless to influence market price. Therefore they do not have any incentive to indulge in competitive behavior against their fellow producers in the same industry.

2. A profit-maximizing firm will produce at an output where (a) price is at least as great as average variable cost, (b) marginal cost equals marginal revenue, and (c) the marginal cost curve cuts the marginal revenue curve from below.

3. The two critical assumptions of the theory of perfect competition are that firms are price takers and that the industry displays freedom of entry and exit. A firm that is a price taker will adjust to different market conditions by varying its output.

4. The perfectly competitive firm's short-run supply curve is the same shape as its MC curve above AVC. The perfectly competitive industry's short-run supply curve is the horizontal sum of its firms' supply curves (i.e., the horizontal sum of the firms' marginal cost curves).

5. When perfectly competitive firms are in short-run equilibrium, they must, if they are producing at all, be covering their variable costs. But they may be making losses (price less than average total cost), making profits (price greater than average total cost), or just covering all costs (price equal to average total cost).

6. In the long run, profits or losses will lead to the entry or exit of capital from the industry. Entry of new firms or exit of existing firms will push a competitive industry to a long-run zero-profit equilibrium and move production to the level of minimum average total cost. Long-run equilibrium is discussed at greater length in the appendix to this chapter.

7. The long-run response of a growing, perfectly competitive industry to steadily changing technology is the gradual replacement of less efficient plants and machines by more efficient ones. Older machines will be utilized as long as price exceeds AVC; then they will be discarded and replaced by newer, more modern ones. The long-run response of a declining industry will be to continue to satisfy the remaining demand from its existing machinery as long as price exceeds AVC. Despite the appearance of being antiquated, this is the correct response in the face of steadily falling demand.

8. The great appeal of the theory of perfect competition as a means of organizing production has both noneconomic and economic elements. The noneconomic appeal lies in the decentralized decision making of myriad firms and households. No individual exercises power over the market.

At the same time, it is not necessary for the government to intervene to determine resource allocation and prices; thus there is no need for government agencies to exercise arbitrary or bureaucratic power.

9. The economic appeal of a world of perfect competition arises from the fact that, under certain conditions, it exhibits both productive and allocative efficiency. Productive efficiency is achieved because the same forces that lead to long-run equilibrium lead to production at the lowest attainable cost. Allocative efficiency is achieved because in competitive equilibrium, price equals marginal cost for every product. If this condition is met in all industries, there will be no shift of resources that can increase the satisfaction of any household without decreasing it for some other household. Other terms for allocative efficiency are *Pareto-optimality* and *Pareto-efficiency*.

10. The efficiency of perfect competition should be understood yet interpreted with caution. Four qualifications to its being "ideal" are: (a) costs may be higher under perfect competition than under alternative market structures; (b) perfect competition may not pertain simultaneously everywhere in the economy; (c) private costs may be poor measures of society's costs; (d) efficiency is not the only goal of the members of society. Because of the first three, competitive equilibrium in a particular industry may not even be efficient. Because of the fourth, even an efficient competitive equilibrium may be regarded as less than ideal in its results.

Topics for Review

Competitive behavior and competitive market structure
Behavioral rules for the profit-maximizing firm
Price taking and a horizontal demand curve
Average revenue, marginal revenue, and price under perfect competition
The relation of the industry supply curve to firms' marginal cost curves
Short-run and long-run equilibrium of firms and industries

Productive and allocative efficiency
Pareto-optimality (and Pareto-efficiency)

Discussion Questions

1. Consider the suppliers of the following commodities. What are the elements of market structure that you might want to invoke to account for differences in their market behavior? Could any of these be characterized as perfectly competitive industries?
   a. television broadcasting
   b. automobiles
   c. sand and gravel
   d. medical services
   e. mortgage loans
   f. retail fruits and vegetables
   g. soybeans

2. Which of the following observed facts about an industry are inconsistent with its being a perfectly competitive industry?
   a. Different firms use different methods of production.
   b. There is extensive advertising of the industry's product by a trade association.
   c. Individual firms devote 5 percent of sales receipts to advertising their own product brand.
   d. There are 24 firms in the industry.
   e. The largest firm in the industry makes 40 percent of the sales and the next largest firm sells 20 percent, but the products are identical and there are 61 other firms.
   f. All firms made large profits in 1980.

3. In which of the following sectors of the American economy might you expect to find competitive behavior? In which might you expect to find industries that were classified as operating under perfectly competitive market structures?
   a. manufacturing
   b. agriculture
   c. transportation and public utilities
   d. wholesale and retail trade
   e. criminal activity

4. In the 1930s the U.S. coal industry was characterized by easy entry and price taking. Because of large fixed costs in mine shafts and fixed equipment, however, exit was slow. With declining demand, many firms were barely covering their variable costs but not their total costs. As a result of a series of mine accidents, the federal government began to enforce mine safety standards, which forced most firms to invest in new capital if they were to remain in production. What predictions would competitive theory make about market behavior and the quantity of coal produced? Would coal miners approve or disapprove of the new enforcement program?

5. Suppose entry into an industry is not artificially restricted but takes time because of the need to build plants, acquire know-how, and establish a marketing organization. Can such an industry be characterized as perfectly competitive? Does ease of entry imply ease of exit, and vice versa?

6. What, if anything, do each of the following tell you about ease of entry or exit in an industry?
   a. Profits have been very high for two decades.
   b. No new firms have entered the industry for 20 years.
   c. The average age of the firms in a 40-year-old industry is less than seven years.
   d. Most existing firms are using obsolete equipment alongside newer, more modern equipment.
   e. Profits are low or negative; many firms are still producing, but from steadily aging equipment.

7. In the 1970s grain prices in the United States rose substantially relative to other agricultural products. Explain how each of the following may have contributed to this result; then consider how a perfectly competitive grain industry might be expected to react in the long run.
   a. Crop failures caused by unusually bad weather around the world in several years.
   b. Rising demand for beef and chickens because of rising population and rising per capita income.
   c. Great scarcities in fishmeal, a substitute for grain in animal diets, because of a mysterious decline in the anchovy harvest off Peru.
   d. Increased Soviet purchases of grain from the United States.

Pricing in Monopoly Markets

15

Is AT&T a monopoly? How about IBM, U.S. Steel, the National Football League, or the Coca-Cola Company? Just as the word "competition" has both an everyday meaning and a more specialized technical one, so too does the word "monopoly." Monopoly, as economists use the concept, is a market structure that leads to certain predicted kinds of market behavior.

The word "monopoly" comes from the Greek words *monos polein,* which mean "alone to sell." It is convenient for now to think of **monopoly** as the situation in which the output of an entire industry is controlled by a single seller. This seller will be called the monopolist. Later in this chapter we will define monopoly in a less restrictive way.

A Monopolist Selling at a Single Price

Consider first an industry producing a single product in which a monopolist sets a price and supplies the entire quantity that buyers wish to purchase at that price. In contrast to the competitive firm, the monopolist is a price setter, not a price taker. The monopolistic firm faces a downward-sloping demand curve and can pick any price-quantity combination on the demand curve. The monopolist is sometimes said to be able to *administer* its price. This means that it, unlike the perfect competitor, can and usually does select its own price.

THE MONOPOLIST'S REVENUE CURVES

Because the monopolistic firm is assumed to be the only producer of a particular product, its demand curve is identical with the demand curve for that product. The market demand curve, which shows the aggregate quantity that buyers will purchase at every price, also shows the quantity that the monopolist will be able to sell at any price it sets. Given the market demand curve, the monopolist's average revenue and marginal revenue curves can be readily deduced.

When the seller charges a single price for all

TABLE 15-1
The Relation of Average Revenue and Marginal Revenue: A Numerical Illustration

Price $P = AR$	Quantity q	$TR = p \times q$	$MR = \Delta TR/\Delta q$
$9.10	9	$81.90	
9.00	10	90.00	$8.10
8.90	11	97.90	7.90

Marginal revenue is less than price because price must be lowered to sell an extra unit. A monopolist can choose either the price or the quantity to be sold. But choosing one determines the other. In this example, to increase sales from 10 to 11 units, it is necessary to reduce the price on all units sold from $9 to $8.90. The extra unit sold brings in $8.90, but the firm sacrifices 10¢ on each of the 10 units that it could have sold at $9 had it not wanted to increase sales. The net addition to revenue is the $8.90 minus 10¢ times 10 units, or $1, making $7.90 altogether. Thus the marginal revenue resulting from the increase in sales by 1 unit is $7.90, which is less than the price at which the units are sold.

Marginal revenue is shown displaced by half a line to emphasize that it represents the effect on revenue of the *change* in output.

FIGURE 15-1
The Effect on Revenue of an Increase in Quantity Sold

For a downward-sloping demand curve, marginal revenue is less than price. A reduction of price from p to p_1 increases sales by 1 unit from q to q_1 units. The revenue from the extra unit sold (i.e., its price) is shown as the lighter shaded area. But to sell this unit, it is necessary to reduce the price on each of the q units previously sold. This loss in revenue is shown as the darker shaded area. Marginal revenue of the extra unit is equal to the *difference* between the two areas.

units sold, average revenue per unit is identical with price. Thus the market demand curve is also the average revenue curve for the monopolist. But marginal revenue is less than price because the monopolist has to lower the price that it charges on *all* units in order to sell an *extra* unit. (Figure 15-1). [23] This is an important difference from the case of perfect competition; it is explored numerically in Table 15-1 and graphically in Figure 15-1.

Figure 15-2 illustrates the average and marginal revenue curves for a monopolist, based on a downward-sloping straight-line demand curve.[1]

---

[1] It is helpful (for sketching revenue curves, etc.) to remember that if the demand curve is a downward-sloping straight line, the *MR* curve also slopes downward and is twice as steep. Its price intercept (where $q = 0$) is the same as that of the demand curve, and it cuts the quantity axis (where $p = 0$) at just half the output that the demand curve does. [24]

FIGURE 15-2
Demand, Average Revenue, and Marginal Revenue Curves for a Monopolist

For the monopolist, **MR** does not equal price. The demand curve is the *AR* curve; the *MR* curve is below and steeper than the *AR* curve because the demand curve slopes downward.

Marginal Revenue, Total Revenue, and Elasticity of Demand

A demand curve represents a single relationship between quantity and price, but there are many different ways of looking at this relationship.

Figure 15-3 shows how total revenue and elasticity of demand (η) are related to *AR* and *MR*. Consider first that part of the demand curve where elasticity is greater than one. This means that total revenue rises as quantity increases, and hence the total revenue curve is upward-sloping. Because total revenue is increasing as quantity is increasing, marginal revenue must be positive. Next consider the point at which elasticity of demand is exactly unity. Here total revenue remains constant as quantity sold increases. This

implies that marginal revenue is zero. Consider finally the part of the demand curve where elasticity is less than one. This means that total revenue falls as quantity increases, and hence the total revenue curve is now downward-sloping. This implies that marginal revenue is negative.

FIGURE 15-3
The Relation of Total, Average, and Marginal Revenue to Elasticity of Demand

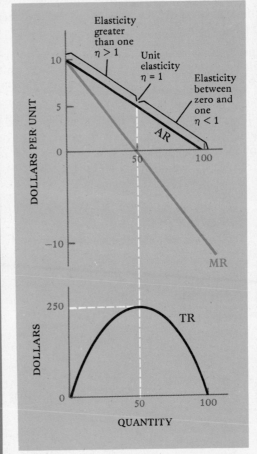

When *TR* is rising, *MR* is greater than zero and elasticity is greater than unity. In this example, for outputs from 0 to 50, marginal revenue is positive, elasticity is greater than unity, and total revenue is rising. For outputs from 50 to 100, marginal revenue is negative, elasticity is less than unity, and total revenue is falling.

Marginal revenue thus goes from positive to negative as the demand curve goes from elastic to inelastic, or (what is the same thing) as the total revenue curve stops rising, reaches its maximum, and begins to fall. (The relation between elasticity and total revenue was examined in Chapter 6.)

This relationship has an immediate and important implication. Since marginal cost is greater than zero, the profit-maximizing monopoly (which produces where MR equals MC) will produce where MR is positive, that is, where demand is elastic.

A profit-maximizing monopolist will never push its sales of a commodity into the range over which the commodity's demand curve becomes inelastic.

The common sense of this is that if demand is inelastic, marginal revenue is negative. Thus the monopolist can both increase revenue and reduce cost by reducing its sales.

PROFIT MAXIMIZATION IN A MONOPOLIZED MARKET

To describe the profit-maximizing position of a monopolist, we need only bring together information about the monopolist's revenues and its costs and apply the rules developed in Chapter 14.

The monopolist produces an output such that marginal revenue equals marginal cost. The price corresponding to that output is given by its demand curve.

This profit-maximizing position is shown in each part of Figure 15-4.

Note for future reference one respect in which this monopolistic equilibrium differs from that of a firm in perfect competition. While a competitive firm produces at an output where $p = MC$, the monopolistic firm produces at an output where p is greater than MC. Later we shall return to discuss some implications of this.

FIGURE 15-4
The Profit-maximizing Position of a Monopolist

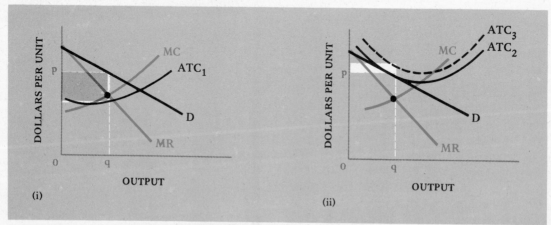

Profit-maximizing output is q, where $MR = MC$; price is above MC. The rules for profit maximization require $MR = MC$ and $p > AVC$. (AVC is not shown in the diagram, but it would be below ATC.) This happens at output q. Whether or not there are profits depends on the position of the ATC curve. In (i) where average total cost is ATC_1, there are profits, as shown by the shaded area. In (ii) where average total cost is ATC_2, profits are zero. If average total costs rose to ATC_3, the monopolist would suffer losses, as shown by the white area in (ii).

The Profits of a Monopolist

The fact that a profit-maximizing monopolist produces at an output where $MR = MC$ says nothing about how large profits will be—or even whether there will be monopoly profits. Profits may exist, as shown in Figure 15-4(i), and indeed they may persist for a long time because entry of new firms does not push price down to the level of average total cost.

But, as Figure 15-4(ii) shows, the profit-maximizing monopolist may be suffering losses too. Nothing guarantees that a monopolist will make profits. If the ATC curve is shifted upward from the level in Figure 15-4(i) while all other curves are left unchanged, profits will shrink as the curve moves up. When the ATC curve gets so high that it just touches the demand curve, as ATC_2 does in Figure 15-4(ii), the monopolist does better at that output than at other levels of output, but it has zero profits.

A Monopolist's Supply Curve?

In describing the monopolist's profit-maximizing behavior, we did not introduce the concept of a supply curve, as we did in the discussion of perfect competition. A supply curve relates the quantity supplied to the price offered. In perfect competition, the industry short-run supply curve is known as soon as the marginal cost curves of the individual firms are known. This is because the profit-maximizing firms equate marginal cost to price. Given marginal costs, it is possible to know how much will be produced at each price.

In monopoly a unique relation between market price and quantity supplied does not exist.

Like all profit-maximizing firms, a monopolistic firm equates marginal cost to marginal revenue; but, unlike firms in perfect competition, for the monopolist marginal revenue does not equal price. Because the monopolist does *not* equate marginal cost to price, it is possible for different demand conditions to give rise to the same output but to differing prices.[2]

EQUILIBRIUM OF THE FIRM AND INDUSTRY

When a monopolist is the only producer in an industry, there is no need for separate theories of the firm and the industry, as is necessary with perfect competition. The monopolist *is* the industry. Thus the profit-maximizing position of the firm shown in Figure 15-4 is the short-run equilibrium of the industry.

In a monopolized industry, as in a perfectly competitive one, profits provide an incentive for new firms to enter. If such entry occurs, the equilibrium position will change and the firm will no longer be a monopolist. **Barriers to entry** are impediments to the entry of new firms into an industry.

If monopoly is to persist in the long run, there must be barriers to the entry of other firms into an industry.

Barriers may come about in many ways. Patent laws, for instance, may create and perpetuate monopolies by conferring on the patent holder the sole right to produce a particular commodity. A firm may be granted a charter or a franchise that prohibits competition by law. Monopolies may also arise because of economies of scale. The established firm that is able to produce at a lower cost than any new, small competitor may well retain a monopoly through a cost advantage.

A monopoly may also be perpetuated by force or by threat. Potential competitors can be intimidated by threats ranging from sabotage to a price war in which the established monopoly has sufficient financial resources to ensure victory.

---

[2] In order to know the amount produced at any given price, it is necessary to know something about the shape and position of the marginal revenue curve in addition to knowing the marginal cost curve. This means that there is not a supply curve independent of the demand curve for the monopolist's product.

It is the barriers to entry in one form or another that allow a monopolist to earn profits that persist in the long run. In perfect competition, an equilibrium in which firms earn profits can occur in the short run but cannot last longer than it takes for entry to force prices down to the level of average total cost. Because there may well be no entry, the short-run profitable equilibrium of a monopolist can continue indefinitely.

THE INEFFICIENCY OF MONOPOLY

In Chapter 14 we saw that (subject to certain qualifications) perfect competition produces efficient results. By leading firms to produce at levels of output at which $p = MC$ and $p = ATC$, it satisfies conditions of both productive and allocative efficiency.

Productive Efficiency or Inefficiency

We cannot make a specific prediction about productive efficiency under monopoly, except to say that (unlike the situation in perfect competition) there is no necessary force to push production to the level where cost of production is a minimum. The output of a monopolized industry will in general be different from that of a competitive industry. While a monopolist will choose to produce its profit-maximizing output at the lowest cost *for that output*, there is no assurance that its chosen output will be the least-cost output. It may be, or it may not be. Figure 15-5 illustrates two possible cases. In Figure 15-5(i) production is at the level of minimum *ATC*; in Figure 15-5(ii) it is not.

Why might a monopolist that wishes to maximize profits not choose the output with the

FIGURE 15-5

Monopolistic Equilibrium With or Without Production at Minimum Average Total Cost

(i) Production at minimum ATC

(ii) Production above minimum ATC

The equilibrium output, where *MR* = *MC*, may occur but need not occur at minimum ATC. The *D*, *MR*, and *MC* curves are identical in the two parts of the diagram. Equilibrium price and output are p_M and q_M in each case. The diagrams differ in the position of average total cost. In (i) minimum *ATC* occurs at the equilibrium output. In (ii) actual average total cost of c_2 is greater than minimum attainable average total cost of c_1, which would require output q_2. Nothing in the theory of monopoly forces equilibrium to occur at minimum average total cost.

lowest per unit cost of production? The answer is that when choosing a level of output, the monopolist affects *both* the level of cost and the price it will receive for that output. A competitive firm, a price *taker,* can always increase profits in the short run by producing at lower average total costs. A monopolist, a price *setter,* faces a downward-sloping demand curve and may profitably accept higher average total costs if price is high enough to offset the increased unit costs. In the example of Figure 15-5(ii), at the output where *ATC* is a minimum, marginal revenue is less than marginal cost. Thus a profit-maximizing monopolist that found itself at that output would choose to decrease output, thereby increasing profits despite increased average total costs.

A monopolistic firm may or may not operate at the output that achieves minimum attainable average total costs.

Allocative Inefficiency (Price Greater than *MC*)

The fact that the monopolist produces where price is greater than marginal cost violates the conditions for allocative efficiency (discussed on page 236). When price equals marginal cost, consumers pay for the last unit purchased an amount just equal to the opportunity cost of producing that unit. But at a monopoly price and output, price is greater than marginal cost. Thus consumers pay for the last unit an amount that exceeds the opportunity cost of producing it. This is illustrated in Figure 15-6. Consumers would be prepared to buy additional units for an amount greater than the cost of producing these units. Recall that opportunity cost is the market value consumers would receive if the resources were used in their best alternative use. Some consumers could be made better off, and none worse off, by shifting extra resources into production of this commodity. In other words, allocative efficiency could be improved by increasing production of the product.

The monopoly output is not allocatively efficient; equivalently, it is not Pareto-optimal.

FIGURE 15-6
The Allocative Inefficiency of Monopoly

Because monopolistic equilibrium occurs where price is greater than marginal cost, it is not allocatively efficient. A monopolist chooses price p_M and output q_M. At that output, consumers put a value of p_M on the last unit produced, but the resources used to produce that last unit have a lower value, c_M, in their best alternative uses. Every unit between q_M and q_1 would cost less to produce than the value consumers place on it. Output q_M is thus allocatively inefficient. The shaded area is sometimes described as the deadweight loss due to the allocative inefficiency of monopoly.

The Inefficiency of Monopoly: A Warning

Just as the conclusion that perfect competition is efficient was subject to some words of warning (see page 237), so too are the conclusions about the inefficiency of monopoly. The detailed comparison of monopoly and competition we defer to Chapter 18, but a preview is in order. Much of the case against monopoly depends on the monopoly's having the same costs as a competitive industry. This assumption has been called into question in the very long run. Specifically, if monopolists engage in more innovation than would firms in a competitive industry, the cost curves of the industry may shift downward enough to offset any short-run inefficiency. (The

The Allocative Inefficiency of Monopoly: A Graphic Interpretation

In the box on p. 237, we gave a graphic interpretation of allocative efficiency. That analysis can be extended here, with reference to the figure below.

Allocative efficiency occurs at the output q_c where $p = MC$. The monopolist restricts output so that price, p_M, is greater than marginal cost. It does so to increase profits: the monopolist gains (at the expense of consumers) by raising price and restricting output. *But the monopolist's gain is smaller than consumers'*

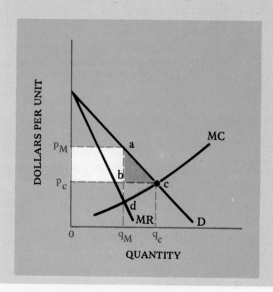

losses. This can be seen in the diagram. First consider the effect on the producer of raising the price from p_c to p_M. On the first q_M units there is a big increase in the producer's profits, shown by the white rectangle $p_c p_M ab$. To be sure, the producer loses some profits on the sales from q_M to q_c. These lost profits are shown by the light shaded area $b c d$. The net gain to the producer is the white rectangle *minus* the light shaded triangle. Now consider consumers. Their loss of consumers' surplus is the white rectangle *plus* the dark shaded triangle abc.

The white rectangle is a pure redistribution from consumers to the monopolist. It reflects extra payments on the first q_M units. Such a redistribution does not affect allocative efficiency. But the two shaded areas are losses to one group that are not gains to the other group. They are a deadweight loss and are a measure of the allocative inefficiency of monopoly.

The monopolist, by restricting output and raising price above the competitive level, gains a larger share of a smaller "pie." The deadweight loss arises because of the decrease in the size of the pie caused by not producing units that consumers value above the opportunity cost of production.

important question of the influence of market structure on innovation is discussed in Chapter 18.)

The Nature and Extent of Monopoly Power

The *theory* of monopoly just developed assumes that the monopolist has no expectation of competition.

It is difficult to imagine a firm without *any* competition. A firm may have a complete monopoly on a particular product at a given moment, but every product has some present or potential substitute for the services it provides. Some products have fairly close substitutes, and even a single seller producing such a product will have close rivals. Other products may have no existing close substitute, but new products may be developed that will compete with it. For these reasons it is useful to recognize monopoly power as a variable that can be relatively slight or nearly complete, rather than as an attribute which either does or does not exist.

Monopoly power exists to the extent that a firm is insulated from loss of customers to other sellers.

How is the extent of monopoly power to be defined? The mere fact that a firm's demand curve slopes downward means that if the firm raises its price, it will lose some sales. But there may be limits on the firm's power over price other than the slope of the market demand curve. Any producer facing a downward-sloping demand curve could choose the price-quantity combination (where $MR = MC$) that appears to maximize its profits. *But this price might not turn out to be the long-run profit-maximizing price* because the choice of a particular price-quantity combination may itself lead to changes in the behavior of other firms that in turn *shift* the original firm's demand curve. If, for example, a firm raises its price and (as an indirect result) its demand curve shifts to the left, its sales and profits will be less than the firm would have expected on the basis of the original demand curve.

Consider an example. The Coca-Cola Company is the sole producer of Cola-Cola and faces a downward-sloping demand curve. But the Coca-Cola Company is not a complete monopolist. To see why, suppose that the demand curve for Coke shows that if the price is cut by 20 percent *and* if all other soft drink suppliers keep their prices at their present levels, sales of Coke will increase by 50 percent. This would almost surely result in an increase in the company's profits. Since the Coca-Cola Company is unquestionably free to cut price by 20 percent, why does it not do so? The answer is that if it did, other soft drink prices would not remain unchanged—and the company knows this. The very action of reducing prices would almost surely cause sellers of other soft drinks to reduce *their* prices. If they did so, Coca-Cola's sales would not increase as much as its *ceteris paribus* demand curve predicts. Sales would not increase by 50 percent; instead they might increase by (say) only 10 percent. In such an event the company's profits would decrease rather than increase. Thus the Coca-Cola Company, while it has a monopoly of Coca-Cola sales, does not

have a monopoly of soft drink sales, although it may well have some market power.

The larger the *shifts* in a demand curve that are induced by a firm's changing its price, the less is that firm's monopoly power. Such shifts have two main sources. The first (as in the Coca-Cola example) is the price reactions of existing producers of substitute products. The second is the entry of new firms who succeed in capturing part of the sales that the monopolist included in "its" demand curve. Such shifts in the demand curve, from either cause, limit the market power of the firm and reduce its profits.

Since no firm is perfectly insulated from all competition for all time, total monopoly power does not exist. Monopoly power is a variable.

It matters a good deal that monopoly power is measured in terms of "more" or "less" rather than "you have it" or "you don't." One consequence is that a monopoly over a single product does not necessarily confer a high degree of monopoly power. A single producer of a product with many close substitutes (e.g., Coke) may have less monopoly power than either of two firms that produce a product with few close substitutes (e.g., soap). A second consequence is that it is not necessarily true that effective monopoly power increases as the number of firms in an industry decreases. For example, less monopoly power may be exercised in an industry where the only two or three firms compete vigorously than in an industry where eight or ten firms cooperate with each other. Such firms could agree among themselves to set a common price and/or to share the market and act in exactly the same way as if they were a single-firm monopoly. Such behavior is known as **collusion.**

MEASURING MONOPOLY POWER

In order to use the theory of monopoly, we must be able to define monopolistic markets. Furthermore, it is a matter of public policy that uncontrolled monopoly power is undesirable. Government agencies such as the Department of Justice and the Federal Trade Commission, which enforce these policies, and the judges who decide the cases, must know where monopoly power exists if they are to control or eliminate it.

Measuring monopoly power is not easy. Ideally, outputs and profits of firms in any industry should be compared with what prices, outputs, and profits would be if all firms were under unified (monopoly) control and were fully insulated from entry. But this hypothetical comparison does not lend itself to measurement.

Concentration Ratios

In practice, two alternative measures are widely used. The first of these is the **concentration ratio,** which shows the fraction of total market sales controlled by the largest group of sellers. Common types of concentration ratios cite the share of total market sales made by the largest four or eight firms. How well concentration ratios measure effective monopoly power is a matter of substantial debate among economists.

A first problem is to define the market with reasonable accuracy. For one example, concentration ratios in national cement sales are low, but they understate the market power of cement companies because heavy transportation costs divide the cement *industry* into a series of regional *markets,* in each of which there are relatively few firms. (We shall discuss problems of market definition further in Chapter 18.)

A second problem is the interpretation of concentration ratios. Are they adequate proxies for the intensity of competition? Clearly, market share is one measure of the *potential* power to control supply and set price. The inclusion in concentration ratios of the market shares of several firms rests on the possibility that large firms will, in one way or another, adopt a common price-output policy that is no different from the policy they would adopt if they were in fact under unified management.

Such common behavior may occur with or without an actual agreement to collude. Lawyers speak of **conscious parallel action** and economists of **tacit collusion** to refer to noncollusive parallel behavior. Concentration ratios measure the *ac-*

tual exercise of monopoly power only if overt or tacit collusion occurs.

High concentration ratios may be necessary for the exercise of monopoly power, but they are not sufficient. They tend to show the potential for monopoly power but not necessarily the actuality.

Profits as a Measure of Monopoly Power

Many economists, following the lead of Professor Joe S. Bain, use profit rates as a measure of monopoly power. By "high" profits, the economist means returns sufficiently in excess of all opportunity costs that potential new entrants desire to enter the industry. Persistently high profits, so goes the logic, are indirect evidence that neither rivalry among sellers nor entry of new firms prevents existing firms from pricing as if they were monopolists.

Using profits in this way requires care because, as we have seen (page 182), profits as reported in firms' income statements are not pure profits over opportunity cost. In particular, allowance must be made for differences in risk and in required payments for the use of owners' capital.

While neither concentration ratios nor profit rates are ideal measures of the degree of market power that a firm, or group of firms, actually exercises, both are of value and are widely used. In fact, concentration ratios and high profit rates are themselves correlated. Because of this, alternative classifications of markets and industries, according to their monopoly power measured in these two ways, do not differ much from one another. In spite of the difficult problems of measuring monopoly power, the theory of monopoly is widely used by economists and policymakers.

Price Discrimination

Raw milk is often sold at one price when it is to go into fluid milk, but at a lower price when it is to be used to make ice cream or cheese. Doctors usually charge for their services according to the incomes of their patients. Movie theaters may have lower admission prices for children than for adults. Railroads charge different rates per ton mile for different products. Electric companies sell electricity more cheaply for industrial than for home use. State universities charge out-of-state students higher tuition than residents. Japanese steel companies sell steel more cheaply in the United States than in Japan.

Such price differences could never persist under perfect competition. Yet many of these examples have existed for decades. Persistent price differences clearly require the exercise of some monopoly power because the seller is exerting influence over the price at which its product is sold. Why should a firm want to sell some units of output at a price well below the price it gets for other units? Why, in other words, does it practice price discrimination?

Price discrimination occurs when a producer sells a specific commodity to different buyers at two or more different prices, for reasons not associated with differences in cost. Not all price differences represent price discrimination. Quantity discounts, differences between wholesale and retail prices, and prices that vary with the time of day or the season of the year are not generally considered price discrimination because the same physical product sold at a different time or place or in different quantities may have different costs. If an electric power company has unused capacity at certain times of day, it may be cheaper to provide service at those hours than at peak demand hours. If the price differences reflect cost differences, they are nondiscriminatory. However, when price differences rest merely on different buyers' valuations of the same product, they are discriminatory. It does not cost a movie theater operator less to fill a seat with a child than an adult, but it may pay to let the children in at a discriminatory low price if few of them would attend at the full adult fare.

WHY PRICE DISCRIMINATION PAYS

Persistent price discrimination comes about either because different buyers may be willing to pay different amounts for the same commodity or because one buyer may be willing to pay different amounts for different units of the same commodity.

Consider differences among buyers. Think of the demand curve for a market containing individual buyers, each of whom has indicated the price he or she is prepared to pay for a single unit. Suppose a single price is charged. For each unit sold, buyers were willing to pay *at least* the price indicated. If the seller can make every buyer pay the maximum he or she is willing to pay, the seller can increase its profits by capturing the amounts in excess of the single price that buyers were willing to pay. In other words, the firm can capture the buyer's consumers' surplus.

WHEN IS PRICE DISCRIMINATION POSSIBLE?

However much the local butcher might like to charge the banker's wife twice as much for hamburger as he charges the taxi driver, he cannot succeed in doing so. Madame Banker can always shop for meat in the supermarket, where her husband's occupation is not known. Even if the butcher and the supermarket agreed to charge her twice as much, she could hire the taxi driver to shop for her. The surgeon, however, may succeed in discriminating (if all reputable surgeons will do the same) because it will not do the banker's wife much good to hire the taxi driver to have her operations for her.

To succeed in price discrimination, a seller must be able to control what is offered to a particular buyer and must be able to prevent the resale of the commodity from one buyer to another.

The first of the two conditions—control over supply—is the feature that makes price discrimination an aspect of the theory of monopoly.

The second of the two conditions—ability to prevent resale—tends to be associated with the character of the product or the ability to classify buyers into identifiable groups. Services are less easily resold than goods; goods that require installation by the manufacturer (e.g., heavy equipment) are less easily resold than are movable goods such as household appliances. An interesting example of nonresalability occurs in the case of plate glass. Small pieces sell much more cheaply per square foot than bigger pieces, but the person who needs glass for a 6' x 10' picture window cannot use four pieces of 3' × 5' glass. Transportation costs, tariff barriers, and import quotas separate classes of buyers geographically and may make discrimination possible.

The examples just discussed relate directly to discrimination among classes of buyers. Discrimination among units of output follows similar rules. The tenth unit purchased by a given buyer in a given month can be sold at a different price than the fifth unit only if the seller can keep track of who buys what. This can be done by the seller of electricity through meter readings or by the magazine publisher, who can distinguish between renewals and new subscriptions. The operator of a car wash and the manufacturer of aspirin find it more difficult, although by such devices as coupons and "one-cent" sales, they too can determine which unit is being purchased.

It is, of course, not enough to be able to separate buyers or units into separate classes. For price discrimination to be profitable, the different groups must have different degrees of willingness to pay. The hypothesis of diminishing marginal utility (see page 132) would lead to the prediction that different valuations are placed by an individual on different units, and differences in income and tastes would lead to the prediction that different subgroups will have different elasticities of demand for a given commodity. Thus the potential for profitable price discrimination is often present. [25]

THE POSITIVE EFFECTS OF PRICE DISCRIMINATION

The positive consequences of price discrimination are summarized in two propositions.

1. **For any given level of output, the most profitable system of discriminatory prices will provide higher total revenue to the firm (and thus also higher average revenue) than the profit-maximizing single price.**

To see that this is reasonable, remember that a monopolist with the power to discriminate *could* produce exactly the same quantity as a single-price monopolist and charge everyone the same price. Therefore it need never get *less* revenue, and it can do better if it can raise the price on even one unit sold.

2. **Output under monopolistic discrimination will generally be larger than under single-price monopoly.**

To see that this is reasonable, remember that a single-price monopolist stops selling at an output where price is greater than MC. Suppose the monopolist is able to sell additional units without reducing the price on all earlier units. Since price is greater than MC on some units not yet sold, it will be profitable to lower the price a bit and sell additional units. It follows that when a firm can price its product unit by unit, it will pay it to produce more than if it were limited to a single price.

THE NORMATIVE ASPECTS OF PRICE DISCRIMINATION

The predicted combination of higher average revenue and higher output does not in itself have any *normative* significance. It will typically lead to a different distribution of income and a different level of output than when the seller is limited to a single price. The ability of the discriminating monopolist to capture some of the consumers' surplus will seem undesirable to consumers but not to the monopolist. How outsiders view the transfer may depend on who gains and who loses.

If discrimination leads a firm to produce a larger output, it will *decrease* the allocative inefficiency of monopoly noted on page 247. The common sense of this is that a monopolistic firm which must charge a single price produces less than the perfectly competitive industry because it is aware that by producing and selling more it drives down the price against itself. Price discrimination allows it to avoid this disincentive. To the extent that the firm can sell its output in separate blocks, it can sell another block without

Is Price Discrimination Bad?

The consequences of price discrimination differ from case to case. No matter what an individual's values are, he or she is almost bound to evaluate individual cases differently.

Secret rebates. A very large oil-refining firm agrees to ship its product to market on a given railroad, provided that the railroad gives the firm a secret rebate on the transportation cost and does not give a similar concession to rival refiners. The railroad agrees and is thereby charging discriminatory prices. This rebate gives the large oil company a cost advantage that it uses to drive its rivals out of business or to force them into a merger on dictated terms. (John D. Rockefeller was accused of using such tactics in the early years of the Standard Oil Company.)

Use of product. When the Aluminum Company of America had a virtual monopoly on the production of aluminum ingots, it sold both the raw ingots and aluminum cable made from the ingots. At one time ALCOA sold cable at a price 20 percent *below* the price it charged for ingots. (Of course, the cable price was above ALCOA's cost of producing cable.) It did so because users of cable could substitute copper cable, but many users of ingot had no substitute for aluminum. In return for its "bargain price" for cable, ALCOA made the purchasers of cable agree to use it only for transmission purposes. (Without such an agreement, any demander of aluminum might have bought cable and melted it down.)

Covering costs. A product that many people want to purchase has a demand and cost structure such that there is no single price at which a producing firm can cover total costs. However, if the firm is allowed to charge discriminatory prices, it will be willing to produce the product and it may make a profit. This is illustrated in the figure.

Because *ATC* is everywhere higher than the demand curve, no single price would lead to revenues equal to costs. A price-discriminat-

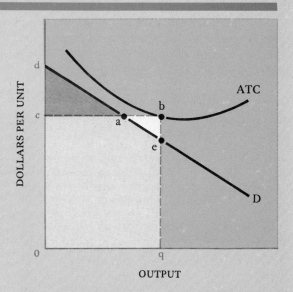

ing monopolist may be able to cover cost. The total cost of output q is the area $0cbq$. The maximum revenue attainable at any output by perfect discrimination is the area under the demand curve. For output q that area, shown as shaded, exceeds total cost since the dark shaded triangle cda is greater than the white triangle abe.

Equitable fares. For many years, British railways were not allowed to discriminate between passengers in different regions. To prevent discrimination, a fixed fare per passenger mile was specified and charged on all lines, whatever their passenger traffic and whatever the elasticity of demand for the services of the particular line. In the interests of economy, branch lines that could not cover costs closed down. This meant that some lines stopped operating even though their users preferred rail transport to any of the available alternatives and even though the strength of their preference was such that they would have willingly paid a price sufficient for the line to yield a profit. Nonetheless, the lines were closed because it was thought inequitable to discriminate against the passengers of these lines. (The policy has recently been dropped.)

spoiling the market for the block already being sold. In the case of *perfect* price discrimination, where every unit of output is sold at a different price, the profit-maximizing firm will produce every unit for which the price charged can be greater than or equal to its marginal cost. It will, therefore, produce the same output as the firm in perfect competition.

Under perfect price discrimination as well as under perfect competition, the price of the last unit sold will equal marginal cost. As a result, allocative inefficiency is avoided.

Economists can specify the different effects of different kinds of pricing behavior. Having specified the differences, people can debate their desirability. Economic analysis can describe the consequences of price discrimination, but it cannot finally evaluate them.

This remark may not satisfy the student who is aware that price discrimination has a bad reputation among economists and lawyers. The very word "discrimination" has odious connotations. Laws make certain kinds of price discrimination illegal. But was discrimination by airlines in giving students lower standby fares really bad? Whether an individual judges price discrimination as "evil" depends on the details of the case as well as on personal value judgments.

PRICE DISCRIMINATION: SYSTEMATIC AND UNSYSTEMATIC

The discussion so far has been concerned with systematic and persistent price discrimination. Systematic price discrimination most often consists of classifying buyers according to their age, location, industry, income, or the use they intend to make of the product, and then charging different prices for the different "classes" of buyers. It may also take other forms, such as charging more for the first unit bought than for subsequent units, or vice versa.

Another sort of price discrimination is common. Any firm that occasionally gives a favorite customer a few cents off, or shaves its price to land a new account, is also engaged in price discrimination. If these practices are used irregularly, they are called unsystematic discrimination. Such discrimination is not really part of the price structure, and we have ignored it here. This does not mean that it is unimportant; on the contrary, unsystematic price discrimination plays a major role in the dynamic process by which prices change in response to changed conditions of supply and demand.

The causes and consequences of systematic as opposed to unsystematic price discrimination are very different.

The law, however, is generally unable to distinguish between the two kinds of price discrimination and so hits at both. Legislation, motivated solely by a desire to attack systematic discrimination, may have unforeseen and possibly undesired effects on unsystematic discrimination. Because unsystematic price discrimination is important for the working of competition, prohibiting it may aid the maintenance of monopoly power.

Summary

1. Our analysis of monopoly begins with two simplifying assumptions: first, that an entire industry is supplied by a single seller, called a monopolist; second, that the monopolist sets a single price and supplies the entire quantity that buyers wish to purchase at that price.

2. Under these circumstances, the monopolist's own demand curve is identical with the market demand curve for the product. The market demand curve is the monopolist's average revenue curve. The marginal revenue resulting from the sale of another unit by a monopolist will always be less than the price obtained for that unit.

3. When the monopolist is maximizing profits (i.e., producing where $MR = MC$), marginal revenue will be positive, and thus elasticity of demand will be greater than unity. The amount of profits that a monopolist earns is not predicted by the theory. The amount may be large, small, zero, or negative in the short run, depending on the relation of demand and cost.

4. The presence of profits in a monopolized industry provides the same incentive to entry as it does in perfect competition. Therefore, for monopoly profits to persist in the long run, there must be effective barriers to entry. Such barriers include patent laws, charters or franchises, economies of scale, and coercive tactics.

5. Monopolists producing where $MR = MC$ and with price greater than MC do not achieve the efficiencies associated with perfect competition. There is no assurance in equilibrium that the output produced is that for which ATC is a minimum. Also, the conditions of allocative efficiency are not met. In restricting output the monopolist does not produce the output that maximizes the sum of consumers' and producers' surplus.

6. There is no such thing as a complete monopoly. Monopoly power is limited by the presence of existing substitute products, by the development of new products, and by the possibility of entry of new firms.

7. Monopoly power exists to the extent that a firm is insulated from loss of customers to other sellers. The degree of monopoly power may best be thought of as a quantitative variable. Two widely used measures of the degree of monopoly power are concentration ratios and the comparison of profits in one industry with those earned in other industries of similar risk and invested capital.

8. Price discrimination occurs when different units of the same commodity are sold for different prices, for reasons not associated with differences in costs. Different buyers may be charged different prices, or the same buyer may be charged different prices on different units of the commodity purchased.

9. The conditions under which a seller can suc-

ceed in charging discriminatory prices are, first, that it can control the supply of the product offered to particular buyers and, second, that it can prevent the resale of the commodity from one buyer to another.

10. Commodities that are highly susceptible to price discrimination include services, equipment requiring installation by the manufacturer, and commodities whose buyers can be isolated geographically by transport costs or international trade barriers.

11. Two predictions about price discrimination are (a) for any given level of output, the best system of discriminatory prices will provide higher total revenue to the firm than the best single price, and (b) output will usually be larger than under a single-price monopoly.

12. The consequences of price discrimination can differ from case to case. Price discrimination affects the distribution of income, the quantities produced, and the allocation of resources. Any individual is almost certain to evaluate individual cases differently, whatever his or her personal set of values. Further, there are important differences in the effects of systematic and unsystematic price discrimination.

Topics for Review

The relationship of price and *MR* for a monopolist
The relationships among *MR, TR,* and elasticity
Allocative inefficiency of monopoly
Measures of monopoly power
Price discrimination
Conditions that make price discrimination both possible and profitable

Discussion Questions

1. Imagine a monopoly firm with fixed costs but no variable or marginal costs—for example, a firm owning a spring of water that produces indefinitely, once certain pipes are installed, in an area where no other source of water is available. What would be the firm's profit-maximizing price? What elasticity of demand would you expect at that price? Would this seem to be an appropri-

ate pricing policy if the water monopoly were municipally owned? Suppose now that entry becomes easy because of the discovery of many additional springs. What price behavior would you expect to occur? What price equilibrium would be predicted?

2. Suppose that only one professor teaches economics at your school. Would you say this professor is a monopolist who can exact any "price" from students in the form of readings assigned, tests given, and material covered? Suppose that two additional professors are hired; has whatever monopoly power that existed been decreased?

3. Each of the following has some "monopoly power": Xerox Corporation, Pepsi-Cola Company, Mobil Oil, OPEC, AT&T. In each case, what do you think is the basis of the monopoly power? How might you decide which of the organizations listed has the greatest degree of monopoly power?

4. Which of these industries—licorice candy, copper wire, outboard motors, coal, local newspapers—would you most like to monopolize? Why? Does your answer depend on several factors or just one or two? Which would you as a consumer least like to have monopolized by someone else? If your answers are different in the two cases, explain why.

5. A movie exhibitor, Aristotle Murphy, owns movie theaters in two Indiana towns of roughly the same size, 50 miles apart. In Monopolia he owns the only chain of theaters; in Competitia there is no theater chain, and he is but one of a number of independent operators. Would you expect movie prices to be higher in Monopolia than in Competitia in the short run? In the long run? If differences occurred in prices, would Mr. Murphy be discriminating in price?

6. Airline rates to Europe are higher in summer than in winter. Canadian railroads charge lower fares during the week than on weekends. Electricity companies charge consumers lower rates, the more electricity they use. Are these all examples of price discrimination? What additional information would you like to have before answering?

7. Discuss how each of the following represents price discrimination. In your view, which are the most socially harmful?

   a. standby fares on airlines that are a fraction of the full fare

   b. standby fares, as above, available only to bona fide students under 22 years of age

   c. first class fares that are 50 percent greater than tourist fares, recognizing that two first class seats use the space of three tourist seats

   d. negotiated discounts from list price, where sales personnel are authorized to bargain hard and get as much in each transaction as the traffic will bear

   e. higher tuition for out-of-state students at state-supported colleges and universities

   f. higher tuition for law students than for history students

Industrial Organization and Theories of Imperfect Competition

16

Texaco, Shell, and Mobil are three of the "major" oil companies. They are not, singly or collectively, monopolists nor are they firms in perfect competition. Yet they are typical of many real firms in our economy. Similar comments apply to the Coca-Cola and Pepsi-Cola companies. Do the two basic theories of pricing behavior we have studied—perfect competition and monopoly—have any relevance to their behavior?

The essential features of perfect competition are that each firm sells a product sufficiently similar to those sold by its numerous competitors that no one firm has any power to influence price (firms are price takers) and that the industry exhibits freedom of entry and exit. The essential features of monopoly are blockaded entry and a demand curve that is substantially the same for the firm and for the industry. Do the theories of perfect competition and monopoly provide a sufficient basis for predictions about price and market behavior in the real economy? Fifty years ago most economists would have said yes; today most would say no, although the matter is still in dispute.

This chapter looks first at some statistics to see how well the assumptions about monopoly and competition *describe* the American economy. This is not the whole of the matter, for it is the method of science to abstract from the full complexity of reality, and it might well be that descriptively unrealistic models were analytically adequate to make predictions that were confirmed by observations. If this were true, one would be able to predict the behavior of all

American industries by classifying each as competitive or monopolistic *for purposes of predicting responses.* Many economists believe that although the models of monopoly and perfect competition are clearly useful, there is a need for other models as well. This chapter suggests some of them.

Structure of the American Economy

Our first task is to analyze how well the models of perfect competition and monopoly describe American firms and industries.

TWO GROUPINGS OF AMERICAN INDUSTRIES

It is relatively easy to divide much of American industry into two broad groups, those with a large number of relatively small firms and those with a few relatively large firms. If these two groups are described by the two market forms we have studied so far, then it must be perfect competition for the first and monopoly for the second.

Sectors with Many Small Firms

Between 40 and 50 percent of the economy's national product is produced by industries made up of a large number of small firms. This includes most agricultural production, most services (travel agents, lawyers, plumbers, television technicians, etc.), most retail trade (stores, gas stations, etc.), most wholesale trade, most construction, and industries whose major business is exchange (real estate agents, stockbrokers, etc.).[1]

The competitive model, with the addition of

---

[1] Although, as we saw in Chapter 7, the size of American farms has increased dramatically in recent years, even the largest farm is small in relation to total market demand. Thus even the largest farmer is a price taker, not a price setter.

government intervention where necessary, does quite well in describing many of these industries. This is obviously so where the business of the industry is exchange rather than production. Foreign exchange markets and stock exchanges are notable examples. Agriculture also fits fairly well in most ways; the individual farmer is clearly a price taker, entry into farming is easy, and exit is possible though not in fact very rapid. Many basic raw materials such as iron ore, tin, and copper are sold on world markets where prices fluctuate continually in response to changes in demand and supply.

Some other industries, however, do not seem to be described by the perfectly competitive model even though they contain many firms. In the retail trades and services, for example, most firms have some influence over prices. The local grocery, supermarket, discount house, and department store not only consider weekend specials and periodic sales important to business success, they spend a good deal of money advertising them. In wholesaling, the sales representative is regarded as a key figure—which would not be true if the firm could sell all it wished at a given market price. Moreover, each store in these industries has a unique location that may give it some local monopoly power over nearby customers.

The first group of industries therefore contains some that are clearly described by the model of perfect competition and many others that are not.

Sectors with a Few Large Firms

About 50 percent of the national product is produced by industries dominated by a few large firms. The names of these firms are part of the average citizen's vocabulary. In this category fall most transportation firms (e.g., the Penn Central Railroad, the Santa Fe Railroad, United Airlines, American Airlines, Greyhound), communications (AT&T, NBC, CBS, Western Union), public utilities (American Electric Power, Consolidated Edison), and much of the largest sector of the American economy, the manufacturing sector.

A casual look at the manufacturing sector can be misleading if one does not distinguish between products and firms. In some manufacturing industries there are many differentiated products produced by only a few firms. In soaps and detergents, for example, a vast variety of products is produced by a mere two firms, Lever Brothers and Procter & Gamble. Similar circumstances exist in chemicals, breakfast foods, cigarettes, and numerous other industries where many more or less competing products are in each case produced by a very few firms. Clearly these industries are not perfectly competitive. Yet neither do they appear to be monopolies, for the few firms typically compete energetically against each other.

Few industries with only a few large firms are easily characterized as monopolies. Many railway companies once enjoyed monopolies of service over rural areas (although seldom between major cities, which were normally served by several companies). In this century, however, both airlines and trucking have provided intense competition to the railroads. In manufacturing, examples of single-firm monopoly outside the regulated areas are few. The Aluminum Company of America was the sole producer of primary aluminum in the United States from 1893 until World War II. Yet even during this period some aluminum was imported and some aluminum scrap was reprocessed, thereby giving ALCOA less than complete control over supply. Nevertheless ALCOA and a few other companies have been described with reasonable accuracy as monopolies. The United Shoe Machinery Company had a monopoly on certain types of shoe machinery until antitrust decrees limited its exercise of monopoly power. The National Cash Register Company, the International Nickel Company, the Climax Molybdenum Company, and International Business Machines all had control, at one time or another, over more than 90 percent of the output of the industries in which they operated.

Monopolies exist in certain utility industries such as power and light, telephone communication, and postal services. Even here, however, the monopoly sometimes exists only because of government regulation. For example, if a legal monopoly were not enforced by the government, postal and parcel delivery services would be fiercely competitive. In other cases a monopoly that seems quite unassailable will not persist over the decades. Technological breakthroughs have already been made that will make voice communication a competitive industry in the foreseeable future. The days of the monopoly of the telephone company are clearly numbered.

Monopoly and perfect competition do not *describe* much of the American economy. Many industries with numerous firms depart from some of the conditions of perfect competition; most industries with no more than a few firms depart from the conditions of monopoly.

PATTERNS OF CONCENTRATION IN MANUFACTURING

Let us take a closer look at American manufacturing. Table 16-1 shows current four-firm concentration ratios in selected industries that together account for about 40 percent of all manufacturing shipments. Notice that, descriptively, few of these industries fit either of the models studied so far. Among the high-concentration industries such as automobiles, aluminum, and cigarettes, the very high concentration is achieved by three or four firms in apparently vigorous rivalry with one another. That these firms have appreciable market power is undoubted; that they may be described by the monopoly model is questionable. The competitive model conceivably fits the two or three industries at the bottom of the list, but even here there are doubts.

Style considerations play a significant role in women's clothing, and many manufacturers believe they have some control over price. Metal stamping firms, print shops, and soft drink bottlers, while very numerous nationally, operate in small regional and local markets in which a small

TABLE 16-1

Concentration Ratios in Selected Manufacturing Industries, 1972

Industry	Four-firm concentration ratio
Automotive	
Vehicles	93
Parts	61
Cigarettes	84
Office machines	60
Tires and tubes	73
Soaps and detergents	62
Aircraft	
Planes	66
Engines and parts	77
Aluminum	
Primary	79
Rolling and drawing mills	73
Radio and television	
Sets	49
Equipment	19
Steel mills and blast furnaces	45
Chemicals	
Organic industrial	43
Plastics	27
Pharmaceutical	26
Machinery	
Farm	47
Construction	43
Metal stamping	9
Nonferrous wire	41
Petroleum refining	31
Foods	
Cereals	90
Bread and cake	29
Fluid milk	18
Canned fruit and vegetables	20
Soft drinks	14
Forest products	
Paper mills	24
Pulp mills	59
Clothes	
Men's and boys' suits and coats	19
Women's and misses' dresses	9
Fur goods	7
Commercial printing, lithography	4

Source: U.S. Department of Commerce, *1972 Census of Manufactures*, 1975.

Concentration ratios vary greatly among manufacturing industries. These data, from the 1972 census of manufactures, show the share of the industries' shipments accounted for by the four largest firms.

number of sellers, in direct rivalry with one another, do not regard themselves as price takers.

INTERMEDIATE MARKET FORMS

The need for intermediate categories to describe the American economy is suggested by Table 16-2, which shows that in more than two-thirds of manufacturing industries, the four largest firms control between 20 and 80 percent of the value of shipments. This is too much to be described as competitive and too little to be described as a monopoly.

The inability of the theories of monopoly and perfect competition to describe the modern economy made economists of 50 years ago uncomfortable. And uncomfortable economists theorize. Some of the resulting theories were appealing in part because they were descriptively realistic. This appeal was expressed by Professor R. L. Bishop when he said that with these alternative theories, economists were at last able to explain "why we are a race of eager sellers and coy buyers, with purchasing agents getting the Christmas presents from the salesmen rather than the other way around."

TABLE 16-2

Manufacturing Industries, Classified by 1972 Concentration Ratios

Concentration ratio (percentage)	Number of industries listed by the census	Percentage of value of total shipments of all manufacturing industries
80–100	22	9
60–79	54	14
40–59	116	21
20–39	170	34
Less than 20	90	22
Total	452	100

Source: U.S. Department of Commerce, *1972 Census of Manufactures*, 1975.

Notice the importance measured both in numbers and in value of shipments of industries in the three middle groups. These data were computed from the 1972 census of manufactures. The concentration ratios are those for the four largest firms in each industry.

Monopolistic Competition

Dissatisfaction with the polar cases of perfect competition and monopoly led in the 1930s to the development of a theory of a new market structure called monopolistic competition. The theory was developed in two classic books, one by the American economist Edward Chamberlin, the other by the British economist Joan Robinson.

The market envisaged in the new theory was similar to perfect competition in that there were many firms with freedom of entry and exit. But it differed in one important respect: Each firm had some power over price because each sold a product that was differentiated significantly from those of its competitors. One firm's soap might be similar to another firm's soap, but it differed in chemical composition, color, smell, softness, brand name, and a host of other characteristics that mattered to customers. This is the phenomenon of **product differentiation.** It implies that each firm has a certain degree of local monopoly power over its own product. This is the "monopolistic" part of the theory. The monopoly power is severely restricted, however, by the presence of similar products sold by competing firms. This is the "competition" part of the theory.

From a theoretical point of view, the major difference between monopolistic and perfect competition lies in the assumptions of homogeneous and differentiated products. Firms in perfect competition sell a **homogeneous product,** which from a practical point of view means a product similar enough across the industry so that no one firm has any power over price. Firms in monopolistic competition sell a **differentiated product,** which from a practical point of view means a group of commodities similar enough to be called a product but dissimilar enough that the producer of each has some power over its own price.

The theory of monopolistic competition was extremely important as a step in the development of models of intermediate market structures. Its main prediction is outlined below, and a more detailed analysis is given in the appendix to this chapter.

The excess capacity theorem. The major characteristics of monopolistic competition are two. First, because each firm has a monopoly over its own product, each is not a price taker. Instead each firm faces a downward-sloping demand curve. But the curve is rather elastic because similar products sold by other firms provide many close substitutes. The downward slope of the demand curve provides the potential for monopoly profits in the short run.

Second, freedom of entry and exit forces profits to zero in the long run. If profits are being earned by existing firms in the industry, new firms will enter. Their entry will mean that the demand for the product must be shared among more brands. Thus the demand curve for any one firm's brand will shift left. Entry continues until profits fall to zero.

The absence of positive profits requires that each firm's demand curve (its average revenue curve) be nowhere above its long-run average cost curve. The absence of losses (losses would cause exit) requires that each firm be able to cover its costs. Thus average revenue must equal average cost at some level of output. Together these requirements imply that when a monopolistically competitive industry is in long-run equilibrium, its firms will be producing where their demand curves are tangent to (i.e., just touching at one point) their average total cost curves.

Two curves that are tangent at a point have the same slope at that point. If a downward-sloping demand curve is to be tangent to the *LRATC* curve, the latter must also be downward-sloping at the point of tangency. In such a situation each firm is producing an output less than the one for which its *LRATC* reaches its minimum point. This is the famous **excess capacity theorem** of monopolistic competition.

Productive efficiency is not achieved under monopolistic competition because firms do not produce at their lowest attainable cost.

This prediction, over which a seemingly endless controversy raged for decades, is illustrated graphically in Figure 16A-2 (page 908) and is discussed further in the appendix to this chapter.

The modern conclusion, however, is that when a choice must be made on how many products to produce, "productive efficiency" is no longer desirable. Let us see why this is so. People have different tastes; some prefer one differentiated product and some another. Each brand of breakfast food, for example, has its sincere devotees. This creates a trade-off between producing more products to better satisfy diverse tastes and producing any given set of products at the lowest possible cost. The larger the number of differentiated products in existence, the further to the left of the least-cost level of output the production of each product will be, but the more it will be possible to satisfy diverse tastes. Under these conditions, consumers' satisfactions are not maximized by increasing production of each product until each is produced at its least-cost point. Instead the number of differentiated products must be increased until the gain from adding one more equals the loss from having to produce each existing product at a higher cost (because less of each is produced). For this reason, among others, the charge that monopolistic competition would lead to a waste of resources is no longer accepted as necessarily, or even probably, true.

Monopolistic competition after 40 years. Monopolistic competition produced a revolution in economists' attitudes. However, there was a long debate over what it actually predicted and how empirically relevant the theory was. Today the debate has subsided somewhat, with the realization that—at least in manufacturing—product differentiation occurs mainly where a small group rather than a large group of firms compete with each other.

Although there are many industries in which a large number of slightly differentiated products compete for the buyers' attention, in most such cases the industries have only a few firms, each of which sells a large number of products. Consider the soap and detergent industry. Among the well-known brands currently on sale in the United States are Cheer, Dash, Dawn, Gain, Oxydol, Tide, Dreft, Ivory Snow, Ivory Liquid, Joy, Cascade, Camay, Lava, Safeguard, Zest,

Mr. Clean, Top Job, Spic and Span, Comet, and Cinch. Surely this is impressive differentiation, and the fact that most of the names are familiar to most Americans shows that they are advertised effectively.

At first glance, the above list of products might appear to provide a perfect example of monopolistic competition. But *every one* of the products named above is manufactured by a single company, Procter & Gamble, which, with Lever Brothers, dominates sales of soaps, cleansers, and detergents in America. Clearly such industries are not the large-group case envisaged by the framers of the theory of monopolistic competition.

Thus it is the small-group case of "differentiated oligopoly" rather than the large-group case of monopolistic competition that seems relevant today.[2] Indeed, in the last half of the 1970s there was a great outburst of theorizing about all aspects of product differentiation. Significantly, the theory that studies market structures where a small number of firms compete to sell a large number of differentiated products has taken the name *monopolistic competition*. The term now refers to any industry in which more than one firm sells differentiated products.

This modern theory is the direct descendant of the earlier theories of monopolistic competition. The focus remains on product differentiation and on industrial structures thought to describe the nature of the modern economy. The new theory is consistent with the famous propositions of Chamberlin and Robinson that it pays firms to differentiate their products, to advertise heavily, and to engage in other forms of nonprice competition. These are characteristics to be found in

[2] At first sight retailing may appear to be closer to the conditions of monopolistic competition than is manufacturing. Certainly every city has a very large number of retailers selling any one commodity. The problem is that they are differentiated from each other mainly by their geographical location, each firm having only a few competing close neighbors. Thus a model of interlocking oligopolies, with every firm in close competition with only a few neighbors, seems to be a better model for retailing than the large-group monopolistic competition model, in which every firm competes directly with a large number of other firms. But this too is subject to current controversy.

the world but not in perfect competition. Most of the modern theory of product differentiation relates to industries with a small number of firms. This is the theory of oligopoly, to which we now turn our attention.[3]

Oligopoly

Manufacturing industries are often characterized by small groups of firms rather than large groups.[4] **Oligopoly** is a market structure in which there are relatively few firms that have enough market power that they may not be regarded as price takers (as in perfect competition) but are subject to enough rivalry that they cannot consider the market demand curve as their own. In most of these cases entry is neither perfectly easy nor wholly blockaded. In many industries, a small number of firms—between three and a dozen—tend to dominate the industry, and newcomers find it hard to establish themselves.

While the American automobile industry is a somewhat extreme example of this, its experience is revealing. Today three large firms and one much smaller firm constitute the industry. No one has successfully entered the industry in the more than 50 years since the Dodge brothers split with Ford and started making their own cars. Henry Kaiser attempted to enter in 1946. His Kaiser-Frazer came on the market, but despite the postwar boom in car sales the company suffered staggering losses and quietly withdrew in 1953. Recently foreign automobile firms have been setting up plants in the United States. These are not new entrants into the world's automobile industry, however, but merely new plants being set up by old established firms.

What makes the automobile industry unusual is the absence of a "competitive fringe." The cigarette industry is similar—there are only eight firms in the entire industry. In contrast, there are 152 petroleum refiners, but the 102 smallest firms together account for only 5 percent of value of output. There are 136 tire and tube manufacturing companies, of which the 100 smallest supply in aggregate less than 2 percent of the market. Oligopoly is not inconsistent with a large number of small sellers when the "big few" dominate the decision making in the industry.

Competition Among the Few: The Theory of Oligopoly

One of the most striking contrasts between perfectly competitive and oligopolistic markets concerns the behavior of prices. In perfect competition prices change daily, even hourly, in response to changes in demand and supply. Oligopolistic prices change less frequently. Manufacturers of radios, automobiles, television sets, and men's suits do not change their prices with anything like the frequency that prices change in markets for basic materials or stocks and bonds. If you price a man's suit or a lady's skirt today in your local store, chances are that the price will be the same when you return to the store tomorrow. Of course prices do change, but in oligopolistic industries prices usually change by relatively large amounts at discrete intervals in time. Book publishers and appliance manufacturers, for example, typically announce list prices for their products and change them infrequently. These prices do not change in response to every small fluctuation in demand and costs, although they do change in response to large or persistent changes.[5]

---

[3] Chamberlin considered the small-group case, but in the historical development of the subject it was his large-group case that was treated as important. The essence of monopolistic competition as understood by Chamberlin, and by the economics profession at the time, was the large-group case.

[4] Oligopolies may be present even in nationally unconcentrated industries. A national concentration ratio is relevant where there is one national market. But if transport costs mean that the country is split up into numerous regional markets, each one may contain a small number of oligopolistic firms.

[5] There tends to be more short-run price competition in the retailing of goods produced by oligopolists than among the oligopolists themselves. For example, the average discount that automobile retailers are prepared to negotiate with their customers may fluctuate continually with market prices even though the prices they pay to the manufacturer may remain stable from month to month.

ADMINISTERED PRICES UNDER OLIGOPOLY

A major difference between perfectly competitive and oligopolistic firms is that the former are price takers while the latter are price setters. A wheat farmer must accept the market price of wheat, but a producer of television sets must *decide* what price to charge for its product. We say that the oligopolistic firm administers its price. An **administered price** is a price that is set by conscious decision of the seller rather than by the impersonal forces of demand and supply.

In determining price an oligopolist has to consider demand, costs, and the prices of competing products.

When all of these influencing factors have been taken into account, the oligopolist must still decide what price to put on its product. Having decided on an administered price, the oligopolistic firm must accept the consequences: its sales will be determined by the demand curve for its product. An increase or decrease in demand is signaled to the firm by a rise or a fall in its sales at the administered price. In contrast, in perfect competition a change in demand is signaled to the firm by a change in its market price.

THEORETICAL APPROACHES TO OLIGOPOLISTIC BEHAVIOR

Homogeneous Products

A pathbreaking attack on the oligopoly problem occurred as long ago as 1838, the work of the French economist A. A. Cournot. He dealt with the special case of an industry containing only two firms, called a **duopoly.** The two firms sold an identical product. He had each choose its profit-maximizing output on the assumption that the other firm would hold its own output constant. He then showed that if each firm in turn adjusted to the last move made by its competitor (on the assumption that the competitor would make no further move), a stable equilibrium would be reached in which the market was divided between the two firms in a definite way. Each firm would charge the same price as the other, and that price would be higher than the perfectly competitive price but lower than the price a monopolist would charge. This finding established oligopoly as a truly intermediate case between perfect competition and monopoly.

Firms in the situation analyzed by Cournot will raise price and lower output when costs rise, and they will usually raise price and raise output when demand increases. Thus changes in price and quantity are in the same direction as under perfect competition, though the magnitude of the changes will be different.

The equilibrium Cournot analyzed has survived in modern theorizing. It is now called a Nash or a Cournot-Nash equilibrium. It is the equilibrium that results when each firm makes its decisions on the assumption that all other firms' behavior will be unchanged.

Nash equilibria can be determined for many oligopolistic situations. Their properties can be compared with the equilibria that would result from perfect competition and from monopoly (usually, higher prices and lower output than under competition; lower prices and higher output than under monopoly). The price-quantity differences can also be studied when equilibrium changes under the impact of shifts in input costs or demand for the industry's output.

Unfortunately the Cournot-Nash assumption, that each firm takes its rival's behavior as given, seems inapplicable to many small-group situations. The Ford Motor Company knows (or quickly learns) that if it slashes the prices of some of its cars, GM, Chrysler, and American Motors will react by adjusting their prices on comparable cars. Similar considerations apply when General Mills considers changing the advertising for one of its breakfast cereals or Lever Brothers the prices of its soaps.

Thus not only must an oligopolistic firm be concerned with how *buyers* of its products will react to changes it makes, it must anticipate how each of a few identified rival *sellers* will react. The firm's policy must depend on how it *thinks* its competitors will react to its moves, and the outcome of the firm's policy will depend on how they do in fact react. Here there is no simple, unique set of rules for the equilibrium either of the firm or of the small group of firms that constitutes the industry. Neither is there a set of simple predictions about how the firms will react, either individually or collectively, to various changes in taxes, costs, and demand. Much depends on the policy that the firm pursues, on the policies that its competitors pursue, on how each reacts to the other's changes, and on how each thinks the other will react.

Economists have sometimes tackled this problem of interactions by assuming that each firm makes its decisions subject to what are called *conjectural variations*. A firm making, say, a price decision conjectures what variations its choice would induce its rivals to make in their prices. The Cournot-Nash equilibrium is the special case where conjectural variations are zero. Firm A sets its price on the conjecture that its rivals will not vary their prices in response to firm A's decision, and its rivals do the same.

Of course a wide range of conjectural variations is possible. For example, firm A might assume that whatever price it sets, its rivals will set the same price. Equilibrium can be shown to exist for many conjectural variations, and the properties of these equilibria (price, quantity, etc.) can be compared with the equilibria that would result if the industry were either perfectly competitive or fully monopolized.

The problem with the conjectural variations approach is that it is difficult to state conjectural variations that are anything other than mechanical rules. Such rules ignore subtle considerations of strategy such as bluff and counterbluff that may be relevant in real situations of small-group competition. More important perhaps, they neglect the learning and adaptation that characterize most real industries.

Differentiated Products

Cournot's analysis dealt with oligopolists selling homogeneous products. Another set of oligopoly problems arises when firms sell differentiated products. For example, one brand of cigarettes sold by the American Tobacco Company differs not only from all other brands sold by that company but from all brands sold by competing companies. With differentiated products, each product is distinct from every other product.

One of the puzzles of such oligopolies is why each firm sells a number of similar products that compete actively with many other products sold by the *same* company. One part of the answer may lie in consumers' tastes; another part may lie in the desire to make more difficult the entry of new firms into the industry. We shall study this question later in this chapter.

EMPIRICALLY BASED APPROACHES TO OLIGOPOLISTIC BEHAVIOR

Because the oligopoly problem is so complex, some economists have sought to build a theory from observations of the behavior of oligopolistic firms. These economists believe that we need to begin with detailed knowledge of the actual behavior of such firms. The knowledge is then used to narrow the range of theoretically possible cases by selecting those that actually occur.

In this section we shall (1) describe one major empirically based hypothesis about oligopoly behavior, (2) describe briefly a number of subsidiary hypotheses concerning forces that pull in opposite directions, and (3) discuss at greater length one or two hypotheses that seem to shed some light on real oligopolistic behavior.

The Hypothesis of Qualified Joint Profit Maximization

While explicit collusion is illegal in the United States, why cannot a small group of firms that recognize their interdependence simply act in a common manner? Such tacit collusion has been called "quasi-agreement" by Professor William Fellner. If all firms behave as though they were branches of a single firm, they can achieve the ends of a monopolist by adopting price and output policies that will maximize their *collective* (joint) *profits*. Every firm is interested, however, in *its own* profits, not the industry's profits, and it may pay one firm to depart from the joint profit-maximizing position, if, by so doing, it can increase its share of the profits.

The hypothesis of qualified joint profit maximization thus rests on the notion that a firm in an oligopolistic industry is responsive to *two* sets of influences.

Any oligopolistic firm wants to cooperate with its rivals to maximize their joint profits; it also wants to receive as large a share of the profits as possible.

Consider the conflicting pressures on an oligopolistic firm when it chooses its price. First, if firms in a group recognize that they are *interdependent* and face a downward-sloping demand curve, they will recognize that their joint profits depend on the price that each of them charges. This pulls each firm to cooperate with its rivals in charging the same price that a single firm would charge if it monopolized the industry.

Second, despite this pull an aggressive seller may hope to gain more than its rivals by being the first to cut price below the monopoly level. But if it does this, other firms may follow and the total profits earned in the industry will fall as prices are pushed below their joint profit-maximizing level. A firm that initiates such a price-cutting strategy must balance what it expects to gain by securing a larger *share* of the profits against what it expects to lose because there will be a smaller total of profits to go around.

The hypothesis of qualified joint profit maximization is that the relative strength of the two tendencies (toward and away from joint profit maximization) varies from industry to industry in a systematic way that may be associated with observable characteristics of firms, markets, and products. Let us consider some examples.

Some Specific Hypotheses About Oligopolistic Behavior

1. *The tendency toward joint maximization is greater for small numbers of sellers than for larger numbers.* Here the argument concerns both ability and motivation. When there are few firms, they will know that there is no chance that any one of them can gain sales without inducing retaliation by its rivals. At the same time, a smaller number of firms can tacitly coordinate their policies with less difficulty than a larger number.

2. *The tendency toward joint maximization is greater for producers of very similar products than for producers of sharply differentiated products.* The argument here is that the more nearly identical the products of sellers, the closer will be the direct rivalry for customers and the less the ability of one firm to gain a decisive advantage over its rivals. Thus, other things being equal, such sellers will prefer joint efforts to achieve a larger pie to individual attempts to take customers away from each other.

3. *The tendency toward joint maximization is greater in a growing than in a contracting industry.* The argument here is that when demand is growing, firms can utilize their capacity fully without resorting to attempts to "steal" their rivals' customers. In contrast, when firms have excess capacity, they are tempted to give discounts or secret price concessions in order to pick up customers. Eventually their rivals will retaliate, and large price cuts may become general.

4. *Tacit price fixing to maximize joint profits will cause nonprice competition that will take the industry away from its joint maximizing position.* The argument here is that when firms seek to suppress their basic rivalry by agreeing, tacitly or explicitly, not to engage in price competition, rivalry will break out in other forms. Firms then seek to maintain or increase their market shares through excessive advertising, quality changes, the establishment of new products, bonuses, giveaways, and a host of other schemes for gaining at the expense of their rivals while leaving the list prices of products unchanged.

5. *The tendency toward joint profit maximizing is greater, the greater are the barriers to entry of new firms.* The high profits of existing firms will attract new entrants, who will drive down price and reduce profits. Less of this will

occur, the greater are the barriers to entry. Thus the greater the entry barriers, the closer the profits of existing firms can be to their joint maximizing level. Such barriers to entry may be natural or created by the firm.

BARRIERS TO ENTRY

Suppose firms in an oligopolistic industry succeed in raising prices above long-run average total costs so that economic profits are earned. Why do these profits not cause further firms to enter the industry? Why does entry not continue until the extra output forces price down to the level where only the opportunity cost of capital is being earned (i.e., economic profits are zero)?

The answer lies in *barriers to entry,* which are anything that puts new firms that wish to enter an industry at a significant competitive disadvantage relative to existing firms in the industry. Barriers are of three sorts: natural barriers, barriers created by the firms already in the industry, and barriers created by government policy. We discuss the first two in this chapter.

Natural Barriers

Natural barriers to entry may result from an interaction between market size—as shown by the market demand curve—and economies of scale—as shown by the firm's long-run average total cost curve (*LRATC*).

One type of natural barrier depends on the shape of the *LRATC* curve and in particular on what is called **minimum efficient scale** (*MES*). This term refers to the smallest size firm that can reap all the available economies of large scale.

Suppose the technology of an industry is such that the typical firm's *MES* is 10,000 units a week at an *ATC* of $10 per unit and that at a price of $10 the total quantity demanded is 30,000 units per week. Clearly there is room for no more than three plants of efficient size—and hence three firms at most will serve this market. The industry will naturally tend to be oligopolistic.

Now say that demand expands to 35,000 units at a price of $10. There is still not room for a fourth plant operating at *MES,* but the existing firms can raise their prices above $10 a unit and earn a profit above total costs.

Natural barriers to entry occur when the output at which *MES* is achieved is large relative to total demand. Under these circumstances a small number of existing firms may earn profits without inducing a further firm to enter the market.

A second type of natural cost barrier occurs when there are **absolute cost advantages.** This means that existing firms have average cost curves that are significantly lower over their entire range than those of potential new entrants. Among possible sources of such an advantage are control of crucial patents or resources, knowledge that comes only from "learning by doing" in the industry, and established credit ratings that permit advantageous purchasing and borrowing. Each of these may be regarded as only a temporary disadvantage of new firms, which, given time, might develop their own know-how, patents, and satisfactory credit ratings.

This kind of barrier, however, makes it possible for existing firms to charge a price such that although existing firms earn profits, new entrants may face losses for some time after entry. This price is known as a **limit price.** The early losses, which persist until the new firms' *ATC*s fall to the level of the going price, can make entry seem sufficiently unprofitable—in spite of the expectation of later profits—to prevent entry.

Firm-created Barriers to Entry

If natural entry barriers do not exist, oligopolistic firms can earn long-run economic profits only if they can create barriers that prevent their profits from attracting new entrants into the industry.

Predatory pricing. One way of doing this is to create a situation that threatens a new entrant with losses in spite of the fact that existing firms are earning profits. For example, prices may be cut to or below cost whenever entry occurs, then raised after the new entrant has given up.

There is much controversy concerning predatory pricing. Some economists argue that pricing policies that appear to be predatory can be explained by other motives and that existing firms only hurt themselves when they engage in such practices instead of reaching an accommodation with new entrants. Others argue that predatory pricing seems to have been observed and that it is in the long-run interests of existing firms to punish new entrants even when it is costly to do so in the short run.

Whatever the outcome of this debate among economists, the courts have taken the position that predatory pricing does occur. A number of firms have been convicted of using it in restraint of trade.

Preemptive expansion in an expanding market. Say the market is growing (demand curve shifting outward) to an extent that there will be room for each of three existing firms to open one more plant operating at *MES* every four years beginning in 1980. If the firms were not worried about entry, each would build a new plant in 1980, 1984, 1988 and so on. But faced with this strategy, a new firm could build a plant in 1983, 1987, and so on — and thus be in possession of a market when the new plant became profitable a year later. The investment in fixed capital represents a commitment to the market. The first three plants that get in will have preempted the new part of the market, and it will not pay anyone else to build yet another plant because four new plants would all lose money.

In order to prevent this from happening, existing firms will be tempted to build their new plants long before the demand expands enough for them to be operated at a profit. Once the plant is built it will not pay a new firm to build a further plant, and the existing firms will remain in possession of the market when demand expands sufficiently to allow the new plant to cover its costs. Existing firms may well be in a much stronger position to expand in anticipation of future demand than po-

tential new firms. This type of entry-preventing strategy — building new capacity to serve an expanding market before it is needed — has been alleged to occur in several oligopoly and monopoly situations.

Advertising. Suppose there are few scale economies so that a new firm can reach minimum costs at an output that is low relative to total industry output. Thus there are only weak barriers to entry. (This may well be the case, for example, in the cigarette and soap industries.) Existing firms can create entry barriers by imposing fixed costs on new entrants. These fixed costs raise the *MES* of all firms, including new entrants.

Advertising is one such policy. Where there is much effective brand-image advertising, a new firm will have to spend a great deal on advertising its product in order to bring it to the public's attention. If the firm's sales are small, advertising costs *per unit sold* will be very large. Only when sales are large, so that the advertising costs can be spread over a large number of units, will costs per unit be brought down to a level low enough that they will not confer a significant competitive disadvantage on the new firm.

Figure 16-1 illustrates how heavy advertising can shift the cost curves of a firm with a low *MES* to make it one with a high *MES*. In essence, what happens is that a scale advantage of advertising is added to a low *MES* of production with the result that the overall *MES* is raised. Thus a new entrant who must both produce and advertise finds itself at a substantial cost disadvantage relative to its established rivals.

A firm with no natural entry barriers may be able to create them by use of nonprice competition. Advertising of course does things other than create barriers to entry. Among them, it may perform the useful function of informing buyers about their alternatives, thereby making markets work more smoothly. Indeed, a new firm may find that advertising is essential, even when existing firms do not advertise at all, simply to call attention to its entry into an industry where it is unknown.

Brand proliferation. Many products have several characteristics, each of which can be varied over a wide range. Thus there is room for a large number of similar products, each with a somewhat different mix of characteristics. Consider the many different kinds of breakfast cereals or cars. The multiplicity of brands is in part a response to consumers' tastes. If you doubt this, try to persuade a sports car addict to switch to a standard four-door sedan, or try to get a lover of Granola to switch to Sugar Puffs, or try to make all the members of one family eat the same cereal every day of the week.

Product proliferation can also serve as a barrier to entry. Because there are some economies of scale in producing every differentiated product, an infinite variety cannot be provided. Even though a small group of consumers could

be found who would prefer each of 10,000 different breakfast cereals, their demands would not be large enough to cover the costs of production. Thus there is room in the market for perhaps only 50 or 60 brands rather than a few thousand. By producing many kinds of cars, cereals, or soaps and adding new ones whenever demand either increases or shifts toward a different mix of characteristics, existing firms can make it more difficult for new firms selling a differentiated product to enter the industry.

Having many differentiated products confers other advantages on existing firms. If the product is one in which consumers switch brands frequently, then increasing the number of brands sold by existing firms will reduce the expected sales of a new entrant. Say that an industry contains three large firms, each selling one brand of cigarettes, and say that 30 percent of all smokers choose brands in a random fashion each year. If a new firm enters the industry, it can expect to pick up 25 percent of these smokers (it has one brand out of a total of four available brands). This would give it 7.5 percent (25 percent of 30 percent) of the total market the first year merely as a result of picking up its share of the random switchers, and it would keep increasing its share year by year thereafter.[6] If, however, the existing three firms had five brands each, there would be fifteen brands already available and a new small firm selling one new brand could expect to pick up only one-sixteenth of the brand switchers, giving it less than 2 percent of the total market the first year, and its gains in subsequent years would also be less.

Applications of the Theory of Entry Barriers

The hypothesis that nonprice competition can create barriers to entry helps to clarify two apparently paradoxical aspects of everyday industrial life: the fact that one firm may sell many dif-

FIGURE 16-1
Advertising Cost as a Barrier to Entry

Large advertising costs can increase the *MES* of production and thereby increase entry barriers. The *ATC* curve shows that the *MES* without advertising is at *q*. The curve *ATC*$_A$ shows that advertising cost per unit falls as output rises. Advertising increases total cost to *ATC*$_1$ and raises *MES* to *q*$_1$. Advertising has given a scale advantage to large sellers and has thus created a barrier to entry.

---

[6] Because it is smaller than its rivals, it will lose fewer customers to them by random switching than it will gain from them.

ferent brands of the same product, and the fact that each firm spends considerable sums on advertising, competing against its own products as well as those of rival firms. The soap and cigarette industries provide classic examples of this behavior; both industries contain only a few firms that sell a large number of differentiated products.

Part of the reason surely lies in differences among consumers' tastes. Yet another part of the reason may lie in the creation of entry barriers. Here the explanation is that technological barriers to entry are weak in these industries: a small plant can produce at an average total cost just about as low as that of a large plant.

Product differentiation and brand-image advertising can be used to create substantial barriers to entry where natural barriers are weak.

To the extent that these practices raise entry barriers, they allow existing firms to move in the direction of joint profit maximization without fear of a flood of new entrants attracted by the high profits.

PRICE INFLEXIBILITY: IS THERE A KINKED DEMAND CURVE?

It has frequently been observed that administered prices change less frequently than do prices determined in competitive markets. One way of putting this is to say that administered prices show some inflexibility in the face of short-term fluctuations in demand and costs.

A sufficient explanation may be found in two forces. The first is the relatively flat short-run average cost curves frequently found for manufacturing firms, which mean that costs per unit remain roughly constant as output varies in response to short-term or cyclical variations in demand. The second is the extra costs of changing administered prices. They include the costs of printing new list prices for the many products of a typical multiproduct firm, the costs of notifying all customers, the accounting difficulty of keeping track of frequently changing prices, and

the loss of customer and retailer loyalty due to the uncertainty caused by frequent changes in prices.

A different kind of explanation that still has some adherents was offered many years ago by Paul Sweezy. His explanation was based on a novel demand curve for the oligopolist firm. This demand curve is based on different conjectural variations for price increases and price decreases. Each oligopolist conjectured that its rivals will match any price decreases it makes but will not follow it in any price increases. If the firm raises its price and no one follows, it will lose market share and its sales will fall off rapidly; its demand curve will be very flat. If the firm lowers its price and everyone follows, it will not gain market share and its sales will expand only in proportion to the expansion in the industry's sales. The demand curve for price cuts will thus be steeper than the demand curve for price increases.

These conjectural variations give rise to the **kinked demand curve** hypothesis, which is explained in Figure 16-2. This kink in the demand curve causes a discontinuity in the marginal revenue curve. [26]

With the kinked demand curve there is an interval in which the firm's profit-maximizing price will be unchanged despite changing economic conditions.

Whether or not the kink is an important element in the theory of oligopoly pricing is still debated; for many economists the evidence seems to relegate the kink to the role of an interesting but infrequent special case. In any event, the kink does not offer a general theory of oligopoly price; it predicts a tendency for a price, once set, to be maintained, but it says nothing about what price is set initially.

OLIGOPOLY AND RESOURCE ALLOCATION

Behavior of oligopolistic industries is much more complex than behavior under perfect competition or under monopoly. If oligopolists made

FIGURE 16-2
The Kinked Demand Curve

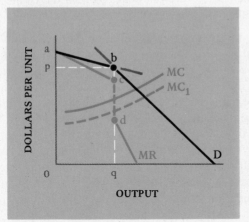

With a kinked demand curve prices tend to be inflexible despite changes in cost. At the market price *p*, the firm sells *q*. It believes that if it lowers price, everyone else will follow suit, and its sales will increase along the demand curve *bD*. But the firm believes that if it raises price, no one else will follow, and its sales will follow the demand curve *ba*. The black curve *abD* is the firm's perception of its own demand curve. The corresponding marginal revenue curve is the *discontinuous* curve *acdMR*. A shift in marginal cost from *MC* to *MC₁* changes neither the price nor the output that maximizes profits.

simplistic Cournot-Nash assumptions, behavior would be relatively easy to predict. As it is, interactions are obvious and oligopolistic firms must — and plainly do — take account of them. The equilibrium reached will then depend on each firm's conjectural variations. No one pattern dominates. However, there can be little doubt that oligopoly is genuinely different from either perfect competition or monopoly.

Firms in oligopolistic markets (as well as monopolies) administer their prices. The market signaling system works slightly differently when prices are determined by the market than when they are administered. Changes in the market conditions for both inputs and outputs are signaled to the perfectly competitive firm by changes in the *prices* of its inputs and its outputs.

Changes in the market conditions for inputs are signaled to the oligopolist by changes in the prices of its inputs. Changes in the market conditions for the oligopolist's product are signaled, however, by a change in sales at the administered price.

The oligopolist that administers its price gets a signal when the demand for its product changes, the signal taking the form of a variation in its sales. The perfectly competitive firm receives a signal of the same change in demand through a change in the market price that it faces.

Rises in costs of inputs will shift cost curves upward, and oligopolistic firms will be led — if the shift is not reversed — to raise price and lower output. Rises in demand will cause the sales of oligopolistic firms to rise. Firms will then respond by increasing output, thereby increasing the quantities of society's resources that are allocated to producing that commodity.

The market system reallocates resources in response to changes in demand and costs in roughly the same way under oligopoly as it does under perfect competition.

Although the market system allocates resources under oligopoly in a manner that is qualitatively similar to what happens under perfect competition, the actual allocation is not likely to be the same. Generally, oligopolistic industries will earn profits and will charge prices that exceed marginal cost (because the firms face downward-sloping demand curves and will equate marginal cost to marginal revenue, not to price). In this respect oligopoly is similar to monopoly.

There is a wide range of oligopolistic behavior. Some oligopolies succeed in coming close to the sort of joint profit maximization that would characterize monopoly. Others compete so intensely among themselves that they approximate competitive prices and outputs. The allocative consequences vary accordingly.

In some respects, oligopolistic industries differ from either perfect competition or monopoly: they may exhibit more price rigidity, more advertising, and more product differentiation. There may also be some tendency for more nonprice competition than consumers want.

Oligopoly is an important market structure in today's economy because there are many industries where the *MES* is simply too large to support a perfectly competitive market. Oligopoly will not, in general, achieve the optimal allocative efficiency of perfect competition. Rivalrous oligopoly, however, may produce more satisfactory results than monopoly. The defense of oligopoly as a market form is that it may be the best of the available alternatives where the *MES* is large. The challenge to public policy is to keep oligopolists competing. Public policies with this objective are discussed in Chapter 18.

Summary

1. A review of the structure of the American economy shows that while there are both large-firm and small-firm sectors, most of the industries involved do not conform descriptively to the models of either perfect competition or monopoly.

2. Monopolistic competition is a market structure in which firms sell a differentiated product. Large-group monopolistic competition does not seem to apply to a significant number of industries in today's world. The theory was, however, extremely important in the development of economics and it is further discussed in the appendix to this chapter.

3. Differentiated products abound, but generally they are produced in industries that contain a small number of firms each one of which sells many such products. This is small-group oligopoly.

4. The basic characteristics of oligopoly are that the firms in an industry recognize that they are interdependent and that anything that one firm does will probably lead to a reaction by rival sellers.

5. Oligopolists must administer their prices. Their prices are not changed with the frequency that prices change in perfect competition.

6. There is no simple set of predictions about the outcome of oligopolistic situations. Everything depends on the strategies adopted by the various rivals. Therefore, instead of a single theory, there are many possible patterns of behavior to understand, explain, and predict. A very general hypothesis of qualified joint profit maximization says that firms who recognize that they are rivals will be motivated by two sets of opposing forces, one set moving them toward joint profit maximization and the other moving them away from it.

7. In order to suggest the way in which observable variables such as size and number of sellers, nature of the product, and conditions of demand may influence the two sets of opposing forces, five specific hypotheses are suggested. The list is illustrative of a much larger list that might be provided.

8. Oligopolies persist because of barriers to entry, which may be natural or created. Natural barriers include large minimum efficient scales and absolute cost advantages. Firm-created barriers may include predatory pricing, preemptive expansion in a growing market, advertising, and brand proliferation.

9. One possible explanation of price rigidity under oligopoly is the kinked demand curve.

10. Under oligopoly the price system works to reallocate resources in response to changes in demand and costs in qualitatively the same way as it does under perfect competition. Oligopoly may not be as efficient as perfect competition, but it is responsive to major changes in economic conditions.

Topics for Review

Concentration ratios
Product differentiation
Administered prices

Barriers to entry
Minimum efficient scale
Absolute cost advantages

Discussion Questions

1. Is the consumer benefited by lower prices, by higher quality, by more product variety, by advertising? If trade-offs are necessary (more of one means less of another), how would you evaluate their relative importance with respect to the following products?
   a. vitamin pills
   b. beer
   c. cement
   d. bath soap
   e. women's dresses
   f. television programs
   g. prescription drugs
2. White sidewall tires cost about $1 per tire more to manufacture than black sidewall tires, and they lower somewhat the durability of tires. At the retail level the extra cost of a white sidewall tire is at least $5 per tire. Yet 70 percent of all passenger car tires manufactured in the United States in 1980 were the white sidewalls. What, if anything, do these facts tell you about the market structure of the manufacture, distribution, or marketing of automobile tires? If white sidewalls are found to be somewhat more likely to suffer blowouts, should their use be prohibited by law?
3. It is sometimes said that there are more drugstores and gasoline stations than are needed. In what sense might that be correct? Does the consumer gain anything from this plethora of retail outlets? How would you determine the optimal number of movie theaters or gasoline stations in a city of 100,000 people?
4. Are any of the following industries monopolistically competitive? Explain your answer.
   a. textbook publishing (fact: there are over 50 elementary economics textbooks in use somewhere in the United States this year)
   b. college education
   c. cigarette manufacture
   d. restaurant operation
   e. automobile retailing

5. It has been estimated that if automobile companies did not change models for 10 years, the cost of production would be reduced by approximately 30 percent. In view of this fact, why are there annual model changes? Which, if any, of the reasons you have suggested depend on the industry's being oligopolistic? Should frequent model changes be forbidden by law?
6. Compare and contrast the effects on the automobile and the wheat industries of each of the following.
   a. The effect of a large rise in demand on quantity sold.
   b. The effect of a large rise in costs on price.
   c. The effect on price of a temporary cut in supplies coming to market due to a three-month rail strike.
   d. The effect on price and quantity sold of a rush of cheap foreign imports.
   e. The effects of a large rise in the price of one of the industry's important imports.
   In the light of your answers discuss general ways in which oligopolistic industries fulfill the same general functions as do perfectly competitive industries.
7. Some analysts of the beer industry believe that the big national companies are going to get bigger and the smaller companies will disappear relatively rapidly. Their reasoning is that big national brewers have decisive advantages over local and regional brewers. What are these analysts assuming about the cost conditions in the beer industry? Is this assumption consistent with the report by *Fortune* which indicated that a small regional brewery has higher labor productivity than the newest but larger plant of Anheuser Busch? If the efficient size of *plant* in the industry is small, might there be reasons to expect multiplant firms to predominate?
8. Many people in advertising have thought that economists, with their emphasis on efficiency in the allocation of resources, have not been duly appreciative of the role of advertising in influencing consumer preferences. What roles does economic analysis give to advertising? Which are regarded as improving resource allocation and which as worsening it?
9. Does the kinked demand curve rest on a state of mind of buyers, of sellers, or on actual market conditions? Would such a state of mind, or such conditions, be more likely in a period of great excess capacity or a period of shortages? Could cost changes ever cause prices to change under the kinked demand theory?

Price Theory in Action

17

Price theory helps us to understand and to make predictions about things that are reported in the newspapers every day: the effect of a grain shortage on the price of chicken feed, for example, and the increased use of car pools when gasoline became hard to find and its price rose. In this chapter we apply price theory to some real-world situations. In the first section the effects of boycotts are examined. In the following section the theories of monopoly and perfect competition are used to study how producers in competitive industries often try, through collective action, to obtain monopolistic profits but fail to do so perfectly. In the final section we examine the impact of a successful cartel, OPEC, on an economy that had come to take cheap and abundant energy for granted.

Boycotts and Their Effect on Market Price

A **boycott** is defined by the dictionary as the process of "engaging in a concerted refusal to have anything to do with something or someone." Boycotts for political, social, and economic ends are familiar. Blacks in the early years of the civil rights movement boycotted segregated buses; President Carter called for a boycott of the 1980 Moscow Olympic Games in order to express American concern over Soviet aggression in Afghanistan.

Many boycotts are intended to have their effect through economic harm imposed on the targets. Some women's groups urge convention boycotts of states that have not ratified the Equal Rights Amendment, in order to hurt the industries of those states and thus generate political support for their cause. Consumers have been urged to boycott grapes and lettuce by farm unions seeking to put pressure on the producers who were their employers. A meat boycott of 1973 was designed to bring down the price of meat. In 1980 automobile workers urged a boycott of foreign made automobiles in an effort to force Japanese manufacturers to use American assembly plants, rather than ship completed cars assembled by Japanese workers in Japan.

There are also sellers' boycotts. When producers of milk and cattle attempt to withhold their products from the market, they too are trying, through a concerted refusal to sell, to influence market results. And embargoes, such as OPEC's withholding of oil from international markets in 1973, are in effect partial boycotts.

A boycott is an attempt to shift to the left the demand or supply curve of a product. If successful, a buyers' boycott will shift the demand curve, a sellers' boycott will shift the supply curve.

A BUYERS' BOYCOTT

Consider, as an example of a strictly economic boycott, an organized attempt of consumers' groups to "do something" about the very high and rapidly rising price of meat. With rising meat prices, boycotts are talked about every couple of years; such a boycott was attempted early in the 1970s.

The background to the 1973 meat boycott was the rising trend in meat consumption. Meat has a high income elasticity of demand, and as Americans became richer they turned increasingly to meat. Between 1955 and 1972 per capita consumption of beef, lamb, and pork doubled, and this led to a steady rightward shift of the demand curve for meat.

In addition, population was growing in the United States, and this too increased the market demand for meat. Of course output was also increasing, but as it went up, the costs of factors of production used in meat production rose. The rising costs led to rising prices. For a while all this occurred gradually, average meat prices rising by 2 to 5 percent per year. Then, in 1972, the pace of price changes suddenly accelerated. A worldwide grain shortage caused the price of cattle feed to escalate, shifting up costs (and supply curves) of cattle and meat production.

Continuing rightward shifts in the demand curve, combined with a sharp leftward shift of the supply curve, are predicted to lead to sharply rising prices. This is precisely what happened. Prices of meat increased at a rate of 5 percent *a month* between December 1972 and the following March. They were a major contributing factor as food prices rose at a rate unprecedented in the memories of most Americans. In the weekly trip to the supermarket, families saw the costs of the cuts of meat they usually bought rising so sharply that they had to make major changes in their purchases.

When the government did nothing, a meat boycott was organized. Americans were urged not to buy meat, starting the first week in April, in order to force prices down. On April 2 the boycott began. The *New York Times* applauded the action editorially on April 3:

Never underestimate the power of the embattled consumer. . . . Millions of Americans are seeking — almost spontaneously — to impose their own discipline on the marketplace by refusing to buy steak, chops or other cuts of meat at the present wildly inflated prices.

Consider this boycott in terms of the competitive theory of supply and demand. See Figure 17-1(i). Suppose first that housewives reduced permanently their purchases of meat and supply curves remained the same. The decrease in demand would lead to a leftward shift in the demand curve and a decrease in price. This is what the boycott leaders wanted. The effect would last as long as the new level of demand and the old supply curve applied. But while boycotts are easily started, they are less easily sustained. What would happen if, after prices fell, consumers ended their boycott and resumed their purchas-

FIGURE 17-1
Boycotts

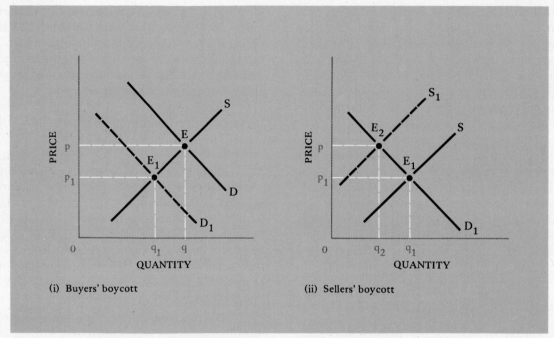

(i) Buyers' boycott

(ii) Sellers' boycott

A buyers' boycott shifts the demand curve leftward; a sellers' boycott shifts the supply curve leftward. (i) With equilibrium at E, a buyers' boycott shifts demand to D_1 and price falls to p_1. When the boycott ends, unless people's tastes have changed, demand rises to D and price will again rise to p. (ii) With equilibrium at E_1, because of the buyers' boycott, producers withhold supplies from the market and shift the supply curve from S to S_1. Price rises to p. As long as both boycotts are in effect, equilibrium is at E_2 and it is quantity, not price, that is greatly changed from the original equilibrium at E.

ing at the old rate? Demand would increase, and prices would go back up.

A temporary consumers' boycott can bring temporary price reductions. For a permanent effect on price, the boycott must produce a permanent reduction in demand.

The 1973 buyers' boycott of meat did not even produce very large short-run price reductions because meat producers countered with a sellers' boycott.

A SELLERS' BOYCOTT

Because many cattle ranchers expected the consumers' boycott to be short-lived, they held cattle off the market in anticipation of the end of the boycott and urged other ranchers to do the same. They did not want to sell at a low price cattle that could be kept on the ranch for a few extra weeks and sold later at a higher price. Of course, if the boycott had been permanent, they would have been forced to sell the cattle sooner or later.

As it was, the temporary withholding of meat (which was in effect a sellers' boycott) had the effect of a compensating leftward shift of the supply curve for meat. The reduction in supply is predicted to lead to price increases. See Figure 17-1(ii).

Indeed, within two weeks the reduction in supply was large enough to offset the reduction in demand and to restore prices to their pre-boycott levels. In the short run, the boycott and withholding led to a decrease in both demand and supply and no reduction in price. Whatever the psychological benefits to either party, neither had gained. Ranchers sold and households ate less meat than they had before the boycott.

A buyers' boycott can be offset by a sellers' boycott, which is likely to occur when sellers expect the buyers' boycott to be temporary. If both boycotts occur, a decrease in quantity sold rather than a decrease in price will result.

Problems in Attempts to Monopolize Perfectly Competitive Industries

Sellers of goods and services often seek collective action to raise what they consider excessively low prices. Cocoa producers in west Africa, wheat producers in the United States and Canada, the Organization of Petroleum Exporting Countries (OPEC), coffee growers in Brazil, taxi drivers in many cities, and labor unions throughout the world have all sought to obtain, through collective action, some of the benefits of departing from perfectly competitive situations. Basically they have sought to form organizations to regulate the output and sales of the goods or services they supply.

The motive behind this drive for monopoly power is easy to understand. The equilibrium position of a perfectly competitive industry is one in which a restriction of output and a consequent increase in price will always increase the profits of all producers. This is particularly obvious when (as is so often the case with agricultural goods) the demand for the product is inelastic at the equilibrium price; then marginal revenue is negative. Because marginal cost is positive, since it surely costs something to produce every extra unit, a reduction in output will not only raise the total revenues of producers, it will also reduce total costs.

It is equally true that the industry's profits can always be increased, even if demand is elastic at the competitive equilibrium price. At such an equilibrium, each firm is producing where marginal cost equals price. Because the market demand curve slopes downward, the industry's marginal revenue is less than price—and thus less than marginal cost. Therefore, in competitive equilibrium, the last unit sold necessarily contributes more to the industry's costs than to its revenue.

In a perfectly competitive industry, profits will increase if the producers enter into an effective agreement to restrict output.

The big "if" is the ability to form and maintain an *effective* agreement. A **cartel** is an organization of producers designed to eliminate competition among its members, usually by restricting output. OPEC is the best known and most effective cartel of modern times. (We examine some aspects of its workings in the final section of this chapter.) Its success comes about because (a) it has been able to prevent cheating, (b) it has been supported by most oil producers, (c) entry into large-scale oil exportation is difficult, and (d) there are relatively few adequate substitutes for oil in the short run. Why each of these features of OPEC is important to its success is illustrated in the following case studies.

CHEATING: THE INSTABILITY OF PRODUCERS' CO-OPS

A **producers' cooperative** or co-op is a joint selling organization for a group of producers. Such a co-op often acts as a cartel and attempts to reduce the output of a commodity by getting each producing firm to agree to restrict its output. While there is an incentive under perfect competition for all producers to enter into such an agreement, there is also an incentive for each producer to violate it.

To see how this would happen, consider a producers' cooperative that raises prices by cutting production. Suppose that every firm except one restricts its output. That one firm will be doubly well off in that it can sell its original output at the new, higher price received by all other firms that

FIGURE 17-2

The Dilemma of Producers' Co-ops

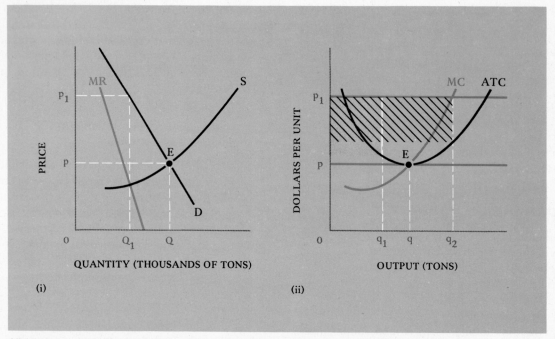

QUANTITY (THOUSANDS OF TONS)

(i)

OUTPUT (TONS)

(ii)

All producers benefit when they restrict output; any one producer will benefit even more if others reduce output but it does not. Market conditions are represented in (i), conditions for an individual producer in (ii). (Note the change of scale.) Before the co-op is formed, the market is in competitive equilibrium at price p and output Q, and the individual producer is producing output q and just covering costs. A co-op is formed and reduces industry output to Q_1 by per-suading each producer to produce only q_1. This output, where supply equals marginal revenue, maximizes joint profits with price p_1. The individual producer earns profits shown by the shaded area.

Once price is raised to p_1, however, the individual producer would like to increase output to q_2 and thus earn the profits shown in the diagonally striped area. But if all producers try to increase their outputs, price will fall back toward p.

have restricted their production. But the same is true for *each* firm.

A co-op organized mainly to restrict output is subject to competing pressures, illustrated in Figure 17-2. Each of the firms is better off if the co-op is formed and is effective; but each firm is even better off if every other firm plays ball while only it does not. Yet if everyone cheats (or stays out of the co-op), everyone will be worse off.

Co-ops will tend to be unstable because of the incentives for individual producers to violate the quotas.

The history of schemes to raise farm incomes by limiting crops bears ample testimony to the accuracy of this prediction. Crop restriction agreements often break down, and prices fall, as individuals exceed their quotas. The great bitterness and occasional violence that is sometimes exhibited by members of crop restriction plans against nonmembers and members who cheat is readily understandable. So far the OPEC countries have resisted the temptation to cheat, perhaps because of their political unity.

PARTIAL PARTICIPATION: MILK WITHHOLDING IN WISCONSIN

The previous discussion revealed the need to police the activities of members of any output-restricting scheme. Another well-documented case shows the problems that occur when the producers' organization covers substantially less than the total number of producers in the industry.

In the late 1960s there were 72,000 dairy farmers in Wisconsin, of whom about 4,300 were members of a militant group known as the National Farmers Organization. The NFO members controlled about 6 percent of the milk produced in the state. Angry about low milk prices and recognizing the inelasticity of the market demand curve, the NFO in 1967 proposed to withhold milk from the market. By dumping it in rivers, fields, and roads, they hoped to dramatize the plight of the dairy farmer and raise the price of milk by 20 percent. The elasticity of demand for milk is approximately 0.5; to achieve a 20 percent price increase would require a reduction in quantity sold of about 10 percent.

The NFO urged all farmers, whether members or not, to join them, but only members withheld supplies, and they withheld *all* their milk. During a three-week period, member farmers removed about 40 million pounds of milk (enough for 18 million quarts), or about 6 percent of the total usually supplied during the three-week period. Even if this withholding action had had the full effect predicted by the theory, given the 6 percent withheld and the elasticity of demand of 0.5, it would have raised prices by 12 percent and *benefited the farmers who were continuing to produce,* not those who were dumping their milk. The participants lost approximately $1.7 million, or an average of $400 each, in the action. The action failed because the total response was too small and too unevenly shared. Just as in the meat boycott, any increase in price would have persisted only as long as reduction in flow continued. Withholding milk for a week or three weeks and then resuming full production would at most drive prices up only until supply increased and brought them down.

A monopoly would seek to decrease the supply as a long-term policy. For a co-op to achieve the same results would require a long-term with-holding, and this could benefit the withholders only if a great majority of producers shared both in the withholding and in the production of what was sent to market. When the NFO failed to enlist the general support of milk producers, its attempts to raise the incomes of its members was doomed to fail.

Whether the NFO was foolish is another matter. If its purpose was to raise the income of its members by direct market action, it clearly (and predictably) failed. If, however, the primary purpose was to achieve a political solution, it may be that the dramatic and expensive action demonstrated the intensity of the members' feelings of grievance. Yet many of the NFO members believed they would succeed because of the laws of supply and demand. Even a neophyte economist could have told them otherwise.

CONTROL OF ENTRY: THE PRICE OF HAIRCUTS

Including all the producers in the industry and being able to police their actions is not enough for the success of a profit-increasing scheme. It is also necessary to prevent new producers, attracted by the monopoly profits resulting from output restriction, from entering the industry.

An example concerns the efforts of men's barbers in a particular city to avoid the rigors of competition. Assume that there are many barber shops and freedom of entry into barbering: anyone who qualifies can set up as a barber. Assume that the going price for haircuts is $5 and that at this price all barbers believe their income is too low. The barbers hold a meeting and decide to form a trade association. They agree on the following points: First, all barbers in the city must join the association and abide by its rules; second, any new barbers who meet certain professional qualifications will be required to join the association before they are allowed to practice their trade; third, the association will recommend a price for haircuts that no barber shall undercut.

The barbers intend to raise the price of haircuts in order to raise their incomes. You are called in as a consulting economist to advise them as to the probable success of their plan. What do you predict?

The first thing you need to know is whether the organization is strong enough to enforce its minimum price on members and to prevent barbers from operating outside the organization. If it is not this strong, you will predict that their plan will not succeed in raising the price above the market level. But suppose you are persuaded that the organization does have the requisite strength to enforce a price rise to, say, $7. What are your predictions about the consequences?

You now need to distinguish between the short-run and the long-run effects of an increase in the price of haircuts. In the short run the number of barbers is fixed. Thus, in the short run, the answer is simple enough: It all depends on the elasticity of the demand for haircuts.

If the demand elasticity is less than 1, total expenditure on haircuts will rise and so will the incomes of barbers; if demand elasticity exceeds 1, the barbers' revenues will fall. Thus you need some empirical knowledge about the elasticity of demand for haircuts. You will probably have to try to gain some idea of demand elasticity by studying the effects of changes in haircut prices either at other times or in other places.

When you propose making such a study, one of the leaders of the organization (who has taken a course in economics) tells you not to waste your time, haircuts are a necessity, and therefore their demand is almost perfectly inelastic. You reject this argument for two reasons. You realize, first, that the time between haircuts is by no means fixed. An increase in the average period between haircuts from four weeks to six weeks would represent a 33 percent fall in quantity demanded. If such a change were occasioned by, say, a 25 percent rise in price, the elasticity of demand over this range would be 1.33. You realize also that people can have their hair cut elsewhere than in a barbershop. The sale of hair clippers for home use keeps rising in America as a direct response to sharp rises in the relative price of haircuts.

Let us suppose, however, that on the basis of

the best available evidence you estimate the elasticity of demand over the relevant price range to be 0.45. You then predict that barbers will be successful in raising incomes in the short run. A 40 percent rise in price will be met by an 18 percent fall in business, so the total revenue of the typical barber will rise by about 15 percent.[1] In predicting the consequences, you will also want to estimate the length of the short run for this industry.

Now what about the long run? If barbers were just covering costs before the price change, they will now be earning profits. Barbering will become an attractive trade relative to others requiring equal skill and training, and there will be a flow of barbers into the industry. As the number of barbers rises, the same amount of business must be shared among more and more barbers, so the typical barber will find business — and thus profits — decreasing. Profits may also be squeezed from another direction. With fewer customers coming their way, barbers may compete against one another for the limited number of customers. The association does not allow them to compete through price cuts, but they can compete in service. They may spruce up their shops, offer their customers expensive magazines to read, and so forth. This kind of competition will raise operating costs.

These changes will continue until barbers are just covering their opportunity costs, at which time the attraction for new entrants will subside. The industry will settle down in a new long-run equilibrium in which individual barbers make incomes only as large as they did before the price rise. There will be more barbers than there were in the original situation, but each barber will be working for a smaller fraction of the day and will be idle for a larger fraction (the industry will have excess capacity). Barbers may prefer this situa-

---

[1] Suppose the quantity of haircuts originally was 1,000. At $5 this produced revenue of $5,000. A rise in price to $7 and a fall in quantity to 820 creates revenue of $5,740, a 14.8 percent increase. More generally, let p and q be the price and quantity before the price increase. Total revenue after the increase is $TR = (1.40p)(.82q) = 1.148pq$.

tion; they will have more leisure. Customers may or may not prefer it: They will have shorter waits even at peak periods, and they will get to read a wide choice of magazines, but they will pay more for haircuts.

But you were hired to report to the barbers with respect to the effect on their incomes, not their leisure. The report that you finally present will say: "You will succeed in the short run (because you face a demand curve that is inelastic), but your plan is bound to be self-defeating in the long run unless you are able to prevent the entry of new barbers."

The important lesson to be learned is this:

Unless producers can control entry, they cannot succeed in keeping earnings above the competitive level in the long run.

If price competition is ruled out, profits will be driven down by the entry of new firms and the resulting creation of excess capacity. Producers' associations that are successful in keeping earnings up are those that are successful in restricting entry.

SUBSTITUTES: THE DECLINE AND FALL OF A PATENT MONOPOLY

The case of the barbers suggests that monopoly profits cannot be maintained unless there are effective barriers to entry. Even if prices are not brought down by new entrants (because of effective group control over price), excess capacity will continue to develop until each firm's profits are reduced to zero. How easy is it to raise barriers to entry to protect monopoly profits? One might think that a patent that confers a legal monopoly to produce a product would be sufficient, but restriction is not that simple.

Profits are a challenge to those who want their share of them; they are the carrot of the free enterprise system, and no producer is immune to potential competition from those who would compete for his or her share of the consumer's dollar. Consider the case of ball-point pens.

In 1945, Milton Reynolds acquired a patent on a new type of pen that wrote with a ball bearing rather then a conventional nib. He formed the Reynolds International Pen Company, capitalized at $26,000, and began production on October 6, 1945.

The Reynolds pen was introduced with a good deal of fanfare by Gimbels, who guaranteed that the pen would write for two years without refilling. The price was set at $12.50 (the maximum price allowed by the wartime Office of Price Administration). Gimbels sold 10,000 pens on October 29, 1945, the first day they were on sale. In the early stages of production, the cost of production was estimated to be around 80¢ per pen.

The Reynolds International Pen Company quickly expanded production. By early 1946 it employed more than 800 people in its factory and was producing 30,000 pens per day. By March 1946 it had $3 million in the bank.

Macy's, Gimbels' traditional rival, introduced an imported ball-point pen from South America. Its price was $19.98 (production costs unknown).

The heavy sales quickly elicited a response from other pen manufacturers. Eversharp introduced its first model in April, priced at $15. In July 1946 *Fortune* magazine reported that Sheaffer was planning to put out a pen at $15, and Eversharp announced its plan to produce a "retractable" model priced at $25. Reynolds introduced a new model but kept the price at $12.50. Costs were estimated at 60¢ per pen.

The first signs of trouble emerged. The Ball Point Pen Company of Hollywood (disregarding a patent-infringement suit) put a $9.95 model on the market, and a manufacturer named David Kahn announced plans to introduce a pen selling for less than $3. *Fortune* reported fears of an impending price war in view of the growing number of manufacturers and the low cost of production. In October, Reynolds introduced a new model, priced at $3.85, that cost about 30¢ to produce.

By Christmas 1946 approximately 100 manufacturers were in production, some of them selling pens for as little as $2.98. By February 1947 Gimbels was selling a ball-point pen made by the

Continental Pen Company for 98¢. Reynolds introduced a new model priced to sell at $1.69, but Gimbels sold it for 88¢ in a price war with Macy's. Reynolds felt betrayed by Gimbels. Reynolds introduced a new model listed at 98¢. By this time, ball-point pens had become economy rather than luxury items but were still highly profitable.

In mid 1948 ball-point pens were selling for as little as 39¢ and costing about 10¢ to produce. In 1951 prices of 25¢ were common. Ever since then the market has been saturated with a wide variety of models and prices, ranging from 19¢ up. Their manufacture is only ordinarily profitable. Ball-point pens were no passing fad, as everyone knows; their introduction has fundamentally changed the writing implement industry.

The ball-point pen example has interested observers in many fields. Lawyers have been concerned about the ease with which patent rights were circumvented. Psychologists have noted the enormous appeal of a new product even at prices that seemed very high. Advertising people have regarded it as a classic case of clever promotion.

From the point of view of economic theory, it illustrates several things:

1. A firm that innovates, taking the risks of introducing a new product, may gain a temporary monopoly. In the short run such a monopoly can charge prices not remotely equal to costs and earn enormous profits.
2. Entry of new firms (even in the face of obstacles) will often occur in response to high profits.
3. Entry will, in time, drive prices down to a level more nearly equal to the costs of production and distribution.
4. The lag between an original monopoly and its subsequent erosion by entry may nevertheless be long enough that the profits to the innovator, as well as to some of the imitators, may be very large.[2]

---

[2] It is estimated that Reynolds earned profits as high as $500,000 *in a single month*—about 20 times its original investment.

The case of the ball-point pen is not an isolated one; it is typical of what happens when a successful innovation brings a new product onto the market. A more recent example is the pocket calculator that has ousted the slide rule as the applied scientist's constant companion. It is so easy to operate that it is carried and used regularly by many who would never have used a slide rule. When first introduced in the early 1970s, pocket calculators were relatively expensive, often costing over $100. They were also relatively crude in their capabilities. Nonetheless they proved popular; sales and profits rose, and firms rushed to enter the lucrative new field. Competition led simultaneously to product improvement and price reduction. Today calculators that perform basic calculations can be bought for about $10, and sophisticated scientific and programmable pocket calculators can be bought for under $50.

OPEC and the Price of Gasoline

In 1970 regular gasoline in Ann Arbor, Michigan, was selling for 29.9¢ a gallon. An enterprising shopper could almost always find a station within 30 miles where the price was in the low twenties owing to a local price war. American automobile manufacturers sold about 10 million new cars that year, mostly big fancy ones. Volkswagens and foreign sports cars (and other imports), while not unknown, especially on the two coasts, amounted to only 5 percent of the total cars sold in the United States.

Early in 1980 regular gasoline in Ann Arbor, Michigan, was selling for 129.9¢ a gallon. There were many fewer gas stations than in 1970, and there were no price wars. American automobiles were selling only at the rate of about 8 million cars per year, even with big discounts thrown in. American cars were smaller and more fuel efficient than the gas guzzlers of a decade earlier, and all but one of the American auto companies were having a hard time. Chrysler was on the edge of bankruptcy, and Ford was reporting large losses. Foreign imports, mostly from Japan, accounted for 22 percent of U.S. sales.

One key to the story behind these facts about the automobile industry is the skyrocketing price of gasoline and the economy's adaptations to it. These factors can be understood largely in terms of the theories of supply and demand, competition and monopoly, with some government intervention thrown in. What happened?

BEFORE OPEC: ENERGY BINGE

During the half century before 1973, Americans increased their consumption of energy at an annual rate of about 5 percent—enough to double consumption every 14 years. That energy came increasingly from oil and gas, the use of which soared (see Figure 13-5, page 208). Much of this surge resulted from the growing use of the mass-produced automobile, which, like Hollywood movies, became a distinctively American contribution to the twentieth century. Automobiles became the symbol of the American dream. As American households became richer they tended to buy larger numbers of ever faster, bigger, and more lavishly equipped cars—to say nothing of trailers, vans, and recreational vehicles. Year by year the demand for gasoline to power these internal combustion engines rose. Yet the price of gasoline remained low, so low that throughout this period the cost of fuel remained a trivial part of the cost of owning and operating a car.

This epoch of ever-increasing demand at a constant price is analyzed in Figure 17-3. The long-run supply curve seemed to be almost perfectly elastic at a low price. For every barrel of oil produced, another was discovered. Although everyone knew this could not go on forever, a rising supply price was far in the future. Indeed, the enormous quantities of oil being discovered and produced in the Middle East so threatened the profitability of American oil producers that the U.S. government imposed quotas that limited

FIGURE 17-3
Gasoline Prices in an Era of Unlimited Supply

With a horizontal long-run supply curve, demand can increase year by year with no increase in price. S is a long-run supply curve that is perfectly elastic at price p_0. Suppose S applies to the United States in the early 1970s. The various demand curves refer to different years; each year the demand curve shifts rightward as gasoline consumption increases. There is no gasoline shortage on the horizon. The U.S. equilibrium in year 0 is E_0, and it is expected to shift to E_1 in year 1, with larger consumption but no increase in price above p_0.

The screened supply curve S' is also perfectly elastic—at a higher price, p'. Suppose it reflects the supply in European countries that have levied a high tax on gasoline. For the same set of demand curves, equilibrium consumption is much lower in European countries than in America, yet there too it increases year by year, with no increase in price, as shown by E_0' and E_1'.

the imports of cheap foreign oil. At the same time the government also gave tax incentives to American oil companies to produce more oil.

The fact that the demand curve shifted rightward year after year was not a cause for alarm; indeed, the reverse was true: Energy fueled the increasing productivity that led to ever-rising material standards of living. America rode on cheap and plentiful oil.

Americans traveling abroad were amused by the small, cramped cars they saw and rented, and

FIGURE 17-4
The Effect of the OPEC Embargo

Non-OPEC supply = S_1

Supply pre embargo = S

A change in gasoline supply, government price control, and short-run demand inelasticity all contribute to a large shortage of gasoline. Before the embargo, supply was S and demand D_1. The oil embargo shifts the supply curve to S_1. A new long-run equilibrium would occur at E, with price rising to p_E and consumption falling to q_E. Government maximum price controls prevented such a price rise. If price is held at p_0, excess demand of q_1q_2 will appear.

Even if the government allows price to rise immediately to p_E, a shortage of q_Eq_3 will occur because the short-run demand curve D_1' is much less elastic than the long-run curve D_1. A short-run price of p_1 would clear the market, but such a high price is not permitted by government, which does not want to allow windfall profits. Yet unless price rises to p_1 there will be excess demand in the short run and the need for some other means of allocation of gasoline.

they were appalled by the high cost of gasoline. The high prices abroad were due to very high taxes on gasoline. (Evidently Europeans did not understand the liberating role the automobile played in the Great Society.) The higher prices led to lower gasoline consumption. Europeans drove smaller cars, waited until they reached a higher level of income before buying a car (or buying a second car), and relied more on bicycles and public transportation. The European situation is also shown in Figure 17-3.

OPEC'S EMBARGO

Although not all U.S. oil came from abroad, a virtually horizontal supply curve of the sort shown in Figure 17-3 was due to the willingness of oil exporters in the Middle East to supply as much oil as the United States and European countries wanted at a fixed price. What would happen if and when the oil exporters changed their mind?

The world found out in 1973, when, in conjunction with the Arab-Israeli war, members of OPEC placed an embargo on exports of Mideast oil. The United States and other oil importers suddenly had to rely on much more limited non-OPEC sources. They discovered that supply from these sources was not perfectly elastic. The change in shape of the supply curve due to OPEC is illustrated in Figure 17-4.

The theory of supply and demand leads to two clear predictions: a sharp rise in gasoline prices due to the upward shift of the supply curve, and a significant reduction in consumption as households adjusted to the new price level. These predictions rest on two assumptions, neither of which was correct in 1974: first, that price was free to rise in response to the embargo-induced scarcity; second, that consumers would reduce consumption rapidly in response to any price increase that occurred.

Gasoline Price Controls

It happened that at the time of the OPEC embargo the federal government was setting maximum prices for gasoline. General price and wage controls had been imposed by the Nixon administration in 1971. Most items had been decontrolled by the time of the embargo, but not gasoline. The result was predictable: a sudden, sharp gas shortage at the controlled prices. Lines developed, and stations ran out of gas and closed down. Rumors that the Amityville Shell station had gas on a summer Friday afternoon led to a colossal traffic jam as thousands of drivers tried to get there to fill their tanks before supplies ran out.

When price does not allocate limited supplies, there is always a need for alternative allocation schemes. Many gas stations would sell only to regular customers. Others sold only a few gallons at a time, thereby increasing the customer's time spent in line. Others exacted hidden prices by selling gas in large quantities only to those who bought tires, batteries, or windshield wipers (at very favorable prices). Travelers spent endless hours searching for gas or sitting in lines. Resort owners found that their guests canceled reservations unless the resort owner could guarantee enough gas to get them back home. As resort owners bought up supplies—some even bought gas stations—the supply available on the general market shrank further. The government was urged to allocate gasoline on a fair and equitable basis, both to dealers and, by issuing ration coupons, to consumers.

While the government did not adopt gasoline rationing, it took some steps. It permitted some price rises, and it attempted to allocate gasoline to the hardest hit areas. It imposed lower speed limits, and it exhorted people to form car pools. Some state governments imposed rationing through odd-even day sales and by closing stations on Sundays. These expedients helped reduce waiting lines. But even after prices had been allowed to rise to what approximated new equilibrium levels, the shortages continued. Why?

Price Increases and Demand Adjustments

In response to a sharp rise in the price of gasoline, households and firms would be expected to consume less of it, as the demand curve shows. Yet price rises had less effect on consumption than suggested by a downward-sloping demand curve such as D_1 in Figure 17-4. The reason is that it takes time to achieve adjustments in quantity demanded in response to a rise in price.

For example, if they had expected gasoline to cost $1.50 a gallon, the suburban Smith family would not have built their life style around two cars that gave only 12 and 15 miles to the gallon. They might not have moved to a location where a 20-mile commute to work and the ferrying of children to school, lessons, doctor's appointments, and parties were required daily. And they certainly would not have bought a fancy recreational vehicle for family vacations. But having done all those things, the Smiths were stuck and had to make the best of it. They began to use their cars more sparingly, but it would have been silly to leave them in the garage and take taxis. (The *variable* cost of using the family car was less than the *total* cost of a taxi ride.) They tried to sell the RV, but the few people who answered their ad in the local paper were willing to pay only a small fraction of the price the Smiths thought was fair.

Up to now we have not needed to distinguish between short-run and long-run adjustments to changes in price. But for a commodity such as gasoline that is consumed along with other, durable goods, *time* is a key element in the adjustment process. It is necessary to recognize short-run demand curves as well as a long-run curve.

The longer the period of time for adjustment, the greater will be the possibilities for substituting for commodities whose relative price is rising. Thus, in general, the longer the period of time, the more elastic the demand curve will be.

In the very short run, the only way to use less gasoline is to drive less. Over a longer time, people have many options. They can change the kind of car they drive. They can move closer to work and make other changes in their lifestyle.

Such adjustments began to occur very quickly. Producers and distributors of small, fuel-saving cars, such as American Motors and Volkswagen, found demand for their products rising; other automobile manufacturers found large cars not selling. The latter stopped production and laid off workers while they strained to shift production into their relatively few plants suitable for producing small cars. Used-car dealers found that their big cars would not sell but their small cars were being snapped up at existing prices—so they changed the structure of their prices.

The full adjustment to smaller, more efficient cars had not been accomplished by the end of the decade, but more of it occurs every year. The adjustment is made more difficult to the extent that the demand for energy continues to grow as part of the long-term trend.

We can capture the spirit of the adjustment problem by using only two demand curves, a relatively elastic long-run demand curve and a relatively inelastic short-run curve. See Figure 17-4. In economic terms, the short-run demand curve for gasoline was much less elastic than the long-run curve. As shown in the figure, such an inelastic demand curve would lead to shortages in the short run even if price jumped at once to the new long-run equilibrium price, p_E. Not only would the Smiths have to pay the new and outrageous higher price, they could not even then be sure of getting gas at that price!

There is of course *some* price at which demand can be equated with supply even in the short run. But neither the government nor the gasoline station operators were willing to let price rise to that level. The more inelastic the demand curve, the greater the windfall profits will be if price rises are used to eliminate excess demand. The government decided not to allow "profiteering" as a result of the unfortunate OPEC-induced gas shortage. Prices would be allowed to rise, but only by a "reasonable amount" based on cost. The government kept maximum prices on gasoline well below those that would have cleared the market. Private operators were reluctant to charge even as much as the government allowed. Ernie Weaver at the local filling station did not want to sell gas for which he had paid 70¢ a gallon for $1.20 or more a gallon. He believed if he did, his customers would never forgive him for gouging them. Yet even at 85¢ a gallon they complained and asked bitterly whether he was planning to retire soon to Florida.

OPEC: SUPPLY LIMITATION AS A LONG-RUN STRATEGY

The oil embargo created a shortage of oil in the United States, but it did not lead to profits for the oil-producing countries. As we have seen, a sellers' boycott (which is what the embargo was) does not generate any revenues. But the experience showed the oil exporters how dependent Americans (and others) were on their product, and how willing they were to pay more for gasoline. What Ernie Weaver would not do, Sheik Yamani, the oil minister of Saudi Arabia, would do: restrict output, raise price, and earn huge profits.

Oil exporters in Saudi Arabia, Kuwait, and Iran could increase profits by restricting output and raising price, just as others can who cartelize a previously competitive industry. The sons of the sheiks had attended the Harvard Business School and learned all about monopolies and cartels. After the embargo, the oil-producing countries did not return to unlimited supply but instead adopted a regime of carefully controlled supply. Producing a limited supply, combined with the ever-rising demand for oil, will keep prices high. See Figure 17-5. By taking into account how much non-OPEC oil is produced, the members of OPEC can determine how much they should produce to maximize their own profits.

Once or twice a year OPEC members meet to survey world supply and demand and to set prices. This implies that they also set output quotas for their members, for the high prices can be maintained only if excess production is avoided.

THE SITUATION IN 1980

By 1980 crude oil prices stood at roughly ten times the level of 1970, and the oil producers were among the richest nations in the world. The gasoline shortages of the mid 1970s had largely disappeared in response to a combination of substantial price increases, some allocation of gasoline supplies, some significant demand adjustments, and the introduction of some new, non-OPEC supplies. But the tentative and insecure nature of the balance between demand and supply was illustrated in 1979 by a temporary cutoff of Iranian oil supplies. Neither prices nor allocations adapted quickly enough. Almost overnight, shortages and waiting lines reappeared. They were followed by another round of major price increases by members of OPEC.

As long as Americans depend on OPEC oil to meet a significant fraction of their energy needs, OPEC can manipulate its contribution to total world supply so as to serve its best interests.

KINDS OF ENERGY POLICY

There are several alternative approaches to the kind of energy policy issue posed by the story of gasoline prices. Three of them are: (1) to let the market work, accepting whatever levels of price are necessary to equate supply and demand; (2) to impose price controls on energy and then to ration or otherwise allocate the shortages that will inevitably occur; (3) with or without either of the others, to attempt to *shift* the supply curve rightward (stimulate production) and/or *shift* the demand curve leftward (conserve energy).

Each of these approaches has its supporters. The second is sufficiently similar to rent control (discussed in Chapter 8) to require no further discussion. What of the other two?

Can the Free Market Do the Job?

If all controls on energy prices and production were removed, the price system could equate quantity demanded and quantity supplied. High and rising prices would force consumers to conserve energy and to find relatively cheaper sources for the most expensive kinds of energy. At the same time, high prices would promise high profits to producers who find new supplies of conventional energy or new substitutes for them.

The free-market strategy relies, in the first instance, on *movements along* supply and demand curves. For example, allowing price to rise (in response to a shortage) may eliminate the shortage by decreasing quantity demanded—moving up the demand curve. Yet initial changes may induce *shifts* in the curves. For example, a price rise may lead to windfall profits to producers, which in turn may lead to a new entry that will shift the supply curve rightward.

The fact that the free market can do the job

FIGURE 17-5
OPEC as a Cartel

Given a sharply rising non-OPEC supply curve of oil, the members of OPEC can determine equilibrium prices by choosing their contribution to total supply. The curve S_1 represents the non-OPEC supply of the product. If OPEC were prepared to supply unlimited quantities at p_0 the supply curve would be S and the situation shown in Figure 17-3 would be restored. But by fixing its production, OPEC can determine the new total (OPEC + non-OPEC) supply curve S_2. OPEC can, for given demand curves and non-OPEC supplies, pick a price (such as p_2) and determine what quantity to supply (q_1q_2) to make that the equilibrium price. If demand is increasing, as from D_2 to D_3, the same OPEC supply will lead the price to increase from p_2 to p_3.

does not necessarily mean it *should* be the chosen strategy. Key questions concern how quickly such results will occur and how much and what sorts of redistribution of income will result. Many critics of the free-market solution believe it may prove highly unfair in its distributive effects. They also believe it keeps the United States too dependent on foreign oil producers, to the country's political and economic detriment. Supporters of the free-market policy recognize such dangers but believe them to be less significant than the dangers inherent in intervention with the market. They also believe that any adverse redistributive effects could be offset by specific measures (such as taxes and subsidies) that are less costly to the economy than any intervention with the free-market price of energy.

Can Intervention Do the Job?

A more interventionist energy policy means direct government action to shift supply or demand curves relative to what they would otherwise be. On the supply side, for example, the government can give exploration subsidies for oil. As a result, at any given price a larger quantity would be found and produced than before — that is, the supply curve would shift to the right. Other elements of a supply-side policy include providing incentives to hasten research in solar or geothermal energy and subsidizing greater use of the abundant supplies of coal.

On the demand side, people can be motivated to consume less energy by means other than allowing producer's prices to rise — e.g., by taxing energy consumption heavily. (For consumers, a 50¢ per gallon tax is like a 50¢ price rise; it moves them up along their demand curves.) Other policies may shift the demand curve leftward. These include rules that compel auto manufacturers to produce more fuel-efficient engines, and subsidies that encourage home insulation, public transportation, and car pooling.

Supporters of interventionist policies believe they will work more fairly than simply letting prices rise. Critics believe that while a wise government might do a better job than the free market, our own government's performance is likely to be much worse.

THE DEBATE ABOUT STRATEGY

The current discussion is in part over which policy to follow and in part about whether there really is a major problem to solve.

When President Carter described the energy crisis as the "moral equivalent of war," he failed to persuade many people of either the urgency of the problem or its genuineness. Since then most Americans have come to believe in the problem, yet many think it will go away if only the energy companies would stop gouging the public.

The view that there is no energy problem is plainly wrong as long as the OPEC countries can control oil production. Oil is at present a key to our energy consumption. Just to stabilize the price of oi given the historical pattern of ever-increasing demand, requires that we increase the supply of oil or oil substitutes *and* reduce the level of demand. If we are unwilling to do those things, we must be prepared to live with steadily rising prices.

Rightward-shifting demand combined with an upward-sloping supply curve inevitably means rising prices or, if prices are held down, ever-increasing shortages.

The way in which the "energy shortage" is resolved involves much more than finding the quickest or fairest way to equate supply and demand. The way in which this is done will also affect the rate of productivity growth, the nature of industrial development, and the quality of life. For one example, if the decision is made not to utilize nuclear energy on the grounds that it involves high safety risks, we will almost surely have higher energy costs and a slower rate of productivity growth than if we do utilize it. If instead we use more high sulfur coal, we will have a dirtier atmosphere. But using nuclear energy, while increasing energy supply, may require safety risks that people find unacceptable and it may generate widespread protests and demonstrations. Finally, much of the dispute about energy policy concerns the issue of the effectiveness of government regulation and intervention, which we will discuss in Chapter 24.

Summary

1. A boycott in which some purchasers refuse to purchase a product sold in a competitive market reduces demand and, as long as it lasts, exerts downward pressure on price. This effect can be offset by a sellers' response — organized or spontaneous — in which supplies are withheld from the market. In either case, when the boycott

ends, the effect on price is reversed. Unless a boycott leads to a permanent change in supply or demand, it does not have a permanent effect on price.

2. Groups supplying goods or services under conditions that approximate those of competitive equilibrium have a strong incentive to organize to restrict output. The reason is that their collective profits will surely increase, since the last units being produced have marginal costs in excess of marginal revenues.

3. To achieve and retain the benefits of monopolization requires more than just agreeing to restrict output. An effective cartel must be able to police and enforce its output quotas because it is in any one producer's interest to cheat. It must also cover most of the output of the industry, control the entry of new producers, and be insulated from too many close substitutes for the product it produces.

4. The NFO's milk-withholding program illustrates the difficulties that face a producers' organization that includes only a fraction of the total producers in the industry. The case of the barbers illustrates the importance of entry control. The ball-point pen case illustrates the problem of substitutes.

5. The OPEC cartel has been remarkably successful so far in raising prices and profits. It includes most large oil exporters; it has prevented cheating; entry into oil production is not easy; and adequate substitutes for the amounts of oil OPEC has held off the market are neither easily or quickly developed.

6. Several aspects of the impact of the rise in the price of gasoline on the American economy and on the automobile industry can be traced, using supply and demand analysis. In the era before OPEC, demand for oil products rose steadily in response to low prices and a seemingly highly elastic supply.

7. OPEC changed the supply situation overnight, by means of an embargo (a sellers' boycott). The embargo, combined with government price controls, led to shortages, long lines, and the clamor for government allocation—all predicted by the theory of a price fixed below the equilibrium level.

8. Following the embargo, OPEC has limited the supply of oil through a cartel output restriction strategy that has converted a horizontal supply curve to a steeply rising one. It has managed the price of oil and received enormous monopoly profits from its sale.

9. Even after the price of gasoline was allowed to rise, the short-run inelasticity of demand (due to the durable nature of gasoline-using machines) and the continuing trend for ever more energy consumption kept gasoline scarce and the equilibrium price rising year by year.

10. Possible policy responses to the cartel-imposed supply limitation include (a) accepting whatever free-market price is necessary to equate demand with the new supply, (b) imposing price controls and allocating the inevitably short supplies, (c) attempting to shift the demand curve leftward (conserving energy) and the supply of non-OPEC production rightward (stimulating production). Either the first or the third policy (or a combination of the two) can eventually work to equate demand and supply. The level of price and the distributive consequences of the policies are not the same, and the differences account for a good bit of the sharp current debate about what sort of energy policy to adopt. Other aspects of the debate concern how much loss of productivity growth, pollution, and government intervention Americans wish to put up with as a consequence of their dependence on OPEC oil.

Topics for Review

Buyers' boycott and sellers' boycott
Long-run effects of a temporary boycott
The motive for output restriction in a competitive industry
Why cartels may fail to raise profits
Long-run and short-run demand elasticity
Alternative energy policies

Discussion Questions

1. There is no law against consumer boycotts. When coffee prices soared in the mid 1970s, each of the following statements was made. Comment on them in terms of the theory of boycotts.
   a. Elinor Guggenheimer (New York City commissioner of consumer affairs): "We've heard all about the cold weather in Brazil and the damaged coffee trees. What we haven't heard is any valid explanation of why the consumer should be forced to bear the impact of this frost. We're going to ask supermarkets and restaurants to stress coffee alternatives, tea and soup. If enough people don't drink coffee, at some point prices will have to be turned around."
   b. William Safire (columnist): "Let the boycott go forward, not only to cut the price, but to put the cartelniks of OPEC on notice: When challenged to economic war, even a little one, the American public is willing to make sacrifices. An effective coffee boycott would send a message to monopolists of oil."
   c. Coffee importer: "The U.S. customer is not the prime factor in the coffee market. The 43 coffee-producing nations couldn't care less if Americans drink coffee, because other people will. Americans can spite themselves, and hurt *me,* but they won't touch Brazil."

2. Technological advances of the 1950s dramatically boosted chicken and egg production in the United States. Petaluma, California, became the center of a booming industry. The Petaluma egg producers tried unsuccessfully and persistently to restrict supply by forming voluntary associations. Why do you think these associations did not succeed? In 1972 the California State Marketing Board did what the private associations failed to do: It compelled cutbacks in production. Why do you suppose it did so, and why was it more successful than the voluntary associations?

3. Profit-making blood banks account for about 10 percent of all blood used in transfusions in the United States. They buy blood from commercial donors and sell blood to hospitals. The Food and Drug Administration wants to put them out of business, but the Council on Wage and Price Stability—also a government agency—wants to encourage more commercial blood donation. Private provision under appropriate safeguards, COWPS suggests, may be the most appropriate way of assuring adequate supplies of quality blood at low prices. Discuss whether or not competition ought to be permitted in blood supply.

4. Use price theory in discussing the following news stories.
   a. The analysis sent out by a leading stock brokerage firm: "Prices of digital watches are following the pattern of pocket calculators—down 25 percent a year. This is just what we expected; it is normal. Expect squeezed profit margins and some bankruptcies."
   b. Donald Hollister, inventor of a new long-lasting light bulb that won't burn out for at least 10 years: "Even if this catches on, I expect to do well, but not to make a million dollars. The idea is too simple."
   c. "Barbers are providing special inducements to long-haired youths: free beard trims with every haircut."
   d. Newspaper report from Greensville, South Carolina, about the growth of "gut row": "It's a bit mind boggling to see so many fast-food restaurants in one place. All the national chains are there—Burger King, McDonald's, Shakey's Pizza—and you have your choice of chicken, seafood, barbecue or even native favorites like sausage biscuits. It's great for the family, but nobody's making any money."

5. In 1973 the OPEC cartel agreed to raise petroleum prices. OPEC was to do this by having each member nation raise the tax it charged producers on each barrel. In 1973 the Persian Gulf members of OPEC increased the taxes charged from less than $2 to over $7 a barrel. By 1980 the price of oil was over $20 a barrel. International cartels are notorious for their instability; in what ways is OPEC stronger than a cartel based on agreements among individual firms in different countries?

6. Comment on the following statements about OPEC and the "energy crisis."
   a. The Japanese minister of trade and industry, Komoto, responding to an OPEC price increase: "An outrageous act that ignores economic principles and is therefore regrettable."
   b. Milton Friedman (in 1976): "OPEC will break up within the next year because it will not be able to withstand the competitive pressure resulting from the vast sources of oil being discovered in many areas."
   c. "The only barrier to solving the energy crisis caused by OPEC is the American public's view that there is no real problem."
   d. "Nuclear energy, polluting coal, skyrocketing gasoline prices—these are the things that are wrong with America today."

Monopoly Versus Competition

18

Monopoly has been regarded with suspicion for a very long time. Even today in some quarters it takes a large share of the blame for inflation, for the energy shortage, for discrimination in employment, and for inequalities in income. It is widely believed that modern economic theory has *proved* that monopoly allows the powerful producer to exploit the consumer, while the competitive system always works to the consumer's advantage. In *The Wealth of Nations* (1776), Adam Smith—the founder of classical economics—developed a ringing attack on monopolies and monopolists. Since then most economists have criticized monopoly and advocated freer competition. In Chapters 14 and 15 we saw that perfect competition has appealing features and that it is efficient in ways that monopoly is not.

Is a preference for competition and a distrust of monopoly justified? This chapter carries further the comparison of monopoly and competition in terms of their predicted effects, then it looks at the principal policies for dealing with monopoly in the United States. Throughout the discussion, "monopoly" refers to monopoly power, not merely to the case of a single seller. "Competition" refers both to the market structure known as perfect competition and to competitive behavior of firms in a variety of market structures. The context will make it clear which meaning is intended.

Comparisons Between Monopoly and Competition

THE EFFECT OF CHANGES IN COST ON PRICE AND QUANTITY PRODUCED

Cost savings mean fewer resources are used in production than would otherwise be the case. If such cost savings occur, how and to what extent are they passed on to consumers?

Consider the case of an invention that lowers the marginal cost of production. In a perfectly competitive industry, the fact that each firm's marginal cost curve shifts downward means that the industry supply curve (which is the sum of the marginal cost curves) also shifts downward. As a result of the invention, any given output will be provided at a lower price than before and any given price will call forth a higher output. The cost-saving invention lowers price and raises output. Figure 18-1(i) illustrates this. The effect of an identical change in marginal cost on the price and output of the monopolist is shown in Figure 18-1(ii). The downward-shifting marginal cost curve intersects the marginal revenue curve at a higher level of output than it did previously. Because the demand curve is unchanged, it follows that the price must fall. So the benefit from

FIGURE 18-1

The Effect on Price of a Reduction in Marginal Cost

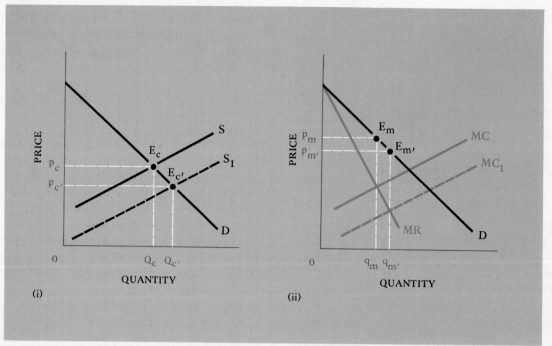

(i)

(ii)

A reduction in marginal cost leads to a greater decrease in price and a greater increase in quantity in a competitive industry than in a monopolized one. The demand curve is the same in both parts of the diagram, and the competitive short-run supply curve (S) is the same as the monopolist's marginal cost curve (MC). When marginal cost decreases, the curves shift downward to S_1 and MC_1. The new competitive output is where D and S_1 cross. The new monopolistic output is where MC_1 and MR cross. Because MR declines more steeply than D, the increase in output (and the consequent decrease in price) is less under monopoly than under competition.

any fall in costs will, to some extent, be passed on to consumers as lower prices in both competition and monopoly.

But while prices will fall in both cases, they will not usually fall to the same degree.

Other things being equal, prices and quantities will change less in monopoly than in competition as a response to a change in marginal costs.

The reason for this is that the monopolist is guided by the marginal revenue curve, which is steeper than the demand curve. The same vertical fall in marginal costs leads to a lesser increase in quantity and thus a lesser fall in price.

THE MONOPOLIZATION OF A COMPETITIVE INDUSTRY WITH NO CHANGE IN COSTS

The classical case against monopoly is to a great extent based on this prediction:

If a perfectly competitive industry should be monopolized, and if the cost curves of all productive units are unaffected by this change, the price will rise and the quantity produced will fall.

Assume that a competitive industry is monopolized as the result of a single firm's buying out all the individual producers and operating each one as an independent plant. Further assume that cost curves are not affected by this change. This means that the marginal costs will be the same to the monopolist as to the competitive industry.

When the industry is monopolized, it becomes profitable to drive price up by restricting output for precisely the same reasons it pays a producers' co-op to do so (see page 277). As long as neither market demand nor costs change, it will always pay the monopolist who charges a single price to restrict output below, and to raise price above, their perfectly competitive levels (see Figure 18-2).

The consequences of this change in equilibrium price and quantity were presented in Chapters 14 and 15: (1) at competitive but not monopolistic equilibrium, the level of average

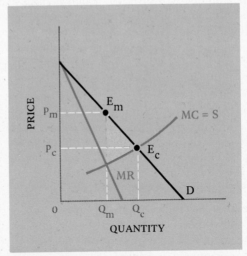

FIGURE 18-2
The Monopolization of a Competitive Industry

When a competitive industry is monopolized, output falls and price rises and a deadweight loss occurs. The competitive industry's supply curve and the monopolist's marginal cost curve are identical. The industry faces demand curve D. A competitive industry would produce Q_c at price p_c. The monopolist reduces output to Q_m because units between Q_m and Q_c add more to its cost than to its revenue. The shaded area shows that consumers were willing to pay more for each unit of lost output than its marginal cost of production. This deadweight loss of monopolization is a source of allocative inefficiency.

cost is necessarily the lowest attainable, given the technology of the society, and (2) at competitive but not monopolistic equilibrium, $p = MC$, and thus allocative efficiency is achieved.

Under these circumstances, the monopolization of a competitive industry surely introduces allocative inefficiency, and it may lead to productive inefficiency.

THE EFFECT OF MARKET STRUCTURE ON COST

What if costs are not the same for the monopolist as for the competitive industry? Costs may be affected when an industry is monopolized or when a large number of small firms is replaced by a small number of large firms. If any savings occur from combining numerous competing groups into a single integrated operation, the costs of producing any given level of output will be lower than they were previously. If this cost reduction occurs, it will be possible for output to be increased and price to be lowered as a result of the replacement of a perfectly competitive industry by a firm with monopoly power. This may occur in two very different ways.

Advantages of Large Scale

The cost advantage of having one railroad between two points rather than 50 railroads (or one water company in a city, or one telephone system in a country) is obvious. In such situations, it would be inefficient to have a large number of firms each producing a small output at a high cost per unit. If such a situation existed, any firm that grew bigger than its rivals would soon find itself in a position to cut price below its rivals' costs and monopolize the industry. This situation is called **natural monopoly**. It exists where the size of the market allows only one firm of efficient size.

Natural monopoly is just the extreme version of a much more common situation in industrialized countries, in which advantages of scale will make perfect competition wholly unattainable because there is room for only a small number of firms of efficient size.

Today the effective choice is usually not between monopoly and perfect competition but between more or less oligopoly.

Whenever there are long-run advantages of large-scale production, of marketing and distribution, of learning by doing, or of innovation or invention, the minimum efficient size of firms will tend to be large.

When MES is large, it is likely that productive efficiency will be improved, rather than worsened, by a shift from competition to a more concentrated market structure.

Lower Levels of Cost of Producing a Given Output

Even if there are no advantages of large-scale *plants*, large *firms* may be able to achieve economies, and thus lower costs, by multiproduct production and associated large-scale distribution, national advertising, and large-scale purchasing. Such economies have been described as **economies of scope** rather than of scale. When such cost reduction occurs, it is possible for output to be increased and price to be lowered as a result of the monopolization of a perfectly competitive industry. The possibility of such a situation is illustrated in Figure 18-3.

Saying that monopoly *may* lead to lower costs does not mean that departures from competition

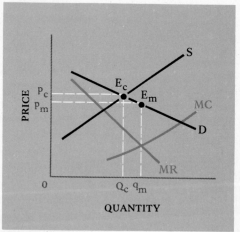

FIGURE 18-3

A Case in Which Monopolization Leads to Lower Prices

If monopolization lowers costs sufficiently, it may lead to greater output and lower price than competition. *D* and *S* are the demand and supply curves of a competitive industry that is in equilibrium at E_c with p_c and Q_c. If costs are unaffected by monopolization, *S* will become the monopolist's marginal cost curve and the monopolist will restrict output and raise price. However, if the monopolization reduces costs to MC, the equilibrium will be at E_m, with p_m less than p_c and q_m greater than Q_c.

must lead to lower costs. A large firm that is protected from competition by an entry barrier may reduce the efficiency of production and so shift marginal and average cost curves upward. In such a case (compared to the competitive industry) monopolization will certainly raise price and lower output.

It is thus possible for changes in market structure to change costs in either direction. The key empirical question is, in what circumstances do large firms in less competitive market structures achieve lower levels of cost than an industry composed of large numbers of small firms? Much of the answer depends on how market structure affects the rate of innovation.[1]

THE INCENTIVE TO INNOVATE

As far as profits are concerned, firms in any market structure have an incentive to innovate in order to find a cost-saving process or a more popular new product. There has been extended debate over which kinds of market structure are most conducive to innovation.

Innovation Under a Monopoly

A monopolist can always increase its profits if it can reduce costs. And because it is able to prevent the entry of new firms into the industry, the additional profits will persist into the long run. Thus, from the standpoint of maximizing profits, the monopolist has both a short-run and a long-run incentive to reduce costs by innovation.

Innovation requires research and development, and that costs money. The monopolistic firm may have an advantage over the competitive firm in that funds for research and development are more readily available to it. In the first place, it may have profits to invest in such ventures even though credit is tight. In the second place, tax laws that permit writing off business expenses may make research and development rel-

atively cheap. Suppose that this year a monopolist expects to make $2 million profit, on which it will have to pay taxes of approximately $1 million. If it spends the $2 million on research and development, it will show no profits for tax purposes this year and the firm will save $1 million in taxes. In effect, it can get $2 million worth of research for only $1 million. Successful research will eventually lead to future profits and will strengthen the firm's position as a monopolist. Of course, in later years it will have to pay taxes on the profits it earns—unless they are again spent on research and development.

Some critics of monopoly concede that innovation occurs but argue that monopolists engage in the wrong kinds of innovation. Monopolists may be expected to give special attention to kinds of innovation that increase or preserve the barriers to entry of potential competitors, as well as undertaking innovations that reduce costs to consumers in the long run.

Innovation Under Competition

The firm in perfect competition has the same profit incentive to innovate as the monopolist, but only in the short run, not in the long run. In the short run, a reduction in costs will allow the firm that was just covering costs to earn profits. In the long run, other firms will be attracted into the industry by these profits. Existing firms will copy the cost-saving innovation, new firms will enter the industry using the new techniques, and the profits of the innovator will eventually disappear.

The effectiveness of profits as an incentive to reduce costs for a firm will depend on the magnitude of the extra profits and the length of time over which they persist.

If it takes only a few months for existing firms and new entrants to copy and install any new invention, then the innovating firm's profits will be above normal for only a short time and the extra profits actually earned may not be sufficient to compensate for the risks and the costs of devel-

---

[1] At this time we suggest you read again the discussion of invention and innovation on pages 210–214.

oping the new innovation. In such cases the direct incentive to innovate will be absent from a competitive industry. Alternatively, if it takes several years for other firms to copy and install the cost-saving innovation, then the profits earned over these years by the innovating firm might be more than sufficient to compensate for all costs and risks and might yield a handsome profit as well. In this case the incentive to innovate is present in a competitive industry.

The Greater Incentive to Innovate?

Might competition be *more* conducive to innovation than monopoly? Some think so. A monopolist who does not innovate may be missing larger profits, yet it can still have some long-run profits. But, the argument runs, if the competitive firm does not innovate, some of its competitors are likely to do so and it will find itself in a position in which it cannot even keep up with its competitors, thus incurring losses and eventual bankruptcy.

A very different view was that of the distinguished Austrian (and later American) economist Joseph A. Schumpeter. In brief, his argument was that only the incentive of profits leads entrepreneurs to take the great risks involved in innovation, and that monopoly power is much more important than competition in providing the climate under which innovation occurs. The profits of the monopolist provide the incentive for other people to try to get their share. This might involve imitating the monopolist's product (thereby eroding the monopoly market), or it might involve trying to come up with a new product that would better serve the underlying wants that make the monopolist rich. As a result no monopoly will last forever; it will not even last very long if it fails to innovate and to anticipate its future competition. Schumpeter called the process of one monopoly being replaced by another the *process of creative destruction*. In *Capitalism, Socialism and Democracy* (1942) he said:

What we have got to accept is that it has come to be the most powerful engine of that progress and in par-

ticular of the long-run expansion of total output not only in spite of, but to a considerable extent through, this strategy which looks so restrictive when viewed in the individual case and from the individual point of time. In this respect, perfect competition is not only impossible but inferior, and has no title to being set up as a model of ideal efficiency. It is hence a mistake to base the theory of government regulation of industry on the principle that big business should be made to work as the respective industry would work in perfect competition.

Innovation Under Oligopoly

Many students of industrial organization have theorized that intermediate market structures, such as oligopoly, might lead to more innovation than either competitive or monopolistic industries. They argue that the oligopolist is faced by clear and present competition from existing rivals and cannot afford the more relaxed life of the monopolist who might choose not to maximize profits. At the same time, however, the oligopolist expects to keep a good share of the profits it earns because of the barriers to entry and its ability to avoid excessive price competition with existing rivals.

The empirical evidence is broadly consistent with this hypothesis. Professor Jesse Markham of Harvard University recently concluded a survey of empirical findings by saying:

If technological change and innovational activity are, as we generally assume, in some important way a product of organized R&D activities financed and executed by business companies, it is clear that the welfare payoffs that flow from them can to some measurable extent be traced to the doorsteps of large firms operating in oligopolistic markets.

Everyday observation provides some confirmation of this finding. Leading U.S. firms that operate in highly concentrated industries, such as Kodak, IBM, du Pont, AT&T, Xerox, General Electric, and General Motors, have been highly innovative over many years.

While Schumpeter's hypothesis, applied to oligopoly, has substantial credibility, it is also true that the relationship is far from perfect. Some highly oligopolistic American industries, such as steel, appear to have lagged far behind their foreign competitors. Evidently the long, sustained absence of competition led them to become complacent and relatively inefficient. (A Schumpeterian might respond that the result is due to such things as tariff protection and other *governmental* impediments to creative destruction.)

Patents and the Incentive to Innovate

Economists who believe that competitive market structures best serve consumers by assuring them low prices, but who worry about the possible lack of incentives to innovate under competition, believe that other institutions, such as the patent laws, can provide the necessary incentives. Patent laws confer a temporary monopoly on the use of an invention. The intent of patent protection is to lengthen the short-run period during which whoever controls the invention can earn supernormal profits as a reward for inventing it. This is meant to act as a spur to invention and innovation. Whether or not existing patent laws have that effect is subject to substantial debate among economists.

Public Policy Toward Monopoly: Antitrust

The theory of monopoly leads to three principal predictions. (1) Where monopoly power exists in an industry, it will lead to a restriction on the flow of resources into the industry and thus to the employment of fewer resources than would be used under competitive conditions. (2) Consequently firms with monopoly power will be able to charge higher prices and will be able to earn profits in excess of opportunity costs. (3) Their owners will command a larger share of the national income than they would under conditions of competition. In short, an economy characterized by firms with monopoly power will lead to a

different allocation of resources and a different distribution of income than will an economy composed largely of competitive industries.

The distributional aspects of monopoly are important. In the industrial sectors of the economy, corporate managers and stockholders are typically of above average income. Thus the higher salaries and higher dividends of corporate monopoly tend to lead to a more unequal distribution of income. Monopoly power, when exercised by those who are relatively poor rather than relatively rich, has frequently been supported rather than opposed by the government. For example, the efforts of farmers to increase farm income have been not only condoned but actively promoted by public policies of crop restriction, price supports, and exemption from antitrust laws of producers' cooperatives. Labor unions are also exempt from antitrust prosecutions, and the efforts of unions to achieve some degree of monopoly power over the supply of labor were also supported actively by those public policies that encouraged the growth of unions.

Antitrust laws attempt to prohibit the acquisition or exercise of monopoly power by business firms.

The first American antitrust law, the Sherman Antitrust Act, was passed in 1890, in an era when economists believed both that perfect competition produced ideal results and that perfect competition was the feasible alternative to monopoly. American antitrust laws prohibit monopoly, attempts to monopolize, and contracts, combinations, and conspiracies in restraint of trade. They give the courts the power to stop such practices and to dissolve into a number of independent companies a company that has violated the law.

While modern economists are no longer so confident about the feasibility of perfect competition and the evils of monopoly power, competition (and the laws that promote it) is still regarded as playing a key role in the successful working of the market economy. The antitrust laws originally adopted in 1890 and 1914 have been amended and added to, yet the original statutes still play a vital role in American policy toward industry.

THE NATURE OF ANTITRUST POLICY

The dominant theme of antitrust policy has been to foster competition against those who would seek to restrain trade.[2]

Anticompetitive results and monopoly power may be achieved or perpetuated in many ways:

1. by firms conspiring among themselves (colluding) to restrict output or raise prices, or otherwise failing to compete with one another
2. by firms adopting practices "in restraint of trade," such as contracts that bind a purchaser to buy all its supplies from a single seller
3. by a firm employing "predatory" practices against rival sellers in an effort to force them into bankruptcy, "good behavior," or merger
4. by a merger of existing firms into a new and larger firm
5. by one firm acquiring control of other firms through purchasing their stock or acquiring their physical assets
6. by a firm finding monopoly "thrust upon it" (in the words of the distinguished American jurist Learned Hand) either by its natural efficiency as a single producer or by successful innovation.

Each of the first five ways has been the object of antitrust legislation. The basic tools of antitrust policy are the laws designed to eliminate practices leading to monopoly. Such practices may be either criminal or civil offenses. In criminal law, a firm found guilty may be fined and its officers may be fined and/or sentenced to jail. While criminal cases can be brought only by the government, civil cases can be brought either by the government or by private litigants.

In civil cases, a firm found in violation of the law may be required by the court to abandon cer-

tain practices, or it may be forced to dissolve itself into a number of separate companies. In the legal phrase, a firm found violating the law must "cleanse itself" of its violation in a manner prescribed by the court. In private cases, a firm may be obliged to pay injured parties an amount up to three times the amount of damages caused by the violation. "Treble damages" were designed to provide a substantial incentive to private firms to root out violations of the law that might escape the notice of government prosecutors.

WHO MAKES OUR ANTITRUST POLICIES?

Antitrust laws prohibit certain forms of activity. Since they are laws, they are enforced in the courts, and enforcement in the main follows the usual legal procedures. There are both federal and state antitrust laws, the federal being far the more important. Government cases originate either within the antitrust division of the Department of Justice or within procedures of the Federal Trade Commission (FTC). Many cases never go to trial because they are settled by agreement between the Department of Justice or the FTC and the companies. Justice Department and private cases go to trial before federal district courts. FTC cases are heard first by the commission. In all cases appeal is to the appropriate Circuit Court of Appeals and then to the Supreme Court. Supreme Court decisions, here as elsewhere, stand until modified by other decisions of this highest court.

The overall effect of antitrust policy at any time rests on three things: the nature of the laws themselves, the courts' interpretation of them, and the vigor with which prosecutions are brought by the government and by private plaintiffs. All three have changed over time, and as a result the overall antitrust climate has changed.

Principal Laws Promoting Competition

The Sherman Antitrust Act (1890) was enacted in response to the great growth in the size of firms during the last half of the nineteenth century. Section 1 of the act declared illegal every

---

[2] There are also noneconomic motives for dealing with the "monopoly problem." Many people fear the political influence of those who have substantial economic power.

Principal Antitrust Provisions

Sherman Antitrust Act (26 Stat 209, 1890, as amended)

§1. Every contract, combination in the form of trust or otherwise, or conspiracy, in restraint of trade or commerce among the several States, or with foreign nations, is hereby declared to be illegal. . . . Every person who shall make any contract or engage in any combination or conspiracy shall be deemed guilty of a felony and on conviction thereof, shall be punished by a fine not exceeding one million dollars if a corporation, or, if any other person, one hundred thousand dollars, or by imprisonment not exceeding three years, or by both . . . in the discretion of the Court.

§2. Every person who shall monopolize, or attempt to monopolize, or combine or conspire with any other person or persons, to monopolize any part of the trade or commerce among the several States, or with foreign nations, shall be deemed guilty of a felony . . .

§8. That the word "person," or "persons," wherever used in this act shall be deemed to include corporations. . . .

Clayton Antitrust Act (38 Stat 730, 1914, as amended)

§2. (Including Robinson-Patman Amendments, 1948).

(a) That it shall be unlawful for any person engaged in commerce, in the course of such commerce, either directly or indirectly, to discriminate in price between different purchasers of commodities of like grade and quality . . . where the effect of such discrimination may be substantially to lessen competition or tend to create a monopoly in any line of commerce. . . . *Provided,* That nothing herein contained shall prevent differentials which make only due allowance for differences in the cost . . . resulting from the differing methods or quantities in which such commodities are . . . sold or delivered. . . .

§3. That it shall be unlawful for any person engaged in commerce, in the course of such commerce, to lease or make a sale or contract . . . on the condition, agreement, or understanding that the lessee or purchaser thereof shall not use or deal in the . . . commodities of a competitor . . . where the effect of such . . . agreement . . . may be to substantially lessen competition or tend to create a monopoly in any line of commerce.

§7. (As amended by Celler-Kefauver Act of 1950.)

That no corporation engaged in commerce shall acquire . . . the whole or any part . . . of another corporation engaged also in commerce, where in any line of commerce in any section of the country, the effect of such acquisition may be substantially to lessen competition, or to tend to create a monopoly. . . .

§16. That any person, firm, corporation, or association shall be entitled to sue and have injunctive relief, in any court of the United States having jurisdiction over the parties, as against threatened loss or damage by a violation of the antitrust laws. . . .

Federal Trade Commission Act (38 Stat 717, 1914, as amended)

§5. (a)

(1) Unfair methods of competition . . . and unfair or deceptive acts or practices in or affecting commerce, are hereby declared unlawful.

(6) The Commission is hereby empowered and directed to prevent . . . using unfair methods . . . or deceptive acts or practices in commerce.

§5. (l)

Any person . . . who violates an order of the commission to cease and desist . . . shall pay a civil penalty of not more than $10,000 for each violation . . . each day of continuance . . . shall be deemed a separate offense.

contract, combination, or conspiracy in restraint of trade. Section 2 made it illegal to monopolize or to attempt to monopolize. It also prohibited conspiracies or combinations that resulted in monopolization. The language of the Sherman Act was strong, but it was vague. It was some time before the courts defined the act's scope more specifically.

The Clayton Antitrust Act (1914) was an attempt to be more precise and to strengthen the powers of the antitrust prosecutors by allowing them to strike at potentially anticompetitive practices "in their incipiency." It also identified certain practices as illegal "where the effect may be substantially to lessen competition." Its most important provisions were Section 7, applying to acquisition of stock in a competing company; Section 2, limiting the practice of price discrimination; and Section 3, regulating exclusive dealing and tying contracts. (A tying contract requires a buyer to purchase other items in order to purchase the item it wants.) An important provision in the Clayton Act specifically exempted collective bargaining by labor unions from the antitrust provisions.

Although the Clayton Act made it illegal to take control of another firm by purchasing its stock when the adverse effect on competition was substantial, the act neglected to prohibit taking control by purchasing the firm's plant and equipment. Thus, although it dealt with the trust, or "loose-knit" combination of competitors, it neglected the merger, or "close-knit" combination. In 1950 this loophole was closed by passage of the Celler-Kefauver Act, which applied the same provisions to asset acquisitions as had previously applied only to acquisitions of stock.

The Federal Trade Commission Act (1914) created an independent commission to investigate industrial practices and to police unfair and predatory practices. Although initially the FTC had substantial powers to issue "cease and desist orders" without being subject to judicial review, the Supreme Court denied it this power in 1919. The FTC has not played the vital fact-finding role its proposers envisaged, though it continues to perform a number of functions and to exercise some policy influence in the antitrust field. It does a fair amount of policing of unfair trade practices, which are defined by Section 5 of the act. Further, by virtue of an unwritten agreement with the antitrust division, it exercises primary supervision in a number of industries.

The Hart-Scott-Rodino Antitrust Improvement Act (1976) amended both the Sherman and Clayton acts in ways that increased penalties and made mergers somewhat easier to attack.

Trends of Judicial Interpretation

The first important series of antitrust prosecutions occurred at the beginning of the twentieth century. Two major decisions were issued in 1911 when, in forcing the Standard Oil Company and the American Tobacco Company to divest themselves of a large share of their holdings of other companies, the Supreme Court enunciated the "rule of reason." Not all trusts, but only *unreasonable* combinations in restraint of trade, merited conviction under the Sherman Act.

The rule of reason received a narrow interpretation in the famous U.S. Steel case (1920). The Court found that the company had not violated the law, even though it found that the organizers of the company had *intended* to monopolize the industry, and even though the company had earlier conspired to fix prices. The Court held that U.S. Steel had not succeeded in *achieving* a monopoly (indeed, its vain attempts at price fixing proved that!). The fact that it was a big company controlling half the industry and with potential monopoly power was, the Court ruled, beside the point. The decision said in part, "The law does not make mere size an offense. It . . . requires overt acts."

The U.S. Steel decision and a series of related ones reached a climax in the International Harvester case (1927). Here the Court not only reiterated that mere size was not an offense but added that neither was the existence of unexerted monopoly power, no matter how impressive that power. These decisions reflected the business-oriented mood of the country during the 1920s, a mood shared by a highly conservative Supreme Court. Under this interpretation, which lasted until World War II, the antitrust laws were virtually unenforceable so far as attacks on the structure of heavily concentrated industries were concerned.

A sharp break in this situation occurred in a series of cases prosecuted in the late 1930s, which reached the Court both before and just after World War II. A landmark decision in *United States* v. *Socony-Vacuum Oil Co.* (1940) enunciated a strong rule against price fixing: "Under the Sherman Act a combination formed for the purpose and with the effect of raising, depressing, fixing, pegging or stabilizing the price of a commodity in interstate commerce is illegal *per se*." Thus where price fixing was concerned no test of reasonableness or sound social purpose would be applied.

An even more basic attack on the rule of reason was enunciated in the Aluminum Company of America (ALCOA) case. Prosecution of the case began in 1937, but the decision was not handed down until 1945. The decision reversed the U.S. Steel and International Harvester decisions and found ALCOA to be an illegal monopoly even though it had engaged in no unreasonable behavior. The decision suggested that beyond some point mere size would in itself be an offense if the defendants had not done everything possible to avoid becoming dominant. This reversal was possible because the mood of the country — and the composition of its courts — had changed sharply.

This case and others led some people to speak of the "new Sherman Act." Subsequent decisions have modified the strongly anti-big-business aspects of the ALCOA case, but the retreat from ALCOA has stopped well short of the Harvester and U.S. Steel decisions. The conduct of firms with massive market power, such as IBM, Kodak, and AT&T, is closely scrutinized to distinguish between competitive and monopolistic behavior.

The modification of Section 7 of the Clayton Act in 1950, together with the onset of the "Warren Court," ushered in a period of virtually unbroken triumphs for the government in its antitrust cases. Four members of that Court, Chief Justice Earl Warren and Associate Justices Hugo Black, William Brennan, and William O. Douglas, formed a solid antitrust block and needed but one more vote to command a majority. They usually found it.

Every **horizontal merger** (i.e., between two companies selling the same or similar products) the Warren Court considered was found to constitute a substantial lessening of competition and was declared illegal. In the Von's Grocery case (1965), a merger of two supermarkets was ruled illegal even though the merged firms would have had only a 7.5 percent share of the local (Los Angeles) market.

In the **vertical merger** field (i.e., between a supplier and a customer), the merger of Brown Shoe Company with a chain of retail stores (Kinney) was found illegal even though Kinney sold less than 2 percent of the nation's shoes and Brown supplied only 8 percent of Kinney's needs.

Conglomerate mergers (i.e., between firms that are neither horizontally nor vertically related and are therefore not in the same market) had long been considered outside the reach of antitrust laws unless specific anticompetitive practices were involved. However, in a series of decisions since 1965, the Court has opened the door to attacking them under Section 7 of the Clayton Act.

The Warren Court has been replaced by the Burger Court, four of its nine members having been appointed by President Nixon and one by President Ford. This Court's views on antitrust matters are much more tolerant of business practices that involve some limitations on trade, so long as they are normal business practices. In particular, this Court has been reluctant to expand the list of actions that are illegal per se.

The pendulum has swung away from the position (as stated by Justice Potter Stewart in a dissenting opinion) where "the government always wins."

Periods of Vigorous Prosecution

Courts, whatever their predilections, decide only those cases that come before them. Whether to prosecute, and which cases to prosecute, is largely decided by the antitrust division, whose head is a presidential appointee.

When the Sherman Act was passed in 1890, it was adopted with little discussion and attracted remarkably little attention. It was not until Theodore Roosevelt succeeded William McKinley in the White House that "trustbusting" became an activity of note. Roosevelt, who had stormed San Juan Hill in the Spanish American War, tried to storm the hill of big business. In 1903 he set up the antitrust division in the Department of Justice. His administration initiated the series of major prosecutions that led to the Standard Oil, American Tobacco, and U.S. Steel decisions.

The rule of reason, World War I, and a sharply conservative turn in American attitudes during the 1920s led to 25 years of unaggressive antitrust, from 1912 to 1937. Despite business's fears about Franklin Roosevelt's radicalism, no administration before or since has given such encouragement to policies in restraint of trade! Roosevelt's first administration (1933–1937) was so concerned with stemming the Great Depression that under the National Recovery Administration it fostered industry councils that were encouraged to fix prices and limit outputs in an attempt to restore stability to demoralized markets.

The appointment of Thurman Arnold in 1937 to the leadership of the antitrust division marked the beginning of a most vigorous period of antitrust activity. The Department of Justice, no doubt partly because of a marked change in the composition of the Supreme Court, attempted to bring cases that would reopen issues that had been foreclosed by the rule of reason. The fruits of this activity included the ALCOA and Socony-Vacuum decisions.

Antitrust policy was pushed to the sidelines by the overriding problems of World War II, the postwar readjustment, and the Korean War. It did not begin to re-emerge until the 1950s. A relatively vigorous antitrust policy was pursued during the Eisenhower, Kennedy, and Johnson administrations. It reached a climax in the mid sixties in the decisions of the Warren Court.

Although the Nixon, Ford, and Carter administrations have been more conservative, antitrust prosecutions by the antitrust division, by the FTC, and by private plaintiffs have remained active. In recent years the courts, rather than the prosecutors, have resisted an even more vigorous antitrust enforcement policy. Many liberals, anxious to recapture the attitudes of the Warren Court, have sought new legislation that would expand the reach of the antitrust laws to deal more directly with concentrated market structures. Important cases now in the courts include actions against IBM, AT&T, and ready-to-eat cereal manufacturers, as well as a massive FTC investigation of the automobile industry.

THE SUCCESS OF ANTITRUST POLICY

Although the Sherman Act is 90 years old, the combination of reasonably permissive (from the government's point of view) interpretation by the courts and reasonably active governmental activity has been present only for the last 35 years. *Antitrust, in this sense, is in its early development.* Economists do not generally agree as to whether the *structure* of American industry has been influenced very much by antitrust policy. American industry remains highly concentrated (see Chapter 16), but empirical studies show no tendency for the concentration either to increase or to decrease drastically. Would the pattern be very different if there had been no antitrust laws, or if the existing laws had been more vigorously enforced? We do not know for sure.

Many economists and antitrust lawyers believe that U.S. antitrust laws have been quite successful in inhibiting price fixing and certain restrictive practices. At the same time, the laws have done little to alter the basic structure of the economy. Whether this constitutes a signal success or a brave failure depends on one's diagnosis of the health of the enterprise system. Here people disagree sharply.

ECONOMICS AND THE LAW

Economic concepts such as competition, monopoly, and markets lie at the heart of antitrust policy, and economists are employed in the Justice Department, by the FTC, and by lawyers for private companies. Market definition, for example, plays a critical role in antitrust merger litigation: Section 7 of the Clayton Act requires evaluation of a merger by asking whether "in any line of commerce, in any section of the country the effect of such acquisition may be substantially to lessen competition or to tend to create a monopoly."

"Line of commerce" and "section of the country" involve product and geographic market definitions because competition occurs only within sensibly defined markets. A great many antitrust cases have turned on market definition, and some have even utilized such economic concepts as cross elasticity of demand.

Here are a few questions the courts have asked and answered: Is cellophane in the same market as wax paper, Saran wrap, and other flexible wrapping materials? (Yes, said the Supreme Court.) Are glass jars and tin cans in the same market? (Yes, said the Supreme Court.) Are insulated aluminum and copper cable in the same market? (Yes, said the District Court; no, said the Supreme Court.) Are New York and Philadelphia banks in the same market and thus in competition with one another? (No, said the courts in 1963.) Do different grades of coal in Illinois constitute an economic market? (No, said the District Court, in part because it found the relevant market to be energy. The Supreme Court did not reverse the decision.) Even though courts decide these matters, the matters themselves involve economic questions, and economic studies or witnesses were introduced by both parties in each of these litigations.

But while antitrust policies use economic theory and economic expertise, our antitrust laws ignore certain distinctions that economists think are important. In particular, the role of big business, even monopoly, in promoting dynamic advances, as argued by Professor Schumpeter, has many adherents yet is largely ignored by antitrust policies. Some decisions have protected smaller competitors against larger, more efficient

rivals. The distinction between injury to competition and injury to *competitors* has not always been made clearly by the courts. Finally, the courts have had a difficult time in coming to grips with oligopoly. Should it be regarded favorably because it is much more competitive than monopoly — or unfavorably because it is much less competitive than perfect competition?

Economists themselves are divided as to whether these distinctions are important. Some believe that public policy ought to be based on things such as size and market share, without regard for actual conduct or performance. Others offer their own "rule of reason," called "workable competition." They argue that the real choice is between more or less oligopoly and that the positive effects of a given market share, or merger, on prices, on profits, and on costs should be determined in each individual case. This seems so reasonable; why do some people object? They object because they believe that workable competition will lead to endless studies and no action. Because economists do not speak with a unified voice on such matters, it is perhaps not surprising that the basic nature of the antitrust program continues to be set by the lawyers.

Public Policy Toward Monopoly: Public Utility Regulation

NATURAL MONOPOLY

Natural monopoly arises because of economies of scale (as was discussed on page 294). Policymakers have not wanted to compel the maintenance of a large number of small, inefficient producers when a single firm would be much more efficient; neither have they wanted to give the natural monopolist the opportunity to restrict output, raise price, and appropriate as profits the gains available by virtue of large-scale production.

FIGURE 18-4
The Problem of Natural Monopoly

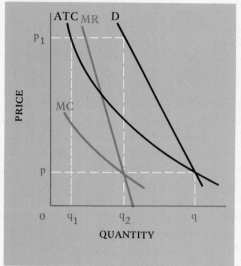

Cost conditions in a situation of natural monopoly are such that a single firm is required to achieve the economies of scale, but a monopolist finds it profitable to restrict output to maximize profits. Because *ATC* declines sharply, efficiency is served by having a single firm. Clearly, one firm producing at q would be more efficient than several firms each producing q_1 at a cost of p_1 per unit. But an unregulated monopoly would restrict output to q_2 and charge price p_1, thereby depriving consumers of the advantages of large-scale production.

The public utility concept grew out of the recognition by economists that when there are major economies of large-scale production, protection of the public interest by competition is impractical if not impossible.

The dilemma of natural monopoly is illustrated in Figure 18-4. To achieve low costs, a single large producer is necessary, but an unregulated profit-maximizing monopoly would restrict output, raise price, and fail to provide the large volume of output at a low price that the technology makes possible.

One possible response to this dilemma is for government to assume ownership of the single firm and instruct (or delegate to) the managers of the nationalized industry how much to produce and what price to charge, in each case being guided by the national interest. Many countries have done precisely that with telephone and railroad services, among others. The characteristic American response since the late nineteenth century, when the modern regulatory commissions first appeared, has been to allow private enterprise but to regulate its behavior.

Public utility regulation gives to appropriate public authorities (usually specially constituted regulatory commissions such as the Interstate Commerce Commission and the Wisconsin Public Utilities Commission) control over the price and quantity of service provided by a natural monopoly, with the object of achieving the efficiency of a single seller without the output restriction of the monopolist.

In return for giving a company a franchise or license to be the sole producer, the public utility regulators reserve the right to regulate its behavior.

Regulation of this kind began with the establishment of the Interstate Commerce Commission (ICC) in 1887. Its primary function was to regulate railroad rates. Public utility regulation has since spread to other forms of transportation (airlines, trucking, pipelines) as well as to the standard utilities: telephone, electricity, water, and gas.

Although regulatory commissions were first created to deal with natural monopoly problems, most regulatory activity is no longer of that kind. Motor carriers, for example, have none of the characteristics of natural monopoly. The Food and Drug Administration (FDA) and the Securities and Exchange Commission (SEC) are concerned mainly with consumer protection. The Environmental Protection Agency (EPA) and the Occupational Safety and Health Administration (OSHA) affect all industries, competitive or not. Many activities of the Federal Communications Commission and the Federal Aviation Administration concern the orderly use of airwaves and skyways—the prevention of chaotic competition. We limit our discussion in this chapter to natural monopoly regulation; some discussion of other regulatory activities will be found in Chapter 24.

THE THEORY OF NATURAL MONOPOLY REGULATION

What price should a regulatory commission permit? It might wish to set price equal to marginal cost (the way it would be in perfect competition), but such a price and quantity would surely lead to losses, for marginal cost is necessarily below average cost when average cost is falling. This is illustrated in Figure 18-5. Some means of continuing subsidization of these losses would be required.

An alternative is to permit the company to charge a price that allows it to cover all its costs and earn a fair return on its investment. In essence, this is the objective of most regulatory commissions with regard to pricing in natural monopoly situations. The theory is extraordinarily simple. The problems of putting the theory into practice are difficult.

PROBLEMS OF IMPLEMENTING THE THEORY

Regulation has aimed at setting prices high enough to permit firms to cover all their costs yet low enough to achieve the large sales required to reap the scale economies that characterize natural monopoly situations. If a regulatory commission knew what the demand curve and the cost curves looked like, it could simply pick the point on the demand curve that corresponded to the lowest price that covered average total costs. But a diagram like that of Figure 18-5 is not usually available. In the absence of reliable demand and cost information, commissions have tended to judge prices according to the level of profits they produce. Generally, having set prices, regulatory agencies permit price increases when profits fall below "fair" levels and require price reductions if profits exceed such levels.

FIGURE 18-5
Pricing Strategy for a Regulatory Commission

Average cost pricing is the goal of regulatory commissions, which seek the lowest prices possible without losses for natural monopolies. Although perfect competition leads to production where price equals marginal costs, here the price cannot be set at p_1, where demand equals marginal cost, because the firm would necessarily suffer losses (the shaded area). Price p covers all costs (including the opportunity cost of capital). The corresponding output q achieves most of the cost advantages of large-scale output.

While it is true that if the appropriate price is charged, economic profits will be zero, the reverse is not necessarily true. Profits can be zero because of inefficient operation, misleading accounting, or pricing at the lowest attainable level of average cost. Thus commissions that rely on profits as their guide to pricing must monitor a number of other aspects of the regulated firm's behavior.

The Definition of Costs

If a company is to be allowed to charge a price determined as "cost plus a fair profit" (as the regulators say), and if that price is below the profit-maximizing one, it is clearly in the firm's interest to exaggerate reported costs if it can. One major activity of regulatory commissions has been to define rules of allowable costing, as they affect both permissible rates of depreciation and reasonable expenses and expenditures. Freezing the rate of return removes the profit motive for keeping costs down. But although the firm does not care, the public presumably does, and thus cost supervision is an important activity of public utility regulation. Without it, the regulated industries' managers might have no incentive to be efficient and might simply let costs drift upward.

The Rate Base

Average total cost includes an appropriate rate of return on the capital invested in the business. Suppose it is agreed that a firm should be allowed to earn a rate of return of 8 percent on its capital. The **rate of return** is defined as the ratio of profits to invested capital. What is the value of the capital to which 8 percent is to be applied? The allowable amount is called the **rate base**. There has been no more controversial area than this in public utility regulation. Should the original cost or the reproduction cost of the firm's assets be used? It does not make much difference unless prices are changing, but in the inflationary situation of the last 35 years, reproduction cost is uniformly higher than original costs and thus leads to higher bases, higher permitted profits, and higher rates to users. If the major concern is to generate profits to buy replacement equipment, reproduction cost is appropriate. If the major concern is to generate profits to compensate past capital investments, original cost may be appropriate. Regulatory commissions (and the courts) have vacillated on this issue.

The precise nature of regulatory rules is important because the rules affect the incentives of those regulated. Economists Harvey Averch and Leland Johnson have shown that a regulated utility has a lesser incentive to resist high capital costs than an unregulated one, and that in some circumstances it pays the unregulated utility to buy relatively unproductive equipment. This is true because if profits depend on the rate base, it

often pays the firm to increase its rate base. Thus the notion of "necessary and prudent investments" enters into regulatory rules. This tendency for one regulation to lead to a need for yet further regulation has been called the tar-baby effect, after a fictional creature made of tar which overcame an attacker by enmeshing it.

A Fair Return

The permitted rate of return that is implicit in the theory of public utility regulation is the opportunity cost of the owners' capital, with allowances for risk. Regulatory commissions have paid some attention to overall earnings rates in the economy, and the level of permitted earnings has changed slightly over time. But equity and tradition have played a much larger role than considerations of opportunity cost, and regulatory commissions have been slow to adjust permitted rates of return to changing market conditions. For decades permitted rates of return of 6 to 9 percent were employed. But when market interest rates soared to double-digit figures during the late 1970s, the traditional levels were not sufficient to induce new investment. Yet regulatory commissions have been reluctant to permit the large increases in prices that would result from sharp increases in the permitted rate of return.

Risk

Regulated public utilities typically enjoy monopoly positions with respect to what are often essential services. This tends to make them less vulnerable to loss of business than other enterprises that face more direct competition. But they are not free of risk. If a utility is losing money because the demand for its product is declining, and if no adjustment of prices or service can save it, it will eventually discontinue service via bankruptcy or will "sell out" to the public, to be run as a subsidized public enterprise. Investors in many American railroads have found this out the hard way.

Even for a utility that stays in business, there

is risk. While it is common to speak of the regulatory rate of return as "guaranteed," this is not accurate. In principle, it is a maximum "target" rate of return. Actual earnings may be larger or smaller over the short run because of economic factors and regulatory lags. If actual earnings are larger, the regulatory commission will refuse to grant price increases and may even seek to lower prices and reduce future profits. If actual earnings are lower, the regulatory commission will permit price increases.

It is possible for a utility to earn more than the maximum target rate if it is in an industry where its unregulated profits would be growing. For example, suppose the permitted rate of return is 10 percent and a certain company earns 15 percent in one year. No one confiscates its "excess" return, and it may take the regulatory commission six months or more to reduce rates to the point where earnings are again 10 percent. If this situation tends to recur, the average profit over time will be in excess of 10 percent — possibly well in excess. Of course, in a declining industry or in a rapid inflation the reverse situation can occur, and a firm may find its profits falling short of the permitted rate. Even though its petition to raise prices is approved, the process takes time and the end result is likely to be an average profit rate less than the official permitted rate.

The Curtailment of Service

Because profits are not guaranteed, a regulated utility in a declining industry may have a serious problem. If it is failing to make profits equal to the permitted rate, it may apply for permission to increase its prices, but if its demand is elastic, a rise in rates will lead to a reduction in revenues and may reduce profits. Privately owned urban transit systems and passenger rail lines have proven unprofitable because of secularly declining demand as people shifted to substitutes: private cars and airplanes. Given elastic demand curves, when transport companies raise fares (hoping to increase revenues), they find they only lose more customers to other means of transport.

At this point a bus company, for example, may look to its costs to see how it can avoid losses. Often it finds that some parts of its service (such as routes to outlying neighborhoods) no longer cover the variable costs of providing them, and it proposes to the regulatory authority that this service be dropped. Often the regulators say no. The reason is that they see other considerations in abandoning the bus service (such as increased congestion in the downtown area as even more people used their own cars) that loom large to the regulators but not to the bus company.

The regulators want the regulated company to "cross-subsidize" the less popular routes with profits from the more popular routes; at the same time, they do not want to force the company into bankruptcy. Thus, each time a curtailment of service is proposed, regulators must make the difficult determination of whether the company is merely trying to increase its profits and is shirking its public service responsibility or whether it is truly in trouble.

EVALUATING PUBLIC UTILITY REGULATION

The moral of the public utility experience is that what looks like a simple and straightforward theory of regulating natural monopoly turns out in practice to be highly complex. In large part this is because regulated companies adapt their behavior to the rules that are imposed on them — and thus begins a chain of adaptation and change by regulators and regulated that produces a complex and cumbersome apparatus. Moreover, the need for due process in decisions that affect property rights has made procedures and decisions legalistic and resource-using.

Regulation brings both costs and benefits. Today's great debate is, "Do the benefits justify the costs?" The debate is its most heated with respect to environmental and safety regulatory activities of the EPA and OSHA, but it extends to public utility regulation as well. The costs of regulation include more than the costs of running regulatory commissions and the costs imposed on the courts by seemingly endless appeals. Regulatory costs are also imposed on businesses that must strive to comply with paperwork.

Professor Richard Posner of the University of Chicago estimated that milk price regulation added about 10 percent to milk prices. The president's Council of Economic Advisers estimated that regulation accounted for a rise of about one point per year in the cost of living. Murray Weidenbaum of Washington University and Willard Butcher of Chase Manhattan Bank put the cost of regulation even higher: as much as $100 billion per year. Whether these estimates are realistic is debated. And there are, of course, benefits. Ralph Nader and others counter the Weidenbaum "costs" with equally impressive (and equally controversial) dollar estimates of "benefits."

The alleged benefits and costs are difficult—if not impossible—to measure with any precision. Much of the debate is ideological, notwithstanding its expression in terms of dollar estimates of benefits and costs. Is keeping the cost to consumers of electricity artificially low a benefit or a cost? It surely benefits some consumers, yet it just as surely involves some resource misallocation. Are the accidents avoided by industrial safety standards worth the extra expenditures they require? Victims of such accidents may answer differently than those who pay more for the products. These questions are not readily answered on a scientific basis.

Some, including Professor George Stigler of the University of Chicago, believe that the evidence shows that the levels of prices, quantities, and profits are about the same under public utility regulation as they would have been without it; they even go so far as to suggest that unregulated monopoly would have performed better.

The experience with airline deregulation suggests that it is difficult to evaluate results. Starting in 1978, the Civil Aeronautics Board (CAB) removed regulations on airline rate making and on protecting individual airline routes. The initial responses seemed almost miraculous: tumbling air fares, supersaver discounts, increased air service on popular routes, increased passenger travel, and a boom in the industry. But a year later fares were *up* 25 to 40 percent over the regulated levels, some of the major carriers were having severe financial troubles, service to certain locations had been curtailed, and the euphoria of a year earlier was gone.

Evaluation is difficult here because expenses have increased, especially the price of jet fuel. Has deregulation of the airlines been a success? It will be many years before enough experience exists to permit a definitive evaluation of the benefits and costs of airline deregulation. Without hard evidence, one can find assertions on each side. To the president of United Airlines the answer was that while fares had risen, they had risen much less than would have been the case with regulation—that is, deregulation was a success. To the senior vice-president of American Airlines deregulation was raising costs and thus prices by encouraging excess capacity on most routes—that is, deregulation was a failure.

Considering regulation generally, there seems in 1980 to be a remarkable consensus that regulation has failed to live up to the expectations held for it. Perhaps the most widely held view is that regulation, even when effective at first, becomes too rigid and unresponsive to change and as a result fails to recognize and to permit such competition as is possible. Given changing technology, yesterday's natural monopoly of a single railroad may become but one mode of transportation in a competitive transportation industry. Wire telephone communications are no longer unique, given radio and satellites. Even the Post Office is not the only way to send written messages and parcels from one place to another. Thus the scope of natural monopoly regulation keeps changing. But regulators tend to cling to, and in some cases are legally committed to, rules and assumptions that may no longer fit the world they are regulating.

Changes in regulation in some form or another seem likely to occur over the next decade in response to this growing consensus. Some favor rapid deregulation and reliance on market forces.

Others believe that the deficiencies lie in the structure of regulation and that changing the way regulation is carried out will improve matters. Still others think that the failures of regulation require nationalization or new legislation defining a novel approach to what regulators should do.

Which of many proposed directions for regulatory reform will be followed is unclear at this stage. In 1980, Congress passed and the president signed a bill that will gradually eliminate virtually all regulation of motor carriers. As of this date Congress has decreased the regulatory authority of the CAB, the ICC and the FTC. However, the present regulatory commissions are not without political support in Congress and are generally staunchly defended *by the regulated industries themselves*. For some, this last point is the most telling criticism of all.

Summary

1. Comparison of the models of perfect competition and monopoly reveals that prices will change less in response to cost changes in monopoly than in competition and that if costs, demand, and products are unchanged, the monopolization of a previously competitive industry will lead to a rise in price and a decline in output. In such circumstances, monopoly may lead to both productive and allocative inefficiency.

2. Levels of cost are not independent of market structures. If there are advantages of large scale in production, distribution, marketing, or purchasing, the minimum efficient size of the firm may be too large to be compatible with conditions of perfect competition. In such cases a shift from competition to a more concentrated market structure — oligopoly or monopoly — may lead to lower costs and increased efficiency. Because costs are not independent of market structure, the prima facie case in favor of competition and against concentration of market power is weakened. Most economists believe that substantial competition is compatible with efficient operation of American industry and that it is desirable to foster at least that amount of competition.

3. A major issue in the evaluation of different market structures concerns the incentive provided for invention and innovation. Joseph Schumpeter believed that the incentive to innovate was so much greater under monopoly that monopoly was to be preferred to perfect competition. While few modern economists go that far, the empirical evidence suggests that technological change and innovation are to a measurable extent traceable to the efforts of large firms in oligopolistic industries.

4. The policy implications of the classical view of monopoly and competition led American legislators of the late nineteenth century in two directions: public utility regulation to deal with natural monopoly and antitrust laws to deal with other kinds of monopoly.

5. The basic tool of antitrust policy is the series of laws that seeks to eliminate practices that lead to monopoly. The overall effect of antitrust policy at any time rests on three things: the nature of the laws themselves, the attitude and interpretation of the courts, and the vigor with which prosecutions are brought by the government and by private plaintiffs. A conjunction of conditions favoring a vigorous and aggressive antitrust policy has been present only in the period since World War II.

6. Economists' opinions as to what antitrust law ought to be are divided between a view based largely on the mere existence of market power and a discretionary view that attempts to evaluate the workability of competition. Many believe that antitrust laws have been more nearly successful in inhibiting restrictive practices than in altering the basic structure of the economy.

7. The original philosophy of public utility regulation was to grant a monopoly where necessary to achieve the advantages of large-scale production but to prevent the monopolist from restricting output and raising price. The most common regulatory approach has been to regulate prices. This is done by watching profits: allowing price increases only if necessary to permit the regulated utility to earn a fair return on its capital and requiring price decreases if profits rise above the approved level.

8. Implementation of this straightforward theory encounters difficulties because any set of rules becomes a set of signals that induces patterns of response from those regulated. Thus it has been necessary for regulators to define carefully "proper" costs, how the costs should be measured, the appropriate rate base, what constitute "necessary and prudent" additions to capital equipment, and what constitutes a fair return. They have also been forced to determine when and whether utilities can discontinue providing services to groups in the community from whom (private) revenues do not cover (private) variable costs.

9. The entire regulatory apparatus has come under close scrutiny in recent years. A first step toward deregulation was the passage in 1978 of the Airline Deregulation Act, which will gradually phase out the existence of the Civil Aeronautics Board, which has controlled both rates and routes. A second step was the 1980 passage of a bill to deregulate motor carriers.

10. Regulation is costly, but it may be beneficial. Whether overall public utility regulation has had much effect and, if it has, whether on balance the effect has been beneficial is a matter of lively current debate and research.

Topics for Review

Effects of monopolizing a competitive industry
Competition and allocative efficiency
The effect of market structure on costs
Purposes of antitrust legislation
Natural monopoly
Difficulties of public utility regulation
Deregulation

Discussion Questions

1. "I think there are some people, in and out of government, who get a little confused and associate bigness with badness. Success alone is now evidence enough to warrant intensive scrutiny by the government to determine how the success can be remedied—as if it were some sort of disease. The age of Orwell's doublethink, prophesied for 1984, has come early. For now, to win is to lose. The real losers are the consumers. They lose the advantages of free competition; new and better products, lower prices and wider choices." Comment on these views of GM Chairman Murphy.

2. Economists Armen Alchian and Reuben Kessel have advanced the hypothesis that monopolists choose to satisfy more of their nonmonetary aims than do perfect competitors. Consider three aims:
   a. exercising the prejudices of the monopolists against certain racial minorities
   b. enjoying a good life with big expense accounts
   c. promoting their political philosophies by advertising and broadcasting
   What theoretical arguments could support the Alchian-Kessel hypothesis? Would the same arguments apply to oligopolists?

3. Evaluate the wisdom of having the antitrust division use profits as a measure of monopoly power in deciding whether to prosecute a case. Would such a rule be expected to affect the behavior of firms with high profits? In what ways might any changes be socially beneficial and in what ways socially costly?

4. Price fixing agreements are (with some specific exemptions) violations of the antitrust laws. Consider the effects of the following. In what way, if at all, should they be viewed as being similar to price fixing agreements?
   a. a manufacturer "recommending" minimum prices to its dealers
   b. manufacturers publishing product price lists that are changed only every three months
   c. a trade association that publishes "average industry total costs of production" every month

5. The Department of Justice merger guidelines permit a "failing company" defense to an otherwise illegal acquisition but reject an "efficiency" defense. Thus a merger that keeps a failing and presumably inefficient firm in business is permitted, but one that achieves a more efficient level of production is not. What arguments can you develop that support or oppose this policy?

6. Under what circumstances might some aspect of market structure or market conduct be treated as illegal per se — that is, without considering the effect in the particular case?

7. The WREDD Brick Company, the second largest of five suppliers of bricks in the Zackville area, plans to merge with one of the following companies:
   a. the Good Old Brick Company, Zackville's largest
   b. the largest lumber company in town
   c. the smallest brick supplier in town
   d. the All Brick Construction Company
   e. the Bank of Zackville
   f. Sam's Used Car Lot

   Classify each potential merger as horizontal, vertical, or conglomerate. How might each merger affect competition? Which would seem to you most objectionable? Least objectionable? Why?

8. One of the most controversial proposals before Congress asks for the "vertical disintegration" of the oil companies. "If you break up the oil companies, you'll pay through the hose," says an oil company ad. "Bringing down oil prices must start with the vertical separation of oil exploration, production, transmission, refining and retail sale," says a consumer advocate. What are the implicit assumptions underlying each of these views?

9. "In a competitive market the least-cost production techniques are revealed by entry and exit, while in public utility regulation they are revealed by commission rate hearings. It is easier to fool the commission than the market. Therefore, wherever possible, competition should be permitted." Discuss.

10. It is often asserted that when a regulatory agency such as a public utilities commission is established, it will ultimately become controlled by the people it was intended to regulate. This argument raises the question of who regulates the regulators. Can you identify why this might happen? How might the integrity of regulatory boards be protected?

Who Runs the Firm and for What Ends?

19

Once upon a time most Americans had great faith in the ability of private firms to produce the goods and services on which the nation's prosperity was founded. America had the highest living standard in the world, and it seemed to be living proof that American-style private capitalism not only worked, it worked much better than any known alternative.

Today the public's perception seems to have changed. Attitude surveys show that private firms no longer enjoy the public's full confidence. Many people question both the morality of business behavior and the ability of business to act as the prime mover of a successful capitalist system. Today many Americans are in the anomalous position of believing in the free-market private enterprise system in general while harboring deep suspicions about whether our major corporations can or will make it work.

Important questions are involved here. Does the continuing success of the American economy depend on the initiative of healthy, independent, private firms? Does it depend instead on increased public scrutiny and control of the behavior of these firms? Is the economy's apparent failure to perform as well in the past decade as it did in previous decades due to a failure of private firms? Or is it perhaps due to increasing government interference with their activities?

What light does the theory we have studied so far shed on these important questions? In economic theory firms are users of factors of production and producers of commodities. They face cost and demand curves that are largely determined by forces beyond their control. They seek to maximize their profits by keeping their costs as low as possible and producing to satisfy consumers' demands. They care only about profits, and their decisions are uninfluenced by their internal structure. Thus they contribute to our high living standards by producing, as cheaply as possible, goods that satisfy consumers' demands.

An important body of criticism disputes this standard theory of the firm. It says instead that actual firms have the power to control their market conditions and that they use that power. They manipulate demand by advertising, and they are not under heavy competitive pressure to produce efficiently by holding costs down. Firms, the critics continue, do not even seek to maximize profits. Instead they seek other goals that are determined by their internal structure, and these goals often cause them to behave in ways that are socially undesirable. If true, such criticisms would support the views that firms hinder rather than advance consumer welfare and that they need to be forced by government to act in the social interest.

In past chapters we studied the traditional view that firms serve the interests of consumers. In the present chapter we will study some criticisms of that view. We begin with those that strike at the very core of the standard microeconomic theory.

Do Firms Manipulate the Market?

In conventional theory, demand curves depend decisively on consumers' tastes and incomes and are to a significant degree independent of the actions of firms. Firms are assumed to be in business to make money, which they do by producing and selling the goods and services that consumers want. The successful firm is the one that best satisfies consumers' demands, while the firm that consistently does not do this will eventually fail. The ultimate source of all profits is consumers' desires. (Even monopoly profits depend on consumers' willingness to buy the product

that the monopolist controls.) The need for firms to respond to consumers' desires is an important part of any argument for the free enterprise system. If firms did not so respond, there would be little justification in allowing them to exert major influences on the allocation of the country's resources.

THE HYPOTHESIS THAT FIRMS CONTROL THE MARKET

A very different hypothesis is given its most prominent expression by Harvard professor John Kenneth Galbraith and consumer advocate Ralph Nader. In this view it is *not* consumers' real wants that create the market signals that in turn provide the profit opportunities that motivate business behavior. Instead, large corporations have great power to create and manipulate demand. Firms must plan and invest for an uncertain future, and the profitability of the enormous investments that they make is threatened by the unpredictability of events. Firms try to make the future less unpredictable by actively manipulating market demand and by co-opting government agencies that are supposed to control their activities.

Manipulation of Demand

The most important source of unpredictable events that may jeopardize corporate investments is unexpected shifts in market demand curves. To guard against the effects of unexpected declines in demand, corporations spend vast amounts on advertising that allows them to sell what they want to produce rather than what consumers want to buy. At the same time, corporations decide not to produce products that consumers would like to buy. This reduces the risks inherent in investing in wholly new and untried products and avoids the possibility that successful new products might spoil the market for an existing product.

According to this hypothesis, we consumers are the victims of the corporations; we are pushed around at their whim, persuaded to buy things we do not really want, and denied products we would like to have. In short we are brainwashed ciphers with artificially created wants, and we have no real autonomy with respect to our own consumption.

Corruption of Public Authorities

A second threat to the long-range plans and investments of corporations comes from uncontrollable and often unpredictable changes in the nature of government interference with the freedom of the corporation. This political threat is met by co-opting or corrupting the members of Congress, who pass laws affecting corporations, and the government agencies that are supposed to be regulating them. Corporation managers, according to the theory, indirectly subvert public institutions, from universities to regulatory agencies.

Government, instead of regulating business and protecting the public interest, has become the servant of the corporation. It supplies the corporate sector with such essential inputs as educated, trained, healthy, socially secure workers. Government also serves the giant corporation through policies concerning tariffs, import quotas, tax rules, subsidies, and research and development. These policies protect the industrial establishment from competitive pressures and reinforce its dominance and profitability.

Corruption of Our Value System

The managers of modern firms have great power. The corporations they manage earn large profits that can be reinvested to further the achievement of the values of the ruling group, which Galbraith calls the technostructure. The values of this "ruling class" emphasize industrial production, rapid growth, and materialistic aspirations at the expense of the better things of life (such as cultural and aesthetic values) and the quality of the environment.

More important, the industrial managers join with the military in a military-industrial complex that utilizes, trains, and elevates the technicians to positions of power and prestige not only in industry but in the armed services, in the defense establishment, and in the highest positions of government. In so doing, the corporations and their managers threaten to dominate if not subvert our foreign policies as well as our domestic policies.

The New Industrial State

The foregoing is an outline of what Galbraith calls the New Industrial State.[1] If Galbraith's theories of the behavior of modern corporations were substantially correct, we would have to make major revisions in our ideas of how free-market economies work.

According to the concept of the New Industrial State, the largest corporations (1) tend to dominate the economy, (2) largely control market demand rather than being controlled by it, (3) co-opt government processes instead of being constrained by them, and (4) utilize their substantial discretionary power against the interests of society.

THE EVIDENCE FOR THE HYPOTHESIS

Superficially, many facts of the American economy lend support to Galbraith's hypothesis. Corporations do account for approximately two-thirds of all business done in the United States today, and large corporations dominate the corporate sector. Of nearly 200,000 manufacturing corporations, roughly 1 percent of them have

---

[1] These views did not originate with the publication in 1967 of Galbraith's book by that title nor with the formation of "Nader's Raiders." Much earlier James Burnham wrote *The Managerial Revolution* and Robert Brady sounded an alarm in *Business as a System of Power*. Thorstein Veblen had predicted the technocratic takeover of society in *The Engineers and the Price System* in 1921, and Karl Marx predicted the subversion of the government bureaucrat by the businessman more than a century ago.

$10 million or more in assets. These large corporations hold approximately 85 percent of manufacturing assets. The 200 to 250 largest corporations—one-tenth of 1 percent of all manufacturing corporations—control approximately 50 percent of the total assets of manufacturing.

The giant corporations are well known: General Motors, Exxon, Dow Chemical, U.S. Steel, Sears Roebuck, General Electric, and so on. Many are highly profitable, and most are so widely owned that management, rather than stockholders, exercises effective control. If power comes with size, a "few" people—several thousand strategically placed executives of a few hundred leading corporations—have great power over economic affairs. Moreover, these people are primarily white, male, wealthy, and politically conservative.

As for political influence, individual corporations and trade associations have lobbyists and exercise whatever persuasion they can. Executives of many of these corporations serve on public commissions and frequently take important government positions. They make large contributions to political campaigns. Political influence is exercised at all levels of government; indeed, there have been cases where entire city governments have been effectively in the pockets of local corporations.

The political activities of corporations are not confined to the United States. In the 1970s the Lockheed Corporation was implicated in scandals involving million-dollar bribes to secure foreign orders. The list of persons involved included (among many others) a former Japanese prime minister, the husband of the ruling queen of the Netherlands, and several former Italian Christian Democratic cabinet ministers. There is no doubt that corporations have succeeded in corrupting governments at the highest levels (or at least in harnessing the corruption that was already there) and have achieved through political channels results they might never have achieved in the marketplace.

The great corporations, along with many smaller firms, spend vast amounts on advertising—as the hypothesis predicts. In 1979 total advertising expenditure accounted for approximately $2\frac{1}{2}$ percent of the value of the contribution of the private sector to the GNP. These expenditures are obviously designed to influence consumers' demand, and there is little doubt that if firms such as Lever Brothers, Gulf Oil, Schlitz, and IBM were to cut their advertising, they would lose sales to their competitors.

It is also true that much environment pollution is associated with industries that consist of well-known large firms. If automobiles, electric power, steel, oil, industrial chemicals, detergents, and paper are the primary sources of our pollution, surely Ford, Consolidated Edison, Bethlehem Steel, Texaco, Monsanto, Procter & Gamble, and International Paper are significantly to blame. Each of these is among the 100 largest nonfinancial corporations.

DOUBTS ABOUT THE HYPOTHESIS

Sensitivity to Market Pressures

Even the largest, most powerful industries are not immune to market pressures. Ford's Edsel was a classic example of the market's rejecting a product. The penetration of small foreign cars into the American market forced the automobile industry into first the compact car and then the still cheaper subcompacts. In spite of this, massive losses were suffered by American automobile manufacturers as consumers turned in very large numbers to foreign cars whose low costs and high gas mileages they preferred even in the face of heavy advertising of American cars. The decline of railroads for passenger travel is manifest in many ways, as the troubled financial history of once great railroading corporations shows. The Pullman Company was the nation's tenth largest firm in 1909; today it is not even in the top 300. The rise of air and motor travel and the decline of railroading were accompanied by a rise in the use of oil and a decline in the use of coal. More recently, the surge in demand for electric power and the shortage of oil have revitalized the coal industry.

Changes in demand and in taste can be sudden and dramatic, but mostly they are gradual, continuous, and less noticeable month by month than decade by decade. On the average about two new firms enter the top 100 every year, and as a consequence two others leave. This means a significant change over a decade.

Turnover in the list of leading companies is continuous and revealing. Only two, U.S. Steel and Exxon (Standard Oil of New Jersey), were in the top 10 both in 1909 and in 1979. Consider these giants of 1909, none of them among the largest 250 today: International Mercantile Marine (today United States Lines), United States Cotton Oil, American Hide and Leather, American Ice, Baldwin Locomotive, Cudahy, International Salt, and United Shoe Machinery. They have slipped or disappeared largely because of the relative decline in the demand for their products. Today's giants include automobile, oil, airline, and electric power companies—for the obvious reason that demand for these products is strong.

Are these demand shifts explained by the corporate manipulation of consumers' tastes through advertising or by more basic changes? Advertising has two major aspects: it seeks to inform consumers about the available products, and it seeks to influence consumers by altering their demands. The first aspect, informative advertising, plays an important part in the efficient operation of any free-market system; the second aspect is one through which firms seek to control the market rather than to be controlled by it.

Clearly, advertising does influence consumers' demand. If GM were to stop advertising, it would surely lose sales to Ford, Chrysler, and foreign imports, but it is hard to believe that the automotive society was conjured up by Madison Avenue. When you are persuaded to "fly the friendly skies of United," your real alternative is hardly a Conestoga wagon, a bicycle, or even a Greyhound bus; more likely you are forgoing American, Eastern, or Northwest Airlines. Careful promotion can influence the success of one rock group over another, but could it sell the waltz to today's teenager? Advertising—taste making—unquestionably plays a role in shaping demand, but so too do more basic human attitudes, psychological needs, and technological opportunities.

Certainly advertising shifts demands among very similar products. It is hard to believe, however, that the American economy or the average American's system of values would be fundamentally changed if there were available one more or one less make of automobile or television set or brand of shoes. A look at those products that have brought basic changes to the economy—and perhaps to our value systems—suggests that these products succeeded *because consumers wanted them,* not because Madison Avenue brainwashed people into buying them. Consider a few major examples.

The automobile transformed American society and is in demand everywhere, even in Communist countries where only informative advertising exists. The Hollywood movie had an enormous influence in shaping our world and in changing some of our values; it was—and still is—eagerly attended throughout the world, whether or not it is accompanied by a ballyhoo of advertising. The jet airplane has shrunk the world: It has allowed major league sports to expand beyond the northeastern and midwestern United States (and those cities that could be reached by an overnight bus or rail journey); it has made the international conference a commonplace; and it has made European, Hawaiian, and Caribbean vacations a reality for many. For better or worse, the birth control pill has revolutionized many aspects of behavior in spite of the fact that it has never been advertised in the mass media. Television has changed the activities of children (and adults) in fundamental ways and has brought viewers a sense of immediacy about distant events that newspapers could never achieve.

The new products that have significantly influenced the allocation of resources and the pattern of society, such as those mentioned above, have succeeded because consumers wanted them; most of those that failed did so because they were not wanted—at least not at prices that would cover their costs of production.

The evidence suggests that the allocation of resources in the American economy owes more to the tastes and values of consumers than it does to corporate advertising and related activities.

Who Controls the Government?

Is government subservient to big business? Lobbying is a legal, large-scale activity employed by many groups. Big business has its influence, but so do farmers, labor unions, and small business. Certainly American corporations have sometimes exercised illegal and improper influence on both domestic and foreign governments.

Cases of corrupt behavior have been documented at all levels of government; it does not follow, however, that government is subservient to the corporations and that decision making by the former is *dominated* by the wishes of the latter. It is easy to assert that "everyone knows that the oil lobby dominates Congress," but such assertions do not resolve empirical questions. Lobbying and influence may well help to explain why for years the United States imposed quotas on foreign oil imports, but lobbying by the oil companies did not prevent a delay of the Alaska pipeline for many years, the reduction in special tax relief, restrictions imposed on offshore oil drilling, or the final passage of a windfall profits tax. Relaxation of many antipollution restrictions came because of the oil shortages of the 1970s, not political pressure. Government contracts bolster the aerospace industry, yet Lockheed's deep financial trouble in the 1970s came in part as a result of government decisions. Tobacco companies have seen government agencies first publicize the hazards of their principal product and then restrict their advertising. Airlines finally lost their decade-long battle to prevent the introduction of the cheap transatlantic air fares pioneered by England's Sir Freddie Laker.

These examples show that while business often succeeds in attempts to protect its commercial interests through political activity, it does so within limits. Where the truth lies between the extremes of "no influence" and "no limits" is a subject of current research. Yet it does seem safe to say that, first, corporations have a lot of political influence and, second, there are some serious constraints on the ability of corporations to exert political influence over all levels of American government.

Neglect of the Public Interest?

One aspect of the Galbraithian critique has found a receptive public: the apparent disregard by large corporations of the adverse effects of productive activities on the environment. The problems of pollution, which we will discuss in Chapter 24, arise from the activities of both small and large corporations and the activities of government units and citizens. Do such polluting activities represent irresponsible behavior by corporations that can be changed by such things as Campaign GM (an effort to make General Motors responsible), or does their correction require direct policy action in the form of rules, regulations, penalties, and tax incentives?

Consumerism is a movement that asserts a conflict between the interests of firms and the public interest. Consumerists hold that the conflict should be removed by pressuring firms to be motivated by the public interest rather than by their stockholders' desires for maximum profits.

Consumerists believe, for example, that GM's directors must be made to recognize that automobiles pollute and cause accidents, and that GM's resources should be invested in the development and installation of safety and antipollution devices. This, they argue, is proper use of GM's funds, even if GM's stockholders do not see it that way and even if automobile purchasers do not want to pay for the extra safety and antipollution devices.

What are the main arguments *for* this view? First, that only the company can know the potentially adverse effects of its actions. Second, that by virtue of holding a corporate charter, the corporation assumes the responsibility to protect the general welfare while pursuing private profits.

What are the main arguments *against* the consumerist view? Managers of companies have neither the knowledge nor the ability to represent the general public interest; they are largely selected, judged, and promoted according to their ability to run a profit-oriented enterprise, and the assumption that they are especially competent to decide broader *public* questions is unjustified. Moral, as distinct from economic, decisions—such as whether or not to make or use nerve gas, to make or use internal combustion engines, to manufacture or smoke cigarettes, and to manufacture or utilize DDT or aerosol sprays—cannot properly be delegated to corporations or their executives. Some are individual decisions; others require either the expertise or the authority of a public regulatory agency. Whoever makes decisions on behalf of the public must be politically responsible to the public.

Those opposing the consumerist view hold that most required changes in corporate behavior should be accomplished not by exhorting business leaders to behave responsibly, nor by placing consumer representatives on the corporation's board of directors, but by regulations or incentives that force or induce the desired corporate behavior. Let corporations pursue their profits—subject to public laws. For example, Congress can require that all cars have seat belts or have antipollution valves or meet specific standards of emission levels. Another alternative is to open the way for lawsuits that would either enjoin certain behavior or force corporations to pay for the damages their products cause.

The controversy over policy alternatives is current and important. Much of the credit for the dialogue belongs to Galbraith and Nader. It is essential to recognize that the policy issues at stake —whether and how to change the behavior of corporations—can arise whether corporations are primarily responding to market signals or are impervious to them. If the public does not approve the results of corporate behavior, it will want to control the behavior, whatever the cause, provided the costs—including undesirable side effects—do not exceed the benefits.

Who Controls the Modern Firm?: Alternative Maximizing Theories

Galbraith's is not the only modern criticism of the theory of firm behavior. Most other critics, however, accept (what Galbraith denies) that industries face market demand curves that the firms can influence only slightly. The critics then go on to suggest that firms will behave in ways different from those suggested by profit maximizing. In effect, these theories view firms as maximizers—of something other than profits.

Corporations play a dominant role in much of American industry, and large corporations have dominant market shares in many industries. But who or what *is* the corporation? In some corporations, a small group or family provided most of the original capital, and the firm grew with little or no sale of equities to the public. Modern American examples are the Ford Motor Company, which until 1956 was wholly owned by the Ford family; the Great Atlantic and Pacific Tea Company, which until recently was controlled by the Hartford family; E. I. du Pont de Nemours and Company (du Pont family); and the Aluminum Company of America (Mellon family). At the other extreme, the giant American Telephone and Telegraph Company is owned by more than 3 million shareholders, no one of whom owns as much as 1 percent of the 700 million outstanding shares.

Between these extremes lie the majority of corporations. The characteristic pattern of corporate ownership is that tens of thousands or hundreds of thousands of shareholders own minute fractions of the total, while dominant groups (often including other corporations) hold from 3 percent to 20 percent of the voting stock.

In major areas of the business world the days of the single proprietor who is both owner and manager of a company are gone forever. Diversification of ownership is a major characteristic of the modern corporation. Does it matter? Traditional profit maximizing theory answers no. The three hypotheses considered below suggest that the answer is yes.

THE HYPOTHESIS OF MINORITY CONTROL

It is quite possible for the owners of a minority of the stock to control a majority of the shares that are voted and thus to exercise effective control over the decisions of the corporation.

This possibility arises because not all shares are actually voted. Each share of common stock has one vote in a corporation. Shares must be voted at the annual meeting of stockholders, either in person or by assigning a **proxy** to someone attending. Any individual or group controlling 51 percent of the stock clearly controls a majority of the votes. But suppose one group owns 30 percent of the stock, with the remaining 70 percent distributed so widely that few of the dispersed group even bother to vote; in this event, 30 percent may be the overwhelming majority of the shares *actually voted*. In general, a very small fraction (sometimes as little as 5 percent) of the shares actively voted may exercise dominant influence at meetings of stockholders.

The hypothesis of minority control is that a well-organized minority often controls the destiny of the corporation against the wishes of the majority.

Dispersed ownership and minority control are well established in the corporate sector. But the hypothesis requires more than that a minority control the voting shares; it requires that stockholders be able to exert a significant influence on the firm's behavior *and* that the controlling minority have interests and motives different from the holders of the majority of the firm's stock. If all stockholders are mainly interested in having the firm maximize its profits, then it does not matter, as far as market behavior is concerned, which set of stockholders actually influences the firm's policy. There is no accepted evidence to show that controlling groups of stockholders generally seek objectives different from those sought by the holders of the majority of the firm's stock. Of course, disagreements between stockholder groups sometimes arise. A colorful phenomenon in corporation history is the **proxy fight,** in which competing factions of stockholders (or management) attempt to collect the voting rights of the dispersed and generally disinterested stockholders.

THE HYPOTHESIS OF INTERCORPORATE CONTROL GROUPS

As early as the passage of the Clayton Act in 1914, Congress had recognized the possibility that an individual might exercise an anticompetitive influence on the behavior of corporations by holding directorships in two or more of them.[2] Congress feared that a small group of people, through the control of boards of directors, could come to control major competitors and alter their market behavior.

The hypothesis of intercorporate control groups is that otherwise independent companies are subject to common control through interlocking directorates.

The factual basis of this hypothesis is that some individuals are directors of many companies. These interlocking directorships have been widely studied; for example, the directorships of the 74 largest companies in 1965 included 182 individuals, each of whom was a director of at least two companies in the group. If each member of a small group holds directorships in several companies, the group could control the boards of directors of many different companies without being so obvious as to have the identical

---

[2] Section 8 of the act forbids interlocking directorships among competing firms under certain conditions, but the provision is seldom applied.

set of persons on each and every board. By controlling the boards of directors, this group might be able to exert effective and relatively unostentatious control over the companies themselves in ways that they, rather than the stockholders, choose.

For the hypothesis of intercorporate control groups to have implications for behavior requires more than interlocking directorates; it requires that boards of directors be able to control the policies of corporations in ways that would not be approved by managers or by stockholders.

There is much evidence about interlocks, but there is no substantial evidence that the common directors exert any significant influence altering the firm's behavior from what it would be if no such interlocking existed. Why, then, do they occur? There are many good reasons, even if such directors do not significantly alter firm behavior. For example, certain bank officers appear on many different boards of directors to represent their bank's interest in companies to which they have loaned money. Other people are wanted for the prestige of their names.

THE HYPOTHESIS OF THE SEPARATION OF OWNERSHIP FROM CONTROL

A different consequence of diversified ownership was suggested in the 1930s by A. A. Berle and Gardiner Means. They hypothesized that, because of diversified ownership and the difficulty of assembling stockholders or gathering proxies, the managers rather than the stockholders or the directors exercise effective control over the corporation.

The hypothesis of the separation of ownership from control is that managerial control occurs and leads to different behavior than would stockholder control.

In the modern corporation the stockholders elect directors, who appoint managers. Directors are supposed to represent stockholders' interests and to determine broad policies that the managers will carry out. In order to conduct the complicated business of running a large firm, a full-time professional management group must be given broad powers of decision. Although managerial decisions can be reviewed from time to time, they cannot be supervised in detail. In fact the links are typically weak enough that top management often does truly control the destiny of the corporation over long periods of time.

As long as directors have confidence in the managerial group, they accept and ratify their proposals, and stockholders elect and reelect directors who are proposed to them. If the managerial group behaves badly, it may later be removed and replaced—but this is a disruptive and drastic action, and it is infrequently employed.

Within wide limits, then, effective control of the corporation's activities resides with the managers, who need not even be stockholders. Although the managers are legally employed by the stockholders, they remain largely unaffected by them. Indeed, the management group characteristically asks for, and typically gets, the proxies of a large enough number of stockholders to elect directors who will reappoint it—and thus it perpetuates itself in office.

Professors Berle and Means made a pioneering study of the ownership of the 200 largest nonfinancial corporations in 1929. They showed that corporations in which no dominant ownership group could be identified as having as much as 10 percent of the stockholdings accounted for 60 percent of the total assets owned by all 200 corporations studied. The percentage of assets thus held is even higher today—above 80 percent. What is the significance of this?

The hypothesis of the separation of ownership from control requires not only that the managers be able to exert effective control over business decisions, but that they wish to act differently from the way the stockholders and directors wish to act. If the managers want to maximize the firm's profits—either because it is in their own interests to do so or because they are legally compelled or voluntarily choose to reflect the stockholders' interest—then it does not matter that they have effective control over decisions.

How Far Can Corporations Depart from Profit-maximizing Behavior?

Many of the criticisms of modern microeconomic theory assume that firms seek to do things other than maximize their profits. If the present management elects not to maximize its profits, this implies that some other management could make more money by operating the firm. A major restraint on existing managements is the threat of a stockholder revolt or a takeover bid. As we shall see in Chapter 22, the maximum amount one can afford to pay for any asset depends on how much it is expected to earn. If I can make an asset produce more than you, I can rationally outbid you for it.

A management that fails to come close to achieving the profit potential of the assets it controls becomes a natural target for acquisition by a firm that specializes in taking over inefficiently run firms. The management of the acquiring firm makes a **tender offer** (or **takeover bid** as it is sometimes called) to the stockholders of the target firm, offering them what amounts to a premium for their shares, a premium it can pay because it expects to increase the firm's profits. Managers who wish to avoid takeover bids cannot let the profits of their firm slip far from the profit-maximizing level—because their unrealized profits provide the incentives for takeovers.

Some, though by no means all of the so-called conglomerate firms, have specialized in this kind of takeover. In the last decade the example par excellence of this has been International Telephone and Telegraph, which acquired (among other companies) Avis Car Rental, Continental Baking, Sheraton Hotels, Canteen Food Service, and Hartford Life Insurance. In each case it substantially increased the operating profits of the acquired company after the takeover.

The pressure of the threat of takeovers must be regarded as limiting the discretion of corporate management to pursue goals other than profit maximization.

Only if the managers wish to pursue different goals than those of the owners will the behavior of the firm be different according to whether the managers or the owners exercise effective control. Consider then a theory that takes the separation of ownership and control as its starting point and proceeds on the assumption that managers are motivated by desires other than to maximize the profits of the firm.

The Sales Maximization Hypothesis

The theory that firms seek to maximize not their profits but their sales revenue was first advanced by Professor William Baumol of Princeton University. Firms, it is assumed, wish to be as large as possible. Faced with a choice between profits and sales, they would choose to increase sales rather than profits.

This theory begins with the separation of management and ownership. In the giant corporation the managers need to make some minimum level of profits to keep the shareholders satisfied; after that they are free to seek growth unhampered by profit considerations. This is a sensible policy on the part of management, the argument runs, because salary, power, and prestige all vary with the size of a firm as well as with its profits. Generally the manager of a large, normally profitable corporation will earn a salary considerably higher than that earned by the manager of a small but highly profitable corporation.

The sales maximization hypothesis says that managers of firms seek to maximize their sales revenue, subject to a profit constraint.

Sales maximization subject to a profit constraint leads to the prediction that firms will sacrifice some profits by setting price below, and output above, their profit-maximizing levels.

Do Firms Maximize Anything?: Nonmaximizing Theories of the Firm

Many students of large and complex organizations have been critical of economic theory for regarding modern corporations as "simple profit-maximizing computers." They believe that firms are profit oriented in the sense that, *ceteris paribus*, they prefer more profits to less. They do not believe, however, that firms are profit maximizers.

Maximization has two aspects. A firm is a *local maximizer* if it maximizes profits that can be earned with its present range of commodities and its present markets. A firm is a *global maximizer* if it surveys and chooses from all possible courses of action, which will include new products, new markets, and radically new sales and production techniques. It is fairly easy to gather evidence showing that most firms are not global maximizers; it is more difficult to do the same for local maximization.

NONMAXIMIZATION DUE TO IGNORANCE

A common but misguided line of criticism holds that firms are unable to maximize profits because they cannot equate marginal cost with marginal revenue. This criticism is based on the observation that many accounting practices are not set up to provide managers with marginal information. Indeed, most managers have never even heard of the concepts of marginal cost and marginal revenue. Thus, these critics conclude,

firms cannot be maximizing profits because they cannot be using the necessary marginal concepts.

The constructs of the theory of the firm are merely tools employed by economists to predict the consequences of certain behavior patterns. They are not meant to describe how firms reach decisions. Economic theorists use the mathematical concepts of marginal cost and marginal revenue to discover what will happen as long as, by one means or another—by guess, hunch, clairvoyance, luck, or good judgment—firms approximately succeed in maximizing profits. The predictions of the theory are thus independent of the thought processes by which the managers of firms actually reach their decisions.

A famous analogy concerns the determination of how safe it may be for a driver to pass a truck on a two-lane road. The analyst must consider a complex equation relating the automobile's speed, the truck's speed, the car's ability to accelerate, the possibility of an oncoming car (and its speed and distance), weather conditions, and so on. But the driver, unlike the analyst, need not solve a mathematical equation to make his or her decision. Yet if the driver and analyst are competent, both will reach the same decision.

What is at issue, then, is not whether firms calculate and equate marginal magnitudes. The question is whether or not they continually indulge in behavior that tends to choose the most profitable of the available alternatives.

NONMAXIMIZATION BY CHOICE

Alternatives to profit maximization are usually based on observations of actual firms. The observations and the theories all have in common the implication that firms *choose* not to be profit maximizers.

Full-cost Pricing

Most manufacturing firms are price setters: they must quote a price for their products rather than accept a price set on some impersonal competitive market. Profit-maximizing theory requires that these firms change their prices in response to every change in demand and costs that they experience. Yet students of large firms have long alleged that this much price flexibility is not observed. In the short run, prices of manufactured goods do not appear to vary in response to every shift in the firm's demand. Instead they appear to change rather sluggishly.

This short-run behavior is consistent with the hypothesis of **full-cost pricing**, which was originally advanced in the 1930s by Robert Hall, a British economist, and Charles Hitch, an American, following a series of detailed case studies of actual pricing decisions made in and around Oxford, England. Case studies in the intervening decades have continued to reveal the widespread use of full-cost pricing procedures.

The full-cost pricer, instead of equating marginal revenue with marginal cost, sets price equal to average cost at full-capacity output, plus a conventional markup.

The **markup** may be either so much per unit or a percentage of average costs. Price having been set, sales are determined by what can be sold at that price.

The firm changes its prices when its average costs change substantially (as a result of such events as a new union contract or a sharp change in the prices of key raw materials), and it may occasionally change its markup. However, its short-run pricing behavior is rather conventional and is not characterized even by local profit maximization.

Modern supporters of profit-maximizing theory accept the full-cost evidence but argue that it reveals only the administrative procedure by which prices are set from day to day. They hold that management makes frequent changes in markups in an attempt to maximize profits. Thus they believe that, while firms may be full-cost pricers from day to day, they are profit maximizers with respect to their average experience over, say, a year.

Modern critics of profit-maximizing theory accept the evidence that full-cost prices are some-times changed in the profit-maximizing direction. They hold, however, that the prevalence of conventional full-cost practices shows that prices are typically not at their profit-maximizing level. They also hold that the prevalence of full-cost pricing shows that firms are creatures of custom that make fairly small, profit-oriented changes at fairly infrequent intervals.

Organization Theory

According to profit-maximizing theory, firms constantly scan available alternatives and choose the most profitable ones. A common criticism of this theory is that behavior is influenced seriously by the organizational structure of the firm. **Organization theory** argues that in big firms decisions are made after much discussion by groups and committees and that the structure of the process affects the substance of the decisions.

The central prediction of organization theory is that different decisions will result from different kinds of organizations, even when all else is un changed.

One proposition that follows from this theory is that large and diffuse organizations find it necessary to develop standard operating procedures to help them in making decisions. These decision rules arise as compromises among competing points of view and, once adopted, are changed only reluctantly. An important prediction following from this hypothesis is that the compromises will persist for long periods of time despite changes in conditions affecting the firm. Even if a particular compromise were the profit-maximizing strategy in the first place, it would not remain so when conditions changed. Thus profits will not usually be maximized.

Another prediction is that decision by compromise will lead firms to adopt conservative policies that avoid large risks. Smaller firms not faced with the necessity of compromising competing views will take bigger risks than larger firms.

Organization theorists have suggested an alternative to profit maximization that they call **satisficing.** Satisficing theory was first suggested by Professor Herbert Simon of Carnegie-Mellon University, who in 1978 was awarded the Nobel Prize in economics for his work on firm behavior. Speaking of his theory, he wrote, "We must expect the firm's goals to be not maximizing profits but attaining a certain level or rate of profit, holding a certain share of the market or a certain level of sales."

According to the satisficing hypothesis, firms will strive to achieve certain target levels of profits, but having achieved them, they will not strive to improve their profit position further. This means that the firm could produce any one of a range of outputs that yield at least the target level of profits rather than the unique output that maximizes profits.

EVOLUTIONARY THEORIES

The modern evolutionary theories advanced by such economists as Richard Nelson and Sidney Winter of Yale University build on the earlier theories of full-cost pricing and satisficing. Nelson and Winter argue that firms do not—indeed, could not—behave as profit maximizing predicts. They accept that firms desire profits and even strive for profits; what they deny is that firms maximize globally or even locally.

Evolutionary theorists have gathered much evidence to show that tradition seems to be paramount in planning. The basic effort at the early stages of planning is directed, they argue, toward the problem of performing reasonably well in established markets and maintaining established market shares. They quote evidence to show that suggestions, made by planners in preliminary planning documents, to do something entirely new in some areas, even on a 10-year horizon, are usually weeded out in the reviewing process. They believe that most firms spend very little effort on *planning* to enter entirely new markets, and still less on direct efforts to leave or even reduce their share in long-established markets.

These attitudes were illustrated by one firm who, although faced with obviously changing circumstances, reported that "We have been producing on the basis of these raw materials for more than 50 years with success, and we have made it a policy to continue to do so."

Concepts of Evolutionary Theory

The evolutionary theory of the firm draws many analogies with the biological theory of evolution. Here are two of the most important.

The genes. In biological theory, behavior patterns are transmitted over time by genes. Rules of behavior fulfill the same function in the evolutionary theory of the firm. In Sidney Winter's words:

That a great deal of firm decision behavior is routinized . . . is a "stylized fact" about the realities of firm decision process. Routinized . . . decision procedures . . . cover decision situations from pricing practices in retail stores to such "strategic" decisions as advertising or R and D effort, or the question of whether or not to invest abroad.

Winter talks of firms "remembering by doing" according to repetitive routines. He adds that government policymakers tend to have unrealistic expectations about firms' flexibility and responsiveness to changes in market incentives. These expectations arise from the maximizing model, whose fatal flaw, Winter alleges, is to underestimate the importance and difficulty "of the task of merely continuing the routine performance, i.e., of preventing undesired deviations."

The mutations. In the theory of biological evolution, mutations are the vehicle of change. In the evolutionary theory of the firm this role is played by innovations. Some innovations are similar to those discussed in Chapter 13, the introduction of new products and new production techniques. However, a further important class of innovations in evolutionary theory is the introduction of new rules of behavior. Sometimes innovations are thrust on the firm; at other times the firm consciously plans for and creates innovations.

According to maximizing theory, innovations are the result of incentives—the "carrot" of new profit opportunities. In evolutionary theory, the firm is much more of a satisficer, and it usually innovates only under the incentive of the "stick" either of unacceptably low profits or some form of external prodding. Firms change routines when they get into trouble, not when they see a chance to improve an already satisfactory performance. For example, in the growing markets of the 1960s many firms continued all sorts of wasteful practices that they shed fairly easily when their profits were threatened in the more difficult 1970s.

THE SIGNIFICANCE OF NONMAXIMIZING THEORIES

An impressive array of evidence can be gathered in apparent support of various nonmaximizing theories. What would be the implications if they were accepted as being better theories of the behavior of the economy than profit maximization?

If nonmaximizing theories are correct, the economic system does not perform with the delicate precision that follows from profit maximization. But the system described by evolutionary theory *does* function. Firms sell more when demand goes up and less when it goes down. They also alter their prices and their input mixes when hit with the "stick" of sufficiently large changes in relative input prices.

Evolutionary theory does not upset the broad case for the price system: that it produces a coordinated response from decentralized decision makers to changes in tastes and costs.

But profit-oriented nonmaximizing firms will also exhibit a great deal of inertia. They will not respond quickly and precisely to small changes in market signals from either the private sector or government policy. Neither are they likely to make radical changes in their behavior even when the profit incentives to do so are large.

Nonmaximizing models imply sensitivity of the price system to large but not to small changes in signals caused by changes in demand, costs, or public policy.

A Final Word: The Importance of Profits

Economics is a continually developing subject; its theories are under constant scrutiny and even attack. Some of the major debates concerning the profit-maximizing theory of the firm have been reviewed in this chapter. On the one hand, the Galbraithian view that firms create their own market conditions seems difficult to maintain in the face of the evidence. On the other hand, it seems unlikely that simple profit-maximizing theory will be rich enough to capture all aspects of corporate behavior. Thus it may benefit by expansion to include elements of such theories as satisficing, sales maximization, and evolutionary behavior.

Profits, however, are unmistakably a potent force in the life—and death—of firms. The resilience of profit-maximizing theory and its ability to predict how the economy will react to some major changes (such as the recent dramatic increases in energy prices) suggests that firms are at least strongly motivated by the pursuit of profits and that, other things being equal, they prefer more profits to less profits.

If profit-maximizing theory should eventually give way to some more organizationally dominated theory, the new theory will still be a profit-oriented theory. The search for profits and the avoidance of losses is a potent force that drives the economy even when firms do not turn out to be continual profit maximizers.

Summary

1. A sweeping attack on the traditional theory of the behavior of the firm is made by Galbraith, along with Nader and others. He argues that large corporations manipulate markets, tastes, and governments rather than respond to market and governmental pressures. While there is evidence about the undoubted size and influence of large corporations, there is also much evidence of market influence on corporate behavior.

2. In recent years, serious concern has developed over whether corporations should represent the interests of their owners and managers or whether they should be responsible to a broader public interest. Consumerists argue for the latter point of view; others prefer to rely on markets and government control to protect the public interest.

3. The widespread ownership of the modern corporation leads to the question, who really controls the modern corporation? Attempts to answer this question have led to alternative theories that firms maximize something other than profits. Three important hypotheses have been advanced.

a. A minority group of stockholders often controls the corporation against the wishes of the majority. The fact of minority control is widely accepted, but there is little evidence to suggest that the minority usually coerce the majority.

b. A small group of people effectively control a large section of the economy through the mechanism of interlocking directorates. This hypothesis is not widely accepted (although interlocking directorships do exist).

c. Because of the widespread ownership of the corporation, stockholders cannot exert effective control over the managers; thus the latter have the real control of the organization and operate it for their advantage rather than that of their stockholders. This hypothesis has some serious, but by no means universal, support.

4. All these hypotheses suggest that firms may seek to maximize something other than profits. One standard alternative is Professor Baumol's hypothesis of sales maximization: firms seek to be as large as possible (judged by sales revenue),

subject to the constraint that they achieve a minimum rate of profit.

5. An alternative set of hypotheses denies that firms maximize profits in either the local or the global sense of maximization.

a. The full-cost hypothesis states that firms determine price by adding a customary—and infrequently changed—markup to full costs. This makes their pricing behavior relatively insensitive to short-term fluctuations in demand.

b. Organization theorists also see firms as insensitive to short-term fluctuations in market signals. Their reason lies in the decision-making structure of large organizations, which must rely on routines and rules of thumb rather than on fresh calculations of profitabilities as each new situation presents itself.

c. Evolutionary theorists build on full-cost and organizational theories. They see the firm as a profit-oriented entity in a world of imperfect information, making small, profit-oriented changes from its present situation but being more resistant to large, "structural" changes. Resources are still reallocated by evolutionary firms as demand and costs shift but usually more in response to the "stick" of threatened losses than the "carrot" of possible extra profits.

6. Under both maximizing and nonmaximizing theories, profits are an important driving force in the economy and changes in demand and costs cause changes in profits, which cause firms to reallocate resources. The speed and precision, but not the general direction of the reallocations, are what is different between maximizing and nonmaximizing theories.

Topics for Review

The New Industrial State
The long-run sensitivity of firms to market pressures
Consumerism
Alternative maximizing theories

Ownership, management, and control of corporate decisions

Sales maximization

Nonmaximizing theories

Full-cost pricing

Satisficing

Evolutionary theories

Discussion Questions

1. In 1976 the automobile manufacturers introduced their 1977 models. GM and American Motors (AMC) put major emphasis on smaller, more economical cars, and Ford and Chrysler stayed with their 1976 model sizes. Read the following news headlines (which appear in chronological order) and then discuss the light they shed on the hypothesis that firms control the market.
   a. "GM's 1977 Line Runs Ahead of the Pack. The big question: Do people want small cars?"
   b. "Ford, Chrysler, beam; AMC in trouble on sales."
   c. "GM's Fuel-Saving Chevette: Right Car at the Wrong Time."
   d. "Price Cuts and Rebates Lift Sales of Small AMC and GM Cars."
   e. "GM Confirms Plans to Drop the Subcompact Vega."
   What do these further events reveal about the same hypothesis? "In 1979 all auto firms sold all the small cars they could produce. But they were left with sizable unsold inventories of large cars, and as a result they are preparing to alter their production mix in favor of small cars."

2. "Because automobile companies were interested only in profits, they would not produce the safer, less polluting, but more expensive cars that the public really wanted. Legislation was necessary, therefore, to force producers to meet consumer needs." Discuss.

3. Assume that each of the following assertions is factually correct. (The first is a matter of current controversy; the rest are unquestioned.) Taken together, what would they tell you about the prediction that big business is increasing its control of the U.S. economy?
   a. The share of total manufacturing assets owned by the 200 largest corporations has been rising steadily for the last 25 years.
   b. The number of new firms begun every year has grown steadily for the last 25 years.
   c. The share of manufacturing in total production has been decreasing for 40 years.
   d. Profits as a percent of national income are no higher now than half a century ago.

4. "Our economy, like an engine, must have fuel to operate. And the fuel our economy runs on is profit. Profits keep it going—and growing. But there is strong evidence that the economy's fuel supply is running low. Profits of U.S. corporations today are about 5 percent on sales—less than the 1965 rate.
   "We Americans have become accustomed to a quality of life that can survive only through profits. For profits not only create jobs and goods, they furnish essential tax revenues. Federal, state, and local taxes finance the countless programs that our citizens demand—from paving the roads on which we drive to building our country's defense forces . . . to helping millions of Americans who need some form of assistance."
   Comment on this excerpt from an Allied Chemical Corporation advertisement.

5. "The business of the businessman is to run his business so as to make profits. If he does so, he will serve the public interest better than if he tries to decide what is good for society. He is neither elected nor appointed to that task." Discuss.

6. "Our list prices are really set by our accounting department: they add a fixed markup to their best estimates of fully accounted cost and send these to the operating divisions. Managers of these divisions may not change those prices without permission of the Board of Directors, which is seldom given. Operating divisions may, however, provide special discounts if necessary to stay competitive." Does this testimony by the president of a leading manufacturing company support the full-cost pricing hypothesis?

7. The leading automobile tire manufacturers (Goodyear, Firestone, etc.) sell original equipment (OE) tires to automobile manufacturers at a price below the average total cost of all the tires they make and sell. This happens year after year. Is this consistent with profit-maximizing behavior in the short run? In the long run? If it is not consistent, what does it show? Do OE tires compete with replacement tires?

Part Six

Factor Pricing and the Distribution of Income

The Distribution of National Income

20

PROBLEMS OF DISTRIBUTION

Are the poor getting poorer and the rich richer as Karl Marx thought they would? Are the rich becoming relatively poorer and the poor relatively richer as Alfred Marshall hoped they would? To what extent do such social changes as the increased number of working women or altered public policies on poverty change the distribution of income? Should we reject the view held by Pareto that inequality of income is a social constant determined by forces that are possibly beyond human understanding and probably beyond human influence?

The founders of classical economics, Adam Smith and David Ricardo, were concerned with the distribution of income among what were then the three great social classes: workers, capitalists, and landowners. To deal with this question they defined three factors of production: labor, capital, and land. The return to each of these factors was the income of each of the three classes in society. Smith and Ricardo were interested in what determined the income of each group relative to the total national income, and in how a nation's economic growth affected this income distribution. Their theory predicted that as society progressed landlords would become relatively better off and capitalists would become relatively worse off. Karl Marx provided different answers to the same questions: He concluded that as growth occurred capitalists would become relatively better off and workers relatively worse off (at least until the whole capitalist system collapsed).

TABLE 20-1

The Functional Distribution of National Income in the United States, 1978

Type of income	Billions of dollars	Percentage of total
Employee compensation	$1304	75.6
Corporate profits	168	9.7
Proprietors' income	117	6.8
Interest	110	6.4
Rental income	26	1.5
Total	$1725	100.0

Source: Survey of Current Business, December 1979.

Total income is classified here according to the nature of the factor service that earned the income. While these data show that employee compensation is more than three quarters of national income, they do not show that workers and their families receive only that fraction of national income. Many households will have income in more than one category listed in the table.

TABLE 20-2

Incomes of American Families,[a] **1978**

Income class (thousands of dollars)	Percentage of families
Less than 9.0	20.8
9.0 to 14.9	19.8
15.0 to 19.9	16.9
20.0 to 24.9	14.5
25.0 to 49.9	24.3
50.0 or more	3.6

[a] The census definition of a family is two or more persons related by blood, marriage, or adoption and residing together.
Source: Current Population Reports, Series P-60, No. 120.

Although median family income in 1978 was about $17,600, many received much less and some a great deal more.

TABLE 20-3

Inequality in Family Income Distribution, 1978

Family income rank	Percentage share of aggregate income
Lowest fifth	5.2
Second fifth	11.6
Middle fifth	17.5
Fourth fifth	24.1
Highest fifth	41.6
	100.0
Top 5 percent	15.6

Source: Current Population Reports, Series P-60, No. 120.

While far from showing overall equality, income distribution is relatively equal for the middle 60 percent of the distribution. If the income distribution were perfectly equal, each fifth of the families would receive 20 percent of aggregate income. The present distribution is virtually unchanged from that of 20 years ago.

These and similar nineteenth century debates focused on the distribution of total income among the major factors of production, now called the **functional distribution of income.** Table 20-1 shows data for the functional distribution of income in the United States in 1978. Although functional distribution categories (wages, rent, profits) pervade current statistics, much of the attention of non-Marxist economists has shifted to another way of looking at differences in incomes.

Around the beginning of the present century, Pareto studied what is now called the **size distribution of income,** the distribution of income between different households without reference to the social class to which they belonged. He discovered that inequality in income distribution was great in all countries and, more surprising, that the degree of inequality was quite similar from one country to another. Tables 20-2 and 20-3 show that even in the United States in 1978 there were many families with very low incomes and there was much inequality in the distribution of income.

Inequality in the distribution of income is shown graphically in Figure 20-1. This curve of income distribution, called a **Lorenz curve,** shows how much of total income is accounted for by given proportions of the nation's families. For example, in 1978 the bottom 20 percent of all U.S. families earned only 5.2 percent of all in-

FIGURE 20-1

A Lorenz Curve of Family Income in the United States

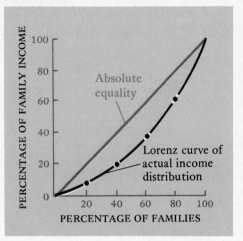

The size of the shaded area between the Lorenz curve and the diagonal is a measure of the inequality of income distribution. If there were complete income equality, the bottom 20 percent of income receivers would receive 20 percent of the income, etc., and the Lorenz curve would be the diagonal line. Because the lower 20 percent receive only 5 percent of the income, the actual curve lies below the diagonal. The lower curve shows actual American data. The extent to which it bends away from the straight line indicates the amount of inequality in the distribution of income.

come earned. The farther the curve bends away from the diagonal straight line, the more unequal is the distribution of income.

There are good reasons why much of the attention of modern economists is devoted to the size distribution rather than the functional distribution of income. After all, some capitalists (such as the owners of small retail stores) are in the lower part of the income scale, while some wage earners (such as skilled athletes) are at the upper end of the income scale. Moreover, if someone is poor, it matters little whether that person is a landowner or a worker. Today many who want to decrease inequality focus on influences other

than which factor of production is owned by the income earner. Among other influences are race, sex, age, education, occupation, and region of residence.

We shall look closely at the poverty problem in Chapter 23. In order to understand this and other problems concerning the distribution of income, we must first study how the income of households is determined and what forces cause it to change.

It is tempting to give superficial explanations of differences in income with remarks like, "People are paid what they are worth." But the economist must ask, Worth what to whom? What gives a particular man his value? His wife, his mother-in-law, and his employer may all respond differently. Sometimes people say, "People earn according to their ability." But incomes are distributed in a very much more unequal fashion than any *measured* index of ability, be it IQ, physical strength, or typing skill. In what sense is Tom Watson five times as able a golfer as Curtis Strange? His average score is only 1 percent better, yet he earns five times as much. In what sense is Barbara Walters four times as able a reporter as Jane Pauley?

If answers couched in terms of worth and ability are easily refuted, so are answers such as, "It's all a matter of luck" or "It's just the system." We want to discover whether the theories of economics provide explanations of the distribution of income that are more satisfactory than the shallow ones mentioned above.

THE THEORY OF DISTRIBUTION

Every element of income has, in a purely arithmetical sense, two components: the quantity of the income-earning service that is provided and the price per unit paid for it. The amount a worker earns in wages depends on the number of hours worked and the hourly wage received. The amount a group of workers (say, union members) earns depends on how many of them there are and how much each earns. The amount of dividends a stockholder receives depends on the number of shares of stock he or she owns and the dividends that each share pays.

Because factor prices are one of two elements that determine factor incomes, a theory of factor prices is essential to a theory of distribution.

The theory of factor prices is just a special case of the theory of price; it depends on the demand for and the supply of factors.

As with the theory of product prices studied in Chapter 5, the theory of distribution is concerned with *relative* prices. One factor becomes "more expensive" when its price rises relative to that of other factors. In an inflationary world, most prices will be rising, but not at the same rate. So some factors will be becoming relatively more expensive, some relatively cheaper. We shall use the phrase "rise in price" to mean a rise in relative price, and the phrase "fall in price" to mean a fall in relative price. (See pages 74–75 for fuller discussion.)

In this chapter we consider competitive markets. Price theory states that the competitive market price of any commodity or factor is determined by demand and supply. The competitive market determination of the equilibrium price and quantity—and thus the money income—of a factor of production is illustrated in Figure 20-2. Look again at Figure 5-8(i), page 74, to see why this analysis is familiar.

To elaborate on the theory of factor pricing, we need a theory of the demand for factors and a theory of their supply. From them we can derive a theory of the determination of competitive equilibrium prices and quantities. In Chapter 21 we will determine the effect of various departures from competitive conditions such as those brought about by employers' associations and labor unions.

The Demand for Factors

The demand for a factor of production is said to be a **derived demand** because a firm requires

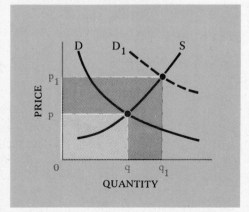

FIGURE 20-2

The Determination of Factor Price and Income in a Competitive Market

Demand and supply for factors determine prices and quantities of factors in competitive factor markets. With demand and supply curve D and S, the price of the factor will be p and the quantity employed q. The total income earned by the factor is the lighter shaded area. A shift in demand from D to D_1 raises equilibrium price and quantity to p_1 and q_1. The income earned by the factor rises by the darker shaded area.

labor, raw materials, machines, and other factors of production, not for their own sake, but in order to produce the goods and services that it sells.

The demand for any factor of production depends on the existence of a demand for the goods that it helps to make.

Examples of derived demand are easy to find. The demand for computer programmers and technicians is growing as industry and government use more and more electronic computers. The demand for carpenters and building materials rises or falls with the level of house building. Anything that increases the demand for new housing—population growth, lower interest rates on mortgages, and so on—will increase the demand for the factors required to build houses. Typically, one factor will be used in making many commodities. Steel is used in dozens of industries, as are the services of carpenters.

The total demand for a factor will be the sum of the demands for it in every activity in which it is used.

THE DOWNWARD SLOPE
OF THE DEMAND CURVE[1]

The demand curve for a factor of production shows how the quantity demanded of that factor will vary as its price varies, the prices of all other factors remaining constant. Although demand curves for factors generally slope downward, they do so for somewhat different reasons than do demand curves for commodities.

What would happen to quantity demanded if there were a rise in the price of a factor? Because demand is a derived demand, the effect must be traced to the commodities that the factor is used to make. One effect is related to the link between a factor's price and the price of the good or service it helps to produce. Consider for example a rise in the wages of carpenters, which increases the cost of producing houses. The rise in cost shifts the supply curve of houses upward. This leads to a rise in the price of houses and to a decrease in the number of houses sold. If fewer houses can be sold, fewer will be built and lesser quantities of factors will be needed. Thus there will be a decrease in the quantity demanded of the factors used to produce houses.

The second effect relates to substitution among factors: When the price of a factor goes up, relatively cheaper factors will be substituted for the factor whose price has risen. For example, if carpenters' wages rise relative to those of factory workers, some prefabricated door and window frames made by factory workers will be used in place of on-the-job carpenters. This is simply the principle of substitution in operation.

---

[1] A more formal derivation of the demand curve for a factor is presented in the appendix to this chapter.

Demand curves for factors slope downward because of (1) the effect of factor price changes on the costs and prices of the commodities the factor makes and (2) the substitution of relatively cheaper for relatively more expensive factors.

WHAT DETERMINES THE ELASTICITY
OF FACTOR DEMANDS?

The greater the change in quantity of a factor demanded for a given change in its price, the greater is the elasticity of demand for the factor. Both of the considerations that lead to downward-sloping demand curves play a role in determining elasticity.

The Demand for the Commodities
That Use the Factor

Other things being equal, elasticity of demand for a factor will be larger, the more elastic is the demand for the commodity that the factor helps to make. If an increase in the price of the commodity causes a large fall in the quantity demanded (i.e., the demand for the commodity is very elastic), there will be a large decrease in the quantity of the factor now needed. But if the increase in the price of the commodity causes only a small fall in its quantity demanded (i.e., the demand for the commodity is inelastic), there will be only a small decrease in the quantity of the factor now required.

The Importance of the Factor
in Total Costs of Production

The elasticity of demand for a factor will be greater, the larger is the fraction of total costs that are payments to the factor. Suppose that wages are 50 percent of the costs of producing a good while raw materials account for 10 percent. A 10 percent rise in the price of labor would raise the cost of producing the commodity by 5 percent (10 percent of 50 percent), but a 10 percent rise in the price of raw materials would raise the cost of the commodity by only 1 percent (10 percent of

10 percent). Thus a 10 percent increase in labor's price would cause a larger increase in the cost of the commodity than a 10 percent rise in the price of raw materials. The larger the increase in cost, the larger the increase in the commodity's price—and hence the larger the decrease in the quantity demanded of the commodity and the factors used to make it.

Substitution of One Factor for Another

Obviously, the greater the substitution of one factor for another in response to changes in relative factor prices, the greater is the elasticity of factor demand. The ease of substitution depends on the substitutes available and technical conditions of production. A contractor in Anaheim, California, may normally use Anaheim laborers. But should they demand higher wages, the contractor might well be able to bring workers from nearby Azusa or Cucamonga at only the additional cost of daily transportation. It is well known that a bushel of wheat can be produced by combining land either with a lot of labor and a little capital or with a little labor and a lot of capital, and that manufactured goods can be made either by capital-intensive or by labor-intensive techniques. In other cases, short-run substitutions are not simple to make. Recent rises in the price of gasoline have not led quickly to massive substitutions of other fuels.

While it is easy to think of barriers to substitution, they can be exaggerated. Even in the short run it is possible to vary factor proportions in surprising ways. For example, in automobile manufacture and in building construction, glass and steel can be substituted for each other simply by varying the dimensions of the windows. Grain in the form of gasohol can substitute for oil as automobile fuel.

Nor are such direct (if dramatic) short-run substitutions the end of the story. In the long run a factory that has a particular technique embodied in its equipment (and thus cannot easily vary factor proportions in the short run) can be replaced. Plant and equipment are continually being re-placed, and more or less capital-intensive methods can be adopted in new plants in response to changes in factor prices. Similarly, engines that use less gasoline per mile (or that use a cheaper fuel) will surely be developed if the price of gasoline remains high.

Determinants of Factor Demand: Summary

The derived nature of the demand for factors, in addition to leading to the prediction of a downward-sloping demand curve, leads to the following predictions about elasticity of demand.

The elasticity of demand for a factor will vary directly with:

1. the elasticity of demand of the final product it makes
2. the proportion of the total cost of production accounted for by the factor
3. the ease with which other factors may be substituted for it.

THE MARGINAL PRODUCTIVITY THEORY OF DISTRIBUTION

Demand for factors is a derived demand. This leads to a proposition that has played an important role in the history of economics.

The conditions for maximizing profits in the short run were discussed in Chapter 14. When one factor is fixed while another is allowed to vary, the profit-maximizing firm increases its output to the level at which the last unit produced adds just as much to costs as to revenue, that is, until marginal cost equals marginal revenue. In other words, the firm will increase production up to the point at which the last unit of the variable factor employed adds just as much to revenue as it does to costs.

All profit-maximizing firms will hire units of the variable factor up to the point at which the marginal cost of the factor equals the marginal revenue produced by the factor.

This implication of profit-maximizing behavior

is true of all profit-maximizing firms, whether they are selling under conditions of perfect competition, monopolistic competition, oligopoly, or monopoly. It is merely a logical deduction from two assumptions: (1) that the firm is a profit maximizer and (2) that the firm *buys* its factors in markets in which it is a price taker. (Note that the second assumption says nothing about the firm's behavior in the market in which it *sells* its product.)

Because we use the term "marginal revenue" to denote the change in revenue resulting when the rate of product sales is increased by 1 unit, we shall use another term, **marginal revenue product** (*MRP*), to refer to the change in revenue caused by the sale of the product contributed by *an additional unit of the variable factor*. We may now state more concisely the equilibrium condition stated above:

The marginal cost   The marginal
of the variable   = revenue product   [1]
factor   of that factor

If the firm is unable to influence the price of the variable factor by buying more or less of it (i.e., if the firm is a price taker when *buying* factors), then the marginal cost of the factor is merely its price. The cost, for example, of adding an extra ton of coal is the price that must be paid per ton of coal purchased. In these circumstances, we may state the condition of [1] in this form:

$$w = MRP \qquad [2]$$

where w is the price of the factor.

A profit-maximizing firm that is a price taker in factor markets hires a factor up to the point at which its price equals its marginal revenue product.

This is an equilibrium condition for a profit-maximizing firm that does not influence the price of a factor by buying more or less of it. It is sometimes called the **marginal productivity theory of distribution** because it says that, in equilibrium, factors of production will receive a price equal to the value of output that is added by the hiring of an additional (marginal) unit of the factor. This comes about by firms adjusting the quantity of the variable factor they hire at the established market price.

This important yet frequently misunderstood proposition means that, under the circumstances specified, all units of a factor will be paid a price equal to the marginal revenue product of the factor. It applies in long-run equilibrium to all factors because in the long run all factors are variable.

IMPORTANT MISCONCEPTIONS ABOUT MARGINAL PRODUCTIVITY THEORY

In certain quarters "marginal productivity theory" is almost a dirty word, for it seems to say that all factors, including labor, are paid on the same basis and that each unit is paid exactly the value of what it produces. The theory has been criticized on the grounds that it is inhumane and that it implies that the market leads to factor prices that, however low they might be, are "just" because every unit is paid the value of its contribution. Both criticisms rest on misconceptions of what the theory says and implies.

Is Marginal Productivity Theory Inhumane?

Marginal productivity theory does not take into account the differences between human services and other services. Thus the theory is sometimes called inhumane because it treats human labor as it treats a ton of coal or a wagonload of fertilizer. One must be careful to distinguish one's emotional reaction to a procedure that treats human and nonhuman factors alike from one's evaluation of it in terms of economics. Anyone who accepts this criticism must explain carefully why separate theories of the pricing of human and nonhuman factors are needed in order to make predictions about behavior.

The marginal productivity theory is only a theory of the *demand* for a factor. It predicts only what profit-maximizing employers would like to buy. It predicts that desired purchases of a factor depend on the price of the factor, the technical conditions of production, and the demand for the product made by the factor. *Supply* conditions undoubtedly differ between human and nonhuman factors, but these differences are accommodated within the theory of distribution, as we shall see. No evidence has been gathered to indicate that it is necessary to have separate theories of the demand for human and nonhuman factors of production.

Does the Theory Define a Just Distribution of Income?

In a world of perfectly competitive factor markets, the theory predicts that in equilibrium all factors receive payment equal to the values of their marginal products. Some eminent economists in the past spoke as if this led to a just distribution because factors were rewarded according to the value of their own contributions to the national product. "From each according to his ability; to each according to his own contribution" might have been the slogan for this group. One of its most famous exponents was the American economist John Bates Clark (1847–1938). Many critics of the low levels of wages that then prevailed reacted passionately to a theory that was claimed to justify them.

It is not necessary here to enter into normative questions of what constitutes a just distribution of income. It is, however, worth getting the facts straight. According to the marginal productivity theory, each worker does not receive the value of what he or she personally contributes to production. The worker receives instead the value of what one more worker would add to production if that worker were taken on while all other factors were held constant. If one million similar workers are employed, then each of the one million will receive a wage equal to the extra product that would have been contributed by the millionth laborer if he or she had been hired while capital and all other factors remained un-

changed. Whether such a distribution of the national product is or is not "just" may be debated. The marginal productivity theory does not, however, contribute to that debate; it does *not* say that each unit of a factor receives as income the value of its own contribution to production. Indeed, where many factors cooperate in production, it is generally impossible to divide total production into the amounts contributed by each unit of each factor of production.

Whether payment according to marginal product is more or less just than payment according to some other criterion has not been generally agreed. However, it is possible both to hold that marginal productivity tends to determine how people get paid and to believe that government policies that change the distribution of income are desirable. Many economists hold both positions.

The Supply of Factors

Some factors, such as exhaustible natural resources, exist in limited quantities. This is true of natural gas and coal, even of sand and gravel. Other factors, such as timber products, beef, machines, and many human services, are renewable. Is it these characteristics or others that make some factors scarce and some plentiful? If we are prepared to pay more for a factor, will we get more of it? What in fact do we need to know to define the supply schedules for factors of production?

Two important economic questions concern the supplies of factors: First, to what extent do economic forces determine the total supply of a factor to the whole economy? Second, to what extent do economic forces determine the supply available to a particular sector of the economy (say, one industry) that wants to purchase only a part of the total supply?

If the total amount of a factor available is too small or too large relative to demand, will such shortages or surpluses correct themselves? If not, what can be done to correct the imbalance?

What Is a Person Worth?
The Economics of Superstar Salaries

Joe Namath, an aging but flamboyant quarterback with injured knees, was paid $450,000 to play for the New York Jets in 1976, a season in which they won only three of their fourteen games (for the second year in a row). At the end of the dismal season, the Jets owners gladly accepted the resignation of the club's coach but wanted Broadway Joe to play again in 1977 at the same salary. Sportscasters and fans agreed that the team played better and had more chance of winning with their second-string quarterback, who was paid less than one-tenth of Namath's salary. Yet the Jets continued to want to play—and pay—Joe Namath. Was this sound economics?

It was. The principal products the Jets sell are football tickets and television rights to their games. Despite their poor won-lost record, the Jets were in those days a major drawing card not only in New York but throughout the country. Joe Namath was a main reason for this, remembered as the David who in 1969 led the Jets of the scorned American Football League to victory over the mighty National Football League Champion Baltimore Colts, quarterbacked by John Unitas. Eight years later thousands of extra fans paid to see the Jets because of Namath. On the road during 1976, the Jets attracted roughly 10,000 more fans per game (in the same stadiums) than did the Buffalo Bills with 1976's reigning superstar, O. J. Simpson. For the season the Jets were estimated to have earned about $240,000 in their share of extra ticket sales for seven games away from home—just because of Namath. At home Namath was credited with attracting more than 10,000 extra fans per game, and this was worth at least another $350,000 in ticket sales to the football club. Add in the additional value in television rights, and Joe was plainly a bargain: his *MRP* was more than his wage. When Namath left the Jets, attendance fell.

When ABC lured Barbara Walters away from NBC with a five-year contract at a million dollars a year, it was economic calculation that was at work, not sympathy for the women's movement. ABC's share of the television news audience had slipped from 23 rating points in 1973 to 19 points in 1976.

Was Barbara worth her million? The critics thought not, but the fact is that if she has raised the rating of ABC by even one point, she will have paid her way. Halfway through her five-year contract, it looks like a financial success for her and for the network.

Before the 1979 baseball season, Pete Rose *at age 37* ("over the hill" for an athlete) signed a four-year contract at $800,000 per year, the highest baseball salary ever paid up to that time. His new employers expected (and have not been disappointed) that the fans who appreciated the acquisition of "Charlie Hustle" would pay to see him play. If they did, it would not matter whether he got 200 hits or batted .300.

Arnold Palmer made golf prizes swell and earnings of professional golfers soar by a magnetic personality that made golf a major spectator sport and brought national television coverage. Nancy Lopez-Melton is now doing the same for women's golf.

Notice that it is not the direct product produced that is responsible for high salaries. It is not yards gained or birdies scored that made Namath and Palmer rich, nor is it interviews conducted or hours on the air that led to Barbara Walters' high salary. It is tickets sold, or advertising sold, that converts the physical feats of these people into marginal revenue product. Will the extraordinary skills of Russian gymnasts or Japanese volleyball players one day make athletes in those sports worth their weight in gold? That will depend on some entrepreneur's ability to generate a market for their product. Whatever happened to Mark Spitz and Eric Heiden?

Can a particular firm or industry meet its requirements even when there is an overall shortage of the factor?

THE TOTAL SUPPLY OF FACTORS

It might seem plausible to assume that the total supplies of factors available to the economy are fixed and not subject to economic influences. After all, there is an absolute maximum to the world's land area; there is an upper limit to the number of workers; there is only so much coal, oil, copper, and iron ore in the earth. In none of these cases, however, are we near the upper limits. The *effective* supplies of land, labor, and natural resources are thus not fixed in any meaningful sense. What, then, causes variations in the supply of a factor of production available to the *whole economy?*

The Total Supply of Labor

The total supply of labor means the total number of hours of work that the population is willing to supply. This quantity, which is often called the **supply of effort,** is a function of the size of the population, the proportion of the population willing to work, and the number of hours worked by each individual. These components in turn are affected by many forces.

Population. Populations vary in size, and the variations may be influenced to some extent by economic factors. There is some evidence that the birth rate is higher in good times than in bad. Much of the variation in population, however, is explained by sociological and biological reasons rather than economic reasons.

Labor force participation. The number of people in the labor market, the **labor force,** varies considerably in response to economic and social conditions. Generally, a rise in the demand for labor and an accompanying rise in the earnings of labor will lead to an increase in the proportion of the population willing to work. Persistent unemployment may lead unemployed workers to become discouraged about finding a job and to withdraw from the labor force.

Social or legal changes can cause major variations in participation rates. The women's liberation movement, for example, has sharply increased labor force participation in the United States. Recent congressional action prohibiting mandatory retirement before age 70 may increase the labor force further, if more of the aged who previously were obliged to retire at 65 decide to stay on the job.

Hours worked. Generally, a rise in real wages such as has occurred in most Western countries over the last two centuries leads people to consume more goods — and to consume more leisure. This means that over time, as wages rise, people are willing to work fewer hours per week, a fact that *ceteris paribus* will lead to a decline in the supply of labor. But incentives such as overtime pay can be used to persuade employees to work more.

Tax rates. Many believe that today's high income taxes tend to reduce the supply of effort by lowering the incentive for people to work. They protest that it is not worth their while to work because of the crushing tax burdens they have to shoulder. Yet such objective evidence as exists suggests that high taxes do not always reduce the supply of effort. To the extent that they do, the aggregate effect may be small. A good deal of research has shown that while some people may work less hard in response to rising taxes, others feel poorer and thus work more to maintain their after-tax incomes. The most recent research suggests at most a small net disincentive up to a level of marginal tax rates of 50 percent, such as exists today in the United States.

At tax rates of 75 percent or more, important distortions may occur. In Britain, where marginal tax rates used to rise to 85 percent at levels of income that would be regarded as moderate in the United States, a "brain drain" occurred in many professional, scientific, and managerial occupations. Low salaries combined with very high tax rates on "extra" earnings to produce dramatic evidence that workers can "vote with their feet" against high taxes on earnings. Such mobility was no doubt made easier by the existence of jobs in other English-speaking countries, principally the United States and Canada.

To reduce the supply of effort is not the only possible response to tax rates regarded as confiscatory. Citizens may vote for politicians who promise to reduce taxes; or they may simply not pay income taxes. Tax avoidance, including outright cheating, may become common and even socially acceptable. The British government estimates that roughly 8 percent of the entire national income arises in cash transactions that avoid taxes because they are never reported. The growth of this "black economy" in Britain is widely believed to have been motivated by the high marginal tax rates. And the desire to avoid taxes may explain the recent rapid growth of bartering in the United States, now estimated to account for $15 to $20 billion of transactions annually.

Inflation, unemployment, and the fear of poverty. Unsettled conditions in the economy and the uncertainties they create tend to increase the supply of effort. People believe they need larger cushions against possible disaster. Rapid inflation during the late 1970s led to a noticeable break in the previous trend toward voluntary earlier retirement. It is not hard to understand why. While the incomes of the employed tend to rise along with a general inflation, most pensions do not. Inflation at a 10 percent annual rate for 14 years reduces the purchasing power of a pension fixed at $20,000 per year to $5,000. After 21 years its purchasing power would be only $2,500. Those who in a noninflationary world would have been glad to retire at age 60 on $20,000 per year will think twice before doing so if they recognize that they may be reduced to poverty by inflation should they be lucky enough to live to be 80.

This problem would be bad enough, and would in itself lead to deferred retirements, if workers could be sure of what the inflation rate would be during their retirement years. The problem is much worse because the future is in doubt. The inflation rate might average as little as 4 percent a year, or it might reach 20 percent, as it did in Italy and England during the 1970s. At 20 percent per year inflation, purchasing power is halved every 3.5 years. That will reduce the purchasing power of a $20,000 pension to $2,700 after 10 years and a mere $366 after 20 years! Even if the higher inflation rate is not probable, many will be unwilling to take a voluntary action, such as early retirement, that would prove disastrous if it should happen.

Chronic unemployment poses a similar threat. Many of the employed believe they should earn as much as they can when work is available in order to build up their reserves against the possibility of future layoffs.

These effects will occur whether or not the fears prove to be real. What matters is what people *think* might happen.

Welfare payments, unemployment insurance, etc. Do welfare payments and other aid to the poor make them less willing to take jobs? Some significant disincentives to working have been found, but they do not seem to have a major effect when the financial aids are structured so as to leave those who can work with some incentive to do so. Many of those receiving payments are unable to work. Most who can work find it worthwhile to do so for their sense of participation in society as well as for the extra income. However, for a sizable—and much noticed—number, there is no doubt that welfare has become a substitute for work. And some welfare rules actually discourage work by making welfare recipients turn over as much as two-thirds of any income they might earn.

The Total Supply of Arable Land

If the term "land" is used to refer to the total area of dry land, then the total supply of land in a country will be almost completely fixed. It was nineteenth century practice (following Ricardo) to define land as the *original and inexhaustible powers of the soil*. But dust bowls were a phenomenon unknown to Ricardo, who also did not know that the deserts of North Africa were once fertile plains. Clearly the supply of fertile land is not inexhaustible; considerable care and effort is required to sustain the productive power of land. If the return to land is low, its fertility may be destroyed within a short time. Moreover, scarcity and high prices may make it worthwhile to increase the supply of arable land by irrigation and other forms of reclamation.

The Total Supply of Natural Resources

People worry—usually when it is too late—about exhausting natural resources. The great iron ore deposits of the Mesabi Range were exhausted in 1965, and America's known supplies of oil and gas had shrunk by 1979 to less than an 11-year supply.[2]

The problem of actual exhaustion of natural resources does not arise as often as one might think. There is frequently a large undiscovered or unexploited quantity of a given resource or of an adequate substitute. The exhaustion of high-grade iron ore reserves in the United States did not end steel production—partly as a result of the discovery of ways to use low-grade iron ores once thought worthless, and partly because new supplies in Labrador and the Caribbean have been developed.

Guessing what will prove to be an effective substitute resource may be difficult. Will solar energy or nuclear fusion one day provide a permanent solution to the energy crisis? A writer in the *Cornell Law Quarterly* in 1930 worried about the upcoming shortage of gasoline. He believed that ordinary alcohol was the answer, and for that reason he urged the repeal of Prohibition! Gasohol may yet prove him to have been a prophet 50 years before his time.

Emerging shortages may lead to their own corrections. As long as oil remains sufficiently valuable, it will pay to find more of it. If the cost of finding oil becomes too high, the supplies that it is economically feasible to find will decrease—at those prices. Before that event, however, free-market prices would surely rise. A sufficient increase in the price of oil would make it economically worthwhile to process the vast quantities of previously unexploited shale oil. Consumers will feel the scarcity in terms of higher prices, and this will lead them to use less oil; this in turn will decrease the rate of exhaustion of known reserves.

One of the dangers of government regulation is that it may prevent these self-correcting responses. In the United States the Federal Power Commission kept the field price of natural gas artificially low. This encouraged consumption, discouraged exploration, and depleted reserves.

Ultimately, of course, there is an upper limit, and resources can be totally exhausted; worse, they can be contaminated or otherwise despoiled so as to render them useless long before they have been consumed.

The Total Supply of Capital

Capital is a man-made factor of production, and its supply is in no sense fixed. The supply of capital in a country consists of the stock of existing machines, plant, equipment, and so on. This capital is used up in the course of production, and thus the stock is diminished by the amount that wears out each year. However, the stock of capital is increased each year by the production of new capital goods. Taking the long view and ignoring cyclical fluctuations, there has been a fairly steady tendency in all developed countries for the stock to increase over time.

---

[2] It should not be inferred that supplies of oil and gas will be exhausted by 1990. The known supply was reported to be at most 20 years in every year from 1920 to 1950; in other words, each year as much was discovered as was used. What *is* new in recent years is that discovery has lagged behind production, and thus the number of years of known supply has been shrinking.

THE SUPPLY OF FACTORS TO PARTICULAR USES

Plainly it is easier for some users to acquire more of a scarce factor of production than it is for all users to do so simultaneously. Most factors have many uses; a given piece of land can be used to grow any one of several crops, or it can be subdivided for a housing development. A machinist in Detroit can work in a variety of automobile plants, or in a dozen other industries, or even in the physics laboratories at Wayne State University. A lathe can be used to make many different products and requires no adaptation when it is turned from one use to another.

The total supply must be allocated among all the different uses to which it can possibly be put. If the factor's owners are concerned only with making as much money as they can, they will move their factor to that use at which it earns the most money. Such a movement out of one use and into another would continue until the earnings of each of the units of one kind of factor in all of its various possible uses were the same. Because owners of factors are known to take other things besides money into account—such as risk, convenience, and a good climate—it is not sufficient to consider only monetary incentives; we must consider the sum of monetary and nonmonetary rewards.

The Hypothesis of Equal Net Advantage

The **hypothesis of equal net advantage** says that owners of factors will choose that use of their factors that produces the greatest net advantage to themselves. (Net advantage includes both monetary and nonmonetary rewards.)

This hypothesis plays the same role in the theory of distribution as the assumption that firms seek to maximize profits plays in the theory of production. It leads to the prediction that the units of one kind of factors of production will be allocated among various uses in such a way that their owners receive the same net return in every use.

People often worry about this hypothesis because we do not know how to measure nonmonetary advantages.[3] The hypothesis can be made operational, however, if we assume (as is no doubt often the case) that the differences in nonmonetary advantages between two uses of a factor remain relatively constant or change only slowly over time. We can then predict that variations in monetary advantages will widen or narrow the gap and that some resources will flow in response to the change.[4]

A change in the relative rate of pay of a factor between two uses will lead to a shift of some but not all units of that factor to the use whose rate of pay has increased.

This prediction implies a rising supply curve for a factor in any particular use. When the price of a factor rises, more of it will be supplied. Such a supply curve (as all supply curves) can *shift* in response to changes in other variables. One of the variables that can shift the supply curve is a change in the size of nonmonetary benefits.

Factor Mobility

When considering the supply of a factor to a particular use, the most important concept is **factor mobility.** The term is used in the sense of shiftability in use. A factor that shifts easily between uses in response to small changes in incentives is

---

[3] An example will suggest why. It used to be said that faculty members at the University of Wisconsin paid $2,000 a year for the privilege of teaching at that beautiful campus on the shores of Lake Mendota. The story is still told, but with recent salary trends in mind the figure has been upped to $8,000. We know of no way to estimate the value of Lake Mendota to the Madison faculty; we can observe only that they appear to be willing to accept less pay to work there. But imputing a value to the lake by determining how much less pay they are willing to accept depends on the hypothesis being true—and thus gives no basis for testing it and no way of discovering if it is wrong.

[4] To return to Lake Mendota, if we assume that its value is stable, then a widening salary differential between the University of Wisconsin and other universities would lead to the predictions that (1) some people, formerly content, would now leave the university to take higher paying jobs elsewhere and (2) the university would have more trouble recruiting new staff.

said to be highly mobile. In such a case the factor will be in very elastic supply in any one of its uses because small increases in the price offered will attract a large flow of the factor from other uses. A factor that does not shift easily from one use to another, even in response to large changes in remuneration, is said to be highly immobile. In this case the factor will be in very inelastic supply in any one of its uses because even a large increase in the price offered will attract only a small inflow from other uses.

Mobility of land. Land, which is physically the least mobile of factors, is one of the most mobile in an economic sense. Consider agricultural land. Within a year at most, one crop can be harvested and a totally different crop planted. A farm on the outskirts of a growing city can be sold for subdivision and development on short notice.

Once land is built upon, as urban land usually is, its mobility is much reduced. A site on which a hotel has been built can be converted into an office building site, but it takes a large differential in the value of land use to make it worthwhile because the hotel must be torn down.

Although land is highly mobile between alternative uses, it is completely immobile as far as location is concerned. There is only so much land within a given distance of the center of any city, and no increase in the price paid can induce further land to locate within that distance. This locational immobility has important consequences, including high prices for desirable locations and the tendency to build tall buildings that economize on the use of land where it is very scarce, as in the centers of large cities.

Mobility of capital. Most capital equipment, once constructed, is comparatively unshiftable (immobile) among uses. A great deal of machinery is utterly specific: once built, it must either be used for the purpose for which it was designed or else not used at all. (It is the immobility of much fixed capital equipment that makes the exit of firms from declining industries a slow and difficult process.) Of course many kinds of capital equipment are mobile—a shed may be used for

many purposes, and a lathe can be used to make hundreds of products.

Over long periods of time the allocation of a country's capital stock among uses does change substantially. When capital goods wear out, firms might simply replace them with identical goods. But the firm has many other options: It may buy a newly designed machine to produce the same goods, it may buy machines to produce totally different goods, or it may spend its resources in other ways. Such decisions lead to changes in the long-run allocation of a country's stock of capital among various uses.

Labor mobility. Labor is unique as a factor of production in that the supply of the service implies the physical presence of the owner of the source of the service. Absentee landlords can obtain income from land located in remote parts of the world while continuing to live in the place of their choice. Investment can be shifted from iron mines in northern Minnesota to mines in Labrador while the owners of the capital commute between New York and the French Riviera. But when a worker employed by a firm in Pittsburgh decides to supply labor service to a firm in Chicago, the worker must physically travel to Chicago. This is all quite obvious, but it has an important consequence.

Because of the need for physical presence, non-monetary considerations are much more important in the allocation of labor than in the allocation of other factors of production.

People may be either satisfied with or frustrated by the kind of work they do, where they do it, those they do it with, and the social status of their occupations. Since these considerations influence their decisions about what they will do with their labor services, they will not move every time they can earn a higher wage.

Nevertheless, according to the hypothesis of equal net advantage, occupational and job movement will occur when there are changes in the wage structure. The mobility that does occur depends on many forces. For example, it is not difficult for a secretary to shift from one com-

Labor Mobility and Immobility

Labor mobility—between places, between jobs, between occupations, and even between social classes—has been studied extensively. The studies show, among other things, that:

1. Labor mobility of every kind increases as the time allowed for movement increases.
2. Labor is more mobile between jobs in the same location than between different locations because movement of the family and loss of social contacts are deterrents.
3. Labor is more mobile between jobs in the same occupation than between occupations because of the time required to acquire new skills.
4. Education is more important than family background in determining occupation. While it is still an advantage to have a successful parent (successful in the sense of the parent's having an occupation at the high end of the income scale), it is not nearly as important as it was 50 years ago. What is helpful in today's America is having the education that a successful parent helps one acquire.
5. While relative wages do matter, job opportunities are often even more important in

influencing labor movement, both among places and among occupations.

While there are many "man-made" encouragements to labor mobility, such as education, training, and employment agencies, there are also barriers. Many organizations, private and public, adopt policies that affect personnel and impede their mobility as workers. When labor unions negotiate seniority rights for their members, they protect older employees from being laid off but they also make them reluctant to change jobs. When an employer provides employees with a pension plan, the employees may not want to forfeit this fringe benefit by changing jobs.

Unions may also limit entrance into an occupation. Licensing is required in dozens of trades and professions. Barbers, electricians, doctors, and, in some places, even peddlers must have licenses. There is, of course, a perfectly legitimate reason for requiring licenses in those cases in which the public must be protected against the incompetent or the quack or the nuisance. Licensing, however, can have the effect of limiting supply. Discrimination based on racial prejudice and other similar attitudes further limit the mobility of labor.

pany to another or to take a job in New York City instead of in Jersey City, but it can be difficult for a secretary to become an editor or a fashion model in a short period of time. There are three considerations here: ability, training, and inclination. Lack of any one will stratify some people and make certain kinds of mobility difficult for them.

One important key to labor mobility is time. In the short term it is often difficult for people to change occupations; in the long term it is much easier.

Some barriers may seem insurmountable for a person once his or her training has been completed. It is not easy, and it may be impossible, for a farmer to become a surgeon or a truck driver to become a professional athlete, even if the relative wage rates change greatly. But the children of farmers, doctors, lawyers, and athletes, when they are deciding how much education or training to obtain, are not nearly as limited in their choices as their parents, who have completed their education and are settled in their occupations.

For this reason the labor force is not static. At one end of the age distribution people enter the labor force from school; at the other end they leave it via retirement or death. The turnover due to these causes is about 3 or 4 percent per year. Over a period of 20 years, a totally different occupational distribution could appear by redirecting new entrants to jobs other than the ones left vacant by workers leaving the labor force, without a single individual ever changing jobs. The role of education in adapting people to available jobs is very great. In a society in which education is provided to all, it is possible to achieve large increases in the supply of any desired labor skill within a decade or so.

The Price of Factors in Competitive Markets

We have now developed theories of both the demand for and the supply of factors of production. These theories predict a downward-sloping demand curve and an upward-sloping supply curve. This is all that is needed for a theory of factor pricing in competitive markets. If factor prices are free to vary, prices and quantities employed will tend toward the point at which quantity supplied equals quantity demanded. Furthermore, shifts in either the demand for or the supply of factors will have the same effects on prices, quantities, and factor incomes as are predicted by standard price theory.

The theory of factor prices is absolutely general. If one is concerned with labor, one should interpret factor prices to mean wages; if one is thinking about land, factor prices should be interpreted to mean land rents, and so on.

FACTOR PRICE DIFFERENTIALS

Prices of different units of factors such as labor or land vary. Consider the prices of a number of closely related factors such as different kinds of labor. If all these factors were identical and if all benefits were monetary, then all their prices would tend toward the same level. Factors would tend to move from low-priced occupations to high-priced ones. The quantities supplied would diminish in occupations in which prices were low, and the resulting shortage would tend to force prices up; the quantities of factors supplied would increase in occupations in which prices were high, and the resulting surplus would force factor prices down. The movement would continue until there were no further incentives to transfer—that is, until factor prices were equalized. Factor price differentials are commonly seen and may be divided into two distinct types.

Dynamic Differentials

Some factor price differentials reflect a temporary state of disequilibrium. These are self-eliminating and are called **dynamic differentials.** They could equally well be called disequilibrium differentials. They are brought about by circumstances such as the growth of one industry and the decline of another. Such differentials themselves lead to reallocations of factors, and these reallocations will in turn act to eliminate the differentials.

Consider the effect on factor prices of a rise in the demand for air transport and a decline in the demand for railroading. The theory predicts an increase in the airline industry's (derived) demand for factors and a decrease in the railroad industry's demand for factors. Relative factor prices are thus predicted to go up in the airline industry and down in railroading. The differential in factor prices will itself foster a net movement of factors from the railroad industry to the airline industry, and this movement will cause the dynamic price differentials to lessen and eventually disappear. How long this process takes will depend on how easily factors move from one industry to the other—that is, on the extent of factor mobility.

Equilibrium Differentials

Some factor price differentials may persist in equilibrium without generating forces that eliminate them. These **equilibrium differentials** are related to differences in the factors themselves (e.g., land of different fertilities or labor of different abilities), to differences in the cost of acquiring skills, and to different nonmonetary advantages of different factor employments.

It is usual to pay academic research workers less than they could earn in the world of commerce and industry because there are substantial nonmonetary advantages attached to the former. If labor were paid the same in both employments, many people would try to move out of industry and into academic employment. Excess demand for labor in industry and excess supply in universities would then cause industrial wages to rise relative to academic ones until the movement of labor stopped.

Equilibrium differentials may also be caused by differences in skills. If there is a chronic shortage of skilled workers, the skilled worker will earn more than the unskilled worker. Although there will be some movement from unskilled to skilled jobs, it is not likely to be sufficient to eliminate this differential. People will not acquire scarce skills, even if they are able to do so, unless the differentials in wages remain large enough to pay for the costs and time spent in acquiring them.

It is important to realize that the high pay of the skilled relative to that of the unskilled merely reflects relative demand and supply conditions for the two types of labor. There is nothing in the nature of competitive markets that ensures that skilled workers always get high pay just because they are skilled. When, for example, the demand for expert harness makers declined, they were in excess supply and their wages came down. History is full of examples of highly skilled workers who lost their privileged position when there was a change in the supply of or the demand for their services. Many think it both unjust and incomprehensible that since World War II truck drivers have been earning more money than schoolteachers. Whatever the justice of the matter, it is certainly not incomprehensible; at the same wage there would be excess demand for truck drivers and excess supply of school teachers.

The two kinds of differentials are closely linked to factor mobility and the hypothesis of equal net advantage. Dynamic differentials lead to, and are eroded by, factor movements; equilibrium differentials are explained in part by different nonmonetary benefits and in part by lack of mobility.

Dynamic differentials tend to disappear over time; equilibrium differentials persist indefinitely.

TRANSFER EARNINGS AND ECONOMIC RENT

The amount that a factor must earn in its present use to prevent it from transferring to another use is called its **transfer earnings.** Any excess that it earns over this amount is called its **economic rent.** The distinction is critical in predicting the effects of changes in earnings on the movement of factors.

The concept of economic rent, a surplus over transfer earnings, is analogous to the notion of economic profit as a surplus over opportunity cost.

Origins of the Concept of Economic Rent

The present concept of economic rent arose out of a policy controversy. In the early nineteenth century, when classical economics was in full bloom, there was a controversy about the high prices of wheat in England. The high price was causing great hardship because bread was a primary source of food. Some argued that "corn" (then the generic term for all grains) had a high price because landlords were charging very high rents to tenant farmers. In order to meet these land rents, the prices that farmers charged for their corn also had to be raised to a high level. In short, it was argued that the price of corn was high because the rents of agricultural land were high. Those who held this view advocated restricting the power of the landlords and somehow forcing them to behave more reasonably.

Others—including, notably, David Ricardo—held that the situation was exactly the reverse.

The price of corn was high, they said, because there was a shortage of corn caused by the Napoleonic wars. Because corn had a high price, it was profitable to produce it and there was keen competition among farmers to obtain land on which to grow corn. This competition in turn forced up the rents of corn land. If the price of corn were to fall so that corn growing became less profitable, then the demand for land would fall and the price paid for the use of land (i.e., its rent) would also fall. Those holding this view advocated removing the tariff so that imported corn could come into the country, thereby increasing the supply and bringing down both the price of corn and that of the land on which it was grown.

Stated formally, the essentials of Ricardo's argument were these: Land was regarded as having only one use, the growing of corn. The supply of land was regarded as unchangeable — that is, in perfectly inelastic supply. Nothing had to be paid to prevent land from transferring to a use other than growing corn because it had no other use. No self-respecting landowner would leave land idle as long as he could obtain some return, no matter how small, by renting it out. Therefore, all the payment to land — that is, rent — was a surplus over and above what was necessary to keep it in its present use. Given the fixed supply of land, the price depended on the demand for land, which was *derived* from the demand for corn. Rent, the term for the payment for the use of land, thus became the term for a surplus payment to a factor over and above what was necessary to keep it in its present use.

The Modern View of Economic Rent

Later two facts were realized. First, land itself often had alternative uses, and from the point of view of any one use, part of the payment made to land would necessarily have to be paid to keep it in its present use. Second, factors of production other than land also often earn a surplus over and above what is necessary to keep them in their present use. Television stars and great athletes, for example, are in short and fairly fixed supply,

and their potential earnings in other occupations are probably quite moderate. But because there is a huge demand for their services, as television stars or athletes, they may receive payments greatly in excess of what is needed to keep them from transferring to other occupations.

Thus it appears that all factors of production are pretty much the same; part of the payment made to them is a payment necessary to keep them from transferring to other uses, and part is a surplus over and above what is necessary to keep them in their present use. This surplus is now called economic rent whether the factor is land or labor or a piece of capital equipment.

The Division of Factor Earnings Between Rents and Transfer Earnings

In most cases, the actual earnings of a factor of production will be a composite of transfer earnings and economic rent. It is possible, however, to imagine cases in which all earnings are *either* transfer earnings *or* economic rent. The possibilities are illustrated in Figure 20-3. When the supply curve is perfectly elastic (horizontal), the whole of the price paid is a transfer earning: if the purchasing industry does not pay this price, it will not obtain any quantity of the factor. When the supply curve is perfectly inelastic (vertical), the whole of the payment is an economic rent: even a price barely above zero would not lead suppliers to decrease the quantity supplied. After all, some price is better than none. The price actually paid allocates the fixed supply to those most willing to pay for it.

The more usual situation is that of a gradually rising supply curve. In this case, a rise in the price serves the allocative function of attracting more units of the factor into the employment, but the same rise in the factor's price provides an extra economic rent to all units of the factor already employed. (The owners of these units were willing to supply them at the original price.)

This is quite a general result. If a factor becomes scarce in any or all of its uses, its price will rise. This will serve the allocative function of

FIGURE 20-3

The Division of Factor Payments Between Economic Rent and Transfer Earnings

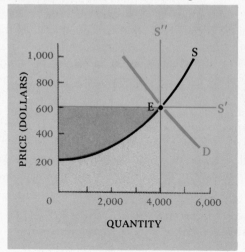

The division of total factor payments between economic rent and transfer earnings depends on the shape of the supply curve. A single demand curve is shown with three different supply curves. In each case the competitive equilibrium price is $600 and 4,000 workers are hired and the total payment to labor ($2,400,000) is represented by the entire shaded area.

(a) When the supply curve rises to the right (the black curve, S) part of the payment is rent, part transfer earnings. The 4,000th worker is just receiving transfer earnings because if the wage falls below $600 a month, he or she will not work. However, other workers would stay in the industry at a lower wage. If a separate bargain were made with each worker so that each was paid only its transfer earnings, the total payment would be the area under the black supply curve, shown as the lighter shaded area. Because the same wage must be paid to everyone, however, the total wage payment is larger, and the extra payment, shown as the darker shaded area, represents economic rent.

(b) When the supply curve is horizontal (the colored line, S') the whole payment is transfer earnings because even a small decrease in price offered would lead all units of the factor to move elsewhere.

(c) When the supply curve is vertical (the colored line, S") the whole payment is rent because a decrease in price would not lead any unit of the factor to move elsewhere.

attracting additional units, but it will also give an economic rent to all units of the factor already in that employment, whose transfer earnings were already being covered.

POLICY IMPLICATIONS OF THE DISTINCTION BETWEEN RENTS AND TRANSFER EARNINGS

Using Wage Increases to Increase the Quantity of a Factor Supplied

If the U.S. government wants more physicists, should it subsidize physicists' salaries? As we have seen, such a policy may well have an effect on supply. It will persuade some students uncertain about whether to become engineers or physicists to become physicists. Whether it is an efficient use of the money will depend on the slope of the supply curve. Clearly, however, raising all physicists' salaries may mean that a great deal of money will have to be spent on extra payments to those who are already physicists. These payments will be economic rents, for existing physicists have demonstrated that they are prepared to be physicists at their old salaries. If these rents are a large part of the total subsidy, an alternative policy may produce more physicists per dollar. One such alternative is to subsidize scholarships and fellowships for students who will train to become physicists. The National Science Foundation and the Atomic Energy Commission did precisely this. The effect of such subsidies is to shift the supply curve of physicists to the right.

If the supply curve is quite inelastic, an increase in the quantity supplied may be achieved more easily and at less cost by policies designed to shift the supply curve to the right than by the policy of raising price and moving up the original supply curve. See Figure 20-4.

Precisely this issue was encountered in the discussion of the draft versus the volunteer army in Chapter 7. The "premium" earned by willing soldiers under the volunteer army is an economic rent.

Urban Land Values and Land Taxes

The high payments made for the services of urban land are largely economic rents. The land is scarce relative to the demand for it, and it commands a price very much above what it could earn in agricultural uses. The payment it receives is thus well in excess of what is necessary to prevent it from transferring from urban uses back to agricultural uses. A society with rising population and rising per capita real income tends also to have steadily rising urban land prices. This fact has created a special interest in taxes on land values.

Suppose there is a tax on the economic rent of land. If the same tax rate is applied to all uses of land, the relative profitability of different uses will be unaffected and a landlord will not be tempted to change the allocation of land among uses. Land will not be forced out of use because land that is very unprofitable will command little rent and so pay little tax. Thus there will be no change in the supply of goods that are produced with the aid of land, and because there is no change in supply, there will be no change in prices.

Furthermore, the tax cannot be passed on to consumers. Farmers will be willing to pay just as much (and no more) as they would have offered previously for the use of land. Agricultural prices and rents will be unchanged, and the whole of the tax will be borne by the landlord. The net rents earned by landlords will fall by the full amount of the tax. Therefore a tax on land rents *that are truly economic rents* falls solely on landowners and is not passed on to the users of land or the consumers of the produce of land.

This is the kind of argument that lay behind the popular appeal of the so-called single-tax movement, of which Henry George (1839–1897) was the guiding genius and his book *Progress and Poverty* (1880) the bible. The book was an all-time best-seller among books on economic issues, and George ran for Mayor of New York City in 1886 and very nearly won, campaigning as a one-issue candidate. The single-tax move-

FIGURE 20-4
Alternative Ways to Increase the Quantity of a Factor Actually Provided

A subsidy that shifts the supply curve may achieve an increase in quantity actually provided without giving economic rents to those previously employed. With demand and supply curves D and S the factor market is in equilibrium at E. An increase in demand to D_1 would bring about an increase in quantity from q to q_1 but only with a sharp rise in factor price from p to p_1. This price rise would give substantial rents to those already employed, as shown by the shaded area. An alternative policy that gives subsidies to new entrants shifts the supply curve to S_1. It provides the additional quantity qq_2 without increasing the payments to units already employed.

ment has only faded in the period since World War II. The chief difficulties with the proposal are that not all land rents are economic rents, not all economic rents are land rents, and the revenues from a land tax would surely not be enough to make it the only tax needed in today's world.

WHAT QUESTIONS DOES THE THEORY ANSWER?

Consider again the questions discussed in the early paragraphs of this chapter. The theory of distribution we have here developed concentrates on the pricing of factors in many of the markets of the economy. We certainly can reject the view that the size distribution of income is beyond understanding, or beyond influence, even if many aspects of what determines incomes remain obscure. We know that when something improves the productivity of a factor, the factor's price will tend to increase. We know that factor mobility and immobility play an important role in the supply of factors to particular uses and thus to the pay of factors in those uses. We know how and why factor price differentials arise. We know that some differentials persist as equilibrium differentials and that others are the signals that lead to their own erosion.

Implicit in this is a large part of the explanation of why some people earn large salaries and incomes and others do not. Thus this theory has a great deal to say about the *size distribution* of income. It is also well understood today that government policies of taxation and expenditure can affect the distribution of income. Income inequality has been diminishing in the United States as a result of systematic attention to problems of poverty, discrimination, and immobility of labor. Although the specific impact of particular programs is often in doubt (and sometimes disappointing), there is no doubt about the government's overall ability to change the distribution of income.

But while the theory answers many questions, it leaves others unanswered. The theory of distribution worked out in this chapter is based on the marginal analysis developed in the last half of the nineteenth century. It emphasizes the determination of both factor and product prices in millions of individual markets. Yet market economies are complex, and it is not easy to go from what happens in one market to what happens in the economy. Consider an example: If the government attempts to increase the income of the poor by giving them amounts of money to be used for rent, how much does this benefit them and how much the landlords from whom they rent? The answer will depend on how much rents

go up as well as on the effect on the prices of the other items the poor buy.

What does this market-oriented theory of distribution contribute to the broad questions about functional distribution of income considered by Marx and raised before him by Ricardo and Smith? What for example can we say about what determines the share of total income earned by labor? Can we say anything about the distribution of income among labor (wages), capital (interest and profits), and land (rent)? Our theory about individual markets offers few general predictions about the functional distribution of income. It holds that to discover the effect of some change, say a tax or a new union, on the functional distribution between wages, profits, and rent, we would need to be able to discover not only what would happen in each individual market of the economy but also to aggregate to find the overall result.[5] Clearly, we are a long way from being able to do all this with our present state of knowledge.

It may well be that general predictions about the effects of events, such as the rise of unions, on overall distribution cannot be easily derived. Many economists would argue that economic theory has little to say about great issues raised by the classical economists on the level of labor and capital's overall shares of the total national product. They could also argue that the ability of marginal productivity theory to deal with detailed questions of distribution is nonetheless a remarkable triumph.

One reason that questions concerning the overall functional distribution of income are difficult, and perhaps impossible, to answer is that the broad categories such as "labor" are themselves highly diverse: a theoretical physicist, a

---

[5] To do this accurately we would, among other things, need to know the degree of monopoly and monopsony in each market, we would need to be able to predict the effect on oligopolists' prices and outputs of changes in their costs, and we would need to have a theory of the outcome of collective bargaining in all market situations. We would also need to know how much factor substitution would occur in response to any resulting change in relative factor prices. Finally, we would need a general equilibrium theory linking all of these markets together.

baseball superstar, and a bus driver all receive labor income. It makes sense to talk about laws governing distribution into three main factor shares if labor, capital, and land are each relatively homogeneous and each subject to a common set of influences not operating on the other two factors. In fact, however, there may well be as much difference between two different types of labor as between one kind of labor and one kind of machine. Thus there is no more reasons to expect that there should be simple laws governing the overall functional distribution of income between land, labor, and capital than to expect that there should be simple laws governing the overall distribution of income between blondes and brunettes or Methodists and Baptists.

Summary

1. The functional distribution of income refers to the shares of total national income going to each of the major factors of production. It focuses on sources of income. The size distribution of income refers to the shares of total national income going to various groups of households. It focuses only on the size of income, not its source.

2. The income of a factor of production can be broken into two elements: (a) the price paid per unit of the factor and (b) the quantity of the factor used. The determination of factor prices and quantities is an application of the same price theory used to determine product prices and quantities.

3. The demand for any factor is *derived* from the commodities the factor is used to make. Factor demand curves slope downward because a change in a factor's price will affect the cost of production (and thus product price, quantity produced, and the need for factors) and because of the ability to substitute cheaper for more expensive factors.

4. The elasticity of factor demand will tend to be greater, (a) the greater is the elasticity of demand of the products it makes, (b) the greater is the proportion of the total cost of production accounted for by the factor, and (c) the easier it is to substitute one factor for another.

5. A profit-maximizing firm will hire units of any variable factor until the last unit hired adds as much to costs as it does to revenue. If factors are bought in a competitive market, the addition to cost will be the price of a unit of a factor. From this comes the important condition that in competitive equilibrium the price of a factor will equal its marginal revenue product. This is the marginal productivity theory of distribution.

6. The total supplies of most factors are variable over time and respond to some degree to economic influences. The most important influences are not the same for labor, arable land, natural resources, and capital.

7. The hypothesis of equal net advantage is a theory of the allocation of the total supply of factors to particular uses. Owners of factors will choose the use that produces the greatest net advantage, allowing for monetary and nonmonetary advantages of a particular employment.

8. Factor mobility (shiftability in use) is important. Land is mobile between uses but cannot change its geographical location. Capital equipment is durable, but firms regularly replace discarded or worn out machinery with totally different machines and so change the composition of the nation's capital stock gradually but steadily. Labor mobility is greatly affected by nonmonetary considerations. The longer the period of time allowed to elapse, the more mobile is the labor force.

9. In competitive factor markets, prices are determined by demand and supply, but factor price differentials occur. Dynamic differentials in the earnings of different units of factors of production serve as signals of a disequilibrium and induce factor movements that eventually remove the differentials. Equilibrium differentials reflect differences among units of factors as well as non-

monetary benefits of different jobs; they can persist indefinitely.

10. Transfer earnings are what must be paid to a factor to prevent it from transferring to another use. Economic rent is the difference between a factor's transfer earnings and its actual earnings. Whenever the supply curve is upward-sloping, part of the factor's earnings is transfer earnings and part is rent.

11. The existence of rents in a factor's price has a potentially important policy implication: If supply is inelastic, raising the factor's price may be a relatively expensive way to induce increases in the quantity of the factor supplied.

12. The theory of distribution developed in this chapter successfully predicts changes in factor earnings that occur for particular groups in response to changes in the market conditions that affect them. However, it has little to say about changes in the broad functional distribution of income among labor, land, and capital.

Topics for Review

Factor demand as a derived demand
Marginal revenue product
The marginal productivity theory of distribution
  ($w = MRP$)
Factor mobility
The hypothesis of equal net advantage
Dynamic and equilibrium differentials in factor prices
Transfer earnings and economic rent

Discussion Questions

1. Other things being equal, how would you expect each of the following to affect the size distribution of after-tax income? Do any of them lead to clear predictions about the functional distribution of income?
   a. an increase in unemployment
   b. rapid population growth in an already crowded city
   c. an increase in food prices relative to other prices
   d. an increase in social security benefits and taxes
2. Consider the effects on the overall level of income inequality in the United States of each of the following.

   a. labor force participation of women increases sharply due to many women shifting from work in the home to full-time paid jobs
   b. increasing use by California agricultural producers of Mexican farm workers who are in the United States illegally
   c. Increasing numbers of minority groups members studying law and medicine
3. The demands listed below have been increasing rapidly in recent years. What derived demands would you predict have risen very sharply? Where will the extra factors of production demanded be drawn from?
   a. the demand for electric power
   b. the demand for medical services
   c. the demand for international and interregional travel
4. Can the following factor prices be explained by the marginal productivity theory of distribution?
   a. The actor James Garner is paid $25,000 for appearing in a ten-second commercial. The model who appears in the ad with him is paid $250.
   b. First prizes in a recent tennis tournament were: men's singles, $40,000; women's singles, $30,000; men's doubles, $15,000; women's doubles, $6,000; mixed doubles, $4,800.
   c. The same jockey is paid 50 percent more money for winning a ¾ mile race with a $150,000 first prize than a 1½ mile race with a $100,000 prize—on the same horse.
   d. The head football coach at Michigan State University is paid *not* to coach in the third year of a three-year contract.
5. Overall participation in the work force has remained at about the same proportion of the total population for the last 20 years, but its composition has changed substantially. Among the features of the labor force over this period are:
   a. Virtually all married men between 25 and 45 years of age have participated in the work force in each year.
   b. The percentage of women aged 40 and over has risen sharply.
   c. The percentage of men over 55 has dropped.
   d. The percentage of both men and women under 25 has declined.
   Hypothesize about the social and economic changes that might explain these conditions. How do they relate to the theory of distribution?
6. What, if anything, do each of the following have to do with factor mobility?
   a. A newspaper advertisement by the New Jersey De-

velopment Council: "Open your new plant in the Garden State. Our sizable labor force of skilled and unskilled workers is a major benefit for any employer. New Jersey workers are experienced, easy to find, easy to train. And just as important for your profit picture, they like it in New Jersey and don't move away."

b. Trailways Bus Company offered one-way bus tickets to anywhere in the United States at half price to anyone in Detroit who had been unemployed for six months or more. Hundreds of people bought these "opportunity fare" tickets.

c. Rising housing prices and very high interest rates on residential mortgages in one section of the country.

7. A recent study showed that after taking full account of differences in education, age, hours worked per week, weeks worked per year, etc., professionally trained people earned approximately 15 percent less if they worked in universities than if they worked in govern-ment service. Can this be accounted for by the theory of distribution?

8. Distinguish between economic rent and transfer earnings in each of the following payments for factor services.

a. the $200 per month a landlord receives for the use of an apartment leased to students

b. the salary of the president of the United States

c. the $800,000 annual salary of Pete Rose

d. the salary of a window cleaner who says, "It's dangerous, dirty work, but it beats driving a truck."

9. Which of the following are dynamic and which equilibrium differentials in factor prices?

a. the differences in earnings of football coaches and wrestling coaches

b. a "bonus for signing on" offered by a construction company seeking carpenters in a tight labor market

c. differences in monthly rentals charged for three-bedroom houses in different parts of the same metropolitan area

Collective Bargaining, Discrimination, and the Determination of Wages

21

Why do automobile workers get the same pay for the same work, no matter where they work in the United States? Why do carpenters get different wages in different locations? Why do railroad employees, who work in a declining industry, get higher rates of pay than equally skilled workers in many expanding industries? How does a worker in a plant employing 5,000 people "ask for a raise"? How does a worker let her employer know that she would be glad to trade so many cents per hour in wages for a better medical insurance scheme? Why do strikes occur?

The competitive theory of factor price determination, the subject of the preceding chapter, yields many useful and confirmed predictions about factor prices, factor movements, and the distribution of income. Indeed, for the pricing of many nonhuman factors, there is little need to discard or to modify the competitive model. Much of what is observed about labor markets is also consistent with the theory. But not all of it is.

Labor is in many ways the exceptional factor of production. The factors that govern working conditions and pay are critically important to workers and their families. When employees and employers negotiate the price to be paid to the factor of production called labor, they are negotiating about something that is vital to most households. It is not surprising that people are sometimes prepared to fight over such negotiations. Considerations other than material advantage enter the relationship between employer and employee, for it is a relationship between people who look for loyalty, fairness, appreciation, and justice along with paychecks and productivity and who, if they believe these are denied them, can often respond with aggression, malice, and hatred.

Labor unions, employers' associations, and the institutions and customs that influence collective bargaining are features of the real world. They have developed in response to the exceptional conditions that govern the bargaining between free people about the terms on which one will work for another. These institutions are important because they influence the wages and working conditions that are finally agreed on.

Because labor markets are characteristically imperfectly competitive, and sometimes monopolistic, the theory of factor price determination must be extended somewhat before it can be applied to the full range of problems concerning the determination of wages.

Theoretical Models of Wage Determination

In a labor market, firms are the buyers and workers, either individually or through a labor union, are the sellers. Noncompetitive elements can enter on either or both sides of the market. The outcome of the wage bargain will be affected by the market situation.

Two extreme but relevant cases are, first, the one in which there are so many employers that no one of them can influence the wage rate by varying its own demand for labor and, second, the one in which there is a single purchaser of labor, either a single firm or an association of several firms operating as a single unit in the labor market. In the former case, labor is said to be purchased under competitive conditions; in the latter case, under monopsonistic conditions. **Monopsony** means a single buyer; it is the equivalent, on the purchasing side, of a monopoly (a single seller). What is the effect of introducing a union into each of these extreme situations?

A UNION IN A COMPETITIVE LABOR MARKET

Where there are many employers and many unorganized workers there is a competitive factor market of the kind discussed in the previous chapter. Under competitive conditions, the wage rate and level of employment are set by supply and demand.

When a union enters such a market and sets a wage for the industry above the competitive level, it is establishing a minimum wage below which no one will be allowed to work. This changes the supply curve of labor. The industry can hire as many units of labor as are prepared to work at the union wage. Each firm in the industry will have to pay that wage; the union will not let the wage rate fall. Thus the industry (and each firm) faces a supply curve that is horizontal at the level of the union wage up to a quantity of labor willing to work at that wage. This is shown in Figure 21-1. The intersection of this new supply

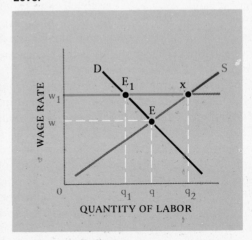

FIGURE 21-1
Union Wage Setting Above the Competitive Level

The union can raise the wages of those who continue to be employed in a competitive labor market at the expense of the level of employment. The competitive equilibrium is at E; the wage is w and employment is q. If a union enters this market and sets a wage of w_1, a new equilibrium will be established at E_1. The supply curve has become w_1xS. At the new wage, w_1, there will be q_2 workers who would like to work, but the industry only wishes to hire q_1. Employment will be q_1. The decrease in employment due to the wage increase over the competitive level is q_1q, and the level of unemployment is q_1q_2.

curve and the demand curve establishes a wage rate and level of employment that differ from the competitive equilibrium.

The major effects of the union's wage setting are:

1. It will raise the wage rates of those who remain employed in the industry.
2. It will lower the actual amount of employment in the industry.
3. It will create a surplus of labor that would like to but cannot obtain jobs in the industry affected.
4. It will create an incentive for some workers to try to evade the fixed wage by offering to work at wages below the union level.

Ample evidence confirms these theoretical predictions. The unemployment that results presents a problem for the union, which is supposed to represent *all* the employees in the industry or occupation. A conflict of interest has been created between employed and unemployed union members. Pressure to cut the wage rate may develop among the unemployed, but the union must resist this pressure if the higher wage is to be maintained.

The loss of employment opportunities may well be permanent, and the unemployment may be quite long lasting. Often the actions of unions will force up the wages of those whose wages would be high in any case. This means that some displaced workers will have difficulty finding jobs that are equivalent in pay, particularly when their skills are not readily transferable to other jobs. For this reason the union jobs are likely to be prized, and many of the displaced may prefer to wait for openings caused by death or retirement rather than seek employment in other occupations.

A MONOPSONISTIC LABOR MARKET WITHOUT A UNION

Consider a labor market in which there are many unorganized workers but only a small number of firms. For simplicity, imagine a case in which the firms form an employers' hiring association in order to act as a single unit so that there is a monopsony in the labor market.

The employers' association realizes that, faced with a rising supply curve for labor, it can pick a wage rate and take the quantity of labor offered, or it can pick the quantity of labor to hire and pay the wage rate required to bring forth that quantity of labor. While the employers' association can offer any wage rate that it chooses—the laborers must either work at that rate or find a different job—the wage rate chosen will affect the profitability of its operations. For any given quantity that the monopsonist wishes to purchase, the labor supply curve shows the price per unit that it must offer; to the monopsonist, this is the *average cost curve* of the factor. In deciding how much labor to hire, however, the monopsonist will be interested in *marginal cost* because it is aware that it can bid up the wage against its own interest.

Whenever the supply curve of labor slopes upward, the marginal cost of employing extra units will exceed the average cost.[1] It exceeds the wage paid (the average cost) because the increased wage rate necessary to attract an extra worker must be paid to everyone already employed. [27] The profit-maximizing monopsonist will hire labor up to the point where the marginal cost just equals the amount it is willing to pay for an additional unit of labor, which is shown by the demand curve. [28] This is illustrated in Figure 21-2.

Monopsonistic conditions in the factor market will result in a lower level of employment and a lower wage rate than would rule when the factor is purchased under competitive conditions.

The common sense of this result is that the

---

[1] If, for example, 100 units of labor are employed at $2 per hour, then total cost is $200 per hour and average cost per hour is $2. If 101 units are employed and the wage rate is driven up to $2.01, then total labor cost becomes $203.01 an hour. Although average cost is only $2.01, the total cost has been increased by $3.01 as a result of hiring one more laborer. Thus the marginal cost of the extra labor is $3.01.

FIGURE 21-2
Monopsony in a Labor Market

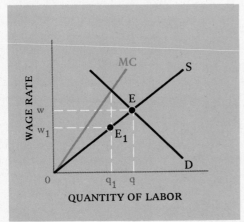

A monopsonist lowers both the wage rate and employment below their competitive levels. *D* and *S* are the competitive demand and supply curves. In competition equilibrium is at *E*, the wage rate is *w*, and the quantity of labor hired is *q*. The marginal cost of labor (*MC*) to the monopsonist is above the average cost. The monopsonistic firm will maximize profits at E_1. It will hire only q_1 units of labor. At q_1 the marginal cost of the last worker is just equal to the value to the firm of that worker's output, as shown by the demand curve. The wage that must be paid to get q_1 workers is only w_1.

FIGURE 21-3
A Wage-setting Union Enters a Monopsonistic Labor Market

By presenting a monopsonistic employer with a fixed wage, the union can raise both wages and employment over the monopsonistic level. The monopsony position before the union enters is at E_1 (from Figure 21-2), with a wage rate of w_1 and q_1 workers hired. A union now enters and sets the wage at *w*. The supply curve of labor becomes *wES*, and wages and employment rise to their competitive levels of *w* and *q* without creating a pool of unemployed workers. If the wage is raised further, say to w_2, the supply curve will become w_2xS and the quantity of employment will fall below the competitive level to q_2 while a pool of unsuccessful job applicants of q_2q_3 will develop.

monopsonistic firm is aware that by trying to purchase more of the factor it is driving up the price against itself. It will therefore stop short of the point that is reached when the factor is purchased by many different firms, no one of which can exert an influence on the wage rate.

A UNION IN A MONOPSONISTIC MARKET

What if a wage-setting union enters a monopsonistic market and sets a wage below which labor will not work? There will then be no point in the employer's reducing the quantity demanded in the hope of driving down the wage rate, nor will there be any point in holding off hiring for fear of driving the wage up. Here, just as in the case of a wage-setting union in a competi-

tive market, the union presents the employer with a horizontal supply curve (up to the maximum number who will accept work at the union wage). The union raises wages above the monopsony level. This result is demonstrated in Figure 21-3.

Because the union turns the firm into a price taker in the labor market, it can prevent the exercise of the firm's monopsony power and raise both wages and employment to the competitive levels.

The union may not be content merely to neutralize the monopsony power. It may choose to raise wages further. If it does, the argument will

Minimum Wages Set by Government Decree

When unions set wages for their members, they are in effect setting a minimum wage. Governments can cause similar effects by legislating specific minimum wages.

In the United States, in 1981, the federal minimum wage was $3.35 per hour. It covered about 80 percent of the labor force. For a very large fraction of all employment covered by the law, this minimum wage is below the actual market wage. When this is true, the wage is said to be not "binding." But many workers are in occupations or industries where the free-market wage rate would be below the legal minimum, and there the minimum wage is said to be binding, or effective.

The occupations and industries in which minimum wages are effective are the lowest paying in the country; they usually involve unskilled or at best semiskilled labor. In most of them the workers are unorganized. Thus the market structures in which effective minimum wages apply are either those where competitive conditions pertain or where employers have and can exercise monopsony power. The effects of minimum wages are different in the two cases.

Effective minimum wages in a competitive market. Here the results are precisely the same as those for a union setting a wage in a competitive industry, as shown in Figure 21-1. *The minimum wage will increase the wages of those employed, decrease employment, increase unemployment, and create incentives to evade the law by working below the legal minimum wage.*

Effective minimum wages in a monopsonistic market. Here the results are the same as those for a union setting a wage in a monopsonistic market, as shown in Figure 21-3. *The minimum wage, when set at the competitive level, will raise both wages and employment.* The minimum wage can protect the unorganized worker against monopsony power in the same way a union can.

It is possible that minimum wages will be set above the competitive level. If so, while wages of those employed will be raised, no prediction can be made as to whether employment will increase or decrease compared to the monopsony level. (It depends both on how high the wage is and on the shapes of the curves.)

These predictions concern individual industries but do not answer questions about all industries. Until relatively recently, large fractions of total employment were exempted from coverage. When that was the case, those who might have become unemployed in "covered" occupations might find jobs in uncovered occupations. As the coverage of the minimum wage increases, this becomes less likely.

A great deal of empirical work has been done on the actual effect of minimum wages on employment. Some unemployment is caused by minimum wages, particularly among youths aged 16 to 19: it is estimated that rates of youth unemployment of 16 percent would be reduced to 12 or 13 percent in the absence of a minimum wage. It is also clear that some new employment is almost surely created in monopsonistic industries. Most studies show that on balance employment is lower and unemployment higher as a result of minimum wages.

The employment effect is, however, only one element in deciding whether, overall, minimum wages are beneficial or harmful.

It is clear that minimum wage laws raise the incomes of many workers at the very lowest levels of employment. Because union "wage-structures" maintain differentials between skill classes, an increase in minimum wages also raises wages in a large number of occupations that are already above the minimum.

Thus, there are gainers and losers, and they may be expected to evaluate minimum wages differently. Professional economists do too. The issue is one that is actively debated today.

be exactly the same as that surrounding Figure 21-1. If the wage is raised above the competitive level, the employer will no longer wish to hire all the labor offered at that wage. The actual amount of employment will fall, and unemployment will develop. This too is shown in Figure 21-3. Notice, however, that the union can raise wages substantially above their competitive level before employment falls to a level as low as it was in the pre-union monopsonistic situation.

Labor Market Institutions

So far we have dealt with the simple case of a union that fixes a wage and allows employment to be determined by demand. Other methods of raising wages are available, and unions have goals other than high wages. Before we consider these further, we need to review some institutional and historical details about labor markets. In the process, we shall be able to use the theory already developed to understand some past events and some present institutions.

Potential Monopsonists: Employers' Associations

A large firm has some degree of monopsony power just by virtue of its size and the number of employees with which it deals. It recognizes that its actions affect the wage rate, especially the rates received by those kinds of labor that are in some way limited to the industry in which the firm operates. This limitation will result when one large firm's need for this kind of labor represents a large fraction of the total demand for it. If steelworkers were not organized, the U.S. Steel Corporation would be in a position to exploit substantial monopsony power in its dealings with them because U.S. Steel represents a large share of the demand for whatever special talents may be required for making iron and steel.

Employers' associations are groups of employers who band together for a number of purposes, one of which may be to agree on a common policy in labor negotiations. If all steel companies

offer the same terms, they can exercise even more monopsony power than any one of them could on its own. The steelworker who did not wish to accept the common conditions would have no alternative but to seek work in another industry. Today formal employers' associations that appoint official bargaining representatives exist on a local level in many industries, including the hotel, restaurant, newspaper printing, and construction industries. There are regional or national associations in the garment manufacturing, hosiery, textile, coal mining, and furniture manufacturing industries, among others.

At least as important as formal associations are informal ones in which the several firms in an industry follow the lead set by a key firm. The industrywide pattern characterizes many manufacturing industries today. The automobile industry, for example, achieves nationwide agreement with its workers without the formal apparatus of an employers' association.

Potential Monopolists: Unions

No one bothers to define unions any more, perhaps because everyone knows what they are, or perhaps because a union is so many things: a social club, an educational instrument, a political club, one more source of withholding money from a worker's pay, a bargaining agent for an individual worker, and, to some, a way of life. For the purposes of our discussion of labor markets, a **union** (or **trade union** or **labor union**) is an association of individual workers that speaks for them in negotiations with their employers.

Unions today have two different principles of organization: the craft (or trade) union and the industrial union. In the **craft union,** workers with a common set of skills are joined in a common association, no matter where or for whom they work. The craft principle of organization was and is the hallmark of the American Federation of Labor (AFL). The **industrial union** is organized along industry lines: All workers in a given plant or industry are collected into a single union. This is the pattern developed by the member unions of the Congress of Industrial Organizations (CIO).

Among the prominent industrial unions are the United Automobile Workers and the United Steelworkers.

The two principles of unionism conflict. Should a carpenter employed in the steel industry be represented by the carpenters' union or the steelworkers' union? Disputes over which union shall have the right to *organize* (i.e., bring into their union) a particular group of workers are known as **jurisdictional disputes.** They have led to prolonged, bitter, and bloody battles of union against union, and they have played an important role in American labor history. In the United States, since the merger of the AFL and CIO in 1955, jurisdictional disputes have become much less common.

The important level for most of the economic functions of the union is the national level. The national officers do the bargaining, set the policies, and set the tone. Individual workers, however, belong to a local to which they pay dues (a part of which goes to the national). There are about 200 national unions, which have over 75,000 locals. The local for a craft union is geographical—the Chicago chapter of the carpenters, say. The local for an industrial union is a plant or a company—the Ford local of the United Automobile Workers, for example.

The **federation** is a loose organization of national unions. Before 1955, the AFL and CIO were two separate organizations; today there is one federation, the AFL–CIO. The federation has little real power yet serves an important role as a voice of organized labor. Its function in recent years has been largely a public relations and political one; it has thrown its support behind certain candidates, its representatives have testified before Congress, appeared on *Meet the Press,* and so on.

Kinds of Bargaining Arrangements: Open, Closed, and Union Shops

In an **open shop** a union represents its members but does not have exclusive bargaining jurisdiction for all workers in the shop. Membership in the union is not necessary to get or to keep a job.

Unions vehemently oppose such an arrangement, and economic theory explains why. If, on the one hand, the employer yields to union demands and raises wages, the nonmembers get the benefits of the union without paying dues or sharing the risks or responsibilities. If, on the other hand, the firm chooses to fight the union, it can run its plants with the nonunion employees, thereby weakening the power of the union in the fight.

If the union succeeds in raising wages above their competitive level, there will be an excess supply of labor (see Figure 21-1). With an open shop, there is nothing to prevent unemployed nonunion workers from accepting a wage below the union one and so undermining the union's power to maintain high wages.

If all members of an occupation must join the union in order to get a job, the union can prevent its members from accepting less than the union wage and so have the power to maintain high wages in spite of the existence of excess supply. This arrangement is called a closed shop. In a **closed shop** only union members may be employed, and the union controls its membership as it sees fit. Employers traditionally regard this as an unwarranted limitation of their right to choose their employees. Since passage of the Taft-Hartley Act in 1948, its use has been virtually prohibited in the United States.

The **union shop** is a compromise between a closed shop and an open shop. It is the most common union arrangement in the United States today. In a union shop a firm may hire anyone it chooses at the union wage, but every employee must join the union within a specified period. This leaves employers free to hire whomever they wish but gives the union the power to enforce its union wages because workers are prevented from accepting employment at lower wages.

Weapons of Conflict: Strikes, Picket Lines, Boycotts, Lockouts, Strikebreakers, Blacklists

The **strike,** the union's ultimate weapon, is the concerted refusal to work by the members of the union. It is the strike or the threat of a strike that backs up the union's demands in the bargaining process. Workers on strike are, of course, off the payroll, so many unions set aside a portion of the dues collected to have a fund for paying striking workers.

Picket lines are made up of striking workers who parade before the entrance to their plant or firm. Other union members will not, by time-honored convention, "cross" a picket line. Thus, if bricklayers strike against a construction firm, carpenters will not work on the project, although they themselves may have no grievance against the firm, nor will any teamster deliver supplies to a picketed site. Pickets represent an enormous increase in the bargaining power of a small union. (Much of the bitterness against jurisdictional disputes arises from the fact that an employer may be unable to settle with either union without facing a picket line from the other union.)

A **labor boycott** is an organized attempt to persuade customers to refrain from purchasing the goods or services of a firm or industry whose employees are on strike. The boycotts organized by Cesar Chavez's United Farm Workers Union against grapes, lettuce, and most recently bananas are prominent examples.

The **lockout** is the employer's equivalent of the strike. By closing the plant the employer locks out the workers until such time as the dispute is settled. **Strikebreakers** (scabs) are workers brought in by management to operate the plant while the union is on strike. A **blacklist** is an employers' list of workers who have been fired for playing a role in union affairs that was regarded by the employer as undesirable. Other employers are not supposed to give jobs to blacklisted workers.

Collective Bargaining

The process by which unions and employers (or their representatives) arrive at and enforce their agreements is known as **collective bargaining.** This process has an important difference from the theoretical models with which we began this chapter. There we assumed that the union set the wage and the employer decided how much labor to hire. In collective bargaining the wage is negotiated. In terms of Figure 21-3, it may be that the employer wants the wage to be w_1 and the union wants w_2. Depending on each side's market power and their bargaining strength, the final agreed wage may be anywhere in between. In collective bargaining, there is always a substantial range over which an agreement can be reached, and in particular cases the actual result will depend on the goals and strengths of the two bargaining parties and on the skill of their negotiators.

The Evolution of the Modern Union

When representatives of the United Automobile Workers sat down with representatives of the General Motors Company in 1979 to discuss wages, contributions to pension funds, number and length of holidays, and other issues, they were engaged in what has been termed "mature collective bargaining." At the end of the negotiations, the newspaper and television coverage showed the smiling representatives shaking hands. Each of the approximately 460,000 workers in the GM plants then knew the conditions under which he or she would work for the next three years. Should an employee have a grievance at any time, he or she reports it to the union representative (called a **shop steward**), and a carefully designed procedure is set in motion to settle the dispute.

Unionism today is both stable and accepted. It was not always so. Within the lifetime of many of today's members, unions were fighting for their lives and union organizers and members were risking theirs. In the 1930s the labor movement evoked the loyalties and passions of people as a great liberal cause, in ways that seem quite extraordinary today. Indeed unions today often appear as conservative (even reactionary) groups of hard hats. Why the change and how did it come about?

Poverty, United States, 1903

Stories of the workers' very real suffering during the Industrial Revolution and the years that followed could fill many volumes, but an example will at least illustrate some of the horrors that lay behind the drive for change and reform. (The quotation comes from *Poverty*, by Robert Hunter, published in 1904.)

In the worst days of cotton-milling in England the conditions were hardly worse than those now existing in the South. Children—the tiniest and frailest—of five and six years of age rise in the morning and, like old men and women, go to the mills to do their day's labor; and when they return home, they wearily fling themselves on their beds, too tired to take off their clothes. Many children work all night—"in the maddening racket of the machinery, in an atmosphere insanitary and clouded with humidity and lint." It will be long before I forget the face of a little boy of six years, with his hands stretched forward to rearrange a bit of machinery, his pallid face and spare form showing already the physical effects of labor. This child, six years of age, was working twelve hours a day in a country which has established in many industries an eight-hour day for men. The twelve-hour day is almost universal in the South, and about twenty-five thousand children are now employed on twelve-hour shifts in the mills of the various Southern states. The wages of one of these children, however large, could not compensate the child for the injury this monstrous and unnatural labor does him; but the pay which the child receives is not enough, in many instances, even to feed him properly. If the children fall ill, they are docked for loss of time. . . . The mill-hands confess that they hate the mills, and no one will wonder at it. A vagrant who had worked in a textile mill for sixteen years once said to a friend of mine: "I done that [and he made a motion with his hand] for sixteen years. At last I was sick in bed for two or three days with a fever, and when I crawled out, I made up my mind that I would rather go to hell than go back to that mill."

The Urge to Organize

Trade unionism had its origin in the pitifully low standard of living of the average nineteenth century worker and his family. Much of the explanation for the low standard of living throughout the world lay in the small size of the national output relative to the population. Even in the wealthiest countries, an equal division of national wealth among all families in 1850 would have left each one in poverty by our present standards.

Poverty had existed for centuries. It was accentuated, however, by the twin processes of urbanization and industrialization. The farmer who was moderately content working the land usually became restive and discontented when the family moved into a grimy, smoky nineteenth century city, lived in a crowded, unsanitary tenement, and took a job in a sweatshop or a factory. The focus of resentment was usually the employer.

The employer set the wages, and the wages were low. The boss was often arbitrary and seldom sympathetic. And the boss was usually conspicuously better off than his employees. Unhappy workers had, of course, the right of all free people to quit their job—and starve. If they grumbled or protested, they could be fired—and worse, blacklisted, which meant no one else would hire them.

Out of these conditions and other grievances of working men and women came the full range of radical political movements. Out of the same conditions also came a pragmatic American form of collective action called **bread-and-butter unionism,** whose goals were higher wages and better working conditions rather than social and political reform.

The early industrial organizer saw that ten or a hundred employees acting together had more influence than one acting alone and dreamed of the day when all would stand solid against the employer. (The word "solidarity" occurs often in the literature and songs of the labor movement.) The union was the organization that would provide a basis for confronting the monopsony power of employers with the collective power of the workers. But it was easier to see solidarity as a solution than it was to achieve it. Organizations of workers would hurt the employer, and employers did not sit by idly; they too knew that in union there was strength. "Agitators" who tried to organize other workers were fired and blacklisted; in some cases they were beaten and killed.

REQUIREMENTS OF A SUCCESSFUL UNION

In order to realize the ambition of creating some effective power over the labor market, a union had to gain control of the supply of labor and have the financial resources necessary to outlast the employer in a struggle for strength. There was no right to organize. The union had to force an employer to negotiate with it, and few employers did so willingly. Unions started in a small way among highly skilled workers and spread slowly.

There are good theoretical reasons that help explain why the union movement showed its first real power among small groups of relatively skilled workers. First, it was easier to control the supply of skilled workers than unskilled ones. Organize the unskilled, and the employer could find replacements for them. But skilled workers —the coopers (barrelmakers), the bootmakers, the shipwrights—were another matter. There were few of them, and by controlling the conditions of apprenticeship they controlled the access to their trade. The original craft unions were, in effect, closed shops: One had to belong to the union to hold a job in the craft, and the union set the rules of admission.

Second, a union of a relatively few highly skilled specialists could attack the employers where they were vulnerable. Because a particu-

lar skilled occupation may be difficult to do without in an industrial process, other factors cannot easily be substituted for it. Because labor in a particular skilled occupation is likely to account for a relatively low proportion of total costs, the effect on the employer's overall costs of giving in to a small group's demand for a wage increase is much less than the effect of giving in to an equivalent demand from the numerous unskilled workers.

In other words, the difficulty of substituting other factors and a relatively small contribution to total costs combined to create an inelastic demand for skilled labor (see page 334). This inelastic demand for their services gave the unions of skilled workers an advantage in fighting the employer not enjoyed by other groups of workers. In the early days, unions needed every advantage they could get since anti-unionism was for some a matter of principle, a crusade, and a way of life.

Even where unions gained a foothold in a strategic trade, they had their ups and downs. When employment was full and business booming, the cost of being fired for joining a union was not so great because there were other jobs. However, during periods of depression and unemployment the risks were greater. An individual worker knew that if he or she caused trouble, unemployed members of the trade would be there to take the job. Solidarity could yield to hunger. Membership in trade unions showed a clear cyclical pattern, rising in good times and falling in bad.

THE HISTORICAL DEVELOPMENT OF AMERICAN UNIONS

The beginnings: before 1933. The American Federation of Labor, founded in 1886 by Samuel Gompers, a cigar maker from England, was totally committed to organizing the skilled trades, to pursuing bread-and-butter issues, and to restricting labor supply. It is no coincidence that Gompers, himself an immigrant, led the AFL in

FIGURE 21-4

FIGURE 21-4

Union Membership as a Percentage of the Labor Force in the United States, 1900–1978

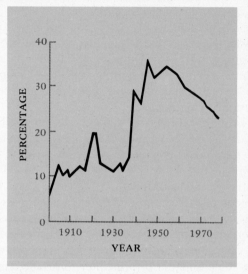

The great spurt in union membership occurred after passage of the Wagner Act (1935) and before the end of World War II. As a result of the great expansion in the labor force since 1960, the *number* of union members has increased slightly, but union membership as a percentage of the labor force has steadily declined. The percentages are of total nonagricultural employment.

vigorous opposition to further immigration: restriction of supply was the key to preserving union power.

Because it was impossible to control supply, the prospects for unionization were bleak for the unskilled. Their hope lay in political reform, in socialism, in cooperatives, or in revolution. The Knights of Labor, organized in 1869, sought one big union for all workers. At its peak in 1886, it had 700,000 members. But the political climate was hostile, and the Knights collapsed in 1887 as a result of many causes, including some unsuccessful strikes of unskilled workers. The depression of 1887 finished this ambitious venture in political rather than bread-and-butter unionism.

The AFL avoided noble causes and continued its steady growth among the skilled until the end of World War I. In 1900 it had just over half a million members (2 percent of the labor force), and by 1920 it had 5 million members, 10 percent of the labor force. By 1922, in the face of depression and the strong anti-labor attitude of government and business alike, union membership had declined to 8 percent, and by 1933, after a decade of gradual decline, to about 6 percent of the labor force.

The New Deal: 1933–1945. The dramatic effect of the New Deal on union membership is seen in Figure 21-4. What happened? First, the monstrousness of the Great Depression created a climate of public opinion openly hostile to big business. Second, the Wagner Act (1935) guaranteed the *right* of workers to organize and to elect, by secret ballot, an exclusive bargaining agent by majority vote of the employees. And, third, the unskilled were organized in industrial unions. The Wagner Act provided the means to control the supply of even unskilled labor.

The great industrial unions in steel and in automobiles, following the leadership of John L. Lewis of the United Mine Workers, organized, split from the conservative AFL, formed the CIO, and struck for recognition. Using bold tactics such as the sit-down strike, where employees occupied the plants and prevented employers from operating with strikebreakers, the CIO won recognition and members. It doubtless benefited from an atmosphere of public opinion in which there was no disposition on the part of the government or the courts to try to stop them. Thus the unions won—first by force and even violence, finally by law—the recognition that was required to permit workers through unions to articulate their grievances and to bargain to relieve them.

After World War II. The New Deal period and its legislation were unmistakably pro-labor. There was widespread recognition that labor had been an abused underdog, and Congress had a mandate to redress the balance. By the end of World War II, attitudes had changed for several reasons, including an increasing number and the changing character of strikes. The long series of strikes during the organizing period, undertaken to compel employers to recognize and deal with unions, were received with a good deal of public sympathy. But the jurisdictional strikes between rival AFL and CIO unions were less comprehensible to public and employer alike. An unprecedented wave of strikes in 1946 led to the loss of over 100 million worker days (about 1 percent of estimated working time), more than four times the loss of any previous year.

These strikes are widely regarded as having created the climate of public opinion that led Congress to pass the Taft-Hartley Act in 1948, despite all-out labor opposition. Among its many provisions, unfair labor practices on the part of unions as well as management were defined and prohibited, use of the closed shop was limited, and strikes that "imperiled the national health and safety" were subject to an 80-day cooling off period. The most controversial feature of the act was the encouragement it gave to states to pass **right-to-work laws.** These laws permit the open shop—the right to work without belonging to a union. In virtually every recent Congress, supporters of organized labor have attempted to repeal this provision, so far without success.

Since 1950 union membership has continued to grow in absolute numbers to over 20 million, but in spite of that growth the percentage of the labor force in unions has declined steadily. Part of the reason is continued employer opposition; part is the absence of employment growth in traditionally unionized industries and in industries with large concentrations of employees. The biggest growth in recent unionization has been among government employees as a result of new, permissive legislation. The biggest question mark is the future of unionism among employees in white-collar, professional, and service fields. Some observers believe that if inflation continues for very long, it will accelerate a trend toward unionization in these traditionally unorganized occupations.

The main development in the nature of union-ization over the last three decades has been the stabilizing of union-management relations in industry after industry. Strikes still occur, and always will, for they are a key part of the poker game of collective bargaining. The number and duration of strikes today are relatively minor compared with those of the 1930s and late 1940s. It has been more than 20 years since strikes resulted in the loss of even one-half of 1 percent of all working time, and typically the work time lost amounts to only two- or three-tenths of 1 percent. Particular strikes—for example, among teamsters, teachers, police officers, or coal miners—can cause real disruption and arouse public opinion. The strikes that do occur, however, are directed overwhelmingly toward specific issues and negotiations rather than recognition or jurisdiction, and the violence and passions of a generation ago are largely gone. Labor unions are now part of the establishment.

Methods and Objectives of the Modern Union

Union constitutions are extremely democratic documents. All members have one vote, officers are elected by the vote of the membership, the rights of individual workers are fully protected, and so on. In practice, however, the relation between the members of a union and its national officers is closer to that of the relationship between stockholders and managers of a giant corporation than to that of the American people and their government. Unions tend toward one-party democracy in most cases. Union leaders are highly paid professionals whose business is to run the union, while the main business of union members is to earn a living on the job. The union members' indifference is understandable; they are paying dues that permit the union to pay generous salaries to union leaders to look out for the rank and file's interests—and as long as the leadership "delivers," all goes well. But delivers what and to whom?

RESTRICTING SUPPLY TO INCREASE WAGES

At the beginning of this chapter we saw that if a union raises the wage above the competitive level, it will create a pool of people eager to work at the going wage rate but unable to find employment. An alternative is to determine the quantity of labor supplied and let the wage be determined on the open market. This is illustrated in Figure 21-5. The union can restrict entry into the occupation by methods such as lengthening apprenticeship periods and restricting openings for trainees. Such tactics make it more difficult and more expensive to enter the occupation.

Under these restrictive conditions, the quantity supplied is reduced at any given wage rate

FIGURE 21-5
Raising Wages by Restricting Entry

By restricting entry into an occupation, a union can shift the supply curve and raise wages. A competitive industry would be in equilibrium at E. When the supply curve shifts to S_1, the wage rises to w_1 and employment falls to q_1. Compare this to the strategy of simply imposing the wage w_1. In each case q_1 workers obtain employment at q_1. By shifting the supply curve, no pool of unsuccessful job applicants is created (as it was when a wage of w_1 was imposed without shifting the supply curve from S).

and the supply curve of labor shifts to the left. This has the effect of raising wages without anyone's ever having to negotiate a rate above what would naturally emerge from the free operation of the competitive market. Furthermore, there is no pool of unemployed wanting to work at the new higher wage but unable to find employment. Thus there is no wage-reducing pressure from unemployed persons who are trained for the occupation but are unable to find jobs.

The choice unions may face between the tactics of wage setting and supply restriction will be affected by the relative ease of enforcing one or the other kind of arrangement and the public acceptability of its tactics. In this respect unions are no different than professional groups, who may treat unions with utter disdain. Consider the professions of medicine and law. Since professional standards may be regarded as necessary to protect the public from incompetent practitioners, doctors and lawyers have found it publicly acceptable to limit supply by controlling entry into their profession.

Doctors are in short supply—and doctors' incomes are the highest of any profession—because of barriers to entry, including the difficulties of getting into an approved medical school, long years of low-paid internship and residency, and various certification rules. Whatever the need for high standards of entry into medical practice, there is no doubt that doctors' earnings are high *because* the barriers to entry into the profession prevent increases in the number of those admitted to medical practice. Most investigators have concluded that restrictions on entering medicine are much greater than they need be to protect the public and that earnings are substantially higher as a result.

Lawyers, by contrast, have been less successful in limiting entry into their profession. The major law schools admit only a small portion of the qualified applicants, and they have not expanded sufficiently to keep pace with the sharply increased demand for admission. But new law schools, often of lower quality than the older ones, have sprung up to serve the growing excess demand. The new schools have proved financially beneficial to the institutions or individuals who organized them. Their graduates have, for the most part, gained access to the profession, often with the aid of "cram schools" that prepare them for the bar exams.

Lawyers, faced with an inability to limit competition by limiting entry into the profession, have turned to "wage setting"—having their state bar associations prescribe and enforce minimum fees for services such as drawing a will, probating an estate, and representing a client in court. They have also tried to label advertising and other forms of competition for clients as unethical. As the theory predicts, many lawyers are underemployed in the sense that they have fewer clients than they could comfortably handle.[2] In contrast, doctors are typically overworked.

Restriction of supply will tend to raise wages. Raising wages without restricting supply will lead to unemployment or underemployment.

COMPETING GOALS

Wages Versus Employment

A union that sets wages above the competitive level is making a choice of higher wages for some and unemployment for others. Should the union strive to maximize the earnings of the group that remains employed? If it does, some of its members will lose their jobs and the union's membership will decline. Should it instead maximize the welfare of its present members? Or should it seek to expand employment opportunities (perhaps by a low-wage policy) so that the union membership grows?

Different unions decide these questions differently. The United Mine Workers Union employed a high-wage, shrinking-employment strategy for decades, and both employment and union membership declined. The longshoremen's union has achieved high wages but chooses to ration

the available jobs among its members rather than reduce its membership. It thus spreads the underemployment around. In the garment trades, the demand for labor is relatively elastic and the major unions have traditionally accepted lower wages than they could have attained in order to protect the employment of their members. The key construction unions in New York City during that city's 1975 fiscal crisis accepted a 25 percent cut in their wage rate on rehabilitation construction because of a high—30 percent—unemployment rate among their members.

Wages versus employment poses a long-term problem as well as a short-term problem. Unionization and rising wages in fruit picking have led to mechanization and a drop in the demand for labor. In the auto industry, the high-wage policy of the United Automobile Workers has encouraged the major manufacturers to increase automation. There are 100,000 fewer jobs in the industry today than ten years ago, although more cars are made. The attempt to get a four-day, 32-hour work week is a work-spreading response to the extra unemployment among the union's membership.

Wages Versus Job Security

People who were in their teens during the Great Depression still dominate the leadership of American unions. Not surprisingly, they have a strong defensive attitude toward their jobs. They lived through a period when unemployment was above 20 percent of the total labor force and nearer 50 percent in many of the hardest hit areas. They saw people grow up, marry, and raise children on relief or part-time work.

In a period of heavy unemployment, installation of a labor-saving machine in a factory is likely to mean unemployment for those whose jobs are lost by the change. It is little wonder that new machines were opposed bitterly and that job-saving restrictive practices were adhered to with tenacity.

The heritage of this fear survived in featherbedding practices such as the standby musician

---

[2] See the discussion of barbers in Chapter 17.

at the television studio and the meticulous division of tasks in the building trades. But in the long run mechanization increases productivity—and consequently the wages and profits that are earned. After World War II the attitude of many unions slowly changed from one of resisting technological change to one of collaborating with it and trying to reduce some of its costs to individuals who are adversely affected. The return of higher unemployment rates in recent years has, however, led again to increased resistance to rapid innovation. In any event, history shows that innovation may be delayed but cannot be stopped.

Wages Versus Fringe Benefits

Today indirect, or **fringe benefits**—such as company contributions to union pension and welfare funds, sick leave, and vacation pay, as well as required payments toward social security and unemployment compensation insurance—are estimated to make up almost a third of the total compensation of industrial workers. Why do unions and employers not simply agree to a wage and let it go at that? Why should the average employed automobile worker have earned $19,800 in wages in 1980 but cost the company $31,700?

Fringe benefits appeal to employees in part because they are not subject to income taxes. Pension funds and medical benefits let employees provide for their future and that of their families more cheaply than they could by purchasing private insurance, and their benefits often protect them even when they lose their jobs.

There may also be advantages to employers in giving indirect or fringe benefits. One advantage is that some forms of fringe benefits, such as pension funds, tend to bind the worker more closely to the company, thereby decreasing the turnover rate among employees. If employees stand to lose part of their benefits by changing jobs, they will not be so ready to move.

Fringe benefits provide scope for bargaining. A union official may have promised the rank and file not to settle for less than $1.50, and the employer's representatives may have assured management that they would stand firm at $1.00. In negotiation they may agree on 90¢ in wage increases and 70¢ in fringe benefits. Both negotiators may claim success, whereas either would feel reluctant to accept a straight $1.25 wage increase. Collective bargaining is more successful when neither side feels it has done too badly.

Discrimination in Labor Markets

In 1973 the American Telephone and Telegraph Company settled an antidiscrimination suit. It paid $15 million in back pay and an additional $23 million a year in raises to women and minority males against whom it had allegedly discriminated in job assignments, pay, and promotions. Since then United Airlines has paid more than $1 million to settle complaints about discrimination in the pay of airline stewardesses, and Consolidated Coal has paid fines for denying women access to high-paying underground jobs. The construction industry has agreed to quotas for black workers to remedy the past exclusion of blacks from a variety of occupations. In 1979 the federal government filed five suits against Sears, Roebuck & Company, charging it with discrimination against women, blacks, and Hispanic persons. These suits or settlements, and others, focus on what many had long suspected—that discrimination by race and by sex have often occurred in the American job market.

The economic effects of discrimination against minorities and women take many forms. Discrimination does not wholly explain, but it surely contributes to, higher unemployment rates (fact: black unemployment rates are more than twice white unemployment rates) and to lower rates of pay (fact: female hourly earnings are 25 percent below male hourly earnings). Both lower wages and greater unemployment lead to lower incomes for the workers involved.

They may also lead to different attitudes toward the workplace and toward society. Discrimination affects not only the workers discriminated against but their children, whose aspirations and willingness to undertake the education or training required to "succeed" may be adversely affected. Indeed, it may change the definition given to success. The costs of all this are borne by the groups discriminated against, but also by society as a whole.

The problems of racial discrimination and sex discrimination are different from one another, and so is the nature of the policies required to eliminate them. With respect to the economics of discrimination, there are similarities as well as differences. It is helpful to look first at how either kind of discrimination produces its effects.

A MODEL OF THE EFFECTS OF DISCRIMINATION

We begin by building a simplified picture of a world without discrimination and then introduce discrimination. While this reverses the contemporary problem (predicting the effect of removing discrimination), it provides insight into the effects of discrimination. We are concerned here with discrimination between two sets of workers who are in every sense equally qualified. Our discussion is phrased in terms of black versus white, but it applies equally to female versus male, alien versus citizen, Catholic versus Protestant, or any other prejudicial basis for dividing workers.

Suppose there are two groups of equal size in a society. One is white; the other is black. Except for color, the groups are the same — each has the same proportion who are educated to various levels, each has identical distributions of talent, and so on. Suppose also that there are two occupations. Occupation E (for elite) requires people of above average education and skills, and occupation O (ordinary) can use anyone, but if wages in the two occupations are the same, employers in occupation O will prefer to hire the above average worker. There is no racial discrimination; everyone is color-blind. The nonmonetary advantages of the two occupations are equal.

The competitive theory of distribution suggests that the wages in E occupations will be bid up slightly above those in O occupations in order that the E jobs attract the workers of above average skills. Whites and blacks of above average skill will flock to E jobs while the others, white and black alike, will have no choice but to seek O jobs. Because skills are equally distributed, each occupation will have half whites and half blacks.

Now we introduce discrimination in its most extreme form. All E occupations are hereafter open only to whites; all O occupations are open to either whites or blacks. The immediate effect is to reduce by 50 percent the supply of job applicants for E occupations (they must be *both* white and above average) and, potentially, to increase by 50 percent the supply of applicants for O jobs (this group includes all blacks and the below average whites).

Wage Level Effects

Suppose, first, that there are no barriers to mobility of labor, that everyone seeks the best job he or she is eligible for, and that wage rates are free to vary so as to equate supply and demand. The analysis is shown in Figure 21-6. Wages rise sharply in E occupations and fall in O occupations. The take-home pay of those in O occupations falls, and while the O group still includes both whites and blacks, it is now approximately two-thirds black.

Discrimination, by changing supply, can decrease the wages and incomes of a group that is discriminated against.

In the longer run, further changes may occur. Notice that total employment in E industries falls. Employers may find ways to utilize slightly below average labor and thus lure the best qualified white workers out of O occupations. While this will raise O wages slightly, it will also make them increasingly "black occupations." An important long-run effect may be that blacks will learn that it no longer pays to acquire above

FIGURE 21-6
Economic Discrimination: Wage Level Effects

(i) Elite market (E)   (ii) Ordinary market (O)

If market E discriminates against one group and market O does not, the supply curve will shift upward in E and downward in O, and wages will rise in E and fall in O. Market E requires above average skills, while market O requires only ordinary skills. When there is no discrimination, demands and supplies are D_E and S_E in market E, and D_O and S_O in market O. Initially, the wage rate is w and employment is q in each market. When all blacks are barred from E occupations, the supply curve shifts to S_E' and the wage earned by the remaining workers, all of whom are white, rises to w_1. Blacks put out of work in the E occupation now seek work in the O occupation. The resulting shift in the supply curve to S_O' brings down the wage to w_2 in the O occupations. Since all blacks are in O occupations, they have a lower wage rate than many whites. The average white wage is higher than the average black wage.

average skills since they are forced by discrimination to work in jobs that do not use them. Yet if they never acquire the skills, they will be locked into the O occupations even if the discriminatory policy is reversed. And their children may conclude that education is for whites only.

Employment Effects

For a number of reasons, labor market discrimination may have adverse employment effects that are even more important than effects on wage levels. Labor is not perfectly mobile, wages are not perfectly flexible downward, and not everyone who is denied employment in an E occupation for which he or she is trained and qualified will be willing to take a "demeaning" O job.

If wages cannot fall to the market-clearing level (say, because of minimum wage laws), the increase in supply of labor to O occupations will cause excess supply and result in unemployment of labor in O occupations. Since, in our model, blacks dominate these occupations, blacks will bear the brunt of the extra unemployment. This is illustrated in Figure 21-7(i). A similar result will occur if labor is not fully mobile between occupations, say because many of the O occupation jobs are in parts of the country to which the workers discriminated against are unable or unwilling to move. See Figure 21-7(ii). Potential O workers who cannot move to where jobs are available become unemployed or withdraw from the labor force.

A different mechanism can produce the identical result if those persons who lose their E jobs

FIGURE 21-7
Economic Discrimination: Employment Effects

(i) Wage rigidities (or minimum wage)   (ii) Immobile labor (or withdrawal from labor force)   (iii) Declining demand

Increasing supply and/or decreasing demand in occupations in which those discriminated against are the major sources of labor can increase unemployment. In each part of the diagram, the curves D_0 and S_0' are those from Figure 21-6(ii); they show the market for O workers after the discriminatory policies are put into effect. In each case the wage w_2 would clear the market and provide employment of q_2.

(i) If the wage rate cannot fall below w_3, perhaps because of a minimum wage law, employment will fall to q_3 and unemployment will occur in the amount shown by the colored arrow.

(ii) If some of the potential workers in O occupations

are unable or unwilling to take employment in O jobs, the supply curve will not be S_0' but S_0''. While O wages will rise somewhat to w_3, employment will be only q_3 and a number of workers, shown by the colored arrow, will not be employed. Whether they are recorded as "unemployed" or as having withdrawn from the labor force will depend on the official definitions.

(iii) If demand is declining in O occupations over time, say from D_0 to D_0', either wages and employment will fall to w_4 and q_4 or wages will be maintained but employment will fall to q_3. The colored arrow illustrates the latter case, where the fall in employment is $q_2 q_3$.

as a result of discrimination withdraw from the labor force. They may do just this if they have the skill and training to do the more respectable and more rewarding E jobs. Indeed, it may be less demeaning to accept unemployment compensation or even welfare than to accept the only jobs that the discriminatory society offers them.

In the long term these unemployment effects may be increased by sociological and economic forces. Children of those discriminated against may well take as role models those who have made a life outside the labor force. Technological changes in the economy tend to decrease the demand for less skilled labor of the kind required in O occupations, which become increasingly

oversupplied. This possibility is sketched in Figure 21-7 (iii).

All these theoretical possibilities have their counterparts in the real world. We shall discuss them briefly with respect to both black/white and female/male differences in the United States.

BLACK-WHITE DIFFERENTIALS IN LABOR MARKETS

The differences in employment and pay rates for blacks and for whites are dramatic and easily measured. By 1980, after more than two decades of vigorous equal employment activity, the median black family had earnings less than 60 per-

Is Economic Discrimination Possible in Competition?

Some argue that the simple E and O model suggested in the text is impossible in a world of competition. Their argument says that E employers would not be so foolish as to refuse to hire qualified black workers whose marginal product exceeded their wage. Any firm that violated the taboo and hired blacks would reduce costs, make profits, and be able to take business from any prejudiced competitor. This argument further says that economic discrimination might exist as a result of monopolies but that it could not exist in a perfectly competitive world.

A monopolistic firm, the argument runs, is in a sheltered position; it can afford to invest some of its owners' monopoly profits in indulging their prejudices by hiring only white employees even if a black could do a given job better than a white. In a truly competitive situation, however, a firm could not afford to discriminate. The fierce winds of competition lead to the survival of only the fittest and thus force firms that want to survive to make choices based solely on considerations of profit. So, the argument goes, if we could only make the economy more competitive and less monopolistic, we would eliminate economic (as contrasted to social or political) discrimination. It is an intriguing idea; is it correct?

If only one employing firm were color prejudiced in a world of otherwise unprejudiced individuals, that firm would suffer by giving in to its prejudices. To maximize profits it needs both to minimize cost—which means hiring the most productive workers available at the going wage rate regardless of color—and to equate marginal cost with marginal revenue without distinguishing between "white marginal revenue" and "black marginal revenue." To distinguish between labor inputs or potential customers on the basis of color would not be profit-maximizing behavior, and the firm that did so discriminate could be driven to bankruptcy by its more efficient competitors.

But consider the other extreme. Assume that there is a single unprejudiced employer in a society of otherwise prejudiced persons. Will it pay the unprejudiced firm to ignore the prejudices of others? If it violated the society's prejudices, the firm's white customers might be so incensed that many would cease to buy from the firm—after all, they have lots of other suppliers to turn to. They may value their prejudices even if it costs them a few cents on the dollar. Similarly, if the employer hired those workers whose productivity was highest regardless of color, it might find that indignant (and prejudiced) white workers would respond with slowdowns and strikes. In that event, production would fall off and costs per unit would rise. In such a world, competition forces the unprejudiced firm to discriminate!

Finally, consider the more realistic case where some people are strongly prejudiced, some are slightly prejudiced, and some have no prejudice at all. A world of perfectly competitive profit maximizers would not eliminate discrimination as long as enough consumers were prejudiced. Most people do not care whether their automobiles are produced with white or black labor; nor do they seem to care about the color of the hands that shine their shoes. But enough people have prejudices about the color of the hands that cut their hair to reduce greatly the demand for black barbers in white areas and to punish severely any integrated barbershop proprietor who hires black barbers. Similarly, discrimination will not be eliminated if a sufficient number of white workers with a choice of where and how to work have racial prejudices about who should be their co-workers. If there is a significant demand for prejudice in a competitive market, there will be a supply of it.

Economic discrimination is not only possible, it may be profitable when there are prejudiced people in the society.

cent of those of the median white family. This figure reflected fewer jobs, lower paying jobs, and more frequent part-time employment. Unemployment among blacks normally runs at more than twice the level for whites—roughly, 13 percent to 6 percent in relatively good times—and in sharp recessions the ratio increases. Among blacks 16 to 19 years old the official unemployment rate was 36 percent in 1979, while a rate adjusted to include those who have given up looking for work after repeated turndowns was 53 percent!

We are talking here about averages. Of course there are some blacks who do as well as or better than their white counterparts in employment opportunities and in pay. But this is true of too few to raise the average black to the economic position of the average white.

Even employed blacks are often disadvantaged. Blacks tend to have less seniority than whites of similar ages, often because of past discrimination. The seniority they do have tends to be in the less skilled, lower paid job categories. Blacks as a group have poorer health, shorter life expectancy, and shorter working lives.

All these characteristics contribute to lower economic status, but not all of them necessarily represent racial discrimination. Many of the disadvantages remain even when there is equal pay for equal work. Whites and blacks have, on average, different educational backgrounds and different sorts of professional or vocational training. Since these too affect employment opportunities and actual pay rates within occupations, is it not possible that they, rather than discrimination, account for the differentials?

To answer this question it is necessary to note that discrimination might be present not only directly (e.g., refusing to hire blacks because they are black) but also indirectly (e.g., refusing to hire blacks because they are not well trained, when training has been denied them because they are black).

Direct discrimination has decreased over the last 25 years. Direct employment discrimination against black athletes ended in that period, and

federal laws have resulted in equal pay for equal work in many industrial jobs. But blatant discrimination undoubtedly survives in some occupations, and a preference for whites still exists in many others.

Indirect discrimination is harder to measure. It is well known that education, training, and aspiration each play an important role in labor market success, and individuals differ in these respects for reasons other than race or sex. White male farm workers earn much less per hour and per lifetime than white male doctors, for reasons not related to discrimination. But prior discrimination may account for differences between blacks and whites in such nondiscriminatory characteristics as occupation and education. One need only recognize that if racial and sexual prejudice and discrimination vanished from the world today, its effects would be felt for generations. A black man whose grandfather and father were illiterate farm workers because they were denied a decent education even after they were freed from slavery is unlikely to have had the opportunity or motivation to get much education himself. For one thing, he will have been needed on the farm to help feed the family. More important, he may have been raised in a culture that failed to see in education either the path to economic opportunity or a desirable end in itself. Even when employers are prepared to treat all applicants equally, blacks are often less skilled in hearing about, applying for, and interviewing for many good jobs.

The Persistence of Black Unemployment

The 1950s and 1960s saw a direct attack on blacks' labor market disabilities as part of a larger federal commitment to affirmative action to reverse the effects of discrimination.

Despite expenditures under the Comprehensive Employment Training Act (CETA) and other federal programs (now running at more than $12 billion per year), employment of blacks has not increased relative to employment of whites. There are a number of well-identified but not easily corrected reasons for this continuing problem. Special training programs do not have much effect on those unused to learning or without basic learning skills. Reinforcing this situation is the steady decline in employment opportunities in the unskilled and semiskilled jobs traditionally open to those with limited education. This decline reflects both increased automation in such heavy industries as automobiles and steel and the rising importance of service industries (as compared to manufacturing).

A further cause is the lesser geographic mobility of poor blacks as many available jobs have tended to move from the central cities to the suburbs and from the older population centers of the North to the sun belt. Among additional reasons are rising minimum wages, which reduce employment opportunities in some unskilled occupations, and some disdain on the part of modern blacks for the lowest paying jobs as being beneath the dignity of people who wish to be treated equally. Finally, it seems unmistakable that the greater labor force participation of women and the deferral of retirement among older workers have increased the competition for jobs. Unfortunately, blacks have often been losers in that competition.

FEMALE-MALE DIFFERENTIALS IN LABOR MARKETS

Women have fared somewhat better under affirmative action than have blacks. Traditionally denied employment in many "male" occupations, adult women in the last three decades have increased their labor force participation from 30 percent in 1950 to more than 50 percent in 1980. (This is still short of the 80 percent participation rate of adult males.) Moreover, the female unemployment rate is only 1 or 2 percent higher than the rate for males. Women have steadily increased their participation in "higher status" occupations, including managerial, sales, scientific, and technical jobs. They have thus done much better than blacks in getting and keeping jobs.

But getting jobs is not the whole story. It has long been clear that women and men make and are offered different occupational choices, that proportionately fewer women than men reach higher paying jobs in the occupations in which both work, and that whose who do, do so more slowly. As a result, average earned income of females in the labor force is well below that of males of similar ages. A number of careful studies have established that in the 1970s labor market earnings were approximately 25 percent lower for employed women than for employed men of the same age and race.

To what extent do these differences reflect discrimination against women and to what extent such other sex-linked characteristics as the voluntary choice of different lifetime patterns of labor force participation? The statistics show that, on average, women have fewer years of education, training, and work experience than men of the same age. The average working female is less mobile occupationally and geographically than her male counterpart. At least some of these facts reflect voluntary choice; for example, many women decide to withdraw from the labor force, or to work only part-time, in order to have and raise children.

Yet direct discrimination against women has been important in labor markets and continues to play a role today. Indeed, some direct discrimination by employers is vigorously defended as being "protective." A striking example came to public attention recently. Four West Virginia women told of having themselves sterilized in order to keep their well-paying jobs in a plant operated by the American Cyanamid Corporation. That company has a policy of removing women of child-bearing age from, or not hiring them for, jobs that expose them to lead or other substances that could damage a fetus. (The Equal Employment Opportunity Commission insists that the solution should be to make the workplace safe for the worker, not to adapt the worker to the unsafe workplace.)

The extent of direct discrimination in an occupation may be measured by taking groups with similar characteristics and comparing their employment and pay status. For example, comparing starting salaries in college teaching of new Ph.D.s from the same graduate schools in a given subject and a given class of institutional employment, Professors Frank Stafford and George Johnson found the average pay of females was about 6 percent below that of males (with allowance for differences in age and prior experience). They attributed this part of a larger male-female pay differential to direct discrimination.

Women have also suffered indirect discrimination. They have been refused admission or discouraged from seeking entry into certain occupations; for example, they have traditionally been pushed into nursing rather than medicine, social work rather than law, and secretarial rather than managerial training programs. Similarly, there is ample evidence that many women in dual career marriages are under substantial pressure to put their husband's job needs first. Girls raised in a culture in which their education seems less important than that of their brothers, or where they are raised to think of themselves as potential homemakers and are urged to prepare themselves to attract and serve a husband, are less likely to acquire the skills or the opportunities for many high-paying forms of employment that are wholly within their capabilities.

Discrimination against women in job opportunities is being eliminated much more quickly than discrimination against racial minorities; the effect of Women's Liberation on attitudes — male as well as female — has been very great in a very short time. Between 1971 and 1979 the fraction of earned doctorates awarded to women rose from 14 to 25 percent and by 1980 nearly half of the new graduate enrollments were women, so this upward trend is likely to continue. In 1979, 15 percent of first professional degrees (law, medicine, etc.) were awarded to women — compared to 6.5 percent eight years earlier. Current enrollments in these fields are roughly 30 percent women. These trends reflect affirmative action on the part of schools, changed attitudes on the part of women, and brighter employment prospects for women than even ten years before.

What accounts for the greater success in eliminating the economic impact of sex discrimination than that of racial discrimination? The economic and educational backgrounds of males and females of the same generation have been much more nearly equal than between blacks and whites of either sex. Moreover, cultural and motivational barriers to women can apparently be changed in a single generation, while such a change may take longer for blacks. It is perhaps also true that sex prejudices in the labor market are less deeply ingrained than racial prejudices. Yet the continuing pay disadvantages of women in the labor force are likely to persist as long as women are less mobile and choose to interrupt their work during child-rearing years.

WHO LOSES FROM DISCRIMINATION?

Obviously, the victims lose as a result of labor market discrimination. To the extent that they are denied employment or receive lower pay than they otherwise would, minorities and women are punished for their race or sex. But it would be a mistake to think that they are the only losers. Society loses too because of the efficiency losses that discrimination causes, and in other ways.

Efficiency losses arise for several reasons. If women or blacks are not given equal pay with white males for equal work, the labor force will not be allocated so as to get the most out of society's resources. When people are kept from doing the jobs at which they are most productive and must instead produce goods or services that society values less, the total value of goods and services produced is reduced. And when prejudice increases unemployment, it reduces the nation's total output.

The gainers from discrimination are those who earn the higher pay that comes from limiting supply in their occupations, those who get the jobs that blacks and women would otherwise have held, and the bigots who gain pleasure from not having to work with "them" or to consume services provided by "them." But if the total output of society is less, the net losses will have to be borne by the society as a whole.

Beyond the efficiency losses that discrimination imposes on society are further economic and social costs. Increased welfare or unemployment payments may be required, and the costs of enforcing antidiscrimination laws must be paid. The costs of discrimination also include increased crime, hostility, and violence. These things are all by-products of unemployment, poverty, and frustration. Discrimination, if not attacked and rolled back, has one more cost, perhaps the most important: a sense of shame in a society that does not do what is necessary to eliminate the barriers to equal treatment.

Summary

1. A wage-setting union entering a competitive market can raise wages, but only at the cost of reducing employment and creating a pool of unsatisfied former workers who would like to work at the going wage but are unable to gain employment.

2. A wage-setting union entering a monopsonistic market may increase both employment and wages over some range. If, however, it sets the wage above the competitive level, it too will create a pool of unsatisfied workers who are unable to get the jobs they want at the going wage.

3. An employers' association is a group of employers who band together for the purpose of adopting a common policy in labor negotiations. A union is an association of workers that speaks for the workers in negotiations with their employers. Unions are subdivided into craft unions and industrial unions. In general, individual union members belong to a local union to which they pay dues (part of which goes to the national union). The local union belongs to a national or international union. A federation is a loose organization of national unions.

4. Three kinds of bargaining arrangements are (a) the open shop, where, though a union represents its members, union membership is not a condition of getting or keeping a job; (b) the closed shop, where only workers who are already union members may be employed; and (c) the union shop, where the employer is free to hire anyone, but where all new employees must join the recognized union within a specified period.

5. American unionism developed first in the skilled trades, along craft lines, where it was possible to control supply and prevent nonunion members from undercutting union wages. Widespread organization of the unskilled did not occur until after the legal right to organize was established by the Wagner Act in 1935. The emergence of mature collective bargaining is a relatively recent development in the stormy and sometimes bloody history of American labor unions.

6. Unions must decide on their goals. There is a basic conflict between the goals of raising wages by restricting supply (thereby reducing the union's employed membership) and preserving employment opportunities for members and potential members. Other trade-offs concern wages and job security, and wages and fringe benefits.

7. Discrimination by race and by sex has played a role in labor markets, as it has in other aspects of American life. Direct discrimination can affect wages and employment opportunities by limiting the supply in the best-paying occupations and increasing it in less attractive occupations. Economic theory leads to the predictions that groups subject to discrimination will earn lower wages and/or suffer higher levels of unemployment than their counterparts who do not suffer discrimination. These predictions are borne out in the labor force experiences of blacks (and other minorities) and women.

8. Precisely how much of the wage and employment differentials between whites and blacks and males and females is due to discrimination is a matter of continuing research. Indirect discrimination has had an effect through limiting the opportunities for education and training available to those subject to discrimination and through lowering people's aspirations in their choices of training and of careers.

9. Affirmative action programs over the past two decades have been more successful in reversing the effects of discrimination against women than against blacks.

10. Discrimination imposes costs on the victims of discrimination. In addition it leads to inefficiency and loss of output and is costly in other ways.

Topics for Review

Monopsony power
Union power
Collective bargaining
Goals of unions
Economic discrimination
Wage effects and employment effects of economic discrimination
Direct and indirect discrimination

Discussion Questions

1. American unions have traditionally supported laws
   a. restricting immigration
   b. expelling illegal aliens
   c. raising the minimum wage and extending its coverage

   Do these positions benefit or hurt (1) the American consumer, (2) American workers as a whole, (3) unionized workers with seniority in their jobs?

2. A union that has bargaining rights in two plants of the same company in different states almost always insists on "equal pay for equal work" in the two plants. It does not always insist on equal pay for men and women in the same jobs. Can you see any economic reasons for such a distinction?

3. Predict the effect of each of the following on the wages of employees in the affected industries. What, if anything, can you say about total earnings of all employees in each case?
   a. an increase in the production of coal due to the increasing shortage of other fossil fuels
   b. passage of a law permitting public employees to bargain collectively and to strike

   c. reducing the apprenticeship period for entry into a skilled trade from five years to two years
   d. making a Ph.D. degree compulsory for all junior college teachers.

4. "The labor of a human being is not a commodity or article of commerce," the Clayton Act states. The context of this statement was a provision that gave labor unions some measure of exemption from antitrust action. Why should wage fixing not be in violation of the antitrust laws when price fixing is?

5. Why were craft unions more successful than industrial unions in the late nineteenth century in the United States? What happened to change this in the 1930s?

6. A labor union that has a union shop contract with a particular employer is in some ways in the same position as a firm that has a monopoly of key raw materials used by the firm. Do you see any differences? Contrast the considerations that enter into the question of the best price (or wage) to charge. Who do you think is in a stronger position to bargain with General Motors, the United Auto Workers or the Goodyear Tire and Rubber Company?

7. Interpret the following statements or practices in terms of the theory of distribution:
   a. a requirement that every passenger train carry a fireman though there may be nothing for him to do
   b. a requirement that one must pass an English language proficiency test to be a carpenter in New York City
   c. a statement of an official of a textile workers union in Massachusetts: "Until we have organized the southern textile industry, we will be unable to earn a decent wage in New England."

8. Suppose it is accepted that, on average, unions have raised the wages of their members. Can this be reconciled with the low and declining percentage of employees who are union members?

9. Interns and residents in many American hospitals are seeking to unionize in an attempt to raise their pay and to shorten the period before they are full-fledged medical practitioners. If they succeed, what effect will this have on the incomes of doctors?

10. "The great increase in the number of women entering the labor force for the first time means that relatively more women than men earn beginning salaries. It is therefore not evidence of discrimination that the average wage earned by females is less than that earned by males." Discuss.

11. "One can judge the presence or absence of discrimination by looking at the proportion of the population

in different occupations." Does such information help? Does it suffice? Consider each of the following examples. Relative to their numbers in the total population, there are:

a. too many blacks and too few Jews among professional athletes

b. too few male secretaries

c. too few female judges

12. "Of nearly 40 million working women, 40 percent are in traditionally female occupations—secretaries, nurses, cashiers, waitresses, elementary school teachers, beauticians, maids, and sales clerks, for example. While this may result from past sex stereotyping, the notion that only a woman can do these jobs may also benefit women by preserving employment opportunities for them, given the high unemployment rates among black males and teenage males." Discuss this argument.

Interest and the Return on Capital

22

To many Marxists, the capitalist is a villain. To many socialists, the capitalist is at best a dispensable drone. To many liberals, capitalists are an important part of the production process, as necessary as farmers and factory workers. To many conservatives, the capitalist is a hero who steers the economy through the risky channels that lead to ever higher living standards.

A capitalist is nothing more than someone who owns capital, which we have defined as all man-made aids to further production. A key characteristic of capital is that it is durable. This means that it has two prices associated with it. The first is the price at which ownership of the capital good may be purchased. The second is the price at which its services may be hired for a period of time. This is called the rental price of capital.

At the outset let us deal with three common misconceptions.

First, capital itself is neither villain nor dispensable drone in the productive process. None but the most extreme and unrealistic members of the back-to-nature school would disagree. A primitive society in which there are no capital goods—no spear, no lever, no stone for grinding grain, no jug for carrying water—has never occurred in recorded human history.

Second, payment for the use of capital, while not necessary, serves such important functions that it would be hard to eliminate it without serious consequences. Early Communist rulers thought differently. Such payments were officially barred during the years following the Russian Revolution of 1917. The trouble with doing this, however, is that capital is scarce;

most producers would like to have more of it than they have. If capital has no price, the available supply must somehow be allocated among the competing demands for it. The state, of course, can allocate it. But how? Any state that is interested in maximizing production will want to allocate scarce capital to its most productive uses. One effective way of doing this is to assign a "price" to capital that is meant to reflect its productivity and to allow firms to use more capital only if the capital earns enough to cover this price. Today all Communist states do this. Furthermore, their planners give a good deal of attention to setting the correct price for capital.

Third, capital does not need to be in private hands, with the price paid for capital being income for its private owners. In many Communist countries capital is owned by the state, and payments for its use go to the state rather than to private "capitalists." The desirability of private versus public ownership of the "means of production" (the term often used in socialist and Communist literature to describe capital) is still debated hotly, a matter that economic analysis has not resolved.

Capital is indispensable in any modern economy, and its efficient use requires that it be priced. When capital is privately owned, payment of its price contributes to the income of its owners; when it is publicly owned, payment of its price contributes to the revenues of the state.

The Productivity or Efficiency of Capital

In what sense is capital productive? To be productive it must lead to higher output than could be possible without it. Rarely if ever does anyone make a consumer good with the aid of only such simple tools as nature provides. Productive effort goes first into the manufacture of capital—the tools, machines, and other goods that are desired not for themselves but as aids to making other commodities. The capital goods are then used to make consumers' goods. The use of capital renders production processes roundabout. Instead of making what is wanted directly, producers engage in the indirect process of first making capital goods that are then used to make consumer goods.

In many cases production is very roundabout indeed. For example, a worker may be employed in a factory that makes machines that are used in mining coal; the coal may be burned by a power plant to make electricity; the electricity may provide power for a factory that makes machine tools; the tools may be used to make a tractor; the tractor may be used by a potato farmer to help in the production of potatoes; and the potatoes may be eaten by consumers. This kind of indirect production is worthwhile when the farmer, using a tractor, can produce more potatoes than could be produced by applying all the factors of production involved in the chain directly to the production of potatoes (using only such tools as were provided by nature). In fact, the roundabout capital-using method of production very often leads to more output than the direct method. The difference between the flows of output that would result from the two methods is called either the **productivity of capital** or the **efficiency of capital.**

The extra output, however, is not achieved without cost.

Generally speaking, a decision to increase the amount of capital available entails a present sacrifice and a future gain.

The present sacrifice occurs because resources are diverted from producing consumption goods to producing capital goods. The future gain occurs because in the long run production will be higher with the new capital than without it (even after allowing for maintenance and replacement of capital goods).

THE RATE OF RETURN ON CAPITAL

Whenever capital is productive, its use must yield a return in excess of the amounts required to cover the costs associated with all other fac-

Human Capital

While capital goods are usually discussed in terms of tangible assets such as buildings or machines, the notion of a capital asset as something that produces an increase in the stream of future output suggests another sort of capital good. Consider a high school graduate who has enough schooling to get and keep a job. Instead of taking a job, however, she elects to go to college, and possibly to graduate or professional school. During her college career, her contribution to society's current output is small (only a summer job perhaps), but because of her education, her lifetime contribution to production may be substantially larger than it would have been had she taken a job after high school.

The choice of whether to take a job now or to continue one's education has all the basic elements of an investment decision, and it is useful to regard the student as making an investment to acquire capital. Because the capital is embodied in a person—in terms of greater skills, knowledge, and the like—rather than in a machine, this is known as acquiring **human capital.** Major elements of human capital are health and education of all sorts. An ex-

tended education program requires, for example, that resources be withdrawn from the production of goods for current consumption; the resources include materials in the school, the services of the teachers, and the time and talents of the pupils. The education is productive if the difference between the value of the lifetime output of the trained worker and the lifetime output of the untrained one exceeds the value of the resources—teachers, buildings, and so on—used up in training her. If so, education increases the value of total production of the economy.

The payoff to education as an investment in human capital has been studied extensively, and many investigators have concluded that investment in higher education pays, in the sense just defined. Of course, education also has other payoffs; it may be valued for cultural or social reasons, and it may bestow benefits or costs on individuals other than those who are educated. But the fact that it may be more than a capital investment does not prevent it from being an investment. The same is true of a painting by Rembrandt.

tors of production. This return is merely a measure of the productivity or efficiency of capital. How is it determined? Take the receipts from the sale of the goods produced by a firm and subtract the appropriate costs for purchased goods and materials, for labor, for land, and for the manager's own contributed talents. Subtract also an allowance for the taxes the firm will have to pay, and what is left may be called the **gross return to capital.**

It is convenient to divide gross return into four components.

1. **Depreciation** is an allowance for the decrease in the value of a capital good as a result of using it in production.

2. The **pure return on capital** is the amount that capital could earn in a riskless investment in equilibrium.

3. The **risk premium** compensates the owners for the actual risks of the enterprise.

4. **Economic profit** is the residual after all other deductions have been made from the gross return. It may be positive, negative, or zero.

The items in this list are related as follows. The productivity of capital is its gross return minus its depreciation. This is also called the net return on capital and it is composed of items 2, 3, and 4 in the list. The opportunity cost of capital is composed of the first three items. In equilibrium the gross return on capital must be just enough to cover its opportunity cost, but item 4 will be zero. In a market economy, positive and negative economic profits are a signal that resources should be reallocated because earnings exceed opportunity costs in some lines of production and fall short of them in other lines. Profits are thus a phenomenon of disequilibrium.

In order to study the return to capital in its simplest form, we consider an economy that is in equilibrium with respect to the allocation of existing factors of production among all their possible uses. Thus economic profits are zero in every productive activity. This does not mean that the owners of capital get nothing; it means rather that the gross return to capital does not now include a profit element that signals the need to reallocate resources.

To simplify further at the outset, we assume that there is no risk in this economy. Consequently the gross return to capital does not include a risk premium.

We have now simplified to the point where the net return to capital is all pure return (item 2 on the previous list), while the gross return is pure return plus depreciation (items 1 and 2). What determines the size of the pure return on capital? Why is it high in some time periods and low in others? What causes it to change?

In discussing such questions, it is usual to deal with a rate of return *per dollar* of capital. This concept requires placing a money value on a unit of capital (the "price of capital goods") and a money value on the stream of earnings resulting from the productivity of capital. If we let X stand for the annual value of the gross return on a unit of capital, and P for the price of a unit of capital, the ratio X/P may be defined as the **rate of return on capital.** As a preliminary to understanding the determinants of the rate of return on capital, we must define two key concepts: marginal efficiency of capital and present value.

The Marginal Efficiency of Capital

It is convenient to think of society as having a quantity of capital that can be measured in physical units. The term **capital stock** refers to this total quantity of capital.[1] As with any other factor of production, there is an average and a marginal productivity of capital. The marginal productivity of capital is the contribution to output of the last unit of capital added to a fixed quantity of other factors.

Marginal productivity is a physical measure, the amount of output per unit of capital. To obtain a value measure we value the output and the capital at their market prices and express one as a ratio of the other. This gives the monetary return on the marginal dollar's worth of capital and it is called the **marginal efficiency of capital** *(MEC)*.[2] A schedule that relates the rate of return on each additional dollar of capital stock to the size of the capital stock is called the **marginal efficiency of capital schedule.** The *MEC* schedule is constructed on the assumptions that the society's population is fixed and that *technology is unchanging*. These assumptions are made in order to focus on changes in the quantity of capital, other things remaining equal. As more and more capital is accumulated, with unchanging technical knowledge and population, the ratio of capital to labor increases. This is called **capital deepening.** To see why it occurs, consider the difference between a single firm and the whole economy.

When a single firm wants to expand output, it can buy another piece of land, build a factory identical to the one it now has, and hire new labor to operate the new plant. In this way, the

[1] The idea of stock of capital being measured by a single number is a simplification. Society's stock of capital goods is made up of factories, machines, bridges, roads, and other man-made aids to further production. For expository purposes, it is useful to assume that all these can be reduced to some common unit and summed to obtain a measure of the society's *physical* stock of capital.

[2] Like the other *marginal* concepts that we have encountered, the *MEC* is the ratio of two changes. In this case, it is the change in the return of capital divided by the change in the capital stock that brought it about.

firm can replicate what it already has. Since each worker in the new factory can be given the same amount of capital to work with as each worker in the old factory, output per worker and per unit of capital can remain unchanged as output rises. Increasing the quantity of capital without changing the proportions of factors used is called **capital widening.**

For the economy as a whole, capital widening is possible only as long as there are unemployed quantities of labor and other factors of production. Additional workers, for example, must be drawn from somewhere. In a fully employed economy, what one small firm can do the whole economy cannot do. If the size of the capital stock is to increase while the total labor force remains constant, the amount of capital per worker must increase. Capital deepening must occur.

What is the effect of capital deepening on the marginal efficiency of capital? Because capital is subject to diminishing returns, as are all other factors of production, the amount of output per unit of capital will fall as capital deepening occurs. Each unit of capital has, as it were, fewer units of labor to work with than previously. As more and more capital deepening occurs, the marginal return to capital declines. The *MEC* schedule when plotted graphically is thus downward-sloping (see Figure 22-1).

A Recapitulation of Terminology

The theory of capital can seem quite bewildering on first acquaintance because there are so many terms that mean almost the same thing. Let us review the standard terminology. The *productivity* and the *efficiency* of capital are the same thing; they are measured for a firm by the *return on its capital.* This return is usually measured as an amount per dollar's worth of capital, which makes it a *rate of return on capital.* This rate may be calculated as an average over all capital, in which case it is called the *average efficiency of capital* (or *average rate of return*); or it may be calculated on the last unit of capital, in which

FIGURE 22-1
The Marginal Efficiency of Capital

The *MEC* curve shows the relation between the size of the capital stock and the rate of return on the marginal unit of capital. The *MEC* schedule slopes downward because of the hypothesis of diminishing returns applied to capital. Each successive unit of capital adds less to output than each previous unit. Thus the curve, which relates the value of the additional output of each additional dollar's worth of capital added to the capital stock, is downward-sloping.

case it is called the *marginal efficiency of capital* (or *marginal rate of return*). The *MEC* schedule relates the rate of return on the marginal unit of capital to the total capital stock. It shows that as the total stock grows the marginal return on each additional unit declines.

The Present Value of Future Returns

The efficiency of capital takes the form of producing a stream of output extending into the future that, as it is sold, yields a stream of gross returns to the firm. How is the price of capital related to the efficiency of capital? To know what price a firm would be willing to pay for a piece of capital, we must be able to put a present value on the stream of gross returns that the capital will yield to the firm.

We assume first that the price level is constant; later we consider the effects of inflation.

The value of a single future payment. How much would you be prepared to pay *now* to acquire the right to receive $100 in cash in one year's time? Say the interest rate on savings accounts is 5 percent. How much would you have to deposit in a savings bank now in order to have $100 a year from now? It would surely not be profitable for you to pay more than such an amount. Alternatively, what is the most you could borrow today in return for your promise to repay $100 in one year if the interest rate is 5 percent?

Both approaches can be reduced to the question, how much money *now* is equivalent to $100 in one year's time if the interest rate is 5 percent? Letting X stand for this unknown amount, we can write $X(1.05) = \$100$. Thus $X = \$100/1.05 = \$95.24$, which tells us that the value today of $100 next year is $95.24 if the interest rate is 5 percent. That sum is said to be the present value of $100 next year. In general, the term **present value (PV)** refers to the value now of a payment, or payments, to be made in the future.

The particular numerical value depends on the interest rate used to "discount" (i.e., reduce to its present value) the $100 to be received one year hence. If the interest rate is 7 percent, the present value of the $100 receivable next year is $100/1.07 = \$93.45$. In general, the present value of X dollars one year hence at an interest rate if i per year is

$$PV = \frac{X}{(1 + i)}$$

(Note that in this expression a rate of interest of 5 percent is written $i = .05$, so that $1 + i$ is 1.05.)

One hundred dollars two years hence has a present value (at an interest rate of 5 percent) of

$$\frac{\$100.00}{(1.05)(1.05)} = \$90.70$$

because $90.70 put in a savings bank now would be worth $100 in two years. In general, we may write, for the present value of X dollars after t years at i percent,

$$PV = \frac{X}{(1 + i)^t}$$

The present value of a given sum will be smaller, the further away is the payment date and the higher is the rate of interest.

The value of an infinite stream of payments. So much for a single sum payable in the future; now consider the present value of a stream of income that continues indefinitely. At first that might seem very high since as time passes the total received grows without reaching any limit. Consideration of the previous section suggests, however, that a person will not value highly payments that are far in the future. To find the present value of $100 a year, payable forever, we need only ask how much money would have to be invested now at an interest rate of i percent per year to obtain $100 each year. This is simply $i \times X = \$100$, where i is the interest rate and X the sum required. This tells us that the present value of the stream of $100 forever (called an **annuity** of $100) is

$$PV = \frac{\$100}{i}$$

If the interest rate were 10 percent ($i = .10$), present value would be $1,000, which is another way of saying that $1,000 invested at 10 percent would yield $100 per year, forever. Notice that *PV* here, as above, is *inversely* related to the rate of interest. The higher the interest rate, the less is the present value of any stream of payments that goes on forever.

If you can buy an asset at its present value, the investment will yield neither gain nor loss. For example, if you buy an annuity conferring the right to receive $100 a year forever for $1,000, and borrow the capital at an interest rate of 10 percent, annual receipts ($100) and interest payments ($100) will be exactly offsetting.

THE VALUE OF AN ASSET

Many assets are valued only because of the streams of income they are expected to produce.[3]

[3] Assets can yield utilities in forms other than income streams. A painting, a house, and valuable jewelry are cases in point. They may be regarded as yielding a stream of utilities each of which could be given a monetary value.

For any such asset, its value will tend to be equal to the present value of the income stream produced. This is often called the **capitalized value** of the asset producing the income stream.

Every expected income stream can be reduced to a present value. In the previous section we considered finding the present values of amounts at specific future dates and of infinite streams of income. All actual streams of income can be treated as the sum or difference of such streams and amounts; thus the present value of *any* stream of future payments can be computed.[4] As a result, the capitalized value of an asset can always be computed.

What then determines the market price of any existing asset that will produce a stream of output over time? The asset might be a piece of land, a machine, a contract for a baseball player's services, or an apartment house. The asset produces a stream of output, and market conditions will determine the price of this output. This allows us to convert the stream of output into an equivalent stream of money. But we know how to calculate the present value of a stream of money, and this is what people will be willing to pay for it. Thus:

The equilibrium market price of the asset will be equal to the capitalized value of the asset—which is equal to the present value of the stream of gross returns associated with it.

A Theory of Interest Rate Determination

Given the concepts just discussed, we can develop a theory that relates *MEC* for the economy as a whole to the rate of interest. It is helpful to begin with the behavior of an individual firm.

---

[4] For example, receiving $100 per year for three years can be considered either as the present value of $100 next year plus the *PV* of $100 two years hence plus the *PV* of $100 three years hence, or as the *difference* between the *PV* of $100 received each year from now to infinity and the *PV* of $100 received from year four to infinity.

THE DEMAND FOR ADDITIONAL CAPITAL BY A FIRM

Suppose that for $8,000 a firm can purchase a machine that yields gross returns of $1,000 a year into the indefinite future. Also suppose that the firm can borrow (and lend) money at an interest rate of 10 percent. The present value of the stream of returns produced by the machine is $1,000/0.10 = $10,000; the present value of $8,000 now is of course $8,000. Clearly the firm can make money by purchasing the machine.

Another way to see this is to suppose that the firm has only two uses for its money: to buy the machine or to lend out the $8,000 at 10 percent interest. It will pay to buy the machine, for the firm can do so and earn $1,000 a year net, while if it lends the $8,000 at 10 percent, it will earn only $800 per year.

To restate the argument in more general terms: If X is the annual stream of gross returns produced by the machine, if P is its purchase price, and if i is the interest rate that correctly states the opportunity cost of capital to the firm, then the capital good should be purchased if

$$\frac{X}{i} > P$$

The term X/i is the present value of the stream of returns produced by the capital good; in other words, the capitalized value of the asset.

It pays to purchase a capital good whenever the present value of its future stream of gross returns is greater than the purchase price of the capital good.

This relationship can be looked at in another way by rearranging terms in the above algebraic inequality to yield:

$$\frac{X}{P} > i$$

The expression X/P shows the annual gross returns produced by the capital good as a fraction of the price of the good. Earlier we defined this as the rate of return on the capital and called it *MEC*. In this form the condition is restated to say:

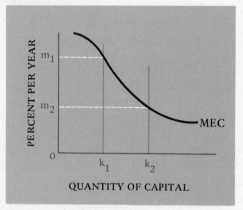

FIGURE 22-2
The Equilibrium Rate of Interest for a Fixed Capital Stock

The rate of interest tends toward the MEC. When the economy has a stock of capital of k_1, the rate of interest will tend toward m_1. If the stock of capital grows to k_2, the interest rate will tend to fall to m_2. Alternatively, k_1 and k_2 could be the capital stock in two otherwise similar economies. The interest rate would be higher in the economy where capital was scarce than in the economy where capital was plentiful.

It pays to purchase a capital good whenever its MEC is greater than the interest rate that could be earned on the money invested in it.[5]

The firm will go on investing in new capital equipment as long as its rate of return, the *MEC*, exceeds the opportunity cost of capital, *i*. *MEC* declines as the firm's capital stock rises, and the firm will reach equilibrium with respect to its capital stock when *MEC* is equal to *i*.

THE ECONOMY AS A WHOLE

Assume for the moment that the interest rate is free to vary and that the only demand to borrow money is from firms seeking funds to invest in new capital equipment. The whole economy has an *MEC* schedule showing how the return on the marginal dollar of new capital declines as the capital stock grows. This *MEC* schedule represents the market demand curve for capital (since each firm will wish to acquire capital until *MEC* = *i*).

A Fixed Stock of Capital

Since the existing stock of capital can be changed only very slowly, we may take the stock as fixed over short-term periods. This stock will have an *MEC* that determines the amount that can be made by investing in a bit more capital. If the rate of interest were lower than this, there would be a rush to borrow money for profitable investment and the rate would be bid up. When the capital stock, technical knowledge—and hence the *MEC*—are given, the interest rate will tend to equal the *MEC* in equilibrium. This is illustrated in Figure 22-2.

A Growing Stock of Capital

Over time, firms and households save and invest in new capital equipment, causing the capital stock to grow. This is shown in Figure 22-2 by a rightward shifting of the vertical line indicating the given capital stock. This has the effect of reducing both the marginal efficiency of capital and the equilibrium interest rate, as shown in Figure 22-2. In an economy with static technology and fixed supplies of land and labor, capital accumulation will tend to lower the marginal efficiency of capital and the rate of interest.

The growth of technical knowledge provides new productive uses for capital. This tends to push the *MEC* schedule outward and *ceteris paribus* will raise *MEC and* the rate of interest.

The accumulation of capital tends to lower the interest rate and the marginal efficiency of capital. The growth of technical knowledge tends to raise both rates.[6]

---

[5] In this chapter we assume that the rate of interest reflects the opportunity cost of capital to the firm. We saw on page 179 that this may not always be the case. When the market rate of interest and the firm's own opportunity cost of capital diverge, the *MEC* must be equated to the latter, not the former.

[6] Graphs illustrating the two effects will be found on page 813.

The Pure and the Market Rates of Interest

The above discussion refers to what is called the **pure rate of interest.** This is the rate of interest that would rule in equilibrium in a riskless economy when all lending and borrowing is to provide funds for investing in productive capital. The discussion allows us to isolate the influences that the size of the capital stock and the efficiency of capital exert on the interest rate.

The actual interest rate ruling at any moment of time is called the **market rate of interest.** This rate will be influenced by the pure rate, but it will diverge from the pure rate because it is influenced by additional forces that do not influence the pure rate.

FURTHER DETERMINANTS OF THE MARKET RATE OF INTEREST

Other Demands for Money to Borrow

Households borrow money to buy goods on time and to buy houses and financial assets such as stocks and bonds. State and local governments borrow to build highways and schools. The federal government borrows to finance part of its expenditures. Each of these is a major component of the aggregate demand for funds to borrow.

Government Control of Interest Rates

Not only is the government a borrower of funds, it also affects the supply of funds available for lending. (We shall see how it does this when we study monetary policy in Chapter 35.) Governments commonly influence the rate of interest for purposes of public policy.

Bank Administration of Interest Rates

The rate of interest does not fluctuate in response to every minor fluctuation in demand and supply. As a result, the interest rate is not always determined in such a way as to equate i with MEC. Banks, for example, consider many factors when they fix the rate of interest that they charge on loans. They are reluctant to change these rates every time changes occur in the demand for money to borrow. If there is an excess demand for loanable funds (perhaps because the MEC is much greater than the interest rate), banks, rather than raise the interest rate, will often ration the available supply of funds among their customers. In doing this they follow such criteria as the borrower's credit rating, how long the banker has known the borrower, and the amount of business the borrower does. This is called **credit rationing.** It is commonly found in lending institutions in most Western countries. When the market rate of interest is below the pure return on capital, money will appear "tight" — hard to borrow — to the typical business person.

Expectations About Business Conditions

In discussing the willingness of firms to borrow money and invest it in capital goods, we have stressed the relation between the rate of interest and the marginal efficiency of capital. Even though capital is physically productive in the sense that more can be produced with it than without it, no one will wish to invest in new equipment if there is no demand for the products produced by the capital goods. In times of severe business depression, the demand to borrow and invest money may fall to very low levels as a result of a declining demand by households for consumption goods.

Market expectations are incorporated in the marginal efficiency framework by recognizing that the efficiency of capital is measured in terms of the *values* (not the quantities) of goods it produces and that these values depend on people's willingness to buy the goods. The MEC is probably very elastic in a fully employed economy so that a small reduction in the rate of interest will lead to a large increase in investment in new capital. When a depression develops, however, and the output of existing capital cannot be sold, it might not be worth borrowing money for new investment even at very low rates of interest. In either case it is expectations about future events that matter.

The Rate of Inflation

An inflation means that the purchasing power of money is falling. When this occurs, it becomes very important to distinguish between the real rate and the money rate of interest. The **money rate of interest** is measured simply in dollars paid. If you pay me $8 interest for a $100 loan for one year, the money rate is 8 percent.

Consider further my $100 loan to you at 8 percent. The real rate that I earn depends on what happens to the overall level of prices in the economy. If the price level remains constant over the year, then the real rate that I earn will also be 8 percent. This is because I can buy 8 percent more real goods and services with the $108 that you repay me than with $100 that I lent you. However, if the price level were to rise by 8 percent, the real rate would be zero because the $108 you repay me will buy the same quantity of real goods as did the $100 I gave up. If I were unlucky enough to have lent money at 8 percent in a year in which prices rose by 10 percent, the real rate would be minus 2 percent.

The real rate of interest concerns the ratio of the purchasing power of the money returned to the purchasing power of the money borrowed, and it may be different from the money rate. The **real rate of interest** is the *difference* between the money rate of interest and the rate of change of the price level.

If lenders and borrowers are concerned with the real costs measured in terms of purchasing power, the money rate of interest will be set at the real rate they require plus an amount to cover any *expected* rate of inflation. Consider a one-year loan that is meant to earn a real return to the lender of 5 percent. If the expected rate of inflation is zero, the money rate set for the loan will also be 5 percent. However, if a 10 percent inflation is expected, the money rate will have to be set at 15 percent.

To provide a given expected real rate of interest, the money rate will have to be set at the desired real rate of interest plus the expected annual rate of inflation.

This point is often overlooked; as a result people are surprised at the high money rates of interest that exist during periods of rapid inflation. For example, when the Federal Reserve System (the U.S. monetary authority) raised money rates of interest drastically in 1979, many commentators expressed shock at the "unbearably" high rates. Most of them failed to notice that with inflation running at about 12 percent, an interest rate of 15 percent represented a real rate of only 3 percent. Had the Fed given in to the heavy pressure to hold interest rates to the more "reasonable" level of 10 percent, it would have been imposing a negative real rate of interest. Lenders would then have been rewarded for lending their money by receiving back less purchasing power in interest plus principal than the purchasing power of the principal they parted with initially.

When an inflation is fully expected, the money rate can be set to give any desired real rate of interest. Problems arise, however, when the inflation rate changes unexpectedly. Consider a loan contract that the parties wish to carry a 3 percent real rate of interest. If a 7 percent inflation rate is expected, the money rate will be set at 10 percent. But what if the inflationary expectations turn out to be wrong? If the inflation rate is only 4 percent, the real rate of interest will be 6 percent. If the inflation rate is 12 percent, the real rate of interest will be minus 2 percent.

Unexpected changes in the rate of inflation cause the real rate of interest on contracts already drawn up to vary in unexpected ways. An unexpected fall in the inflation rate is beneficial to lenders; an unexpected rise is beneficial to borrowers.

The Significance of Multiple Influences

Because the market rate of interest is influenced by many factors other than the demand to borrow money for new investment, the market rate can diverge from the pure rate set by the *MEC*. If the market rate is well below the *MEC*; there will be a heavy desire to borrow and invest in new capital; the stock of capital will then grow, and the *MEC* will begin to fall toward the market rate of interest. However, if the market rate is held above the *MEC*, there will be little or no desire to borrow to invest in new capital. Capital may not even be replaced as it wears out. As the capital stock shrinks, the *MEC* will rise toward the market rate of interest.

In general there is a tendency for the interest rate and the marginal efficiency of capital to be drawn toward each other.

Since the stock of capital (and thus the *MEC*) can change only slowly, most of the short-term adjustment is done by the interest rate. If however, the interest rate were fixed, the *MEC* would change to adjust to it. One way or the other, there is a tendency for the two rates to come together.

A COMPLICATION: MANY RATES OF INTEREST

In the real world there are many different rates of interest. Speaking in terms of a single rate can be a valid simplification for many purposes because the whole set of rates *tends* to move upward or downward together. Concentrating on one "typical" rate as "the" rate of interest in such cases is quite acceptable. For some purposes, however, it is important to take into account the multiplicity of interest rates.

At the same time that you receive an interest rate of 6 or 7 percent on deposits at a savings and loan association, you may have to pay 11 or 12 percent to borrow from that savings and loan association to buy a house. Interest rates on consumer installment credit of 16 percent and 20 percent are observed. A small firm pays a higher interest rate on funds it borrows from banks than does a giant corporation. Different government bonds pay different rates of interest, depending on the length of the period for which the bond runs. Corporate bonds tend to pay higher interest than government bonds, and there is much varia-

tion among bonds of different companies. Considering the extreme mobility of money, why do such differences exist? Why do funds not flow between different uses to eliminate these differences? The answer is that money does flow quite rapidly between alternative assets in response to relevant interest differentials, but differences prevail because quoted interest rates are composites of many things.

Differences in risk. Corporate bonds generally have higher interest rates than U.S. government bonds because they carry a greater degree of risk. At one point in 1970, bonds of Ling-Temco-Vought (LTV) were selling at a price that made their "interest rate" more than 50 percent per year at the same time that some U.S. government bonds were yielding only 8 percent. Why? Investors were sure of the ability of the U.S. government to pay both the interest and the principal on its bonds, but they were less sure about LTV, which was having financial difficulties in 1970. Much of the high interest rate on LTV bonds was a risk premium. By 1976 the effective rate of interest on LTV bonds had declined to about 12 percent. Clearly investors had become much happier with LTV's financial position and were no longer demanding the enormous risk premium that they required in 1970.

Secured loans, where the borrower pledges an asset as collateral, tend to have lower interest rates than unsecured loans, other things being equal. Loans secured by houses (mortgages) tend to have lower interest rates than loans secured by automobiles, in part because it is harder to run away with a house than with a car and in part because a car can depreciate much more rapidly and unpredictably than a house.

Differences in duration. The *term* (duration) of a loan may likewise affect its price. The same bank will usually pay a higher rate of interest on a certificate of deposit that cannot be redeemed at the bank (without penalty) for at least one year than on a straight savings account, which can be withdrawn in a matter of minutes. Yet many savers prefer savings accounts because they want to be able to withdraw their money on short notice. Except when interest rates are thought to be temporarily abnormally high, borrowers are usually willing to pay more for long-term loans than for short-term loans because they are certain of having use of the money for a longer period. Lenders usually require a higher rate of interest the longer is the time before the borrower must repay. Other things being equal, the shorter the term of a loan, the lower are the interest rates.

Differences in costs of administering credit. There is great variation in the cost of different kinds of credit transactions. It is almost as cheap (in actual dollars) for a bank to lend United Airlines $1 million that the airline agrees to pay back with interest after one year as it is for the same bank to lend you $4,000 to buy a new car on an installment loan that you agree to pay back over two years in 24 equal installments.

The loan to you requires many more bookkeeping entries than the loan to the airline. In addition, it is easier, and therefore less costly, to check United Airlines' credit rating than it is to check yours. The difference in the cost *per dollar* of each loan is considerable. The bank may very well make less profit per dollar on a $4,000 loan at 20 percent per year than on a $1 million loan at 10 percent per year. In general, the bigger the loan and the fewer the payments, the less the cost per dollar of servicing the loan. Why then do banks and finance companies usually insist that you repay a loan in frequent installments? They worry that if you do not pay regularly, you will not have the money when the loan comes due.

In the market for borrowed funds there will be a structure of interest rates for credit transactions of different kinds.

Individual rates will be set that take into account such factors as risk premiums, duration of loan, and costs of administration. Nevertheless, it is useful and usual to talk about movements of interest rate structures up and down as changes in "the" interest rate. This simplification is most useful when the entire structure of rates moves up or down together so that changes in a single typical rate can capture changes in all rates.

Sources of Funds for Investment

So far in this chapter we have considered financing investment only with borrowed money. But loans are just one of several sources of finance available to firms for new investment. Most firms use several sources; a profit-maximizing firm that is free to do so will obtain funds from each source until the marginal cost of the last dollar obtained from each is the same.[7] (Otherwise the firm could reduce costs by shifting from higher-cost sources of funds to lower-cost sources.) The analysis of the first part of the chapter can now be generalized. When the *MEC* exceeds the cost of obtaining funds for new investment, firms will try to raise funds not only by borrowing but by tapping their other main sources of funds. When the *MEC* is less than the opportunity cost of capital, the demand for new investment funds from all sources will be low or nonexistent.

FINANCING THE MODERN CORPORATION

The most important ways in which firms obtain funds for new investment are (1) offering shares, stocks, or equities (as they are variously called) for private or public sale; (2) borrowing by the sale of bonds; (3) borrowing from banks; and (4) reinvesting the firm's profits.

The money that a firm raises for carrying on its business is sometimes called its **money capital** as distinct from its **real capital**, the physical assets that constitute plant, equipment, and inventories. Money capital may be broken down into **equity capital**, provided by the owners, and **debt**, which

---

[7] If a firm could get all the funds it wished from each source at constant marginal costs, it would use only the cheapest source. But firms usually face rising marginal costs of funds from each source, and thus they typically obtain funds from many sources.

consists of the funds borrowed from persons who are not owners of the firm.

The use of the term "capital" to refer to both an amount of money and a quantity of goods can be confusing, but it is usually clear from the context whether a sum of money or a stock of equipment is being referred to. The two uses are not independent of each other, for much of the money capital raised by a firm will be used to purchase the capital goods that the firm requires for production.

STOCKS AND STOCKHOLDERS

The owners of the firm are its **stockholders**—persons who have put up money to purchase shares in the firm. They make their money available to the firm and risk losing it in return for a share in the firm's profits. Stocks in a firm often proliferate into a bewildering number of types. Basically, however, there is common stock and preferred stock.

Common stock usually carries voting rights and has only a residual claim on profits. After all other claims have been met, the remaining profits, if any, belong to the common stockholders. There is no legal limit to the profits that may be earned by the company and therefore no limit to potential dividends that may be paid out to common stockholders. Firms are not obliged by law to pay out any fixed portion of their profits as dividends, and in fact the practice among corporations as to the payout ratio varies enormously. Firms sometimes pay out a large fraction and hold back only enough to meet contingencies; at other times they pay small or no dividends in order to reinvest retained funds in the enterprise.

The basic difference between **preferred stock** and common stock is that preferred stock carries with it a right to a preference over common stock to any profits that may be available after other obligations have been met. If profits are earned, the corporation is obliged to pay a dividend to preferred stockholders, but there is a stated maximum to the rate of dividends that will be paid per dollar originally invested.

BONDS AND BONDHOLDERS

Bondholders are creditors, not owners, of the firm. They have loaned money to the firm in return for a **bond,** which is a promise to pay a stated sum of money each year by way of interest on the loan and to repay the loan at a stated time in the future (say 10, 20, or 30 years hence). This promise to pay is a legal obligation on the firm's part whether or not profits have been made. If these payments cannot be met, the bondholders can force the firm into bankruptcy. Should this happen, the bondholders have a claim on the firm's assets prior to that of the stockholders. Only when the bondholders and all other creditors have been repaid in full can the stockholders attempt to recover anything for themselves.

A major disadvantage to the corporation of raising capital through the sale of bonds is that interest payments must be met whether or not there are profits. Many a firm that would have survived a temporary crisis had all its capital been share capital has been forced into bankruptcy because it could not meet its contractual obligations to pay interest to its bondholders.

LOANS FROM FINANCIAL INSTITUTIONS

Much of a firm's short-term and some of its long-term monetary needs are met through bank loans. This is true of giant corporations as well as of small businesses. Indeed, making commercial and industrial loans is one of the major activities of the banking system (which we shall discuss in Chapter 33). Banks, however, limit the amounts they are willing to lend companies, typically to specified fractions of the companies' total financial needs.

Many small businesses that are not well established cannot sell stocks to the public, nor can they raise all the funds they require from banks. Such companies often seek funds from other financial institutions such as insurance companies and small loan companies, usually at higher rates of interest. Several government agencies, such as the Small Business Administration, have been established to help them get access to funds at "reasonable" rates. Generally, term (i.e., short-term) borrowing tends to be expensive. Firms prefer to raise money capital in other ways for long-term purposes.

REINVESTED PROFITS

Another important source of funds for the established firm is the reinvesting, or plowing back, of the firm's own profits. One of the easiest ways for the firm to raise money is to retain some of its own profits rather than pay them out as dividends. Reinvestment has become an extremely important source of funds in modern times; about $30 billion per year is plowed back into U.S. firms. The shareholder who does not wish his or her profits to be reinvested can do very little about it except to sell the stock and invest in a company with a policy of paying out a larger fraction of its dividends.

SECURITIES MARKETS (STOCK MARKETS)

When a household buys shares newly issued by a company, it hands over money to the company and becomes one of its owners. The household cannot get its money back from the company except in the unlikely event that the company is liquidated. If the household wishes to get its money back, it can only persuade someone else to buy its shares in the company.

Similarly, when a household buys a bond from a company, it cannot get its money back from the company before a specified date. If I bought a 1998 bond in 1978, the bond will be redeemed by the company (i.e., the loan will be paid back) only in 1998. If I wish to get my money back sooner, all I can do is sell the bond.

An organized market where stocks and bonds are bought and sold is a **stock market** or a **securities market.** Such markets include not only the well-known New York Stock Exchange and the American Stock Exchange but also the whole network of "over-the-counter" markets handled by brokers and specialists. The selling of existing shares on the stock market indicates that the company's existing ownership is being trans-ferred; it does not indicate that the company is raising new money from the public.

Securities markets are important because by providing for the ready transfer of corporate securities they make it possible for individuals to invest without committing themselves for long periods.

Because of the existence of securities markets, people are willing to put their savings in securities that are not themselves directly or quickly redeemable. For example, if I want to invest in a particular stock or bond that pays an attractive yield, I may do so even though I know that I will want to withdraw my money after only a year. Given a securities market, I can be confident that I can sell the stock or bond a year from now.

But while securities markets provide for the quick sale of stocks and bonds, they do not guarantee that the securities will sell at the same price at which they were bought. The price at any time is the price that equates the demand and supply for a particular security, and rapid fluctuations in stock prices are common.

Prices on the Stock Market

Figure 22-3 shows the wide swings in a well-known index of stock market prices. In January 1977 the Dow Jones index showed the average price of leading U.S. industrial stocks to be well above the figure for mid 1975. People who bought a representative selection of industrial stocks in 1975 and held them to January 1977 saw the average value of their holdings rise by about 25 percent (and of course they earned dividends as well).

After that prices fell. By March 1978 the index was well below what it had been in January 1977. Investors who bought stocks in 1975 and held them until 1978 first saw the paper value of their stocks rise by one-fourth and then saw these gains quickly disappear. Those who had bought stocks near the top of the market saw their value cut by over 25 percent within 14 months.

What causes such rapid gains and losses, and what do they have to do with the kind of investment we have been talking about in this chapter? When investors buy a company's stock, they are

FIGURE 22-3
Fluctuations in an Index of Stock Prices, 1960–1980

Stock market fluctuations are sharp and irregular. The chart shows monthly variations in the Dow Jones Industrials Index of 30 leading stocks.

buying rights to shares in the stream of dividends to be paid out by that company. They are also buying something they can sell in the future at a gain or loss. The value of that stock depends on two things: first, what people expect the stream of future dividend payments to be and, second, what capital gain or loss people expect to realize when the stock is sold.

Both things make dealing in stocks an inherently risky operation. Will the company in which you are investing pay more or less dividends over future years? Will the company's value rise or fall so that you can sell your share in it for more or less than what you bought it for? While dividend policies of most established companies tend to be fairly stable, stock prices are subject to wide speculative swings.

Speculative Swings

Expectations about future stock prices are important. They can be based on such factors as present earnings, careful estimates of future earnings, or the vague feeling that stock prices will be rising or falling.

In major stock market booms, people begin to expect rising stock prices and hurry to buy while stocks are cheap. This action bids up the prices of shares and creates the capital gains that justify the original expectations. This is the phenomenon of *self-realizing expectations*. Everyone gets rich on paper in the sense that the market value of their holdings rises. Money making now looks easy to others, they also rush in to buy, and new purchases push up prices still further. At this stage, attention to current earnings all but ceases. If a stock can yield, say, a 50 percent capital gain in one year, it does not matter much if the current earnings represent only a small percentage yield on the purchase price of the stocks. Everyone is "making money," so more people become attracted by the get-rich-quick opportunities. Their attempts to buy bid up prices still further, and current earnings represent an ever-diminishing percentage yield on the current price of the stocks.

Capital gains are so attractive that investors may buy stocks on margin—that is, borrow money to buy them, using the stocks themselves as security for the loans. In doing this, many investors may be borrowing money at a rate of interest considerably in excess of the rate of yield on current dividends. If $50,000 is borrowed at 10 percent (interest, $5,000 per year) to buy stocks yielding a current dividend return of only 4 percent (dividend, $2,000 per year), never mind, says the investor's logic, the stocks can be sold in a year or so for a handsome capital gain that will more than repay the $3,000 of interest not covered by dividends. Some people have the luck or good judgment to sell out near the top of the market, and they actually make money. Others wait eagerly for ever greater capital gains, and in the meantime they get richer and richer — on paper.

Eventually something breaks the period of unrestrained optimism. Some investors may begin to worry about the very high prices of stocks in relation not only to current yields but to possible future yields even when generous allowances for growth are made. Or it may be that the prices of stocks become depressed slightly when a sufficiently large number of persons try to sell out in order to realize their capital gains. As they offer their securities on the market, they cannot find purchasers without some fall in prices. Even a modest price fall may be sufficient to persuade others that it is time to sell. But every share that is sold must be bought by someone. A wave of sellers may not find new buyers at existing prices, and prices will come down. Panic selling may now occur.

A household that borrowed $50,000 to buy stocks near the top of the market may find the paper value of its holdings sliding below $50,000. How will it repay its loan? Even if it does not worry about the loan, its broker will. The household may sell now before it loses too much, or its broker may "sell the customer out" to liquidate the loan before it is too late. All this brings prices tumbling down and provides another example of self-realizing expectations. If enough people think prices are going to come down, their attempt to sell out at the present high prices will itself create the fall in prices the expectations of which caused selling.

This is a very simple and stylized description of a typical speculative cycle, yet it describes the basic elements of market booms and busts that have recurred throughout stock market history. It happened in the Jay Cooke panic of 1873 and in the Grover Cleveland panic of 1893. What was possibly the biggest boom of all began in the mid 1920s and ended on Black Tuesday, October 29, 1929. The collapse was dramatic: The average price of 50 leading stocks in November 1929 was about 50 percent below the September peak. Nor did it stop there. For three long years, stock prices continued to decline until the average value of stock sold on the New York Stock Exchange had fallen from its 1929 high of $89.10 a share to $17.35 a share by late 1933.

Are these booms and busts only ghosts from a lurid and reckless past? Until 1969, many would have said that the modern investor was too sophisticated for it ever to happen again. But look again at Figure 22-3. The Dow Jones index of the prices of leading industrial stocks tumbled by 30 percent between December 1968 and April 1970 — in just over a year. The market then recovered, and by January 1973 prices had reached an all-time high. This "boom" was followed by an even bigger "bust": In the two-year period prices fell to less than 60 percent of their January 1973 values. More recently, a sustained decline in prices from January 1977 to March 1978 took about 25 percent of the value of stocks in the Dow Jones index.

Stock Markets: Investment Marketplaces or Gambling Casinos?

Stock markets fulfill many important functions. It is doubtful that the great aggregations of capital needed to finance modern firms could be raised under a private ownership system without them. There is no doubt, however, that they also provide an unfortunate attraction for many naive investors whose get-rich-quick dreams are more often than not destroyed by the fall in prices that follows the occasional booms they help to create.

To some extent, public policy has sought to curb the excesses of stock market speculation through supervision of security issues. This is handled by the Securities and Exchange Commission, which was set up in 1934. It seeks, among other things, to prevent both fraudulent or misleading information and trading by "insiders" (those in a company with confidential information). Moreover, the government can limit the ability of speculators to trade on margin (see pages 662–663).

All in all, the stock market is both a real marketplace and a place to gamble. As in all gambling situations, those who are less well informed and less clever than the average tend to be losers in the long term.

Summary

1. Capital goods are man-made aids to production; they include machines, buildings, trucks, and human capital. When production with capital is more efficient than production without it (even when full allowance is made for the resources needed to produce and maintain the capital goods), capital is said to be *productive* or *efficient*.

2. The gross return to capital is the excess of a firm's revenue over the amount payable to factors of production other than capital, and after allowance for taxes. This can be divided into depreciation, a pure return on capital, a risk premium, and economic profits.

3. The marginal efficiency of capital schedule is downward-sloping because there are diminishing returns as more capital is added to fixed quantities of other resources with constant technical knowledge.

4. A piece of capital equipment is valued because it promises an expected stream of future income to its owners. The value of this capital equipment is the present value of the stream of gross returns it is expected to produce. A single payment of X after t years has a present value of $X/(1 + i)^t$. A stream of returns of X dollars per year in perpetuity has a present value of X/i.

5. A profit-maximizing firm will invest in a machine whenever the present value of the future stream of expected gross returns—the capitalized value of the machine—exceeds the purchase price of the machine or (what is the same thing) whenever the rate of return on the capital exceeds the rate of interest that correctly reflects the opportunity cost of capital to the firm. At equilibrium, the firm will purchase capital equipment until the marginal rate of return is equal to the rate of interest.

6. The amount of investment that firms wish to undertake will depend on the relation between the market rate of interest and the *MEC*.

7. The society as a whole will tend to acquire capital stock as long as the *MEC* is greater than the opportunity cost of money invested in capital, *i*. If there is competition among borrowers and lenders of money, the rate of interest will tend toward the *MEC*.

8. There are important influences on the market rate of interest other than those connected with the efficiency of capital: (a) expectations about price level changes, (b) expectations about the future state of the economy, (c) demands for funds to borrow for purposes other than investment in capital goods, (d) government control of interest rates as a tool of monetary policy, (e) bank administration of interest rates.

9. At any moment in time there is a whole structure of interest rates. Individual rates depend on the riskiness, duration, and liquidity of a loan and also on the cost to the lender of processing the loan and collecting payments of interest and principal.

10. Corporations can raise money in four main ways: by selling shares in the firm; by selling bonds; by borrowing from banks or other financial institutions; and by reinvesting (or plowing back) their own profits.

11. Securities (stock) markets allow firms to raise new capital from the sale of newly issued securities and allow the holders of existing securities to sell their securities to other investors.

12. Prices on the stock market tend to reflect the public's expectations both of firms' future earnings and of future changes in prices (for whatever reason). This necessarily puts a strong speculative dimension into security prices and large speculative swings do occur. Such swings are accentuated by the phenomenon of self-realizing expectations.

Topics for Review

The productivity or efficiency of capital
The marginal efficiency of capital and the *MEC* schedule

The gross return, the net return, and the pure return on capital

The present value of future returns and the capitalized value of assets

The inverse relationship between interest rates and the prices of assets

Reasons for the multiplicity of market interest rates

Equity capital and debt

Functions of securities markets

Self-realizing expectations

Discussion Questions

1. The Atlas Company has calculated that it has the following opportunities to invest
   a. $20,000 to make a critical replacement of an inadequate machine, with an estimated rate of return of 200 percent
   b. $100,000 in an additional machine, with an estimated return of 10 percent
   c. $50,000 for plant expansion, with a return of 25 percent

   How much would the company probably be willing to invest at an interest rate of 20 percent? of 10 percent? What assumptions are you making about risk in your answers?

2. Each of the following is sometimes described as an "investment" in everyday usage. Which represent investments in capital in the economist's sense?
   a. building of the Aswan Dam by the government of Egypt
   b. acquisition of a law degree at Harvard
   c. purchase of a newly discovered Picasso painting. (Does it matter to your answer if the purchaser is the Metropolitan Museum or a private collector?)
   d. purchase by one company of the stock or assets of another company

3. The future profits of Skeeter, Inc., a going concern, are estimated at $100,000 annually for the indefinite future. What is the present value of the business at interest rates of 5 percent, 10 percent, and 25 percent? What factors will determine the appropriate rate of capitalization to use for a prospective buyer of Skeeter, Inc.?

4. Irving Fisher (1867–1947), a distinguished Yale economist, said the durability of capital goods and consumer goods was affected by the rate of interest. Assume that the more durable a house, the higher is its present cost of construction. Would you expect rising interest rates to lead to more or less durable houses being built? Would you expect rising interest rates to foster or discourage sales of mobile homes?

5. How might each of the following affect the pure rate of return on capital? How might they affect the market rate of interest?
   a. a major innovation in a specific industry
   b. an increase in the rate of inflation
   c. a wave of corporate bankruptcies
   d. a substantial increase in economic activity due to renewed confidence in the business outlook

6. Suppose you are offered, free of charge, one of each of the following pairs of assets. What considerations would determine your choice?
   a. a perpetuity that pays $20,000 a year forever; an annuity that pays $100,000 a year for only 5 years
   b. owning an oil-drilling company that earned $100,000 after corporate taxes last year; owning a bond that paid $100,000 interest last year
   c. owning a municipal bond that provides for a tax-free interest payment of $1,000 per year; owning a U.S. government bond that provides a taxable interest payment of $1,500 per year

7. Many stores, including the large mail-order chains, sell for cash or credit at the same prices. If you do not pay your bill completely within 30 days (and you are encouraged to make partial payments) a service charge of 1.5 percent per month of the unpaid balance is added to the bill. What circumstances make it desirable
   a. to pay cash
   b. to pay the bill within the next month
   c. to pay in "easy monthly installments"

   Explain whether unpaid bills by customers represent a capital investment by the firm. Is the 1.5 percent per month paid by customers on their unpaid bills a pure return on the money that the firm has tied up?

8. In 1974 interest rates on industrial bonds hit the highest levels in 45 years. In 1975 they fell sharply and then gradually crept upward during 1976. Suppose you had accurately predicted all this in late 1973. How might you have "cashed in" on your foresight by buying or selling bonds? Would you expect all bonds to respond in a similar way to these changes in interest rates? Would the person who owned a bond purchased in 1972, whose due date was 1986, be affected by these changes in interest rates?

9. Update Figure 22-3 on the Dow Jones Industrials Index. Looking at data in the *Economic Report of the President* (or the *Survey of Current Business*), can you "explain" the changes that have occurred in the years since 1980? What data did you look at in attempting to explain what happened? What other data, not in the president's report, might have been useful?

Poverty, Inequality, and Mobility

23

National income divided by the total population is the average income for all Americans. Some individuals and groups get much more than the average, and others get much less. Distribution theory attempts to explain, among other things, why this happens.

Possibly the most discussed aspect of distribution theory concerns the proportion of national income that goes to the very poor. Who are the poor? Why are they poor? What can—or should —we do about it? Poverty and the means used to prevent and alleviate it played a very large part in the political debates of the 1960s and 1970s. The intensity of the debates shows no sign of waning. We discuss the problem of poverty in the first part of this chapter; in the second part we examine the relevance of the theory of distribution for understanding income differences.

The Distribution of Income Between Rich and Poor: The Problem of Poverty

The theory of distribution offers a number of reasons for the variations in what different individuals can earn. People differ in the talents they possess and the factors they own; consequently both the quantity of factor services they can sell and the price they can receive will vary. Some factor owners are in a position to respond quickly to, and thus to take advantage of, changing opportunities. Others are immobile and will suffer when events leave them in markets where no one wants what they have to sell. To what extent do such reasons account for the continuing presence of poverty in the United States?

THE CONCEPT OF POVERTY

One possible definition of poverty is to be poorer than most of your fellow citizens. There will, of course, always be 10 percent of the population that is poorer than the other 90 percent. If poverty is regarded as a matter of low relative income, it is here to stay, for we inescapably have the (relatively) poor among us.

Clearly poverty must mean more than low relative income. Some minimum family income standard is required to define the **poverty level** below which a family is said to be poor. Such a standard specifies a dollar amount based on estimates of need and the cost of living. In 1978 the American poverty level was defined by the Department of Commerce as $6,662 per year for a nonfarm family of four. Every year this figure is increased by the amount of increase in the Consumer Price Index.

The concept of poverty is more than a statistical cutoff point defined by a Washington bureaucrat. It reflects the expectations and aspirations of society as a whole—and of the poor themselves—as to what constitutes an acceptable minimum standard of living. For example, in 1969 the farm poverty level was raised from 70 percent to 85 percent of the nonfarm level.

Less than 100 years ago, poverty would have been defined as the lack of the minimum amounts of food, shelter, and clothing needed to sustain life. Once this condition faced (or threatened) a large portion of the world's urban and rural masses. Total output was so low that all but a privileged minority lived at or near this level, and any flood or famine or crop failure plunged thousands into starvation. Poverty in this sense is still present in the world, even in the United States. Starvation, hunger, and malnutrition are suffered by millions of individual Americans, and some Americans born in 1981 will starve to death.

Yet in most advanced industrial countries, as in the United States, output has risen until the typical industrial worker enjoys a high material standard of living, and the provision of *subsistence requirements* of food, shelter, and clothing is a major problem for only a small number of families. If this is so—if mere subsistence does not define the poverty level—what does it mean to say (as the Department of Commerce did in 1978) that 24.5 million Americans live in poverty?

Consider the income of a member of a family just at the poverty level. Income of $6,662 for a family of four is $1,665 per person. This will not seem like a great deal to most of you, but it is above the per capita income of three-quarters of the world's population. This should not lead anyone to minimize poverty problems; the black American living in Harlem and working as a porter at LaGuardia airport needs more clothes, transportation, and other basics than an Indonesian peasant. Visit the slums of any American city and you will not lightly dismiss poverty.

But $6,662 for a family of four buys enough food, shelter, and clothing to get by. What it does not provide is enough money for the necessities and also for the full range of commodities that 90 percent of us take for granted, such as having a refrigerator, hot water, and a television set that works and attending an occasional movie. Many of the poor are understandably bitter and resentful that they and their children are outsiders looking in on the comfortable way of life shown in ads and on television.

THE EXTENT OF POVERTY

The extent of poverty may be measured either by the number and percentage of persons in households having incomes below this level or by measuring the **poverty gap:** the number of dollars required to raise everyone's income to this level. In 1978 roughly 25 million persons (11 percent of the population) were classified as poor, and the poverty gap was approximately $20 billion.

These figures are themselves controversial. Critics such as Stanford University economist

Martin Anderson and the University of Virginia's Edgar Browning argue that they neglect such extras as illegal income, unreported income, and noncash benefits such as food stamps and subsidized housing. An accurate measure, they say, might count those really in poverty as only 7 million and lower the poverty gap to somewhere between $5 to $8 billion.

Whatever the deficiencies of these numbers as absolutes, they are useful for tracing changes in the magnitude of the poverty problem. Both the number and the percentage who are poor change. In 1933, President Franklin D. Roosevelt spoke of a third of a nation as being in poverty. By 1959, the official definitions placed 22 percent of the nation below the poverty line. Figure 23-1 charts the course of poverty in America since that date. The steady downward trend from 22 percent to just over 12 percent in the decade from 1959 to 1969 is impressive. The decline to 11 percent over the next nine years is much less impressive.

While the failure to continue a downward trend in the percentage of Americans in poverty during the 1970s is disappointing for those who would like to eradicate poverty, the long-term trend over the last century is impressive.

Historically, the greatest source of relief of poverty has come through economic growth.

If productivity growth can be restored to even 2 percent per year, living standards will double again in the next 35 years. This will surely reduce further the number of people living in poverty. But it is a mistake to expect too much from growth, first because (as we saw in Chapter 13) productivity growth has slowed, and second because some forms of poverty seem immune to growth.

Today, after a century of rapid growth, the poor — like death and taxes — are still with us. It is safe to predict that if we rely only on growth of average income, they will be with us a century hence. For the poverty problem is no longer rooted in low *average* productivity but in the fact that particular groups have been left behind in

FIGURE 23-1

Percentage of Americans Below the Poverty Level, 1959–1978

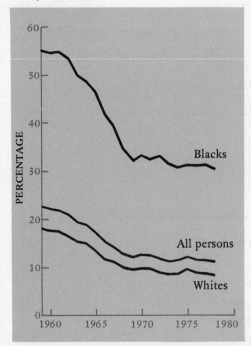

Poverty declined sharply during the 1960s but declined much less during the 1970s. The poverty level is adjusted annually to incorporate changes in the Consumer Price Index. For 1978 a nonfarm family of four with an income below $6,662 was considered poor. The frequency of poverty is much higher for blacks than for whites, and there is no suggestion in the chart that this condition is likely to change soon.

the general rise of living standards. It is no consolation — indeed it adds to the gall — that they are poor in an increasingly affluent society.

WHO ARE THE POOR?

There are poor among people of all ages, races, and educational levels, among the working as well as the unemployed and the retired. Yet some groups have very much higher incidences of poverty than others, as Figure 23-1 suggests with respect to blacks. Table 23-1 shows that

TABLE 23-1

The Incidence of Poverty Among American Families, 1978

Characteristic	Percentage of population who fall below the poverty line
All families	9
Race	
White	7
Black	28
Spanish origin	20
Youth and race	
Children under 18 years	
of age and living in families	16
White	11
Black and other	41
Employment status of	
family head	
Employed (including	
armed forces)	5
Unemployed	25
Not in the labor force	22
Education of family heads	
over 24 years of age	
Elementary school only	32
1–3 years high school	14
4 years of high school	7
Some college	3

Source: U.S. Department of Commerce, Bureau of the Census, *Current Population Reports,* Series P-60, No. 120.

Race, employment status, education, and age all affect the likelihood of poverty. The percentages show the fraction of families in the designated class whose incomes fall below the poverty level. Thus, while only 3 percent of family heads with some college education were below the poverty level, 41 percent of nonwhite children living in families were so classified. (The data do not include persons living outside of families. The poverty rate for all persons is 11 percent.)

poverty is also particularly high among those under 18 years of age (particularly if they are black), those unemployed or not in the labor force, and those with limited education.

Table 23-2 considers the problem somewhat differently. Instead of focusing on the prevalence of poverty among certain subgroups in the population, it looks at those who are poor and de-

scribes some of their characteristics. A great many of the poor are employed, many are aged, and many did not complete high school. Many are members of small families. These data may help dispose of two superficial caricatures: One is the slothful father faking a disability because he is too lazy to do an honest day's work; the other is the family with so many children that an ordinarily decent wage is spread so thin that the whole household is reduced to poverty. Of course, individual households that come close to these extremes can be found, but most poor households do not.

WHY ARE THERE POOR?

To answer the question, we need to recognize that the poor come from many groups and that the causes of their poverty are various. The fact that many of the poor are over age 65 shows that age and illness force people out of the labor market; the fact that so many of those who are poor are under age 18 reflects both the plight of the children in families without a working head (often families with a father who died or deserted) and the high school dropout's difficulties in finding employment. Other important groups include the rural poor, who strive in vain to earn a decent living from marginal or submarginal farmlands; the urban working poor, who simply lack the skills to command a wage high enough to support themselves and their families above the poverty level; the immobile poor, who are trapped by age and outdated skills in areas and occupations where the demand for their services is declining faster than their number; and, most important, the minority poor—blacks, Indians, Puerto Ricans, Chicanos, Chinese—who constitute only one-eighth of the population but are almost one-third of the poor, and who often suffer the additional barriers of discrimination.

Thus there can be no simple answer to the question: What causes poverty in the midst of plenty? It is partly a result of mental and physical handicaps, partly of low motivation, and partly of the raw deal that fate gives to some—such as the

TABLE 23-2

Selected Characteristics of American Families Below Poverty Level, 1978

Characteristic	White (percentage)	Black (percentage)
Employment status of family head		
Employed (including armed services)	45	31
Unemployed	7	9
Not in labor force	48	60
	100	100
Age of head		
Under 25 years	12	16
25–44 years	47	50
45–64 years	26	23
65 years and over	15	11
	100	100
Education of family heads over 24 years of age		
Elementary school	36	34
1–3 years high school	20	34
4 years of high school	29	22
Some college	15	10
	100	100
Size of family		
2 or 3 persons	60	47
4 or 5 persons	29	34
6 or more	11	19
	100	100

Source: U. S. Department of Commerce, Bureau of the Census, *Current Population Reports*, Series P-60, No. 120.

Employment status, age, education, and size of family all affect the likelihood of poverty. Nearly half the whites and one-third of the blacks who are in poverty are in families whose head is employed, and over one-half of both blacks and whites are in families whose heads did not finish high school.

children of the young father who dies unexpectedly, having been meaning to take out that life insurance policy almost any day. Partly it is a result of current and past prejudice. Partly it is a result of unwillingness or inability to invest in the

kind of human capital that does pay off in the long run. Partly it is a result of the market's valuing the particular abilities that an individual does have at such a low price that, even in good health and with full-time employment, the income that can be earned leaves that person below the poverty line.

The extent of poverty is also affected greatly by the performance of the economy. A recession, with its increase in unemployment, pushes additional millions into poverty. (The recession of 1974 did this to 4 million people.) Inflation continually erodes the resources of those on fixed incomes, and the recent rapid inflation has far outstripped increases in welfare payments and the earnings of many families at or near the poverty level.

Fluctuations in the number classified as poor as a result of swings in the economy highlight the important distinction between the *occasionally poor* and the *persistently poor*. It is much easier to withstand six months (or even several years) of poverty due to a bout of unemployment or illness than it is to be permanently poor. For the latter condition erodes hope and warps one's entire outlook on life. While perhaps one-third of those officially classified as being in poverty at any time are only temporarily poor—and thus not really forced to adjust to poverty—half of the rest are virtually permanently poor, according to a recent study by the University of Michigan Survey Research Center.

The study defines the persistently poor as those who have been in poverty for *nine consecutive years*. They are the hard-core poor; they will not be rescued by an upswing in the economy, by another decade of economic growth, or even by somewhat bigger welfare payments and less inflation. A shocking statistic from the Michigan study is that more than three-quarters of the persistently poor are black. Blacks represent 11 percent of the total population, 31 percent of those below the poverty level, and 77 percent of the persistently poor. This statistic, like those in Table 23-1, shows that the poverty problem of blacks is particularly acute.

Profiles of Poverty

Each of the following newspaper sketches concerns a person or family living below the poverty level. Only the names are fictitious.

■ A 34-year-old mother of four children ranging in age from 5 to 15 waited in the Nassau County, N.Y., Social Services building recently for recertification for welfare.

Divorced last year from her husband, who "lived at home on and off," Glenda Rodriguez has been on welfare for 10 years. She is entitled to $450 a month in welfare grants; of that, $271 goes for rent and $67 for heating. She works as a part-time waitress whenever she can and earns $60 in a good week.

For every $60 she earns, however, her welfare grant is reduced by $40.

"Right now, I don't know how I'll make it the next two days until Friday," she said. "I owe the oil company $400—money I haven't been able to pay. We're not starving, but my kids get a little tired of eating eggs and franks."

"I'm working and I'm trying to give my children a little better life, rather than being completely on assistance," she said, "but I'm not getting any place. I'm in the hole each month."

■ Eddie Mason, 19 years old, drank cheap wine and smoked marijuana recently in an abandoned building on Jones Street in St. Louis's slums as he told a visitor, "I've been to the employment office and they've got jobs there only in the suburbs, and I don't have a car. It wouldn't be worth my time to pay bus fare, taxes, lunch, and stuff for a job way out in the suburbs that pays $2.65 an hour."

Mr. Mason lives with his mother and admits to just enough petty thievery "to stay alive."

■ The slightly built woman, holding two small children by the hand, walked into the cafeteria near the Welfare Office, where she had been waiting all morning, and gazed at the menu posted on the wall.

The warmth and smell of the food set the children to clamoring: "Mamma, I want . . ." and "Mamma, can I have . . . ?" She hushed the children and looked at the prices: tuna salad, $1.65; two eggs, 96 cents, with ham or bacon, $1.42; deli sandwich, $1.65; hamburger, 85 cents; cheeseburger, $1.

Checking her purse, she bought two frankfurters at 60 cents each, two containers of milk at 33 cents each, and, for herself, a cup of coffee, 32 cents.

"I don't know what I'm going to do if I'm not approved for welfare," she told the visitor at the table where she was drinking her coffee and wiping sauerkraut from her children's clothes. She said she lived in Freeport with her sick husband, an unemployed carpenter.

"Things have been bad in the past," she said, "what with the high cost of everything—food, rent, clothing. But it's never been like this. We've never had to ask for help before."

■ The old man is sitting at the bus stop, "just resting." He's very old, but he's not slow witted. He's hunched a little forward, hands cupped on the top of the cane that he holds between his knees.

He wants to talk, and in a little time he covers a lot of ground. Private Julius Goldman in World War I, master sergeant in World War II, and 1929 and the depression in between. Kids, inflation, retirement, a dead wife, more inflation. The way it is and the way it was.

He is a pet food devotee. Heat it; it tastes like hash.

BLACK POVERTY

In spite of some genuinely comfortable incomes —roughly 10 percent of black families had incomes of more than $25,000 in 1978—black families tend to have much lower incomes than white families of the same size. Overall, the median income of black families is only about 64 percent of that of white families.

As recently as 1963, more than half the nation's blacks lived in poverty; in 1978 the proportion was approximately one-third.

This results from two related circumstances. First, blacks have many of the characteristics associated with poverty: many of them farm in the rural South or live in areas of the North where jobs are disappearing; a disproportionate number are less well educated than the average American; working blacks have the bad luck to be heavily concentrated in industries with declining demands for labor; their health has often been seriously impaired by malnutrition or untreated diseases; a disproportionate number of black households do not have a male head. The second factor is discrimination, whose effects were discussed in Chapter 21. The two factors interact with and reinforce each other. Whatever the combination of reasons, and despite attempts to deal with them as a matter of public policy, the gap in incomes remains and does not show signs of diminishing. (See Figure 23-2.)

There is one hopeful sign in the recent data: the large and significant difference in educational levels is being reduced. In 1960 only 42 percent of blacks between the ages of 20 and 24 had completed four years of high school; in 1978, 73 percent of the same age group had done so. More education does not translate into higher incomes at once; incomes earned as a result of education rise only after the newly educated group finish their education and find better paying jobs. And education alone is not enough. If more and better employment opportunities are not opened to blacks, the increase in income that should follow

FIGURE 23-2

The Income Gap Between Whites and Blacks

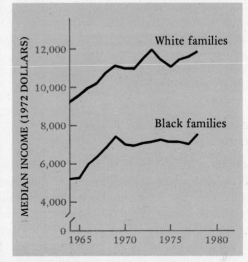

The average income difference between white and black families shows no sign of decreasing. The figures show the median income of black and white families measured in 1972 dollars (to eliminate the influence of inflation). Blacks tend on average to have less than two-thirds as much income as whites.

an increase in educational attainments will not come about in full measure.

"WAGING WAR" ON POVERTY

Eliminating poverty is easier than eliminating air pollution or cancer, for which cures are as yet unknown. For an amount estimated at about $20 billion per year in 1980 dollars, every family now below the poverty level could be given a sufficient income supplement to bring it to that level. Congress could, in other words, close the poverty gap. Although $20 billion is a lot of money, it is less than 20 percent of the national defense budget, and it represents only about 1 percent of the total income earned in the nation.

Poverty, once an ineradicable scourge of humanity along with pestilence and famine, is now within the realm of control in America. Traditionally, and currently, energies have been divided between attacking the causes of poverty and attempting to help some of the poor through payments of money to ease their poverty. Surprisingly perhaps, a good deal of the debate about attacking poverty does not concern whether we can afford it or how best to do it, but whether we *ought* to do it.

The Case Against an All-out War on Poverty

Everyone concedes that there are poor people who deserve to be helped. They are those who despite their best efforts have not been able to escape the ravages of illness, blindness, desertion, age, or obsolescence. There are as well the helpless children of the poor, who should not be made to suffer endlessly for the failings or misfortunes of their parents. But there are also the "undeserving poor," those who could work but will not as long as someone else will support them and their families.

Not only is it unnecessary and perhaps immoral to support such people, the argument says, but their number will grow rapidly if we choose to adopt more generous programs for relieving existing poverty. Even if we could afford to eliminate poverty, the attempt to do so would be self-defeating. For in doing so, the argument continues, we would destroy the incentives of those now supporting themselves just above the level at which the government would support them. They would stop working and end up on welfare as quickly as others were raised above the poverty level.

These critics point to the decline in the work ethic that accompanies increased welfare payments, unemployment compensation, and the issuance of food stamps. There is some factual basis for this argument. Today many gladly accept unemployment compensation, welfare payments, and free goods and services—and indeed expect them, as a matter not of charity but of basic rights. Almost every program has had its scandals, and all too many people can identify

others who are relying on public assistance when in fact they could support themselves.

Disincentive effects. The first part of the case against a general attack on poverty thus concerns disincentive effects. The most direct disincentive effect is on the willingness to keep working or to accept work when to do so will disqualify the person from receiving welfare or unemployment benefits.

A second such effect is on the beneficiaries of government welfare payments: Children who grow up knowing they have a welfare safety net under them may not develop the attitudes or gain the skills needed to climb above the level of the net. This effect may be particularly noticeable in those who, because of the limitations of their abilities, could never in any case hope to climb far above the level provided by the welfare safety net.

A third possible disincentive effect relates to those who will be asked to pay the extra taxes that must be levied if welfare spending increases. As more people go on welfare, fewer will be left to pay the taxes, so tax rates must rise. If, in response, taxpayers work less, the total amount of income available for redistribution will shrink.

There can be no quarrel with the logical proposition that each of these effects may occur, and each of them can be documented by case studies. Some were discussed in Chapter 20. But the important question is whether the effects are merely occasional horror stories or whether they are frequent and quantitatively significant. Opponents of an all-out attack on poverty believe that these magnitudes are, and will be proven to be, very large.

Opportunity costs. Some maintain that we cannot afford to eliminate poverty, given all the competing uses of public money. They contend that welfare spending is already at cripplingly high levels.

Advocates of the view that total government spending is already too large often argue that there are few other items over which so much discretion may be exercised. On the one hand, less could no doubt be spent on such items as defense or schools. Many believe, however, that significant cuts in these items are either impractical or undesirable. On the other hand, a genuine option does exist with welfare expenditures. One of the few realistic hopes of keeping government spending under control, so goes this view, lies in holding a tight rein on the expansion of welfare costs and in particular eliminating payments to the dishonest and lazy who are receiving payments without real need.

The Case for an All-out Attack on Poverty

The war on poverty has its supporters as well as its opponents. Welfare cheaters, supporters agree, should be identified, exposed, and eliminated from welfare rolls wherever possible. But the abuses should not be allowed to confuse the issue. It was one thing to put up with poverty when we had no alternative; it is another to do so when we are rich enough to spend billions on cosmetics, sports, and other frills—to say nothing of space exploration and foreign "diplomacy."

The shame of poverty, the argument says, is not that of the victim but of the society that lets it continue. One great advance of modern civilization has been to lift the stigma from those who are less able and less fortunate. It is to our credit that we have replaced the poorhouse with programs of social insurance as a matter of right, not charity. To let a few cheaters plus some unsupported fears about destruction of the will to work be the excuse for not "coming to peace with poverty" is, they say, a real immorality in modern society.

Of course, any scheme that reduces welfare payments by 65 cents or 75 cents for every dollar that the recipient earns means a 65 percent or 75 percent tax on earnings and may well provide a short-term disincentive to work. But this is the fault of the scheme, not of the people who are only responding rationally to it. Schemes that reduce this marginal disincentive feature can be designed.

Resolving the Debate?

Thus there is disagreement about the desirable direction of change in welfare expenditures. Choosing whether to expand or to contract poverty programs depends in part on value judgments of what is good and right and worth doing, and in part on positive factual assessments of what can be done and how much it will cost. Positive economic research can help to narrow the range of these uncertainties, even if it cannot dictate what we should finally do. Today a great deal of research is devoted to studying the effects of welfare expenditure on incentives—both of the recipients and of the taxpayers who must foot the bill.

THE NATURE OF CURRENT PROGRAMS

The implicit distinction between the deserving and undeserving poor has played an important part in the development of existing programs. The two underlying assumptions are, first, that the able-bodied should work and, second, that heads of households should support their families whenever possible. A three-pronged strategy has developed: (1) to provide job opportunities for all who are able to work; (2) to provide social insurance, related to work, for temporary unemployment and for retirement; and (3) to provide monetary assistance only to those poor who are unable to work for reasons of age, health, or family status.

Providing Employment Opportunities

Families with an employed member have very much less chance of being below the poverty level than those without one. One aspect of fighting poverty is to encourage economic growth and avoid general unemployment. Another is to fight discrimination that denies employment opportunities to minority group members, among whom poverty is many times more prevalent than among whites.

But about 40 percent of all poor families have

a full-time working head; for these working poor, the problem is the lack of skills that command a decent wage, not an absence of demand for the skills they have. Programs of education, training, and retraining are designed to lessen these causes of poverty. Such programs have proved both expensive and limited in the number of persons they can reach. Educational opportunities for the children of the poor may free them from inheriting poverty, but such progress is measured from generation to generation, not from year to year.

Social Insurance

The second prong of traditional antipoverty legislation is social insurance. The Social Security Act, first passed in 1935, pays Old Age and Survivors Insurance (OASI) to millions of Americans who are "old" and to the widows and orphans of eligible workers. Over $100 billion was paid in 1979. Such expenditures keep millions off the poverty roles and for many others reduce the size of the poverty gap.

Medicare and Medicaid tend to prevent or lessen the poverty of the aged who incur major medical expenses. Another $10 billion annually is paid in unemployment insurance—much of which prevents or mitigates poverty.

Successive increases in eligibility for coverage and in the size of benefits, including increases to match rises in the cost of living, promise to make social insurance an increasingly effective antidote to poverty for the majority of Americans.

Categorical Assistance

The poorest of the poor are those who have never worked or for whom employment is not the answer. So-called categorical assistance programs are designed to identify categories of the poor who cannot use labor market participation to avoid poverty, either directly by way of earnings or indirectly by way of employment-related social insurance. The most important are the aids to almost 5 million aged, blind, and disabled persons under the Supplemental Security Income

(SSI) program and the aid to 11 million families with dependent children (AFDC). All the programs have certain common characteristics. They are administered by the states, which share some of the costs with the federal government. States individually determine both eligibility and levels of payment. Eligibility is limited to demonstrated cases of need; maximum payments under each of these programs are reduced when the family has other income.

In addition to these long-standing programs, a series of special programs were instituted as part of the so-called War on Poverty of the Kennedy and Johnson administrations. Grants for food stamps, rent supplements, disadvantaged youth, and alleviating rural poverty are examples of special programs initiated during the Kennedy-Johnson years. Only a few survived in the Nixon and Ford administrations. The Carter administration made two principal proposals. The first was to guarantee income at 65 percent of the poverty level. The second was to decrease payments when the family had other income by a maximum of only 50 cents on the dollar. However radical this may sound, it still would have subjected the poor to an effective 50 percent tax on earnings. As of 1980, these proposals had not been adopted by Congress.

SCOPE AND ADEQUACY OF PRESENT PROGRAMS

After a decade of steady decreases in government spending for the poor, the programs leveled out in the 1970s. By 1978 the government was spending about $170 billion in transfer and welfare payments, of which perhaps half went to people who, without the payments, would have been below the poverty level. Other things being equal, the poverty gap would be much larger without these programs.

Eighty-five billion dollars a year is a lot of money but a hard figure to relate to. To gain some perspective, think of it as roughly 7 percent of total personal consumption expenditures; as about 20 percent of government purchases of goods and services; or as about $450 for every person in every family above the poverty level. Whether in these terms we are spending a lot or a little depends on individual values and on other pressures on the government budget.

One item in the overall program of government financial assistance that has been of increasing concern to Congress is the rising burden of social security payments required under present laws. In an attempt to decrease the number eligible for payments, changes in the law have been enacted that delay retirement for those able and willing to work. (Of course, when older workers displace younger workers, the decrease in social security payments to some may be partially offset by increased unemployment insurance or welfare payments to others.)

Proposed Changes in the Form of Antipoverty Programs

Quite apart from the question of more or less is the question of *how* to spend allocated funds. One concern is redesigning programs to eliminate avoidable disincentive effects. If transfer payments are reduced dollar for dollar when outside income is earned, the effect will be a 100 percent tax on earned income. Not long ago, such implicit 100 percent tax rates were common. Most have already been reduced to an average of about 65 percent, and the Carter administration's proposals to Congress would reduce them further, to a maximum of 50 percent.

Perhaps the most far-reaching proposal is to shift from state and locally funded and administered programs to a federal program. Proposals to "federalize welfare" arise in part from the fact that state and local governments face a far greater fiscal crisis than does the federal government (for reasons to be discussed in Chapter 25) and in part from the great differences in treatment of the poor from city to city and state to state. The poor are not distributed evenly throughout the United States—42 percent live in the South, many of the rest in northern urban slums. Much of the state and local tax base is generated in political jurisdictions in which poverty is not a major problem. Thus the tax bur-

den of fighting poverty locally falls very unevenly. Differences in ability and willingness to pay lead to great differences in programs. For example, in 1979 a woman with no income and three dependent children in Newark, New Jersey, who was eligible for aid could receive $4,488 per year; in Biloxi, Mississippi, she would get at most $1,440. While each amount is below the poverty line, the difference in the realized levels of poverty are enormous—and they are not explained by differences in the cost of living.

The case for federalization rests on defining poverty as a national problem. If it is that, there is little reason for the level of relief or the tax burden to vary as greatly as it does from state to state. The case against federalization rests on the advantages of pluralism and local control. There are great differences in costs of living and in local standards of what constitute an adequate minimum standard of living; such differences cannot easily be taken into account (as a political matter) by federal bureaucrats or by Congress. Yet to provide equal welfare payments in Newark and Biloxi would be every bit as unjust as the present scheme.

A second major proposal calls for a shift from categorical assistance to general assistance. Basically, it argues for aid to the poor based on level of income rather than on *categories* of eligibility. Thus it would no longer matter why someone is poor, only that he or she is poor. Put differently, general assistance attempts to erase any implicit distinctions between the deserving and the undeserving poor.

The Relevance of Distribution Theory

A large part of the problem of poverty is due to the pricing of the labor services that people have to offer. Factor pricing, and hence the distribution of income, is a by-product of the market-allocation system. This allocation helps to determine both the quantities of the various goods and services that are produced and the methods by which they are produced.

Does the theory of distribution studied in this part satisfactorily explain the allocation process in our economy? For the answer to be yes, it is necessary to give affirmative answers to two more basic questions. First, do market conditions of demand and supply play important roles in determining factor earnings? Second, do factors move in response to changes in factor earnings?

Some would answer no to each question. They argue that prices of products and factors bear little relation to market conditions because prices and wages are administered by oligopolies and giant unions. Such administered prices and wages are sticky downward and tend to rise annually at a bit more than the general rate of inflation. Products with above average price increases are produced by firms with above average market power, and the most powerful unions get the biggest wage increases. Entry barriers in industry and mobility barriers for factors of production, the argument continues, prevent significant movements of resources in response to product and factor price differentials that exist or develop. Thus, they argue, the theory of distribution we have studied is irrelevant to the real world.

Some of the views expressed in the previous paragraph are closely related to those discussed on pages 313–317. In the following sections of this chapter, we examine whether market forces do in fact play the roles predicted by the theories of competition and monopoly in determining factor prices and the allocation of resources.

DO MARKET CONDITIONS DETERMINE FACTOR EARNINGS?

Factors Other Than Labor

Many, if not all, nonhuman factors are sold on competitive markets. The theory predicts that changes in the earnings of these factors will be associated with changes in market conditions.

Overwhelmingly the evidence supports this prediction of the theory, as shown by the examples that follow.

The market theory of factor pricing provides a good explanation of raw material prices and hence of the incomes earned by their producers. The prices of plywood, tin, rubber, cotton, and hundreds of other materials fluctuate daily in response to changes in their demand and supply. The responses of factor markets to the many shortages that seemed to characterize the American economy in the 1970s provide dramatic confirmation. When the price of agricultural commodities shot up following a grain shortage, farm income soared. When oil became scarce, prices rose and oil producers and owners of oil properties found their profits and incomes rising rapidly. Not only did the relative prices of oil products rise, so also did the relative prices of commodities, such as chemical fertilizers and air travel, that make use of petroleum products.

Land in the heart of growing cities provides another example. Such land is clearly fixed in supply, and values rise steadily in response to increasing demand for it.[1] Very high land values even make it worthwhile to destroy durable buildings in order to convert the land to more productive uses. Several of New York's old and once favorite hotels have been pulled down, to be replaced by high-rise office buildings. The skyscraper is a monument to the high value of urban land. In many smaller cities, the change from shopping downtown to shopping in outlying shopping centers has lessened the demand for land downtown and influenced relative land prices. The increase in the price of land on the periphery of every growing city is a visible example of the workings of the market.

Similar results occur in markets that are far from being perfectly competitive. In 1979 the price of power in virtually all forms rose sharply in response to the extra energy shortage caused by the change in government in Iran. Oligopo-

---

[1] A friend is fond of saying, "Nobody buys land any more; its price is much too high because everybody wants it."

lists producing key metals such as zinc, molybdenum, steel, and aluminum have not hesitated to increase prices as their costs of production rose or when demand outran their production. Further examples can be found in almost every issue of the *New York Times* and the *Wall Street Journal,* but the point should now be clear:

The prices and earnings of nonhuman factors are successfully predicted by market theories of factor pricing.

Labor

When we apply the theory to labor, we encounter two important sets of complications. First, labor being the human factor of production, nonmonetary considerations loom large in its incentive patterns, and thus market fluctuations may have less effect. Second, the competitive and noncompetitive elements of labor markets occur in different proportions from market to market. These complications make it harder to answer the question, Do market conditions determine factor earnings? Monopolistic elements and nonmonetary rewards, both difficult to measure, must be carefully specified if the theory that labor earnings respond to market forces is to be testable. Nevertheless, there is a mass of evidence to go on.

Market fluctuations in demand and supply. Do earnings respond to normal fluctuations of demand and supply as the theory predicts? The evidence shows that they often do. The competitive theory predicts that a decline in the demand for a product will cause a decline in the derived demand for the factors that make the product and thus a decline in their owners' incomes. A rise in the demand for a product will have the opposite effect. Cases come easily to mind.

With the advent of the automobile, many skilled carriage makers saw the demand for their services decline rapidly. Earnings fell, and many older workers found that they had been earning substantial economic rents for their scarce but highly specific skills. They suffered large income cuts when they moved to other industries. Workers who acquired skills wanted in the newly expanding automotive industry found the demands for their services and their incomes rising rapidly.

More recently there has been a large increase in the earnings of first class professional athletes in most sports. In part this has been caused by rising demand due to expansion in the number of major league teams. In part it has resulted from increased revenues to the teams and leagues from televising sports, which has increased the marginal revenue product of the athletes. And in part it has been the result of athletes' acquiring the right to offer their services to more than one employer, thereby reducing the ability of employers to hold down wages by acting as monopsonists.

Doctors as a group have also gained from an increase in demand for their services. With the rise in real incomes in the twentieth century, the typical household has spent an increasing proportion of its income on medical services. The resulting rise in demand has greatly increased the incomes of physicians relative to the incomes of many other groups in the society.

College professors are an example of a group that gained as a result of changes in labor markets during the 1960s but fell back in the 1970s. The relative earnings of a college professor were much higher by 1970 than they had been 20 years earlier. This was particularly so at the starting end of the scale, where intense competition for the scarce supply of good students who had just obtained Ph.D.s forced up their price throughout the 1960s to levels that would have seemed princely only 15 years before. In response to the higher incomes, many more college graduates went on to get advanced degrees, and a rising proportion stayed on to teach and do research in universities.

The supply of new Ph.D.s began to arrive on the market in 1969–1970, and for the first time in ten years the starting salaries of Ph.D.s hired for the fall of 1970 were not significantly higher than the salaries for those hired the previous year. By 1973 the average percentage increase in academic salaries was not only below the average percentage increase in all American incomes but was insufficient even to keep pace with the increase in the cost of living. The relative downward pressure on college professors' salaries continued throughout the 1970s and shows no sign of abating as additions to supply continue to outstrip additions to demand. These relative changes in factor compensation have occurred even in an occupation where nonmonetary benefits loom large. The reason is that the nonmonetary benefits exist both when demand is strong relative to supply and when it is relatively weak.

Another group that has been suffering the chill winds of the consequences of factor price determination on competitive markets is college graduates. During the 1970s the earnings of college graduates fell relative to other workers, and employment opportunities dropped sharply, especially for new graduates. The downturn is explained by slackening demand due to changes in industrial structure (e.g., substituting sophisticated computers for college-trained persons) and continued growth of supply.

Price changes induced by market conditions have little to do with abstract notions of justice or merit. If you have some literary talent, why can you make a lot of money writing copy for an advertising agency on Madison Avenue but very little money writing poems? It is not because an economic dictator or group of philosophers has decided that advertising is more valuable than poetry. It is because in the American economy there is a large demand for advertising and only a tiny demand for poetry.

Effects of monopoly elements in labor markets. A strong union—one able to bargain effectively and to restrict entry of labor into the field —can cause wages to rise well above the competitive level. Highly skilled plasterers, plumbers, and electricians have all managed to restrict entry into their trades and as a result maintain wages well above their transfer earnings. Many similar cases have been documented. Unions can and do succeed in raising wages and incomes when they operate in small sections of the whole economy; the high earnings attract others to enter the occupation or industry, and the privileged position can be maintained only if entry can be effectively restricted.

Not only can monopoly elements raise incomes above their competitive levels, they can also prevent wages from falling in response to decreases in demand. Of course, if the demand disappears more or less overnight, there is nothing any union can do to maintain incomes. But the story may be different when, as is more usually the case, demand shrinks slowly but steadily.

Consider coal mining in the years since World War II. From 1945 to 1960 production of coal declined as oil, gas, and electricity were steadily substituted for it. The coal that was produced was used largely by electric utilities, and it was mined by ever more capital-using and labor-saving techniques. Both these forces led employment to shrink steadily.

What would competitive theory predict about wages? Coal mining was plainly a declining labor market from 1945 to 1960; competitive theory would predict low wages and low incomes, followed by exit of the most mobile coal miners under this forceful disincentive, and hard times for those who decide to stick it out.

As Table 23-3 shows, this was *not* the pattern in coal. The wages of coal miners rose steadily in real terms, maintaining their parity with wages in manufacturing. Employment did fall; by 1960 it was 44 percent of the level in 1945. By 1968, 260,000 fewer miners were employed than in 1945, and those who did not find other occupations contributed to the generally depressed conditions in Appalachia. But those who kept jobs did relatively well.

What happened was that a powerful union, the United Mine Workers, prevented wages from falling. Did the union behavior contradict the predictions of theory? Not at all; by raising wages despite falling demand, the union actually accelerated the decline in employment. Notice

TABLE 23-3
Coal Mining Production, Employment, and Wages, 1945–1978

	Index of coal production (1945 = 100)	Index of employment in coal mining (1945 = 100)	Average hourly earnings (1972 dollars)	Average hourly earnings as a percentage of those in manufacturing
1945	100	100	$1.19	118
1950	89	96	1.94	135
1955	80	57	2.47	134
1960	72	44	3.15	139
1965	89	34	3.49	134
1968	94	33	3.86	128
1973	102	41	5.75	141
1978	113	52	9.57	155

A powerful union can keep wages high in a period of declining demand, but only at the expense of employment. From 1945 to 1960 coal production was a declining industry. A powerful union kept real wages rising steadily and above wages in the much healthier manufacturing sector. The combination of declining production and high wages led to declining employment. After 1960 the demand for coal expanded; eventually it increased enough to lead to both rising wages and rising unemployment. But in 1978, with production above 1945 levels, employment was only about half what it was in 1945.

that employment fell more than production after 1950, and then kept falling when production rose. Aggregate wage payments (wages *times* employment) fell sharply—in 1968 they were 55 percent of their 1945 level. Economic theory suggests that lower wages *or* declining employment opportunities (or both) will serve to decrease labor earnings and trigger movements of factors out of the industry. The lower employment that accompanied the "high wage" policy of the United Mine Workers Union discouraged the young from waiting for jobs in the industry. As workers left the industry because of retirement, ill health, or death, they were not replaced.

Some people argue that the "restrictive behavior" of the union in this industry has led to a more orderly, humane, and civilized phasing out than would have occurred had the adjustment been left to a competitive market. In the latter case, those who remained in the industry, and who were needed by it, would have suffered depressed conditions in order that the disincentive could operate on those who did leave and on those who might otherwise have entered.

Since 1968 the demand for coal miners has rebounded as the demand for coal to produce electricity has surged. As a result—as theory predicts—employment rose sharply *and* wages in coal mining shot up relative to those of all U.S. industry. Consequently, labor earnings in coal mining rose sharply.

All the above examples support the general proposition:

Earnings of labor respond to significant changes in market conditions.

DO FACTORS MOVE IN RESPONSE TO CHANGES IN EARNINGS?

The theory of factor supply says that factors will move among uses, industries, and places, taking both monetary and nonmonetary rewards into account. They will move in such a way as to equalize the net advantages to the owners of factors. Because there are impediments to the mobility of factors, there may be lags in the response of factors to changes in relative prices, but in due course adjustments will occur. We now ask, Does the world behave in the way the theory predicts?

Factors Other Than Labor

The most casual observation reveals that the allocative system works pretty much as described by the theory with respect to land, materials, and capital goods.

Land is transferred from one crop to another in response to changes in the relative profitabilities of the crops. Land on the edge of town is transferred from rural to urban uses as soon as it can earn substantially more as a building site than as a cornfield. Materials and capital goods move from use to use in response to changes in relative earnings in those uses.

This is hardly surprising. Nonmonetary benefits do not loom large for factors other than labor, and the theories of both competition and monopoly predict that quantities supplied will respond to increases in earnings generated by increased demand.

In the case of nonhuman factors, there is strong evidence that the theory is able to predict events with reasonable accuracy.

Labor

Labor mobility can occur in many dimensions. Labor can move among occupations, industries, skill categories, and regions. These categories are not exclusive; to change occupation from a farm laborer to a steelworker, for example, a person will also have to change industries and probably towns.

The mobility of labor is as well documented as it is impressive. When wages on the West Coast soared during World War II, workers flocked there to take lucrative jobs in the rapidly expanding aircraft and shipbuilding industries. When new oil fields were discovered in Alaska and northern Canada, high wages attracted welders, riveters, and the many other types of labor that the oil fields required. During the period 1950–1970 black workers migrated steadily from South to North in search of jobs. Since 1970, and especially since 1975, this flow has slowed and stopped; indeed, it has been reversed as the movement of industry to the sun belt has created new jobs in the South.[2]

Overall, major reallocations of labor have occurred. The fraction of the labor force in agriculture declined from 23 percent in 1930 to 3.4 percent in 1979. Within the nonagricultural labor force, sharp reallocations have also occurred, as shown in Figure 23-3. Movements *within* sectors and among firms have been even greater.

There are, of course, barriers to labor mobility. Unions, pension funds, and other institutions can and do inhibit labor mobility substantially. By influencing supplies of labor in various markets, they exert considerable influence on labor earnings. It is easier to move from one occupation to another within one industry when there is a single industrial union than it is when each occupation in the industry is organized in its own craft union. It is easier to move between two industries in the same occupation when both are organized by craft unions than it is when each has its own industrial union.

Although various barriers to the entry of labor exist in particular markets, few seem able to withstand for long the pressures of severe excess demand. Prejudice against females, for example, did not hold up under the excess demand for labor during World War II. Once millions of men had been absorbed by the armed forces, occupations traditionally closed to women suddenly opened up. Employers, with profits at stake, quickly decided they would rather have Rosie for a riveter than no riveter at all. This occurred without social pressures arising out of concern for discrimination against women. Once the excess demand had disappeared after the war, however, many of the old prejudices reasserted themselves—and barriers were not again lowered until they were directly assaulted.

---

[2] During the 1960s it was often argued that the northward migration of the unemployed was motivated not by job opportunities but by the more generous welfare benefits offered in northern states and cities. The reversal of the labor flow, despite the continuing differential in welfare benefits, is taken by a recent Department of Commerce study as conclusive refutation of that argument.

FIGURE 23-3
The Changing Composition of the Nonagricultural Labor Force

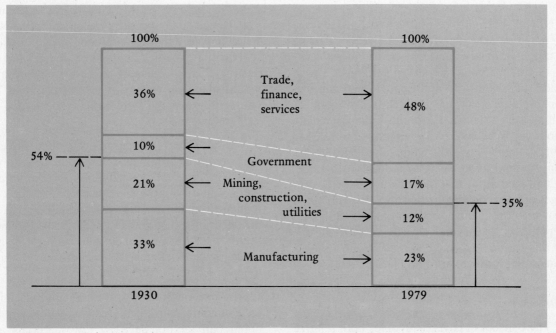

In half a century, a major shift has occurred in labor utilization. In 1930, 54 percent of the nonagricultural labor force was in the heavy industrial (largely blue collar) sectors. As shown by the bottom two blocks, this figure had decreased to 35 percent by 1979. The shift was to the service-oriented (largely white collar) sectors of government, trade, finance, and other services.

Excess supply also tends eventually to generate out-migration of labor. Yet it may not occur quickly enough to prevent substantially depressed conditions. Consider regional mobility. On the one hand, the regional distribution of population has been shifting toward the sun belt and other centers of rapid economic growth in the United States; on the other hand, depressed Appalachian areas have remained regions of excess labor supply for over 25 years, since coal mines in Pennsylvania and West Virginia began to shut down.

Although it is relatively easy to get *some* out-migration, it is difficult to get large-scale transfers in a short period of time. When demand falls rapidly, pockets of poverty tend to develop. In Appalachia, labor has been leaving yet poverty has increased. The reason for this is that the rate of exit has been slower than the rate of decline of the economic opportunities in the area. Indeed, the exit itself causes further decline: when a family migrates, both the supply of labor and the demand for labor decline. This is because all the locally provided goods and services that the family consumed before they migrated now suffer a reduction in demand.

Such lagging mobility creates a cruel policy dilemma. On the one hand, it is desirable to ease the poverty of those who cannot move; on the other, policies designed to do just that reduce the incentives to move to areas with available jobs.

In all these cases, the theories of competitive and monopolistic factor markets go a long way in explaining what we see and in predicting many of the consequences of changes in market conditions on labor mobility, and the consequences of barriers to mobility on the welfare of those trapped by immobility.

Not all behavior is neatly explained by the theory. For example, despite the recent decline in academic salaries and job opportunities, many more students today persist in getting Ph.D.s in fields such as history and English than can reasonably expect to find jobs that will require or utilize their training. Economists can speculate about such behavior—for example, by saying that for many students, graduate education is a consumption good as well as an investment in human capital, or that the nonmonetary advantages of an academic position are large enough to be worth the gamble of finding a job. But such hypotheses go beyond straightforward theory. At this stage we have to be satisfied with a theory that explains much, but not all, behavior.

Summary

1. The concept of poverty involves both relative and absolute levels of income and reflects the aspirations of society as well as the income needed for subsistence alone. Today roughly 11 percent of all Americans are classified as living in poverty. Since the aggregate poverty gap is small relative to national income, the possibility exists of eradicating poverty in the United States.

2. Economic growth, though it has led to a reduction of poverty, will by itself never eradicate it, for many of those most in need do not share directly in the fruits of growth. Thus public programs are thought to be required.

3. Poverty is particularly acute among such minority groups as blacks. This reflects in part the minority group's lower average stock of human capital—especially education and training—and in part the discrimination that has prevented utilizing more fully the skills and talents that the group's members have. Recent years have seen no significant decrease in the relative income disadvantage of blacks to whites or in their labor market disabilities.

4. Poverty programs are a matter of lively current debate. Some people believe that it is possible and desirable to make further major reductions in poverty now. They place particular importance on an income supplement to the poor regardless of why they are poor. Others believe that further expensive attacks on poverty are undesirable both because of the additional burden it would place on the average taxpayer and because of the disincentive effects generated by welfare programs.

5. Methods currently used to reduce poverty include antidiscrimination laws that seek to expand employment opportunities for blacks and other minority groups; retraining programs intended to match people with available jobs; social insurance that helps the able-bodied to meet the risks of unemployment and retirement; and categorical assistance designed to serve those unable to care for themselves.

6. Market conditions exercise a powerful influence on factor earnings. This is most evident for nonhuman factors such as raw materials and land. For labor, the influence of nonmonetary factors is greater because the owners of labor must accompany their labor services to work. Nevertheless, market forces exert powerful influences on earnings of labor.

7. There is much evidence of the movement of factors in response to changes in earnings. Factor mobility is typically greater for nonhuman factors than it is for labor. Even where impediments to mobility exist, factors (including labor) tend to move in response to persistent differences in earnings or employment opportunities.

Topics for Review

Poverty and the poverty gap
Correlates of poverty
Occasional poverty and persistent poverty
Possible disincentive effects of alleviating poverty
Social insurance
Categorical assistance and general assistance

Discussion Questions

1. In what ways are the problems of poverty in the United States likely to be different from the problems of poverty in an underdeveloped poor country, such as Bangladesh? In what ways are they easier to solve in one place than in the other?

2. The official poverty level used in the United States is based only on money income. It does not take into account food stamps or subsidized housing. It does not consider the assets of the family. It does not consider whether families with low incomes have wealthy relatives. Do these omissions lead to an exaggerated view of the poverty problem? Should the poverty line rise if average income of the American people rises, with no increase in the prices of individual items of consumption?

3. Suppose that your objectives are (first) to eradicate poverty and (second) to reduce unemployment. Evaluate the probable effectiveness of each of the following in meeting each objective.
   a. increasing welfare payments
   b. increased labor union membership
   c. creating a program of public works to hire the poor
   d. ending employment discrimination against blacks

4. A proposed program of rental allowances to the poor has been attacked in Congress as giving money to slumlords instead of to the poor and thereby worsening the distribution of income. Evaluate this position. Argue the case for and against assistance that is tied to a particular kind of expenditure rather than giving the money to the poor to spend as they think best.

5. Egalitarian U has the policy of paying all faculty members of the same rank and years of experience the same salary regardless of field. Further, it grants promotion strictly on the basis of years of service at EU. Elitist Tech has a nominal salary scale but meets offers made from outside to members of the faculty whom it especially wants to keep. Where would you rather be a student? Where would you rather teach? Does it matter in answering these questions whether your field is medieval history or chemical engineering?

6. Is the Empire State Building immobile? Is the Empire State Building more mobile among uses than the use of the land it sits on? How about the uses of the pyramids of Egypt? What resources can you think of that are immobile over a time span as long as 25 years? In general, are a factor's earnings likely to be greater or smaller if its mobility is relatively low?

7. The supply of regular New York taxicabs is rigidly controlled by a licensing system that keeps the number of cabs well below what it would be in a free-market situation. A "medallion" issued for a nominal fee by the city confers the right to operate a cab. The medallion, however, is freely salable; in 1980 its price was $68,000. Evaluate the effect on the price of the medallion of
   a. an increase in average incomes of New Yorkers
   b. increased operation of "gypsy cabs" (cabs without medallions)
   c. increases in parking lot fees and parking violation fines in New York
   d. a new law that bans private passenger autos from midtown during business hours

8. Suppose that you had been on the margin about whether to buy a medallion and become a licensed cab operator in 1980. A 50 percent increase in taxi fares was then authorized. How, if at all, would this affect your decision? Toronto uses a similar scheme, but the price of a medallion there is only about one-half as much as it is in New York. What might account for this difference?

9. It has been estimated that it costs employers $20,000 to move an executive from one city to another. Is this a barrier to labor mobility? Despite the cost, some 200,000 executives were moved (at company expense) in 1979. It this consistent with the theory of distribution? Executives involved in the moves were asked whether they liked having to move; 69 percent said they did not, yet 78 percent said they could have remained in their old jobs if they had so chosen. Are these replies consistent with one another and with the theory of distribution?

Part Seven

The Market Economy:
Problems and Policies

Microeconomic Policy I: Benefits and Costs of Government Intervention in the Market Economy

24

There are two caricatures of the American economy. One pictures the United States as the last stronghold of free enterprise, with millions of Americans in a mad and brutal race for the almighty dollar. In the other, American business people, workers, and farmers are seen strangling slowly in a web of red tape spun by the spider of government regulation. Neither is realistic.

Many aspects of economic life in the United States, perhaps more than in most other countries, are determined by the operation of a free-market system. In the United States, private preferences, expressed through private markets and influencing private profit-seeking enterprises, determine much of what is produced, how it is produced, and the incomes of productive factors.

But even casual observation makes it clear that public policies and public decisions play a very large role. Not only do laws restrict what people and firms may do, but taxes and subsidies influence their choices. Much public expenditure is not market determined, and this leads to a distribution of national product very different from what would exist in a system that relied entirely on private markets. The United States is in fact a mixed economy.

Although all economies are mixed, the mixture varies greatly among economies and over time. Whether the existing mixture is wrong—and if so, in which direction—is debated sharply today. One reason for the mixture (and the debate) relates to what an unkind critic called the economists' two great insights: markets work, and markets fail. A second reason is what the critic might call the political scientists' great insights: government intervention can work, and it can fail. In this chapter we discuss the role of the government in economic markets. Why is it there at all? What does it do well, and what badly? Do we need more or less government intervention?

Market Success

THE INTERDEPENDENT ECONOMY

The nation's economy consists of thousands upon thousands of individual markets. There are markets for agricultural goods, for manufactured goods, and for consumers' services; there are markets for semi-manufactured goods, such as steel and pig iron, which are outputs of some industries and inputs of others; there are markets for raw materials such as iron ore, trees, bauxite, and copper; there are markets for land and for thousands of different types of labor; there are markets in which money is borrowed and in which securities are sold.

An economy is not a series of markets functioning in isolation but an interlocking system in which an occurrence in one market will affect many others. The coordination of what occurs in the many markets is brought about by the price system. Changes in surpluses and scarcities are reflected in price and quantity changes that signal to decision makers what is happening throughout the economy. The responses to these signals cause the signals to change. Such changes trigger other changes. Like a pebble thrown into a pond, one change in one market sends ripples (and sometimes waves) through many other markets.

HOW MARKETS COORDINATE

Any change, such as an increase in demand for beef, requires many further changes and adjustments. Should production of beef change? If so, by how much and in what manner? Someone or something must decide what is to be produced, how, and by whom, and what is to be consumed and by whom. Such decisions can be made by an army of planners who sit in a central office and order more to be produced of this and less of that. Or they can be made by a large number of decentralized decision makers (households and firms), all responding to a series of economic signals given to them by the economy's markets.

How the price system gets these decisions made has been examined at several places in this book (for example, with respect to carrots and brussels sprouts in Chapter 4, agriculture in Chapter 7, and ball-point pens in Chapter 17). When shortages occur in a market, price rises and windfall profits develop; when gluts occur, price falls and windfall losses develop. These are *signals,* for all to see, that arise from the overall conditions of total supply and demand.

Individual households and firms respond to common signals according to their own best interests. There is nothing planned or intentionally coordinated about their actions, yet when (say) a shortage causes price to rise, individual buyers begin to reduce the quantities they demand and individual firms begin to increase the quantities they supply. As a result the shortage will begin to lessen. As it does, prices begin to come back down, and windfall profits are reduced. These signals in turn are seen and responded to by firms and households. Eventually, when the shortage has been eliminated, there will be no windfall profits to attract further increases in supply. The chain of adjustments to the original shortage is completed.

Notice that in the sequence of signal-response-signal-response no one had to foresee at the outset the final price and quantity. Nor did any government agency have to specify who would increase production and who would decrease consumption. Some firms responded to the signal for "more output" by increasing production, and they kept on increasing production until the signal got weaker and weaker and finally disappeared. Some buyers withdrew from the market when they thought prices were too high, and perhaps they re-entered gradually, when they wanted to, as prices became "more reasonable."

Households and firms responding to market signals, not government bureaucrats issuing orders, "decided" who would increase production and who would limit consumption. No one was forced to do something against his or her best judgment. Voluntary responses collectively produced the end result.

To say that the price system coordinates is not to imply that it is perfect. It coordinates responses even to prices "rigged" by monopolistic producers or by government controls. The signal-response process occurs in a price system even when the "wrong" signals are sent.

When an international cartel of uranium producers decided to reduce production and raise price, they created a current shortage (and a fear of worse future shortages) among those electricity utilities that depend on uranium to fuel nuclear power plants. The price of uranium shot up from under $10 per pound to over $40 in less than a year. This enormous price rise greatly increased efforts among producers outside the cartel to find more uranium and to increase their existing production by mining poorer grade ores previously considered too expensive to mine. The increases in production from these actions slowly began to ease the shortage. On the demand side, high prices and short supplies led some utilities to cancel planned nuclear plants and to delay the construction of others. Such actions implied a long-run substitution of oil or coal for uranium. (Only the fact that the OPEC cartel had also sharply raised the price of oil prevented an even more rapid reversal of the previous trend from oil to nuclear-powered generators.) With the prices of both uranium and oil quadrupling, the demand for coal increased sharply, and its price and production rose. Thus the market mechanism generated adjustments to the relative prices of different fuels, even though some prices were set by cartels rather than by the free-market forces of supply and demand. It also set in motion reactions that place limits on the power of the cartel.

This example and countless others illustrate the great discovery of the early economists.

The *unplanned* price system, like an *invisible hand* (Adam Smith's famous phrase), coordinates the responses of individual decision makers who seek only their own self interests. Because they respond to signals that reflect market conditions, their responses are coordinated without any conscious central planning of who may or must do what.

WHAT DO MARKETS DO WELL?

The free-market system has several great virtues: it provides *automatic coordination* without the need for devoting resources to central planning; it is *impersonal* in denying to any individual or firm great power over others; it leads (under well-defined circumstances) to an *efficient allocation of resources;* and it automatically sets in motion forces that *correct any disequilibrium* that may develop. We have just reviewed how markets coordinate; let us review briefly the other points.

Impersonal Decision Making

Suppose (to take an extreme example) that 10,000 families from neighboring areas decide that at existing prices they all want to move into single-family houses in the hills of Berkeley, California, overlooking San Francisco Bay. However, that beautiful residential area is already heavily populated. There are at most (say) 1,000 vacant houses or building sites. Obviously, not all of the present and potential residents can live there. Which ones will be able to do so, and which ones will be disappointed?

Market allocation. How would the market system make the allocation? The first impact of the great increase in demand would be a sharp rise in the asking prices of houses in the Berkeley hills. This would persuade some Berkeley residents, who probably had had no intention of moving, to sell their houses and move to other areas. The same rises in price would discourage many who had hoped to move into the Berkeley hills. The rising prices will also lead some owners of vacant lots to sell or develop them.

One way or the other—by reducing quantity demanded and by encouraging an increase in quantity supplied—the market will make the allocation. Of the 10,000 families who originally wanted to move in, 3,000 may end up living there, while 2,500 old residents move away and 500 of the vacant houses or lots become occupied. Which 3,000 moved in? Those who valued it the most. Which 2,500 moved out? Those who valued the extra money more than the privilege of staying in Berkeley. The market has sorted them out without anyone's having to issue orders ("you go, you stay") and without the need for a court or a board to hear appeals from those who object to the orders.

Non-market allocation. Had prices not been free to rise, some other system for allocating supply would have been needed. Suppose prices had been frozen by law in order to "keep Berkeley housing within the reach of the ordinary family." There would have been dozens of applicants for any house that became available. The sellers would then have had great power to decide to whom to sell (and thus whom to turn down). They might have exercised their prejudices, or they might have found ways to get a secret payoff.

Alternatively, the Berkeley City Council might set up a Berkeley Authorized Waiting List (BAWL) to determine the order in which people would be permitted to become residents. This would give some public official the duty (or perhaps the privilege) of judging the relative worthiness of potential Berkeleyites and ranking them accordingly. It would also provide opportunities for bribery of those with allocative authority.

Whether allocative authority rests with private individuals or with government officials, excess demand at the fixed price implies personalized power of some people over others. Many who fear the exercise of centralized or personalized power regard the avoidance of this kind of arbitrary power a major advantage of market allocation.

Allocative and Productive Efficiency in Equilibrium

As we saw in Chapter 14, competitive markets reach equilibrium at prices equal to both marginal costs of production and minimum average total cost. In so doing they achieve allocative and productive efficiency. (We saw in Chapter 18 that this conclusion depended on the level of costs in competitive markets being no higher than that in noncompetitive markets; we shall consider other qualifications shortly.) Early economists who believed that free markets were synonymous with perfectly competitive markets consequently believed in the efficiency of free markets.

Modern economists, aware of more qualifications concerning the possibilities of a perfectly competitive economy, nevertheless believe that free markets frequently achieve or approximate the competitive result of prices equal to marginal cost and minimum average cost. When they do this, real-world markets achieve or approximate economic efficiency.

In a market economy, market prices signal households about the relative costs *to them* of consuming different commodities. The same prices signal firms about the costs and profitability *to them* of producing the commodities by utilizing different combinations of the factors of production.

The price system links households satisfying their wants and the basic resources of the society. Firms are intermediaries that use resources to produce the commodities that satisfy households' wants.

The linkage that the price system provides will be efficient whenever three conditions are met:

1. Costs faced by firms are the opportunity costs to society of the resources required to produce commodities.

2. Prices at which firms sell their output are equal to marginal costs.
3. Entry and exit of new firms forces prices to the lowest attainable levels of average total cost.

Freely operating markets frequently (but not always) come close to satisfying these conditions.

Self-correction of Disequilibrium

The allocative efficiency discussed above, and in Chapters 14 and 18, concerned the *equilibrium* conditions of a competitive market economy. But the economic system is repeatedly thrown out of equilibrium by continual change. If in this situation the economy does not "pursue" equilibrium, there will be little comfort in saying that if only it reached equilibrium, things would be bright indeed. (We all know someone who would have been a great surgeon if only he or she had gone to medical school.)

An important characteristic of the price system is its ability to set in motion forces that tend to correct disequilibrium.

To review the advantages of the price system in this respect, imagine operating without a market mechanism. Suppose that planning boards make all market decisions. The Board in Control of Women's Clothing hears that pantsuits are all the rage in neighboring countries. It orders a certain proportion of clothing factories to make pantsuits instead of the traditional women's skirt. Conceivably the quantities of pantsuits and skirts produced could be just right, given shoppers' preferences. But what if the board misguessed, producing too many skirts and not enough pantsuits? Long lines would appear at pantsuit counters while mountains of unsold skirts piled up. Once the board saw the lines for pantsuits, it could order a change in quantities produced. Meanwhile, it could store the extra skirts for another season—or ship them to a country with different tastes.

Such a system can correct an initial mistake, but it may prove inefficient in doing so. It may use a lot of resources in planning and administration that could instead be used to produce commodities. Further, many consumers may be greatly inconvenienced if the board is slow to correct its error. In such a system the members of the board may have no incentive to admit and correct a mistake quickly. Indeed, if the authorities do not like pantsuits, the board may get credit for having stopped that craze before it went too far!

In contrast, suppose that in a market system a similar misestimation of the demand for pantsuits and skirts was made by the women's clothing industry. Lines would develop at pantsuit counters, and inventories of skirts would accumulate. Stores would raise pantsuit prices and run skirt sales. Pantsuit manufacturers could earn large profits by raising prices and running extra shifts to increase production. Some skirt producers would be motivated to shift production quickly to pantsuits and to make skirts more attractive to buyers by cutting prices. Unlike the planning board, the producers in a market system would be motivated to correct their initial mistakes as quickly as possible. Those slowest to adjust would lose the most money and might even be forced out of business.

QUALIFICATIONS ABOUT MARKET SUCCESS

Many nineteenth century economists advocated a policy of **laissez faire**: government should not interfere with the operation of markets. They did so because they believed the price system actually achieved all of the four beneficial results we have just reviewed.

Each of the virtues of market systems that we have examined *may* occur; that does not mean that each *does* occur in every free-market situation. The price system coordinates responses, but the price system has not proved to be the only possible, or necessarily the best, system for regulating an economy. There is a difference between the word "automatic," which we have used, and the phrase "perfectly functioning," which we have not used.

The price system as it actually operates may not yield ideal results. It may not be efficient for a number of reasons, including the presence of monopoly. It may not prove impersonal, as when large firms and large unions have and exercise market power. It may not respond quickly to inefficiencies where there are impediments to the mobility of resources.

In addition, static allocative efficiency may not be a wholly satisfactory goal. One reason, examined in Chapter 18, concerns Schumpeter's insight that dynamic changes in the level of innovation can greatly affect long-run efficiency. A different reason is that a particular allocation of resources, even when it is efficient, will only by accident accord to most people's sense of what is just or fair. A free-market economy distributes output as well as produces it. There are many very different possible allocations of resources, any one of which, once achieved, would meet the test of Pareto-optimality (that no shift of resources would make someone better off without making someone else worse off). The actual distribution of income of a freely functioning competitive system reflects its past: It tends to perpetuate inequalities in the distribution of income and the ownership of assets. Executives and their children exert more influence on market allocations than do taxi drivers and their children.

When a market system "succeeds" in allocating resources efficiently but distributes income in a way that the majority consider highly unfair or unjust, the members of the society are unlikely to believe that the market has succeeded. The supporters of laissez faire focused on the virtues that a market system might achieve and neglected or played down its limitations. The more important these limitations are—in other words, the greater the failures of the market system—the greater will be the incentive to depart from laissez faire.

Market Failure

The United States does not have a laissez faire economy. What has led a majority of Americans to believe that a pure private enterprise system is not the best of all possible worlds? What has led them to lessen their reliance on the unrestricted workings of the free market and, in many cases, to impose regulations on markets or to substitute collective action for individual action? What leads many Americans today to question whether we have gone far enough—or too far —away from free markets?

Whenever market performance is judged to be faulty, it is the practice to speak of **market failure.** The word "failure" in this context probably conveys the wrong impression.

Market failure does not mean that nothing good has happened, only that the *best attainable outcome* has not been achieved.

As a result of market failure, many people believe it desirable to modify, restructure, complement, or supplement the unrestricted workings of the market. There are several major sources of market failure, and it is important to understand how they arise. As we have seen, there are two somewhat different senses in which the phrase is used. One is the failure of the market system to achieve efficiency in the allocation of society's resources, the other is its failure to serve social goals other than efficiency. We shall discuss both.

EXTERNALITIES AS A SOURCE OF INEFFICIENCY

Cost, as economists define it, concerns the value of resources used up in the process of production. According to the opportunity cost principle, value is the benefit the resources would produce in the best alternative use. But who decides what resources are used and what is their opportunity cost? When a timber company buys a forest, it perhaps regards the alternative to cutting the trees this year as cutting them next year or five years hence. But citizens in the area may value the forest as a nature sanctuary or a recreation area. The firm values the forest for the trees; the local residents may value the trees for the forest. The two values need not be the same.

These differences in point of view lead to the important distinction between private cost and social cost.

Private cost measures the value of the best alternative uses of the resources available to the producer.

As we noted in Chapter 11, private cost is usually measured by the market price of the resources that the firm uses.

Social cost measures the value of the best alternative uses of resources that are available to the whole society.

For some resources the best measure of the social cost may be exactly the same as the private cost: the price set by the market may well reflect the value of the resources in their best alternative use. For other resources, as will soon be clear, social cost may differ sharply from private cost. Discrepancies between private and social cost lead to market failure from the social point of view. The reason is that efficiency requires that prices cover social cost, but private producers, adjusting to private costs, will neglect those elements of social cost that are not included in private costs. When an element of (social) cost is not part of a private firm's profit and loss calculation, it is *external* to its decision-making process.

Discrepancies between social and private cost lead to **externalities,** which are the costs or benefits of a transaction that are incurred or received by members of the society but are not taken into account by the parties to the transaction. They are also called **third-party effects** because parties other than the two primary participants in the transaction (the buyer and the seller) are affected. Externalities arise in many different ways.

Harmful Externalities

Pollution. A major source of differences between private cost and social cost arises when firms use resources they do not regard as scarce.

This is characteristic of most examples of pollution. When a paper mill produces pulp for the world's newspapers, more people are affected than its suppliers, employees, and customers. Its water-discharged effluent hurts the fishing boats that ply nearby waters, and its smog makes many resort areas less attractive, thereby reducing the tourist revenues that local motel operators and boat renters can expect. The firm neglects these effects because its profits are not affected by the external effects of its actions, but they are affected by how much paper it produces.

This example and hundreds more concern the production of goods and services by private firms. They also concern the use of society's basic resources such as timber, coal, labor, iron ore, water, and air. The pollution connected with production is not an accidental event, as is the periodic breaking up of oil tankers off the world's beaches or the blowout of oil in the Gulf of Mexico. The pollution is the result of calculated decisions as to what and how to produce or consume.

Common-property resources. The world's oceans once teemed with fish, but today a worldwide fish shortage is upon us. There seems to be no doubt that overfishing has caused the problem. How could this happen?

Fish are one example of what is called a **common-property resource.** No one owns the oceans' fish until they are caught. Thus a fisherman can sell them only when he has caught them. Even if he realizes that doubling the catch this year will hurt next year's catch, he cannot afford to hold back unless everyone does the same.

Even if the effects of the decline in the fishing industry are regarded as problems for that industry alone (which of course they are not; unemployed fishermen and unavailable fish impose costs on all of us), the effects represent an externality to the individual act of fish production. When one fisherman takes one too many unspawned fish, he affects every other fisherman's catch next year. Yet this effect—a cost to someone else—does not play a role in the fisherman's private calculation of the cost of catching that fish. Thus there is a discrepancy between private and social cost, an externality.

Congestion. Collisions between private planes and commercial airliners are headline news when they occur. They cannot occur unless *both* planes are in the air; this is what creates the externality. Suppose that the probability of a midair plane crash is roughly proportional to the number of planes in the air. Suppose too that I have the choice of flying from Phoenix to Los Angeles in my own plane or on a commercial airliner that has 100 of its 150 seats filled. In choosing to fly by myself, I decide that the extra "cost" to me of taking the risk of a midair collision can be compensated for by taking out some extra life insurance.

What I have neglected is part of the social cost of my action: the increased risk for every other person in the air on my route of flight that results from one more plane in the air. Since I do not consider your increased risk, my private decision may have been the wrong social decision.

Notice that in the case of congestion no individual need be at fault. If ten planes, or cars, or people, occupy a space large enough for only nine, any one of them may be regarded as the "one-too-many."

Neglect of future consequences of present actions. When private producers ignore or undervalue future effects on others, they neglect an externality. A business facing bankruptcy tomorrow may be motivated to cheat on safety standards in order to cut costs today, even if it would hurt the firm's reputation in the long term and impose heavy future costs on others.

One dramatic example of the neglect of future effects concerns DDT. DDT was invented in 1874, but its insecticidal properties were not discovered until 1939, and it was not until World War II had moved to the mosquito-ridden Pacific three years later that its full powers were revealed.

After the war it was found to be equally effec-

tive in controlling agricultural pests, particularly the cotton boll weevil. When in 1948 the Swiss chemist Paul Mueller won the Nobel prize for his discovery of its value as a pesticide, few doubted his contributions to the world's well-being. The use of DDT grew steadily in the United States and throughout the world until, in the peak year of 1958, 78 million pounds were used in the United States alone.

Gradually it was confirmed that DDT did more than kill unwanted insects. Once sprayed, the chemical did not break down for years. It entered the food chain and worked its way up from insects to birds and fish, to small mammals, and to larger and larger birds and mammals, including human beings. Arctic penguins, though thousands of miles from any sprayed areas, have measurable amounts of DDT in their bodies. DDT has thinned the egg shells of large birds to the point where breakage threatens many species, among them the peregrine falcon, the osprey, and the eagle.

In 1962 Rachel Carson began the public debate about DDT in her book *The Silent Spring,* in which she labeled DDT an "elixir of death." In 1969—21 years after the Nobel prize was awarded—formal attempts to ban the use of DDT began. DDT had come of age. The "future" costs that were neglected in the forties and fifties are being paid today.

Beneficial Externalities

Externalities can be for good as well as for ill. When I paint my house, I enhance my neighbors' view and the value of their property. When an Einstein or a Rembrandt gives the world a discovery or a work of art whose worth is far in excess of what he is paid to produce it, he confers an external benefit. Educating my children may make them better citizens and thus benefit third parties, even if they do not prove to be latter-day Nightingales or Mozarts. Individuals will tend to engage in too little of activities that produce beneficial externalities because they bear all of the costs but others reap part of the benefits.

Externalities, whether adverse or beneficial, make privately efficient market results socially inefficient.

MARKET IMPERFECTIONS AND IMPEDIMENTS AS A SOURCE OF INEFFICIENCY

The efficiency of the price system depends on firms and households receiving and responding to the signals provided by prices, costs, and profits. Forces that seriously change these signals or prevent the required response to them may cause a market to fail to perform efficiently. Consider a few examples.

Barriers to Mobility

One kind of market impediment is factor immobility. If increases in a factor's pay do not lead to increases in supply (for any of the reasons discussed in Chapters 21 and 23), the market will fail to reallocate resources promptly in response to changing demands. Monopoly power creates market imperfections by preventing enough resources from moving in response to the market signals of high profits. In this case, barriers to entry rather than factor immobility frustrate the flow of resources. Another kind of market imperfection is ignorance or deception; signals can work only if they are received.

Collective Consumption Goods

Certain goods and services, if they provide benefits to anyone, necessarily provide them to a large group of people. Such goods are called **collective consumption goods.** National defense is the prime example of a collective consumption good. An adequate defense establishment protects everyone in the country whether they want it or not, and there is no market where you can buy more of it and your neighbor less. The quantity of national defense provided must be decided collectively. Other examples of collective consumption goods include the beautification of a city, a levee to protect a city from a flood, and a hurricane-warning system. In general, market systems cannot compel payment for a collective consumption good since there is no way to prevent a person from receiving the services of the good if he or she refuses to pay for it.

Excessive or Prohibitive Transactions Costs

If a firm's products are not marketable, say because of an institutional barrier, they will not be produced even though people value them more than their costs. Costs of negotiating and completing a transaction, such as the costs of billing or the bad-debt cost of those who never pay, are examples of **transactions costs.** They are always present to some degree, and they are a necessary cost of doing business. If buyers cannot be made to pay for the product, for example, the producer will not be motivated to provide it. For a private firm to stay in business, it must be able to recover both production and transactions costs. If transactions costs are higher than they need to be because of imperfections in the private market, some products that it is efficient to produce will not be produced, and the market will have failed. Consider an example.

Could a private entrepreneur provide a road system for Los Angeles, paying for it by collecting tolls? The answer is surely no (at least with today's technology). It would be prohibitively expensive, both in money and in delays, to erect and staff a toll booth at every freeway exit. The users of a road system may be more than willing to pay the full costs of its construction and maintenance, but without an inexpensive way to make them pay, no private firm can produce the road. The government, collecting revenue by means of a gasoline tax, can do what the private market fails to do. (Whether it can do so without making a different mistake—producing more of the product than users are willing to pay for—is discussed below.)

The warning about technology merits an additional comment. Technology changes rapidly.

For example, the electronic metering of road use may make the toll booth unnecessary just as the postage meter has made licking stamps unnecessary. Thus what a private market cannot do today, it may be able to do efficiently tomorrow.

Market imperfections may lead to market failure by preventing firms and households from completing many transactions that are required for efficient resource allocation.

THE NEGLECT OF NONMARKET GOALS AS A SOURCE OF MARKET FAILURE

The two sources of market failure we have discussed—externalities and market impediments—concern the inability of the free market to achieve efficient resource allocation. Exclusive reliance on markets, even when markets are allocatively efficient, may lead to the neglect of other goals that seem important to society. The market can be said to have failed when this occurs.

Public Provision May Lead to Different Preferred Goods

Police protection, even justice, might be provided by private market mechanisms. Watchmen, Pinkerton detectives, and bodyguards all provide policelike protection. Privately hired arbitrators, "hired guns," and vigilantes of the Old West represent private ways of obtaining "justice." Yet the members of society may believe that a public police force is preferable to a private one and that public justice is preferable to justice for hire.

For another example, public schools may be better or worse than private schools, but they are likely to be different, particularly because persons other than parents, teachers, and owners influence their policies. Much of the case for public education rests on the advantages to you of having other people's children educated in a particular kind of environment that is *different* from what a private school would provide. Of course,

you can debate whether the differences make it better or worse. The market may be said to fail if the public product is better.

Protecting Individuals from the Acts of Others

People can use—even abuse—other people for economic gain in ways that the members of society find offensive. Child labor laws and minimum standards of working conditions are responses to such actions. Yet direct abuse is not the only example of this kind of market failure. In an unhindered free market, the adults in a household would usually decide how much education to buy for their children. Selfish parents might buy no education, while egalitarian parents might buy the same quantity for all their children regardless of their abilities. The members of society may want to interfere in these choices, both to protect the child of the selfish parent and to ensure that some of the scarce educational resources are distributed according to intelligence rather than wealth. All households are forced to provide a minimum of education for their children, and strong inducements are offered—through public universities, scholarships, and other means—for gifted children to consume more education than either they or their parents might voluntarily choose if they had to pay the entire cost themselves.

Paternalism: Protecting Individuals from Themselves

In a significant number of cases, members of society acting through the state seek to protect adult (and presumably responsible) individuals, not against others, but against themselves. Laws prohibiting heroin and other hard drugs and laws prescribing the installation and use of seat belts are intended primarily to protect individuals from their own ignorance or shortsightedness.

Intervention of this kind with the free choices of individuals is called **paternalism.** Whether or not such actions reflect real values of the majority of the society, or whether they simply reflect overbearing governments, there is no doubt that the market will not provide this kind of protection. Buyers do not buy what they do not want, and sellers have no motive to provide it. Thus if the members of society insist on such "protection," markets may be said to fail to provide it.

The Existence of "Social Obligations"

In a market system you can pay someone to do things for you. If you can persuade someone else to clean your house in return for $25, presumably both parties to the transaction are better off: You would prefer to part with $25 rather than clean the house yourself, and your household help prefers $25 to not cleaning your house.

Normally society does not interfere with people's ability to negotiate mutually advantageous contracts when there are no external effects. Such freedom is not allowed, however, where an activity is regarded as a social obligation. Prime examples are military service in wartime and jury duty, in which those selected are not permitted to hire substitutes.[1] Similarly, one may not legally sell one's vote to another.

Compassion

A free-market system rewards certain groups and penalizes others. The workings of the market may be stern, even cruel; consequently society often chooses to intervene. Should heads of households be forced to bear the full burden of their misfortune if, through no fault of their own, they lose their jobs? Even if they lose their jobs through their own fault, should they and their families have to bear the whole burden, which may include starvation? Should the ill and aged be thrown on the mercy of their families? What if they have no families? Both private charities and a great many government policies are concerned

with modifying the distribution of income that results from such things as where one starts, how able one is, how lucky one is, and how one fares in the free-market world.

Even if the price system allocated goods and services with complete efficiency, this would not assure market success if members of society have other goals that they wish to serve by the allocation of resources.

Responding to Market Failure

While private collective action can sometimes remedy the failures of private individual action (private charities can help the poor; volunteer fire departments can fight fires), by far the most common remedy for market failure is reliance on government intervention.

It is useful to ask several questions about possible government policies designed to correct market failure. First, what tools does the government have? Second, when and how vigorously should the tools be used? Third, under what circumstances is government intervention likely to fail?

THE TOOLS OF MICROECONOMIC POLICY

The legal power of the government to intervene in the workings of the economy is limited only by the Constitution (as interpreted by the courts) and by the willingness of Congress to pass laws and the executive branch to enforce them. There are numerous ways in which one or another level of government can prevent, alter, complement, or replace the workings of the unrestricted market economy. It is convenient to group these methods into four broad categories:

1. *Public provision.* Goods and services may be publicly provided in addition to or instead of private provision.
2. *Redistribution.* Public expenditures and taxes may be used to provide a distribution of in-

---

[1] This has not always been the case; during the Civil War a man could avoid the draft by hiring a substitute to serve in his place.

come and output different than that which the private market provides.

3. *Rule making*. Rules and regulations may be adopted to compel, forbid, or specify within acceptable limits the behavior that private decision makers may engage in.

4. *Structuring incentives*. Government may alter market signals to persuade rather than force decision makers to adopt different behavior, either by one of the above methods or in some other way.

Each of the four methods is frequently used, and each has great capacity to change whatever outcomes the unregulated market would provide. The first two will be discussed in detail in Chapter 25; the remainder of this section concerns the last two, rule making and structuring incentives.

Rule Making

Rules require, limit, or compel certain activities and market actions. It is helpful to distinguish between *proscriptive* and *prescriptive* rules.

Proscriptive rules. These regulations are like the Ten Commandments; they tell people and firms what they can and cannot do. Such rules require parents to send their children to school and to have them inoculated against measles and diphtheria. Laws that prohibit gambling and pornography attempt to enforce a particular moral code on the whole society. In Chapter 18 we discussed an important form of policy by prohibition — antitrust policy.

There are many other examples: Children cannot legally be served alcoholic drinks. Prostitution is prohibited in most places, even between a willing buyer and a willing seller. In most states you must buy insurance in case you should do damage with your private motor car. A person who offers goods for sale, including his or her own house, cannot refuse to sell because of a dislike for the customer's color or dress. There are rules against fraudulent advertising and the sale of substandard, adulterated, or poisonous foods.

Such rules only set limits to the decisions that firms and households can make; they do not replace those decisions. But the allowed limits can be changed. An important means of government regulation is to change old rules or add new ones that redefine the boundary between forbidden and permitted behavior.

Prescriptive rules. Prescriptive rule making substitutes the rule maker's judgment for the firm's or the household's judgment about such things as prices charged, products produced, and methods of production. It tends to restrict private action more than proscriptive regulation does because it replaces private decision making rather than limiting it to an acceptable set of decisions. Regulation of public utilities is an important example of prescriptive regulation (see Chapter 18). But prescriptive regulation goes far beyond the natural monopoly regulation we have discussed.

Federal regulatory commissions regularly decide such matters as who may broadcast and on what frequencies; which airlines may fly which routes; what rates bus lines and pipeline operators may charge for different kinds of services; what prices may be paid for gasoline; how much foreign sugar may be imported into the United States; and how many miles to the gallon the average automobile sold by General Motors in 1982 must deliver.

Effectiveness. Rule making often appears to be a cheap, simple, and direct way of compelling desirable behavior in the face of market failure. But the simplicity is deceptive. Rules must be enforceable and enforced, and once enforced they must prove effective if they are to achieve the results hoped for by those who made them. These conditions are often difficult and expensive to achieve.

Consider the requirement for the installation of an antipollution device that will meet a certain standard in reducing automobile exhaust emissions. Such a law may be the outcome of congressional debate on pollution control—and having passed the bill, Congress will turn to other things. Yet certain problems must be solved before the rule can achieve its purposes. It may be relatively easy to enforce the law at the manufacturers' level because they are few in number. (This is not automatically true; witness the Ford Motor Company's fine of $7 million for "rigging" pollution tests in the 1970s.) But even with perfect compliance by the manufacturer, the device will not work well unless it is kept in working order by the individual driver. And it would be expensive to inspect every vehicle regularly and to force owners to keep the devices at the standard set by law. Even a well-designed rule will work only until those regulated figure out a way to evade its intent while obeying its letter. There will be substantial incentive to find such a loophole, and resources that could be used elsewhere will be devoted to the search—and to counteracting such avoidance or evasion.

Structuring Incentives

Government can change the incentives of households and firms in a great variety of ways. It can fix minimum or maximum prices (as we saw in the discussions of agriculture and rent control in Chapters 7 and 8). It can adjust the tax system to offer many exemptions and deductions. Tax-deductible mortgage interest and real estate taxes, for example, can make owned housing relatively more attractive than rental housing. Such tax treatment sends the household different signals than those sent by the free market. Scholarships to students to become nurses or teachers may offset barriers to mobility into those occupations. Fines and criminal penalties for violating the rules imposed are another part of the incentive structure.

An important means of influencing incentives is to change the prices that firms and households pay in such a way as to eliminate externalities. Because externalities are a major source of market failure, much attention has been given to means of inducing decision makers to take them

into account. Charging a producing firm for the pollution it causes can motivate the firm to alter its production in a socially desirable way. Procedures that make firms take account of the extra social costs they impose are said to **internalize** the external effects of production. How exactly does this work?

First we need to define terms. The **net private benefit** (*NPB*) of a unit of production is the difference between that unit's contribution to a firm's revenue and its contribution to the firm's cost. In other words, it is the contribution to profit of that unit. If we think of each unit of production as contributing to social welfare (and call that contribution **social benefit**) and to cost (*social cost,* defined on page 424), we can define the difference between social benefit and social cost as **net social benefit** (*NSB*).

Net social benefit is the key concept in judging efficiency. A unit should be produced if, but only if, its *NSB* is greater than or equal to zero.

In general *NSB* will be equal to *NPB*, plus beneficial externalities, minus adverse externalities. In the following discussion, we consider an adverse externality (such as pollution) so that *NSB* is less than *NPB*.

A private firm responding only to private benefits and costs will produce up to the point at which marginal *NPB* becomes zero. But at that output marginal *NSB*, being less than *NPB*, is necessarily negative: too much has been produced from the social point of view. This market failure can be avoided by the procedure shown in Figure 24-1. Once the firm has been forced to pay for what were previously externalities, the new net private benefit is exactly the same as net social benefit. That is, *NPB* = *NSB*. Thus the firm will be motivated to produce only as long as marginal *NSB* is not negative.

Internalization avoids the market failure caused by externalities.

There are many ways to internalize external costs. Consider two. If the amount of the external cost imposed per unit of output is known, it is

FIGURE 24-1
The Consequence and Correction of Externalities

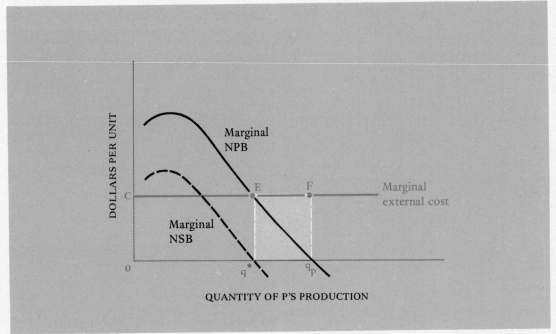

Internalizing an externality can correct market failure. The *NPB* earned by a private firm, *P*, is shown by the solid black curve. The firm is motivated to produce all units that make a positive contribution to its profits. Its equilibrium output is q_p, where *NPB* is zero. This production imposes an external cost of $C per unit on outsiders (call them *S*), as shown by the colored line. Subtracting this additional social cost from the *NPB* yields the *NSB*, the curve shown by the dashed black line. The socially optimal output is q^* where marginal *NSB* equals zero. At this output, *NPB* is just equal to marginal external cost. (Note that the only way to avoid all the external costs is for *P* to produce nothing.) At q^* the outsiders, *S*, are still having costs inflicted on them by *P*, but *S*'s costs *plus* *P*'s private costs are just equal at the margin to *P*'s profit from production.

Suppose the firm is required to pay an "effluent tax" of $C per unit. Its *NPB* now becomes the dashed black line. The externality has been *internalized*, and the profit-maximizing firm reduces its output from q_p to q^*. It does this because any units produced beyond q^* would now subtract from total profits; given the tax, marginal profits are negative beyond q^*.

possible to impose an **effluent charge,** or pollution tax, that compels the producer to pay a tax on every unit of polluting production. Such a charge might lead the producer to find a way to produce without polluting. Another way to internalize external costs is to give legal standing to private citizens to sue for damages against polluters or to seek court injunctions against polluting activities. The legal action makes it costly for polluters; there will be damage payments if they lose and legal payments win or lose.

GOVERNMENT ATTEMPTS TO CORRECT MARKET FAILURE: BENEFITS AND COSTS

Consider the following argument: (1) The market system is working imperfectly; (2) government has the legal means to improve the situation; (3) therefore the public interest will be served by government intervention.

This appealing argument is deficient because it neglects two important considerations. First,

Avoiding Undesirable Externalities and the Coase Theorem

Look again at Figure 24-1 where a producer, P, is inflicting external costs on S. P will produce q_p instead of the socially optimal output, $q\star$. Consider five alternative ways the output $q\star$ might be achieved.

I. Direct Determination of Quantity Produced

1. The government might nationalize the industry and direct it to produce $q\star$.
2. The government might determine $q\star$ and then try to impose that output on the private producer. This could be attempted by either (a) fining the firm heavily if its output exceeds $q\star$ or (b) giving the firm a subsidy if its output does not exceed $q\star$. To be effective, the fine or subsidy must exceed the profits resulting from producing beyond $q\star$.

II. Government Intervention to Internalize the Externality

3. The government can place an effluent tax on P of $\$C$ per unit. This forces P to take the full social costs into account and P is then motivated to produce at $q\star$.
4. P can be made legally liable to compensate S. Firm P could be forced to pay $\$C$ per unit (to S) in addition to its private costs of production. P would then be motivated to produce at $q\star$.

III. Private Agreement Between P and S

5. Even if P has no liability to compensate S, and even if the government does not levy a tax on P, the socially optimal result can still occur. This is because it will pay S to bribe P to produce at $q\star$. Since every unit P produces imposes a cost of $\$C$ on S, it is worthwhile for S to bribe P any amount up to $\$C$ for every unit by which P will reduce production. Each unit produced between $q\star$ and q_p adds less than $\$C$ to P's profits. Thus P should be prepared to stop producing those units in return for a bribe equal to or

greater than its marginal profit. Thus S can bribe P to reduce output from q_p to $q\star$. Below $q\star$, however, the marginal private profit to P is greater than the cost that P's production imposes on S. Thus S cannot persuade P to produce less than $q\star$ since at outputs less than $q\star$ the minimum bribe P would accept is more than $\$C$.

Each scheme will produce the same socially optimal output $q\star$. Each, however, yields a different distribution of costs and benefits. We leave it as an exercise for the reader to discover how P and S would rank each scheme.

Each scheme will have a different cost of enforcement and a different probability of evasion. Each will also have a different degree of flexibility in the face of changing conditions. But in spite of their differences, each scheme can ensure that there is an optimal quantity of resources allocated to the production of the commodity.

Professor Ronald H. Coase of the University of Chicago once put these propositions in a most startling way. He assumed that there were no transactions costs. Then, he pointed out, it does not matter which party, P or S, is fined or made legally liable for preventing an undesirable result. Since it is in their combined interest to avoid production beyond $q\star$, it will pay them jointly to avoid the result. Therefore laws and court proceedings fixing legal liability for a vast range of events such as pollution damage, defective products, and so on may be irrelevant to efficient allocation of resources.

Critics of Coase have been quick to point out that in many cases transactions costs are not negligible, considerations of equity or income distribution are paramount, or one party is so much better able to identify and control adverse effects that the party should be made responsible on the grounds of efficiency. In these cases, laws still affect the allocation of resources as well as the distribution of gains and losses.

government intervention is costly. For that reason not every market failure is worth correcting; the benefit of the correction must be balanced against the cost of achieving it. Second, government intervention may be imperfect. Just as markets sometimes succeed and sometimes fail, so government intervention sometimes succeeds and sometimes fails.

To evaluate governmental intervention it is necessary to compare the benefits and the costs of the intervention. In many cases each is large.

Large benefits do not justify government intervention, nor do large costs make it unwise. What matters is the relative size of benefits to costs.

The *benefits* of government intervention are the value of the market failures averted. If pollution imposes external costs of $X, then government action that prevents that amount of pollution will avoid $X of social costs. In other words, it provides public benefits of $X.

The *costs* of government intervention are not stated so concisely because they are of several different kinds whose *sum* is the total cost of intervention.

Government Expenditures on Corrective Activities: Internal Costs

When government inspectors visit plants to see whether they are complying with federally imposed standards of health, industrial safety, or environmental protection, they are imposing costs on the American public. When regulatory bodies develop rules, hold hearings, write opinions, or have their staff prepare research reports, they are incurring costs. When the antitrust division has 40 lawyers spend 10 years preparing for and engaging in antitrust prosecution of IBM, they are incurring costs. The costs of the judges and clerks and court reporters who hear and transcribe and review the evidence are likewise costs imposed by regulation. All these activities use valuable resources, resources that could have provided very different goods and services.

The aggregate size of federal expenditures for activities that regulate market behavior alone are large indeed: in 1979 they were estimated at $4.8 billion. Such costs have grown greatly in the last several decades. They represent one cause of the growth in the size of government in the economy. However, they are only the most visible part of the total costs of government regulatory activities.

Costs Imposed on Those Regulated: Direct External Costs

The nature and size of the extra costs borne by firms subject to government intervention are themselves of several kinds, and they vary with the type of regulation. A few examples are worth noting.

Changes in costs of production. Antipollution regulations forced producers not to burn high sulfur coal. As a result, extra fuel costs were imposed on many firms. Such cost increases are directly attributable to regulation.

For 50 years (since the mid 1920s) the prices of automobiles relative to other consumer goods were falling because of continuing technological advances in automobile engineering. Recent federal safety and emission standards have added so much to the cost of producing automobiles that in the 1970s Americans had to adjust to a steadily rising trend in the relative prices of autos.

Costs of compliance. Government regulation and supervision generate a flood of reporting and related activities that are often summarized in the phrase "red tape." The number of hours of business time devoted to understanding, reporting about, and contesting regulatory provisions is enormous. Affirmative action, occupational safety, and environmental control have greatly increased the size of nonproduction payrolls. The legal costs alone of a major corporation can run into tens of millions of dollars per year. While all of this provides lots of employment for lawyers and economic experts, it is costly because there are other tasks that such professionals could do that would add more to the production of consumer goods and services.

Losses in productivity. Quite apart from the actual expenditures, the regulatory climate may reduce the opportunity or the incentive for experimentation, innovation, and the introduction of new products. Requiring advance government clearance before a new method or product may be introduced (on grounds of potential safety hazards or environmental impact) can eliminate the incentive to develop it. The requirement for advance approval by a regulatory commission before entry is permitted into a regulated industry can discourage potential competitors. (We discussed the role of regulation in productivity growth in Chapter 18.)

Costs Imposed on Third Parties: Indirect External Costs

It has been estimated that because of regulatory activities the growth rate of output per person in the United States has been decreasing by about 0.4 percent per year. If this does not sound like much, consider that this lost growth amounts to a loss of 50 percent in real living standards every century. Such lost purchasing power is an externality of government intervention. It may seem paradoxical that government intervention to offset adverse externalities can create new adverse externalities, but it is plain that it can.

Consider an example. Government regulations designed to assure that all new drugs introduced are both effective and safe, have the incidental effect of delaying the introduction of drugs which are both effective and safe by an average of about nine months. The benefits of these regulations are related to the unsafe and ineffective drugs kept off the market. But nothing is without cost. Here the cost includes the unavailability for about nine months of all those safe and effective drugs whose introduction was delayed.

Government Failure and the Theory of Government Intervention

All costs of intervention discussed in the previous section would be present with a government that had perfect foresight in defining goals, an unerring ability to choose the least costly means of achieving them, and intelligent and dedicated officials whose concern was to do those things — and only those things — that achieved the greatest possible efficiency of the economy.

CAUSES OF GOVERNMENT FAILURE

Government intervention usually falls short of the high standard just described. This is not because bureaucrats are worse than other people, more stupid, more rigid, or more venal. Instead, it is because they are like others, with the usual flaws and virtues. Here are six reasons why government intervention can be *imperfect* (i.e., "fail") in achieving its potential.

Imperfect knowledge or foresight. Regulators may not know enough to set correct standards. For example, natural gas prices may, with the best of intentions, be set too low. The result will be too much quantity demanded and too little quantity supplied, with no automatic correction built in. Or the automobile emission standards for 1983 may be too demanding, thereby proving unexpectedly expensive to achieve — or too lax, thereby leading to unexpected excessive pollution.

Rigidities. Regulatory rules and allocations are hard to change. Yet technology and economic circumstances change continually. Regulations that at one time protected the public against a natural monopoly may perpetuate an unnecessary monopoly after technological changes have made competition possible. Giving AT&T a monopoly in long-distance communication, and specifying its price structure, made sense when the technology for transmitting messages (use of cable) led to natural monopoly. After a communications satellite had been placed in orbit there was room for many competitors, but the regulatory commission was not free simply to open up the industry to anyone. Too many people had invested in the telephone industry and accepted limited profits on the expectation of continued regulation.

Inefficient means. Government may fail to choose the least costly *means* of solving a problem. It may decree a specific form of antipollution device that proves less effective and more expensive than another. A strict rule that proves all but impossible to enforce may be passed, when a milder one would have achieved higher compliance at lower enforcement cost.

Myopic regulation. Regulation may become too restricted and too narrowly defined because the regulators are forced to specialize. Specialization may lead to expertise in a given area, but the regulators may lack the breadth to relate their area to broader concerns. Officials charged with the responsibility for a healthy *railroad* industry (dating from the time when railroads were the dominant means of transportation) may fail to see that the encouragement of trucking, even at the expense of the railroads, may be necessary for a healthy *transportation* industry.

Political constraints. Political realities may prevent the "right" policy from being adopted, even when it has been clearly identified. This is particularly true in a government such as ours that is based on checks and balances. Suppose a technically perfect tax (or farm, or tariff) policy is designed by the experts. It will surely hurt some groups and benefit others. Lobbyists will go to work. The policy is likely to be modified by the cabinet, mutilated by the Senate, rebuilt in a different image by the House, and finally passed by the Congress in a form the experts know is inadequate. Although the president may be aware of

its flaws, he will sign it into law because it is "better than nothing." This scenario occurs because the political process must respond to political realities. "After all," the official may reason as he yields to the demands of the widget lobby (against his best judgment about the public interest), "if I'm defeated for reelection (or not reappointed), I won't be here to serve the public interest on even more important issues next year." (Next year he will have to support widgets out of a sense of consistency!)

Decision maker's objectives. Public officials almost always wish to serve the public interest. But they have their careers, their families, and their prejudices as well. Their own needs are seldom wholly absent from their consideration of the actions they will take. Similarly, their definition of the public interest is likely to be influenced heavily by their personal views of what policies are best.

A close relationship often exists between the regulators and those they regulate. Many government regulators come from industry and plan to return to it. The broadcasting official who serves five years on the Federal Communications Commission and hopes to become a network vice-president after that term of office may view the networks' case in a not wholly disinterested way. Indeed, regulators may protect an industry in ways that would be quite illegal if done from within the industry.

THE REALITY OF GOVERNMENT FAILURE

Regulation is difficult, for it requires all kinds of market decisions without the benefit of self-correcting market signals. The government regulator can decide to build a highway system and raise the money to pay for it, and once built, it will be heavily used. But would the users have been willing to pay as much for the highway as it actually cost? There is no market to answer this question.

Indeed, there is good reason to expect that the

public sector will provide too much of the road network (or other public good), with the result that the marginal cost exceeds the marginal benefit. The reason is political. The beneficiaries are likely to know which politicians voted for the road network in their city, and they will reelect them, whereas, taxpayers pay for so many things that they do not identify the extra taxes that the road network imposes on them.

Evaluating the costs and the probable effectiveness of government intervention requires a comparison of the unregulated economic system as it is working (not as it might work ideally) with the pattern of government intervention as it is likely to perform (not as it might perform ideally). Government failure, like market failure, is a fact of life. It can be caused by stupidity or by corruption, but those flaws are not necessary. The ordinary knowledge and skill and foresight of honest bureaucrats will not by themselves avoid the myriad problems of regulation.

THE THEORY OF GOVERNMENT INTERVENTION TO CORRECT MARKET FAILURE

Economic principles are useful in making decisions concerning the optimal correction of market failure in a particular case. In order to develop these principles, we shall look at the question of preventing pollution.

There are people who are wholly unconcerned about pollution and regard the current fuss as the troublemaking activities of a pampered generation. There are others who regard every form of pollution as a national scandal and some forms as threatening an imminent crisis of survival. A more balanced view recognizes that "pollution" covers many externalities, ranging from threats to our survival to minor nuisances. Virtually all activity leaves some waste product; to say that all pollution must be removed whatever the cost is to try for the impossible and to ensure a vast commitment of society's scarce resources to many projects that will yield a low social value. But somewhere between trying for the impossible

and maintaining a callous indifference to the problem lies a middle ground. Economics helps to define it.

We approach the problem by assuming that government intervention is perfect and imposes no indirect costs. Later we shall relax these artificial assumptions.

Costless, "Perfect" Intervention

We start with the easiest case: Government intervention is costless except for the direct costs imposed by changes in the nature of production, and government intervention is completely honest, wise, and efficient. All the government must do is identify the best form of pollution control, determine the right amount of it, and institute the appropriate means of achieving it. How should it proceed?

First it must choose among alternative antipollution strategies. Suppose a particular factory is releasing all kinds of soot and noxious gases into the atmosphere through its chimneys. The government's experts identify four ways to avoid or reduce the effects of the pollution: (1) shut down the plant or reduce its hours of operation; (2) move everyone out of the area being polluted; (3) require the company to install filters on its smokestacks in order to clean up its exhaust; (4) change the firm's method of production to one that produces cleaner discharges. After detailed study, the experts recommend the third course of action: to filter the exhausts.[2]

The next question concerns how much pollution to eliminate. The experts advise that it is easy and cheap to get rid of virtually all the soot by installing a mechanical filter. But the gases, especially sulfur dioxide (SO_2), are more of a problem. Simple recirculation of the gases would reduce the discharge of SO_2 by 50 percent; after that, the cost doubles for each further 10 percent

---

[2] This is not always the best solution, of course. This first-stage determination among alternative means is of prime importance in achieving the correct solution. A major source of "government failure" is choice of the wrong technique of control.

reduction in the remaining SO_2. At most it would be possible to eliminate 99.44 percent of all SO_2, but the cost would be vast. In economic terms, the marginal costs of removal rise sharply as the amount of SO_2 eliminated rises from 50 percent to 99.44 percent.

What percentage of the gases should be eliminated? The answer depends on the marginal benefits relative to marginal costs. The benefits of pollution control are the external effects avoided. They are not expected to rise as the amount of discharge decreases; after all, the atmosphere can handle a certain amount of discharge with no problem. The optimal amount of prevention will occur where the marginal costs of further prevention equal the marginal benefits. This is illustrated by the black curves in Figure 24-2.

The optimal amount of pollution prevention will be less than the maximum possible when pollution is costly to prevent. Thus the optimal amount of pollution is not equal to zero.

This important proposition can be generalized: The optimal amount of government intervention to avoid market failure will be lower, the greater are the costs imposed.

The Effect of Other Costs of Intervention

Next we add to our consideration the fact that government intervention brings with it enforcement costs—costs to the government, to the firm, and to third parties—of the kinds already discussed. These costs have to be added to the direct costs we have just considered.

Suppose first that the enforcement costs are known accurately and are of a lump-sum nature; that is, they are independent of whether 70 percent or 90 percent of the pollution is to be removed. Whether the intervention is now justified depends on the total size of the costs, relative to the benefits of the optimal pollution prevention policy. Say the net benefits before considering enforcement costs are estimated at $2 million. What if the enforcement costs would be $3 million? It would be better to live with the pollution

FIGURE 24-2
The Optimal Amount of Pollution Prevention

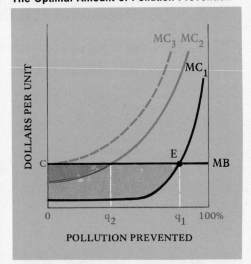

The optimal quantity of pollution prevention occurs where marginal benefits from prevention equal marginal costs of prevention. *MB* represents the marginal benefit achieved by pollution prevention, assumed in this example to be constant at $C per percentage point. MC_1 represents the marginal costs of preventing pollution; it rises sharply as more ahd more pollution is eliminated. The optimal level of pollution control is q_1, where $MB = MC_1$. Notice that not all pollution is eliminated. For all units up to q_1, marginal benefits from pollution prevention exceed marginal costs. Net benefits are shown by the total shaded area. Any further pollution elimination would add more to costs than to benefits.

If the marginal cost curve shifts upward to MC_2, due, say, to the addition of enforcement costs, the quantity of optimal prevention will decrease to q_2 and the net benefits will be reduced to the darker shaded area. If costs increase to MC_3, the optimal amount of prevention becomes zero.

than to prevent it! For prevention activities use up resources that the public values at $3 million to achieve benefits that the public values at only $2 million. However, if the lump-sum costs were less than the benefits—say, $500,000—it would pay to prevent the pollution, for the net gain would be $1.5 million.

What if, instead of lump-sum costs, the enforcement costs are variable rising with the level of control sought? The marginal costs of enforcement must be added to the marginal direct costs of prevention, thereby shifting upward the marginal costs of prevention. This is shown by the colored marginal cost curves in Figure 24-2. The addition of such costs will surely decrease the amount of prevention that is optimal. If the costs are large enough, they may even make any prevention uneconomical.

The Effect of Government Failure

Finally, suppose that the government makes a mistake in regulation. Say the government mistakenly specifies a method of pollution control that is less effective than the best method. This will increase the cost of achieving any given level of prevention. If the government insists on the level of control appropriate to the correct method but requires the incorrect method, it can convert a social gain from control into a social loss. This is illustrated in Figure 24-3.

GOVERNMENT INTERVENTION IN THE UNITED STATES TODAY

The theoretical principles for determining the optimal amount of intervention that we have just developed are individually accepted by virtually everyone. What they add up to, however, is more controversial.

Does government intervene too little or too much in response to market failure? This question reflects one aspect of the ongoing argument about the role of government in the economy. Much of the rhetoric of our concern with ecology urges government intervention against heartless, profit-mad, giant corporations that pervert the environment for their own crass purposes. The apparent reluctance of the American public to believe in an energy shortage rests in good part on the suspicion that the oil and gas companies are somehow manipulating their supplies (and the American public) for private profit. Such feelings lead to the demand for more—and more stringent—government regulation.

FIGURE 24-3
The Effects of Government Failure

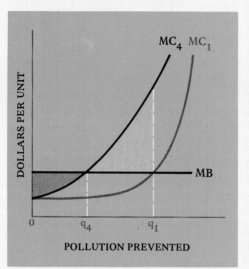

Choice of the wrong method of control will reduce the optimal amount of intervention and may convert the gains from intervention into losses. The MB and MC_1 curves are similar to those in Figure 24-2. One common form of government failure is to specify the wrong method of intervention. Suppose the government specifies a method of pollution control that leads to the costs shown by MC_4. This is inefficient because costs at every level of pollution prevention are higher than necessary. Under such a method, the optimal level of prevention falls to q_4 with net benefits shown by the dark shaded area. Government failure reduces the appropriate amount of prevention that is optimal. The government will compound its failure if it insists on the level of prevention q_1 while requiring use of the inefficient method. The cost of every unit of pollution prevented beyond q_4 is in excess of its benefits, as shown by the light shaded area. Indeed, the result is worse than no intervention at all (the light shaded area is larger than the dark shaded area). While the best possible government intervention would have produced a net gain, government failure produces a net loss.

At the same time, the heavy hand of government regulation is seen as contributing greatly to both inflation and recession by burdening private companies with regulations that add to costs and impede innovation and by keeping prices and wages artificially high. Even perfect intervention would be costly, but imperfect intervention makes it much too costly. In this view, the deregulation of the airlines was a gift to the American consumer and it foreshadows the deregulation of motor transport, communications, and other regulated industries. In some quarters the government (rather than the oil companies or OPEC) is seen as the villain in the energy shortage: its rigid and unresponsive price controls and allocations of gasoline, oil, and natural gas, and its quotas on imported oil early in the 1970s, were the cause of the shortages that now plague us.

The Role of Analysis

Economic analysis and measurement can help to eliminate certain misconceptions that cloud and confuse the debate. We have noted one such misconception: the optimal level of pollution (or of any other negative externality) is not, as some urge, zero. Another mistake is to equate "market failure" with the greed of profit-motivated corporations. Externalities do not require callous, thoughtless, or deliberately deceptive practices of private, profit-seeking firms; they occur whenever the signals to which decision makers respond do not include social as well as private benefits and costs. Such situations are not limited to private firms in a capitalistic system. Cities and nationalized industries pollute just as much as privately owned industries when they are operated in the same way, as they typically are. A third mistake is to think that the profits of a corporation tell something about neglected externalities. It is possible for a profitable firm (such as GM) or an unprofitable one (such as Chrysler) to spend too little on pollution control or on safety, but it is also possible for it to spend too

much. The existence of profits provides no clue as to which is the case.

The Role of Ideology

While positive analysis has a role to play, there are several reasons why ideology plays a bigger role in the evaluation process here than in many other areas.

First, measuring the costs of government intervention is difficult, particularly with respect to indirect costs, because some of the trade-offs are inherently uncertain. How important and how unsafe is nuclear power? Does the ban on DDT cause so much malnutrition as to offset the gains in the ecology it brings? What cannot be readily measured can be alleged to be extremely high (or low) by opponents (or supporters) of intervention. The numerous findings by well-known scholars on both sides of each of these subjects has led one economist to the cynical conclusion that "believing is seeing."

Second, classifying the actual pattern of government intervention as successful or not is another matter touched by ideology. Has government safety regulation been (choose one) useful if imperfect, virtually ineffective, or positively perverse? All three views have been expressed and "documented."

A third difficulty arises in defining what constitutes market failure. Does product differentiation represent market success (by giving consumers the variety they want) or failure (by foisting expensive and useless variations on them)?

In the United States at the start of the 1980s it seems safe to conclude that confidence in the existing mix of free-market and government regulation is at a relatively low ebb. Not only are specific policy suggestions hotly argued, so is the whole philosophy of intervention. There is as yet no consensus as to what is wrong; the pressures for changes are strong in *both* directions.

Summary

1. The various markets in the economy are coordinated by the price system. Changes in prices and profits, resulting from emerging scarcities and surpluses, lead decision makers in far-flung markets to make adaptations in response to a change in any one market of the economy. Such responses tend to correct the shortages and surpluses as well as to change the market signals of prices and profits.

2. The case for the free market is that, in addition to providing automatic coordination, it often provides an impersonal, efficient, and self-correcting way of making the decisions about what to produce and how to distribute the fruits of production. Such virtues of the competitive free market led many nineteenth century economists to believe that government should not interfere in any way with the free-market determination of prices and quantities.

3. Markets do not always work perfectly. Market failure may occur for three main kinds of reasons: (a) externalities arising from differences between private and social costs and benefits, (b) market imperfections and impediments, and (c) the existence of goals that the market process neglects.

4. Pollution is an example of an externality. An important source of pollution is producers' use of water and air that they do not regard as scarce. Since they do not pay all the costs of using these resources, they are not motivated to avoid the costs. Individual use of common-property resources, congestion, and neglect of future consequences are other sources of externalities.

5. Market imperfections and impediments are anything that prevents the prompt movement of resources in response to market signals; they include monopoly, ignorance, and sources of labor immobility. They also include the inability in some situations of private firms to collect revenues for goods produced, and the existence in other situations of transactions costs of private production and sale of commodities that are much higher than costs of public provision.

6. Nonmarket goals that may lead to market failure include values placed on public provision for its own sake, on protection of individuals from themselves or from others, on recognition of social obligations, and on compassion.

7. Microeconomic policy concerns activities of the central authorities that alter the unrestricted workings of the free-market system in order to affect either the allocation of resources among uses or the distribution of income among people. Major tools of microeconomic policy include (a) public provision, (b) redistribution, (c) rule making, and (d) structuring incentives. The first two are the subject of Chapter 25. Both prescriptive and proscriptive rule making occur in a variety of forms. Incentives can be structured in a number of ways including the use of fines, subsidies, taxes, and effluent charges. All are designed to lead private decision makers to internalize externalities or to give weight to nonmarket goals.

8. There are costs as well as benefits of government intervention, and they must be considered in choosing whether, when, and how intervention is appropriate. Among these costs are the direct costs of government incurred; the costs imposed on those regulated, direct and indirect; and the costs imposed on third parties. These costs are never negligible and are often large. In addition to these costs there is the fact that government intervention may fail; if it does, the costs of intervention may be incurred without the benefits of avoiding market failure being fully realized.

9. The optimal degree of government intervention is determined by considering the magnitude of market failure, the likelihood that government intervention will correct the failure, and the costs of intervention. It is neither possible nor efficient to correct all market failure; neither is it always efficient to do nothing. Just how and where to change the proportions of free-market decision

making and government intervention in that decision making is an area of continuing economic and political debate.

Topics for Review

The difference between central planning and market coordination
How the price system coordinates
Differences between private and social valuations
Causes of market failure
Externalities
Internalizing externalities
Net social benefit (*NSB*) and net private benefit (*NPB*)
Benefits and costs of government intervention
Causes of government failure
The optimal amount of pollution

Discussion Questions

1. For each of the following events, indicate how you might expect the market economy to respond.
   a. The decision of an automobile manufacturer to build a large assembly plant employing 5,000 workers near a town with only 11,000 total population, situated 40 miles from the nearest city.
   b. Discovery of a new means of making bricks that reduces their cost by 50 percent.
   c. A further doubling of the price of gasoline as a result of OPEC's latest oil summit meeting.
2. The Aswan Dam has been called Egypt's "wall against hunger," by virtue of its provision of both irrigation water and electric power to the Nile Valley. Among its less salutary side effects are:
   a. The reduced flow of water and silt in the river have allowed the Nile Delta to be overrun by sea water, leaving harmful salts.
   b. Lake Nasser, in back of the dam, has become a breeding place for malaria mosquitoes.
   c. Homes of 122,000 Nubian villagers have been inundated, along with countless antiquities for 310 miles upstream from the dam.
   Should the dam have been built? Discuss the issues involved, using the concepts of private and social costs and externalities.

3. Each of the following activities has known harmful effects: (a) cigarette smoking, (b) driving a car at 55 mph, (c) private ownership of guns, (d) drilling for offshore oil. In each case, identify whether there is a divergence between social and private costs.
4. Develop the case for (or against) government interference in the areas of education, medicine, airport construction and location, egg production, logging, electricity generation, and the location of a privately financed toll highway. Which of these do you think least suitable for government action?
5. Should the free market be allowed to determine the price for the following, or should government intervene?
   a. transit fares
   b. heating oil
   c. plastic surgery for victims of fires
   d. garbage collection
   e. postal service to newspapers and magazines
   f. fire protection for churches
   g. ice cream
6. The president of Goodyear Tire and Rubber Company complained that government regulation had imposed $30 million per year in "unproductive costs" on his company. These costs of compliance were broken down:
   a. environmental regulation, $17 million
   b. occupational safety and health, $7 million
   c. motor vehicle safety, $3 million
   d. personnel and administration, $3 million
   How would one determine whether these costs were "productive" or "unproductive"?
7. Suppose the facts asserted below are true; should they trigger government intervention? If so, what policy alternatives are available?
   a. The Concorde jet is twice as fast, twice as noisy on takeoff and landing, and carries half the passengers of jumbo jets.
   b. Hospital costs have been rising at about four times the rate of increase of personal income, and proper treatment of a serious illness has become extraordinarily expensive.
   c. The cost of the average one-family house in Washington, D.C., is now over $120,000, an amount that is out of the reach of most government employees.
   d. Cigarette smoking tends to reduce life expectancy by eight years.
   e. Saccharin in large doses has been found to cause cancer in Canadian mice.

8. Consider the possible beneficial and adverse effects of each of the following forms of government interference.
   a. Charging motorists a tax for driving in the downtown areas of large cities—and using the revenues to provide peripheral parking and shuttle buses.
   b. Prohibiting doctors from purchasing malpractice insurance.
   c. Mandating no-fault auto insurance, in which the car owner's insurance company is responsible for damage to his or her vehicle no matter who causes the accident.
   d. Requiring automobile manufacturers to warrantee the tires on cars they sell instead of (as at present) having the tire manufacturer be the warrantor.

9. Consider the problem of motorcycle noise pollution. What is the "optimal level of permissible noise"? How might it be determined? A given level of noise permitted might be achieved in a variety of ways; name several, including at least one that does not regulate the motorcyclist in any way. Which is the fairest way? Which is the most effective way?

10. Consider the following (alleged) facts about pollution control and indicate what, if any, influence they might have on policy determination.

a. In 1979 the cost of meeting federal pollution requirements was $61 per person.
b. More than a third of the world's known oil supplies lie under the ocean floor, and there is no known blowout-proof method of recovery.
c. Sulfur removal requirements and strip mining regulations have led to the tripling of the cost of a ton of coal used in electrical generation.
d. Every million dollars spent on pollution control creates 67 new jobs in the economy.

11. During a Pittsburgh air pollution alert a newspaper reporter interviewed a 69-year-old retired steelworker. He said: "I've got a heart condition myself, and I know that when I look out the window and see the air like it was this morning, I've got to stay inside. Yesterday, I tried to drive to the store, and I couldn't see 50 feet ahead of me, it was so thick, so I just came home. I remember that when I was young, we never thought about pollution. Everybody was working, and everybody had money, and the smokestacks were smoking, and the air was dirty, and we were all happy. I think the best air we ever had in Pittsburgh was during the Depression. That's when nobody was working." Comment on this statement in terms of the issues discussed in this chapter.

Microeconomic Policy II: Public Finance and Public Expenditure

25

All governments spend money, and they must raise revenue in order to do so. The American federal government is no exception. To do what the Constitution mandates, it must spend and tax. But government spending and government taxation today go far beyond the minimum required to provide such essentials as a system of justice and protection against foreign enemies. Spending and taxing are also key tools of both macroeconomic and microeconomic policy.

In this chapter we look at these as tools of microeconomic policy. Government expenditure and government taxation inescapably affect both the allocation of resources and the distribution of income. Often they are used intentionally to try to correct for market failures.

There is no simple and sharp functional distinction between expenditure and tax policies. One way to deal with polluted rivers, for example, is by public expenditure to clean them up. An alternative is to use taxes to penalize pollution or to give tax concessions to firms that install pollution-abating devices. Tax concessions that seek to induce market responses are now called **tax expenditures** — that is, sacrifices of revenue by the taxing authorities that are designed to achieve purposes that the government believes are desirable.

In this chapter we are concerned both with the overall impact of public expenditure and taxation on microeconomic decisions and with the deliberate use of these tools for effecting such decisions.

Taxation as a Tool of Micro Policy

There is a bewildering array of taxes, some highly visible (such as sales taxes and income taxes) and others all but invisible to the con-

TABLE 25-1

Government Tax Receipts, by Source

Kind of tax	Federal		State		Local		All government	
	Billions of dollars	Percentage	Billions of dollars	Percentage	Billions of dollars	Percentage	Billions of dollars	Percentage
Personal income	156.7	41	25.5	16	3.8	3	186.0	28
Corporate income and related	54.9	14	9.2	6	0.0	0	64.1	10
Social security and related	98.5	26	32.4	21	2.8	2	133.7	20
Subtotal (income and related)	310.1	81	67.1	43	6.6	5	383.8	58
Excise and sales	23.2	6	52.4	34	8.2	7	83.8	13
Property	0.0	0	2.3	1	60.3	51	62.6	9
All others	48.8	13	34.0	22	44.3	37	127.1	20
Total	382.1	100	155.8	100	119.4	100	657.3	100

Source: Facts and Figures on Government Finance, 20th Biennial Edition (New York: Tax Foundation, 1979).

The federal government places major reliance on income taxes; state governments on excise and sales taxes; and local governments on property taxes. Different levels of government rely on different kinds of taxes. The most important are highlighted by the percentages printed in color. The data are for fiscal year 1977.

sumer because they are imposed on raw materials producers or manufacturers at an early stage. People are taxed on what they earn, on what they spend, and on what they own. Firms are taxed as well as households. And taxes are not only numerous, they take a big bite. Aggregate taxes amount to roughly one-third of the total value of goods and services produced in the United States each year. The diversity and importance of various taxes are shown in Table 25-1.

TAXES AND THE DISTRIBUTION OF INCOME

A government that taxes the rich and exempts the poor is redistributing income. How much redistribution is achieved by U.S. taxes today?

Progressivity

Rhetoric about income distribution and tax policy often invokes the important but hard to define concepts of "equity" and "equality." Equity —fairness—is a normative concept; what one group thinks is fair may seem outrageous to another. But equality is a straightforward concept —or is it?

To tax people equally might mean several things. It might mean that each person should pay the same tax, which would be very hard on the unemployed worker and very easy on Reggie Jackson. It might mean that each should pay the same proportion of his or her income, say a flat 25 percent, whether rich or poor, living alone or supporting eight children, healthy or suffering from a a disease that requires heavy use of expensive drugs. It might mean that each should pay an amount of tax such that everybody's income after taxes is the same—which would remove any incentive to earn above average income. Or it might mean none of these things.

People may not agree on what redistributions are fair, but they can agree on what redistributions actually occur. To get precise measurements of what happens, the distributional effects of taxes are usually discussed using the concept of **progressivity of taxation,** the ratio of taxes to income at different levels of income.

A **proportional tax** takes amounts of money from people in direct proportion to their income.

A **regressive tax** takes a larger percentage of income from people, the lower their income.

A **progressive tax** takes a larger percentage of income from people, the larger their income.

A tax system is said to be progressive if it decreases the inequality of income distribution and to be regressive if it increases the inequality.

It is easier to assess the progressivity or regressivity of particular taxes than of the tax system as a whole.

The Regressivity of Sales and Excise Taxes

If two families each spend the same proportion of their income on a certain commodity that is subject to a sales or an excise tax, the tax will be proportional in its effects on them. If the tax is on a commodity, such as food, that takes a larger proportion of the income of lower-income families, it will be regressive; if it is on a commodity such as jewelry, where the rich spend a larger proportion of their income than the poor, it will be progressive.

Commodities with inelastic demands provide easy sources of revenue. In many countries commodities such as tobacco, alcohol, and gasoline are singled out for very high rates of taxation. But these commodities usually account for a much greater proportion of the expenditure of lower-income than higher-income groups, and taxes on them are thus regressive.

The sales and excise taxes used in the United States today are as a whole regressive.

The Regressivity of Property Taxes

The progressivity of the property tax has been studied extensively. It is well known that the rich live in more expensive houses than the poor, but all that this establishes is that the rich tend to pay more dollars in property tax than do the poor. Because the rich tend to live in different communities than the poor and thus pay taxes at different rates, and because they tend to spend a different proportion of their income for housing, the question of the progressivity or regressivity of the property tax is difficult and controversial. Most studies have shown that the proportion of income spent for housing tends to decrease with income. Many but not all public finance experts believe that the property tax tends to be regressive in its overall effect.

The Progressivity of Personal Income Taxes

The personal tax rate is itself a function of taxable income, and it is useful to distinguish between two different rates. The **average tax rate** paid by an individual or by a couple is their income tax divided by total income. The **marginal tax rate** is the amount of tax the taxpayer would pay on an additional dollar of income.

Table 25-2 shows the applicable rates on federal income tax in 1980, and Figure 25-1 shows the fraction of taxable income paid in taxes.

In structure, the federal personal income tax is quite progressive because the average rate rises steadily with income. However, because of the special definitions given to net income by the tax laws, the overall effect of the federal income tax is actually less progressive than Table 25-2 suggests. To arrive at taxable income, total income is modified by certain exemptions from income, by capital gains provisions, and by permitted deductions from gross income. Moreover, income earned by personal services, as distinct from property, is subject to a maximum marginal tax rate of 50 percent, instead of the 70 percent shown in the table.

Despite modifications, the federal income tax is progressive in effect as well as in structure.

The Unknown Progressivity of Corporate Income Tax

The federal corporate income tax is, for practical purposes, a flat-rate tax of 48 percent of profits

TABLE 25-2

The Rate Structure of the Federal Income Tax, 1980

(1) Taxable income after deductions and exemptions	(2) Personal income tax	(3) Average tax rate, percentage (2) ÷ (1)	(4) Marginal tax rate, percentage (tax on extra dollar)[a]
$ 2,400	$ 0	0	0
3,400	0	0	14
6,000	374	6.2	16
10,000	1,062	10.6	18
15,000	2,055	13.7	21
20,000	3,225	16.1	24
30,000	6,238	20.8	37
50,000	14,754	29.5	49
75,000[b]	27,778[b]	37.0[b]	54[b]
100,000	41,998	42.0	59
150,000	73,528	49.0	64
200,000	107,032	53.5	68
250,000	141,724	56.7	70
1,000,000	666,724	66.7	70
10,000,000	6,966,724	69.7	70

[a] The marginal tax rate on personal service income is limited to a maximum of 50 percent.

[b] For incomes above $50,000, actual taxes and tax rates will be less than the amounts shown if part of the income is earned by personal services.

Both marginal and average tax rates rise with income; thus the tax is progressive in structure. These data give the amount of federal tax to be paid at different income levels by a married couple in 1980. The marginal tax rate rises with income and reaches 50 percent at $50,000. However, these rates are based on taxable income, not total income received. Because of a variety of deductions and exemptions, the effective average tax rates on income received are much lower than those shown in column (3).

as defined by the taxing authorities. It is difficult to determine its effects on income distribution, for there is great controversy over the extent to which it is "shifted" to consumers.[1] So far as the tax falls on stockholders, they as a group tend to be wealthier than individuals who do not own stock, and there is thus a tendency toward pro-

---

[1] The question of tax incidence—that is, who really pays a tax imposed on any one group—is discussed later in this chapter.

gressivity. But within the stockholder group, lower-income stockholders bear a disproportionate share of the tax relative to wealthy stockholders. If a dollar were paid out in dividends instead of taxes, rich stockholders would keep a much smaller share than poorer stockholders because of their high marginal personal tax rates.

The Progressivity of the Tax System

To assess the way in which the whole tax system, as distinct from any one tax, affects income distribution is more difficult. One aspect concerns the mix of taxes of different kinds. Federal taxes (chiefly income taxes) tend to be somewhat progressive. State and local authorities rely heavily on property and sales taxes and thus have tax systems that are regressive.

The matter of assessing progressivity is even more complex than this. Is progressivity defined for the individual or for the family? When a couple with two children pays the same tax as a childless couple with the same income, is this proportional or regressive taxation? If the *family* is the relevant unit, it is proportional taxation. If the *person* is the relevant unit, equal tax rates on families of different sizes having the same income would be regressive. As it is, a household with children pays less *income* tax than a household without children but with the same income. (This does not mean, as childless people often assume, that the household with children pays less total taxes. For other taxes, such as sales taxes, tend to fall more heavily on large families than on small ones.)

The difficulty of determining progressivity is increased by the fact that income from different sources is taxed at different rates. For example, in the federal individual tax, income from royalties on oil wells is taxed more lightly than income from royalties on books; profits from sales of assets (called capital gains) are taxed more lightly than wages and salaries; and some bond interest is tax exempt while most interest income is taxed. To evaluate progressivity, one needs to

FIGURE 25-1
Taxable and After-tax Income for a Married Couple in 1980

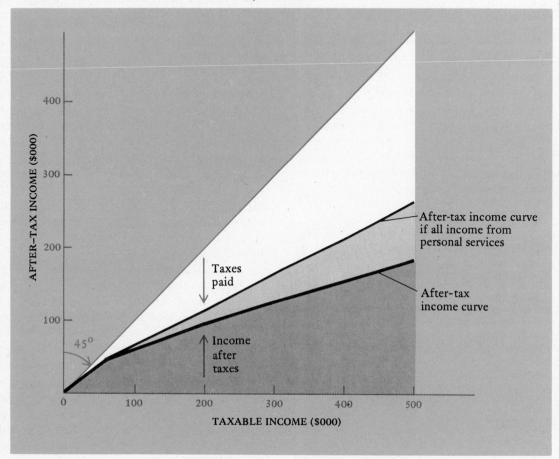

The tax rate schedule is quite progressive for the first $50,000 of taxable income and much less for higher incomes. If taxes were zero, after-tax income would equal taxable income, as shown by the colored 45° line. If taxes were proportional, the after-tax income curve would be a straight line from the origin. The actual after-tax income curve (neglecting the per- sonal service adjustment) is the heavy black curve. Its curvature away from the 45° line represents progres- sivity. (Because personal service income is taxed at a maximum rate of 50 percent, the after-tax income may be greater than shown by the heavy black line; it is shown by the thin black line.)

know the way in which different levels of income correlate with different sources of income.

The combined effect of all U.S. taxes, federal, state, and local, is virtually proportional today for families with incomes between $5,000 and $50,000 and progressive only above $50,000. For families of very low income, the tax struc- ture is regressive.

CAN PROGRESSIVITY BE INCREASED?

Many observers have argued that to achieve overall proportionality in the tax structure is in itself a significant accomplishment. Some argue that, given the enormous fraction of national in- come that is taxed away, more progressivity can- not be achieved. (The greater the fraction of the population's money taxed away, the harder it is to do so progressively.) Whether or not more progressivity is desirable, is more progressivity possible?

Taxes can be levied on assets, on incomes, and on expenditures. Inheritance taxes and gift taxes are taxes on assets; such taxes do not—and cannot—play a large continuing role in the overall revenue picture. Taxes on incomes are important and can be quite progressive. Taxes on expenditures—especially sales and excise taxes —are related to the dollar value of expenditures, not the incomes of those spending the money; they are known to be regressive.

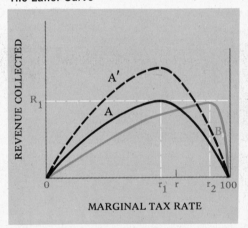

FIGURE 25-2
The Laffer Curve

Increases in tax rates beyond some level will decrease rather than increase tax revenue. The solid black curve A shows that as tax rates are increased from zero up to r_1 tax revenues increase, but beyond r_1 further increases in rates lead to less revenue. Curve B is different; it does not reach its maximum until rate r_2. While both A and B are Laffer curves and each predicts the same maximum revenue yield, the policy implications are very different for the two curves. If actual tax rates are r and the objective is to maximize revenue, rates should be reduced if A is correct and increased if B is correct.

Structural changes in the tax laws may shift these curves. For example, by eliminating tax loopholes the A curve might be shifted to A', thereby increasing the revenue yield at every level of tax rates.

Substantial progressivity in income taxes is required merely to achieve proportionality in the overall tax pattern.

Will Increasing Reliance on Income Taxes Increase Progressivity?

It may seem obvious that, since income taxes are progressive and expenditure taxes are regressive, to shift more of the tax burden to income taxes must increase progressivity. Surprisingly, some economists have argued that this is not the case. While a shift to more reliance on income taxes will raise both the average rate and the marginal rate of tax on incomes, it may or may not raise the total amount of revenue actually collected. Whether it does depends on the incentive effects of tax rates.

A graph that relates the government's income tax yield to the level of marginal tax rates has recently gained attention as the **Laffer curve,** named after economist Arthur Laffer. Its essential feature is that tax revenues reach a maximum at some rate of taxation well below 100 percent. The general shape of the Laffer curve is a matter of simple logic: at a zero tax rate, no revenue will be collected. Similarly, at a 100 percent tax rate, revenues will again be zero because no one will bother to earn taxable income just to support the government. For some intermediate rates, people will both earn income and pay taxes. Thus the revenue collected must reach a maximum at tax rates somewhere between zero and 100 percent. For rates higher than the rate that produces this maximum, every increase in tax rates will lead to a decrease in tax revenues. (See Figure 25-2.)

Just where this maximum occurs—whether at a tax rate of 60 percent or 80 percent or 95 percent—is an important empirical matter. Laffer and others think tax policy has already carried progressiveness too far. They believe that the United States is at or past the rate at which higher tax rates yield more revenue. As a result, they say, any attempt to increase progressivity by raising income tax rates would be self-defeating. Many other economists disagree. While they

The Laffer Curve 600 Years Before Laffer

In the fourteenth century the Arabic philosopher Ibn Khaldun wrote:

It should be known that at the beginning of the dynasty, taxation yields a large revenue from small assessments. At the end of the dynasty, taxation yields a small revenue from large assessments. . . .

When the dynasty follows the ways of group feeling and (political) superiority, it necessarily has at first a desert attitude. The desert attitude requires kindness, reverence, humility, respect for the property of other people, and disinclination to appropriate it, except in rare instances. Therefore, the individual imposts and assessments, which together constitute the tax revenue, are low. When tax assessments and imposts upon the subjects are low, the latter have the energy and desire to do things. Cultural enterprises grow and increase, because the low taxes bring satisfaction. When cultural enterprises grow, the number of individual imposts and assessments mounts. In consequence, the tax revenue, which is the sum total of (the individual assessments), increases.

When the dynasty continues in power and their rulers follow each other in succession, they become sophisticated. The Bedouin attitude and simplicity lose their significance, and the Bedouin qualities of moderation and restraint disappear.

As a result, the individual imposts and assessments upon the subjects, agricultural laborers, farmers, and all the other taxpayers, increase. Every individual impost and assessment is greatly increased, in order to obtain a higher tax revenue. Customs duties are placed upon articles of commerce. Gradual increases in the amount of assessments succeed each other regularly, in correspondence with the gradual increase in the luxury customs and many needs of the dynasty, and the spending required in connection with them. Eventually, the taxes will weigh heavily upon the subjects and overburden them. Heavy taxes become an obligation and tradition, because the increases took place gradually, and no one knows specifically who increased them or levied them. They lie upon the subjects like an obligation and tradition.

The assessments increase beyond the limits of equity. The result is that the interest of the subjects in cultural enterprises disappears, since when they compare expenditures and taxes with their income and gain and see the little profit they make, they lose all hope. Therefore, many of them refrain from all the activity. The result is that the total tax revenue goes down.

Finally, civilization is destroyed, because the incentive for cultural activity is gone. It is the dynasty that suffers from the situation, because it (is the dynasty that) profits from cultural activity.*

* *From the Muqaddimah: An Introduction to History*, translated from the Arabic by Franz Rosenthal. Bollingen Series XLIII. Copyright © 1958 and 1967 by Princeton University Press. Reprinted by permission of Princeton University Press.

might concede that some countries (such as the United Kingdom) may have reached such a point, they argue that this has happened only because their residents can migrate to countries with lower taxes, such as the United States. They believe that the current U.S. top marginal tax rates of 50 percent on personal service income and 70 percent on other income are still short of being self-defeating in terms of tax revenue. That is, they believe that Professor Laffer has identified a potential rather than an actual problem.

Increasing Progressivity by Changing the Income Tax Structure

If the government raises income taxes for one group and lowers them for another in a way that leaves the total tax yield constant, the *structure* of the income tax will have been changed. Much repeated demand for "tax reform" relates to proposed changes in the structure of income taxes. Most economists believe that such changes can be made (whether or not they consider them desirable) and that if they were made,

TABLE 25-3

One Version of the Negative Income Tax with a 50 Percent Marginal Tax Rate

(1) Family income	(2) Tax	(3) Family income after tax
$ 0	$−3,200	$3,200
800	−2,800	3,600
1,600	−2,400	4,000
2,400	−2,000	4,400
3,200	−1,600	4,800
4,000	−1,200	5,200
4,800	− 800	5,600
5,600	− 400	6,000
6,400	0	6,400

Instead of having a zero income tax up to some level and a positive tax thereafter, there is a continuous variation of tax with income. Under this plan a family with no income is entitled to $3,200. For every dollar the family earns between $0 and $6,400, its receipts from the government are reduced by 50 cents. Column (2) shows the "tax" at different levels of income. Column (3) shows the total income available for spending. The "break-even" income is $6,400, at which the family neither receives a grant nor pays a tax. On incomes above $6,400, taxes are paid.

they would increase the progressivity of the total tax system. Here are two important and widely advocated proposals.

The negative income tax (NIT). A tax can be negative if at some level of income the government pays "the taxpayer" instead of the other way around. The so-called **negative income tax** is a policy tool designed to increase progressivity and combat poverty by making taxes negative at very low incomes. Such a tax would extend progressivity to incomes below those where people currently have income tax liability.

There are many versions of NIT proposals; the one described here will illustrate the basic idea. The underlying belief is that a family of four is entitled to a minimum annual income—say, $3,200. The aim is to guarantee this income without eliminating the incentive to become self-supporting. This is done by combining a grant with a tax. At a break-even level the family will neither receive money from the government nor

pay any tax. Below this income level the family will be paid by the government (i.e., the family pays a "negative tax"). Above this break-even level it will pay a positive tax. An example, based on a grant of $3,200 and a marginal negative tax rate of 50 percent, is given in Table 25-3.

Supporters of the negative income tax believe that it would be a particularly effective tool for reducing poverty. It provides a minimum level of income as a matter of right, not of charity, and it does so without removing the incentive to work of those eligible for payments. Every dollar earned adds to the after-tax income of the family. As a potential replacement for many other relief programs, it promises to avoid the most pressing cases of poverty with much less administrative cost and without the myriad exceptions that are involved in most programs. An incidental advantage is that it removes whatever incentive people might have to migrate to states with better welfare programs, but it does not discourage migration to places where work may be available.

The net cost of such a negative income tax scheme would depend on which other programs of aid to the needy were curtailed and on the effect on the incentives of those covered. Current cost estimates of the plan described here are about $7.4 billion a year. To institute the same type of program with a basic income of $5,000 for a family of four (still below the poverty level) would cost $27.5 billion per year. To bring every family up to the 1978 poverty level of $6,662 would cost much more—about $56 billion per year.

Comprehensive income taxation (CIT). Joseph Pechman of the Brookings Institution has taken the lead in arguing that it is possible to raise more revenue from the income tax, increase its progressivity, and at the same time *reduce* the disincentive effects by reducing both average and marginal tax rates!

This sounds like magic, but it is a matter of simple arithmetic. The **tax base** is the total amount of taxable income. Under present definitions taxable income is much less than total income because there are all sorts of deductions and exemptions. If all income were taxed, regardless of source, it would be possible to raise more revenue by applying lower rates to this larger tax base. The idea of **comprehensive income taxation** is to eliminate virtually all the so-called loopholes, the deductions and exemptions that make taxable income less than total income. By eliminating some or all personal deductions, homeowner preferences, special treatment of capital gains, and exemptions for dependents, old age, and blindness, the tax base could be increased by up to 70 percent. It would then be easy to reduce tax *rates* in all income brackets.

Under these schemes it would be possible to achieve substantially more progressivity without increasing anyone's marginal tax rate at all. For example, imagine a definition of the CIT where comprehensive income is 150 percent of present taxable income. Rates could be left unchanged for high-income taxpayers and greatly reduced for middle- and low-income taxpayers in such amounts as to maintain the same total tax revenue but to increase progressivity.

Alternatively, some rates could be decreased by a little and others by a great deal—as long as the average decrease was one-third. Needless to say, even if everyone's tax *rates* went down under CIT, not everyone's tax *payments* would do so: what some regard as an unfair loophole may be for others their toehold on economic prosperity.

Political Barriers to Using Tax Policy to Redistribute Income

The purely political barriers to tax reform are formidable. Any single reform is likely to impose large costs on a relatively well-identified group, while the benefits it gives would be more widely diffused.

The ten people who would each lose a million dollars from a particular tax reform are much more interested in the issue than the 10 million people who would each gain a dollar. The ten, not the 10 million, would hire lobbyists and make

campaign contributions. Legislators must respond to these pressures if they want long public careers. With *expenditure* programs the political pressures are reversed. The beneficiaries of a program to increase social security payments, provide medical care, or give aid to the cities are much more intensely and immediately involved than the millions of others whose taxes will rise a little bit to pay for it. The 100,000 who would gain a hundred dollars each from a particular expenditure policy are much more likely to be heard than the 10 million whose taxes would rise by a dollar each. (Even when people demand lower taxes, they vote out of office politicians who refuse to provide the services the taxes would make possible.) The result is that political pressures make redistribution by expenditures more attractive than by tax reform.

HOW MUCH PROGRESSIVITY IS DESIRABLE?

Suppose increased progressivity could be achieved; would we want it? Many say no.

One obvious objection to tax reform designed to increase progressivity is that not everyone wants more progressivity. A second is that many who do not oppose more progressivity do not want changes that make it easier for the government to raise more money. Such people fear schemes such as NIT and CIT precisely because they do not generate tax revolts. They point to the introduction of "pay as you go" (withholding) taxes in the 1940s. The argument used then to persuade people to accept withholding was that it was more convenient and less painful to have one's employer collect the taxes on income as it was earned than to have to come up with a lump sum on a date such as April 15. But, they argue, the reality has been that governments discovered they could exploit the system: they kept raising taxes until the same level of pain was suffered all year round.

A third source of opposition to increasing progressivity by means of tax reform is that every aspect of present tax policy was introduced to benefit some group whose members believe they have valid claims to special treatment. Consider some of the "loopholes" that the CIT would reduce or eliminate. Tax deductibility of charitable and educational contributions provide incentives for gifts to churches, universities, and private charities and foundations. Tax-exempt municipal bonds help hardpressed cities raise money. After all, every deduction or exemption was enacted by Congress for a purpose and with some political support.

More progressivity conflicts with other goals. Further, more progressivity may conflict with what is seen as fair. Much erosion of the tax base has arisen from adjustments made in the name of equity. Special tax treatment of the aged seems fair to many, in view of the probable needs by the aged for extensive medical treatment. More favorable tax treatment of families with children than of childless couples seems fair to some on the basis of need but unfair to those who think population is already too high.

Finally, the case against tax policy as a means of achieving redistributive goals has some support even among those who favor more redistribution of income from rich to poor. They argue that it is misleading, unnecessary, and poor tactics politically to pay so much attention to *tax* progressivity. After all, how the money is spent is just as important, and often less controversial, than how it is collected. A regressive tax, say a sales tax, may provide funds for increasing welfare payments and thus in effect redistribute income to the poor. Social security taxes are regressive; social security payments are progressive. It is the combined overall effect of the two that is regarded as important, and it is easier to get Congress to enact progressive expenditure programs than progressive taxes.

TAX STRUCTURE AND THE ALLOCATION OF RESOURCES

The tax system influences the allocation of resources by changing the *relative* prices of different goods and factors and the *relative* profit-

ability of different industries and of different uses of factors of production. These changes in turn affect resource movements.

While it is theoretically possible to design a *neutral* tax system—one that leaves all relative prices unchanged—American tax policy, both intentionally and unintentionally, is certainly not neutral. It leads to a different allocation of resources than would occur without it.

Intended Effects

The tax structure is often used deliberately to change incentives and thus to affect resource allocation. Taxing gasoline to discourage energy consumption is one example; effluent charges on polluters are another. And tax provisions may be used as a carrot as well as a stick. One way is to allow the deduction of some expenditures from income before computing the amount of taxes payable or tax credits for some portion of expenditures. Every $100 spent by a wealthy family in the 70 percent marginal tax bracket on an item that is tax deductible costs only $30 in after-tax income. Every $100 they spend on items that are not tax deductible costs the full $100 in after-tax income. This encourages them to spend money on charitable and educational contributions. Interest payments for a mortgage are tax deductible under the U.S. tax code, while payments for rental housing are not deductible. This encourages home ownership by lowering the cost of buying a house relative to the cost of renting one. When corporations are allowed "accelerated depreciation" or "investment credits" on certain investments, it encourages them to make such investments in larger amounts.

Unintended Allocative Effects

Not all effects of the tax system are intended. To the extent that high income taxes discourage work, or induce people to spend money on tax avoidance, we are plainly reaping unintended and undesirable by-products of a tax system.

Consider further the tax incentives to home

ownership, which were surely intended. An incidental result of providing such incentives through the income tax is that the incentive effect is much less for a poor person than for a rich one. The value of the deduction for interest is much greater to a taxpayer in the 70 percent marginal tax bracket than to someone in the 20 percent bracket. When a bank charges each of them 10 percent interest, the richer taxpayer really pays only 3 percent interest; the poorer one pays 8 percent interest if he or she itemizes deductions. For people who take the standard deduction, the actual interest rate remains 10 percent. Thus the lower one's income, the less the incentive is to obtain a property stake in the society. This is surely an unintended effect.

The major unresolved question about taxes and allocation is empirical: Just how different is the allocation because of tax policy? Perhaps surprisingly, there is no consensus on this question. The reason is that we are not sure who really pays the taxes that are levied. This is called the problem of **tax incidence.**

TAX INCIDENCE

When a tax is imposed on a firm, does the firm pay the tax, or does it pass it on to the consumer in the form of higher prices? To see why this is a difficult question to answer, consider two examples.

Do Landlords or Tenants Pay the Property Tax?

Landlords characteristically protest that the crushing burden of property taxes makes it impossible for them to earn a reasonable living from renting buildings to tenants who abuse the property. Tenants typically reply that landlords shirk their responsibilities for building maintenance and that the whole burden of the tax is passed on to the tenants in the form of higher rents. Both sides cannot be right in alleging that they each bear the entire burden of the tax! They are arguing about the incidence of the property tax.

To examine the incidence, suppose that a city imposes a property tax. Each of the thousands of landlords in the city decides to raise rents by the full amount of the tax. There will be a decline in the quantity of rental accommodation demanded as a result of the price increase. (For one reason, higher rents will induce some renters to economize on space now that it has become more expensive.)

The decline in the quantity demanded without any change in the quantity supplied will cause a surplus of rental accommodations at the higher prices. Landlords will find it difficult to replace tenants who move out, and the typical unit will remain empty longer between tenancies. Prospective tenants will find many alternative sites from which to choose and will become very particular in what they expect from landlords.

Some prospective tenants, seeing vacant apartments, will offer to pay rents below the asking price. Some landlords will accept the offer rather than earn nothing from vacant premises. Once some landlords cut their rentals, others will have to follow suit or find their properties stay unrented for longer periods of time.

As the rent received by landlords falls, there will be a supply reaction. There will be a movement down the supply curve when, for example, some homeowners become less willing to rent out parts of their homes. More important, there will be a shift of the supply curve. When apartment buildings are replaced (as they are continuously in a big city), it will not pay to build them quite as high as before. This shift in supply prevents the price from falling to its pretax level.

Eventually rentals will reach a new equilibrium at which the quantity demanded equals the quantity supplied. This equilibrium price for rental housing will be higher than the original pretax rent but lower than the rent that passes the entire tax on to the tenants. (See Figure 25-3.)

The burden of the property tax is shared by landlords and tenants.

Just how it is shared by the two groups will

FIGURE 25-3
The Incidence of a Tax on Rental Housing

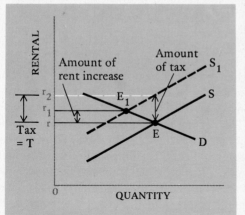

If the equilibrium rent rises by some amount less than the amount of the tax, landlords and tenants will share the burden. The supply schedule S reflects landlords' willingness to supply apartments. When a tax of T is imposed, the supply curve shifts upward, to S_1, indicating an increase of T in the price needed to call forth each quantity supplied. Equilibrium shifts from E to E_1, and rents have risen only to r_1. Of the total tax, tenants have paid rr_1 per unit and landlords r_1r_2.

depend on the elasticity of the demand and supply curves. If the demand curve is very flat, the landlord will pay most of the tax; if it is very steep, the tenant will.[2]

Notice that this result does not depend on who writes the check to pay the tax bill. In many European countries, the tenant rather than the landlord is sent the tax bill and pays the tax directly to the city; even in this case, however, the landlord bears part of the burden. As long as the existence of the tax reduces the quantity of rental accommodations demanded below what it otherwise would be, the tax will depress the amount received by landlords. In this way landlords will bear part of its burden.

[2] We suggest you draw a series of diagrams to see how this works. In each case, shift the supply curve up by the same vertical amount — to represent the property tax — and see what proportion of the increase is reflected in the new equilibrium price.

Notice also that this result emerges even though neither landlords nor tenants realize it. Because rents are changing for all sorts of other reasons, no one will have much idea of what equilibrium rentals would be in the absence of the tax. It does not do much good just to look at what happens immediately after tax rates are changed because, as we have already seen, landlords may begin by raising rents by the full amount of the tax. Although they think they have passed it on, this creates a disequilibrium, and in the final position prices will have risen by less than the full tax.

Do Taxes on Profits Affect Prices?

Economic theory predicts that a general percentage tax on pure profits will have no effect on price or output, and thus the full incidence of such a tax will fall on producers. To see this quickly, suppose that one price-quantity combination gives the firm higher profits (without considering taxes) than any other. If the government imposes a 20 percent profits tax, the firm will have only 80 percent as much profits after tax as it had before; *this will be true for each possible level of output*. The firm may grumble, but it will not be profitable for it to alter its price or output.

Notice that this argument is independent of the tax rate. [29] It applies equally whether the tax rate is 10 percent or 75 percent.

A tax on corporation income. American corporate income taxes are taxes on profits as defined by the tax laws. The definitions make them a tax on a combination of pure profits plus some of the return to capital and risk taking.

Because such a profits tax will reduce the returns to these important factors of production, it can have significant effects on the allocation of resources and on the prices and output of goods. Suppose a risky industry requires, say, a 20 percent return on its capital to make prospective owners willing to take the risk of investing in the industry. Suppose that every firm is earning 30 percent on its investment before taxes. A 50 percent corporate income tax will reduce the return to 15 percent, below the point that makes investment attractive, and resources will leave the industry. Obviously price and output changes will occur. As firms leave the industry, and as supply decreases, prices will rise until the remaining firms can earn a sufficient level of after-tax profits so that they are once again compensated for the risks involved. Thus customers must bear part of the burden of the tax through a price increase.

A tax on profits, as defined by the taxing authorities, will have an effect on prices and outputs and thus will be shared by the consumer.

Public Expenditure as a Tool of Micro Policy

Public expenditure is large and growing. It affects both the distribution of income and the allocation of resources. In recent years, spending by federal, state, and local government units in the United States—that is, by the public sector—has amounted to about 36 percent of the nation's expenditures. Defense, international relations, education, and social security are the largest items; collectively they make up half the total. Public welfare, highways, and interest on the public debt add up to another 22 percent of the total. The remainder covers everything else, from police protection and sanitation to general administration of government and space research. About half the expenditure is made by the federal government; the remaining half is divided nearly equally between state governments and local governments.

Figure 25-4 shows the changing importance of different types of federal government expenditures. Until 1974 the largest category of federal expenditures (and still the dominant type for state and local government expenditures) was for provision of goods and services that the market fails to provide or is not allowed to provide. Foremost among these (in volume of expenditure) are the defense and defense-related activi-

ties of the federal government; expenditures on police services, education, roads, conservation, and urban redevelopment are similar in character.

Although such purchases of goods and services are large (about $178 billion in 1980), they have remained roughly constant in real terms over the last 25 years. They have been overtaken by transfer payments as the largest form of government expenditure. Transfer payments and grants-in-aid have been steadily increasing in importance; together they account for virtually all recent growth in constant dollar government expenditure. This has led to important changes in both the distribution of income and the allocation of resources.

PUBLIC EXPENDITURES AND REDISTRIBUTION OF INCOME

The federal government, as Table 25-1 indicates, raises more than half its revenues by income-related taxes. When these federal receipts are transferred back to individuals or to state and local governments, they have a substantial redistributive effect.

Federal Transfer Payments to Individuals

Transfer payments are defined generally as payments to private persons or institutions that do not arise out of current productive activity. (They do not include intergovernment transfers.) Welfare payments are transfers; so, too, are social security payments, pensions, veterans' benefits, fellowships, unemployment insurance, and Medicare payments. Some federal transfers are made to foreigners as part of aid programs. Some transfer payments are private, such as private pensions and charitable contributions by individuals and corporations. Many are made by state and local governments, often using funds they have received as federal grants-in-aid. The greatest part, which we consider here, is paid by the federal government to individuals. In 1980 they amounted, in the aggregate, to $200 billion.

FIGURE 25-4
The Changing Form of Major Federal Expenditures

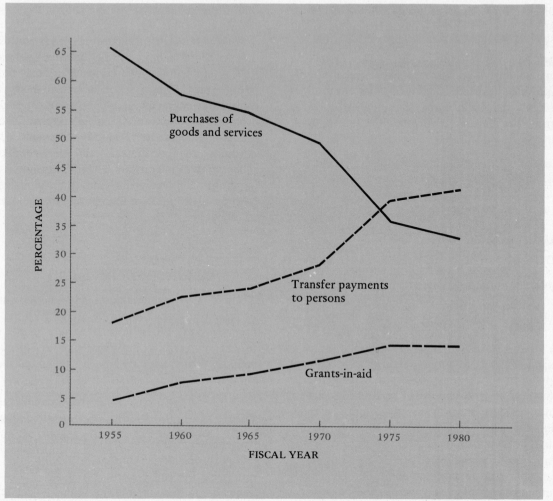

Transfer payments to persons and grants-in-aid to state and local governments have been growing steadily in importance. In 1955 two-thirds of all federal expenditures were for purchases of goods and services. By 1980 the fraction was only one-third. Transfer payments to persons in the United States and grants-in-aid to state and local governments have increased from less than one-fourth to more than one-half of the total. The three categories of expenditure graphed account for almost 90 percent of total federal expenditures. The largest item not shown on the graph is net interest paid by the government.

The bulk of these transfer payments are part of public income-maintenance programs of the kind examined in Chapter 23.

The growth of transfer payments reflects several developments. First, the coverage and level of social security (including Medicaid and Medi-care) is steadily increasing. Second, the attention to reducing poverty, discussed in Chapter 23, has been responsible for much of the increase. Third, the persistent unemployment during the 1970s greatly increased unemployment compensation payments.

While some transfer payments go to people with above average incomes, most do not. Certainly transfer payments have had some tendency to redistribute income to the poor.

The percentage of all personal income received in the form of government transfer payments has increased sharply, from under 5 percent in 1955 to 7 percent in 1965 and more than 13 percent in 1979.

Grants-in-aid as Forms of Redistribution

In addition to the federal government, there are 50 state governments, 3,000 county governments, 8,000 municipalities, and 17,000 townships in the United States. Further, there are about 20,000 districts for schools and another 20,000 for miscellaneous purposes such as sewage. Each of the more than 80,000 governmental units spends public money, and each must get the money to spend. Not all units have equal access to revenue, and this fact necessitates both the division of responsibilities and intergovernmental grants-in-aid.

Grants-in-aid from federal to state and local governments have been among the most rapidly increasing forms of public expenditure. They were more than five times as large, in constant dollars, in 1979 as they had been 20 years earlier; by way of contrast, total federal expenditure in constant dollars approximately doubled. The growth in grants-in-aid is a response to a growing inability of state and local communities to manage their finances.

Grants-in-aid are of two general types: categorical and general. At present, 90 percent of all federal grants are **categorical grants-in-aid,** that is, for specific categories of assistance such as highways, education, and welfare payments. Not only are such grants restricted as to use, they usually require some degree of state or local matching. General grants-in-aid without restriction or matching requirements are now called **revenue sharing.**

Many grant-in-aid programs were not designed primarily for redistribution. Do they, incidentally, have a big effect on the distribution of income? Economists are now looking at this question; they do not yet know the answer. Some categorical assistance goes for inequality-reducing welfare payments and other programs of aid to the poor. But grants for highways, hospitals, and research probably tend to increase the inequality of income distribution. Revenue sharing money goes to state and local governments whose uses of the funds vary enormously and therefore have no single pattern of impact.

Many public finance specialists believe that grants-in-aid to states tend not to decrease inequality of income distribution and may increase it, while grants to the cities tend to reduce inequality.

The Overall Redistributive Effects of Government Expenditures

Since tax policy tends to be roughly proportional in its overall effect, the overall progressivity of government policies depends on the overall progressivity of government expenditures. Here the large and growing role of transfer payments to the poor and the use of many grants-in-aid to the cities (for programs that ultimately help the poor) probably assure that overall there is some net redistribution of income from high-income and middle-income groups to the poor. But it is not very large.

Changes in the degree of income inequality from decade to decade are extremely small, despite growing government expenditures.

The Lorenz curve on page 332 does not look appreciably different than one based on data from 1940.

Why does government expenditure not have a bigger effect on income distribution? One view says that government programs are really less progressive than we had thought because progressive programs are offset by regressive ones. Another view is that market forces exert steady

Distribution Versus Efficiency

Economists recognize that government actions can affect both the efficient allocation of resources and the distribution of income. Because it is possible to talk about *efficient* and *inefficient* allocations, but not about "better" or "worse" distributions of income, without introducing normative considerations, much of positive economics concerns efficiency and neglects redistribution of income. Many policy disagreements can be understood in terms of a difference in emphasis on these things.

From an efficiency point of view alone, the correct policy was to let domestic oil prices in all oil-importing countries rise along with the world price. Instead, many governments held the price down. For they were concerned, among other things, with the effect of rising prices on the windfall profits earned by large oil companies and on the welfare of poorer citizens. "We just cannot let the poor find their heating bills rise so much and so fast while the profits of the oil companies soar" was a common reaction.

Here is a genuine conflict for which economics cannot provide a solution—because in the end the answer must rest on value judgments. However, economics can make the consequences of various choices apparent, and it can suggest policy alternatives. The consequence of holding down the price of oil (out of concern for the effect of higher prices on the poor) in the manner discussed in Chapter 17, was an inefficient use of the countries' resources. Total production was reduced, and some new investment was misdirected into high-cost (rather than low-cost) methods of production. Thus in the long run average standards of living were reduced. Whether the reduction in the average was a reasonable price to pay for shielding the poor is an open question; yet it is unlikely that the question was ever posed or the calculations made.

Can one have both efficiency and desired redistributions? One way is to let the price system do the job of signaling relative scarcities and costs, thereby ensuring some efficiency in the allocation of resources, but at the same time to use taxes or expenditures to transfer income to achieve redistributive goals. This method does not seek to help the poor (or other underprivileged groups) by subsidizing oil or any other price. Rather, it seeks to provide these groups with sufficient income by direct income transfers. Then it leaves producers and consumers free to respond to relative prices that approximately reflect relative opportunity costs.

Advocates of this method argue that it is surer, more direct, and less costly in its side effects than the method of subsidizing the prices of particular goods. Moreover, the price-subsidy method surely ends up subsidizing some who are rich and missing some who are very poor. Subsidizing gasoline prices, for example, benefits the Cadillac owner and does nothing for those too poor to own a car. Thus even in redistribution it is haphazard.

Supporters of redistribution through the price system usually counter with one or both of two arguments. The first says that it is well and good to say we *could* let oil prices rise and simultaneously subsidize the poor and tax the rich, but the political process makes it unlikely that we *will* do so. Thus holding prices down may be the best or even the only practical way to get a fair distributive result.

The second argument claims that certain commodities such as food, heat, medical care, and housing are basic to a civilized life and should be provided to households cheaply, whatever their real opportunity cost. Supporters reject the view that a minimum living standard can be provided simply by allowing a minimum income and letting the recipients spend it at market-determined prices. They believe that the inefficiencies resulting from prices that do not reflect opportunity costs are a price worth paying to ensure that everyone can afford these basics.

pressure toward more inequality, which government programs merely offset.

To understand the second view—that one must run just to stay even with inequality—imagine that the government today created complete equality in wealth and income. Inevitably market forces would produce inequality by next year, as some people and firms worked hard and long and succeeded while others took it easy or failed, as some invested wisely while others squandered their resources on a binge. Most economists agree that there is a limit to how much inequality can be eliminated; there is controversy as to how close we are to that limit. (And beyond that there is controversy as to how close it is desirable to get to "as much equality as possible," both on ethical grounds of justice and economic grounds of incentives.)

GOVERNMENT EXPENDITURE AND RESOURCE ALLOCATION

Governments spent nearly $200 billion in 1980 to provide goods and services. In these activities governmental units act like firms, using factors of production to produce outputs. They produce outputs rather than leave them to the free market because the people, acting through their state legislatures, Congress, and city councils, have decided that they should. They are responding to the various sources of market failure discussed in Chapter 24. By and large these outputs are of collective consumption goods, of goods with strong externalities, or of services whose benefits are not marketable. In so doing governments are plainly changing the allocation of resources.

From time to time, major new initiatives are undertaken that have the purpose and the effect of a sharp further change in resource allocation. A current example is the proposals to provide some kind of heavily subsidized medical care in order to increase the quantity of such care that people consume. This is, of course, an attempt to change the allocation of society's resources. (A second example, coping with urban problems, will be discussed later in the chapter.)

SUBSIDIZING HEALTH CARE

For more than a decade a great controversy has raged over American health care. Why are medical and hospital costs so high? Why are they rising so rapidly? Can these high costs be avoided? If they cannot, who should bear them? Can government do anything to make better quality health care available to more Americans?

Health care has become extremely expensive. A hospital stay costs more than $200 a day. Major surgery such as a heart operation can easily cost $25,000. A single major operation not covered by insurance can be a desperate financial drain not only to the aged and the poor but to middle-income households. And if a single operation can be a serious financial burden, a prolonged illness can be a financial disaster that eats up life savings and pushes into poverty even the most prudent middle-income household. Clearly, some form of insurance is needed for adequate protection, yet the cost of private medical and hospital insurance is also high and rising because the health costs that insurance companies must pay are high.

Medical and hospital costs were not always as relatively high as they are today. Where they were about 10 percent of GNP in 1980, they were only 6.2 percent in 1965 and 4.5 percent in 1950. The rapidly rising portion of national income that goes to health care reflects both the increasing quantity of medical and hospital care per person and the rising real costs of specific items. For example, a hospital bed that costs over $200 today cost only $40 in 1950, measured in constant 1980 dollars. In other words, the *real* cost has increased fivefold.

The Rising Unit Cost of Medical and Hospital Care

Why have the costs of an illness, a hospital stay, and an operation risen so sharply relative to the costs of most other goods and services?

A first reason is that health care is highly labor-intensive. Costs have risen much faster in industries that depend heavily on labor services than in more capital-intensive industries. The number of temperatures taken, beds made, and meals served per employee do not increase much over time. Lack of dramatic increases in the productivity of nurses, cooks, laboratory technicians, and other medical service personnel have combined with minimum wage laws, unionization, and rising wages in alternative employments to increase greatly the total medical and hospital operating costs. (Hospital employees today are as a result much better off than those of earlier decades, but patient care has had to bear the extra cost.)

A second reason is that the average "unit" of medical care has risen in quality year by year. Health care is more costly than it was 20 years ago in part because it is better than it was 20 years ago. Training of physicians, available knowledge, techniques, and equipment all have improved over time. As a result it becomes possible not only to provide quicker, surer cures for common and recurring ailments, but to guard against ailments and complications that, although uncommon, are serious for those affected. The hospital "bed" of 1980 is a very much safer place to be than the bed of 1960. But such safeguards are costly. It is expensive to have equipment and trained staff standing by in the 999 cases where they are not needed in order to be able to treat the one case in a thousand where the emergency arises.

Third, a number of influences prevent offering patients a wide variety of price-quality alternative forms of health care and instead tend to provide the highest quality, highest cost options. If patients had to pay their own bills, and if they could make fully informed choices, many might prefer to pay less and not have equipment available that will be used in only one complication in a thousand or even ten thousand. Lots of people, too, might be satisfied to have a less well-trained doctor (whose knowledge, say, was equivalent to that of the best trained doctor available when their parents were young) if his or her fees were only half of those of doctors with the most advanced training. Of course everyone

wants the best of everything, *ceteris paribus,* but the relevant question always concerns costs: Is the extra quality worth the extra cost?

A wide range of quality and price is not available. For one reason, doctors and hospital administrators are not highly motivated to provide low-cost alternatives. The individual doctor wants the best equipment available; if equipment and techniques exist that will save patients' lives, then it seems wrong not to have them available. After all, doctor and patient *both* want to succeed in saving the patient's life and curing illnesses.

Many patients do not have to pay the specific cost of a particular treatment. They have "prepaid" their medical costs in the form of insurance which they have bought or which their employer provides. When they get sick, they want the best available care—that is what the insurance promised to provide. The insurance companies that pay the bills will resist high costs only when they cannot pass them along in premiums. Here the mystique of medicine and the ignorance of most of us combine to make us uncritical about the perhaps excessively high quality of the protection that we agree our insurance should provide for us.

In the matter of health care you may be tempted to say "nothing but the best"; yet the best medical care, like the best automobile, is costly, perhaps too costly for most buyers. One serious result of offering only the best is that some will choose—or literally be forced—to have nothing, when they would have chosen the second best were it available. Most of the added cost of the "best" does not, however, really affect health or the probability of survival. Professor Victor Fuchs has shown that the correlation between higher medical expenditures and better health is very low.

Even when the extra cost really does pay off in a saved life, we must ask how much we would pay to have (say) nine instead of ten people in one thousand die from a particular disease? Surely no one would want to spend a billion dollars per life saved. We would say the opportunity cost of saving that life was too high. Yet no one really asks the question, which costs are worth incurring? Often doctors and hospitals make the decision implicitly by ordering the best of everything—and then pass the costs on to their patients, who are given little or no choice between cost and quality.

The Rising Quantity of Medical and Hospital Care per Person

Since medical care is a commodity, one would have expected rising prices per unit to have led, *ceteris paribus,* to decreases in quantity demanded. In fact the quantity of health care consumed per person has *increased* steadily. This is in part an income effect: as per capita income rises, people are prepared to consume more and better health care. In economic terms, health care has proven to be income-elastic.

Most of the explanation, however, lies in the widespread acceptance of the notion that health care ought to be made available to more and more people as a matter of right, whether or not patients are able or willing to pay the costs of providing it. The major argument here is that health care is necessary to a person's survival. The spectacle of untreated illness and unnecessary death no more belongs in a modern high-income society than does the spectacle of masses of starving poor. The latter has been banished; according to this view, it is high time that the former be eliminated as well.

Critics of this view maintain that although some food and some health care is absolutely vital, much of it is elective. To say that no one should starve is not to say that everybody should receive all the free food they can eat. Some people put up with dandruff, skin rashes, nagging sinuses, grumbling stomachs, and a host of other health complaints while others rush to have them "attended to." Such non-vital attention accounts for a large part of our demand for health care. If it is provided free, or subsidized, or offered at no *marginal* cost to users, it will be consumed far

past the point where its marginal utility is equal to the costs of providing it.

In the United States the growing provision of health care services by direct public action and by comprehensive insurance coverage has had the effect of keeping the marginal payments below the marginal cost of provision. This has meant much more consumption of health care services than if consumers had had to pay the full marginal cost.

Should the Government Encourage More Health Care Than the Private Market Would Provide?

Before discussing *how* best to increase health care, it is worth asking *why*. What makes health care (as distinct from, say, bread, raincoats, or owner-occupied housing) a likely candidate for public provision or subsidization?

There are many serious health situations, from the heart attack to the premature birth of quintuplets, the emergency care of accident victims, and the effects of lingering, crippling, and disabling diseases, that are not in any sense discretionary. Suppose we agree that these situations provide a compelling case for subsidizing some medical care. It is necessary to concede, however, that most health care expenditures are for much less dramatic events—a sprained ankle, chronic arthritis, normal pregnancy and delivery, tonsillitis, measles, lower back pains, and so on. These things do not seem to be obvious candidates for subsidy. Thus one can rationally support some government subsidy of medical services without supporting unlimited provision.

How Much Health Care Should the Government Provide or Subsidize?

The current health care debate is not about whether the government should play no role in health care provision (as was the case in the United States 50 years ago) but rather about whether to increase present levels.

In 1979 the federal government paid directly

for about 25 percent of all medical and hospital costs. This amounted to $50 billion, a significant annual sum by any standard. Yet the U.S. government's portion was far smaller than that of the governments of Britain, Sweden, and Italy. Should we be increasing, decreasing, or staying put in this regard?

Almost everyone agrees that a way should be found to provide some minimum level of health care to all who need it. When only a small number could not afford that minimum, and the costs of providing it were not too large, private charity and the contributed services of doctors coped with the problem.

Minimum levels of health care have now far outstripped the capacity of private charity. One reason for this is the rising cost of medical and health services. A second is the steadily rising notion of the minimum level of care to which all are entitled. *Public* provision on a large scale began by defining three groups within the population for subsidy: (1) veterans, whose health problems are arguably a by-product of service to the nation; (2) the very poor, who not only lack income but also tend to get locked into poverty by ill health; and (3) the elderly, who encounter ill health just when retirement and inflation have reduced their ability to pay for expensive medical services. In the last 40 years these public programs have been built into or parallel to programs of social security (Medicare) and public welfare (Medicaid).

The current discussion concerns whether to extend such programs from the limited *categories* of beneficiaries to the population as a whole. Many individuals support such an expansion because they believe they will get something for nothing by shifting the cost to someone else. Yet the cost must be borne. Although some individuals or small groups may be able to evade some or all of the cost, most of it must eventually fall on ordinary middle-income people. If the government foots the bill, it will have to increase taxes — and, as we have seen, taxes are roughly proportional over a very wide range of income.

The central disadvantage of public provision is that it does not lend itself to rationing a costly commodity to uses that justify the costs. In a free-market economy, use is rationed by each individual's decision whether or not to pay the price. If the individual does not pay a marginal price because of a government subsidy, there will be no incentive to economize on use. Either the government must increase supply to meet the demand (which can put enormous burdens on a government already under heavy pressure to balance its budget and to cut taxes), or it must find other ways to ration demand. In countries with national health services, such as Britain and Italy, such rationing is accomplished in part by long lines in doctors' offices and waiting lists of up to three years for "elective" surgery (defined as anything not vital to work and survival).

Policy Options in Providing Needed Additional Health Care

Suppose we had a consensus as to the appropriate quantity of medical and hospital care, and suppose that this quantity is more than people can afford to buy in the free market. The government might attempt to fill the gap in many different ways: (1) by reimbursing part or all of medical bills; (2) by subsidizing doctors and hospitals to charge lower prices; (3) by subsidizing insurance companies to provide affordable insurance that will pay the bills; (4) by direct provision of health service; and (5) by imposing controls on the costs incurred and the prices charged. Each policy has its supporters in the current debate.

The economic issue underlying the choice is the effectiveness of a given scheme in achieving the "right" distribution of the total quantity supplied. Unless there is some marginal charge for medical services equal to the marginal costs of providing them, there will be no direct incentive to avoid uneconomic uses. The absence of such marginal charges today applies not only to government provision of services but to most insurance plans, private and public.

In essence, most insurance schemes charge everyone the average cost of health care. Consequently an individual has no incentive to economize on elective care. The person might as well accept an expensive treatment even when it has only a small chance of improving his or her health. "After all," one may argue, "what have I got to lose?" Many insurance plans try to provide incentives to economize by not covering all things. Some of the incentives, however, work in perverse ways. For example, plans that cover doctors' bills only for hospital stays (on the ground that these are the more serious illnesses) lead patients to opt for expensive hospitalization even when much less expensive outpatient medical care would have done just as well.

It is possible, within a scheme of overall subsidization, to provide the needed marginal incentives. Insurance could be structured to provide patients with an incentive to economize *at the margin* on medical care. For example, such schemes might include deductible clauses. "Elective" care might get a lower rate of coverage than care under a defined class of "necessary" treatments. Only 80 percent of the costs up to, say, $5,000 or $10,000 might be covered, then 100 percent thereafter (to give an incentive to economize at the margin except where costs were already so high as to reduce the chance that the treatment was really elective). There might also be a minimum noninsurable charge to be paid by the patient for each separate routine visit to a doctor or hospital. (Emergency visits, suitably defined, would be exempted.) It might also be possible to grant government-subsidized loans, repayable at low interest over ten years, to cover extraordinary medical expenses.

Government intervention might make the system work better by providing a larger range of price-quality choice. The control of the American medical profession over standards might be reviewed to see whether the standards are unnecessarily high. Increased use of paramedics, midwives, and nursing homes for routine medical problems might be possible. Obviously, persons with only half the training of doctors could not solve all medical problems, but they might be able to cope with health care problems that account for well over half of today's visits to doctors.

Recent U.S. Health Care Proposals

The drive to reduce the size of the federal budget that characterized the early months of 1980 did not augur well for any increase in government programs. But as recently as 1979 major new programs were proposed, and they may be expected to emerge again in the 1980s.

In 1979 the Carter administration proposed a plan that would add roughly 12 percent to total expenditures on health care, three-fourths of it to be financed by increased tax-supported subsidies, the remainder by employer and employee contributions. The major features of the plan were that it would provide all "necessary medical care" to persons below the poverty level, pregnant women, and infants and also provide a subsidy to insurance programs so that no family would be required to pay more than $2,500 per year in medical costs. It would thus provide first-dollar coverage for the poor and for pregnancy and 100 percent major medical coverage above $2,500 for all. However, it would put upper limits on the amount the government or subsidized insurers would pay hospitals for their services; it would set maximum fees that doctors could collect for specified services; and it would limit hospital construction. In essence, the plan would seek to offset incentives for overuse by direct price and quantity controls.

A somewhat more expensive plan supported by Senator Edward Kennedy would provide full coverage for all hospital costs, regardless of the patient's income or age. This plan would shift much more of the cost both to the government and to insurance and actually reduce the fraction of the costs now being paid by patients from the present 50 percent to about one-third of all payments. Recognizing that this would increase the incentives to overuse, strict cost controls would be imposed on hospital charges and on all physicians' fees.

Neither the Carter plan nor the Kennedy plan attempts to raise the marginal costs of nonessential health care service. Instead, each relies on some government supervision of charges. Such regulations have their cost both in terms of enforcement and in terms of the inefficiencies and rigidities they impose. One group of economists believes that such cost controls will suffice and will not themselves prove too expensive and too rigid. Another group believes that the reliance on price and cost controls would present an unmanageable bureaucratic burden and prove ineffective. This group would insist on building in marginal incentives to avoid excess expenditures. The way to do that is to make every use of medical or hospital services costly at the margin.

URBAN PROBLEMS

Some of the biggest news stories of the 1970s concerned the feared bankruptcy of such cities as New York, Philadelphia, and Cleveland. President Ford, many political observers believe, lost his bid for reelection in 1976 because of his treatment of New York City's plea for federal help. (On October 30, 1975, the New York *Daily News* carried the page one banner headline, FORD TO CITY: DROP DEAD). Ford failed to carry New York the following November; if he had done so, he would have defeated Jimmy Carter.

The crisis of the cities is in part a fiscal crisis because of the limited ability of local governments to raise revenues equal to their necessary expenditures. The purely fiscal crisis can be solved by financial help to the cities from state and federal governments. But underlying the fiscal crisis are some "real" problems that inhere in the changing character of the central cities. If urban decline is to be reversed, major changes in the allocation of resources will be required.

The Economics of Urban Decay

The root cause of the changing character of the nation's biggest cities is the change in who lives in them.

The selective flight to the suburbs (and beyond) that has triggered the urban crisis is a function of many circumstances—among them, different preferences of different groups in the population,

rising incomes, and sometimes prejudice. To understand why more and more families choose to trade the traditional advantages of the big city for cleaner neighborhoods, safer streets, and whiter schools, it is helpful to explore the dynamics of suburban migration. Much of it can be understood in economic terms. The scenario that follows suggests some causes of the urban crisis.

The flight of the wealthy. As the relatively wealthier residents of a densely populated city find their incomes rising, they choose increasingly to spend extra income on bigger houses, more spacious lots, and tree-lined streets. Very high real estate prices in the central cities make extra space a luxury, but low-cost land exists just outside the central cities. Thus suburban communities begin to be formed. As more upper-income residents move out, the concentration of lower-income residents in the city increases.

The disenchantment of the middle classes. The services required by the poor are of a different type from those sought by the middle class. More money goes to welfare, social work, and police and less to civic symphonies, schools, parks, and amenities. At the same time, the average income per capita that is subject to taxation declines as the relatively wealthy move beyond the reach of city tax authorities. Remaining middle-class residents discover that they are paying more taxes but receiving fewer services of the kind they value. They find the museums closed and the park toilets unclean. Their schools curtail the "frills" in the curriculum, such as interscholastic athletics, foreign languages, and music and art. Life in the city costs more but offers less.

Meanwhile, empty expensive houses tend to be converted to cheaper housing as three or four families move in where one used to live. The housing also deteriorates because it does not pay landlords to maintain it at its former standard. If the poor are black or Chicano, their increasing presence in the schools, the streets, and the parks does not go unnoticed by whites.

Upper-middle-class residents who remain will

see their tax burdens rising, their neighborhoods becoming more crowded, the older sections of "their" city deteriorating, the racial composition of their schools changing, and the crime rate increasing. Some will move into more expensive neighborhoods or send their children to private schools; more and more will flee to the suburbs.

Shifting employment opportunities. Many will discover that they do not even have to commute, because jobs move to the suburbs, too. Stores and banks follow their customers, first by establishing branches in suburban shopping centers, later by closing central-city branches. Industry, too, moves outward, partly because of the available labor force, partly in response to the interstate highway system and the trucking industry. These give suburban plants ready access to their suppliers and markets that formerly only the inner-city rail centers provided. Industry also moves to avoid rising taxes. (In the 1960s and 1970s three-fourths of all new industrial expansion in the United States occurred in the suburbs. In New York City alone 600,000 jobs were lost during the 1970s.)

The inner city becomes a ghetto. When the jobs go, not all the workers will follow. Many inner-city residents, held together by the bonds of race, language, or poverty as well as by lack of cars and lack of middle-class aspirations, stay put. Unemployment increases, more families need welfare, housing deteriorates further, clean streets seem less important—and, of course, the tax base continues to shrink.

A reform mayor raises the sales tax or proposes a city income tax and finds that these measures only hasten the exodus. At this stage the city may actually be underpopulated. Existing residents abandon the worst neighborhoods as they deteriorate—and move to and begin the downgrading of more expensive housing. The worst slums may become homes for new immigrants from rural areas, the South, or Puerto Rico, or they may be abandoned and begin to crumble. Rats, disease, crime, and decay spread.

However bleak this story seems, it comes close to representing the plight of many American cities today. One might attack urban decay by channeling efforts and funds into rebuilding the city itself. Alternatively, one might attack the problems of poverty, unemployment, and prejudice that contribute so heavily to urban deterioration. Cities, without help, can do neither.

The Fiscal Crisis of the Cities

If greater spending on municipal services and urban renewal might halt the decline of the cities, why do cities not solve their problems by more spending? The answer lies in four forces: (1) the fact that tax revenues of local governments are relatively unresponsive to growth in average income, (2) the limited ability of cities to borrow, (3) the rapidly rising demand for local government services, and (4) the rising cost per unit of providing these services. Together they contribute to local governments' steadily worsening financial situation and their urgent demand for federal assistance.

Tax revenues. Whether government tax revenues rise as fast as the average income of residents depends on the government's ability to use income taxes. The larger the percentage of income raised by income taxes, the stronger the fiscal position of any government unit will be as income rises. While 81 percent of federal tax receipts and 43 percent of state tax receipts today come from income taxes, only 5 percent of local taxes are so raised.

Local governments cannot readily increase their reliance on income taxes. As the percentage of personal income taken by the federal government has grown, the resistance of taxpayers to higher taxes of any kind has grown—and this is especially true of further taxes on income. Many state and local governments have tried to impose (or increase) income taxes; however, the electoral defeats of officials who advocated these taxes, and the interstate and intercity competition to attract residents and industries by having lower taxes than neighboring jurisdictions, have severely limited the additional revenue that state and local governments have been able to raise in this way.

State and local governments thus rely heavily on property, sales, and excise taxes. Revenues from these taxes rise more slowly than income in the short run, and in the long run they rise only at the same rate as the income levels *of the population in their jurisdictions*. In many of the largest cities average income (and thus per capita tax revenue) is in fact falling because of the movement of many higher-income families to the suburbs and the higher unemployment rates in the cities.

The limited ability of cities to borrow. Cities, unlike the federal government, cannot spend more than they raise in taxes, receive as gifts, or borrow, for they cannot print money. In some states, cities are constitutionally limited in their ability to borrow; even where this is not the case, prudence limits what is possible.

Cities borrow for three reasons: (1) to finance long-term capital investment projects such as schools or hospitals, (2) to smooth out seasonal fluctuations in the patterns of expenditures and receipts, and (3) to cover current account deficits. The first two reasons are wholly responsible. The third is irresponsible and unacceptable to bondholders because the revenue to repay the bonds is nowhere provided for. Because of this, it cannot long continue.

What happens when a city sells bonds (borrows) to cover a continuing deficit? As these bonds come due, money will be needed to repay the bondholders, but there will be no current surplus available. The obvious solution is to borrow still more. Then rumors of trouble will start, and they will lead to the downgrading of the bonds. Investors will become unwilling to buy new issues to replace the old ones. Once this happens, the city has lost its ability to borrow even for legitimate purposes.

Demand for government services rises more rapidly than average income. Local govern-ment expenditures have been rising more rapidly than their residents' incomes. One reason is the high income elasticity of demand for city services. As societies become wealthier, their residents want more parks, more police protection, more and better schools and colleges, and more generous treatment of their less fortunate neighbors. This alone, combined with the limited tax sources available, would create budgetary problems for local governments in a period of rising incomes and rising expectations—a fact that many mayors have learned the hard way. Taxpayers increasingly want the social services that governments provide, but they do not want to accept the taxes required to pay for them. Elected officials arouse the public wrath when they fail to provide wanted programs, but they also do so when they provide the services and then raise taxes.

A second and more important rise in the quantity of local government services required has to do with the changing character of central-city populations and the increased demands for local government expenditures associated with these changes. The selective outward migration from the cities to the suburbs has led to ever-increasing proportions of low-income groups in the central cities. This in turn has led to more poverty, more crime, and more demand for the public services to cope with them.

The rising relative cost of local government services. Government services tend to use much labor of a kind whose productivity (output per work hour) has increased much less rapidly than its cost. Thus cost per unit of output has risen. While the national average of output per work hour in manufacturing has risen over 50 percent in the last decade, the size of the beat covered by a police officer, the number of students taught by each schoolteacher, and the number of families that can be handled effectively by a social worker have not risen in proportion. Because wage levels tend to rise with national average productivity, the costs of services in the low-productivity sectors have soared. Overall it is estimated that, on average, state and local expenditures have risen at 1.67 times the rate of increase of national income.

The inevitable crisis. The four forces just described lead inevitably to a crisis.

Rising quantities and rising unit costs of government services cause local government expenditures to rise more than their revenues.

Eventually the city's reserves will be used up. It must then either reverse the causes of its decline, get help from the outside, or default on its obligations.

Coping with the Urban Crisis

Once the interrelated processes of urban decay and movement out of the cities has begun, the city has passed the point of self-help. Only a massive dosage of money will now help. The city recognizes that it can recover its tax base if it can annex suburban areas, but those who have escaped the city's problems will reject the overtures for annexation, and their political influence in the state governments is sufficient to prevent forced annexation. The city itself, hopeless, now tries to persuade the state or federal government to channel funds to it. Substantial funds are required simply to maintain the status quo, and programs for urban reconstitution or reconstruction must compete with other demands on public budgets.

The rising level of federal contributions to state and local government during the 1970s was a response to this problem. That it has not been solved was made clear by New York City's fiscal crisis of 1975, by the sharply worsening plights of Philadelphia, Chicago, Detroit, and other cities, and by the urgency with which the nation's mayors keep clamoring for ever more help. Congress and the president, trying to control overall levels of expenditure, are reluctant to pour ever more money into the cities — especially when many believe that local governments have been less diligent than they should have been in managing their own affairs.

Is There a Long-run Solution?

Cities play too vital a role in the nation's political and economic life to let them wither and their millions of inhabitants be overwhelmed by poverty, disease, and crime. Yet what is to be done?

One solution is a more or less permanent "subsidy" of the cities by taxes levied on those who live elsewhere. A great expansion in unconditional revenue sharing would give revenues to state and local governments on a per capita basis, in effect making residents of wealthy states and rich suburbs pay some part of the costs of areas densely populated by the poor.

An alternative approach favored by many is increasingly to federalize aid to the poor wherever they reside by guaranteeing a minimum family income sufficient to permit escape from slum conditions. Others hope to provide this minimum income not by grants to individuals, categorical or otherwise, but by manipulation of the tax structure — specifically, by introducing a negative income tax.

Mayors of large cities, and many economists who specialize in urban economics, believe that the needed support to the cities is appropriately provided by state and federal governments because the key problems of the cities are those of race, poverty, and unemployment, which are *national* problems. The fact that these problems are most severe among city dwellers does not make them city problems, to be ignored by those who live in the suburbs or smaller cities, towns, and villages.

If this argument is accepted, regular and permanent transfers of money to the cities or their residents will become not charity to an imprudent relative but a regular part of public attention to persistent national problems. However, this point of view does not represent the view held by a majority of Congress or by the American public at large. They appear to regard urban crises as the product primarily of irresponsible city governments, and aid to the cities as a temporary necessity that perhaps has to be given "this time" but not next. The conflict between these views is emerging as a key in the policy debate of the 1980s.

As is usually the case in real debates, there is some truth in both extreme views. New York, for example, greatly compounded its problems by some irresponsible expenditure policies and fiscal maneuvering. But even a most prudent city administration is going to have desperate trouble making ends meet in the 1980s, for the basic problems are still there.

Evaluating the Role of Government

Most everyone would agree that the government has some role to play in the economy because of the myriad sources of possible market failure. Yet there is no consensus that the present level and role of government intervention is about right.

One aspect of the contemporary debate – the efficient level of government intervention – was discussed at the end of Chapter 24. There we asked when and to what degree government ought to attempt to modify private market behavior – say, by affecting the way a paper mill discharges its wastes. Other issues arise when government provides goods and services that the private sector does not and will not provide.

DO BENEFITS OF GOVERNMENT PROGRAMS EXCEED COSTS?

The federal government has developed techniques of evaluation designed to provide estimates of benefits and costs in order to determine whether the former exceed the latter. If they do, the program is said to be *cost effective,* and thus to be justified. For some government programs, such as flood control, there are well-defined benefits and costs. It is thus relatively easy to decide whether the project is justified. But consider the evaluation of a program such as the great space adventure of the 1960s – placing a

man on the moon before the end of the decade. The budgetary costs were easily defined. At its peak in 1966, the program absorbed about $6 billion per year. Unmistakably, the project succeeded; it met its stated objective. But was the "giant step for mankind" worth the billions it cost? The benefits certainly included the psychological lift that the moon walks may have given the American people and the substantial advances in technology and knowledge that the space program is known to have spawned. The real costs are those things that all that expenditure may have replaced. But what was the alternative? More arms to Vietnam? Massive urban redevelopment? A return of funds to private spenders to use as they saw fit? Most of us will evaluate the worth of the space program very differently, depending on what we see as the alternative uses of the resources involved.

Such questions can never be answered unambiguously. As a result the evaluation of government programs is inherently political and controversial. Economic analysis of benefits and costs is involved, but it does not play the sole or even the dominant role in answering some big questions.

THE BALANCE BETWEEN PRIVATE AND PUBLIC SECTORS

When the government raises money by taxation and spends it on an activity, it increases the spending of the public sector and decreases that of the private sector. Since the public sector and the private sector spend on different things, the government is changing the allocation of resources. Is that good or bad? How do we know if the country has the right balance between the public and private sectors? Should there be more schools and fewer cars, or more cars and fewer schools?

Because automobiles and houses are sold on the market, consumer demand has a significant influence on the relative prices of these commodities, and (through prices) on the quantities produced and, thence, on the allocation of the nation's resources. This is true for all goods produced and sold on the market. But there is no market that provides relative prices for automobiles versus public schools; thus the choice between allowing money to be spent in the private sector and spending it for public goods is a matter to be decided by Congress and other legislative bodies.

John Kenneth Galbraith in a 1958 best seller, *The Affluent Society,* proclaimed the "liberal" message that a correct assignment of marginal utilities would show them to be higher for an extra dollar's worth of expenditure on parks, clean water, and education than for an extra dollar's worth of expenditure on television sets and deodorants. In this view, the political process often fails to translate preferences for public goods into effective action; thus more resources are devoted to the private sector and fewer to the public sector than would be the case if the political mechanism were as effective as the market.

The "conservative" view has a growing number of supporters who agree with Professor James Buchanan that society has already gone beyond the point where the value of the marginal dollar spent by the government is greater than the value of that dollar left in the hands of households or firms that would have spent it had it not been taxed away. Because bureaucrats, the conservatives argue, are spending other people's money, they regard a few million (or billion) dollars here or there as a mere nothing. They have lost all sense of the opportunity cost of public expenditure; thus they tend to spend far beyond the point where marginal benefits equal marginal costs.

This debate is not readily settled on a scientific basis because of the difficulty of measuring benefits when the things produced (e.g., clean air or the preservation of the Everglades) are not readily marketable. The so-called taxpayers' revolt, symbolized by the passage of Proposition 13 in California and similar measures intended to limit the powers of government to collect taxes,

suggests that many people agree with the conservative position. The clamor for ever more public aid to help hard-pressed citizens points to the liberal position. The struggle between them continues.

WHAT IS THE ROLE OF GOVERNMENT TODAY?

We have been looking at the role of the government in the market economy throughout the microeconomic part of this book. Now, at the end, let us pause for perspective. One of the most difficult problems for the student of the U.S. economic system is to maintain perspective about the scope of government activity in the market economy. There are literally tens of thousands of laws, regulations, and policies that affect firms and households. Many believe that a significant amount of deregulation would be possible and beneficial.

But private decision makers still have an enormous amount of discretion about what they do and how they do it. One pitfall is to become so impressed (or obsessed) with the many ways in which government activity impinges on the individual that one fails to see that these only make changes—sometimes large but often small—in market signals in a system that basically leaves individuals free to make their own decisions. In the private sector most individuals choose their occupations, earn their livings, spend their incomes, and live their lives. In this sector firms, too, are formed, choose products, live, grow, and sometimes die.

A different pitfall is to fail to see that some, and perhaps most, of the highly significant amounts paid by the private sector to the government as taxes also buy goods and services that add to the welfare of individuals. By and large the public sector complements the private sector, doing things the private sector would leave undone or do very differently. To recognize this is not to deny that there is often waste, and sometimes worse, in public expenditure policy. Nor does it imply that whatever is, is just what people want. Social policies and social judgments evolve and change.

Yet another pitfall is failing to recognize that the public and private sectors compete in the sense that both make claims on the resources of the economy. Thus government activities are not without opportunity costs, except in those rare circumstances in which they use resources that have no alternative use.

Public policies in operation at any time are not the result of a single master plan that specifies precisely where and how the public sector shall seek to complement, help along, or interfere with the workings of the market mechanism. Rather, as individual problems arise, governments attempt to meet them by passing ameliorative legislation. These laws stay on the books, and some become obsolete and unenforceable. This is true of systems of law in general. As a result it is easy to find outrageous examples of inconsistencies and absurdities in any system. A distinguished professorship at Harvard gives its incumbent the right to graze a cow in Harvard Yard; laws still exist that permit the burning of witches.

Many anomalies exist in our economic policies; for example, laws designed to support the incomes of small farmers have created some agricultural millionaires, and commissions created to assure competition often end up creating and protecting monopolies. Neither individual policies nor whole programs are above criticism.

In a society that elects its policymakers at regular intervals, however, the majority view on the amount and type of government interference that is desirable will have some considerable influence on the interference that actually occurs. This now seems sure to be one of the major political issues of the 1980s. Fundamentally, a free-market system is retained because it is valued for its lack of coercion and its ability to do much of the allocating of society's resources. But we are not mesmerized by it; we feel free to intervene in pursuit of a better world in which to live. We also recognize, however, that some intervention has proven excessive and/or ineffective.

Summary

1. Two of the most powerful tools of microeconomic policy are taxation and public expenditure.

2. While their main purpose is to raise revenue, taxes represent a means of redistributing income. Federal taxes overall are progressive because of their heavy reliance on income taxation; state and local taxes are on balance regressive, particularly because of their heavy reliance on property and sales taxes.

3. The total American tax structure is roughly proportional except for very low-income groups (for whom it is regressive) and very high-income groups (for whom it is progressive). Either a negative income tax or a move in the direction of comprehensive income taxation would increase progressivity. Whether this is feasible politically, or desirable, is a subject of sharp current debate.

4. Evaluating the effects of taxes on resource allocation requires first determining tax incidence — that is, determining who really pays the taxes. For most taxes, the incidence is shared. Excise taxes, for example, affect prices and are thus partially passed on, but part is absorbed by producers. The actual incidence depends on such economic considerations as demand and supply elasticities.

5. A large part of public expenditure is for the provision of goods and services that private markets fail to provide. Direct and indirect subsidies, transfer payments to individuals, and grants-in-aid to state and local governments are all rising sharply.

6. The major redistributive activities of the federal government take the form of direct transfer payments to individuals and grants-in-aid to state and local governments for economic welfare payments. While the public sector has a tendency to redistribute some income from high-income and middle-income groups to the poor, the change in income inequality from decade to decade has been small.

7. Government expenditure of all kinds has a major effect on the allocation of resources. The government determines how much of our total output is devoted to national defense, education, and highways. It is also influential in areas where private provision of goods and services is common. Government subsidization of health care has led such expenditures to more than double as a fraction of total GNP in 30 years, and a sharp further increase in this fraction will result if the proposed expansions of government support for health care are enacted.

8. The debate about subsidization of health care raises key questions that surround all new major government expenditure programs. Why does the government have to intervene? How much of the subsidized commodity should be produced? What are the costs of providing it and who should pay them? What is the least inefficient form of government intervention?

9. Grants-in-aid to state and local government are a key form of public expenditure policy; they lead to a different allocation of resources than would occur without them. The need for such grants-in-aid is dramatically revealed by the plight of the nation's cities.

10. The urban crisis is in large part a result of the selective migration of residents to the suburbs and out of reach of the urban taxing authorities. Such migration develops a dynamic that feeds itself, and increasingly the central cities have become occupied by the poor, with rising needs and a shrinking tax base. This leads to the urban fiscal crisis, for which state or federal assistance may be the only solution.

11. Evaluating public expenditures involves reaching decisions about absolute merit (do benefits exceed costs?), about the relative merit of public and private expenditures, and about the desirable size of government.

12. The U.S. economy is a mixed economy and a changing one. Each generation faces anew the choice of which activities to leave to the unfet-

tered market and which to rely on public expenditures or taxes to encourage or repress. It is clear that many people today are dissatisfied with the present role of government in the economy.

Topics for Review

Tax expenditures
Progressivity and regressivity of taxes
Tax incidence
Transfer payments to individuals
The debate about public subsidization of health care
The uses of grants-in-aid to state and local governments
The sources of urban crises
Choosing between private and public expenditures

Discussion Questions

1. The American taxpayer is assaulted by dozens of different taxes with different incidence, different progressivity, and different methods of collection. Discuss the case for and against using at most two different kinds of taxes. Discuss the case for a single taxing authority that would share the revenue with all levels of government.

2. Under federal tax law, municipal bond interest is tax exempt. Who benefits from this provision? What are its effects on the distribution of income and the allocation of resources? In what sense is this a "tax expenditure"?

3. "Taxes on tobacco and alcohol are nearly perfect taxes. They raise lots of revenue and discourage smoking and drinking." In this statement, to what extent are the two effects inconsistent? How is the incidence of an excise tax related to the extent to which it discourages use of the product?

4. How might each of the following affect the incidence of a real estate property tax imposed on central city rental property?

   a. The residents of the community are largely blacks who face racial discrimination in neighboring areas.

   b. The city installs a good, cheap rapid-transit system that makes commuting to the suburbs less expensive and more comfortable.

   c. The income tax laws are changed to eliminate the deductibility of property taxes from taxable income for those who itemize deductions.

5. Under the federal tax laws, all state and local income taxes can be deducted from income in computing the federal tax liability. Suppose two local communities each impose a 10 percent tax on personal incomes. Richville is composed of families who earn $100,000 per year or more. Uniontown consists mainly of workers' families who earn about $10,000 per year. Who really pays the taxes in each case? What, if anything, prevents Richville from raising its taxes?

6. Classify each of the following programs as "transfer payment," "grant-in-aid," "purchase of goods and services," or "none of the above." Which ones clearly tend to decrease the inequality of income distribution?
   a. payments of wages and family living allowances to soldiers serving overseas
   b. unemployment insurance payments to unemployed workers
   c. payments to states for support of highway construction
   d. a negative income tax
   e. pensions of retired Supreme Court justices
   f. an excess-profits tax on oil companies

7. Comment on each of the following.
   a. "Everybody is entitled to the right to live. The only way this can be assured is to make medical care available free to anyone who needs it."
   b. "Subsidizing medical and hospital care removes the only effective restraint to overcharges by doctors and hospitals."
   c. "Health care insurance provided by employers removes any disincentives to efficient provision of medical services, while assuring that everyone will be able to get essential services."
   d. "If doctors were limited to incomes of $50,000 per year, medical costs would come down."

8. Comment on each of the following.
   a. "New York's financial problem is not a natural disaster or an act of God. It is a self-inflicted act by the people who have been running New York City."
   b. "It is not New York City policy but U.S. policy that encouraged over a million Puerto Ricans to come to New York and caused dramatic changes in the city's population. Between 1970 and 1975 the white population *decreased* by 600,000 while the nonwhite *increased* by over 100,000. Because the new New Yorkers were characteristically poor, undereducated, and often non-English speaking, they added extraordinary costs to the city's welfare, schools, and other programs. These are properly *national* problems, not *city problems*."
   c. "New York should declare war on the United States—and then lose. In that way it would qualify for the economic aid the United States gives to its former enemies."
   d. "Poverty, discrimination, and unemployment are federal, not state and local, problems. If the federal government solved these problems, urban crises would disappear."

9. If governments tend to step in when markets fail, why are not similar functions performed similarly in different countries? Medical care, sport fishing rights, steel production, broadcasting, telephone service, and garbage collection are provided publicly in some Western countries and privately in others. What accounts for the diversity?

10. Evaluate each of the following statements about the role of government in the economy.
    a. "Big government, not big business, is this country's problem. We are convinced that government should not try to perform economic functions that the marketplace performs more efficiently and more equitably. In our view, the proper and most productive role of government lies in balancing off various national needs, formulating policies, setting objectives, establishing appropriate incentives to the private sector to achieve those objectives, monitoring progress toward objectives, and, perhaps most important, providing leadership."
    b. "Government spending threatens our way of life. If such spending continues at the rate of the last 20 years, by the year 2000 half the people of this nation will be living off the other half."
    c. "It is private spending that has gone unchecked in an orgy of mindless consumption. That and so-called defense expenditures swallow our national income and make ours an overfed, overentertained, polluted, and impoverished society."

Part Eight

National Income
and Fiscal Policy

Aggregate Demand and Aggregate Supply

26

Inflation, unemployment, recession, and *economic growth* have become household words. Governments worry about how to reduce inflation and unemployment, how to prevent recessions, and how to increase growth. Firms are concerned with the effects of inflation on their assets and how to raise their productivity; many of them have good cause to fear recessions. Households wish to avoid the unemployment that comes in the wake of recessions and would like to protect themselves against the hazards of inflation.

What Is Macroeconomics?

As we saw in Chapter 4, the whole of economics can be divided into two main branches, microeconomics and macroeconomics[1]. Each of the concerns listed above plays a major role in macroeconomics. But what exactly *is* macroeconomics?

MICRO AND MACRO COMPARED

Microeconomics is concerned with the behavior of individual markets. A typical microeconomic problem is to explain the behavior of automobile prices. For decades car prices fell in relation to the prices of most other commodities. Recently this trend has been reversed, with automobiles becoming increasingly expensive relative to other commodities. In microeconomics we seek to understand the causes and the effects of such changes in *relative* prices.

Macroeconomics deals with the overall behavior of the whole economy. A typical macroeco-

---

[1] Macro and micro derive from the Greek words *makros* and *mikros,* which mean, respectively, long or large and short or small.

nomic problem is to account for the behavior of the price level as measured by the Consumer Price Index (CPI). Why is the average rate at which all prices rise quite low in some decades and quite high in others?

SOME MAJOR MACROECONOMIC ISSUES

We live in an inflationary world. Why did the pace of inflation accelerate during the early 1970s to rates never before seen in peacetime in most advanced Western nations? If Americans and Canadians thought that inflation rates in the range of 10 percent were serious, what was it like to live in Japan, Italy, or Great Britain, where inflation rates were much higher?

The economy proceeds in fits and starts rather than in a smooth upward trend. Why did the 1930s see the greatest economic depression in recorded history, with up to a quarter of the labor force unemployed in America and the other major countries of the world? Why were the 25 years following World War II what now appears in retrospect to have been a period of sustained secular boom with only minor interruptions from modest recessions? Why did the mid 1970s see the onset of the worst worldwide recession and slowest recovery since the 1930s?

Alternating bouts of inflationary boom and deflationary slump have caused many policy headaches in the past. Why was the recession of the mid 1970s accompanied not only by its familiar companion, high unemployment, but also by an unexpected fellow traveler, rapid inflation? Is the new disease of stagflation—simultaneous high unemployment and rapid inflation—here to stay?

The long-run trend of most advanced (and many less advanced) economies has been a rising total and per capita output accompanied by rising living standards. Does the recent slowdown of worldwide growth rates represent a change in underlying growth trends, or is it just a reflection of the prolonged cyclical downturn of the last half of the 1970s? Can governments do anything to change growth rates? If so, should they intervene

to accelerate economic growth, as one group advocates, or to slow it, as another group advocates?

KEY MACRO VARIABLES: DEFINITION AND BEHAVIOR

Many of the key variables whose behavior we study in macroeconomics are related to the price level, employment, and total output. Let us define some of these variables and see how they have behaved over the past half century.

The Price Level

The price level can be measured by any index of the economy's prices.[2] The three most common indexes are the CPI, which covers commodities bought by the "typical consumer"; the Producer Price Index, which covers wholesale prices; and the GNP deflator, which covers everything produced in the economy. The price level is usually denoted by the symbol P.

The annual rate of inflation is the percentage change in some price index from one year to the next. When the rate is measured by the CPI, the formula is:

$$\text{rate of inflation} = \frac{\text{this year's CPI} - \text{last year's CPI}}{\text{last year's CPI}} \times 100$$

The rate of inflation can be measured between various points in the two years. It is common to use year-end (CPI on December 31) or mid-year (CPI on July 1) figures or annual averages (average monthly CPI) in the above formula. Figure 26-1 shows the rate of inflation as measured by the rate of change of annual averages in the CPI.

Output Variables

There are several related measures of the country's total output. The one most commonly

[2] Price indexes are discussed on pages 29–33.

FIGURE 26–1
Annual Inflation Rate in the United States, 1930–1979

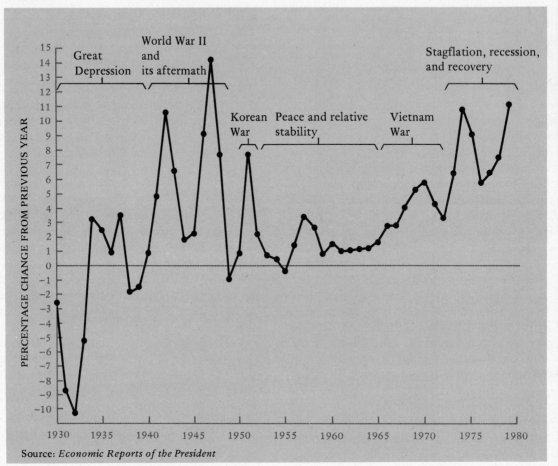

Source: *Economic Reports of the President*

The rate of inflation has varied from –10 percent to +14 percent over the period since 1930. Prices fell dramatically during the onset of the Great Depression. They rose sharply during and after World War II and during the Korean War. Although variable, there was no discernible trend in the inflation rate from the end of the Korean War to the mid 1960s. The period starting in the mid 1960s, however, experienced a strong upward trend in the inflation rate, interrupted by short-term fluctuations.

used is called **gross national product (GNP).** Its definition and calculation are discussed in the next chapter; here we merely note that it seeks to measure the total market value of the nation's output.

GNP may be measured in current dollars. This tells us the total value of the nation's output in prices ruling at the moment. It is then called **nominal GNP** or **current dollar GNP,** and its changes reflect changes both in quantities produced and in market prices.

GNP may also be measured in constant dollars. In this case the quantities produced in each year are valued in terms of prices ruling in some base year, such as 1972. It is then called **real GNP** or **constant dollar GNP,** and its changes reflect only quantity changes.

Total output is often denoted by the symbol Y.

When used in this chapter, Y and the term *national product* refer to the nation's GNP measured in constant dollars, a measure of the total quantity of output produced in the economy.

Figure 26-2 shows real GNP produced by the American economy since 1929. The series shows two kinds of movement. The major movement is a trend-increase in real output. The real output of the American economy rose by over 400 percent in the half century from 1929 to 1979. This trend represents the economic growth of the American economy. A secondary movement in the GNP series is that of the short-term fluctuations resulting from the cyclical behavior of the economy. The overall growth of the economy so dominates the GNP series that the cyclical behavior is hardly visible in this figure. Cyclical patterns are more readily apparent in a series called the GNP gap.

Potential GNP and the GNP Gap

To define the GNP gap, we first need to define one new concept. **Potential GNP** or **full-employment GNP** is what the economy would produce if its productive resources were fully employed at their normal intensity of use. It may be measured either in current or in constant dollars, and it is given the symbol Y_F. *Actual GNP* is what the economy does in fact produce. When measured in current dollars it is *nominal income;* when measured in constant dollars it is *real income.* The **GNP gap** is the difference between the two: potential GNP minus actual

FIGURE 26–2
United States GNP, 1929–1979, in Constant (1972) Dollars

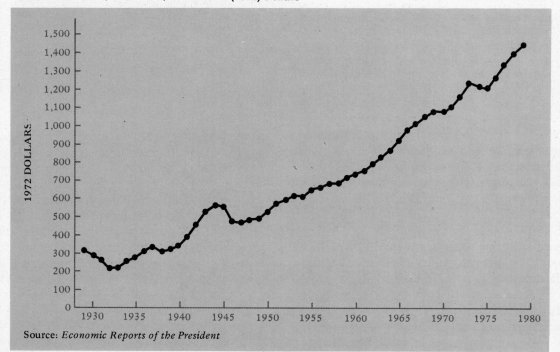

Source: *Economic Reports of the President*

Constant dollar GNP measures the quantity of total output produced by the nation's economy over the period of a year. National product has risen steadily since the early 1930s, with only a few interruptions. This represents the economic growth of the American economy. Shorter-term fluctuations have occurred, but they are obscured by the long-term growth trend.

FIGURE 26-3
The GNP Gap

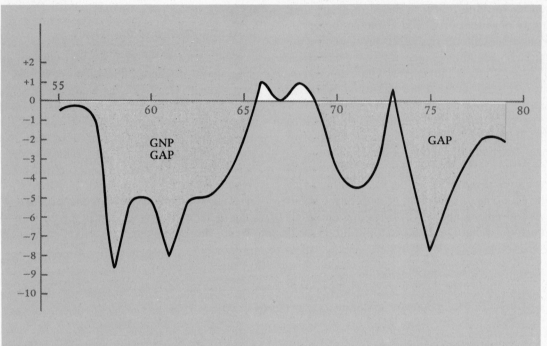

The GNP gap measures the difference between the economy's potential output and its actual output; it is expressed here as a percentage of potential output. The cyclical behavior of the economy is clearly appar-ent from the behavior of the GNP gap. Slumps in eco-nomic activity cause large gaps, booms reduce the gap. The shaded area under the curve represents the deadweight loss from unemployment.

GNP. The GNP gap represents useful output—valuable goods and services—that *could have been* produced if the economy were fully employed but that actually goes unproduced. This is often referred to as the "deadweight loss" of unemployment.

Slumps in business activity are associated with large GNP gaps, booms with small ones. In a major boom the gap can even become negative, indicating that actual GNP exceeds the economy's potential GNP! This surprising result occurs because potential GNP is defined for a normal rate of utilization of factors of production, and there are many ways in which normal rates of utilization can be exceeded. Labor may work harder or work longer hours; factories may work an extra shift or not close for normal repairs and

maintenance. (This is only a temporary expedient, but it is an effective one in the short term.)

Figure 26-3 shows the GNP gap for the American economy expressed as a percentage of potential GNP. The fluctuations in economic activity are readily apparent from the fluctuations in the size of the gap. The deadweight loss from unemployment over any time span is indicated by the overall size of the gap over this span (i.e., by the shaded area under the curve between the two points in question).

Labor Variables

Employment denotes the number of adult workers (defined in the U.S. to be workers over 15 years old) who hold full-time civilian jobs.

Unemployment denotes the number of persons who are not employed and are actively searching for a job. The civilian **labor force** is the total number of the employed, other than those serving in the armed services, plus the unemployed. The **unemployment rate,** usually denoted by the symbol U, is unemployment expressed as a percentage of the labor force:

unemployment rate $(U) =$

$$\frac{\text{unemployed}}{\text{number in the labor force}} \times 100$$

Figure 26-4 shows labor force, employment, and unemployment in America. In spite of the much-discussed occurrences of business booms and slumps and inflations and deflations, the

FIGURE 26–4

Labor Force, Employment, and Unemployment in the United States, 1929–1979

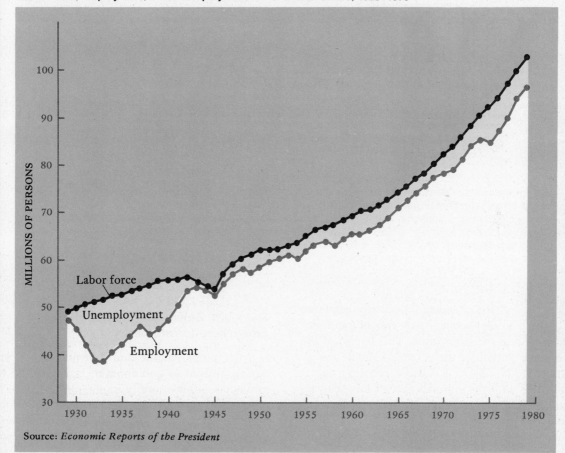

Source: *Economic Reports of the President*

The labor force and employment have grown since the 1930s with only a few interruptions. The size of the American labor force has doubled since 1930, and so has the number of the employed. Unemployment, the gap between the labor force and employment, has fluctuated but has not again reached the magnitude suffered in the 1930s. (Up to 1946 the definition of labor force includes persons 14 years of age and over; from 1947 it includes only persons 16 years of age and over.)

FIGURE 26–5
Percentage of the Labor Force Unemployed in the United States, 1929–1979

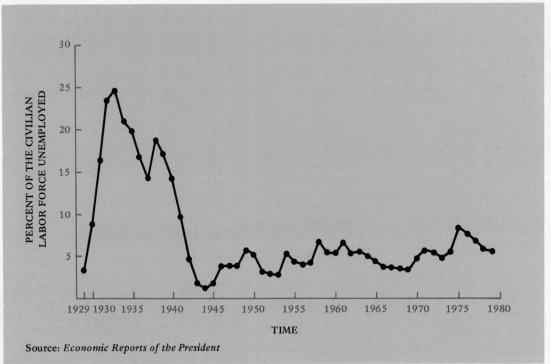

Source: *Economic Reports of the President*

The unemployment rate responds to the cyclical behavior of the economy. Booms are associated with low unemployment, slumps with high unemployment. The Great Depression of the 1930s produced record unemployment figures for an entire decade. During World War II unemployment rates fell to very low levels. The depression in the mid 1970s produced unemployment rates second only to those of the 1930s; these rates were extremely large by the standards of the post-World War II behavior of the American economy.

main trend of the economy has clearly been one of growth in employment that roughly matches the growth in the labor force. This is part of the economic growth of the economy. Some unemployment, however, is always present, and it fluctuates with the ebb and flow of business activity. This is part of the short-term cyclical behavior of the economy.

As with the GNP, the long-term growth trend dominates the employment figures. The unemployment *rate* graphed in Figure 26-5 gives a better picture of the effects of the shorter-term cyclical behavior of the economy on unemployment.

Relations Between Output and Employment Variables

Output, employment, and unemployment are closely related to one another. If more is to be produced, either more workers must be used in production or existing workers must produce more. The first change means a rise in employment, the second a rise in output per person employed, which is called a rise in productivity. Increases in productivity are a major cause of economic growth.

A rise in unemployment will occur if output falls and some people lose their jobs as a result.

It will also occur if, with the same amount of employment, the labor force grows. For example, the number of people finishing school to enter the labor force might exceed the number leaving the labor force because of retirement and death.

Changes in productivity and the labor force dominate the long-term behavior of such variables as output and employment. (They are discussed in Chapter 43, on economic growth.) But productivity and the labor force generally change only a little from one year to the next, and thus they have little effect on the short-term behavior of the economy. We assume for the time being that the labor force and productivity are constant, in order to concentrate on the shorter-term cyclical behavior. Assuming them to be constant is a reasonable approximation to reality *for purposes of analyzing* the short-term behavior of the economy.

When the labor force and productivity are constant, unemployment varies inversely with output while employment varies directly with output.

Aggregate Demand and Aggregate Supply

We want to investigate the causes of changes in the price level and in real national product (and, through national product, changes in employment and unemployment). One way to do this is by using the concepts of demand and supply.

In Chapter 5 we saw that the interaction of demand and supply in competitive markets determines prices and quantities for individual commodities. If we had a single demand curve and a single supply curve for the whole economy, we could determine the economy's price level and its total national product just as we can determine price and quantity for a single product such as wheat or breakfast cereal.

This possibility is illustrated in Figure 26-6, which assumes the existence of an aggregate demand curve and an aggregate supply curve for the entire economy. The **aggregate demand curve**

(*AD*) shows a relation between the total amount of all output that will be demanded by purchasers and the price level of that output. The **aggregate supply curve** (*AS*) shows a relation between the total amount of output that will be produced and the price level of that output.

In fact, aggregate demand and aggregate supply curves can be derived, though it takes some time and care to do so. For the moment let us see what we can do with these curves if we simply assume that they exist.

THE SHAPES OF THE AGGREGATE CURVES

The aggregate demand curve typically slopes downward to the right, as shown by the *AD* curve in Figure 26-6. This shape means that, *ce-*

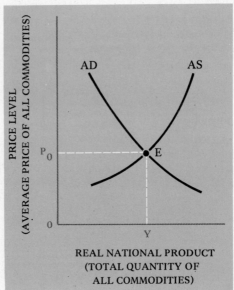

FIGURE 26–6
The Price Level and National Product for the Whole Economy

Aggregate demand and aggregate supply determine the price level and national product for the entire economy. Equilibrium is at *E* with the price level P_0 and a national product of *Y*. At higher price levels aggregate supply exceeds aggregate demand; at lower price levels aggregate demand exceeds aggregate supply.

teris paribus, the higher the price level, the smaller the total quantity demanded will be; and the lower the price level, the larger the total quantity demanded will be.

The aggregate supply curve shown in Figure 26-6 describes a short-term relation between the price level and national product. Its upward slope indicates that, *ceteris paribus*, the higher the price level, the greater the quantity supplied will be (at least over the short term). There are three interesting possibilities for the shape of this curve. At one time or another each of the three possibilities has been relevant. We can capture them by drawing, as in Figure 26-7, a composite aggregate supply curve with three ranges.

To the left of Y_0 the AS curve is horizontal. Over that range national product can be increased without any increase in the price level. This indicates that national product will vary without significant accompanying variations in the price level. This range may be called Keynesian because it is associated with the pioneering work of John Maynard Keynes, who studied the behavior of economies with heavy unemployment. This is the depression case, in which there is substantial unemployment of all kinds of resources. Output can be increased without running into shortages and bottlenecks.

At Y^* the AS curve is vertical, indicating that production cannot be expanded beyond Y^*, even if prices rise. Output Y^* is the maximum that can be produced when all of the economy's resources are fully employed. The vertical portion of AS is labeled classical because the so-called classical economists studied the economy under conditions of full employment of all resources. They assumed that in such circumstances no more output can be squeezed out of existing resources. If there is an increase in aggregate demand, prices will rise but output cannot increase.

Between Y_0 and Y^* there is an intermediate range over which AS slopes upward. In this range there is scope for some increase in output, but as output rises, shortages will develop. The excess demand for commodities that are in short supply will force up the average of all prices along with output. In the intermediate range of the AS curve, therefore, prices and output vary directly with each other.

It is a mistake to think that each economy has a unique aggregate supply curve or that its shape is always the same. The aggregate supply curve expresses a short-term relation between the price level and national income that is suitable for analyzing short-term fluctuations in the level of business activity. The relevant aggregate supply curve may sometimes look like the curve in Figure 26-6 and sometimes like only one of the segments of the curve in Figure 26-7.

The composite curve of Figure 26-7 catches a simplified essence of three situations: *depression*, where the price level is relatively constant; *full employment*, where output cannot be increased; and a period of *modest slack* in the economy, where output and the price level tend to change together.

FIGURE 26–7
A Composite Aggregate Supply Curve

A composite aggregate supply curve can be seen as composed of the three distinct ranges. Over the Keynesian (horizontal) range the price level is constant but real national product can vary. Over the classical (vertical) range real national product is constant while the price level can vary. Over the intermediate range real national product and the price level vary with each other.

SHIFTS IN THE AGGREGATE CURVES

What will happen to total output and the price level if one or both of the aggregate curves shift? Shifts in aggregate demand and aggregate supply are often called demand shocks and supply shocks respectively.

Increases in Aggregate Demand

Figure 26-8 shows how increases in aggregate demand affect the economy over the three ranges of the single composite *AS* curve. Over the Keynesian range, where there is general unemployment of resources, a rise in aggregate demand raises output without raising the price level. In this case any government (or private) policy that increases demand will increase output and employment while decreasing unemployment.

Increases in aggregate demand over the intermediate range of the *AS* curve affect both price and output. The economy is close enough to full-capacity output that increases in output can be made only at the cost of some inflation. The further one moves to the right along the *AS* curve, the steeper it becomes. As a result, the effect of successive increases in aggregate demand is felt more and more on prices and less and less on output.

Finally, in the classical range there is full employment of all factors of production. Increases in aggregate demand leave output unchanged but cause prices to rise. This is the range of a pure demand inflation. All increases in demand in this range are inflationary and bring no offsetting gain in terms of extra output or employment.

Shifts in Aggregate Supply

Figure 26-9 shows the effects of an upward shift in the *AS* curve with no change in *AD:* the price level rises and output falls. This combination of events is now called stagflation. This rather inelegant word was derived by running together "stagnation" (less than full employment) and

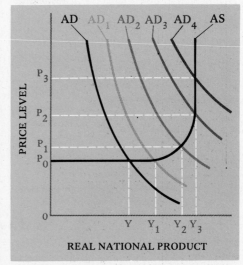

FIGURE 26-8
The Effects of Increases in Aggregate Demand

Increases in aggregate demand may cause an increase in output alone, an increase in both output and prices, or an increase in prices alone. An increase in aggregate demand from *AD* to AD_1 increases total output from *Y* to Y_1, leaving the price level unchanged. An increase to AD_2 raises output from Y_1 to Y_2 and raises the price level from P_0 to P_1. An increase to AD_3 brings a smaller increase in output (from Y_2 to Y_3) and a larger increase in the price level (from P_1 to P_2). An increase to AD_4 raises the price level from P_2 to P_3 but leaves output constant at Y_3.

"inflation" (a rise in the price level). **Stagflation** therefore refers to inflations that occur when national income is below its full-employment level. In Figure 26-9 the price level rises while national product actually falls (which implies a growing GNP gap).

AGGREGATE DEMAND AND SUPPLY IN ACTION

The tools of aggregate demand and aggregate supply can be used to give a brief overview of some of the major macro events of the last 50 years. (These events will be studied in more detail in Chapter 37.)

The Effect of Shifts in Aggregate Supply

Upward shifts in aggregate supply raise prices but lower output. The original curves are *AD* and P_0AS. The aggregate supply curve then shifts upward to P_1AS. The shift causes output to fall from *Y* to Y_1 and the price level to rise from P_0 to P_1. Here a rising price level is associated with a falling level of output.

The 1930s. In the Great Depression of the 1930s, the economy could be thought of as being on the Keynesian portion of a relatively stable *AS* curve. The *AD* curve, however, was shifting. This exposed the economy to a series of demand shocks that changed national product, employment, and unemployment. Economists looked for ways in which government policy could be used to shift the *AD* curve to the right and thus raise output and employment.

The 1940s. During World War II the vast government purchases of war supplies increased *AD* and pushed the economy to full employment. After that the economy was in the classical (vertical) portion of the aggregate supply curve. Full employment and inflationary pressures prevailed. After 1941 the inflation rate was held to the low figures shown in Figure 26-1 by direct wage and price controls. When the controls were removed, the excess aggregate demand made its presence felt in the dramatic postwar inflation

that greatly increased the price level. Economists studied ways of restraining aggregate demand in order to control inflation.

1950–1965. Aggregate demand fluctuated mainly over the intermediate range on a relatively stable *AS* curve. Increases in aggregate demand tended to increase both national product and the price level. Because of the downward inflexibility of prices, however, decreases in aggregate demand tended to lower national product and employment while leaving the price level unchanged. Economists looked for ways to reduce the demand shocks so that output, employment, and prices could be made as stable as possible.

1965–1973. The buildup of defense spending to finance the accelerating war in Vietnam hit the economy with a severe demand shock that took it again into the classical range of full employment and rising prices. Although there were lapses from full employment, the period was mainly one of excess demand. It culminated in the boom of 1972–1973, when excess demand throughout the world created strong worldwide inflationary pressure. The U.S. inflation rate hit the double-digit range for the first time since 1947. Economists suggested ways in which aggregate demand could be reduced in order to alleviate the growing inflationary pressure.

1974–1980. The boom of the first part of the decade ended in 1974 with the onset of the most severe recession since the 1930s. By itself this would have taken the economy back into the Keynesian range of the *AS* curve, with low national product and stable prices. Just at that time, however, the economy was hit with severe supply shocks. Serious crop failures combined with the sale of surplus wheat to the USSR raised food prices greatly. OPEC policies forced up not only the price of energy but the prices of fertilizer, plastics, synthetic rubber, and dozens of other products produced from petroleum. High prices and shortages of oil caused buyers to shift to such alternative energy sources as coal, and this in turn drove their prices up. All these forces pushed the aggregate supply curve upward because they increased the price level.

The leftward shift in the *AD* curve combined with an upward shift in the *AS* curve brought about a serious stagflation. For the first time the economy experienced simultaneously the twin "evils" of falling output and rising prices.

The mid 1970s were the first time in the last half century that a major part of the explanation of the behavior of prices and output lay in an upward-shifting aggregate supply curve. The public was so used to the behavior of the economy under the impact of demand-side shocks that behavior under severe supply-side shocks seemed incomprehensible, even paradoxical. Economists were so used to explaining observed events by demand-side shocks that many of them did not at first appreciate what was happening. Some announced the collapse of conventional macroeconomic theory; others claimed to see a complete change in all economic behavior. Although plausible at the time, such reactions can now be seen to have been excessive—once the part played by aggregate supply is appreciated.

THE SHAPES OF THE AGGREGATE CURVES EXPLAINED

Up to now we have assumed that we could draw aggregate demand and supply curves for the whole economy analogous to the curves we know we can draw for individual competitive markets. If we could simply aggregate all the demand and supply curves in individual markets to obtain aggregate demand and supply curves, there would be little left to do but to apply our aggregate tools to those aspects of macro behavior in which we were interested. Unfortunately, life is not so simple. Let us see why we cannot take such an approach.

The Fallacy of Composition

If we assumed that we could add up market demand curves for each individual commodity to obtain a downward-sloping aggregate demand curve, we would be committing the *fallacy of composition*. This is to assume that what is correct for the parts must be correct for the whole.

Consider a simple example of the fallacy. Any art collector can go into the market and add to a collection of nineteenth century French paintings provided only that he or she has enough money. But to assume that because any one person can do this, everyone could do so simultaneously is plainly wrong. The stock of nineteenth century French paintings in the world is totally fixed. All of us cannot do what any one of us may be able to do.

How does the fallacy of composition relate to demand and supply curves?

The Shape of the Aggregate Demand Curve

The demand curve for an individual commodity slopes downward for two basic reasons. First, as the price of a particular commodity rises, consumers buy less of it and more of now relatively cheaper substitutes. Second, as the price of one commodity rises, each consumer's given money income will buy a smaller total amount of goods, so a smaller quantity of the commodity in question will be bought.

Neither of these explanations will do for the aggregate demand curve, which relates total quantity to the price level. A rise in the price level means a rise in all prices. This has two consequences. First, total demand does not fall as a result of substitution among commodities in the way that demand for one commodity falls when *only* its price changes. Second, a change in the price level means a change both in prices of commodities and in prices of factors of production, which includes wages and salaries. Thus a rise in the price level does not necessarily lead to a general loss of purchasing power. This is because it also leads to a rise in the average money incomes of households. When people have more income, they can increase their money expenditure. For example, a 10 percent rise in all prices, causing a 10 percent rise in all money incomes, might be expected to cause a 10 percent rise in money expenditure and leave the quantities of goods bought and sold unchanged.

The reason why the *aggregate* demand curve slopes downward is to be found in the effects of money on interest rates and of interest rates on total purchases, topics not discussed until later in this book. The main forces are suggested below; the reasons will be apparent later when the necessary links in the argument have each been studied.

When the price of everything rises, firms need more money to finance their payrolls and other purchases of factors of production. And households need more money in the bank to cover their expenses between each payday and the next. *Ceteris paribus*, this extra need for money creates a shortage of money. When money is in short supply, interest rates tend to rise. Firms that borrow money to invest in plant and equipment and households that borrow money to buy houses are sensitive to rising interest rates. As rates go up they wish to spend less on capital goods, housing, and other classes of expenditure that are sensitive to interest rates. But this means a decline in the aggregate quantity demanded of the nation's output. This then is the main reason why the aggregate demand curve slopes downward.[3]

A rise in the price level creates a shortage of money, which drives up interest rates. This in turn discourages interest-sensitive expenditures. Thus, *ceteris paribus*, the higher the price level, the lower the quantity demanded of the nation's output.

The full explanation can be found in Chapter 34.

The Shape of the Aggregate Supply Curve

If we tried to derive an aggregate supply curve by adding up the changes in the quantity supplied of each commodity when its price rises, *ceteris*

paribus, we would again be committing the fallacy of composition. This is because the things held constant along an individual supply curve do not remain constant when *all* prices change. The explanation of the shape of the composite aggregate supply curve turns out to be simpler than that of the aggregate demand curve.

The Keynesian portion. The horizontal shape of the *AS* curve in the Keynesian portion is a result of two forces. First, there are unemployed supplies of all resources, so output can be increased without placing *upward* pressure on prices. Second, prices are relatively rigid downward, and thus they do not fall enough to have an important influence in spite of excess supply in both labor markets and goods markets.

The absence of upward pressure on prices when there is excess supply is not surprising. But why do prices and wages not fall when firms have excess capacity and there are many unemployed workers? Why does competition among unemployed labor for the available jobs not force wages down? Why does competition among firms, all of whom would like to sell more, not force prices of commodities down?

Certainly prices would fall in perfectly competitive markets. Indeed, the prices of some basic raw materials—tin, copper, and iron, for example—do fall during a depression. But it is a matter of common observation that during a depression there is substantial *downward rigidity* in wages and in the prices of manufactured goods. In spite of a sizable excess supply of labor, money wages do not fall. Since wages are a major part of most firms' costs, this rigidity holds costs up and makes firms less likely to cut prices in the hope of gaining new sales. Further, most manufactured goods are not sold on perfectly competitive markets but are produced by large firms that set their own prices. Such firms are reluctant to get into price wars with their rivals; instead they are inclined to hold prices relatively stable and cut production when demand for their product falls in a recession.

Of course all prices are not completely inflexible downward. Figure 26-1, for example, reveals

---

[3] There are other reasons. For example, a rise in the American price level, *ceteris paribus*, reduces foreign demand for American exports and leads Americans to buy foreign imports rather than increasingly expensive American commodities. Both of these changes reduce the demand for American output.

that the price level was not constant during the Great Depression. It fell dramatically in the three years 1931–1933. After 1933, however, there were no further major reductions in the price level even in the face of an enormous GNP gap. Between 1933 and 1939 the price level sometimes rose and sometimes fell, but its average change over that whole period of depression was a *rise* of just less than 0.5 percent per year.

The Keynesian (horizontal) portion of the aggregate supply curve is not intended, then, to be an exact description of an economy in depression. It is meant instead to capture in simple form the essential condition that has prevailed in every subsequent recession and depression: the price level does not fall significantly in the presence of those GNP gaps that the economy has actually experienced.

The classical portion. The classical (vertical) portion of the aggregate supply curve is derived from the simplifying assumption that when all resources are fully employed, real output reaches its "full-employment ceiling," which cannot be exceeded. As with the Keynesian portion of the *AS* curve, this is a simplification that is meant to capture a slightly more complex reality. In fact it is almost always possible to squeeze more output out of the economy. After all, three shifts a day could be worked, and every able-bodied man, woman, and child could be employed.

Although there is no absolute full-employment ceiling to output, the vertical section of the *AS* curve catches the reality that under normal conditions there is some level of output beyond which output will not respond significantly to further increases in aggregate demand.

The intermediate portion. The intermediate portion occurs because economic growth imposes a constant need for change in the economy. This means that all sectors of the economy are never in perfect balance with each other at any moment in time. Some industries will be enjoying rapidly rising demands; they will be struggling to increase capacity in order to keep pace. Other industries will find their demands growing slowly or even declining; they will have a higher margin of extra capacity. Similarly, labor in some skill and industry classifications and geographical areas will be in very short supply while other labor will be in more abundant supply relative to the demand for it.

These inevitable imbalances in the economy mean that as production expands toward its full-employment level, shortages and bottlenecks will first appear in some but not all product and labor markets. Prices and wages will begin to rise in these markets while there is still some slack in other markets of the economy. As total output continues to increase, more and more shortages and capacity limits will be encountered, so more prices will start to rise and it will become harder and harder to obtain further increases in output. Thus the economy does not run into a capacity constraint abruptly, like a car hitting a brick wall. Instead, like a car running up an ever steepening hill, real progress becomes harder and harder to achieve as output expands further and further. Output increases by smaller and smaller amounts and more and more prices are forced up, so the aggregate supply curve becomes steeper and steeper the higher output is within this range.

The ratchet effect. There is a further basic and very important property of any *AS* curve that must be understood. The problem arises because the Keynesian portion of the aggregate supply curve depends on the assumption that prices are rigid downward: when demand falls, firms reduce output but do not reduce prices.

To see the importance of this downward rigidity of prices consider Figure 26-8 once again. Assume that aggregate demand shifts rightward enough to cause the price level to rise and then shifts leftward back to its original position (say, from *AD* to AD_4 and back to *AD* again). Given downward rigidity of prices, the price level cannot fall back to its original level. The original aggregate demand curve will now be associated with a higher price level. (This is not shown in Figure 26-8, which is suitable for analyzing a sequence of *increases* in aggregate demand but not decreases.)

FIGURE 26-10
The Ratchet Effect on Aggregate Supply

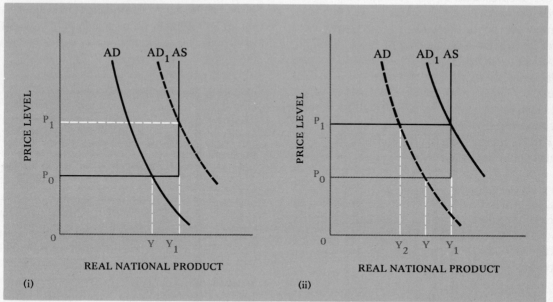

(i)

(ii)

A rise in aggregate demand raises the price level, but a fall in AD does not lower the price level. Suppose the economy begins in (i) on the Keynesian (horizontal) range of the aggregate supply curve, with aggregate demand AD, at price level P_0 and a national product of Y. A large demand shock then shifts aggregate demand to AD_1, the price level to P_1, and national product to Y_1. Because the price level is inflexible downward, the Keynesian portion of the aggregate supply curve now shifts upward to P_1. This indicates that once the price level has risen to P_1, prices will never again fall to P_0. The new aggregate supply curve is shown in (ii) by the heavy AS line, the old curve by the screened line.

Now suppose aggregate demand shifts back to AD. In (ii) this lowers national product to Y_2 but leaves the price level at P_1. (If the aggregate supply curve had not ratcheted upward, the fall in aggregate demand from AD_1 back to AD would have reduced national product only to Y while returning the price level to P_0.)

We must now amend our aggregate supply analysis in order to deal with declines as well as increases in aggregate demand. A simplification will help: we reduce our composite aggregate supply curve to include just the Keynesian and the classical cases. This suppression of the intermediate case leaves us with the two extremes shown in Figure 26-10: depression where output can be varied at constant prices and full employment where output cannot rise but the price level can.

The change required to deal with decreases in AD is shown in Figure 26-10. (It should be studied carefully.) Because the price level can rise but does not normally fall by any significant amount, the Keynesian (horizontal) portion of the AS curve is always at the *current* price level. Whenever the price level rises, the Keynesian portion rises as well. We speak of it being "ratcheted" up, a ratchet being a device that allows a wheel to turn one way but not the other. The downward rigidity of prices requires the ratcheting up of the Keynesian portion of the AS curve whenever the actual price level rises.

Starting from equilibrium positions on the classical portion of the aggregate supply curve, a rise in aggregate demand will raise the price level, leaving national product unchanged. This leads to a new Keynesian portion of the aggregate supply curve so that a fall in aggregate demand will lower national product, leaving the price level unchanged.

THE GAME PLAN

In this chapter we have only *assumed* most characteristics of the aggregate demand and supply curves. But if we are to use these tools of analysis, we need to understand their shapes more fully and what causes them to shift. For this it will be necessary to understand their components.

In Chapter 27 we consider the meaning of the basic concept of national product. In Chapters 28 and 29 we see what determines the position of the aggregate demand curve and what causes it to shift. We will then be able to study in Chapters 30 and 31 those forces that arise from private market decisions and from government fiscal policy decisions that affect the economy by shifting the aggregate demand curve.

In Chapters 32–35 we consider the role of money in the economy. In Chapter 34 we study the shape of the aggregate demand curve and explain more fully why it slopes downward to the right. In Chapter 35 we see how changes in the government's monetary policy can influence real national income and the price level by shifting the aggregate demand curve.

In Chapter 36 and 37 we use the tools of aggregate demand and aggregate supply to understand more fully the causes of the macroeconomic ills of the last 10 to 15 years. We also assess some of the proposed cures for these ills. In Chapter 38 we look briefly at some of the major policy controversies whose outcome will seriously affect the economy's macro performance and the welfare of all its citizens.

Summary

1. Macroeconomics studies the behavior of such broad aggregates and averages as the price level, national product, potential GNP, the GNP gap, employment, and unemployment.

2. The dominant theme of the economy is the growth of real output and employment. In order to isolate shorter-term cyclical factors, we assume that the labor force and productivity are constant. Then we focus attention on the GNP gap and the unemployment rate.

3. Two major tools of macroeconomics are the aggregate demand and aggregate supply curves. Typically the aggregate demand curve slopes downward, indicating a lower demand for the nation's output the higher the price level.

4. Three typical situations can be captured in a composite aggregate supply curve with three sections. The first section is the Keynesian (horizontal) portion, where the price level is fixed and output can vary. The second section is the intermediate portion, over which both the price level and output can vary. The third section is the classical (vertical) portion, over which output is fixed but the price level can vary. These stylized versions are intended to capture the essence of depressionary mild slack and full-employment situations without pretending to be exact descriptions of each.

5. Most of the year-to-year experience of the economy has been generated by a shifting aggregate demand curve acting on a relatively stable aggregate supply curve. This tends to associate inflations with periods of high and rising output and stable prices with periods of low and falling output.

6. Supply-side shocks that came into prominence in the 1970s tend to associate rising prices with periods of falling output. This association can be readily understood in terms of a shifting aggregate supply curve acting on a relatively stable aggregate demand curve.

7. The slope of the aggregate demand curve will be explained in full in later chapters. It arises from the fact that an increase in the price level, *ceteris paribus*, creates a shortage of money that drives up interest rates. Higher interest rates in turn cause firms to demand less capital goods and households to demand less new housing. Both represent a fall in the demand for the nation's output.

8. Each segment of the composite aggregate supply curve has its own explanation. The Keynes-

ian portion arises because prices and wages do not tend to fall by significant amounts even in the face of large GNP gaps. The intermediate portion arises because as output expands, more and more capacity limitations, bottlenecks, and shortages are encountered, making further increases in output even more difficult and forcing still larger increases in prices as output does increase. The classical (vertical) portion arises from the assumption that a full-employment output hits an absolute capacity ceiling.

9. Because the price level is inflexible downward, the aggregate supply curve is subject to a ratchet effect. The Keynesian portion is always at the existing price level. Thus, if the price level rises, the Keynesian portion will move up with it. This means that in the region of full employment, increases in aggregate demand will tend to cause prices to rise while decreases in demand will tend to cause output to fall.

Topics for Review

Measures of the price level and the rate of inflation
National income, potential GNP, and the GNP gap
Employment, unemployment, and the labor force
Aggregate demand and aggregate supply
When high and rising output will be associated with rising prices
When falling output will be associated with rising prices
Keynesian, classical, and intermediate portions of an aggregate supply curve
Downward inflexibility of prices
The ratchet effect

Discussion Questions

1. Classify as micro or macro (or both) the issues raised in the following newspaper headlines.
   a. "Lettuce crop spoils as strike hits California lettuce producers."
   b. "Price of bus rides soars in Centersville as city council withdraws transport subsidy."
   c. "A fall in the unemployment rate signals the beginning of the end of the recession in the Detroit area."
   d. "Silicon chip technology brings falling prices and growing sales of minicomputers."
   e. "Wage settlements in key industries seen by the president to pose inflationary threat."

   f. "Rising costs of imported raw materials cause most American manufacturers to raise prices."
   g. "Index of Industrial Production falls by 4 points."
2. Explain each of the following by shifts in either (or both) the aggregate demand and aggregate supply curve. (Pay attention to the initial position before the shift(s) occurs.)
   a. Output and unemployment rise while prices hold steady.
   b. Prices soar but employment and output hold steady.
   c. Inflation accelerates even as the recession in business activity deepens.
   d. The inflation rate falls, but at the expense of employment.
3. Which of the following statements are examples of the fallacy of composition?
   a. "There is no real problem of unemployment today because help-wanted columns are full of unfilled jobs."
   b. Because 10 percent of a random sample of the U.S. population is Hispanic, 10 percent of the whole U.S. population is probably Hispanic.
   c. There is no shortage of machinists in Plainsville—anyone who needs a machinist can get one quickly if willing to pay above-market wages.
   d. If I am guaranteed a right in America, everyone is guaranteed that right.
4. In 1979–1980, the British government greatly reduced income taxes but restored the lost government revenue by raising excise and sales taxes. This led to a short burst of extra inflation and a fall in employment. Explain this in terms of shifts in aggregate demand and/or supply.
5. For each of the following events, indicate whether it is the cause or the consequence of a shift in aggregate demand or supply. If it is a cause, what do you predict will be the effect on the price level and on real national income?
   a. Unemployment increase in 1979 in the United States.
   b. OPEC once again raises oil prices.
   c. Country X is suffering a rapid inflation under conditions of approximately full employment.
   d. In country Y, income and employment continue to fall while the price level is quite stable.
   e. The recovery of the economy has led to a large increase in income and employment.
   f. The new administration decreases taxes sharply in an effort to stimulate the economy.

The Concepts of National Product and National Income

27

In the preceding chapter we saw how we could use the tools of aggregate demand and aggregate supply to explain the macro behavior of the economy. An important part of this explanation depends on the position of the aggregate demand curve. In order to understand why this curve is where it is, and what makes it shift, we need to look at the individual components of aggregate demand. In this chapter we see how the component parts of aggregate demand are defined and measured.

The aggregate demand curve, like the aggregate supply curve, relates the price level to the economy's total output, or *real national product*. This is the total market value of all goods and services produced in the economy during a year.

Closely related to real national product is the generic concept of *real national income*. This is all the income generated by the production of the national product. Clearly, much of the market value of output goes to pay the wages of workers who help to make the output; some goes as gross profit to firms that produce the commodities; and another portion goes to pay sales taxes that give governments a claim on some of the market value of production.

National Income Accounting

National income accounting is the set of rules and techniques for measuring the total flow of output (goods and services) produced and the total flow of incomes generated by this production. Let us see exactly what national income includes, how it is measured, and what it can tell us.

A standard convention of double-entry book-keeping is that all value produced must be accounted for by a claim that someone has to it. National product is the market value of all the production in the economy over a year, while national income is the value of all the claims generated by that production. Thus it is a matter of accounting convention that these two values be equal.

National product and national income are alternative ways of looking at one magnitude: the market value of the nation's output.

Because both concepts have the same total value, we can use the terms national income and national product interchangeably whenever we are interested only in their total value. National product emphasizes the economy's output; national income emphasizes the income generated by producing that output. In Chapter 26 we spoke of national product to emphasize the quantity-of-output aspect of the aggregate demand and supply diagrams. In theoretical work the total value of output is more often referred to as national income.

Corresponding to the two concepts of national product and national income are two ways of arriving at the total value of the nation's output.

THE OUTPUT-EXPENDITURE APPROACH TO NATIONAL INCOME

Value of Expenditure and Value of Output

The output-expenditure approach to measuring the total value of output calculates the total expenditure needed to purchase the nation's output. If all production were sold directly to households, one could in theory add up all household expenditure on currently produced commodities to get the total value of the nation's output. In our complex economy, however, many groups other than households purchase the marketed part of the economy's output, while another part is not sold at all (because it is held by firms for future sale). In these circumstances, it is often simpler to calculate the market value of producers' total output directly rather than calculate the expenditure on that output by those who purchase it. Both approaches will yield the same total because they merely measure opposite sides of the same transactions. (When the bookstore sells you a book for $19.95, *its sale* and *your purchase* are each $19.95.)

The Problem of Double Counting

When we seek to arrive at the total value of output by looking at the output or sales of individual firms, we run into a complication caused by stages of production. Firms usually carry the production of something to a certain stage and then sell it to other firms. They in turn carry production further and then sell to another set of firms. From raw material to final product, many firms may be involved in the various stages of production. Under these circumstances we cannot calculate the total output of the economy by simply adding up the outputs of all firms. For the total value of sales of all firms would be greater than the total value of production available for use. Furthermore, the total value of sales depends on how many firms are involved in the stages of production of a commodity, while the value of the commodity finally produced does not.

Suppose, for example, we took the value of all farmers' sales of wheat and added to it all sales of flour by flour mills, all sales of bread by wholesale bakeries, and all sales of bread by retail stores. Our total figure would be much larger than the value of the final product, the bread produced by the economy. For we would have counted the value of the wheat four times, the flour three times, the bread produced by the bakery twice, and the service of the retail store once.

This is the problem of *double counting* (though for obvious reasons "multiple counting" would be a better term). To avoid it, national income accountants use the important concept of value added. Each firm's **value added** is the value of its output *minus* the value of the inputs that it purchases from other firms. Thus a flour mill's value added is the value of its output of flour

Value Added Through Stages of Production

Because the output of one firm often becomes the input of other firms, the total value of goods sold by all firms greatly exceeds the value of the output of final goods. This general principle is illustrated by a simple example in which firm R starts from scratch and produces goods (raw materials) valued at $100; the firm's value added is $100. Firm I purchases raw materials valued at $100 and produces semimanufactured goods that it sells for $130. Its value added is $30 because the value of the goods is increased by $30 as a result of the firm's activities. Firm F purchases the semi-manufactured goods for $130, works them into a finished state, and sells them for $180. Firm F's value added is $50. The value of the final goods, $180, is found either by counting only the sales of firm F or by taking the sum of the values added by each firm. This value is much smaller than the $410 that we would obtain if we merely added up the market value of the commodities sold by each firm.

	Transactions Between Firms at Three Different Stages of Production			
	Firm R	Firm I	Firm F	All Firms
A. Purchases from other firms	$ 0	$100	$130	$230 = Total interfirm sales
B. Purchases of factors of production (wages, rent, interest, profits)	100	30	50	180 = Value added
Total A + B = value of product	$100	$130	$180 = Value of final goods and services	$410 = Total value of all sales

minus the value of the grain it buys from the farmer and minus the values of any other inputs (such as electricity and fuel oil) that it buys from other firms.

In macroeconomics a firm's output is its value added; the sum of all values added is the value of all goods and services produced by the economy.

Value added is discussed further in the box.

The concept of value added suggests an important distinction between intermediate and final products. **Intermediate products** are goods and services used as inputs in a further stage of production. In the previous example, grain, flour, electricity, and fuel oil were all intermediate products used at various stages in the process that led to the production of the final product, bread. **Final products** are what the economy produces, after eliminating double counting due to stages of production. They include all consumer commodities such as television sets and taxi rides, all capital goods such as factories and machine tools, plus all government production such as police protection and public parks.

Categories of Expenditure

When charting the course of total aggregate expenditure in the economy, it is useful to divide the total into several categories. Four major categories are consumption, investment, government, and net exports. Although each of these may be subdivided into finer groupings, the fourfold classification is extremely useful.

Consumption expenditure. **Consumption** covers all goods and services produced and sold to households during the year (with the exception of residential housing, which is counted as investment). It includes services such as haircuts, medical care, and legal advice; nondurable goods such as fresh food and newspapers; and durables such as cars, television sets, and air conditioners. This class of expenditure represents output of the economy that is applied directly to satisfying the wants of consumers. It is usually denoted by the symbol **C**.

Investment expenditure. **Investment** is the production of goods not for present consumption. Such goods are called **investment goods.** They are produced by firms, and they may be bought either by firms or by households. Most investment is done by firms, and for the present we shall concentrate solely on such investment. Firms can invest either in inventories or in capital goods such as plant and equipment.

Virtually all firms hold stocks of their inputs and their own outputs. Such stocks are called **inventories.** Inventories of inputs allow production to continue at the desired pace in spite of short-term fluctuations in the deliveries of inputs bought from other firms. Inventories of outputs allow firms to meet orders in spite of temporary fluctuations in the rate of output or sales.

Inventories are an important part of the productive process. They require an investment of the firm's money since the firm has paid for but not yet sold the goods. An accumulation of inventories counts as current investment because it represents goods produced but not used for current consumption. A drawing down—often called a decumulation—counts as *dis*investment because it reduces the stock of goods produced in the past.

All production uses capital goods: man-made aids to production such as hand tools, machines, and factory buildings. The economy's total quantity of capital goods is called the **capital stock.** The act of creating new capital goods is an act of investment.

The total investment that occurs in the economy is called **gross investment.** Gross investment may be thought of as divided into two parts, replacement investment and net investment. The amount of replacement investment required to maintain the existing capital stock intact is called the **capital consumption allowance** or simply

depreciation. Net investment is gross investment minus the capital consumption allowance. It is net investment that increases the economy's total stock of capital, while the replacement investment keeps the existing stock intact by replacing what has been used up.

Total investment expenditure is denoted by the symbol **I**.

Government expenditures on goods and services. When the government produces goods and services that households want, such as roads and air traffic control, it is engaged in useful activity. It is obviously adding to the sum total of valuable output in the same way as do private firms that produce the trucks and airplanes that use the roads and air lanes. With other government activities the case may not seem so clear. Should expenditures by the federal government to send a rocket to the moon or to pay a civil servant to file and refile papers from a now defunct department be regarded as contributions to GNP? Should payments by governments to the aged be part of national income? If so, what is the "product" produced? Everyone knows somebody who believes that many (or even most) activities "up in Washington" or "down at City Hall" are wasteful if not downright harmful. But most of us also know someone else who believes that it is governments (not private firms) that are producing the really important things of life, such as pollution control.

The national income statistician avoids speculation about which government expenditures are or are not worthwhile and instead counts everything that produces goods or services and uses factors of production. Just as the national product includes, without distinction, the output of both gin and Bibles, it includes all the bombers and all the upkeep of parks, along with the services of internal revenue agents, CIA agents, and even members of Congress. Government expenditure that is included is given the symbol **G**.

Government transfer payments. There is an important exception to the rule that all government expenditure is included in national income. When a government agency makes welfare payments to a mother of five children whose husband has deserted her, income is transferred to the welfare recipient but the government does not receive, nor does it expect to receive, any marketable services from the deserted mother in return for the welfare payments.[1] The expenditure itself adds neither to employment of factors nor to total output. This is true whether the government raises the welfare money by taxes, by borrowing, or by creating new money. Government payments to households that are not made in return for the services of factors of production are called government transfer payments, or simply **transfer payments.** Such payments do not lead directly to any increase in output, and they are not included in the nation's national income.

The government expenditure that is part of national income does not include transfer payments.

National Income in a Closed Economy

A **closed economy** is one that does not engage in foreign trade. Of course no totally closed economy exists today. Nonetheless, for economies where foreign trade is relatively unimportant, and for problems where foreign trade is irrelevant, it is a valuable simplification to use a model of a closed economy. In such an economy the main elements of aggregate expenditure are the three already discussed.

In a closed economy national income equals the aggregate expenditure (AE) needed to purchase the output of consumption, investment, and government goods and services: GNP = AE = C + I + G.

National Income in an Open Economy

Net exports. An economy that engages in foreign trade is called an **open economy.** Allowing for foreign trade introduces a complication into the relatively straightforward procedures we have considered so far.

One country's national product is the total value of final commodities produced in that country. If you spend $6,000 to buy an American car whose synthetic rubber tires are made from Libyan oil, not all of that $6,000 will represent the output of American producers. Because the oil was produced abroad, it is part of the national product of another country. If your cousin spends $4,000 on a Japanese car, only a small part of that value will represent expenditure on American production. Some of it goes for the services of the U.S. dealers and U.S. transportation; the rest is the output of Japanese firms and expenditure on Japanese products.

Similarly, when an American firm makes an investment expenditure on an American-produced machine tool made partly with imported raw materials, only part of the expenditure is on American production. The rest is expenditure on the production of the countries supplying the raw materials. The same is also true for government expenditures on such things as roads and dams: some of the expenditure is for imported materials, only part of it for domestically produced goods and services.

Since consumption, investment, and government expenditures all have an import content, it is necessary to subtract total domestic expenditure on imports (given the symbol M) to arrive at the total that goes to purchase domestically produced goods. The result, $C + I + G - M$, is domestic expenditure on domestically produced commodities.

There is a second consideration. If American firms sell goods to German households, the goods are a part of German consumption expenditure as well as a part of American national product. Indeed, all goods and services produced in America and sold abroad must be counted as part of American output (they create incomes for the Americans who produce them). To arrive at the total value of expenditure on American national product, it is necessary to add in the value of American exports. They are denoted by the symbol X.

[1] In looking after her children the mother is performing a useful and valuable function. What she is not doing is producing a commodity that adds to total *marketed* production. The treatment of transfer payment recognizes that fact; it does not imply a value judgment that the mother's activities have a low or zero usefulness in any fundamental sense.

FIGURE 27-1

Two Ways of Accounting for GNP

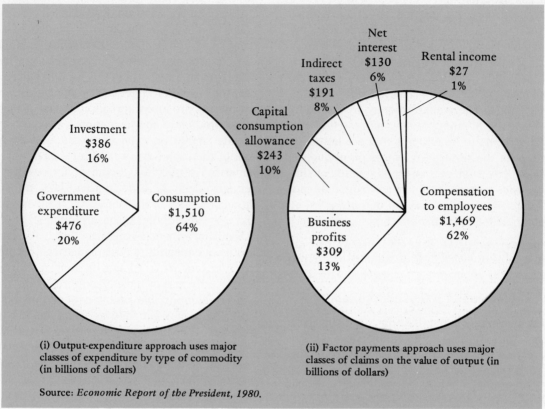

(i) Output-expenditure approach uses major classes of expenditure by type of commodity (in billions of dollars)

(ii) Factor payments approach uses major classes of claims on the value of output (in billions of dollars)

Source: *Economic Report of the President, 1980.*

America's 1979 GNP of $2,369 billion can be classified into expenditure or factor payment classes. Only three items are shown in the output-expenditure classification since 1979 net exports of $3.5 billion were too small to show. In the factor payments classification, compensation to employees includes wages and salaries plus employers' contributions to social insurance, private pension, and other similar schemes; business profits includes profits of incorporated and unincorporated business; and the capital consumption allowance is that part of the earning of business required to replace capital worn out during the year.

From the output-expenditure approach, the total value of expenditure that measures total national income and national product in an open economy is $AE = C + I + G + (X - M)$.

The term in parentheses is called **net exports**. It is exports, which are added to domestic expenditure, minus imports, which are subtracted from domestic expenditure. This national income measure is called **gross national product (GNP)**. We had used this term earlier; now we have seen how it is defined and constructed.

The importance of net exports. The value of net exports is usually small in relation to the total value of either **X** or **M**. Thus the correction to national income made to allow for foreign trade will not usually be large. However, a change in **X** will cause the national income to change in the same way as would a change in **C, I,** or **G**.

Figure 27-1(i) shows American gross national product for 1979 calculated according to the output-expenditure approach. The box provides further details on how the various components are defined and calculated.

Components of Income in the Output-Expenditure Approach

Personal consumption. The expenditures included under personal consumption in the output-expenditure approach represent almost all purchases by households of currently produced goods and services *except* purchases of houses. Why are house purchases excluded from personal consumption? Purchase of old housing should be excluded from any category of the GNP because it is a mere transfer of assets, the assignment among persons of property rights in already produced goods. Expenditure on new housing construction, however, is part of the GNP, but it is included under investment.

Housing is an important element of the expenditure of all households; therefore national income accountants include under personal consumption both rent paid (by households that do not own their housing) and an estimated imputed value for owner-occupied housing that is the equivalent of rent.

The difference between the treatment of houses and that of household purchases of other durable goods such as automobiles and washing machines is arbitrary.

Gross private domestic investment. The primary components of investment are residential housing, plant and equipment, and the net change in business inventories. Remember that "gross" means that these are total amounts spent for construction and producers' durables, whether (1) as replacement of outmoded or worn-out machines and buildings or (2) as net additions to the capital stock.

In dealing with inventories, only net changes are included because only in this way is double counting avoided. Remember that GNP aims to measure the value of goods produced but is largely computed by measuring the *sales* by firms. An accounting identity

$$\text{sales} \equiv \begin{array}{c}\text{opening}\\\text{inventory}\\\text{of goods}\\\text{on hand}\end{array} + \begin{array}{c}\text{production}\\\text{for the year}\end{array} - \begin{array}{c}\text{closing}\\\text{inventory}\\\text{of goods}\\\text{on hand}\end{array}$$

can be transformed into

$$\text{production} \equiv \text{sales} + (\text{closing inventory} - \text{opening inventory})$$

The term in parentheses measures the net change in inventories; it must be added to sales to obtain the value of all of production.

Net exports. Net exports means the difference between exports and imports of goods and services. The reason the national income accountants include only the excess over imports is explained on pages 495–496.

Exports as shown include not only merchandise exports but also military sales to foreign governments, income received from foreign investments, and sales of other services. Imports include merchandise plus American military expenditures overseas, tourist expenditures, purchase of such foreign services as shipping and insurance, income paid on foreign investments in the United States, and pensions paid to overseas Americans.

Government purchases of goods and services. In principle, there are many ways in which one might account for government activity. Governments might, for example, be viewed as giant firms that hire factors of production and produce products that are "sold" to consumers for taxes. In fact, the national income statisticians reject this notion, and also the notion that government expenditures should be divided between consumption and investment. Instead, they simply set up a separate category called "government purchases of goods and services." Almost all government expenditures for goods and services are thus included. (We say "almost all" because certain government enterprises, such as the post office, which sell output to households and firms, are treated as business firms.)

Transfer payments such as social security payments, unemployment insurance, relief payments, and veterans' pensions are excluded. An important additional exclusion is interest on the national debt. This exclusion implicitly (and arbitrarily) assumes that such payments are transfer payments that do not reflect use of a factor of production—in contrast to interest paid to households by firms that have borrowed the money.

THE FACTOR PAYMENTS (FACTOR INCOME) APPROACH

The second approach to measuring national income and national product is usually called the factor payments approach and sometimes the factor income approach.

National income accountants distinguish four main components of factor incomes: (1) **rent,** which is the payment for the services of **land** and other factors that are rented; (2) **wages and salaries** (often referred to simply as wages), which are the payment for the services of **labor;** and (3) **interest** and (4) **profits,** both of which are payments for the services of **capital.** In order to obtain its capital goods, a firm requires money. This is made available by those who lend money to the firm and by those who put up their own money and risk its loss as the firm's owners. Interest is earned by those who lend money to the firm, and profits are earned by those who own the firm.[2] Some profits are paid out as **dividends** to the owners of the firm, the rest are retained for use by the firm. The former are called **distributed profits** and the latter **undistributed profits.**

We saw earlier that accounting practice is to account for all value produced by claims against that value. The factor payments approach to measuring national income accounts for final output in terms of the various claims to the value of that output. Owners of factors of production have claims in terms of wages, rent, interest, and profits that they earned producing the output. The claims are measured before taxes. For example, total wages in the factor payments accounts include *all* wages earned, of which part will be received by suppliers of labor and part will go to the government as income taxes. A government claim on the market value of goods produced in the form of indirect taxes must, however, be entered in the accounts. If a good's sale

value of $10 includes $3 of business excise taxes, only $7 will be available for payments to factors of production. The payments approach must in this case record $3 as the government's claim to part of the market value of the good.

The box describes the components of income in the factor payments approach and how they are defined. Figure 27-1(ii) shows American national income in 1979 from the factor payments approach. By virtue of accounting conventions, total national income classified by factor payment categories is the same as total national income classified by output-expenditure categories.

RELATED MEASURES OF NATIONAL INCOME

Gross national product is the most comprehensive of the several national income concepts. It measures the sum of all values added in the economy.

The next most comprehensive measure is **net national product (NNP).** This is GNP minus the capital consumption allowance (defined on page 499). NNP is thus a measure of the net output of the economy after deducting from gross output an amount necessary to maintain intact the existing stock of capital.

Two other important measures are personal income and disposable income. The interrelationship of the four measures is shown in Table 27-1.

Personal income is income earned by or paid to individuals, before allowance for personal income taxes. Some personal income goes for taxes, some for saving, and the rest for consumption. A number of adjustments to NNP are required to arrive at personal income. The most important are: (1) subtracting from NNP the business earnings retained by corporations, (2) subtracting from NNP the taxes paid by business, and (3) adding to NNP the government transfer payments and government payments of interest to households. The first two represent parts of the value of output not paid to persons;

---

[2] The concepts of rent, wages, interest, and profits used in macroeconomics do not correspond exactly to the microeconomic concepts that go under the same names. The details of the differences need not detain us in an introductory treatment, but readers should keep in mind that differences exist.

Components of Income in the Factor Payments Approach

Wages and other compensation of employees. In this category are all payments to and on behalf of employees, including take-home pay, income taxes withheld, social security contributions, and contributions to pension funds. Obviously, only some of these payments go to households; some go to governments, some to trust funds, some to unions, and so on; but in total they represent the "labor cost" of production.

Corporate profits. All corporate profits before income taxes are treated as factor payments because they represent claims on the value of production by the owners of corporations. Dividends become actual payments to owners for the use of their capital and for risk taking. Undistributed profits are treated as payments to owners for the same purposes, and corporate income taxes are regarded as payments to governments that must be included.

The income of proprietors. Unincorporated enterprises such as small businesses, professions, partnerships, and farms generate income flows to their owners, and these incomes, before taxes, are included. Approximately one-quarter of the total is farm income.

Rental income. Rental income includes rents paid to persons, plus the estimated imputed rent for owner-occupied housing that was added to consumption in the expenditures approach. "Rents" also include royalties from patents and copyrights.

Net interest. Net interest is defined arbitrarily as interest earned by persons in the United States, *less* interest paid by the U.S. government and less consumer interest payments.

Indirect business taxes. All taxes paid by businesses must be included. We have in earlier categories included social security and withholding and income taxes paid by corporations and unincorporated enterprises. We now add all the sales and excise taxes paid by businesses.

Many people find it baffling that such taxes are treated as part of national income. In a purely double-entry bookkeeping sense they must be included. The value of a final good is, *by definition*, equal to profits plus taxes plus all other costs. Therefore, taxes must be included to make the factor payments approach yield the value of final output.

Capital consumption allowance. This item reflects an estimate of the depreciation of the nation's capital stock. It is a "payment" imputed out of the value of production, and its purpose is to recognize the contribution made by the nation's capital stock to current production of goods and services.

Miscellaneous adjustments. A number of small additional items are required to make the accounts balance. These include government subsidies to business (subtracted); surpluses of government enterprises (added; they are like business profits); business transfer payments (added because they use part of business sales dollars); inventory valuation adjustments (added or subtracted depending on the nature of the adjustment). Finally, after all the above, a small "statistical discrepancy" is usually required to make the accounts balance.

The Significance of Arbitrary Decisions

National income accounting uses many arbitrary decisions. Goods that are finished and held in inventories are valued at market value, thereby anticipating their sale even though the actual sales price may not be known. In the case of a Ford in a dealer's showroom, this practice may be justified because the *value* of this Ford is perhaps virtually the same as that of an identical Ford that has just been sold to a customer. But what is the correct market value of a half-finished house or an unfinished novel? Accountants arbitrarily treat goods in process at cost (rather than at market value) if the goods are being made by business firms; they ignore completely the value of the novel-in-progress. While these decisions are arbitrary, so would any others be.

Clearly, practical people must arrive at some compromise between consistent definitions and measurable magnitudes. The imputation of a market value to an owner-occupied house, but not to the services of the housewife who occupies and often owns the house, probably is justified only by such a compromise.

The definition of final goods provides further examples. Business investment expenditures are treated as final products, as are all government purchases. Intermediate goods purchased by business for further processing are not treated as final products. Thus, when a firm buys a machine or a truck, the purchase is treated as a final good; when it buys a ton of steel, however, the steel is treated not as a final product but as a raw material that will be used as an input into the firm's production process. (But if the steel sits in an inventory, it is regarded as a business investment and thus *is* a final good.)

Such arbitrary decisions surely affect the size of measured GNP. Does it matter? The surprising answer, for many purposes, is no. In any case, it is an error to believe that just because a statistical measure falls short of perfection (as all statistical measures do) it is useless. Very crude measures will often give estimates to the right order of magnitude, whereas substantial improvements in sophistication may make only second-order improvements in these estimates. In the third century B.C., for example, the Alexandrian astronomer Eratosthenes measured the angle of the sun at Alexandria at the moment it was directly overhead 500 miles south at Aswan, and he used this angle to calculate the circumference of the earth to within 15 percent of the distance as measured today by the most advanced measuring devices. For the knowledge he wanted—the approximate size of the earth—his measurement was decisive. To launch a modern earth satellite it would have been disastrously inadequate.

Absolute figures mean something in general terms, although they cannot be taken seriously to the last dollar. In 1979 GNP was measured as $2,369 billion. It is certain that the market value of all production in the United States in that year was not $100 billion, nor was it $10,000 billion. It was not $500 billion, but it might well have been $2,500 billion or $2,200 billion had different measures been defined with different arbitrary decisions built in.

International and intertemporal comparisons, though tricky, may be meaningful when they are based on measures all of which contain roughly the same arbitrary decisions. American per capita GNP is roughly three times the Spanish and 60 percent higher than the Japanese. Other measures might differ, but it is unlikely that any measure would reveal that either the Spanish or the Japanese per capita production was higher than the per capita production in the United States. But the statistics also show that GNP per capita was 4 percent higher in Switzerland than in Sweden, a difference too small to have much meaning. American output has been growing at 2.8 percent per year since World War II; it is unlikely that another measure of output would have indicated a 6 percent increase. Further, the Japanese output has been growing at about 9 percent per year. It is inconceivable that another measure would change the conclusion that Japanese national output rose faster than American national output in recent decades.

TABLE 27–1

Various National Income Measures, 1979 (billions of dollars)

A. Gross national product (GNP)	$2,369
Less: Capital consumption allowance	243
B. Net national product (NNP)	2,126
Less:	
1. Retained earnings	126
2. Business taxes (including social security)	379
3. Miscellaneous adjustments	2
Plus:	
4. Transfer payments to individuals	304
C. Personal income	1,923
Less: Personal tax payments	300
D. Disposable income	1,623

Source: Economic Report of the President, 1980.

Each of the four related national income measures focuses on a different aspect of the national output. GNP measures the market value of total output. NNP measures the net value of output after an allowance for maintaining the capital stock. Personal income measures income earned or received by persons, before personal income taxes. Disposable income is a measure of after-tax income of persons; it is the amount they have available to spend or to save.

the third represents payments to households that households have available to spend or to save even though they are not part of GNP.

Disposable income is a measure of the amount of current income that households have to spend or to save. It is calculated as personal income minus personal taxes.

For most purposes personal income is less useful than disposable income. Because disposable income measures are published only every three months, forecasters who need monthly data may use personal income instead.

The relation between GNP and disposable income is important:

Disposable income is GNP *minus* any part of it that is not actually paid over to households, *minus* the personal income taxes paid by households, *plus* transfer payments received by households.

Interpreting National Income Measures

The information provided by measures of national income can be extremely useful for many purposes, but unless it is carefully interpreted it can also be seriously misleading. Furthermore, each of the specialized measures – GNP, NNP, personal income, disposable income, and others that we shall consider shortly – gives slightly different information, so each may be the best statistic for studying a certain range of problems.

MONEY VALUES AND REAL VALUES

The GNP measures the total *money* value of final goods produced during a year. Thus it has a price and a quantity component, and a particular change in the GNP can be caused by many different combinations of price and quantity changes. A 10 percent rise in GNP might, for example, have been caused by a 10 percent rise in prices, all quantities remaining unchanged; a 10 percent rise in output, all prices remaining unchanged; or smaller increases in both prices and quantities. For some purposes the money value of national income is just the measure required. Sometimes, however, we wish to know what is happening to the *quantity* (rather than the *value*) of output. To do this we need to separate

TABLE 27-2
GNP in Current and Constant Dollars

Year	(1) GNP in billions of current dollars	(2) GNP in billions of 1972 dollars	(3) Implicit GNP deflator 1972 = 100
1935	72	261	27.6
1945	212	559	38.0
1955	399	655	61.0
1965	688	926	74.3
1975	1,529	1,202	127.2
1979	2,369	1,431	165.5

Source: Economic Report of the President, 1980.

Current dollar GNP tells us about the money value of output; constant dollar GNP tells us about changes in physical output. The GNP in current dollars gives the total value of all final output in any year, valued in the selling prices of that year. The GNP in constant dollars gives the total value of all final output in any year, valued in the prices ruling in one particular year, in this case, 1972. The ratio *GNP in current dollars/GNP in constant dollars* is the implicit GNP deflator. (It is in effect a price index with current-year quantity weights.)

changes in the GNP caused by variations in market prices from changes caused by variations in the quantities of output. Changes of the latter kind are defined as "real" or "constant dollar" changes to distinguish them from mere "money" or "nominal" changes.

Over any long period, changes in the GNP reflect both real quantity changes and money price changes. In 1929 American GNP was $103 billion; in 1979 it was $2,369 billion. When GNP is measured at prices prevailing during the same year, it is said to be measured in **current dollars.** How much of this increase resulted from a change in the volume of goods and services produced and how much from a general rise in prices?

To answer such questions, the GNP is calculated in **constant dollars;** that is, the quantities produced each year are valued at the prices ruling in an arbitrary *base year.* The resulting figures constitute a series called **real GNP** or **constant dollar GNP.** GNP measured in constant

1972 dollars means that the quantities produced in each year are each multiplied by their 1972 prices and then summed. The constant dollar figures give a measure of changes in the quantity of output because they tell what the total value of actual output would have been if prices had not changed.

Table 27-2 gives the GNP measured in both ways for selected years since 1935.[3]

TOTAL OUTPUT AND PER CAPITA OUTPUT

The rise in real GNP during this century has had two main causes: first, an increase in the amounts of land, labor, and capital used in production; second, an increase in output per unit of input. In other words, more inputs have been used, and each input has become more productive. For many purposes we want the measure of total output: for example, to assess a country's potential military strength or to know the total size of its market. For other purposes, however, we prefer per capita measures, which are obtained by dividing a total measure such as GNP by the relevant population.

There are many useful per capita measures. GNP divided by the total population gives a measure of how much GNP there is on average for each person in the economy; this is called **per capita GNP.** GNP divided by the number of persons employed tells us the average output per employed worker. GNP divided by the total

---

[3] Comparison of the two sets of figures yields an "index number" of price changes that is called the implicit GNP deflator, or usually just the **GNP deflator.** It is defined as

$$\frac{\text{GNP in current dollars}}{\text{GNP in constant dollars}} \times 100$$

This is the most comprehensive measure of price changes available in that it covers all the goods and services produced by the entire economy. The value of the deflator in any particular year, such as 1979, is obtained by valuing 1979 output first at current prices and then at base year (say, 1972) prices. Since the former is 166 percent of the latter, the change must be due to the price changes between the base year and the current year: average prices have risen 66 percent over the period.

number of hours worked measures output per hour of labor input. A widely used measure of the purchasing power of the average person is disposable income per capita, in constant dollars. This measure is shown in Figure 27-2.

OMISSIONS FROM MEASURED NATIONAL INCOME

Finally, we come to a series of omissions from the GNP, and thus also from the NNP, disposable income, and other measures based mainly on parts of the GNP. The importance of these omissions can be judged only when we know the purpose for which the income data is to be used.

Illegal Activities

The GNP does not measure illegal activities even though many of them are ordinary business activities which produce goods and services that are sold on the market and generate factor incomes. The liquor industry during Prohibition was an important example because it accounted for a significant part of the nation's total economic activity. Today the same is true of many forms of illegal gambling, prostitution, and the illicit production and distribution of soft and hard drugs. If we want an accurate measure of the *total* demand for factors of production in the economy or of *total* marketable output—whether or not we as individuals approve of particular products—we should include these activities. Probably the main reason for leaving them out is that, because they are illicit, it would be hard to find out enough about them to include them even if we wanted to.[4]

_____

[4] Some of them do get included because people often report their earnings from illicit activities as part of their earnings from legal activities in order to avoid the fate of Al Capone. He, having avoided conviction on many counts, was finally caught for income tax evasion. Don Corleone, the godfather in Puzo's famous novel about the Mafia, undoubtedly reported part of his illegal earnings as belonging to his legal business. Thus total GNP would come closer to reflecting all income earned in the nation, but it would overstate the contribution of olive oil importing and understate the contribution of gambling and similar enterprises.

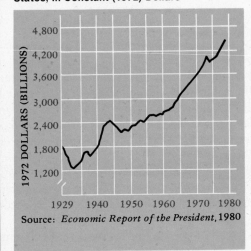

FIGURE 27-2

Disposable Income Per Capita in the United States, in Constant (1972) Dollars

Source: *Economic Report of the President,* 1980

Disposable income per capita in constant dollars provides a measure of the real purchasing power available to the average American household. Disposable income per capita fell during the early 1930s and late 1940s but it has risen in every decade since the thirties, including the 1970s. It underestimates the average living standard because it leaves out the contribution of government expenditure to such items as police, fire, justice, defense, and recreation.

Unreported Activities

An important source of omission from the measured GNP is the so-called underground economy. People make perfectly legal transactions such as repairing a leak in your roof but are paid in cash or in kind in order to avoid income taxes. Such transactions go unreported and hence unrecorded in the country's GNP. Their potential importance is shown by the fact that estimates of the value of income earned in the American underground economy run as high as 15 percent of American GNP. Since these are ordinary market activities, their omission is an important source of error in published GNP figures. Increases in activities that go unreported are one reason why the rate of growth of total and per capita GNP and hence of living standards may be underestimated by currently published data.

Nonmarketed Economic Activities

When a bank employee hires a carpenter to build a bookshelf in her house, the value of the bookshelf enters into the GNP; if the teller or her husband builds the bookshelf, the value of the bookshelf is omitted from the GNP. In general, any labor service that does not pass through a market is not counted in the GNP. Such omissions include, for example, the services of housewives, any do-it-yourself activity, and voluntary work such as canvassing for a political party, helping to run a day-care center, or leading a boy scout troop.

Does the omission of nonmarketed economic activities matter? Once again, it all depends. If we wish to measure the flow of goods and services through the market sector of the economy, or to account for changes in the opportunities for employment for those households who sell their labor services in the market, most of these omissions are desirable.

If, however, we wish to measure the overall flow of goods and services available to satisfy people's wants, whatever the source of the goods and services, then all the omissions are undesirable and potentially serious.

In most advanced industrial economies the nonmarket sector is relatively small, and it can be ignored even if GNP is used for purposes for which it would be appropriate to include nonmarketed goods and services. The omissions become serious, however, when GNP or disposable income figures are used to compare living standards in very different economies. Generally, the nonmarket sector of the economy is larger in rural than in urban settings and in underdeveloped than in developed economies. Be a little cautious, then, in interpreting data from a country with a very different climate and culture. When one hears that the per capita GNP of Nigeria is $150 per year, one should not imagine living in Washington, D.C., on that income. Certainly the average Nigerian is at a low level of real income compared to an urban American, but the measured GNP figure does not allow for the fact that many of the things that are very costly to an American—such as fruit and a warm house—are provided free to many Nigerians by wild fruit trees and a warm climate and by a host of nonmarketed goods and services.

Factors Affecting Human Welfare but Not Included in the Value of Output

Many things that contribute to human welfare are not included in the GNP. Leisure is one example. In fact, although a shorter work week may make people happier, it will tend to reduce measured GNP.

GNP does not allow for the capacity of different goods to provide different satisfactions. A million dollars spent on a bomber or a missile makes the same addition to GNP as a million dollars spent on a school, a stadium, or candy bars—expenditures that may produce very different amounts of consumer satisfaction.

GNP does not measure the quality of life. To the extent that material output is purchased at the expense of overcrowded cities and highways, polluted environments, defaced countrysides, maimed accident victims, longer waits for public services, and a more complex life that entails a frenetic struggle to be happy, GNP measures only part of the total of human well-being.

WHICH MEASURE IS BEST?

We have seen that there are several distinct income measures. To ask which is *the* best is something like asking which is *the* best carpenter's tool. The answer is that it all depends on the job to be done.

The use of several measures of national income rather than one is common because different measures provide answers to different questions. GNP answers the question, What was the market value of goods and services produced for final demand? NNP answers the question, By how much did the economy's production exceed the amount necessary to replace capital equipment used up? Disposable income answers the question, How much income do consumers have to allocate between spending and saving? In addition, real (constant dollar) measures eliminate purely monetary changes and allow comparisons of purchasing power over time; per capita measures shift the focus from the nation to the average person.

Which measure we use will depend on the problem at hand. For example, if we wish to predict households' consumption behavior, disposable income is what we need. If we wish to account for changes in employment, GNP is wanted (since all production requires labor inputs).

For yet other purposes, such as providing an overall measure of economic welfare, we may wish to supplement or modify conventional measures of national income.[5] Even if we do, we are unlikely to discard GNP (and its progeny) entirely in favor of such a measure. Economists and politicians interested in the ebb and flow of economic activity that passes through the market and in the rise and fall in employment opportunities for factors of production whose services are sold on the market will continue to use GNP as the measure that comes closest to telling them what they need to know.

Summary

1. National product is the total market value of goods and services produced in the economy during a year; national income is the total of all income claims generated over the same period of time. By virtue of standard accounting conventions, national product and national income have the same value.

2. National income may be calculated either by the output-expenditure approach or by the factor payments approach. Both approaches yield the same value, for they are just two ways of accounting for the total value of output.

3. The value of the output of final goods and services can be found by taking the sum of the *values added* in the economy. Value added is the market value of the firm's output minus the cost of inputs purchased from other firms.

4. Using the output-expenditure approach, GNP $= AE = C + I + G + (X - M)$. C represents consumption expenditures of households and I represents investment in capital goods such as plant equipment, residential construction, and inventory accumulation. Gross investment can be split into replacement investment (necessary to keep the stock of capital intact) and net investment (net additions to the stock of capital). G represents government expenditures except transfer payments. $(X - M)$ represents the excess of exports over imports; it will be negative if imports exceed exports.

5. The factor payments approach to GNP divides total GNP according to who has a claim to the value arising from the production and sale of commodities. Wages, interest, rents, profits, taxes, depreciation (called capital consumption allowance), and indirect taxes are the major categories.

6. Several related but different national income measures are used in addition to the GNP. Net national product (NNP) measures total output after deducting an allowance for output needed to keep the capital stock intact. Personal income is income actually paid to households before any allowance for personal taxes. Disposable income gives the amount that is actually available to households to spend or to save.

7. GNP measured in constant dollars expresses the value of output measured in the prices ruling

---

[5] Measures that come closer to measuring economic welfare than GNP have been calculated. One was developed by Professors William Nordhaus and James Tobin. It tries to measure consumption of things that provide utility to households rather than total production; it gives value to such nonmarketed activities as leisure and makes subtractions for such "disutilities" as pollution and congestion.

in some particular base year. Because it removes the effects of price changes, it provides a measure of real income.

8. GNP and related measures of national income must be interpreted with regard for their limitations. GNP excludes production resulting from activities that are illegal, take place in the underground economy, or do not pass through markets (such as that produced by do-it-yourself activities). Moreover, GNP does not measure everything that contributes to human welfare.

9. Notwithstanding its limitations, GNP remains the best measure available for estimating the total economic activity that passes through the markets of our economy and for accounting for changes in the employment opportunities that face households who sell their labor services on the open market.

Topics for Review

National income, GNP, NNP, personal income, and disposable income

Output-expenditure and factor payments approaches to measuring national income

Final goods and value added

GNP = **AE** = **C** + **I** + **G** + **(X − M)**

Major characteristics of GNP

Limitations of GNP as a measure of economic welfare

Discussion Questions

1. If Canada and the United States were to join together as a single country, what would be the effect on their total GNP (assuming that output in each country is unaffected)? Would any of the components in their GNPs change significantly?

2. "Every time you rent a U-haul, brick in a patio, grow a vegetable, fix your own car, photocopy an article, join a food co-op, develop film, sew a dress, avoid purchasing a convenience food, stew fruit, or raise a child, you are committing a productive act, even though these activities are not reflected in the gross national product." To what extent are each of these things "productive acts"? Are any of them included in GNP? Where they are excluded, does the exclusion matter?

3. What would be the effect on the measured value of America's *real* GNP of (a) the destruction of a thousand homes by flood water; (b) passage of a constitutional amendment making abortion illegal; (c) a complete cessation of all imports from South Africa; and (d) the outbreak of a new Arab-Israeli war in which American troops became as heavily involved as they were in Vietnam. Speculate on the effects of each of these events on the true well-being of the American people.

4. A Social Security Administration study, using 1972 data, found the "average American housewife's value" to be $4,705. It arrived at this total by adding up the hours she spent cooking, multiplied by a cook's wage, the hours spent with her children, multiplied by a babysitter's wage, and so on. Should the time a parent spends taking children to a concert be included? Are dollar amounts assigned to such activities a satisfactory proxy for market value of production? For what, if any, purposes should such values be excluded from national income?

5. Use the endpaper at the back of this book to calculate the percentage increase over the most recent two decades of each of the following magnitudes: (a) GNP in current dollars; (b) GNP in constant dollars; (c) disposable income in constant dollars; and (d) disposable income per capita in constant dollars. Can you account for the relative size of these changes?

6. Consider the effect on measured GNP and on economic well-being of each of the following: (a) a reduction in the standard work week from 40 hours to 30 hours; (b) the hiring of all welfare recipients as government employees; (c) further increases in oil prices that lead to a general inflation; and (d) an increase in the salaries of priests and ministers as a result of the increased contributions of churchgoers.

What Determines National Income?

28

We saw in Chapter 26 how the interaction of the aggregate demand and aggregate supply curves determines national income, Y, and the price level, P. This is illustrated once again in Figure 28-1. Why is the aggregate demand curve where it is in that figure? It determines national income at Y, on the Keynesian portion of the aggregate supply curve; but why was it not in some other position, determining national income at, say, Y_1 or Y_2?

To provide answers to these questions, we need to develop a new relation called the **aggregate expenditure function.** This relates real national income to the aggregate real amount that all decision makers desire to spend on purchasing the nation's output. (Unless otherwise specified, real national income can be taken from now on to be measured by real GNP.)

Desired Expenditure

In the preceding chapter we discussed how national income statisticians measure actual aggregate expenditure, **AE**, and its components, consumption, **C**, investment, **I**, government, **G**, and net exports, **(X − M).**

In this chapter we are concerned with desired expenditure. Of course, everybody would like to spend more or less unlimited amounts—if only they had the money. However, desired expenditure does not refer to what one would like to do under imaginary circumstances. It refers instead to what you and everybody else want to spend, given the resources at your, and their, command.

FIGURE 28-1
The Determination of National Income by Aggregate Demand and Aggregate Supply

REAL NATIONAL INCOME

On the Keynesian portion of the aggregate supply curve, national income is determined by the aggregate demand curve. With aggregate demand and supply curves of *AD* and *AS*, national income is Y. If only Y_1 were produced, demand would exceed output and output would rise. If Y_2 were produced, demand would be less than output and output would fall. These forces are shown by the arrows pointing toward the equilibrium position at *E*.

Everyone who has money to spend makes expenditure decisions. It is impossible—and unnecessary—to look at each of the millions of such individual decisions. To simplify, we divide decision makers into four main groups: domestic households, firms, central authorities (called governments), and foreign purchasers of domestically produced products. Their actual purchases account for the four main categories of expenditure studied in the previous chapter: consumption, investment, government expenditure, and exports. Their desired purchases may be divided in the same fashion. As in the preceding chapter, we must allow for the fact that some of the commodities desired by each of these groups

will have an import content. Thus we subtract import expenditure to obtain total desired expenditure on domestically produced goods and services:

$$AE = C + I + G + (X - M)$$

We have indicated actual aggregate expenditure and its components by the boldface letters **AE, C, I, G,** and **(X − M)**. Now we use lightface letters to indicate desired amounts of expenditure in the same categories.

Desired expenditure need not equal actual expenditure, either in total or in each individual category. For example, if households want to buy commodities that firms will not or cannot produce, households will not be able to buy as much as they want. In this case, desired consumption expenditure, C, will exceed actual consumption expenditure, **C.** (One reason for this might be that because all resources are fully employed, firms cannot increase output even though the demand for more output exists.) For a second example, firms may not intend to invest in inventory accumulation this year but may nonetheless do so unintentionally. If they produce goods for sale and demand is unexpectedly low, the unsold goods that pile up on their shelves will represent undesired (and unintended) inventory accumulation. In this case actual investment expenditure, **I,** will exceed desired investment expenditure, I.

The distinction between actual and desired expenditures is important.

National income accounts measure *actual expenditures* in each of the categories, C, I, G, and (X − M). The theory of national income determination deals with *desired expenditures* in each of the categories, C, I, G, and (X − M).

To develop a theory of national income, we need to know what determines each of the components of aggregate desired expenditure. We begin in this chapter by treating all the components except consumption expenditure as constants. This allows us to study national income determination under the simplest possible conditions. In subsequent chapters we shall look at the determinants of desired I, G, and (X − M).

DESIRED CONSUMPTION EXPENDITURE

Households decide how much of their income they wish to spend on consumption, and they save the rest. **Saving** is defined as all income that is not consumed. It follows that households have to make a single decision: how to split their disposable income between consumption and saving. Household consumption expenditure is the largest single component of actual aggregate expenditure. But what determines the amount that households want to spend on goods and services for their consumption and how much they want to save? One major determinant turns out to be household disposable income. As disposable income rises, households have more money to spend on consumption—and the evidence is that they do just that. We therefore treat consumption expenditure as varying with disposable income.

The Consumption Function

The term **consumption function** describes the relationship between consumption expenditure and all the factors that determine it. It is, as we shall see, one of the most important relations in macroeconomics.[1] The macro consumption function explains the aggregate desired consumption expenditure of all households in the economy.

Consumption as a Function of Disposable Income

We have noted that one important force influencing desired consumption expenditure is household disposable income, to which we now give the symbol Y_d. Other forces, such as interest rates and inflationary expectations, also exert an

[1] The concept of a functional relationship is discussed on page 24.

influence, but they may be set aside for the moment. In the simple theory of the consumption function, we focus on changes in disposable income to explain changes in consumption. An example of a schedule relating disposable income to desired consumption expenditure is presented in the first two columns of Table 28-1.

Average and marginal propensities to consume. To discuss the consumption function concisely, economists use some technical vocabulary.

The **average propensity to consume (APC)** is total consumption expenditure divided by disposable income. The calculation of *APC* for the consumption schedule illustrated in Table 28-1 will be found in the third column of the table.

The **marginal propensity to consume (MPC)** relates the *change* in consumption to the *change* in disposable income that brought it about. It is the change in disposable income divided into the resulting consumption change: $MPC = \Delta C / \Delta Y_d$ (where the Greek letter Δ means "a change in"). Table 28-1 shows the calculations of the *MPC* in the last column. [30]

These propensities can be calculated either for desired expenditure, as in Table 28-1, or for actual expenditure, as when national income data are used.

The shape of the consumption function. Empirical studies of year-to-year changes in disposable income and consumption (i.e., when each observation consists of income and consumption expenditure over the same year) for a period of ten years or so have found a close relation between the two. In general, years with higher than average levels of income tend to be years with higher than average levels of consumption, and vice versa. Figure 28-2 shows the general shape of such a consumption function. [31] Its essential features are:

1. There is a break-even level of income that is the level of disposable income at which households just consume all their income.

TABLE 28-1

The Calculation of the Average Propensity to Consume (APC) and the Marginal Propensity to Consume (MPC) (billions of dollars)

Disposable income (Y_d)	Desired consumption (C)	APC = C/Y_d	ΔY_d (Change in Y_d)	ΔC (Change in C)	MPC = $\Delta C / \Delta Y_d$
$ 0	$ 100	0			
			$ 100	$ 80	0.80
100	180	1.80			
			300	240	0.80
400	420	1.05			
			100	80	0.80
500	500	1.00			
			500	400	0.80
1,000	900	0.90			
			1,000	800	0.80
2,000	1,700	0.85			
			1,000	800	0.80
3,000	2,500	0.83			
			1,000	800	0.80
4,000	3,300	0.83			

The APC measures the proportion of disposable income that households desire to spend on consumption; the MPC measures the proportion of any *increment* to disposable income that households desire to spend on consumption. The data are hypothetical. The APC calculated in the third column exceeds unity below the break-even level of income because consumption exceeds income. Above the break-even level the APC is less than unity and declines steadily as income rises. The last three columns are set between the lines of the first three columns to indicate that they refer to changes in the levels of income and consumption.

In this example, the MPC calculated in the last column is constant at .8 at all levels of Y_d. This indicates that 80¢ of every additional $1 of income is spent on consumption and 20¢ is used to increase saving (or decrease dissaving).

2. Below the break-even level, households consume in excess of their current disposable income. They do this by borrowing or by using up past savings, which is known as **dissaving**.[2]
3. Above the break-even level of income, households consume only part of their disposable income and save the rest.
4. Any increase in household income causes consumption expenditure to rise but by less than the rise in income. For example, every increase in household income of $1 might cause households to raise their consumption expenditure by 80¢, as is the case with the consumption function in the first two columns of Table 28-1.[3]

Using the concepts of the average and marginal propensities to consume, we can restate the four properties as two summary propositions:

[2] Clearly this cannot go on forever, which is one reason why dissaving cannot be a feature of long-term behavior; but it can go on for some time, and it does appear to be a feature of short-term behavior.

[3] This fourth assumption was described by John Maynard Keynes (widely regarded as the first to stress the consumption function) in his classic *The General Theory of Employment, Interest, and Money:* "The fundamental psychological law, upon which we are entitled to depend with great confidence both *a priori* from our knowledge of human nature and from the detailed facts of experience, is that men are disposed, as a rule and on the average, to increase their consumption as their income increases, but not by as much as the increase in their income."

1. There is a break-even level of disposable income at which *APC* = 1. Below this level *APC* is greater than unity; above it *APC* is less than unity.
2. *MPC* is greater than zero but less than unity for all levels of income.

It follows that an increase of $1 in disposable income will lead to an increase of less than $1 in both desired consumption expenditure and desired saving.

Figure 28-2 shows a graph of the consumption function plotted from the first two columns of Table 28-1. The figure makes it clear that the slope of the consumption function ($\Delta C/\Delta Y_d$) is the *MPC*. The upward slope of the consumption function indicates that *MPC* is positive. However, the slope is less than unity, indicating that *MPC* is less than unity.

The 45° Line

Figure 28-2 also shows a construction that will prove very useful. This is a line that connects all points where desired expenditure (measured on the vertical axis) equals disposable income (measured on the horizontal axis). Since both axes are measured in the same units, this line has an upward slope of unity, or (what is the same thing) it makes an angle of 45° with both axes. This line is called the **45° line,** and to remind us of its definition it is labeled $AE = Y_d$.

The 45° line proves handy as a reference line. For example, in Figure 28-2 it helps locate the break-even level of income at which consumption expenditure equals disposable income. Graphically, this is where the consumption line cuts the 45° line.

The Saving Function

Because households have only one decision to make on how to divide their income between consumption and saving, it follows that if we know the dependence of consumption on disposable income, we will also know the dependence of saving on disposable income. Table 28-2 illustrates this.

We may define two saving concepts that are exactly parallel to the consumption concepts of *APC* and *MPC* already defined. The **average propensity to save** (*APS*) is the proportion of disposable income that households desire to devote to savings. It is total desired saving divided by total disposable income: $APS = S/Y_d$. The **marginal propensity to save** (*MPS*) relates the *change* in total desired saving to the *change* in disposable income that brought it about: $MPS =$

FIGURE 28-2

The Consumption and Saving Functions

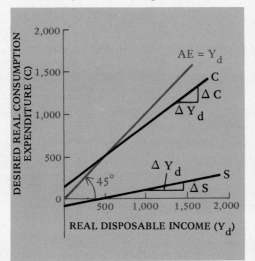

Both consumption and saving rise as income rises. This diagram plots the data from Table 28-2. The *C* and *S* lines relate desired expenditure on consumption and on saving to disposable income. The slope of the lines are $\Delta C/\Delta Y_d$ and $\Delta S/\Delta Y_d$, which are the *MPC* and the *MPS* respectively. At the break-even level of income, the consumption line cuts the 45° line and the saving line cuts the horizontal axis. Since saving is all disposable income not spent on consumption ($S = Y_d - C$), the vertical sum of the *S* and *C* lines must by definition coincide with the 45° line; that is, at each level of income, disposable income must be accounted for by the amount saved plus the amount consumed.

$\Delta S/\Delta Y_d$. Calculations from Table 28-2 will allow you to confirm for yourself that, in the example given, *MPS* is constant at .2 at all levels of income, while *APS* rises with income. (For example, *APS* is zero at $Y = \$5,000$ and .175 at $Y = \$4,000$. [32]) Figure 28-2 also graphs the saving schedule given in Table 28-2. The slope of the savings line $\Delta S/\Delta Y_d$ is the *MPS*.

Consumption as a Function of National Income

We have seen that desired consumption is related to *disposable* income. For a theory of the determination of national income, however, we need to know how consumption varies with national income.

The Long-term Consumption Function

The text deals with what is called a short-term consumption function. This is suitable for describing how consumption varies from year to year as income varies. It is based on empirical observations of cyclical variations in consumption and income.

Some empirical studies of the consumption function have used ten-year averages of consumption expenditure and income. Thus the time-series data used consisted of decade-by-decade averages of consumption and disposable income. When plotted on a graph, one point would relate average consumption in, say, 1900–1909 to average income in that period; another point would relate average consumption in 1910–1919 to average disposable income in that period; and so on. The characteristic of such data is that they average out the effects of cyclical fluctuations in national income and focus attention on the long-run reaction of consumption to long-run trend changes in national income.

Such studies suggest that there is a highly stable long-term division of national income between consumption and saving—in other words, that the consumption expenditure of American households tends to be a stable fraction of their disposable income. In technical terms, the *APC* tends to be constant over time; so too does the *MPC*. Further, *MPC* tends to be approximately equal to *APC* in these long-term studies. [33] The figure shows

a long-run consumption function that exhibits these properties.

Thus the consumption function described in the text is a short-term function suitable for analyzing cyclical fluctuations in the economy that take only a few years to work themselves out. The consumption function illustrated here is suitable for analyzing the behavior of the economy under long-term growth conditions over a span of many decades.

The major difference between the two functions is that the proportion of income devoted to consumption declines as income rises on the short-term function but remains constant on the long-term function.

A long-term consumption function

TABLE 28-2
Consumption and Saving Schedules (billions of dollars)

Disposable income	Desired consumption expenditure	Desired saving
$ 0	$ 100	−$100
100	180	− 80
400	420	− 20
500	500	0
1,000	900	+ 100
2,000	1,700	+ 300
3,000	2,500	+ 500
4,000	3,300	+ 700

Saving and consumption account for all household disposable income. The first two columns repeat the data from Table 28-1. The third column is disposable income minus desired consumption. The three columns thus show desired consumption and desired saving at each level of income. Consumption and saving each increase steadily as disposable income rises. In this sample the break-even level of disposable income is $500 million. At an income of $100 million, $180 million is spent on consumption. Since this must involve new borrowing or the consumption of past saving, households in aggregate are dissaving. As income rises, dissaving decreases for income levels up to $500 million and saving increases above $500 million.

The transition from a relation between *consumption and disposable income* to one between *consumption and national income* is easily accomplished since, as we saw above, disposable income and national income are themselves related to each other.

The relation between disposable income and national income. We saw on pages 498 and 501 the several adjustments required to derive disposable income from GNP. Since transfer payments, the major addition, are smaller than total taxes, the major subtraction, the net effect is for disposable income to be much less than GNP. (It was just less than 70 percent of GNP in 1979.)

The general relation between disposable income and national income can be approximated by assuming Y_d to be an unchanging proportion of Y. The relation might, for example, be $Y_d =$

$.7Y$. More generally, we can write $Y_d = mY$, where m is the proportion of national income that becomes disposable income.

Substitution of national income for disposable income in the consumption function. If we know how consumption relates to disposable income and how disposable income relates to national income, it will be an easy matter to derive the relation between consumption and national income.

To illustrate, assume that disposable income is always 70 percent of national income. Then, whatever the relation between C and Y_d, we can always substitute $.7Y$ for Y_d. Thus, if consumption were always 90 percent of Y_d, then C would always be 63 percent (70 percent of 90 percent) of Y. [34]

This relation is further illustrated in Table 28-3. Note from the table that since we can write desired consumption as a function of Y as well as of Y_d, we can define marginal and average propensities to consume from Y as well as from Y_d.

TABLE 28-3
Consumption as a Function of Disposable Income and National Income (billions of dollars)

(1) National income (Y)	(2) Disposable income ($Y_d = .7Y$)	(3) Desired consumption ($C = 100 + .8Y_d$)
100	70	156
1,000	700	660
2,000	1,400	1,220
3,000	2,100	1,780
4,000	2,800	2,340

If desired consumption depends on disposable income, which in turn depends on national income, desired consumption can be written as a function of either income concept. The data are hypothetical. They show deductions of 30 percent of any change in national income to arrive at disposable income from national income. Deductions of 30 percent of Y imply that the remaining 70 percent of changes in Y becomes disposable income. The numbers also show consumption as 80 percent of disposable income. By relating columns 2 and 3, one sees consumption as a function of disposable income. By relating columns 1 and 3, one sees consumption as a function of national income.

The new propensities tell us the proportion of total national income that goes to desired consumption (C/Y) and the proportion of any change in national income that goes to a change in desired consumption $(\Delta C/\Delta Y)$.

We now have a function showing how desired consumption expenditure varies as national income varies. The relation is defined for real income and real expenditure (i.e., income and expenditure measured in constant prices). This means that for every given level of real income, measured in terms of purchasing power, households will spend a given fraction of that purchasing power and save the rest.

OTHER CATEGORIES OF DESIRED EXPENDITURE

Having discussed the determinants of desired consumption expenditure in some detail, we now consider briefly the categories I, G, and $(X - M)$.

Desired Investment Expenditure

Firms plan how much to invest in new capital equipment and in inventories. In this chapter it is convenient to study how the level of national income adjusts to a fixed level of planned investment. So we assume that firms plan to make a constant amount of investment in plant and equipment each year and that they plan to hold their inventories constant. (In Chapters 29 and 30 we shall drop these assumptions and study the important effects on national income caused by changes in the level of investment.)

Desired Government Expenditure

Government expenditures on currently produced goods and services are part of aggregate expenditure on the nation's output. At the outset we take desired and actual government expenditure as a constant. Governments intend to spend, and succeed in spending, so many billions of dollars on goods and services. This amount is assumed not to change as the circumstances of the economy change. This assumption allows us to see in this chapter how national income adjusts to a constant level of government expenditure. (In Chapter 31 we shall see how national income responds to changes in desired and actual government expenditure.)

Desired Net Exports

For purposes of our simple theory, American exports may be taken as a constant because they depend on decisions taken by foreign purchasers of our goods and services. Imports, however, depend on domestic purchases. Since all categories of expenditure have an import content, imports will rise when any other category of expenditure, C, I, or G, rises. Because consumption rises with income, imports of materials that go into the production of domestically produced consumption goods must also rise with income. But since imports rise as income rises, we must expect net exports $(X - M)$ to *fall* as income rises. All this says is that, with exports constant, *net* exports will fall as income rises because imports rise. This then reduces aggregate desired expenditure on domestically produced commodities below what it would be if there were no expenditure on imports. The calculation of a net export function is illustrated in Table 28-4.

TABLE 28–4
A Net Export Schedule (billions of dollars)

National income (Y)	Exports (X)	Imports (M = .1Y)	Net exports
1,000	240	100	140
2,000	240	200	40
2,400	240	240	0
3,000	240	300	−60
4,000	240	400	− 160
5,000	240	500	−260

Net exports fall as national income rises. The data are hypothetical. They assume that exports are constant and that imports are 10 percent of national income. Net exports are then positive at low levels of national income and negative at high levels.

TABLE 28–5
The Equilibrium of National Income: Expenditure Equals Income (billions of dollars)

National income (Y)	Desired consumption (C = 100 + .6Y)	Desired investment (I = 250)	Desired government expenditure (G = 410)	Net exports (X − M = 240 − .1Y)	Desired Aggregate expenditure (AE = C + I + G + [X − M])	
$ 100	$ 160	$250	$410	$230	1,050	Pressure on income to increase
400	340	250	410	200	1,200	
500	400	250	410	190	1,250	
1,000	700	250	410	140	1,500	↓
2,000	1,300	250	410	40	2,000	Equilibrium income
3,000	1,900	250	410	−60	2,500	↑
4,000	2,500	250	410	−160	3,000	Pressure on income to decrease
5,000	3,100	250	410	−260	3,500	

National income is in equilibrium where aggregate desired expenditure equals national income. The data are hypothetical. Aggregate desired expenditure is found by adding desired expenditures on consumption, investment, government purchases, and net exports. When national income is below its equilibrium level, aggregate desired expenditure exceeds the value of current output. This creates an incentive for firms to increase output and hence for national income to rise. When national income is above its equilibrium level, desired expenditure is less than the value of current output. This creates an incentive for firms to reduce output and hence for national income to fall. Only at the equilibrium level of national income is aggregate desired expenditure exactly equal to the value of the current output.

THE AGGREGATE DESIRED EXPENDITURE FUNCTION

Total desired expenditure on the nation's output is the sum of desired consumption, investment, government expenditure, and net exports. How do *changes* in national income affect total desired expenditure? To answer this question, we require the **aggregate expenditure function,** which relates the level of desired expenditure to the level of income. Table 28-5 illustrates how such a function can be calculated, given the consumption function and the levels of desired investment, government expenditure, and net exports at each level of income.

The aggregate expenditure function tells how much domestic governments, firms, and households and foreigners would like to spend on purchasing final domestic output at each level of income.

The function is illustrated by the first and sixth columns of Table 28.5.

Since for the present we assume that I, G, and X are constant, C and (X − M) are the only items of AE that vary systematically with income. But this is enough to make total desired expenditure vary with national income.

Just as we could define propensities to consume and to save that accounted for all household income, so we can define propensities to spend and not to spend that account for the whole of national income. The fraction of any addition to national income that all spending units would like to spend is measured by $\Delta AE/\Delta Y$ and is called the economy's marginal propensity to spend. The remainder is the fraction that spending units do not wish to spend. This is the marginal propensity not to spend (or the marginal propensity to withdraw). It is measured by $1 - \Delta AE/\Delta Y$. Assume for example that decisions of all spending units cause an increase of 80¢ in desired spending whenever national income rises by $1. The marginal propensity to spend is .8 (i.e., .80/1.00), while the marginal propensity to withdraw is .2 (i.e., 1.00 − .80).

Autonomous and Induced Components of Aggregate Expenditure

On page 23 we defined autonomous variables as those exerting an influence on other variables while they themselves are *not influenced* by any other variable in the theory. They are determined from outside the theory. We also defined induced variables as those that are *influenced* by other variables within the theory.

In the elementary theory of national income investment, government expenditure and exports are assumed to be autonomous while consumption expenditure and imports (and hence net exports) are assumed to be induced.

Determining Equilibrium National Income

We are now in a position to see how equilibrium national income is determined. To do this, we study the conditions that must be fulfilled if national income is to be in equilibrium. Conditions that must hold if something is to be in equilibrium are called **equilibrium conditions.**

DESIRED EXPENDITURE EQUALS NATIONAL INCOME IN EQUILIBRIUM

Table 28-5 illustrates the determination of equilibrium national income. It is based on hypothetical data where consumption is $100 + .6Y$, imports are $.1Y$, and I, G, and X are constant at values of $250, $410, and $240 respectively (all figures are in billions of dollars).

Suppose that firms are producing final output of $1,000, and thus national income is $1,000. According to Table 28-5, total desired expenditure, $C + I + G + (X - M)$, is $1,500 at that level of income. If firms persist in producing a current output of only $1,000 in the face of aggregate desired expenditure of $1,500, one of two things must happen.[4]

[4] Remember that for the moment we are operating on the Keynesian portion of the *AS* curve. This rules out, just for the moment, the possibility of increases in prices, which is another possible reaction to a shortage.

One possibility is that households, firms, and governments will be unable to spend the extra $500 that they wish to spend, so shortages and lines of unsatisfied customers will appear. These provide a signal to firms that they can increase their sales if they increase their production. When they do so, national income will rise.

The second possibility is that spending units will succeed in meeting their desired expenditures by purchasing goods produced in the past. Indeed, the only way that plans to purchase more than is currently being produced can be fulfilled is by purchasing inventories of goods produced in the past. In the present case, if plans to buy $1,500 worth of commodities were fulfilled in the face of current output of only $1,000, then inventories would have to be reduced by $500. As long as inventories last, this situation could persist with more goods being sold than were currently being produced. Sooner or later, however, inventories would run out. But long before this happened, firms would take steps to increase their output. This would allow their extra sales to be made without a further decumulation of inventories, and it would increase national income. Thus the final response to an excess of aggregate desired expenditure over current output is a rise in national income.

At any level of national income at which aggregate desired expenditure exceeds total output, there will be pressure for national income to rise.

Now consider the $4,000 level of national income in Table 28-5. At this level of income, desired expenditure on domestically produced goods is only $3,000. If firms persist in producing a total output of $4,000 worth of goods, $1,000 worth must remain unsold. Therefore inventories must rise. Firms will, however, be unwilling to allow inventories of unsold goods to rise indefinitely; sooner or later they will cut back on the level of output to make it equal to the level of sales. When they do, national income will fall.

At any level of income for which aggregate desired expenditure falls short of total output, there will be a strong tendency for national income to fall.

Now look at the national income of $2,000 in the table. At this level, and only at this level, total desired expenditure is exactly equal to national income. Purchasers are able to buy just the total value of commodities that they wish to buy without causing inventories to be depleted, and firms are just able to sell all of their current output so that their inventories are neither rising nor falling. There is no incentive for firms to change their total output. Thus national income will tend to remain steady; it is in equilibrium.

The equilibrium level of national income occurs where aggregate desired expenditure is exactly equal to total output.

Total output, or national product, is the same as national income. Thus it is an equilibrium condition that desired expenditure equal actual national income.

The results just obtained are quite general and do not depend on the numbers chosen for this specific illustration. A glance at Table 28-5 will show that there is *always* a tendency for national income to be pushed in the direction of its equilibrium value. Only when aggregate desired expenditure is equal to income is there no tendency for national income to change.

A GRAPHICAL ILLUSTRATION OF EQUILIBRIUM

Figure 28-3 shows the equilibrium level of national income. The *AE* line is the graph of the aggregate expenditure function. It shows expenditure rising with income but not as much as income rises because a $1 increase in income leads to an increase in consumption expenditure of less than $1 (and also to an increase in imports). The 45° line is the graph of the equilibrium condition that aggregate desired expenditure, *AE*, should equal national income, *Y*.

The intersection of the two lines determines equilibrium income. This is the level of income where desired expenditure is just equal to total national income, which is the total value of final output.

Graphically, equilibrium occurs at the level of income at which the aggregate desired expenditure line intersects the 45° line.

We have now developed a simple but very powerful theory of the determination of equilibrium national income. It gives a general result that holds for this and for all more complex cases: national income is in equilibrium where aggregate desired expenditure is equal to national income because in that case desired purchases will exactly equal total production.

A word of caution. It is important to note that equilibrium income is not the same thing as full-employment income. The latter is the national income that would be produced if there were full employment. The former is the level of income at which desired expenditure equals total income. Nothing in our model guarantees that they will be the same, and equilibrium income may be above or below full-employment income. The relation between the two defines the GNP gap and helps to determine the amount of unemployment. The further below full-employment income is equilibrium income, the larger is the GNP gap and the more unemployment there will be at equilibrium.

The Relation Between Aggregate Demand and Aggregate Expenditure

We now have two important and powerful graphical tools at our command: the aggregate demand-aggregate supply diagram and the aggregate expenditure-45° line diagram. Let us call them "*AD-AS*" and "*AE*" for short. Both show the determination of equilibrium real national income. The *AD-AS* diagram relates *Y* to the price level while the *AE* diagram relates *Y* to desired

FIGURE 28–3
Equilibrium National Income

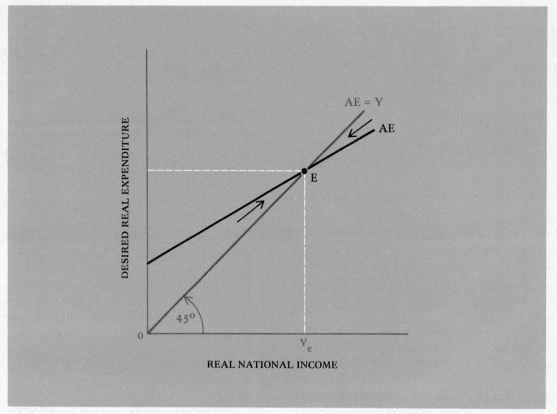

The equilibrium level of national income occurs at *E*, where the aggregate desired expenditure line intersects the 45° line. If national income is below Y_e, desired expenditure will exceed national income and production will rise. This is shown by the left-hand arrow. If national income is above Y_e, desired expenditure will be less than national income and production will fall. This is shown by the right-hand arrow in the figure.

expenditure. These diagrams will be used, starting in the next chapter, to shed light on the economy's macroeconomic behavior. But let us first be clear on how the two are related.

Since both diagrams have real national income on their horizontal axes, they can be stacked one above the other, as in Figure 28-4. The levels of national income determined in each can then be compared. Each graph, however, has a different vertical axis. The *AD-AS* diagram relates income to the price level, while the *AE* diagram relates income to desired expenditure.

Consider the *AE* diagram. Equilibrium na-

tional income is Y_e and, as the graph shows, lower levels of income have desired expenditure in excess of actual income while higher levels of income leave desired expenditure below actual income. The argument for why the economy moves to Y_e (see pages 516–517) assumes that firms adjust their output to demand at current prices: if desired expenditure exceeds current output, firms will produce more; if it is less than current output, firms will produce less. The equilibrium income determined by the *AE* diagram thus assumes that firms will produce whatever is demanded at the going price level, *P*. It assumes, therefore, that the economy is operating on the Keynesian portion of an aggregate supply curve. (Under these circumstances we say that there are no "supply constraints" on national income.)

The *AE* diagram analyzes the determination of equilibrium income on the assumption that firms are able and willing to produce whatever is demanded at the going price level.

This is in fact a demand-determined equilibrium with passive adjustment on the supply side.

The *AD* curve in Figure 28-4(ii) shows the same equilibrium income, Y_e, as in (i). In (ii) Y_e is associated with the price level P_0.

The *AD* curve shows for each price level the equilibrium income that would equate desired expenditure with actual income if firms were willing to produce whatever was demanded at that price level.

Thus the *AD* curve shows the national income that would establish demand-side equilibrium at each price level, on the assumption that the economy is on the Keynesian portion of an aggregate supply curve at that price level.

Which diagram is most useful? When there are no supply constraints, the *AE* diagram is the more revealing way of seeing the forces that push the economy toward its equilibrium income. The *AD-AS* diagram is the more revealing when supply-side constraints are encountered. To see why, look at Figure 29-7 on page 533. If the relevant curves are AD_1, *AS*, and AE_1 and the price level is P_0, then national income would be in equilibrium at Y_1 *if firms were willing and able to produce that much.* But the *AD-AS* diagram shows that output Y_1 is more than the economy can produce. In other words, there is a supply-side constraint. If we had only the *AE* diagram, we would not be able to tell what would happen. The *AD-AS* diagram tells us that the price level will rise because *AD* and *AS* intersect at a price above P_0. (We defer a full analysis of this case.)

In the following chapter we study the factors that can cause equilibrium to change by shifting the *AD* and *AE* curves. In beginning the analysis, it is helpful to deal with an economy that is

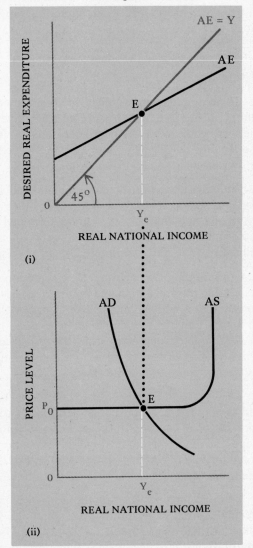

FIGURE 28–4

The *AD-AS* and *AE* Diagrams Related

Equilibrium national income occurs where the aggregate desired expenditure function cuts the 45° line *and* where the aggregate demand and aggregate supply curves intersect. The *AE* diagram (i) shows the demand forces that drive national income to its equilibrium level when there are no supply constraints in the economy. The equilibrium income determined in the *AE* diagram yields a point on the aggregate demand curve. This curve shows for each price level the level of national income for which desired expenditure would equal income.

operating on the Keynesian portion of an aggregate supply curve so that at the outset we do not have to worry about encountering supply-side constraints. Under these circumstances, the *AE* diagram is our major analytical tool.

Summary

1. Desired expenditure includes desired consumption, desired investment, desired government expenditure, and desired net exports. It is the amount that decision makers want to spend on purchasing the national product.

2. With the exception of consumption and imports, the components of desired expenditure are assumed to be constant; they are determined by forces outside the simple theory of income determination.

3. Consumption expenditure is a function of disposable income with a marginal propensity to consume of less than unity. Since disposable income is a function of national income, it follows as well that consumption can be expressed as a function of national income. Both consumption and imports rise as income rises.

4. The aggregate expenditure (AE) function shows how aggregate desired expenditure varies with national income. It slopes upward with a slope less than unity, indicating that a rise in national income of $1 leads to a rise in desired expenditure of less than $1.

5. National income is in equilibrium when aggregate desired expenditure equals national income. At that point purchasers wish to buy neither more nor less than what is being produced. At incomes above equilibrium, desired expenditure falls short of national product and output will sooner or later be curtailed. At incomes below equilibrium, desired expenditure exceeds national product and output will sooner or later be increased.

6. Graphically, equilibrium national income occurs where the aggregate expenditure curve cuts the 45° line and where the aggregate demand curve cuts the aggregate supply curve.

Topics for Review

The consumption function
Average and marginal propensities to consume and save, and to spend and not to spend
The aggregate expenditure function
The 45° line
Equilibrium national income

Discussion Questions

1. "The concept of an equilibrium level of national income is useless because the economy is never in equilibrium. If it ever got there, no economist would recognize it anyway." Discuss.

2. Interpret each of the following statements either in terms of the *shape* of a consumption function or the *values* of *MPC* and/or *APC*.
   a. "Tom Green has lost his job and his family is existing on its past savings."
   b. "The Grimsby household is so rich that they used all the extra income they earned this year to invest in a wildcat oil-drilling venture."
   c. "The widow Harris can barely make ends meet by clipping coupons on the bonds left to her by dear Henry, but she would never dip into her capital."
   d. "We always thought Hammerstein was a miser, but when his wife left him he took to wine, women, and song."

3. Can you think of any reasons why an individual's marginal propensity to consume might be higher in the long run than in the short run? Why it might be lower? Is it possible for an individual's average propensity to consume to be greater than unity in the short run? In the long run? Can a country's average propensity to consume be greater than unity in the short run? In the long run?

4. Along the 45° line on the basic diagram, what relationship holds between total expenditures and total income? In determining equilibrium graphically, are we restricted to choosing identical vertical and horizontal scales?

5. Explain carefully why national income changes when aggregate desired expenditure does not equal national income. Sketch a scenario that fits the cases of too much and too little desired expenditure. What factors might influence the speed with which national income moves toward its equilibrium level?

6. Explain how a sudden unexpected fall in consumer expenditure would initially cause an *increase* in investment expenditure by firms.

Changes in National Income

29

In Chapter 28 we investigated the conditions for national income to be in equilibrium. Recall that when equilibrium is obtained, there is no tendency for national income either to rise or to fall. National income does not, however, remain in a position of unchanging equilibrium; in fact, it changes continuously.

Why National Income Changes

In this chapter we study why income changes. As a preliminary to this study, we re-emphasize the important distinction between movements along curves and shifts of curves.

MOVEMENTS ALONG CURVES VERSUS SHIFTS OF CURVES

If desired expenditure rises, it makes a great deal of difference whether the rise is in response to a change in national income or to an increased desire to spend *at each level of national income* including the present one. The former change is represented by a movement along the aggregate expenditure function; it is the response of desired expenditure to a change in income. The latter change is represented by a shift in the expenditure function that occurs in response to a change in the proportion of income that people desire to spend at each level of income. It is the type of change that can itself disturb an existing equilibrium and cause national income to move from one equilibrium level to another. Figure 29-1 illustrates this important distinction.

FIGURE 29–1

Movements Along Curves and Shifts of Curves

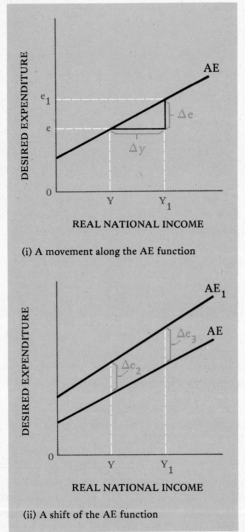

(i) A movement along the AE function

(ii) A shift of the AE function

A movement along the aggregate expenditure function occurs in response to a change in income; a shift of the *AE* function indicates a different level of desired expenditure at each level of income. In (i), a change in income of ΔY, from Y to Y_1, changes expenditure by Δe, from e to e_1. In (ii), a shift in the expenditure function itself raises the amount of expenditure associated with *each* level of income. At Y, for example, AE is increased by Δe_2; at Y_1, AE is increased by Δe_3. (If the shift is a parallel one, then $\Delta e_2 = \Delta e_3$.)

The response of expenditure to a change in income is indicated by a movement along the expenditure function and is shown graphically by the slope of the expenditure curve.

The response of any expenditure to a change in income is called a **marginal propensity.** In Chapter 28 we defined the marginal propensities to save, consume, and spend out of national income as the changes in saving, in consumption, and in total spending that were brought about by a change in national income: $\Delta S/\Delta Y$, $\Delta C/\Delta Y$, and $\Delta AE/\Delta Y$. Graphically, marginal propensities are shown by the *slopes* of the relevant curves.

Marginal propensities relate to movements along curves and tell us how much a particular component of desired expenditure responds to a change in income.

Flows of expenditure can change for a second reason: the curves *themselves* may shift, indicating a new level of expenditure for *each* level of national income. One such shift is illustrated in Figure 29-1(ii).

The main causes of upward shifts in the aggregate expenditure function are:

1. An increase in the amount that firms wish to spend on investment at each level of income.
2. An increase in the amount that governments wish to spend on currently produced goods and services at each level of income.
3. An increase in the amount that households wish to spend on consumption at each level of disposable income. This is the same thing as a decrease in the amount that households wish to save at each level of disposable income.
4. Anything that shifts the function relating disposable income to national income in such a way that households get a larger disposable income at each level of national income—for example, a reduction in tax rates.
5. An increase in exports, X, so there is more foreign expenditure on domestically produced output at each level of national income.
6. A decrease in imports, M, causing a shift of consumption, investment, or government ex-

penditure away from foreign produced goods and toward goods produced domestically. *Ceteris paribus*, either (5) or (6) will increase net exports, $X - M$.

What effects will each of these shifts have on equilibrium national income?

SHIFTS IN THE DESIRED EXPENDITURE FUNCTION

The desired expenditure function shifts directly when one of its components shifts and indirectly when something else shifts, and that in turn causes a component of desired expenditure to shift.

Direct Shifts in Aggregate Expenditure

What will happen to national income if there is a shift in the consumption expenditure of households, in the investment expenditure of private firms, in government expenditure, or in exports? What will happen if, say, households permanently increase their levels of consumption spending at each level of income? if the Ford Motor Company increases its rate of annual investment by $25 million in order to meet the threat of small car imports? if the U.S. government increases its defense spending? or if U.S. exports of prefabricated housing soar? Fortunately, the same analysis can be used to study all four changes.

Each of the changes shifts the entire aggregate expenditure function upward.[1] A constant shift, indicating the same additional expenditure at all levels of income, shifts AE parallel to itself. Such shifts are illustrated in Figure 29-2. A change in the propensity to consume out of disposable or national income, however, changes the slope of the AE line. (Recall that the slope is the marginal

---

[1] It is extremely important to remember that we are dealing with continuous flows measured as so much per period of time. An upward shift in the expenditure function means that *in each period* expenditure is more than it was previously.

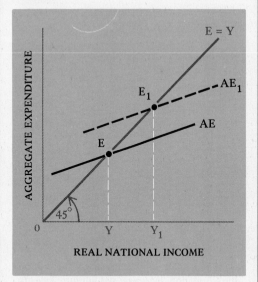

FIGURE 29–2

Parallel Shifts in the Aggregate Expenditure Function

Parallel upward shifts in the *AE* function increase equilibrium income; parallel downward shifts decrease equilibrium income. Initially the aggregate expenditure function is *AE*, with national income *Y*. A parallel upward shift in *AE*, say to *AE₁*, increases equilibrium income to *Y₁*. A downward shift in the function from *AE₁* to *AE* lowers equilibrium income from *Y₁* to *Y*.

Such parallel shifts mean that the same change in desired expenditure takes place at each level of national income.

propensity to spend out of national income.) Such a shift is illustrated in Figure 29-3.

All upward shifts in *AE* increase equilibrium national income. After the shift, at the original level of income, desired expenditure exceeds income, and this causes income to rise. As income rises, expenditure rises, but by less than the rise in income that induced it. The rise in income continues until expenditure is once again equal to (the now higher level of) income. In other words, the upward shift of the expenditure function induces a movement along the new function until the flow of desired expenditure is again equal to national income.

What will happen to national income if there is

FIGURE 29-3

Changes in the Slope of the Aggregate Expenditure Function

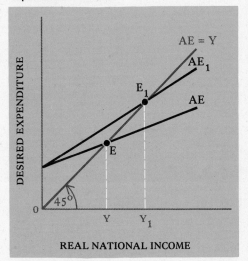

Increases in the slope of the aggregate expenditure function increase equilibrium income; decreases in the slope decrease equilibrium income. Initially the aggregate expenditure function is AE, with national income in equilibrium at Y. The propensity to spend out of national income then increases, shifting the expenditure function to AE_1. Equilibrium income increases to Y_1. The opposite change, a fall in the propensity to spend out of national income, is shown by a shift of the expenditure function from AE_1 to AE and of equilibrium income from Y_1 to Y.

The shift from AE to AE_1 can be caused by a rise in the propensity to consume or a fall in tax rates that raises the proportion of national income going to disposable income. The shift from AE_1 to AE can be caused by a fall in the propensity to consume or a rise in tax rates.

a fall in consumption, investment, exports, or government spending? What will happen if, say, households permanently decrease their rate of spending at each level of income? if a loss of markets to foreign cars causes the American automobile industry to reduce their investment expenditure permanently? if exports of refrigerators to Mexico fall because of increases in Mexican tariffs? or if the government drastically

reduces expenditure on urban renewal? Each of these changes shifts the aggregate expenditure function downward. A constant shift, indicating the same reduction in expenditure at all levels of income, shifts AE parallel to itself. A fall in the propensity to consume out of national income reduces the slope of the AE function. Figures 29-2 and 29-3 show that both kinds of shifts cause national income to fall.

We have now derived two important predictions of the theory of national income.

1. **A rise in the amount of desired consumption, investment, government, or export expenditure associated with each level of income will increase equilibrium national income, other things being equal.**
2. **A fall in the amount of desired consumption, investment, government, or export expenditure associated with each level of income will lower equilibrium national income, other things being equal.**

Indirect Shifts in Aggregate Expenditure

So far we have considered the effects of direct changes in components of aggregate expenditure, consumption, investment, government expenditure, and exports. However, there are other flows that exert an indirect effect on expenditure. Consider the effects of changes in saving, taxes, and imports.

Increases in saving. What will happen to national income if domestic households go on a saving kick? Perhaps they just do not like this year's models of gas-guzzling cars, and they elect to save the money they originally intended to spend on car purchases. A rise in saving means a fall in consumption. This causes a downward shift in the aggregate expenditure function and, as we have seen, that causes a fall in national income.

Increases in imports. What will happen if, instead of saving the money they do not spend on American cars, domestic households turn in-

TABLE 29–1
Shifts in the Function Relating Consumption to National Income

(1) National income (Y)	(2) Disposable income ($Y_d = .7Y$)	(3) Consumption ($C = .9Y_d$)	(4) Consumption ($C = .8Y_d$)	(5) Disposable income ($Y_d = .6Y$)	(6) Consumption ($C = .9Y_d$)
100	70	63	56	60	54
500	350	315	280	300	270
1,000	700	630	560	600	540

The consumption function shifts if either the propensity to consume out of disposable income changes, or the relation between disposable and national income changes. The table is based on simplified hypothetical data where C is always a constant fraction of Y_d and Y_d is always a constant fraction of Y. Initially, $Y_d = .7Y$ and $C = .9Y_d$. This yields a schedule relating consumption to national income that is given in columns 1 and 3. An increased saving propensity is indicated in column 4, where C falls to $.8Y_d$. This yields the new consumption schedule given in columns 1 and 4. In-creased tax rates, which lower the proportion of national income passing into disposable income, are illustrated in column 5. With the initial consumption function of $.9Y_d$, this yields the consumption schedule given in columns 1 and 6. Comparison of columns 3 and 4 shows that a fall in the propensity to consume shifts the schedule rating consumption to disposable income and to national income downward; comparison of columns 3 and 6 shows that a rise in tax rates shifts the schedule relating consumption to national income downward.

creasingly to gas-saving foreign cars? Or if firms and governments buy from abroad commodities they formerly purchased at home? Any of these changes causes a fall in aggregate expenditure on domestic production. The result is a fall in equilibrium national income.

Increases in tax rates. Finally, what will be the effect of a rise in tax rates? Suppose rates are raised so as to take an extra 10 percent of national income at all levels of income in taxes. This will reduce the disposable income associated with each level of national income. If 80 percent of disposable income is consumed, consumption expenditure will fall by 8 percent of national income at each level of national income. This will shift the consumption schedule in Table 29-1 from that shown by columns 1 and 3 to that shown by columns 1 and 6.

Reductions in saving, imports, and tax rates. Not surprisingly, the opposite changes have the opposite effects. A fall in desired saving at each level of income means more consumption expenditure at each level of income. A fall in imports means more spent on home production at

each level of income. A fall in tax rates means more disposable income and hence more expenditure at each level of income. All these changes raise the aggregate expenditure function, either by shifting it parallel to itself or by changing its slope. They thus cause an increase in equilibrium national income, as shown in Figures 29-2 and 29-3.

We have now derived two additional predictions of the theory of national income.

3. A rise in tax rates, saving, or imports will lower the level of national income, other things being equal.
4. A fall in tax rates, saving, or imports will raise the level of national income, other things being equal.

These predictions translate directly into predictions about unemployment and employment: anything that raises national income raises employment and lowers unemployment; anything that lowers national income has the opposite effect.[2]

---

[2] This assumes, as we did on page 481, that the labor force and productivity are constant.

The Paradox of Thrift

These predictions have one important and rather surprising application. It is frequently assumed by analogy with the individual household that for the whole economy thrift is always good and prodigality always bad; that the former leads to increased wealth and prosperity and the latter to eventual bankruptcy. But is a penny saved really as good as a penny earned?

Prediction 3 (above) tells us what we should expect to happen if all households try simultaneously to increase the amount that they save. *The increase in thriftiness will decrease the equilibrium level of national income!* The upward shift in the savings schedule causes a fall in the aggregate expenditure function, which reduces national income.

The contrary case, a general decrease in household thriftiness and an increase in consumption, causes an upward shift in the aggregate expenditure function, which increases national income.

We have now derived the predictions of the so-called paradox of thrift.

Other things being equal, the more frugal and thrifty are spending units, the lower will be the level of national income and total employment. The more prodigal and spendthrift are spending units, the higher will be the level of national income and employment.

The prediction is not in fact a paradox. It is a straightforward, and important, corollary of prediction 3 that in turn follows logically from the theory of the determination of national income. It seems paradoxical to those who expect the way in which a single household should act if it wishes to raise its wealth and its future ability to consume ("save, save, and save some more") to be directly applicable to the economy as a whole. Indeed, the expectations that lead to the "paradox" are based on the fallacy of composition (see page 485), the belief that what is true for the parts is necessarily true for the whole.

The paradox of thrift applies to governments as well as to households. If governments decide to save more, they must raise taxes or cut expenditure. Both alternatives will shift the aggregate expenditure function downward and reduce equilibrium national income. If governments decide to save less (that is, to become more spendthrift), they must lower taxes and/or raise spending. This will shift the expenditure function upward and raise equilibrium national income.

The policy implication of this prediction is that substantial unemployment is correctly combated by encouraging governments, firms, and households to *spend* more, not by encouraging them to save more. In times of unemployment and depression, frugality and parsimony will only make things worse. This prediction goes directly against the idea that we should tighten our belts when times are tough. The idea that it is possible to spend one's way out of a depression touches a very sensitive point in the consciences of people raised in the belief that success is based on hard work and frugality and not on prodigality; as a result, the idea often arouses great emotional hostility.

The implications of the paradox of thrift were not generally understood during the Great Depression of the 1930s. Country after country adopted policies that were, in the light of today's knowledge, disastrously misguided. President Franklin D. Roosevelt, in his first inaugural address (1933), urged:

Our greatest primary task is to put people to work . . . [this task] can be helped by insistence that the Federal, State, and local governments act forthwith on the demand that their costs be drastically reduced. . . . There must be a strict supervision of all banking and credits and investment.

Across the Atlantic, King George V told the House of Commons in 1931 that, "The present condition of the national finances, in the opinion of His Majesty's Ministers, calls for the imposition of additional taxation, and for the effecting of economies in public expenditure." At the time, unemployment in America stood at 23 percent of the labor force and that in Britain at 21 percent!

You should not read on until you are sure that you know what national income theory predicts to be the outcome of the policies recommended in the 1930s. The suffering and misery of that unhappy decade would have been greatly reduced if those in authority had known even as much economics as is contained in this chapter.

Assumptions Underlying the Paradox of Thrift

The striking prediction of the paradox of thrift depends critically on two basic assumptions.

The first assumption is that the economy is on the Keynesian portion of an aggregate supply curve so that output varies directly with aggregate demand and aggregate desired expenditure. However, if the economy is on the classical portion of an aggregate supply curve, a fall in saving will increase aggregate demand, but this will not increase output and employment.

The second assumption is that the volume of investment is at least partly independent of the volume of saving. There is no reason, according to the theory, why the amount that firms spend on investment at any level of income should bear any particular relation to the amount that households save. If the Smiths and the Greens save more, the theory assumes that there is no reason why the Johnsons or Acme, Inc., should decide to increase their investment expenditure to offset the effects of their neighbors' saving. Under these circumstances, an increase in saving necessarily reduces aggregate desired expenditure.

If this second assumption is incorrect, none of the predictions of the paradox of thrift need hold. If changes in household saving cause changes in investment, there would be offsetting shifts in *both* consumption and investment whenever the desire to save changed. If, for example, households saved an extra $1 billion, their consumption expenditure would fall; but they might lend the money to firms that would spend the extra $1 billion on investment. Thus, while the composition of expenditure would change, there would

be no change in total expenditure and hence no downward pressure on national income.

The predictions of the paradox of thrift, and most other predictions of the elementary theory of national income, depend critically, then, on the assumptions that saving and investment decisions are made to a great extent by different groups in society and that there is no mechanism whereby a change in the amount that is desired to be saved at a particular level of income will cause a change in the amount that is desired to be invested at the same level of income.

The Multiplier: A Measure of the Magnitude of Changes in Income

We have seen the direction of the effect on national income of various changes in the aggregate expenditure function. What can we know about the *magnitude* of these changes?

What if there is an upward shift in any of the elements of autonomous expenditure? Say government expenditure or private investment increases by $10 billion; by how much will national income change?

Economists must know the answer to this question in order to determine the effects of changes in expenditures in both the private and the public sectors. At the beginning of the 1980s, those wishing to balance the federal budget called for cutting as much as $20 billion from federal expenditure. To predict the effect of this policy on unemployment, one had to know by how much national income would decrease as a result.

During a depression, government measures are often taken to stimulate the economy. If these measures have a larger effect than estimated, demand may rise too much and full employment may be achieved with demand still rising. This will have an inflationary effect because no further increase in output can occur to meet further increases in demand. If, on the other hand, the government greatly overestimates the effect of its measures, much time will have been wasted. There is also a danger that the policy will be discredited as ineffective, even though the correct diagnosis is merely that too little of the correct thing was done.

DEFINITION OF THE MULTIPLIER

A central prediction of national income theory is that an increase in autonomous expenditure, whatever its source, will cause an increase in national income that is greater than the initial increase in expenditure. The change in autonomous expenditure might come, for example, from an increase in private investment, from new government spending, or from additional exports. The **multiplier** is the ratio of the change in national income to the initial change in expenditure that brings it about.

The importance of the multiplier in national income theory makes it worthwhile to use more than one approach to develop it and to show why its value exceeds unity.

THE MULTIPLIER: AN INTUITIVE STATEMENT

What would happen to national income if the government increased its expenditure on road building by $1 billion per year with no corresponding rise in taxes (so that initially the other components of aggregate expenditure were left unaffected)?[3]

National income will initially rise by $1 billion because of the increase in government spending. The road program will create $1 billion worth of new income and a corresponding amount of employment for those households and firms on which the money is spent. Yet that is not the end of the story. The increase in national income of $1 billion will cause an increase in disposable income, which will cause an induced rise in con-

sumption expenditure. Owners of factors of production that gain new income directly from the government's road program will spend some of it on food, clothing, entertainment, cars, television sets, and other consumption commodities. When output expands to meet this demand, employment will increase in all the affected industries. When the owners of factors that are newly employed to produce consumption commodities spend their extra incomes, output and employment will rise further; more income will then be created and more expenditure induced. Indeed, at this stage we might begin to wonder whether the increase in income will ever come to an end. This question will be more easily answered if we look at a second way to describe the process of income expansion.

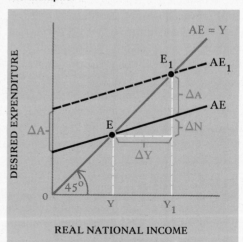

FIGURE 29–4
The Multiplier

An increase in autonomous expenditure increases national income by a multiple of the initial increase. Initial equilibrium income is Y, where the expenditure function AE cuts the 45° line. Autonomous expenditure now increases by ΔA, taking the new expenditure function to AE_1 and equilibrium income to Y_1. The increase in income of ΔY is equal to the increase in autonomous expenditure of ΔA plus the increase in induced expenditure of ΔN. Since ΔN is positive, ΔY exceeds ΔA. The multiplier, which is the ratio $\Delta Y/\Delta A$, is thus greater than one.

---

[3] For simplicity we assume that there is no import content to road building.

The Multiplier: A Numerical Approach

Suppose that the economy behaves in this simple way: whenever national income rises by $1, disposable income rises by 60¢ and induced consumption expenditure rises by 50¢. This economy's marginal propensity to spend out of national income is .5.

Now suppose that autonomous expenditure increases because the government spends an extra $1 billion a year on new roads. National income initially rises by $1 billion. But that is not the end of it; there is a second round of spending. The factors of production involved directly and indirectly in road building receive an extra $600 million as disposable income, and they spend an extra $500 million each year on domestically produced goods and services. This $500 million generates $300 million of new disposable income and $250 million of new consumption expenditure (the remaining $50 million is saved), which is a third round of additions to aggregate expenditure.

And so it continues, each successive round of new income generating 50 percent as much in new expenditure. Each additional round of expenditure creates new income and yet another round of expenditure.

The table below carries the process through ten rounds. Students with sufficient patience (and no faith in mathematics) may compute as many rounds in the process as they wish; they will find that the sum of the rounds of expenditures approaches $2 billion, which is twice the initial injection of $1 billion. [35] The multiplier is thus 2, given these numerical assumptions about the relations between national income and disposable income and induced expenditure.

	Increases in disposable income	Increases in expenditure
	(millions of dollars per year)	
		$1,000.00
Assumed increase in government expenditure per year		
2nd round (increase in disposable income and expenditure)	$ 600.00	500.00
3rd round (increase in disposable income and expenditure)	300.00	250.00
4th round (increase in disposable income and expenditure)	150.00	125.00
5th round (increase in disposable income and expenditure)	75.00	62.50
6th round (increase in disposable income and expenditure)	37.50	31.25
7th round (increase in disposable income and expenditure)	18.75	15.63
8th round (increase in disposable income and expenditure)	9.38	7.81
9th round (increase in disposable income and expenditure)	4.69	3.91
10th round (increase in disposable income and expenditure)	2.34	1.95
Sum of 1st 10 rounds		1,998.05
All other rounds		1.95
Total		$2,000.00

THE MULTIPLIER: A GRAPHICAL ANALYSIS

Figure 29-4 illustrates the multiplier graphically. The increase in autonomous expenditure of ΔA initially raises national income by that amount. Then the increase in national income induces more consumption expenditure, and this further raises national income. As income rises, consumption expenditure rises by less than income.

FIGURE 29-5

The Size of the Multiplier

(i) A flat AE line yields a small multiplier

(ii) A steep AE line yields a large multiplier

The steeper the expenditure function, the larger the marginal propensity to spend and the larger the multiplier. In both parts of the figure national income, initially at Y, is disturbed by an increase in autonomous expenditure of ΔA.

In (i), the aggregate expenditure function is flat (a low marginal propensity to spend) and there is only a small increase in induced expenditure of ΔN_1. The increase in national income of ΔY_1 is only slightly larger than the increase in autonomous expenditure that brought it about. The multiplier is small.

In (ii), the AE function is steep (a high marginal propensity to spend) and there is a large increase in induced expenditure of ΔN_2. The increase in national income of ΔY_2 is much larger than the increase in autonomous expenditure that brought it about. The multiplier is large.

Income will stop rising when desired aggregate expenditure is once again equal to national income.

A high marginal propensity to spend means a steep AE curve. The resulting induced consumption expenditure caused by the initial increase in income is large, with the result that the final rise in income is correspondingly great. A low marginal propensity to spend means a relatively flat AE curve. The resulting induced consumption expenditure caused by the initial increase in income is small. The result is that the final rise in income is not much larger than the initial rise in autonomous expenditure that brought it about. Both cases are shown in Figure 29-5.

The multiplier is given the symbol K. It is defined as the final change in income divided by the change in autonomous expenditure that brought it about. In symbols,

$$K = \frac{\Delta Y}{\Delta A}$$

Using the symbols of Figure 29-4, we can break up ΔY, the change in Y, into the change in autonomous expenditure, ΔA, and the induced change in expenditure, ΔN. Substituting $\Delta Y = \Delta A + \Delta N$ in the above expression yields

$$K = \frac{\Delta A + \Delta N}{\Delta A}$$

This shows that it is the induced change in expenditure, ΔN, that makes the multiplier greater than unity. As the induced component to expenditure becomes smaller (the AE line becomes flatter), the multiplier becomes smaller. Indeed, if ΔN were zero, the multiplier would be one. The common sense of this is that if there were no induced expenditure, those who initially received the government's expenditure of $1 billion per year would spend none of their extra income. There would then be no repercussions; income would rise by the $1 billion of ΔA but no further.

The size of the induced component depends, *ceteris paribus*, on the marginal propensity to spend. If it is high, people who receive the initial $1 billion of extra income will in turn raise their spending a lot. If it is low, they will raise their spending only a little.

The larger is the marginal propensity to spend (the steeper the aggregate expenditure function), the larger is the value of the multiplier.

THE SIZE OF THE MULTIPLIER

We have seen that the multiplier depends on the slope of the aggregate expenditure function. It turns out that the precise relation is

$$K = \frac{1}{1-n}$$

where n is the slope of the expenditure function, that is, the marginal propensity to spend. **[36]** The term $1 - n$ is the marginal propensity not to spend, or what we called the marginal propensity to withdraw (see page 515). For example, if 80¢ of every $1 of new national income is spent ($n =$ .8), then 20¢ (1.00 − .80) is the amount not spent of every $1 of new income. If we refer to $1 - n$ as w, we can write the size of the multiplier as

$$K = \frac{1}{w}$$

The multiplier is the reciprocal of the marginal propensity to withdraw (or not to spend).

If w is very small, the multiplier will be very large (because extra income induces much extra expenditure). The largest possible value of w is unity, indicating that all extra income is not spent. In this case, as we have already argued, the multiplier has a value of unity, indicating that the increase in income is confined to the initial increase in autonomous expenditure.

HOW LARGE IS THE MULTIPLIER IN THE UNITED STATES TODAY?

The predictions and the policy implications of a multiplier of 1.5 or 2 are very different from those of a multiplier of 5 or 10. Will $10 billion of new investment expenditure increase national income by $15 billion or by $50 billion? Clearly this is an important question.

If the marginal propensity to spend out of national income is known or can be estimated, the magnitude of the effect on income of a shift in any component of aggregate expenditure can be estimated.

Many studies of the American economy have been made that suggest that as a rough order of magnitude the GNP multiplier is between 1.5 and 2. This may not sound very precise. But only about three decades ago economists thought the multiplier might be as high as 5 or 10. Today we are confident that an increase in autonomous expenditure of $10 billion per year will lead to an increase in GNP of roughly $15 to $20 billion— maybe only $14 billion, or maybe as much as $22 billion—but we are certain that (other things remaining approximately equal) it will not increase GNP by so much as $50 billion or so little as only $11 billion. For practical purposes, this acquired knowledge makes an enormous difference in our ability to control the economy.

Inflationary and Deflationary Gaps

Up to now we have considered equilibrium positions on the Keynesian portion of the aggregate supply curve. Now we want to look at situations in which the price level can rise. This will take us to positions off the Keynesian portion of the *AS* curve. To simplify matters at the outset, we employ the version of the aggregate supply curve introduced in Figure 26-10, on page 488.

The *kinked aggregate supply curve* contains only a Keynesian portion and a classical portion, as shown by the AS curves in Figures 29-6 and 29-7. National income, Y_F, at which the kink occurs, can be identified as full-employment national income.

The kinked aggregate supply curve makes a sharp distinction between situations of unemployment, where the price level is fixed and real national income is variable, and situations of full employment, where real national income is fixed at its full-employment level while the price level is variable.

FIGURE 29–6

The GNP Gap and the Deflationary Gap

(i)

(ii)

REAL NATIONAL INCOME

The GNP gap measures the shortfall of equilibrium national income below full-employment national income; the deflationary gap measures the shortfall of aggregate desired expenditure below full-employment income. Aggregate expenditure and aggregate demand, AE and AD, produce equilibrium income of Y, which falls short of full-employment income, Y_F. The GNP gap is $Y_F - Y$. The deflationary gap is the amount by which the aggregate expenditure function would have to be shifted upward to create full employment. This would require shifting AE to AE_F, which would shift AD to AD_F.

In analyzing situations of unemployment and full employment, three gaps are used by policy analysts such as the president's Council of Economic Advisers. These are considered below.

Situations of Unemployment

When national income is below its full-employment level, two gaps may be calculated. The first gap, which we encountered in Chapter 26, measures the extent of the shortfall in national income.

The extent to which actual national income is below its full-employment level is called the GNP gap.

This can be shown in both an *AD-AS* diagram and an aggregate expenditure diagram, such as in the two parts of Figure 29-6. The GNP gap measures the lost output that could have been produced if full employment had been achieved.

The second gap measures the extent of the shortfall in desired expenditure. When national income is in equilibrium at less than full employment, a sufficiently large upward shift in the aggregate expenditure function would raise national income to its full-employment level.

The extent to which the aggregate expenditure schedule would have to shift upward to produce the full-employment level of national income is called the **deflationary gap**.

Because this gap refers to a shortfall of aggregate expenditure, it can be shown only in part (i) of Figure 29-6.

Situations of Full Employment

Now consider inflationary situations. If aggregate desired expenditure exceeds the economy's full-employment output at the current price level, there will be inflationary demand pressure in the economy. Such a situation is shown in Figure 29-7 when the aggregate expenditure curve has shifted to AE_1 in part (i) and the aggregate demand function to AD_1 in part (ii) while the price level is still at P_0.

FIGURE 29–7
The Inflationary Gap

(i)

(ii)

The inflationary gap is the amount by which the aggregate expenditure curve must be shifted downward to produce equilibrium at full-employment income at the present price level. Aggregate expenditure and aggregate demand are AE_1 and AD_1 and the price level is P_0. At full-employment income, aggregate desired expenditure exceeds income by the amount of the inflationary gap. To produce equilibrium at Y_F and P_0, the aggregate expenditure curve would have to be shifted downward to AE_F (which would shift the aggregate demand curve to AD_F).

If aggregate desired expenditure exceeds output at the full-employment level of income, there is inflationary pressure. Enough output to satisfy demand at current prices cannot be produced.

The extent to which the aggregate expenditure schedule would have to shift downward to produce the full-employment level of national income without inflation is called the inflationary gap.

This gap is shown in part (i) of Figure 29-7.[4]

USING THE CONCEPTS OF THE "GAPS"

The modern theory of income determination is an elaboration of the original model put forward by John Maynard Keynes in *The General Theory of Employment, Interest and Money,* first published in 1936. In the original Keynesian model, the emphasis was on situations of unemployment rather than full employment. This was not surprising since Keynes was concerned to find cures for the Great Depression, which had had disastrous consequences for the tens of millions of workers who made up the massive armies of unemployed in Western industrial nations. Indeed, the Depression was helping to undermine the very social fabric of Western democracies; finding a cure for it was then the most pressing social problem.

The extension of the theory to cover problems of full employment and demand inflation did not come until World War II, when those problems replaced the nightmare of persistent, massive unemployment in the minds and consciences of people. The concept of the inflationary gap proved the vehicle for extending the theory beyond the conditions that it was originally designed to explain.

---

[4] There is a fourth gap, shown in Figure 29-7. When the price level is P_0 but aggregate expenditure is AE_1, there is enough desired expenditure to purchase Y_1 of national output if only it could be produced. The gap $Y_1 - Y_F$ measures the inability of current full-employment capacity to produce the level of output that would yield an equilibrium (desired expenditure equals income) at the current price level. This gap does not play any great part in current policy discussion because the amount that could be bought, if only it could be produced, is of no great importance to any macro policy.

The concepts of both inflationary and deflationary gaps prove useful in discussing policy questions of how to achieve stability in the economy. That discussion can be foreshadowed by noting that one way to combat unemployment is to estimate the size of the deflationary gap and attempt to eliminate it by policies that shift the aggregate expenditure curve upward. Similarly, one way to combat inflation is to estimate the size of the inflationary gap and attempt to eliminate it by policies that shift the aggregate expenditure curve downward. Such policies are discussed in detail in Chapter 31.

Summary

1. A movement along an expenditure curve represents an induced change in expenditure in response to a change in national income. A shift of an expenditure function represents a change in expenditure associated with each level of national income.

2. Movements along curves are described by marginal propensities. They give the change in expenditure as a proportion of the change in income that brought it about. The marginal propensity gives the slope of the expenditure function over the range for which it is measured.

3. Equilibrium national income is increased by an upward shift in the consumption, investment, government, or export expenditure associated with each level of national income. National income is decreased by the opposite changes.

4. Equilibrium national income is decreased by an increase in saving, imports, or taxes associated with each level of income. National income is increased by the opposite changes.

5. The above predictions have an important counterintuitive application: the paradox of thrift. What is true for the individual is not true for the nation. If everyone reduces consumption and increases saving, national income will fall. Leading governments demonstrated ignorance of this by their economic policies during the Great

Depression, when they tried to fight the Depression by cutting their expenditures because their tax revenues had fallen.

6. The magnitude of the effect on national income of shifts in autonomous expenditure (such as I, G, and X) is given by the multiplier. This is defined as $K = \Delta Y / \Delta A$, where ΔA is the change in autonomous expenditure. The elementary theory of national income gives the value of the multiplier as $1/(1 - n) = 1/w$, where n is the marginal propensity to spend and w is the marginal propensity to withdraw (or not to spend). Thus the larger the propensity to spend, the larger the multiplier.

7. It is a basic prediction of national income theory that the multiplier is greater than unity. Its actual size is an important magnitude. As a rough order of magnitude for the United States today, the GNP multiplier is taken to be about 2. (An increase in autonomous expenditure of $\$X$ billion will tend to lead to an increase in GNP of about $\$2X$ billion.)

8. The GNP gap is the difference between actual national income and full-employment or potential national income. It represents a waste in terms of lost production because all of the nation's resources are not fully employed.

9. The inflationary and deflationary gaps measure the level of aggregate desired expenditure relative to the level required to achieve full employment. An inflationary gap means that aggregate desired expenditure is more than sufficient to produce full-employment national income at constant prices. A deflationary gap means that it is insufficient to do so.

Topics for Review

Shifts of and movements along expenditure curves
The effect on national income of changes in the amounts of I, G, X, S, T, and M associated with each level of income
The paradox of thrift
The multiplier

The relation between the size of the multiplier and the slope of the expenditure schedule

The kinked aggregate supply function

The GNP gap

Inflationary and deflationary gaps

Discussion Questions

1. In what direction would each of the following change national income, *ceteris paribus?* Which expenditure flows would be affected first? Would other elements of expenditure also change? Be sure to distinguish between movements along curves and shifts of curves.
   a. the production and sale of fighter planes to Israel
   b. a decrease in personal income tax withholding for low-income taxpayers
   c. the institution of a new federal program of $2 billion of payments to the elderly
   d. a spurt in consumer spending for CB radios accompanied by a reduction in savings
   e. a decision to end the space-shuttle program
2. The fallacy of composition is defined as a fallacy in which what is true of a part is inaccurately assumed to be true also of the whole. Can the "paradox" in the paradox of thrift be explained by applying this point of logic? Explain.
3. Predict whether each of the following events will, *ceteris paribus,* increase, decrease, or leave unchanged the size of the multiplier:
   a. a shift from foreign travel to holidays at home
   b. an expansion of federal expenditures on the interstate highway program
   c. decisions by corporations to pay out a smaller percentage of their earnings in dividends and to increase their bank balances whenever national income falls
   d. widespread adoption by cities of a city income tax
4. If you were running a country's economic stabilization program, would you prefer the country to have a large or a small multiplier?
5. The president of the Chamber of Commerce of Southeastern Connecticut commented on the effects in his area of a 22-week strike at a shipyard where the lost payroll was $2 million per week: "You don't just figure $2 million a week times 22 weeks, you have to multiply that by four or five. That shipyard is the prime source of money in this region. Money comes into the region from Washington and then the shipyard worker's wife takes it to the grocery, and the grocery clerk takes it to the gas station, and so on until it leaves the area in taxes or some other way." Interpret his statement in terms of the analysis of this chapter.
6. Homer Hardcrust, chairman of the Council of Economics Advisers, proposes that because of the economic situation the government should prepare an austerity program and cut down government expenditures to set an example for private households. Under what economic conditions might Hardcrust's advice make sense? Under what conditions would it worsen the situation?
7. "We now have approximately 70 percent of our industrial capacity being used; which means that 30 percent or so is not being used. With eight million people unemployed, that's another tremendous untapped reservoir of workers and capacity that can be tapped before you have pressures of an inflationary type." Does the speaker (President Carter, at a news conference) express views consistent with the kinked aggregate supply curve?

Cycles and Fluctuations in National Income

30

Changing, always changing; this is the dominant characteristic of the GNP for as far back as records exist. Long-term growth and short-term fluctuations are the two major components of the GNP changes that we observe. Long-term growth is seen in the steady upward trend in the potential GNP—the GNP that can be produced when the economy is at full employment. (Long-term growth will be studied in Chapters 43 and 44.) Shorter-term fluctuations are seen in oscillations of actual GNP around the level set by potential GNP. Such oscillations are related to changes in aggregate demand and aggregate supply. They lead to changes in what is actually produced, and these changes in turn cause variations in the amount of employment and unemployment. Short-term fluctuations in GNP are the subject of the present chapter.

THE HISTORICAL RECORD

Figure 30-1 shows the year-to-year changes in real GNP. What produces such changes? If, on the one hand, aggregate demand shifts to the left because of decreases in desired consumption, investment, government expenditure, or net exports without a compensating change in any of the other components, aggregate expenditure will fall. Total output will soon be reduced in response, and employment and actual GNP will fall. If, on the other hand, aggregate demand shifts to the right, aggregate expenditure will rise. This will cause a rise in real output, and employment and real GNP will rise—at least until all available factors of production become fully employed.

Fluctuations in aggregate demand have usually been the major reason for short-term fluctuations in GNP. Events of the mid 1970s, however, have made the citizens of advanced industrial countries acutely aware of supply-side causes. If supplies of such critical raw materials as oil or iron ore are drastically reduced, output will fall and unemployment will rise even though there is enough demand to buy the whole of the economy's potential GNP. If goods cannot be produced, they cannot be sold.

In Chapter 29 we developed a theory of how national income changes in response to changes in the various components of aggregate expenditure. If there were merely occasional sharp shifts in these components, we would expect national income to show occasional sharp changes followed by long periods of little or no change. This is not, however, the picture suggested by Figure 30-1; instead the short-term situation is one of continual change but at a varying rate. This general picture is confirmed for a much longer period by the data in Figure 30-2. Evidently there are factors at work causing the economy to display continual short-term fluctuations around its long-term rising growth trend.

The short-term behavior of the economy cannot be fully caught by a single statistic. Figure 30-3 shows three important economic series; each series, as well as each of a dozen other widely used series, tells us something about the general variability of the economy. It is obvious that some series vary more than others and that they do not all move together.

Traditionally fluctuations such as those illustrated in Figure 30-2 have been called **business cycles.**

There is a fairly general consensus among students of economic fluctuations that:

1. There is a common pattern of variation that more or less pervades all economic series.
2. There is substantial difference from cycle to cycle in duration and in amplitude.
3. There are differences among economic series in their particular patterns of fluctuation.

IS THERE A PRINCIPAL CAUSE OF CYCLES?

Professor Alvin Hansen, one of the most distinguished American students of business cycles, once reported that between 1795 and 1937 there were 17 cycles, of an average duration of 8.35 years. A shorter "inventory cycle" of 40 months' duration was also found, as well as longer cycles associated with building booms (15 to 20 years). The Russian economist Kondratieff identified long waves of 40 to 50 years associated with the introduction of major innovations. Some economists have recently argued for the existence of a four-year political business cycle associated with the quadrennial presidential elections.

Why does the U.S. economy undergo business fluctuations? It seems apparent from the behavior of the economy that some elements of aggregate expenditure must be changing continuously. Such a situation causes the equilibrium

---

FIGURE 30-1
Annual Changes in Real GNP

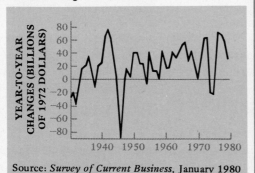

Source: *Survey of Current Business,* January 1980

Real national income changes continually from one year to the next. Despite a strong upward trend shown by the fact that most changes are increases, real national income does not rise steadily year after year. Generally, two or three years of very rapid increase tend to be followed by two or three years of slow increase, or even decline, in GNP.

FIGURE 30-2
American Business Activity Since 1870

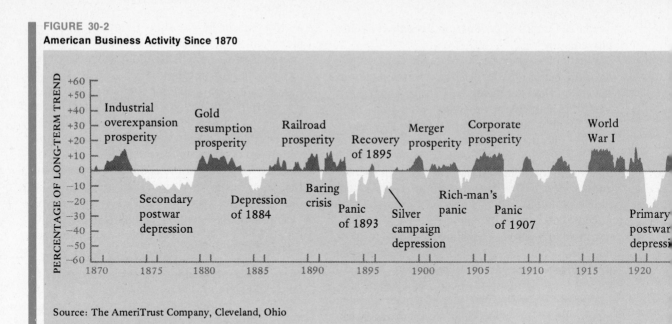

Source: The AmeriTrust Company, Cleveland, Ohio

Cyclical ups and downs have dominated the short-term behavior of the U.S. economy at least since 1870. This chart is constructed by taking some single index of general economic activity, fitting a trend line to it, and plotting deviations of the index from its trend value. It shows well the tendency for an economy to fluctuate. There is no great

level of national income to be changing continuously as well and causes the actual level of national income to be moving in pursuit of this equilibrium income.

What are the possible sources of these continuous disturbances? The theory of income determination suggests four main candidates—shifts in each of the four main components of aggregate expenditure.

Historically, foreign trade has been too small a proportion of American national income to have caused the historical pattern of fluctuations actually observed. It can, however, be the continuing source of disturbances to small sectors of the economy—those sectors concerned with exporting and importing. In particular periods, too, a foreign trade shock, such as the OPEC oil embargo, can jolt the entire economy. Oil imports were a major contributor to the 1974–1975 recession.

Each of the other three components of ag-gregate expenditure—consumption, investment, and government expenditures—are large enough that shifts in them can have a large impact on the equilibrium level of national income. Moreover, each of them can shift in response to outside exogenous shocks, to endogenous forces within the economy, and to government policy measures.

Shifts in Consumption

About two-thirds of total expenditure in the United States is made up of consumption expenditures. If households were to reduce their consumption expenditure by 3 percent, this would amount to a reduction of 2 percent in total expenditure. Combined with a multiplier of 2, this would cause the GNP to decline by 4 percent. Perhaps this does not sound like very much, but if employment were to change merely in proportion to income, this could change a situation of 4 percent unemployment (a level considered to be

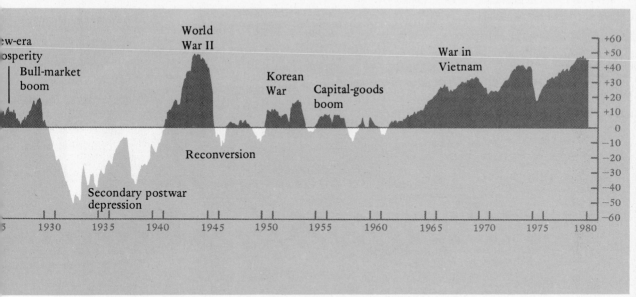

significance to being above or below zero because the zero line is based on an arbitrary trend. But major booms and depressions are unmistakable.

full employment or even above full employment and one not achieved since 1953) to one of 8 percent, which was exceeded in only one year from 1948 to 1980. Clearly, even relatively small percentage fluctuations in consumption can have big effects on the economy. Such fluctuations have occurred in the past. What causes them?

In discussing the effects of shifts in the consumption function on GNP, it is useful to distinguish between factors that change the function relating household consumption to household disposable income, and factors changing the relation between disposable income and GNP. (We first encountered the distinction on page 525.)

SHIFTS IN THE RELATIONSHIP BETWEEN CONSUMPTION AND DISPOSABLE INCOME

From time to time tastes change; when they do, consumption levels and patterns may change. A large number of households may decide that they do not take to this year's American-make car models and elect to save (or spend on an imported car) the money they were expected to spend on a new American car this year. If this happens, the consumption function will shift downward this year. Incomes earned in Detroit (and many other places) will fall, and unemployment will rise. The unemployed auto workers will cut their spending on other products, and a multiplier process will be set up that will magnify and spread the original cut in spending on new automobiles into a general fall in income and employment.

While the demand for an individual commodity (such as cars) often shifts sharply from year to year, the aggregate proportion of consumer income going to current expenditure tends to be relatively more stable. The division between consumption and saving does however shift. What are some of the reasons for this?

FIGURE 30-3
Three Indicators of Economic Activity, 1950–1979

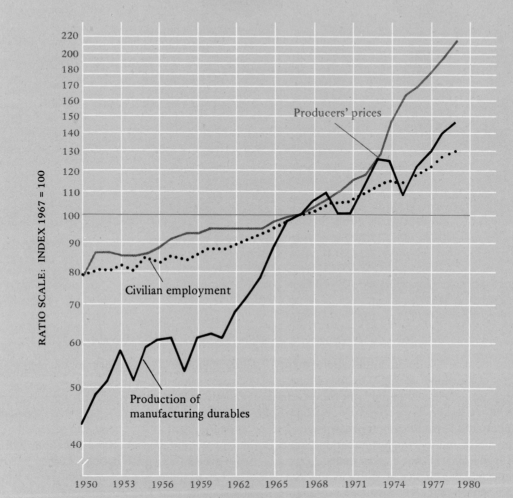

Source: *Economic Report of the President,* 1980

Short-term variability and a long-term upward trend characterize many indices of American economic activity, including these three. All three series are index numbers with 1967 = 100, so all pass through 100 at 1967. All series exhibit short-term variability, though in varying degree. Producers' prices were much more stable than production of durables in 1950–1970 but were more volatile during the 1970s. Civilian employ-ment does not fluctuate greatly because even a large change in unemployment, say from 4 percent to 8 percent of the labor force, makes a relatively small percentage change in employment: from 96 percent to 92 percent. Employment growth over time reflects both population growth and the increasing employment of women.

Expectations About the Future

Many kinds of consumer expenditures — such as food, clothing, and automobile repair — are hard to postpone. Many others are discretionary. The latter include purchases of durable goods such as television sets and new cars and luxuries such as restaurant meals and long vacation trips. It is now well known that consumers' discretionary expenditures respond to the general economic and political climate.

Measures such as the Survey of Consumer Attitudes (of the Institute of Social Research at the University of Michigan) prove helpful in predicting aggregate consumer expenditure and savings patterns. If consumers are apprehensive about the economic future, particularly about the possibility of unemployment, they tend to postpone purchases and increase savings. Generally, when consumers are optimistic, they are willing to buy and to dissave by extending their credit purchases.

Inflationary expectations have proven very troublesome to consumers. On the one hand, if households expect prices to rise rapidly, they may rush to buy new goods they know they will have to purchase sometime in the relatively near future. In such circumstances purchase at today's prices may be an attractive use of accumulated savings. However, inflationary expectations also cause insecurity about the adequacy of the household's future income and may lead to a decrease in purchases in order to increase savings.

If many consumers are led to postpone durable purchases — which on average account for about 15 percent of all consumer expenditures — this will lead to sharp downward shifts in consumption expenditures and leftward shifts in the aggregate demand function. When such postponements occur, the age of the existing stock of durables grows. Once the end of the period of pessimism comes, there is likely to be a sudden outburst of expenditures out of accumulated savings. The consumption function may shift sharply upward for a year or two until the backlog of demand is exhausted.

Terms of Credit

Most durable consumer goods and many nondurable ones are purchased on credit, which may range from a few months to pay for a stereo or a new suit to up to five years to pay for an automobile. If credit becomes more difficult or more costly to obtain, many households will postpone their planned, credit-financed purchases. If the amount of the typical down payment rises, or if monthly carrying charges rise, some consumers will postpone replacing a television set or do without the recreational vehicle they had planned to buy. Instead they may add the purchase price to their savings deposit at the bank (which is probably advertising new, higher rates of interest).

Notice here that government policymakers can, by controlling the cost and availability of credit, shift the consumption function and thereby affect aggregate demand.

Changes in Income Distribution

Because the consumption function relates *aggregate* consumption expenditures of the nation's households to their aggregate disposable income, the consumption function can change without the habits of any individual changing. For example, if income is transferred from a rich family that saves 40 percent of its marginal income to a poor family that spends every dollar it gets, the consumption function will shift up, indicating more consumption and less saving at the same level of aggregate disposable income.

More generally, since different households have different marginal propensities to consume, aggregate consumption depends not only on aggregate income but also on the distribution of this income among households. Thus a change in the distribution of income will cause a change in the aggregate *level* of consumption expenditure that is associated with any given *level* of national income. In other words, there will be a shift in the consumption function.

Here too the government can have a significant role, either through its transfer payments to households or through changes in the structure of taxes.

SHIFTS IN THE RELATIONSHIP BETWEEN DISPOSABLE INCOME AND NATIONAL INCOME

Even if the relationship between disposable income and consumption does not change, a change in the relationship of Y_d to GNP will shift the consumption function relating consumption to GNP. For example, if households consume 90 percent of their disposable income and if disposable income is 70 percent of GNP, then consumption will be 63 percent of GNP. Suppose that with no change in the 90 percent propensity to consume out of Y_d, personal income tax reductions increase disposable income from 70 to 80 percent of GNP. Consumption is thereby increased from 63 to 72 percent of GNP. This shift in consumption will increase aggregate demand.

An increase in tax rates lowers the aggregate demand function by lowering the ratio of disposable income to national income. A decrease in tax rates has the opposite effect.

If the government cuts taxes during an election year, in order to win votes, the effect will be to shift the consumption function upward. This may well trigger a cyclical boom.

Investment and Its Determinants

A leading candidate for principal source of disturbance is investment expenditure. Consider the period 1929–1932. In 1929 total investment expenditure of firms and households in the American economy was $16.2 billion, almost double the amount of expenditure needed to replace the capital goods that were used up that year in the process of producing a GNP of $103 billion. The American economy in 1929, then, was adding rapidly to its stock of capital equipment. Three years later, in 1932, total investment expenditure was $1 billion. This was less than one-sixth of the amount needed merely to keep the stock of

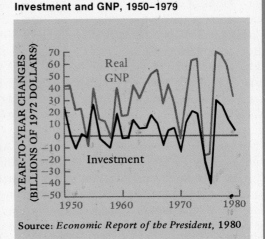

FIGURE 30-4

Year-to-year Changes in Real Gross Private Investment and GNP, 1950–1979

Source: *Economic Report of the President,* 1980

The fluctuations in gross private investment are sharp and closely related to changes in national income. The screened line repeats the change of real GNP from Figure 30-1. The heavy line shows changes in investment. Changes in private investment are very closely related to changes in national income.

capital intact. The American economy in 1932, with its GNP reduced to $58 billion, was rapidly reducing its stock of capital equipment.

Investment expenditure is both volatile and closely correlated with changes in GNP. This is shown in Figure 30-4.

Investment expenditures play a key role in most theories of cyclical fluctuations.

Table 30-1 shows this in some detail for the severe recession that beset the U.S. economy between the end of 1973 and the middle of 1975. While fixed investment was only about 15 percent of GNP over this period, *changes* in such investment were about one-third as large as changes in GNP, and in seven of the eight quarters they moved in the same direction.

WHY DOES INVESTMENT CHANGE?

It is useful to know that changes in investment are one of the prime causes of short-term fluctuations, but we do not have the whole story unless

TABLE 30-1

Fixed Investment and GNP During the 1974 Recession (billions of 1972 dollars)

Quarter	Total		Quarter-to-quarter change	
	Gross private fixed domestic investment	GNP	Gross private fixed domestic investment	GNP
1973: 4th	$188	$1,241		
1974: 1st	184	1,230	$– 4	$–11
2nd	179	1,221	– 5	– 9
3rd	171	1,213	– 8	– 8
4th	161	1,192	–10	–21
1975: 1st	150	1,161	–11	–31
2nd	147	1,177	– 3	+16
3rd	150	1,209	+ 3	+32
4th	152	1,219	+ 2	+10

There is a close correlation between changes in fixed investment and changes in GNP. Investment expenditure, although only a small fraction of total expenditure, is a volatile component of it. The data in the last two columns lend support to the theory that a decline in investment expenditure was a major cause of the 1974 recession.

we know why investment fluctuates. In discussing the theory of income determination in Chapters 28 and 29 we talked simply of shifts in investment, not of the underlying causes of such shifts. It would be quite possible for two economists to accept all that has been said so far in this chapter and yet believe in different causes of cyclical fluctuations.

One theory might be that investment depends mainly on business firms' anticipations of the future state of their markets. When there is confidence in the future, investment will be high; when there is pessimism, investment will be low. To go further in understanding fluctuations we would have to appeal to psychology to explain variations in business attitudes. The economist alone could not go beyond studying the consequences of exogenous, unexplained shifts in the investment function.

A second theory might be that monetary factors provide the major explanation of fluctuations in investment.[1] When credit is easily obtainable, interest rates are low and banks and other financial institutions are eager to lend money to investors; when credit is tight, interest rates are high and loans are hard to obtain. The

first theory is close to that advocated by Keynes; the second is close to the one advocated by many monetarists.

While each dollar of investment has the same consequences for aggregate demand, different types of investment respond to different sets of causes. Thus it is useful to discuss separately the determinants of investment in plant and equipment, changes in inventories, and residential construction.

INVESTMENT IN INVENTORIES[2]

Inventory changes represent only about 5 percent of private investment in a typical year. Their average size is not an adequate measure of their importance because they are one of the more volatile elements of total investment and therefore contribute importantly in shifts in the investment schedule.

[1] The monetary sector is studied in detail in Part Nine.

[2] As we saw in Chapter 26, there are two kinds of changes in inventories. Intended changes are a *cause* of cyclical fluctuations and are discussed here. Unintended changes are a *consequence* of fluctuations due (for example) to firms' finding their inventories rising in a recession because they do not have customers for their current production and thus their goods pile up in warehouses. Because it is impossible to isolate these changes in the statistics, we have excluded changes in inventories from Table 30-1.

Firms characteristically hold substantial inventories of raw materials, goods in process, and goods already produced but unsold. It is almost impossible to imagine a manufacturing firm doing business successfully without some minimum holdings of inventories. In fact, most firms choose to hold inventories well above the necessary minimum level. They do this for many reasons; for one, it is usually cheaper to hold production constant in the face of daily, weekly, or even monthly fluctuations in sales than to adjust levels of production frequently. Although many things can influence the desired size of a firm's inventory holdings, the two most important factors are the size of a firm's sales and the rate of interest.

Empirical studies show that the stock of inventories held tends to rise as a firm's rate of production and sales rises. But while the size of inventories is related to level of sales, the *change* in inventories (which is a form of investment) is related to the *change* in the level of sales.

A firm may wish to hold inventories of 10 percent of its sales: if sales are $100,000, it will wish to hold inventories of $10,000; if its sales increase to $110,000, it will want to hold inventories of $11,000. When a firm with $10,000 in inventories wishes to increase its inventories by 10 percent, it will require an additional $1,000 in inventories. *Over the period during which the stock is being increased,* there will be a total of $1,000 new inventory investment.

The higher the level of production and sales, the larger the desired stock of inventories. Changes in the rate of production and sales cause temporary bouts of investment (or disinvestment) in inventories.

When a firm has money tied up in inventories, that money cannot be doing something else. The rate of interest represents the cost of borrowing this money, and obviously the higher is the rate of interest, the higher will be the cost of holding an inventory of a given size. Suppose a firm holds the level of inventories it desires, given its level of sales and the cost of holding inventories. Now suppose the rate of interest rises from 8 percent to 18 percent. As it does, the cost of holding inventories rises and, *ceteris paribus*, firms would be expected to hold smaller inventories. Producers can do this by letting their rate of output fall temporarily below their rate of sales. Alternatively, a fall in interest rates makes it less costly to have funds invested in inventories, and then firms are expected to let inventories expand somewhat.

By causing firms to change the level of inventories that they desire to hold, a change in the rate of interest can lead to a flurry of investment or disinvestment as firms adjust their inventory levels to the new levels they plan to hold.

The higher the rate of interest, the lower the desired stock of inventories. Thus changes in the rate of interest cause temporary bouts of investment (or disinvestment) in inventories.

INVESTMENT IN RESIDENTIAL CONSTRUCTION

In recent years the value of expenditures on residential structures has varied between one-fifth and one-third of all gross private investment in the United States and has accounted for 4 to 5 percent of GNP. Figure 30-5 shows the course of residential construction in the United States since 1929. Notice the substantial fluctuations from year to year. Because expenditures for housing construction are both large and variable, they exert a major impact on the economy.

To what does residential construction respond? Many of the influences on residential construction are noneconomic, dependent on demographic or cultural considerations such as new family formation. A rapidly expanding population will require more new construction than will a static population. Changes in marriage age also affect the demand for housing: if marriages are postponed, as during World War II, so too is family formation—and the demand for new housing units declines. But while demographic and cultural considerations affect people's hopes for

The Cost of Buying a House on Time

Few people who buy a house can pay cash, and most purchases are financed by borrowing money on a *mortgage*. A mortgage is a loan to the house purchaser (sometimes of as much as 85 or 90 percent of the purchase price, but 60 to 75 percent is common). In return, the borrower promises to make fixed monthly payments that cover interest on the money borrowed and to repay the amount borrowed over some agreed period, commonly 20 years. (The monthly payments often include an amount to cover insurance and taxes, but this is ignored in what follows.) The house itself acts as security for the loan. Loans of this type are said to be *amortized*, which means that fixed payments cover the interest on the principal outstanding *and* repay the principal over a stated period.

Because the loan stretches over a long period, a great deal of the total amount paid by the borrower is interest on the outstanding loan. For example, on a 20-year mortgage for $10,000 at a nominal annual interest rate of 8 percent per year (a monthly rate of 8/12 of 1 percent), a total of $20,075 would be paid in 240 monthly installments of $83.65 each. This is $10,000 to repay the principal of the loan and $10,075 of interest. At a 12 percent nominal annual rate (a monthly rate of 1 percent) the total payments would be $26,426, making $16,426 total interest as well as $10,000 to repay the principal.

Because interest is such a large part of the total payments on a mortgage, small changes in the rate of interest cause relatively large changes in the annual payments. For instance, a rise in the rate of interest from 8 percent to 10 percent increases the monthly payments on a 20-year mortgage by nearly 15.4 percent (from $8.37 to $9.66 per thousand dollars borrowed).

The interest on a mortgage is calculated on the amount of the loan still outstanding. After each payment the amount outstanding is reduced so that, with fixed annual payments, most of the total amount paid goes to paying interest in the early years and to repaying principal in later years. It follows that the purchaser's equity in the house builds up slowly at first, then more and more rapidly as the terminal date approaches.

Note in the table that when half the life of the mortgage has passed, only about a quarter of the principal has been repaid. In the first year of the mortgage, $993 goes as interest and only $165 to reduce the principal on the loan. In the last year, only $60 is interest and $1,098 goes to repay the principal.

Breakdown of payments in selected years on a 20-year mortgage for $10,000 at 10 percent (all figures to the nearest dollar)

Year	Payments made over the year	Interest paid over the year	Principal (amount of loan) repaid over the year	Equity (amount of loans repaid over all previous years)
1	$1,158	$993	$ 165	$ 165
2	1,158	975	183	349
5	1,158	912	246	1,020
10	1,158	753	405	2,698
15	1,158	491	667	5,458
19	1,158	164	994	8,902
20	1,158	60	1,098	10,000

FIGURE 30-5
Components of Real Gross Private Domestic Investment, 1929–1979

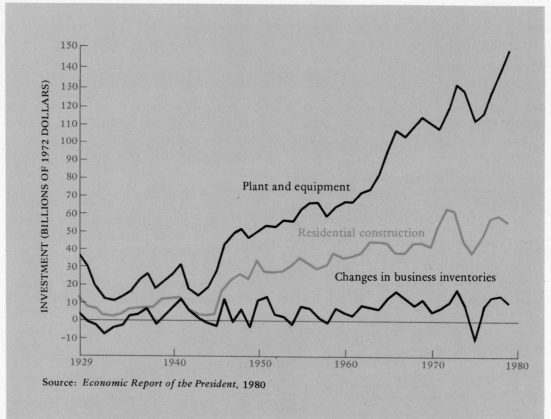

Source: *Economic Report of the President,* 1980

Each of the components shows enough variation to be a significant source of business fluctuations. Each component shows its own pattern of year-to-year fluc-tuations. Sometimes one, sometimes another, and sometimes all together account for the sharp changes in total investment shown in Figure 30-4.

housing, households must not only want to buy houses, they must be able to do so. Thus periods of high employment and high average family earnings tend to lead to increases in house build-ing, and unemployment and falling earnings to decreases in such building.

The vast majority of houses are purchased with money borrowed on mortgages that run 20, 30, or even 40 years. Interest on the borrowed money typically accounts for about one-half of the purchaser's annual mortgage payments (the other half being repayment of principal). A rise in the rate of interest charged on mortgages from 10 percent to 16 percent can lead to an increase of more than 40 percent in the monthly payment necessary to buy a given house. It is for this reason that sharp variations in interest rates exert a substantial effect on the demand for hous-ing.

Expenditures for residential construction tend to vary directly with changes in average income and inversely with interest rates.

INVESTMENT IN PLANT AND EQUIPMENT

Investment in plant and equipment is the largest component of domestic investment. Why does a business firm decide to build a new factory? Why does a firm decide to engage in major modernization this year rather than next?

Successful firms invest in plant and equipment not only because they like being surrounded by impressive pieces of hardware but because they want to sell at a profit the goods that the equipment can produce. But profitability—and thus the level of investment in plant and equipment—depends on a variety of economic variables. The rate of innovation is one. New innovations typically require new plant and equipment, and in some instances (e.g., the basic changes that followed the introduction of railroads) innovation brings fundamental changes in the nature of the capital stock and leads to vast amounts of new investment.

Expectations also play a role. The decision to invest *now* is to a great extent an act of faith in the future. If businesses guess wrong, the penalties can be great. Business managers do their best to predict the extent of their firms' markets, but many things can influence those markets other than the tastes of households. A new Congress may adopt different taxing and spending policies that affect a business profoundly. An Arab oil embargo can shift the demand for large and small cars, for coal, for skis, for stay-at-home recreational activities, and for a host of other goods and services. Particularly in the short run, expectations can have a decisive influence on the timing of business investments. Sometimes a form of group psychology takes over and general optimism (or pessimism) can lead to a burst of investment spending (or cutbacks in investment). If such expectations prove false, corrective adjustments will occur later; meanwhile, volatile investment behavior will be observed.

Some economists, and many business analysts, lay great stress on the effect of profits on investment. It is assumed that business firms are not able (or do not wish) to borrow all the funds they require, but that they may use their own funds to finance their investment projects. Profits thus become a key explanatory factor in investment because retained profits provide an important source of investable funds.

Many economists believe that the two major influences on the level of plant and equipment investment are the rate of interest and *changes* in the level of national income.

Plant and Equipment Investment and the Rate of Interest

It will pay a business firm to borrow money to finance its investment projects as long as the return on the investment (including an allowance for the riskiness of the project) exceeds the rate of interest. Thus a particular investment in a new machine becomes more attractive (other things being equal) the lower the rate of interest. To go from this conclusion to a prediction about how actual aggregate investment in plant and equipment responds to changes in the interest rate is more complicated.

The aggregate quantity of a society's capital goods is called its capital stock. Changes in the potential profitability of plant and equipment will lead to desired changes in capital stock, but capital goods cannot be produced (or worn out) overnight. Investment concerns actual expenditures for investment goods, not the desired level of the stock of capital. A desired increase in capital goods generates investment when the capital goods are actually produced. Suppose, for example, that in response to a fall in interest rates there is an increase of $10 billion in the desired capital stock. If the capital stock is raised by $10 billion within a year, net investment will rise to $10 billion for a year and then fall to zero. In this case a fall in the interest rate will lead only to a one-year increase in the amount of investment.

But the timing of investment will depend on how fast the stock of capital can be built up to its new desired level. The actual volume of investment in plant and equipment that takes place each year is limited by the capacities of the capital-goods and the construction industries.

Assume that in response to a fall in interest rates the firms in the economy decide that they want a total of 30,000 newly built and equipped factories in operation next year, but that factories can only be built and equipped at the rate of

10,000 a year. It will take three years before the desired addition to the capital stock is achieved. If, at the end of the first year, a rise in the rate of interest decreases the desired overall addition to the capital stock from 30,000 to 20,000 factories, this new change will have no effect on investment in year 2 because the capital-goods industries would still have to work to capacity to fill back orders.

Thus, while we expect the capital stock (and thus investment) to be related to long-term changes in the level of interest rates, we cannot make precise predictions about the relationship of investment in a particular year in response to a change in the interest rate.

Substantial variations in the interest rate can have a major effect on the length of the backlog of orders for capital equipment rather than on the level of investment in a particular year.

Changes in National Income

The need for plant and equipment is obviously influenced by the demand for the goods the plant and equipment are designed to produce. If there is a rise in demand that is expected to persist and that cannot be met by increasing production with existing industrial capacity, then new plant and equipment will be needed. The production of such plant and equipment is investment. Once the new plants have been built and put into operation, however, the rate of new investment will fall. This further illustrates an important characteristic of investment already encountered in the case of inventories: if the desired stock of capital goods increases, there will be an investment boom while the new capital is being produced. But if nothing else changes, and even though business conditions continue to look rosy enough to justify the increased stock of capital, investment in new plant and equipment will cease once the larger capital stock is achieved. This aspect of investment leads to the accelerator theory of investment, which requires a close look.

THE ACCELERATOR THEORY OF INVESTMENT

Because changes in the desired stock of capital goods lead to spurts in investment activity, the pattern of investment from year to year may prove quite changeable. According to the accelerator theory (usually called the **accelerator**), investment is related to the rate of change of national income. When income is increasing, it is necessary to invest in order to increase the capacity to produce consumption goods; when income is falling, it may not even be necessary to replace old capital as it wears out, let alone to invest in new capital.

The main insight which the accelerator theory provides is the emphasis on the role of net investment as a phenomenon of *disequilibrium* — something that occurs when the stock of capital goods differs from what firms and households would like it to be. Net investment will not occur when the desired quantities of inventories, buildings, or equipment has been achieved. Anything that changes the desired quantities can generate investment. The accelerator focuses on one such source of change, changing national income. This gives the accelerator its particular importance in connection with *fluctuations* in national income. As we shall see, it can itself contribute to those fluctuations.

How the Accelerator Works: A Numerical Example

To see how the theory works, it is convenient to make the simplifying assumption that there is a particular capital stock needed to produce a given level of an industry's output. (The ratio of the value of capital to the annual value of output is called the **capital-output ratio.**) Given this assumption, suppose that the industry is producing at capacity and the demand for its product increases. If the industry is to produce the higher level of output, its capital stock must increase. This necessitates new investment.

Table 30-2 provides a simple numerical ex-

TABLE 30-2
An Illustration of the Accelerator Theory of Investment

(1) Year	(2) Annual sales	(3) Change in sales	(4) Required stock of capital, assuming a capital-output ratio of 5/1	(5) Net investment: increase in required capital stock
1	$10	$0	$ 50	$ 0
2	10	0	50	0
3	11	1	55	5
4	13	2	65	10
5	16	3	80	15
6	19	3	95	15
7	22	3	110	15
8	24	2	120	10
9	25	1	125	5
10	25	0	125	0

With a fixed capital-output ratio, net investment occurs only when it is necessary to increase the stock of capital in order to change output. Assume that it takes $5 of capital to produce $1 of output per year. In years 1 and 2, there is no need for investment. In year 3, a rise in sales of $1 requires investment of $5 to provide the needed capital stock. In year 4, a further rise of $2 in sales requires an additional investment of $10 to provide the needed capital stock. As columns (3) and (5) show, the amount of net investment is proportional to the *change* in sales. When the increase in sales tapers off in years 7–9, investment declines. When, in year 10, sales no longer increase, net investment falls to zero because the capital stock of year 9 is adequate to provide output for year 10's sales.

ample of the accelerator that, worked through step by step, leads to three conclusions:

1. Rising rather than high levels of sales are needed to call forth net investment.
2. For net investment to remain constant, sales must rise by a constant amount per year.
3. The amount of net investment will be a multiple of the increase in sales because the capital-output ratio is greater than one.[3]

The data in Table 30-2 are for a single industry, but if many industries behave in this way, one would expect aggregate net investment to bear a similar relation to changes in national income. This is what the accelerator theory predicts. [37]

[3] In the example in the table the capital-output ratio is 5. Why should anyone spend $5 on capital stock to get $1 of output? It is not unreasonable to spend $5 to purchase a machine that produces only $1 of output *per year*, provided that the machine will last enough years to repay the $5 plus a reasonable return on this investment.

The accelerator theory says nothing directly about replacement investment, but it does have implications for such investment. When sales are constant (no net investment required), replacement investment will be required to maintain the capital stock at the desired level. When sales are increasing from a position of full capacity, both net investment and replacement investment will be required. When sales are falling so that the desired capital stock is below the actual capital stock, not only will net investment be zero but there will be a tendency to postpone replacement investment as well until the capital stock falls to the desired levels.

Limitations of the Accelerator

Taken literally, the accelerator posits a mechanical and rigid response of investment to changes in sales (and thus, aggregatively, to changes in national income). It does this by assuming a proportional relationship between changes in income and the size of the desired capital stock, and by assuming a fixed capital-output ratio. Each assumption is invalid to some degree.

Changes in sales that are thought to be temporary in their effect on demand will not necessarily lead to new investment. It is usually possible to increase the level of output for a given capital stock by working overtime or extra shifts. While this would be more expensive per unit of output in the long run, it will usually be preferable to making investments in new plant and equipment that would lie idle after a temporary spurt of demand had subsided. Thus expectations about what is the required capital stock may lead to a much less mechanistic response of investment to income than the accelerator suggests.

A further limitation of the accelerator theory is that it takes a very limited view of what constitutes investment. The fixed capital-output ratio emphasizes investment in what economists call **capital widening,** the investment in additional capacity that uses the same ratio of capital to labor as existing capacity. It does not explain **capital deepening,** which is the kind of increase in the amount of capital per unit of labor expected in response to a fall in the rate of interest. Neither does the theory say anything about investments brought about as a result of new processes or new products. Furthermore, it does not allow for the fact that investment in any period is likely to be limited by the capacity of the capital-goods industry.

For these and other reasons, the accelerator does not by itself give anything like a complete explanation of variations in investment in plant and equipment, and it should not be surprising that a simple accelerator theory provides a relatively poor overall explanation of changes in investment. Yet accelerator-like influences do exist, and they play a role in the cyclical variability of investment.

Government and Cyclical Fluctuations

Governments frequently alter their revenues and expenditures in an intentional response to cyclical swings in the economy. In the next chapter we shall consider such use of government expenditure and tax policies for the purpose of stabilizing the economy. In Chapter 35 we shall look at use of monetary policy for the same purpose. Such policies play important roles in the actual pattern of cyclical fluctuations observed.

Government expenditures and taxes are also altered for many other reasons, since public officials often respond to those groups in our society that look to governments to provide goods, services, and wealth transfers to them. When this happens changes in government expenditures can become the initiating cause of cyclical fluctuations.

GOVERNMENT EXPENDITURES ON GOODS AND SERVICES

Look again at Figure 30-2. It is obvious that every war in this century has been accompanied by a rapid expansion of economic activity. Wars result in an enormous increase in federal government expenditures as people and materials are shifted from civilian to military uses. This shift is usually reversed in the postwar period. For example, federal government purchases of goods and services (measured in constant dollars at 1972 prices) rose from $26 billion in 1940 to $268 billion in 1944 and then fell to $36 billion by 1947. Changes in government purchases of goods and services during 1941–1946 were the principal cause of changes in GNP during that period.

Such expenditures played a similar though less dramatic role during the Vietnam War, rising from $100 billion in 1965 to $128 billion in 1968 and falling back to roughly $100 billion by the end of 1972. The extra expenditures, on top of a full-employment civilian economy, opened up a large inflationary gap and were a major cause of the subsequent inflation.

Aside from periods of major wars, American government expenditures have not often actually been destabilizing. For peacetime periods before 1940, government expenditures were both small and relatively stable. Since 1972 they have been large and stable, at about $100 billion per year in constant dollars at 1972 prices. Thus, whatever their potential for being a major source of cyclical instability, they have not proven to be such except during wars. Indeed, many economists believe that the growth in the size of the government sector in the last half century has been an important source of added stability in the economy, since public expenditures tend to be less volatile than private ones, thus tending to stabilize the economy.

GOVERNMENT TRANSFER PAYMENTS

Large as the government's purchases of goods and services are, its transfer payments to individuals are larger yet, amounting to roughly one-eighth of personal income. Sharp fluctuations in such transfer payments too could theoretically be a highly destabilizing factor via their effects on personal consumption and investment. Here the empirical evidence suggests that expenditures of these kinds tend to be sharply *counter-cyclical,* rising relative to national income when national income is falling. The reason is clear: many of these expenditures, such as those for unemployment insurance and welfare, rise when unemployment rises and fall when unemployment declines.

Elements of a Theory of Fluctuations

We have seen that the components of aggregate demand such as consumption and investment may be influenced by factors such as expectations, interest rates, and government policies. If any of these factors change, investment or consumption may change, and if investment or consumption change, national income will change as well. This might be the end of the story if we were trying to explain occasional erratic changes in national income. Most economic time series, however, display more or less continuous upswings and downswings. The evidence suggests that, whatever the initiating cause of a distur-

bance, the movements of the economy, up or down, tend to acquire a momentum of their own. After a while such cumulative movements appear to run their course and generate the seeds of their own reversal. Not all cycles are alike in duration or intensity, but each appears to have tendencies toward cumulative movements that eventually reverse themselves. This was true long before governments attempted to intervene and stabilize the economy, and it is true still. In the following discussion we consider the cyclical tendencies in an economy where government is not actively intervening.

THE TERMINOLOGY OF BUSINESS FLUCTUATIONS

Although recurrent fluctuations in economic activity are neither smooth nor regular, a vocabulary has developed to denote their different stages. Figure 30-6 shows a stylized cycle that will serve to illustrate some terms.

Trough. The trough is, simply, the bottom. If the trough is sufficiently severe, it may be called a **depression.** A trough is characterized by unemployment of labor and a level of consumer demand that is low in relation to the capacity of industry to produce goods for consumption. There is thus a substantial amount of unused industrial capacity. Business profits will be low, and in many individual cases they will be negative. Confidence in the future will be lacking and, as a result, firms will be unwilling to take risks in making new investments. Banks and other financial institutions will have surplus cash that no one whom they consider to be a reasonable credit risk wishes to borrow.

Expansion or recovery. When something sets off a recovery, the lower turning point of the cycle has been reached. The symptoms of an expansion are many: worn-out machinery will be replaced; employment, income, and consumer spending all begin to rise; expectations become more favorable as a result of increases in production, sales, and profits. Investments that once seemed risky may now be undertaken as the

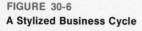

FIGURE 30-6
A Stylized Business Cycle

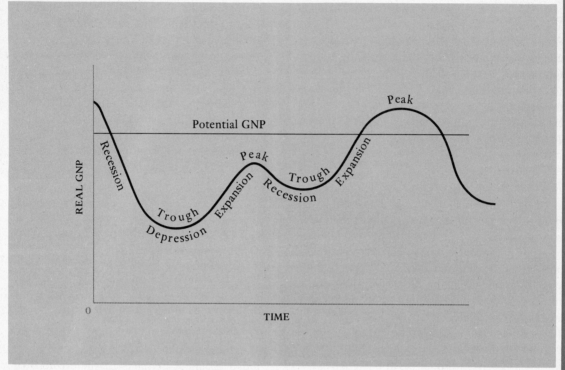

While the phases of business fluctuations are described by a series of commonly used terms, no two cycles are the same. Starting from a lower turning point, or trough, a cycle goes through a phase of expansion, reaches an upper turning point, or peak, and then enters a period of recession. Cycles differ from one another in the severity of their troughs and peaks and in the speed with which one phase follows another. Severe troughs are called depressions. Peaks are called inflations when a rapidly rising price level is a dominant symptom.

climate of business opinion begins to change from pessimism to optimism. As demand expands, production will be expanded with relative ease merely by reemploying the existing unused capacity and unemployed labor.

Peak. The peak is the **upper turning point.** At the peak there is a high degree of utilization of existing capacity, labor shortages begin to occur, particularly in certain key skill categories, and shortages of certain key raw materials develop. Bottlenecks appear with increasing frequency. It now becomes difficult to increase output because the supply of unused resources is rapidly disap-

pearing; output can be raised further only by means of investment that increases capacity. Because of such investment expenditure, investment funds will be in short supply. Because such investment takes time, further rises in demand are now met more by increases in prices than by increases in production. As shortages develop in more and more markets, a situation of general excess demand for factors develops. Costs rise but prices rise also, and business remains generally very profitable.

Losses are infrequent because a money profit can be earned merely by holding on to goods whose prices are rising and selling them later at higher prices. Expectations of the future are favorable, and more investment may be made than is justified on the basis of current levels of prices and sales alone.

Recession. Beyond the upper turning point, the economy turns downward. When the contraction is sustained, it is called a **recession.** Suppose that for some reason demand falls off and as a result production and employment fall. As employment falls, so do households' incomes; falling income causes demand to fall further, and more and more firms get into difficulties. Prices and profits fall. New investments that looked profitable on the expectation of continuously rising demand and prices suddenly appear unprofitable; investment is reduced to a low level, and it may not even be worth replacing capital goods as they wear out because unused capacity is increasing steadily.

CUMULATIVE MOVEMENTS AND TURNING POINTS

Many events occur in the economy at once, and all may contribute to rises and falls in national income. Our purpose at the moment is to show how it is that cumulative self-reinforcing and self-reversing movements can occur. This may be done concisely by putting together two now-familiar concepts—the multiplier and the accelerator. A simple theory emerges that, while not a complete theory of cyclical fluctuations, emphasizes many important interactions.

The Interaction of the Multiplier and the Accelerator

The combination of the multiplier and the accelerator can cause upward or downward movements in the economy to be cumulative. Imagine that the economy is settled into a depression with heavy unemployment and that there then occurs a revival of investment demand. Orders are placed for new plant and equipment, and this creates new employment in the capital-goods industries. The newly employed workers spend most of their earnings; this creates new demand for the consumer goods that they buy. A multiplier process is now set up with new employment and incomes created in the consumer goods industries.

The spending of the newly created incomes in turn causes further increases in demand. At some stage the increased demand for consumer goods will create, through the accelerator process, an increased demand for capital goods. Once existing equipment is fully employed in any industry, extra output will require new capital equipment—and the accelerator theory takes over as the major determinant of investment expenditure. Such investment will increase or at least maintain demand in the capital-goods sector of the economy. So the process goes on, the multiplier-accelerator mechanism continuing to produce a rapid rate of expansion in the economy.

The Upper Turning Point

A very rapid expansion can continue for some time, but it cannot go on forever because eventually the economy will run into bottlenecks (or ceilings) in terms of some resources. For example, investment funds may become scarce, and as a result interest rates will rise. Firms now find new investments more expensive than anticipated, and thus some will be unprofitable to make. Or suppose that what limits the expansion is exhaustion of the reservoir of unemployed labor. Once this has happened, further expansion of the economy requires growth of the labor force or growth of labor productivity. The full-employment ceiling guarantees that any sustained rapid growth rate of real income and employment will eventually be slowed. At this point the accelerator again comes into play. A slowing down in the rate of increase of production leads to a decrease in the investment required in new plant and equipment. This causes a fall in employment in the capital-goods industries and, through the multiplier, a fall in consumer demand. Once consumer demand begins to fall, investment in plant and equipment will be reduced to a low level because firms will already have more productive capacity than they can use. Unemployment begins to mount, and the upper turning point has been passed.

The Lower Turning Point

A rapid contraction, too, is eventually brought to an end. Consider the worst sort of depression you can imagine, one in which every postponable expenditure of households, firms, or governments is postponed. Even then aggregate demand will not fall to zero. For there is a minimum level of consumption expenditure that households will be obliged to make to sustain life. Even if aggregate demand consisted only of consumption, it would not fall to zero because households can and will use up savings, or go into debt, to buy the necessities of life. Moreover, transfer payments to households in the form of unemployment compensation and welfare payments will increase and will provide the funds to support consumption expenditures.

Nor is consumption the only element of aggregate demand. Government expenditure will not fall to zero. Civil service salaries and national defense expenditures will continue. Moreover, the political pressure for governments to increase their expenditures will surely grow and may be effective. Even business investment, in many ways the most easily postponed component of aggregate demand, will not fall to zero. In our most severe depression, between 1930 and 1932, investment fell drastically, but at the depth of the Depression it was still nearly $1 billion. In the industries providing food, basic clothing, and shelter, demand may remain fairly high in spite of quite large reductions in national income. These industries will certainly be carrying out some investment to replace equipment as it wears out, and they may even undertake some net investment.

Taken together, the minimum levels of consumption, investment, and government expenditure will assure a minimum equilibrium level of national income that, although well below the full-employment level, will not be zero. There is a floor! (This may be small comfort, however; it is possible for the economy to settle into a period of heavy unemployment for a long time, and if it does, many will suffer great hardship.)

Sooner or later, though, an upturn will begin. If nothing else causes an expansion of business activity, there will eventually be a revival of replacement investment because as existing capital wears out the capital stock will eventually fall below the level required to produce current output. At this stage new machines will be bought to replace those that are worn out.

The rise in the level of activity in the capital-goods industries will cause, by way of the multiplier, a further rise in income. The economy has turned the corner. An expansion, once started, will trigger the sort of cumulative upward movement already discussed.

THE VARIETY OF CYCLICAL FLUCTUATIONS

The previous section suggests why an economy that is subjected to periodic external shocks will tend to generate a continuously changing pattern of fluctuations, as first cumulative and then self-reversing forces come into play. But no two cycles are the same. In some the recession phase is short; in others a full-scale period of stagnation sets in. In some cycles the peak phase develops into a severe inflation; in others the pressure of excess demand is hardly felt and a new recession sets in before the economy has fully recovered from the last trough. Some cycles are of long duration, some are very short.

Our discussion of cumulative movements, floors and ceilings, and turning points only hints at what happened in actual cyclical movements; this is as far as the theory can be carried without the use of complex dynamic models. But this type of theory can fit either a very modest fluctuation such as the recession of 1957–1958, a bigger fluctuation such as that of 1973–1975, or the massive disaster that was the 1930s. Cycles differ from one another in terms of the origin and the magnitude of the initiating shock. Sometimes, but not always, economists can identify the initiating causes. (The causes of the Great Depression remain shrouded in controversy despite nearly four decades of study.) Inventories are believed by many economists, and housing by some, to lead to their own special patterns of fluctuation. Presidents, bent on reelection for themselves and their parties, may affect the course of a cycle by timing expenditures or tax cuts in order to create a favorable economic climate at election time.

Inventory Cycles

There are, as we have seen, good reasons to suppose that the required size of inventories is related to the level of firms' sales, and sales are related to the level of national income. If firms maintain anything like a rigid inventory-to-sales ratio, this will cause an accelerator-like linkage between investment in inventories and *changes* in national income.

Look back at the fluctuating investment in business inventories shown in Figure 30-5. Many observers believe that these sharp and somewhat periodic fluctuations lead to an "inventory cycle" of roughly 40 months' average duration.

A Building Cycle?

Economists have noted some long-run, wavelike movements of roughly 20 years' duration in the statistics for expenditures on residential construction. These are sometimes referred to as "building cycles." Some economists suggest an accelerator-like explanation that runs from external events to demographic changes, to changes in the demand for housing and other buildings, and thence to changes in construction activity.

A major war, by taking males away from home, tends to retard family formation and thereby tends to depress the demand for private housing. After the conclusion of the war there is typically a great increase in marriages and household formation, a large increase in the demand for housing, and a boom in the construction industry. Typically, too, there are the postponed babies and an increase in the birth rate.

Depending on the capacity of the building industry, the boom may last many years before the desired increases in the stock of buildings of various kinds are achieved, but eventually the demand will taper off and the construction boom will have ended. Then, approximately 20 years after the end of the war that triggered the boom, there is likely to be a further boom in the number of marriages and births as the new generation starts its process of family formation. Wars are not the only source of such population-induced cycles; a severe depression will lead to a similar postponement of family formation.

The evidence concerning construction expenditures over the past century is thought by many economists to provide support for the theory just outlined, a theory very much like the accelerator, though with changes in demographic factors (rather than changes in income) providing the impetus.

FLUCTUATIONS: A CONSENSUS VIEW?

Economists once argued long and bitterly about which was the best explanation of the recurrent cyclical behavior of the economy. Today most agree that there need not be one cause or one class of causes for business cycles. In an economy that has tendencies for both cumulative and self-reversing behavior, any sort of large shock, whether from without or within the system, can initiate a cyclical swing. Wars are important; so, too, are major technical inventions. A major automobile strike could curtail production and bring on a recession. A sharp increase in interest rates and a general tightening of credit can cause a sharp decrease in investment. Expectations can be changed by a political campaign or a development in another part of the world. The list of possible initial impulses, autonomous or induced, is long. It is probably true that the characteristic cyclical pattern includes many outside shocks that initiate, sometimes reinforce, and sometimes dampen the cumulative tendencies that exist within the economy.

Cycles differ also in terms of their internal structure. In some, full employment of labor may be the bottleneck that determines the ceiling. In others, high interest rates and shortages of funds for business expansion may nip an expansion and turn it into a recession while unemployment of labor is still an acute problem. These and other differences occupy the attention of economists concerned with understanding the cyclical economy.

An important part of controlling cycles is to anticipate correctly when a turning point is near. Control requires more than understanding; it requires countercyclical policies. Into this picture we must now bring the central authorities, who seek to influence the pattern of business fluctuations. The federal government tries both to prevent extremes of expansion and contraction from developing and to mitigate the most undesirable effects of those peaks and troughs that do occur.

Summary

1. Short-term fluctuations in GNP are usually, though not always, the result of variations in aggregate demand. Overall, these fluctuations show a fairly clear pattern that is sometimes described as cyclical. In spite of the overall pattern, the evidence is that the cycles are irregular in amplitude, in timing, in duration, and in the way they affect particular industries and sectors of the economy.

2. An important source of fluctuations is shifts in the consumption function due to changes in income distribution, availability of credit, stocks of durable goods, and expectations about the future course of the economy.

3. Even if the relation of consumption to disposable income does not change, the government can shift the consumption function related to GNP by changing personal tax rates. An increase in personal taxes lowers disposable income relative to GNP and can decrease the level of consumption at every level of GNP.

4. Investment is large enough and volatile enough to cause fluctuations in aggregate demand. Most economists regard shifts in investment as a major cause of business fluctuations. Saying that, however, does not commit one to a particular theory of *why* aggregate demand and investment fluctuate. The three principal components of private investment are changes in business inventories, residential construction, and investment in plant and equipment. Each responds to somewhat different influences.

5. Changes in business inventories, the smallest of the three major components of investment expenditure, often account for an important fraction of the year-to-year changes in the level of investment. They are thought to respond both to changes in the level of production and sales and to the rate of interest.

6. Residential construction, a major component of investment, shows a wavelike motion of its own. House building responds to economic (as well as noneconomic) influences, varying directly with the level of national income and inversely with the rate of interest. The rate of interest is important because interest payments are a large fraction of the mortgage payments that greatly affect a household's ability to purchase a house.

7. Investment in plant and equipment depends on a number of variables—among them innovation, changes in the level of national income, expectations about the future, the level of profits, and the rate of interest.

8. The accelerator theory relates net investment to changes in the level of national income on the assumption of a fixed capital-output ratio. Its central prediction is that rising income is required to maintain a positive level of investment. Its central insight is that net investment is

a disequilibrium phenomenon that occurs when the capital stock is different from the desired capital stock.

9. The accelerator does not provide a complete theory of investment. It neglects capital deepening and the influence of variables other than the rate of change of national income. Moreover, the actual world is not one with a fixed capital-output ratio. Nevertheless, an accelerator-like mechanism may help explain some of the fluctuations in total investment, in inventory changes, and in construction activity.

10. Government expenditure, both on goods and services and on transfer payments, can have a large effect on aggregate demand and thus can affect cyclical fluctuations. Government purchases of goods and services tend to be dramatically destabilizing during wartime but relatively stable during peacetime. Transfer payments tend to be countercyclical.

11. Economists break down a stylized cycle into four phases — trough, expansion, peak, and recession — which have certain characteristic features, although no two real-world cycles are exactly the same.

12. The elements of a theory of fluctuations are summarized in terms of a set of tendencies for *cumulative movements* and a set of ceilings or floors that lead to *turning points*. A theory that predicts cumulative but eventually reversing movements is a theory of fluctuations. Such a theory explains some characteristics of all cycles, but it fails to explain the great variety among cycles, which differ from one another in the nature of the initiating shock, in their internal structure, and, as a consequence, in their duration and amplitude.

Topics for Review

Business cycles and business fluctuations
Causes of shifts in the consumption function
Components of investment
The accelerator

Phases of the cycle
Cumulative upward and downward movements in economic activity
The interaction of the multiplier and the accelerator
Different kinds of cycles

Discussion Questions

1. "In most years changes in government expenditure are larger than changes in inventories, and consumption is larger than investment in both plant and equipment and housing combined. Therefore, the theorists who say that investment is the main culprit in causing cycles are neglecting the facts of our economy." Reply to this charge.

2. How and in what direction might each of the following shift the function relating consumption expenditure to disposable income?
   a. introduction of free medical care
   b. a change in attitudes so that we become a nation of conspicuous conservers rather than conspicuous consumers, taking pride in how little we eat or spend for housing, clothing, and so on
   c. increases in income taxes
   d. news that due to medical advances everyone can count on more years of retirement than ever before
   e. a spreading belief that all-out nuclear war is likely within the next ten years
   f. sharp increases in the down payments required on durable goods

3. Suppose the government wished to reduce private investment in order to reduce an inflationary gap. What policies might it adopt? If it wished to do so in such a way as to have a major effect on residential housing and a minor effect on plant and equipment expenditures, which measures might it use?

4. What effect on total investment — and on which category of investment — would you predict as a result of each of the following?
   a. widespread endorsement of ZPG (zero population growth) by young couples
   b. a sharp increase in the frequency and duration of strikes in the transportation industries
   c. forecasts of record levels of real national income over the next five years
   d. tax reform that eliminated deductions for property taxes in computing taxable personal income

5. Recently, when interest rates rose sharply, home construction fell dramatically but sales of mobile homes increased. How does the rise in the sale of mobile

homes relate to the notion that investment responds to the rate of interest?

6. Empirical studies show that as the volume of a firm's sales increases, the size of its inventories of raw materials tends to increase in proportion. It is common for business firms to speak of such inventories in terms of "a 20-day supply of coal" rather than "52,000 tons of coal" or "$280,000 worth of coal." Why should relative size be more important than absolute quantity or dollar value?

7. Which "cause" of business investment is being relied on in each of the following quotes?

   a. An aluminum industry spokesman, justifying a 50¢ a pound increase in aluminum prices: "We must have it to build the new capacity we need."

   b. "The two major classes of consumer expenditures most closely related to the onset of a recession are housing and auto expenditures. Buying attitudes toward both markets have eroded seriously during the past year."

   c. Bethlehem Steel, in a newspaper ad: "We need lower taxes not cheaper money or government deficits to help lower barriers to capital formation."

   d. "The Carter administration is using a credit crunch to bring on a recession and reduce inflation."

8. Since different series behave differently, does it make sense to talk about a business cycle? Predict the comparative behavior of the following pairs of series in relation to fluctuating changes in GNP:

   a. purchases of food, purchases of consumer durables

   b. tax receipts, bankruptcies

   c. unemployment, birth rates

   d. employment in New York, employment in Michigan

   Check your predictions against the facts for the last two decades.

Fiscal Policy

Fiscal policy involves using government expenditure and tax policy to shift the aggregate demand and aggregate expenditure functions toward desired positions. Since government spending increases aggregate expenditure and taxation decreases it, the *directions* of the required shifts are easily established. But, as we shall see, the *timing* and the *magnitude* of changes in tax and expenditure policies pose more difficult issues.

Any policy that attempts to stabilize national income at or near a desired level (usually full-employment national income) is called **stabilization policy.** This chapter deals first with the theory of fiscal policy as a tool of stabilization policy and then with the actual experience of using it.

There is no doubt that the government can exert a major influence on aggregate expenditure and hence on the size of national income. Prime examples occur during major wars when governments engage in massive military spending and abandon fiscal caution. As we noted in Chapter 30, U.S. federal expenditure during World War II (measured in 1972 dollars) rose from $26 billion, or 7.7 percent of GNP, in 1940 to $268 billion, or 47.3 percent of GNP, in 1944. At the same time, the unemployment rate fell from 14.6 to 1.2 percent. Economists agree that the increase in the government's aggregate expenditure caused the fall in unemployment and the associated rise in GNP. Similar experiences occurred during the rearmament of most European countries before, or just following, the outbreak of World War II in 1939.

When used appropriately, fiscal policy can be an important tool for influencing the economy. In the heyday of fiscal policy in the 1940s, 1950s, and 1960s, many economists thought that the economy could be regulated adequately solely by varying the size of the government's taxes and expenditures. That day is now past. Today most economists are aware of the limitations of fiscal policy, and there is much discussion of other tools of stabilization that can complement fiscal policy or possibly even replace it.

The Theory of Fiscal Policy

Not so many years ago people generally accepted, and indeed many still fervently believe, the argument that prudent government should always balance its budget. The argument is based on an analogy with what seems prudent behavior for the individual. It is a foolish individual whose current expenditure consistently exceeds his or her current revenue so that he or she goes steadily further into debt. From this observation it is argued that if avoiding a steadily rising debt is good for the individual, it must also be good for the nation.

But the paradox of thrift, discussed in Chapter 29, suggests that analogy between the government and the household may be misleading. When a government follows a balanced budget policy, as most governments tried to do even during the Great Depression of the 1930s, it must restrict its expenditure during a recession because its tax revenue will necessarily be falling at that time. During a recovery, when its revenue is high and rising, it increases its spending. In other words, it rolls with the economy, raising and lowering its expenditure in step with everyone else.

By the mid 1930s, many economists had concluded that the government, by going along with the crowd, was not making the most of its potential to control the economy in a beneficial manner. Why, they asked, should not the government try to stabilize the economy by doing just the op-

posite of what everyone else was doing—by increasing its demand when private demand was falling and lowering its demand when private demand was rising? This policy would hold aggregate demand constant even though its individual components were fluctuating.

When Milton Friedman said, "We are all Keynesians now," he was referring to (among other things) the general acceptance of the view that the government's budget is much more than just the revenue and expenditure statement of a very large organization. Whether we like it or not, the sheer size of the government's budget inevitably makes it a powerful tool for influencing the economy.

THE BUDGET BALANCE

The **budget balance** refers to the difference between all government revenue and all government expenditures. For this purpose government expenditure includes both purchases of currently produced goods and services and transfer payments. Thus the budget balance is the difference between all the money the government pays out and all the money it takes in as revenue.

There are three possibilities for the relation between these two flows. If current revenue is exactly equal to current expenditure, the government has a **balanced budget**; if revenues exceed expenditures, there is a **budget surplus**; if revenues fall short of expenditures, there is a **budget deficit**.

If the government raises its spending without raising taxes, its extra expenditure may be said to be *deficit financed*. If the extra spending is accompanied by an equal increase in tax revenue, we speak of a *balanced budget change in spending*.

Financial Implications of Budget Deficits and Surpluses

When the government spends more than it raises, where does the money come from? If the government raises more than it spends, where does the money go? The difference between expenditure and current revenue shows up as changes in the level of the government's debt. When expenditures exceed revenues, the balance must be borrowed from someone; when revenues exceed expenditures, the balance pays off some of the loans made in the past.

A deficit requires an increase in borrowing, for which there are two main sources: the central bank and the private sector of the economy—banks and other financial institutions, firms, and households.[1] The government borrows money from these sources by selling treasury bills or bonds to them. A **treasury bill** is a promise to repay a stated amount 90 days from the date of issue. It is sold in return for a smaller amount paid to the government now. The difference between the two sums represents the interest on the loan. A government bond is also a promise to pay a stated sum of money in the future, but in the more distant future than a bill—possibly as much as 20 years from now.

A surplus allows the government to reduce its outstanding debt. Treasury bills and bonds may be redeemed from tax revenue when they fall due rather than from money raised by selling new bills and bonds.

When the government makes new loans from or repays old loans to the private sector, this action merely shifts funds between the two sectors. When the government "borrows" from the central bank, however, the central bank creates new money. Since, unlike the private sector, the central bank can create as much money as it wishes, there is no limit to what the government can "borrow" from the central bank.

FISCAL POLICY WHEN PRIVATE EXPENDITURE FUNCTIONS DO NOT SHIFT

A relatively easy problem faces fiscal policy-makers when private-sector expenditure func-

[1] In the United States the central bank is the Federal Reserve System, which will be described and discussed in Chapter 33.

tions for consumption, investment, and net exports are given and unchanging. What is needed then is a once-and-for-all fiscal change that will remove any existing inflationary or deflationary gap.

Changes in either expenditure or tax rates. The necessary policies were established in Chapter 29: a reduction in tax rates or an increase in government expenditure shifts the aggregate expenditure function upward; an increase in tax rates or a cut in government expenditure will shift the aggregate expenditure function downward.

The key proposition in the theory of fiscal policy follows these results.

Government taxes and expenditure can be used to remove inflationary and deflationary gaps by shifting the aggregate expenditure and aggregate demand functions.

The necessary policies are described and illustrated in Figures 31-1 and 31-2.

Balanced budget changes in expenditure and tax rates. The changes analyzed so far would move government expenditure and tax rates in opposite directions. Another policy available to the government is to make a balanced budget change in both expenditures and taxes.

Consider a balanced budget increase in expenditure. Say the government increases personal income tax rates enough to raise an extra $1 billion that it then spends on purchasing goods and services. Aggregate expenditure will be unaffected by this change only if the $1 billion that the government takes from the private sector would have been spent by the private sector in any case. If this is the case, the government's policy will reduce private expenditure by $1 billion and raise its own expenditure by $1 billion. Aggregate expenditure, and hence national income and employment, will remain unchanged.

But this is not the usual case. When an extra $1 billion in taxes is taken away from households, they usually reduce their spending on

FIGURE 31-1

Policies to Eliminate a Deflationary Gap

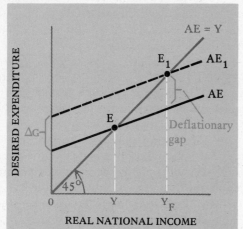

(i) An increase in government expenditure

(ii) A cut in tax rates

FIGURE 31-2

Policies to Eliminate an Inflationary Gap

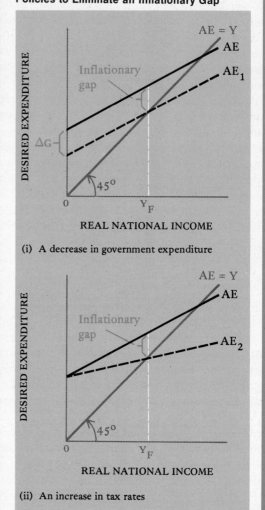

(i) A decrease in government expenditure

(ii) An increase in tax rates

Policies that shift the aggregate expenditure function upward can be used to eliminate deflationary gaps. In each part the original aggregate expenditure function, *AE*, produces the deflationary gap shown by the braces. In (i) an increase in government expenditure, ΔG, shifts *AE* to AE_1. This eliminates the deflationary gap and raises equilibrium income from *Y* to Y_F.

In (ii) a cut in tax rates raises the percentage of national income that goes to disposable income. This causes a corresponding increase in the amount of consumption expenditure associated with each level of national income and thus pivots *AE* to AE_2. That eliminates the deflationary gap and raises equilibrium income from *Y* to Y_F.

Policies that shift the aggregate expenditure function downward can be used to eliminate inflationary gaps. In each part the original aggregate expenditure function, *AE*, produces the inflationary gap shown by the braces. In (i) a cut in government expenditure, ΔG, shifts *AE* to AE_1 and removes the inflationary gap.

In (ii) a rise in tax rates reduces the proportion of national income that goes to disposable income. This causes a corresponding decrease in the amount of consumption expenditure associated with each level of national income and thus pivots *AE* to AE_2. That eliminates the inflationary gap.

domestically produced goods by less than $1 billion. If, say, the marginal propensity to consume out of disposable income is .75, consumption expenditure will fall by only $750 million. If the government spends the entire $1 billion on domestically produced goods, aggregate expenditure will increase by $250 million. In this case the balanced budget increase in government expenditure has an expansionary effect because it shifts the aggregate expenditure function upward.

A balanced budget increase in government expenditure will have an expansionary effect on national income, and a balanced budget decrease will have a contractionary effect.

The **balanced budget multiplier** measures these effects. It is the change in income divided by the balanced budget change in government expenditure that brought it about. Thus, if the extra $1 billion of government spending financed by the extra $1 billion of taxes causes national income to rise by $500 million, the balanced budget multiplier is .5; if income rises by $1 billion it is 1.

In general, the balanced budget multiplier is much lower than the multiplier that relates the change in income to a deficit-financed increase in government expenditure with tax rates constant. For with a deficit-financed increase in expenditure, there is no increase in taxes and hence no consequent decrease in consumption expenditure to offset the increase in government expenditure. With a balanced budget increase in expenditure, however, the offsetting increase in taxes and decrease in consumption does occur.

FISCAL POLICY WHEN PRIVATE EXPENDITURE FUNCTIONS ARE SHIFTING

Thus far we have considered fiscal policy intended to remove an inflationary or deflationary gap when the expenditure function was given (and unchanged by anything other than the fiscal policy itself). But as we saw in Chapter 30, private expenditure functions change continually. Investment expenditure shifts a great deal with business conditions, and consumption functions sometimes shift upward as the public goes on a spending spree or downward as people become cautious and increase their saving. This makes stabilization policy much more difficult than it would be if it were necessary only to identify a stable inflationary or deflationary gap and then take steps to eliminate it once and for all.

What can the government reasonably expect to achieve by using fiscal policy when private expenditure functions are shifting continually? Fiscal policy might be altered often in an effort to stabilize the economy completely, or it might be altered less frequently as a reaction to gaps that appear to be large and persistent.

Fine Tuning

In the heyday of Keynesian fiscal policy in the 1950s and 1960s, many economists advocated the use of fiscal policy to remove even minor fluctuations in national income around its full-employment level. Fiscal policy was to be altered frequently, and by relatively small amounts, to hold national income almost precisely at its full-employment level. This is called **fine tuning** the economy. Fiscal fine tuning was never really possible in the United States because of the length of the so-called **decision lag,** the period of time between perceiving a problem and making the desired reaction to it. Many things contribute to the length of this lag. Experts must study the economy and agree among themselves on what fiscal changes are most desirable. They must persuade the president to call for the action they endorse. The president must then temper their advice with what he believes to be politically possible as well as desirable. Then Congress must be persuaded to enact the necessary legislation. A majority of the legislators must be convinced to vote for the measure, either because it is in the country's interests or because it would be politically advantageous to do so. The time required for this process can be very long.

While the American form of government makes the decision lag rather long, both the British system—used in the rest of the English-speaking world—and the systems used in most European countries make the decision lag very short. In these countries the decision lag is only the time taken for the cabinet (the executive branch) to become informed and to reach a decision. Such decisions are subject to legislative approval, and the government falls when, as rarely happens, it is defeated on a major piece of financial legislation. The government can usually count on effecting tax and expenditure changes once the cabinet has agreed on them.

In countries where political institutions keep the decision lag short, fine tuning has been attempted. Careful assessment of the results shows that their successes, if any, fell far short of what was hoped for them. The basic reason for this lies in the complexity of any economy. Although economists and policymakers can identify broad and persistent trends, they do not have detailed knowledge of what is going on at any moment in time, of all the forces that are operating to cause changes in the immediate future, and of all the short-term effects of small changes in the various government expenditures and tax rates. Because of these imperfections in detailed knowledge, efforts at fine tuning often did as much to encourage minor fluctuations in the economy as to remove them. As a result of these experiences, fine tuning is out of favor at present.

The Removal of Persistent Gaps

In addition to more or less continuous fluctuations, the economy occasionally develops severe and persistent inflationary or deflationary gaps. One such inflationary gap developed in the late 1960s as Vietnam War expenditures accelerated. A deflationary gap developed after 1973 when America, along with many other Western countries, experienced the deepest and longest-lasting depression since the 1930s. Another one opened up in 1980. Gaps such as these persist long enough for their major causes to be studied and

understood and for fiscal remedies to be carefully planned and executed.

Many economists who do not believe in fine tuning believe that fiscal policy can aid in removing persistent gaps.

Tools of Fiscal Policy

The major fiscal tools that governments can use can be classified in many ways; one important classification is based on the division between automatic and discretionary tools.

AUTOMATIC TOOLS OF FISCAL POLICY: BUILT-IN STABILIZERS

As a result of factors discussed in Chapter 30, the aggregate demand and aggregate expenditure functions are continually fluctuating. A stabilization policy for fine tuning the economy would thus require a policy that was itself ever changing. If such a conscious fine tuning policy is impossible, must we throw up our hands and say that nothing can be done through fiscal policy except in the face of major and long-lived inflationary or deflationary gaps?

Fortunately, this is not the case. Much of the adjustment of fiscal policy to an ever-changing economic environment is done automatically by what are called built-in stabilizers. A **built-in stabilizer** is anything that reduces the marginal propensity to spend out of national income and hence reduces the value of the multiplier (see page 531). Built-in stabilizers thus reduce the magnitude of the fluctuations in national income caused by autonomous changes in such expenditures as investment. Furthermore, they do so without the government's having to react consciously to each change in national income as it occurs.

The three principal built-in stabilizers are taxes, government expenditure on goods and services, and government transfer payments.

TABLE 31-1
The Effect of Tax Rates on the Marginal Propensity to Consume Out of National Income

Marginal rate of tax	National income changes by $1,000 million (The *MPC* out of disposable income is .8)				
	Change in national income (millions) ΔY	Change in tax revenue (millions) ΔT	Change in disposable income (millions) ΔY_d	Change in consumption (millions) ΔC	Marginal propensity to consume out of national income $\Delta C/\Delta Y$
.2	$1,000	$200	$800	$640	.65
.4	1,000	400	600	480	.48

The higher is the marginal rate of tax, the lower is the marginal propensity to consume out of national income. When national income changes by $1,000, disposable income changes by $800 when the tax rate is 20 percent and by $600 when the tax rate is 40 percent. Although the *MPC* out of disposable income is the same in both examples, consumption changes by $640 in the first case and by only $480 in the second. These calculations illustrate that households' *MPC* out of their disposable income is unchanged. An increase in tax rates will lower the *MPC* out of national income on which the size of the multiplier depends.

Taxes

Direct taxes act as a built-in stabilizer because they reduce the marginal propensity to consume out of national income. Consider an example. If there were no taxes, every change in national income of $1 would cause a change in disposable income of nearly a dollar.[2] With a marginal propensity to consume out of Y_d of (say) .8, consumption would change by 80¢. With taxes, however, disposable income changes by less than $1; hence consumption expenditure will change by *less than* 80¢ when national income changes by $1 (even though the *MPC* out of Y_d is still .8).

Direct taxes reduce the fluctuations in disposable income associated with a given fluctuation in national income. Hence, for a given *MPC* out of disposable income, they reduce the *MPC* out of national income.

This is illustrated in Table 31-1. The lower is the *MPC* out of national income, the lower will be the multiplier (as we saw on pages 530–531). Thus higher tax rates will reduce the fluctuations in national income associated with autonomous shifts in expenditure functions.

Tax rates have increased greatly over this century. Although citizens complain about the burden of high taxes—perhaps with good reason—few are aware that the high taxes help to stabilize the economy and reduce the large swings in national income and employment that once plagued all industrial economies.

To see the common sense of this, consider the extreme case in which the marginal tax rate is 100 percent. If there is an autonomous rise of $1 billion in investment expenditure, none of the $1 billion will reach households as disposable income. There are no induced rounds of secondary expenditure; the rise in national income is limited to the initial $1 billion in new investment, and the multiplier is unity. Similarly, a drop in investment expenditure of $1 billion reduces incomes earned in the investment industry by $1 billion and hence reduces government tax revenue by $1 billion. But it does not affect disposable income. Thus there are no secondary rounds of induced contractions in consumption experience to magnify the initial drop in national income caused by the investment decline.

[2] Undistributed profits and other minor items would still hold disposable income below national income. We ignore these in the text because taxes are the major source of the discrepancy between Y_d and Y.

Government Expenditure

Government expenditure on goods and services tends to be relatively stable in the face of cyclical variations in national income. Much expenditure is already committed by earlier legislation, so only a small proportion can be varied at the government's discretion from one year to the next. And even this small part is slow to change.

In contrast, private consumption and investment expenditure tend to vary with national income. The consumption function is an expression of the tendency for consumption expenditure to rise and fall as national income rises and falls. And as we saw in Chapter 30, investment expenditure tends to vary with national income; it is high in booms and low in slumps.

The twentieth century rise in the importance of government in the economy may have been a mixed blessing. One benefit, however, has been to put a large built-in stabilizer into the economy. It has transferred expenditure from the private sector (where it varies cyclically) to the public sector (where it does not). The value of the multiplier has been reduced as a result.

Steady government expenditure acts as a built-in stabilizer by reducing the marginal propensity to spend out of national income.

Transfer Payments

Social insurance and welfare services. Welfare payments rise with the unemployment and hardship that accompany falling national income. Many welfare schemes are financed by taxes based on payrolls or earnings, and these taxes yield less when income is low. Thus welfare schemes act to make net additions to disposable income in times of slumps. They also serve as net subtractors in times of boom and full employment, when payments are low and revenues high.

The Old-Age, Survivors, and Disability Insurance program (popularly called social security) is financed by taxes (called social security premiums) that are paid jointly by employers and employees. Unemployment insurance is financed by a payroll tax on employers. During periods of depression, these tax collections decrease while payments to individuals under the programs rise. Thus both Old-Age, Survivors, and Disability Insurance and unemployment insurance support disposable income when national income falls and hold it down when national income rises.

Agricultural support policies. When there is a slump in the economy, there is a general decline in the demand for all goods, including agricultural produce. The free-market prices of agricultural goods fall, and government agricultural supports come into play. This means that government transfers which support agricultural disposable income will rise as national income falls.

Transfer payments act as built-in stabilizers; they tend to stabilize disposable income, and hence consumption expenditure, in the face of fluctuations in national income.

Assume a reduction in autonomous expenditure of $10 billion that, in the absence of transfer payments, would reduce disposable income by $6 billion. With an *MPC* out of disposable income of .8, this $6 billion reduction would cause an initial induced fall in consumption expenditure of $4.8 billion. Now assume instead that the fall in national income is accompanied by an increase in transfer payments of $4 billion. Instead of falling by $6 billion, disposable income now falls by only $2 billion. With the *MPC* out of Y_d still at .8, the initial induced fall in consumption expenditure is only $1.6 billion instead of $4.8 billion.

The smaller is the induced fall in consumption expenditure, the smaller will be the multiplier and hence the smaller the final reduction in national income as it responds to the initial fall in autonomous expenditure.

The Origin of Built-in Stabilizers

Most built-in stabilizers are fairly new phenomena in this country. Fifty years ago high marginal rates of taxation, high and stable government expenditures, farm stabilization policies, and large unemployment and other social security payments were unknown in the United States. Each of these built-in stabilizers was the unforeseen by-product of policies originally adopted for other reasons. The progressive income tax arose out of a concern to make the distribution of income less unequal. The growth of the government sector has been the result of many factors other than a desire for cyclical stability. Social insurance and agricultural support programs were adopted more because of a concern with the welfare of the individuals and groups involved than with preserving the health of the economy. But unforeseen or not, they work. (Even governments can be lucky.)

The Council of Economic Advisers has estimated that with the present tax system and schedules of unemployment compensation benefits, a decline in GNP automatically produces a reduction in government receipts and an increase in transfer payments that limits the decline in after-tax income to about 65¢ for each $1 of reduction of GNP. Thus about a third of any decline is automatically offset by these two stabilizers alone.

The Partial Nature of the Job Done by Built-in Stabilizers

No matter how lucky governments have been in finding built-in stabilizers, these cannot reduce fluctuations to zero. Stabilizers work by producing stabilizing reactions to changes in income. But until the income change occurs, the stabilizer is not even brought into play.

The evidence of the U.S. economy as reviewed in the previous chapter suggests two important conclusions. First, fluctuations have been less extreme since 1945 than they were earlier. This is due in part to the operation of powerful built-in stabilizers not on the scene before World War II. Second, the magnitude of the post-1945 fluctuations has nonetheless been sufficient to cause policymakers serious concern.

DISCRETIONARY FISCAL POLICY

Short-term, minor fluctuations that are not removed automatically by built-in stabilizers cannot, with present knowledge and techniques, be removed by consciously fine tuning the economy. We have already noted, however, that larger and more persistent gaps sometimes appear. In these cases there is time for the government to operate a **discretionary fiscal policy,** that is, to institute changes in taxes and expenditures that are designed to offset gaps. To do this effectively, the administration needs to make periodic conscious decisions to alter fiscal policy. The Council of Economic Advisers must study current economic trends and predict the probable course of the economy. If the predicted course is unsatisfactory, Congress must be persuaded to enact the necessary legislation.

In considering discretionary fiscal policy, we shall deal with three main questions. First, does it matter whether government expenditure or government tax revenue is varied to achieve the desired budget deficit or surplus? Second, why is it important that the fiscal change be easily reversible? Third, does it matter whether households and firms regard the government's fiscal changes as being temporary or as being long-lived?

The Choice Between Changes in Tax Rates and Changes in Government Expenditures

There is often sharp debate on whether taxes or expenditures or both should be used to achieve any stabilizing changes that are thought to be desirable. What issues are involved in these debates? What factors affect the choice between changes in government expenditure and changes in tax rates?

Location of effects. The multiplier effects of an increase in aggregate expenditure tend to spread over the whole economy, causing a rising demand for virtually every commodity. If a slump is general, with widespread unemployment, this will be an advantage. If, however, a slump is severely localized, with a major depression in a particular industry (such as automobiles) or area (such as Appalachia), then it may be desirable to achieve a disproportionate effect in the depressed industry or area. In this case, raising government expenditure has a distinct advantage over cutting taxes. A tax cut would have its initial impact on the entire economy, but by careful choice of projects much of the initial effect of extra expenditure can be channeled into the depressed industry or area. Thus, if specific impact effects are important, increased government expenditure will have an advantage over tax cuts.

Time lags. We have discussed the decision lags of discretionary fiscal policy. Although they are long under the American political system, there is no reason why they should be of significantly different lengths for changes in government expenditure and in tax rates.

However, there is a second type of lag, one that may differ for changes in taxes and changes in expenditure. After a fiscal change has been authorized, there will necessarily be some lag before it actually goes into effect. This is an **execution lag.** Once Congress has passed appropriations for a new road-building program, for example, it will be some time before substantial income payments are made to private firms and households. Routes must be surveyed; land must be acquired, often by condemnatory procedures; public protests must often be heard; bids must be called for and contracts let. All this can take considerable time. However, the execution lag can be very short for tax cuts. Once tax reduction legislation has been passed by Congress, rates of withholding can be reduced quickly. Only a few weeks after the tax cut is passed, wage earners may find themselves with more take-home pay.

The Need for Reversibility

To see what is involved in the issue of reversibility, assume that national income is *normally* at or near full-employment income. Then a *temporary* slump in private investment opens up a large deflationary gap. The gap persists. Eventually the government decides to adopt some combination of tax cuts and expenditure increases to push the economy back toward full employment. If this policy is successful, private investment can be expected to recover to its pre-slump level. If the government does not then reverse its policy, an inflationary gap will open up as the combination of recovered investment expenditure and continuing fiscal stimulus takes national income into the inflationary range. This is illustrated in Figure 31-3.

Alternatively, assume that starting from the same situation of nearly full employment, an *abnormal* investment boom opens up an inflationary gap. Rather than let the inflation persist, the government reduces expenditure and raises taxes to remove the gap. Then, when the investment boom is over, investment expenditure will return to its original level. If the government does nothing, a deflationary gap will open up and a serious slump ensue. This too is analyzed in Figure 31-3.

Fiscal policies designed to remove persistent inflationary or deflationary gaps resulting from abnormally high or low levels of private expenditure will destabilize the economy unless they can be fairly rapidly reversed once private expenditure returns to its more normal level.

In the American economy, where decision lags on changes in spending or taxes are measured in years, rapid reversals are not easily accomplished. This fact is a powerful argument against fiscal policy. Even if the inflationary and deflationary gaps persist long enough for fiscal changes to be agreed to and made, subsequent rapid changes in private expenditure may require a quick reversal of the fiscal stance—a reversal that cannot easily be made, given the present slow political decision-making process.

FIGURE 31-3
Effects of Fiscal Policies That Are Not Reversed

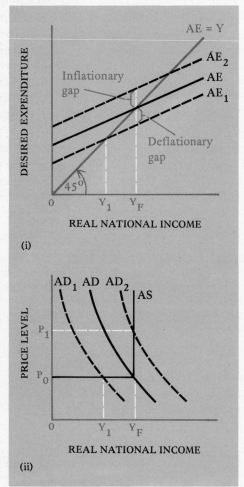

REAL NATIONAL INCOME

(i)

PRICE LEVEL

REAL NATIONAL INCOME

(ii)

Fiscal policies that are initially appropriate may become inappropriate when the private expenditure function shifts. The normal levels of the aggregate demand and aggregate expenditure functions are assumed to be AD and AE, leaving income normally at Y_F.

First, a persistent slump in private investment shifts aggregate demand to AD_1 and aggregate expenditure to AE_1, producing income of Y_1 and the deflationary gap indicated by the brace. The government now cuts taxes and raises expenditure to restore aggregate demand and aggregate expenditure to AD and AE and national income to Y_F. Later, private investment recovers to its original level, pushing aggregate demand and aggregate expenditure to AD_2 and AE_2. Unless the fiscal policy is quickly reversed, an inflationary gap (indicated by the brace) will open up and the price level will rise to P_1.

Second, starting from income Y_F, a persistent investment boom takes AD and AE to AD_2 and AE_2. In order to stop the price level from rising in the face of the inflationary gap, the government raises taxes and cuts expenditure, thereby shifting the curves back to AD and AE. Eventually, however, the investment boom comes to a halt and the curves shift down to AD_1 and AE_1. Unless the fiscal policy can be rapidly reversed, a deflationary gap (indicated by the brace) will open up and equilibrium income will settle down at Y_1.

The Choice Between Changes Seen by Households as "Temporary" or as "Longlasting"

Consider the attempt to remove a persistent inflationary or deflationary gap through changes in tax rates. Such a gap, though persistent, is unlikely to be a permanent feature of the economy. The relevant tax changes should therefore be advocated only for "the duration," that is, for as long as the administration thinks the gaps would persist without the tax changes.

It might have seemed reasonable at the time, for example, to expect the inflationary gap of the late 1960s to persist only as long as the Vietnam War. A discretionary fiscal policy designed to remove that gap could take the form, say, of a surcharge on income taxes for a two-year period. For another example, the recession that began in 1974 was fought by "temporary" tax rebates that had to be renewed by Congress every six months — with the clear implication that taxes would return to their "normal" levels when recovery was well under way.

Such tax changes cause changes in household disposable income and, according to the Keynesian theory of the consumption function, would cause changes in consumption expenditure. Consumption expenditure would increase as tax rebates rose in times of deflationary gaps and would decrease as tax surcharges rose in times of inflationary gaps. This theory of the effects of short-term tax changes relies on the assumption that household consumption depends on current disposable income.

Permanent-income theories. Many recent theories of the consumption function have emphasized what is called a household's expected *lifetime income* or *permanent income* as the major determinant of consumption. According to such theories, households have expectations about their lifetime incomes and adjust their consumption to those expectations. When temporary fluctuations in income occur, households maintain their long-term consumption plans and use their stocks of wealth as a buffer to absorb income fluctuations. Thus when there is a purely temporary rise in income, households will save all the extra income; when there is a purely temporary fall in income, households will maintain their long-term consumption plans by using up part of their wealth accumulated through past saving. The two most important theories of this type are the *life-cycle* and the *permanent-income* hypotheses. The first is associated principally with Franco Modigliani and the second with Milton Friedman.[3]

To the extent that this kind of influence is at work, it may have serious consequences for short-lived tax changes. A temporary rebate raises a household's disposable income, but households, recognizing it as temporary, might not revise their expenditure plans and instead save the extra money. Thus the hoped-for increase in aggregate expenditure would not occur. Similarly, a temporary rise in tax rates reduces

disposable income, but that may merely cause a fall in saving. Thus total expenditure is again unchanged, and a temporary surcharge fails to reduce the inflationary gap.

If households' consumption is more closely related to lifetime income than to current income, tax changes that are known to be of short duration may have relatively small effects on current consumption.[4]

The advantage of having households perceive as permanent any tax cut or tax surcharge conflicts with the need for the reversibility of cuts and surcharges if they are not to destabilize the economy at a later date. This problem reduces the effectiveness of changes in tax rates as a stabilizing tool.

Fiscal Policy in Action

We have seen that governments inevitably have a major impact on GNP through their fiscal behavior. The very size of a government's budget guarantees that. However, the conscious use of the budget to influence GNP that constitutes fiscal policy is by no means inevitable. Fiscal impact is unavoidable, but fiscal policy is a matter of choice.

Before we look at some of the experience of fiscal policy in the United States, let us consider how we are to assess the direction of current fiscal policy.

JUDGING THE STANCE OF FISCAL POLICY

Governments seek to shift aggregate demand by consciously changing their fiscal policy stance. The "stance" of fiscal policy refers to its expan-

[3] Professor Friedman was awarded the 1976 Nobel Prize in economics for his work on the theories of money and stabilization policy.

[4] The permanent-income theory is not as immediately applicable to fiscal policy as it may seem. This is because fiscal policy seeks to affect *expenditure* (on consumption and investment goods) while permanent-income theories seek to explain the consumption of goods and services—which in the case of durables is spread over the whole life of the durable. This important matter is discussed further in Appendix A to this chapter.

sionary or contractionary effects on the economy. An expansionary fiscal policy is one that increases aggregate demand and thus tends to increase national income; a contractionary fiscal policy reduces aggregate demand and thus tends to lower national income. Now, how can we judge changes in the stance of fiscal policy from one year to the next?

In popular discussion, a change in the government's current deficit or surplus is often taken as an indicator. When the deficit rises (i.e., tax yields fall and/or government expenditure rises), this is widely taken to indicate an expansionary change in fiscal policy. When the deficit falls (i.e., tax yields rise and/or government expenditure falls), this is widely taken to indicate a contractionary policy. This argument is based on a comparison of government expenditure and tax revenue.

But tax revenues are the result of the interaction of tax rates, which the government does set, and the level of national income, which is influenced by many forces that are beyond the government's control. Thus to judge changes in the stance of fiscal policy from changes in the government's budget deficit or surplus can be very misleading. It confuses endogenous changes due to changes in national income with exogenous changes due to changes in the stance of fiscal policy.

The major tools of fiscal policy are government expenditure and *tax rates*. The budget deficit or surplus is the relation between government expenditure and *tax revenues*.

The distinction between the two causes of changes in the budget balance is easily seen in what is called the government's **budget surplus function.** This function, which relates the surplus (government revenue minus government expenditure) to national income, is graphed in Figure 31-4. Endogenous changes in the government's budget balance due to changes in national income are shown by movements along a given surplus function. Changes in the budget balance due to policy-induced changes in government expenditure or in tax rates are shown by shifts in the surplus function. Such shifts indicate a different budget balance at *each* level of national income.

When measuring changes in the stance of fiscal policy, it is common to calculate changes in the estimated budget balance at some base level of national income. Holding income constant ensures that measured shifts in the budget balance are due to policy-induced shifts of the surplus function rather than income-induced movements along the function. The base most commonly used is full-employment national income, and the measure calculated is called the **full-employment surplus** (*FES*). This is an estimate of government tax revenues minus government expenditures, not as they actually are, but as they would be if full-employment national income had obtained (i.e., if the GNP gap had been zero). In this usage a full-employment budget deficit (expenditures exceed revenues) is regarded as a negative full-employment surplus.

Changes in the full-employment surplus are an indicator of changes in the stance of fiscal policy.[5]

Figure 31-4 analyzes the use of the full-employment surplus, as well as the errors that can arise from use of the current surplus as an indicator of the stance of fiscal policy.

FISCAL POLICY BEFORE 1946

In 1932 Franklin Roosevelt was elected to the U.S. presidency on a platform of fighting the Great Depression with vigorous government policies. Not until America entered World War II, nearly a decade later, was massive unemployment ended. Did the experience of the 1930s prove the failure of fiscal policy?

There is a widespread misconception that Roosevelt believed in deficit financing and that massive fiscal policy was tried during the 1930s and failed. Professor E. Cary Brown of MIT,

---

[5] The full-employment surplus is the simplest adequate measure, and it is vastly superior to the current surplus for estimating year-to-year changes in the stance of fiscal policy. More sophisticated measures exist and are often used in detailed empirical work.

FIGURE 31-4

The Budget Surplus Function

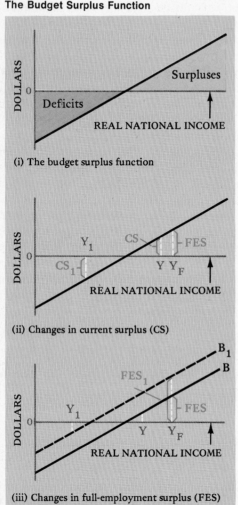

(i) The budget surplus function

(ii) Changes in current surplus (CS)

(iii) Changes in full-employment surplus (FES)

Changes in national income cause changes in the current surplus by moving the economy along its surplus function; changes in the stance of fiscal policy shift the surplus function. The budget surplus function expresses the difference between government's tax revenues and its expenditures at each level of national income. The curve shown in (i) assumes that as income fluctuates tax revenues fluctuate more than expenditure. Thus deficits are associated with low levels of income and surpluses with high levels.

In (ii) a fall in national income from Y to Y_1 causes the budget to go from a current surplus of CS to a current deficit of CS_1 with no change in government expenditure or tax rates—that is, the fiscal policy stance is unchanged. The unchanged fiscal stance is correctly measured by the constant full-employment surplus, FES.

In (iii) there is a contractionary change in the stance of fiscal policy: a government expenditure cut and/or a tax rate increase shifts the surplus function from B to B_1, indicating that there is a larger budget surplus *at each level of national income*. This change is correctly measured by the rise in the full-employment surplus from FES to FES_1. The misleading effects of judging changes in the policy stance from changes in the current surplus can be seen by noting that if national income had fallen from Y to Y_1 at the same time that the surplus function shifted from B to B_1, the current balance would have gone from surplus to deficit in spite of the rise in the full employment surplus.

after a careful study, concludes: "Fiscal policy seems to have been an unsuccessful recovery device in the 'thirties—not because it did not work, but because it was not tried." In 1933, at the depth of the Depression, the federal government was spending $2 billion for purchases of goods and services, only slightly more than the $1.3 billion it spent in 1929. This was a small drop in a very large bucket—considering that GNP fell from $103 billion in 1929 to $46 billion in 1933!

Professor Brown finds that the impact on aggregate demand of public expenditure was about what would be expected today, but that it was too small to do much good. Given the deficits achieved, it would have taken a multiplier of 25 for the American economy to have come within striking distance of full employment; in fact, the multiplier in the 1930s was approximately 2. Expenditures were wastefully small, not (as many people thought at the time) wastefully large. For President Roosevelt and his advisers hoped that a small increase in government expenditure would induce a flow of new private investment that would eliminate the need for further public stimulus. This small-scale "pump priming" did not work. Today it seems hopelessly naive to have expected that it would.

Once the massive, war-geared expenditure of the 1940s began, income responded sharply and unemployment all but evaporated. Government expenditures on goods and services, which had been running at under 15 percent of GNP during the 1930s, jumped to 46 percent by 1944, while unemployment reached the incredible low of 1.2 percent of the civilian labor force.

The increase in aggregate demand changed a deflationary gap into an inflationary one, but the government was in no position to curtail its expenditures. It urged citizens to be patriotic and buy War Bonds instead of goods. It resorted to price controls, rationing, and a series of priorities for defense materials to mask the inflationary pressures. These substantially restrained the inflationary forces, though prices did rise by almost one-third during 1940–1945.

The performance of the American economy from 1930 to 1945 is quite well explained by modern income theory. It is clear that the government did not effectively use fiscal measures to stabilize the economy. War cured the depression because war demands made acceptable a level of government expenditure sufficient to remove the deflationary gap. Had the first Roosevelt administration been able to do this, it might have ended the waste of the Depression many years sooner.

FISCAL POLICY AFTER WORLD WAR II

The most pressing economic problem of 1946 was the inflationary gap. People rushed to spend their wartime savings on new cars and houses that had been unavailable during the war and on new products such as television sets that had been developed during the war. The large volume of accumulated purchasing power, combined with the time lag required to convert the economy from wartime to peacetime production, caused a large gap between aggregate demand and aggregate supply. Wartime price controls and rationing were removed. Between 1946 and 1948, prices rose more than they had in the entire wartime period.

The postwar years were characterized by steady growth of real GNP and, once the postwar inflation had ended, only gradual inflation. As the 1950s wore on, however, the economy's economic growth became increasingly sluggish. Unemployment began an upward creep from 2.9 percent in 1953 to 6.7 percent in 1961. Many worried that the combination of general prosperity, rising prices, and rising unemployment represented a new set of structural problems that could not easily be solved by using the existing tools of macroeconomic policy.

FISCAL POLICY IN THE 1960s

The 1960s saw two major experiments with fiscal policy. In terms of achieving their objectives, the first was a success and the second a failure.

The "New Economic Policy" and the 1964 Tax Cuts

President Kennedy and his Council of Economic Advisers took the view that the economy's problems could be alleviated by using the existing tools of macroeconomic policy. They diagnosed the problem as one of "fiscal drag" and proposed a major cut in tax rates to deal with it.

Fiscal drag. This important problem, first diagnosed in the early 1960s, is one that requires periodic attention. **Fiscal drag** is a rising full-employment surplus produced by economic growth acting on stable government expenditure and fixed tax rates.

Throughout the 1950s full-employment GNP was rising 2 to 3 percent per year because of economic growth. This increased aggregate supply. But since higher output means higher income earned, aggregate demand was also shifting out-

FIGURE 31-5
Fiscal Drag

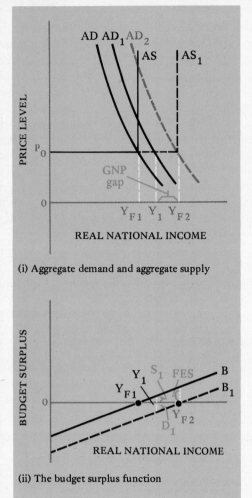

(i) Aggregate demand and aggregate supply

(ii) The budget surplus function

Economic growth tends to produce a rising full-employment budget surplus and a rising GNP gap. Although economic growth is a continuous process, the figure deals with a single rise in national income. Economic growth raises full-employment income from Y_{F1} to Y_{F2}, shifting the aggregate supply curve from AS to AS_1. This produces the full-employment budget surplus shown in (ii). Because of the budget surplus, aggregate demand shifts right only from AD to AD_1 and therefore by less than does aggregate supply. This produces an equilibrium national income of Y_1 and the GNP gap shown. One cure is to cut tax rates, thereby shifting the budget surplus function from B to B_1 in (ii) and aggregate demand from AD_1 to AD_2 in (i).

Note that even though the tax cuts turn the current budget surplus of S_1 into a current deficit of D_1 at the level of income Y_1, the deficit disappears once income rises to its new equilibrium level of Y_{F2}.

ward. With both demand and supply increasing, it might seem that maintaining full employment would be no problem. There was a problem, however, and it lay with the tax system.

With tax rates constant, rising national income causes rising tax revenues. These revenues are money that does not become disposable income for households. If the government spent all its extra tax revenue, aggregate demand would not be depressed. With a relatively stable level of government expenditure, however, rising tax revenues exert a drag on the growth of aggregate demand by taking income away from households that would have spent it and transferring it to governments that do not.

The results are analyzed in Figure 31-5 (i). The growing full-employment surplus meant that aggregate demand was not growing as fast as aggregate supply, thereby opening a growing GNP gap, as shown in Figure 31-5 (ii).

To prevent an ever stronger depressing effect being exerted on national income by a growing full-employment surplus, it is necessary to reduce the surplus periodically either by increasing government spending or by reducing tax rates.

The full significance of the long-term problem of fiscal policy in a growing economy was not appreciated until the 1960s. When it was, the Kennedy and Johnson administrations advocated a large cut in tax rates to remove the fiscal drag. Their concern was not with cyclical stabilization of the economy but with solving a problem associated with long-term economic growth. As long as economic growth continues, periodic adjustments to remove fiscal drag will be needed.

Earlier in this chapter we noted that decision lags made it difficult to fine tune the American economy through discretionary fiscal policy. Certainly the possibility of effective fine tuning was made to look unlikely by the decision lag on the tax cut that was finally enacted in 1964 after fully *two years* of heated congressional debate.

When it was finally enacted, the predicted effects occurred. The tax cuts increased disposable income, causing an increase in consumption expenditure which in turn caused an increase in national income and employment.

The Vietnam Inflation and the 1968 Tax Surcharges

By the time the full effects of the tax cut were felt, the large increases in military expenditures due to the escalation of the war in Vietnam were also exerting a substantial expansionary effect on the economy. A growing inflationary gap now replaced the deflationary gap of the late 1950s and early 1960s. The large 1967 deficit (owing to increased defense expenditures on top of a heavy domestic budget) came with GNP already at the full-employment level and produced a large inflationary gap in 1968.

The fiscal response to these danger signals was slow in coming. Again, decision lags were long. Presidential advisers had foreseen the developing inflationary gap two years earlier, and President Johnson made his first request to Congress a full 18 months before the tax increase was finally enacted.

By mid 1968, however, a temporary tax surcharge bill was approved by Congress. This bill raised effective tax rates for a period of about 18 months and produced a substantial budget surplus. (In terms of Figure 31-5, the policy shifted the surplus function from B_1 to B in an effort to shift the aggregate demand function to the left.) The object was to slow inflation by removing the inflationary gap. The restraining effect was disappointingly small; inflation hardly slowed its trend toward ever higher rates.

The apparent failure of the contractionary budgetary policy of 1968–1969 caused much debate among economists. The general judgment, after long discussions, seems to be that the "failure" of the 1968–1969 tax surcharges to restrain inflation revealed the shortcomings of the fine tuning but did not show fiscal policy to be generally impotent. Numerous factors had offset the effects of the surcharge: (1) federal government expenditure rose more than expected; (2) state and local fiscal changes were expansionary; (3) there was an unexpected surge in the demand for automobiles, which caused an upward shift in the consumption function; (4) there was an unexpected increase in investment expenditure; (5)

the knowledge that the tax surcharge was temporary may have caused households to make only small downward revisions in their expected permanent incomes and hence only very small reductions in their consumption. Another factor, understood now but unappreciated then, is that inflationary expectations, once entrenched, are not easily shaken—especially by a transitory tax surcharge.

FISCAL POLICY IN THE 1970s

In the 1970s the American economy underwent a series of cyclical swings that fiscal policy sometimes aggravated and sometimes resisted. The stance of fiscal policy in each of these years can be judged from the full-employment surpluses shown in Table 31-2.

TABLE 31-2

Actual and Full-employment Budget Balances for the Federal Government (billions of dollars)

Year	Actual budget surplus[a]	Full-employment budget surplus[a] FES
1969	8.5	3.0
1970	−12.1	− 2.6
1971	−22.0	− 9.2
1972	−17.3	−21.5
1973	− 6.7	− 9.8
1974	−10.7	9.3
1975	−70.6	−18.2
1976	−53.6	−13.4
1977	−46.3	−18.6
1978	−27.7	−11.6
1979	− 9.7	9.9

Source: *Economic Report of the President,* 1980.
[a] A minus indicates a deficit.

Wide swings in the full-employment surplus in the 1970s indicate wide swings in the stance of fiscal policy. Because the economy operated at less than full employment during most of the 1970s, actual budget surpluses were less than full employment surpluses in most years. The very large actual deficits in the mid 1970s were mainly an endogenous response to low levels of national income during the recession. Variations in the FES show the variability of the stance of fiscal policy. It was most expansionary in 1972 and 1977 and most contractionary in 1974 and 1979.

Fiscal Expansion, 1970–1972

After a mild recession in 1970–1971, an inflationary gap emerged once again as the economy expanded into a major boom in 1971–1972. Fiscal policy contributed substantially to the boom. Lower taxes and increased expenditures were the rule in the election year of 1972. Estimates show that whereas the GNP grew at 6 percent per year over 1971–1972, it would have grown at only 2 percent per year in the absence of fiscal stimulation. In a major study of the period, Professor Alan S. Blinder of Princeton University concludes that "fiscal stimulus transformed 1972 from a year of healthy growth into an unsustainable and inflationary boom."

The government's behavior during 1972 prompted charges that it was generating a **political business cycle:** cyclical swings in the economy generated by fiscal and monetary policy for the purpose of winning elections. Economists may never know the Nixon administration's real motives in generating this fiscal stimulus. Yet there is no doubt that during an election year the economy was manipulated into a rapid boom with rising GNP and falling unemployment.

Fiscal Contraction, 1973–1974

The election was in November 1972; in early 1973 fiscal policy swung from being expansionary to being contractionary. Professor Blinder's calculations estimate that with a neutral fiscal policy there would have been a 3 percent rate of growth of GNP from the first quarter of 1973 to the first quarter of 1974. With the contractionary fiscal policy, the rate of growth of real GNP was zero.

The contractionary swing in stance of fiscal policy in 1973 was planned. In 1974 there was an even larger change in the stance, and this time it was unplanned. By 1974 the inflation had become very rapid. During an inflation prices and money incomes rise rapidly. Progressive income tax rates then yield more and more revenue even though there is no change in the structure of tax rates.

Fiscal drag develops when full-employment national income measured in current dollars rises because of inflation, just as it develops when full-employment national income measured in constant dollars rises because of economic growth.

The inflation continued well after the economic downturn in 1974, and the fiscal drag due to inflation more than offset the expansionary effects of the built-in stabilizers. As a result, discretionary changes in fiscal policy were enacted in 1975 to try to offset the severe recession that developed.

Fiscal Expansion, 1975–1978

The next four years saw a gradual recovery, with the GNP gap narrowing and unemployment falling. At first the policy seemed successful; the inflation rate measured by the full CPI fell to 7 percent in 1975 and 4.6 percent in 1976. Indeed, if one takes out food prices (which are dominated by short-term supply fluctuations) and energy prices (which are dominated by foreign events), the inflation rate as measured by the rest of the CPI remained quite stable at around 6 percent for the three years 1975, 1976, and 1977. This was clearly an improvement over the double-digit inflation of 1974.

Yet two worrying questions remained. First, since the inflation rate did not fall to near zero in the face of the most severe slump since the 1930s, was inflation now a permanent phenomenon? (We shall consider this question in Part 10.) Second, would the rate accelerate back to double-digit levels when recovery took the economy within striking distance of full employment?

Unfortunately, the second question was answered with a resounding yes. As the recovery proceeded, the inflation rate rose to 9.6 percent in 1978 and 13.3 percent in 1979. By mid 1980 the recovery was over but the inflation rate was hovering around 10 percent.

Fiscal Contraction, 1978–1980

The administration's fiscal policy was one of slowly increasing stimulus from 1975 through 1977. Then, as the inflation rate accelerated once again, inflation rather than unemployment came to be perceived as the major enemy. The full-employment deficit was first reduced and then turned into a surplus in 1979.

As the new decade began, the 1980 *Economic Report of the President* was dominated by concern over inflation. The control of inflation was stated to be the major goal of macroeconomic policy. Contractionary fiscal and monetary policies were called for to reduce aggregate demand in the hope that this would reduce inflation. By the middle of 1980 the policy had achieved its first goal; a downturn had occurred, and a recession had begun.

The experience of the 1970s as well as that of earlier decades indicates an impressive ability to manipulate aggregate demand. The stance of fiscal policy has been changed many times, sometimes in pursuit of stabilization policy, sometimes for political motives, and sometimes because of automatic effects (e.g., when real growth or rapid inflation introduces fiscal drag). Each time the response has been in the direction predicted by economic theory.

The 1980s began with a further demonstration that policymakers, aided by modern macroeconomic theory, know how to manipulate aggregate demand. The Carter administration had little trouble in inducing a recession at the beginning of the year. What no one knew was how much effect the decline in economic activity would have on the inflation rate.

Can Fiscal Restraint Cure Inflation?

A restrictive fiscal policy that raises taxes and lowers government expenditure can lower the aggregate expenditure function. This can remove an inflationary gap or create a deflationary gap. If the inflation is due to excess demand, a restrictive fiscal policy can control the inflation by removing the excess demand. The inflation of the last half of the 1970s and the early 1980s, however, proceeded without excess demand. Much of the blame seemed to lie with an upward-shifting aggregate supply curve rather than with the aggregate demand curve. Since fiscal policy works through the demand side of the economy, its scope for controlling the current supply-side inflation is limited.

PROPOSALS CONCERNING THE BUDGET BALANCE

Although few people see a restrictive fiscal policy as the solution to the present inflation, many argue that governments should not add to inflationary pressures by spending more than they raise in taxes. Thus the call has gone out for fiscal restraint as one, possibly small, part of a more general anti-inflationary package.

An Annually Balanced Budget?

Much current rhetoric of fiscal restraint calls for a balanced budget. Some people would even make an annually balanced budget an object of policy or an obligation enforced by an act of Congress.

The discussion earlier in this chapter suggests that an annually balanced budget would be extremely difficult—perhaps impossible—to achieve. With fixed tax rates, tax revenues fluctuate endogenously as national income fluctuates. We have seen that much government expenditure is fixed by past commitments and that most of the rest is hard to change quickly. Thus an annually balanced budget may be quite unfeasible, particularly with the long decision lags inherent in the American system of government. But suppose an annually balanced budget, or something approaching it, were feasible. What would its effects be? Would they be desirable?

We saw earlier that a large government sector whose expenditures on goods and services are not very sensitive to the cyclical variations in national income is a major built-in stabilizer. To insist that annual government expenditure be tied to annual tax receipts would be to abandon the present built-in stability provided by the government. Government expenditure would then become a major *destabilizing* force. Tax revenues necessarily rise in booms and fall in slumps; an annually balanced budget would force government expenditure to do the same. Changes in national income would then cause induced changes not only in household consumption expenditure but also in government expenditure. This would greatly increase the economy's marginal propensity to spend and hence increase the value of the multiplier.

An annually balanced budget would accentuate the swings in national income that accompany changes in such autonomous expenditure flows as investment and exports.

A Cyclically Balanced Budget?

Annually balanced budget proposals are aimed at two major problems: first, to avoid the alleged inflationary consequences of chronic budget deficits; second, to prevent stabilization policy from leading to a continual increase in the size of the government sector. How could the growth in the public sector occur? During a slump the government increases expenditures to stimulate the economy, but during a boom the government allows inflation to occur rather than cut expenditure. In the next slump, government expenditure is raised once again. The more ready willingness to follow an expansionary fiscal policy in slumps than to follow a contractionary policy in booms can lead to a long-term increase in the size of the government sector.

The annually balanced budget would prevent both these occurrences—but at the cost, as we have seen, of destabilizing the economy.

An alternative policy, one that would prevent continual deficits and could inhibit the growth in the size of the government sector, would be to balance the budget over a number of years, say, over a five-year or a seven-year period. This would be more feasible than the annually balanced budget, and it would not make government expenditure a destabilizing force. The policies are illustrated in Figure 31-6.

Although more attractive in principle than the annually balanced budget, a cyclically balanced budget would carry problems of its own. Congress might well spend in excess of revenue in (say) 1982, leaving the next Congress the obligation to spend less than current revenue in 1983 and 1984. Could such an obligation to balance over a period of several years be made binding? It could be made a legal requirement through an act of Congress. But what the Congress does, the Congress can undo. (This has been the history of attempts to limit the size of the national debt by legal restriction.) A constitutional amendment might only mandate an action that was impossible or manifestly foolish to achieve; the response would surely be a mixture of window dressing and a redefinition of terms that produces a paper balance without any change in the substance of present tax and spending policies.

The problems of achieving a cyclically balanced budget or a budget balanced over any reasonable time span remain unsolved. Clearly, however, the cyclically balanced budget is both more feasible and more desirable than the annually balanced budget.

Yet there is serious doubt that the idea of a balanced budget over any time period is a sensible one. Many economists believe that a superior alternative to insisting on a precise balance is to pay attention to the balance without making a fetish of never adding to the national debt. We shall see in the next section that there is no reason why a country cannot live satisfactorily forever with a growing national debt.

THE NATIONAL DEBT[6]

We may worry about the impact on inflation of the government's deficit or surplus in any one

[6] The issues dealt with here are considered in more detail in Appendix B to this chapter.

FIGURE 31-6
Balanced and Unbalanced Budgets

(i) A cyclically unbalanced budget

(ii) A cyclically balanced budget

(iii) A constantly balanced budget

An annually (constantly) balanced budget is a destabilizer; a cyclically balanced budget is a stabilizer. The flow of tax receipts is shown varying over the business cycle while government expenditure is shown at a constant rate.

In (i) deficits (dark areas) are common and surpluses (light areas) are rare because the average level of expenditure exceeds the average level of taxes. This policy will tend to stabilize the economy against cyclical fluctuations, but the average fiscal stance of the government is expansionary. This has been the characteristic U.S. budgetary position over the last several decades.

In (ii) government expenditure has been reduced until it is approximately equal to the average level of tax receipts. The budget is now balanced cyclically. The policy still tends to stabilize the economy against cyclical fluctuations because of deficits in slumps and surpluses in booms. But the average fiscal stance is neither strongly expansionary nor strongly contractionary.

In (iii) an annually balanced budget has been imposed. Deficits have been prevented, but government expenditure now varies over the business cycle, tending to destabilize the economy by accentuating the cyclical swings in aggregate expenditure.

year. Should we also worry about the cumulative effect of decades of budget deficits that have outweighed budget surpluses? The cumulative effect shows up in a rising national debt.

Does an increasing debt matter? Would an ever-increasing debt lead to an ultimate collapse of the free enterprise economy? Does the debt represent a burden we are passing on to our heirs? It is to these and related questions that we now turn.

The national debt represents money that the federal government has borrowed by selling bonds to households, firms, and financial institutions. In this sense, the national debt is owed by all of us to some of us.

The Size of the Debt

The national debt in December 1979 was $844 billion, more than $3,836 for every man, woman,

FIGURE 31-7
Trends in the National Debt

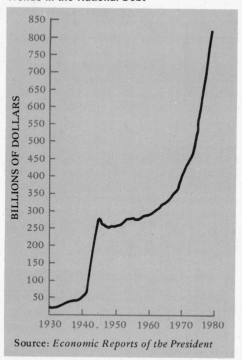

Source: *Economic Reports of the President*

The trend in the national debt has been upward at least since 1930. The national debt has risen in most years since 1930. The rise has been relatively gradual except during World War II and since 1972. Since that time the rise has been very rapid when measured in current dollars.

and child in the country. Just over 40 percent of the debt was held by the government itself and by Federal Reserve banks.[7] Interest payments on this part of the debt are only bookkeeping transactions. The debt actually held by the private sector is about $540 billion, or more than $2,455 per person.

These "per person" figures are often quoted in an attempt to shock the reader, but they require interpretation. For a government, as for a household, the significance of debt depends on what it

[7] Federal Reserve banks buy government bonds in the course of operating monetary policy (see Chapter 35). Government departments can acquire government bonds when they have funds that they do not require for short, or even long, periods of time.

represents and on whether the income is available to pay the interest. No one would be shocked, for example, to find that an average American family of four had a mortgage of $35,000 on a $60,000 home.

Consider the actual size of the public debt. Figure 31-7 shows the growth of national debt in the United States; the trend of the debt has been steadily upward. But as national income grows, the scale of government activity can be expected to grow. Just to maintain its relative share of the GNP, government spending would have to increase at the same rate as the GNP. If a constant proportion of government expenditures was financed by borrowing, government debt would be growing at the same rate as the GNP. This suggests that debt statistics should be looked at in the perspective of national income data.

How large is the debt as a fraction of the total value of the economy's annual production? How large are interest payments as a fraction of GNP? What proportion of the tax load is incurred because interest has to be paid on the national debt? Figure 31-8 shows these data.

Is There a Limit to the Size of the Debt?

Congress sets "permanent" and "temporary" new limits to the national debt. But whenever the debt reaches the limits, the limits are raised. Such permanent and temporary limits are pure window dressing; they are raised by Congress as the need to borrow more arises. Our concern here is not with statutory limits but with economic ones.

The Keynesian view. To the extent that the money raised by borrowing is spent on items that add to national income, the borrowing creates the extra income out of which extra taxes can be raised to pay the interest. To the extent that the money is spent on items that do not add to national income, it will be necessary to increase existing taxes in order to provide funds to meet the interest payments. Up to a point, this will not cause serious problems because the process of paying interest on the debt involves only a transfer from some citizens (taxpayers) to other citizens (holders of government bonds).

FIGURE 31-8
The Relative Significance of the National Debt

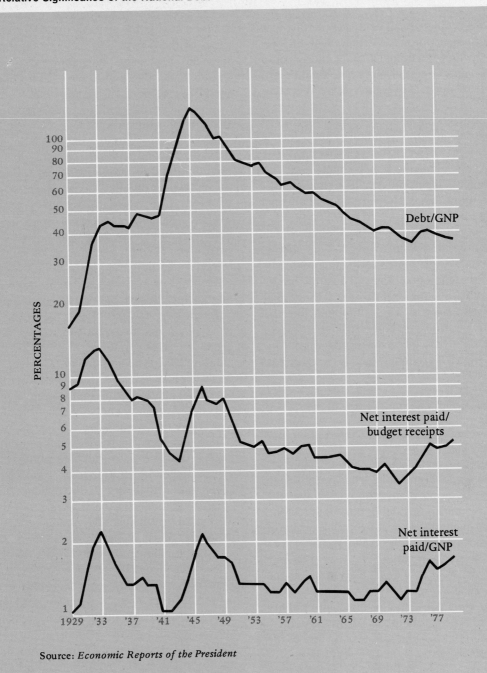

Source: *Economic Reports of the President*

The national debt itself and interest payments on it have not risen in proportion to the GNP since the end of World War II. Three significant ratios are plotted here on a ratio scale. The national debt, after rising sharply through the Great Depression and World War II, was a declining fraction of GNP until 1973, after which there was a slight rise. Interest payments reached 2 percent of GNP in 1946, but for the last 20 years they have remained at under 1.5 percent. Such interest payments required the use of over 20 percent of all federal budget receipts during the early 1930s but now require less than 7 percent. Clearly the picture of a spendthrift government adding recklessly to the burden of the national debt is wrong.

If, however, the national debt grew so fast that the interest payments on the debt took up an ever larger proportion of national income, there would be an ever-increasing tax burden to finance the interest payments. Clearly, then, there is a grain of truth in the worry over the size of the interest payments on the national debt. Yet this worry applies only to those expenditures that do not themselves help to create the extra income out of which interest payments can be met. And the worry becomes significant only if such new non-income-creating debt is a large fraction of current national income.

Such a situation existed in the United States during the crisis periods of World Wars I and II. Both periods were, by historical standards, very short. At no other time has the United States long sustained a situation in which the national debt was increasing at a rate anything like the rate at which national income was increasing. In fact, total debt as a percentage of national income has shown a declining trend, as seen in Figure 31-8.

A good measure of whether the size of the debt is approaching dangerous levels is the willingness of borrowers to hold government bonds at various rates of interest.

Well before a government reaches an absolute debt limit (in terms of its ability to raise the money to pay the interest on its bonds) the public would lose confidence in its debt. The price of bonds would fall and interest rates would rise as borrowers asked a premium for risk. The fact that U.S. government bonds are regarded as the least risky type of investment available provides compelling evidence that the financial community is not concerned about the size of the debt.

The basic points of the Keynesian view of the national debt are that (1) the size of the debt is of no great practical importance and (2) the debt should be increased or decreased according to the needs of full-employment policy.

A non-Keynesian view. An alternative view is based on what has come to be called *fiscal con-*servatism. Fiscal conservatives accept many parts of the Keynesian view but maintain that they are irrelevant. The conservatives believe that deficits have important harmful effects that are not recognized by Keynesians.

The main premise of this alternative theory is that governments are not passive agents who do what is necessary to create full employment and maximize social welfare. Instead, governments are composed of individuals, such as elected officials, legislators, and civil servants, who, like everyone else, seek mainly to maximize their own well-being. And their welfare is best served by government's having a big role and a satisfied electorate. Thus they tend to favor spending and to resist tax increases. This creates a persistent tendency toward deficits that is quite independent of any consideration of a sound fiscal policy.

In the conservative view, the government is an irresponsible body by economists' standards because it seeks to increase its own welfare by creating a large budget deficit. The theory of national income predicts that whenever the economy is at or near full-employment income, the large-deficit policy will be undesirable because it will create an inflationary gap.

The non-Keynesian theory takes a broad historical perspective. It says that in the eighteenth century, spendthrift European rulers habitually spent more than their tax revenues and so created inflationary gaps. The resulting inflations were harmful because they reduced the purchasing power of savings and disrupted trade. By the end of the nineteenth century, the doctrine was well established that a balanced budget is the citizen's only protection against profligate government spending and consequent wild inflation. Thus the balanced budget doctrine was not silly and irrational, as Keynes made it out to be. Instead, it was the symbol of the people's victory in a long struggle to control the spendthrift proclivities of the nation's rulers.

The Keynesian revolution swept away that view. Budget deficits became, according to Keynesians, the tool by which benign and enlightened central authorities sought to ensure full employment. But, say the anti-Keynesians, deficit spending let the tiger out of the cage. Released from the nearly century-old constraint of balancing the budget, governments went on a series of wild spending sprees. Inflationary gaps, deflationary gaps, or full employment notwithstanding, governments spent and spent and spent. Deficits accumulated, national debts rose, and inflation became the rule.

Inflation robbed the people of the real value of their savings by lowering the purchasing power of money saved. In the end, the inflations even defeated the full-employment goal; when governments were finally forced to reduce inflation, they imposed massive deflationary gaps in order to reduce inflations that had developed a momentum of their own. Today we see the legacy of these disastrous policies: the simultaneous occurrence of high inflation, high unemployment rates, and large budget deficits.[8]

The debate reflects deeply held views about the role of government, the nature and motivation of public officials, and the desirability of stabilization. Keynesians tend to regard government officials as well-meaning and substantial government intervention as essential to an effective and humane society. Fiscal conservatives regard public officials as self-serving and of limited competence and see public intervention, however well motivated, as probably inept and ultimately destabilizing. Both recognize that an interventionist government will play a large role in economic affairs. Conservatives regard that prospect with concern, Keynesians with relative equanimity.

Summary

1. Fiscal policy uses government expenditure and tax policies to influence the economy by shifting the aggregate expenditure function.

When private expenditure functions are fixed, it is a relatively simple matter to increase expenditure, to cut tax rates, or to make a balanced budget increase in expenditure in order to remove a deflationary gap (and to make the opposite changes to remove an inflationary gap).

2. Fiscal policy is more difficult when, as is almost always the case, private expenditure functions are continually shifting. Fine tuning, the attempt to hold the aggregate expenditure function virtually constant by offsetting even small fluctuations in private expenditure, has been largely discredited. Yet large and persistent gaps can be offset by fiscal policy.

3. Short-term stabilization by fiscal policy works largely through such automatic stabilizers as tax revenues that vary directly with national income, expenditures on goods and services that do not vary directly with national income, and transfer payments that vary inversely with national income.

4. Discretionary fiscal policy is used to attack large and persistent gaps. The choice between tax and expenditure changes turns, among other things, on the nature of the decision and execution lags and on the need for generalized or localized impact effects.

5. Fiscal stabilization policy needs to be reversible. Otherwise the economy may overshoot its target once private investment recovers from a temporary slump or falls back from a temporary boom. Also without full reversibility, fiscal policy may cause a secular upward shift in the proportion of the GNP accounted for by government as expenditure is raised in recessions and not cut in expansions. Tax changes also need to be perceived as relatively long-lived if they are to induce major changes in household spending patterns. (Temporary changes may merely affect the current saving rate and not expenditure.) This possibility is further discussed in Appendix A to this chapter.

---

[8] The pro-Keynesian view can be found in almost any modern textbook on macroeconomics. The view of the fiscal conservatives is well presented in J. M. Buchanan, J. Burton, and R. E. Wayne, *The Consequences of Mr. Keynes* (London: Institute of Economic Affairs, 1978).

6. Changes in the stance of fiscal policy may be reasonably judged by changes in the full-employment surplus. This is the balance between revenues and expenditures as they would be if full employment prevailed.

7. Fiscal policy was never seriously used to cope with the Great Depression of the 1930s; when it was used to create full employment in the 1940s, it was an accidental by-product of the war effort. Throughout the 1950s a growing fiscal drag made the achievement of full employment more and more difficult. The drag was successfully removed by the 1964 tax cuts. In 1968 fiscal policy was unsuccessful in dampening the inflationary spiral that had been induced by the deficit financing of the Vietnam War. The 1968–1969 experiment is now viewed as a case of "too little and too late."

8. In the 1970s fiscal policy oscillated between expansionary and contractionary stances. This gave rise to the charge of government's engineering a political business cycle with expansions just before elections and contractions just after.

9. An annually balanced budget would be virtually unfeasible; even if it were possible, it would destabilize the economy. A cyclically balanced budget would act as a stabilizer while also curbing the secular growth of the government sector. However, there is no reason why a healthy economy cannot live with a national debt that is steadily growing (e.g., by keeping its ratio to national income constant) and thus with a secularly unbalanced budget.

10. American national debt and debt service have risen and fallen as a percentage of national income, but they have not shown a long-term trend to grow inexorably. Issues concerning the burden of the debt are considered in Appendix B.

11. Keynesians take a relatively sanguine view of the national debt. As long as it does not grow wildly as a proportion of national income, they view its short-term fluctuations and its long-term upward trend in absolute terms as a stabilizing device. Fiscal conservatives mistrust government and view insistence on a balanced budget as the only effective means of curtailing reckless government spending that wastes scarce resources and feeds the fires of inflation.

Topics for Review

Fiscal policy
Budget balance, balanced and unbalanced budgets, surpluses and deficits
Fine tuning
Built-in stabilizers
Discretionary fiscal policy
Decision lags and execution lags
The stance of fiscal policy
The actual budget balance and the full-employment surplus
Fiscal drag
The Keynesian and the fiscal conservative views of budget deficits

Discussion Questions

1. On presidential economics:
   a. President Carter in 1977 said, "There will be no new programs implemented under my administration unless we can be sure that the cost of those programs is compatible with my goal of having a *balanced budget* before the end of that term." Does this mean President Carter rejected fiscal policy? What might it mean?
   b. President Ford in 1975 maintained that his proposed package of a $28 billion cut in federal expenditure and a $28 billion tax cut "as a short-term measure would not affect the economy in any significant way." Does this mean that President Ford believed the balanced budget multiplier was zero? If so, why then might he have proposed the package? If not, what might he have meant?
   c. Why is it so much easier for presidential candidates to advocate balanced budgets than it is for incumbent presidents to achieve them?
2. A study by the Public Interest Research Group in Michigan (PIRGIM) found that every $1 billion in new federal expenditure produced 55,000 jobs, but $1

billion in state and local expenditure created 100,000 jobs. If the study is correct, would a sound fiscal policy (other considerations aside) dictate more and more grants to state and local governments and less and less federal expenditure? Why or why not?

3. J. K. Galbraith said, about coping with a deflationary gap by means of a tax rebate: "Those who advocate a tax cut do so in deeply conditioned disregard of its economic ineffectiveness, its demonstrated political disutility, and its patently reactionary social effects." What might Professor Galbraith have had in mind by his statement?

4. Which of the following would be built-in stabilizers?
   a. food stamps for the needy
   b. cost of living escalators on government contracts and pensions
   c. income taxes
   d. free college tuition for unemployed workers after six months of unemployment, provided that they are under 30 years old and have had five or more years of full-time work experience since high school

5. When the government subsidizes particular industries or regions rather than industry in general, is this a sure sign of "playing politics" with fiscal policy?

6. In his first inaugural address, President Franklin D. Roosevelt expounded the doctrine of "sound finance"—that the government's budget should always be balanced. Government spending, however, rose faster than taxes could be increased, and deficits resulted. Would the effect of the New Deal on employment have been more or less favorable if Roosevelt had been successful in keeping the budget balanced throughout his first term?

7. The Employment Act of 1946 made no explicit mention of price stability as an objective of national income policy. Why do you suppose this was so? Can fiscal policy affect the price level as well as the level of employment?

8. How does growth in full-employment income produce fiscal drag? How may inflation produce fiscal drag? Is not fiscal drag just another name for a built-in stabilizer?

9. Consider the typical annual expenditures and revenues of the organizations listed below. Comment on the appropriate debt policy for each, taking into account their respective goals, life spans, and resources.
   a. family household
   b. private corporation (differentiate between a rapidly growing and a mature firm)
   c. a village of 5,000 inhabitants
   d. New York City
   e. New York State
   f. the U.S. government
   g. the United Nations

10. The national debt is essentially the net result of past and present fiscal policy; that is, the net debt increases when the government runs a budget deficit. Does increasing the national debt make a nation poorer? What effect, if any, does the national debt have on the distribution of income?

11. If Congress passed a law limiting government borrowing from the public in each year to X percent of the national income in that year, would this tend to stabilize or destabilize the economy? Does it matter how large X is? Would such a law be either necessary or sufficient to assure that the government debt did not become excessive?

12. Between 1973 and 1974 the full-employment surplus went from a deficit of nearly $10 billion to a surplus of nearly $10 billion while the actual surplus went from a deficit of almost $7 billion to a deficit of almost $11 billion. What was the change in the stance of fiscal policy? What do you think happened to national income? What do you think might have happened to national income and to the actual budget surplus if the stance of fiscal policy had remained constant?

13. A late 1979 *Financial Post* article heralded "How a Slump May Fuel the Deficit." Why do deficits rise in slumps? Does this signal a change in the stance of fiscal policy?

Part Nine

Money, Banking, and
Monetary Policy

The Nature and History of Money

32

Everyone understands the importance of money, or the lack of it, to his or her own welfare. Most people believe that money is one of the more important things in life and that there is never enough of it. Money gives an individual command over goods, but increasing the world's money supply would not change the quantity of goods available. Inflation is on all our minds these days, and everyone knows that inflation and money are somehow related to one another.

What, then, is the significance of money to the economy as a whole, and why are economists concerned about it? Indeed, what is money, and how did it come to play its present role?

The Importance of Money

THE "REAL" AND MONEY PARTS OF THE ECONOMY

Very early in the history of economics changes in the quantity of money were seen to be associated with changes in the price level. Eighteenth and nineteenth century economists developed the first comprehensive theories of the functioning of the economy, with money playing a special part in those theories. The economy was conceived of as being divisible into a "real part" and a "monetary part."

The allocation of resources is determined in the real part of the economy by demand and supply. This allocation depends on the structure of *relative* prices. Whether a lot of beef is produced relative to pork depends on the relation between the prices of the two commodities. If the price of beef is higher than the price of pork and both commodities cost about the same to produce, the incentive exists to produce beef rather than pork. This argument depends on the relationship between the prices of the two commodities, not on the money price of each. At prices of 50¢ a pound for pork and $1.50 for beef, the *relative* incentive will be the same as it would be at $1 for pork and $3 for beef. As with beef and pork, so with all other commodities: the allocation of resources between different lines of production depends on relative prices.

According to the early economists, the price *level* was determined in the monetary part of the economy. An increase in the money supply led to an increase in all money prices. In the beef and pork example, an increase in the total money available might raise the price of pork from 50¢ to $1 a pound and the price of beef from $1.50 to $3, but in equilibrium it would leave relative prices unchanged. Hence it would have no effect on the real part of the economy, that is, on the amount of resources allocated to beef and to pork production (and to everything else). If the quantity of money were doubled, the prices of everything bought would double; and money income would also double, so everyone earning an income would be made no better or worse off by the change. Thus, in equilibrium, the real and the monetary parts of the economy were believed to have no effect on each other.

Because early economists believed that the most important questions—How much does the economy produce? What share of it does each group in the society get?—were answered in the real sector, they spoke of money as a "veil" behind which occurred the real events that affected material well-being. The doctrine that the quantity of money influences the level of money prices but has no effect on the real part of the economy is called the doctrine of the **neutrality of money.**

Modern economists still accept the insights of

the early economists that relative prices are a major determinant of the real allocation of resources and that the quantity of money has a lot to do with determining the absolute level of prices. They do not however accept the neutrality of money, as we shall see in Chapter 34.

In this chapter we look first at the experience of price level changes—one aspect of the importance of money—and then at the nature of money itself.

THE EXPERIENCE OF PRICE LEVEL CHANGES

Figure 32-1 shows the course of American producer (or wholesale) prices from 1785 through 1979. Considerable year-to-year fluctuations are apparent. Major wars have been associated with sharp inflations and, up until World War II, they were all followed by sharp deflations. In spite of the large fluctuations that occurred during the nineteenth century, the price trend during that period was neither upward nor downward. World War II was the first war in American history not followed by a major deflation. The price level rose rapidly from 1946 until the end of the Korean War in 1952. It then became relatively stable for a while, rising by only 13 percent between 1952 and 1967, an average of less than 1 percent per year. During the last dozen years we have experienced a significant new round of inflation, one that started gradually but quickly accelerated. Producer prices rose 128 percent between 1967 and January 1, 1980.

Although admittedly a long time, even two centuries may still not be long enough to give a clear perspective of long-term price fluctuations. Indeed, nineteenth century price levels were not typical. The experience of the period since 1946 looks much more dramatic and unusual when compared only with the nineteenth century than when considered in longer perspective. An indication of the course of price levels in England over seven centuries is given in Figure 32-2. The

FIGURE 32-1

An Index of Producer Prices in the United States, 1785–1979 (1967 = 100)

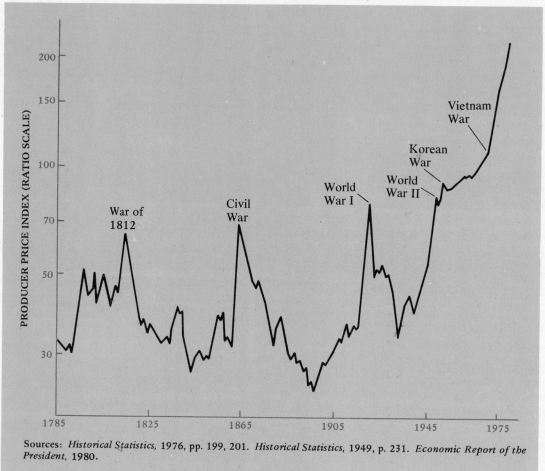

Sources: *Historical Statistics,* 1976, pp. 199, 201. *Historical Statistics,* 1949, p. 231. *Economic Report of the President,* 1980.

Persistent peacetime inflation has only recently become a problem in America. While the price level has fluctuated throughout American history, no long-term trend was visible during the period from the Revolutionary War to 1930. Every major war produced an inflation that was subsequently reversed. The data are plotted on a ratio scale in which equal vertical distances represent equal percentage changes.

figure shows that there was an overall inflationary trend but that it was by no means evenly spread over the centuries. Some further idea of the variability of price levels can be obtained from Table 32-1, which looks at the same price level over various periods within the seven centuries.

The period since World War II has seen fairly

general inflationary tendencies throughout the world. Table 32-2 shows the average rate of change in the price level of 20 countries over 15 years. Notice the great range and variability of experience from country to country; notice too that the rate of inflation increased in most countries. While OPEC is often identified as a major source of the worldwide inflationary trend, note

FIGURE 32-2
A Price Index of Consumables in Southern England, 1275–1959

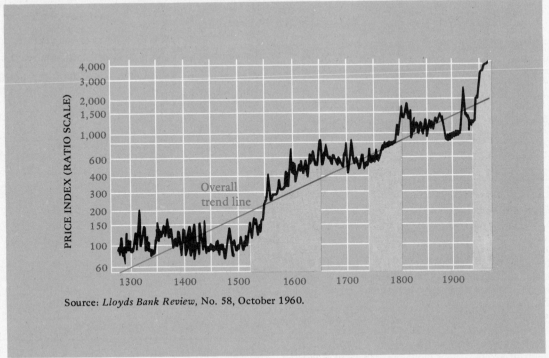

Source: *Lloyds Bank Review*, No. 58, October 1960.

Over the last seven centuries long periods of stable prices have alternated with long periods of rising prices. This remarkable price series shows an index of the prices of food, clothing, and fuel in southern England from 1275 through 1959. The trend line shows that the average change in prices over the whole period was .5 percent per year. The shaded areas indicate periods of unreversed inflation. The series also shows that even the perspective of a century can be misleading because long periods of stable or gently falling prices tended to alternate with long periods of rising prices.

that the current increase in inflation started in most countries before 1973 and the OPEC embargo.

WHY INFLATIONS MATTER

Modern economists have devoted much effort to identifying and measuring the consequences of inflation. Even the early economists, with their strict division between the economy's real and monetary sectors, were strongly opposed to rapid inflations or deflations because of the harm that could be done during the transition from one price level to another. Indeed, it may take years

to move from one equilibrium price level to another, and in the course of the movement many people may be hurt. The consequences of an inflation depend significantly on whether or not it is anticipated.

The Effects of Unanticipated Inflations

Unanticipated inflations cause more upset than do anticipated inflations. Contracts freely entered into when the price level was expected to remain constant will yield hardships for some and unexpected gains for others once the unanticipated inflation begins.

TABLE 32-1

Seven Centuries of English Prices

Period	Number of years in period	Percentage change in price level over whole period	Average annual percentage change over period
1275–1525	250	+ 29	+ 0.12
1526–1650	125	+550	+ 4.40
1651–1744	94	− 38	− 0.40
1745–1813	69	+263	+ 3.81
1814–1893	80	− 51	− 0.64
1894–1920	27	+183	+ 6.78
1921–1932	12	− 59	− 4.92
1933–1960	28	+322	+11.50

Source: Lloyds Bank Review, No. 58, October 1960.

Long periods of relatively stable prices have alternated with long periods of continuous inflation. The table shows percentage changes in the price level over selected time periods. (The data come from the series graphed in Figure 32-2.) Notice, first, the very long periods during which the change in the price level averaged less than 1 percent per year. Most of the unreversed rises in the price level before 1960 occurred in three periods: 1526–1650, when Spanish gold and silver flowed into Europe; 1750–1800, when banking spread from London into the English provincial cities, greatly increasing the supply of bank money; and 1939–1950, when there was massive deficit financing of World War II and its aftermath. The recent period of inflation (since 1960) is not included in the data.

A first effect of a continuing inflation is to influence the allocation of resources by changing *relative* prices (including *relative* wages), often in haphazard fashion. In a market economy, changes in relative prices are supposed to signal resource shifts in response to changing patterns of demand and supply. In an inflationary period other influences may play a major (and potentially distorting) role.

For example, workers in occupations with strong unions will be able to keep their wages rising as fast as prices; they may even be able to do better than they would have done if prices had never risen. In other occupations, wages and salaries will be very slow to adjust. Employees in these occupations will lose substantially because of the inflation. Schoolteachers often find them-

TABLE 32-2

Inflation Rates of Selected Countries, 1963–1978

Country	Average annual rate of increase of consumer prices		
	1963–1968	1968–1973	1973–1978
Argentina	25.5	33.4	170.2
Canada	3.1	4.6	9.2
Chile	28.1	74.6	199.1
China (Nationalist)	4.0	4.8	12.5
Denmark	6.3	6.4	11.0
Ecuador	3.8	8.1	14.7
France	3.2	6.1	10.7
Iran	1.6	5.1	15.3
Italy	3.5	5.7	16.4
Japan	5.1	7.2	11.3
Mexico	3.1	6.3	20.1
Netherlands	4.7	6.9	7.8
Norway	4.2	6.9	9.5
South Korea	14.9	9.9	17.9
Switzerland	3.5	5.6	4.0
Syria	3.2	5.5	11.8
United Kingdom	3.8	7.5	16.1
United States	2.6	5.0	8.0
West Germany	2.5	4.6	4.8
Yugoslavia	15.7	14.2	17.0

Source: Computed from IMF, *International Statistics Yearbook* 1979.

Inflation rates vary greatly among countries, yet the worldwide trend is one of increased inflation. Annual rates of increase in prices, of the size shown in the table, cause substantial changes in price levels over five-year periods. In Chile between 1973 and 1978, prices on average tripled every year. In West Germany prices rose 27 percent in five years. In the United States prices were roughly 50 percent higher in 1978 than in 1973. The trend to increasing inflation of the 1970s afflicted most countries.

selves in this group. Not only do these individuals suffer, but the change in relative wages will affect the allocation of resources. For example, the fall in the real income of teachers relative to that of plumbers is likely to reduce the supply of new entrants into the teaching profession below what it would have been in the absence of inflation.

A second effect of unanticipated inflations is to redistribute wealth from lenders to borrowers, whereas unanticipated deflations do the opposite. To see why this is true, suppose that Mr. Jones lends Ms. Smith $100 at 5 percent interest for one year. If the price level rises by 10 percent over the year, Jones will actually earn a negative rate of interest on the loan. The $105 Jones gets back from Smith can buy fewer goods than the $100 Jones originally parted with. As well as doing without the money for a year, Jones is worse off in terms of purchasing power at the end of the year than at the beginning.

Jones's loss, however, is Smith's gain. Smith did not even have to use the $100 in any productive business enterprise to show a gain. All she needed to do was to buy and hold goods whose prices rose merely by the average rate of inflation. At the end of the year Smith can sell the goods for $110, pay back the $100 she borrowed plus $5 interest, and show a gain of $5 for having done nothing more than hold goods instead of money. This sort of redistribution occurs not just on borrowing and lending contracts but on any form of contract that is stated in terms of monetary units.

A third effect of inflation, whether anticipated or unanticipated, is to reduce the living standards of those on fixed incomes. Consider the case of Mr. and Mrs. Prudent, who invested in an annuity designed to provide them with a fixed annual dollar income after retirement. The Prudents saved enough throughout their working years to give themselves a retirement income of $10,000 a year. They figured that with the children no longer at home and with their durable goods already purchased, $10,000 would allow a good standard of living for their retirement years. However, if the price level doubles just before the Prudents retire, the purchasing power of their money income will be halved. They will still get $10,000 a year, but it will buy only half as many goods as they had expected it to buy.

Furthermore, if the price level continues to rise slowly, say at 3 percent per year, the Prudents will have to cut their real purchases of goods and services by a steady 3 percent each year. If they should live for 23 years after retirement, their living standard will have been halved

once again. By that time they will be able to buy only as many goods per year as if they had saved just enough to provide themselves an income of $2,500 a year. Instead of having a modest but satisfactory living standard, the Prudents will have been made progressively worse off, until finally they will have been reduced to poverty.

This kind of situation was not far from the experience of those who saved during the years before World War II and then retired into the creeping inflation of the 1950s and 1960s. It understates the plight of retirees facing the sharp inflation that characterized the 1970s. As the 1980s begin—with double-digit inflation—the nightmare of inflation eroding retirement incomes affects not only the Prudents but the Welloffs.

The reduction in the purchasing power of money savings is one of the most dramatic and obvious effects of an inflation. It helps to explain the hostility to inflation felt by anyone who has suffered seriously from one.

The Effects of Anticipated Inflations

To the extent that inflations are anticipated, some of the haphazard effects can be avoided by drawing up contracts in real terms or with "escalator clauses" or "indexing" that build changes in average price levels into such things as social security benefits and specific wage and price contracts. Escalator contracts are common in labor agreements, in long-term raw material contracts, and in many government procurement agreements.

Even without a formal contract in real terms, it is possible to allow for the effects of an inflation. Wage and price contracts are major examples. If, say, a 10 percent inflation is expected over the next year, a money wage that rises by 10 percent over that period may represent the minimum demand of a union intent on preserving or increasing the purchasing power of its members. A banker will demand 9 percent interest for the use of money if 3 percent is the real rate of interest and 6 percent is the anticipated rate of inflation.

Hyperinflation

Can a sharp inflation continue year after year without triggering an explosive inflation that wholly destroys the value of a currency? The answer appears to be yes — at least some of the time. Inflation rates of 50, 100, and even 200 percent or more a year have occurred year after year and proven quite manageable as people adjust their contracts to real terms. While there are strains and side effects, the evidence shows such situations to be possible without hyperinflation.

Does this mean there is nothing to fear from rapid inflation? The historical record is not entirely reassuring. There have been a number of so-called hyperinflations in which at some point prices began to rise at an ever-accelerating rate until the nation's money ceased to be a satisfactory store of value even for the short period between receipt and expenditure. Consider the index of wholesale prices in Germany during and after World War I:

Date	Wholesale price index (1913 = 1)
Jan 1913	1
Jan 1920	13
Jan 1921	14
Jan 1922	37
July 1922	101
Jan 1923	2,785
July 1923	74,800
Aug 1923	944,000
Sept 1923	23,900,000
Oct 1923	7,096,000,000
15 Nov 1923	750,000,000,000

The index shows that a good purchased with one 100 mark note in July 1923 would have required *ten million* 100 mark notes for its purchase only four months later!

While Germany had experienced substantial inflation during World War I, averaging more than 30 percent per year, the immediate postwar years of 1920 and 1921 gave no sign of an explosive inflation. Indeed during 1920 price stability was experienced. But in 1922 and 1923 the price level exploded. On November 15, 1923, the mark was officially repudiated, its value wholly destroyed. How could this happen?

When an inflation becomes so rapid that people lose confidence in the purchasing power of their currency, they rush to spend it. But people who have goods become increasingly reluctant to accept the rapidly depreciating money in exchange. The rush to spend money accelerates the increase in prices until people finally become unwilling to accept money on any terms. What was once money then ceases to be money.

The price system can then be restored only by official repudiation of the old monetary unit and its replacement by a new unit. This destroys the value not only of monetary savings but of all contracts specified in terms of the old monetary units.

There are approximately a dozen documented hyperinflations in world history, among them the collapse of the *continental* during the American revolution, the *ruble* during the Russian revolution, the *drachma* during and after the German occupation of Greece in World War II, the *pengo* in Hungary during 1945 and 1946, and the Chinese national currency during 1946–1948. Every one of these hyperinflations was accompanied by great increases in the money supply; new money was printed to give governments purchasing power they could not or would not obtain by taxation. And every one occurred in the midst of a major political upheaval in which grave doubts existed about the stability and future of the government itself.

Is hyperinflation likely in the absence of civil war, revolution, or collapse of the government? Most economists think not. And it is clear that inflation rates of 5 or 10 or 20 percent per year — which many Americans find so upsetting — do not mean the inevitable or likely onset of a disastrous hyperinflation, however serious their distributive and social effects may be.

While some people may be able to avoid the effects of inflation when they see it coming, many people can not do so much of the time. One of the most troubling aspects of the rapid increase in the inflation rate at the start of the 1980s was the unavailability to ordinary people of "inflation proof" havens for their savings. Thus many of those who correctly anticipated a continued inflation were unable to protect themselves against it.

Even a fully foreseen inflation has real effects. Many practices—such as business accounting conventions, definitions of allowable expenses given in tax laws, and many private pension schemes—make use of money definitions that cannot be altered even in the face of an inflation that is fully foreseen. In addition, not everyone can find a way to adjust to an anticipated inflation without incurring substantial transactions costs—for example, paying commissions for buying and selling property. These transactions costs may be particularly high for those with relatively small amounts to protect.

Does Everyone Lose by Inflations?

Contrary to popular opinion, inflation does not generally make everyone or even the vast majority worse off. This is because inflation does not normally have major effects on the economy's total output.

The popular image of the average person's being slowly impoverished as money prices rise steadily faster than his or her money income is mistaken. This is in sharp contrast to the overall effects of a serious recession. A recession typically will lower average living standards because many of the country's resources—its labor, factories, and raw materials—lie idle.

The main undesirable domestic effects of inflation, whether foreseen or unforeseen, are distributive: contracts stated in money terms do not have the effects in terms of real purchasing power that was expected of them. Since contracts are two-sided, one person's losses are another's gains.

Thus *typical* households and firms are wrong when they say that inflation is pricing everything out of their reach.[1] When income-earning households and firms say that inflation is ruining them, what they are probably thinking is how much better off they would be if they had this year's money income to spend at the prices ruling several years ago. But this is impossible, for that much output is not available. Few would prefer the prices of, say, ten years ago and their money incomes of the same period because real income rose over the decade, inflation notwithstanding. Of course, some groups are seriously hurt by inflation, but the *average* household and the *average* firm are not hurt because in most years money income rises significantly faster than money prices.

In saying that the main effects of inflation are redistributional, we do *not* say that inflation is unimportant. Redistributions of income can be very important. After all, the causes of the distribution of income among social classes were *the* major problem faced by the classical economists. The call for a major redistribution from capitalists to workers was, and still is, an important part of Marxian economics. Rapid inflations cause major, arbitrary, and socially destructive redistributions. The continual erosion of the purchasing power of fixed money incomes is tragic to those who suffer it, and such erosion is only one of the many serious negative redistributive effects of inflation.

Other effects of inflation may also be serious. For example, social and personal tensions arise from the race to keep up with the rise in prices and from the knowledge that some gain from inflation at the expense of others.

---

[1] Some goods may go nearly out of reach if their *relative* prices rise. For example, the rise in the relative price of prime cuts of beef over the last 20 years (because of rapidly rising demand as real income has risen) certainly has been dramatic, yet this has not been due to inflation, but rather to a change in relative prices. Even if the overall price level had remained constant in America, prime cuts of beef would have risen in price. Householders would have found it just as expensive to buy a steak *relative to their overall budget* as they do in today's inflationary world.

The Nature of Money

Inflation is a monetary phenomenon in the sense that a rise in the general level of prices is the same thing as a decrease in the purchasing power of money. But what exactly *is* money? There is probably more folklore and general nonsense believed about money than about any other aspect of the economy. In the remainder of this chapter we describe the functions of money and outline the history of money. One purpose of this account is to remove some misconceptions.

WHAT IS MONEY?

Traditionally in economics **money** has been defined as any generally accepted medium of exchange—anything that will be accepted by virtually everyone in exchange for goods and services.

Money has several different functions: to act as a medium of exchange, as a store of value, and as a unit of account.

Different kinds of money vary in the degree of efficiency with which they fulfill these functions, and different definitions of money may be required for different purposes.

A Medium of Exchange

An important function of money is to facilitate exchange. Without money the economic system, which is based on specialization and the division of labor, would be impossible, and we would have to return to primitive forms of production and exchange. It is not without justification that money has been called one of the great inventions contributing to human freedom.

If there were no money, goods would have to be exchanged by barter, one good being swapped directly for another. We discussed this cumbersome system in Chapter 4; the major difficulty with barter is that each transaction requires a *double coincidence of wants*. For an exchange to occur between A and B, not only must A have what B wants, but B must have what A wants. If all exchange were restricted to barter, anyone who specialized in producing one commodity would have to spend a great deal of time searching for satisfactory transactions.

The use of money as a generally accepted **medium of exchange** removes these problems. People can sell their output for money and subsequently use the money to buy what they wish from others. The double coincidence of wants is unnecessary when money is used as a medium of exchange. Efficient production demands specialization, and this in turn requires that people satisfy most of their desires by consuming goods produced by others. In any complex economy, such exchanges entail the use of some kind of money.

The difficulties of barter force people to become more or less self-sufficient. With money as a medium of exchange, everyone is free to specialize; with specialization in the direction of one's natural talents and abilities, the production of all commodities can be increased.

To serve as an efficient medium of exchange, money must have a number of characteristics: it must be readily acceptable; it must have a high value for its weight (otherwise it would be a nuisance to carry around); it must be divisible because money that comes only in large denominations is useless for transactions having only a small value; and it must not be readily counterfeitable because if money can be easily duplicated by individuals, it will lose its value.

The nature of what serves as a medium of exchange changes over time. Recently there has been considerable talk about a checkless society. In this society, one's salary is fed into the memory of a giant computer. Purchases are paid for by inserting an identity card into the seller's recording device, which immediately tells the central computer to reduce the credit in the buyer's account and increase the credit in the seller's account. Such a society would dispense with cash and checks but not with money. Credit in the computer constitutes each individual's medium of exchange. Call it what you like, for all practical purposes it is money.

During the 1970s there was a sharp rise in barter transactions. One week a gasoline station might supply gasoline to another, only on the promise of the receiver to pay back the same number of gallons of gasoline out of its next week's allotment. And there were such offers as, I'll paint your house if you'll fix my daughter's teeth. These examples do not represent a reversal of the forces that led to the need for and the convenience of using money. The first example reflects only the belief that in a period of gasoline shortage and rationing, dollars may not be as satisfactory a medium of exchange for gasoline as the promise of gasoline at another time. The second example, and the widely reported development of barter clearing houses, almost surely indicates the desire to avoid or evade taxation. If you hire me (a painter) to paint your house, and I hire you (a dentist) to do orthodonture, the Internal Revenue Service will surely find out about it. If we engage in barter, the IRS will still want to know about it, for the transaction is legally subject to tax, but it is much less likely to find out.

A Store of Value

Money is a handy way to store purchasing power when the price level is relatively stable. With barter, some other good must be taken in exchange; with money, goods may be sold today and money stored until it is needed. This provides a claim on someone else's goods that can be exercised at a future date. The two sides of the transaction can be separated in time with the obvious increase in freedom that this confers.

To be a satisfactory store of value, however, money must have a relatively stable value. When prices are stable, it is possible to know exactly how much command over real goods and services has been stored up when a certain sum of money has been accumulated. When prices change rapidly, there is no way of knowing how many goods can be bought when previously ac-

cumulated money is spent. This reduces the usefulness of money as a store of value.

Although money can serve as a satisfactory store of accumulated purchasing power for a single individual, it cannot do so for the society as a whole. If a single individual accumulates a pile of dollars, he or she will, when the time comes to spend it, be able to command the current output of some other individual. The whole society cannot do this. If all individuals were to save their money and then retire simultaneously to live on their savings, there would be no current production to purchase and consume. The society's ability to satisfy wants depends on goods and services being available; if some of this want-satisfying capacity is to be stored up for the whole society, goods that are currently producible must be left unconsumed and carried over to future periods.

A Unit of Account

Money may also be used purely for accounting purposes without having a physical existence of its own. For instance, a government store in a truly communist society might say that everyone had so many "dollars" to use each month. Goods could then be assigned prices and each consumer's purchases recorded, the consumer being allowed to buy until the allocated supply of dollars was exhausted. These dollars need have no existence other than as entries in the store's books, yet they would serve as a perfectly satisfactory unit of account. Whether they could also serve as a medium of exchange between individuals depends on whether the store would agree to transfer dollar credits from one customer to another at the customer's request. Banks will transfer dollars credited to demand deposits in this way, and thus a bank deposit can serve as both a unit of account and a medium of exchange. Notice that the use of *dollars* in this context suggests a further sense in which money is a unit of account. People think about values in terms of the monetary unit with which they are familiar.

A further but related function of money is sometimes distinguished: that of a "standard of deferred payments." Payments that are to be made in the future, on account of debts and so on, are reckoned in money. Money is used as a unit of account with the added dimension of time because the account will not be settled until some time in the future.

DO WE NEED MONEY?

Many radical social reformers have seen money as the root of society's evils and have dreamed of the day when the institution of money would be eradicated. Whenever this hope has been combined with a "back to the land" social program and the simple, self-sufficient life for everyone, the goals are at least consistent. For the self-sufficient community that is small enough to base all transactions on barter can dispense with money.

Sometimes the dream of abandoning money is combined with the ideas of a modern industrial socialist state that enjoys a high standard of living without private ownership. Here the goals are contradictory: efficient production demands a specialization of tasks, and this requires that people satisfy most of their wants by consuming goods produced by others. A sophisticated economy also requires that people be able to consume on a different time path than they produce, that is, to borrow now and repay later, or to save now for later needs. In any complex economy, such exchanges require that some kind of money be used.

THE ORIGINS AND GROWTH OF METALLIC MONEY

The origins of money are lost in antiquity; most primitive tribes known today make some use of it. The ability of money to free people from the cumbersome necessity of barter must have led to its early use as soon as some generally acceptable commodity appeared. All sorts of commodities have been used as money at one time or another, but gold and silver proved to have great advantages. They were precious because their supply was relatively limited, and they were in constant demand by the rich for ornament and decoration. They had the additional advantage that they do not easily wear out. Thus they tended to have a high and stable price. They were easily recognized and generally known to be commodities that, because of their stable price, would be accepted by most people. They were also divisible into extremely small units (gold, to a single grain).

Precious metals thus came to circulate as money and to be used in many transactions. Before the invention of coins it was necessary to carry precious metals around in bulk. When a purchase was to be made, the requisite quantity of the metal would have to be weighed carefully on a scale. A sack of gold and a highly accurate set of scales were the common equipment of the merchant and trader.

Such a system, though better than barter, was cumbersome. Coins eliminated the need to weigh the metal at each transaction. The prince or ruler weighed the metal and made a coin out of it to which he affixed his own seal to guarantee the amount of precious metal it contained. A certain coin was stated on its face to contain exactly 1/16 of an ounce of gold. If a commodity was priced at 1/8 of an ounce of gold, two coins would be given over without weighing the gold. This was clearly a great convenience as long as traders knew that they could accept the coin at its "face value." The face value itself was nothing more than a guarantee that a certain weight of metal was contained therein.

The prince's subjects, however, could not let a good opportunity pass. Someone soon had the idea of clipping a thin slice off the edge of the coin. If he collected a coin stamped as containing half an ounce of gold, he could clip a slice off the edge and pass the coin off as still containing half an ounce of gold. ("Doesn't the stamp prove it?" he would argue.) If he got away with this, he would have made a profit equal to the market value of the clipped metal.

Whenever this practice became common, even

the most myopic traders noticed that things were not what they seemed in the coinage world. It became necessary to weigh each coin before accepting it at its face value; out came the scales again, and most of the usefulness of coins was lost. To get around this problem, the idea arose of minting the coins with a rough edge. The absence of the rough edge would immediately be apparent and would indicate that the coin had been clipped. The practice, called milling, survives on some coins as an interesting anachronism to remind us that there were days when the market value of the metal in the coin (if it were melted down) was equal to the face value of the coin.

Not to be outdone by the cunning of his subjects, the prince was quick to seize the chance of getting something for nothing. Because he was empowered to mint the coins, he was in a very good position to work a *really* profitable fraud. When he found himself with bills that he could not pay and that it was inexpedient to repudiate, he merely used some suitable occasion—a marriage, an anniversary, an alliance—to remint the coinage. The subjects would be ordered to bring their gold coins into the mint to be melted down and coined afresh with a new stamp. The subjects could then go away the proud possessors of one new coin for every old coin that they had brought in. Between the melting down and the recoining, however, the prince had only to toss some inexpensive base metal in with the molten gold to earn a handsome profit. If the coinage were debased by adding, say, one pound of new base metal to every four pounds of old coins, five coins would be made for every four turned in. For every four coins brought in, the prince could return four and have one left for himself as profit. With these coins he could pay his bills.

The result was inflation. The subjects had the same number of coins as before and hence could demand the same quantity of goods. When the prince paid his bills, however, the recipients of the extra coins could be expected to spend some or all of them, and this would represent a net increase in demand. The extra demand would bid up prices. Debasing the coinage thus led to a rise in prices. It was the experience of such inflations that led early economists to propound the *quantity theory of money and prices*. They argued that there was a relation between the average level of prices and the quantity of money in circulation, such that a change in the quantity of money would lead to a change in the price level in the same direction.

The early experience of currency debasement led to a famous economic "law" that has stood the test of time. The hypothesis is that "bad money drives out good." It has come to be known as **Gresham's law** after the Elizabethan financial expert Sir Thomas Gresham, who first explained the workings of the law to Queen Elizabeth.

To see how the law works, assume there are two kinds of gold coins, Royals and Sovereigns. Royals have not been debased—the gold in the coin is actually worth its face value. Sovereigns have been debased to the point that the gold in the coin is worth only 80 percent of its face value. If you possessed one of each type of coin, each with the same face value, and had a bill to pay, what would you do? Clearly, you would pay the bill with the debased Sovereign and keep the undebased Royal. You part with less gold that way. If you wanted to obtain a certain amount of gold bullion by melting down the gold coins (as was frequently done), which coins would you use? Clearly, you would use Royals because you would part with less "face value" that way—for according to face value, five Sovereigns are equal to five Royals, but if you melt them down it takes only four Royals to get the same amount of gold as is contained in five Sovereigns. The debased coins would thus remain in circulation and the undebased coins would disappear. Whenever people got hold of an undebased coin, they would hold on to it; whenever they got a debased coin, they would pass it on.

THE EVOLUTION OF PAPER MONEY

Another important step in the history of money was the evolution of paper currency. Artisans

Where Has All the Coinage Gone?

American tourists traveling in Chile or another country with rapid inflation often wonder aloud why paper currency is used even for transactions as small as the purchase of a newspaper or a pack of matches. Metallic currency in such places is often very scarce and sometimes nonexistent. Similarly, the silver dollar, half-dollar, quarter, and dime have disappeared from the American scene. The reason for these things is a nice example of Gresham's law.

Consider a country that has three different "tokens," each of them legal tender in the amount of 25 cents. One is a silver quarter with ten cents worth of recoverable silver in it; a second is made of cheaper metals with five cents worth of recoverable metal in it; the third is a 25-cent bill, a brightly colored piece of paper money that says plainly on its face "legal tender for all debts public and private."

If prices are stable and the government produces all three forms of money, there is no reason why they should not all circulate freely and interchangeably. Each is legal tender, and each is worth more as money than as anything else.

However, suppose an inflation starts and prices — including proportionally the prices of silver and other metals — begin to rise sharply.

By the time prices have tripled, the silver quarters will have disappeared because the silver in each one is now worth 30 cents, and people will hoard them or melt them down rather than spend them to buy goods priced at only 25 cents. While not everyone will do this, coins passing from hand to hand will eventually reach someone who withdraws them from circulation.

What about the coins made of cheaper metal? Since prices have tripled, they now contain metal worth 15 cents, still less than their face value. Will they too disappear? They will if there is a further inflation of, say, 100 percent. They may even disappear without such a further inflation if people begin to expect one. Suppose people believe there is a reasonable chance that metal prices will soon double again. It will be worth holding on to the coins and using paper money instead. Why spend coins that may in the foreseeable future be more valuable than their face value when you can spend paper that isn't worth anything at all *except* as money?

Thus inflation — and even the expectation of inflation — may make some money "good" and some "bad" in Gresham's sense. If it does, the bad will displace the good.

who worked with gold were called goldsmiths. Naturally they kept very secure safes in which to store their gold.[2] Among the public the practice grew up of storing gold with the goldsmith for safekeeping. In return, the goldsmith would give the depositor a receipt promising to hand over the gold on demand. If the depositor wished to

make a large purchase, he or she could go to the goldsmith, reclaim the gold, and hand it over to the seller of the goods. Chances were that the seller would not require the gold but would carry it back to the goldsmith for safekeeping.

Clearly, if people knew the goldsmith to be reliable, there was no need to go through the cumbersome and risky business of physically transferring the gold. The buyer need only transfer the goldsmith's receipt to the seller, who would accept it, secure in the knowledge that the gold-

---

[2] All the basic ideas about paper money can be explained by concentrating on the goldsmiths, though there were earlier sources of paper money in various negotiable evidences of debt.

smith would pay over the gold whenever it was needed. If the seller wished to buy a good from a third party who also knew the goldsmith to be reliable, this transaction too could be effected by passing the goldsmith's receipt from the buyer to the seller. The convenience of using pieces of paper instead of gold is obvious.

Thus, when it first came into being, paper money was a promise to pay on demand so much gold, the promise being made first by goldsmiths and later by banks. Banks too became known for their vaults ("safes") where the precious gold was stored and protected. As long as the institutions were known to be reliable, their pieces of paper would be "as good as gold." Such paper money was *backed* by precious metal and was *convertible* on demand into this metal. When a country's money is convertible into gold, the country is said to be on a *gold standard*.

In nineteenth century America, private banks operating under either federal or state charters commonly issued paper money nominally convertible into gold. **Bank notes** represented banks' promises to pay. In areas such as the American West, where banks were small and often proved unreliable in meeting demands for payment in gold, bank notes had a shady reputation. The gold bag and scales persisted in America well into the second half of the nineteenth century, even after paper money became widely accepted in most parts of the country.

Fractionally Backed Paper Money

For most transactions, individuals were content to use paper currency. It was soon discovered that it was not necessary to keep an ounce of gold in the vaults for every claim to an ounce circulating as paper money. It was necessary to keep some gold on hand because, for some transactions, paper would not do. If a man wished to make a purchase from a distant place where his local bank was not known, he might have to convert his paper into gold and ship the gold. Further, he might not have perfect confidence in the bank's ability to honor its pledge to redeem the

notes in gold at a future time. His alternative was to exchange his notes for gold and store the gold until he needed it.

For these and other reasons, some holders of notes demanded gold in return for their notes. However, some of the bank's customers received gold in various transactions and stored it in the bank for safekeeping. They accepted promises to pay (i.e., bank notes) in return. At any one time, then, some of the bank's customers would be withdrawing gold, others would be depositing it, and the great majority would be trading in the bank's paper notes without any need or desire to convert them into gold. Thus the bank was able to issue more money redeemable in gold than the amount of gold held in its vaults. This was good business because the money could be profitably invested by purchasing securities that yielded a return and granting interest-earning loans to households and firms.

This discovery was made by the early goldsmiths. From that time to the present, banks have had many more claims to pay outstanding against them than they actually had in reserves available to pay those claims. In such a situation we say that the currency is *fractionally backed* by the reserves.

In the past the major problem of a fractionally backed, convertible currency was that of maintaining its convertibility into the precious metal by which it was backed. The imprudent bank that issued too much paper money found itself unable to redeem its currency in gold when the demand for gold was even slightly higher than usual. This bank would then have to suspend payments, and all holders of its notes would suddenly find them worthless. The prudent bank, which kept a reasonable relation between its note issue and its gold reserve, found that it could meet the normal everyday demand for gold without any trouble.

It was always the problem with fractionally backed currency that if all noteholders demanded gold at once, they could not all be satisfied. Thus, if the public ever lost confidence and en masse demanded redemption of their currency, the banks would be unable to honor their

Should Currency Be Backed by Gold?

The gold standard imposed an upper limit on the quantity of convertible currency that could be issued. When the United States abandoned the gold standard in 1934, many in Congress feared that the Federal Reserve Bank would issue too much currency, so Congress imposed the requirement that the Fed hold a certain fraction of gold backing (called the "gold cover") for currency.* If the gold backing had been taken seriously, gold would have placed an upper limit on the quantity of currency. Below that limit the central bank would have had discretionary power. Until this provision was repealed in 1968, the gold supply thus put an apparent upper limit on the quantity of currency that the Fed might issue. But at the time our gold holdings were vastly in excess of the amount required to back all of the currency the public wanted to hold. Thus in practice the theoretical limit placed on currency by gold never became binding. Indeed, the removal of the gold cover occurred in 1968 when a shortage of gold for international payments led to the possibility that the requirement for gold backing might become binding. Like the ceiling on the national debt, the gold cover was designed to make people feel better, not to affect policy.

Does it matter that the central bank is not limited to its ability to issue currency? Consider the gold standard again. Gold derived its value because it is scarce relative to the demand for it (the demand being derived from both its monetary and its nonmonetary uses). Tying a currency to gold meant that the quantity of money in a country was determined by such chance occurrences as the discovery of

* The gold itself is in government vaults, most of it at Fort Knox, Kentucky, and at the Federal Reserve Bank of New York. The central bank merely held gold certificates asserting that the gold was there.

new gold supplies. This was not without advantages, the most important being that it provided a check on governments' ability to cause inflation. Gold cannot be manufactured at will; paper currency can. There is little doubt that in the past, if the money supply had been purely paper, many governments would have attempted to pay their bills by printing new money rather than by raising taxes. Such increases in the money supply, in periods of full employment, would lead to inflation in the same way that the debasement of metallic currency did. Thus the gold standard provided some check on inflation by making it difficult for the government to change the money supply. Periods of major gold discoveries, however, brought about inflations of their own. In the 1500s, for example, Spanish gold and silver flowed into Europe from the New World, bringing inflation in their wake.

A major problem caused by a reliance on gold is that it is usually desirable to increase the money supply when real national income is increasing. This cannot be done on a gold standard unless, by pure chance, gold is discovered at the same time. The gold standard took discretionary powers over the money supply out of the hands of the central authorities. Whether or not one thinks this is a good thing depends on how one thinks the central authorities would use this discretion. In general, a gold standard is probably better than having the currency managed by an ignorant or irresponsible government, but it is worse than having the currency supply adjusted by a well-informed and intelligent one. "Better" and "worse" in this context are judged by the criterion of having a money supply that varies adequately with the needs of the economy but does not vary so as to cause violent inflations or deflations.

pledges and the holders of their notes would lose everything. The history of nineteenth and early twentieth century banking on both sides of the Atlantic is replete with examples of banks ruined by "panics," sudden runs on their gold reserves. When this happened, the bank's depositors and the holders of its notes would find themselves holding worthless pieces of paper.

The so-called central bank was a natural outcome of this sort of banking system. For where were the commercial banks to keep *their* reserves? Their own vaults, although safer than those of their customers, were not safe against a really determined attempt at robbery. Where were the commercial banks to turn when they had good investments but were in temporary need of cash? If they provided loans for the public against reasonable security, why should not some other institution provide loans to them against the same sort of security? Central banks evolved in response to these and other needs.

The Development of Fiat Currencies

As time went on, note issue by private banks became less common and central banks took control of the currency. Central banks in turn became governmental institutions. In time *only* central banks were permitted to issue notes. Originally the central banks issued currency that was fully convertible into gold. In those days, gold would be brought to the central bank, which would issue currency in the form of "gold certificates" that asserted the gold was there on demand. The gold supply thus set some upper limit on the amount of currency. But central banks could issue (as bank notes) more currency than they had gold because not all of the currency was presented for payment at any one time. Thus even under a gold standard central banks had substantial discretionary control over the quantity of currency outstanding.

During the period between World Wars I and II, virtually all the countries of the world abandoned the gold standard. The reasons for this need not be gone into here (they will be men-

tioned in Chapter 42). The result of abandoning the gold standard was that currency was no longer convertible into gold—or anything else. Money that is not convertible by law into anything valuable depends upon its acceptability for its value. Money that is declared by government order (or fiat) to be legal tender for settlement of all debts is called a **fiat money.**

Today virtually all currency is fiat money.

Look at any bill in your wallet—it is not convertible into anything. Until recently much American currency bore the statement: "The United States of America Will Pay to the Bearer on Demand Twenty Dollars" (or whatever the currency was worth). The notes were signed by both the secretary of the Treasury and the treasurer. If you took this seriously and demanded $20, you could have handed over a $20 bill and received in return a different but identical $20 bill! Today's Federal Reserve $20 notes simply say, "The United States of America," "Twenty dollars," and "This note is legal tender for all debts, public and private." It is, in other words, fiat money pure and simple.

The meaning of the phrase **legal tender** is that if you are offered something that is legal tender in payment for a debt and you refuse to accept it, the debt is no longer legally collectible.

Not only is our currency fiat money, so is our coinage. Modern coins, unlike their historical ancestors, rarely contain a value of metal equal to their face value; indeed, the value of the metal is characteristically a minute fraction of the value of the coin. In 1966, faced with a shortage of silver for commercial purposes, the United States Treasury removed the silver from the 25¢ piece. Quarters, however, continued to be traded four to the dollar. Modern coins, like modern paper money, are merely tokens.

Why Is Fiat Money Valuable?

In the early days of the gold standard, paper money was valuable because everyone believed it was convertible into gold on demand. Experience during periods of crisis, when there was often a temporary suspension of convertibility into gold, and of panic, when there were bank failures, served to demonstrate that the mere *promise* of convertibility was not sufficient to make money valuable. Gradually the realization grew that neither was convertibility necessary.

Paper money is valuable when it will be accepted in payment for goods and for debts and is not valuable when it will not be accepted.

Today our paper money and our coinage is valuable because it is generally accepted. Because everyone accepts it as valuable, it *is* valuable; the fact that it can no longer be converted into anything has no effect on its functioning as a medium of exchange.

Many people are disturbed to learn that present-day paper money is neither backed by, nor convertible into, anything more valuable — that it is nothing but pieces of paper whose value derives from common acceptance and from confidence that it will continue to be accepted in the future. People believe their money should be more substantial than that; after all, what of "dollar diplomacy" and the "bedrock solidity" of the Swiss franc? But money is in fact only pieces of paper. There is no point in pretending otherwise.

If paper money is acceptable, it is a medium of exchange; if its purchasing power remains stable, it is a satisfactory store of value; and if both of these things are true, it will also serve as a satisfactory unit of account.

DEPOSIT MONEY

By the twentieth century private banks had, by law, lost the authority to issue money by issuing bank notes. Yet they did not lose the power to create money in the form of deposit money. Just *how* this is done will be discussed in Chapter 33; here we ask what is deposit money?

Banks' customers frequently deposit coins and paper money with the banks for safekeeping, just as in former times they deposited gold. Such a deposit is recorded as an entry on the customer's account. If the customer wishes to pay a debt, he or she may come to the bank and claim the money in dollars, then pay the money over to another person. This person may then redeposit the money in a bank.

Like the gold transfers, this is a tedious procedure, particularly for large payments. It is more convenient to have the bank transfer claims to this money on deposit. The common "check" is an instruction to the bank to make the transfer. As soon as such transfers became easy and inexpensive, and checks became widely accepted in payment for commodities and debts, the deposits became a form of money called **deposit money.**

When individual A deposits $100 in a bank, his account is credited with $100. This is the bank's promise to pay $100 cash on demand. If A pays B $100 by giving her a check that B then deposits in the same bank, the bank merely reduces A's account by $100 and increases B's by the same amount. Thus the bank still promises to pay on demand the $100 originally deposited, but it now promises to pay it to B rather than to A. What makes all of this so convenient is that B can actually deposit A's check in any bank, and the banks will arrange the transfer of credits.

Checks are in some ways the modern equivalent of old-time bank notes issued by commercial banks. The passing of a bank note from hand to hand transferred ownership of a claim against the bank. A check on a deposit account is similarly an order to the bank to pay the designated recipient, rather than oneself, money credited to the account. Checks, unlike bank notes, do not circulate freely from hand to hand; thus checks themselves are not currency. The balance in the demand deposit *is* money; the check transfers money from one person to another. Because checks are easily drawn and deposited, and because they are relatively safe from theft, they are widely used. In 1980 approximately 40 billion checks were drawn in the United States. During the 1970s the number of checks drawn increased at about 7 percent per year.

Thus, when commercial banks lost the right to issue notes of their own, the form of bank money changed but the substance did not. Today banks have money in their vaults (or on deposit with the central banks) just as they always did. Once it was gold, today it is the legal tender of the times—paper money. It is true today, just as in the past, that most of the bank's customers are content to pay their bills by passing among themselves the bank's promises to pay money on demand. Only a small proportion of the transactions made by the bank's customers is made in cash.

Today, just as in the past, banks can create money by issuing more promises to pay (deposits) than they have money available to pay out.

Demand Deposits

A customer's deposit in a bank can be kept in one of two basic forms, as a demand deposit or as a time deposit. A **demand deposit** means that the customer can withdraw the money on demand (i.e., without giving any notice of intention to withdraw). Demand deposits are transferable by check. Such a check instructs the bank to pay without a delay a stated sum of money to the person to whom the check is made payable. Until very recently banks in the United States were prohibited from paying interest on demand deposits.

Time Deposits

A **time deposit** is an interest-bearing deposit that is legally withdrawable only after a certain amount of notice, such as 30 days for a passbook account and up to six months on certificates of deposit. Although banks, savings and loan associations, and other savings institutions do not usually enforce this delay, they could legally do so if proposed withdrawals threatened their re-

serves. Until quite recently it was impossible to pay a bill by writing a check on a time deposit. A depositor wishing to use a time deposit to pay a bill had to withdraw money from a savings (time) account and then either pay the bill in cash or deposit the funds in a demand account and write a check on the demand account.

The Disappearing Distinction Between Demand and Time Deposits

When interest rates on time deposits amounted to only a few percent, people were content to keep their savings in time deposits and their reserves of cash for ordinary transactions in demand deposits. Then, as interest rates available on time deposits and other safe liquid investments grew, it became more and more expensive (in terms of lost interest) to keep cash in demand deposits, even for a week or two. Starting in the early 1970s, a series of devices were invented that tended to make it easier to convert interest-bearing deposits into demand deposits transferable by check.

One of the first was the **negotiable order of withdrawal (NOW),** a checklike instruction to the savings institution to transfer funds from the depositor's time deposit to the recipient of the NOW. Use of NOW accounts began in Massachusetts in 1973 and have spread widely since legal barriers to them were removed by federal legislation in 1980. A similar device is the **automatic transfer service (ATS),** which allows depositors to maintain both a demand and a time deposit at the bank and to make all deposits to the time deposit. The bank automatically transfers funds to the demand deposit as needed to cover checks when they are written. This permits the customer to maintain only a small minimum amount (for example, $200) in the demand deposit account. All the rest earns interest. The ATS comes close to being a demand deposit that pays interest and/or a time deposit that can be transferred without delay by check.

New devices such as NOW and ATS accounts have all but obliterated the distinction between time and demand deposits.

NEAR MONEY AND MONEY SUBSTITUTES

Over the past two centuries what has been accepted by the public as money has expanded from gold and silver coins to include, first, bank notes and then bank deposits subject to transfer by check. Until recently, most economists would have agreed that money stopped at that point. No such agreement exists today, and an important debate centers on the definition of money appropriate to the present world.

If we concentrate only on the medium-of-exchange function of money, there is little doubt about what is money in America today. Money consists of notes, coins, and deposits subject to transfer by check or checklike instruments. No other asset constitutes a generally accepted medium of exchange; indeed, even notes and checks are not universally accepted—as you will discover if you try to buy a pack of cigarettes with a $1,000 bill (or even a $100 bill in a corner grocery store) or if you try to walk out of a store on a Saturday afternoon with a mink coat after having offered your personal check in exchange. But these exceptions are unimportant.

The problem of deciding what is money arises because cash, which best fulfills the medium-of-exchange function, may provide relatively poor ways to meet the store-of-value function (see Table 32-3). Interest-earning assets will do a better job of meeting this function of money than will currency or demand deposits that earn no interest. At the same time, however, they are less capable of filling the medium-of-exchange function. NOW and ATS accounts provide a better store of value than currency and demand deposits, without too much loss of the medium-of-exchange function. Once it is recognized that there is a trade-off between these functions, it is possible to consider other monetary assets.

Near Money

Assets that fulfill adequately the store-of-value function and are readily converted into a medium of exchange but are not themselves a medium of exchange are sometimes called **near money**. Deposits at a savings and loan association are a characteristic form of near money. When you have a deposit at a savings and loan association, you know exactly how much purchasing power you hold (at today's prices) and, given modern banking practices, you can turn your deposit into a medium of exchange—cash or a checking deposit—at a moment's notice. Additionally, your deposit will earn some interest during the period that you hold it. Why then does not everybody keep their money in such deposits instead of in demand deposits or currency? The answer is that the inconvenience of continually shifting money back and forth may outweigh the interest that can be earned. One week's interest on $100 (at 5 percent per year) is only about 10¢, not enough to cover carfare to the bank or the cost of mailing a letter. For money that will be needed soon, it would hardly pay to shift it to a time deposit.

In general, whether it pays to convert cash or demand deposits into interest-earning savings deposits for a given period will depend on the in-

TABLE 32-3
The Dollar as a Store of Value Since 1959

$1 put aside in	Had the purchasing power 5 years later of	Its average annual loss of value was
1959	$.94	1.2%
1964	.85	3.2%
1969	.74	6.0%
1974	.68	7.6%

The dollar has become an increasingly less satisfactory store of value over the last two decades. The second column shows the purchasing power, measured by the Consumer Price Index, of $1 five years after it was saved (assuming it earned no interest). In order for it to have maintained its real purchasing power, it would have had to earn the annual percentage return shown in the last column. The growth in the required return explains the increasing use of near moneys and money substitutes that (unlike currency and demand deposits) earn interest.

convenience and other transaction costs of shifting funds in and out and on the amount of interest that can be earned.

There is a wide spectrum of assets in the economy that pay interest and also serve as reasonably satisfactory temporary stores of value. The difference between these assets and savings deposits is that their capital values are not quite as certain as are those of savings deposits. If I elect to store my purchasing power in the form of a government bond that matures in 30 days, its price on the market may change between the time I buy it and the time I want to sell it—say 10 days later. If the price changes, I will suffer or enjoy a change in the purchasing power available to me. But because of the short horizon to maturity, the price will not change very much. (After all, the government will pay the bond's face value in a few weeks.) Such a security is thus a reasonably satisfactory short-run store of purchasing power. Indeed, any readily salable capital asset whose value does not fluctuate significantly with the rate of interest will satisfactorily fulfill this short-term, store-of-value function.

Money Substitutes

Things that serve as a temporary medium of exchange but are not a store of value are sometimes called **money substitutes.** Credit cards are a prime example. With a credit card many transactions can be made without either cash or a check. The evidence of credit, the credit slip you sign and hand over to the store, is not money because it cannot be used to make further transactions. Furthermore, when your credit card company sends you a bill, you have to use money in (delayed) payment for the original transaction. The credit card serves the short-run function of a medium of exchange by allowing you to make purchases even though you have no cash or bank deposit currently in your possession. But this is only temporary; money remains the final medium of exchange for these transactions when the credit account is settled.

CHANGING CONCEPTS OF WHAT IS MONEY

What is an acceptable enough medium of exchange to count as money has changed and will continue to change over time. NOW and ATS accounts have broadened the spectrum. New monetary assets (such as certificates of deposit and money-market fund shares) are continuously being developed to serve some, if not all, the functions of money, and they are more or less readily convertible into money. There is no single, timeless definition of what is money and what is only near money or a money substitute. Indeed, as we shall see, our monetary authorities use several different definitions of money, and these definitions change from year to year.

Summary

1. Early economic theory regarded the economy as being divided into a real part and a money part. The real part was concerned with production, the allocation of resources, and the distribution of income—determined only by relative prices. The monetary part merely determined the level of prices at which real transactions took place. This was determined by the quantity of money. Double the quantity of money, and in the new equilibrium all money prices would double but relative prices and the entire real sector would be left unaffected. Modern economists recognize interconnections between the two parts, as will be discussed in Chapter 34.

2. Inflation has been a common but by no means constant state of affairs in world history. Although inflation is widespread in the world today, the rate of inflation varies greatly from country to country.

3. Three of the major effects of unanticipated inflations are (1) to influence the allocation of resources and the distribution of income by haphazardly changing relative prices and wages, (2) to influence the real outcome of borrowing and

lending agreements and other contracts expressed in money terms, and (3) to reduce the living standards of people living on fixed incomes. Some but not all of these adverse effects may be avoided if the rate of inflation is accurately anticipated.

4. Traditionally in economics, money has referred to any generally accepted medium of exchange. A number of functions of money may, however, be distinguished—the major ones are the medium of exchange, the store of value, and the unit of account.

5. Money arose because of the inconvenience of barter, and it developed in stages from precious metal to metal coinage, to paper money convertible to precious metal, to token coinage and paper money fractionally backed by precious metals, to fiat money, and to deposit money. Societies have shown great sophistication in developing monetary instruments to meet their needs.

6. Today there is debate about what constitutes money. Concentrating on the medium-of-exchange function, money is restricted to notes, coins, and deposits subject to transfer by check. It is difficult, however, to separate the medium-of-exchange function from the function of providing a temporary store of purchasing power between the selling and the buying of goods. Any readily salable asset that has a secure capital value can be a satisfactory store of purchasing power. In an inflationary world, any asset that does not increase in value will be a poor store of value. When the asset earns an interest return, it has an advantage over cash and demand deposits (as long as the interest earned exceeds the costs and trouble of transferring into and out of the asset). Savings and loan deposits are an example of such a near money.

7. The question of what is money is further complicated by the existence of money substitutes. For example, credit cards allow purchases and sales to be made without the use of currency or checks. While credit cards substitute for

money at the time of purchase, the accounts must eventually be settled using money.

8. Just as monetary instruments change over time in response to new needs, so does the most useful definition of what is money.

Topics for Review

Real and monetary parts of the economy
Effects of anticipated and unanticipated inflations
Functions of money
Gresham's law
The gold standard and convertible money
Fully backed, fractionally backed, and fiat money
Legal tender
Deposit money and the use of checks
Demand and time deposits
Near money and money substitutes

Discussion Questions

1. "For the love of money is the root of all evil" (I Timothy 6:10). If a nation were to become a theocracy and money were made illegal, would you expect the level of national income to be affected? How about the productivity of labor? Might classical economists have answered this question differently than modern ones?

2. Which of the following groups, if any, might be expected to *benefit* from a rapid unforeseen inflation: (a) landlords, (b) storekeepers with large inventories, (c) printers of price lists, (d) homeowners with mortgages, (e) old-age pensioners, (f) tenants, (g) a government whose tax revenue comes mostly from a progressive income tax, (h) bondholders.

3. Consider each of the following with respect to its potential use as a medium of exchange, a store of value, and a unit of account. Which would you think might be regarded as money? (a) a $100 Federal Reserve note, (b) an American Express credit card, (c) a painting by Picasso, (d) a NOW account, (e) a U.S. Treasury certificate of indebtedness payable in three months, (f) a savings account at a savings and loan association in Las Vegas, Nevada, (g) one share of American Telephone & Telegraph Company stock, (h) a lifetime pass to Pittsburgh Steelers football games.

4. We often read that money serves three purposes: (a) as a medium of exchange, (b) as a unit of account,

and (c) as a store of value. Does something that serves as a country's medium of exchange necessarily serve as a unit of account? Is any one of the three absolutely essential?

5. When in 1976 the Austrian government minted a new 1,000 schilling gold coin—worth $59 face value—the one-inch diameter coin came into great demand among jewelers and coin collectors. By law, the number of such coins to be minted each year is limited. Lines of people eager to get the coins formed outside the government mint and local banks.

   "There is exceptional interest in the new coin," said a Viennese banker. "It's a numismatic hit and a financial success." It has disappeared from circulation, however. Explain why.

6. In Canada, American and Canadian coins often circulate side by side, exchanging at their face values, even though notes often are of unequal value. Someone who receives a U.S. coin has the option of spending it at face value or taking it to the bank and converting it to Canadian money at the going rate of exchange. When the rate of exchange was near "par," so that $1 Canadian was within plus or minus 3¢ of $1 U.S., the two monies circulated side by side. When the Canadian dollar fell to $0.845 U.S., predict which money disappeared from circulation according to Gresham's law. Why did a 2¢ differential not produce this result?

7. Some years ago a strike closed all banks in Ireland for several months. What do you think happened to money, near money, and money substitutes during the period?

8. During hyperinflations in several foreign countries after World War II, American cigarettes were sometimes used in place of money. What made them suitable?

9. During inflations, money is not a perfect store of value and many people seek to buy other assets better suited to that purpose. From January 1979 to March 1980, the purchasing power of the American dollar declined by 20 percent. In January 1979 silver was selling for about $10 an ounce and gold for $270 an ounce. In March 1980 an ounce of silver sold for $20 and gold for $480 an ounce. Are gold and silver better stores of value than dollars? Before you answer, you should take into account the fact that silver reached $50 an ounce and gold $950 in January 1980.

10. Take some five-year period during the last ten years and (using library sources) calculate which of the following was the best store of value over that period: (a) the dollar, (b) the Dow Jones industrial average, (c) gold, (d) a Georgia Power 11¾%, '05 bond. How confident are you that the one was the best store of value over those five years will be the best over the *next* 18 months?

The Banking System and the Money Supply

33

The total stock of money in the economy at any moment is called the **money supply** or the **supply of money.** Economists and financial analysts tend to use a number of different definitions for the money supply, each of which is regularly reported in the *Federal Reserve Bulletin*. The definitions change from time to time as new monetary instruments come to be important.

In the spring of 1980 these classifications were in use: **M-1A,** the narrowest, defines money as currency plus demand deposits. **M-1B** defines money as M-1A plus NOW, ATS accounts, and similar accounts at credit unions and mutual savings banks. **M-2** is M-1B plus savings and smaller time deposits of all kinds, including money-market fund shares. **M-3** is M-2 plus large denomination **certificates of deposit (CD).** CDs are savings deposits, the evidence for which is a slip of paper, or certificate, rather than an entry in the saver's passbook. The most important is the large denomination, negotiable CD, which is designed to attract funds from large businesses. These pay a much higher rate of interest than ordinary savings deposits.

M-1A and M-1B concentrate on the medium-of-exchange function. The others add in highly liquid assets that serve the temporary store-of-value function and are in practice quickly convertible into a medium of exchange at a known price ($1 on deposit in a savings account is always convertible into a $1 demand deposit or $1 in cash). Table 33-1 shows the principal elements in the money supply.

In our economy the quantity of money is affected both by the private commercial banking

TABLE 33-1

Money Supply in the United States, December 1979 (billions of dollars)

Currency	$108	
Demand deposits	273	
M-1A		$ 381
NOW, ATS, and other checkable deposits	16	
M-1B		397
Savings deposits	415	
Other small time deposits[a]	714	
M-2		1,526
Large time deposits[a]	253	
M-3		1,779

Source: *Federal Reserve Bulletin*, February 1980, page A-14, table 1-21.

[a] A time deposit is small if under $100,000, large if $100,000 or more.

There are several widely used measures of the money supply. The traditional, narrow view of the money supply concentrates on currency and demand deposits (M-1A) and checkable substitutes such as NOW and ATS (M-1B). M-2 and M-3 add in near moneys that serve the store-of-value function and can be readily converted into demand deposits or cash on a dollar-for-dollar basis.

system and by the actions of the central bank. The commercial banks affect the money supply as an incidental but very important feature of how they do business. In so doing, of course, they respond to what is happening in the economy — to the level of business activity, to interest rates, and to the demands of their customers for cash and for loans. The central bank, which in the United States is the Federal Reserve System, influences the money supply as a matter of deliberate monetary policy.

The Commercial Banks

Modern commercial banking systems are of two main types. In one system, there is a small number of banks, each with a very large number of branch offices; in the other system, there are many independent banks. The banking systems of Britain and Canada are of the first type, with only a few banks accounting for the overwhelming bulk of the business. The American system is of the second type. In 1980 there were approximately 15,000 independent banks, some (such as the Bank of America) with hundreds of branches and others with only a single office. Branch banking in the United States is governed by state law. Interstate branching is not allowed. In some states, such as New York and California, banks are permitted to branch statewide. Illinois and Missouri, among others, are "unit-bank" states and permit no branching. Other states, such as Pennsylvania, permit limited branching into areas near the home office. The functioning of the banking system is, however, essentially the same in all these systems.

The basic unit of the American banking system is the ordinary **commercial bank,** which is a privately owned, profit-seeking institution. All commercial banks have common attributes: They hold deposits for their customers, permit certain deposits to be transferred by check from an individual account to other accounts held in any bank in the country, make loans to households and firms, and invest in government securities.

It is these common features, in particular the holding of demand deposits, that distinguish commercial banks from other financial institutions, each of which may perform some but not all of these functions. Many other institutions such as credit unions, savings and loan associations, and mutual savings banks accept time deposits and grant loans for specific purposes. Finance companies make loans to households for practically any purpose. The post office and Western Union will transfer money; American Express will issue travelers' checks. Credit card companies will extend credit so that purchases can be made on a buy-now, pay-later basis.

Commercial banks differ from one another in many ways. Some are very large (in 1980 the Bank of America had deposits in excess of $86 billion) and others are very small; some are located in big cities, others in small towns; some hold charters from the federal government (national banks), others from state governments (state banks). Nearly 40 percent of the commercial banks, including most of the larger ones, are members of the Federal Reserve System—nicknamed the Fed.[1] All national banks must be members, and any state bank may join the system by agreeing to abide by its regulations. However, nonmember banks are indirectly tied into the system since they are invariably *correspondents* of larger member banks. The nonmember banks keep their reserves on deposit with member banks, depend on them for loans when they are pressed for cash, and rely on them for a variety of other services that the Federal Reserve System provides for its members. In practice, then, all commercial banks, members and nonmembers alike, have always come under the effective regulatory influence of the Fed. (New banking legislation passed in March 1980 greatly reduced the difference in regulatory rules applying to member and nonmember banks.)

The common regulatory framework is one reason why it is usual to speak of the banking *system,* as distinct from (and in addition to) the commercial banking industry.

INTERBANK ACTIVITIES

A second reason for speaking of a banking system is that commercial banks have a number of interbank cooperative relationships that are encouraged by special banking laws because they facilitate the smooth functioning of money and credit markets.

Check Clearing and Collection

Bank deposits are an effective medium of exchange only because banks accept each other's checks. If you live in Columbus, Ohio, and receive a check drawn on a Chicago bank, you are likely either to cash it or to deposit it in a

Columbus bank. If the rules of the banking business were different, so that you had to go in person to Chicago and present it to the bank on which it was drawn, you would be so inconvenienced that you would be unwilling to accept checks for most transactions. Fortunately, banks accept one another's checks. But the problem of presenting checks for payment remains. If a depositor in bank A writes a check to someone who deposits it in bank B, bank A now owes money to bank B.

There are, of course, millions of such transactions in the course of a day, resulting in an enormous sorting and bookkeeping job. Multibank systems make use of a **clearing house** where interbank debts are settled. At the end of the day, all the checks drawn by bank A's customers and deposited in bank B are totaled and set against the total of all the checks drawn by bank B's customers and deposited in bank A. It is necessary only to settle the difference between the two sums. The actual checks are passed through the clearing house back to the bank on which they were drawn. Both banks are then able to adjust the individual accounts by a set of book entries; a flow of cash between banks is necessary only when there is a net transfer of cash from the customers of one bank to those of another. For member banks in the United States, much of this clearing function is performed by the Federal Reserve System.

The Sharing of Loans

Large though the resources of a single bank may seem to an individual, they are often not large enough to permit that bank to meet all the credit needs of a giant industrial customer such as Sears, Roebuck or General Motors who may want to borrow as much as $100 million at one time. For such enormous loans, a group of banks may join together and offer a pool loan, agreeing on common terms and dividing the loan up into manageable segments.

On a different scale, it is not uncommon for a smaller bank to be approached by a customer for

[1] We shall examine the functioning of the Federal Reserve System later in the chapter.

a loan larger than it can comfortably or safely make. A bank in, say, Peoria, Illinois, will then ask a larger bank (probably in St. Louis or Chicago) to participate in the loan at some agreed percentage. Such "participating loans" represent, in effect, interbank lending. Along with pool loans, they serve to make available to a customer anywhere the resources of the entire banking system.

Bank Credit Cards

A relatively new form of interbank cooperation is the bank credit card. VISA and Master Charge are the two most commonly used credit cards in America; both are run by large groups of banks. Either card permits the holder to charge purchases of goods and services. The participating banks promptly pay the merchants and bill the credit card holder, who has the option of paying at once or paying later at the cost of a prespecified rate of interest.

COMMERCIAL BANKS AS PROFIT-SEEKING INSTITUTIONS

Banks are private firms that start with invested capital and seek to "make money" in the same

sense as do firms making neckties or bicycles. (Banks, as we shall see, do not set out to "make money" in the literal sense; nonetheless they do so as a by-product of their attempt to make profits for their owners.)

A commercial bank provides a variety of services to its customers: a safe place to store money; the convenience of demand deposits that can be transferred by personal check; a safe and convenient place to earn a modest but guaranteed return on savings; and often financial advice and estate management services. The bank earns some revenue by charging for these services, but such fees are a small part of the bank's total earnings. The largest part (typically about five-sixths) of a bank's earnings is derived from the bank's ability to invest profitably the funds placed with it.

Principal Assets and Liabilities

Table 33-2 is the combined balance sheet of the commercial banks in the United States. The bulk of a bank's liabilities are deposits that are owed to its depositors. The principal assets of a bank are the *securities* it buys (including government bonds), which pay interest or dividends, and the *loans* it makes to individuals to buy houses, cars,

TABLE 33-2
Consolidated Balance Sheet of U.S. Commercial Banks, January 30, 1980 (billions of dollars)

Assets		Liabilities	
Reserves (cash assets including deposits with Federal Reserve banks)	$ 166.5	Deposits	
		Demand	$ 380.5
		Savings	201.3
Loans	930.7	Time	481.3
U.S. government securities	94.3		
Other securities	192.7	Borrowings	179.5
Other assets	83.7	Other liabilities	121.1
		Capital accounts	104.2
	$1,467.9		$1,467.9

Source: Federal Reserve Bulletin, March 1980.

Reserves are only a small fraction of deposit liabilities. If all the banks' customers who held demand deposits tried to withdraw them in cash, the banks could not meet this demand without liquidating $214 billion of other assets. This would be impossible without assistance from the Fed.

television sets, and securities and to businesses to build factories, buy machines, and finance the purchase of goods and raw materials. A bank loan is a liability to the borrower (who must pay it back) but an asset to the bank. The bank expects not only to have the loan repaid but to receive interest that more than compensates for the paperwork involved and the risk of nonpayment.

Most money deposited with banks is "at work," having been invested in loans or securities. Banks earn money by lending and investing the money left with them so as to earn more than it costs them to attract the deposits. Deposits are the lifeblood of a commercial bank. Without them, the bank has nothing to lend or invest except the small amount of its initial capital.

Most bank services are designed to attract or keep deposits. In the case of time deposits, a bank pays the depositor an interest rate (from 5.25 to 11 percent in 1980, depending on the term of the deposit and on the amount of money deposited) in the expectation that it can earn more than that by reinvesting the money. In the case of demand deposits, banks until 1980 were not permitted to pay interest to their depositors, but they could and did provide free checking, monthly statements, and postage-paid deposit-by-mail envelopes. NOW and ATS accounts have created something very much like an interest-paying demand deposit. And new legislation passed in 1980 phases out interest rate limitations over the next six years.

Competition for Deposits

Competition for deposits is active among banks and between banks and other financial institutions. Savings and loan associations (S & Ls) and mutual savings banks are important competitors of commercial banks for time deposits. These nonbank savings institutions specialize primarily in mortgage lending secured by residential real estate; their rapid postwar growth has reflected the high and growing demand for home financing. Competitive bidding for funds by various kinds of financial institutions was traditionally heavily regulated. But the 1980 banking law provided for the gradual phasing out of such restrictions as maximum interest rates on savings and time deposits. Money-market funds, high-interest CDs, advertising, personal solicitation of accounts, giveaway programs for new accounts and new deposits to existing accounts, and new and improved services are all forms of competition for funds. Among the special services are payroll-accounting and pension-accounting schemes for industrial customers. The "lock box" is another kind of service: banks establish locked post office boxes to which retail customers of large companies send their payments. Most gasoline companies have credit card customers remit to a lock box. The bank opens the remittances, deposits them to the company's account, and forwards notices of payment to the company. Among other features, this speeds the receipt of funds to the company and decreases the need to borrow money for working capital. All these services are costly to the bank, but they serve as inducements to customers in order to gain deposits.

RESERVES

The Need for Reserves

All bankers would as a matter of convenience and prudence keep *some* cash on hand against their deposits in order to be able to meet depositors' day-to-day requirements for cash. But the reserves required for these needs are far less than 100 percent. Just as the goldsmiths of old discovered that only a fraction of the gold they held was ever withdrawn at any given time, and just as banks discovered that only a fraction of convertible bank notes was actually converted, so, soo, have banks discovered that only a fraction of their deposits will be withdrawn in cash at any one time. Most deposits of any individual bank remain on deposit with it; thus an individual bank need only keep fractional reserves against its deposits.

Many of the funds withdrawn by the depositor from one bank do not leave the banking system, even though they leave the bank. Even if Ms. Jones withdraws $5,000 from her bank to buy a new car, the chances are great that the car dealer will deposit the check received from Jones in its own account. Thus the banking system as a whole will simply have transferred its deposit liabilities from one depositor to another and from one bank to another. For this reason, the banking system as a whole can operate with fewer reserves than would be needed by any one bank standing alone. While one bank may be losing reserves, others may be gaining them; the bank experiencing a shortage can borrow from those banks with excess reserves.[2]

The reserves needed to assure that depositors can withdraw their deposits on demand will be quite small in normal times.

The psychological effect of a bank's refusing to give a depositor cash can be devastating. Until relatively recent times, such an event—or even the rumor of it—could lead to a "run" on the bank as the bank's depositors rushed to withdraw their money. Faced with such a panic, the bank would have to close until it had borrowed funds or liquidated enough assets to meet the demand or until the demand subsided. But the closing of even one bank often led nervous depositors to demand cash from other banks. Bankers could not instantly turn their loans into cash since the borrowers had the money tied up in such things as buildings. They could not even quickly sell their securities since many of the potential purchasers found their money was tied up in the closed banks. Thus, in a domino effect, once many banks closed, a wave of foreclosures, bankruptcies, and further bank failures would ensue. Moreover, as many banks tried to sell their securities at the same time, the prices of the securities often fell disastrously, and the result-

ing decline in the value of the banks' assets added to the risk of their insolvency.

To avoid panics, reserves must be large enough to meet extraordinary demands for cash.

The need of the commercial banking system for reserves against depositors' panics has been diminished by governmental policies. In the first place, the central bank can provide commercial banks with needed cash either by lending them money or by buying the securities they want to sell. In the second place, the government provides Federal Deposit Insurance, which guarantees that depositors will get their money back even if a bank fails completely. Such insurance decreases the likelihood of a widespread panic because one bank's failure is much less likely to lead to a run on other banks. Most depositors will not withdraw their money as long as they are *sure* they can get it when they need it.

Actual and Required Reserves

Look again at Table 33-2 and observe that the banking system's cash reserves are just a fraction of its deposits. If the holders of even 45 percent of its demand deposits had demanded cash sometime in January 1980, the commercial banking system would have been unable (without outside help) to meet the demand, for its total cash assets were less than $167 billion.

The American banking system is a **fractional reserve system,** with banks holding reserves of much less than 100 percent of their deposits. The size of the reserves reflects not only the judgment of bankers, it also reflects the legal requirements imposed on the banks by the Fed.

A bank's **reserve ratio** is the fraction of its deposits that it holds as reserves either as cash or as deposits with the central bank. Those reserves that the Federal Reserve System requires the bank to hold are called **required reserves.** Any reserves held over and above required reserves are called **excess reserves.** Reserves are required by the Fed both to assure the stability of the banking system and as part of its policy arsenal

---

[2] There is an active market, the federal funds market, in which excess reserves are loaned among banks on a short-term basis. In the first week of 1980, for example, $30 billion worth of transactions occurred in this market.

in attempting to control the money supply, as we shall discuss at the end of this chapter.

The Creation and Destruction of Deposit Money by Commercial Banks

The fractional reserve system creates the leverage by which privately owned and operated banks and other financial institutions can create new money.

If banks can increase their reserves, they can increase their deposits even more. Since deposits are money, banks can thus increase the money supply.

In a real sense, that is all there is to money creation. Yet the process is worth examining in some detail. We shall limit our attention to commercial banks and their creation of demand deposits.

Some Simplifying Assumptions

To focus on the essential aspects of how banks create money, assume that banks can invest in only one kind of asset, loans, and that there is only one kind of deposit, a demand deposit.

Three other assumptions listed below are provisional; later, when we have developed the basic ideas concerning the bank's creation of money, these assumptions will be relaxed.

Fixed required reserve ratio. It is assumed that all banks have the same required reserve ratio, which does not change. In our numerical illustration we shall assume that the required reserve ratio is 20 percent, that is, that banks must have at least $1 of reserves for every $5 of deposits.

No excess reserves. It is assumed that all banks want to invest any reserves they have in excess of the legally required amount. This implies that they always believe there are safe investments to be made when they have excess reserves.

No cash drain from the banking system. It is assumed that the public holds a fixed amount of currency in circulation, an amount that will not change with changes in the total money supply. Thus changes in the money supply will take the form of changes in deposit money. If extra money is created, the money will be deposited in a bank; if money is destroyed, bank deposits will be decreased.

Armed with these assumptions, we shall now examine money creation, starting with the simplest possible situation and progressing to two more complex but more realistic ones. The three situations are: (1) a single new deposit in a system that has only one bank, (2) a single new deposit in a system with many banks, and (3) many new deposits in a many-bank system. Surprisingly, perhaps, the results are exactly the same in all three cases.

A MONOPOLY BANK, A SINGLE NEW DEPOSIT

Suppose that the entire country is served by a single multibranch bank, called a *monopoly bank* because it has no competitors. The balance sheet of this monopoly bank appears in Table 33-3.

The monopoly bank's assets consist of $200 of reserves, held partly as cash on hand and partly as deposits with the central bank, and $900 of loans outstanding to its customers. Its liabilities are $100 to those who initially contributed capital to start the bank and $1,000 to current deposi-

TABLE 33-3
The Monopoly Bank's Initial Balance Sheet

Assets		Liabilities	
Cash and other reserves	$ 200	Deposits	$1,000
Loans	900	Capital	100
	$1,100		$1,100

The monopoly bank has a reserve of 20 percent of its deposit liabilities. The commercial bank earns money by finding profitable investments for much of the money deposited with it. In this balance sheet, loans are its earning assets.

TABLE 33-4

The Monopoly Bank's Balance Sheet After an Immigrant Deposits $100

Assets		Liabilities	
Cash and other reseves	$ 300	Deposits	$1,100
Loans	900	Capital	100
	$1,200		$1,200

The immigrant's deposit raises deposit liabilities and cash assets by the same amount. Since both cash and deposits rise by $100, the cash reserve ratio, formerly .20, now increases to .27. The bank has more cash than it needs to provide a 20 percent reserve against its deposit liabilities.

tors. The bank's ratio of reserves to deposits is $200/1,000 = .20$, exactly equal to its minimum requirement.

An immigrant arrives in the country and opens an account by depositing $100 with the monopoly bank. This is a wholly new deposit for the bank, and it results in a revised balance sheet (Table 33-4). As a result of the immigrant's new deposit, both cash assets and deposit liabilities have risen by $100. More important, the reserve ratio has increased from .20 to $300/1,100 = .27$. The monopoly bank now has excess reserves—with $300 in reserves it could support $1,500 in deposits.

The monopoly bank knows that any new deposit it creates will remain in the system. It is in a position to say to the next business executive who comes in for a loan, "We will lend your firm $400 at the going rate of interest." The bank does so by adding that amount to the firm's deposit account. The bank does not care how the executive spends the money, for whoever receives the firm's checks will deposit them in the same bank (since there is no other).

Table 33-5 shows what happens when such new deposits are created. The new immigrant's deposit initially raised cash assets and deposit liabilities by $100. The new loans create an additional $400 of deposit liabilities. This restores the reserve ratio to its legal minimum ($300/1,500 = .20$), and no further expansion of deposit money is possible. As the bank's customers do

business with each other, settling their accounts by checks, the ownership of the deposits will be continually changing. But what matters to the bank is that its total deposits will remain constant.

The extent to which the bank can increase its loans *and thus its deposits* and thus the money supply depends on the reserve ratio. Because in this case the ratio is $1/5 (= .20)$, the bank is able to expand deposits to five times the original new acquisition of money. In general, if the reserve ratio is r, a bank can increase its deposits by $1/r$ times any new reserves. This general relationship proves true of a banking system whether or not there is a monopoly bank. [38]

The "multiple expansion of deposits" that has just been worked through applies in reverse to a withdrawal of funds. Suppose a depositor in a monopoly bank withdraws $50 (in the form of a $50 bill) and spends it in a new shop, whose owners decide to frame the bill and display it on their wall. The bank has lost both cash and a deposit. Its revised balance sheet is shown in Table 33-6. As a result of the loss of $50 cash and $50 deposits, the bank's reserve ratio has fallen to $250/1,450 = .17$. This is below the legal minimum, and the bank will have to take steps to restore the required ratio.

Say that the bank calls for the repayment of some loans made to its customers and repayable at short notice, hoping thereby to raise its cash position to restore the required ratio. What happens, however, is that the loans are not repaid by cash but by the customers' drawing checks on

TABLE 33-5

The Monopoly Bank's Balance Sheet After Making a $400 Loan

Assets		Liabilities	
Cash and other reserves	$ 300	Deposits	$1,500
Loans	1,300	Capital	100
	$1,600		$1,600

The loan restores the reserve ratio of .20. By increasing its loans by a multiple of its new cash deposit, the bank restores its reserve ratio of .20.

TABLE 33-6
The Monopoly Bank's Balance Sheet After a $50 Cash Withdrawal

Assets		Liabilities	
Cash and other reserves	$ 250	Deposits	$1,450
Loans	1,300	Capital	100
	$1,550		$1,550

A cash withdrawal lowers the bank's reserve ratio. The cash withdrawal reduces both cash assets and deposit liabilities by the same amount. The reserve ratio, which was .20 before the withdrawal, is now only .17.

their accounts in favor of the bank. This means that deposit liabilities are reduced by the repayment of the loan, but cash is unchanged. To restore the correct reserve ratio, it will be necessary to reduce deposits — by calling in loans and not making new ones until deposits are once again only five times reserves.

The revised balance sheet when this has been achieved appears in Table 33-7. The bank lost $50 in cash from the initial withdrawal of funds. To maintain a reserve ratio of .20, it was necessary that deposits fall by $250. The initial withdrawal trimmed deposits by $50, but the remaining $200 cut had to be made by reducing outstanding loans. The new position restored the reserve ratio to $250/$1,250 = .20.

To summarize the example, the result of the withdrawal of $50 is that the quantity of deposit money shrinks by $250 and the volume of loans

TABLE 33-7
The Monopoly Bank's Balance Sheet After the Reserve Ratio Has Been Restored

Assets		Liabilities	
Cash and other reserves	$ 250	Deposits	$1,250
Loans	1,100	Capital	100
	$1,350		$1,350

A multiple contraction of loans is necessary to restore the reserve ratio after a cash withdrawal. A withdrawal of $50 in cash reduces deposits by $50. A further contraction of $200 in loans and deposits is necessary to cause deposits to fall by five times the fall in cash. This restores the reserve ratio of .20.

available to the bank's customers shrinks by $200.

MANY BANKS, A SINGLE NEW DEPOSIT

Deposit creation is more complicated in a multibank system than in a single-bank system, but *the end result is exactly the same.* It is more complicated because, when a bank makes a loan, the recipient of the loan may pay the money to someone who deposits it not in the original bank but in another bank. How this works is most easily seen under the extreme assumption that every new borrower immediately withdraws the borrowed funds from the lending bank and pays someone who in turn deposits the money in another bank or banks.

Suppose that the Immigrants Bank and Trust Company is initially in the position of the monopoly bank (shown in Table 33-3), which is repeated in Table 33-8. Now suppose that, as before, an immigrant makes a wholly new deposit of $100. The bank's position after the deposit is shown in Table 33-9. This is exactly the same position given in Table 33-4, when the monopoly bank received the immigrant's deposit. The reserve ratio is once again 300/1,100 = .27, but here the similarity to the monopoly bank ends.

The Immigrants Bank cannot use its excess reserves to support $400 of new loans. When the bank makes new loans to its customers, they will

TABLE 33-8
The Initial Balance Sheet of the Immigrants Bank and Trust Company (IB&T Co.)

Assets		Liabilities	
Cash and other reserves	$ 200	Deposits	$1,000
Loans	900	Capital	100
	$1,100		$1,100

The initial position is the same as that of the monopoly bank in Table 33-3. Although the balance sheet of the IB&T Co. is initially the same as that of the monopoly bank, the crucial difference is that the IB&T Co. is one of many banks in a multibank system, while the monopoly bank was itself the whole banking system.

TABLE 33-9

The Balance Sheet of the IB&T Co. After a $100 Cash Deposit

Assets		Liabilities	
Cash and other			
reserves	$ 300	Deposits	$1,100
Loans	900	Capital	100
	$1,200		$1,200

The immigrant's deposit raises deposit liabilities and cash assets by the same amount. Since both cash and deposits rise by $100, the cash reserve ratio, formerly .20, now increases to .27. The bank has more cash than it needs to provide a 20 percent reserve against its deposit liabilities.

TABLE 33-10

The IB&T Co. Balance Sheet After a New Loan and Cash Drain of $80

Assets		Liabilities	
Cash and other			
reserves	$ 220	Deposits	$1,100
Loans	980	Capital	100
	$1,200		$1,200

The bank lends its surplus cash and suffers a cash drain. The bank keeps $20 as a reserve against the new deposit of $100. It lends $80 to a customer who writes a check to someone who deals with another bank. When the check is cleared, the IB&T Co. has suffered an $80 cash drain, has increased its loans by $80, and has restored its reserve ratio to .20.

make payments to other persons who will deposit the checks in their own banks. Because of this, the Immigrants Bank will suffer a cash drain — that is, the checks drawn against it will not be offset by deposits of checks drawn against other banks, and it will lose cash to other banks. But even though it cannot expand loans and deposits by as much as the monopoly bank, it can do something. It has more reserves than required, and even on the extreme assumption that every dollar that it lends will be withdrawn and deposited in another bank, there is an opportunity to make some profitable loans with the excess reserves on hand.

With its present level of deposits at $1,100, the bank needs only $220 of reserves (.20 × $1,100 = $220), so it can lend the $80 excess that it has on hand. Table 33-10 shows the position after this has been done and after the new deposit has been withdrawn to be deposited to the account of a customer of another bank. The Immigrants Bank once again has a 20 percent reserve ratio.

So far deposits in the IB&T Co. have increased by only the initial $100 of new immigrant's money with which we started, as shown in Table 33-9. (Of this, $20 is held as a cash reserve against the deposit and $80 has been lent out to a customer.) But other banks have received new deposits of $80 as the persons receiving payment from the initial borrower deposited those payments in their own banks. The receiving banks (sometimes called "second-

generation banks") receive new deposits of $80, and when the checks clear, they have new reserves of $80. Because they require an addition to their reserves of only $16 to support the new deposit, they have $64 of excess reserves. They now increase their loans by $64. After this money is spent by the borrowers and has been deposited in other, third-generation banks, the balance sheets of the second-generation banks will have changed, as in Table 33-11.

The third-generation banks now find themselves with $64 of new deposits. Against these they need hold only $12.80 in cash, so they have

TABLE 33-11

Changes in the Balance Sheets of Second-generation Banks

Assets		Liabilities	
Cash and other			
reserves	+$16	Deposits	+$80
Loans	+ 64		
	+$80		+$80

Second-generation banks receive cash deposits and expand loans. The second-generation banks gain new deposits of $80 as a result of the loan granted by the IB&T Co., which is used to make payments to customers of the second-generation banks. These banks keep 20 percent of the cash they acquire as their reserve against the new deposit, and they can make new loans using the other 80 percent. When the customers who borrowed the money make payments to the customers of third-generation banks, a cash drain occurs.

TABLE 33-12
Many Banks, a Single New Deposit

Bank	New deposits	New loans	Addition to reserves
Immigrants Bank	$100.00	$ 80.00	$ 20.00
Second-generation bank	80.00	64.00	16.00
Third-generation bank	64.00	51.20	12.80
Fourth-generation bank	51.20	40.96	10.24
Fifth-generation bank	40.96	32.77	8.19
Sixth-generation bank	32.77	26.22	6.55
Seventh-generation bank	26.22	20.98	5.24
Eighth-generation bank	20.98	16.78	4.20
Ninth-generation bank	16.78	13.42	3.36
Tenth-generation bank	13.42	10.74	2.68
Total first 10 generations	446.33	357.07	89.26
All remaining generations	53.67	42.93	10.74
Total for banking systems	$500.00	$400.00	$100.00

The banking system as a whole can create deposit money whenever it receives new reserves. The table shows the process of the creation of deposit money on the assumptions that all the loans made by one set of banks end up as deposits in another set of banks (called the "next-generation banks"), that the required reserve ratio (r) is .20, and that there are no excess reserves. Although each bank suffers a cash drain whenever it grants a new loan, the system as a whole does not, and the system ends up doing in a series of steps what a monopoly bank would do all at once; that is, it increases deposit money by 1/r, which in this example is five times the amount of any increase in reserves that it obtains.

excess reserves of $51.20 that they can immediately lend out. Thus there begins a long sequence of new deposits, new loans, new deposits, and new loans. The stages are shown in Table 33-12. The series in the table should look familiar, for it is the same converging series we met when dealing with the multiplier.

The banking system has created new deposits and thus new money, although each banker can honestly say, "All I did was invest my excess reserves. I can do no more than manage wisely the money I receive."

If r is the reserve ratio, the ultimate effect on the deposits of the banking system of a new deposit will be 1/r times the new deposit. [39] This is exactly the same result reached in the monopoly bank case.[3]

[3] Indeed, the process might have been the same. Look again at Table 33-4. If the monopoly bank had merely loaned its excess reserves of $80, it would have soon received a new deposit of $80 in one of its branches. This in turn would give it excess reserves of $64, which it could loan—and so on.

MANY BANKS, MANY DEPOSITS

The two cases discussed above, the monopoly bank and the single new deposit in a many-bank situation, serve this purpose: they show that under either set of opposite extreme assumptions, the result is the same. So it is, too, in intermediate situations where banks suffer some, but less than a total, cash drain to other banks. A far more realistic picture of the process of deposit creation is one in which new deposits (or new withdrawals) tend to accrue simultaneously to all banks, perhaps because of changes in the monetary policy of the government. Say, for example, that the community contains ten banks of equal size and that each received new deposits of $100 in cash. Now each bank is in the position shown in Tables 33-4 and 33-9, and each can begin to expand deposits based on the $100 of excess reserves. (Each bank does this by granting loans to customers.)

Because each bank does one-tenth of the total

banking business, an average of 90 percent of any newly created deposit will find its way into other banks as the customer pays other people in the community by check. This will represent a cash drain from the lending bank to the other banks. However, 10 percent of each new deposit created by every other bank should find its way into this bank. All banks receive new cash and all begin creating deposits simultaneously; no bank should suffer a significant cash drain to any other bank.

Thus all banks can go on expanding deposits without losing cash to each other; they need only worry about keeping enough cash to satisfy those depositors who will occasionally require cash. The expansion can go on with each bank watching its own ratio of cash reserves to deposits, expanding deposits as long as the ratio exceeds 1/5 and ceasing when it reaches that figure. The process will come to a halt when each bank has created $400 in additional deposits, so that for each initial $100 cash deposit, there is now $500 in deposits backed by $100 in cash. Now *each* of the banks will have entries in its books similar to those shown in Table 33-5.

The general rule, if there is no cash drain, is that a banking system with a reserve ratio of *r* can change its deposits by 1/*r* times any change in reserves.

EXCESS RESERVES AND CASH DRAINS

Two of the simplifying assumptions made earlier can now be relaxed.

Excess reserves. If banks do not choose to invest excess reserves, the multiple expansion discussed will not occur. Turn back to Table 33-4. If the monopoly bank had been content to hold 27 percent reserves, it might well have done nothing more. Other things being equal, banks will choose to invest excess reserves because of the profit motive. But there may be times when they believe the risk is too great. It is one thing to be offered 12 percent or even 24 percent interest on a loan, but if the borrower defaults on the

payment of interest and principal, the bank will be the loser. Similarly, if the bank expects interest rates to rise in the future, it may hold off making loans now so that it will have reserves available to make more profitable loans after the interest rate has risen.

There is nothing automatic about credit expansion; it rests on the decisions of bankers. If banks do not choose to use excess reserves to expand their investments, there will not be an expansion of deposits.

Banks tend to hold larger excess reserves in times of business recession, when there is a low demand for loans and very low interest rates, than they do in periods of boom, when the demand for loans is great and interest rates are high.

The significance of relaxing this assumption about excess reserves is that it cuts the automatic link between the creation of excess reserves and money creation.

Excess reserves make it *possible* for the banks to expand the money supply, but only if they want to do so.

The money supply is thus at least partially determined by the commercial banks in response to such forces as changes in national income and interest rates. However, the upper limit of deposits is determined by the required reserve ratio and by the reserves available to the banks, both of which are under the control of the central bank.

Cash drain. Suppose firms and households find it convenient to keep a fixed *fraction* of their money holding in cash (say 5 percent) instead of a fixed *amount* of dollars. In that case an extra $100 in money supply will not all stay in the banking system; only $95 will remain on deposit, while the rest will be added to money in circulation. In such a situation any multiple expansion of bank deposits will be accompanied by a cash drain to the public that will reduce the maximum expansion below what it was when the public was content to hold all its new money as bank deposits. Table 33-13 shows the position of a mo-

TABLE 33-13

The Monopoly Bank's Balance Sheet After a Credit Expansion and an Accompanying Cash Drain

Assets		Liabilities	
Cash and reserves	$ 280	Deposits	$1,480
Loans	1,300	Capital	100
	$1,580		$1,580

The maximum possible deposit expansion is reduced by a cash drain. This example differs from that shown in Table 33-5 because, after a new deposit of $100 and a new loan of $400, 5 percent of the newly created money is withdrawn as cash to be held by the public. Cash and deposits each fall by $20 and the reserve ratio falls below 20 percent.

nopoly bank after a credit expansion of $400 and a cash drain of $20.

The story of deposit creation when there is a cash drain to the public might go like this: Each bank starts creating deposits and suffers no significant cash drain to other banks. But because approximately 5 percent of newly created deposits is withdrawn to be held as cash, each bank suffers a cash drain to the public. The expansion continues, each bank watching its own ratio of cash reserves to deposits, expanding deposits as long as the ratio exceeds 1/5 and ceasing when it reaches that figure. Because the expansion is accompanied by a cash drain, it will come to a halt with a smaller deposit expansion than in the no cash drain case.[4]

Central Banks

All advanced free-market economies have, in addition to commercial banks, a central bank. At first central banks were private profit-making institutions that provided services to ordinary banks, but their potential to influence the behavior of commercial banks and through them that of the whole economy led them to develop close ties with central governments. In Europe these

---

[4] It can be shown algebraically that the percentage of cash drain must be added to the reserve ratio to determine the maximum possible expansion of deposits. [40]

---

ties eventually became formalized as central banks were taken over by governments. The central bank is an instrument of the government, whether or not it is in fact publicly owned. The Bank of England—the "Old Lady of Threadneedle Street"—is one of the oldest and most famous central banks; it began to operate as the central bank of England in the seventeenth century. In the United States the central bank is called the Federal Reserve System, and it was organized in 1914.

The similarities of central banks in the functions they perform and the tools they use are much more important than their differences in organization. Although our attention is given to the operations of the Federal Reserve System, the basic situation is not different for the Bank of England, the Bank of Greece, or the Bank of Canada.

BASIC FUNCTIONS OF A CENTRAL BANK

A **central bank** serves four main functions: as a banker for commercial banks, as a bank for the government, as the controller of the nation's supply of money, and as a supporter of financial markets.

The first three functions are revealed by a study of the balance sheet of a central bank. Table 33-14 is such a balance sheet.

Banker to Commercial Banks

The central bank accepts deposits from commercial banks and will, on order, transfer them to the account of another bank. In this way the central bank provides each commercial bank with the equivalent of a checking account and with a means for settling debts to other banks. The deposits of the commercial banks with the central bank appear in Table 33-14. Notice that the reserves of the commercial banks deposited with the central bank are *liabilities* of the central bank (because it promises to pay them on demand), just as the money reserves of an individual or corporation deposited with a commercial bank are the liabilities of the commercial bank.

Historically, one of the earliest services provided by central banks was that of "lender of last resort" to the commercial banking system. Central banks would lend money to commercial banks that had sound investments (such as government securities and safe loans to individuals) but were in urgent need of cash. If such banks could not obtain ready cash, they might be forced into insolvency because they could not meet the demands of their depositors, in spite of their being basically sound. Today's central banks continue to be the lender of last resort. In a year such as 1980, when the Fed was seeking to hold down the money supply, such loans were discouraged. In other years they have been much larger than the 2.5 percent of reserves they were in 1980.

The rate of interest the Fed charges on loans to its member banks is called the **discount rate.** Commercial banks sometimes borrow from the central bank when they wish to build up their reserves. More frequently, they sell government securities or borrow on the federal funds market.

Banker to the Government

Governments, too, need to hold their funds in an account into which they can make deposits and on which they can write checks. The U.S. Treasury keeps its checking deposits at the Federal Reserve banks, replenishing them from much larger tax and loan accounts kept at commercial banks. When the government requires more money than it collects in taxes, it too needs to borrow, and it does so by selling securities. Most are sold directly to the public, but when the central bank buys a government bond on the open market, it is indirectly lending to the government. As of January 1980, the Federal Reserve System held over $16 billion in U.S. government securities.

Regulator of the Money Supply

One of the most important functions of a central bank is to control the money supply. From Table 33-14 it is clear that the overwhelming proportion of a central bank's liabilities (its promises to pay) are either Federal Reserve notes (money) or the deposits of commercial banks, which provide reserves for demand deposits (money) owned by households and firms.

The central bank can affect the levels of its assets and liabilities in many ways, and as its liabilities rise and fall, so does the money supply. Here is a simple example. Suppose that the cen-

TABLE 33-14

Federal Reserve Banks, Consolidated Balance Sheet, January 30, 1980 (billions of dollars)

Assets		Liabilities	
Gold certificates		Federal Reserve Notes outstanding	$108.9
and other cash	$ 11.2	Deposits of member	
U.S. government		bank reserves	31.2
securities	116.3	Deposits of U.S.	
Loans to commercial		Treasury	2.9
banks	0.8	Other liabilities	9.0
Other assets	27.0	Capital	3.3
	$155.3		$155.3

Source: *Federal Reserve Bulletin,* February 1980.

The balance sheet of the Fed shows that it serves as banker to the commercial banks and the U.S. Treasury and as issuer of our currency; it also suggests the Fed's role as regulator of money markets and the money supply. The principal liabilities of the Fed are the basis of the money supply. Federal Reserve notes are currency, and the deposits of member banks give commercial banks the reserves they use to create deposit money. The Fed's principal assets, holdings of U.S. government securities, arise from its open market operations designed to regulate the money supply and also from direct purchases from the Treasury.

Currency Control as a Means of Controlling the Money Supply

Controlling the quantity of currency it issues might seem to be the most obvious way for the government to control the money supply. After all, the amount of coinage is controlled directly by the Treasury, and the rest of the currency in circulation is in the form of central bank notes. Look at the next piece of paper money you see; if you live in the United States the odds are great that it will have the words "Federal Reserve Note" on it. Virtually all the currency in circulation is in the form of Federal Reserve notes.

The Treasury and the Fed would seem to be able to control the amount of currency in circulation by issuing more of it or by withdrawing some of it from circulation. In fact they are unwilling to tell the public how much of its money to hold in cash. They are not able to make the public hold more cash than it wants as long as banks will accept deposits. They could not make the public hold less cash than it wanted without serious risk to the stability of the monetary system.

Suppose that with a given money supply the public decided it wished to hold a higher proportion in currency and a lower proportion in deposits (as it does, for example, every Christmas season). If the Fed wished to prevent this, it would have to take steps to reduce the cash available to commercial banks so that they could not, or would not, turn their customers' deposits into cash. Because commercial banks have a legal obligation to pay cash whenever it is demanded by their customers, a failure to do so would mean widespread bank insolvency and a consequent financial panic. (Even that would not work for very long; Federal Deposit Insurance payments would give depositors the cash they were legally entitled to receive.)

The Fed can and does influence the *total* money supply (currency plus demand deposits). But it does not seek to influence how the total is divided between currency and deposits. Thus the proportion changes, as habits and customs change with respect to paying bills.

---

tral bank buys $100 million worth of newly printed bonds from the Treasury. The bank's assets (government securities) rise by $100 million, and so do its liabilities (Treasury deposits). The government has an extra $100 million of purchasing power to spend. As easy as printing money, you say. Indeed, it is the same thing.

Regulator of Money Markets

The central bank frequently enters money markets for reasons other than controlling the money supply. It may, as an arm of the government, attempt to keep interest rates low in periods when the government is increasing its debt, so as to reduce the government's cost of financing a given size deficit.

Central banks also assume a major responsibility to support the country's financial system and to prevent serious disruption by wide-scale panic and resulting bank failures. Various institutions are in the business of borrowing on a short-term and lending on a long-term basis. One example is savings and loan associations, which take in short-term deposits from the public and lend on long-term mortgages. Large, unanticipated increases in interest rates tend to squeeze these institutions. The average rate that they earn on their investments rises only slowly as old contracts mature and new ones are made, but they must either pay higher rates to hold on to their deposits or they must accept wide-scale withdrawals that could easily bring about their insolvency. The central bank can help such institutions by lending them money or by using its control over interest rates to ease their plight.

Conflicts Among Functions

The several functions of the central bank can each be performed, but they are not always mutually compatible. When the Fed seeks to bring about a tight money supply and causes interest rates to rise, it is causing the credit squeeze that makes life uncomfortable for banks and other financial institutions and makes borrowing expensive for the government. When the Fed chooses to ease those problems, say by lending money to banks, it is relaxing its tight-money policy.

The central bank must strive to balance these conflicting objectives. When it wishes to raise interest rates to control the money supply, it must do so by an amount and on such a timetable as to prevent financial panic or disasters in money markets. While in theory there is a compromise that is the ideal balance of all the objectives, there is a major debate about whether an actual central bank can find and follow it. Many critics think that it cannot, that periodically central banks cause problems by their monetary mismanagement.

THE FEDERAL RESERVE SYSTEM

The most important thing about the Federal Reserve System is this:

In its role as the central bank of the United States, the Federal Reserve System is the arm of the U.S. government responsible for its monetary policy.

This is stressed because things are not always as they seem; the organizational structure of the system appears, at first glance, to consist of a number of privately owned banks over which commercial banks rather than the government have control.

The basic elements in the Federal Reserve System are (1) the board of governors, (2) the Federal Advisory Council, which has no real powers, but whose 12 members advise the board of the views of commercial bankers, (3) the 12 Federal Reserve banks, (4) the Federal Open Market Committee, and (5) the more than 5,700 member commercial banks.

The board of governors. The board consists of seven members appointed by the president and confirmed by the Senate. Appointment is for 14 years. The length of term is important because each member of the board serves beyond the term of the president making the appointment. The board members are top-level public servants who often, but not inevitably, come from the world of business or banking. In 1980 two of its members, Henry Wallich and Nancy Teeters, were professional economists. The board is responsible to Congress but works closely with the Department of the Treasury. The board supervises the entire Federal Reserve System and exercises general policy control over the twelve Reserve banks.

The chairman of the board, currently Paul A. Volcker, is in a powerful position to influence the country's monetary policies.

The Reserve banks. Twelve Federal Reserve banks serve the 12 districts into which the country is divided. The Federal Reserve banks are located in Boston, New York, Philadelphia, Cleveland, Richmond, Atlanta, Chicago, St. Louis, Minneapolis, Kansas City, Dallas, and San Francisco. Each bank is nominally owned by the member banks in its district. A commercial bank that is a member of the system is required to purchase Reserve bank stock to an amount equal to 3 percent of the member bank's own capital. The commercial banks receive a flat 6 percent dividend on this investment. Each Federal Reserve bank has nine directors: three bankers elected by the member banks; three representatives of business, agriculture, or industry; and three public members appointed by the board of governors.

Although technically privately owned and operated, the Federal Reserve banks are actually operated under guidelines set down by the board of governors in what it deems to be the public interest.

The Federal Reserve banks have a strong tradition of service to the banking community within the policy lines laid down by the board of governors. Revenues that they earn in excess of

TABLE 33-15(a)

Balance Sheet for a Loaned-up Banking System with a 20 Percent Reserve Ratio

Assets		Liabilities	
Reserves	$1,000	Deposits	$5,000
Loans	4,100	Capital	100
	$5,100		$5,100

Increasing the required reserve ratio forces a loaned-up bank to reduce its deposits — and thus decreases the supply of deposit money. The banking system in part (a) has a ratio of reserves to deposits of .20. If the Fed now raises the required reserve ratio to .25, the reserves of $1,000 will support deposits of only $4,000. As shown in (b), the banking

TABLE 33-15(b)

Balance Sheet for a Loaned-up Banking System After a Change in Reserve Ratio to 25 Percent

Assets		Liabilities	
Reserves	$1,000	Deposits	$4,000
Loans	3,100	Capital	100
	$4,100		$4,100

system can reduce its deposits by reducing its loans. A reduction in reserve requirements from .25 to .20 would permit a banking system in the position of (b) to expand its loans and deposits to those of (a) with no increase in its dollar reserves.

expenses and of fixed minimum profits are turned over to the U.S. Treasury. Most Reserve banks, along with the office of the board of governors, engage in research and publish many bulletins of interest to the financial communities they serve.

The Open Market Committee. The Open Market Committee has 12 members: the seven members of the board of governors plus five presidents of Reserve banks. This committee determines the open market policy of the system, which deals principally with how many government securities the Reserve banks should buy or sell on the open market.

Central Banks and the Money Supply

Deposit money is a large part of the money supply, no matter how the supply of money is defined. Demand deposits of commercial banks account for 70 percent of M-1A, the narrowest definition of money, and roughly 20 percent of M-3, the broadest measure in widespread use (see Table 33-1). The ability of commercial banks to create deposit money depends on their reserves, as we have seen. The ability of the central bank to affect the money supply is critically related to its ability to affect the size and adequacy of the reserves of commercial banks. We shall discuss three means of doing so.

CHANGING THE REQUIRED RESERVE RATIOS

One way to control the money supply is by altering the required minimum reserve ratios. Suppose the banking system is loaned-up; that is, it has no excess reserves. If the Fed increases the required reserve ratio (say from 20 percent to 25 percent), the dollar amount of reserves held by the commercial banks will no longer be adequate to support their outstanding deposits. Commercial banks will then be forced to reduce their deposits until they achieve the new, higher required reserve ratio.[5] This decrease in demand deposits is a decrease in the money supply. The process is illustrated in Table 33-15.

The effect of a reduction in required reserve ratios is also shown in the table. Of course, if banks choose not to increase their loans, they will not need to respond to a decrease in required reserves, since those requirements are only minimum requirements. The first effect of a decrease in required reserves is to create excess reserves. In normal times the profit motive will lead most banks to respond by increasing loans and deposits — and thus will lead to an increase in the money supply.

---

[5] They will do this by gradually decreasing their loans and/or selling some of their securities. In the short term they may borrow from the Fed to give themselves time to meet the increased reserve requirements without disrupting financial markets.

Increases in required reserve ratios force banks with no excess reserves to decrease deposits and thus reduce the money supply. Decreases in required reserve ratios permit banks to expand deposits and thus may increase the money supply.

CHANGES IN THE DISCOUNT RATE

The central bank can use the terms on which it will lend funds to the commercial banks to affect the money supply. Such borrowing by member banks is said to take place at the Fed's discount window. Increases in the discount rate discourage such borrowing and cause banks that desire or need extra reserves to get them instead by selling bonds or liquidating loans. These latter activities, as we shall see, contract the money supply. Decreases in the discount rate make borrowing from the Fed cheaper and (other things being equal) encourage credit expansion and increases in the money supply.

OPEN MARKET OPERATIONS

The most important tool that the central bank has for influencing the supply of money is the purchase or sale of government securities on the open market. At the start of 1980 the Federal Reserve held more than $116 billion in government securities. In December 1960 it held only $25 billion. At the end of 1972 it held about $70 billion. In a typical year, the Fed buys and sells $15 to $25 billion worth of government securities. What is the effect of these purchases and sales?[6]

Purchases and sales of government securities in financial markets by the central bank are known as **open market operations.** There are active and well-organized markets for government

---

[6] It is necessary for some purposes to distinguish between the Federal Reserve banks' occasional purchase of government securities directly from the Treasury and their purchase or sale of such securities on the open market. The two are different kinds of transactions and have different effects. We are now talking about the latter.

securities, just as there is a stock market. You or I, or General Foods, or the Bank of America, or the Federal Reserve Bank of New York can enter this market and buy or sell negotiable government securities at whatever price supply and demand establishes. When the Fed buys or sells securities, it does not know from whom it buys or to whom it sells them. Moreover, it does not care. The effects on the money supply of the purchase or sale are the same no matter who is on the other side of the transaction.

Purchases on the Open Market

When a Federal Reserve bank buys a bond from a household or firm, it pays for the bond with a check drawn on the central bank and payable to the seller. The seller deposits this check in its own bank. The commercial bank presents the check to the Fed for payment, and the central bank makes a book entry increasing the deposit of the commercial bank at the central bank.

Table 33-16 shows the changes in the balance sheets of the several parties in response to a Federal Reserve bank purchase of $100 in government securities from a household. After these transactions, the commercial banks have excess reserves and are in a position to expand their loans and deposits. The household that sold the bond to the Fed receives a check from the Fed in payment. When the household deposits this check in its own commercial bank account, its bank is placed in the same position as was the bank in Table 33-4 that received the new deposit from the immigrant.

What if the seller of the security is a commercial bank instead of a private household or firm? It trades one asset (a security) for another asset (an increased deposit with the central bank). The increased central bank deposit, but not the security, is part of its reserves. Table 33-17 summarizes the changes that would take place. The commercial banks again find themselves with excess reserves and so can expand the money supply by expanding loans and deposits or by purchasing securities.

TABLE 33-16

Balance Sheet Changes Caused by an Open Market Purchase from a Household

Private household		
Assets		Liabilities
Bonds	−$100	No change
Deposits	+ 100	

Commercial banks		
Assets		Liabilities
Reserves (deposits with central bank)	+$100	Demand deposits	+$100

Central bank		
Assets		Liabilities
Bonds	+$100	Deposits of commercial banks	+$100

The money supply is increased when the Fed makes an open market purchase from a household. When the Fed buys a $100 bond from a household, the household gains money and gives up a bond. The commercial banks gain a new deposit of $100—and thus new reserves of $100. Commercial banks can now engage in a multiple expansion of deposit money of the sort analyzed earlier in the chapter.

When the central bank buys securities on the open market, the reserves of the commercial banks are increased. These banks in turn can expand deposits, thereby increasing the money supply.

If the central bank buys many securities in the open market, the entire banking system will gain new reserves. Whether the seller is a household, a firm, or a bank, the purchase by the Federal Reserve of securities on the open market sets in motion a series of book transactions that increase the banking system's reserves and thus make possible a multiple expansion of credit.

Sales on the Open Market

When the central bank sells a $100 security to a household or firm, it receives in return the buyer's check drawn against its own deposit in a commercial bank. The central bank presents the check to the private bank for payment. Payment is made by a book entry reducing the private bank's deposit at the central bank.

Now the central bank has reduced its assets by the value of the security it sold and reduced its liabilities in the form of the deposits of commercial banks. The household or firm has increased its holding of securities and reduced its cash on deposit with a commercial bank. The commercial bank has reduced its deposit liability to the household or firm and reduced its reserves (on deposit with the central bank) by the same amount. Each of the asset changes is balanced by a liability change. Indeed, everything balances.

But the commercial bank finds that by suffering an equal change in its reserves and deposit liabilities, its ratio of reserves to deposits falls. The changes are the opposite of those shown in Table 33-16. If the reserve ratio was previously at the minimum acceptable level, the commercial bank will have to take immediate steps to restore its reserve ratio. The necessary reduction in deposits can be effected by not making new investments when old ones are redeemed (e.g., by not

TABLE 33-17

Balance Sheet Changes Caused by an Open Market Purchase from a Commercial Bank

Commercial banks		
Assets		Liabilities
Reserves	+$100	No change
Bonds	− 100	

Central bank		
Assets		Liabilities
Bonds	+$100	Deposits of commercial banks	+$100

The money supply is increased when the Fed makes an open market purchase from a commercial bank. When the Fed buys a $100 bond directly from a commercial bank, there is no change in the assets or liabilities of households, but commercial banks gain an increase in their deposits with the Fed of $100; these are direct additions to their reserves. Commercial banks can now engage in a multiple expansion of deposit money of the sort analyzed earlier in the chapter.

granting a new loan when old ones are repaid) or by selling (liquidating) existing investments.

To understand this, set up the balance sheet changes that correspond to the verbal description of this case and work through what would have happened if the central bank had sold the security directly to a commercial bank. In this case there should be a reduction in the commercial bank's reserves by the value of the securities sold by the central bank and (if reserves are pushed below acceptable levels) pressure to contract the volume of demand deposits in order to reestablish an acceptable reserve ratio.

When the central bank sells securities on the open market, the reserves of the commercial banks are decreased. These banks in turn are forced to contract deposits, thereby decreasing the money supply.

The question arises, What if the public does not want to play ball? How can the central bank force the public to buy securities? The answer, of course, is that there is always a price at which the public will buy. The central bank in its open market operations must be prepared to have the price of the securities fall if it insists on suddenly selling a large volume of them. As we shall see, a fall in the price of securities is the same thing as a rise in interest rates, so if the Fed wishes to curtail the money supply by selling bonds, it may well drive up interest rates.

Notice in Table 33-14 that the Fed's holdings of government securities are large relative to the reserves of commercial banks. By selling securities it can contract those reserves very sharply if it chooses. Similarly, by buying securities it can expand them. In its open market operations the central bank has a potent weapon for affecting the size of member bank reserves—and thus for affecting the money supply.

Summary

1. The money supply—the stock of money in the country at a specific moment—can be defined in various ways. M-1A is currency plus demand deposits, the narrowest definition in common use. (M-1A was about $400 billion in 1980.) M-3, the widest commonly used definition, adds in all time and savings deposits. (M-3 was about $1,800 billion in 1980.)

2. The banking system in the United States consists of two main elements: commercial banks and the Federal Reserve System, which is the central bank. Each has an important effect on the money supply.

3. American commercial banks are profit-seeking institutions that allow their customers to transfer demand deposits from one bank to another by means of checks. They create and destroy money as a by-product of their commercial operations—by making or liquidating loans and various other investments.

4. Because most customers are content to pay their accounts by check rather than by cash, the banks need not keep anything like a 100 percent reserve against their deposit liabilities. Consequently, banks are able to create deposit money. When the banking system receives a new cash deposit, it can create new deposits to some multiple of this amount. The amount of new deposits created depends on the legal minimum reserves the Federal Reserve enforces on the banks, the amount of cash drain to the public, and whether the banks choose to hold excess reserves.

5. There is nothing automatic about the expansion of the money supply when reserves of commercial banks increase. If bankers do not choose to use excess reserves to expand their investments, there will be no expansion. In normal times it is profitable for bankers to keep excess reserves small, but in times of depression they may not find the investment risks worth taking.

6. All advanced free-market economies have a central bank that serves as banker for commercial banks, banker for the government, controller and regulator of the money supply, and regulator and supporter of money markets.

7. The central bank of the United States is the

set of Federal Reserve banks and its board of governors. Although nominally private, the Reserve banks are in fact parts of a system that functions as a central bank. Effective power is exercised by the board of governors, whose seven members are appointed by the president of the United States for 14-year terms.

8. The Fed can affect the money supply in many ways, each of which affects the reserves of the commercial banking system. Among them are changing required reserves, changing the rate of interest at which it will lend to commercial banks, and open market operations.

9. The major policy instrument used by the Fed is open market operations. Purchases of bonds on the open market are expansionary because they create new deposits that permit (but do not force) a multiple expansion of bank credit. Sales on the open market reduce bank reserves and force a multiple contraction of bank credit on the part of all banks that do not have excess reserves.

Topics for Review

The money supply
The banking system
Assets and liabilities of a commercial bank
The creation and destruction of deposit money
Reserve ratio, required reserves, and excess reserves
Functions of a central bank
The discount rate
Open market operations

Discussion Questions

1. How would you expect the following to change the relative size of M-1A, M-1B, M-2, and M-3?
   a. allowing interest payments on demand deposits
   b. prohibiting NOW and ATS accounts
   c. setting the same maximum interest rate on time deposits in savings and loan associations as in commercial banks (savings and loans are now higher)

   d. printing twice as much currency as is now printed annually

2. Commercial banks in the United States are no longer allowed to issue their own bank notes. How do they now create money? (Explain the process carefully.) How do they make profits? Is it possible for them to create money without being aware of it?

3. The *Wall Street Journal* asked: "Why do we have reserve requirements anyway? . . . Even if there were no reserve requirements, a prudent banker would hold reserves, but the amount each would hold would be a function of his personal assessment of risk." What are your thoughts on these points raised by the *Wall Street Journal*? Might reserves be lower without regulation? Is regulation of reserve requirements just one more example of a spreading government bureaucracy that interferes with the efficient working of the market?

4. If all depositors tried to turn their deposits into cash at once, they would find that there are not sufficient reserves in the system to allow all of them to do this at the same time. Why then do we not still have panicky runs on the banks? Would a 100 percent reserve requirement be safer? What effect would such a reserve requirement have on the banking system's ability to create money? Would it preclude any possibility of a panic?

5. The reciprocal of the required reserve ratio indicates the maximum multiple expansion of demand deposits that can take place with an increase in member bank reserves. Why is the actual expansion likely to be less than the maximum?

6. What would be the effect on the money supply of each of the following?
   a. a decline in the public's confidence in the banks
   b. a desire on the part of banks to increase their levels of excess reserves
   c. the monopolizing of the banking system into a single super bank
   d. the increased use of credit cards
   e. allowing banks to pay any level of interest they wish on demand deposits

7. "Federal Reserve notes are money, right? 'Good as gold', they tell you. *Don't you believe it!* The Federal Reserve banks know better. They list their gold certificates as *assets*, but they list their Federal Reserve notes as *liabilities*." Is there a sensible explanation for this confusing state of affairs?

The Role of Money in Macroeconomics

34

At one time or another most of us have known the surprise of opening our wallet or purse to discover that we had either more or less money than we thought. There can be as much pleasure in deciding how to spend an unexpected windfall in the first case as there can be pain in deciding what intended expenditure to eliminate in the second case.

What determines how much money people hold in their purses and wallets and how much they keep in the bank? What happens when everyone discovers that they are holding more, or less, money than they believe they need to hold?

These turn out to be key questions for our study of the influence of money on output and prices. The answers will help us to establish links between the money supply and the aggregate expenditure and aggregate demand functions.

The Demand for and the Supply of Money

KINDS OF ASSETS

At any moment in time households have a given stock of wealth. This wealth is held in many forms. Some of it is money in the bank or in the wallet; some is in short-term securities such as CDs, money market shares, and treasury bills; some is in long-term bonds; and some is in real capital, which may be held directly (in the form of family businesses) or indirectly (in the form of shares of stock that indicate ownership of a corporation's assets). All these ways of holding wealth may be grouped into three main categories: (1) assets that serve as a medium of exchange, that is, paper money, coins, and bank checking deposits; (2) other financial assets, such as bonds earning a fixed rate of interest, that will yield a fixed money value at some future *maturity* date and that can usually be sold before maturity for a price that fluctuates on the open market; and (3) claims on real capital (physical objects such as factories and machines).

In this chapter we are concerned with the amount of wealth everyone in the economy wishes to hold in the form of money balances. This total is called the **demand for money.** We can discover what determines this important magnitude by looking at the division of wealth between the holding of money on the one hand and the holding of other financial assets and real capital on the other. The amount of money balances held in the economy is a *stock* quantity. It is so many billions of dollars. (It is *not* a flow of so much per unit of time.)

"Money" and "Bonds"

There are many different kinds of financial assets. They differ from each other in the rate of interest they yield and in their **liquidity:** the degree of ease and certainty with which an asset can be turned into a given amount of the economy's medium of exchange. The spectrum of financial assets reaches from perfectly liquid currency that earns no interest at one end to relatively illiquid long-term bonds that earn a substantial interest rate at the other end.

To simplify our discussion, it is helpful to assume that only two kinds of financial assets exist: *money,* which is perfectly liquid but earns no interest return, and *bonds,* which are less liquid but earn an interest return. Here the term *bonds* stands for all interest-earning financial assets plus claims on real capital such as equities.

The Rate of Interest and the Price of Bonds

A bond is a promise by the issuer to pay a stated sum of money as interest each year and to repay the face value of the bond at some future "redemption date," often many years distant. The time until the redemption date is called the **term to maturity** or often simply the **term** of the bond. Some bonds, called perpetuities, pay interest forever and never repay the principal.

The price of any bond reflects the value of the stream of future payments that its owner will receive.

The relationship between interest rates and bond prices is most easily seen in the case of a perpetuity. Assume that such a bond will pay $100 per year to its holder. The *present value* of this bond depends on how much $100 per year is worth, and this in turn depends on the rate of interest. (The discussion of the concept of present value in Chapter 22, pages 383–385, may profitably be read at this time.)

A bond that will produce a stream of income of $100 a year forever is worth $1,000 at 10 percent interest because $1,000 invested at 10 percent per annum will yield $100 interest per year forever. But the same bond is worth $2,000 when the interest rate is 5 percent per year because it takes $2,000 invested at 5 percent per annum to yield $100 interest per year. The lower the rate of interest obtainable on the market, the more valuable is a bond paying a fixed amount of interest.

Similar relations apply to bonds that are not perpetuities, though the calculation of present value must allow for the lump-sum repayment of principal at maturity. In general, the present value of any asset that yields a stream of money over time is inversely related to the interest rate.

This proposition has two important implications: (1) if the rate of interest falls, the value of an asset producing a given income stream will rise; and (2) when the market price of an asset producing a fixed income is forced up, this is equivalent to a decrease in the rate of interest earned by the asset.

Thus a promise to pay $100 one year from now is worth $92.59 when the interest rate is 8 percent and only $89.29 when the interest rate is 12 percent. For $92.59 at 8 percent interest ($92.59

× 1.08) and $89.29 at 12 percent interest ($89.29 × 1.12) are both worth $100 in one year's time.

The rate of interest and bond prices vary inversely with each other.

A redeemable bond differs from a perpetuity in that its present value becomes increasingly dominated by the fixed redemption value as the redemption date approaches. Take an extreme case: if a bond will be redeemable for $1,000 in a week's time, its present value will be very close to $1,000 no matter what the interest rate. Thus its value will not change much even if the rate of interest leaps from 5 percent to 10 percent during that week.

The closer to the present date is the redemption date of a bond, the less the bond's value will change with a change in the rate of interest.

For example, a rise in the interest rate from 8 to 12 percent will lower the value of $100 payable in one year's time by 3.6 percent, but the same rise will lower the value of the same sum payable in ten years time by a full 37.9 percent.[1]

WHAT DETERMINES THE SUPPLY OF MONEY?

As used in this chapter, the supply of money is M-1A: the total quantity of currency and checkable bank deposits available to be held as money balances. In January 1980, M-1A was approximately $380 billion. We saw in the previous chapter that deposit money is created by the commercial banking system, but only within limits set by their reserves, which are under the control of the Fed. Thus the ultimate control of the money supply is in the Fed's hands. In Chapter 35 we shall look at the degree to which the Fed can in fact control the money supply with a view to manipulating the economy. In this

[1] The example assumes annual compounding. The first case is calculated from the numbers of the previous example: $(92.58 - 89.29)/92.58$. The ten-year case uses the formula present value = principal$/(l + r)^n$, which gives $46.30 with 8 percent and $28.75 with 12 percent. The fall in value is thus $(46.30 - 28.75)/46.30 = 0.379$.

chapter we shall simplify by assuming that the money supply can be precisely controlled by the Fed. This makes it an exogenous variable, to be determined by the Fed's policy decisions.

Let us see first how the economy adjusts to a given money supply.

WHAT DETERMINES THE DEMAND FOR MONEY?

When we say that on January 2, 1980, the demand for money was $380 billion, we mean that on that date everyone wished to hold money balances that totaled $380 billion. But why do firms and households wish to hold money balances at all?

There is a cost in holding any money balance. The money could instead be used to purchase bonds; it would then earn interest as a return. The opportunity cost of holding any money balance is the rate of interest that could have been earned if the money had instead been used to purchase bonds.

Clearly money will be held only when it provides services that are valued at least as highly as the opportunity cost of holding it. The services provided by money balances are, first, to finance purchases and sales; second, to provide a cushion against uncertainty about the timing of cash flows; and third, to provide a hedge against uncertainty over the prices of other financial assets. The desire to hold money to obtain each of these services is summarized by the so-called **transactions motive, precautionary motive,** and **speculative motive** for holding money. We may now see how these motives together determine the demand for money.

The Demand for Money and National Income I: The Transactions Motive

The majority of the transactions that take place in any economy require money. Money passes from households to firms to pay for the goods and services produced by firms; money passes from firms to households to pay for the factor services supplied by households to firms. To finance their transactions, both firms and households hold money balances.

In an imaginary world, where the receipts and disbursements of households and firms were perfectly synchronized, it would be unnecessary to hold transactions balances. If every time a household spent $10 it received $10 as part payment of its income, no transactions balances would be needed. In the real world, however, receipts and disbursements are not perfectly synchronized.

Consider, for example, the balances held because of wage payments. Assume, for purposes of illustration, that firms pay wages every Friday and that households spend all their wages on the purchase of goods and services, with the expenditure being spread out evenly over the week. Thus on Friday morning firms must hold balances equal to the weekly wage bill; on Friday afternoon households will hold these balances. Over the week, households' balances will be drawn down as a result of purchasing goods and services. Over the same period, the balances held by firms will build up as a result of selling goods and services until, on the following Friday morning, firms will again have amassed balances equal to the wage bill that must be met on that day.

On the average over the week, firms will hold balances equal to half the wage bill, and so will households; thus, in this example, total money balances held will be equal to the total weekly wage bill. Notice that while the money circulates so that each group holds a varying balance over the week, the combined demand for balances summed for the two groups remains constant.

The size of the balances held for transactions purposes is influenced, therefore, by the size of the wage bill. If the wage bill doubles, either because twice as many people are employed at the same rate or because the same number is employed at twice the wage rate, the balances held must double.

Our argument has been conducted in terms of the wage bill, but a similar analysis holds for payments for all factor services. The need for transactions balances depends on the money value of all kinds of transactions. This in turn depends on the money value of national income.[2] If money national income doubles, the money value of transactions will tend to double, as will the demand for money to finance the transactions.

The Demand for Money and National Income II: The Precautionary Motive

Many goods and services are sold on credit. The seller can never be certain when payment for those goods will be made, and the buyer can never be certain of the day of delivery and thus of the day on which payment will fall due. In order to operate without a series of cash crises caused by receipts being abnormally low and/or disbursements being abnormally high, firms and households carry money balances as a precaution. The larger are the precautionary balances, the greater is the degree of protection against running out of money because of temporary fluctuations in cash flows.

How serious this risk is depends on the penalties for being caught without sufficient money balances. A firm is unlikely to be pushed into insolvency, but it may have to incur considerable costs if it is forced to borrow money at high interest rates for short periods in order to meet a temporary cash crisis.

The transactions motive arises because a firm knows that payments and receipts will not synchronize perfectly. The precautionary motive arises because the firm is uncertain about the *degree* to which payments and receipts will synchronize.

The protection provided by a given quantity of precautionary balances depends on the volume of payments and receipts. A $100 precautionary

---

[2] The difference between total transactions and national income arises from the problem of "double counting" (see page 492). In economies where both magnitudes have been estimated, the value of total transactions runs from five to ten times as large as national income.

balance provides a large cushion (50 percent) for a person whose volume of payments per month is $200, and a very small cushion (1 percent) for a firm whose monthly volume is $10,000. Haphazard fluctuations of the sort that give rise to precautionary balances may be expected to vary directly with the firm's cash flow. To provide the same degree of protection as the value of transactions rises, more money is necessary. Thus the firm's precautionary demand for money will rise as national income rises.[3]

The transactions and precautionary motives cause the demand for money to vary directly with the value of national income measured at current prices.

The Demand for Money and Wealth: The Speculative Motive

Households that hold bonds will have to sell some if they wish to consume in excess of their current income or if some temporary excess of payments over receipts exceeds their money holdings. At one extreme, if a household or firm held all its wealth in bonds, it would earn interest on all that wealth, but it would have to sell some bonds the first time its payments exceeded its receipts. At the other extreme, if a household or firm held all its wealth in money, the money would earn no interest, but the household or firm would never have to sell bonds to meet excesses of payments over current receipts. Wealth holders usually do not adopt either extreme position; instead, they hold part of their wealth as money and part as bonds. (Do not forget that "bonds" are here defined to include such interest-earning assets as deposits in savings accounts, certificates of deposit, and treasury bills.)

A household that holds bonds and money runs the risk that an unexpected gap between its receipts and its payments will force it to sell some bonds. If the price of bonds were fixed, there would be no risk in selling. But the price of bonds fluctuates from day to day on the open market. A household that may have to sell bonds to meet a need for money takes the risk that the price of bonds may be unexpectedly low at the time it sells them. Of course, if the household is lucky, the price may be unexpectedly high. But because no one knows in advance which way the price will go, firms and households must accept a risk whenever they hold in the form of bonds wealth that they may need to spend. Many firms and households do not like risk — economists say they are *risk adverse*. This leads them to hold more money than they otherwise would, in order to reduce the risk of having to sell bonds in the future at a price that cannot be predicted in advance.

The motive that leads firms to hold more money in order to avoid the risks inherent in a fluctuating price of bonds was analyzed first by Keynes, who called it the **speculative motive.** The modern analysis of this motive, sketched in the preceding paragraph, is the work of Professor James Tobin of Yale University.

Firms and households tend to insure against this risk by holding some fraction of their wealth in money and the rest in earning assets. Thus the demand for money depends on wealth and varies directly with wealth. For example, Ms. B. O'Reiley might elect to hold 5 percent of her wealth in money and the other 95 percent in bonds. If Ms. O'Reiley's wealth is $50,000, her demand for money will be $2,500. If her wealth increases to $60,000, her demand for money will rise to $3,000. Although an individual's wealth may rise or fall rapidly, the total wealth of a society changes only slowly. For the analysis of short-term fluctuations in national income, the effects of changes in wealth are fairly small, and we shall ignore them for the present. (Over the long term, however, variations in wealth can have a major effect on the demand for money.)

There is a second important aspect of the speculative demand for money. This leads to the ex-

---

[3] Institutional arrangements affect the precautionary demands. In the past, for example, a traveler would have had to carry a substantial precautionary balance in cash, but today a credit card covers most unforeseen expenses that may arise while traveling.

tremely important relation discussed in the next section.

The Demand for Money and the Rate of Interest

An important force acting on the decision of how to divide wealth between bonds and money is the cost of holding money. Wealth held in cash earns no interest; hence the reduction in risk involved in holding more money also carries a cost in terms of interest earnings forgone.

The speculative motive leads a household or firm to add to its money holdings until the reduction in risk obtained by the last dollar added is just balanced (in the wealth holder's view) by the cost in terms of the interest forgone on that dollar.

Because the cost of holding money balances is the interest that could have been earned if wealth had been held in bonds instead, the demand to hold money will vary inversely with the interest rate. When the rate of interest falls, the cost of holding money falls. This leads to more money being held both for precautionary motives (to reduce risks caused by uncertainty about the flows of payments and receipts) and for speculative motives (to reduce risks associated with fluctuations in the market price of bonds). When the rate of interest rises, the cost of holding money rises. This leads to less money being held for speculative and precautionary motives.

There is an important general conclusion of this analysis:

The demand for money varies inversely with the rate of interest.

The Total Demand for Money: Recapitulation

The demand for money is defined as the total amount of money balances that everyone in the economy wishes to hold. Our discussion of the motives for holding money leads to the conclusion that the demand for money, which is the demand to hold a stock of money balances,

varies directly with national income and wealth and inversely with the rate of interest.

Variations in wealth are an important influence on variations in the demand for money in the long term; they are relatively unimportant in the short term, however, because society's total wealth changes only slowly.

Figure 34-1 shows the influences of national income and the rate of interest, the two variables that account for most of the short-term variations in the quantity of money demanded. Following Keynes, the function relating money demand to the rate of interest is called the **liquidity preference (LP) function.** Since this function merely shows how the demand for money varies with the rate of interest, it is often labeled M^D, for money demand, rather than LP, for liquidity preference. Whichever name is used the relation described is: how the quantity of money people wish to hold varies as the rate of interest varies.

The Determination of Monetary Equilibrium: The Transmission Mechanism

A **monetary disequilibrium** is a situation where the demand for money does not equal the supply of money. A **monetary equilibrium** is a situation where the two magnitudes are equal. In Chapter 5 we saw that when there is disequilibrium in a competitive market for some commodity such as carrots, the price will change to bring about an equilibrium. What will do the same job with respect to money demand and money supply?

The answer is that the rate of interest will change to eliminate the excess demand for money. But as we saw in Chapter 30, desired investment expenditure is sensitive to the interest rate. Here, then, is a link between monetary factors and real expenditure flows.

The mechanism by which excess demand for or supply of money affects the aggregate expenditure function is called the transmission mechanism. In the next two sections we study its two parts, first, the link between monetary disequili-

FIGURE 34-1
The Demand for Money as a Function of Income and Interest Rates

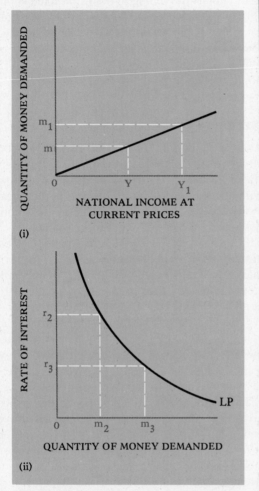

(i)

(ii)

The quantity of money demanded varies directly with national income and inversely with the rate of interest. In (i) the demand for money varies directly with money national income. As income rises from Y to Y_1, firms and households increase their demand for money from m to m_1.

In (ii) the demand for money varies inversely with the rate of interest along the liquidity preference function. As the rate falls from r_2 to r_3, firms and households increase their demand for money from m_2 to m_3.

(Note that the quantity of money is a variable in both parts of this figure but that it appears once on the horizontal axis and once on the vertical axis.)

brium and the interest rate and, second, the link between the interest rate and the aggregate expenditure function.

FROM MONETARY DISEQUILIBRIUM TO CHANGES IN THE RATE OF INTEREST

To study how monetary disequilibrium affects the rate of interest, we look separately at situations of excess demand and excess supply.

An Excess Demand for Money

We saw that firms and households must decide how much of their wealth to hold as money and how much to hold as bonds. When a single household or firm finds that it has less money than it wishes to hold, it need only sell some bonds and add the proceeds to its money holdings. This transaction simply redistributes given stocks of bonds and money between two individuals; it does not change the total supply of either money or bonds. Now assume that everyone in the economy has an excess demand for money balances. All try to sell bonds to add to their money balances. But what one person can do, everyone cannot do. At any moment in time, the society's total stocks of money and bonds are fixed; there is just so much money and so many bonds in existence. If everyone tries to sell bonds, there will be no one to buy them. The price of bonds will fall.

We saw earlier that a fall in the price of bonds is the same thing as a rise in the rate of interest. (For example, if a "bond" offering a single payment of $100 in one year's time falls in price from $95 to $90, this implies a rise in the rate of interest from 5.3 to 11.1 percent.) As the interest rate rises, people will economize on money balances because the opportunity cost of holding them is rising; that is, money balances move upward along the liquidity preference curve in response to a rise in the rate of interest. Eventually the interest rate will rise high enough that people will no longer try to add to their money balances by selling bonds. When there is no longer an excess supply of bonds, the interest

FIGURE 34-2

The Effects of Monetary Disequilibrium on the Interest Rate

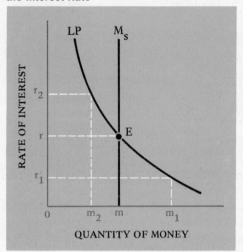

QUANTITY OF MONEY

The interest rate rises when there is an excess demand for money and falls when there is an excess supply of money. The fixed quantity of money, m, is shown by the completely inelastic supply curve M_S. The demand for money is LP. Equilibrium is at E with a rate of interest of r.

If the interest rate is r_1, there will be an excess demand for money of m_1m. Bonds will be offered for sale in an attempt to increase money holdings. This will force the rate of interest up to r (the price of bonds falls), at which point the quantity of money demanded has fallen to equal the fixed quantity supplied of m.

If the interest rate is r_2, there will be an excess supply of money of mm_2. Bonds will be demanded in return for excess money balances. This will force the rate of interest down to r (the price of bonds rises), at which point the quantity of money demanded has risen to equal the fixed supply of m.

In other words, because the money supply is fixed by the Fed, the rate of interest will fluctuate until people are willing to hold that fixed supply. If they want to hold more, their attempts to get it by selling bonds will drive up the interest rate. If they want to hold less, their attempts to buy bonds with their unwanted holdings will drive down the interest rate.

An Excess Supply of Money

Assume now that firms and households hold larger money balances than they would like. A single household or firm would purchase bonds with its excess balances; it would then reach monetary equilibrium by reducing its money holdings and increasing its bond holdings.

But what one household or firm can do, all cannot do. When all households enter the bond market and try to purchase bonds with unwanted stocks of money, they bid up the price of existing bonds—which entails a fall in the interest rate. As the rate falls, households and firms become willing to hold larger quantities of money; that is, the quantity of money demanded moves downward along the liquidity preference curve in response to a fall in the rate of interest.

This rise in the price of bonds continues until firms and households stop trying to convert bonds into money. It continues, then, until everyone is content to hold the existing supplies of money and bonds. Thus the whole economy arrives at equilibrium because the price of bonds rises (the rate of interest falls) until the quantities of money and bonds demanded equal their fixed supplies. This is also shown in Figure 34-2.

An excess supply of money causes firms and households to try to buy bonds. This lowers interest rates until the quantity of money demanded equals the constant money supply.

Monetary Equilibrium

We have discussed the two cases of monetary disequilibrium, excess monetary demand and excess monetary supply. Clearly the condition for

rate will stop rising. The demand for money again equals the supply.

The net effect of the original excess demand for money will have been an increase in the rate of interest, as illustrated in Figure 34-2.

An excess demand for money causes firms and households to try to sell bonds to add to their money balances. This raises interest rates and lowers the quantity of money demanded until it equals the fixed money supply.

monetary equilibrium is that the rate of interest be such that everyone is willing to hold the existing supplies of money and bonds. While a single individual can reach equilibrium holdings of money and bonds by adjusting the quantities held at existing market prices, the whole economy can reach equilibrium only by having bond prices (i.e., the rate of interest) adjust so that people are willing to hold the existing fixed quantities of money and bonds.

FROM CHANGES IN THE RATE OF INTEREST TO SHIFTS IN AGGREGATE EXPENDITURE

The second link in the transmission mechanism from money to aggregate expenditure is one that relates interest rates to expenditure. We saw in Chapter 30 that investment, which includes expenditure on inventory accumulation, residential construction, and plant and equipment, responds to changes in the rate of interest. Other things being equal, a decrease in the rate of interest makes borrowing cheaper and will set off a bout of new investment expenditure.[4]

Economists hypothesize an inverse relation between the rate of interest and the quantity of investment. This relation is shown by a downward-sloping curve, indicating that the lower is the rate of interest, the higher will be investment expenditure. This relation between investment and the rate of interest is called the **marginal efficiency of investment (MEI) function.** A graph of it is shown in Figure 34-3(ii).

THE TRANSMISSION MECHANISM SUMMARIZED

The transmission mechanism provides a connection between monetary forces and real expenditure forces. A monetary disequilibrium sets up a chain of events that will eventually cause the aggregate expenditure function to shift. The working of this mechanism may be summarized:

The transmission mechanism works from an excess demand or excess supply of money, to changes in the demand or supply of bonds, to changes in bond prices and interest rates, to changes in investment expenditure, to shifts in the aggregate investment function.

Because a change in the money supply changes interest rates—and thereby changes investment and national income—the influence of money spreads throughout the whole economic system. The money supply is linked to aggregate demand and aggregate expenditure by the interest rate.

The Theory of Monetary Policy

Monetary policy attempts to influence the economy by altering the money supply and interest rates. Monetary policy is administered by the country's central bank, which in the United States is the Fed. When the Fed changes the money supply, it creates the type of monetary disequilibrium whose effects we have just studied.[5]

POLICY-INDUCED MONETARY DISEQUILIBRIUM

Say that the economy is in equilibrium, with desired aggregate expenditure equal to income at less than full-employment national income and with the demand for money equal to its supply. Then the Fed increases the money supply, which creates an excess supply of money. Firms and households now hold larger money balances than they require, and they will try to buy bonds with the extra money balances. This action forces up the price of bonds, which means a fall in the rate of interest. Desired investment rises along the

---

[4] In Chapter 30 we saw that purchases of durable consumer goods also respond to changes in interest rates. In this chapter we concentrate on investment expenditure, which may be taken to stand for *all interest-sensitive expenditure.*

[5] As we shall see, the Fed can in principle affect the money supply or interest rates; it cannot, however, expect to have an independent influence on both.

FIGURE 34-3

The Effects of Changes in the Money Supply on Investment Expenditure

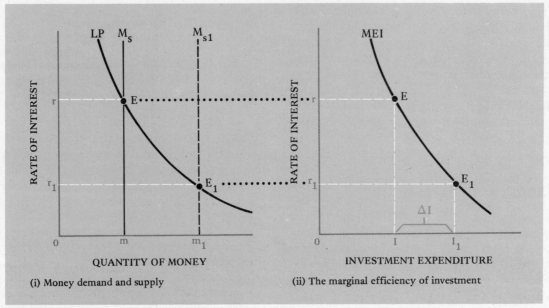

(i) Money demand and supply

(ii) The marginal efficiency of investment

Increases in the money supply reduce the rate of interest and increase desired investment expenditure. The economy is in equilibrium at E with a quantity of money of m (yielding inelastic money supply curve, M_S), an interest rate of r, and investment expenditure of I. The Fed then increases the money supply to M_{S1}. This forces the rate of interest down to r_1 and increases investment expenditure by ΔI, to I_1. This is the effect of an expansionary monetary policy.

A contractionary monetary policy reduces the money supply from M_{S1} to M_S. This raises interest rates from r_1 to r and lowers investment expenditure by ΔI, from I_1 to I.

MEI curve. These changes, shown in Figure 34-3, are merely an application of the transmission mechanism.

The increase in desired investment expenditure shifts the *AE* and *AD* functions. The aggregate expenditure curve shifts upward, indicating more desired expenditure at each level of national income. The aggregate demand curve shifts rightward, indicating a higher demand for output at each price level. These shifts raise equilibrium national income, as shown in Figure 34-4.

What happens when the Fed decreases the money supply? This creates an excess demand for money because firms and households no longer have the money balances they wish to hold at the existing level of interest rates. In an effort to replenish their inadequate holdings of money, firms and households will seek to sell bonds. But all cannot succeed in doing this; their efforts to sell will drive the price of bonds down, which means an increase in the interest rate. The increased interest rate will cause a reduction in investment expenditure. This in turn shifts the aggregate expenditure function downward and the aggregate demand curve leftward. These shifts lower equilibrium income.

Monetary policy seeks to create a monetary disequilibrium that will work through the transmission mechanism to shift the aggregate expenditure and aggregate demand functions and so change equilibrium national income. An increase in the money supply is expansionary, a decrease is contractionary.

THE STRENGTH OF MONETARY POLICY

So far we have seen that increases in the quantity of money tend to increase national income, while decreases in the quantity of money tend to decrease national income. How strong is this relation? If, for example, the Fed engineers an immediate 10 percent increase in the money supply, by how much will income rise?

The magnitude of the changes in national income caused by changes in the money supply depends on the shapes of the schedules for liquidity preference and marginal efficiency of investment. The influences of the shapes of the two schedules may be summarized:

1. **A change in the money supply will have a larger effect on interest rates, the steeper (less interest elastic) is the *LP* function.**[6]
2. **A change in the rate of interest will have a larger effect on investment, and hence on national income, the flatter (more interest elastic) is the *MEI* function.**[7]

The combination that produces the largest effect on national income for a given change in the money supply is a steep *LP* function and a flat *MEI* function. This combination makes monetary policy a powerful means of influencing the economy.

The combination that produces the smallest effect is a flat *LP* function and a steep *MEI* function. This combination makes monetary policy relatively ineffective. All this is illustrated in Figure 34-5.

Not surprisingly, much of the controversy about the effectiveness of monetary policy as a means for influencing national income has centered on the shapes of these two functions. We shall discuss this controversy further in Chapter 38.

FIGURE 34-4

The Effects of Changes in the Money Supply on National Income

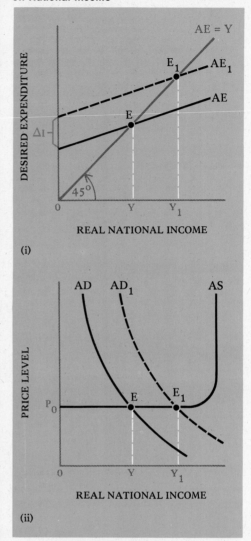

REAL NATIONAL INCOME

(i)

REAL NATIONAL INCOME

(ii)

Changes in the money supply cause shifts in the aggregate expenditure and aggregate demand functions. An expansionary monetary policy increases the money supply. In Figure 34-3 it increased desired investment expenditure by ΔI. Here it raises the aggregate expenditure function by ΔI (which is the same as ΔI in Figure 34-3), from AE to AE_1. It also shifts the aggregate demand curve outward from AD to AD_1. Equilibrium income rises from Y to Y_1.

A contractionary monetary policy decreases the money supply. When the supply of money falls (from M_{S1} to M_S in Figure 34-3), investment falls by ΔI thereby shifting aggregate expenditure from AE_1 to AE. This reduces equilibrium income from Y_1 to Y.

FIGURE 34-5
The Strength of Monetary Policy

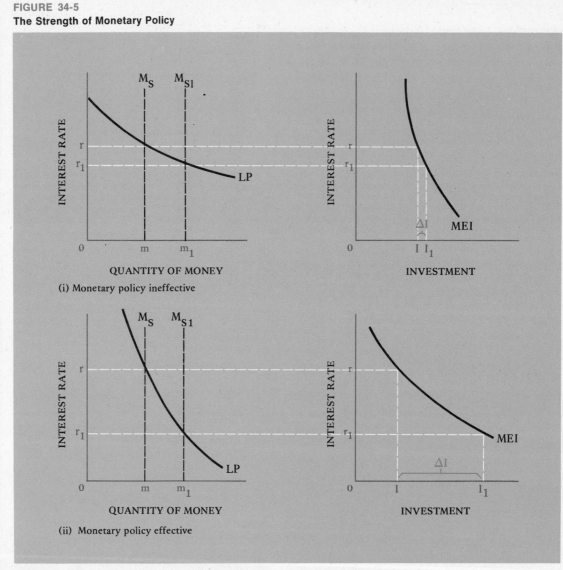

(i) Monetary policy ineffective

(ii) Monetary policy effective

Monetary policy is most effective when the *LP* curve is very inelastic and the *MEI* curve is very elastic. In both (i) and (ii) the same increase in the money supply from M_S to M_{S1} lowers the rate of interest from r to r_1. This fall in the rate of interest leads to an increase in investment, ΔI, from I to I_1. The shapes of the curves in (i) cause monetary policy to have a small effect on investment—and thus on aggregate expenditure; the shapes of the curves in (ii) cause monetary policy to have a large effect.

Changes in the Price Level

With what we know now, we can begin to study the theory of inflation systematically. Here we confine that study to certain basic points, leaving the full story to be taken up in Part Ten. Our ultimate goal is to discover the *causes* of changes in the price level. The best place to start, however, is with some *consequences* of changes in the price level.

THE SHAPE OF THE AGGREGATE DEMAND CURVE

Our first task is to see the effects on aggregate expenditure and hence on equilibrium national income of changes in the price level. The chain of causes that links changes in the price level to changes in the aggregate expenditure function, though long, is already largely familiar. In brief, a rise in the price level creates monetary disequilibrium, then the process of the transmission mechanism links monetary disequilibrium to a shift in the aggregate expenditure function. Let us follow the steps in detail.

We begin at a position of equilibrium, where at the current price level, P, aggregate desired expenditure equals income, Y, and the demand and supply of money are equal. P and Y yield one point on the aggregate demand curve.

Now let the price level rise to some higher level, P_1. For any given *real* national income, the money value of total sales must rise in proportion to the rise in the price level. If real income is constant while the price level rises by, say, 10 percent, then the market value of national income must rise by 10 percent.

The rise in the money value of all transactions leads to an increase in the quantity of money needed for transactions purposes. This causes a rise in the demand for money.

A rise in the demand for money, with an unchanged supply of money, creates an excess demand for money. This monetary disequilibrium sets the transmission mechanism in opera-

FIGURE 34-6

The Effects of Changes in the Price Level on Investment Expenditure

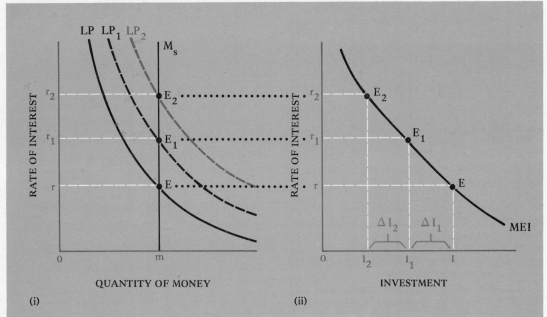

An increase in the price level raises the rate of interest and lowers investment expenditure. The economy is in equilibrium at *E*, with a liquidity preference schedule and money supply of *LP* and M_S, a rate of interest of *r*, and investment expenditure of *I*. An increase in the price level raises the money value of transactions and increases the demand for money to LP_1. This raises interest rates to r_1 and lowers investment expenditure by ΔI_1, to I_1.

A further increase in the price level shifts the liquidity preference function to LP_2, raises the interest rate to r_2, and lowers investment expenditure by ΔI_2, to I_2.

FIGURE 34-7
The Slope of the Aggregate Demand Curve

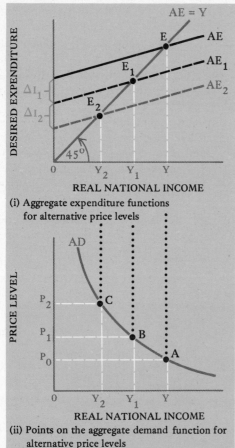

(i) Aggregate expenditure functions for alternative price levels

(ii) Points on the aggregate demand function for alternative price levels

The aggregate demand curve's slope occurs because an increase in the price level lowers aggregate expenditures and hence lowers equilibrium income. Initially the price level is P_0, the aggregate expenditure function is AE, and equilibrium income is Y. This yields point A on the AD curve in (ii).

A rise in the price level to P_1 shifts the aggregate expenditure function downward by ΔI_1 (see Figure 34-6), to AE_1. Equilibrium national income is now Y_1. This yields point B on the AD curve.

A rise in the price level to P_2 shifts the aggregate expenditure function downward by ΔI_2 (see Figure 34-6), to AE_2. Equilibrium income is now Y_2. This yields point C on the AD curve.

Repeating the process for every price level traces out the curved line of the aggregate demand function shown in (ii).

tion. The excess demand for money leads to (1) an attempt to sell bonds to replenish money balances, (2) a fall in bond prices, which entails a rise in interest rates, and (3) a fall in desired investment, which means a downward shift in the aggregate expenditure function. This process is described further in Figure 34-6.

The new equilibrium national income that results from these changes is less than the original equilibrium income. The higher price level, P_1, and the lower income, Y_1, yield a second point in an aggregate demand function that slopes upward to the left. These reasons for the slope of the AD curve are explained further in Figure 34-7.

The inverse relation between the price level and equilibrium real income shown by the AD curve occurs because *ceteris paribus* a rise in the price level raises the demand for money, and this shifts the aggregate expenditure function downward and lowers equilibrium national income.

Notice the qualification, "Other things being equal." It is important for this argument that the nominal money supply remain constant. The monetary disequilibrium occurs because the demand for money increases when the price level rises *while the money supply is held constant.* The attempt to add to money balances by selling bonds is what drives the interest rate up and reduces desired expenditure, thereby reducing equilibrium national income.

EQUILIBRIUM NATIONAL INCOME AND THE PRICE LEVEL

The aggregate demand curve shows points where desired expenditure equals income and the demand for money equals its supply. If firms are willing and able to produce whatever is demanded at some price level, the aggregate demand curve will determine the equilibrium level of national income at that price level. This is the case on the perfectly elastic Keynesian portion of the aggregate supply curve.

What if an *upward-sloping AS* curve lies to the left of the *downward-sloping AD* curve at the

A Common Error in Explaining the Shape of the Aggregate Demand Curve

Beginners sometimes offer a plausible but erroneous argument to account for the slope of the *AD* function. They argue that a rise in the price level will obviously lower the aggregate expenditure function because people will be able to buy less with their money incomes as prices rise. Thus the *AD* curve will slope upward to the left.

This appealing argument confuses real and nominal values. The aggregate expenditure function is expressed in real units; it shows how real expenditure (measured in constant prices) is related to real national income (measured in constant prices). An inflation that raises the money value of prices also raises the money value of most incomes. If both money prices and money incomes rise in the same proportion, the aggregate expenditure function will remain unchanged. Inflation does not shift the aggregate expenditure function through its effects on the purchasing power of money incomes that are fixed for the whole economy. (Of course, some unfortunate people are on incomes fixed in money terms, but the vast majority of income earners find the prices of what they sell to earn their incomes rising along with the prices of what they buy to spend their incomes.)

Perhaps the easiest way to see that inflation does not necessarily shift the aggregate expenditure function downward by reducing real expenditure directly is to note that if *real* national income is constant everyone cannot be worse off. Since total real income is fixed at any point in the aggregate expenditure function, one person's loss must be someone else's gain. Thus inflation will *not* directly shift the aggregate expenditure function downward, because a given level of *real* income (and a given interest rate) will be associated with a given level of *real* desired expenditure whatever the price level.*

The correct reason why a rise in the price level lowers aggregate expenditure is that it raises interest rates, and this lowers investment expenditure.

* Inflation will shift the aggregate expenditure function downward through its effects on money incomes only if it redistributes income systematically from people with higher marginal propensities to consume to people with lower propensities. (We ignore this redistributive effect here because there is no evidence that it exerts a systematic and continuous force on the expenditure function in one direction or the other.)

current price level, as shown at P_1 in Figure 34-8? This situation is not an equilibrium. When firms produce all they are willing to produce at the going price level, aggregate desired expenditure exceeds output. Thus there is excess demand, and the price level will rise. As this happens, aggregate quantity supplied increases along the *AS* curve while aggregate quantity demanded decreases along the *AD* curve (for the reasons just analyzed). This will continue until an equilibrium is reached.

THE MONETARY ADJUSTMENT MECHANISM

The foregoing analysis has a very important but subtle implication for the theory of inflation:

A sufficiently large rise in the price level will eliminate any inflationary gap, provided the nominal money supply is held constant.

To see this, it is convenient to use the kinked aggregate supply curve used earlier and now

FIGURE 34-8

Determination of National Income and the Price Level

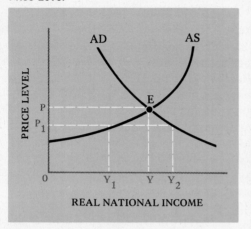

When the *AD* curve slopes downward and the *AS* curve slopes upward, they jointly determine national income and the price level. The initial price level is P_1. The level of income that would leave desired expenditure equal to national income is Y_2. Suppose, however, the output Y_1 is all that firms are willing to produce at a price level of P_1. But at that level of national income aggregate desired expenditure exceeds total output, and the excess demand will cause the price level to rise. As this occurs, the aggregate quantity supplied increases along *AS* while aggregate quantity demanded decreases along *AD*. Equilibrium is reached at a price level of P and a national income of Y, where aggregate demand equals aggregate supply.

shown in Figure 34-9. Assume that an expenditure boom has created an inflationary gap. Under the impact of excess aggregate demand, the price level will rise. The shortage of money caused by the rise in the money value of transactions raises interest rates so that at any level of real income, desired real expenditure will be reduced. The falling desired real expenditure as the price level rises is shown by a movement upward to the left *along* the *AD* curve. This reduces the inflationary gap. Eventually, when the price level is high enough, the inflationary gap disappears and the price level stops rising.

This mechanism, described further in Figure 34-9, may be called a *monetary adjustment*

mechanism. It works through the monetary transmission mechanism described above.

The monetary adjustment mechanism will eliminate any inflationary gap, provided that the money supply is held constant.

The reason is that the ensuing inflation causes a shortage of money that will sooner or later cause interest rates to rise enough to eliminate the excess demand.

The theory just outlined shows that inflationary gaps tend to be self-correcting. They will cause the price level to increase, but those increases set in motion a chain of events in the markets for financial assets that will eventually remove the inflationary gap. (If this were not so, there would be no automatic mechanism to stop any demand inflation once it had begun.)

The self-correcting mechanism is the reason why price levels and the money supply have been linked for so long in economics. Many things can cause the price level to rise for some time. Yet whatever the reason for the rise, unless the money supply is expanded, the price level increase itself sets up forces that will reduce the aggregate expenditure function. Sooner or later these forces will remove any initial inflationary gap and so bring any demand inflation to a halt.

Inflations that are caused by upward shifts in the aggregate supply curve may continue after the inflationary gap is removed. If so, the monetary adjustment mechanism will continue to operate, producing falling aggregate expenditure, falling national income, and rising unemployment.[8]

FRUSTRATION OF THE MONETARY ADJUSTMENT MECHANISM

The self-correcting mechanism for removing an inflationary gap can be frustrated indefinitely

[8] This possibility was first discussed on page 483 (see Figure 26-9 and its caption). By explaining the slope of the aggregate demand curve, the monetary adjustment mechanism explains why, *ceteris paribus,* inflations that are caused by upward shifts in the aggregate supply curve are associated with falling national income and rising unemployment.

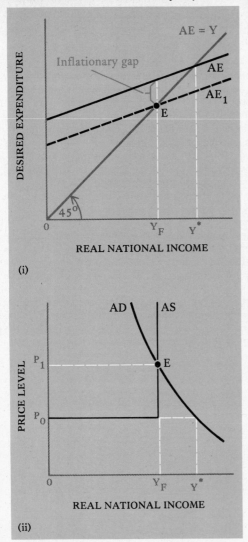

FIGURE 34-9
The Elimination of an Inflationary Gap

(i)

(ii)

A rise in the price level will eliminate an inflationary gap. The economy's curves are AE, AD, and AS: the price level is P_0. Income would be in equilibrium if Y^* could be produced. But full employment output is only Y_F, so there is an inflationary gap in (i) and excess aggregate demand of $Y^* - Y_F$ in (ii).

The inflationary gap causes the price level to rise to P_1. The monetary adjustment mechanism (working through a rising demand for money, a falling price of bonds, a rising interest rate, and falling investment) lowers aggregate expenditure to AE_1, eliminating the inflationary gap and producing equilibrium at Y_F.

The same process is shown in (ii): the economy moves upward along its AD curve until at price level P_1 aggregate demand equals aggregate supply at full-employment income. The excess aggregate demand has been eliminated.

if the money supply is increased at the same rate that prices are rising. Say that the price level is rising 10 percent a year under the pressure of a large inflationary gap. Demand for money will also be rising at about 10 percent per year. Now suppose that the Fed increases the money supply at 10 percent per year. No excess demand for money will develop, for the extra money needed to meet the rising demand will be forthcoming. The real interest rate will not rise, and the inflationary gap will not be reduced.[9] This process is analyzed in Figure 34-10.

If the money supply increases at the same rate that the price level rises, no excess demand for money will emerge, and the monetary adjustment mechanism that automatically removes an inflationary gap will be frustrated.

An inflation is said to be *validated* when the money supply is increased as fast as the price level so that the monetary adjustment mechanism is frustrated. A validated inflation can go on forever.

A FEW IMPLICATIONS

There is tremendous debate about the relevance of the monetary adjustment mechanism for policy. A group of economists called monetarists make it the centerpiece of their policy recommendations. They maintain that central banks can and should hold the money supply constant in the face of increases in the price level and that this behavior is both necessary and sufficient to control inflation.

Opponents of the monetarist view are divided into several groups. A few say that it is not within the power of central banks to control the money supply. (This denies the analysis of the control of the money supply presented in

[9] With a continuing inflation we need to distinguish between the real and nominal rates of interest (see pages 388–389). The real rate (on which expenditure depends) will be unchanged, but the nominal rate will rise by the rate of inflation. Thus, if the real rate of interest is 3 percent, the nominal rate will be 3, 5, and 10 percent when the inflation is expected to continue at a rate of 0, 2, and 7 percent respectively.

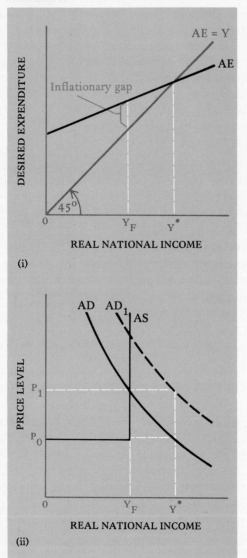

FIGURE 34-10

Frustration of the Monetary Adjustment Mechanism

An inflationary gap can persist forever if the money supply increases as fast as the price level rises. Initially the aggregate curves are *AE*, *AD*, and *AS* and the price level is P_0. National income would be in equilibrium at Y^* if that quantity could be produced. But full-employment income is only Y_F, so there is an inflationary gap, shown in (i). The price level now rises, but the Fed increases the money supply, so no excess demand for money develops. The real interest rate does not rise, so aggregate desired expenditure remains unchanged in real terms. Since the *AE* curve does not shift, the inflationary gap remains unchanged in spite of the rise in the price level.

The same process is shown in (ii). The rise in the price level tends to shift the economy upward to the left along any given *AD* curve, thereby tending to reduce the excess aggregate demand. But the increase in the money supply shifts the aggregate demand curve outward, thereby tending to increase excess aggregate demand. If the two forces just balance each other, by the time the price level has risen to P_1 the aggregate demand curve will have shifted to AD_1, leaving the excess aggregate demand unchanged.

Chapter 33.) Others say that, given the government's political and economic objectives, it is quite unrealistic to expect the Fed to attempt to hold the money supply constant in the face of an inflation even though the Fed is able to do so. Still others say that while an inflation might be stopped by the monetary adjustment mechanism, the economic and social costs of doing so would be too great. Therefore, say the last group, the central bank *should* frustrate the monetary adjustment mechanism, and the government should find other ways of bringing inflation under control. We shall return to these very important debates in Part Ten.

Summary

1. The value of money balances people wish to hold is called the demand for money. It is a stock (not a flow), and it is measured as so many billions of dollars.

2. For simplicity, we divide all forms of holding wealth into money, which is a medium of exchange and earns no interest, and bonds, which earn an interest return but can be turned into money only by selling them at a price that is determined on the open market.

3. The price of bonds varies inversely with the rate of interest. A rise in the rate of interest lowers the prices of all bonds. The longer its term to maturity, the greater the change in the price of a bond for a given change in the interest rate.

4. The reasons for holding money balances in spite of the opportunity cost of bond interest forgone are described by the transactions, precautionary, and speculative motives. They have the effect of making the demand for money vary *directly* with national income valued in current dollars and with wealth, and *inversely* with the rate of interest.

5. Monetary disequilibrium causes the interest rate to change. When there is an excess demand for money balances, people try to sell bonds. This pushes the price of bonds down and the interest rate up. When there is an excess supply of money balances, people try to buy bonds. This pushes the price of bonds up and the rate of interest down. Monetary equilibrium is established when people are willing to hold the fixed stocks of money and bonds at the current rate of interest.

6. A change in the interest rate causes desired investment to change along the *MEI* function. This shifts the aggregate desired expenditure function and causes equilibrium national income to change.

7. Points (5) and (6) together describe the transmission mechanism that links money to national income. An excess demand for money tends to reduce national income; an excess supply of money tends to increase it.

8. Monetary policy seeks to influence national income by creating a monetary disequilibrium that will work through the transmission mechanism. An increase in the supply of money creates excess supply, which is expansionary. A decrease in the supply of money creates excess demand, which is contractionary.

9. A given change in the money supply will have larger effects on national income, the steeper is the *LP* function and the flatter is the *MEI* function.

10. A rise in the price level raises the demand for money. The resulting monetary disequilibrium causes the interest rate to rise and aggregate expenditure to fall. This lowers equilibrium national income.

11. *Ceteris paribus,* each price level is associated with an equilibrium real national income such that desired expenditure equals income and the demand for money equals the supply. Each price level and its corresponding equilibrium real national income gives one point on the aggregate demand curve.

12. The whole aggregate demand curve slopes upward to the left because the higher the price level, the lower is equilibrium national income. The explanation lies with the monetary adjustment mechanism: the higher the price level, the higher the demand for money, the higher the rate of interest, the lower the aggregate expenditure function and thus the lower equilibrium income.

13. The monetary adjustment mechanism that causes the aggregate demand curve to slope upward to the left means that a sufficiently large rise in the price level will eliminate any inflationary gap. However, this mechanism can be frustrated if the Fed increases the money supply as fast as the price level is rising.

Topics for Review

Interest rates and bond prices
Transactions, precautionary, and speculative motives for holding money
Monetary disequilibrium and equilibrium
The transmission mechanism
The liquidity preference (LP) function
The marginal efficiency of investment (MEI) function
The strength of monetary policy
The shape of the aggregate demand function
The monetary adjustment mechanism and its frustration
A validated inflation

Discussion Questions

1. Describing a possible future "cashless society," a public report recently said: "In the cashless society of the future, a customer could insert a plastic card into a machine at a store and the amount of the purchase would be deducted from his 'bank account' in the computer automatically and transferred to the store's account. No cash or checks would ever change hands." What would such an institutional change do to the various motives for holding money balances? What functions would remain for commercial banks and for the central bank if money as we now know it disappeared in this fashion? What benefits and disadvantages can you see in such a scheme?

2. What motives do you think explain the following holdings?
   a. the currency and coins in the cash register of the local supermarket at the start of each working day
   b. the payroll account of the Ford Motor Company in the local bank
   c. certificates of deposit that mature after one's retirement

   d. the holdings of government bonds by private individuals

3. What would be the affects on the economy if Congress were to vote a once-and-for-all universal social dividend of $5,000 paid to every American over the age of 17, to be financed by the creation of new money?

4. What sort of situation might lead a society to have a very flat liquidity preference schedule and a very steep marginal efficiency of investment schedule? Is this a good combination for those who wish to affect the level of income by changing the money supply?

5. One relationship encountered in this chapter and elsewhere is the inverse one between bond prices and interest rates. Be sure that you can explain just why this occurs. Is this a special feature of bonds, or does it apply to the value of other earning assets as well?

6. Suppose you are sure that the Fed is going to engage in policies that will decrease the money supply sharply starting next month. How might you make speculative profits by purchases or sales of bonds now?

7. In the days of the gold standard the money supply was tied rigidly to the quantity of refined gold. What would be the effects of new discoveries of gold if (1) the economy were in the midst of a severe recession and (2) the economy were producing its full-employment national income?

8. What do you expect to happen to interest rates if the Fed reduces the money supply? What would happen if, starting from a situation of 10 percent rates of inflation and of monetary expansion, the Fed cut the rate of monetary expansion to 5 percent?

9. Trace out the full sequence of events by which the monetary adjustment mechanism would work if, in the face of a constant money supply, workers and firms insisted on actions that raised prices continually at a rate of 10 percent per year. "Sooner or later in this situation something would have to give." What possible things could "give"? What would be the consequence of each "giving"?

10. If the monetary adjustment mechanism is always present in any economy, why hasn't it prevented the inflations of the 1970s and 1980s?

Monetary Policy

35

We have seen that the Fed in pursuit of its monetary policy can regulate the quantity of money and that the quantity of money can affect the aggregate expenditure function. This chapter looks at the use of monetary policy in the United States.

Objectives and Instruments of Monetary Policy

Policy Variables

Monetary policy is employed with certain ultimate objectives of policy in view. The variables that the authorities are interested in controlling—the objects of their policy—are called **policy variables.** The major policy variables that we shall consider in this chapter are the level of real national income and the rate of change of the price level. The Fed can seek to remove inflationary and deflationary gaps by its monetary policy and thus seek to keep national income at its full-employment level.

The third major policy variable that is sometimes important is the rate of interest. For a number of reasons the Fed may be concerned about the rate of interest quite separately from any effects that the rate may have on national income. First, the higher is the rate of interest, the higher will be the cost of servicing the national debt. The government thus has an obvious concern to keep the interest rate it pays as low as possible, and the Fed may sometimes wish to assist the government in holding the rate down. Second, the Fed may want to prevent interest rates from changing too rapidly and thereby causing severe financial strain on those who are vulnerable to rapid changes in interest rates. (The reasons why this may be a matter of serious concern are discussed on page 659.) Third, the Fed may be concerned with the American balance of payments. If American interest rates are high relative to those in the rest of the world, there may be an influx of foreign capital to take advantage of the high U.S. rates. If American rates are low relative to those in the rest of the world, there may be a large outflow of capital from the United States to foreign financial centers. Rapid movements of international funds can be upsetting to the economy (as we shall see in Chapter 42). The Fed may thus desire to check U.S. interest rates in order to influence international capital flows.

Instrumental Variables

Having selected its policy variables and formulated targets for their behavior, the Fed must decide how to achieve the targets. How can the policy variables be made to perform in the way that the Fed wishes?

The variables that the Fed can control directly for the purpose of influencing other policy variables indirectly are called its **instrumental variables.** The Fed's two major instrumental variables are the rate of interest and the money supply. Both can be manipulated by the Fed, and the manipulations can be used to exert ultimate influence on national income.

The level of national income is a policy variable. The money supply is an instrumental variable. The rate of interest may be either a policy variable—when the Fed has definite objectives for interest rates—or an instrumental variable—when the Fed causes changes in interest rates with a view to affecting national income.

CONTROLLING THE INTEREST RATE THROUGH MONETARY POLICY

If the Fed wishes to take the interest rate as its policy variable, control will be relatively straight-forward. The Fed can influence interest rates by its open market operations. When the Fed buys bonds on the open market, it is supplying money to the market. This will push up the price of bonds or—the same thing—push down interest rates. When the Fed sells bonds, this takes money out of the market; the price of bonds will fall, and interest rates will rise.

CONTROLLING NATIONAL INCOME THROUGH MONETARY POLICY

If the Fed wishes to make real national income or the inflation rate its main policy variable, its task will not be as easy as when the rate of interest is its policy variable. The Fed must work through such instrumental variables as the money supply and the rate of interest.

Assume that in pursuit of an expansionary policy the Fed wishes to increase aggregate demand. It will enter the open market and buy bonds. This expands the reserves of the commercial banks and leads to an increase in the money supply in the manner analyzed on pages 617–621. The increase in the money supply forces the rate of interest down and leads to an increase in investment expenditure. This shifts the aggregate expenditure function upward, which is the result desired.

Execution Lags in Monetary Policy

While there is strong evidence that actual reactions are similar to those just described, the complexities of the real world cause the full effect of the Fed's policy to occur only after quite long time lags. Lags have several important sources.

1. The Fed's open market operations affect the reserves of the commercial banks. The full increase in the money supply occurs only when the banks have granted enough new loans and made enough investments to expand the money supply by the full amount permitted by existing reserve ratios. This process can take quite a long time.

2. The division of all assets into money and

bonds was useful in Chapter 34 for seeing the underlying forces at work in determining the demand for money. In fact, however, there is a whole series of assets—from currency and demand deposits to time deposits, to treasury bills and short-term bonds, to very long-term bonds and equities—that offer alternative ways of holding wealth. Wealth holders will typically hold a portfolio that includes money and quantities of some or all of the other assets. When households find themselves with larger money balances than they require, they will transfer some money into short-term bonds, and the extra demand will cause the price of the bonds to rise. The rise in the price of short-term bonds will make longer-term bonds seem more attractive, and households will move into them, making their price rise in turn. Thus a chain of substitutions occurs, with short-term and long-term interest rates changing as households try to hold less money and more interest-earning assets. The change in longer-term interest rates will in turn affect interest-sensitive expenditures. This process of adjustments along a chain of assets and interest rates can take considerable time to work out.

3. When interest rates fall, investment expenditure is expected to rise. However, it takes time for new investment plans to be drawn up, approved, and put into effect. It may easily take up to a year before the full increase in investment expenditure builds up in response to a fall in interest rates.

4. When they occur, the increased investment expenditures will set off a multiplier process that increases national income by some multiple of the initiating increase in investment expenditure. This too takes some time to work out.

Similar considerations apply to contractionary monetary policies that seek to shift the aggregate expenditure function downward. Furthermore, although the end result is fairly predictable, the speed with which the entire expansionary or contractionary process works itself out can vary from time to time in ways that are hard to predict in advance. In one case the spectrum of interest rates may adjust quickly and investment may respond to the changes in a matter of months. In another case interest rates may adjust more slowly and investment may take over a year to respond fully to the stimulus of changed interest rates. Although some of the effects of expansionary and contractionary monetary policies may be felt quite quickly, their full effects typically take from one to two years to work through the entire economy.

Monetary policy is capable of exerting expansionary and contractionary forces on the economy, but it operates with a time lag that is long and unpredictably variable.

Fine Tuning with Monetary Policy

We have seen that it may take from one to two years for Congress to reach a decision to change tax rates or government expenditure after the administration has come to the conclusion that a change in the stance of fiscal policy is desirable. This is not the case with monetary policy. The Fed's open market committee meets monthly; once it is convinced that a change in the stance of monetary policy is needed, it can direct its open market operators to begin purchasing or selling bonds immediately.

The decision lag is very short for monetary policy; as a result, American discretionary fine tuning has been left mainly to monetary rather than fiscal policy.

Fine tuning looks inviting to the Fed because of the short decision lags involved. To see why monetary fine tuning may not be so simple, assume that the execution lag is 18 months. If on December 1 the Fed decides that the economy needs stimulus, it can be increasing the money supply within days, and by the end of the year a significant increase may be registered.

But because the full effects of this policy take much time to work out, the Fed's policy may prove to be destabilizing. Perhaps by the fall of next year a substantial inflationary gap will have developed. The open market committee may then call for a contractionary policy, but the full effects of the monetary expansion initiated nine

A Conflict Between the Money Supply and the Rate of Interest as Instrumental Variables

Suppose the Fed takes the level of national income as its policy variable and is interested in controlling the interest rate and the money supply only as instrumental variables that are linked to national income. The Fed chooses either the rate of interest or the money supply as its instrumental variable.

Since the two potential instrumental variables are not independent of each other, it might not seem to matter which the Fed selects. For example, if the Fed wishes to remove an inflationary gap by forcing interest rates up, it will sell securities and thus drive their prices down. These open market sales will also contract the money supply. Thus it is largely immaterial whether the Fed seeks to force interest rates up or to contract the money supply; doing one will accomplish the other. Similarly, driving interest rates down by open market purchases of government securities will tend to expand the money supply as the public gains money in return for the securities it sells to the Fed.

In spite of the interrelation between these two instrumental variables, many economists have argued that it is important that the Fed use the money supply rather than interest rates as its main instrumental variable. They maintain that it is much easier to assess the trends of the economy and to assess the current stance of the Fed's policy when the money supply is used as the instrumental variable and targets are set for its behavior.

The argument proceeds in three steps.

1. In times of business expansion, both interest rates and the money supply will be rising. Interest rates rise because of a heavy demand to borrow money and because of an increasing shortage of loanable funds. The money supply expands because banks let their excess reserves fall to very low levels in order to meet the pressing demands for loans from firms and households that are their customers.

2. A restrictive monetary policy requires that the Fed increase the rate of interest and reduce (or slow the rate of expansion of) the money supply. Thus, if the Fed seeks to restrain a business expansion that is threatening to get out of hand and produce a serious inflationary gap, it will wish to *accentuate* the rising trend in interest rates but to *reverse* the rising trend in the money supply. By selling bonds on the open market it does both.

3. It is easier, however, to determine whether the Fed's current policy is contractionary, expansionary, or neutral when it is working through the money supply rather than through interest rates. When a typical rate of interest rises to 9 percent during an expansion, we may be uncertain how much of this is due to the Fed's tightening of monetary policy and how much of it would have happened anyway. Indeed, the more rapid is the expansion, the more rapidly will interest rates tend to be rising without assistance from the Fed. But when the annual rate of increase in the money supply is, say, 20 percent, this is unambiguously expansionary and it clearly shows that a much more restrictive policy is required to restrain the business expansion.

In the past the Fed has taken interest rates as its main instrumental variable. It would appear that this has sometimes led to uncertainty even within the Fed about how restrictive or expansionary was the current stance of its monetary policy.

In the 1970s there was a shift from interest rates to the money supply as the major instrumental variable.

months earlier is just being felt—so an expansionary monetary stimulus is adding to the existing inflationary gap.

If the Fed now applies the monetary brakes by contracting the money supply, the full effects of this move will not be felt for another 18 months. But that time a contraction may have already set in because of the natural cyclical forces of the economy. If so, the delayed effects of the Fed's monetary policy may turn a minor downturn into a major recession.

The long execution lag of monetary policy makes monetary fine tuning difficult, and it may make it destabilizing.

Of course, when a persistent gap has existed and is predicted to continue for a long time, the full effects of monetary policy may be in the appropriate direction even when they occur after their usual long time lag.

A CONFLICT BETWEEN NATIONAL INCOME AND THE RATE OF INTEREST AS POLICY VARIABLES

The Fed cannot set policies with respect to both national income and the interest rate and expect to achieve them both by its open market operations. Assume, for example, that the Fed picks a rate of interest that it wishes to maintain. The Fed must now enter the open market and buy or sell whatever quantity of bonds is necessary to stabilize the interest rate at its desired level. If the Fed has to buy bonds to stop the rate of interest from rising above its target level, it will be expanding the money supply. If the Fed has to sell bonds to stop the rate of interest from falling below its target level, it will be contracting the money supply. In either case the Fed's policy with respect to the interest rate *determines* what it must do to the money supply. By choosing the rate of interest as the target variable, the Fed loses control over the money supply—the money supply will rise or fall depending on whether the Fed is acting to prevent the interest rate from falling below or rising above its target value.

What are the consequences of a Fed policy to stabilize, or at least to reduce the fluctuations in, the rate of interest? Normally in the upswing of a business cycle interest rates rise as funds for investment become scarce. The rise in interest rates causes a reduction in all interest-sensitive expenditure, and this helps to restrain the boom. However, when the Fed is committed to a policy of holding the rate of interest constant, it must supply all the funds that are demanded at the fixed rate of interest but not supplied by the private sector. The Fed's policy will cause the money supply to expand and will prevent interest rates from rising to restrain investment demand. This will cause the boom to be stronger than it otherwise would have been.

An analogous result occurs in the downswing of a cycle. Normally in a recession the falloff in the demand to borrow money leads to a fall in the rate of interest, and this helps to increase all interest-sensitive expenditure and thereby reduce the severity of the recession. However, if the Fed is committed to holding the rate of interest constant, it will have to enter the market and sell bonds to keep their price from rising. This reduces the money supply and prevents interest rates from falling. The policy of stabilizing the rate of interest thus tends to make the downswing more severe than it otherwise would have been.

When the rate of interest is the target variable, the money supply varies with the business cycle. Cyclical swings are larger than they would be if the Fed left interest rates free to vary.

Monetary Policy in Action

Having studied the objectives and instruments of monetary policy, we may now consider how monetary policy has actually worked in the period since World War II. Monetary policy is formulated by the Federal Open Market Committee (FOMC), which was described on page 626. The FOMC generally meets about every four weeks; its decisions are embodied in a directive issued to the Federal Reserve Bank of New York. Open market operations are conducted in the New York Fed by the manager of the system's Open Market Account.

THE ACCORD

The use of monetary policy as a tool of stabilization policy in the postwar period began in 1951 with the famous Treasury-Federal Reserve Accord. Under this agreement the Federal Reserve discontinued the practice, which had been carried on throughout World War II, of supporting the prices of treasury securities to facilitate financing of the war effort. This practice had meant that the Fed held the interest rate down — thereby keeping the cost of servicing the debt low[1] — and that it supplied new money to buy any part of a government debt issue that the public would not buy at the fixed rate of interest. The effect of this policy was that the Fed had no control over the money supply — which expanded rapidly, with serious inflationary consequences, whenever the government demand to borrow was too heavy to be met by private lending at the going rate of interest.

THE SHIFT FROM INTEREST RATES TO THE MONEY SUPPLY AS THE MAIN POLICY VARIABLE

The basic concern of monetary policy since the accord has been the achievement of objectives such as full employment and price stability. To make them operational, however, the FOMC must translate these broader economic goals into targets concerning the monetary and credit variables over which the Fed has a direct influence.

Prior to 1970, the operating instructions of the

FOMC were generally couched in terms of money-market conditions, that is, short-term interest rates, member bank borrowings from the Federal Reserve, and the net excess reserve position of member banks.[2] Some references were made to monetary aggregates, but these were generally confined to statements concerning the desired behavior of bank credit.

In the 1970s monetary aggregates came to play a more prominent role, and the emphasis shifted from targets specified in terms of money-market conditions to target rates of growth of the money supply. The measure used for this purpose has generally been the narrowly defined money supply, M-1, but broader definitions have also been taken into account.[3] The shift to greater emphasis on controlling the money supply on the part of the Federal Reserve reflected the growing influence on the monetarist view on the economics profession.

THE USE OF MONETARY POLICY SINCE THE ACCORD

Figure 35-1 shows the behavior of M-1, the narrowly defined money supply, and relates it to unemployment and the rate of inflation for the period since the accord. Two things stand out. First, monetary policy has shown sharp, short-period changes — from being quite expansive to being highly restrictive. Second, there has been a steady upward trend in the rate of monetary expansion.

The Variability of Monetary Policy

From 1952 to 1967 the inflation rate was relatively low — under 3 percent — but unemployment frequently rose well above 4 percent. The Fed took national income as one of its main target

---

[1] During World War II this was a dominant objective of the Fed. Between 1941 and 1945 the federal government debt rose from about $50 billion to about $250 billion. This enormous debt offering was kept inexpensive to the Treasury by the Fed's keeping the interest rate on three-month treasury bills at .375 percent and on three-to-five-year bonds at under 1.5 percent.

[2] Net excess reserves are defined as total reserves *minus* legally required reserves *minus* borrowing from the Fed. These are sometimes also called free reserves.

[3] In this chapter we use the M-1 series so that we can make historical comparisons. As we explained at the beginning of Chapter 33, the Fed now uses a revised measure, M-1A, of the narrowly defined money supply.

FIGURE 35-1
Changes in the Money Supply Related to Inflation and Unemployment

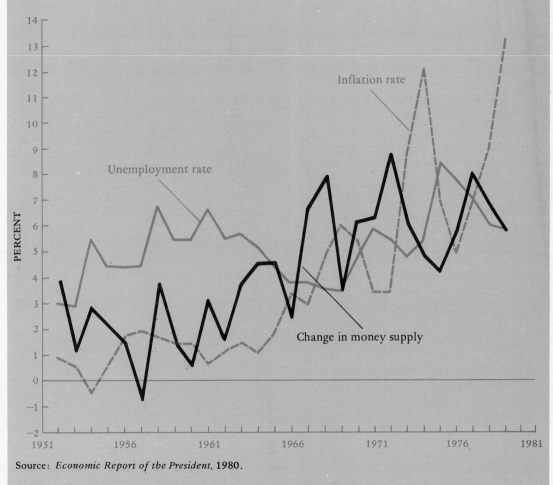

Source: *Economic Report of the President*, 1980.

The rate of monetary expansion has shown substantial short-term variability combined with a strong long-term upward trend. *Change in money supply* is the percentage change in M-1, December to December; *Inflation rate* is the percentage change in the Consumer Price Index, December to December; *Unemployment rate* is the percentage of the civilian labor force unemployed.

variables with a view to influencing unemployment. The sharp variations in the rate of monetary expansion resulted to a great extent from the Fed's attempt to use monetary policy to fine tune the economy.

The 1954 recession led to an expansionary monetary policy; by 1956 unemployment had been reduced to a low level but an inflationary gap had opened up. In response, the Fed tightened monetary policy, and in 1957 the quantity of money was actually decreased.[4] From 1960 to 1964 unemployment, which rose sharply in 1957

[4] M-1 normally is increased over time in order to finance the growing level of full-employment national income without putting deflationary pressures on the economy. Thus any rate of increase of less than 2 or 3 percent is plainly deflationary.

and 1958, stayed above the 5 percent level, and this led the monetary authorities to progressively more expansionary policies (with the exception only of 1962), until by the middle of the decade the annual rate of monetary expansion exceeded 4.5 percent.

In 1966, with unemployment falling sharply in response to the strong recovery of the economy, the Fed applied the monetary brakes. The so-called credit crunch of 1966 cut the rate of monetary expansion in half. But the policy was quickly reversed, and by 1968, in response to the government's need for cheap financing of the escalating war in Vietnam, monetary expansion was at nearly 8 percent, a level unprecedented in the years since the accord.

Because of the lags in monetary policy, the full effects of the 1968 expansionary stance were felt just in time to help offset the contractionary fiscal policy of 1969 (see page 575).

The sharp inflationary gap of 1969 led to another abrupt policy reversal, with the rate of monetary expansion falling to 3.5 percent in 1969. But the restrictive policy was short-lived, and a very expansionary policy was followed over the next three years. The peak rate of monetary expansion was close to 9 percent in 1972. It is clear that both monetary and fiscal policy (see page 576) combined to turn the upswing of the early 1970s into an unsustainable boom that had its end in the almost unprecedented inflation rate of 1973–1974.

Alarmed by the inflation, and with the presidential election past, the Fed once again reversed direction in 1973 and steadily reduced the rate of monetary expansion until it reached 4 percent in 1975. At the same time, a severe recession had set in and monetary restraint certainly helped to accentuate it. In 1976 and 1977 the Fed pursued a mild expansionary policy. By the end of 1978, however, inflation had once more become a prime concern and mildly contractionary policies were pursued.

In mid 1979 the brakes were applied more strongly: the rate of monetary growth was reduced and interest rates were driven to unprecedented levels. By early 1980 it was clear that the policy had worked; a downturn had been induced, and the economy was well into a recession. Once again the impressive ability of the government to manipulate aggregate demand had been demonstrated. Yet how much of the fall in demand would cause an undesirable fall in output and a rise in unemployment, and how much of it would cause a desirable fall in the inflation rate, were hotly debated.

Most observers agree that monetary policy was perverse throughout the 1970s. A series of alternating expansionary and contractionary policies, rather than stabilizing the economy's natural cyclical swings, added to them.

Several senior economists have spoken of "this incredible series of self-inflicted wounds." Professor Alan Blinder of Princeton University, in a detailed study of the mid 1970s, says that monetary policy in the period "bears eloquent witness to the monetarists' incessant complaint that policy is too variable, too apt to swing from one extreme to another. It is true that whenever monetary policy departed notably from what a fixed rule would have called for, it did so in the wrong direction and made things worse than they need to have been."

The Rising Trend of Monetary Expansion

As the solid black line in Figure 35-1 shows, fluctuations in monetary expansion have occurred around a rising trend. This has been accompanied by a similar rising trend in prices, and it leads to an unmistakable correlation between the rate of monetary expansion and the rate of inflation. Yet correlation does not in itself prove causation, and there is some debate about the causes of the American inflation in recent years.

Whether monetary expansion was the main cause of the inflation of the 1970s and 1980s, as monetarists believe, or mainly a passive reaction to it, as some others believe, there is no doubt that the inflation of the 1970s was validated by monetary expansion. Most economists think there is little chance of reducing inflation to the relatively modest levels of the 1950s and 1960s until the rate of monetary expansion is reduced to the more modest annual amounts of those years.

A Monetary Rule?

The dismal record of monetary policy in the 1970s lends force to the monetarist economists' persistent criticisms of monetary fine tuning.

The monetarists argue that (1) monetary policy is a potent force of expansionary and contractionary pressures; (2) monetary policy works with lags that are both long and variable; and (3) the Fed is in fact given to sudden and strong reversals of its policy stance. Consequently monetary policy has a destabilizing effect on the economy, the policy itself accentuating rather than dampening the economy's natural cyclical swings.

Monetarists argue from this position that the stability of the economy would be much improved if the Fed stopped trying to stabilize it. What then should the Fed do? Since growth of population and productivity leads to a rising level of output, the Fed ought to provide the extra money needed to allow the holding of additional transactions, precautionary, and speculative balances as real income and wealth rise over time.

According to the monetarists, the Fed should expand the money supply year in and year out at a constant rate equal to the rate of growth of real income. When the growth rate shows signs of long-term change, the Fed could adjust its rate of monetary expansion, but it should not alter this rate with a view to stabilizing the economy against short-term fluctuations.

Theorists have conducted a long debate over this monetarist recommendation. The outcome is that, at least in many standard models of the economy, cyclical fluctuations can be made smaller with the best fine tuning policy than they are with a constant-rate rule. However, whatever the conclusion drawn from the theoretical debate:

Experience of the 1970s convinced many that whatever may be true of the best conceivable monetary policy, the policy we actually had made cyclical fluctuations much larger than they would have been under a constant-rate rule.

USE OF TOOLS OTHER THAN OPEN MARKET OPERATIONS

The major instrument the Fed uses to control both interest rates and the money supply is its open market operations. The Fed has a number of other tools at its disposal, but their use has been hedged by the plethora of detailed controls to which the banking industry was subject. Whatever the original reasons for these measures, in recent times most of them have served only to protect the profits of special interest groups and to destabilize the monetary system in undesirable ways.

Consider two examples.

Smaller banks were generally subject to lower reserve requirements than were larger banks. Because reserves are funds held idle that could otherwise be used to make profitable loans, small banks welcomed this implicit subsidy that allowed them to earn interest on a larger proportion of their assets than could their larger competitors.

Second, many kinds of deposits were subject to interest rate ceilings. When the spectrum of interest rates rose in times of tight money, the rates of savings and other deposits subject to such regulations would stop at their ceilings while other rates went on rising. As the interest differential widened, depositors would withdraw their funds from regulated types of accounts and place them in unregulated types where interest rates were free to rise. Typically this caused a drain of deposits out of commercial banks, whose deposits were regulated, and into nonbank financial institutions, whose interest rates on deposits were often either unregulated or regulated less stringently. When interest rates fell, savings deposits would again become competitive and funds would flow back into commercial banks. The sudden shifts of funds could put the system under great stress, for under the fractional reserve system, a bank that loses deposits is in a difficult position.

Under the Depository Institutions Deregulation and Monetary Control Act of 1980, most of these regulations are being phased out during the first half of the 1980s. The general purpose of the act is "to facilitate the implementation of monetary policy, to provide for a gradual elimination of all limitations on the rates of interest which are payable on deposits and accounts, and to authorize interest-bearing transactions accounts."

The act will make the banking system much more competitive. It will also free monetary policy from having to offset distortions caused by such regulations as interest rate ceilings on some types of deposits.

Reserve Requirements

In Chapter 33 we illustrated the importance of the reserve ratio in the expansion and contraction of credit. In 1934 the Federal Reserve Board was given authority by Congress to set (within limits) required reserve ratios for both demand and time deposits. The Fed has frequently changed reserve requirements within the allowable limits, and Congress has from time to time changed the limits.

Bankers usually believe their reserve requirements are set higher than is required for safe operation. The reason for this is clear. It is unthinkable that the central bank would set reserve ratios below safe standards and thereby encourage reckless lending; but it is quite reasonable for it to set reserves "too high" (by safety standards) in order to give it the freedom to maneuver in *both* directions should it want to use variations in reserve requirements as a tool of control.

In recent times the use of reserve ratio changes has fallen out of favor. The chief argument against manipulating the reserve ratio is that it is a ponderous weapon for changing excess reserves, while open market policy can be applied flexibly to achieve the same effects. The chief arguments for using reserve ratio changes are that they cause less disruption in the market for government securities than do open market operations and that even small changes serve effectively to "announce" the board's views about

the desirable changes in the credit positions of member banks.

The 1980 act set the same reserve requirements for all banks, large or small and members of the Federal Reserve System or not. The reserve requirements set were 3 percent against demand deposits (and other accounts subject to direct or indirect transfer by check) up to $25 million and a ratio to be set by the Fed (between the limits of 8 and 14 percent) on demand deposits in excess of $25 million. The ratio on time deposits is to be set by the Fed between limits of 3 and 9 percent.

The Fed was also given the power to require that all banks hold up to 4 percent additional reserves, provided that "the sole purpose of such requirement is to increase the amount of reserves maintained to a level essential for the conduct of monetary policy." This instrument is copied from one the Bank of England has long used to prevent deposit expansion when commercial banks unexpectedly find themselves with excess reserves at a time when the central bank does not deem monetary expansion desirable.

The Discount Rate

The discount rate is the rate at which the Fed will lend funds to member banks who need to replenish their reserves. As a matter of policy, the Fed discourages long-term borrowing from it by commercial banks, and the reserve banks tend to accommodate requests at their "discount window" only on a short-term basis. This suggests a relatively minor role for the discount rate as a policy weapon.

Discounts rarely reach 5 percent of reserves, which makes them *quantitatively* a minor influence compared to open market policy. The importance of the discount rate lies in the signal it gives about the trend of interest rates in general and the ease or tightness of credit.

When the discount rate changes, so (with a very short lag) do the rates banks charge their customers. In response to rises in the discount rate, the stock market often plunges because investors

TABLE 35-1
Average Interest Rates, Selected Years

Year	Average discount rate (Federal Reserve Bank of New York)	Prime rate on commercial paper (4–6 months)	Three-month treasury bills[a]	Grade A corporate bonds
1929	5.16	5.85	—	4.73
1931	2.12	2.64	1.40	4.58
1935	1.50	0.75	0.14	3.60
1939	1.00	0.59	0.02	3.01
1942	1.00[b]	0.66	0.33	2.83
1945	1.00[b]	0.75	0.38	2.62
1948	1.34	1.44	1.04	2.82
1951	1.75	2.16	1.55	2.86
1955	1.89	2.18	1.75	3.06
1958	2.15	2.46	1.84	3.79
1961	3.00	2.97	2.38	4.35
1964	3.55	3.97	3.55	4.40
1967	4.19	5.10	4.32	5.51
1970	5.95	7.72	6.46	8.04
1972	4.50	4.69	4.07	7.21
1974	7.83	9.87	7.89	8.57
1976	5.50	5.35	4.99	8.43
1977	5.46	5.60	5.27	8.02
1978	7.49	7.99	7.22	8.73
1979	10.28	10.91	10.04	9.63

Source: Economic Report of the President, 1972 and 1980.

[a] First issued in December 1929, these issues were tax exempt before March 1, 1941.

[b] From October 30, 1942, to April 24, 1946, a preferential rate of .5 percent was in effect for advances secured by government securities maturing in one year or less. The purpose was to encourage banks to buy government securities for financing the war.

Interest rates show considerable variation over the years. Although interest rates vary substantially over the years, the various rates all tend to move together. Notice the low of .02 percent on three-month treasury bills in 1939, which seems almost incredible in light of more recent experience. Notice too the unprecedentedly high interest rates in 1979 as monetary policy moved to a very contractionary stance.

believe it signals tight money and reduced investments by firms in the period ahead.

Table 35-1 shows the average discount rate for selected years since 1929. It indicates that the discount rate has varied substantially and that it moves in a rough way with other rates of interest.[5] The table does not indicate whether the discount rate follows or leads changes in other interest rates, but, in one sense at least, the Fed's discount rate follows other developments. Open market operations that apply the monetary brakes by selling bonds tend to push up interest rates. Then, to discourage banks from turning to its discount windows, the Fed must raise the discount rate. But sharp changes in the discount rate often lead other rates in the economy by creating expectations about the relative abundance or scarcity of funds. During World War II and the postwar period, the discount rate was little used because the Fed was cooperating with the Treasury in an attempt to keep down the interest cost on the federal debt. During the 1960s discount policy reemerged as a major weapon, as Table 35-2 indicates.

[5] Considerations of risk, duration, and tax status, of course, affect different rates differently. For example, the interest rate on corporate bonds during the Great Depression was high because they were considered risky. Today they are considered safer. Because treasury bills were considered virtually riskless and were tax exempt, they could be sold at very low interest rates during the Depression, when banks had large excess reserves that they were reluctant to lend to private firms because of the risk of nonrepayment.

TABLE 35-2
Changes in the Discount Rate, Federal Reserve Bank of New York, 1960–1979

Date		Rate	Date		Rate
1960	In effect January 1	4		May	5.75
	June	3.5		May	6.00
	August	3	1974	April	8.00
1963	July	3.5		December	7.75
1964	November	4	1975	January	7.25
1965	December	4.5		February	6.75
1967	April	4		March	6.25
	November	4.5		May	6.00
1968	March	5	1976	January	5.50
	April	5.5		November	5.25
	August	5.25	1977	August	5.75
	December	5.5		October	6.00
1969	April	6	1978	January	6.50
1970	November	5.75		May	7.00
	December	5.5		July	7.25
1971	January	5.25		August	7.75
	January	5		September	8.00
	February	4.75		October	8.50
	July	5		November	9.50
	November	4.75	1979	July	10.00
	December	4.5		August	10.50
1973	January	5		September	11.00
	February	5.5		October	12.00

Source: Federal Reserve Bulletin.

The discount rate is changed frequently. During 1974 the discount rate rose to a post-World War II record of 8 percent. A slight easing of monetary policy was evident through 1975 and 1976. In 1978 the rate was changed more frequently than ever before. The steady rise of the rate from 6.5 percent in January 1978 to 12 percent in October 1979 indicates a change in the stance of monetary policy from being mildly expansionary to being quite contractionary.

Selective Credit Controls

Monetary policy seeks to make money and credit scarce or plentiful in general and leaves it to the financial system of the private sector to cope with these conditions. **Selective credit controls,** on the other hand, seek to let the Fed decide where the initial impact of tight or plentiful credit will be felt. Among the selective controls that have been used at some time during the postwar period are margin requirements, installment-credit control, mortgage control, and maximum interest rates.

These controls can be very powerful. Increasing the down payment required for an installment-plan purchase, for example, can cause a major fall off in demand until households accumulate the new larger down payments. Many of them have been used in the United States in the past, and all of them are now in use somewhere in the Western world. In the United States, however, only margin requirements are used today, installment-credit controls having been dropped after World War II and mortgage controls after 1953.

Margin requirements. Stock market speculation can be controlled by the Federal Reserve through its power to regulate the **margin requirement,** which is the fraction of the price of a stock that must be put up by the purchaser. (The balance may be borrowed from the brokerage firm through which the purchaser buys the security.) Since 1960 the margin requirement has varied between 50 percent and 90 percent. Such variations can have a substantial selective effect on stock market activity that is independent of the general credit picture. Thus, if the Federal Reserve wishes to impose moderate credit restraint generally but is particularly apprehensive about stock market speculation, it may combine a moderate amount of open market selling with a sharp increase in margin requirements.

Moral Suasion

If the commercial banking system is prepared to cooperate, the Federal Reserve banks can operate a tight-money policy merely by asking banks to be conservative in granting loans; when the need for restriction is over, the commercial bankers can then be told that it is all right to grant loans and extend deposits up to the legal maximum. The use of "moral suasion" does not depend on mere jawboning. Member banks depend on the Federal Reserve banks for loans, and in the long term noncooperation with the Fed's "suggestions" can prove costly to a bank.

In countries such as Canada and Great Britain, where there are only a few banks, control by moral suasion is presumably easier than it is in the United States, where there are thousands of independent banks. After all, an official of the Bank of England could have a long telephone conversation with a senior official of every important British bank in the course of a morning. Such quick personal contact with the whole system would be quite impossible in the American banking system, but to talk to 20 leading bankers could accomplish a good deal.

MONETARY POLICY: SOME INTERIM CONCLUSIONS

There is general agreement among economists that rapid changes in the money supply have major effects on aggregate demand. Most econo- mists agree that slowing the rate of monetary expansion is a necessary condition for avoiding rapid inflations.

Many economists also hold that changes in the money supply could be used, if we knew enough, to help in the government's efforts to stabilize the economy by avoiding the extremes of large inflationary and deflationary gaps.

There is disagreement, however, on a number of important issues that we summarize here and discuss in more detail in Part 10.

1. Is control of the money supply a sufficient means of controlling inflation? Some economists answer yes; others think not and look to causes of inflation in addition to excessive monetary expansion.

2. How strong is the influence of monetary policy on aggregate expenditure? Do small changes in monetary magnitudes yield large changes in aggregate expenditure, or are large changes in monetary magnitudes needed to induce even small changes in aggregate expenditure? We discussed this issue in Chapter 34, and we shall return to it in Part Ten.

3. If stabilization policy is to be used, what are the appropriate relative roles of monetary and fiscal policies? At one extreme, some economists give monetary policy a relatively minor role as a supplement to fiscal policy; at the other extreme, some economists give it the exclusive role, arguing that fiscal policy is effective only to the extent that it causes change in the money supply.

4. Although the experience of the 1970s convinced many economists that monetary policy had in fact been a serious destabilizer, controversy continues on the conclusion to be drawn from this unhappy experience. Should we give up trying to follow a discretionary monetary stabilization policy and instead adopt a fixed rule of monetary expansion, or should we merely try to do better with discretionary policy next time?

In this chapter we have emphasized the areas of general agreement on the workings of monetary policy; in Part Ten we shall study many of the major areas of disagreement.

Summary

1. The ultimate objectives of the Fed's monetary policy are called its policy variables. Both real national income and the inflation rate are policy variables. So too may be interest rates.

2. Where the Fed cannot influence its policy variables directly, it must work through instrumental variables that it can control and that will in turn influence its policy variables. The money supply is an instrumental variable. The rate of interest is also an instrumental variable when the Fed manipulates it with a view to influencing real national income.

3. When the interest rate is a policy variable, it is easily controlled through open market operations. National income as a policy variable can also be influenced by open market operations, but less directly than can the interest rate. To reduce national income, the Fed sells bonds on the open market, thereby driving up the rate of interest and reducing the quantity of money. To increase national income, the Fed buys bonds on the open market, thereby driving down the rate of interest and increasing the quantity of money.

4. Because decision lags are long for fiscal policy and short for monetary policy, the main burden of American attempts to fine tune the economy through discretionary stabilization policy have fallen on monetary policy. However, long execution lags make monetary policy potentially destabilizing.

5. The Fed cannot have wholly separate monetary policies with respect to national income and the interest rate because the two are related. For example, a policy of stabilizing interest rates will accentuate fluctuations in national income.

6. The modern use of monetary policy in the United States dates from the 1951 accord between the Treasury and the Fed, under which the Fed's main objective ceased to be minimizing the cost of financing the government's debt by controlling interest rates. In the 1950s and the 1960s the rate of interest was the main instrumental variable through which the Fed sought to influence national income. In the 1970s the emphasis shifted to the money supply.

7. The Fed has sometimes been criticized for alternating its policy stance between expansionary and contractionary pressures on national income too quickly and thereby contributing to cyclical swings in the economy. In the 1960s and 1970s a series of strong and abrupt changes in the stance of monetary policy often combined with long execution lags to make actual monetary policy exert a destabilizing force on the economy.

8. In addition to control of the money supply and interest rates through open market operations the Fed has several other important tools of control: It can vary reserve requirements or the discount rate, and it can use a number of selective controls on credit. It can also use moral suasion.

9. It is generally agreed that rapid changes in the money supply and interest rates can have large effects on the economy. There is disagreement, however, on how much monetary policy can and should be used as a device for stabilizing the economy or coping with temporary bouts of rising prices.

Topics for Review

Policy and instrumental variables
Conflicts between the rate of interest and national income as policy variables
Decision and execution lags of monetary policy
Monetary policy as a destabilizing force
Alternative instruments of monetary policy

Discussion Questions

1. In the study of banking history we often see the term *elastic currency*. For example, to provide an elastic currency was a purpose behind the creation of the Federal Reserve System. What do you think this term might mean, and why might it be emphasized?

2. Early in 1977 the *New York Times* reported, "A year ago, it was widely believed that interest rates would bottom out early in 1976 and head higher. Instead, they have declined with few interruptions all year long and have dropped to their lowest levels in three years or more. The man Wall Street credits for this achievement is Arthur F. Burns, 72-year-old chairman of the Federal Reserve Board." How might Dr. Burns have been responsible for this result? What does it imply about the money supply?

3. The Federal Reserve Board runs a facility in Culpeper, Virginia, which costs $1.8 million per year to maintain and to guard against robbery, according to Senator William Proxmire of Wisconsin. Inside this "Culpeper switch," a dugout in the side of a mountain, the government has hidden $4 billion in new currency for the purpose, it says, of "providing a hedge against any nuclear attack that would wipe out the nation's money supply." Comment on the sense of this policy.

4. Describe the chief weapons of monetary policy available to the Federal Reserve and indicate whether, and if so how, they might be used for the following purposes:
   a. to create a mild tightening of bank credit
   b. to signal that the Board of Governors favors a sharp curtailment of bank lending
   c. to permit an expansion of bank credit with existing reserves
   d. to supply banks and the public with a temporary increase of currency for Christmas shopping

5. It is often said that an expansionary monetary policy is like "pushing on a string." What is meant by such a statement? How does this contrast with a contractionary monetary policy?

6. In what situations might the following pairs of objectives come into conflict?
   a. keeping the cost of government finance low *and* using monetary policy to change aggregate demand
   b. signaling a tighter monetary policy by raising interest rates *and* accommodating the public's desire for money
   c. maintaining stable interest rates *and* controlling inflation

7. In February 1980 *Newsweek* reported that, "In the fight on inflation, the Fed admits it has underestimated the U.S. monetary supply" and quoted a Fed official as saying, "There is no doubt that [monetary] policy has not been as restrained as was intended." Why should underestimating the money supply make monetary policy less anti-inflationary than was intended?

8. "High interest rates portend a serious slump" said *Business Week* in March 1980. Why should this be so? Is there any reason for the sequence of the two news items quoted in questions 7 and 8?

9. Writing in 1979, Nobel Laureate Milton Friedman accused the Fed of following "an unstable monetary policy," arguing that while the Fed "has given lip service to controlling the quantity of money . . . it has given its heart to controlling interest rates." Why might the desire to stabilize interest rates create an "unstable" monetary policy?

Part Ten

Macroeconomic Policy in Action: The Control of Inflation and Unemployment

The Nature of Unemployment and Inflation

36

The president, the cabinet, the Council of Economic Advisers, the Open Market Committee of the Federal Reserve System, and many others have a hand in setting macroeconomic policy in the United States. Macroeconomic policymakers must meet mighty challenges whatever free-market society they may operate in. They will want to take the economy as close as possible to full-employment national income and at the same time ensure both a high growth rate in national income and a low rate of inflation. Sometimes these policy objectives will conflict; when they do, painful choices may have to be made.

Policymakers' problems are further complicated by disagreement among economists over their diagnoses of the causes of the economy's present ills. Indeed, many believe that macroeconomics itself is in a genuine crisis.

A decade or so ago there was consensus that the macro behavior of the economy was fairly well understood and that policy goals could be achieved by using the available tools. Policy conflicts might arise from the nature of the economy, at times making it impossible to achieve all goals simultaneously. Hard choices among alternative goals might then be necessary, but once the choices were made, policymakers thought they had sufficient knowledge to achieve their chosen goals through the use of macro policy.

Today this consensus no longer exists.[1] There

[1] The disagreements among economists are serious, and their outcome will profoundly affect the average citizen. Many issues go well beyond introductory economics; while they can be outlined here, their full nature cannot well be appreciated without the benefit of intermediate and perhaps advanced courses in macroeconomics and monetary theory.

is disagreement over the causes of the severe inflations that hit Western countries in the 1970s. Ten years ago economists spoke confidently about the choice *between* unemployment and inflation; today high unemployment *and* high rates of inflation often exist simultaneously.

In this part of the book we concentrate on the twin policy objectives of low unemployment and stable prices. We begin by considering unemployment and the inflation rate separately, asking why each is a cause for concern, why it changes, and how it can be controlled by the central authorities. Our discussion will bring together material that has been introduced in widely separated parts of this book. In the next chapter we shall deal with the experience of inflation and unemployment over the last half century. In Chapter 38 we shall consider some of the policy issues and debates concerning the control of inflation and unemployment in the United States today.

Unemployment

Keynes distinguished between voluntary and involuntary unemployment. Voluntary unemployment occurs when there is a job available but the unemployed person is not willing to accept it at the going wage rate for that job. Involuntary unemployment occurs when a person is willing to accept a job at the going wage rate but no such job can be found. Clearly when we are concerned about the undesirable social effects of unemployment in terms of lost output and human suffering, it is involuntary unemployment that concerns us most.

WHY POLICYMAKERS ARE CONCERNED

The social and political importance of the unemployment rate is enormous. It is widely reported in newspapers and on television; the government is blamed when it is high and takes credit when it is low; it is often a hot issue in elections; and few macroeconomic policies are formed without some consideration of their effect on it. No other summary statistic, with the possible exception of the Consumer Price Index, carries such weight as both a formal and an informal objective of policy as does the percentage of the civilian labor force unemployed.

There are two main reasons for worrying about unemployment: it produces economic waste and it causes human suffering. The economic waste is fairly obvious. Human services are the least durable of economic commodities. If a fully employed economy with a constant labor force has 100 million people willing to work in 1980, their services must either be used in 1980 or wasted. When the services of only 90 million are used because 10 percent of the labor force is unemployed, the potential 1980 output of 10 million workers is lost forever. In an economy characterized by scarcity, where there is not nearly enough output to meet everyone's needs, this waste of potential output seems undesirable to most people.

Then there is the human cost of unemployment. The severe hardship and misery that can be caused by prolonged periods of unemployment were discussed earlier; they are heavy costs. Yet it is wrong to think that if the number of unemployed rises by, say, 100,000, this means that 100,000 workers join the ranks of the permanently unemployed. Modern research has shown that short-term variations in the unemployment rate, at or near the full-employment level, reflect, to a great extent, changes in the duration of short-term unemployment. Moreover, some people decide to stay unemployed rather than accept a job at a lower pay level than the one they lost because they believe that the difference between what they could earn and their unemployment benefits is too small. Such people choose the alternative of unemployment.

However, when a deep recession is followed by a long trough and only a slow recovery, as was the case in the mid 1970s, long-term unemployment increases. People begin to exhaust their unemployment insurance and must fall back on savings, welfare, or charity. When this happens, the human suffering caused by unemployment increases. Nearly half the large number of persons who fell below the poverty level for the first time in 1976 did so because they had run out of unemployment insurance and were still unable to find a job because of a persistently high level of general unemployment.

Before we can make a value judgment about the human costs of a rise in unemployment, we need to know how the increase is distributed both between long-term and short-term unemployment and between those for whom there is no work alternative and those for whom there is a nonpreferred employment alternative.

CAUSES OF UNEMPLOYMENT

In discussing the causes of unemployment, it is helpful to distinguish among several kinds of unemployment.

Frictional Unemployment

Unemployment associated with normal labor turnover is called **frictional unemployment.** This is the amount of unemployment that occurs when full-employment income, Y_F, is being produced.

People leave jobs for all sorts of reasons and then take time to find new jobs; old persons leave the labor force and young persons join it, but new workers may not fill the jobs vacated by those who have left. All this movement takes time. The result is a pool of persons who are frictionally unemployed in the process of finding new jobs.

Frictional unemployment is unavoidable in any free society; it may run as high as 3 or 4 percent of the American labor force.

National income theory seeks to explain the causes of, and cures for, unemployment in excess of unavoidable frictional unemployment.

Structural Unemployment

Structural changes in the economy can be a cause of unemployment. As economic growth proceeds, the mix of required inputs changes, as do the proportions in which final goods are de-

manded. These changes require considerable readjustments in the economy. **Structural unemployment** occurs when the adjustments do not occur fast enough, so that severe pockets of unemployment occur in areas, industries, and occupations in which the demand for factors of production is falling faster than is the supply. In the United States today, for example, structural unemployment exists in New England and in the automobile industry.

Structural unemployment can increase either because the pace of change accelerates or because the pace of adjustment to change slows down. Examples of the former are the increased adjustments required by the rapid increases in energy prices occurring in recent years. Examples of the latter would be government policies that increasingly discourage movement among regions, industries, and occupations. Policies that prevent firms from replacing some labor with new machines may protect employment in the short term. However, if they lead to the decline of an industry that cannot then compete with more innovative foreign competitors, the policies can in the end cause pockets of severe structural unemployment.

Structural unemployment may be said to exist when there is a mismatching between the unemployed and the available jobs in terms of regional location, required skills, or any other relevant dimension.

As with many distinctions, the one between structural and frictional unemployment becomes blurred at the edges. In a sense, structural unemployment is really long-term frictional unemployment. Consider a change that requires a reallocation of labor. When the reallocation occurs quickly, we call the unemployment frictional while it lasts; when the reallocation occurs slowly—possibly only after the person who has lost a job dies or retires from the labor force and has been replaced by a new person with different and more marketable skills—we call the unemployment structural.

One useful measure of the total of frictional

plus structural unemployment is the percentage of the labor force unemployed when the number of unfilled job vacancies is equal to the number of persons seeking jobs. When the two magnitudes are equal, there is a job opening to match every person seeking a job. The unemployment that then occurs must be either frictional or structural.

Deficient-demand Unemployment

Unemployment that occurs because there is insufficient aggregate demand to purchase full-employment output is called **deficient-demand unemployment.** One useful measure of this kind of unemployment is the difference between the number of persons seeking jobs and the number of unfilled job vacancies (i.e., total unemployment *minus* frictional and structural unemployment) expressed as a percentage of the labor force. This measure shows the excess of the supply of workers looking for jobs over the number of jobs available. It will be positive when there is deficient aggregate demand and negative when there is excess aggregate demand.

Deficient-demand unemployment refers to the unemployed who would have jobs if the economy were producing its full-employment output.

At a time of heavy unemployment, frictional, structural, and deficient-demand causes will all be operative. It is not usually possible to say that one particular worker is unemployed because of deficient demand and another for structural reasons, nor is it possible to say what proportion of the total unemployment is accounted for by each cause. Nonetheless, all three causes can operate and contribute to the total volume of unemployment.

Search Unemployment

We have seen that national income theory is concerned with the causes of and cures for involuntary unemployment in excess of unavoidable frictional and structural unemployment. Unfor-

tunately, in practice it is not easy to draw lines between the several types of involuntary unemployment or between those who are voluntarily unemployed and those who are involuntarily unemployed.

How should we classify an unemployed woman who refuses to accept a job at a lower skill level than the one for which she feels she is qualified? What if she turns down a job for which she is trained because she hopes to get a higher wage offer for the same job from another firm? People who could find work of the type for which they are fitted yet remain unemployed in order to search for a better offer are said to be in **search unemployment.**

In one sense they are voluntarily unemployed because they could find some job; in another sense they are involuntarily unemployed because they have not yet succeeded in finding a job for which they are suited at a rate of pay that they believe exists somewhere. Those in search unemployment can be said to have been frictionally unemployed if they find an acceptable job within a reasonable period of time; they can be said to be in structural unemployment if a long search reveals that there are not enough jobs to employ everyone with their particular training and experience.

Search unemployment occurs in a grey area between voluntary and involuntary unemployment and between frictional and structural unemployment. It exists when workers who could take jobs remain unemployed in order to look for something better.

Workers do not have perfect knowledge of all available jobs and rates of pay, and they may be able to gain information only by searching the market. In the face of this uncertainty, it may be quite sensible to refuse a first job offer, for it may prove to be a poor offer in the light of further market information. How long it will pay to remain in search unemployment depends on the economic costs of being unemployed.

Sufficient search unemployment to allow unemployed people time to find an available job that best uses their talents and training is socially desirable. Too much search—for example, holding off, to be supported by others, in the hope of stumbling into a job better than that for which one is really suited—is clearly undesirable and an economic waste. Here again search unemployment is a grey area: some is useful and some is wasteful.

Two recent developments apparently have increased the amount of search unemployment in many Western economies. First, there has been a large increase in the number of households with more than one income earner. When both husband and wife work, it is possible for one to support both while the other looks for "a really good job" rather than accept the first job offer. Second, unemployment insurance reduces the income loss caused by being unemployed and may enable a person to prolong the search for the "right job."

MEASURED AND NONMEASURED UNEMPLOYMENT

The number of unemployed persons is estimated from the Current Population Survey, which is conducted each month by the Bureau of the Census. Persons who are currently without a job but who say they have actively searched for one during the sample period are recorded as unemployed. The total number of estimated unemployed is then expressed as a percentage of the civilian labor force (employed plus unemployed) to obtain the figure for percentage unemployment.

This measured figure for unemployment may not reflect the number of people who are truly unemployed. *It may overestimate or underestimate the number who would accept the offer of a job for which they are qualified if one were forthcoming at the wage rate presently being paid to those who are employed.*

On the one hand, the measured figure may overstate unemployment by including people who are not involuntarily unemployed. For example, unemployment compensation provides

protection against genuine hardships, but it also induces some to stay out of work and collect unemployment benefits for as long as they last. Such people have in fact voluntarily withdrawn from the labor force, but they will usually show up in the statistics as being in the ranks of the unemployed because, for fear of losing their benefits, they tell the person who surveys them that they are actively looking for a job.

On the other hand, the measured figure may understate involuntary unemployment by omitting people who would accept a job if one were available. For example, if a slump lasts long enough that jobs cannot be found even when unemployment benefits are exhausted, some people will become discouraged and stop seeking work. These people have voluntarily withdrawn from the labor force and will not be recorded as unemployed; they are, however, truly unemployed in the sense that they would willingly accept a job if one were available.

TOOLS FOR THE CONTROL OF UNEMPLOYMENT

Reducing Unemployment

Frictional unemployment is inevitable in any changing economy. A certain minimum amount of unemployment must be accepted as being "in the nature of things." Yet any policy measure that makes it easier or quicker to move between jobs can reduce the volume of frictional unemployment somewhat.

Structural unemployment may be attacked by policies for retraining and relocating labor. These can be used as part of a general effort to increase the speed with which the supplies of various types of labor adjust to the changing pattern of demands.

Unemployment that is due to deficient aggregate demand can be attacked by increasing aggregate demand. This may be done by any of the expansionary fiscal and monetary policies discussed in Parts Eight and Nine.

Genuine search unemployment may be reduced, first, by making it easier for individuals to locate job openings and, second, by increasing the chance that individuals will accept an offer received early in their search period. The first can be done, for example, by providing market information on job availability; the second requires increasing the cost of search to the unemployed individual. A reduction in the unemployment benefits, for example, would increase the income loss associated with continued search and make it more likely that individuals will reduce the time they spend in search unemployment. This may not always be desirable; as we have observed, a certain amount of search unemployment is useful in ensuring that people find a job for which they are well suited. Phony (no intention of accepting a job) and unreasonable (looking for too good a job) search unemployment might be reduced by more careful screening of persons before they are allowed to collect unemployment benefits.

Coping with Unemployment

Unemployment can never be reduced to zero. Frictional unemployment is inevitable; some deficient-demand unemployment will always exist at the troughs of business cycles; some structural unemployment must exist as the structure of the demand for labor changes faster than the supply of labor can adapt to it. All kinds of unemployment have costs in terms of the output that could have been produced by the unemployed workers. Yet reducing unemployment is also costly. For example, retraining and reallocation schemes designed to reduce structural unemployment will use scarce resources.

It would be neither possible nor desirable to reduce unemployment to zero. The causes could never be removed completely, and to reduce the amount of unemployment stemming from those causes is a costly process.

Unemployment insurance is one method of helping people to live with the unemployment that is inevitable. Certainly unemployment insur-

ance has benefits in reducing significantly the human costs of the bouts of unemployment that are inevitable in a changing society. Nothing, however, is without cost. While alleviating the suffering from some kinds of unemployment, unemployment insurance itself contributes to other kinds of unemployment by encouraging voluntary and search unemployment.

Supporters of unemployment insurance emphasize its benefits. Critics emphasize its costs. As with any policy, a rational assessment of the value of unemployment insurance requires a balancing of its undoubted benefits against its undoubted costs. Most Americans seem convinced that, when this calculation is made, the benefits greatly exceed the costs.

EXPERIENCE OF UNEMPLOYMENT

Figure 26-5 (see page 480) shows the behavior of the unemployment rate since the end of World War II. Until 1970 the rate fluctuated cyclically but showed no clear rising or falling trend. During the 1950s the average rate was 4.5 percent, and during the 1960s it was 4.8 percent —not a significant difference. During the 1970s, however, the cyclical fluctuations appeared to be superimposed on a rising trend. From 1970 to 1976 the *low* figure for unemployment of 4.9 percent was above the *average* for the two decades of the 1950s and 1960s of 4.7 percent.[2] This low of 4.9 percent was achieved during the boom of 1972–1973, but the subsequent recession carried the rate to a high of 8.5 percent in 1975, the highest unemployment figure since the Great Depression of the 1930s. The slow recovery that lasted for the remainder of the decade gradually reduced the unemployment rate. Nevertheless, at the beginning of the new decade it stood at 6.2 percent and was once again rising.

Clearly the level of unemployment that will persist when all deficient-demand unemployment is removed has risen in recent years. Just how

---

[2] Figures in this section are based on annual averages of unemployment.

FIGURE 36-1

Variations in Unemployment Rates, 1969 and 1979

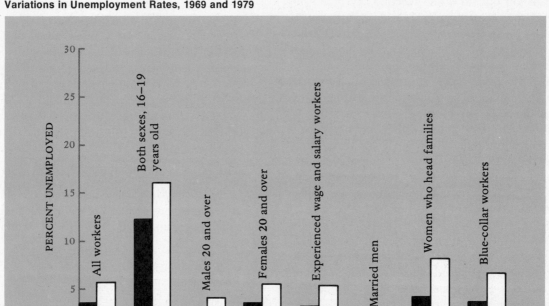

Unemployment was very unevenly divided between various sex and skill groups in 1969 and again in 1979. The 1969 and 1979 overall unemployment rates of 3.5 and 5.8 percent concealed large variations in unem-ployment rates for different groups. In 1979, for ex-ample, 16–19 year olds had an unemployment rate of 16.1 percent while married men had a rate of only 2.7 percent.

much deficient-demand unemployment remains when the overall rate is 6 percent is a matter of current debate. While some believe the answer is almost none, the Council of Economic Advisers says it is almost 1 percent. Others believe it may be as much as 1.5 percent.

Expressed as percentage points, these may not seem like big differences, but a reduction of one percentage point in the unemployment rate means about one million more people in jobs rather than in the ranks of the unemployed. It is important to settle the issue of how much defi-cient-demand unemployment exists because to apply the cure of raising aggregate demand when

there is no deficient-demand unemployment would add greatly to inflationary pressure while doing little to reduce unemployment.

As suggested earlier, the duration of unem-ployment shows a marked cyclical pattern. The average number of weeks that a newly unem-ployed person remained without a job varied from a low of about 8 weeks in the boom of 1969 to a high of about 16 weeks in 1976.

Figures 36-1 and 36-2 show the very uneven distribution of unemployment among various groups in the economy. Such an unequal dis-tribution has existed at least since World War II, and it strongly suggests an important structural

FIGURE 36-2
Unemployment by Age, Sex, and Race

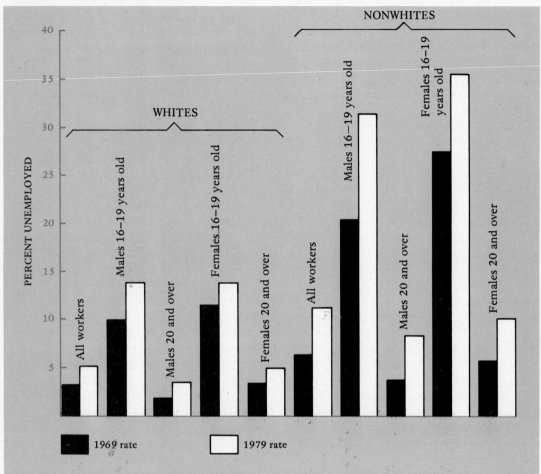

Classifications by age, sex, and race reveal enormous differences in unemployment rates among various groups. In 1979 unemployment rates ranged from a high of 35.7 percent for young nonwhite females to a low of 3.6 percent for white males age 20 and over. Similar inequalities were apparent in 1969 even though the overall rate of unemployment was lower.

component to unemployment. It also shows that even when the overall unemployment rate is satisfactorily low, disturbingly high rates will persist among large groups. Influencing aggregate demand in order to lower the overall unemployment rate is a desirable policy goal, yet it is not the only one. Another pressing policy problem is to reduce the pockets of very high unemployment that persist even when national income is at or near its full-employment level.

Inflation

THE DEFINITION OF INFLATION

In 1965 an article in the authoritative *Encyclopedia of Social Sciences* defined inflation in the way economists had always defined it, as a rise in the price level. Then, in the early 1970s, a new distinction was adopted by many economists: a rise in the price level that did not go on continuously was called *a rise in the price level;*

the term *inflation* was reserved for a rise in the price level that went on continuously. Today there is confusion in communication. More or less half the economics profession and virtually all the general public use the old definition of inflation as a rise in the price level. The other half of the economics profession (and almost no one else) uses the more restrictive definition of inflation as covering only a *sustained* or *continuous* rise in the price level.

In this book we use the older definition, and talk about inflations that are fast or slow, short-lived or long-lived, or that have any other set of characteristics. There is of course no right or wrong about definitions, which are to be judged instead on whether or not they are convenient. There is some value in using the continuous definitions in theoretical work. When talking to the public, however, using the monetarist definitions would cause confusion. We would have to keep saying, for example, that "only some of the current rise in prices is an inflation, while the rest is merely a rise in the price level," and "we won't know if the current rise in the price level is an inflation or not until we see if it is sustained."

No matter of substance depends on the terms that we select to refer to clearly defined concepts. When we point out that, where we use the terms "sustained inflation" and "nonsustained inflation" (or their equivalents), others use the terms "inflation" and "a rise in the price level," our purpose is only to guard against your being confused when you encounter the different usages. Our selection of terms reflects only a desire to keep our language as close as possible to common usage.

WHY POLICYMAKERS ARE CONCERNED[3]

By and large, governments do not have policies about the price level per se. No one feels that the price level ruling in America in 1776 was intrinsically better or worse than that ruling in 1976.

Standards of living depend on the purchasing power of money income, and if all money incomes and all prices doubled overnight, the living standards of income earners would be left unchanged. What does matter is what happens while the price level is changing—that is, the process of inflation or deflation. Whatever the present level of prices, there will be many economic consequences if it rises or falls sharply over the course of the next few years. Since sustained deflations have not occurred in the twentieth century, we confine our attention to increases in the price level, that is, to periods of *inflation.*

There is a very strong belief among the general public that inflation is seriously eroding the average American's living standards. There is, however, no evidence that this is so. If inflation is to lower living standards over the long term, it has to lower either the level or the rate of growth of potential national income or else raise the GNP gap. Many economists have studied the effects of inflation, but no one has yet established any of these alleged effects.[4]

Since inflation seems neither to affect the level or the rate of growth of full-employment national income nor to raise the average GNP gap, it follows that inflation does not reduce *average* living standards. A main consequence of inflation is the *redistribution* of income, benefiting some people and hurting others.

The redistributions of income caused by inflations are often large and haphazard, and they produce serious social tensions.

This is one major reason for avoiding inflations.

Many people whose real incomes fell during the late 1970s are skeptical of the proposition that inflation does not lower total income. The problem is that the proposition refers to the effects of inflation *ceteris paribus,* while in the real world many things are changing at once. Of course, inflation may accompany a fall in living

---

[3] This matter is discussed at greater length in Chapter 32, pages 591–595.

[4] But it can raise the GNP gap temporarily, as we shall see later.

standards—as, for example, when the price level rises during a recession. Yet here the cause of the fall in living standards is the drop in real output associated with the downturn in the business cycle, not the rise in the price level.

A rise in prices may also be the mechanism by which a fall in living standards due to some other cause is accomplished. When, for example, OPEC increased oil prices enormously, the living standards of major oil-importing nations had to fall. The mechanism by which this was brought about in most countries was a rise in prices relative to earnings. But other mechanisms are possible, and the cause of the fall in living standards was in fact the rise in the price of oil imports, not the inflation that accompanied it. The rise in oil prices was bad news, but the inflation was merely the bearer of that news, not the news itself.

Perhaps the most telling point against the general perception that inflation is lowering average living standards is made by the figures for per capita real disposable income. In spite of those things that were not constant in the 1970s—in spite of OPEC, agricultural price rises, and other supply shocks—the per capita disposable income measured in 1972 dollars rose every year but one during the 1970s. At the end of the decade, the average person had 25 percent more real purchasing power in the form of disposable income than he or she had had at the beginning.

CLASSIFICATION OF THE CAUSES OF INFLATION

Most economists agree that there are at least two senses in which inflation is a monetary phenomenon. First, very rapid inflations in many countries, particularly those of South America, have been caused by rapid expansions of the money supply. Such expansions have been due to large and persistent government budget deficits that were often incurred to finance development projects that governments could or would not pay for out of tax receipts. Second, whatever its causes,

inflation cannot continue for a sustained period without increases in the money supply.

Beyond this agreement, there is serious controversy over the causes of the mild inflations experienced by the countries of North America and Western Europe in the 1950s and 1960s and of the somewhat more rapid inflations of the 1970s. Several theories—demand-pull, wage cost-push, import cost-push, price-push, structural rigidity, expectational, and inertial—have been advanced as explanations.

The theories fall into three main groups: (1) those that find the initiating forces of inflation in shifts of the aggregate demand curve, (2) those that find it in shifts of the aggregate supply curve, and (3) those that find it in endogenous shifts of aggregate supply induced by shifts in aggregate demand. We call the three groups demand-side theories, supply-side theories, and demand-supply theories. Although some supporters speak as though these theories were in inevitable conflict, this is not necessarily so. More than one cause may be operating, and the issues dividing advocates of different theories are often ones of emphasis among the various causes.

Different theories of inflation are not necessarily competing theories of inflation; the causes that several theories emphasize may all be operating at the same time.

DEMAND-PULL THEORIES OF INFLATION

The usual collective name for all demand-side theories is the **demand-pull** theory. This theory explains price level changes by inflationary and deflationary gaps. It says that price level changes are accounted for by changes in aggregate demand. A rise in aggregate demand in a situation of more or less full employment will create excess demand in many individual markets, and prices will be bid upward. The rise in demand for goods and services will cause a rise in demand for factors, and their prices will be bid upward as well. Thus inflation in the prices both of consumer goods and of factors of production is

FIGURE 36-3
Demand-side Inflation

Increases in aggregate demand can cause inflationary gaps that in turn cause the price level to rise. With the aggregate demand curve AD and the aggregate supply curve P_0AS, the economy is in equilibrium at E with price level P_0 and national income Y_F. A rise in aggregate demand to AD_1 creates an inflationary gap. The price level then rises to P_1, at which point the economy is in equilibrium at E_1 on its new aggregate supply curve, P_1AS.

caused by a rise in aggregate demand when the economy is at full employment.

Virtually all economists agree that excess aggregate demand can be, and often has been, a major cause of inflation.

Demand-pull theories are illustrated in Figure 36-3.

All demand-pull theories agree in finding the immediate cause of inflation to be shifts in aggregate demand that cause inflationary gaps. They differ, however, on just what it is that causes the aggregate demand curve to shift. Monetarists see the main cause as increases in the money supply. Neo-Keynesians accept monetary expansion as one major cause but also hold that temporary bouts of demand inflation can be caused by shifts in the consumption, investment,

or government expenditure functions without the money supply necessarily having to increase.

SUPPLY-SIDE THEORIES OF INFLATION

Supply-side theories look to shifts in the aggregate supply curve as the initiating cause of inflation. The resulting inflations are also called cost-push or supply-shock inflations. As the aggregate supply curve shifts upward, equilibrium moves upward and to the left along the given aggregate demand curve. Thus the price level rises while real national income falls, as shown in Figure 36-4.

The various theories of supply-side inflation differ from one another in what they assume to be the main cause of the upward shift in the aggregate supply curve: wages, domestic prices, import prices, or structural rigidities.

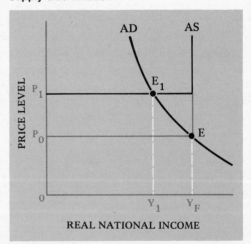

FIGURE 36-4
Supply-side Inflation

Supply-side inflation causes upward shifts in the aggregate supply curve; this raises the price level and lowers real income. The economy is in equilibrium with aggregate demand curve AD, aggregate supply curve P_0AS, equilibrium price level P_0, and national income Y_F. An upward shift in the aggregate supply curve to P_1AS raises equilibrium to E_1. The price level then rises to P_1 while national income falls to Y_1.

Wage Cost-push Inflation

The **wage cost-push** theory of inflation says that rises in wage costs not themselves associated with excess demand are the *initiating* cause of inflation. Powerful unions are seen as demanding increases in wages even when there is no excess demand for labor. Employers, the theory says, generally accede to these demands and pass the increased wage costs on to the consumer through higher prices. Thus the root cause of the inflation is union power combined with weak employer resistance to labor's demands. Consequently the upward push to prices originates from the cost side rather than from the demand side of the economy.

Price-push Inflation

The **price-push,** or administered price theory of inflation, is similar to the wage cost-push theory. The price-push theory predicts the same sequence of events as does the wage cost-push theory, but with firms rather than unions as the main culprits. The theory says that sellers have monopoly power and would like to raise prices but are restrained from doing so for fear of anti-trust action, adverse public opinion, or regulatory review of their prices. Under these circumstances, cost increases can provide the necessary excuse for price increases. During wage negotiations, for example, sellers grant wage increases and then use them as an excuse to raise prices by more than is required to offset the rise in wage costs.

Import Cost-push Inflation

An **import cost-push** inflation is a rise in a country's price level due to a rise in the prices of important imports. The theory relies on linkages among countries that arise from international trade. A demand-pull inflation in country A raises all its prices, including those of its exports. If country B uses country A's exports, A's demand-pull inflation becomes B's import cost-push inflation. A's export prices may also rise for reasons other than a general inflation in A. When OPEC increased the price of oil, this caused significant import cost-push inflations in the oil-importing countries.

Except for unusual disturbances, such as those created by OPEC, this theory does not account for world inflation. Basically all it does is to place the initiating cause of an inflation in some other country. Country B can import country A's inflation through a rise in its import prices; but why did A have an inflation in the first place? The import cost-push theory explains the transmission of inflation from initiating countries to receiving countries, but it does not explain the cause of inflation in the initiating countries.

Structural Rigidity Inflation

The **structural rigidity** theory of inflation assumes that resources do not move quickly from one use to another, and that it is easy to increase money wages and prices but hard to decrease them. Given these conditions, when patterns of demand and costs change, real adjustments occur very slowly. Shortages appear in potentially expanding sectors and prices rise because the slow movement of resources prevents these sectors from expanding rapidly enough. Contracting sectors keep factors of production on part-time employment or even in full unemployment because mobility is low in the economy. Because their wages and prices are rigid, there are no significant wage and price reductions in these potentially contracting sectors. Thus the mere process of adjustment in an economy with structural rigidities causes inflation to occur. Prices in expanding sectors rise, and prices in contracting sectors stay the same; on average, therefore, prices rise.

Many economists believe that the structural rigidity theory explains why the inflation rate, instead of falling to zero in the face of a persistent deflationary gap in the late 1950s and early 1960s, remained in the 1 to 2 percent range. Although this theory cannot be a major part of the explanation of the very high inflation rates of the 1970s and early 1980s, it suggests that a zero inflation rate may be an unachievable target. If there is anything in the structural rigidity theory, then the minimum inflation rate compatible with a changing economy may be 1 to 2 percent rather than zero.

DEMAND-SUPPLY THEORIES OF INFLATION

Theories in this group see inflation as being initiated by aggregate demand shifts but persisting because of aggregate supply shifts long after the aggregate demand curve has been stabilized. The process is analyzed in Figure 36-5.

There are two main theories of this type, the expectational and inertial theories.

Expectational Inflation

The **expectational** theory of inflation depends on a general set of expectations of price and wage increases. Suppose, for example, that both unions and firms expect that a 10 percent inflation will occur next year. Unions will tend to start negotiations from a *base* of a 10 percent increase in money wages (which would hold their real wages constant). They will argue that firms will be able to meet the extra 10 percent on the wage bill out of the extra revenues that will arise because product prices will go up by 10 percent. *Starting from this base,* unions will then negotiate in an attempt to obtain some desired increase in their real wages. Firms will also be inclined to begin bargaining by conceding at least a 10 percent increase in money wages, since they expect that the prices at which they sell their products will rise by 10 percent. The real substance of the debate between unions and employers will thus center on how much money wages can rise in excess of 10 percent. Here such factors as profits, productivity, and bargaining power will be important.

Since both labor and management expect an inflation of 10 percent (or any other figure), their

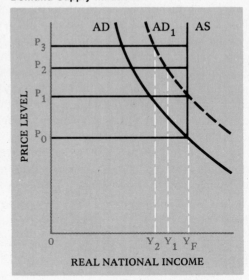

FIGURE 36-5
Demand-Supply Inflations

Demand-pull inflations that produce entrenched inflationary expectations can turn into supply-side inflations once demand increases come to a halt. Suppose increases in aggregate demand have been shifting the aggregate demand curve continually to the right, causing a continuing demand inflation with output constant at Y_F. When the aggregate demand curve has increased from AD to AD_1, taking the price level from P_0 to P_1, the curve is then stabilized so that further demand inflation does not occur. If inflationary expectations are firmly entrenched, firms and unions may continue to raise prices and wages, shifting the horizontal portion of the aggregate supply curve upwards to P_2 and eventually to P_3. This causes a supply-side inflation with prices rising, while output falls from Y_F to Y_1 to Y_2 along the fixed aggregate demand curve AD_1.

behavior in wage and price setting will tend to bring that rate of inflation about, whatever the state of monetary and fiscal policy.

Expectational inflation does not break out all by itself, for expectations do not arise out of thin air. It is possible, however, that an expectational inflation may take over from a demand-pull inflation once excess demand is reduced or eliminated. Say, for example, that the government has been generating a demand-pull inflation of 10 percent per year for two or three years as a result of spending well in excess of its tax revenue and creating new money to finance its budget deficit. Firms and unions may now expect this rate to continue; if so, they will grant 10 percent wage and price increases at a minimum. Suppose then that the government eliminates its budget deficit and stabilizes the money supply but that the expectations of 10 percent inflation persist. Wage and price increases of at least 10 percent will occur in the *expectation* of continuing inflation. At this point what was a demand-pull inflation becomes an expectational inflation.

The danger of expectational inflation is that it may cause a demand-pull inflation (or any other kind) that has lasted for several years to persist long after the original causes of the inflation have been removed.

Once inflationary expectations become established, it may not be an easy matter to force decision makers to revise these expectations downward notwithstanding changed government fiscal and monetary policies.

Expectational inflation depends on forward-looking comparisons. Wage and price setters form expectations about what they expect the general price level will be and then set their own money price or wage in relation to the price level they expect to exist over their planning horizon.

An appropriate way for the government to attack expectational inflation, therefore, is to take action that lowers people's expectations about a future rise in the price level.

One major difference between expectational inflation and wage cost-push inflation is that the former can only sustain an ongoing inflation while the latter can initiate a new one. If the economy were settled in a period of stable prices, an expectational inflation would not break out spontaneously. The theory of wage cost-push inflation says that labor can force up wages (and hence costs and prices) even in the absence of excess demand. Thus wage cost-push (if it exists)

could turn a period of stable prices into one of rising prices, forcing up wage rates and hence prices spontaneously.

Inertial Inflation

Expectational inflation tends to be emphasized by monetarists. Neo-Keynesians emphasize a similar but by no means identical theory. **Inertial inflation** is the tendency for an inflation rate, once established, to persist on its own inertia even when the original cause has been removed. The forces of inertia are somewhat wider than mere expectations of further inflation.

According to the inertial theory, firms and workers are concerned with relative wages and prices. They look at what has happened to closely related wages and prices when determining their own. If they see that closely related prices and wages have risen by 6 percent, they will tend to use 6 percent as a base for negotiating their own increases. If everyone does the same when setting wages and prices, an inflationary spiral will be hard to break once it has begun. The inflation rate will come down only when a recession becomes so severe that a majority of wage and price setters are willing to cut their wages and prices relative to those closely related wages and prices to which they pay most attention. If enough people try to do this, the overall rate of wage and price inflation will slow.

According to such advocates of the inertial theory as James Tobin of Yale University, a large and persistent deflationary gap must be present before much impact can be made on inertial inflation. Even then, they argue, the rate will come down only very slowly because wage and price setters are cautious about cutting their relative wages and prices even when markets are slack.

Inertial inflation depends on backward-looking comparisons. Wage and price setters look at recent wage settlements and price decisions for closely related labor groups and products when setting their own wages and prices.

Slowing inertial inflation requires more than just changing people's expectations of the general rate of inflation. Market conditions must be created where wage and price setters wish to lower their own wages or prices relative to closely related wages and prices that have already been set.

The differences between expectational and inertial inflation are relatively minor under the older theory of how expectations are formed. This theory, which is called the theory of **adaptive expectations,** assumes that people's expectations of the future inflation rate are based on observed inflation rates in the recent past. This puts substantial inertia into the formation of expectations concerning the future inflation rate, and makes the expectational and inertial theories of inflation quite similar.

The newer theory of expectations formation, however, gives rise to a sharp distinction between the two. This theory, which is called **rational expectations,** assumes that people look to monetary and fiscal policy and the general state of the economy to predict the future inflation rate. On average, people get their predictions correct. Of course mistakes are made, but these are random errors, not the sort of systematic errors that would occur if people predicted the future merely by projecting past rates of inflation.

With rational expectations, expectational inflation is substantially different from inertial inflation. A change in government policy that is anti-inflationary will lead people's expectations of inflation to fall and they will correspondingly moderate their own price and wage increases, the sum of which determines the actual inflation rate. Thus with rational expectations, expectational inflation is appropriately countered by anti-inflationary fiscal and monetary policy. But inertial inflation depends on comparisons with other existing wages and prices. If recent price and wage contracts were in the 6 to 8 percent inflation range, new contracts will tend to follow along — and so will the earlier contracts when they come to be renegotiated. Inertial inflation is not easily broken by a mere change in macroeconomic policy. Firms and unions looking backwards at recently set wages and prices will continue their inflationary behavior even though the Fed adopts a significant anti-inflationary monetary policy.

A Dominant Cause?

Few economists would rule out all structural influences, but virtually no one believes the structural rigidity theory to be the major explanation of today's inflation. Many economists believe that all significant inflations have their initiating causes in excess aggregate demand. Others believe that some of the mild inflations of the 1950s, 1960s, and early 1970s were initiated through wage cost-push or price-push. Most agree that import cost-push inflation contributed to the more rapid inflation rates of the 1970s and early 1980s. Most economists agree that an inflation once started often generates inflationary expectations and inertias that can cause the inflation to persist for some time after the initiating causes have been removed.

Debate continues among economists who accept the demand-pull explanation. Monetarists place most emphasis on increases in the money supply as the cause of the excess aggregate demand. Neo-Keynesians look to other contributory causes, such as temporary bursts in investment and government spending.

When explaining why inflation persists when there is neither demand-pull nor import-price inflation, monetarists stress expectational inflation while neo-Keynesians stress inertial inflation. The monetarist view makes this type of inflation responsive to anti-inflationary policy since, according to the theory of rational expectations, people will lower their inflationary expectations when they see government policy become more anti-inflationary. The Keynesian view is more gloomy. Inertial inflation may drive up the price level (and reduce national income) from the aggregate supply side long after the government's anti-inflationary policies have stopped the outward movement of the aggregate demand curve.

Of course there does not have to be a single cause of inflation, and certainly the weight of different causes can vary from time to time and place to place. For this reason people who look for a single dominant cause of inflations *may* be missing the real issue, the balance between various causes at different times and places.

THE CONTROL OF INFLATION: VALIDATED AND UNVALIDATED INFLATION

When inflation is allowed to persist because the government permits the money supply to expand at the same rate as the inflation, economists speak of the inflation as being *validated* by increases in the money supply. When an inflation occurs that is not accompanied by an increase in the money supply, it is *unvalidated*. The consequences of validated and invalidated inflation were discussed on pages 645–647; this discussion should now be reviewed. The earlier discussion established that:

A continuing inflation not validated by increases in the money supply moves the economy upward to the left along its aggregate demand curve, first removing any inflationary gap and then producing ever-falling levels of output and ever-rising levels of unemployment.

The distinction between validated and unvalidated inflation has an important consequence for controlling inflation. Demand-pull inflations caused by increases in the money supply (such as the government's financing a budget deficit by creating new money) can go on indefinitely because they bring their own monetary validation with them. However, all other kinds of inflation will eventually lead to falling output and rising unemployment *if* the money supply is held constant. Sooner or later, output will become low enough and unemployment high enough that prices and wages will stop rising.

In summary, the initial consequences of bringing a cost-push, price-push, or expectational inflation to a halt by refusing to increase the money supply will be a fall in output and a rise in unemployment. If the push or expectational factors prove stubborn, the inflation may persist for some time in the face of these undesirable consequences.

Rising prices and rising unemployment present policymakers with a serious dilemma. Should they let the recession persist, knowing that if it is deep enough and sufficiently long-lasting, it will break the inflationary spiral? Or should they validate the inflation by increasing the money supply and so remove the disincentives provided by the recession to making further increases in wages and prices? Neither alternative is attractive to politicians whose constituents expect them to reduce inflation *and* unemployment.

EXPERIENCE OF INFLATION

Figure 26-1 (see page 476) shows the inflation rate over the last 50 years, as measured by the Consumer Price Index. Like the unemployment figures, inflation rates showed no tendency to increase until the late 1960s. The average rate of inflation in the 1950s was 2.2 percent, and from 1960 to 1967 it was 1.8 percent. The dramatic rise in the inflation rate began with the acceleration of expenditures for the Vietnam War. This drove the inflation rate to 4.7 percent in 1968 and to over 6 percent in 1969. The rate subsided somewhat in the early 1970s, but its low of 3.4 in 1971 and 1972 still exceeded the average rate of each of the previous two decades. Then the inflation rate jumped to 8.8 percent in 1973 and 12.2 percent in 1974. The latter was a truly exceptional rate for a peacetime year in the United States.

In the course of 1974 the economy encountered an upper turning point and passed from boom to recession. As the slump developed in late 1974 and in 1975, the inflation rate fell. It was 7 percent in 1975 and 4.8 percent in 1976. Even in the depths of the most serious trough in business activity since the Great Depression of the 1930s, however, the inflation rate remained stubbornly above the rate achieved in the previous trough and well above the average rate for the previous two decades. As the economy slowly recovered, the inflation rate rose steadily. It was 6.8 percent in 1977, 9 percent in 1978, and 13.3 percent in 1979.

These inflation figures are based on December-to-December increases in the Consumer Price Index. Recently economists have become aware of the extent to which short-term changes of the CPI are dominated by changes in the money prices of a few commodities whose *relative* prices are temporarily rising. Concentration on such short-term changes in the CPI can muddle assessments of the efficacy of anti-inflationary policies.

Government fiscal and monetary policy that is directed at the control of inflation can be expected to influence the trend of all prices. However, it cannot influence cyclical and short-term fluctuations in relative prices. From one year to the next, these relative price effects can be the dominating influence on movements in the CPI. From decade to decade, however, short-term movements are unimportant because greater-than-average rises due to temporary shortages cancel out less-than-average rises due to temporary surpluses.

Yet, as we have seen, this is not so from one year to the next. As a result, a successful government anti-inflationary policy that reduces the trend rate of inflation may be discredited when the measured rate rises because of a temporary fluctuation in a few prices such as those for food or energy.

To get a better measure of the impact of policy on the inflation rate, economists sometimes omit from the price index certain prices that cannot be affected by monetary and fiscal policy. Changes in the amended index are then said to measure the underlying rate of inflation. Two common omissions are food and energy prices.

The rationale for removing food prices is that in the short term they are dominated by demand and supply fluctuations that have nothing to do with inflationary forces, while over the long term they follow the rest of the CPI. The rationale for

excluding energy prices is that they are determined in part by local shortages and in part by OPEC policy over which the government has no control. Yet long-term trend changes in energy prices are a contributory force to inflation, and their omission is thus more debatable than that of food in calculating the underlying rate of inflation. Table 37-2 (see page 702) shows the rate of inflation as measured by the complete CPI and then by the CPI without food, which provides one measure of the underlying rate of inflation.

A Link Between Inflation and Unemployment

So far in this chapter we have considered inflation and unemployment separately. Until the 1960s most economists and policymakers viewed them as independent policy goals and accepted the twin objectives of full employment *and* stable prices. The early Keynesian policies for achieving full employment without inflation were based on the kinked aggregate supply curve shown in Figures 36-3 and 36-4. We have seen that this curve creates a sharp distinction between how the economy reacts to a rise in aggregate demand when there is unemployment (real national income rises and prices remain constant) and when there is full employment (real national income remains constant and prices rise).

Throughout the 1950s, however, evidence accumulated that when the economy expanded out of a slump, the price level began to rise before full-employment income was reached. Furthermore, Y_F did not appear to be the absolute barrier to further output, of the kind suggested by the kinked aggregate supply curve. Indeed, it always seemed possible to squeeze a little more output from the economy by sufficiently large increases in aggregate demand. This is true because factories can be run at more than normal capacity and labor can work at more than normal hours. But such increases in output *above* Y_F always seemed to be associated with inflations.

This experience suggested that, when the economy is close to full employment, shifts in aggregate demand affect *both* output and prices.

THE INTERMEDIATE SECTION OF THE AGGREGATE SUPPLY CURVE

Economists sought to capture this behavior by introducing an intermediate section into the aggregate supply curve. We first saw this section in Chapter 26; it is shown again in Figure 36-6. When the intermediate section is introduced, full-employment income, Y_F, is no longer defined as the maximum output the economy can produce.

Full-employment or potential national income must be redefined as *normal* capacity output. At this output there is no upward *demand* pressure on prices. Instead there is just enough demand to employ plant and equipment at normal capacity and to employ a normal-size labor force at normal hours.

Over the intermediate portion of the aggregate supply curve, the initial effect of a rise in aggregate demand is a rise in both prices and output. This is shown in Figure 36-6.

Upward Shifts in Aggregate Supply

Yet this is not the end of the story. If it were, a once-and-for-all rise in the price level of a few percentage points would be the only penalty for a permanent increase in the flow of output. However, Figure 36-6 shows only the *initial* effects of an increase in aggregate demand that puts the equilibrium position on the intermediate portion of the aggregate supply curve. The full effects follow because *whenever the economy comes to rest on the intermediate portion of the aggregate supply curve, the curve itself starts to shift upwards*.

Why do the upward shifts in aggregate supply occur? One major reason lies in the way that markets adjust to excess demand. When the aggregate demand curve rises sufficiently to take equilibrium income above Y_F, manufacturing

FIGURE 36-6
Simultaneous Changes in Output and Prices

Over the intermediate section of the aggregate supply curve, the initial effect of any increase in aggregate demand is an increase in both output and prices. A rise in aggregate demand from *AD* to *AD₁* to *AD₂* takes national income from Y_F to Y_1 to Y_M and the price level from P_0 to P_1 to P_2. National income, Y_M, is the absolute maximum output that can be squeezed from the economy when everyone is working well beyond normal capacity. However, these effects on output and prices are only the initial or impact effects; they do not represent stable equilibrium positions.

firms raise their output and seek to get more labor inputs by working their existing work force longer hours and hiring new workers. They also increase their demand for raw materials and other inputs. This expansion of output creates excess demand in some markets for labor and raw materials. Excess demand in turn causes input prices to rise. Manufacturing firms find their cost curves shifting upward, so they must raise prices to cover the extra costs. The initial increase in output and prices is represented by a movement along the aggregate supply curve into its intermediate range. The continuing rise in costs and prices *shifts* the whole aggregate supply curve upward.

As long as firms are producing beyond normal

FIGURE 36-7

An Upward-shifting Aggregate Supply Curve

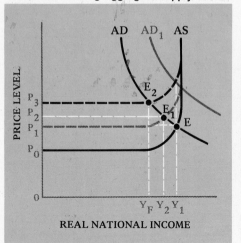

When equilibrium lies in the intermediate portion of the aggregate supply curve, the curve itself shifts upward. An increase in aggregate demand to AD has taken national income to Y_1 and the price level to P_1 on the intermediate portion of the aggregate supply curve P_0AS. The aggregate supply curve then shifts to P_1AS, reducing national income to Y_2 and raising the price level to P_2. This shifts the aggregate supply curve to P_2AS. As long as national income exceeds Y_F, the price level goes on rising and the aggregate supply curve goes on shifting upward. The final equilibrium is at Y_F with a price level of P_3.

If the aggregate demand curve were shifted outward by monetary policy, reaching AD_1 when the aggregate supply curve reached P_3AS, national income would be held constant at Y_1 in spite of the rise in the price level. Since the aggregate supply curve goes on shifting upward as long as Y exceeds Y_F, holding income at Y_1 requires continued upward shifts in aggregate demand and continued inflation.

capacity, however, there will be *continued* upward pressure on wage and material costs that will force the aggregate supply curve continually upward. The upward-shifting aggregate supply curve is shown in Figure 36-7. Do not worry about the aggregate demand curve in the figure (the significance will be explained later.) Just notice the upward shifts in the aggregate supply curve that occur whenever equilibrium is on the intermediate portion of the curve.

The Phillips Curve

The tendency for the price level to *continue* to rise whenever national income exceeds Y_F is more easily seen on a new diagram showing what is called a **Phillips curve,** which is named after its modern discoverer, the late Professor A. W. Phillips of the London School of Economics.[5] This curve is shown in Figure 36-8. The AS curve relates national income to the *price level.* The Phillips curve relates national income to the *rate of change of the price level.*

The slope of the curve to the left of Y_F indicates the same downward inflexibility of the price level as is shown by the horizontal position of the aggregate supply curve. The aggregate supply curve is horizontal at the current price level while the Phillips curve, which measures inflation, is horizontal on the income axis (i.e., at a zero rate of inflation). These are two ways of showing that the price level does not fall even though national income is below Y_F.

The shape of the Phillips curve to the right of Y_F shows that the inflation rate will be positive for incomes above Y_F. This is of course the same thing as saying the AS curve relating income to the price level will be shifting upwards continually for national incomes in excess of Y_F. The increasing height of the Phillips curve as national income rises further above Y_F indicates the further hypothesis that the greater is the inflationary gap the more rapidly will the price level be rising.

In summary:

(i) The downward inflexibility of the price level

[5] Phillips drew graphs of British data from 1862 to 1958, showing the rate of change of *money wages* and the percentage of *unemployment*. Figure 36-8 shows the rate of change of prices and the level of national income. This has the effect of making the curve slope upward to the right instead of upward to the left as did Phillips' original curve. The basic behavior being described by the two curves is, however, identical. (Unemployment and national income are inversely related, while the rate of increase of money wages and money prices are directly related to each other.)

in the face of deflationary gaps is shown both by a horizontal *AS* curve at the current price level, and by a horizontal Phillips curve lying on the income axis (inflation = zero) when national income is less than Y_F.

(ii) The tendency for prices to rise continually in the face of inflationary gaps is shown both by the tendency for the aggregate supply curve to shift upward and by the position of the Phillips curve above the income axis (thus showing positive inflation rates) when national income exceeds Y_F.

Unvalidated Demand Inflation: National Income Tends to Full-employment Income

The effects of an inflation caused by excess demand but unvalidated by further increases in the money supply are shown in Figure 36-7. An increase in aggregate demand has taken national income into the intermediate portion of the aggregate supply curve so that current income exceeds full-employment income. But as long as an inflationary gap persists, the continued upward pressure on prices continues to shift the aggregate supply curve upward. But the inflation is not validated, so the upward-shifting aggregate supply curve moves the economy upward and to the left along its fixed aggregate demand curve, as shown in the figure. Prices rise and output falls. The rise in the price level halts when national income has returned to normal capacity output at Y_F, so that the inflationary gap is eliminated.

When the process comes to a halt, the economy is back at full-employment national income, Y_F, but with a higher price level, as is shown in Figure 36-7.

Increases in *output* caused by a movement into the intermediate section of the aggregate supply curve are transitory.

In Figure 36-8 the same process is shown by movements along the Phillips curve. The original rise in aggregate demand took national income to Y_1. At this point on the Phillips curve the price

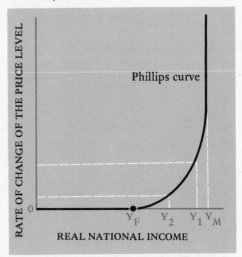

FIGURE 36-8
The Phillips Curve

The Phillips curve relates national income to the rate of change of the price level rather than to the price level itself. Here the vertical axis represents the rate of change of the price level, not the price level itself (as it would be in an aggregate supply diagram). The Phillips curve lies on the axis for national incomes below Y_F, indicating the same downward inflexibility of prices as shown by the Keynesian portion of the *AS* curve. To the right of Y_F the Phillips curve rises ever more steeply, indicating that more output can be obtained only at the cost of an increasingly rapid inflation rate. National income of Y_M is the absolute maximum that can be squeezed out of the economy.

When aggregate demand and aggregate supply intersect to yield national income Y_1 (see Figure 36-7) the inflation rate is given by the height of the Phillips curve at that income. As the rising price level reduces national income, income falls first to Y_2 (which produces a lower but still positive rate of inflation) and then to Y_F. At Y_F there is no further demand-inflation and the price level remains constant.

level is rising at a fairly fast rate. Equilibrium national income falls back towards Y_F (passing through Y_2 when the aggregate supply curve is P_1AS in Figure 36-7). As income falls, the inflationary pressure is reduced until finally, when income reaches Y_F, the inflationary gap has been removed and the price level becomes stable.

FIGURE 36-9

Short-run and Long-run Aggregate Supply Curves

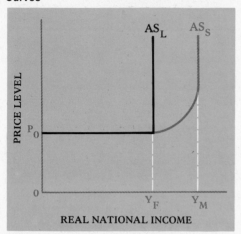

The long-run aggregate supply curve is kinked at full-employment national income. In the long run, the aggregate supply curve is the heavy black curve AS_L, where P_0 is the current price level. This means that any output up to full-employment national income, Y_F, is possible, but no more. In the short run, the aggregate supply curve is P_0AS_s, where the intermediate portion indicates that it is possible to produce more than Y_F.

When output exceeds Y_F, the pressure of excess demand causes the price level to rise continuously, thereby shifting AS_s upward. A stable price level is not therefore consistent with output in excess of Y_F.

The Long-run Aggregate Supply Curve: National Income and a Constant Price Level

The analysis just conducted means that the upward-sloping aggregate supply curve is a *short-run curve*. It shows how output and the price level can vary together under the impact of a rise in aggregate demand. We have seen, however, that when the economy comes to rest at a point on the intermediate portion of the aggregate supply curve, prices will go on rising and that this will lead to an upward *shift* in the whole short-run aggregate supply curve.

A *long-run* aggregate supply curve shows combinations of national income and the price level that can persist. The long-run aggregate supply curve is vertical at full-employment income, indicating that a stable price level cannot be achieved at higher levels of income. There is also a short-run aggregate supply curve that allows national income to rise temporarily above Y_F. The relationship is shown in Figure 36-9.

VALIDATED DEMAND INFLATION: AN UNEMPLOYMENT-INFLATION TRADE-OFF?

The Phillips curve suggested a permanent trade-off between the rate of inflation and the amount of national income. If, for example, equilibrium national income exceeds Y_F, the price level will be rising. We saw earlier (Figure 36-7) that the rise in the price level will shift the economy upward to the left along its fixed aggregate demand curve until national income falls back to Y_F, at which point all demand pressures will be removed from the price level.

However, if the Fed increases the money supply as fast as the price level is rising, that will shift the aggregate demand curve to the right. It can hold national income constant at some value in excess of Y_F, as shown by the screened curve in Figure 36-7. This keeps national income at Y_1 in spite of the rising price level. On the Phillips curve the economy remains at the point on the curve corresponding to national income Y_1. National income is stabilized at a level in excess of full-employment and the inflation rate is constant.

The Phillips curve thus suggests a long-term trade-off between national income and the rate of inflation. If the Fed increases the money supply as fast as the price level is rising, the aggregate demand curve will shift upward as fast as the aggregate supply curve is shifting upward. Equilibrium national income will thus remain constant and, according to the Phillips curve, a constant rate of inflation will be the price paid for holding national income above Y_F.

VALIDATED DEMAND INFLATION AND ACCELERATING INFLATION

Most economists who accept the expectational theory of inflation—that expectations of future inflation are an important cause of current inflations—deny the existence of the long-term trade-off between inflation and national income just described. They argue that the economy could not be held at some point on the Phillips curve of Figure 36-8, with a constant rate of inflation and national income greater than Y_F, unless people did *not* expect that rate of inflation. Once they do come to expect it, wages and prices will rise in response to *both* the general excess demand and to inflationary expectations.

To illustrate, assume that (with *no* inflationary expectations) the general excess demand associated with Y_1 in the figure makes all sellers decide to raise their relative prices by 5 percent. Since they expect the general price level to remain constant, they all raise their money prices by 5 percent. But because everyone's money prices actually do rise, no one succeeds in raising relative prices; they have instead generated a 5 percent inflation.

Now everyone tries again and all they do once again is to generate a further 5 percent inflation. Sooner or later, if this process continues, everyone comes to expect a continuing 5 percent inflation. When this happens sellers who want to raise their relative prices by 5 percent must increase their money prices by 10 percent—5 percent to keep abreast of the general inflation and 5 percent to raise relative prices. But this round of increases only generates a 10 percent inflation. Once people become adjusted to the 10 percent figure, they will raise their money prices by 15 percent in a vain effort to raise their relative prices. (The effort is vain because *every* price cannot rise relative to the average of all prices.)

According to this theory—often called the Phelps-Friedman theory—the general excess demand created when national income exceeds Y_F leads everyone to try to raise relative prices.

This generates a general inflation, and once this comes to be expected, prices will rise ever faster in an effort to keep ahead of the general price rise. According to this theory, the attempt to hold national income above Y_F leads to an ever-accelerating rate of inflation.[6]

Summary

1. Unemployment may be voluntary or involuntary. Involuntary unemployment is a serious social concern both because it causes economic waste measured in terms of lost output and because it is a source of human suffering.

2. There are several kinds of unemployment: frictional unemployment, due to the time taken in moving from job to job as a result of normal labor turnover; structural unemployment, caused by the need to reallocate resources between occupations, regions, and industries as the structure of demands and supplies changes; deficient-demand unemployment, caused by too low a level of aggregate demand; and search unemployment, caused by the need to discover the state of the labor market by searching for alternative employment opportunities.

3. Unemployment can be reduced by raising aggregate demand, by making it easier to move between jobs, and by raising the cost of staying unemployed.

4. Unemployment insurance helps to alleviate the human suffering associated with inevitable unemployment. It also increases unemployment by encouraging voluntary and search unemployment.

5. Control of inflation is a major goal of macroeconomic policy. Inflation redistributes income in haphazard ways, and this is sufficient to make it a matter of serious concern. There is no strong evidence that mild inflations change the average living standard of the population.

[6] The Phelps-Friedman theory is discussed in more detail in the appendix to this chapter.

6. Inflation has many alleged causes. Demand-pull inflation occurs when there is an inflationary gap. Wage cost-push and price-push inflations occur when unions and price-setting firms raise wages and prices independently of the state of aggregate demand. Import cost-push inflation occurs when rising prices of major imports pushes up the domestic price level. Expectational inflation occurs when wages and prices rise in the expectation that a current inflation will continue. Inertial inflation occurs when wage and price setters look to other wages and prices in making their own decisions and are cautious about reducing their relative wages or prices.

7. A validated inflation, one in which the money supply increases in step with the rise in prices, can go on indefinitely with no necessary fall in output. An unvalidated inflation will be accompanied by rising rates of interest and falling levels of output. Sooner or later output will fall and unemployment will rise to levels sufficient to bring the unvalidated inflation to a halt.

8. Some prices fluctuate greatly in the short run for causes that cannot be influenced by macroeconomic policy. To obtain a more reliable indication of the effects of anti-inflation policy, some of these prices are sometimes removed from the CPI.

9. When aggregate demand increases enough to take national income above Y_F, that is, into the intermediate portion of the aggregate supply curve, the initial effect is a rise in national income and a rise in the price level. However, the excess demand causes the price level to go on rising, and this causes an upward shift in the aggregate supply curve. If the aggregate demand curve is constant, this process will continue until national income falls back to Y_F.

10. The tendency for the price level to rise continuously when national income exceeds Y_F is shown by the Phillips curve, which relates national income to the rate of inflation. The curve suggests a trade-off: higher levels of national income are achievable at the cost of higher rates of inflation. To hold income above Y_F, the Fed will have to increase the money supply at the same rate as the price level is rising.

11. The accelerationist theory denies the existence of a stable trade-off between national income and the rate of inflation. It says instead that whenever the Fed takes action to hold national income above Y_F, the rate of inflation will accelerate continuously. This theory is discussed in the appendix to this chapter.

Topics for Review

Frictional, structural, deficient-demand, and search unemployment

Voluntary and involuntary unemployment; measured and unmeasured unemployment

Demand-pull, wage cost-push, import cost-push, price-push, structural rigidity, expectational, and inertial inflations

Validated and unvalidated inflation

Discussion Questions

1. To what extent is today's unemployment a serious social problem? If people could vote to choose between 10 percent unemployment combined with zero inflation and 2 percent unemployment combined with 10 percent inflation, which alternative do you think would win? Which groups might prefer the first alternative, and which groups the second?

2. The director of the National Urban League recently suggested that he believed the true unemployment figure for the United States was "at least double" the officially reported figure. What are possible sources of "hidden unemployment"? On the other side, are there possible reasons for expecting some exaggeration of the number of people reported as unemployed? Would you expect the relative strength of these opposing forces to change over the course of the business cycle? What would you expect if a short recession turned into a long and deep depression?

3. On what source or sources of unemployment do the following statements focus their attention?
   a. "We can reduce unemployment without increasing inflation by targeting unemployment programs toward those groups and to those geographical areas where unemployment is especially high."

b. "We have never had full employment in this country and never will have. Even during World War II the unemployment rate was nearly 2 percent."

c. "If people on unemployment compensation were required to take a job when it is offered to them, the unemployment rate would drop 30 percent within three months."

d. "The cure for unemployment is spending. Public spending or private spending, foolish spending or shrewd spending, it doesn't really matter. Spend, spend, spend. Employ, employ, employ."

4. On what source or sources of inflation do the following statements focus their attention?

a. "The one basic cause of inflation is the government's spending more than it takes in. The cure is a balanced budget."

b. "The breaking out of major labor negotiations in steel, autos, and other basic industries will lead to double-digit wage increases and a serious inflationary effect."

c. "Wage settlements are high. The widespread publicity they are receiving will make it difficult to wind down inflation."

d. "While the CPI rose by .7 percent last month, most of the increase was in a very few sectors where bottlenecks are developing."

5. "Inflations cannot long persist, whatever their initiating causes, unless the inflations are validated by increases in the money supply." Why is this so? Does it not imply that control of inflation is merely a matter of not allowing increases in the money supply to rise faster than the rate of increase of real national income?

6. Look up the rate of increases of the money supply and the CPI over the last 3 years and decide whether or not the current inflation is being validated.

7. Discuss the following views on the effects of inflation.

a. "Now the beast [of inflation] is easily visible, a luminescent specter, a killer, a threat to society, public enemy No. 1"—Robert D. Hersy Jr., 1979.

b. "Inflation—has become the national obsession, the catchall scapegoat for individual and societal economic difficulties, the symptom that diverts attention from the basic maladies"—James Tobin, 1980.

8. William Nordhaus of Yale University recently described inflation as an "inertial process like people standing up at a football game. When some people jump up to see better, other people can't see unless they stand up, too. When everybody is up, people as a group can't see as well as they did when they were all sitting; in fact, they probably see worse and are more uncomfortable. But the problem is how to get them all to sit down together." What view of inflation is Professor Nordhaus embracing?

9. In a 1978 article on the harmful impact of inflation on consumers the *New York Times* reported on the case of Mrs. Valentine Jones, who had to pay $55.99 to replace a car battery that she had bought nine years before for $41.00. "Inasmuch as she and her two sons live on a Social Security check of $200 a month," reported the article, "the extra $15 makes a difference. It's going to hurt."

What do you think her social security check would have been nine years before, assuming she lived then under similar circumstances? Do you think that Mrs. Jones would prefer to go back to 1969 with the social security payments of that time and a $41 battery? In what sense has inflation "ravaged" Mrs. Jones' living standards, as the article alleged?

10. In an article on the harmful effects of inflation, a reporter wrote "with the rise in mortgage interest rates to 10 percent heaven only knows the price of what was once idealized as 'the $100,000 house.'" At the time the inflation rate was 9 percent. Did this 10 percent interest rate represent a heavy burden of inflation on the new home owner? What do you think the mortgage interest rate would have been if the inflation rate had been zero? What would have been a heavier real burden on the purchaser of a new house?

11. In an article entitled "On the Rise, A New Breed of Debtors," a recent newspaper article suggested that because of the ravages of inflation many people were going into debt to make ends meet. What would be a rational debt policy—to borrow or to lend—if you thought the rate of inflation was going to be at least as high as the current rate of interest? Does your answer suggest possible reasons for the "rise in the new breed of debtors" other than an inability to make ends meet?

Macroeconomic Experience

37

The problems of the present are rooted in the events of the past. With the tools at our command we can now examine, and understand at least in broad outline, the experience of the last half century.

THE 1930s: DEPRESSION ECONOMICS

The late 1920s were a boom period in the United States. Employment was high, output was high and rising—the automobile industry, for example, was in a strong growth period—and optimism was the rule of the day. Then came the great stock market crash of 1929, dashing many hopes for unlimited prosperity.

Much more important to the average American was the economic collapse that by 1932 had taken the economy to the depths of the most serious depression in American history, the Great Depression. Unemployment became a grave social problem in the aggregate and a personal tragedy for those most seriously affected by it. At its peak in 1933, unemployment reached 25 percent of the labor force! And it never fell below 15 percent during the rest of the decade. The price level fell somewhat from 1928 to 1933 in the face of a heavy excess supply of labor and capital; it then rose slowly during the gradual recovery of the late 1930s. Nevertheless, it is a fair approximation to characterize the period from 1932 to 1939 as one of stable prices and heavy unemployment.

In short, the economy was operating on the Keynesian portion of its aggregate supply function. In fact, it was the experience of that troubled decade that led Keynes to develop his model of the behavior of the economy under conditions of excess supply and downwardly rigid prices. In such circumstances, changes in national income are determined by aggregate demand alone, as shown in Figure 37-1.

Under these depressionary conditions, an increase in capacity that raises full-employment output by extending the horizontal portion of the aggregate supply curve has no effect on equilibrium national income. Because there is not enough demand to employ existing capacity, the creation of additional capacity serves no current purpose.

FIGURE 37-1
Depression Macroeconomics

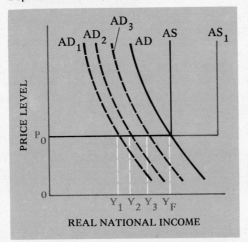

When there is a substantial GNP gap, fluctuations in aggregate demand determine fluctuations in national income. With aggregate demand and supply of *AD* and *AS*, the late 1920s were a period of more or less full employment. The Great Depression caused a sharp drop in aggregate demand (to AD_1 in the figure) and opened the large GNP gap ($Y_F - Y_1$). The slow recovery through the 1930s took aggregate demand to positions such as AD_2 and AD_3, thereby narrowing the GNP gap (to $Y_F - Y_2$ and $Y_F - Y_3$).

In these circumstances equilibrium income is said to be demand determined. An increase in full-employment national income, shown by the rightward shift of the aggregate supply curve to AS_1, has no effect on equilibrium income.

For this reason many early Keynesians paid little attention to the long-term effect of investment on aggregate supply. Although not an unreasonable thing to do when analyzing severe deflationary conditions, the neglect was serious when the economy was operating at full employment. When national income is already at full employment, income cannot be increased by raising aggregate demand. What is needed is a rightward extension of the aggregate supply curve. A major long-term cause of such extensions is investment.

The early 1930s saw aggregate demand at a low level, with a very large GNP gap. In the course of the decade, demand recovered and income rose slowly. There was a further setback in the recession of 1937, but by the end of the decade the GNP gap had narrowed substantially.

The main problem facing the economy throughout the decade of the 1930s was a deficiency of aggregate demand.

In these circumstances, any policy that increased demand would have helped to alleviate the depression. This was Keynes' great insight.

THE 1940s: FULL EMPLOYMENT AND INFLATION

With the outbreak of World War II, governments threw fiscal caution to the winds as they spent huge amounts that were much in excess of their tax receipts. Aggregate demand rose steadily, first eliminating the GNP gap and then opening a large inflationary gap, as shown in Figure 37-2. Price controls and rationing were used to slow the inflation that resulted from the excess demand.

Price controls, which were becoming increasingly difficult to enforce, were removed when the war ended. The inflationary gap then made its full effects felt, and the price level rose by 33 percent in three years. But by the end of the decade prices once again appeared to be fairly steady, and the period of demand inflation seemed to be at an end.

FIGURE 37-2
Wartime Demand Inflation

REAL NATIONAL INCOME

When there is sufficient aggregate demand, real national income is determined by full-employment aggregate supply while aggregate demand determines the equilibrium price level. Government expenditures during World War II quickly took aggregate demand to AD, which restored full employment. As expenditures increased further, they took aggregate demand to AD_1, opening up a substantial inflationary gap. Once aggregate demand was sufficient to purchase the economy's full-employment output, real national income was determined by the position of the aggregate supply curve. Further increases in aggregate demand could then affect only the price level.

The inflationary gap was contained by wartime price controls, so the price level rose only a little, to P_1. When controls were removed after the war, the price level rose to its equilibrium at P_2, changing the aggregate supply curve to P_2AS.

The experience of the 1940s suggested several conclusions that are illustrated in Figure 37-2. First, the quick recovery to full employment in wartime America convinced most observers that Keynes was right. A major depression caused by deficient aggregate demand had been cured by measures that increased aggregate demand. This conclusion led to the passage of the 1946 Full Employment Act, which accepted the maintenance of full employment as a goal of federal pol-

icy and set up the president's Council of Economic Advisers to advise on appropriate full-employment policy.

A second conclusion drawn by most economists was that excess demand at full-employment income was a major cause of inflation. (This had been known before, but the experience of World War II reconfirmed it.) Demand inflation was recognized as a major concern whenever aggregate demand threatened to exceed aggregate supply at full-employment national income.

The third lesson that many economists learned was that price controls designed to suppress a demand-pull inflation were a temporary expedient at best. As time passed controls became increasingly hard to enforce; when they were removed, the excess aggregate demand took the price level to where it would have been had the controls never existed.

The conclusion from World War II experience was that price controls might postpone a demand inflation, but they would have no long-term effect on the price level when the inflationary pressure originated in excess demand.

This was a recognition that price controls attack the symptoms but not the cause of demand-pull inflation. (Note that a demand-pull inflation is often simply called a demand inflation.)

THE 1950s: THE GOAL OF FULL EMPLOYMENT WITHOUT INFLATION

The governments of most Western countries entered the postwar period committed to the goals of full employment and stable prices. Aggregate demand was to be manipulated in order to keep demand equal to full-employment aggregate supply at the prevailing price level (see Figure 37-3). Fluctuations in private-sector demand were to be offset by compensating fluctuations in the public sector in order to hold aggregate demand approximately constant at its full-employment level. This was the policy of fine tuning the economy, discussed on page 563.

Many Western countries pursued an active stabilization policy in which both fiscal and monetary changes were made frequently in an effort to fine tune. In the United States, stabilization policy was left largely to the Fed's monetary policy. (See Chapter 35 for a discussion of how it unfolded.) The economy seemed stable enough that a major injection of fiscal stabilization policy appeared to be unnecessary.

The 1950s opened with a major bout of demand inflation brought on by heavy expenditures associated with the Korean War. The price level rose about 10 percent in two years. This was a wartime demand inflation similar to that experienced during and after World War II; although its consequences might be disturbing, its causes were well understood.

After this inflation had run its course, the economy settled down at an average performance that seemed (particularly in retrospect) to come quite close to the twin goals of full employment and stable prices. The average rate of unemployment in 1953–1959 was 4.8 percent, while the average rate of inflation was around 1 percent per year.

The fluctuations in demand caused some mild fluctuations in income and employment. They also caused a slow upward shift in the price level. Although a worry at the time, this price experience would be regarded as virtual stability by today's standards.

Toward the end of the decade, one new problem was causing concern. There was a tendency for the price level to rise despite a significant GNP gap. Thus, for example, when aggregate demand was at AD_1 in Figure 37-3, the price level might be rising at 1 to 2 percent per year. This seemed to imply a spontaneous upward shift in the horizontal portion of the aggregate supply curve (say from P_0 to P_1 in the figure) *not associated with any excess demand.*

Various explanations were put forward. The most commonly given were the structural rigidity and the wage cost-push hypotheses (discussed on pages 678–679). The inflation was very mild and the debate on its causes inconclusive.

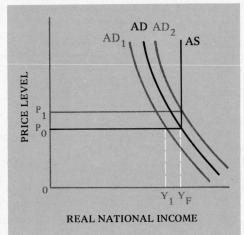

FIGURE 37-3
Full Employment and Relatively Stable Prices

If aggregate demand and supply can be held at *AD* and *AS*, the goals of full employment and stable prices can both be achieved. From the end of the Korean War to the end of the 1950s, full employment and stable prices seemed to be within grasp. Inevitably there were some fluctuations, making aggregate demand oscillate— say between AD_1 and AD_2. This led to fluctuations in national income between Y_1 and Y_F and to unreversed increases in the price level when an inflationary gap appeared. This caused a slow upward drift in the horizontal part of the aggregate supply curve. One such upward shift is shown from P_0 to P_1.

However, this was the first real evidence of a force that later became a plaguing policy problem: inflations originating in shifts in the aggregate supply curve.

THE 1960s: INFLATION-UNEMPLOYMENT TRADE-OFFS AND MORE DEMAND INFLATION

The Trade-off Relation

As the 1950s wore on, it became increasingly evident that the view of the economy given by the kinked aggregate supply curve in Figure 37-3 was inadequate. With such an aggregate supply curve, increases in aggregate demand affect only

TABLE 37-1

Employment, Unemployment, and Inflation in the United States, 1947–1970

Unemployment[a]	Number of years	Average unemployment[a]	Average employment[a]	Average annual rate of inflation of CPI (percent)
Less than 4.0	9	3.5	96.5	4.8
4.0–4.9	5	4.4	95.6	2.5
5.0 or more	10	5.8	94.2	0.7

Source: Economic Report of the President, 1976.
[a] As a percentage of the civilian labor force.

On average, inflation and unemployment were negatively related over the years 1947–1970. During this period higher levels of unemployment tended to be associated with stable or only slowly rising prices. Lower levels of unemployment tended to be associated with higher rates of inflation. The data are plotted in Figure 37-5 on page 700.

national income when Y is less than Y_F and only the price level when Y equals Y_F. Full employment and stable prices are attainable simultaneously provided only that the aggregate demand curve can be made to intersect the aggregate supply curve at the latter's kink.

The experience of the late 1950s forced economists to regard the kinked aggregate supply curve as an inadequate description of the supply side of the economy. An intermediate section was suggested, over which the price level and national income could vary simultaneously, as shown in Figure 36-6 on page 685. However, the realization that the aggregate supply curve would continue to shift upward when equilibrium was on its rising portion and that the aggregate demand curve would have to be shifted right by monetary policy to prevent national income from falling, led to the formulation of the Phillips curve, shown in Figure 36-8 on page 687.

The Phillips curve is often called a trade-off curve because it shows an apparent trade-off between income and inflation: a higher level of real national income can be obtained, but at the cost of more inflation. (Since a rise in national income entails a fall in unemployment, the trade-off was often expressed in terms of an unemployment-inflation trade-off rather than an income-inflation trade-off. But the two relations are interchangeable over the short term because national income and unemployment vary inversely with each other.)

The 1960s were the era of the Phillips curve trade-off. Economists sought to measure the inflation-unemployment trade-off curve for various economies while policymakers discussed which point on the curve the economy should be made to operate at. Table 37-1 shows the trade-off for the U.S. economy that existed on the basis of data for the 1950s and 1960s. In general, conservatives favored points close to Y_F, where the inflation rate was very low, while liberals favored points further to the right along the curve, where higher output and lower unemployment were obtained at the cost of a higher inflation rate.

Inflation-Unemployment Experience

The 1960s began with a mild deflationary gap that threatened to become chronic. It was diagnosed by most economists as a case of fiscal drag caused by a rising full-employment budget surplus associated with economic growth. We studied this problem in Chapter 31 (see page 573).

A long debate ensued in the early 1960s. Keynesian economists diagnosed the unemployment as a case of deficient-demand unemployment and advocated a permanent tax cut as remedy. Structuralists, led by Charles Killingsworth of Michigan State University and John Kenneth Galbraith of Harvard, blamed the unemployment on a structural mismatching between the characteristics of the unemployed and the requirements of available jobs. They claimed that the tax cut would not reduce unemployment and, further, that the resulting rise in aggregate demand would cause an inflation. In other words, they believed that output was supply constrained —that shifting aggregate demand would not raise output. While there was plenty of unemployed labor, they maintained that it was the wrong kind of labor and that an expansion of output would quickly be brought to a halt by a shortage of the right kind (in particular, highly skilled workers).

After two years of debate in academic journals and before congressional committees, the tax cut was finally passed in 1964. Aggregate demand increased, national income rose, and unemployment fell by about the amount predicted by the Keynesian economists. This victory for the Keynesians marked the birth of what in the United States came to be called the New Economics—though it was rather old to the rest of the world, where aggregate demand had been manipulated regularly by many governments at least since World War II.

The full effects of the tax cuts were still working themselves out when the Johnson administration increased the American military presence in Vietnam. The president was unwilling to ask Congress to raise taxes to pay for the growing Vietnam War, so military spending was mainly deficit financed.

The result of the large increase in government expenditure, unmatched by an increase in taxes, was just what economic theory predicts: aggregate demand rose greatly; full employment was restored quickly; and consequently a serious inflationary gap opened up and an inflation ensued.

America was launched on the period of high rates of inflation that has persisted for nearly two decades.

The final major macro policy event of the late 1960s was a belated attempt to take some of the inflationary steam out of the economy by means of temporary tax increases in 1968. We considered the failure of these measures in Chapter 31 (see page 575). Economists long debated the correct lesson to be drawn from this policy failure. Did it show that aggregate demand cannot be influenced by fiscal policy? Most economists reject this conclusion. Instead they believe it showed that delicate fine tuning is fraught with difficulties for at least two reasons: first, because the economy can be sluggish in reacting to deflationary fiscal changes; second, because unexpected and unpredictable changes in aggregate expenditure can easily swamp the effects of relatively small, planned fiscal changes designed to fine tune the economy.

As the 1960s closed, the economy seemed to be firmly on a path of persistent excess demand and rising inflation.

THE 1970s: INFLATION, STAGFLATION, AND THE "FAILURE OF CONVENTIONAL WISDOM"

The 1970s opened with an expanding economy buoyed by continued Vietnam War expenditures. After a slight recession in 1971, a boom developed through 1973 that took on extraordinary proportions. Shortages and bottlenecks quickly appeared, and the inflation rate, which had moderated to just over 3 percent at the end of 1971, reached 9 percent by the end of 1973 and was still rising.

Wage and Price Controls Again

Although by 1971 unemployment was above the levels previously associated with full employment, an inflationary gap seemed to be developing, with an inflation rate at what was then regarded as the very high level of 4 to 5 percent. In an attempt to halt inflation without making deflationary fiscal changes, the Nixon administration introduced wage and price controls. Here was a classic attempt to stop a demand inflation by applying direct controls. The subsequent course of events was just what macroeconomic theory predicts; the situation is analyzed in Figure 37-4.

FIGURE 37-4

Wage and Price Controls and Excess Demand

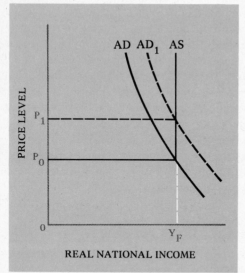

Wage and price controls can delay a demand inflation only for as long as they are in place. When aggregate demand rises from *AD* to *AD₁*, an inflationary gap develops. In the absence of controls the price level would rise from P_0 to P_1. Effective controls hold the price level at P_0 but do not eliminate the inflationary gap. Once the controls are removed the price level rises to its equilibrium value, P_1. The controls have delayed but not altered the final response of the price level to the excess aggregate demand.

The controls in action. The controls were divided into several phases. Phase I (which lasted for two months) imposed a complete freeze on virtually all wages and prices in the economy. Phase II (fourteen months) attempted to hold wage increases to 5.5 percent per year and price increases to no more than was necessary to cover any increase in costs. Phase III (five months) began in mid January 1973. At that time the economy was expanding rapidly and a need was recognized for a more flexible program that would permit substantial changes in relative prices.

When it became apparent that Phase III was not restraining inflation, a new freeze was introduced in June 1973 with the announcement that it was temporary and was to be followed by a further set of Phase IV controls. Phase IV controls proved ineffective, however, and they petered out. By April 1974, when Congress let the control authority expire, its later phases were acknowledged failures.

Extensive research into the effects of this experiment with wage and price controls suggests that the entire costly effort had little or no effect on wages but it did hold down price inflation by perhaps as much as 2 percentage points. The restraint on prices was achieved by forcing narrower profit margins. Not surprisingly, once the controls were lifted, profit margins were restored. Thus the episode had little or no lasting effect on the price level.

By delaying the demand inflation, however, the controls contributed significantly to the unprecedented inflation rate of 1974. One cause of the accelerating inflation during that period was the "price bubble" that occurred as prices rebounded after decontrol to make up for the effects of their temporary restraint.

Lessons of the controls. This saga of a long and in the end unsuccessful attempt to control a demand-pull inflation by means of wage and price controls forced many to relearn the lesson that an earlier generation of economists had learned from the World War II price controls. The use of wage and price controls in the face of an inflationary gap usually involves most of the stages in this sequence:

1. The successful application of blanket controls on everything.
2. The need to regulate price changes brought about by innumerable unavoidable circumstances, since it would be inviting chaos to freeze relative prices permanently.
3. The exemption of many wages and prices for seemingly valid special reasons.
4. The spread of exceptions (since all prices and costs are interrelated), leading to a growing web of exceptions, complex regulations, and

diminishing effectiveness in controlling overall price rises.

5. The abandonment of the system, followed by a price bubble that takes prices to about where they would have been in the absence of the entire effort at control.

The American experience of 1971–1974 was no exception to these general rules.

The Elusive Trade-off

By the early 1970s a major doctrine of macroeconomic policy, the existence of a stable inflation-income or inflation-unemployment trade-off, was being seriously questioned. Toward the end of the 1960s and during the early 1970s the Phillips curves of most countries began to shift upward. In other words, any level of national income and unemployment was associated with a higher rate of inflation than previously. For example, the U.S. recession at the beginning of the 1970s left the inflation rate at just over 3 percent, a rate that before the Vietnam War was associated only with peaks of business activity and large inflationary gaps. The boom that then developed took the inflation rate to 8.8 percent by the end of 1973, a rate unprecedented in peacetime America.

The breakdown of the American Phillips curve relation is shown in Figure 37-5. The colored curve shows the relatively stable inflation-income trade-off as it appeared to policymakers in the late 1960s. The dots show the 1970s. They show that the decade's experience was always above the earlier curve, indicating unprecedentedly high inflation associated with any given level of pressure of demand.

It was clear by the early 1970s that something was very wrong with the simple theory of the stable Phillips curve trade-off. As so often happens, a newer theory was at hand to explain the failure of the simple Phillips curve. In 1968 Professor Edmund S. Phelps of Columbia University and Professor Milton Friedman of the University of Chicago had mounted a major attack on the Phillips curve trade-off, an attack based on the expectational theory of inflation (explained in Chapter 36 and its appendix). Their argument said that an attempt to hold national income *above* its full-employment level would lead not to a stable rate of inflation but to an ever-accelerating rate. They called the rate of unemployment associated with full-employment income the **natural rate of unemployment.** An alternative statement of their theory's major prediction was that an attempt to hold unemployment *below* its natural rate would lead to an accelerating rate of inflation.

The Phelps-Friedman theory is important for at least two reasons. First, it produced a major change in the way macro policy problems are viewed. It suggested that the trade-off between unemployment and inflation was merely transitory. Attempts to hold output above Y_F (and hence unemployment below its natural rate), while leading to temporary gains in employment output, are likely to lead to ever-accelerating rates of inflation.

Second, the theory provided an explanation for bouts of stagflation: strong inflationary expectations can sustain the inflation rate and rising expectations can even increase it temporarily in the face of declining demand and output and hence rising unemployment.

1974–1975: Stagflation and Supply Shocks

Before 1973 the major force driving economic fluctuations had always been aggregate demand. When demand was high, output would be high, unemployment low, and strong inflationary pressures would exist. When aggregate demand was low, output would be low, unemployment high, and inflationary pressures weak or nonexistent. These associations had become the conventional wisdom about how the economy must behave. They were so widely accepted as the natural state of things that ordinary citizens, most policymakers, and many economists were mystified when quite a different association of events occurred.

FIGURE 37-5
U.S. Stagflation in the 1970s

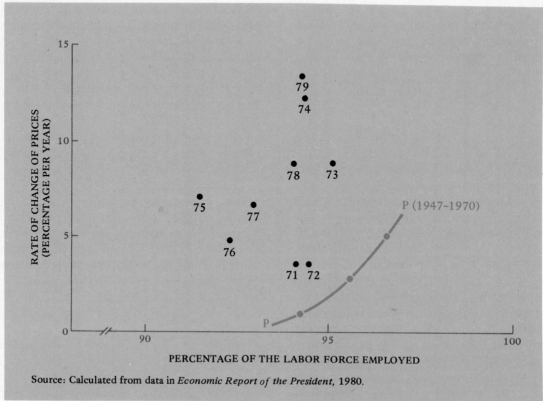

Source: Calculated from data in *Economic Report of the President*, 1980.

The 1970s were unusual in combining high rates of unemployment with high rates of inflation. The three colored dots are plotted from Table 37–1. They show the average rates of inflation associated with the indicated rates of employment between 1947 and 1970. The colored curve is thus a rough Phillips curve for the economy of that period. The black dots show the rates of employment and inflation for each of the years 1971 to 1979. The year 1974 was the year of the most ex-treme stagflation. The employment rate fell from 95.1 to 94.4 percent while the rate of inflation rose from 8.8 to 12.2 percent! In 1975 the employment rate fell to its all-time low since World War II of 91.5 percent while the inflation rate remained at the high rate of 7 percent. With the recovery of 1976–1978 the inflation rate first fell and then rose steadily. The rate finally soared in 1979 (partly under the impact of major increases in oil prices).

In 1974 and 1975 the economies of all Western countries fell into the deepest recession since the Great Depression of the 1930s. Unemployment peaked at 9 percent of the labor force in May 1975. During those years the economy encountered the new economic disease of stagflation: falling output and rising unemployment combined with high and sometimes rising inflation rates. Inflation peaked at an annual rate of 12 percent in July, 1975.

Aggregate supply shifts. For the first time in recent history the economy was being affected significantly by shifts in *aggregate supply* not caused by excess aggregate demand. The most severe of the shifts in aggregate supply—often called supply-side shocks—came with the OPEC oil embargo in 1973, which was followed by major increases in OPEC's prices. Oil prices at the wellhead were quadrupled in a matter of months. Not only fuel but a host of other petroleum-based products from plastics to fertilizers suddenly rose in price. The rising prices of these vital materials meant rising costs for many firms. Rising costs were passed on by raising the prices of finished goods, which in turn caused an upward shift in the aggregate supply curve.

The other major supply-side shock that hit the economy at this time came from the agricultural sector. A series of crop failures drove up many food prices. At the same time, the sale to the USSR of large stocks of American wheat and other agricultural commodities removed the depressing effect on prices that large buffer stocks had exerted, and this too led to price rises. Again the price level rose for causes associated with supply rather than demand shifts.

Aggregate demand shifts. The supply-side shocks were reinforced by severe contractionary shifts in aggregate demand. The effect of OPEC was to transfer large amounts of income from American purchasers to sellers of petroleum products. Had the sellers spent the money in the same way that Americans would have, aggregate demand would have been unaffected. But much of the new oil income was spent on short-term financial securities, gold, and land rather than on currently produced goods and services. Thus the effect on aggregate demand was the same as if the American propensity to save had risen: there was a reduction in the amount of income spent on current production. This caused a leftward shift in the aggregate demand curve (or, the same thing, a downward shift in the aggregate expenditure curve).[1]

The net stagflationary effects of this upward

[1] There were further reasons for the fall in aggregate demand. First, the world hit a serious recession in 1974, so demand fell everywhere. Second, the Fed reinforced the worldwide trend by applying the monetary brakes in the United States with great severity. Worried by the rise in the inflation rate, the Fed had moved toward a more restrictive monetary policy in 1973, and this move continued into 1974. Since monetary policy works with long lags, it is fairly clear that the effects of the 1974 restrictions shifted the aggregate demand curve left and contributed further to the severe stagflation that was setting in.

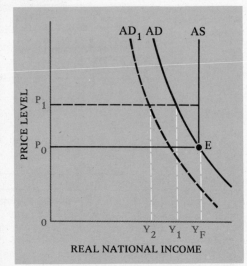

FIGURE 37-6
Stagflation

Upward shifts in aggregate supply cause rising prices and falling output. Initially aggregate demand is *AD* and aggregate supply is P_0AS, producing equilibrium at *E*. The aggregate supply curve now shifts upward to P_1AS. This reduces national income from Y_F to Y_1 and raises the price level from P_0 to P_1 along the given aggregate demand curve, *AD*. If aggregate demand shifts simultaneously to AD_1, the fall in output will be even larger than it would otherwise have been (from Y_F to Y_2). This is roughly what happened in America from 1973 to 1975.

shift in aggregate supply and fall in aggregate demand are shown in Figure 37-6.

The shocks to the economy accounted for much of the stagflation. During 1974, however, there were other important influences. Professor Alan Blinder of Princeton University has described the situation.

The causes of the inflationary surge, and also the recession that followed, seem to have been a trio of relative price shocks. The soaring price of food was the main impetus that pushed inflation rates up initially from 3–4 percent in 1972 and 6–7 percent in 1973. [Then came] energy prices, which had their biggest impact in late 1973 and early 1974 and continued to reverberate through the wage-price spiral well into 1975.

TABLE 37-2
Output and Inflation Rates

	GNP gap as a percentage of potential GNP	Annual percentage change in Consumer Price Index		
		All items	Excluding food	Excluding food and energy
1973	−0.7[a]	6.2	3.9	3.5
1974	3.7	11.0	9.9	8.3
1975	7.6	9.1	9.3	9.2
1976	5.1	5.8	6.6	6.6
1977	3.0	6.5	6.5	6.2
1978	1.7	7.7	7.2	7.3
1979	2.0	13.3	11.4	9.7

[a] Minus indicates a negative GNP gap (actual national income exceeded potential income).

The overall inflation rate responded in the 1970s both to demand and supply shocks. Stagflation is most obvious in 1974–75, when extremely high inflation rates coexisted with a high, and rising, GNP gap. The impact of supply shocks on the inflation rate can be seen by comparing the three different inflation rates in the table. In 1974, for example, the inflation rate of 11 percent would have been only 8.3 percent had it not been for the supply shocks of rising food and energy prices. In 1979 the inflation rate of 13.3 percent would only have been 9.7 percent without the direct contribution of unusually rapid rises in food and energy prices.

But it took a stunning surge in the prices of items other than food and energy to sustain the momentum of double-digit inflation through the balance of 1974. The demise of wage-price controls is the leading candidate to explain this sharp acceleration of non-food, non-energy . . . .

Thus price controls turned out in retrospect to be the stagflationary shock *par excellence* . . . and the ill-timed demise of controls helped cause the Great Recession. In sum . . . the 1971–74 controls program constituted a remarkable act of national self-flagellation. More remarkable still is the American public's eagerness [as shown by several opinion polls] to try for a repeat performance at any time.[2]

The interpretation suggested here makes the great inflation and stagflation of 1972–1975 the result of a set of serious, once-and-for-all shocks, not the result of inflationary fiscal and monetary policies. Monetary policy was validating the underlying rate of 4 to 6 percent, but it is hard to blame the acceleration of two-digit inflation on it.

[2] Alan S. Blinder, *Economic Policy and the Great Stagflation* (New York: Academic Press, 1980), first paragraph, page 102; second paragraph, page 132.

Slow Recovery and Fears of Accelerating Inflation

The years 1974 and 1975 saw major stagflation. The explanation is to be found in supply-side shocks and in the persistent inflationary expectations that held the inflation rate up in spite of a low level of aggregate demand. By the end of 1975, however, the inflationary rate was moderating rapidly. Then began a long period when the rate settled in the range of 6 to 7 percent.

During this period there were major changes in food prices that were determined by short-run changes in market conditions. The underlying rate of inflation is probably better gauged by looking at an inflation rate that excludes food prices. As Table 37-2 shows, this rate remained in the 6 percent range in 1976 and 1977 and then crept up to the 7 percent range as the slow recovery of the economy proceeded into 1978.

Why, in the face of so severe a recession, did the inflation rate stay stubbornly at above 6 percent, a rate never achieved at the height of any peacetime boom before the mid 1970s? There were not enough supply-side shocks coming from exogenous rises in costs to explain this persistent inflation.

Expectational and inertial inflation are accepted as the major culprits. If everyone saw an effective 6 percent inflation rate and expected it to continue, and if sellers were cautious about reducing their relative prices, everyone would raise their own prices by about 6 percent. This would continue to generate the 6 percent inflation that everyone had come to expect and accept. And once such expectational and inertial forces become well established, they are hard to break, even by a severe recession.

An alternative (or additional) explanation was the wage cost-push theory. This theory assumes that unions exert an upward pressure on wages independent of aggregate demand. That pressure raises firms' costs and hence their prices. The aggregate supply curve shifts upward as a result, thereby generating a supply-side inflation. Yet wage cost-push seems an unlikely candidate for major culprit because wages throughout most of the period were lagging behind rather than leading prices. Indeed, real wages (money wages divided by the price index) were falling much of the time.

Whether it was cost-push, as some believed, or expectational and inertial, as many believed, the inflation of 1976–1978 was clearly generated from the supply side. National income was well below its full-employment level, as is shown in Table 37-2. How such an inflation can be halted is a matter of current debate, to be reviewed in the next chapter.

Whatever its causes, the underlying inflation rate of about 6 percent was being validated by the Fed. The money supply was expanding fast enough to accommodate such an inflation without its causing a money shortage that would bring into play the monetary adjustment mechanism we discussed on page 683.

By 1978 the economy was within striking distance of its full-employment output, and the inflation rate rose to over 7 percent. In 1979, in spite of a slight fallback in income away from its full-employment level, the inflation rate jumped to 13.3 percent (11 percent when food prices are excluded) and was rising rapidly at the end of the year.

Part of this inflation was due to further supply-side shocks as OPEC raised world prices of oil and decontrol in the United States at last allowed domestic prices to rise nearer to the world level. A very rapid rise in interest rates, a part of the Fed's anti-inflationary package, also caused a temporary rise in the measured inflation rate. As in 1974–1975, the rise to two-digit inflation was due mainly to transitory supply-side shocks.

After allowing for all transitory factors, however, the underlying inflation rate seemed to have accelerated over 1978–1979 without the economy's having reached full employment. Going into the 1980s, the president's Council of Economic Advisers estimated that the underlying rate of inflation was not far from 10 percent.

1979–1980: Policy-induced Recession

Worried by the accelerating inflation rate, the Carter administration moved throughout 1979 to institute contractionary fiscal and monetary policies. Major efforts to cut government expenditures were announced; more important, monetary policy became extremely restrictive. Interest rates soared to record heights, close to 20 percent. Money became very scarce, and the monetary adjustment mechanism was clearly working to reduce aggregate expenditure. By mid 1980 a recession was in progress. People no longer debated whether the policy measures would cause a downturn; instead they discussed how deep the recession would be. The effects of the decline in aggregate demand on output and employment were in the predicted direction; what effect this would have on moderating price inflation remained to be seen.

THE CONTROL OF AGGREGATE DEMAND AND THE CONTROL OF INFLATION

The experience of this latest policy reinforced a lesson that had become increasingly obvious in the 1970s. Armed with the tools of economic theory, policymakers are able to influence aggregate demand. Some details remain to be settled regarding the relative powers of fiscal and monetary policy, but there is no doubt that, using a mixture of the two, governments can manipulate aggregate demand. Modern economic theory is not the irrelevant white elephant some commentators would make it out to be; it is a potent tool — far more potent than any current rival — for understanding and controlling the macro behavior of the economy.

If this is the case, why does macro policy encounter so many problems? The difficulty is not in manipulating demand; this we know how to do, at least within a reasonable margin of error. The grave uncertainty lies in how the impact of a change in aggregate demand will be divided between quantity changes and price changes.

Say that the government engineers a 10 percent increase in aggregate expenditure. At one time this might lead to a 10 percent increase in real output with prices constant; at another time it might lead to a 10 percent increase in prices with real output constant; at still other times it might lead to any number of different combinations of price and output changes that combine to make up a 10 percent increase in national income valued at current prices.

The great problem of macroeconomics in the 1980s arises from the fact that, while governments can cause changes in aggregate demand, they are uncertain about how the effects of such changes will be divided between quantities and prices.

It is on this issue that current controversies turn. Our present inability to understand fully and to predict accurately the division of effects between real and monetary variables lies at the root of policymakers' failure to control the inflation rate as readily as they can control aggregate demand.

Thus we still ask: Why did the inflation rate not fall below 6 percent in the recession of the mid 1970s? Why did the rate accelerate at the end of the decade? Will the recession engineered in 1980 slow the inflation rate? What is wrong? What can be done? These current policy debates are the subject of the next chapter.

Summary

1. The 1930s were the decade of the Great Depression, when Keynesian economics was born. Declining aggregate demand and the relative downward inflexibility of prices (after the first shock of recession had passed) combined to create a problem of massive unemployment.

2. During World War II, massive deficit-financed government expenditure first restored full employment and then opened a serious inflationary gap whose effects were partially masked by price controls. After the war, price controls were removed and inflation took the price level to its new and higher equilibrium.

3. In the 1950s governments sought to produce both full employment and stable prices. Although their policies were not completely successful, the unemployment rate and the inflation rate were both very modest by the standards of the 1970s and 1980s.

4. The 1960s were the era of the Phillips curve trade-off: policymakers thought they could reduce the unemployment rate more or less to any desired level if they were willing to accept the associated stable inflation rate. The decade opened with unemployment and a deflationary gap that was remedied by the 1964 tax cuts. The deficit financing of the Vietnam War then opened up an inflationary gap. The decade closed with the unsuccessful attempt to dampen inflationary forces through temporary tax increases in 1968–1969.

5. The early 1970s saw growing demand inflation that was restrained only partially and temporarily by wage and price controls. A series of relative price shocks associated in turn with agriculture, energy, and the decontrol of manufactured goods prices took inflation into the two-digit range toward the end of the boom and held it there during the first year of the great mid-decade slump. After a year, the inflation rate fell back to its underlying rate of about 6 percent. The slow recovery brought the economy to within striking distance of full employment in 1978; after a very gradual increase, the inflation rate accelerated again into the two-digit range at the turn of the decade.

6. The experience of the last 50 years shows that policymakers have impressive ability to manipulate aggregate demand. Where we lack understanding and control, however, is in knowledge of how the effects of a change in aggregate demand will be distributed between changes in output, real income, and employment on the one hand and changes in prices on the other.

Topics for Review

The effects on the economy of demand-side shocks
The effects on the economy of supply-side shocks
The effects of price controls in inflationary-gap situations
Causes of stagflation

Discussion Questions

1. "We have nothing to fear but fear itself" — Franklin Roosevelt, Inaugural Address, 1933. With hindsight might Roosevelt have better said, "We have nothing to fear but the fear of spending"?

2. In a recent issue of *Business Week* MIT economist Franco Modigliani was quoted as saying, "The view that saving is a nuisance that threatens full employment is dead. As far as I am concerned it should have been dead in the mid 1950s." Under what circumstances might increased savings threaten full employment? Under what circumstances might they help the economy to reach full employment?

3. What theory or theories of inflation are suggested by each of the following quotations?
   a. "Congress would be ready to move [on wage-price controls] if we get some direct message from the White House" — Representative "Tip" O'Neill, Speaker of the House, in mid 1980.
   b. "Carter Sees Controls as Inflationary — President Warns of Anticipatory Wage-Price Rise" — *New York Times*, 1980.
   c. "Government causes inflation and therefore government is the only one to cure it by fiscal policy" — Ronald Reagan, January 1980.
   d. "The nation's spiraling inflation reflects a global depletion of physical resources and therefore cannot be cured by traditional fiscal and monetary tools" — a study issued in 1980 by the Worldwatch Institute.
   e. "February Producer Prices Up a Sharp 1.5 Percent — Rise in Costs of Energy Largest in 6 Years" — *New York Times*, 1979.

4. A recent newspaper article on inflation warned, "It is a mistake to think that every higher price is due to inflation." Give some examples of higher prices that have increased the CPI without being a part of a general inflationary process.

5. A recent newspaper discussion of inflation gave the following arguments *for* and *against* reductions in specific taxes.

   For:
   a. "Cuts in social security payroll taxes would reduce employment costs, thereby helping to slow down price inflation."
   b. "Faster depreciation write-offs would provide greater incentives for new equipment and technology investments, thus boosting efficiency and productivity."

   Against:
   c. "Pumping more money and more purchasing power into the economy through a tax cut without cutting federal spending would do little to restrain inflation [indeed it would increase it]."
   d. "A better approach would be to attack inflation by achieving a budget surplus and paying off the federal debt."

   Match each one of the above statements with the following theoretical category that best describes it.
   (i) Shift the aggregate demand curve to the right.
   (ii) Shift the aggregate supply curve downwards.
   (iii) Shift the aggregate demand curve to the left.
   (iv) Shift the kink on the aggregate supply curve outwards to the right.

6. Interviewed at the end of 1978, Fred Kahn, President Carter's newly appointed "anti-inflation czar," answered the question "Will President Carter's new [anti-inflation] program succeed?" with a resounding, "It has got to succeed." Taking, say, a two-year time horizon, did it succeed?

Current Issues in Macroeconomic Policy

38

In this chapter we consider the controversies over some alleged causes of and cures for our present macroeconomic ills. In the current disagreement over aspects of macroeconomic policy two extreme views can be seen.[1]

In the first view, held by many monetarists, the free-market economy has strong self-regulating tendencies: if a satisfactory general climate is maintained, the economy will tend naturally toward full employment and a relatively stable price level. At the same time, private initiative, spurred on by the profit motive, will yield a satisfactory growth of real national income.

In this view the government's attempts to stabilize the economy will usually be perverse. They will cause larger recessions on the downside, and bigger inflations on the upside, than would have occurred had government policy been passive. Instead of trying to stabilize the economy, government policy should take a very passive stance. The fiscal stance should be one of low and stable government expenditure and a budget that is balanced cyclically if not annually. The monetary stance should be one of a 3 percent increase in the money supply, year in and year out, to accommodate the increased demand for money associated with a growth of wealth and full-employment income. Against this stable backdrop, the natural corrective forces of the

---

[1] "Extreme" implies only the descriptive statement that the view lies at one end or the other of a spectrum of views. It does not imply a judgmental statement that the view is wrong, subversive, or otherwise undesirable. The history of ideas is full of examples where extreme views proved correct and moderate views wrong (and vice versa).

economy can be relied on to prevent the extremes of serious recessions and serious inflation.

The second view, held by many Keynesians, maintains that the free-enterprise economy has weak self-regulatory powers and may readily settle into prolonged periods of heavy unemployment. As a result of the restrictive practices of monopolies and the tendency of large corporations to avoid risks and adopt safe and cautious policies, the income growth rate will be low. Further, the enormous power of large unions and corporations may cause wage cost-push inflations that cannot be blamed on monetary mismanagement.

In this view, active government intervention is vital. Without such efforts the economy will sometimes undergo wide cyclical fluctuations, with alternating bouts of inflation and unemployment; at other times it will settle into prolonged stable periods of heavy unemployment. To avoid these situations, government must use its instruments of fiscal policy supplemented by monetary policy.

In this chapter we look first at controversies over the control of inflation, then at disputes over stabilization policy in general. We shall consider the two major groups of theories that command widest support and a third that, though less widely accepted among economists, is probably the most popular of the three among the general public!

The first theory, called monetarism, points to variations in the money supply as the major cause of recessions and inflations. The second theory is called neo-Keynesian: "Keynesian" because it is derived from the Keynesian theory of income determination, "neo" because it has been developed and amended by much theoretical and empirical work done in the half century since Keynes wrote. The third theory is called post-Keynesian: "Keynesian" since it finds its roots in Keynesian economics, "post" because it really goes beyond Keynesian theory as it is now understood. It emphasizes things that Keynes discussed at length but which did not find their

way into the subsequent formal development of Keynes' model: power structures and institutional rigidities.

In this chapter we give our attention primarily to monetarism and neo-Keynesianism, but we will speak of post-Keynesian theories from time to time. (Note that neo-Keynesians are often referred to as just Keynesians.)

Control of Inflation in the 1980s

As the 1980s began, the control of inflation seemed to many to be the major macroeconomic problem. There was much agreement among monetarists and neo-Keynesians on the causes of inflation, but there was considerable disagreement on how to control it.

CAUSES OF INFLATION

The consensus on causes is illustrated in Figure 38-1. The inflation of the last half of the 1970s and the early 1980s was occurring in the face of a substantial GNP gap. The inflation was generated by aggregate supply curve shifts and was being validated by monetary policy. By increasing the money supply, the Fed allowed the aggregate demand curve to shift upward at about the same speed as aggregate supply. Aggregate supply was shifting upward in part because of import cost-push inflation and in part because of expectational and inertial forces. Monetarists and neo-Keynesians more or less agree on this much. Post-Keynesians also agree, except that they see upward-shifting aggregate supply as a chronic problem associated with the power of trade unions and oligopolistic firms rather than a transitory problem associated with expectations and inertia.

While all agree that monetary policy contributed to the great inflation of the 1970s and early 1980s, agreement stops there. Monetarists are inclined to blame fluctuations in monetary policy for the fluctuations in the inflation rate. Neo-Keynesians see monetary policy as contributing to the underlying rate but point to nonrecurring

FIGURE 38-1

Inflation in the 1970s and Early 1980s

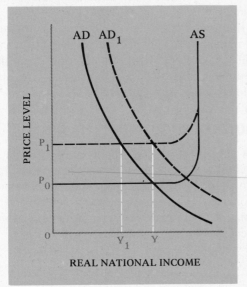

Aggregate supply shifts generated the inflation, and a validating monetary policy permitted accommodating shifts in aggregate demand. Shifts in aggregate supply such as that from P_0AS to P_1AS generated an inflation that would have reduced national income from Y to Y_1 if the aggregate demand curve were fixed. However, the Fed expanded the money supply about as fast as prices rose, so by the time the aggregate supply curve reached P_1AS, the aggregate demand curve had shifted to AD_1. This produced an inflation with a constant GNP gap.

supply shocks as a major cause of short-term variations in the inflation rate over the last decade.

There is also disagreement over the role played by wage cost-push. Monetarists dismiss it as of no importance and so do many neo-Keynesians. Other neo-Keynesians, and most post-Keynesians, think wage cost-push important; their view of inflation is thus the most pessimistic. In existing circumstances they see inflation as more or less inevitable, given powerful corporations and unions and the existing wage-bargaining arrangements. Even if inflation could be halted temporarily, they believe, it would

break out again spontaneously because of continued wage cost-push.

AN APPROPRIATE TARGET RATE OF INFLATION

One major debate centers on the dimensions of a cure for the inflation problem. Must we be satisfied with 2, 3, or 4 percent inflation? Or can we aim at the zero rate that would signal a truly stable price level?

The problem of choosing an appropriate rate lies in the economy's need for continued relative price adjustments. For example, the price of imported oil is being raised periodically by OPEC, and the rising oil price is inevitably taking other energy prices up with it. And in any changing economy, expanding sectors will find their money wages and prices rising in response to their need to expand. When many prices are rising, a zero rate of inflation overall would require compensating reductions in many other prices.

Some monetarists believe there is enough downward flexibility in money wages and prices that the price level—which is after all merely an appropriate average of all prices—can be held constant in spite of increases in some money prices and money wages. Some monetarists and most Keynesians (neo and post) argue that this downward flexibility does not exist. If the money supply were held constant in the face of import cost-push inflation, they believe, other prices would not fall but real income and output would fall. Upward shifts in the aggregate supply curve caused by an increasing price level would shift the economy's equilibrium upward and to the left along its fixed aggregate demand curve. Thus, they argue, the attempt to target for a zero inflation rate would produce a positive inflation rate caused by import cost-push and structural inflation, and this would be accompanied by a growing GNP gap. These economists call for a target rate equal to import cost-push and structural inflation—say, a rate between 2 and 4 percent. They would have the Fed validate this much inflation, which they hope could be combined with full-employment national income.

Whether or not a zero rate of inflation is possible, most people would settle for the 2 to 4 percent rate that is consistent with import cost-push and structural inflation—at least as an interim target.

POSSIBLE CURES FOR INFLATION

What everyone wants to know is, How can the existing inflation be slowed? What are the available cures?

All the major theories agree that monetary restraint is a *necessary condition* for slowing inflation. If monetary policy allows the aggregate demand curve to shift rightward each year, an inflation will be virtually assured. Even if cost-push forces do not raise the aggregate supply curve, the rising aggregate demand curve will soon generate an inflationary gap that will force the price level upward.

Successful control of inflation requires sufficient monetary restraint to prevent the aggregate demand curve from shifting rapidly upward year after year.

Monetarist Cures

Monetarists believe that control of the money supply is a sufficient as well as a necessary condition for controlling inflation. They advocate having the Fed rapidly reduce the rate of monetary expansion to one consistent with the target rate of inflation.

This policy is illustrated in Figure 38-2. (For simplicity, the rate of import cost-push and structural inflation is taken as zero.) The money supply is held constant so that the aggregate demand curve is fixed at *AD*. Expectational inflation causes prices to rise, but now the economy moves up its fixed aggregate demand curve with a rising price level and falling national income.[2] As national income continues to fall, unemploy-

[2] The mechanism operating here is the monetary adjustment mechanism described on page 645. As prices rise and the money supply is held constant, a shortage of money develops. This forces up interest rates and causes investment and other interest-sensitive expenditures to be curtailed.

FIGURE 38-2
The Monetarist Cure for Inflation

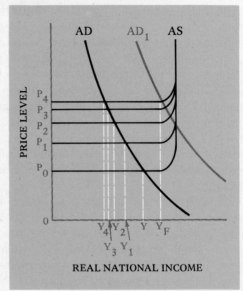

When inflation is being generated by an upward-shifting aggregate supply curve, fixing the aggregate demand curve will cause national income to fall and will eventually bring the inflation to a halt. An ongoing expectational inflation shifts the *AS* curve upward from $P_0 AS$ to $P_1 AS$, $P_2 AS$, and so on. If the money supply is held constant, the aggregate demand curve will not shift upward. National income will then fall from Y to Y_1 to Y_2 to Y_3. As the depression worsens, expectations of further inflation weaken and in each period the rate of price rise slackens. Finally the price level comes to rest at P_4, with the corresponding low level of national income at Y_4.

Aggregate demand may then be cautiously expanded toward AD_1 and, if the inflation was mainly expectational, income will rise toward Y_F, with the price level relatively stable at P_4.

ment and the GNP gap grow. Expectations of further inflation are weakened as the recession deepens. Eventually people come to expect no further price rises, and the inflation comes to a halt.

Evidence from the recent past suggests that the downward revision of inflationary expectations is slow to occur in response even to severe slumps in economic activity. However, monetarists believe that this may be misleading because governments have been so timid and so quick to abandon their policies. They argue that a really sharp recession, with the government demonstrating that it is determined to keep to a policy of monetary restraint, would cause firms and unions to revise their inflationary expectations downward very quickly. Then perhaps a recession involving 8 to 10 percent unemployment for only one or two years would be enough. Although high unemployment is a heavy cost, it is one worth paying, monetarists argue, if inflation can again be brought back to the 0 to 4 percent range.

Once expectational inflation has been removed, the money supply can be expanded cautiously to reduce the severe money shortage. This move will bring interest rates down and increase investment expenditure, thereby shifting the aggregate demand curve outward. National income will rise, and if the original inflation really was expectational, it should be possible to approach full employment without a further outburst of inflation.

Neo-Keynesian Cures

Neo-Keynesians agree that the monetarists' scenario is possible. However, they argue that the cure would be much slower and therefore much more painful than monetarists think. They stress existing evidence that inflationary expectations and inertias are hard to alter. If indeed rising unemployment can do the job, statistical studies based on past experience suggest that four "percentage-point years" of unemployment are needed to force inertial and expectational inflation down by one percentage point; that is, a rise in unemployment of four percentage points for one year or two percentage points held for two years is required to force inflationary expectations and inertia down from, say, 10 percent to 9 percent.

To appreciate the gloomy implications of these figures, assume that with a labor force of 100 million, unemployment is currently 6 percent, and that the actual and the expected inflation rates are 10 percent. In order to force expectational and inertial inflation down to 4 percent, there would have to be 24 "percentage-point years." This means 10 percent unemployment (4 million more unemployed persons) for six years or 12 percent unemployment (6 million more unemployed persons) for four years! This, the neo-Keynesians say, would represent a colossal loss in GNP and heavy suffering among the unemployed.

Many neo-Keynesians seek to avoid the lost output by creating a policy package that includes the same monetary restraint that the monetarists advocate but adds to it temporary policies designed to slow the rise in the aggregate supply curve directly. Such a policy package is illustrated in Figure 38-3.

The policies advocated by the Keynesians are called **incomes policies.** These are any form of direct or indirect intervention by the government into wage-price formation with a view to influencing the rate of inflation (and sometimes the distribution of income as well). Incomes policies vary from direct controls on wages and prices, through tax incentives, to mere "jawboning," which means setting guidelines and relying on voluntary cooperation from the private sector in adhering to them.

Wage and price controls. The most obvious instrument for slowing the upward shift of the aggregate supply curve is direct controls over wages and prices. The rate of monetary expansion would be slowed gradually to validate an inflation rate that fell by, say, two percentage points each year. Wage and price controls would *force* that falling rate of inflation on the economy. Over three years the controls would force the rate down from, say, 10 to 8 to 6 to 4 percent, and the rate of monetary expansion would be slowed correspondingly. Once the target rate of inflation has been achieved and stabilized, the controls can be removed. If everyone then expects the new lower rate to persist, expectational and inertial inflation will have been broken without the recession required by the monetarists' policy that would use monetary restraint alone.

TIPs. Past experience of wage and price controls (see page 697) has made most economists and administrators very reluctant to resort to them. As a result, many Keynesians advocate new methods to achieve the same purpose. The most important are the so-called **tax-based incomes policies (TIPs).** They provide a tax incentive for management and labor to conform to government established wage and price guidelines. Increases in wages and prices in excess of the guideline rates would be heavily taxed, thereby making firms and unions reluctant to engage in inflation-producing behavior.

TIPs rely on tax incentives to secure voluntary conformity with the guidelines; wage and price controls try to force conformity by legal means.

Consider the neo-Keynesian scenario for using TIPs to slow a 10 percent inflation. Each year the Fed slows the rate of growth of the money supply so as to validate, say, 2 percent less inflation than last year at the same level of national income. Each year the government's guidelines are lowered to follow the Fed's monetary policy. The TIPs encourage conformity of wage and price setting with the guidelines so that the inflation rate falls year by year from, say, 10 to 8 to 6 to 4 percent without a reduction in national income.

If it could be initiated without significant cost, the Keynesian package would be superior to that of the monetarists because it avoids the fall in output and the corresponding rise in unemployment. Critics argue, however, that the TIPs would prove to be little different from wage and price controls. They would be a nightmare to design, costly to administer, ineffectual in restraining wages and prices, and they would have similar distorting effects on the economy.

Post-Keynesian Cures

A third position is that of the post-Keynesians. They contend that the upward shift in the aggregate supply curve is caused by wage cost-push, price-push, and various structural rigidities. Unlike inertia and expectations, these

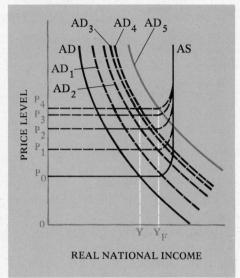

FIGURE 38-3
The Neo-Keynesian Cure for Inflation

When inflation is being generated by aggregate supply shifts, a restrictive monetary policy combined with an incomes policy might halt the inflation without lowering output. An ongoing expectational inflation is met by only a gradual reduction in the rate of monetary expansion so that aggregate demand shifts from AD to AD_1 to AD_2 to AD_3 and finally comes to a halt at AD_4. At the same time, incomes policies slow the upward shift in aggregate supply by direct order (wage and price controls) or by incentives (TIPs) so that it shifts upward from $P_0 AS$ to $P_1 AS$, $P_2 AS$, $P_3 AS$, and comes to a halt at $P_4 AS$. The inflation is slowed and finally halted with no reduction in output.

Once expectations have been stabilized, aggregate demand can be expanded cautiously to AD_5, taking the economy back to full employment at the stable price level P_4.

causes will not go away merely because the inflation rate is forced to a low level for a year or two. Instead, inflationary pressure will always be present when the economy is anywhere near full employment. Post-Keynesians thus advocate *permanent* wage and price controls, or TIPs, as the only way to achieve anything approaching full employment and relatively stable prices.

At the moment there is little evidence to support the post-Keynesian view of the causes

Supply-side Economics

Starting toward the end of the 1970s, a new cry was frequently heard in popular discussion and in serious debate: supply-side economics. Supply-side economics is not new. Indeed, it's what Adam Smith's *Wealth of Nations* was all about. In its modern version, like many general but catchy terms, it sometimes means all things to all people. Here are some of the things it means to some people.

1. In explaining inflation and stagflation, it means an emphasis on the aggregate supply curve. As we have seen at length in these chapters, "supply-side shocks" are now a major part of most people's explanation of what happened in the 1970s.
2. In control of inflation, it means an emphasis on pushing the aggregate supply curve outward rather than reining the aggregate demand curve inward. This proposition concerns short-run stabilization policy.
3. In concern over living standards, it means an emphasis on pushing the aggregate supply curve out to the right rather than on manipulating aggregate demand. The motto here might be, "It is more important to increase full-employment national income than to try to reduce the temporary deviations from it that the market economy produces." This proposition concerns long-run growth policy.

Point 1 is a diagnosis of our past ills. But both 2 and 3 are policy prescriptions to improve things in the future. Both require pushing the aggregate supply curve outward in the manner shown in Figure 37-1 on page 693. The key idea is to provide the appropriate *incentives* for the private sector to do the job. How might this be done?

a. *By encouraging saving.* Keynes emphasized the negative effect of saving on aggregate demand. Supply-side economics emphasizes its positive effect—that of encouraging investment in order to increase productive capacity and hence full-employment national income.
b. *By encouraging labor force participation.* Reducing taxes, so goes the argument, will make people work more and by increasing the labor supply, increase full-employment output.
c. *By encouraging risk taking.* Cutting taxes and regulations will make businesses more willing to invest and to innovate. Risking capital to introduce new products and new methods is, historically, one of the great mechanisms for economic growth. If we can encourage more of it, full-employment national income will grow faster.
d. *By encouraging labor mobility.* Stop lavish welfare schemes that encourage the unemployed to stay in depressed regions. In the absence of state support, they would be forced to move to regions where they could earn their living productively.

of inflation. Therefore, their extreme solution, which would take the United States significantly closer to having a command economy, does not seem to many economists to be appropriate.

Post-Keynesians also stress the political causes of inflation. They study political circumstances that lead governments to adopt policies that either cause or validate inflations. They argue, for example, that whenever a democratic government persistently follows inflationary policies, it is because a coalition of groups believes that, whatever the public rhetoric, it is actually *e. By getting people back to producing goods rather than tax loopholes.* Millions of high-powered lawyers, accountants, and entrepreneurs are currently employed doing nothing other than finding loopholes to protect high-income individuals and firms from heavy tax liabilities. Eliminate high marginal tax rates and it wouldn't be worthwhile for the rich to pay for these people's expensive services and to devote so much of their time to their tax affairs. These resources will then be freed to produce goods and services that contribute to people's want satisfaction.

The number of possible proposals is myriad. They all have the intended effect of increasing full-employment income by increasing the supplies of capital or of labor, or by increasing the rate of technical change.

There is little doubt that many current policies and practices do have the alleged output-restricting effects, so that some changes in policy would do some of the things alleged by supply-side economics. If even a small increase in the growth rate of full-employment income could be achieved, the long-term effects on living standards would be enormous (as Table 43-1 on page 805 and its caption illustrate).

Thus policy 3 is a viable objective. Increasing the growth rate of full employment *will* raise living standards.

The second objective, however, is more debatable. It would, for example, be an enormous achievement to raise the growth rate by $\frac{1}{2}$ a percentage point — and a generation or two down the line the effect on the *level* of income would be large. But two years down the line it is only 1 percent more full-employment output. In the face of an inflationary gap of, say, 10 percent (aggregate demand is 10 percent greater than full-employment aggregate supply at current prices) increasing aggregate supply by 1 percent is not going to do much to the inflation rate. Even the conservative economist Herbert Stein of the *American Enterprise Institute,* who could be expected to be sympathetic to many supply-side measures, warned in early 1980:

Despite the tone of much of the current argument, the propositions of supply-side economics are not matters of ideology or principle. They are matters of arithmetic. So far one must say that the arithmetic of any of the "newer" propositions is highly doubtful. Supply-side economics may yet prove to be the irritant which, like the grain of sand in the oyster shell, produces a pearl of new economic wisdom. But up to this point the pearl has not appeared.*

Whether or not its potential for controlling inflation is overstated, there is no doubt that supply effects are important, and that supply-side economics in one form or another is here to stay.

* *The AEI Economist,* April 1980, published by *American Enterprise Institute.*

gaining from inflation. Thus post-Keynesians predict that inflation will not be controlled until these political circumstances are changed. Some people believe that, in looking for the political roots of inflation, post-Keynesians are on stronger ground than when they present their wage cost-push and price-push theory of the immediate economic causes of inflation.

Some ideas on the control of inflation that cut across the monetarist and Keynesian camps are covered by the term *supply-side economics.* These are briefly discussed in the box.

Controversies over Stabilization Policy

Stabilization policy, as we have seen, involves the use of monetary and fiscal policy to shift the aggregate demand and expenditure functions in order to avoid the extremes of large inflationary and deflationary gaps. Differences between monetarists and neo-Keynesians on this subject have narrowed somewhat over the past 15 years, yet significant differences remain.

CAUSES OF CYCLICAL FLUCTUATIONS

Monetarist Views

Monetarists believe that monetary causes are the major source of serious fluctuations in national income.[3] The modern interpretation of business cycles as having mainly monetary causes relies heavily on the evidence advanced by Milton Friedman and Anna Schwartz in their monumental *A Monetary History of the United States, 1867–1960*. They establish a strong correlation between changes in the money supply and changes in the level of business activity. Major recessions are found to be associated with absolute declines in the money supply, and minor recessions with the slowing of the rate of increase in the money supply below its long-term trend.

The correlation between changes in the money supply and changes in the level of business activity is now accepted by virtually all economists. But there is controversy over how this is to be interpreted; do changes in the money supply cause changes in the level of business activity, or vice versa?

Friedman and Schwartz maintain that changes

[3] The view that fluctuations often have monetary causes is not new. The English economist R. G. Hawtrey, the Austrian Nobel laureate F. A. von Hayek, the Swedish economist Knut Wicksell are prominent among those who earlier gave monetary factors an important role in their explanations of the turning points in cycles and/or the tendency for expansions and contractions, once begun, to become cumulative and self-reinforcing. Modern monetarists carry on this tradition.

in the money supply cause changes in business activity. They argue, for example, that the severity of the Great Depression was due to a major contraction in the money supply. Their analysis runs along the following lines.

The stock market crash of 1929, and other factors associated with a moderate downswing in business activity during the late 1920s, led to a reduction in the public's desire to hold demand deposits and an increase in its desire for cash. The banking system could not meet this increased demand for liquidity without help from the Federal Reserve System.[4] The Fed had been set up to provide just such emergency assistance to basically sound banks that were unable to meet sudden demands by their depositors to withdraw cash. However, the Fed refused to extend the necessary help, and successive waves of bank failures followed as a direct result. During each wave, literally hundreds of banks failed, ruining many depositors and thereby making an already severe depression even worse. In the last half of 1931, almost 2,000 American banks were forced to suspend operations! One consequence of this was a sharp drop in the money supply; by 1933 the money supply was 35 percent below the level of 1929.

For monetarists, fluctuations in the money supply cause fluctuations in national income.

Neo-Keynesian Views

The neo-Keynesians' view on the causes of cyclical fluctuations in the economy has two parts. First, it emphasizes variations in investment as a cause of business cycles and stresses nonmonetary causes of such variations. Many pre-Keynesian economists also took this view.[5]

[4] As we saw in Chapter 33, banks are never able to meet from their own reserves a sudden demand to withdraw currency on the part of a large fraction of their depositors. Their reserves are always inadequate to meet such a demand.

[5] Like the monetarists, the neo-Keynesians are modern advocates of views that have a long history. The great Austrian (and later American) economist Joseph Schumpeter stressed such explanations early in the present century. The Swedish economist Wicksell and the German Speithoff both stressed this aspect of economic fluctuations before the emergence of the Keynesian school of thought.

Second, neo-Keynesians believe that the economy lacks natural corrective mechanisms that will always force it easily and quickly back to full employment. They believe that the economy may settle into an *underemployment equilibrium,* where it may stay for a long time unless it is forced out by an active stabilization policy. If investment opportunities seem unattractive, the equilibrium national income (where aggregate desired expenditure equals income) may leave a large GNP gap. Monetarists charge that there are strong forces, omitted from the Keynesian model, that will drive income back to its full-employment level.[6] Keynesians respond that these forces are weak or nonexistent (and are thus omitted from their model of the determination of national income).[7]

Neo-Keynesians reject what they regard as the extreme monetarist view that only money matters in explaining cyclical fluctuations. Many believe that both monetary and nonmonetary forces are important in explaining the behavior of the economy. Although they accept serious monetary mismanagement as one potential source of economic fluctuations, they do not believe that it is the only, or even the major source of such fluctuations. Thus they deny the monetary interpretation of business cycle history given by Friedman and Schwartz.

As for the 1930s, neo-Keynesians accept the argument that the Fed's behavior was perverse. However, they argue that the cyclical behavior of investment and consumption expenditure was the major cause of the Great Depression. In support of this view, they point out that in Canada, where the central bank came to the aid of the banking system, bank failures were trivial during the Great Depression, and as a consequence the money supply did *not* shrink drastically as it did in the United States. In spite of these markedly different monetary histories, the behavior of the GNP gap, investment expenditure, and unemployment was very similar in the United States and Canada.

Neo-Keynesians accept the correlation between changes in the money supply and changes in the level of economic activity, but their explanation reverses the causality suggested by the monetarists: the neo-Keynesians argue that changes in the level of economic activity tend to cause changes in the money supply. They offer several reasons for this, but only the most important need be mentioned.

Neo-Keynesians point out that from 1945 to the early 1970s most central banks tended to stabilize interest rates as the target variable of monetary policy. To do this they had to increase the money supply during upswings in the business cycle and decrease it during downswings. This created the positive correlation on which the monetarists rely. The central bank followed this monetary policy when an expansion got under way because the demand for money tended to increase, and when there was no increase in the money supply, interest rates would rise. The central bank might prevent this rise in interest rates (by buying bonds offered for sale at current prices), but in so doing it would increase banks' reserves and thereby inject new money into the economy. Similarly, in a cyclical contraction interest rates would tend to fall unless the central bank stepped in and sold bonds to keep interest rates up. And if it did so, this would decrease the money supply.

For neo-Keynesians, fluctuations in national income cause fluctuations in the money supply.

This argument applies to relatively mild cyclical swings; most neo-Keynesians agree that major changes in the money supply induced by the Fed can be a cause of changes in national income.

[6] The two main forces are a fall in the rate of interest, which encourages investment, and a fall in the price level, which encourages consumption by the so-called Pigou effect.

[7] Keynesians believe that the interest elasticity of investment is very low, especially in recessions, when the ability to sell goods at all over the next few years is the main determinant of investment. They also point to evidence that the price level does not fall significantly, so whatever the effects of a fall might be, they are not felt in practice.

Underemployment Equilibrium

Many pre-Keynesian economists took the view that fluctuations in investment expenditure were a major cause of business cycles. However, there was an important difference between those economists and Keynes. The earlier economists might or might not have believed that government policy could shorten significantly a period of depression, but they would almost certainly have believed that in the absence of government intervention, recovery and boom would inevitably follow the period of depression.

What was new in Keynes' *General Theory* was the concept of underemployment equilibrium: the economy could come to rest with substantial unemployment and without significant forces operating to push it back to full employment. This was more than a theory of cyclical alternations of prosperity and depression; it was a theory of the possibility of permanent (or at least very long-lived) depression.

There was—and is—a great deal of controversy about the sense in which we can speak of underemployment *equilibrium*. Consider one of the simplest interpretations.

The short-term equilibrium of the economy occurs at the level of income where desired expenditure equals income. In the face of any change in desired expenditure, the economy will move fairly quickly to a new equilibrium level of national income. Once there, however, national income will remain constant if desired expenditure does not change. This may well be at a level of income below Y_F.

If the economy comes to rest in a state of underemployment equilibrium, there will in fact be forces at work tending to move it back to full employment, but in practice these forces will be so weak and so slow-acting that they can be ignored.*

Since forces tending to move the economy back to full employment probably exist, it might be more accurate to describe a state of underemployment as a state of *underemployment disequilibrium* that is slowly moving toward a full-employment equilibrium. But because these forces act very slowly, they are of little interest in the context of coping quickly with a major depression and its accompanying massive unemployment.

For all practical purposes, we may regard a situation where desired expenditure equals income at less than full-employment income as a short-run equilibrium that can be changed only by a further shift of the expenditure function. Those who, in the 1930s, were content to wait for long-run forces to produce full employment without government intervention could have been confronted with Keynes' famous words: "In the long run we are all dead."

Modern Keynesians might add that the Great Depression came to an abrupt end only after World War II forced the adoption of Keynesian remedies in the form of massive deficit-financed government expenditures. They might well conjecture that without these Keynesian remedies it could have taken another decade for full employment to be produced by the economy's natural forces. Keynes, of course, did not say that the economy would always settle in a position of underemployment equilibrium, only that it *could* settle there.

---

* In Keynes' theory these forces would have been set in motion by a fall in the real wage rate as prices fell more than wages. This would induce employers to hire more labor. Also, if the price level is flexible downward, the monetary adjustment mechanism will shift the aggregate expenditure function upward.

FIGURE 38-4
Monetarist and Neo-Keynesian Views on Interest Sensitivities

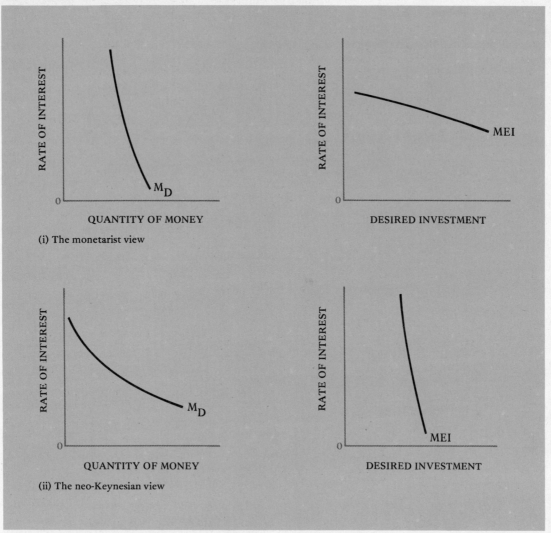

(i) The monetarist view

(ii) The neo-Keynesian view

Monetarists and neo-Keynesians disagree about the interest sensitivities of the demand for money and the marginal efficiency of investment functions. M_D is the demand for money and *MEI* is the marginal efficiency of investment function that relates investment expenditure to the rate of interest. Monetarists hold that the demand for money does not respond much to changes in the rate of interest, while investment expenditure is very sensitive to such changes. Neo-Keynesians hold that the demand for money is very sensitive to changes in interest rates, while investment expenditure is insensitive to such changes.

CONTROL OF CYCLICAL FLUCTUATIONS: MONETARY VERSUS FISCAL POLICY[8]

Monetarists believe that national income can be influenced strongly by monetary policy and only

weakly by fiscal policy. Keynesians believe that fiscal policy may be more potent than monetary policy. The difference in views turns partly on the slopes of two relations that both groups agree do exist. The different views are illustrated in Figure 38-4.

[8] This section may be omitted without loss of continuity.

FIGURE 38-5
Monetarist and Neo-Keynesian Views on Monetary Policy

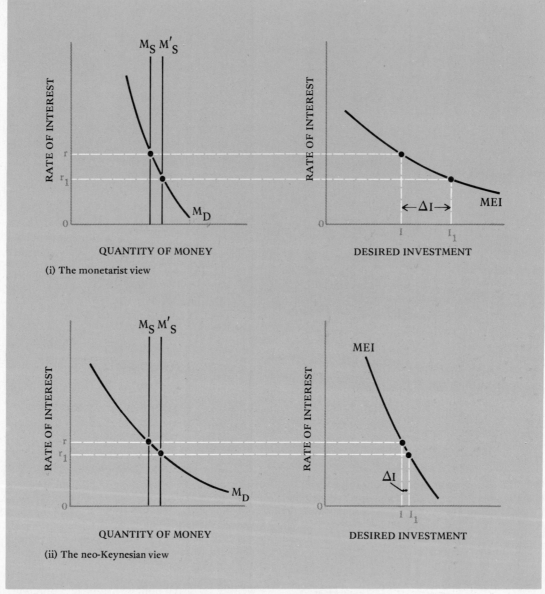

(i) The monetarist view

(ii) The neo-Keynesian view

Monetarist assumptions make monetary policy very effective; neo-Keynesian assumptions make it relatively ineffective. Initially the economy is in equilibrium with an interest rate of r and investment expenditure of I. In both parts the expansionary monetary policy of the Fed shifts the money supply to M'_S. The

rate of interest falls to r_1, and this causes an increase in investment expenditure of ΔI (from I to I_1).

(i) In the monetarist view, ΔI is large. Monetary policy is effective.

(ii) In the neo-Keynesian view, ΔI is small. Monetary policy is ineffective.

The Effect of Changes in the Money Supply

The demand for money. The first relation is the demand for money. Monetarists believe it is insensitive to interest rates; Keynesians think it is sensitive to interest rates because money is a near substitute for a whole range of short-term, interest-earning assets.

An expansionary monetary policy creates an excess supply of money. Firms and households seek to buy bonds with their surplus money, and this lowers the rate of interest. The rate falls until everyone is prepared to hold the increased supply of money. If the monetarists are right, this will require a large fall in the interest rate; if the Keynesians are right, there need be only a small fall.

A contractionary monetary policy creates excess demand by lowering the supply of money. Firms and households seek to restore their money balances by selling bonds, and the rate of interest rises until everyone is satisfied to hold only the reduced money supply. If the monetarists are right, this will require a large rise in the interest rate; if the Keynesians are right, there need be only a small rise.

Investment expenditure. The second relation is the marginal efficiency of investment function. A rise in the rate of interest lowers investment expenditure, and a fall in the rate of interest raises it. Monetarists hold that investment expenditure is highly sensitive to interest rates. Keynesians believe that it is influenced mainly by sales, profits, and expectations and that it does not respond greatly to the rate of interest, at least over the short term.

Implications for the Effectiveness of Fiscal and Monetary Policy

The shapes just discussed have direct implications for the effectiveness of monetary policy, as illustrated in Figure 38-5.

According to the monetarists, changes in the money supply cause large changes in interest rates that in turn cause large changes in expenditure. According to the Keynesians, changes in the money supply cause small changes in interest rates that in turn cause small or negligible changes in expenditure.

The same assumptions about sensitivities to interest rates cause monetarists and Keynesians to disagree over the potency of fiscal policy, as illustrated in Figure 38-6. Consider an increase in government expenditure. This raises national income and creates excess demand for money because of a rise in the demand for transactions balances. The rate of interest rises until everyone is content to hold the existing stock of money. The rise in the interest rate lowers private investment expenditure. (A parallel analysis applies to a decline in government expenditure.)

According to the monetarists, changes in government expenditure will induce large changes in interest rates that in turn cause large offsetting changes in private investment expenditure, leaving a small net effect on aggregate demand. According to the neo-Keynesians, changes in government expenditure cause only small changes in interest rates that in turn cause small or negligible offsetting changes in investment expenditure.

The tendency just discussed is called the **crowding out effect.** It may be defined as the offsetting reduction in private investment that follows an expansionary fiscal policy due to a rise in interest rates. Monetarists believe the crowding out effect is large, so that an increase in government expenditure will crowd out almost as much private expenditure and thus have only a small net expansionary effect on income. Keynesians believe the crowding out effect is small when the economy is suffering from a substantial GNP gap, which is when one would wish to use an expansionary fiscal policy. In this case only a small part of any rise in government expenditure will be offset by a fall in private expenditure. Thus there will be a large net increase in aggregate expenditure and hence a large increase in equilibrium national income.

FIGURE 38-6
Monetarist and Neo-Keynesian Views on Fiscal Policy

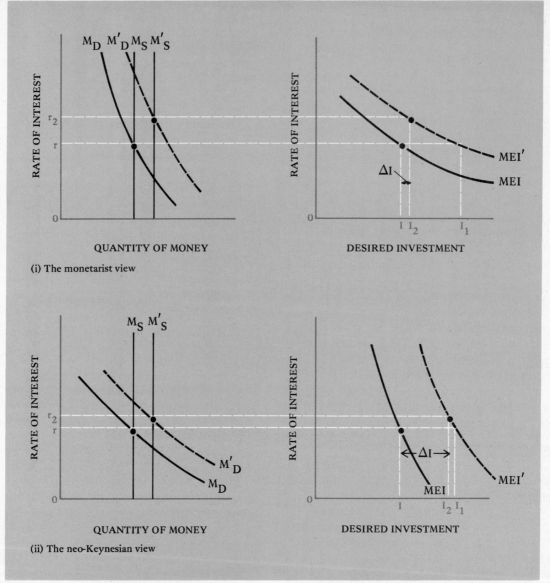

(i) The monetarist view

(ii) The neo-Keynesian view

Neo-Keynesian assumptions make fiscal policy very effective; monetarist assumptions make it relatively ineffective. Initially the economy is in equilibrium with an interest rate of r and investment expenditure of I. Suppose an expansionary fiscal policy increases aggregate demand. The effect on national income is given by the multiplier formula (see page 531) if the interest rate remains at r. But when expenditure rises, the transactions demand for money rises. This shifts M_D to M'_D, and leads to an increase in the rate of interest to r_2. The rise in interest rates leads to a reduction in desired investment expenditure from I_1 to I_2. This "crowding out" of private investment expenditure, caused by a rise in interest rates brought about by the expansionary fiscal policy, reduces the multiplier because the decline in investment partially offsets the rise in government expenditure.

(i) In the monetarist world, the crowding out effect is large so ΔI is small. Fiscal policy is ineffective.

(ii) In the neo-Keynesian world, the crowding out effect is small so ΔI is large. Fiscal policy is effective.

Policy Preferences

When policy intervention is called for, monetarists have a strong preference for monetary policy. Keynesians tend to be less strong in their preferences. They believe that monetary policy can influence national income through its effects on interest rates. Thus they tend to deny that there is serious conflict between monetary and fiscal policies; they see the policies as complements to each other.

Neo-Keynesians tend to place heavier emphasis on fiscal policy. They do this because they believe that monetary policy may prove weak in major depressions, when it is particularly important to have some policy intervention. In addition, they are disturbed by the uneven effects of monetary policy. A restrictive monetary policy, for example, tends to fall particularly heavily on potential home owners, small businesses, and rapidly expanding firms specializing in new products.

When monetary restraints are applied, home building tends to be seriously affected because interest costs are a major part of the total expense of buying a house. Thus a restrictive monetary policy hits at potential home owners, particularly those with modest means who would have the most difficulty in raising a mortgage.

Small firms usually have more trouble getting credit than do large firms. It can be argued that the continual use of monetary policy reinforces the already strong tendency for large firms to dominate the economy. The reason is that new products are often manufactured by small, new, rapidly expanding firms. Since the costs of production must be met before goods are sold, rapidly expanding firms usually find themselves in constant need of credit to meet the gap between paying their costs and receiving money from the sale of their goods. New firms are the source of much economic growth, yet they are the firms that are hardest hit, and sometimes driven into insolvency, by restrictive monetary policies that make it impossible for them to obtain the credit they need.

For all these reasons, neo-Keynesians call for an active stabilization policy with fiscal policy playing a major role and monetary policy playing, at most, a supporting part.

The Micro Foundations of Monetarism and Neo-Keynesianism[9]

Keynes made a vast advance in our study of the overall behavior of the economy by concentrating on a few aggregated functions such as consumption and investment. For a long time Keynesian economics seemed to work well both in explaining the overall behavior of the economy and in suggesting successful policies for controlling inflation and unemployment. As long as it worked reasonably well, few were interested in just how it worked. Then, as control of the economy by means of traditional fiscal and monetary tools seemed to become more and more difficult during the late 1960s and the 1970s, the question of the foundations of the Keynesian theory became more pressing. This concern took the form of asking: What behavior in individual markets for products and factors of production is implied by the Keynesian aggregate relationships? The question involves what are called the *micro foundations* or *micro underpinnings* of macro models.

In the late 1960s and early 1970s the monetarist model made its serious challenge as an alternative model for understanding the macro behavior of the economy and predicting appropriate policies. The explanations of observed events and the prediction of policies for changing them that were suggested by the monetarist model were very different from those of the Keynesian model.

The micro underpinnings are at the heart of the debate between monetarism and neo-Keynesianism. Consequently they are at the frontier of much modern research. The issues are

[9] This section (to page 726) may be omitted without loss of continuity.

important, but they are also difficult; we need to be aware of them in broad outline if not in detail.

ONE MONETARIST MICROECONOMIC MODEL

Many economists accept the main monetarist view that monetary forces are the most important cause acting on inflation and unemployment. These economists differ among themselves on many other matters concerning the behavior of the economy. Thus there is no single, accepted, monetarist microeconomic model of the economy. Many monetarists, however, follow the leads of Milton Friedman in his 1968 Presidential Address to the American Economics Association and of Professor Edmund Phelps in his classic attack on the theory of the stable Phillips curve, also published in 1968. These economists view the markets of the economy as competitive. They realize, of course, that perfect competition does not exist everywhere in the economy, but they believe that the forces of competition are strong—strong enough so that a model based on the theory of perfect competition will be closer to the real behavior of the economy than one based on the theory of oligopoly to which many neo-Keynesians appeal.

According to this prototype model, markets behave more or less as if they were perfectly competitive. In particular, prices and wages are flexible and they adjust to establish equilibrium at all times. When a competitive market is in equilibrium (see Chapter 5), the market is said to have *cleared*, which means that every purchaser has been able to buy all he or she wishes to buy and every seller has been able to sell all he or she wishes to sell at the going price.[10] When each and every market is in equilibrium, there is full employment of all resources. The prices that clear markets are called **market clearing prices.**

According to the monetarists, departure from full-employment equilibrium occurs mainly be-

cause people make mistakes. How does this happen? Assume that each of the economy's markets is in equilibrium; there is full employment, prices are stable, and the actual and expected rates of inflation are zero.

Now let the government increase the money supply at some constant rate, say 5 percent per year. People find themselves with unwanted money balances, which they seek to spend. For simplicity, assume that this leads to an increase in desired expenditure on all commodities: the demand for each commodity shifts to the right, and competitively determined prices rise. Individual decision makers see their selling prices go up and mistake the increase for a rise in their own relative price (because they expect the overall rate of inflation to be zero). Firms will produce more and workers will work more because both groups think they are getting an increased relative price for what they sell. Thus total output and employment rise.

Sooner or later both groups will realize that all prices are rising and that their own relative prices are in fact unchanged. Since relative prices determine behavior, and since relative prices are unchanged, output and employment will fall back to their initial level. The extra output and employment occurred only while people were being fooled; when they realized that all prices were rising at 5 percent, they reverted to their initial behavior. The only difference is that now the actual and expected rate of inflation is 5 percent.

Now assume that the government wishes to continue to have the extra output and employment that was achieved while people were being fooled. To do this, it doubles the rate of increase in the money supply. This increases demand, and prices begin to rise by 10 percent. As long as people expect the overall rate of inflation to be 5 percent, they will make the same mistake they made before. Thinking their own relative price has risen by 5 percent, workers will work harder and firms will produce more. Thus the extra output and employment will be restored, but only because everyone is again being fooled.

Sooner or later people will see that all prices are rising by 10 percent and realize that their

---

[10] Competitive markets clear only at the equilibrium price. At any other price there are either unsatisfied would-be purchasers (excess demand) or unsatisfied would-be sellers (excess supply).

own relative price has never changed. Their behavior will then revert to what it was originally. The extra output and employment is lost once more, and now the actual and expected inflation rate is 10 percent. To achieve the higher output and employment again, the government must now raise the rate of monetary expansion to 15 percent!

If the government tries to maintain the position of higher output, it will have to expand the money supply ever faster to validate an *accelerating* inflation rate. If it does not do so, people will soon realize that relative prices are not changing, and their behavior will revert to what it was originally.

Now return to the initial equilibrium with no monetary expansion and stable prices. Then let the government reduce the money supply at a constant rate so that demand falls off. Prices begin to fall. Firms and workers mistakenly think their own relative prices are falling; firms voluntarily produce less, and laborers voluntarily work less. Output falls and a deflation occurs. Sooner or later people will notice that *all* prices are falling and realize that they have been fooled—their relative price has not changed. Output and employment revert to their original levels, but now the actual and expected rate of "inflation" is −5 percent.

To restore the cut in output and employment, the rate of monetary contraction must be raised to 10 percent. Once again people will be fooled for a while, workers will work less and firms produce less, and sooner or later they will discover the real situation and their behavior will revert to what it was—only now the actual and expected rate of "inflation" is −10 percent!

According to the monetarist theory of the economy, deviations from full employment occur only because people make mistakes that cause markets to clear at more or less than full-employment output. People are not prevented from selling as many commodities or as much labor as they wish; the contraction or expansion in output is *voluntary.*

The major conclusion following from this part of the model is that there is no long-term trade-off between inflation and national income. An attempt to hold income above its full-employment level will lead not to a constant rate of inflation, but to a continuously accelerating inflation. Most economists now accept one version or another of this view that inflation will tend to accelerate if income is held permanently below its full employment level. Most neo-Keynesians do not accept, however, that increases in output above Y_F occur only because workers and firms make mistakes.

The other part of the model is more contentious. The downward flexibility of prices in the competitive model leads to the prediction that as long as national income is below its full-employment level the price level should *fall* at an ever-accelerating rate. Neo-Keynesians say that the observed downward inflexibility of the price level totally refutes this view even as a prototype explanation. Neo-Keynesians also reject the prediction that the main cause of GNP gaps is voluntary reductions in employment and output due to errors in reading the signals provided by the price system.

The Theory of Rational Expectations

This model has recently been augmented by the addition of the theory of *rational expectations,* first discussed in Chapter 36. According to this theory, people learn fairly quickly from their mistakes; while random errors can be made, systematic and persistent errors are not made.

Not all monetarists accept the full theory of rational expectations. For those who do, however, the contrast with the neo-Keynesians is extreme. Not only is there no long-term trade-off between output and employment on the one hand and inflation on the other (with which many neo-Keynesians would agree), but there is no chance for fiscal or monetary policy to stabilize the economy in the face of small or large inflationary or deflationary gaps. Government policy can do harm but cannot do good (except by random chance). Thus even in the face of major recessions, laissez-faire is the best stabilization policy conceivable. Let us see how this result comes about.

The theory says that people learn and will alter their behavior when they find they are making systematic mistakes. Suppose, for example, you always thought that next year's inflation rate would be the same as this year's rate but in fact it always increased by two percentage points over what it was last year. When this year's rate was 2 percent, you expected next year's rate to be 2 percent, but it would turn out to be 4 percent. You then expected the following year's rate to be 4 percent, but it would turn out to be 6 percent. And so it went, with you constantly under-predicting the rate by 2 percent. According to the theory of rational expectations, you would soon notice this and revise your expectations to remove the error. You would then look for the rate to rise by two points each year, and as long as the pattern continued, your expectations would be right on target.

According to the theory of rational expectations, people do not make persistent, systematic errors in predicting the overall inflation rate; however, they may make unsystematic errors.

What are the implications of combining the monetarist micro foundations with the theory of rational expectations? (1) According to the monetarists' micro foundations, deviations from full employment occur only because of errors in predicting the price level (which allows workers and firms to mistake changes in the price level for changes in relative prices). (2) According to the theory of rational expectations, errors in predicting the price level are only random. (3) It follows from (1) and (2) that the economy's deviations from full employment must be random. (4) It follows from (3) that there is no room for systematic stabilization policy; although governments can identify and offset systematic deviations from full employment, it is the essence of random fluctuations that they cannot be predicted well enough to be offset by planned stabilization policy.

The strongest monetarist attack on stabilization policy has two parts. The first is a model of an economy where deviations from full employment occur because of errors. The second is a theory of
people's expectations that predicts that persistent systematic errors — and hence persistent systematic deviations from full employment — will not occur.

According to this view there is no room for active government policy to stabilize the economy. The causes of fluctuations are random (although because of long lags the behavior of the economy may be systematically cyclical). It is in the nature of random fluctuations that they cannot be foreseen and offset. Thus there is no room for stabilization policy to reduce the fluctuations in the economy by offsetting the disturbances that emanate from the private sector.

THE NEO-KEYNESIAN MICRO FOUNDATIONS

The neo-Keynesian micro foundations emphasize the oligopolistic nature of the economy. Large firms are seen as price setters, not price takers. Their short-run cost curves tend to be fairly flat, and they set prices by adding a relatively inflexible markup to their costs.[11] They then sell what they can at the going price. This is not a model of market clearing; firms will usually be able and willing to sell more than their current sales at the going price. Cyclical fluctuations in aggregate demand cause cyclical fluctuations in the demand for each firm's products, which in turn cause individual firms to make cyclical variations in *output and employment* rather than in *price*.

While in the monetarist model fluctuations in aggregate demand have their impact mainly on prices, in the neo-Keynesian model their main impact is on output and employment.

The same is true for labor markets in the neo-Keynesian model. Wages are set with the price level and productivity in view, but they are relatively insensitive to short-term cyclical fluctuations in demand.

---

[11] Complete cyclical inflexibility of markup is not necessary. What matters is that firms do not adjust prices continually so that they are always unwilling to sell further units at the same price.

Let us see how this short-term wage inflexibility may stem from rational behavior on the part of workers. If wage rates fluctuate to clear labor markets, wages will fluctuate over the cycle. *All* workers will then bear the uncertainty associated with the cyclical fluctuations in wages. However, if wages are set in response to long-term considerations but do not vary cyclically so as to clear labor markets, the cyclical fluctuations in demand will cause employment to fluctuate. Since much hiring and firing is done by seniority, employment fluctuations are borne by the 10 or 20 percent of workers who are least senior. The majority of workers will then have little uncertainty in the face of cyclical fluctuations in demand, all the uncertainty having been placed on the *minority* with low seniority. Thus contracts that fix wages over the cycle and allow employment to vary may be preferable to the majority of workers over contracts that allow wages to vary in order to clear the labor market continually and thus prevent unemployment.[12]

In the Keynesian microeconomic view of the world, the economy does not have a unique short-term equilibrium. Because markets do not clear (firms would like to sell more and some workers would work more at current prices), fluctuations in aggregate demand cause output and employment (rather than prices) to fluctuate in the short term.

The Keynesian micro model leaves room for systematic disturbances that cause prolonged deflationary or inflationary gaps. Because of this, there is room for stabilization policy to offset at least those GNP gaps that are large and persistent. Such policies seek to alter aggregate demand using both fiscal and monetary tools.

DIFFERENCES IN THE TWO MODELS

There are many differences in the micro behavior implied by the two models. Let us consider two of them.

[12] Such contracts may be acceptable even to the least senior employees, who know that they bear the uncertainty early in life but realize that when they move up the seniority ladder they will be relatively secure against normal cyclical fluctuations in employment.

Voluntary Versus Involuntary Unemployment

In the monetarist model, all unemployment and output below capacity is voluntary. Workers decide to be unemployed and firms decide to produce less than capacity output as a result of errors they make in predicting the general price level (and therefore the relative price of what they sell).

In the Keynesian model, prices and wages do not fluctuate so as to clear markets. Unemployment and production below capacity is involuntary in the sense that unemployed workers would like jobs at the going wage rate but cannot find them, and firms would like to sell more at going prices but customers are not forthcoming.

Response to Errors Versus Response to Correctly Understood Signals

In the monetarist model, deviations from full-employment income occur only when the price level is being mistakenly predicted. In boom conditions, people are on average underpredicting the price level and consequently mistaking rises in their own money prices for rises in their relative prices. In recessionary conditions, people are overpredicting the price level and thus mistaking reductions in their own money prices for reductions in their relative prices.

In the Keynesian model, deviations from full employment do not imply errors, one way or the other, in predicting the price level. Labor groups and firms set their money prices with longer-run considerations in mind and then sell all they can sell at the going price as demand varies over the cycle.

Current Debate

Major current debate centers around these two prototype models and some of their subtler offshoots. Much of our view on how the economy behaves both at the micro and at the macro level will be influenced by the progress of the debate. So will our views on the place of fiscal and monetary policy as possible measures for alleviating inflationary and deflationary gaps.

How Much Unemployment at Full Employment?

Another example of the current interest in microeconomic underpinnings of macro concepts is the concern over the unemployment that occurs at "full employment." The uncritical macroeconomic approach just *defines* that amount of unemployment as "full employment" and stops worrying about it. But why is it that amount and not a higher or a lower amount? What could be done to change it?

Let us see how this issue arises in a macro model. Everyone, including those who maintain that all recent inflations have been cost-push inflations, agrees that demand inflations can occur. Thus they agree that national income cannot be held above Y_F indefinitely without causing inflation. The goal of stable prices requires that the maximum target for national income be set at Y_F.

The amount of unemployment occurring at Y_F is often called the natural rate of unemployment, a term that is misleading to the extent that it implies that the unemployment is unavoidable.

Look again at Figures 36-1 and 36-2 on pages 674 and 675. There is evidence that the natural rate of unemployment has been rising in many countries since the late 1960s. Even if it is not rising, it is still disturbingly high; when the overall level of unemployment is judged to be at its "natural" rate, some groups will be suffering unemployment rates of 20 to 30 percent! If these unsatisfactory performances in individual labor markets are to be changed, even pure demand-pull inflation theorists will have to find instruments other than aggregate demand stimulation to lower unemployment levels.

Raising aggregate demand will cure unemployment only if there are unemployed supplies of *all* resources ready to work when there is demand for their potential outputs. If firms do not have unused productive capacity, unemployed labor

will not be put to work merely because people have more money to spend.

Demand stimulation can cure deficient-demand unemployment, but it does not provide the major cure for structural unemployment.

Economic theory predicts that to the extent that high unemployment is structural, an attempt to cure it by stimulating aggregate demand will only cause inflation without reducing unemployment. The best that aggregate demand stimulation can do is to raise national income to its full-capacity level, that is, make Y equal to Y_F. It cannot lower the amount of unemployment that is associated with Y_F, that is, frictional and structural unemployment.

An attempt to arrest rising structural unemployment by increasing aggregate demand will lead only to an inflation accompanying the rising level of unemployment.

There is nothing inevitable about the unemployment that occurs at full-employment income. It has frictional and structural causes; it can be reduced by measures to speed up the reallocation of labor among geographical regions, skill categories, industries, and occupations.

THE COMPOSITION OF MACRO VARIABLES

We have seen that macroeconomic policy is concerned with the behavior of key averages and aggregates such as the average level of all prices and the overall level of unemployment. We have also seen that current research is looking at the micro underpinnings of many assumed macro relations. In fact, we care about more than just the macro averages and aggregates—we also care about their composition.

Consider unemployment once again. We worry about more than just the country's overall rate of unemployment. Is the overall rate of unemployment made up of very unequal rates of unemployment, such as those among industries, occupations, or areas? Or is it made up of rates that are very similar across all classifications? We

Structural Unemployment

Structural unemployment relates to growth and change in the economy. These factors can cause dramatic changes in the structure of output over time. But the changes in employment may be even more dramatic. As long as an industry's income elasticity of demand exceeds zero (i.e., as long as the commodity is not an inferior good), output will rise as economic growth proceeds. However, employment will not increase unless demand expands *faster than output per hour of labor*. An industry in which productivity is growing at 3 percent per year while demand is growing at 2 percent per year will find its output expanding but its employment contracting.

The displaced worker who sees that change (or growth) has destroyed his or her job is likely to conclude that growth destroys jobs in general and thereby creates unemployment in the economy. But this is not the case when workers let go in one sector of the economy find employment in another. Relatively few people remain permanently unemployed when they lose a job. Thus the genuine fear should be about the sometimes very heavy short-term costs of moving from one job to another, not about the possibility of there being no jobs at all. Of course, movements of labor may be both slow and costly.

The costs of transitional unemployment are borne unequally by members of society. To those with heavy investments in education and experience in particular occupations, the cost can be enormous. A man of 45 or 50 whose skills are special to a declining industry may, should he lose his job, find the market value of his services cut drastically. Just as the machine that was built to produce a product no one now wants is worthless, so the human capital invested in redundant skills is worthless.

Furthermore, when the declining industry is a major part of the economy of a particular geographical area, the entire area may be declining, and all its residents may suffer because of the decline in total demand for goods and services in the area. Consequently, an unemployed man who wishes to move to an area where jobs are plentiful may be unable to sell his house for anything near what it would cost to buy a house in a growing area. Thus he will not be in a position to buy a comparable house in a new area. The costs of growth and change fall heavily on a small section of the society, and although minor in the aggregate, they are serious to those who bear them.

Every major innovation and every major depression since the Industrial Revolution has rekindled the fear of steadily shrinking employment opportunities. Two pieces of evidence are unmistakable: (1) in all growing Western economies over the last century, lapses from full employment have been temporary; and (2) there has been no long-term tendency for average levels of unemployment to rise over the decades in spite of prolonged periods of sustained growth.

No doubt in today's world the demand for unskilled labor has been shrinking. The theory of competitive price determination predicts that this should lead to a substantial drop in the wages earned by the unskilled. However, we know that there is downward rigidity in wage rates because unions and minimum-wage laws prevent wages from falling nearly as much as they would in a wholly free market. Price theory predicts that this wage rigidity will cause unemployment.

If the labor supply were to respond to the probability of getting jobs, as well as to the wage rates earned by those who get jobs, we would expect a leftward shift in the supply curve for unskilled labor. A sophisticated version of the hypothesis of increasing structural unemployment, then, is that the demand curve for unskilled labor is shifting to the left faster than the supply curve, so that, at more or less constant wages, the gap between supply and demand has been increasing. Only time will tell whether there is validity in this modern version of the old structuralist nightmare.

The Progress of Economics

In this chapter we have discussed a number of current controversies about the behavior of the economy and the evidence relating to them that is now available. General acceptance of the view that the validity of economic theories should be tested by confronting their predictions with the mass of all available evidence is fairly new in economics. At this point you might reread the quotation from Lord William Beveridge given on the endpapers of this book. The controversy that Beveridge describes was the one that followed the 1936 publication of Keynes' *The General Theory of Employment, Interest and Money*. Keynes' work gave rise to the macroeconomics discussed in Part Eight and used so often in subsequent sections of this text. The question of how various parts of macroeconomic theory have been or could be tested has been raised at many points in this book: you might reflect on how very different this approach to the problem of accepting or rejecting theories is from the approach described by Beveridge.

Since 1936 great progress has been made in economics in relating theory to evidence. This progress has been reflected in the superior ability of governments to achieve their policy objectives. The financial aspects of World War II were far better handled than those of World War I. When President Roosevelt tried to reduce unemployment in the 1930s, his efforts were greatly hampered by the failure even of economists to realize the critical importance of budget deficits in raising aggregate demand and in injecting newly created money into the economy. When the Vietnam War forced the government to adopt expansive fiscal and monetary policies, economists had no trouble in predicting the outcome: more involvement abroad was obtained at the cost of heavy inflationary pressure at home.

Such important policy areas as the running of wars, the curing of major depressions, and coping with inflations are where the general tone of theories is tested, even if all their specific predictions are not. In some general sense, then, economic theories have always been subjected to empirical tests. When they were wildly at variance with the facts, the ensuing disaster could not but be noticed, and the theories were discarded or amended in the light of what was learned. Our current inability to avoid the twin problems of inflation and unemployment is a case in point—and it is leading to intensive new research.

The advances of economics in the last 40 years reflect economists' changed attitudes toward empirical observations. Today economists are much less likely to dismiss theories just because they do not like them and to refuse to abandon theories just because they do like them. Economists are more likely to try to base their theories as much as possible on empirical observation and to accept empirical relevance as the ultimate arbiter of the value of theories. As human beings, we may be anguished at the upsetting of a pet theory; as scientists, we should try to train ourselves to take pleasure in it because of the new knowledge gained thereby. It has been said that one of the great tragedies of science is the continual slaying of beautiful theories by ugly facts. It must always be remembered that when theory and fact come into conflict, it is theory, not fact, that must give way.

---

would assess a 6 percent overall unemployment rate in the United States very differently if we knew that it resulted from 6 percent unemployment in all industries, occupations, and geographical areas than if we knew that it resulted—as it actually does—from 25 percent unemployment in some industries, occupations, and areas and only 1 to 2 percent unemployment in others.

Levels of unemployment of 15 to 20 percent are very serious matters indeed. They imply levels of social and personal upheaval that just do not accompany unemployment rates of the order of 4 to 5 percent. The degree of regional and occupational inequality in unemployment rates in the United States has remained quite high throughout the postwar period. While policymakers could be satisfied that the overall rate in the United States was held at a very low level from 1945 until the mid 1970s, there was always reason to be disturbed at the high rates that persisted in some sectors.

Why did these localized high rates occur? How is it that in the midst of the "fully employed" society we had persistent pockets of poverty that would not respond to the cure of raising aggregate demand? Why does the market not adjust to bring about approximate equality in unemployment rates?

Does this market mechanism work at all? How fast does it work? Does the shifting pattern of economic growth continue to disturb markets so that the adjustment mechanism can never catch up? Would things be better if we interfered more in the market mechanism? What government policies would reduce labor-market disequilibria? Would things be better if we interfered less with the market mechanism? How much do restrictive practices and the resistance of unions to the introduction of new technologies contribute to structural unemployment?

A similar set of "disaggregated observations" could be produced for any macro variable, and each would provide a similar set of questions. But to state just one set is enough to show that we have now gone full circle and are back at the *micro*economics with which we began our study in Chapter 5.

There is no sharp distinction between microeconomics and macroeconomics. There are merely higher and lower levels of aggregation and a series of questions appropriate to each level of aggregation, with each series shading into the other.

Summary

1. The consensus is that the inflation of the late 1970s and early 1980s was caused by supply shocks due to expectational, inertial, and import cost-push inflation that was then validated by the Fed.

2. Some monetarists believe there is enough downward flexibility of money prices to allow a target rate of zero inflation. Other monetarists and most neo-Keynesians believe that the target rate must be in the range of 2 to 4 percent to allow for necessary price increases where money prices are relatively inflexible downward.

3. Almost everyone agrees that a necessary condition for the reduction of inflation is a reduction in the rate of monetary expansion.

4. Monetarists would stop inflation solely by reducing the rate of monetary expansion. Neo-Keynesians say this would lead to a large depression. They seek to avoid the loss of output associated with the monetarist cure by adding a policy of wage and price controls, or TIPs, that would slow the inflation rate directly and so avoid the temporary loss of output associated with the monetarist cure.

5. Post-Keynesians believe the inflation is caused by wage cost-push and price-push and thus that it can be controlled only by permanent wage and price controls. They believe all contemporary attempts to control inflation are doomed to failure.

6. Monetarists believe that cyclical fluctuations in the economy stem mainly from monetary causes. Neo-Keynesians tend to emphasize fluctuations in expenditure flows not themselves caused by monetary factors.

7. Monetarists tend to believe that stabilization policy is unnecessary. Neo-Keynesians believe it is essential. Where government intervention is called for, monetarists tend to believe that monetary policy has a large effect while fiscal policy has only a small effect. Neo-Keynesians hold the opposite view.

8. The monetarists' macro model is based on a microeconomic model of competitive, fully clearing markets. The only equilibrium of all markets is one of full employment. Departures from this

norm occur (voluntarily) only because people make mistakes in predicting the price level.

9. The neo-Keynesian model assumes that wages and prices are relatively rigid over the cycle and are certainly not market clearing. Fluctuations in demand cause fluctuations in employment and production because prices are fixed and firms and labor groups will sell what they can at the going price.

10. The theory of rational expectations says that people make only random errors in predicting the price level. Combined with the monetarist theory that deviations from equilibrium occur only because of errors, this predicts that the source of deviation will be random, not systematic. This leaves no place for systematic stabilization policy. Neo-Keynesians reply that even the most casual observations of the economy conflict with this view.

11. The amount of unemployment occurring at full-employment income has been called the natural rate. The economy's aggregate natural rate of 5 to 6 percent conceals vast differences in unemployment by occupational, industrial, educational, racial, and age classifications.

12. Macroeconomic theory is a valuable tool, but it conceals many important microeconomic relations concerned with the dispersion of micro figures around a macro average.

Topics for Review

The appropriate target rate of inflation
Wage and price controls and TIPs
Explanations of the correlation between the quantity of money and national income
Underemployment equilibrium
Keynesian and monetarist micro foundations
The theory of rational expectations
The natural rate of unemployment

Discussion Questions

1. In its 1979 Report the Joint Economic Committee of the Congress urged the administration to fight inflation and combat unemployment by encouraging private sector saving and investment. How might expanded saving and investment help to reduce inflation and/or combat unemployment?

2. "Carter's Inflation Options All Carry Political Costs." Can you suggest the political costs of each of the possible attacks on inflation that a President might recommend?

3. "Kennedy advocates a six months' freeze on wages, prices and profits" reported the press in early 1980. What theories of inflation might Edward Kennedy have been embracing first if he saw the controls being totally removed after six months and second, if he saw the six-months' freeze being followed by a prolonged period of more flexible wage-price controls?

4. Neo-Keynesian and Nobel Laureate Paul Samuelson recently quoted a "conservative economist friend" as saying in mid 1980, "If you're contriving a teensy-weensy recession for us, please don't bother. It won't do the job. What's needed is a believable declaration that Washington will countenance *whatever* degree of unemployment is needed to bring us back on the path to price stability, and a demonstrated willingness to *stick* to that resolution no matter how politically unpopular the short-run joblessness, production cutbacks, and dips in profit might be." Discuss the "conservative friend's" view of inflation. Does experience since 1980 suggest that his advice was followed? If so, what was the consequence?

5. In 1979 in Britain, the newly elected conservative government of Prime Minister Margaret Thatcher embraced the monetarist view of inflation and decided to follow the advice of Professor Samuelson's "conservative friend" quoted in the previous question. Check unemployment and inflation rates and money supply figures in Britain since 1977 to see if she stuck to the advice and if the inflation rate did moderate.

6. A recent ad in the *New York Times* had this to say about inflation. "First [our politicians] blamed wage increases and price hikes for inflation. Then when 'voluntary guidelines' were established, the blame shifted to OPEC oil prices. Both explanations were wrong. Government policy is responsible for inflation—paying for deficit spending by 'creating money out of thin air.'" What theories of inflation are rejected and accepted by the writers of this ad?

7. At a time when the U.S. unemployment rate stood at close to 8 percent, the press reported, "Skilled labor shortage plagues many firms—newspaper ads often draw few qualified workers; wages over time are up." What type of unemployment does this suggest to be important?

Part Eleven

International Trade
and Finance

The Gains From Trade

39

Americans buy Volkswagens, Germans take holidays in Italy, Italians buy spice from Tanzania, Africans import oil from Kuwait, Arabs buy Japanese cameras, and the Japanese depend heavily on American soybeans as a source of food. *International trade* refers to all such exchanges of goods and services that take place across international boundaries. This trade gives rise to a number of characteristic problems. In this chapter we explore the fundamental question of what is to be gained by international trade. In Chapter 40 we deal with the pros and cons of interfering with the free flow of such trade. Chapter 41 will consider the problems caused because different countries use different currencies. Finally, Chapter 42 will be devoted to a brief study of the international monetary systems under which the international exchange of goods and movements of capital have functioned in the twentieth century.

The founders of modern economics were intimately concerned with foreign trade problems. The great eighteenth century British philosopher and economist David Hume, one of the first to work out the theory of the price system as a control mechanism, developed his concepts mainly in terms of prices in foreign trade. Adam Smith and David Ricardo, the two British economists who developed in full the classical theory of the functioning of the economy, were greatly concerned with trade problems. Smith in his *Wealth of Nations* (1776) attacked government restriction of trade. He was personally responsible for many reforms in the control of trade. Ricardo in 1817 developed the basic theory of the gains from trade that is studied in this chapter. The repeal of the Corn Laws—tariffs on the importation of grains into England—and the transformation of Britain in the mid nineteenth century from a country of high tariffs to one of complete free trade were to a significant extent the result of agitation by the economists whose theories of the gains from trade led them to a condemnation of all tariffs.

INTERPERSONAL, INTERREGIONAL, AND INTERNATIONAL TRADE

The advantages realized as a result of trade are usually called the **gains from trade.** The source of such gains is most easily studied by considering the differences between a world with trade and a world without it. Although governments often tend to regard foreign trade differently, economists from Adam Smith on have argued that the causes and consequences of international trade are simply an extension of the principles governing domestic trade. What is the advantage of trade among individuals, among groups, among regions, or among countries?

Consider trade among individuals. If there were no such trade, each person would have to be self-sufficient; each would have to produce all the food, clothing, shelter, medical services, entertainment, and luxuries that he or she consumed. Although a world of individual self-sufficiency is wildly unreal, it does not take much imagination to realize that living standards would be very low in such a world. Trade between individuals allows people to specialize in those activities they can do well and to buy from others the goods and services they cannot easily produce. A bad carpenter who is a good doctor can specialize in medicine, providing a physician's services not only for his or her own family but also for, say, an excellent carpenter without the training or the ability to practice medicine. Thus trade and specialization are intimately connected. Without trade everyone must be self-sufficient; with trade everyone can specialize in what they do well and satisfy other needs by trading.

The same principles apply to regions. Without interregional trade, each region would have to be self-sufficient. With such trade, plains regions can specialize in growing grain, mountain regions in mining and lumbering, and regions with abundant power in manufacturing. Cool regions can produce wheat and crops that thrive in temperate climates, and tropical regions can grow bananas and coconuts.

To generalize, the living standards of the inhabitants of all regions will be higher when the inhabitants of each region specialize in producing the commodities in which they have some natural or acquired advantage and obtain other products by trade, than when all seek to be self-sufficient.

The same applies to nations. A national boundary does not usually define an area that could easily be self-sufficient. Nations, like regions or persons, can gain from specialization and the international trade that must accompany it.

This preliminary discussion suggests one important possible gain from trade.

With trade, each individual, region, or nation is able to concentrate on producing things in which it has an advantage while trading to obtain things that it could not produce efficiently itself.

SOURCES OF THE GAINS FROM TRADE

To concentrate on the sources of gains from trade one at a time, we begin by ruling out any gains in productivity that result from specialization. Assume that each region can produce goods at certain levels of productivity and that these levels are independent of the degree to which it specializes in the production of any good. In these circumstances, what is the gain from regional specialization?

A Special Case: Absolute Advantage

The gains from specialization are clear when there is a simple situation involving absolute advantage. **Absolute advantage** relates to the quantities of a single product that can be produced using the same quantity of resources in two different regions. One region is said to have an absolute advantage over another in the production of commodity X when an equal quantity of resources can produce more X in the first region than in the second.

Suppose region A has an absolute advantage over B in one commodity, while B has an absolute advantage over A in another. This is a case of reciprocal absolute advantage: each country has an absolute advantage in some commodity. In such a situation the total production of both regions can be increased (relative to a situation of self-sufficiency) if each specializes in the commodity in which it has the absolute advantage.

Table 39-1 provides a simple example. Assume that, with a given quantity of resources, America can produce 10 bushels of wheat or 6 yards of cloth, while England (with the same quantity of resources) can produce 5 bushels of wheat or 10 yards of cloth. Suppose at first that America and England were both self-sufficient, each producing wheat and cloth for home markets. Now assume that trade is opened between the two countries and that America moves resources out of cloth and into wheat while England moves resources out of wheat and into cloth. The gains and losses are summarized in the lower half of Table 39-1. Total world production of both wheat and cloth increases when this reallocation of production takes place; there is more wheat *and* more cloth for the same use of resources.

The potential gains from *specialization* make possible gains from *trade*. England is producing more cloth and America more wheat than when they were self-sufficient. America is probably producing more wheat and less cloth than American consumers wish to buy, and England is producing more cloth and less wheat than English consumers wish to buy. If consumers in both countries are to get cloth and wheat in the desired proportions, America must export wheat to England and import cloth from England.

International trade is necessary to achieve the gains that international specialization makes possible.

Because specialization and trade go hand in hand — there is no motivation to achieve the gains from specialization without being able to trade the goods produced for goods desired — the term *gains from trade* is used to embrace both.

A First General Statement: Comparative Advantage

When each country has an absolute advantage over the other in one commodity, the gains from trade are obvious: if each produces the commodity in the production of which it is more efficient than the other, world production will be higher than if each tries to be self-sufficient. But what if America can produce both wheat and cloth more efficiently than England? In essence, this was the

TABLE 39-1
Gains from Specialization with Absolute Advantage

	One unit of resources can produce	
	Wheat (bushels)	Cloth (yards)
America	10	6
England	5	10

Changes resulting from the transfer of one unit of American resources into wheat production and one unit of British resources into cloth production

	Wheat (bushels)	Cloth (yards)
America	+ 10	− 6
England	− 5	+ 10
World	+ 5	+ 4

When there is reciprocal absolute advantage, specialization makes it possible to produce more of both commodities. The top half of the table shows the production of wheat and cloth that can be achieved in each country by using one unit of resources. The lower half shows the changes in production caused by moving one unit of resources out of cloth and into wheat production in America and in the opposite direction in England. There is an increase in world production of 5 bushels of wheat and 4 yards of cloth; worldwide, there are gains from specialization.

question David Ricardo posed over 160 years ago. His answer underlies the theory of comparative advantage that is still accepted by economists as a valid statement of the potential gains from trade.

Assume that American efficiency increases above the levels recorded in the previous example, so that a unit of American resources can produce either 100 bushels of wheat or 60 yards of cloth, but English efficiency remains unchanged. See Table 39-2. Now, surely America, which is better at producing both wheat and cloth than is England, has nothing to gain by trading with such an inefficient foreign country! It *does* have something to gain, however, as is illustrated in Table 39-2. Even though America is ten times as efficient as it was in the situation of Table 39-1, it is still possible to increase world production of both wheat and cloth by having America produce more wheat and less cloth and England produce more cloth and less wheat.

There is a gain from specialization because while America has an absolute advantage over England in the production of both wheat and cloth, its margin of advantage differs in the two commodities. America can produce 20 times as much wheat as England can by using the same quantity of resources, but only 6 times as much cloth. America is said to have a **comparative advantage** in the production of wheat and a comparative disadvantage in the production of cloth. (This statement implies another: England has a comparative disadvantage in the production of wheat and a comparative advantage in the production of cloth.)

A key proposition in the theory of international trade is:

The gains from specialization and trade depend on the pattern of comparative, not absolute, advantage.

A comparison of Tables 39-1 and 39-2 refutes the notion that the absolute *levels* of efficiency of two areas affect the gains from specialization. All that matters is that the margin of advantage that one area has over the other must differ between

TABLE 39-2

Gains from Specialization with Comparative Advantage

	One unit of resources can produce	
	Wheat (bushels)	Cloth (yards)
America	100	60
England	5	10

Changes resulting from the transfer of one-tenth of one unit of American resources into wheat production and one unit of British resources into cloth production

	Wheat (bushels)	Cloth (yards)
America	+ 10	− 6
England	− 5	+ 10
World	+ 5	+ 4

When there is comparative advantage, specialization makes it possible to produce more of both commodities. The productivity of English resources is left unchanged from Table 39-1; that of American resources is increased tenfold. England no longer has an absolute advantage in producing either commodity. Total production of both commodities can nonetheless be increased by specialization. Moving one-tenth of one unit of American resources out of cloth and into wheat and moving one unit of resources in the opposite direction in England causes world production of wheat to rise by 5 bushels and cloth by 4 yards. Reciprocal absolute advantage is not necessary for gains from trade.

commodities. As long as this margin differs, total world production can be increased when each area specializes in the production of the commodity in which it has a comparative advantage.

Comparative advantage is necessary as well as sufficient for gains from trade. This is illustrated in Table 39-3, showing America with an absolute advantage in both commodities and neither country with a comparative advantage over the other in the production of either commodity. America is ten times as efficient as Britain in the production of wheat and in the production of cloth. Now there is no way to increase the production of both wheat and cloth by reallocating resources within America and within England. The lower half of the table provides one example; you should try others. Absolute advan-

TABLE 39-3

Absence of Gains from Specialization Where There Is No Comparative Advantage

	One unit of resources can produce	
	Wheat (bushels)	Cloth (yards)
America	100	60
England	10	6

Changes resulting from the transfer of one unit of American resources into wheat production and ten units of British resources into cloth production

	Wheat (bushels)	Cloth (yards)
America	+100	−60
England	−100	+60
World	0	0

Where there is no comparative advantage, there is no reallocation of resources within each country that will increase the production of both commodities. In this example America has the same absolute advantage over England in each commodity (tenfold). There is no comparative advantage, and world production cannot be increased by reallocating resources in both countries. Therefore specialization does not increase total output.

tage without comparative advantage does not lead to gains from trade.

A Second General Statement: Opportunity Costs

Much of the previous argument has used the concept of a unit of resources and assumed that units of resources can be equated across countries, so that such statements as "America can produce ten times as much wheat with the same quantity of resources as England" are meaningful. Measurement of the real resource cost of producing commodities poses many difficulties. If, for example, England uses land, labor, and capital in proportions different from those used in America, it may not be clear which country gets more output "per unit of resource input." Fortunately, the proposition about the gains from trade can be restated without reference to absolute efficiencies.

TABLE 39-4

The Opportunity Cost of One Unit of Wheat and One Unit of Cloth in America and England

	Wheat	Cloth
America	0.6 yards cloth	1.67 bushels wheat
England	2.0 yards cloth	0.50 bushels wheat

Comparative advantages can always be expressed in terms of opportunity costs that differ between countries. These opportunity costs can be obtained from Table 39-1 or Table 39-2. The English opportunity cost of one unit of wheat is obtained by dividing the cloth output of one unit of English resources by the wheat output. The result shows that 2 yards of cloth must be sacrificed for every extra unit of wheat produced by transferring English resources out of cloth production and into wheat. The other three cost figures are obtained in a similar manner.

To do this, we return to the examples of Tables 39-1 and 39-2 and calculate the opportunity cost of wheat and cloth in the two countries. When resources are assumed to be fully employed, the only way to produce more of one commodity is to reallocate resources and so produce less of the other commodity. Table 39-1 shows that a unit of resources in America can produce 10 bushels of wheat *or* 6 yards of cloth, from which it follows that the opportunity cost of producing one unit of wheat is 0.6 units of cloth while the opportunity cost of producing one unit of cloth is 1.67 units of wheat. These data are summarized in Table 39-4. The table also shows that in England the opportunity cost of one unit of wheat is two units of cloth forgone, while the opportunity cost of a unit of cloth is 0.50 units of wheat. Table 39-2 also gives rise to the opportunity costs in Table 39-4.

The sacrifice of cloth involved in producing wheat is much lower in America than it is in England, and world production can be increased if America rather than England produces wheat. Looking at cloth production, one can see that the loss of wheat involved in producing one unit of cloth is lower in England than in America. England is a lower (opportunity) cost producer of cloth than is America, and world production can be increased if England rather than America

TABLE 39-5
Gains from Specialization When Opportunity Costs Differ

Changes resulting from each country's producing one more unit of a commodity in which it has the lower opportunity cost		
	Wheat (bushels)	Cloth (yards)
America	+1.0	−0.6
England	−0.5	+1.0
World	+0.5	+0.4

Whenever opportunity costs differ between countries, specialization can increase the production of both commodities. These calculations show that there are gains from specialization given the opportunity costs of Table 39-4. To produce one more bushel of wheat, America must sacrifice 0.6 yards of cloth. To produce one more yard of cloth, England must sacrifice 0.5 bushels of wheat. Making both changes raises world production of both wheat and cloth.

produces cloth. This situation is shown in Table 39-5.

The gains from trade arise from differing opportunity costs in the two countries.

The conclusions about the gains from trade in the hypothetical example of two countries and two commodities may be generalized:

1. One country has a comparative advantage over a second country in producing a commodity when the opportunity cost (in terms of some other commodity) of production in the first country is lower. This implies however that it has a comparative disadvantage in the other commodity.
2. Opportunity costs depend on the relative costs of producing two commodities, not on absolute costs. (Notice that the data in both Tables 39-1 and 39-2 give rise to the opportunity costs in Table 39-4.)
3. When opportunity costs are the same in all countries, there is no comparative advantage and no possibility of gains from specialization and trade. (You can illustrate this for yourself

by calculating the opportunity costs implied by the data in Table 39-3.)
4. When opportunity costs differ in any two countries, and both countries are producing both commodities, it is always possible to increase production of both commodities by a suitable reallocation of resources within each country. (This proposition is illustrated in Table 39-5.)

If, but only if, opportunity costs differ among countries, the specialization of each country in producing those commodities in which it has comparative advantages will make it possible to achieve gains from trade.

ADDITIONAL SOURCES OF THE GAINS FROM TRADE: LEARNING BY DOING AND ECONOMIES OF SCALE

So far we have assumed that costs are constant. With constant costs there are gains from specialization and trade as long as there are interregional differences in opportunity costs. If costs are not constant, *additional* sources of gain are possible.

Early economists placed great importance on a factor that we call learning by doing. They believed that as regions specialized in particular tasks, workers and managers would become more efficient in performing them. As people acquire expertise, or know-how, costs tend to fall. Much modern empirical work suggests that this really does happen. If it occurs in our example, output of cloth per worker will rise in England as England becomes more specialized in that commodity, and the same will happen to output of wheat per worker in America. This is, of course, a gain over and above that which occurs when costs are constant.

A further reason why costs might fall as regions specialize concerns economies of large-scale production. If costs fall as output increases, world output can be greater when there is one large cloth industry in England and one large wheat industry in America (rather than two half-size cloth industries and two half-size wheat industries, one in each country).

A Graphic Representation of the Gains from Trade

Suppose America has a competitive advantage in wheat and England a comparative advantage in cloth. Initially each country is self-sufficient. Each country will be operating at a point (such as E and e in the diagrams) on its own production—and consumption—possibility curve (the heavy black line). The production possibility curves are straight lines because the opportunity cost of one commodity in terms of the other is assumed to be the same, no matter what the current levels of output of each commodity. America's curve (AB) is steeper because the opportunity cost of producing cloth instead of wheat is high.

America has a comparative *advantage* in wheat and a comparative *disadvantage* in cloth.

Suppose America were offered the chance of obtaining cloth by trade at the English opportunity cost. It would pay America to produce nothing but wheat and then acquire cloth at the English opportunity cost. This would allow America to attain some point on AC', which is drawn through A (America's fully specialized output of wheat) parallel to CD. Clearly consumption opportunities have increased: America could now reach a point such as E_1, which was unobtainable without

America's consumption possibilities

England's consumption possibilities

TERMS OF TRADE

So far we have seen that world production can be increased when America and England specialize in the production of the commodity in which they have a comparative advantage and then trade with each other. How will these gains from specialization and trade be shared between the two countries? The division of the gain depends on the terms at which trade takes place. The **terms of trade** are defined as the quantity of domestic goods that must be exported to get a unit of imported goods.

The terms of trade reflect the opportunity cost of imports measured in terms of exports.

trade. In such circumstances America would gain by trade and England would break even.

Suppose England were offered the chance of obtaining wheat at the American opportunity cost in terms of cloth sacrificed. It would pay England to produce nothing but cloth and to trade along DA' (drawn parallel to AB) to reach a higher point, say e_1, than was obtainable when wheat had to be produced at the English opportunity cost. In such circumstances England would gain by trade and America would break even.

But this means there is a range of "prices" of cloth in terms of wheat—lower than America's high opportunity cost and higher than England's low opportunity cost—at which each country gains. Represent one such relative price by the slope of the line AT (= DT). If America produces only wheat and England only cloth, and they are willing to trade at this relative price, their consumption possibilities with trade will be shown by the lines AT and DT. America can go to some point such as E_2, which gives it more wheat and more cloth than the self-sufficiency point E, while England can go to some point such as e_2, which gives it more wheat and more cloth than the self-sufficiency point e. Thus the central generalization of the theory of the gains from trade is graphically illustrated: trade allows each country to have more of each commodity than it otherwise would if each country were self-sufficient.

In the example of Table 39-4, the American domestic opportunity cost of one unit of cloth is 1.67 bushels of wheat. If Americans can obtain cloth by international trade at terms of trade more favorable than 1.67 bushels of wheat, they will gain by doing so. Suppose that international prices are such that 1 yard of cloth exchanges for (i.e., is equal in value to) 1 bushel of wheat. At

those prices, Americans can obtain cloth at a lower wheat opportunity cost by trade than by domestic production. Therefore the terms of trade favor selling wheat and buying cloth on international markets.

Similarly, in the example of Table 39-4, English consumers gain when they can obtain wheat abroad at any terms of trade more favorable than 2 yards of cloth per bushel of wheat, which is the English domestic opportunity cost. If the terms of trade are 1 bushel of wheat for 1 yard of cloth, the terms of trade favor English traders' buying wheat and selling cloth on international markets. Both England and America in this example gain from trade: each can obtain the commodity in which it has a comparative disadvantage at a lower opportunity cost through international trade than through domestic production.

In practice an index of the terms of trade is computed as the ratio of two index numbers:

$$\frac{\text{Index of terms}}{\text{of trade}} = \frac{\text{Index of import prices}}{\text{Index of export prices}} \times 100$$

A fall in the index is referred to as a *favorable* change in a country's terms of trade. It means that less has to be exported to pay for a unit of imports than previously. For example, when America's import price index rises from 100 to 120 while its export price index rises from 100 to 125, the terms of trade index falls from 100 to 96. At the new terms of trade, 96 units of exports will buy what formerly required 100 units to buy. An increase in the index of the terms of trade, called an *unfavorable* change, means the country must export more to pay for its now relatively more expensive imports. The sharp rise in oil prices during the 1970s led to large unfavorable shifts in the terms of trade of the oil-importing countries, including the United States.

Summary

1. The principles governing trade between any two groups are the same—for individuals, regions, or nations.

2. One country (or region or individual) has an absolute advantage over another country (or region or individual) in the production of a commodity when, with the same input of resources in each country, it can produce more of the commodity than can the other.

3. In a situation of reciprocal absolute advantage, total production of both commodities will be raised if each country moves resources into the production of the commodity in which it has the absolute advantage. However, the gains from trade do not require absolute advantage on the part of each country, only comparative advantage.

4. Comparative advantage is the relative advantage one country enjoys over another in various commodities. If, for example, America is 10 times as efficient as is England in producing commodity X and 12 times as efficient in producing commodity Y, America has a comparative advantage over England in Y (its margin of advantage over England is larger in Y than it is in X). Three other ways of saying the same thing are: (a) America has a comparative disadvantage in X; (b) England has a comparative advantage in X; (c) England has a comparative disadvantage in Y.

5. World production of all commodities can be increased if each country transfers resources into the production of the commodities in which it has a comparative advantage.

6. The gains from trade result from different opportunity costs in different countries, which in turn lead to differences in comparative advantage.

7. The theory of the gains from trade may be stated thus: Trade allows all countries to obtain the goods in which they do not have a comparative advantage at a lower opportunity cost (in terms of units sacrificed of the commodities in which they do have a comparative advantage) than they would have to accept if they were to produce all commodities for themselves. This allows all countries to have more of all commodi-

ties than they could have if they made themselves self-sufficient.

8. As well as gaining the advantages of specialization arising from comparative advantage, a nation that engages in trade and specialization may realize the benefits of increasing returns to scale and learning by doing.

9. The terms of trade refer to the quantity of imported goods that can be obtained per unit of goods exported. They show the opportunity cost of obtaining goods by trade. The terms of trade determine how the gains from trade are shared. They are measured by an index number showing the ratio of import prices to export prices.

Topics for Review

Interpersonal, interregional, and international specialization
Absolute advantage and comparative advantage
Gains from specialization and gains from trade
Opportunity cost and comparative advantage
Terms of trade
Index of the terms of trade

Discussion Questions

1. Adam Smith saw a close connection between the wealth of a nation and its willingness "freely to engage" in foreign trade. What is the connection?
2. Suppose that the following situation exists. Assume no tariffs, no intervention by the government, and that labor is the only factor of production.

Country	Labor cost of producing one unit of	
	Artichokes	Bikinis
Inland	$20	$40
Outland	$20	$ X

Let X take different values—say $10, $20, $40, and $60. In each case, will there be trade? If so, in which direction?

3. It is probable that the United States with its advanced technology has an absolute advantage in the production of many manufactured products. Suppose it had such an advantage in all manufactured products.

Should it then ever import any manufactured products?

4. Suppose, after 1865, the United States had become two separate countries with no trade between them. What predictions would you make about the standard of living compared to what it is today? Does the fact that Canada, the United States, and Mexico are separate countries lead to a lower standard of living in the three countries than if they were united into a new country called Northica?

5. Uruguay, formerly a significant exporter of raw beef and mutton, found it needed more exports to pay for its greatly increased imports of oil. Because the market for raw meat was limited, it decided to take advantage of a low wage rate by processing its beef, hides, and wool and then exporting these processed goods. The policy has proved a great success. What does this suggest about Uruguay's comparative advantages?

6. If the European Common Market led to such a rise in efficiency that the price of every good manufactured in Germany, France, and Italy fell below the price of the same good manufactured in the United States, what would happen? Would Americans as a whole gain or lose because of this? Might some Americans benefit and some be hurt?

7. Studies of U.S. trade patterns have shown that very high wage sectors of industry are among the largest and fastest growing export sectors. Does this contradict the principle of comparative advantage?

8. Saudi Arabia has a comparative advantage over West Germany in producing oil. In what, if anything, does it have a comparative disadvantage? When Saudi Arabia raises the price of oil, does it change the gains from trade? What does it change?

9. Predict what each of the following will do to the terms of trade of the importing country and the exporting country, *ceteris paribus*.

   a. A blight destroys a good part of the coffee beans produced in the world.

   b. The Japanese cut the price of the steel they sell to the United States.

   c. Competition among the maritime nations of the world leads prices of ocean transport to fall relative to the prices of the commodities transported.

   d. A general inflation of 10 percent occurs around the world.

Barriers to Free Trade

40

There are always difficulties in conducting business in a foreign country. Differences in language, in local laws and customs, and in currency all complicate transactions. In this chapter our concern is not with these difficulties but with the *trade policy* by which governments intentionally erect barriers to the free flow of goods and services among nations. **Protectionism** refers to protecting domestic industries from foreign competition. **Free trade** is a situation in which no protectionism is practiced.

Our major concern in this chapter is with the case for and against protectionism. But we shall begin by looking briefly at alternative *means* of implementing protectionism.

METHODS OF PROTECTIONISM

There are basically three means by which a country might seek to reduce the quantity of some good it imports. (1) It may place a tax on imports of the commodity, called a **tariff.** Such a tax, like any excise tax (see Chapter 25), shifts upward the supply curve of the foreign good and thus tends to raise its price. The tariff causes this shift because it adds to the foreign producer's cost of every unit sold in the country imposing the tariff. (2) It may impose an *import quota* that limits the quantity of the commodity that may be shipped into the country in a given period. Once the quota has been reached, the effective supply curve becomes a vertical line. Until the quota has been reached there is no change in demand or supply. (3) It may take steps to reduce the

FIGURE 40-1

Alternative Means of Decreasing the Quantity of Imports of a Commodity

(i) Tariff   (ii) Quota   (iii) Demand restriction

The government can decrease the quantity of imports below the free-market level by policies that shift either the demand curve or the supply curve to the left or that simply regulate the quantity permitted to enter. In each diagram D and S represent the free-market demand and supply for some imported goods, with p and q being the equilibrium price and quantity. If the government wishes to achieve a smaller quantity of imports, such as q_1, it may do so in various ways.

In (i) it imposes a tariff of T per unit. This shifts the supply curve vertically by the amount of the tariff, to S', and achieves a new equilibrium at E_1.

In (ii) it imposes an import quota, Q_1, as the maximum quantity permitted to enter. This in effect changes the supply curve to the heavy kinked line S'' and leads to equilibrium at E_1.

In (iii) it causes demand to shift leftward by ΔD by a policy such as limiting importers' right to purchase the commodity or the foreign exchange needed to pay for it. In this case a new equilibrium occurs at E_2. In all three parts the equilibrium quantity imported is reduced to q_1.

demand for the imported commodity on the part of its citizens. For example, it may require potential importers to acquire a special license, or it may restrict the ability of its citizens to use their funds to purchase the foreign exchange needed to pay for the commodity. Such steps would shift the demand curve for the import to the left.[1]

The three parts of Figure 40-1 illustrate the three means. Although there are differences in the effects of the different means, almost all the issues can be raised by considering any one of them. We shall concentrate on tariffs.

---

[1] A distinction is frequently made between tariff and non-tariff barriers. The latter includes both the second and third categories mentioned here.

TARIFFS

The usual form of a tariff is a tax that is a specified percentage of the producer's price. This is called an *ad valorem* tariff. Its major purpose is to raise the price of imported goods in order to discourage imports by offsetting (to some extent at least) a cost advantage that foreign producers have over domestic producers of a particular product.[2]

---

[2] Tariffs can also be utilized to raise revenue. In the United States, customs revenues are about $8 billion per year. Although this amount is not negligible, it represents less than 2 percent of federal tax revenue. The protective function of a tariff is opposed to the revenue function because the tariff will not yield much revenue when it is effective in cutting imports. This chapter concentrates on the protective feature of tariffs.

TABLE 40-1

Assumed Comparative Costs of Domestic Versus Foreign Production

Commodity	U.S. price if all production is domestic	Delivered cost of import	Percentage tariff needed to exclude	Delivered cost of imports in U.S. with 20% tariff
Coal (ton)	$ 30	$ 35	none	$ 42.00
Coffee (lb.)	15	2	650+	2.40
Steel (ton)	115	100	15+	120.00

Commodities whose delivered cost to the United States is below the price of domestically produced commodities are potential imports; tariffs change the effective delivered costs of imports. In the example, foreign producers have a comparative advantage at current prices in both coffee and steel production but not in coal. To make all importation uneconomic would require a tariff of at least 15 percent on steel and 650 percent on coffee. A 20 percent tariff would exclude steel but not coffee; however, it would raise coffee prices. A tariff would not affect coal because coal imports are effectively excluded without a tariff. These data are hypothetical.

To see when and how tariffs work, consider three different commodities that Americans might import—coal, coffee, and steel. We shall make the simplifying assumptions shown in Table 40-1 about the price of the commodity in the United States compared to the costs of production in a foreign country plus shipment to the United States.

There is potential demand for the importation of any commodity that can be delivered to a country at a cost lower than the cost at which it can be produced domestically. At any time there is a wide array of potentially importable commodities, some with large cost savings, some with moderate savings, and some with no advantage at all. (In the example, both coffee and steel would be candidates for importation.) A world of free trade would have no tariffs on imports. In such a world, a country would import all those commodities that it could buy from abroad at a delivered price lower than the cost of producing them at home.

Suppose the United States wishes to protect its home industries from any foreign competition. It does not need a tariff on coal; it does need (at the assumed prices and costs) a tariff in excess of 15 percent on steel and a tariff of more than 650 percent on coffee.

Now suppose that a country imposes a 20 percent tariff on all imports. This does not prohibit trade, but by making imported goods more expensive, it affects those items it is profitable to import. Any foreign good that enjoys a cost advantage of less than 20 percent is now effectively prohibited. This is the case of steel in the example. A 20 percent tariff thus provides protection to domestic industries that produce at a cost disadvantage of up to 20 percent. Imported goods that enjoy cost advantages in excess of 20 percent (such as coffee) will still be in demand, but they will not be as big a bargain as previously. Because their price will be higher, a smaller quantity will be demanded than if there were no tariff.

When a country desires to prohibit trade in a specific commodity, it might do so by setting a tariff that is larger than the cost advantage of the lowest-cost foreign producer. When it desires to stimulate competition between domestic and foreign producers, it might set tariffs so as to equalize the present cost advantages. In the example of Table 40-1, a 15 percent tariff on steel would make steel produced in the United States competitive with foreign steel at current costs.

The Debate About Protectionism

In today's world two facts about international trade stand out. First, there is a great deal of it.

Second, virtually every government interferes to some extent with free trade.

The reasons behind these facts need to be examined.

THE CASE FOR FREE TRADE

In Chapter 39 we saw that where opportunity costs differ among countries, some degree of specialization with some consequent amount of trade will raise world standards of living. Free trade allows all countries to specialize in producing commodities in which they have comparative advantages. They can then produce (and consume) more of all commodities than would be available if specialization had not taken place.

Free trade makes it possible to maximize world production and makes it *possible* for every household in the world to consume more goods than it could if free trade did not exist. Yet this does not mean that everyone will be better off with free trade than without it, for the aggregate size of the world's output and the way in which that output is divided are important considerations. It is possible that protectionism will give some people a large enough share of a smaller world output so that they will benefit from protectionism. If we ask if it is possible for free trade to be advantageous to everyone, the answer is yes. But if we ask if it is in fact always mutually advantageous to everyone, that is quite another matter.

There is abundant evidence to show that real differences in comparative costs exist and that there are potential gains from trade because of these differences. There is also ample evidence that trade occurs and that no nation tries to be self-sufficient or refuses to sell to foreigners the items it produces cheaply and well.

The case for free trade is powerful; what needs explanation is not the extent of trade but the fact that it is not wholly free. Tariffs and nontariff barriers to trade still exist 200 years after Adam Smith stated the case for free trade. If there is a valid case for interfering with free trade, where is the balance between the advantages of more or less trade?

THE CASE FOR PROTECTIONISM

Two kinds of arguments for protection are common. The first concerns objectives other than maximizing output; the second concerns the difference between the welfare of a single nation and that of the world.

Objectives Other Than Maximizing Output

It is quite possible to accept the proposition that production is higher with free trade and yet rationally oppose free trade because of a concern with policy objectives other than production and consumption. There are, after all, policy goals other than maximizing real national income.

For example, comparative costs might dictate that a country should specialize in producing a single commodity, say bananas. The government might decide, however, that there are distinct social advantages to encouraging a more diverse economy—one that would give citizens a wider range of occupations. The authorities might decide that the social and psychological advantages of a diverse economy more than compensate for a reduction in living standards by, say, 5 percent below what they could be with complete specialization of production.

Specializing in the production of one or two commodities, although dictated by comparative advantage, may involve risks that a country does not wish to take. One such risk is a technological advance that renders its basic product obsolete. The quartz crystal badly damaged the Swiss watch industry in just this way; between 1974 and 1979 its share of the world market dropped from 40 percent to 30 percent, and 30,000 jobs were lost.

Another risk is cyclical fluctuations in the prices of basic commodities, which may face depressed prices for years at a time, then periods of very high prices. The national income of a country specializing in the production of such commodities will be subject to wide fluctuations. Even though the average income level over a long period might be higher when there is specialization in the production of basic commodities, the serious social problems associated with a widely fluctuating national income may make the government decide to sacrifice some income in order to reduce fluctuations. Such a government might use protectionist policies to encourage the expansion of several cyclically stable industries.

Yet another reason for protectionism may be the desire to maintain national traditions. For example, many Canadians are passionately concerned with maintaining a separate nation with traditions that differ from those of the United States. Many believe that a tariff helps them to do this. They would be prepared, if necessary, to tolerate a 5 or 10 percent differential in living standards in order to maintain this independence.

The most frequently cited noneconomic defense of protectionism concerns national defense. It has traditionally been argued, for example, that the United States needs an experienced merchant marine in case of war and that this industry should be fostered by protectionist policies, even though it is less efficient than the foreign competition.

There is nothing irrational in a country's deciding to accept substantial costs in order to attain objectives other than maximizing living standards. Although most people would agree that, *ceteris paribus,* they prefer more income to less, economists cannot pronounce as irrational a nation that chooses to sacrifice some income in order to achieve other goals.

Protectionism as a Means to Higher National Living Standards

The most important example in this category relates to economies of scale. It is usually called the **infant industry argument.** If an industry has large economies of scale, costs and prices will be high when the industry is small, but they will fall as the industry grows. In such an industry, the country first in the field has a tremendous advantage. A newly developing country may find that

its industries are unable to compete in the early stages of their development with established foreign rivals. A tariff or import quota may protect these industries from foreign competition while they grow up. When they are large enough, they will be able to produce as cheaply as can foreign rivals and thus be able to compete without protection.

A similar argument in favor of protectionism concerns learning by doing. Giving a domestic industry protection from foreign competition may enable it to learn to be efficient and give the labor force the time needed to acquire necessary skills. If so, it may pay the government to protect the industry while the learning occurs.

FREE TRADE VERSUS PROTECTIONISM

From what we have said it appears that there is a strong case for allowing trade in order to realize the gains from trade — and that there may also be reasons for departing from completely free trade.

It is not necessary to choose between free trade on the one hand and absolute protectionism on the other; a country can have some trade and some protectionism too.

Free Trade Versus No Trade

It would undoubtedly be possible, by using greenhouses, to grow oranges, cotton, and other now-imported raw materials and foodstuffs in Norway and to grow coffee beans in the United States. But the cost in terms of other commodities forgone would be huge, for artificial means of production require lavish inputs of factors of production. It would likewise be possible for a tropical country currently producing foodstuffs to set up industries to produce all the manufactured products that it consumes. The cost in terms of resources used, for a small country without natural advantages in industrial production, could be very large. It is thus clear that there is a large gain to all countries in having specialization and trade. The real output and consumption of all countries would be very much lower if each had to produce domestically all the goods it consumed.

In an all-or-nothing choice, virtually all countries would choose free trade over no trade.

Some Trade Versus No Trade

Table 40-2 shows the level of tariffs on selected commodities in force today. Some reflect protectionism, others reflect a use of tariffs to raise revenue. It is clear that these tariffs are not sufficient to offset widely differing cost conditions, the most dramatic of which are those associated with climate. Even the most casual observation reveals major cost differences among countries. Thus there are significant gains from trading for commodities in which a country has a large comparative disadvantage. Careful empirical measurement might put an actual numerical value on the amount of gains, but certainly production and consumption in the world, and in each major trading country, are higher with trade than they would be with no trade.

A Little More Trade Versus a Little Less Trade

Today we have trade between nations, but that trade is not perfectly free. Would we be better off if today's barriers to trade were reduced or increased a little bit? It is quite a jump from the proposition that "Some trade is better than no trade" to the proposition that "A little more trade than we have at present is better than a little less trade." Yet most arguments about commercial policy involve the latter sort of proposition, not the former. Should American automobile and steel manufacturers and workers be given *some* increased protection against Japanese imports is the question debated today, not should Japan be totally excluded from the American market.

Most actual policy disagreements concern the relative merits of free trade versus controlled trade with tariffs on the order of, say, 5, 10, or 15 percent. Such tariffs would not cut out imports of

TABLE 40-2
Tariffs on Selected Commodity Groups (ad valorem rates), 1981

Commodity	United States	European Economic Community	Japan
Weighted average of all manufactured items	4.4	5.5	3.6
Fruits, vegetables	1.7	3.4	14.5
Tea, coffee, spices	5.3	1.8	34.1
Paper, paperboard	0.3	4.0	1.4
Textiles	15.9	9.0	8.0
Transport vehicles	2.5	6.2	2.1
Tobacco	13.0	0.0	54.3
Petroleum and coal products	0.0	6.3	1.4
Oil and natural gas	4.0	0.0	0.0
All commodities (trade weighted)	3.2	3.7	5.4

Source: Post-Tokyo Round tariff rates, courtesy Special Trade Representatives Office, U.S. government.

The United States is a low-tariff country overall, yet tariffs on selected items are plainly designed to be protective of important domestic industries. These tariffs, the lowest in history, result from the GATT Tokyo Round negotiations; they began to take effect in 1981. Notice the U.S. use of tariffs for protection on textiles and tobacco. In Japan the high tariffs on tobacco, tea, coffee, and spices are for revenue since Japan does not produce these commodities.

bananas, coffee, diamonds, bauxite, or any commodity in whose production the United States would be really inefficient. (Yet these are just the commodities that defenders of free trade sometimes use as examples when the hypothesis of the gains from trade is challenged.) When one accepts the hypothesis that some trade is better than no trade, it is not necessary to accept the hypothesis that free trade is better than controlled trade with, say, 15 percent tariffs; nor is one committed to saying that 9 percent tariffs would be better than 10 percent tariffs.

As a simplified version of the sort of argument that really does take place over commercial policy, compare the effects of a 20 percent uniform ad valorem tariff with those of free trade. As a rule, tariffs are seldom advocated to protect industries that are extremely inefficient compared to foreign industries; they are usually advocated to protect industries that can very nearly compete, but not quite. How much would be gained by removing 20 percent tariffs or how much lost by imposing 20 percent tariffs in a situation of free trade?

Tariffs of 20 percent will protect industries that are up to 20 percent less efficient than foreign competitors. If the costs of the various tariff-protected industries were spread out evenly, some would be 20 percent less efficient than their foreign competitors, and others would be only 1 percent less efficient. Their average inefficiency would be about half the tariff rate, so they would be on average about 10 percent less efficient than their foreign competitors.

Suppose that as a result of tariffs, approximately 10 percent of a country's resources are allocated to industries different from the ones to which they would be allocated if there were no tariffs. This means that about 10 percent of a country's resources would be working in certain industries only because of tariff protection. If the average protected industry is 10 percent less efficient than its foreign rival, approximately 10 percent of a country's resources are producing about 10 percent less efficiently than they would be if there were no tariffs. This causes a reduction in national income on the order of 1 percent as a result of tariff protection.

This rough-and-ready calculation is meant simply to illustrate why the gains from removing modest barriers to trade may appear small. That conclusion was established by three careful studies of the effects of tariffs in Great Britain and Europe. Professor P. J. Verdoorn estimated that the gain to the six European Common Market countries from eliminating tariffs on trade among themselves to be about .05 percent of their national incomes. Professor Harry Johnson estimated that the maximum cost to Britain of staying out of the Common Market would have been equal to approximately 1 percent of Britain's national income. And Professor W. Welmesfelder estimated that the gain to Germany from major tariff reductions in 1956 and 1957 would have been less than 1 percent of German national income.

The potential net gains from somewhat freer trade than there is today are not so large as to make it certain that the removal of all remaining barriers is desirable.

Suppose the gains from freer trade would be 1 percent of national income. Is such a sacrifice of national income large or small? As a percentage it seems small, yet in 1980 prices it would be $25 billion *per year* in the United States. That amount every year forever could buy a lot of hospitals, schools, medical research, solar energy research—or even gasoline.

Whether free trade is better than a policy of moderate protectionism depends on the policy goals that a country is trying to attain, the magnitude of the benefits, and the costs of the actions. There is thus a highly important area for study and debate about trade and trade barriers.

There are also many claims that do not advance the debate; fallacious arguments are heard on both sides, and they color much of the popular discussion. These arguments have been around for a long time, but their survival does not make them true.

Fallacious Free Trade Arguments

Free trade always benefits all countries. This is not necessarily so. The potential gains from trade might be offset by costs such as unemployment or economic instability or by the interference with policy objectives other than maximizing income. These factors may render some interference desirable.[3]

Infant industries never grow up. It is argued that to grant protection on an infant industry basis is a mistake because infant industries seldom admit to growing up and will cling to their protection even when they are fully grown. Even

---

[3] To see how sensitive the gains from trade are to other considerations, suppose that totally free trade led to an allocation of resources that was 1 percent more efficient than an allocation resulting from 20 percent tariffs, but led simultaneously to an average level of unemployment 1.2 percent higher. In this case, free trade would bring losses rather than gains.

if this allegation were true, it would not be a sufficient reason for avoiding protectionism. When economies of scale are realized, the real costs of production are reduced and resources are freed for other uses. Whether or not the tariff or other trade barrier remains, a cost saving has been effected by the scale economies.

Fallacious Protectionist Arguments

The exploitation doctrine. According to this view, one trading partner *must* always reap a gain at the other's expense. The principle of comparative advantage shows that it is possible for both parties to gain from trade and thus refutes the exploitation doctrine of trade. When opportunity cost ratios differ in two countries, specialization and the accompanying trade make it possible to produce more of all commodities and thus make it possible for both parties to get more goods as a result of trade than they could get in its absence.

Keep the money at home. This argument says, If I buy a foreign good, I have the good and the foreigner has the money, whereas if I buy the same good locally, I have the good and our country has the money, too. Abraham Lincoln is said to have made this argument, and it is still heard today. It assumes that domestic money actually goes abroad physically when imports are purchased and that trade flows only in one direction.

The argument is based on a misconception. When American importers purchase Italian-made goods, they do not send dollars abroad. They (or some financial agent) buy Italian lire (or claims on them) and use them to pay the Italian manufacturer. They purchase the lire on the foreign exchange market by giving up dollars to someone who wishes to use them for expenditure *in the United States.* Even if the money did go abroad physically—that is, if an Italian firm accepted a shipload of dollars—it would be because that firm (or someone to whom it could sell the dollars) wanted them to spend in the only country where they are legal tender, the United States.

Dollars ultimately do no one any good except as purchasing power. It would be miraculous if green pieces of paper could be exported in return for real goods; after all, the central bank has the power to create as much new money as it wishes. It is only because the green paper can buy American commodities that others want it.

Protection against low-wage foreign labor. Surely, the argument says, the products of Oriental sweatshops will drive our products from the market, and the high U.S. standard of living will be dragged down to that of the impoverished Orient. Arguments of this sort have swayed many voters through the years.

As a prelude to considering them, stop and think what the argument would imply if taken out of the international context and put into a local one, where the same principles govern the gains from trade. Is it really impossible for a rich person to gain from trading with a poor person? Would the local millionaire be better off if she did all her own typing, gardening, and cooking? No one believes that a rich person cannot gain from trading with those who are less rich. Why then must a rich group of people lose from trading with a poor group? "Well," you say, "the poor group will price their goods too cheaply." Does anyone believe that consumers lose from buying in a discount house or a supermarket just because the prices are lower there than at the old-fashioned corner store? Consumers gain when they can buy the same goods at a lower price. If the Koreans pay low wages and sell their goods cheaply, *Korean* labor may suffer, but we will gain because we obtain their goods at a low cost in terms of the goods that we must export in return. The cheaper our imports are, the better off we are in terms of the goods and services available for domestic consumption.

Stated in more formal terms, the gains from trade depend on comparative, not absolute, advantages. World production is higher when any two areas, say the United States and Japan, specialize in the production of the goods for which they have a comparative advantage than when they both try to be self-sufficient.

Might it not be possible, however, that Japan will undersell the United States in all lines of production and thus appropriate all, or more than all, the gains for itself, leaving the United States no better off, or even worse off, than if it had remained self-sufficient? The answer is no. The reason for this depends on the behavior of exchange rates, which we shall study in Chapter 41. As we shall see there, equality of demand and supply on the foreign exchange market ensures that trade flows in both directions.

Imports can be obtained only by spending the currency of the country that makes the imports. Claims to this currency can be obtained only by exporting goods and services or by borrowing. Thus, lending and borrowing aside, imports must equal exports. All trade must be in two directions; we can buy only if we can also sell. In the long run, trade cannot hurt a country by causing it to import without exporting. Trade, then, always provides scope for international specialization, with each country producing and exporting those goods for which it has a comparative advantage.

Exports raise national income, imports lower it. Exports add to aggregate demand; imports subtract from it. Exports thus tend to increase national income, *ceteris paribus,* and imports reduce it, *ceteris paribus.* Surely, then, it is desirable to encourage exports and discourage imports. This is an appealing argument, but it is incorrect.

Saying that exports raise national income means that they add to the value of output, but they do not add to the value of domestic consumption. In fact, exports are goods produced at home and consumed abroad, while imports are goods produced abroad and consumed at home. The standard of living in a country depends on the goods and services available for *consumption,* not on what is produced.

If exports were really good and imports really bad, then a fully employed economy that man-

aged to increase exports without a corresponding increase in imports ought to be better off. Such a change, however, would result in a reduction in current standards of living because when more goods are sent abroad and no more are brought in from abroad, the total goods available for domestic consumption must fall.

What happens when a country achieves a surplus of exports over imports for a considerable period of time? It will accumulate claims to foreign exchange for which there are three possible uses: to add to foreign exchange reserves, to buy foreign goods, and to make investments abroad. Consider each of them.

1. Some foreign exchange reserves are required for the smooth functioning of the international payments system, as we shall see in Chapters 41 and 42. But the accumulation of reserves over and above those required serves no purpose. Permanent excess reserves represent claims on foreign output that are never used.

2. British pounds and Indian rupees cannot be eaten, smoked, drunk, or worn. But they can be spent to buy British and Indian goods that can be eaten, smoked, drunk, or worn. When such goods are imported and consumed, they add to U.S. living standards. Indeed, the main purpose of foreign trade is to take advantage of international specialization: trade allows more consumption than would be possible if all goods were produced at home. From this point of view, the purpose of exporting is to allow the importation of goods that can be produced more cheaply abroad than at home.

3. An excess of exports over imports may be used to purchase foreign assets. Such foreign investments add to living standards only when the interest and profits earned on them are used to buy imports, or when the investment is liquidated. The essence of any investment is to permit the investor to earn profits or interest that can be used to buy goods. Foreign investments permit the later purchase of foreign goods.

The living standards of a country depend on the goods and services consumed in that country.

The importance of exports is that they permit imports to be made. This two-way international exchange is valuable because more goods can be imported than could be obtained if the same goods were produced at home.

Protectionism creates domestic jobs and reduces unemployment. It is sometimes said that an economy with substantial unemployment, such as that of the United States in the 1930s or in 1980, provides an exception to the case for freer trade. Suppose that tariffs or import quotas cut the imports of Japanese cars, Korean textiles, Italian shoes, and French wine. Surely, the argument maintains, this will create more employment for Detroit auto workers, Georgia textile workers, Massachusetts shoe factories, and California farm workers. The answer is that it will—initially. But the Japanese, Koreans, Italians, and French can buy from America only if they earn American dollars by selling goods in America. The decline in their sales of autos, textiles, shoes, and wine will decrease their purchases of American machinery, aircraft, grain, and vacations in America. Jobs will be lost in our export industries and gained in those industries that formerly faced competition from imports.

The likely long-term effect is that overall unemployment will not be reduced but merely redistributed among industries. This explains why industries and unions that compete with imports favor protectionism while those with large exports favor more trade. Economists are highly skeptical about the government's ability to reduce overall unemployment by protectionism.

Subsidizing exports increases employment. Export industries do not necessarily favor free trade; they may argue instead that the government should subsidize them. This argument is closely related to the last point, though it is made by different groups. Assume that there is a rise in exports without a corresponding rise in imports, perhaps because the government pays producers a subsidy on every unit exported. According to the theory of the multiplier, this rise in exports

will increase income and employment. Surely, in a time of unemployment, this is to be regarded as a good thing.

Two points may be made about such a policy. In the first place, the goods being produced by the newly employed workers in the export sector are not available for domestic consumption and so do not directly raise domestic standards of living. Surely it would be better if, instead of subsidizing exports, the central authorities subsidized the production of goods for the home market so that all goods produced—not just those produced in response to increased incomes—would contribute to a rise in domestic living standards. Or, if there is objection to the government's subsidizing private firms, the government could create new employment by building more roads, schools, and research laboratories. Consequently income and employment would go up, but there would be something more tangible to show for it in the first instance than the smoke of ships disappearing over the horizon bearing the subsidized exports to foreign markets.

The second point to be made concerns the foreign effects of a policy that fosters exports and discourages imports in a situation of general world unemployment. Although the policy raises domestic employment, it will have the reverse effect abroad, where it creates unemployment. The foreign countries will suffer a rise in their unemployment because their exports will fall and their imports rise. Not surprisingly, they may be expected to retaliate; as we will see, this has been the historical experience. If all countries try a policy of expanding exports and discouraging imports, the net effect is likely to be a large drop in the volume of international trade without much change in the level of employment in any one country.

Arguments About Barriers to Trade: A Final Word

While there are cases in which a restrictive policy has been pursued following a rational assessment of the approximate cost, it is hard to avoid the conclusion that, more often than not, such policies are pursued for flimsy objectives or on fallacious grounds, with little idea of the actual costs involved. The very high tariffs in the United States during the 1920s and 1930s are a conspicuous example. The current clamor for the government to do something about the competition from Japan, Korea, and other countries of the East may well be another.

Trade Restrictions in the World Today

TARIFFS IN THE UNITED STATES

Figure 40-2 shows how tariffs have been used in U.S. history. The government of the United States has often paid less attention to economists' arguments for freer trade than to the protests of producers who would be hurt by tariff

FIGURE 40-2
Tariffs in the United States, 1828–1979

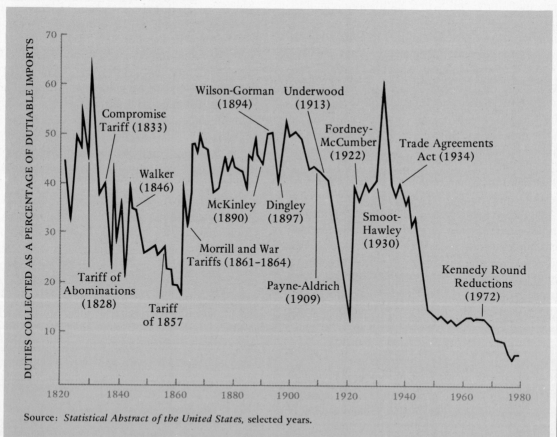

Source: *Statistical Abstract of the United States,* selected years.

U.S. tariffs have been lower in the post-World War II period than in any other period of comparable length in American history. Throughout its history the United States has alternated from being a high-tariff country to being a modest-tariff country. The average rate of tariff has been lower since World War II than ever before. The rate fell below 10 percent in 1971, and it may be expected to fall below the current 6 percent level when the ongoing Tokyo Round tariff reductions take full effect in the mid 1980s.

reductions. Part of the reason was the relative unimportance of trade to the American economy; even today only about 7 percent of the economy's output is exported.[4]

In contrast, trade is extremely important to the economies of many countries. Sweden, Great Britain, and Canada all export between 20 and 25 percent of their GNP. The loss of their foreign trade would have a devastating effect on their standards of living. America would also suffer from the loss of its foreign trade, but to a lesser degree.

Although foreign trade is not a large *fraction* of American national income, it is very important to particular industries. Large quantities of certain materials—petroleum, bauxite, coffee beans, iron ore, lumber, and newsprint—are imported. The loss of any of these supplies would cause serious difficulties in some industries, and some would cause major disruptions in the whole economy—as we have learned from even the temporary interruptions in oil supplies.

The existence of certain domestic industries—such as those producing steel, television sets, clothing, and automobiles—has been severely threatened by foreign competition. This is one indication that even if the existence of foreign trade is not vital to the country as a whole, it does affect particular sectors in important ways. Whether the country as a whole has an interest in protecting such industries is often debated. Yet it is a matter of undeniable political reality that both labor and management representatives of these industries will lobby vigorously for protection. They are often heeded.

Even in areas where foreign trade is not critically important to the U.S. economy, our imports are the exports of other countries. In some cases they are essential to those other countries. For example, nearly two-thirds of Canada's trade is with the United States. Exports to the United States account for about one-sixth of Canadian GNP. A change in U.S. commercial policy that caused only a small ripple in the U.S. economy could cause a tidal wave in Canada.

Other countries are critical of and sensitive to changes in U.S. policy if those changes will have a vital effect on them. They fear that because it does not have a similarly vital effect on the United States, a policy change may sometimes be made without due consideration of its effects on others. It is unpleasant to be in the position of having your welfare affected by decisions that do not matter much one way or the other to the person who makes them. (Americans learned this lesson when OPEC embargoed oil shipments to the United States.) Table 40-3 shows the impor-

[4] Trade is more important in the United States today than it was half a century ago, in the heyday of prohibitive tariffs. In 1929 exports were less than 5 percent of GNP.

TABLE 40-3
Percentages of Trade with the United States, 1978

Country	Percentage of exports to United States	Percentage of imports from United States
Canada	68	68
Mexico	64	60
Nigeria	40	10
Venezuela	36	41
Philippines	34	22
Japan	26	19
Brazil	22	22
Ghana	16	11
New Zealand	15	14
Iran	13	20
Australia	11	22
Thailand	11	14
United Kingdom	9	10
Portugal	7	12
Italy	7	7
Germany	7	7
Denmark	6	5
Sweden	6	7
France	5	7
Netherlands	3	8
Austria	3	3
USSR	3	11

Source: IMF, *Direction of Trade Yearbook,* 1979.

For many countries trade with the United States is a very large part of their total exports, imports, or both. Not surprisingly, the United States is the major trading partner of Canada and Mexico. But the United States as a market for exports or a source of imports is also vitally important to such distant countries as Venezuela, Brazil, Japan, Nigeria, Australia, and Iran.

tance of trade with the United States to the economies of some other countries.

Foreign trade contributes substantially to the standards of living of many countries. Even the United States, with its low dependence on trade, would have its living standard noticeably lowered if it refused to participate in the gains from trade between nations.

NONTARIFF BARRIERS

While the United States is generally a low-tariff country, there are a significant number of nontariff barriers in force at the present time, intended for the protection of particular domestic industries that have recently been losing ground to foreign competition. Some of these restrictions have been negotiated, the U.S. government putting pressure on the other country to limit "voluntarily" its exports to the United States. Others have been imposed unilaterally. Let us consider one example of each.

Negotiated Import Restrictions in Textiles

In the late 1950s the American textile and clothing industries saw their market shares badly eroded by a rising volume of trade from Hong Kong, Korea, the Philippines, and other developing nations. In response to a United States initiative, a series of international meetings was held in 1961 that reached agreements providing for the limitation of imports into the United States in the interest of what was called orderly marketing. In this way, maximum annual quotas were agreed to by each exporting textile-producing country for a 20-year period. As 1981 approached, the agreements were being amended and extended.

Similar orderly marketing agreements have been accepted by foreign countries with respect to footwear in 1977, color television sets in 1977, and citizens band radio sets in 1978. Lobbyists for many other industries have urged similar agreements for their products.

Why, one may ask, would a country such as Korea agree voluntarily to limit its profitable exports to the United States when it needs the revenue and foreign exchange that its exports earn? The answer, one may surmise, is that the United States is so needed and valued an ally that its "requests" have the weight of veiled threats. In any case, the State Department has proven to be quite persistent and persuasive once it has set out to negotiate an agreement.

Unilaterally Imposed Trigger Prices and Antidumping Rules in Steel

The American steel industry has suffered badly from competition from Japan, which (it is charged) is selling steel in the United States at lower prices than it is selling steel at home. This is called **dumping**, and it is a form of price discrimination of the kind studied in the theory of monopoly (see Chapter 15). The steel industry has asked the United States government for help, and it has received it. To understand the issues, we need to understand a bit more about dumping.

Possible motives for dumping. Japanese producers dump steel in the United States because it is profitable for them to do so. There are several reasons why it might pay them to sell more cheaply here than at home.[5]

1. It may be a sensible long-term strategy because of economies of large-scale production and the fact that the Japanese home market is permanently too small to support an industry of efficient size. In such circumstances, to have an efficient industry requires an export market; but to achieve that market, a low-price policy may be required. By selling cheaply abroad, the country can generate sufficient demand to justify an efficient-size industry. Dumping in this case benefits both its domestic and its foreign customers, by making it possible to produce output at the lowest possible cost per unit.

---

[5] The theory of price discrimination, studied in microeconomics, shows that when elasticity of demand differs in two markets, it pays to charge different prices in each market. Here we are concerned about why Japan may wish to sell in the U.S. market at all, given the distance it must ship and the competition it faces from American producers.

2. It may be a sensible middle-term strategy to provide a market for efficiently produced steel for a period — say five or ten years — until Japanese manufacturers will be able to absorb the entire output of Japanese production. In this scenario, home sales would gradually replace export sales. Dumping permits an efficient-size industry now, without waiting for Japanese demand to grow.

3. It may be a sensible cyclical strategy, providing a market for output in periods when Japanese demand is low, and thereby utilizing the capacity required to meet maximum Japanese demands in periods of boom and expansion. In this scenario, sales in the export market are simply sporadic "white sales" that permit Japanese production to continue on an even level over the cycle.

4. It may be a predatory strategy designed to destroy the foreign industry. In this scenario, after foreign plants have shut down and the foreign industry's work force has dispersed, prices can be raised to exploit the foreigner's new dependence on imports.

Effects on the buying country. Suppose America is the "beneficiary" of dumped Japanese steel, that is, steel sold at less than the Japanese home price and (let us suppose) below the average cost of production in the United States. If such sales continue, they will either eliminate the U.S. industry or force it to become competitive by becoming more efficient. However unfair this may sound to American steel makers, it will benefit American steel buyers for as long as they are able to buy cheaper steel. Cheaper steel will lead to less expensive buildings, refrigerators, nails, and all other products that use steel.

No matter what the Japanese producers' motives, the American steel industry and the United Steelworkers of America will want the U.S. government to stop this, for it threatens their profits and their jobs.

Suppose the government chooses to look beyond the political pressures of the moment and to do what is best for the national interest. Here it matters which of the four motivations explains the dumping. If the Japanese are prepared to supply cheap steel on a permanent basis, it would surely benefit Americans to buy Japanese steel and use American resources to produce something in which we have a comparative advantage. This is the case for doing nothing to protect the domestic steel industry and instead helping it to become more efficient or encouraging an orderly shift of workers and resources out of steel production.

However, if cheap Japanese steel would destroy the American industry without replacing the need for it — that is, for any of the last three listed reasons — then sufficient protection to preserve a viable industry may be required. This is the valid case for protectionism.[6]

The problem for policy is to diagnose what is happening and to adopt rules that will preserve needed industries without depriving American buyers of cheaper sources of supply. Currently there is controversy about what is really happening in Japanese steel production; many economists are not persuaded that protection is required to preserve American national interests.

Antidumping provisions and trigger prices. Under current American law, any American producer or the government itself can file suit before the U.S. International Trade Commission, alleging that a foreign producer is dumping. It need not show *harm,* only that the American price is below the foreign producer's home price. Congress has given the commission the power to impose quotas or tariffs on the dumping country when such an allegation is found to be true.

In 1977 the United States announced a series of **trigger prices** for imported steel products. If a foreign producer were to sell below one of those prices, the United States would initiate antidumping proceedings. The trigger prices were set at a level designed to be no lower than the

---

[6] The fact that three of the four motives listed lead to the protectionist position does not mean that they are three times as likely to apply as the other motive.

average total cost of production and shipment of the Japanese steel industry.

Trigger prices—vital protection or unjustified protectionism? If trigger prices had been set at levels just sufficient to prevent pricing below Japanese marginal costs of production and shipment, they could readily be defended as a means of protecting the domestic industry against destructive competition that could not be expected to provide a reliable long-term supply of steel. No producer can permanently sell below marginal costs unless subsidized. There is a valid fear of pricing below marginal costs. Similarly, if foreign producers are unwilling to enter into long-run supply contracts at their bargain prices, it might be inferred that the Japanese supply is subject to interruptions and could not be counted on to replace American production. Thus there is a case for scrutiny of both import prices and supply contracts.

The American rules, however, do not limit their applicability to such legitimate concerns. Two features of the trigger-price system now in effect make it highly protectionist. First, the setting of trigger prices at the level of *average total costs* places them above the marginal costs of an industry subject to decreasing costs. This assures that much price discrimination that may be mutually beneficial to Japanese producers and American buyers will be challenged. Second, the fact that *any* price discrimination is classified as dumping by the U.S. antidumping rules, and thus subject to penalties, means these challenges will be sustained. As a result the trigger prices become in effect minimum prices below which no foreign producer can afford to sell. Thus the provisions inhibit foreign competition and serve as nontariff barriers to trade, both where dumping is beneficial to American interests and where it is not.

Overall Importance of Nontariff Barriers in the United States

American trade policy, all things considered, remains relatively unprotectionist. But in se-lected industries—textiles and steel among them —the combined effect of nontariff and tariff barriers is significant. Many economists who have seen American policy become less and less protectionist over 50 years are concerned that protectionism will spread via nontariff barriers as American policymakers, unable to find a short-run solution to pockets of unemployment, prove unable to resist the protectionist views of the lobbyists for industries hurt by foreign competition.

INTERNATIONAL AGREEMENTS CONCERNING TRADE AND TARIFFS

In the past any country could impose any desired set of tariffs on its imports. But when one country increases its tariffs, the action may trigger retaliatory changes by its trading partners. Just as an arms race can escalate, so can a tariff war; precisely this happened during the 1920s and early 1930s. Extended negotiations may then be required to undo the damage.

Bilateral Agreements

International attempts to roll back tariffs from the high levels of the late 1920s began with the passage of the 1934 Trade Agreements Act in the United States. This act authorized the president to enter into bilateral trade agreements with other countries providing for *reciprocal* decreases in any tariff of up to 50 percent. The act also provided for unconditional most-favored-nation treatment in any such agreement. This meant that if we agreed on a tariff with country X for some commodity today, it would be automatically lowered if tomorrow we agreed to a lower tariff on the commodity with country Y.

There were serious drawbacks to bilateral negotiation. Because of the most-favored-nation clauses, one country was reluctant to make large reductions in tariffs on an important import except in return for a reciprocal reduction in the tariff it paid on an important export. Yet much trade is multinational: A imports from B, which imports from C, which imports from A. In these circumstances *bilateral* negotiations between A and B, B and C, and C and A might each fail to agree to tariff reductions. The solution, obviously, was *multinational* negotiations, but they did not occur on a large scale until after World War II.

The General Agreement on Tariffs and Trade (GATT)

One of the most notable achievements of the post-World War II world in retreating from the high-water mark of protectionism achieved in the 1930s was the General Agreement on Tariffs and trade (GATT). Under this agreement, GATT countries meet periodically to negotiate bilaterally on mutually advantageous cuts in tariffs. They agree in advance that any tariff cuts negotiated in this way will be extended to all member countries. Significant tariff reductions have been effected by the member countries.

The two most recent rounds of GATT agreements have each reduced tariffs by about one-third. The Kennedy Round negotiations were completed in 1967, and new rates were phased in over a five-year period ending in 1972. The most recent Tokyo Round negotiations began in 1975 and were completed in 1979. Final approval by the approximately 100 member nations of GATT was being secured in 1980. The reductions begin to take effect in 1981.

The enormous reductions in *tariffs* that have been the result of GATT are a bit misleading in terms of the freedom of trade because of the growing use of nontariff barriers. Perhaps the most important feature of the Tokyo Round was the agreement, for the first time, on steps to limit the growth of nontariff barriers. It is too early to tell whether these efforts will prove as successful as the tariff reductions.

Regional Common Markets

A common market is an agreement among a group of countries to eliminate barriers to free trade among themselves and to provide a common trading front to the rest of the world.

The most important is the so-called European Common Market. In 1957 the Treaty of Rome joined France, Germany, Italy, Holland, Belgium, and Luxembourg in the European Economic Community (EEC). The original six were joined in 1973 by the United Kingdom, the Republic of Ireland, and Denmark; the entry of Spain, Portugal, and Greece is currently being considered.

The EEC is dedicated to bringing about free trade, complete mobility of factors of production, and the eventual harmonization of fiscal and monetary policies among the member countries. Tariff reductions were made according to a time schedule that eliminated all tariffs on manufactured goods among the original six before 1970. If the development continues, before the end of the century Western Europe will be a single economic community with a free movement of goods, labor, and capital among the member countries.

Other common markets have been formed, such as the Central American Common Market and the East African Community, but none has yet achieved the success of the EEC, and some have collapsed.

Summary

1. Free trade among nations may be restricted intentionally by protectionist policies in the form of tariffs, import quotas, restrictions on the purchase of foreign exchange, and in other ways.

2. The case for free trade is that world output of all commodities can be higher under free trade than when protectionism restricts regional specialization.

3. Protection can be urged as a means to ends other than maximizing world living standards. Examples of such ends are to produce a diversified economy, to reduce fluctuations in national income, to retain distinctive national traditions, and to improve national defense.

4. Protection can also be urged on grounds that it may lead to higher living standards for the protectionist country than would a policy of free trade. Such a result might come about through exploiting a monopoly position or by allowing inexperienced or uneconomically small industries to become sufficiently efficient that they can subsequently compete with foreign industries.

5. Virtually everyone would agree that free trade should be chosen if the only choice were between free trade and *no* trade. However, most real choices facing nations today are not about free trade versus no trade; rather they are about *a little more* trade (caused, say, by a slight lowering of tariffs) versus *a little less* trade (caused, say, by a slight raising of tariffs). Here the choice is not so obvious as that between free trade and no trade. The potential gains from small reductions in barriers to trade must be balanced against other objectives and other effects.

6. Some fallacious free trade arguments are that (a) because it is possible for free trade to be beneficial, free trade will in fact always be beneficial; and (b) because infant industries seldom admit to growing up and thus try to retain their protection indefinitely, the whole country necessarily loses by protecting its infant industries.

7. Some fallacious protectionist arguments are that (a) mutually advantageous trade is impossible because one trader's gain must always be the other's loss; (b) our high-paid workers must be protected against the competition from low-paid foreign workers; (c) imports are to be discouraged because they lower national income and cause unemployment; and (d) buying abroad sends our money abroad, whereas buying at home keeps our money at home.

8. Trade is vitally important in the national incomes of many countries. It is relatively less important to the United States. Nonetheless, trade is vital to particular American industries, and few economists doubt that American living standards would be lowered significantly if America tried to make itself fully self-sufficient.

9. Although America today has very low tariffs, its recent tendency to institute nontariff barriers either by negotiation (as in textiles) or by unilateral policies (as in steel) leads to some uncertainty as to whether the 50-year trend to ever freer trade is being reversed.

10. International agreements and negotiations have succeeded in lowering trade barriers from the very high levels of 50 years ago. In 1934 the United States took the lead in negotiating reciprocal trade treaties containing most-favored-nation clauses. After World War II the GATT began a series of multinational rounds of tariff reduction that have greatly lowered tariffs. GATT is now beginning to attack nontariff barriers as well. Regional common markets, such as the EEC, have created substantial free trade areas.

Topics for Review

Free trade and protectionism
The case for some protectionism
The case for free trade versus no trade
Fallacious arguments about protectionism
Tariff and nontariff barriers to trade
Dumping
Most-favored-nation treatment
Bilateral and multilateral agreements

Discussion Questions

1. Suppose America had imposed prohibitive tariffs on all imported cars over the last three decades. How do you think this would have affected (a) the U.S. automobile industry, (b) the American public, (c) the kinds of cars produced by U.S. manufacturers?

2. George Washington, in his Farewell Address, argued that the United States should foster free trade but at the same time avoid any complex political arrangements with foreign countries. Are free trade and absence of foreign entanglements compatible goals in time of peace? In a world where there is a threat of war?

3. Lobbyists for many industries argue that their products are essential to national defense and therefore require

protection. Suppose that supplies of a certain commodity are indeed essential in wartime. How does restricting imports solve the problem? Are there alternatives to import restrictions? If so, how might the alternatives be evaluated?

4. Import quotas are often used instead of tariffs. What real difference (if any) is there between quotas and tariffs? Explain why lobbyists for some American industries (cheese, sugar, shoes) support import quotas, while lobbyists for others (pizza manufacturers, soft drink manufacturers, retail stores) oppose them. Would you expect labor unions to support or oppose quotas?

5. Listed below are some recent average duties paid in the United States, by commodity classes.

Coffee	0%	Raw wool	15%
Whisky	9	Clothing	25
Iron ore		Television sets	5
and scrap	0	Chemicals	9
Natural rubber	0	Newsprint	0

What economic and political reasons can you see for

duties on some commodities being well above the average rate (7 percent) of duty charged and for others being zero?

6. "The only pro-tariff argument that is likely to be valid for the whole world taken as an economic unit (rather than for a particular nation at a particular time) is the infant industry argument." Explain why you agree or disagree with this statement.

7. The United States has greatly reduced tariffs since Congress passed trade legislation authorizing the president to negotiate tariff concessions with foreign countries. Why might Congress find it desirable to give the president this authority rather than reserve the authority to itself?

8. When France increased tariff restrictions on foreign poultry, seriously hurting American chicken exporters, the United States reversed tariff reductions that had been made on brandy. Does this kind of "trade war" make any sense?

9. "A commodity that does not face foreign competition, either because of trade barriers or because of transport costs, is going to cost domestic buyers too much in the long term." Is this ever true? Is it always true?

Foreign Exchange, Exchange Rates, and the Balance of Payments

41

In the 1970s Americans for the first time found themselves hearing about the dollar and its price on the evening news. "The dollar was down today on world markets" and similarly worded reports became commonplace. In this chapter our concern is with what it means to speak of the "price of the dollar" and what causes that price to change. The discussion will bring together material on three topics studied elsewhere in this book: the theory of supply and demand (Chapter 5), the nature of money (Chapter 32), and the process of international trade (Chapter 39).

THE NATURE OF FOREIGN EXCHANGE TRANSACTIONS

We have seen that money is vital in any sophisticated economy that relies on specialization and exchange. Money consists of any accepted medium of exchange. Yet money as we know it is a *national* matter, one closely controlled by the national governments. Money in the United States is the dollar, money in England is pounds sterling, money in Japan is the yen, and money in Germany is the mark.

Each country has its own monetary system, and all governments regulate the size of the money supply within their own countries. If you live in Sweden, you will earn krona and spend krona; if you run a business in Austria, you will borrow schillings and meet your payroll with schillings. The currency of one country is generally acceptable within the bounds of that country, but it will not usually be accepted by households and firms in another country. The Stockholm bus company will accept krona but not Austrian schillings for your fare. The Austrian worker will not take Swedish krona for wages but will accept schillings. Because Austrian and Swedish firms, governments, and individuals sometimes take part in transactions that cross national boundaries, money necessarily takes on an international aspect. The need to exchange one currency for another arises from the need for the other currency to complete a purchase of goods or services.

In general, trade between nations can occur only if it is possible to exchange the currency of one nation for that of another.

When American producers sell their products, they require payment in dollars. They must meet their wage bills, pay for their raw materials, and reinvest or distribute their profits. If they sell their goods to American purchasers, there will be no problem; the firms will be paid dollars for their output. However, if American producers sell their goods to Indian importers, either the Indians must exchange their rupees to acquire dollars to pay for the goods or the U.S. producers must accept rupees—and they will accept rupees only if they know that they can exchange the rupees for the dollars that they require. The same holds true for producers in all countries; they must eventually receive payment for the goods that they sell in terms of the currency of their own country.

International payments that require the exchange of one national currency for another can be made in a bewildering variety of ways, but in essence they involve the exchange of currencies between people who have one currency and require another. Suppose that an American firm wishes to acquire £3,000 for some purpose (£ is the symbol for the British "pound sterling"). The firm can go to its bank or to some other seller of foreign currency and buy a check that will be accepted in England as £3,000. How many *dollars* the firm must pay to purchase this check will depend on the price of pounds in terms of dollars.

The exchange of one currency for another is part of the process of foreign exchange. The term **foreign exchange** refers to the actual foreign currency or various claims on it, such as bank deposits or promises to pay, that are traded for each other. The **exchange rate** is the price at which purchases and sales of foreign currency or claims on it take place; it is the amount of one currency that must be paid in order to obtain one unit of another currency. For example, if one must give up two dollars to get one pound sterling, the exchange rate (£1 = $2) could be expressed by saying the price of the pound is $2.00 or (the same thing) the price of the dollar is £0.50.

A change in the exchange rate is called an **appreciation of the exchange rate** when the value of the currency in question rises, and a **depreciation of the exchange rate** when the value of the currency falls. For example, when the price of the pound rises from $2 to $2.50 (in other words, the price of the dollar falls from £0.50 to £0.40), the pound has *appreciated* and the dollar has *depreciated*.

Let us see how foreign exchange transactions are carried out. Suppose that an American firm wishes to purchase a British sports car to sell in the United States. The British firm that made the car demands payment in pounds sterling. If the car is priced at £3,000, the American firm will go to its bank, purchase a check for £3,000, and send the check to the British seller. Let us suppose this requires that the firm pay $5,000.[1] (In other words, the exchange rate in this transaction is £1 = $1.67, or $1 = £0.60.) The British firm deposits the check in its bank. The effect of this transaction on banks in the two countries is shown in Table 41-1.

Now assume that in the same period of time a British wholesale firm purchases ten American refrigerators to sell in Britain. If the refrigerators are priced at $500 each, the American seller will have to be paid $5,000. To make this payment, the British importing firm goes to its bank and writes a check on its account for £3,000 and re-

---

[1] Banks charge a small commission for effecting exchanges of currency, but we shall ignore this and assume that parties can exchange moneys back and forth at the going exchange rate.

TABLE 41–1
Changes in the Balance Sheets of Two Banks as a Result of International Trade

U.K. bank			U.S. bank		
Assets	Liabilities		Assets	Liabilities	
No change	(1) Deposits of car exporter	+£3,000	No change	(1) Deposits of car importer	−$5,000
	(2) Deposits of refrigerator importer	−£3,000		(2) Deposits of refrigerator exporter	+$5,000
	Net change	0		Net change	0

International transactions involve a transfer of deposit liabilities among banks. The table records two separate international transactions at an exchange rage of $1 = £0.60: (1) an American purchase of a British car for £3,000 (= $5,000), and (2) a British purchase of American refrigerators for $5,000 (= £3,000). The American's import of a car reduces deposit liabilities to U.S. citizens and increases deposit liabilities to British citizens. The Britisher's import of refrigerators does the opposite. When a series of transactions are equal in value, there is only a transfer of deposit liabilities among individuals within a country. The American refrigerator manufacturer received (in effect) the dollars the American car purchaser gave up to get a British-made car.

ceives a check drawn on a U.S. bank for $5,000 The check is sent to America and deposited in an American bank. The effect of this transaction is also shown in Table 41-1.

The two transactions cancel each other out, and there is no net change in international liabilities. No money need pass between British and American banks to effect the transactions; each bank merely increases the deposit of one domestic customer and lowers the deposit of another. Indeed, as long as the flow of payments between the two countries is equal (Americans pay as much to British residents as British residents pay to Americans), all payments can be managed as in the above examples, and there will be no need for a net payment from British banks to American banks. When the flow of payments is not the same in both directions, things are a little more complicated, as we will see later.

The Theory of Exchange Rates in a Competitive Foreign Exchange Market

Consider, as an example, trade between America and Britain and the determination of the rate of exchange between their two currencies, dollars and pounds sterling. In order to relate this problem to the demand and supply analysis of Chapter 5, we need only to recognize that *in the market for pounds sterling* the American firm that wants pounds is a demander of pounds and the British firm that is selling pounds to buy dollars is a supplier of pounds. We can also look at the *same* transaction in the market for dollars: the American firm is a supplier of dollars, and the British firm is a demander of dollars.

Because one currency is traded for another on the foreign exchange market, it follows that to desire (demand) dollars implies a willingness to offer (supply) pounds, while an offer (supply) of dollars implies a desire (demand) for pounds.

At an exchange rate of £1 = $1.667, a British importer who offers to buy $5.00 with pounds must be offering to sell £3.00. Similarly, an American importer who offers to sell $5.00 for pounds must be offering to buy £3.00. For this reason, a theory of the exchange rate between dollars and pounds can deal either with the demand for and the supply of dollars or with the demand for and the supply of pounds sterling; both need not be considered. We shall concentrate on the demand, supply, and price of dollars (quoted in pounds). The parallel between this and the supply, demand, and price of pounds (quoted in dollars) is explored in the box.

Two Ways of Looking at the Exchange of Dollars for Pounds Sterling

In a world of only two currencies, dollars and pounds, there is only one foreign exchange market, but it can be looked at in two ways: (A) as a market for dollars and (B) as a market for pounds. The two graphs show the alternative perspectives.

In (A) dollars are bought and sold. The price of the purchases is quoted as so many pounds sterling for each dollar. Consider point a on the demand curve $D_£$. This price-quantity pair shows that when each dollar costs £0.52, buyers will purchase $90 million. Point E shows that if the price falls to £0.50, buyers will purchase $100 million. Points a and E are simply points on the demand curve $D_£$ for dollars. Such a demand curve can shift, say to the curve labeled $D'_£$, for which at each price more dollars are demanded. Such a shift might be caused by an increase in interest rates offered by American banks. Point b is on the new demand curve.

At point a, buyers who were willing to pay £0.52 per dollar to acquire $90 million were prepared to give up £46.8 million to do so (90 × .52 = 46.8). They were prepared to supply pounds. The price of pounds in terms of dollars is the reciprocal of the price of dollars in terms of pounds. That is, when $1 = £0.52,

£1 = $1.92. (This is the same as saying that if the price of hamburgers in terms of dollars is $.50, the price of a dollar is 2.0 hamburgers.)

In (B), where the supply and demand for *pounds* is measured in dollars, point a appears as the willingness to supply £46.8 million at a price per pound of $1.92. It is the *same* point a as in (A); it is the opposite side of the same willingness to give up pounds to acquire dollars. Point a is on the demand curve for dollars ($D_\$$) *and* on the supply curve of pounds ($S_£$).

Point E in (B) is the other view of point E in (A); it too is on the supply curve of pounds, $S_£$. Similarly, when the demand curve for dollars shifts to $D'_\$$, this is the same thing as the supply curve of pounds shifting from $S_£$ to $S'_£$. Satisfy yourself that point b is the same point in both diagrams.

Because both (A) and (B) show exactly the same information, we can use either one or convert from one to another. This will seem less confusing if you remember that every time you buy (demand) something, you give up (supply) something else. When a farmer swaps a chicken for your axe, does the farmer acquire an axe or lose a chicken? The answer, of course, is both.

(A) Market for dollars

(B) Market for pounds sterling

THE DEMAND FOR DOLLARS

Sources of a Demand for Dollars

American exports. One important source of a demand for dollars in foreign exchange markets is someone who does not own dollars but wishes to use his or her own currency to buy American-made goods and services. The British importer of refrigerators was such a purchaser; an Austrian couple planning to vacation in the United States is another; the Soviet government seeking to buy American wheat is a third; the Volkswagen company wishing to open bank accounts in several Pennsylvania towns preparatory to building its new plant there is a fourth. All are sources of demand for dollars arising out of international trade. Each potential buyer wants to sell its own currency and buy dollars for the purpose of purchasing American exports.

Long-term capital flows. A second source of a demand for dollars comes from foreigners who wish to purchase American assets. In 1979 a German firm purchased 29 percent of the assets of A&P. This transaction required the purchase of dollars for marks. Billions of "petrodollars" are being invested in American securities and real estate by the oil-rich countries and their residents. In order to buy American assets, holders of foreign currencies must first buy dollars on foreign exchange markets. Such transactions are called *long-term capital movements*.

Short-term capital flows. When interest rates in the United States soared early in 1980, floods of "foreign money" came to the United States to buy short-term treasury bills and notes, certificates of deposit, and so on. The buyers of these securities were seeking a high return on their liquid assets. But first these buyers had to convert their lire, guilder, marks, and francs into dollars. When people sell financial assets in one country for foreign exchange that they they use to buy short-term financial assets in another country, the transactions are called *short-term capital movements,* or sometimes "flights of capital," from one currency to another.

As a medium of exchange. One other type of transaction may be noted. Certain currencies, the most important of them the American dollar, have come to be accepted by nations, banks, and ordinary people as an international medium of exchange: these currencies are readily acceptable among buyers and sellers who might be less willing to trade with each other using less well-known kinds of money. Thus a Norwegian exporter of smoked fish to a Turkish wholesaler may quote prices in dollars and expect payment in dollars. Most of the oil sold by the OPEC countries must be paid for in dollars, whether the purchasing firm or government is in France, Chad, or India. The French purchaser of oil must first convert francs to dollars, then pay the dollars to Saudi Arabia. There is therefore a demand for currencies that act as an international medium of exchange. Some of the trading in the U.S. dollar exists to provide a medium of exchange quite independent of the flow of American imports or exports.

Reserve currency demand. Firms, banks, and governments often accumulate and hold currency reserves just as individuals maintain savings accounts. The government of Nigeria, for example, has foreign exchange reserves. It may decide to increase its holdings of dollars and reduce its holdings of pounds; if so, it will be a demander of dollars (and a supplier of pounds) on foreign exchange markets.

The Aggregate Demand for Dollars

The demand for the dollar by holders of pounds sterling is the sum of the demands for it for each of the purposes discussed above — for purchases of American exports, for long-term capital acquisitions, for short-term capital acquisitions, and for purchases of the dollar to use in other transactions or to add to reserve holdings as a reserve currency. The *total* foreign exchange market demand for dollars in terms of pounds includes the demand of British persons and firms wishing to use dollars to make payments in the United

States. It also includes the demands of other businesses, individuals, and governments who hold pounds and want to sell them for dollars.

Furthermore, since people, firms, and governments in all countries purchase goods from and invest in many other countries, the demand for any one currency will be the aggregate demand of business, individuals, and governments in a number of different countries. Thus the total demand for dollars, for example, may represent Germans offering marks, British offering pounds, Greeks offering drachmas, and so on. The demand for any one currency comes from many sources, and the supply of that currency comes from many holders of that currency, including banks, individuals, and businesses in many different countries.

There are exchange rates between every pair of currencies. A process known as arbitrage keeps them in line. **Arbitrage** is the buying of currencies in markets where they are cheap and selling them where they are expensive in order to make a profit on the transaction. Once the rates between the U.S. dollar and any two foreign currencies have been determined, there will be only one rate between the two foreign currencies that will *not* allow buyers and sellers of foreign exchange to engage in profitable arbitrage.

Consider an example. Suppose that on a particular day the dollar is worth £0.60 and 800 lire. Given the two rates, the only rate between lire and sterling that rules out profitable arbitrage operations is £0.60 = 800 lire, which is the equivalent of £1 = 1,333 lire. Table 41-2 gives an example in which the exchange rate between the pound and the lira is out of line with the other two. Such "disorderly cross-rates" will be quickly eliminated in a free market. Arbitragers will buy lire with dollars and sell lire against pounds. If rates are free to vary, this will tend to bid the rates toward a consistent level where it is no longer possible to make profits by arbitrage.

For our purposes it will be helpful to deal with only one pair of currencies, pounds and dollars. We can do this by imagining that all other demands for dollars have first been converted into

TABLE 41-2

An Example of Rates of Exchange Giving the Possibility of Profitable Arbitrage Operations

One unit of this currency	Exchanges for the stated number of units of this currency		
	Dollar	Lira	Pound
Dollar	1	800	0.60
Lira	0.00125	1	0.000909
Pound	1.67	1,100	1

Disorderly cross-rates mean that a profit can be made merely by buying and selling currencies at existing rates in different markets. In this example, a trader can start with $2 and purchase 1,600 lire. He or she can then use the lire to purchase £1.45, which can be exchanged for $2.42. The profit is $.42 on an investment of $2, or 21 percent. Because the transactions can be effected quickly and with large amounts of money, very large profits can be earned. Because this is possible, however, such rates will not long persist.

pounds. For example, a German wishing to purchase dollars with marks is (for our purposes) assumed to convert the marks to pounds and then to offer the pounds for dollars.

The Shape of the Demand Curve for Dollars

The demand for dollars in terms of pounds is represented by a downward-sloping curve such as that shown in Figure 41-1. This figure plots the price of dollars (measured in pounds) on the vertical axis and the quantity of dollars on the horizontal axis. Moving down the vertical scale, the dollar becomes cheaper (i.e., it is worth fewer pounds); its value is depreciating on the foreign exchange market. Moving up the scale, the dollar becomes more expensive; it is appreciating on the market.

Why does the demand curve for dollars slope downward? Consider the demand derived from purchases of American exports. If the dollar depreciates in value, the sterling price of American exports will fall. The British will buy more of the cheaper U.S. goods and will require more dollars for this purpose. The quantity of dollars demanded will rise. In the opposite case, when

FIGURE 41-1

An Exchange Rate Determined on a Competitive Market

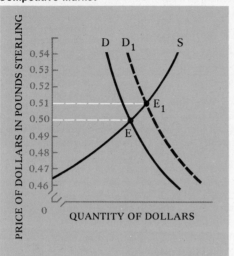

The **equilibrium exchange rate equates demand and supply on the foreign exchange market.** The quantity of dollars demanded is originally equal to the quantity supplied at a price of £0.50 per dollar (or £1 = $2.00). If the demand of dollars rises to D_1 the equilibrium exchange rate will change to £0.51 per dollar—that is, the dollar appreciates in value and the pound depreciates.

the dollar rises in value, the price of American exports rises in terms of foreign currency. The British will buy fewer U.S. goods and thus demand fewer U.S. dollars. Similar considerations affect other sources of demand for dollars. When the dollar is cheaper, American assets or securities become attractive purchases, and the quantity purchased will rise. As it does, the quantity of dollars demanded to pay for the purchases will increase.

The demand curve for dollars on the foreign exchange market is downward sloping when plotted against the sterling price of dollars.

THE SUPPLY OF DOLLARS

Because of the symmetrical nature of foreign exchange markets, the sources of supply of dollars are merely the opposite side of the demand for pounds. (Recall that the supply of dollars seeking pounds is the same as the *demand* for pounds by holders of dollars.) Who wants to sell dollars? Americans seeking to purchase foreign goods and services or assets will be supplying dollars and purchasing pounds, yen, marks, schillings, and pesos for the purpose. Holders of American securities may, in response to some international event, decide to sell their American holdings and shift into another country's assets. If they do, they will try to sell dollars—that is, they will be supplying dollars to the foreign exchange market. Similarly, a country with large dollar reserves of foreign exchange may decide the dollar is "weak" and try to sell dollars in order to buy pounds or marks.

Once again, from many sources and for many purposes, people will be willing to give up dollars and acquire other currencies. Again, for simplicity, we assume they supply dollars to acquire pounds. (They may subsequently use the pounds to buy marks or any other currency.)

What about the shape of the supply curve of dollars? When the dollar depreciates, the effective price of British exports to the United States rises. It takes more dollars to buy the same British good, so Americans will buy fewer of the now more expensive British goods and will spend fewer dollars on them. The amount of dollars being offered in exchange for pounds sterling in order to pay for British exports (American imports) thus falls.

In the opposite case, when the dollar appreciates, British exports to the United States become cheaper, more are sold, and more dollars are spent on them. Thus more dollars will be offered in exchange for pounds in order to obtain the foreign exchange needed to pay for the extra imports. Precisely the same argument used for commodities applies to purchases and sales of assets.

The supply curve of dollars on the foreign exchange market is upward sloping when plotted against the sterling price of dollars.

EQUILIBRIUM EXCHANGE RATES IN A COMPETITIVE MARKET

Consider a rate of exchange that is set on a freely competitive market. Like any competitive price, this rate fluctuates according to the conditions of demand and supply.

Assume that the current price of dollars is so low (say, £0.48 in Figure 41-1) that the quantity of dollars demanded exceeds the quantity supplied. Dollars will be in scarce supply, some people who require dollars to make payments to America will be unable to obtain them, and the price of dollars will be bid up. The value of the dollar vis-à-vis the pound will appreciate. As the price of the dollar rises, the sterling price of U.S. exports to Britain rises and the quantity of U.S. dollars demanded to buy British goods decreases. However, as the dollar price of imports from Britain falls, a larger quantity will be purchased and the quantity of U.S. dollars supplied will rise. Thus a rise in the price of the dollar reduces the quantity demanded and increases the quantity supplied. Where the two curves intersect, quantity demanded equals quantity supplied—and the exchange rate is in equilibrium.

What happens when the price of dollars is above its equilibrium value? The quantity of dollars demanded will be less than the quantity supplied. With the dollar in excess supply, some people who wish to convert dollars into pounds will be unable to do so. The price of dollars will fall, fewer dollars will be supplied, more will be demanded, and an equilibrium will be reestablished.

A competitive foreign exchange market is like other competitive markets in that the forces of demand and supply tend to lead to an equilibrium price in which quantity demanded equals quantity supplied.

CHANGES IN EXCHANGE RATES

What causes exchange rates to vary? The simplest answer to this question is, changes in demand or supply in the foreign exchange market. Anything that shifts the demand curve for dollars to the right or the supply curve for dollars to the left increases the equilibrium exchange rate and thus tends to lead to the appreciation of the dollar. Anything that shifts the demand curve for dollars to the left or the supply curve for dollars to the right decreases the equilibrium exchange rate and tends to lead to the depreciation of the dollar. This is nothing more than a restatement of the laws of supply and demand, applied now to the market for foreign currencies.

But what causes the shifts in demand and supply that lead to changes in exchange rates? There are many causes, some of them transitory and some persistent; we shall mention several of the most important.

A Rise in the Foreign Price of Imports

Consider the effects of a large rise in the price at which some important import is supplied. Assume that the pound price of Scotch whisky increases sharply. Assume also that American drinkers have an inelastic demand for Scotch, so they end up spending more pounds for Scotch whisky than they did before. In order to buy the extra pounds, they must supply more dollars. The supply curve of dollars shifts to the right, and the price of the dollar tends to fall.

A Rise in the Domestic Price of Exports

Suppose the dollar price of something we export rises. What this will do to the demand for dollars depends on the foreign elasticity of demand for the American product. If the demand is elastic, perhaps because other countries supply the same product in world markets, the total amount spent will decrease and thus fewer dollars will be demanded. That is, the demand curve for dollars will shift to the left and the dollar will depreciate. If the demand is inelastic, say because America is uniquely able to supply the product for which there are no close substitutes, more will be spent, the demand for dollars to pay the bigger bill will shift the demand curve to the right, and the dollar will appreciate.

Changes in the Overall Price Levels

Suppose that instead of a change in the price of a specific export, such as tractors, there is a change in all prices due to inflation. What matters here is the change in our price level relative to the price levels of our trading partners. (In our two-country example, "Britain" stands for the rest of the world.)

An equal percentage change in the price level in both countries. Suppose there is a 10 percent inflation in both the United States and Britain. In this case, the sterling prices of British goods and the dollar prices of U.S. goods both rise by 10 percent. At any given exchange rate, then, the dollar prices of British goods and the sterling prices of American goods will each rise by 10 percent. Thus the relative prices of imports and domestically produced goods will be unchanged in both countries. There is now no reason to expect a change in either country's demand for imports at the original exchange rate, so the inflations in the two countries leave the equilibrium exchange rate unchanged.

A change in the price level of only one country. What will happen if there is inflation in the United States while the price level remains stable in Britain? The dollar price of U.S. goods will rise, and American goods will become more expensive in Britain. This will cause the quantity of American exports, and therefore the quantity of dollars demanded by British importers in order to pay for American goods, to diminish.

At the same time, British exports to America will have an unchanged dollar price while the price of American goods sold at home will have been increased by the inflation. Thus British goods will be more attractive compared to American goods (because they have become *relatively* cheaper), and more British goods will be bought in America. At any exchange rate the quantity of dollars supplied in order to purchase pounds will be increased.

An American inflation unmatched in Britain causes the demand curve for dollars to shift to the left and the supply curve of dollars to shift to the right. As a result the equilibrium price of dollars must fall; there is a depreciation in the value of the dollar relative to that of the pound.

Inflation at unequal rates. The two foregoing examples are of course just limiting cases of a more general situation in which each country can experience price level changes at home. The arguments can readily be extended when one realizes that it is the *relative* size of the changes in prices in two countries that determines whether home goods or foreign goods look more or less attractive. If country A is inflating more rapidly than country B, country A's exports will be becoming relatively expensive in B's markets, while imports from country B will be becoming relatively cheap in A's markets. This will shift the demand curve for A's currency to the left and the supply curve to the right. Each change causes the price of A's currency to fall.

If the price level of one country is rising relative to that of another country, the equilibrium value of its currency will be falling relative to that of the second country.

Capital Movements

Major capital flows can exert major influences on exchange rates. For example, an increased desire to invest in British assets will shift rightward the supply of dollars and depreciate the value of the dollar.

A movement of investment funds has the effect of appreciating the exchange rate of the capital-importing country and depreciating the exchange rate of the capital-exporting country.

This statement is true for all capital movements, short term or long term. Since the motives that lead to large capital movements are likely to be different in the short and long terms, it is worth considering each.

Short-term capital movements. A major motive for short-term capital flows is a change in interest rates. International traders hold transactions balances just as domestic traders do. These balances are often lent out on short-term loan rather than being left idle. Naturally, the holders of these balances will tend to lend them, other things being equal, in those markets where interest rates are highest. Thus if one major country's short-term rate of interest rises above the rates in most other countries, there will tend to be a large inflow of short-term capital into that country to take advantage of the high rate, and this will tend to appreciate the currency. If these short-term interest rates should fall, there will most likely be a sudden shift away from that country as a source of transactions balances, and its currency will tend to depreciate.[2]

A second motive for short-term capital movements is speculation about a country's exchange rate. If foreigners expect the dollar to appreciate, they will rush to buy assets that pay off in dollars; if they expect the dollar to depreciate, they will be reluctant to buy or hold American securities.

Long-term capital movements. Such movements are largely influenced by long-term expectations about another country's earnings and the long-run value of its currency. A German investor would be more willing to purchase an American factory if it expected that the dollar profits would buy more German marks in future years than the profits from investment in a German factory. This could happen if the American firm earned greater profits than the German firm, with exchange rates unchanged. It could also happen if the profits were the same but the investor expected the dollar to appreciate relative to the mark.

Capital movements: summary. Anything that leads to an inflow of capital—relatively high interest rates, high earnings expectations, expectations of exchange rate appreciation—increases the demand for a country's currency and tends to appreciate its exchange rate. Anything that leads to an outflow of capital—relatively low interest rates, low earnings expectations, expectations of exchange rate depreciation—decreases the demand for a country's currency and tends to depreciate its exchange rate.

Structural Changes

An economy can undergo structural changes that alter the equilibrium exchange rate. *Structural change* is an omnibus term for a change in cost structures, the invention of new products, or anything else that affects the pattern of comparative advantage. For example, when a country's products do not improve as rapidly as those of some other country, consumers' demand (at fixed prices) shifts slowly away from the first country's products and toward those of its foreign competitors. This causes a slow depreciation in the first country's exchange rate because the demand for its currency is shifting slowly leftward.

Many people believe that U.S. manufacturing today is suffering just such an adverse structural change, its exports of everything from textiles to automobiles being slowly displaced by exports from newly industrializing countries such as Korea, Germany, and Japan. This decreases the demand for dollars. The same forces lead domestic American households to turn ever more toward foreign-made goods, thereby increasing the supply of dollars. Each of these changes tends to depreciate the value of the dollar.

Loss of Confidence in the Dollar as a Reserve Currency

In the period since 1944 many nations, banks, and even private firms have come to hold dollars as a major part of their foreign exchange reserves. In 1970 more than $500 billion was held

---

[2] Such short-term capital flows in a market in which exchange rates and interest rates fluctuated freely would have a tendency to equalize interest rates in different countries. In effect, short-term capital movements would be a form of arbitrage in interest rates. But since central banks often prevent interest rates from fluctuating freely, changes in interest rates invite large volumes of short-term capital flows.

for that purpose. If for any reason these holders come to believe that the dollar will depreciate in world markets, they may decide that it would be shrewd to shift some of their dollar holdings to sterling, marks, or even gold. This happened during the 1970s. Indeed, for the decade overall the holdings of dollars decreased for 76 of 81 countries recently studied. When this happened, the supply of dollars on foreign exchange markets increased and led to a decrease in the equilibrium price of dollars. When there are large dollar holdings, attempts to "get out of dollars" in a hurry can lead to large rightward shifts of the supply curve and rapid depreciation of the price of the dollar.

Central Bank Management of Exchange Rates

So far we have considered exchange rates that are left completely free to be determined by the market forces of demand and supply. Such rates are called free, or flexible, or **floating exchange rates.** In practice, however, exchange rates are seldom left entirely free from influence by the central authorities.

FIXED EXCHANGE RATES

From the end of World War II until the early 1970s, the rates of exchange between most currencies were set, or pegged, within very narrow limits by each country's own central bank. Such rates are commonly called *pegged* or **fixed exchange rates.** When rates are fixed, fluctuations in the demand for and supply of dollars vis-à-vis other currencies are not allowed to affect the actual exchange rate. But of course they will create situations of disequilibrium in which there is excess demand or supply in the foreign exchange market.

While the government can fix the exchange rate of its currency, it cannot usually prevent shifts from developing in the demand for and supply of its currency. Either the government

must take steps to eliminate the excess demand or the excess supply or it must be prepared to change the exchange rate from one fixed level to another. A change in the rate at which a currency is fixed by its government is called a **revaluation of the exchange rate** when the currency is increased in value and a **devaluation of the exchange rate** when the currency is reduced in value.

How can a government manage a fixed exchange rate in order to avoid the need for devaluation or revaluation? Consider further our simple example in which only the United States and Britain trade with each other and there are only *two* currencies and *one* exchange rate between them. In this situation the U.S. and British governments cannot make independent decisions on fixing the exchange rate between their two currencies.

In practice, foreign governments (in our example, the British government) fixed the prices of their currencies in terms of U.S. dollars. Having picked a fixed exchange rate for sterling against the dollar, the British authorities must then manage matters so that the selected rate can actually be maintained. They must be prepared to offset imbalances in demand and supply by government sales or purchases of foreign exchange. In the face of short-term fluctuations in market demand and supply, the central authorities can maintain a fixed exchange rate by entering the market and buying and selling as required to stabilize the price.

As long as the central authorities are trying to maintain an exchange rate *that equates demand and supply on average,* the policy can be successful. Sometimes the authorities will be buying and at other times they will be selling, but their reserves will fluctuate around a constant average level.

However, if there is a permanent shift in one of the curves so that the pegged rate is substantially different from the long-term equilibrium rate, it will be very difficult to maintain the fixed rate. For example, if there is a major inflation in Britain and prices are stable in the United States, the equilibrium value of the British currency will fall. In a free market the pound would depreciate and the dollar appreciate. But we are assuming that this is not a free market. If the Bank of England persists in trying to maintain the original rate, it will have to meet the excess demand for dollars by selling its reserves of dollars. This policy can persist only as long as it has reserves that it is willing to spend to maintain its artificially high price of pounds. The Bank cannot do this indefinitely because sooner or later its reserves will be exhausted.

The management of a fixed rate is illustrated in Figure 41-2. When the rate is not near the free-market equilibrium rate, controls of various sorts may be introduced to attempt to shift the demand curve for foreign exchange so that it intersects the supply curve at a rate close to the controlled rate. This is usually done by restricting imports of goods and services or by restricting the export of capital.

If the authorities cannot shift demand and supply in order to keep the equilibrium rate approximately as high as the fixed rate, they will have no alternative but to devalue the exchange rate when they run out of reserves.

MANAGED FLEXIBLE RATES

In the current system, exchange rates are not stabilized at an announced par value. Nevertheless governments, working through their central banks, intervene from time to time to influence the exchange rate and prevent sharp or sudden changes in it. What tools does the government have for this task?

First, here too it can attempt to influence the long-term equilibrium exchange rate by various forms of payments or trade restrictions. Suppose there is excess supply of one currency and thus downward pressure on the exchange rate. If domestic holders of the currency are forbidden to buy all the foreign currency they wish, this will decrease the supply. Sometimes countries restrict the use of their domestic currency by requiring licenses for the purchase of foreign exchange.

FIGURE 41-2
A Fixed Exchange Rate

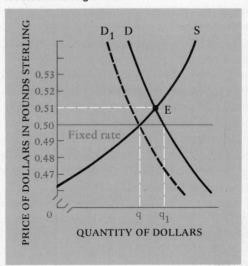

When an exchange rate is fixed at other than the equilibrium rate, there will be either persistent excess demand or excess supply. Suppose demand and supply curves of dollars in the absence of government controls are D and S; equilibrium is at E, with a price of £0.51 per dollar. The equilibrium price of the pound is $1.96. Now the British authorities peg the price of the pound at $2.00; that is, they fix the price of the dollar at £0.50. They have overvalued the pound and undervalued the dollar; as a result, there is an excess of dollars demanded over dollars supplied of qq_1. To maintain the fixed rate, it is necessary to shift either the demand curve or the supply curve (or both) so that the two intersect at the fixed rate. For example, demand might be shifted to D_1 by the British government's limiting imports. If the curves are not shifted, the fixed rate will have to be supported by the British government's supplying dollars in the amount of qq_1 per period out of its reserves.

This is called "blocking" their currency. If imports are restricted, there will be less need to sell the home currency to acquire foreign exchange.

Another method for bringing the market into line with the current exchange rate is to manipulate the short-term interest rate and thus to induce short-term capital into or out of the country. A U.S. government that wishes to increase the demand for dollars can raise interest rates above world market levels. This will induce some foreign investors to shift their excess cash out of pounds and marks and into dollars for the purpose of buying U.S. government bonds or other dollar financial assets. For as long as the inflow persists, the demand for dollars on the foreign exchange market will be high, so the value of the dollar will be held higher than it otherwise would be. But as soon as interest rates fall, a reverse flow will occur and put downward pressure on the dollar.

Another form of intervention is for the central bank to attempt to iron out short-term and medium-term fluctuations in the exchange rate through open market purchases and sales of foreign exchange. If the Fed enters the foreign exchange market to sell dollars and buy foreign exchange, this will cause the dollar to depreciate. If the Fed does the opposite, buying dollars and selling foreign exchange, this will cause the dollar to appreciate. The exchange rate can be stabilized against short-run fluctuations in this way, and it can even be held above its equilibrium value for as long as the Fed wishes to invest its reserves of foreign exchange.

The main difference between managed flexible rates and managed fixed rates is that with the former the government is not committed to defending a publicly announced rate; it can resist changes it thinks are transitory and yield to changes it believes are the result of long-term forces.

The Balance of Payments

THE NATURE OF BALANCE-OF-PAYMENTS ACCOUNTS

In order to know what is happening to the course of international trade, governments keep track of the *transactions* among countries. The record of such transactions is made in the **balance-of-payments accounts.** Each transaction, such as a

shipment of exports or the arrival of imported goods, is classified according to the payments or receipts that would typically arise from it.

Any transaction that is expected to lead to a payment to other nations is classified as a debit (−) item because, *ceteris paribus,* it subtracts from our foreign exchange reserves. American imports and outflows of American capital to purchase foreign assets are debit items. (An outflow of capital is really an *import* of the foreign assets purchased.) Any transaction that is expected to lead to a payment by foreigners to the United States or its residents is classified as a credit (+) item because, *ceteris paribus,* it adds to our foreign exchange reserves. American exports and capital flows into the United States are credit items.

Consider some examples. When a British importer buys an American washing machine to sell in the United Kingdom, this appears as a credit in the U.S. balance of payments because when the machine is paid for, sterling will be sold and dollars purchased. The United States thus gains foreign exchange on the deal. However, when an American shipping firm insures with Lloyds of London a cargo destined for Alexandria, Egypt, this represents a debit in the U.S. balance of payments because when the insurance premium is paid, the shipping firm will have to pay Lloyds in sterling. Because it will purchase and pay out sterling by selling dollars, the United States stands to lose foreign exchange on the deal. Of course, a credit item to one country is a debit item to the other, and vice versa; thus the washing machine transaction is a debit and the insurance transaction a credit in the British balance of payments.[3]

The first thing to notice about the record of international transactions is that the balance of payments refers to actual transactions, not desired transactions. We have seen that at some exchange rate between dollars and pounds it is quite possible for holders of sterling to want to

[3] As we shall see, there is nothing *inherently* good about "credits" or bad about "debits." The purpose of earning foreign exchange (gaining a credit) is to be able to use it (incurring a debit).

purchase more dollars in exchange for pounds than holders of dollars want to sell in exchange for pounds. In this situation quantity demanded exceeds quantity supplied. But it is not possible for sterling holders to buy more dollars than dollar holders will sell; every dollar that is bought must have been sold by someone, and every dollar that is sold must have been bought by someone.

Because the amount of dollars actually bought must equal the amount of dollars actually sold, the balance of payments always balances.

Although the total number of dollars bought on the foreign exchange market must equal the total number sold, this is not true of purchases and sales for each specific purpose or within particular categories. For example, more dollars may well be sold for the purpose of obtaining foreign currency to import foreign cars than are bought for the purpose of buying American cars for export to other countries. In such a case, the United States has a balance-of-payments deficit on the "car account": the value of U.S. imports of foreign cars exceeds the value of U.S. exports of American cars. Most economists are not interested in the balance of payments for single commodities, but they are interested in larger classes of transactions.

MAJOR CATEGORIES IN THE BALANCE-OF-PAYMENTS ACCOUNTS

Table 41-3 presents a typical balance-of-payments account that shows divisions that are of particular interest.

Current Account

The balance of payments on *current account* includes all payments made because of current purchases of goods and services. There is no automatic reason why current account payments should balance (any more than the automobile account should). It is quite possible that more dollars were sold in order to purchase imports than were bought in order to allow foreigners to

TABLE 41-3
Balance-of-payments Categories (billions of dollars)

Current account		
Exports	+ 300	
Imports	− 270	
Trade balance[a]		+ 30
Government grants and other transfers	− 10	− 10
Balance on current account		+ 20
Capital account		
Net change in U.S. investments abroad (increase −, decrease +)	− 60	
Net change in foreign investments in U.S. (increase +, decrease −)	+ 48	
Balance on capital account		− 12
Balance on capital plus current accounts		+ 8
Official financing		
Changes in liabilities to foreign official agencies (increase +, decrease −)	− 6	
Use of official reserves (increase −, decrease +)	− 2	
Balance on official account		− 8
Overall balance of payments		Always zero[b]

[a] We do not distinguish here between visible and invisible items. See footnote 4 on page 774.
[b] In actual balance-of-payments accounts there is often a "statistical discrepancy" item that results from the inability to measure accurately some industrial items. For example, many capital transactions are not recorded.

The overall balance of payments always balances, but the individual components do not have to. The principal categories of greatest interest are shown in color. In this example, the country shows a positive (surplus) trade balance (exports exceed imports) and a smaller positive (surplus) balance on current account. There is a negative (deficit) balance on capital account because capital exports exceeded capital imports. The capital *plus* current account surplus of $8 billion is what is commonly referred to as the "balance of payments." It is exactly matched by the balance in the official accounts.

purchase our exports. If so, the dollars must have come from somewhere, and the excess of sales over purchases on current account must be exactly matched by an excess of purchases over sales on the capital and official accounts.

The current account is often subdivided in a number of different ways. The most quoted is the so-called **balance of trade** (or the trade balance), the difference between the dollar value of exports and imports in a given year. In the table, exports exceeded imports in the year reported, and thus there was a *surplus* in the balance of trade. In other years imports exceed exports and there is a *deficit*, and in some years the balance of trade is virtually zero.

Note that the balance of trade relates only to the *difference* between exports and imports, not to the volume of trade. Thus one could have a $30 billion excess of exports over imports on a volume of exports of $300 billion or on a volume of $50 billion. In either case the same pressure on the exchange rate would be exerted. But the effect of foreign trade on the nation's economy would be very different because such things as the gains from trade depend on the volume of trade.

The gains from trade depend on the volume of trade, not the balance of trade. The effect on foreign exchange markets depends on the balance of trade, not the volume of trade.

The trade balance is sometimes divided further into visible and invisible trade balances.[4] **Visibles** are goods—all those things such as cars, pulpwood, aluminum, coffee, and iron ore that can be seen and touched when they cross international borders. **Invisibles** are services—all those things that cannot be seen or touched, such as insurance, freight haulage, and tourist expenditures. When a U.S. firm buys insurance from Lloyds of London for a shipment of goods consigned to Egypt, the firm consumes a British export just as surely as if it purchased and used a British-made automobile or sent its president on a vacation to

Scotland. Payment for the insurance services, for the automobile, and for the vacation must be made in pounds; each is thus a U.S. import and a British export.

Another invisible item is the payment of interest and dividends on loans and investments made by Americans in foreign countries. An American who holds shares in a British aircraft company will receive dividend payments in pounds. If the American wishes to spend these dividends at home, he or she will need to exchange the pounds for dollars. Interest and dividends on foreign loans and investments thus provide foreign exchange and are entered as credit items on the balance of payments.

The most important items in the current account not included in exports or imports are government current transactions. Among them are military expenditures in foreign lands and so-called unilateral transfers (gifts, pensions, etc.) to persons living abroad.

Capital Account

The *capital account* records transactions related to movements of long-term and short-term capital. The main items here are capital transfers. Consider an American citizen who wishes to invest abroad by lending money to a British industry; he is exporting capital from the United States to the United Kingdom. Suppose that he buys newly issued bonds being sold in London by an expanding British firm. In order to do this, he needs to obtain pounds. He is a demander of foreign exchange and a supplier of dollars; therefore his transaction is a debit item in the American balance-of-payments account.

Changes in the capital account can be subdivided in a number of ways. One way is to focus on whether the change is due to actions of foreign investors or to actions of Americans. An increase in foreign investments in the United States and an equal decrease in U.S. investments abroad have identical effects on the balance of payments—each is a credit item. Yet they may be viewed differently in terms of nationalistic goals: many Americans today, for example, are

[4] We use the term balance of trade to include both *visible* and *invisible* items in the balance-of-payments accounts, as defined in the text. However, the term is often used to refer only to the balance of trade on visible exports and imports. The narrower concept (excluding invisibles) is usually called the *merchandise* trade balance.

concerned about foreigners acquiring large positions of ownership in U.S. corporations and would not be at all concerned if Americans decreased their investments in foreign countries.

A second important distinction is often made between short-term and long-term capital movements. This distinction is important because short-term capital movements tend to be much more volatile than long-term ones and thus are more likely to cause sudden sharp changes in the balance on capital account.

Capital movements often seem baffling to beginners, who find it puzzling that the export of capital is a debit item and the export of a good is a credit item. But the apparent contradiction can be resolved. Consider the export of American capital to invest in a British bond. The capital transaction involves the purchase, and hence the *import,* of a British bond, and this has the same effect on the balance of payments as the purchase, and hence the import, of a British good. Both items involve payments to foreigners and use foreign exchange, and they are thus debit items in the American balance of payments.

Official Financing

The final section in the balance-of-payments account represents transactions in the *official reserves* held by the central authorities. It shows how the balance on the remainder of the accounts was financed. Here there are two main items: changes in liquid liabilities to foreign official agencies and changes in official reserve assets. The first represents the change in liquid claims on official reserves held by foreign central banks. When the United States has a deficit on the rest of the accounts, foreign monetary authorities accumulate these claims. They may then hold on to them or they may demand payment in official reserve assets. To the extent that they hold on to them (as part of *their* foreign exchange reserves), they are lending to the United States and allowing us to use this loan to finance the deficit on the rest of the accounts.

When holders of dollar claims against the United States present them for payment, there is a loss of official reserve assets. Payment may be made in gold, in foreign exchange (our claims on other convertible currencies), or in other accepted media of official international payments (such as SDRs), which we will encounter in Chapter 42.[5]

The Relation Among Current, Capital, and Offical Accounts

The relation among the three divisions of accounts follows from the fact that their sum must be zero.

A deficit on current plus capital accounts must be matched by a net surplus on the official financing accounts—which entails the government's borrowing abroad or decreasing its exchange reserves. A surplus on current plus capital accounts implies a deficit on the official financing accounts. Similarly, deficits on current account can be offset by surpluses on capital account, and vice versa.

To illustrate these relationships, consider a situation in which the value of American exports exceeds the value of American imports. This involves a surplus on the balance of trade, which was the characteristic situation in the years following World War II. In such a situation foreigners will not be able to obtain all the U.S. dollars they need to buy American goods from U.S. sources that wish to supply dollars in return for foreign currency in order to buy foreign goods. Thus the excess of exports over imports can only be paid for if foreigners obtain dollars from other sources.

There are several possibilities. First, U.S. dollars may be provided by American investors eager to obtain foreign currency so that they can buy foreign stocks and bonds. In this case the trade surplus is balanced by a deficit on capital account. Second, the U.S. government, rather than its firms or citizens, may have lent money to

[5] If exchange rates were entirely free to fluctuate and were not managed at all, there would be no "official" settlements, for any imbalance in the current plus capital accounts would cause the exchange rate to vary to eliminate the deficit or surplus (see page 767). But official settlements remain in a world of managed flexible exchange rates.

foreign governments to finance their purchases of American-produced goods or services. This too is a capital account deficit. Third, the U.S. government may have given away money as aid to other countries. Such gifts allow those countries to purchase more from the United States than they sell to us. This is a unilateral transfer; it appears as a debit in the current account. Fourth, foreign governments may have reduced their holdings of U.S. dollars or gold by selling them to persons who wish to buy U.S. goods, accepting their own domestic currency in exchange. This appears in the official financing accounts. One way or another, the trade surplus can occur only when someone else provides the dollars needed to pay for the excess American exports.

Consider another example: the consequence of America's imports exceeding its exports in a given year because of its heavy reliance on imported oil. The foreign currency needed to finance the imports that were in excess of exports had to come from somewhere; it must have been lent by someone or provided out of the government's reserves of gold and foreign exchange. One possibility is that foreign households or firms were investing funds in the United States, which entails selling foreign currency and buying U.S. currency in order to be able to buy American assets of any kind. Such foreign investments can provide the foreign exchange necessary to allow the United States to have an excess of imports over exports. Another possibility is that foreign governments have increased their holding of U.S. dollars by buying dollars and supplying their currency in return to persons wishing to purchase their goods and services. In both cases the American economy is consuming more than it is producing. In other words, it is borrowing from abroad.

BALANCE-OF-PAYMENTS DEFICITS AND SURPLUSES

Meaning of the Concepts

We have already noted that when all the uses to which foreign currency is put and all the sources from which it came are added up, the two amounts are necessarily equal, and thus the overall accounts of all international payments necessarily balance.

Yet it is common to speak of a country as having a balance-of-payments deficit or surplus. What does this mean? These terms usually refer to the balance of the account *excluding* changes in official financing. A **balance-of-payments surplus** means that the authorities are reducing their liquid liabilities to foreign central authorities or else adding to their holdings of official reserves in such forms as gold and foreign exchange. A **balance-of-payments deficit** means that the authorities are adding to their liquid liabilities to foreign central authorities or else reducing their stocks of official reserves.

The statement, for example that America had a balance-of-payments deficit of $14 billion in 1979 means that the U.S. official reserves (net of claims that foreign central authorities held against these reserves) fell by $14 billion because all other transactions were in deficit by that amount.

A balance-of-payments deficit means that the reserves of the central authorities are being run down; a surplus means that reserves are rising.

Consequences of Deficits and Surpluses

People sometimes act as though deficits were bad and surpluses good. A balance-of-payments deficit means that in the aggregate debit items exceed credit items and says nothing about whether this is beneficial or harmful. For example, an investment by an American firm in foreign countries that will yield future profits for American owners is a debit item that will increase a balance-of-payments deficit, yet there is nothing necessarily bad about the investment. On the opposite side, the transfer of ownership of American firms to foreigners is a credit item that will decrease a balance-of-payments deficit, but such loss of control over American firms is not necessarily desirable.

There is nothing inherently good about a balance-of-payments surplus or inherently bad about a balance-of-payments deficit.

When a balance-of-payments deficit is caused by something considered undesirable (such as heavy dependence on Mideast oil), it may be that the government will seek a way to decrease such imports. When the same deficit is caused by something considered desirable (such as contributions to our allies and underdeveloped nations to foster their economic development), the government may be willing to draw down its reserves for the purpose.

Whether desirable or undesirable, permanent deficits on the balance-of-payments accounts cannot be maintained, for the official reserves that are needed to finance such deficits are sure to be exhausted.

It might seem that a permanent surplus could be tolerated, but this is not the case either. If we have a permanent balance-of-payments surplus, some of our trading partners must have a permanent deficit. Unless we are prepared to give them the money, or allow them to increase their debts to us without limit, that too must be ended.

In the long term, when the balance of payments on current plus capital account is out of balance in either direction, something must be done. One approach is to maintain the exchange rate and adopt policies to shift the demand and supply curves to the point where the balance of payments is approximately zero. The government can do this through import or export restrictions, changes in interest rates, or a variety of other methods.

Another way is to allow exchange rates to change. Suppose the United States has a balance-of-payments surplus with respect to Britain. Holders of sterling are trying to make more payments in dollars than holders of dollars wish to make in sterling. If exchange rates are free to vary, the dollar will appreciate and the pound depreciate until the balance of payments is in equilibrium.

If exchange rates are completely free to vary, balance-of-payments deficits and surpluses will be eliminated through exchange rate adjustments.

The concern of economists and policy officials with "the balance-of-payments problem" is largely a carryover from the fact that for most of the hundred years before 1972 the world operated under a regime of fixed exchange rates.

In today's world, while no country need have a balance-of-payments problem, many still have them. As long as governments intervene in foreign exchange markets, there will be balance-of-payments deficits and surpluses. Surpluses will occur whenever the currency is held below its equilibrium level, deficits whenever it is held above its equilibrium level. Persistent deficits will cause persistent loss of reserves; they are evidence that the government is trying to resist longer-term trends.

But there is one great difference between this kind of balance-of-payments problem and that under fixed exchange rates. The central bank always has an available solution to its balance-of-payments problem: it can stop intervening in the market and let the exchange rate find its equilibrium level. This will not only end its balance-of-payments problem, it will end its loss of foreign exchange reserves.

In a world of more or less flexible exchange rates such as has existed since 1972, there are more important problems than the balance of payments—problems such as the extent of trade, the pattern of trade, and the desirability of letting foreigners purchase one's assets.

Summary

1. International trade can occur only when it is possible to exchange the currency of one country for that of another. The exchange rate between two currencies is the amount of one currency that must be paid in order to obtain one unit of another currency. Where more than two currencies are involved, there will be an exchange rate between each pair of currencies.

2. The determination of exchange rates in the free market is simply an application of the laws of supply and demand studied in Chapter 5; the object being bought and sold is a nation's currency.

3. The demand for dollars arises from American exports of goods and services, long-term and short-term capital flows into the United States, and the desire of foreign banks, firms, and governments to use American dollars as an international medium of exchange or as part of their reserves.

4. The supply of dollars to purchase foreign currencies arises from American imports of goods and services, capital flows from the United States, and the desire of holders of dollars to decrease the size of their holdings.

5. A depreciation of the dollar lowers the foreign price of American exports and increases the quantity of dollars demanded; at the same time, it raises the dollar price of imports from abroad and thus lowers the quantity of dollars supplied to buy foreign exchange to be used to purchase foreign goods. Thus the demand curve for dollars is downward sloping and the supply curve of dollars is upward sloping when the quantities demanded and supplied are plotted against the price of dollars measured in terms of a foreign currency.

6. A currency will tend to appreciate on foreign exchange markets if there is a shift to the right of the demand curve or a shift to the left of the supply curve for its currency. Shifts in the opposite directions will tend to depreciate the currency. Such shifts are affected by such things as the prices of imports and exports, the rates of inflation in different countries, capital movements, structural changes, expectations about future trends in earnings and exchange rates, and the level of confidence in the currency as a source of reserves.

7. When exchange rates are pegged or fixed, they must be managed by the countries' monetary authorities. From the end of World War II to the early 1970s most countries maintained fixed exchange rates. Fixed rates pose two main problems: (a) If there are long-term shifts in demand and supply in the foreign exchange market, either the fixed rate must be changed periodically to accommodate such shifts or controls must be used to prevent the disequilibrium in demand and supply from occurring; (b) short-term fluctuations must be ironed out by the central authority's sales and purchases of foreign exchange; these sales and purchases require that a reserve of gold and foreign exchange be held. The world is now on a system where many exchange rates are left to be determined by the forces of demand and supply on a relatively free market.

8. Flexible exchange rates can also be managed in an attempt to reduce fluctuations or to resist long-term trends, but (unlike fixed rates) they need not be managed. The use of interest rates to induce short-term capital movements is an important device for managing exchange rates.

9. Actual transactions among the firms, households, and governments of various countries are kept track of and reported in the balance-of-payments accounts. In these accounts, any transaction that uses foreign exchange is recorded as a debit item and any transaction that produces foreign exchange is recorded as a credit item. If all transactions are recorded, the sum of all credit items necessarily equals the sum of all debit items since the foreign exchange that is bought must also have been sold.

10. Major categories in the balance-of-payments account are the balance of trade (exports minus imports), current account, capital account, and official financing. The so-called balance of payments is the balance of the current plus capital accounts; that is, it excludes the transactions on official account.

11. There is nothing inherently good or bad

about deficits or surpluses. Persistent deficits or surpluses cannot be sustained because the former will eventually exhaust a country's foreign exchange reserves and the latter will do the same to a trading partner's reserves.

12. Balance-of-payment surpluses or deficits can be managed by the government's use of its foreign exchange reserves to buy or sell its currency, by policies that shift the demand and supply for the currency, or by allowing the exchange rate to seek its own level.

Topics for Review

Foreign exchange and exchange rates

Appreciation, depreciation, revaluation, and devaluation of exchange rates

Sources of the demand for and supply of foreign exchange

Effects of capital flows on equilibrium exchange rates

The effects on exchange rates of inflation, interest rates, and expectations about exchange rates

Fixed, freely flexible, and managed flexible exchange rates

The balance of trade and the balance of payments

Current and capital account

The balance of trade and the volume of trade

Discussion Questions

1. What is the probable effect of each of the following on the exchange rate of a country, *ceteris paribus?*
   a. the quantity of oil imports is greatly reduced, but the value of imported oil is higher due to price increases
   b. the country's inflation rate falls well below that of its trading partners
   c. rising labor costs of the country's manufactures lead to a worsening ability to compete in world markets
   d. the government greatly expands its gifts of food and machinery to undeveloped countries
   e. a major recession occurs with rising unemployment
   f. the central bank raises interest rates sharply
2. The president of the Federal Reserve Bank of New York said recently, "Inflation is the enemy in maintaining international trade." What might he have had in mind?

Compare the behavior of fixed versus fluctuating exchange rates in a world:
   a. with no inflation but short-run fluctuations in prices
   b. with a substantial but similar degree of inflation everywhere in the world
   c. with sharply varying degrees of inflation

3. In recent years money wages have risen substantially faster in Canada than in the United States. Many Canadians have expressed the fear that their rapidly rising costs will price them out of U.S. markets. Did this fear make sense when the Canadian exchange rate was fixed relative to the American dollar? Does it make sense today when exchange rates are free to vary on the open market?

4. Suppose that in the foreign exchange market £1 = $2.00, 1 French franc = $.20, and £1 = 12 French francs. How could an arbitrager make a profit? Assuming flexibility in exchange rates, how would such arbitrage eliminate this profit possibility? What would happen if exchange rates were fixed at these levels?

5. Indicate whether each of the following transactions increases the demand for dollars or the supply of dollars (or neither) on foreign exchange markets.
   a. IBM moves $10 million from bank accounts in the United States to banks in Paris to expand operations there
   b. the U.S. government extends a grant of $3 million to the government of Peru, which Peru uses to buy farm machinery from a Chicago firm
   c. Canadian investors, responding to higher profits of U.S. rather than Canadian corporations, buy stocks through the New York Stock Exchange
   d. U.S. oil companies build a pipeline across Canada to transport Alaskan oil to the United States
   e. lower interest rates in New York than in London encourage British firms to borrow in the New York money market, converting the proceeds into pounds sterling for use at home

Do these transactions affect the balance of payments, exchange rates, or both?

6. Does it ever make sense for a central government to intervene in foreign exchange markets rather than let exchange rates find their own level? Does it always make sense? Discuss.

7. "The necessity of the government to balance the balance of payments through the settlement account is a relic of the past. It was a by-product of the adherence to a policy of fixed exchange rates." Do you agree?

8. "If a country solves its balance-of-payments problems, it will have solved its foreign trade problems." Discuss.

International Monetary Systems

42

The nations of the world have tried several different systems of international monetary management. No system has been fully satisfactory, and periods of crisis have alternated with periods of stability. Changes have usually occurred during or after a crisis. The gold standard, the Bretton Woods system, the International Monetary Fund, the Smithsonian agreements, the European snake — all are part of the history of the international monetary systems of the twentieth century.

The issues involved in determining whether and how well international payments schemes work affect ordinary citizens and their standard of living even though the issues are understood by only a small number of international traders, bankers, financiers, and economists. In this chapter we review the principal systems and indicate when and why they ran into trouble. Our study is of more than historical interest, for the hope for a better, more smoothly functioning system than we have today lies in learning the lessons of the historical experience.

The century began with a system of fixed exchange rates under the gold standard which encountered periodic crises in the post-World War I years but did not collapse until the onset of the Great Depression. The 1930s were a period of unsuccessful experimentation with flexible, market-determined exchange rates. This phase was ended by World War II, when governments fixed exchange rates and managed international payments with the successful waging of war as their main policy objective.

In 1944 an era of fixed exchange rates in

peacetime was again instituted, this time by international agreement at a conference in Bretton Woods, New Hampshire. The system lasted for over a quarter of a century, until its shortcomings and periods of crisis seemed to prevail over its advantages and periods of stability. After several attempts to patch up the system in the 1970s, it finally broke down and was abandoned as countries turned one by one to market-determined, flexible exchange rates.

Neither the fixed rates of the gold standard or the Bretton Woods system nor the flexible rates of the 1930s or the 1970s have avoided problems. Yet they had different problems, and it is worth examining each of the major episodes.

Before World War II

THE GOLD STANDARD IN THEORY

The gold standard was not *designed*. Like the price system, it just happened. It arose out of the general acceptance of gold as the commodity to be used as money. In most countries, paper currency was freely convertible into gold at a fixed rate.

The gold standard is an example of a fixed exchange rate system. Rates of exchange between the standard units of currency of various countries were fixed by their values in terms of the standard unit, gold. In 1914 the U.S. dollar was convertible into .053 standard ounces of gold, while the British pound sterling was convertible into .257 standard ounces. This meant that the pound was worth 4.86 times as much as the dollar in terms of gold, thus making one pound worth U.S. $4.86. (In practice, the exchange rate fluctuated within narrow limits set by the cost of shipping gold.)

As long as all countries were on the gold standard, a person in any one country could be sure of being able to make payments to a person in any other country. Someone who was unable to buy or sell claims to the foreign currencies on the foreign exchange market could always convert currency into gold and then ship the gold.

The Gold Flow, Price Level Mechanism

The gold standard was supposed to work to maintain a balance of international payments by forcing adjustments in price levels within individual countries. Consider a country that had a balance-of-payments deficit because the value of what its citizens were importing (i.e., buying) from other countries exceeded the value of what they were exporting (i.e., selling) to other countries. The demand for foreign exchange would exceed the supply on this country's foreign exchange market. Some people who wished to make foreign payments would be unable to obtain foreign exchange. No matter; they would merely convert their domestic currency into gold and ship the gold. Therefore, some people in a surplus country would secure gold in payment for exports. They would deposit this to their credit and accept claims on gold—in terms of convertible paper money or bank deposits—in return. Thus deficit countries would be losing gold while surplus countries would be gaining it.

Under the gold standard, the whole money supply was linked to the supply of gold (see pages 598–600). The international movements of gold would therefore lead to a fall in the money supply in the deficit country and a rise in the surplus country.[1] If full employment prevails, changes in the domestic money supply will cause changes in domestic price levels. Deficit countries would thus have falling price levels while surplus countries would have rising price levels. The exports of deficit countries would become relatively cheaper, while those of surplus countries would become relatively more expensive. The resulting changes in quantities bought and sold would move the balance of payments toward an equilibrium position.

[1] When the person who received gold deposited it in a bank, the bank would be in the position of the IB&T Co. in Table 33-4 on page 617, and a multiple expansion of deposit money would ensue.

ACTUAL EXPERIENCE OF THE GOLD STANDARD

The half century before World War I was the heyday of the gold standard; during this relatively trouble-free period, the automatic mechanism seemed to work well. Subsequent research has suggested, however, that the gold standard succeeded during the period mainly because it was not called on to do much work. Trade flowed between nations in large and rapidly expanding volume, and it is probable that existing exchange rates and price levels were never far from the equilibrium ones. No major trading country found itself with a serious and persistent balance-of-payments deficit, so no major country was called upon to restore equilibrium through a large change in its domestic price level.

Inevitably there were short-run fluctuations, but they were ironed out either by movements of short-run capital in response to changes in interest rates or by changes in national income and employment.

Problems in the 1920s

In the 1920s the gold standard was called on to do a major job. It failed utterly, and it was abandoned. How did this come about? During World War I, most belligerent countries had suspended convertibility of currency (i.e., they went off the gold standard). Most countries suffered major inflations, but the degree of inflation differed from country to country. As we have seen, this will lead to changes in the equilibrium exchange rates.

After the war, countries returned to the gold standard (i.e., they restored convertibility of their currencies into gold). For reasons of prestige, many insisted on returning at the prewar rates. This meant that some countries' goods were overpriced and others' underpriced. Large deficits and surpluses in the balance of payments inevitably appeared, and the adjustment mechanism required that price levels should change in each of the countries in order to restore equilib-

rium. Exchange rates were not adjusted, and price levels changed very slowly. By the onset of the Great Depression, equilibrium price levels had not yet been attained. The financial chaos brought on by the Depression destroyed the existing payments system.

Major Disabilities of a Gold Standard

While inflationary policies combined with an overly rigid adherence to pre-World War I exchange rates led to the downfall of the gold standard, one may ask whether an altered gold standard, based on more realistic exchange rates, might not have succeeded. While some modern economists, notably Robert Mundell of Columbia University, think it would, most believe the gold standard suffered from key disabilities.

Like any other fixed exchange rate system, it required a mechanism for orderly adjustment to changes in the supply and demand for a nation's currency. The price adjustment process worked too slowly and too imperfectly to cope with large and persistent disequilibrium.

Furthermore, gold as the basis for an international money supply suffered several special disadvantages. They included a limited supply that could not be expanded as rapidly as increases in the volume of world trade required, an uneven distribution of existing and potential new gold supplies among the nations of the world, and a large and frequently volatile speculative demand for gold during periods of crisis. These factors could cause large, disruptive variations in the supply of gold available for international monetary purposes.

THE 1930s: EXPERIMENTATION WITH FLUCTUATING RATES

It is doubtful that any fixed exchange rate system could have survived the Great Depression, for the changes in the demand and supply of foreign exchange were large and sudden. The speculative demand for gold rose sharply, as it always does during periods of major uncertainty, and one by one nations simply suspended convertibility of their currencies into gold, thereby abandoning gold as the medium of exchange at home and abroad.

Following the abandonment of the gold standard, various experiments were tried with both fixed and fluctuating rates. Often a rate would be allowed to fluctuate on the free market until it had reached what looked like equilibrium, and then it would be fixed at that level. Sometimes, as with the British pound, the rate was left to be determined by a free market throughout the period.

But the overriding feature of the decade was that considerations of massive unemployment came to dominate economic policies in virtually every country, and all devices, including exchange rate manipulations, seemed fair game for dealing with them. Many governments adopted policies that were acts of desperation and that made long-term sense only if other countries were not also in crisis. They tended not to consider the long-term effects on trade, or on their trading partners, of the policies they adopted, hoping to gain short-term advantages before their policies provoked the inevitable reaction from others.

The use of devaluations to improve domestic unemployment rested on a simple and superficially plausible line of analysis: if a country has unemployed workers at home, why not substitute home production for imports and thus give jobs to one's own citizens instead of to foreigners? One way to do this is to urge people to "buy American." Another, probably more effective way is to lower the prices of domestic goods relative to those of imports. The devaluation of one's currency does this by making foreign goods that much more expensive. (A 10 percent devaluation, *ceteris paribus,* means that it will take 10 percent more domestic money to buy the same imports; this is equivalent to a 10 percent rise in the prices of all foreign goods.)

Of course, if this policy works, other countries will find *their* exports falling and unemployment rising as a consequence. Because such policies

attempt to solve one country's problems by inflicting them on others, they are called **beggar-my-neighbor policies** and are sometimes described as attempts to "export one's unemployment."

In a situation of inadequate world demand, a beggar-my-neighbor policy on the part of one country can work only in the unlikely event that other countries do not try to protect themselves. A situation in which all countries devalue their currencies in an attempt to gain a competitive advantage over one another is called a situation of **competitive devaluations.**

Precisely this happened during the 1930s. One country would devalue its currency in an attempt to reduce its imports and stimulate exports. But because other countries suffered the same kinds of problems of unemployment, they did not sit idly by. Retaliation was swift, and devaluation followed devaluation.

The effect was both futile and perverse, futile because the simultaneous attempts of all countries to cut imports without suffering a comparable cut in exports is bound to be self-defeating.

When unemployment is due to insufficient world aggregate demand, it cannot be cured by measures designed to redistribute among nations the fixed and inadequate total of demand.

And it was perverse because the net effect of restrictions on trade was to decrease the volume of trade and thereby sacrifice the gains from trade without raising worldwide employment.[2]

These policies, along with other restrictive

---

[2] It was perverse in a second way as well. Under a paper currency system, a simultaneous equal devaluation of all currencies would have no effect, beneficial or harmful. If all countries devalue their currencies in the same proportion, they will all be right back where they started, with no change in the relative prices of goods from any country and hence no change in relative prices from the original situation. In a gold standard world such as existed at the start of the 1930s, however, each country devalues by lowering the gold content of its currency. Thus a full round of competitive devaluations of X percent leaves relative exchange rates unchanged, but it raises the price of gold (measured in all currencies) by X percent. The effect of this is to enrich those producing gold and those holding stocks of it and thus to increase their claims on the world's output.

trade policies such as import duties, export subsidies, quotas, and prohibitions, led to a declining volume of world trade and brought no relief from the worldwide depression. Moreover, they contributed to a loss of faith in the economic system and in the ability of either economists or politicians to cope with economic crises.

The Rise and Fall of the Bretton Woods System, 1944–1972

The one lesson that everyone thought had been learned from the competitive devaluations of the 1930s was that neither a system of freely fluctuating exchange rates nor a system of fixed rates with easily accomplished devaluations could prevent disaster in international affairs. In order to achieve a system of orderly exchange rates that would be conducive to the free flow of trade following World War II, representatives of most countries that had participated in the alliance against Germany, Italy, and Japan convened to agree on a system of international payments for the postwar world. The international monetary system that developed out of the agreements reached at Bretton Woods consisted of a large body of rules and understandings for the regulation of international transactions and payments imbalances.

The object of the Bretton Woods system was to create a set of rules that would maintain fixed exchange rates in the face of short-term fluctuations; to guarantee that changes in exchange rates would occur only in the face of long-term, persistent deficits or surpluses in the balance of payments; and to ensure that when such changes did occur they would not spark a series of competitive devaluations.

The basic characteristic of the Bretton Woods system was that U.S. dollars held by foreign monetary authorities were made directly convertible into gold at a fixed price (of approximately $35 an ounce) by the U.S. government while foreign governments fixed the prices at which their currencies were convertible into U.S. dollars. It was this characteristic that made the system a **gold exchange standard:** gold was the ultimate reserve, but the currencies were held as reserves because directly or indirectly they could be *exchanged* for gold.

The rate at which each country's currency was convertible into dollars was pegged. The pegged rate could be changed from time to time in the face of a "fundamental disequilibrium" in the balance of payments. A system with a rate that is pegged against short-term fluctuations but that can be adjusted from time to time is called an **adjustable peg system.**

In order to maintain convertibility of their currencies at fixed exchange rates, the monetary authorities of each country had to be ready to buy and sell their currency in foreign exchange markets to offset imbalances in demand and supply at the pegged rates.[3]

In order to be able to support the exchange market by buying domestic currency, the monetary authorities had to have reserves of acceptable foreign exchange to offer in return. In the Bretton Woods system, the authorities held reserves of gold and claims on key currencies—mainly the American dollar and the British pound sterling. When a country's currency was in excess supply, its authorities would sell dollars, sterling, or gold. When a country's currency was in excess demand, its authorities would buy dollars or sterling. If they then wished to increase their gold reserves, they would use the dollars to purchase gold from the Fed, thus depleting the U.S. gold stock.

The problem for the United States was to have enough gold to maintain fixed-price convertibility of the dollar into gold as demanded by foreign monetary authorities. The problem for all other countries was to maintain convertibility (on a restricted or unrestricted basis, depending on the country in question) between their cur-

---

[3] The exchange rates were not quite fixed; they were permitted to vary by one percent on either side of their par values. Later the bands of permitted fluctuation were widened to 2.25 percent on either side of par.

rency and the U.S. dollar at a fixed rate of exchange.

The Bretton Woods international payments system was an adjustable peg, gold exchange standard where the ultimate international money was gold. Countries held much of their exchange reserves in the form of U.S. dollars, which they could convert into gold, and British pounds sterling, which they could convert into dollars.

THE INTERNATIONAL MONETARY FUND

The International Monetary Fund (also called the IMF and the Fund) was created to manage the system. It had several tasks. First, it tried to ensure that countries kept their exchange rates pegged in the short run. Second, it made loans—out of funds subscribed by member nations—to governments that needed them to support their exchange rates in the face of temporary payments deficits. Third, the Fund was supposed to consult with countries wishing to alter their exchange rates to ensure that the rate was really being changed to remove a persistent payments disequilibrium and that one devaluation did not set off a self-canceling round of competitive devaluations.

PROBLEMS OF AN ADJUSTABLE PEG SYSTEM

Three major problems of the Bretton Woods system, which will recur with any adjustable peg system, were (1) providing sufficient reserves to iron out short-term fluctuations in international receipts and payments while keeping exchange rates fixed; (2) making adjustments of the rates to long-term trends in receipts and payments; and (3) handling speculative crises.

Since many people advocate a return to an adjustable peg system, it will be worth examining each of these problems to learn what must be guarded against if a similar system were to be adopted.

Reserves to Accommodate Short-term Fluctuations

We have seen that each country's monetary authorities had to be prepared to buy or sell foreign exchange to offset imbalances at the fixed exchange rates. To be able to sell, one must have reserves. Even when the exchange rate is an equilibrium rate over several years, there may be considerable imbalances over shorter periods of time.

The amount of reserves that the authorities need to hold depends on their estimate of the maximum amount of foreign exchange they might have to sell to stabilize the exchange rate in the face of a particularly unfavorable period of excess demand. If the authorities run out of reserves, they cannot maintain the pegged rate, so they will want to hold some safety margin over the maximum they expect to use. It is generally believed that the absolute size of any gap they may have to fill with their own foreign exchange sales will increase as the volume of international payments increases.

Since there was a strong upward trend in the volume of overall international payments, there was also a strong upward trend in the demand for foreign exchange reserves.

The crisis in gold reserves. The ultimate reserve in the Bretton Woods gold exchange standard was gold. The use of gold as a reserve caused two serious problems during the 1960s and early 1970s. First, the world's supply of monetary gold did not grow fast enough to provide adequate reserves for an expanding volume of trade. During the 1960s, as a result of a fixed price of gold, rising costs of production, and rising commercial uses, the world's stock of monetary gold was rising at less than 2 percent per year while trade was growing at nearly 10 percent per year. Gold, which had been 66 percent of the total monetary reserves in 1959, was only 40 percent in 1970 and had fallen to 30 percent by 1972; over this period, reserve holdings of dollars and sterling rose sharply. Clearly, the gold backing needed to maintain convertibility of these currencies was becoming increasingly inadequate.

Second, the country whose currency is convertible into gold must maintain sufficient reserves to ensure convertibility. During the 1960s the United States lost substantial gold reserves to other countries that had acquired dollar claims through their balance-of-payments surpluses with the United States. By the late 1960s the loss of U.S. reserves had been sufficiently large to undermine confidence in America's continued ability to maintain dollar convertibility.

By 1970 there was an inadequate world supply of gold for monetary uses, and the United States had too small a proportion of the supply that did exist.

Problems for nations whose currency is held as a reserve. Under the Bretton Woods system the supply of gold was augmented by reserves of key currencies, the U.S. dollar and the British pound sterling. Because the need for reserves expanded much more rapidly than the gold stock in the period since World War II, the system required nations to hold an increasing fraction of their reserves in dollars and sterling. They would be willing to do this only as long as they had confidence in the convertibility of these currencies, but maintaining confidence was made difficult by a continually declining percentage of gold backing for the dollar.

While it is prestigious to have one's currency held as a reserve currency—and even advantageous as long as other countries are willing to increase their holdings of one's paper money without making claims on current output—there are both disadvantages and hazards for the country whose currency is involved.

Such a country is placed under great pressure not to devalue its currency. If it does devalue, owing to a severe balance-of-payments deficit, all countries holding that currency will find the value of their reserves diminished. If it tries to avoid devaluation, the fear that it may be unable to do so will impair the usefulness of the currency as a reserve because other countries will become reluctant to hold it.

The result may well be that too much of the domestic policy of the country whose currency is the reserve becomes subservient to the overriding need to maintain its exchange rate and its gold reserves. These considerations make it more difficult for the country to deal with its own unemployment and inflation. This was the case of Britain throughout much of the Bretton Woods era and of the United States during the early seventies.

Search for a new type of reserves. The desire to provide a supplementary reserve not tied to the currency of a particular country led to the development in 1969 of **special drawing rights** (SDRs) at the IMF. SDRs were designed to provide a supplement to existing reserve assets by setting up a Special Drawing Account kept separate from all other operations of the Fund. Each member country of the Fund was assigned an SDR quota that was guaranteed in terms of a fixed gold value and that it could use to acquire an equivalent amount of convertible currencies from other participants. SDRs could be used without prior consultation with the Fund, but only to cope with balance-of-payments difficulties.

SDRs might have gone a long way toward alleviating the system's difficulties if the system had not been overwhelmed by much more fundamental problems in the early 1970s. In any case SDRs have outlasted the Bretton Woods system that they were first designed to assist.

Adjusting to Long-term Disequilibria

The second characteristic problem of a fixed rate system is the adjustment to changing trends in trade. With fixed exchange rates, long-term disequilibria (what the IMF used to call *fundamental disequilibria*) can be expected to develop because of secular shifts in the demands for and supplies of foreign exchange.

There are three important long-term causes of shifts in demands and supplies in the foreign exchange market. First, different trading countries have different rates of inflation. Persistent differences will cause continuing changes in the equilibrium rates of exchange, as we saw in Chapter 41. If exchange rates are maintained at a fixed level, this will inevitably lead to cumulating excess demands or supplies of particular currencies. Second, changes in the demands for and supplies of imports and exports are associated with long-term economic growth. Because different countries grow at different rates, their demands for imports and their supplies of exports would be expected to be shifting at different rates. Third, structural changes, such as major new innovations or a rise in the price of oil, cause major changes in the pattern and balance of imports and exports among nations.

The associated shifts in demand and supply on the foreign exchange market imply that, even when starting from a current account equilibrium with imports equal to exports at a given rate of exchange, there is no reason to believe that equilibrium will exist at the same rate of exchange 10 or 20 years later (any more than equilibrium relative prices would be expected to remain unchanged over 20 years within any one country).

The rate of exchange that will lead to a balance-of-payments equilibrium will tend to change over time; over a decade the change can be substantial.

Governments may react to long-term disequilibria in at least three ways.

1. The exchange rate can be changed whenever it is clear that a balance-of-payments deficit or surplus is a result of a long-term shift in the demands and supplies in the foreign exchange market, rather than the result of some transient factor. This was the solution envisaged by the framers of the IMF when they allowed member countries, after consultation with the IMF, to change their exchange rates in the face of a "fundamental disequilibrium." During the period of the Bretton Woods system, there were three major rounds of exchange rate adjustments. The first two were led by a devaluation of sterling, the second of the world's two reserve currencies; the third round was led by the devaluation of the U.S. dollar in December 1971.

2. Domestic price levels can be allowed to change in an attempt to establish an equilibrium set of international prices. Changes in domestic price levels have all sorts of domestic repercussions (e.g., reductions in aggregate demand intended to lower the price level are more likely to raise unemployment than to lower prices), and one should have expected governments to be more willing to change exchange rates—which can be done by a stroke of a pen—than to try to change the price level. A deflation is difficult to accomplish, while an inflation is thought to be accompanied by undesirable side effects.

3. Restrictions can be imposed on trade and foreign payments. Imports and foreign spending by tourists and governments can be restricted, and the export of capital can be slowed or even stopped. Surplus countries were often quick to criticize such restrictions on international trade and payments. As long as exchange rates were fixed and price levels proved difficult to manipulate, the deficit countries had little option but to restrict the quantity of foreign exchange their residents were permitted to obtain so as to equate it to the quantity available.

Speculative Crises

The third characteristic problem of a fixed rate system is the handling of speculation in the foreign exchange market. When enough people begin to doubt the ability of the central authorities to maintain the current rate, speculative crises develop. The most important reason for such crises is that equilibrium exchange rates change, and over time they tend to get further and further away from any given set of fixed rates. When the disequilibrium becomes obvious to everyone, traders and speculators come to believe that a realignment of rates cannot long be delayed. Since the *direction* of required adjustments is not in doubt, speculators can earn large profits with virtually no risk. If somehow changes in rates are not made, all they will lose is the interest on their money.

At such a time there will be a rush to buy currencies expected to be revalued and a rush to sell currencies expected to be devalued. Even when the authorities take dramatic steps to remove the payments deficit, there may be doubt as to whether these measures will work before the exchange reserves are exhausted. Speculative flows of funds can reach very large proportions, and it may be impossible to avoid changing the exchange rate under such pressure.

Speculative crises are one of the most intractable problems of any adjustable peg system. The impact of such crises might be reduced if governments had more adequate reserves. When a speculative crisis precedes an exchange rate adjustment, however, more adequate reserves may just mean that speculators will make larger profits since more of them will be able to sell the currency about to be devalued and to buy the currency about to be revalued before the monetary authorities are forced to act.

During the Bretton Woods period, governments tended to resist changing their exchange rates until they had no alternative. This made the situation so obvious that speculators could hardly lose, and their actions set off the final crises that forced exchange rate readjustments. More frequent and surprise changes made before they had become inevitable might have diminished the occurrence of speculative crises. However, they would have removed the day-to-day certainty associated with the system of fixed exchange rates that was its chief advantage. Moreover, a surprise change might lead to suspicion that a devaluation was made to gain a competitive advantage for a country's exports rather than to remove a fundamental disequilibrium. After all, governments were not supposed to devalue until it was *clear* that they were faced with a fundamental disequilibrium. If this was clear to them, it was also likely to be clear to ordinary traders and speculators.

COLLAPSE OF THE BRETTON WOODS SYSTEM

The Bretton Woods system worked reasonably well for nearly 20 years. Then it was beset by a series of crises of ever-increasing severity that reflected the system's underlying weaknesses.

Speculation Against the British Pound

Throughout the 1950s and 1960s the British economy was more inflation prone than the U.S. economy, and the British balance of payments was generally in a less satisfactory state. Holders of sterling thus had reason to worry that the British government might not be able to maintain its pledge to keep sterling convertible into dollars at a fixed rate. When these fears grew strong, there would be speculative rushes to sell sterling before it was devalued. The crises in the 1960s were of this kind. By the mid 1960s it was clear to everyone that the pound was seriously overvalued. Finally, in 1967 it was devalued in the midst of a serious speculative crisis. Many other countries with balance-of-payments deficits followed, bringing about the first major round of adjustments in the pegged rates since 1949.

Speculation Against the American Dollar

The U.S. dollar was not devalued in 1967. The lower prices of those currencies that were devalued in 1967 plus the increasing Vietnam War expenditures combined to produce a growing deficit in the American balance of payments. This deficit led to the belief that the dollar itself was becoming seriously overvalued. People rushed to buy gold because a devaluation of the U.S. dollar would take the form of raising its gold price.[4]

The first break in the Bretton Woods system came when the major trading countries were forced to stop pegging the free-market price of gold. Speculative pressure to buy gold could not be resisted, and the market price was allowed to go free in 1968. From that point there were two prices of gold: one was the official price at which monetary authorities could settle their debts with

---

[4] Under a Bretton Woods type of system, the dollar is devalued by raising the official price at which the Fed will convert dollars into gold.

each other by transferring gold; the other was the free-market price, determined by the forces of private demand and supply independent of any intervention by central banks. The free-market price quickly rose far above the official U.S. price of $35 an ounce.

Once the free-market price of gold was allowed to be determined independently of the official price, speculation against the dollar shifted to those currencies that were clearly undervalued relative to the dollar.[5] The German mark and the Japanese yen were particularly popular targets, and during periods of crisis billions and billions of dollars flowed into speculative holdings of these currencies. The ability of central banks to maintain pegged exchange rates in the face of such vast flights of funds was in question; on several occasions all exchange markets had to be closed for periods of up to a week.

Devaluation of the Dollar

The need for agreement. By 1971 the American authorities had come to the conclusion that the dollar would have to be devalued. This uncovered a problem, inherent in the Bretton Woods system, that had so far gone virtually unnoted. Because the system required that each foreign country fix its exchange rate against the dollar, the American authorities could not independently fix their exchange rate against other currencies.[6] This system had worked reasonably well while the American price level was rela-

tively stable. Countries that were inflating a bit too fast could occasionally devalue their exchange rates, and countries that were inflating even more slowly than the United States could occasionally revalue their exchange rates. Occasional upward and downward readjustments relative to the dollar served to keep the system near equilibrium.

But if the United States began to inflate rapidly (or to do anything else that put it in a serious payments deficit with most other countries), it would become necessary to devalue the U.S. dollar relative to most (or even conceivably all) other currencies. Any other country in this situation would merely unilaterally devalue its currency relative to the U.S. dollar. But the only way that the required U.S. devaluation could be brought about was for all other countries to agree to revalue their currencies relative to the dollar.

Under the Bretton Woods system any country other than the United States could devalue its currency by a unilateral decision, but a U.S. devaluation required the cooperation of all countries against whose currency the dollar was to be devalued.

Speculation and negotiated devaluation. Prompted by continuing speculation against the dollar, President Nixon announced the suspension of the gold convertibility of the dollar in August 1971. He also made known the intention of the United States to achieve a de facto devaluation of the dollar by persuading those nations whose balance of payments were in surplus to allow their rates to float upward against the dollar.

By ending the gold convertibility of the dollar, the U.S. government brought the gold exchange standard aspect of the Bretton Woods system officially to an end.

The fixed exchange rate aspect of the system lasted a little longer.

The immediate response to the announced intention of devaluing the dollar was a speculative run against that currency. The crisis was so severe that for the second time in the year

---

[5] When the free-market price of gold was held the same as the official price, a devaluation of the dollar entailed a rise in the free-market price—and hence profit for all holders of gold. Once the free-market price was left to be determined by the forces of private demand and supply independent of any central bank intervention, there was no reason to believe that a rise in the official price of gold would affect the (much higher) free-market price. Speculators against the dollar then had to hold other currencies whose price was sure to rise against the dollar in the event of the dollar's being devalued.

[6] If, for example, the British authorities pegged the pound sterling at $2.40, as they did in 1967, then the dollar was pegged at £0.417 and the Fed could not independently decide on another rate. Similar considerations applied to all other currencies.

foreign exchange markets were closed throughout Europe. When the markets reopened after a week, several countries allowed their rates to float. The Japanese, however, announced their intention of retaining their existing rate. In spite of severe Japanese controls, $4 billion in speculative funds managed to find its way into yen in the last two weeks of August, and the Japanese were forced to abandon their fixed rate policy by allowing the yen to float upward.

After some very hard bargaining, an agreement between the major trading nations was signed at the Smithsonian Institution in Washington, D.C., in December 1971. The main element of the agreement was that all countries consented to a 7.9 percent devaluation of the dollar against their currencies.

The De Facto Dollar Standard

Following the Smithsonian agreements, the world was on a de facto **dollar standard.** This arrangement still had fixed exchange rate features as long as the dollar was regarded as a safe and stable currency. Foreign monetary authorities held their reserves in the form of dollars and settled their international debts with dollars. But the dollar was not convertible into gold or anything else. The ultimate value of the dollar was given not by gold but by the American goods, services, and assets that dollars could be used to purchase.

One major problem with such a dollar system is that the kind of American inflation that upset the Bretton Woods system is no less upsetting to a dollar standard because the real purchasing power value of the world's dollar reserves is eroded by such an inflation.

The Final Breakdown
of Fixed Exchange Rates

The Smithsonian agreements did not lead to a new period of international payments stability. This doomed the hope that a de facto dollar standard could provide the basis for an international payments system free of major rounds of crisis and devaluation.

The U.S. inflation continued unchecked, and the U.S. balance of payments never returned to the relatively satisfactory position that had been maintained throughout the 1960s. Within a year of the agreements, speculators began to believe that a further realignment of rates was necessary. In January 1973 heavy speculative movements of capital once again began to occur. In February the United States proposed a further 11 percent devaluation of the dollar. This was to be accomplished by raising the official price of gold to $42.22 an ounce and not keeping other currencies tied to the dollar at the old rates. Needless to say, intense speculative activity followed the announcement.

Five member countries of the European Common Market then decided to stabilize their currencies against each other but to let them float together against the dollar. This joint float was called the **snake.** Norway and Sweden later became associated with this arrangement. The other EEC countries (Ireland, Italy, and the United Kingdom) and Japan announced their intention to allow their currencies to float in value. In June 1972 the Bank of England had abandoned the de facto dollar standard with the announcement that it had "temporaily" abandoned its commitment to support sterling at a fixed par value against the U.S. dollar. The events of 1973 led "temporarily" to become "indefinitely."

Fluctuations in exchange rates were severe. By early July the snake currencies had appreciated about 30 percent against the dollar, but by the end of the year they had returned nearly to their February values.

The dollar devaluation formally took effect in October. Most industrialized countries maintained the nominal values of their currencies in terms of gold and SDRs, thereby appreciating them in terms of the U.S. dollar by 11 percent. The devaluation quickly became redundant, for in spite of attempts to restore fixed rates, the drift to flexible rates had become irresistible by the end of 1973.

The Present System: Its Nature and Its Problems

A DIRTY FLOAT

By 1974 many industrial countries—Austria, Canada, Italy, Japan, Switzerland, the United Kingdom, and the United States—were no longer maintaining rates for exchange transactions within announced margins, while other industrial countries—Belgium, Denmark, France, Germany, Luxembourg, the Netherlands, Norway, and Sweden—maintained fixed bands for exchange transactions among their currencies but not against the dollar. A large proportion of the remaining countries maintained stable rates of exchange for their currencies in terms of *one* of the three major currencies (the U.S. dollar, pound sterling, or the French franc). This implied that such a country's rate fluctuated against the major currencies to which its national currency was not tied.

Although such exchange rates are determined on the free market, there is nevertheless substantial intervention in these markets by central banks. Central banks try to reduce short-term fluctuations in rates and sometimes try to resist longer-term trends. The difference between the present system and the previous one is that central banks no longer have announced values for their exchange rates (values that they are committed to in advance to defend even at heavy cost). Central banks do not need to say what their targets are; they may change them with complete flexibility as circumstances change. Sometimes they leave the rate completely free from their own intervention while at other times quite heavy intervention occurs with the object of altering the exchange rate from what its value would be on the free market. Such a system is called a **managed float** or a **dirty float.** The rate floats because it is not pegged at any publicly announced par value. The floating rate, however, is managed (or dirty) because the central bank does intervene in the foreign exchange market to influence the rate.

To manage exchange rates, central banks still hold reserves in the form of gold, foreign exchange, and SDRs (see Table 42-1). The relatively fixed stock of monetary gold is an important part of the total. Dollars continue to play a large role in the reserves of many countries. SDRs and reserves at the IMF, while a small part of the total, raise the possibility that in the future the ultimate real reserve may become the SDR, which is a genuine international paper money. If this happens, the system will have become an "international paper money standard."

The present international monetary system is a dollar standard with managed exchange rate flexibility.

The experiences of the period of managed intervention have been mixed. On the one hand, short-term movements in exchange rates have been more volatile than advocates of flexible rates would perhaps have hoped; on the other, exchange rates have been managed without any rounds of competitive devaluation and have been

TABLE 42-1
Changing Composition of International Reserves (year-end data)

Type of reserve	Billions of dollars		Percentage of total	
	1970	1979	1970	1979
Gold[a]	$39.5	$360.1	41.2	57.2
SDRs and reserves at IMF	10.8	24.2	11.3	3.9
Foreign exchange				
U.S. dollars[b]	34.3	154.7	35.9	24.5
All other	11.1	91.0	11.6	14.4
Total reserves	$95.7	$630.0	100.0	100.0

[a] Valued at market prices. The number of ounces of monetary gold was 1.1 billion in 1970, 0.9 billion in 1979.

[b] Official claims on dollars plus identified holdings. This number greatly underestimates foreign total dollar holdings.

The dollar, though declining in importance, is still a major part of international reserves. The rise in the importance of gold is purely a price effect due to the peak in gold prices reached in 1979 and 1980. The dollar figures do not include vast unofficial holdings of dollars by private persons and firms. The *total* foreign dollar holdings in 1979 was estimated to be above $700 billion.

allowed to change to compensate for substantial national differences in inflation rates.

SURVIVAL OF THE IMF IN A WORLD OF FLOATING EXCHANGE RATES

Although the IMF bitterly resisted the drift toward floating exchange rates, it has now accommodated itself to them and promises to be as effective a means of securing international financial cooperation under a system of managed floating rates as it was under fixed rates.

The changing position of the IMF is illustrated by amendments to its charter that were agreed to in 1976. These amendments, while allowing for the possible return to fixed rates at some possible future date, have legalized floating rates within the framework of the IMF system.

1. With the concurrence of the IMF, any country may adopt a floating exchange rate.
2. The exchange rate management of a floating currency must be subject to IMF surveillance and must not be conducted so as to disadvantage other countries.
3. The agreed practices with respect to floating rates will operate until such time as a general return to par values is attained. If new par values are ever fixed, they will be set in terms of SDRs rather than gold or U.S. dollars.

The acceptance by the IMF of the reality of floating exchange rates is perhaps the best indication that such rates are not a mere transition to a new period of pegged rates.

CURRENT PROBLEMS

The shift from fixed rates to a system of managed flexible rates has not ended the sense of recurring crises in international trade and payments problems—for several reasons.

The Loss of Confidence in the Dollar as a Reserve Currency

Historical background. Balance-of-payments deficits are nothing new to the American econ-omy. In the 1950s and 1960s America ran frequent deficits on the sum of current and capital accounts. Much of this was due to American loans, investments, and contributions to other nations who were rebuilding their economies after World War II. As long as other nations were willing to accumulate dollar holdings, this caused no problem; indeed, the buildup of dollars in foreign exchange reserves provided the growth in reserves that was needed to finance the steadily growing volume of world trade.

As Table 42-1 shows, the number of dollars grew sharply over the decade of the 1970s as governments, banks, corporations, and even individuals held dollars without using them to exercise claims on U.S. output. But every dollar held is a potential dollar offered for sale if the holders decide to reduce their holdings.[7]

The effect of the dollar devaluations of the early 1970s. The two devaluations of the dollar in 1971 (7.9 percent) and 1973 (11 percent) automatically reduced the value of the exchange reserves of everyone who held dollars. Had everyone believed this was a once-and-for-all adjustment, they might well have licked their wounds and gone on as before. But nothing in American policy indicated that the trade deficits and the inflationary problems that caused the dollar problem were at an end. Thus many believed that the past devaluations were but prelude to inevitable future devaluations.

Fears of further devaluation not only made holders of dollars reluctant to increase their dollar holdings year by year (as it was necessary to do to finance the American balance-of-payments deficits without devaluation), but actually led many prudent holders of dollars to want to decrease their reliance on such a shaky reserve. As people tried to get rid of dollars, the exchange rate began to slide (see Figure 42-1). Between 1970 and 1973 the dollar declined 22

[7] Nor could the American economy expand quickly enough to provide goods should the holders attempt to buy American products. Any attempt to spend these large holdings of dollars would have caused massive inflation in the United States.

FIGURE 42-1

The Decline of the Dollar During the 1970s

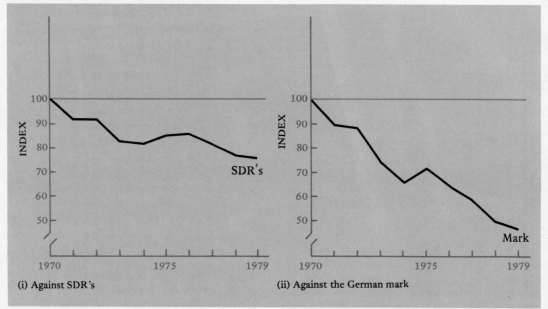

(i) Against SDR's   (ii) Against the German mark

The dollar depreciated sharply on the world's foreign exchange markets during the 1970s. In each part the curve is an index number (1970 = 100) that reflects the price of the dollar (at year-end) relative to other forms of foreign exchange. The price of the SDR in (i) is an average of 16 key currencies and is the best measure of the average devaluation of the dollar. The German mark, shown in (ii), proved the strongest of the world's currencies over the decade. The dollar depreciated 25 percent relative to SDRs and more than 50 percent relative to the mark.

percent against the yen and 30 percent against the mark. From 1973 to early 1980 it dropped an additional 23 percent against the yen and 31 percent against the mark.

As the dollar lost value, everyone who held large quantities of dollars became uncomfortable. The decreasing value of the dollar reduced the adequacy of most countries' reserves and threatened their financial stability.

Attempts to flee from the dollar. Had the dollar been but a small part of the reserve picture, it could have been replaced (as the pound was largely replaced in the late 1960s). But dollars were a key part of the world's foreign exchange reserves, and the system could not have functioned without them or some substitute.

While one country (or one bank) could readily reduce its holdings of dollars by buying gold or other currencies, the whole world could not do so unless an alternative source of international reserves was available. One source of the incredible rise in the price of gold in 1979–1980 from $250 to over $900 an ounce was the attempt of many holders of dollars to flee to gold. Since the monetary gold supply was in fact declining, this merely bid up the price of gold and depressed the price of the dollar. And this shrunk the size of the dollar reserves without letting their holders escape to a safer source of reserve. The volatile price of gold, shown in Figure 42-2, does not make it a very safe reserve.

Such attempted flights from the dollar will end only if the causes of the dollar's decline in price are eliminated, or if an adequate alternative international reserve is created to replace it. Neither

FIGURE 42-2
The Price of Gold

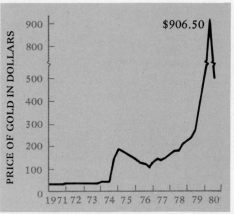

Gold soared in value and proved highly volatile after convertibility of the dollar was ended. The two devaluations of the dollar under the gold exchange standard can be seen in the early 1970s but they are barely visible. The course of gold speculation is seen in the subsequent experience. (Note that the vertical axis is interrupted between $500 and $800.) Gold does not exhibit the sort of price stability desired in an international source of reserve assets.

has occurred. Periodically over the 1970s the discomfort or concern with the dollar edged into panic. Only the concerted willingness of France, Germany, Japan, and Britain to increase their dollar holdings has prevented a major crisis. They have done so in order to support an orderly monetary system, not out of faith in the stability of the dollar.

Continuing causes of the decline of the dollar. A major continuing cause of the decline of the dollar during the late 1970s was the unwillingness or inability of Americans to decrease their dependence on imported oil. In addition, the inflation rate in the U.S. rose more rapidly than did that of many of its trading partners, because of a series of relatively expansionary monetary and fiscal policies. With other nations unwilling to increase their dollar holdings, these factors together put the dollar under continuous downward pressure.

The Lack of an Alternative to the Dollar as a Reserve Currency

Governments operating dirty floats need reserves, just as do governments operating adjustable pegs. The search for an adequate supply of reserves has continued unabated since the demise of the Bretton Woods system. In January 1976, agreement was reached for a 30 percent average increase in the quotas of funds that member countries must provide to the IMF and from which the IMF can make loans to countries wishing to support their exchange rates. But increases of that quantity have not done more than keep up with the growth in the volume of world trade. They have certainly not provided a substitute for the enormous role of the dollar. As the dollar's role as a reserve currency became less popular, several other currencies—first the mark, then the yen—gained temporary prominence as potential reserve currencies.

While it is possible that some other national currencies will take over the reserve currency role played by the dollar, this is not likely. First, such a replacement of the dollar would require a massive shift out of dollars and into the new currency. Unless this were carefully managed, it would result in a sharp depreciation of the dollar that would hurt the United States and all other holders of dollars. Second, no other country is likely to accept for its currency the role of major international reserve. We have seen that the reserve currency role results in major problems and limits the scope of domestic policy action. The American experience has not gone unnoticed.

Why does the world not turn to an international paper reserve system based on SDRs or some similar creation? Such a solution has much support from academic economists, who see an appropriate international institution managing the supply of international currency to accommodate growth and to avoid inflation.

Critics—among them most of the world's central bankers—distrust the concept of an international paper currency and can point to the fact that few countries have managed their own money supplies in an effective way. However difficult the task of the Fed may be, the task of a World Reserve Board would be more difficult.

Some who are skeptical of an international paper monetary standard have urged a return to the gold standard. We have seen that this approach has critical disadvantages. In fact, the IMF and the U.S. government have at various times taken the lead in the attempt to "demonetize" gold completely. The violent fluctuations in gold prices in 1979–1980 have done nothing to decrease the opposition to a return to the gold standard.

For the moment at least, the world cannot agree on an international monetary reserve. Until it does, there will be crises whenever there is a desire to shift from one to another of the multiple sources of reserves: dollars, gold, SDRs, marks, francs, and yen. The speculative opportunities inherent in such a system remain large.

The Changing Pattern and Volume of Trade

Growing world interdependence. As the volume of international trade increases each year, countries quite naturally become more dependent on other countries to supply them with goods and provide them with markets. This situation has a number of favorable consequences in terms of gains from trade, but it is not an unmixed blessing.

One undesirable consequence is that a major shock to one economy quickly spreads to a large fraction of the world. This was the case with the cutoff of Iranian oil in 1979. It is much easier to resolve a crisis in one country than to resolve a simultaneous crisis in a large fraction of the world. Indeed most of the emergency powers of the IMF contemplated only isolated emergencies.

A second aspect of the growing world interdependency is the tighter connection between world and domestic economic policies. It was once possible for a major country such as the United States to be regarded as a closed econ-

omy, one little disturbed by foreign developments. This is no longer true of any major country of the free world. Countries cannot pursue policies designed to solve unemployment, inflation, or lagging growth on the assumption that other countries will be unaffected. Yet the political and economic mechanisms for achieving a mutually consistent set of economic policies on the part of different nations do not exist.

The Impact of OPEC

The most serious event affecting the future payments system — and indeed the whole of international economic relations — was the tenfold increase in the price of oil in the decade following the formation of the OPEC cartel. The price rises have generated an unprecedented imbalance in the international economic system in the form of a massive payments surplus for the oil producers and a corresponding deficit for the oil-importing countries. The excess purchasing power in the hands of oil producers has come to be called **petrodollars.** The size of this excess has been put in the neighborhood of $75 billion to $100 billion *per year* at the start of the 1980s. The cumulative stock of petrodollars may well exceed $500 billion. Petrodollars cause several different kinds of current problems, some of them short term, others long term in nature.

Short-term problems of industrialized countries. In the long term many and perhaps most petrodollars will be used for the purchase of both consumption goods and services and investment goods from industrialized countries. In time these countries will thus find their exports to the oil producers rising to meet their imports from them. But the oil-producing countries cannot spend their oil revenues on goods and services fast enough.[8] Nor can the industrialized oil-con-

---

[8] There is a limit to the speed with which any country can absorb foreign goods, and many oil-producing countries are at that limit. Ships wait months to unload for want of dock capacity, unloaded goods sit in wharfside stockpiles for months — even years — for want of transportation capacity, and so on.

suming countries produce the goods and services at the necessary rate for all the oil revenues to be spent without creating enormous inflationary pressures.[9]

Thus in the short term the OPEC countries have excess dollars. And they have an understandable desire to earn a return on those funds. One way is to invest their surplus revenues in the advanced industrialized nations, thereby returning on capital account the purchasing power extracted from the current accounts of the oil-importing nations. This situation raises many serious problems. One of the most important arises from the potential havoc brought to foreign exchange markets when surplus oil funds are invested in liquid assets and switched between currencies in response to changes in interest rates and expected capital gains arising from possible exchange rate alterations. This happened in both 1979 and 1980.

The world seeks but has not yet found some means for placing the funds in less liquid investments and/or creating sufficient central bank cooperation to allow the funds to be moved without upsetting foreign exchange markets completely.

Another use of surplus petrodollars is speculative, and many observers believe that a good part of the wild rise and sudden fall in gold prices in 1979–1980 was due to just such a use of petrodollars.

Short-term problems of the underdeveloped countries. Consider a country like Kenya for which the OPEC price increase turned a small trade surplus into a massive deficit overnight. The country was unable to generate revenues quickly enough to pay its oil bill, yet it could sharply decrease its use of oil only at the cost of a great slowdown in its domestic economy.

Although there were many dire predictions following the 1973–1974 oil price rise that the inter-

national monetary system could not cope with this new challenge, they were proved wrong. The IMF stepped in with loan arrangements to help those countries most severely affected by the rising oil prices, the repayments of maturing loans were deferred, and the OPEC nations established a fund for short-term loans to such countries. The purely short-term problems can be and were solved through international cooperation and recognition of the need for accommodation on the part of creditor nations.

Longer-term problems of the changing terms of trade for underdeveloped countries. For a country such as the United States, Japan, or West Germany the higher price of oil will eventually be recovered in the higher price of the goods that that country sells to oil producers. But many of the less-developed countries of the world have no export commodities that will loom large enough to owners of petrodollars to offset the rising cost of oil imports. More Saudi Arabians will visit Kenyan game parks and buy more Kenyan coffee, but not enough more. It is probable that the price of what residents of many oil-importing countries must buy has risen permanently relative to the price of what they can hope to sell. In other words, there has been a change in the terms of trade to their long-term disadvantage. This sort of disadvantage is likely to be greatest in countries that are already among the poorer nations of the world. Any decrease in their relative standard of living seems unfortunate to them—and to many observers.

However, this is not an international *payments* problem at all; rather, it concerns the distribution of world wealth. It can be dealt with by gifts or grants to these countries, and some such increases in world contributions have occurred. To attempt to solve this problem as though it were a payments problem, by artificially supporting the currency of the country above its equilibrium value, is undesirable. It implies an indirect subsidy that prevents the efficient use of the country's resources. This occurs because main-

---

[9] Production of the goods produces factor incomes and thus adds to domestic demand, while export of the goods removes them from domestic markets and thus reduces domestic supplies.

taining the exchange rate at a disequilibrium level distorts the price signals of foreign goods relative to domestic goods. Consequently, trade will not follow patterns of comparative advantage.

The Challenge for the 1980s

The 1970s witnessed the replacement of a system of managed fixed exchange rates by a system of managed flexible rates. The problems of the latter have been well defined by the events of the decade, but they cannot be said to have been solved. Officials understand the need both to develop an adequate reserve unit not tied to any national currency and to devise workable guidelines for managing flexible rates.

AN INTERNATIONAL
RESERVE CURRENCY

Many and perhaps most economists believe that a controlled international money supply based on SDRs and expanded to keep pace with the volume of world trade is the best answer to the reserve problem. But an international paper currency, like a national currency, cannot work until there is confidence in it. The turmoil of the last two decades did nothing to create the climate of confidence required for the complete demonetization of gold and the dollar as international media of exchange. Flawed though either gold or the dollar is, each seems better (at this date) to many of the world's bankers than SDRs or similar "pieces of paper."

THE MANAGEMENT OF
EXCHANGE RATES

The managed aspect of managed floating rates poses several potential problems for the international monetary system. They include the possibilities of mutually inconsistent exchange rate stabilization policies, competitive exchange rate depreciation, and instability of exchange rates in the face of speculative pressures. To help avoid these problems, the IMF issued guidelines for exchange rate management in June 1974. The guidelines emphasized the point that exchange rate policy is a matter for international consultation and surveillance by the IMF and that intervention practices by individual central banks should be based on three principles: (1) exchange authorities should prevent sudden and disproportionate short-term movements in exchange rates and ensure an orderly adjustment of exchange rates to longer-term pressures; (2) in consultation with the IMF, countries should establish a target zone for the medium-term values of their exchange rates and keep the actual rate within that target zone; (3) countries should recognize that exchange rate management involves joint responsibilities.

The experiences of the 1970s have underlined one of the most important problems not yet solved: coping with the massive volume of short-term funds that can be switched very rapidly between financial centers. Short-term capital flows forced the abandonment of exchange rates that were agreed on in 1971, and they have caused violent fluctuations in floating rates as recently as 1979.

Various attempts have been made to limit such flows. Italy has adopted a "two-tier" foreign exchange market with one price for foreign exchange to finance current account transactions and another price (and another set of controls) for foreign exchange to finance capital movements. Germany has used direct controls on overseas borrowing. There has also been a considerable extension of arrangements under which central banks in surplus countries lend the funds they are accumulating back to central banks in deficit countries, thereby enhancing the ability of banks to maintain stable exchange rates in the face of short-term speculative flights of capital.

The major problem in managing speculative flows is to identify them accurately. Experience suggests that exchange rate management can smooth out temporary fluctuations but cannot resist underlying trends in equilibrium rates caused by relative inflation rates, structural changes, and persistent nonspeculative capital flows. In the day-to-day management it is not always easy to distinguish among them.

THE NEED FOR COOPERATION

One of the most impressive aspects of the international payments history of the last 30 years has been the steady rise of effective international cooperation. When the gold standard collapsed and the Great Depression overwhelmed the countries of the world, "every man for himself" was the rule of the day. Rising tariffs, competitive exchange rate devaluations, and all forms of beggar-my-neighbor policies abounded.

After World War II the countries of the world cooperated in bringing the Bretton Woods system and the IMF into being. The system itself was far from perfect, and it finally broke down as a result of its own internal contradictions. But the international cooperation that was necessary to set the system up survived the collapse of the system itself. The joint cooperative actions of central banks allowed them to weather in the 1970s speculative crises that would have forced them to devalue their currencies in the 1950s.

Thus the collapse of Bretton Woods did not plunge the world into the same chaos that followed the breakdown of the gold standard. The world was also better able to cope with the terrible strains caused by the sharp rise in oil prices in the 1970s. Enormous oil-related problems remain, and they are matters for continuing international dialogue.

Whatever the problems of the future, the world has a better chance of coping with them — or even just learning to live with them — when its countries cooperate through the IMF and other international organizations than when each country seeks its own selfish solution without concern for the interests of others.

Summary

1. Under the gold standard, the central authorities of each country kept their paper currency convertible into gold at a fixed rate, and the "gold content" of each currency established fixed rates of exchange between all the currencies. Because all currencies were freely convertible into gold, they were also freely convertible into each other.

2. The gold standard was supposed to work through changes in national price levels and from them to changes in the prices of imported and exported commodities. A deficit country would lose gold, its money supply would shrink, its price level would fall; thus imports would become relatively more expensive while exports became relatively cheaper, and both changes would tend to reduce the deficit. A surplus country would gain gold, expand its money supply, experience an inflation that would make its imports relatively cheap and its exports relatively inexpensive, and thus find its surplus being reduced.

3. Before 1914 this system was not required to remove major disequilibria in the balance of payments. In the 1920s the gold standard was required to do so and failed. The major disabilities of a gold standard in the 1920s were that price levels adjusted too slowly and the authorities were unwilling to adopt realistic exchange rates. Any gold standard system suffers from the serious difficulties of a rigid supply and a large and volatile speculative demand for gold.

4. The gold standard was abandoned and many experiments were tried throughout the 1930s. The use of exchange rates and trade restrictions to increase local employment in the face of inadequate aggregate world demand was discredited as a means of dealing with a worldwide unemployment problem.

5. The international payments system existing between 1944 and the early 1970s was called the Bretton Woods system. It put the world on an adjustable peg, gold exchange standard. To maintain their rates of exchange vis-à-vis the dollar, foreign monetary authorities bought and sold reserves of gold and of the two reserve currencies, the British pound sterling and the U.S. dollar. Exchange rates were only to be changed in the face of a fundamental disequilibrium in the balance of payments.

6. The International Monetary Fund (IMF) was the major institution of the Bretton Woods system. It tried to ensure that countries pegged their exchange rates and changed them only in the face of fundamental disequilibrium. To this end it made loans of foreign exchange to countries trying to weather temporary balance-of-payments deficits.

7. Three major problems with any adjustable peg system are (1) to provide sufficient international reserves, (2) to adjust to long-term trends in receipts and payments, and (3) to handle periodic speculative crises. The SDR is a relatively new international paper money meant to provide adequate international reserves not linked to gold or the U.S. dollar.

8. The Bretton Woods system broke down under a series of speculative crises that stemmed from the failure of the system to provide sufficient international reserves, and the need to accommodate devaluations of the U.S. dollar.

9. The two major events in the transition from the Bretton Woods system to the present one were the abandonment of gold convertibility of dollars held by foreign central banks in 1971 and the drift toward flexibility of exchange rates that occurred mainly during 1972 and 1973.

10. The present system is a dollar standard with managed flexibility of exchange rates, often called a dirty float. The system is under very heavy strain because of the current account deficits of so many of the oil-importing countries, because of the enormous supplies of short-term foreign investment held by the oil exporters, and because of the loss of confidence in the dollar as a reserve currency.

11. Current problems are the need to find an ade-quate reserve not tied to a national currency, the accommodation to both the short-term and the longer-term impact of OPEC, and the development of rules for managing flexible exchange rates. The spirit of international cooperation is a constructive step toward finding solutions.

Topics for Review

The gold standard
The Bretton Woods system
A dollar standard
Kinds of foreign exchange reserves
Pegged exchange rates and adjustable pegs
Freely floating exchange rates
Dirty or managed floats
Petrodollars

Discussion Questions

1. What role in international payments does or did gold play under (a) the gold standard, (b) the adjustable peg Bretton Woods system, (c) the present system? In 1974 *Barron's* had an editorial headed, "Monetary Reform and Gold: You Can't Have One Without the Other." Does the gold price experience of the 1970s bear out this editorial opinion?

2. "The price of gold soared as much as $50 an ounce on European bullion markets today. Dealers attributed it to fears that the president's economic policy might touch off more worldwide inflation. The dollar and the pound both declined sharply against the mark and the franc in busy trading on foreign exchange markets."

   This quotation from the *New York Times* was made during the administration of one of the following presidents. Guess which one, and explain your answer.

William H. Taft	1909–1913
Franklin D. Roosevelt	1933–1945
Harry S Truman	1945–1953
John F. Kennedy	1961–1963
Jimmy Carter	1977–1981

3. Might a person who regards inflation as the number one economic danger favor a return to the pre-1914 gold standard? Would you predict noninflationary results if in order to restore the gold standard, the price of gold had to be set at $1600 per ounce, either all at once or gradually?

4. The dollar is no longer convertible into gold because of a change in U.S. policy. Does this lack of conversion make the dollar any less useful as an international medium of exchange?

5. Are Americans benefited or hurt when the dollar is the standard form of international reserves?

6. "Under a flexible exchange rate system no country need suffer unemployment, for if its prices are low enough there will be more than enough demand to keep its factories and farms fully occupied." The evidence suggests that flexible rates have not generally eliminated unemployment. Can you explain why? Can changing exchange rates ever cure unemployment?

7. The OPEC oil price increase has caused grave problems in international payments and increased the need for IMF loans. Why has not market adjustment of exchange rates solved the problem?

Part Twelve

Economic Growth
and Comparative
Systems

Growth in Developed Economies

43

In Chapter 30 we saw that investment can be the cause of economic fluctuations ranging from mild disturbances to major upheavals. Investment has been even more important as the major reason for the economic growth that has raised living standards so rapidly since about 1800. Eightfold or tenfold increases in material living standards have occurred over a single lifetime.

Investment affects growth because it affects the economy's ability to *produce* goods by changing both the quantity and the quality of the capital stock available.

Investment increases the economy's potential, or full-employment, national income.

The theory of economic growth concentrates on the effect of investment on full-employment national income. Contrast this with the theory of fluctuations, which concentrates on the effects of investment expenditure on aggregate demand and hence on the degree to which actual current national income falls short of, or exceeds, potential national income. See Figure 43-1. Put another way, the theory of fluctuations is concerned with the degree of utilization of existing productive capacity, while the theory of growth is concerned with the growth of productive capacity, or full-employment national income.

The Nature of Economic Growth

Economic growth has been a dominant force in industrial nations for 200 years. It has been the source of industrialization's greatest triumph: the raising of the ordinary person's living standards to levels where leisure, travel, and luxury goods are within reach. It has produced standards of living in industrial nations that are the envy of the rest of the world and has led many other nations—with varying degrees of success—to strive to copy that performance. Economic growth has also been the source of spectacular adverse complications such as pollution of the air, water, and land by chemicals, heat, and noise.

Members of developed societies have come to accept growth. Even when they worry about pollution and other undesirable concomitants of growth, they ask, How can we remove this or that harmful side effect of growth? Few people ask, How can we stop growth? and even fewer take those few seriously.

Yet growth, which seems inevitable to most of us, has not always been present, nor is it present everywhere today. During human history there have been periods of increases in living standards followed by long periods with no change. One of the latter was documented by Professor Phelps-Brown of the London School of Economics, who showed that there was no significant increase in the real income of English building-trade workers between 1215 and 1798, a period of almost six centuries. Peasants in many underdeveloped countries today enjoy a living standard probably little different from that of their ancestors a thousand or more years ago.

Recent data show that world output has doubled in the last 15 years. Despite dramatic population growth, worldwide output per person has increased sharply; it was twice as high in 1975 as in 1950.

These figures provide impressive evidence of the mastery of aspects of our environment, but they are enormously misleading in one respect: most of the growth in output has occurred in countries that make up only about one-fifth of the world's population, while much of the population growth has occurred in countries that have not experienced economic growth.

For many countries, and for much of history, the phenomenon of growth has been absent.

In this chapter and the next we ask, Why are there large differences among countries in their growth rates?

THE DEFINITION OF ECONOMIC GROWTH

In a country where GNP has increased tenfold in half a century, and where personal consumption expenditures per capita have doubled in real terms in less than 30 years, it is easy to recognize the phenomenon of growth. It is harder to measure it because of several potential confusions. Because each is found in some contemporary discussions, it is worth bearing them in mind as

FIGURE 43-1
Short-run and Long-run Effects of Investment

Investment affects aggregate demand in the short run and aggregate supply in the long run. An increase in investment expenditure increases aggregate demand from say *AD* to *AD₁* and is thus an important part of the theory of fluctuations. Such an effect is shown by the colored curves. Over the long run, net investment increases the productive capacity of the economy. This leads to an increase in the level of full-employment income and involves a rightward shift in the aggregate supply curve from say *AS* to *AS₁*, as shown by the black curves.

you read of any country's spectacular achievements.

Capacity versus utilization. The increase in an economy's national income over three or four years reflects changes both in its productive capacity and in the percentage of utilization of this capacity.

If there have been large decreases in unemployment, high rates of increase in national income may be observed. But such increases will not be sustainable once full employment is reached. For example, American GNP increased by 50 percent between 1933 and 1936, but this reflected almost entirely the reduction in the GNP gap from the depths of the Great Depression, not growth in full-employment national income.

A great deal of confusion would be avoided if the term "growth rate" were used to refer only to the growth rate of full-employment national income and if comparisons of national income figures for one country over several years were divided into two parts: changes due to such growth and changes due to variations in the GNP gap.

Money versus real output. Part of any increase in the money value of full-employment output may be due to a rise in prices rather than in output. Constant-dollar measures are essential to measure growth, and they are now commonly used by all major statistical agencies in reporting growth rates.

Output, output per person, and output per hour of labor. To determine a nation's growth in the context of its ability to wage war or pollute its environment, we must look at total output. To measure living standards, per capita output is important; a country's average material living standard depends on output per person. (As an example of the relations between these concepts, a doubling of national output combined with a doubling of population would mean no change in per capita output. As will be seen in Chapter

44, population growth is a problem plaguing many countries.)

Output per person may grow at a different rate than the economy's productive capacity per person. As an economy grows, many people choose to spend a shorter portion of their days and lives at work. As standards of living rise, entry into the labor force tends to be delayed by increased schooling, work weeks are shortened to permit greater leisure, and the size of the older non-working population rises because of earlier retirement and longer life spans. To offset this, there may be increases in the labor force participation of women and of men who worked previously in nonmarket sectors of the economy.

In theoretical discussions of growth, it is useful to have an indicator of the ability of an economy to convert its resources into goods and services. A widely used summary measure of this is output per hour of labor, often called simply **productivity.** Obviously, productivity depends not only on labor effort but also on the amount and kind of machinery used, the raw materials available, and so on. The focus of this measure is explained by the special emphasis that human beings place on human labor.

THE CUMULATIVE NATURE OF GROWTH

A growth rate of 2 percent per year may seem insignificant, but if it is continued for a century, it will lead to more than a sevenfold increase in real national income!

The cumulative effect of small annual growth rates is large.

To appreciate the cumulative effect of what seem like very small differences in growth rates, examine Table 43-1. Notice that when one country grows faster than another, the gap in their living standards widens progressively. If two countries start from the same level of income, and if country A grows at 3 percent while B grows at 2 percent per year, A's income per capita will be twice B's in 69 years. You may not think it matters much whether the economy

TABLE 43-1
The Cumulative Effect of Growth

Year	Percentage rate of growth per year				
	1%	2%	3%	5%	7%
0	100	100	100	100	100
10	111	122	135	165	201
30	135	182	246	448	817
50	165	272	448	1,218	3,312
70	201	406	817	3,312	13,429
100	272	739	2,009	14,841	109,660

Small differences in growth rates make enormous differences in levels of potential national income over a few decades. Assume that potential national income is 100 in year zero. At a rate of growth of 3 percent, it will be 135 in 10 years, 448 after 50 years, and over 2,000 in a century. Compound interest is a powerful force!

grows at 2 percent or 3 percent, but your children and grandchildren will!

To dramatize the powerful long-run effects of differences in growth rates, we included in the early editions of this text a table that showed students of the 1960s that, if the then current growth trends continued, America would not long remain the world's richest nation, for Sweden, Canada, Japan, and many others were growing at a much faster rate. Many readers of that era rejected the notion as a textbook gimmick; deep down they *knew* that the material standard of living of the United States was and would remain the highest the world had ever known. Such a table is no longer even interesting, for by 1980 several industrial countries, including Sweden and Canada, had passed the United States in terms of per capita national income and several more were within 10 percent of the U.S. level. In addition, Kuwait and several other oil producers reported higher average incomes.

BENEFITS OF GROWTH

Growth in Living Standards

A country whose per capita output grows at 3 percent per year doubles its living standards about every 24 years. (A helpful approximation device is the "rule of 72." Divide any growth rate into 72 and the resulting number approximates the number of years it will take for income to double.) [41]

A primary reason for desiring growth is to raise general living standards.

The extreme importance of economic growth in raising income can be illustrated by comparing the real income of a father with the real income of the son who follows in his father's footsteps. If the son neither rises nor falls in the relative income scale compared with his father, his share of the country's national income will be the same as his father's. If the son is 30 years younger than his father, he can expect to have a real income nearly twice as large as that which his father enjoyed when his father was the same age. These figures assume that the father and son live in a country such as the United States where the growth rate has been 2 or 3 percent per year. If they live in Japan, where growth has been going on at a rate of about 8 percent per year, the son's income will be about 10 times as large as his father's.

For those who share in it, growth is a powerful weapon against poverty. A family earning $5,500 today can expect $8,200 within ten years (in constant dollars) if it just shares in a 4 percent growth rate. The transformation of the life style of blue-collar workers in America as well as in Germany and Japan in a generation provides a notable example of the escape from poverty that growth makes possible.

Of course, not everyone benefits equally from growth. Many of the poorest are not even in the labor force and thus are least likely to share in the higher wages that, along with profits, are the primary means by which the gains from growth are distributed. For this reason, even in a growing economy redistribution policies will be needed if poverty is to be averted.

Growth and Income Redistribution

Economic growth makes many kinds of redistributions easier to achieve. For example, a rapid

An Open Letter to the Ordinary Citizen from a Supporter of the Growth-Is-Good School

Dear Ordinary Citizen:

You live in the world's first civilization that is devoted principally to satisfying *your* needs rather than those of a privileged minority. Past civilizations have always been based on leisure and high consumption for a tiny upper class, a reasonable living standard for a small middle class, and hard work with little more than subsistence consumption for the great mass of people. In the past, the average person saw little of the civilized and civilizing products of the economy, except when he or she was toiling to produce them.

The continuing Industrial Revolution is based on mass-produced goods for you, the ordinary citizen. It ushered in a period of sustained economic growth that has raised consumption standards of ordinary citizens to levels previously reserved throughout history for a tiny privileged minority. Reflect on a few examples: travel, live and recorded music, art, good food, inexpensive books, universal literacy and a genuine chance to be educated. Most important, there is leisure to provide time and energy to enjoy these and thousands of other products of the modern industrial economy.

Would any ordinary family seriously doubt the benefits of growth and prefer to be back in the world of 150 or 500 years ago, in its same relative social and economic position? Most surely the answer is no. But we cannot say the same for those with incomes in the top 1 or 2 percent of the income distribution. Economic growth has destroyed much of their privileged consumption position: they must now vie with the masses when visiting the world's beauty spots and be annoyed, while lounging on the terrace of a palatial mansion, by the sound of charter flights carrying ordinary people to inexpensive holidays in far places. The rich resent their loss of exclusive rights to luxury consumption. Some complain bitterly, and it is not surprising that they find their intellectual apologists.

Whether they know it or not, the antigrowth economists—such as Harvard's Ken Galbraith, Cambridge's Joan Robinson, and the LSE's Ed Mishan—are not the social revolutionaries they think they are. They are counterrevolutionaries who would set back the clock of material progress for the ordinary person. They say that growth has produced pollution and wasteful consumption of all kinds of frivolous products which add nothing to human happiness. But the democratic solution to pollution is not to go back to where so few people consume luxuries that pollution is trivial; it is to accept pollution as part of a transitional phase connected with the ushering in of mass consumption, to keep the mass consumption, and to learn to control the pollution it tends to create.

It is only through further growth that the average citizen can enjoy consumption standards (of travel, culture, medical and health care, etc.) now available to people in the top 25 percent of the income distribution—which includes the intellectuals who earn large royalties from the books they write denouncing growth. If you think that extra income confers little real benefit, just ask those in that top 25 percent to trade incomes with the average citizen. Or see how hard *they* struggle to reduce their income taxes.

Ordinary citizens, do not be deceived by disguised elitist doctrines. Remember that the very rich and the elite have much to gain by stopping growth—and even more by rolling it back—but you have everything to gain by letting it go forward.

Onward!

I. Growthman

growth rate makes it much more feasible politically to alleviate poverty. If existing income is to be redistributed, someone's standard of living will actually have to be lowered. However, when there is economic growth, and when the increment in income is redistributed (through government intervention), it is possible to reduce income inequalities without actually having to lower anyone's income. It is much easier for a rapidly growing economy to be generous toward its less fortunate citizens—or neighbors—than it is for a static economy.

Growth and Life Style

A family often finds that a big increase in its income can lead to a major change in the pattern of its consumption—that extra money buys important amenities of life. In the same way, the members of society as a whole may change their consumption patterns as their average income rises. Not only do markets in a country that is growing rapidly make it profitable to produce more cars, but the government is led to produce more highways and to provide more recreational areas for its newly affluent (and mobile) citizens. At yet a later stage, a concern about litter, pollution, and ugliness may become important, and their correction may then begin to account for a significant fraction of GNP. Such "amenities" usually become matters of social concern only when growth has assured the provision of the basic requirements for food, clothing, and housing of a substantial majority of the population.

National Defense and Prestige

When one country is competing with another for power or prestige, rates of growth are important. If our national income is growing at 2 percent, say, while the other country's is growing at 5 percent, the other country will only have to wait for our relative strength to dwindle. Moreover, a country will find the expenses of an arms race or a program of foreign aid easier to bear, the faster its productivity is growing.

More subtly, growth has become part of the currency of international prestige. Countries that are engaged in persuading other countries of the might or right of their economic and political systems point to their rapid rates of growth as evidence of their achievements.

COSTS OF GROWTH

The benefits discussed above suggest that growth is a great blessing. It is surely true that, *ceteris paribus,* most people would regard a fast rate of growth as preferable to a slow one, but other things are seldom equal.

Social and Personal Costs of Growth

Industrialization, unless carefully managed, causes deterioration of the environment. Unspoiled landscapes give way to highways, factories, and billboards; air and water become polluted; and in some cases unique and priceless relics of earlier ages—from flora and fauna to ancient ruins—disappear. Urbanization tends to move people away from the simpler life of farms and small towns and into the crowded slum-ridden, and often darkly evil life of the urban ghetto. Those remaining behind in the rural areas find that rural life, too, has changed. Larger-scale farming, the decline of population, and the migration of children from the farm to the city all have their costs. The stepped-up tempo of life brings joys to some but tragedy to others. Accidents, ulcers, crime rates, suicides, divorces, and murder all tend to be higher in periods of rapid change and in more developed societies.

When an economy is growing, it is also changing. Innovation leaves obsolete machines in its wake, and it also leaves partially obsolete people. No matter how well trained you are at age 25, in another 25 years your skills may well be partially obsolete. Some will find that their skills have become completely outdated and unneeded. A rapid rate of growth requires rapid adjustments, which can cause much upset and misery to the individuals affected. The decline in the number

An Open Letter to the Ordinary Citizen from a Supporter of the Growth-Is-Bad School

Dear Ordinary Citizen:

You live in a world that is being despoiled by a mindless search for ever higher levels of material consumption at the cost of all other values. Once upon a time, men and women knew how to enjoy creative work and to derive satisfaction from simple activities undertaken in scarce, and hence highly valued, leisure time. Today the ordinary worker is a mindless cog in an assembly line that turns out ever more goods that the advertisers must work overtime to persuade the worker to consume.

Statisticians and politicians count the increasing flow of material output as a triumph of modern civilization. Consider not the flow of output in general, but the individual products that it contains. You arise from your electric-blanketed bed, clean your teeth with an electric toothbrush, open with an electric can opener a can of the sad remnants of a once-proud orange, you eat your bread baked from super-refined and chemically refortified flour, and you climb into your car to sit in vast traffic jams on exhaust-polluted highways. And so it goes, with endless consumption of high-technology products that give you no more real satisfaction than the simple, cheaply produced equivalent products used by your great-grandfathers: soft woolly blankets, natural bristle toothbrushes, real oranges, old-fashioned and coarse but healthy bread, and public transport that moved on uncongested roads and gave its passengers time to chat with their neighbors, to read, or just to daydream.

Television commercials tell you that by consuming more you are happier. But happiness lies not in increasing consumption but in increasing the ratio of *satisfaction of wants* to *total wants*. Since the more you consume the more the advertisers persuade you that you want to consume, you are almost certainly less happy than the average citizen in a small town in 1900 whom we can visualize sitting on the family porch, sipping a cool beer or a lemonade, and enjoying the antics of the children as they play with scooters made out of old crates and jump rope with pieces of old clothesline.

Today the landscape is dotted with endless factories producing the plastic trivia of the modern industrial society. They drown you in a cloud of noise, air, and water pollution. The countryside is despoiled by strip mines, petroleum cracking plants, and dangerous nuclear power stations that produce the energy that is devoured insatiably by modern factories and motor vehicles.

Worse, our precious heritage of natural resources is being fast used up. Spaceship earth flies, captainless, in its senseless orgy of self-consuming consumption.

Now is the time to stop this madness. We must stabilize production, reduce pollution, conserve our natural resources, and seek justice through a more equitable distribution of existing total income.

A long time ago Malthus taught us that if we do not limit population voluntarily, nature will do it for us in a cruel and savage manner. Today the same is true of output: if we do not halt its growth voluntarily, the halt will be imposed on us by a disastrous increase in pollution and a rapid exhaustion of natural resources.

Citizens, awake! Shake off the worship of growth, learn to enjoy the bounty that is yours already, and reject the endless, self-defeating search for increased happiness through ever-increasing consumption.

Upward!

A. Nongrowthman

of unskilled jobs makes the lot of untrained workers much more difficult. When they lose jobs, they may well fail to find others—particularly if they are over 50.

It is often argued that costs of this kind are a small price to pay for the great benefits that growth can bring. Even if that is true in the aggregate (which is a matter of debate), these personal costs are very unevenly borne. Indeed, many of those for whom growth is most costly (in terms of jobs) share least in the fruits of growth. Yet it is also a mistake to see only the costs—to yearn for the good old days while enjoying higher living standards that growth alone has made possible.

The Opportunity Cost of Growth

In a world of scarcity, almost nothing is free. Growth requires heavy investments of resources in capital goods as well as in activities such as education. Often these investments yield no *immediate* return in terms of goods and services for consumption; thus they imply sacrifices by the current generation of consumers.

Growth, which promises more goods tomorrow, is achieved by consuming fewer goods today. For the economy as a whole this is the primary cost of growth.

An example will suggest the magnitude of this cost. Suppose the fictitious economy of USSA has full employment and is experiencing growth at the rate of 2 percent per year. Its citizens consume 85 percent of the GNP and invest 15 percent. The people of USSA know that if they are willing to decrease immediately their consumption to 77 percent, they will produce more capital and thus shift at once to a 3 percent growth rate. The new rate can be maintained as long as they keep saving and investing 23 percent of the national income. Should they do it?

Table 43-2 represents the choice in terms of time paths of consumption. How expensive is the "invest now, consume later" strategy? On the assumed figures, it takes ten years for the actual

TABLE 43-2
The Opportunity Cost of Growth

In year	(A) Level of consumption at 2% growth rate	(B) Level of consumption at 3% growth rate	(C) Cumulative gain (loss) in consumption
0	85.0	77.0	(8.0)
1	86.7	79.3	(15.4)
2	88.5	81.8	(22.1)
3	90.3	84.2	(28.2)
4	92.1	86.8	(33.5)
5	93.9	89.5	(37.9)
6	95.8	92.9	(40.8)
7	97.8	95.0	(43.6)
8	99.7	97.9	(45.4)
9	101.8	100.9	(46.3)
10	103.8	103.9	(46.2)
15	114.7	120.8	(28.6)
20	126.8	140.3	19.6
30	154.9	189.4	251.0
40	189.2	255.6	745.9

Transferring resources from consumption to investment goods lowers current income but raises future income. The example assumes that income in year zero is 100, and that consumption of 85 percent of national income is possible with a 2 percent growth rate. It is further assumed that to achieve a 3 percent growth rate, consumption must fall to 77 percent of income. A shift from (A) to (B) decreases consumption for 10 years but increases it thereafter. The cumulative effect on consumption is shown in (C); the gains eventually become large.

amount of consumption to catch up to what it would have been had no reallocation been made. In the intervening ten years a good deal of consumption was lost, and the cumulative losses in consumption must be made up before society can really be said to have broken even. It takes an additional nine years before total consumption over the whole period is as large as it would have been if the economy had remained on the 2 percent path. [42]

A policy of sacrificing present living standards for a gain that does not begin to be reaped for a generation is hardly likely to appeal to any but the altruistic or the very young. The question of how much of its living standards one generation is prepared to sacrifice for its heirs (who are in any case likely to be richer) is troublesome. As one critic put it, Why should we sacrifice for them? What have they ever done for us?

Many governments, particularly those seeking a larger role in world affairs, have chosen to force the diversion of resources from consumption to investment. The Germans under Hitler, the Russians under Stalin, and the Chinese under Mao Tse-tung adopted four-year and five-year plans that did just this. Many less-developed countries are using such plans today. Such resource shifts are particularly important when actual growth rates are very small (say, less than 1 percent), for without some current sacrifice there is little or no prospect of real growth in the lifetimes of today's citizens. The very lowest growth rates are frequently encountered in the very poorest countries. This creates a cruel dilemma, discussed in Chapter 44 as the vicious circle of poverty.

GROWTH AS A GOAL OF POLICY: DO THE BENEFITS JUSTIFY THE COSTS?

Suppose that the members of a society want to increase their output of goods by 10 percent in one year. There are many ways they can do this.
1. They may be able to find idle and unutilized resources and put them to work.
2. They may be able to schedule extra shifts and overtime labor.
3. They may, by exhortation or by an appropriate incentive system, induce people to work much harder.
4. They may (if they have time) increase the supply of machines and factories.
5. They may utilize new techniques that permit them to get more output from the same inputs.

In the short run, the first three approaches seem the more promising; in fact, when nations face such crises as wars, these devices are used to achieve rapid increases in output. But the gains to be achieved by utilizing unemployed resources, extending the hours of use of employed ones, or "working harder" are limited. Eventually they will be used up. When there are no longer unutilized resources or underutilized capacity, further increases in output become more difficult to achieve.

In the long term, it is the last two approaches that bring the sustained increases in living standards that have eliminated the 14-hour day and the six-day work week and made possible both leisure and high material standards of living.

But do the already developed countries need yet more growth? Most people think they do. Poverty is now a solvable problem in the United States as a direct result of its enhanced average living standards. Clearly, people in the top quarter of the present income distribution have more opportunities for leisure, travel, culture, fine wines, and gracious living than have persons with much lower incomes. Most of those now in the bottom half of the income distribution would like these opportunities too. Only growth can give it to them.

Today, many countries that have not yet—or have only newly—undergone sustained periods of economic growth in modern times are urgently seeking to copy those that have in order to obtain the benefits of growth.

Most nations and most people today wish to pursue the goal of growth for the benefits it brings, despite its costs.

How seriously the costs are taken depends in part on how many of the benefits of growth have already been achieved. With mounting population problems, the poor countries are increasingly preoccupied with creating growth. With mounting awareness of pollution, the rich countries are devoting ever more resources to overcoming the problems caused by growth—at the same time that they are understandably reluctant to give up further growth.

Indeed, a similar conflict can often be seen within the same country at one time: a relatively poor community fights to acquire a new paper mill for the employment and income it will create; another, relatively affluent community deplores the ruin of its beaches and its air by an existing mill.

Theories of Economic Growth

Economists today recognize that many different factors may contribute to—or impede—economic growth. Although our present knowledge of the relative importance of these factors is far from complete, modern economists look at the problems of growth more optimistically than did the classical economists of a century and more ago. Of particular importance is the nature and source of the investment opportunities that, when utilized, lead to growth. The differences between the classical and contemporary points of view can best be understood by considering a revealing though unrealistic case.

GROWTH IN A WORLD WITHOUT LEARNING

Suppose that there is a known and fixed stock of projects that might be undertaken; suppose nothing ever happens to increase either the supply of such projects or knowledge about them. Whenever the opportunity is ripe, some of the investment opportunities are utilized, thereby increasing the stock of capital goods and depleting the reservoir of unutilized investment opportunities. Of course, the most productive opportunities will be used first.

Such a view of investment opportunities can be represented by a fixed marginal efficiency of capital schedule of the kind met in Chapter 22. Such a schedule is graphed in Figure 43-2; it relates the stock of capital to the productivity of an additional unit of capital. The productivity of a unit of capital is calculated by dividing the annual value of the additional output resulting from an extra unit of capital by the value of that unit of capital. Thus, for example, a marginal efficiency of capital of .2 means that $1 of new capital adds 20¢ per year to the stream of output.

The downward slope of the *MEC* schedule indicates that, with knowledge constant, increases in the stock of capital bring smaller and smaller increases in output per unit of capital. That is,

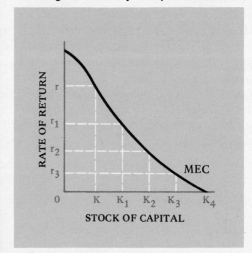

FIGURE 43-2
The Marginal Efficiency of Capital Schedule

A declining *MEC* schedule shows that successive increases to the capital stock bring smaller and smaller increases in output and thus a declining rate of return. A fixed *MEC* schedule can represent the theory of growth in an economy with some unutilized investment opportunities but no learning. Increases in investment that increase the capital stock from K to K_1 to . . . K_4 lower the rate of return from r to r_1 to . . . zero. Because the productivity of successive units of capital decreases, the capital-output ratio rises.

the rate of return on successive units of capital declines. This shape is a consequence of the law of diminishing returns.[1] If, with land, labor, and knowledge constant, more and more capital is used, the net amount added by successive increments will diminish and may eventually reach zero. Given this schedule, as capital is accumulated in a state of constant knowledge the society will move down its *MEC* schedule.

In such a "nonlearning" world, where new investment opportunities do not appear, growth occurs only so long as there are unutilized opportunities to use capital effectively to increase output. Growth, in a nonlearning world, is a transitory phenomenon that occurs as long as the

[1] This hypothesis was discussed on pages 190–192.

society has a backlog of unutilized investment opportunities.

So far we have discussed the *marginal* efficiency of capital. The *average* efficiency of capital refers to the average amount produced in the whole economy per unit of capital employed. It is common in discussions of the theory of growth to talk in terms of the *capital-output ratio,* which is the reciprocal of output per unit of capital. In a world without learning, the capital-output ratio is increasing.

In a world without learning the growth in the capital stock will have two important consequences:

1. Successive increases in capital accumulation will be less and less productive, and the capital-output ratio will be increasing.
2. The marginal efficiency of new capital will be decreasing and will eventually be pushed to zero as the backlog of investment opportunities is used up.

GROWTH WITH LEARNING

The steady depletion of growth opportunities in the previous model resulted from the fact that new investment opportunities were never discovered or created. However, if investment opportunities are created as well as used up with the passage of time, the *MEC* schedule will shift outward over time and the effects of increasing the capital stock may be different. This is illustrated in Figure 43-3. Such outward shifts can be regarded as the consequences of "learning" either about investment opportunites or about the techniques that create such opportunities. When learning occurs, what matters is how rapidly the *MEC* schedule shifts relative to the amount of capital investment being undertaken. Three possibilities are shown in Figure 43-3.

Gradual Reduction in Investment Opportunities: The Classical View

If, as in Figure 43-3(i), investment opportunities are created but at a slower rate than they are

used up, there will be a tendency toward a falling rate of return and an increasing ratio of capital to output. The predictions in this case are the same as those given above (in color) for the world without learning, though the cause is different: too slow, rather than no, discovery of new investment opportunities.

This figure illustrates the theory of growth held by most early economists. They saw the economic problem as one of fixed land, a rising population, and a gradual exhaustion of investment opportunities. These conditions, they believed, would ultimately force the economy into a static condition with no growth, very high capital-output ratios, and the marginal return on additional units of capital forced down toward zero.

Constant or Rising Investment Opportunities: The Contemporary View

The pessimism of the classical economists came from their failure to anticipate the possibility of really rapid innovation—of technological progress that could push investment opportunities outward as rapidly or more rapidly than they were used up, as shown in parts (ii) and (iii) of Figure 43-3.

In a world with rapid innovation:

1. Successive increases in capital accumulation may prove highly productive, and the capital-output ratio may be constant or decreasing.
2. In spite of large amounts of capital accumulation, the marginal efficiency of new capital may remain constant or even increase as new investment opportunities are created.

The historical record suggests that outward shifts in investment opportunities over time have led to the reality of sustained growth. Evidently modern economies have been successful in generating new investment opportunities at least as rapidly as old ones were used up. Modern economists devote more attention to understanding the *shifts* in the *MEC* schedule over time and less to its shape under a nonlearning situation.

FIGURE 43-3
Shifting Investment Opportunities: Three Cases

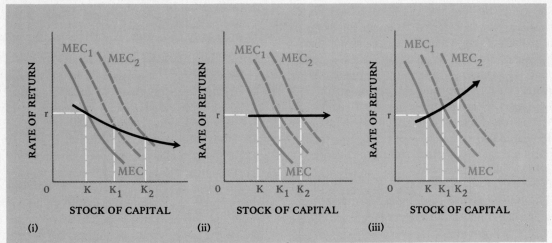

When both knowledge and the capital stock grow, the actual marginal efficiency of capital depends on their relative rates of growth. In each case, the economy at period 0 has the *MEC* curve, a capital stock of *K,* and a rate of return of *r.* In period 1 the curve shifts to *MEC₁* and there is investment to increase the stock of capital by *KK₁.* In period 2 the curve shifts to *MEC₂* and there is new investment of *K₁K₂.* It is the relative size of the shift of the *MEC* curve and the additions of the capital stock that are important.

In (i) investment occurs more rapidly than increases in investment opportunities and *r* will fall along the black curve. In (ii) investment occurs at exactly the same rate as investment opportunities and *r* is constant. In (iii) investment occurs less rapidly than increases in investment opportunities and *r* will rise.

A CONTEMPORARY VIEW OF GROWTH

The classical economists had a relatively simple theory of growth because they viewed a single mechanism—capital accumulation—as decisively important. Contemporary theorists begin by recognizing a number of factors that influence growth, no one of which is necessarily dominant.

Quantity of Capital per Worker

Human beings have always been tool users. It is still true that more and more tools tend to lead to more and more output. As long as a society has unexploited investment opportunities, productive capacity can be increased by increasing the stock of capital. The effect on output per worker of "mere" capital accumulation is so noticeable that it was once regarded as virtually the sole source of growth.

But if capital accumulation were the only source of growth, it would lead to movement down the *MEC* schedule and to a rising capital-output ratio and a falling rate of return on capital. The evidence does not support these predictions. The facts suggest that investment opportunities have expanded as rapidly as investments in capital goods, roughly along the pattern of Figure 43-3(ii). While capital accumulation has taken place and has accounted for much observed growth, it cannot have been the only source of growth.

Quality of Capital

New knowledge and inventions can contribute markedly to the growth of potential national income, even without capital accumulation. In order to see this, assume that the proportion of the society's resources devoted to the production of capital goods is just sufficient to replace capital as it wears out. Thus, if the old capital were merely replaced in the same form, the capital stock would be constant and there would be no increase in the capacity to produce. But if there is a growth of knowledge so that as old equipment wears out it is replaced by different, more productive equipment, national income will be growing.

Increases in productive capacity that are intrinsic to the form of capital goods in use are called **embodied technical change.** The historical importance of embodied technical change is clearly visible: the assembly line and automation transformed much of manufacturing, the airplane revolutionized transportation, and electronic devices now dominate the communications industries. These innovations plus less well-known but no less profound ones — for example, improvements in the strength of metals, the productivity of seeds, and the techniques for recovering basic raw materials from the ground — create new investment opportunities.

Less visible but nonetheless important changes occur through **disembodied technical change.** These concern innovations in the organization of production that are not embodied in the form of the capital goods or raw materials used. One example is improved techniques of managerial control.

Most innovations involve both embodied and disembodied changes: new processes require new machines, which make yet newer processes economical. Computerization promises many such changes in the years ahead. One of them, which many regard with a mixture of awe and apprehension, is a cashless society in which banks become parts of vast information networks that receive one's pay, pay one's bills, and invest one's savings. But whatever the form of innovation, the nature of the goods and services consumed and the way they are made changes continually as innovations occur. Major innovations of the past century have resulted from the development of the telephone, the linotype, the automobile, the airplane, plastics, the assembly line, coaxial cable, xerography, computers, transistors, and silicon chips. It is hard for us to imagine life if we had none of them.

The Quality of Labor

The "quality" of labor — or human capital — has several aspects. One involves improvements in the health and longevity of the population. Of course, these are desired as ends in themselves, yet they have consequences for both the size of the labor force and its productivity. There is no doubt that they have increased productivity per worker-hour by cutting down on illness, accidents, and absenteeism. At the same time, the extension of the normal life span with no comparable increase in the working life span has created a larger group of nonworking aged that exercises a claim on total output. Whether health improvements alone have increased output per capita in the United States is not clear.

A second aspect of the quality of human capital concerns technical training, from learning to operate a machine to learning how to be a scientist. Training is clearly required to invent, operate, manage, and repair complex machines. More subtly, there are often believed to be general social advantages to an educated population. It has been shown that productivity improves with literacy and that, in general, the longer a person has been educated, the more adaptable he or she is to new and changing challenges — and thus, in the long run, the more productive. But education may also increase feelings of alienation in a society that is thought to be arbitrary or unjust.

The Quantity of Labor

The size of a country's population and the extent of participation in the labor force are important in and of themselves, not merely because they affect the quantity of a factor of production. For this reason, it is less common to speak of the quantity of people available for work as a source of, or detriment to, growth than it is to speak of the quantity of capital or iron ore in the same way. But, clearly, for any given state of knowledge and supplies of other factors of production, the size of the population can affect the level of output per capita. Every child born has both a mouth and a pair of hands; over a lifetime, each person will be both a consumer and a producer. Thus, on average, it is perfectly possible to speak of overpopulated or underpopulated economies, depending on whether the contribution to production of additional people would raise or lower the level of per capita income.

Because population size is related to income per capita, it is possible to define a theoretical concept, *optimal population,* that maximizes income per capita.

Many countries have had, or do have, conscious population policies. America in the nineteenth century sought immigrants, as did Australia until very recently. Germany under Hitler paid bonuses for additional Aryan children and otherwise offered incentives to create Germans. Greece in the 1950s and 1960s tried to stem emigration to Western Europe. All are examples of countries that believed they had insufficient population, though the motives were not in every case purely economic. In contrast, many underdeveloped countries of South America, Africa, and Asia desire to limit population growth.

Institutional Considerations

Almost all aspects of a country's institutions can foster or deter the efficient use of a society's natural and human resources. Social and religious habits, legal institutions, and traditional patterns of national and international trade are all important. So too is the political climate. In Chapter 44 many of these institutions will be discussed as potential barriers to development.

Is There a Most Important Source of Growth?

The modern theory of growth tends to reject a dominant source of growth and to recognize that several different influences singly and in interaction affect the growth rate.

Among the major contributors to rapid economic growth are a capital stock that is steadily growing and improving in quality, a healthy and well-educated labor force, and a rate of population growth that is small enough to permit per capita growth in capital.

These factors are more likely to be utilized effectively in some institutional settings than in others.

A complete theory of growth would do more than list a series of influences all of which affect the growth rate. It would include assessments of (1) their relative importance, (2) the trade-offs involved in having more of one beneficial influence and less of another, and (3) the interactions among the various influences. This poses a formidable empirical challenge to research that is just beginning to be accepted.

While much remains to be learned, an important tentative conclusion of such scholars as E. F. Denison and Robert Solow is that improvements in the *quality* of capital, human as well as physical, have played a larger role than increases in the *quantity* of capital in the economic growth of the United States since 1900. Whether quality rather than quantity of capital is also the more important source of growth for countries with very different cultural patterns, more acute population problems, or more limited natural resources is a matter of continuing research.

ARE THERE LIMITS TO GROWTH?

Those opposed to growth argue that sustained growth for another century is undesirable; some even argue that it is impossible. Of course all terrestrial things have an ultimate limit. Astronomers predict that the solar system itself will die as the sun burns out in another 6 billion or so years. To be of practical concern a limit must be within some reasonable planning horizon. Best-selling books of the 1970s by Jay Forrester [*World Dynamics* (1973)] and D. H. Meadows et

A Case Study of Rapid Growth: Japan, 1953–1971

The real national income of Japan was 5.4 times as large in 1973 as it was in 1953. Japan's economic growth rate was more than double the average rate in ten North American and European countries and greatly exceeded the rate in any of them. What accounts for the extraordinarily rapid growth of Japan's economy? To answer that question, two economists, Edward F. Denison and William K. Chung, analyzed and measured the sources of economic growth in Japan from 1953 to 1971 and compared the results with those for ten Western countries. They also measured the difference between levels of output per worker in the United States and Japan in 1970 and identified its sources and magnitude. The results were published in 1976.*

They find that no single factor was responsible for Japan's high postwar growth rate. Rather, the Japanese economy benefited from several major sources of growth: an increase in quantity of labor, an increase in quantity of capital, improved technology in production, and economies of scale. Japan gained more in each of these respects than did any of the ten other countries studied. In addition, Japan had the greatest reallocation of labor from agriculture to industry of all the countries studied ex-

* Edward F. Denison and William K. Chung, *How Japan's Economy Grew So Fast: The Sources of Postwar Expansion* (Washington, D.C.: Brookings, 1976).

cept Italy. Since productivity is generally higher in industry than in agriculture, a shift of this kind raises average productivity and thereby contributes to growth even without an increase in output per person in either sector.

The overall growth record of Japan is as good as it is partly because of a low *level* of productivity. It is easier to improve from a low base than a high one. At the end of the period productivity was still more than 40 percent lower in Japan than in the United States, even after eliminating the effects of differences between the countries in working hours, in composition and allocation of the labor force, in amounts of capital and land, in size of markets, and in the cyclical positions of the two economies. There is thus an obvious potential for still further Japanese growth relative to the United States.

Can Japan's growth rate be sustained? The authors stressed the probability of a declining growth rate as various ways of securing fast growth by "catching up" are successively exhausted. Nevertheless, they considered a fairly high rate of long-term growth in Japan—between 5 and 8 percent per year—likely for the rest of this century. (This prediction proved accurate for the 1970s.) By the year 2000 Japan may well be enjoying the highest standard of living of any industrialized country in the world.

al. [*The Limits to Growth* (1974)] predicted the imminence of a growth-induced doomsday. Living standards were predicted to reach a peak about the year 2000 and then, in the words of Professor Nordhaus, a leading critic of these models, to "descend inexorably to the level of Neanderthal man." What can be said about this debate?

The Uncontroversial Fact of Increasing Pressure on Natural Resources

The years since World War II have seen a rapid acceleration in the consumption of the world's resources, particularly fossil fuels and basic minerals. World population has increased from under 2.5 billion to over 4 billion in that period, and this alone has increased the demand for all the world's resources. But the single fact of population growth greatly understates the pressure on resources.

Calculations by Professor Nathan Keyfitz of Harvard, and others, focus on the resources used by those who can claim a life style of the level enjoyed by 90 percent of American families. This so-called middle class, which today includes about one-sixth of the world's population, consumes 15 to 30 times as much oil per capita and, overall, at least five times as much of the earth's scarce resources per capita as do the other "poor" five-sixths of the population.

The world's poor are not, however, content to remain forever poor. Whether they live in the USSR, Brazil, Korea, or Kenya, they have let their governments understand that they expect policies that generate enough growth to give *them* the higher consumption levels that all of *us* take for granted. This upward aspiration is being fulfilled to a degree. The growth of the middle class has been nearly 4 percent per year—twice the rate of population growth—over the postwar period. The number of persons realizing middle-class living standards is estimated to have increased from 200 million to 700 million between 1950 and 1980.

This growth is a major factor in the recently recognized or projected shortages of natural resources: the increases in demand of the last three decades have outstripped discovery of new supplies and caused crises in energy and mineral supplies as well as food shortages. Yet the 4 percent growth rate of the middle class, which is too fast for present resources, is too slow for the aspirations of the billions who live in underdeveloped countries and see the fruits of development all around them. Thus the pressure on world resources of energy, minerals, and food is likely to accelerate even if population growth is reduced.

Another way to look at the problem of resource pressure is to note that present technology and resources could not possibly support the present population of the world at the standard of living of today's average American family. Such a shift in level of living, if made overnight, would more than double the world's demand for resources. The demand for oil would increase fivefold to tenfold. Since these calculations (most unrealistically) assume no population growth anywhere in the world and no growth in living standards for the richest sixth of the world's population, the fact of insufficient resources is plain.

Doomsday Predictions

Those most opposed to growth combine the undoubted acceleration of resource utilization with a series of assumptions: first, that there is no technical progress; second, that no new resources are discovered or rendered usable by new techniques; and third, that there is no substitution of more plentiful resources for those that become scarce. Under these circumstances, exhaustion of one or more key resources is predictable. If, in addition, population growth continues at historical rates, this exhaustion will occur relatively quickly—certainly within the next century. And if the increasing production continues to pollute the atmosphere faster than the pollutants can be absorbed, the capacity to produce will be diminished and the quality of life further damaged.

These are the basic assumptions of the doomsday models. Doom can come in several ways (or in any combination of them): natural resource depletion, famine due to overpopulation, or an increasing and ultimately fatal pollution of the earth and its atmosphere.

The many possible routes to disaster mean that no single restraint will suffice to prevent it. If both natural resource usage and pollution are controlled, doom will result from overpopulation. Population control will prove self-defeating because it leads to an increase in the per capita food supply and in the standard of living—which in turn generates forces to trigger a resurgence in population growth.

The only way to prevent disaster, some doomsday models suggest, is to stop economic growth at once through a comprehensive plan to curtail drastically natural resource use (by 75 percent), pollution generation (by 50 percent), investment (by 40 percent), and the birth rate (by 30 percent). Since the countries of the world are not likely to agree on the stern measures needed to meet these targets, a descent down the slippery slope of declining living standards during our own lifetimes is inevitable—and disaster looms for our grandchildren.

A Reply to Doomsday

Critics reply that predictions of an imminent doomsday are as old as human life itself and about as reliable as predictions of the arrival of universal peace and goodwill on earth. They recognize the pressures on the world's resources, and they concede that at present rates of utilization we would clearly run out of specific resources—particularly oil, gas, and certain minerals—in the foreseeable future.

But, they argue, all economic history shows the key assumptions of the doomsday models to be invalid. Nothing could be clearer than that technology changes. People are ingenious in finding ways not only to economize on the use of scarce resources but to substitute materials that are common for those that become scarce. Just as ample taconite replaced scarce iron ore in making steel, just as ample coal replaced scarce charcoal in making iron and steel, and just as synthetic rubber replaced natural rubber in making tires, so it is reasonable to expect new energy sources to be developed to replace fossil fuels. The potential supplies of nuclear and solar energy are inexhaustible, and one day we will be able to harness them.

Can it be doubted, they ask, that a society that has developed birth control pills and explored Mars can solve the problems of overpopulation and control of pollutants?

A Tentative Verdict

Most economists agree that conjuring up absolute limits to growth based on the assumptions of constant technology and fixed resources is not warranted. Yet there is surely cause for concern. Most agree that any barrier can be overcome by technological advances—but not in an instant, and not automatically. Clearly there is a problem of timing: how soon can we discover and put into practice the knowledge required to solve the problems that are made ever more imminent by growth in population, growth in affluence, and by the growing aspirations of the billions who now live in poverty? There is no guarantee that a whole generation may not be caught in transition, with social and political consequences that promise to be enormous even if they are not cataclysmic. The nightmare conjured up by the doomsday models may have served its purpose if it helps to focus our attention on these problems and their imminence.

Summary

1. Investment that causes short-term fluctuations in national income by affecting aggregate demand also makes possible long-term economic growth by increasing a nation's capacity to produce. Such growth is frequently measured using rates of change of potential real national income per person or per hour of labor.

2. The cumulative effects of even small differences in growth rates become large over periods of a generation or more.

3. The most important benefit of growth lies in its contribution to the long-run struggle to raise living standards and escape poverty. Growth also makes more manageable the policies that would redistribute income among people. Economic growth can likewise play an important role in a country's national defense or in its struggle for international prestige.

4. Growth, while often beneficial, is never costless. The opportunity cost of growth is the diversion of resources from current consumption to capital formation. For some individuals who are left behind in a rapidly changing world the costs are higher and more personal. The optimal rate of growth involves balancing benefits and costs. Few wish to forgo the benefits growth can bring, but few wish to maximize growth at any cost.

5. Understanding growth involves understanding both the utilization of existing investment opportunities and the process of creating new investment opportunities. The source of economic growth was once thought to be almost entirely capital accumulation and the utilization of a backlog of unexploited investment opportunities. Today most economists recognize that many investment opportunities can be *created,* and much attention is given to the sources of outward shifts in the *MEC* schedule.

6. In addition to mere increases in quantity of capital per person, any list of factors importantly affecting growth includes the extent of innovation, the quality of human capital, the size of the working population, and the whole institutional setting.

7. The critical importance of increasing knowledge and new technology in sustaining growth is highlighted by the great drain on existing natural resources of the explosive growth of the last two or three decades. Without continuing new knowledge, the present needs and aspirations of the world's population cannot be met.

Topics for Review

The role of investment in increasing potential national income

The cumulative nature of growth

Benefits and costs of growth

Effects of capital accumulation with and without new knowledge

Embodied and disembodied technical change

Factors affecting growth

Limits to growth

Discussion Questions

1. We usually study and measure economic growth in macroeconomic terms. But in a market economy who makes the decisions that lead to growth? What kind of decisions and what kind of actions cause growth to occur? How might a detailed study of individual markets be relevant to understanding economic growth?

2. Why is rising productivity a more significant contributing factor for economic growth than simply increasing the quantity of productive resources? Define *productivity.* List all the factors that increase the productivity of labor and the productivity of capital. Comment on the differences and similarities of the two lists.

3. *Family Weekly* recently listed (among others) the following "inventions that have changed our lives": microwave ovens, digital clocks, bank credit cards, freeze-dried coffee, tape cassettes, climate-controlled shopping malls, automatic toll collectors, soft contact lenses, tubeless tires, and electronic word processors.

   Which of them would you hate to do without? Which, if any, will have a major impact on life in the twenty-first century? If there are any that you believe will not, does that mean they are frivolous and unimportant?

4. The Overseas Development Council, in 1977, introduced "a new measure of economic development based on the physical quality of life." Its index, called PQLI, gives one-third weight to each of the following three indicators: literacy, life expectancy, and infant mortality. While countries such as the United States and the Netherlands rank very high on either the PQLI or on an index of per capita real national income, some relatively poor countries, such as Sri Lanka, rank much higher on the PQLI index than much richer countries such as Algeria and Kuwait. Discuss the merits or deficiences of this measure.

5. "The case for economic growth is that it gives man greater control over his environment, and consequently increases his freedom." Explain why you agree or disagree with this statement by Nobel laureate W. Arthur Lewis.

6. Growth in income per capita is a necessary condition for a rising standard of living in a country. Is it also a *sufficient* condition for making everyone better off? Why may not everyone benefit from economic growth?

7. GNP in real terms in the United States doubled be-

tween 1959 and 1980. Over this period the annual percentage rate of increase in GNP in constant dollars was 3.5 percent per year. Evaluate this measure of growth with respect to how well it reflects changes in (a) the material well-being of the average resident of the United States and (b) the nation's capacity to produce goods and services. In each case suggest what additional information you would like to know.

8. You discover that a particular economy has achieved a rapid increase in the size of its capital stock over several decades with no appreciable change in the rate of return to capital. What, if anything, can you conclude about its rate of innovation? Its rate of growth?

9. Consider a developed economy that decides to achieve a zero rate of growth for the future. What implications would such a "stationary state" have for the processes of production and consumption?

10. Suppose solar energy becomes the dominant form of energy in the twenty-first century. What changes will this make in the comparative advantages and growth rates of Africa and Northern Europe?

Growth and the Less-developed Countries

44

In our civilized, comfortable urban life, most of us lose sight of the fact that, in terms of the life span of the earth, it is a very short time since human beings lived as other animals, scratching an existence as best they could. It is only about 10,000 years since human beings became food producers rather than food gatherers. It is only within the last few centuries that a significant proportion of the world's population could look forward to anything but a hard struggle to wrest an existence from a reluctant nature. The concept of leisure combined with high consumption standards as a right to be enjoyed by all is new in human history.

The Uneven Pattern of Development

Table 44-1 repays careful study. It shows how few people have made the transition from poverty to relative comfort. There are more than 4.5 billion people alive today, but the wealthy parts of the world, where people work no more than 40 or 50 hours per week and enjoy substantial leisure and a level of consumption at or above half of that attained by the citizens of the United States, contain only about 18 percent of the world's population. Many of the rest struggle for subsistence. About 2 billion exist on a level at or below that enjoyed by peasants in ancient Egypt or Babylon.

Data of the sort shown in Table 44-1 cannot be

TABLE 44-1
Income and Population Differences Among Groups of Countries, 1977

Classification (based on GNP per capita in 1976 U.S. dollars)[a]	Number of countries (1)	GNP (billions) (2)	Population (millions) (3)	GNP per capita (4)	Percentage of the world's GNP (5)	Percentage of the world's population (6)	Growth rate[b] (7)
I Less than $175	22	$ 130	968	$ 135	1.7	23.1	1.5
II $175–349	19	84	347	242	1.1	8.3	4.8
III $350–699	22	481	1254	384	6.4	29.9	5.2
IV $700–1,399	25	478	442	1,081	6.4	10.5	4.0
V $1,400–2,799	19	416	183	2,276	5.4	4.4	4.7
VI $2,800–5,599	12	2,314	574	4,028	30.6	13.7	3.5
VII $5,600 or more	18	3,669	426	8,606	48.4	10.1	4.6
Totals	137	$7,572	4194	$1,805	100.0	100.0	

Source: U.S. Arms Control and Disarmament Agency, *World Military Expenditures 1968–1977; International Financial Statistics; Statistical Abstract.*

[a] The groups represent arbitrary groupings in which real GNP per capita doubles with each progression.

[b] Average annual percentage rate of growth of real GNP per capita, 1968–1977.

Over half of the world's population live in poverty; many of the very poorest are in countries that have the lowest growth rates and thus fall ever farther behind. The unequal distribution of the world's income is shown in columns 5 and 6. Groups I–III, with over 60 percent of the world's population, earn less than 10 percent of world income. Groups VI–VII, with 24 percent of the world's population, earn 79 percent of world income. Column 7 shows that the poorer countries are not closing the gap in income between rich and poor countries.

accurate down to the last $100.[1] Nevertheless, the *development gap*—the discrepancy between the standards of living in countries at the two ends of the distribution—is real and large.

There are many different ways to look at the inequality of income distribution among the world's population. One is shown in Figure 44-1, which plots the Lorenz curve of the world's income distribution. The farther the curve bends away from the straight line, the greater is the inequality in income distribution. To give perspective on the great disparity in income among countries, the middle line shows the Lorenz curve of income distribution among people in the United States. It is much closer to equality than the world distribution.

[1] There are many problems in comparing national incomes across countries. For example, home-grown food is vitally important to living standards in underdeveloped countries, but it is excluded—or at best imperfectly included—in the national income statistics of most countries. So is a warm climate. But these data do reflect enormous real differences in living standards that no statistical discrepancies can hide.

Another approach is to look at the geographic distribution of income per capita, as shown in Figure 44-2. Recent political discussions of income distribution have distinguished between richer and poorer nations as "North" versus "South." The map reveals why.

The Consequences of Underdevelopment

The human consequences of very low income levels can be severe. Someone studying the effect of rainfall variations would find that for a rich country such as the United States, the variations would be reflected in farm output and farm income: for each inch of rainfall below some critical amount, farm output and income would vary in a regular way. In poor countries such as India, variations in rainfall are reflected in the death rate. Indeed, many live so close to subsistence that slight fluctuations in the food supply bring death by starvation to large numbers. Other less dramatic characteristics of poverty include inadequate diet, poor health, short life expectancy, illiteracy, and—very important—an attitude of helpless resignation to the caprice of nature.

These facts make the problems of economic growth very much more pressing in poor countries than in rich ones. Reformers in underdeveloped countries—often called **less-developed countries (LDCs)**—feel a sense of urgency not felt by their counterparts in rich countries. Many now living at the bare subsistence margin can look forward to improvements in their lot only if their country experiences an immediate and rapid rate of economic growth. Yet, as the first row of Table 44-1 shows, the development gap for the very poorest countries has been widening. As will be seen, this is a problem of both output and population. It is also an international political problem.

Incentives for Development

Obviously "underdevelopment" is nothing new.[2] Concern with it as a remediable condition, however, is recent; it has become a compelling policy issue only within the present century. Probably the dominant reason for this newfound concern has been the extraordinary success of planned programs of "crash" development, of which the Soviet experience is the most remarkable (see Chapter 45) and the Chinese the most recent. Leaders in other countries ask, If they can do it, why not us?

"Demonstration effects" should not be underestimated. It has been said that the real secret of the atomic bomb was that it *could* be made, not how. Much the same is true of economic development. In the last 35 years there have been many examples of rapid and more or less planned

---

[2] The terminology of development is often confusing. "Underdeveloped," "less developed," and "developing" do not mean the same thing in ordinary English, yet each has been used to describe the same phenomenon. For the most part we shall refer to the underdeveloped countries as the less-developed countries, the LDCs for short. Some of them are making progress, that is, developing; others are not. All of these are terms used by development economists, and should be understood as such.

FIGURE 44-1

Lorenz Curves Showing Inequalities Among the Nations of the World and Within the United States

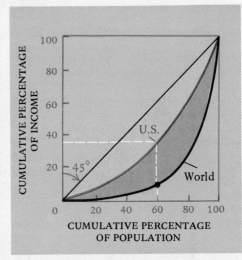

The inequality in the distribution of income is much less within the United States than it is among all the nations of the world. In a Lorenz curve, a wholly equal distribution of income would be represented by the 45° line: 20 percent of the population would have 20 percent of the income, 50 percent of the population would have 50 percent of the income, and so on. The very unequal distribution of world income is shown by the black curve. For example, 60 percent of the world's population live in countries that earn only 10 percent of the world's income, as shown by the black dot.

Contrast this with the distribution of income within the United States: the poorest 60 percent of the American population earn 36 percent of the nation's income. This is not equality, but it is much less unequal than the differences between rich and poor countries.

---

economic development. In a world that each year is made smaller by communication and transportation improvements, these developments are visible to all. It is bad enough to be poor, but to be poor when others are escaping poverty is intolerable. Suddenly people see that it is possible to achieve better lives for themselves and their children.

FIGURE 44-2
Countries of the World, According to Per Capita GNP, 1976

Key:
Per Capita GNP

■ $1,400 or more   ■ $350–$1,399   ☐ Less than $350   ☐ No available data

There is a sharp geographic division between North and South in the level of income per capita. The nations of the world are classified here according to three levels of measured per capita GNP. The poorest, shown in light gray, represents 31 percent of the world's population. The middle group, shown in dark gray, represents about 41 percent of world population. The wealthiest group, shown in black, includes all of North America, Europe, the Soviet Union, and Japan yet includes only 28 percent of the world's people. Areas shown in white are those for which data are unavailable. See Table 44-1 for more detail.

A second push toward development has come from the developed countries, with their policies to aid less-developed countries. We shall discuss such programs and their motivation later.

A third pressure for development results from the emergence of a relatively cohesive bloc of LDCs within the United Nations. The bloc is attempting to utilize its political bargaining power to achieve economic ends.

Both from within and without the LDCs the passive acceptance of underdeveloped status has ended. LDCs want to achieve major increases in living standards within a generation.

What are the causes of underdevelopment, and how may they be overcome?

Barriers to Economic Development

When income per head is taken as an index of the level of economic development, a country may develop by any set of devices that causes its aggregate income to grow faster than its population. However, there are many impediments to such growth.

POPULATION GROWTH

Today many LDCs have more national income than before, but they also have more mouths to feed. Thus their standard of living is no higher than it was a hundred or even a thousand years ago. The average Burmese and the rural Ethiopian are as hungry today as their great-grandparents were. The growth problem faced by underdeveloped countries is how to get off the treadmill and onto the escalator. Will modest gains in the capital stock eventually add up to enough to produce sustained growth? Not necessarily; it is the amount of output *per person* that determines whether living standards will rise. There is all too often a losing race between output and population.

Population growth is a central problem of economic development. If population expands as fast as national income, per capita income will not increase. When population expands rapidly, a country may by great effort raise the quantity of capital only to find that a corresponding rise in population has occurred, so that the net effect of its "growth policy" is that a larger population is now maintained at the original low standard of living. Much of the problem of the very poorest countries is due to population growth. They have made appreciable gains in income, but most of the gains have been eaten up (literally) by the increasing population. Table 44-2 shows this.

The population problem has led economists to talk about the "critical minimum effort" that is required not merely to increase capital but to increase it fast enough so that the increase in output outraces the increase in population. The problem arises because population size is not independent of the level of income. When population control is left to nature, nature solves it in a cruel way. Population increases until many are forced to live at a subsistence level; further population growth is halted by famine, pestilence, and plague. This grim situation was perceived early in the history of economics by Thomas Malthus.

In some ways, the population problem is more severe today than it was even a generation ago because advances in medicine and in public health have brought sharp and sudden decreases in death rates. It is ironic that much of the compassion shown by wealthier nations for the poor and underprivileged people of the world has traditionally taken the form of improving their health, thereby doing little to avert their poverty. We praise the medical missionaries who brought modern medicine to the tropics, but the elimination of malaria has doubled population growth in Sri Lanka. Cholera, once a killer, is now largely under control. No one argues against controlling disease, but other steps must also be taken if the child who survives the infectious illnesses of infancy is not to die of starvation in early adult-

TABLE 44-2
The Relation of Population Growth to Per Capita GNP, 1968–1977 (percentages)

Group[a]	Classification of countries (GNP per capita, 1976 U.S. dollars)		Average annual rate of growth of			Population growth as a percentage of real GNP growth
	Average income level	Percentage of population	Real GNP	Population	Real GNP per capita	
I	less than $175	23.1	4.0	2.6	1.4	65
II–IV	$175–1,399	48.7	6.8	2.1	4.7	30
V–VII	$1,400 or more	28.2	4.4	0.5	3.9	10

Source: Calculated from sources in Table 44-1.
[a] Groups from Table 44-1.

Growth in per capita real income depends on the difference between growth rates of real national income and population. The very poorest countries have *both* a relatively low growth rate of income and a relatively high growth rate of population. The middle group shows rising living standards despite large population growth by virtue of a high growth rate of income. The wealthiest countries owe much of their growth in living standards to a low rate of population increase.

FIGURE 44-3
World Population Growth, 1400–2000

The current growth in the world's population is explosive. The solid line reflects present measurements. The dashed line involves projections from observed trends. It took about 50,000 years from the emergence of modern human beings for the world's population to reach 1 billion. It took 100 years to add a second billion, 30 years to add the third billion, and 15 years to add the fourth billion. If present trends continue, the 1975 population of 4 billion will double by 2005.

hood. In Pakistan the population is growing at a rate of 3.4 percent per year; thus a rise in production of more than 3 percent per year is required for Pakistan to "break even."

Figure 44-3 illustrates actual and projected world population growth. The population problem is not limited to underdeveloped countries, but about seven-eighths of the expected growth in the world's population is in Africa, Asia, and Latin America, those areas where underdevelopment is the rule rather than the exception.

NATURAL RESOURCES

A country with ample fertile land and a large supply of easily developed resources will find growth in income easier to achieve than one poorly endowed with such resources. Kuwait has an income per capita above that of the United States because by accident it sits on top of the world's greatest known oil field. Oil is transforming living standards in Kuwait. But a lack of oil proved a devastating setback to many LDCs when the OPEC cartel increased oil prices tenfold during the 1970s. Without oil their development efforts would be halted, but to buy oil took so much scarce foreign exchange that it threatened to cripple their attempts to import needed capital goods.

Natural resource endowments can be the product of people as well as of nature. In fact, a nation's supplies of land and natural resources are often readily expandable in their effective use, if not in their total quantity. Badly fragmented land holdings may result from a dowry or inheritance system. For example, when farm land is divided into very small parcels, it may be much more difficult to achieve the advantages of modern agriculture than it is when the land is available in huge tracts for large-scale farming.

Lands left idle because of a lack of irrigation or spoiled by excessive irrigation or lack of crop rotation are well-known examples of barriers to development. Ignorance is another. The nations of the Middle East sat through recorded history alongside the Dead Sea without realizing that it was a substantial source of potash. Not until after World War I were these resources utilized; now they provide Israel with raw materials for its rapidly growing fertilizer and chemical industries.

INEFFICIENCY IN THE USE OF RESOURCES

Low levels of income and slower than necessary growth rates may result from the inefficient use of resources as well as the lack of key resources.

It is useful to distinguish between two kinds of inefficiency. An hour of labor would be used inefficiently, for example, if a worker, even though working at top efficiency, were engaged in making a product that no one wanted. Using society's resources to make the wrong products is an example of **allocative inefficiency.**

In terms of the production possibility boundary encountered in Chapter 1, allocative inefficiency represents operation at the wrong place on the boundary. Allocative inefficiency will occur if the signals to which people respond are distorted—both monopoly and tariffs are commonly cited sources of distortions—or if market imperfections prevent resources from moving to their best uses.

A second kind of inefficiency has come to be called *X*-inefficiency, following Professor Harvey Leibenstein. **X-inefficiency** arises whenever resources are used in such a way that even if they are making the right product, they are doing so less productively than is possible. One example would be workers too hungry or too unmotivated to concentrate on their tasks.

The distinction between allocative inefficiency and *X*-inefficiency is illustrated in Figure 44-4. All economies suffer from *X*-inefficiency because all are to some extent captives of their customs, their institutions, and their histories. But LDCs may be particularly vulnerable because of such factors as illiteracy, poor health, and lack of skills. They may also have cultural attitudes that give greater weight to friendship, loyalty, and tradition than to productivity. However admirable those qualities may be, they may not promote the most efficient use of resources.

INADEQUATE HUMAN RESOURCES

A well-developed entrepreneurial class, motivated and trained to organize resources for efficient production, is often missing in underdeveloped countries. This lack may be a heritage of a colonial system that gave the local population no opportunity to develop; it may result from the fact that managerial positions are awarded on the basis of family status or political patronage; it may reflect the presence of economic or cultural attitudes that do not favor acquisition of wealth by organizing productive activities; or it may simply be due to the nonexistence of the quantity or quality of education or training that is required.

Poor health is likewise a source of inadequate human resources. When the labor force is healthy, less time is lost and more effective effort is expended. The economic analysis of medical advances is a young field, however, and there is a great deal to be learned about the size of the drag of poor health on the growth of an economy.

INSTITUTIONAL AND CULTURAL BARRIERS

The progress of economic development is reflected in the increasing flow of goods and services from a nation's farms and factories to its households. Yet the ability to sustain and expand these flows depends on many aspects of economic and social organization.

FIGURE 44-4
Allocative Inefficiency Versus X-inefficiency

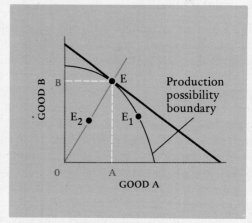

Allocative inefficiency places the society at the wrong point on its production possibility boundary, while X-inefficiency places the society inside its boundary. The thinner black curve represents a society's production possibilities between two goods, A and B. The slope of the thicker black line represents the opportunity cost of good B in terms of good A. The efficient output of A and B is represented at point *E*. *E*₁ is inefficient in the allocative sense: society is operating on its production possibility boundary but producing too much A and too little B for the given opportunity cost. In contrast, at *E*₂ the proportions of B and A are the same as at *E*, but the society is operating inside its boundary. This is *X*-inefficiency.

Infrastructure

Certain key supporting services—sometimes called the **infrastructure**—such as a transportation and communications network are necessary to efficient commerce. Roads, bridges, railroads, and harbors are needed to transport people, materials, and finished goods. The most dramatic confirmation of their importance comes in wartime, when belligerents always place high priority on destroying each other's transportation facilities.

Reasonable phone and postal services, water supply, and sanitation are essential to economic development. The absence, whatever the reason, of a dependable infrastructure can impose severe barriers to economic development.

Financial Institutions

The lack of an adequate and trusted system of financial institutions is often a barrier to development. Because investment has a key role in growth, banks are needed to help overcome the shortage of funds for investment. It may take as much as $10 of capital to increase full-employment national income by $1 per year. If this is so, it will take $66 *billion* of capital to raise average income per year by $100 in a country of 66 million—such as Mexico in 1980.

One source of funds for investment is the savings of households and firms. When banks and banking do not function well and smoothly, the link between private saving and investment may be broken and the problem of finding funds for investment greatly intensified.

Many people in LDCs do not trust banks, sometimes with good reason, more often without. Either they do not maintain deposits or they panic periodically, drawing them out and seeking security for their money in mattresses, in gold, or in real estate. The tendency to flee from money is made stronger when, as in recent years, a sharp inflation threatens the value of money holdings. When this happens, increases in savings do not become available for investment in productive

capacity. When banks cannot count on their deposits being left in the banking system, they cannot engage in the kind of long-term loans needed to finance investments.

Developing countries must not only create banking institutions, they must create enough stability and reliability that people will trust their savings to those who wish to invest.

Cultural, Social, and Religious Barriers

Traditions and habitual ways of doing business vary among societies, and not all are equally conducive to productivity. Max Weber argued that the "Protestant ethic" encourages the acquisition of wealth and is consequently more likely to encourage growth than is an ethic that directs activity away from the economic sphere.

Often in the LDCs personal considerations of family, of past favors, or of traditional friendship or enmity are more important than market signals in explaining behavior. One may find a too-small firm struggling to survive against a larger rival and learn that the owner prefers to remain small rather than expand because expansion would require use of nonfamily capital or leadership. To avoid paying too harsh a competitive price for built-in inefficiency, the firms' owners may then spend half their energies in an attempt to influence the government to prevent larger firms from being formed or to try to secure restrictions on the sale of output—and they may well succeed. Such behavior is very likely to inhibit economic growth.

When people believe that who your father is is more important than what you do, it may take a generation to persuade employers to change their attitudes and another generation to persuade workers that times have changed. Structuring incentives is a widely used form of policy action in market-oriented economies, but this may be harder to do in a personalistic society than in a market economy. If people habitually bribe the tax collector rather than pay taxes, they will not be likely to respond to policies that are supposed to work by raising or lowering taxes. All that will change is the size of the bribe.

In a society in which children are expected to stay in their fathers' occupations, it is more difficult for the labor force to change its characteristics and to adapt to the requirements of growth than in a society where upward mobility is itself a goal.

There is lively current debate on how much to make of the significance of differing cultural attitudes. Some believe that traditional and cultural considerations dominate peasant societies to the exclusion of economic responses; others suggest that any resulting inefficiency may be relatively small.

If it is true that social, religious, or legal patterns make growth more difficult, this need not mean that they are undesirable. Instead it means that the benefits of these patterns must now be weighed against the costs, of which the effect on growth is one. When people derive satisfaction from a religion whose beliefs inhibit growth, when they value a society in which every man owns his own land and is more nearly self-sufficient than in another society, they may be quite willing to pay a price in terms of growth opportunities forgone.

Whether a society's customs reflect cherished values or only such things as residual influences of a colonial history or an oligarchical political structure is important to the policymakers who must decide whether the cost in terms of efficiency should be paid. In any case, cultural attitudes are not easily changed.

THE CHALLENGE TO DEVELOPMENT POLICY

The many barriers to economic development—population growth, lack of natural and human resources, inefficient use of resources, and institutional and cultural restraints—singly or in combination can keep a country poor.

Economic development policy involves identifying the particular barriers to the level and kind of development desired and then devising policies to overcome them. Planners can seek funds for investment, and they can attempt to identify cultural, legal, social, and psychological barriers to growth. They can undertake the programs of education, legal reform, resource development, negotiation of trade treaties, or actual investment that smooth the way to more rapid growth.

All this is more easily said than done. Further, as the dozens of "development missions" sent out by the World Bank and other international, national, and private agencies have discovered, the problems and strategies vary greatly from country to country. Economic development as a field of expertise is in its infancy. However, there are common basic choices that all developing countries must face, and there are a number of alternative development strategies that may be pursued.

Some Basic Choices

HOW MUCH GOVERNMENT CONTROL?

How much government control over the economy is necessary and desirable? Practically every shade of opinion from "The only way to grow is to get the government's dead hand out of everything" to "The only way to grow is to get a fully planned, centrally controlled economy" has been seriously advocated. The extreme views are easily refuted by historical evidence. Many economies have grown with very little government assistance; Great Britain, Holland, Singapore, and Hong Kong are all examples. Others, such as the Soviet Union and Poland, have sustained growth with a high degree of centralized control. In other countries there is almost every conceivable mix of government and private initiative in the growth process. Many possible combinations of state and private initiative have been used successfully. On the question of what will prove the best mix at a particular time and in a particular place, there is likely to be much disagreement.

The Case for Planning

**Active government intervention in the manage-
ment of a country's economy often rests on the
real or alleged failure of market forces to produce
satisfactory results. The major appeal of such intervention is that it is expected to accelerate the
pace of economic development.**

Any of the barriers to development may be
lowered by enlightened actions of the government. Consider, for example, how the central authorities might seek to ease a shortage of investment funds. In a fully employed free-market
economy, investment is influenced by the quantity of savings households and firms make, and
thus the division of resources between consumption and saving is one determinant of the rate of
growth.

When living standards are low, people have
urgent uses for their current income. When savings decisions are left to individual determination, savings tend to be low, and this is an impediment to investment and growth. In a variety of
ways, central authorities can intervene and force
people to save more than they otherwise would.
Compulsory saving has been one of the main
aims of most development plans of centralized
governments such as those of the USSR and
China.

The goal of such plans is to raise savings and
thus lower current consumption below what it
would be in an unplanned economy. While
forced savings plans are largely associated with
totalitarian regimes, a frequent subject of planning in less centrally controlled societies is increasing the savings rate through tax incentives
and monetary policies. The object is the same: to
increase investment in order to increase growth,
and thus to make future generations better off.

Central governments of an authoritarian sort
can be particularly effective in overcoming some
of the sources of X-inefficiency. A dictatorship
may suppress social and even religious institutions that are barriers to growth, and it may hold
on to power until a new generation grows up that
did not know and does not value the old institu-

tions. It is much more difficult for a democratic
government, which must command popular support at each election, to do currently unpopular
things in the interests of long-term growth.
Whether the gains in growth that an authoritarian
government can achieve are worth the political
and social costs is, of course, an important value
judgment.

The Case for Laissez Faire

Most people would agree that government must
play an important part in any development program and especially in education, transportation,
and communication. But what of the sectors usually left to private enterprise in advanced capitalist countries?

The advocates of laissez faire in these sectors
place great emphasis on human drive, initiative,
and inventiveness. Once the infrastructure has
been established, an army of entrepreneurs will
do vastly more to develop the economy than will
an army of civil servants. The market will provide the opportunities and direct their efforts,
and individuals will act energetically within it
once their self-interest is understood. People
who seem irretrievably lethargic and unenterprising when held down by lack of incentives
will show amazing bursts of energy when given
sufficient self-interest in economic activity.

Furthermore, the argument goes, individual
capitalists are far less wasteful than civil servants
of the country's capital. A bureaucrat investing
capital that is not his own (raised perhaps from
the peasants by a state marketing board that buys
cheap and sells dear) may choose to enhance his
own prestige at the public's expense by spending too much money on cars, offices, and secretaries and too little on truly productive activities.
Even if the bureaucrat is genuinely interested in
the country's well-being, the incentive structure
of a bureaucracy does not encourage creative
risk taking. If his ventures fail, his head will
likely roll; if they succeed, he will receive no
profits—and his superior may get the medal.

WHAT SORTS OF EDUCATION?

Most studies of underdeveloped countries suggest that undereducation is a barrier to development and often urge increased expenditures on education. This poses a choice: whether to spend educational funds on erasing illiteracy and increasing the level of mass education or on training a small cadre of scientific and technical specialists. The problem is serious because education is expensive and does not pay off quickly.

To improve basic education requires a large investment in school building and in teacher training. This investment will result in a visible change in the level of education only after ten or more years, and it will not do much for productivity over that time span.

The opportunity cost of basic education expenditures always seems high. Yet it is essential to make them because the gains will be critical to economic development a generation later.

A great many developing countries have put a large fraction of their educational resources into training a small number of highly educated men and women — often by sending them abroad for advanced study — because the tangible results of a few hundred doctors or engineers or Ph.D.s are relatively more visible than the results from raising the school-leaving age by a year or two, say, from age 10 to age 12. It is not yet clear whether this policy pays off, but it is clear that it has some drawbacks.

Many of this educated elite are recruited from the privileged classes on the basis of family position, not merit; many regard their education as the passport to a new aristocracy rather than as a mandate to serve their fellow citizens; and an appreciable fraction emigrate to countries where their newly acquired skills bring higher pay than at home. Of those who return home, many seek the security of a government job, which they may utilize to advance their own status in what is sometimes a self-serving and unproductive bureaucracy.

WHAT POPULATION POLICY?

The race between population and income has been a dominant feature of many underdeveloped countries. There are only two possible ways for a country to win this race. One is to make such a massive push that it achieves a growth rate well in excess of the rate of population growth. The other is to control population growth. The problem *can* be solved by restricting population growth. This is not a matter of serious debate, though the means of restricting it are, for there are considerations of religion, custom, and education involved.

The consequences of different population policies are large. Sweden and Venezuela have similar death rates. Yet the birth rate in Sweden is 12 per thousand, and in Venezuela it is 42. These variations in birth rates have economic consequences. In Venezuela the net increase of population per year is 33 per thousand (3.3 percent), but it is only 3 per thousand (0.3 percent) in Sweden. If each country were to achieve an overall rate of growth of production of 3 percent per year, Sweden's living standards would be increasing by 2.7 percent per year while Venezuela's would be falling by 0.3 percent per year. In 1977 Sweden's income per capita ($8,400) was three times as high as Venezuela's ($2,600) — and Venezuela is the wealthiest country in South and Central America. The gap will widen rapidly if present population trends continue.

Different countries have adopted very different positions with respect to population. Kenya, with a birth rate of 50 per thousand, until very recently rejected any serious national policy of population control. Mexico, with nearly as high a birth rate in the early 1970s, began to dispense free contraceptives and family planning information and has seen its annual rate of population growth drop from 3.2 percent to 2.5 percent in less than five years.

The Chinese — today a quarter of the world's population — have reduced their rate of population increase from more than 3 percent to 1.2 percent in the last 25 years by promoting later marriages and exhorting parents to value daughters as well as sons and thus to be content with fewer children. In 1980 China began more aggressive steps in an announced attempt to achieve zero population growth by the year 2000. It has introduced new regulations to limit families to one or at most two children. Those that comply will receive bonuses and preferential treatment in housing and education for their offspring. (Housing space will be allocated to all families as though they had two children.) Families that do not comply with the policy will have their salaries decreased and will be promoted more slowly.

Aggressive population control policies do not always work. Indira Gandhi, in her first term as prime minister of India, imposed male surgical sterilization in the mid 1970s. It succeeded in the short run—at its peak nearly 1 million vasectomies per month were being performed—but failed in the longer run because a political storm of opposition toppled her government. Consequently, any national program of population control has become a liability too heavy for the leading Indian political parties to support.

Positive economics cannot decide whether population control is desirable, but it can describe the consequences of any choice. Economic development is much easier to achieve with population control than without it.

HOW TO ACQUIRE CAPITAL?

A country can raise funds for investment in three distinct ways: from the savings (voluntary or forced) of its domestic households and firms, by loans or investment from abroad, and by contributions from foreigners.

Capital from Domestic Saving: The Vicious Circle of Poverty

If capital is to be created at home by a country's own efforts, resources must be diverted from the production of goods for current consumption.

This means a cut in present living standards. If living standards are already at or near the subsistence level, such a diversion will be difficult. At best, it will be possible to reallocate only a small proportion of resources to the production of capital goods.

Such a situation is often described as *the vicious circle of poverty:* because a country has little capital per head, it is poor; because it is poor, it can devote only a few resources to creating new capital rather than to producing goods for immediate consumption; because little new capital can be produced, capital per head remains low, and the country remains poor.

The vicious circle can be made to seem an absolute constraint on growth rates. Of course it is not; if it were, we would all still be at the level of Neanderthal man. The grain of truth in the vicious circle argument is that some surplus must be available somewhere in the society to promote saving and investment. In a poor society with an even distribution of income, where nearly everyone is at the subsistence level, saving may be very difficult. But this is not the common experience. Usually there will be at least a small middle class that can save and invest if opportunities for the profitable use of funds arise. Also in most poor societies today the average household is usually above the physical subsistence level. Even the poorest households will find that they can sacrifice some present living standards for a future gain. After all, presented with a profitable opportunity, villagers in Ghana planted cocoa plants at the turn of the century even though there was a seven-year growing period before any return could be expected!

The last example points to an important fact: in underdeveloped countries one resource that is often *not* scarce is labor hours. Profitable home or village investment that requires mainly labor inputs may be made with relatively little sacrifice in current living standards. However, this is not the kind of investment that will appeal to planners mesmerized by large, spectacular, and symbolic investments such as dams, nuclear power stations, and steel mills.

Imported Capital

Another way of accumulating the capital needed for growth is to borrow it from abroad. When a poor country, A, borrows from a rich country, B, it can use the borrowed funds to purchase capital goods produced in B. Country A thus accumulates capital and needs to cut its current output of consumption goods only to pay interest on its loans. As the new capital begins to add to current production, it becomes easier to pay the interest on the loan and also to repay the principal out of the increase in output. In this way income can be raised immediately and the major sacrifice postponed until later, when part of the increased income that might have been used to raise domestic consumption is instead used to pay off the loan. This method has the great advantage of giving a poor country an initial increase in capital goods far greater than it could possibly have created by diverting its own resources from consumption industries.

However, many countries, developed or undeveloped, are suspicious of foreign capital. They fear that foreign investors will gain control over their industries or their government. The extent of foreign control depends on the form that foreign capital takes. When foreigners buy bonds in domestic companies, they do not own or control anything; when they buy common stocks, they own part or all of a company, but their control over management may be small. If a foreign company (perhaps a multinational corporation) establishes a plant and imports its own managers and technicians, it will have much more control. Finally, if foreign firms subsidize an LDC government in return for permission to produce, they may feel justified in exacting political commitments.

Whether foreign ownership of one's industries carries political disadvantages sufficiently large to outweigh the economic gains is a subject of debate. In Canada, for example, there is serious political opposition to having a large part of Canadian industry owned by U.S. nationals. Many other countries suppress these fears and actively seek more foreign investment than they are getting.

The economic choices are quite clear:

Accumulating a given amount of capital through domestic saving requires greater current sacrifice but later pays a higher return. Foreign financing requires small present sacrifices but involves holding down living standards later in order to make the interest payments to foreign investors.

When both ways of financing are equally possible, the choice between them raises an important intergenerational question: to what extent should the sacrifices required to pay for growth be met now rather than ten years from now? One suspects that, political considerations aside, most people would prefer to postpone the cost by using borrowed capital.

Getting foreign capital is easier said than done in the early stages of development. America and Canada were once underdeveloped in the sense of being underpopulated, with many unused resources, but they were latent giants that promised rich returns to foreign investors. It is harder to see similar investment opportunities in Pakistan, say, where overpopulation has been a problem for centuries and where the soil has been severely salt-damaged by centuries of irrigation without proper drainage. The ability of such a country to borrow from private sources is small. Foreign capital plays a role, but it is capital provided by foreign governments and international agencies, not by private investors.

Contributed Capital

From the viewpoint of the receiving country, contributed capital might seem ideal. It has the advantage of enabling the country to shift to more rapid growth without either sacrificing consumption now or having to repay later. Investment funds for development are being received today by underdeveloped countries from the governments of the developed countries acting both unilaterally (as in the U.S. Agency for International Development and a similar Soviet

"Aid," "Trade," or "Restitution"

The motivations behind international giving have become the subject of debate. Do developed nations give aid for humanitarian reasons, because it serves their political objectives, or because it is economically self-serving? Obviously all three motives can play a role, but which one dominates? Should LDCs demand aid, accept it gratefully, or reject it?

LDCs more or less chronically lack capital and lack wealth. Typically they have large and mounting foreign debts as a result of past borrowing. In these circumstances, one might think that foreign aid, whether from a single country or from an international forum, would be eagerly sought and gratefully received. This is not always so; there is some significant resistance to accepting aid.

The slogan "Trade, not aid" reflected political opposition to U.S. economic aid in certain recipient countries in the 1950s. Yugoslavia turned down much aid proffered by the Soviets after 1948, and China accepted no foreign aid after 1960. In 1975 Colombia made the decision to forgo further U.S. aid on the grounds that it bred an unhealthy economic dependency.

The primary explanation of this attitude lies in a country's noneconomic goals. It may suspect the motives of the givers and fear that hidden strings may be attached to the offer. Independent countries prize their independence and want to avoid either the fact or the appearance of being satellites. Pride—a desire to be beholden to no one—is also a factor.

One response was to do without aid, no matter how badly it was needed. Another, increasingly the pattern in the 1970s, was to reject "aid" but to demand "wealth transfers," not as a matter of charity but as a matter of "restitution" or redress for past sins by colonial powers against their former colonies. The obvious problem of asserting such claims against noncolonial powers such as the United States and the USSR has been no deterrent. There is a generalized sense that the inhabitants of the "North" exploited the nations of the "South" in past centuries and that present generations should redress the balance. The paradoxical aspect of this is that while "restitution, not charity" makes LDCs willing to accept aid, precisely that claim decreases the willingness of developed countries to offer it.

What *are* the motives of givers of aid? The Scandinavian Nobel Prize winning economist Gunnar Myrdal has argued that humanitarian considerations have played a large role. The evidence for the existence of humanitarian motives is in part the success of voluntary appeals in developed countries for food, funds, and clothes for persons in stricken areas of the world. As per capita incomes have risen in the Western world, so have contributions, private as well as public. It is the policy of the governments of most of the so-called Western democracies to devote some resources to alleviating poverty throughout the world.

Professor Edward S. Mason, among others, has argued that such aid can best be understood by looking to political and security motives. He points to the substantial U.S. congressional preference for military assistance over economic assistance, the denial of aid to countries such as Sri Lanka that traded with Communist countries, the fostering of Tito's Yugoslavia *because of* its anti-Soviet stand—all of which reveal a strong political motive. Many critics of OPEC think its contributions are designed to quiet opposition among LDCs to the oil price hikes that have proved so profitable to the oil producers and so painful to oil users, LDCs and developed countries alike.

Should motives and attitudes, either of givers or of receivers, matter? After all, it is economically beneficial to receive aid when you are poor. Economists cannot say that fears, aspirations, pride, and "face" are either foolish or unworthy; they can only note that they do have their cost.

program) and through international agencies such as the World Bank, the Export-Import Bank, and the OPEC Fund established in January 1980.

Contributed capital has played a significant role in post-World War II economic development. For example, American foreign aid expenditures in the decade after the war were $90 billion, and even today they amount to more than $3 billion per year. The $3 billion is more than 1 percent of the GNP of the 2 billion people who live in the most underdeveloped nations of the world. The OPEC Fund started with an initial capital of $4 billion and is expected to grow rapidly.

The Soviet Union has given substantial aid to less-developed countries. Russian aid to China in the 1950s was essential to that country's development of heavy industry. In addition to funds, the USSR transported capital in the form of more than 150 complete plants and sent thousands of technician specialists to China to help plan, build, and run factories. China today is itself a significant donor to a few ideologically sympathetic countries, including Tanzania and Albania.

Alternative Development Strategies

In the search for development, individual LDCs have a number of policy options. The choice among them is in part a matter of what the planners believe will work, in part a question of the nature of the society that will be created once development has occurred.

The noneconomic aspects of the choice of a development strategy may be illustrated by the Greek government's explicit decision in the mid 1960s to change the direction of its growth. At that time Greece was achieving rapid growth in income per capita largely because of a booming tourist trade and the emigration of many young Greeks to West Germany to work in factories there. The emigrants had been earning incomes

in Greece that were substantially below the Greek average, and their remittances home to their families increased both domestic income and foreign exchange reserves. Although it was helpful to the Greek rate of growth to continue to rely on tourism and emigration as bulwarks of the economy, this policy threatened an image of life that visualized "Greece for the Greeks." Even at the prospect of some loss in growth, Greek planners recommended the restriction of emigration, the moderation of the size of the tourist role in the economy, and the development of new industry for the Greek economy.

There may be economic reasons for choosing a different pattern of growth than the free market would provide. One role of planning is to direct growth in a different direction, one that the planners guess will have the greatest chance of long-run success.

Unplanned growth will usually tend to exploit the country's present comparative advantages; planners may choose a pattern of growth that involves trying to change the country's future comparative advantage.

One reason for doing so is the belief that planners can evaluate the future more accurately than the countless individuals whose decisions determine market prices. A country need not passively accept its current comparative advantages. Many skills can be acquired, and fostering an apparently uneconomic domestic industry may, by changing the characteristics of the labor force, develop a comparative advantage in that line of production.

The Japanese had no visible comparable advantage in any industrial skill when Commodore Matthew Perry opened that feudal country to Western influence in 1854, but they became a major industrial power by the end of the century. Their continuing gains relative to the United States in fields such as steel, automobile manufacture, and communications do not need to be called to anyone's attention today. Soviet planners in the 1920s and 1930s chose to create an industrial economy out of a predominantly agricultural one and succeeded in vastly changing the mix between agriculture and industry in a single generation (see Chapter 45).

These illustrations suggest why the big choice may be that of a development strategy. Governments must choose between agricultural and industrial emphases; between different kinds of industrial development; and between more or less reliance on foreign trade. Several possibilities have been widely advocated, and each has been tried. None is without difficulties.

AGRICULTURAL DEVELOPMENT

Everyone needs food. An LDC may choose to devote a major portion of its resources to stimulating agricultural production, say, by mechanizing farms, irrigating land, and utilizing new seeds and fertilizers. If successful, the country will stave off starvation for its current population, and it may even develop an excess over current needs and so have a crop available for export. A food surplus can earn foreign exchange to buy needed imports.

Among the attractions of the agricultural strategy are that it does not require a great deal of technical training or hard-to-acquire know-how, nor does it place the country in direct competition with highly industrial countries.

India, Pakistan, Taiwan, and other Asian countries have achieved dramatic increases in food production by the application of new technology—and new seed—to agricultural production. Increases of up to 50 percent have been achieved in grain production, and it has been estimated that with adequate supplies of water, pesticides, fertilizers, and modern equipment, production could be doubled or even tripled. This has been labeled the "green revolution." When the Nobel Prize Committee gave the 1970 *peace* prize to the American plant pathologist Norman Borlaug, it recognized the potential importance of these developments in alleviating, for at least a generation, the shortage of food that the population explosion was expected to bring.

The possibilities of achieving such dramatic gains in agricultural output may seem almost irresistible at first glance, yet many economists think they should be resisted—and they point to a series of problems.

One problem is that a vast amount of resources is required to irrigate land and mechanize production, and these resources used alternatively could provide industrial development and industrial employment opportunities. Thus there is a clear opportunity cost. Critics of the agricultural strategy argue that the search for a generation free from starvation will provide at best only a temporary solution because population will surely expand to meet the food supply. Instead, they argue, underdeveloped countries should start at once to reduce their dependence on agriculture. Let someone else grow the food; industrialization should not be delayed.

A second problem with the agricultural strategy is that the great increases in world production of wheat, rice, and other agricultural commodities that the "green revolution" makes possible could depress their prices and not lead to increased earnings from exports. What one agricultural country can do, so can others, and there may well be a glut on world markets. This is the heart of the argument of the distinguished Latin American economist Raúl Prebisch. He maintains that underdeveloped countries, overspecialized in the production of agricultural commodities, are sure to suffer steadily worsening terms of trade relative to manufacturing outputs. Prebisch believes that current market prices fail to anticipate fully this worsening in the terms of trade for agriculture and thus that planners should intervene and shift the country out of what is sure to be a long-run overreliance on agriculture.

A third problem has arisen (most acutely in India and Pakistan) where increasing agricultural output has been accompanied by decreasing labor requirements in agricultural production without a compensating increase in employment opportunities elsewhere. Millions of tenant farmers—and their bullocks—have been evicted from their tenant holdings by owners who are buying tractors to replace them. Many have found no other work.

Where there is already large-scale unemployment, devoting resources to labor-saving innovations makes little sense unless at the same time new jobs are developed for the displaced labor.

Despite the worldwide need for food, the agriculture strategy of development has not proven to be a surefire path to economic development.

SPECIALIZATION IN A FEW COMMODITIES

Many LDCs have existing unexploited resources such as copper, uranium, or opportunities for tourism. The principle of comparative advantage provides the traditional case for the desirability of relying on such resources. By specializing in producing those products in which it has the greatest comparative advantage, the country can achieve the most rapid growth in the short run. To neglect these opportunities will result in a lower living standard than would result from specialization accompanied by increased international trade.

These are cogent reasons in favor of *some* specialization. But specialization involves risks, and the risks may be worth reducing even at the loss of some income. Specialization here, as with agriculture, makes the economy highly vulnerable to cyclical fluctuations in world demand and supply. When a recession in developed countries decreases overseas travel, an LDC that has relied on tourism for needed foreign exchange is in immediate trouble.

The problem is not only cyclical. When technological or taste changes render a product partially or wholly obsolete, a country can face a major calamity for generations. Just as individual firms and regions may become overspecialized, so too may countries.

IMPORT SUBSTITUTION INDUSTRIALIZATION

International trade may bring great benefits, but it also entails risks. During the Great Depression the collapse in world agricultural prices caused the value of the exports of agricultural countries to decline drastically relative to the prices of goods those countries imported. During World War II many countries found that the manufactured goods they wished to import were simply unavailable. In each of those situations dependence on foreign trade for necessities did not seem wholly attractive. More recently, the rising prices of fuel and other imports have created enormous balance-of-payments problems for many LDCs. Such countries must either reduce imports or increase exports.

In order to conserve scarce foreign exchange reserves (and protect itself from interruptions in supply), a country can attempt to reduce its reliance on foreign trade by using its resources to produce domestic substitutes for some of the goods presently imported.

Much of the industrialization by LDCs in the 1950s and 1960s was directed toward **import substitution industry (ISI),** which is producing for sale in the home market goods that were previously imported. Because countries characteristically suffer from a significant comparative disadvantage when they produce goods for the first time, it proved necessary both to subsidize the home industry and to restrict imports to allow the infant ISI time to develop.

Implementing an import substitution policy is relatively easy. It can be done by imposing import quotas and raising tariffs. Such actions provide incentives for the development of domestic industry by carving out a ready-made market and by providing a substantial price umbrella that promises high profits to successful local manufacturers and to foreign investors who might enter with both capital and know-how. Subsidies, government loans, and other forms of encouragement have also been used in many cases. A study of import substitution industries in seven countries found that the effective rate of protection or subsidy varied from 25 to more than 200 percent.

The ISI strategy also has problems. It may well foster *inefficient* industries by virtue of the amount of protection granted, and in the long run countries do not become rich by being inefficient. It may well aggravate inequalities in income distribution by raising the prices of manufactured goods relative to agricultural goods and by favoring profits over wages. Another difficulty with the ISI strategy is that the opportunities for import substitution are limited; once the country runs out of imports to substitute for, what then?

The success of ISI is now in question. Taiwan followed it and has come to be one of the great successes of economic development of the recent past. Its income per capita has averaged a rate of increase of over 6 percent during the whole of the last two decades. Yet in India, Pakistan, Mexico, and Argentina it has not been a success. Mexico has succeeded, but largely by shifting from ISI to an export-oriented strategy.

ISI is now regarded as a strategy of limited promise unless it can lead to the ultimate establishment of efficient industries.

INDUSTRIALIZATION FOR EXPORT

Most development economists believe that industrialization ought to be encouraged only in areas where, once the protected phase of the development period is past, the country will have a reliable and efficient industry that can compete in world markets.

Obviously, if Tanzania or Peru could quickly develop steel, shipbuilding, and manufacturing industries that operated as efficiently as those of Japan or West Germany, they too might share in the rapid economic growth enjoyed by those industrial countries. Indeed, if a decade or two (or even three) of protection and subsidization could give infant industries time to mature and become efficient, the price might be worth paying. After all, both Japan and Russia were underdeveloped countries within living memory.

The greatest problem with such a strategy is that there is a good chance of failure. Even when the country has the basic natural resources, it may be backward enough that it is unlikely it will have the labor or managerial talent to achieve success within a reasonable time. India may create a steel industry and have its productivity

increase year by year, but it must do more: it must catch up to the steel industries of other countries in order to compete in world markets.

The catch-up problem is a race against a moving target. Suppose you are committed to making a given industry competitive in ten years. In such a situation, it is not sufficient to make gains in productivity; they must be made at a rate fast enough to overcome a present disadvantage against an improving opponent. Suppose you must improve by 50 percent to achieve the present level of a competitor who is improving at r percent per year. If you want to catch up in ten years, you must improve at $r + 4$ percent per year. [43] If r is 6 percent, you must achieve 10 percent. To achieve 6 percent or 7 percent may be admirable, but you will lose the race just the same.

Thus, while this route to development is available, it depends both on having the required resources and on overcoming the difficulties that contribute to X-inefficiency. This often means devoting resources for a long period to education, training, development of an infrastructure, and overcoming the various cultural and social barriers to efficient production.

While this is hard, it is not impossible. Indeed, there have been some spectacular success stories: Brazil, Korea, Hong Kong, and Taiwan are charter members in a new category, "newly industrializing countries" that are providing vigorous competition in manufactured goods in world markets. Their success has led to a further (and bitterly resented) problem for the industrialization strategy. When an LDC succeeds, it is likely to find the developed countries trying to protect *their* home industries from the new competition.

During the 1950s the American textile industry began to suffer from the success of the industrialization of LDCs. American textile manufacturers and workers sought tariffs, import quotas, or an agreement on the part of the newly industrialized LDCs to voluntary export quotas. John Kennedy campaigned with a promise to "do something for textiles," and when he became president in 1960, he negotiated such an agreement. Similar pressures exist today with respect to American imports of steel, autos, television sets, shoes, and many other commodities. Yet these are the fruits of successful industrialization by LDCs.

The greatest success in development has been achieved by nations that have succeeded in developing efficient industrial export industries.

Having recognized this fact, it is easy to be led astray by it. LDCs sometimes pursue certain lines of production on a subsidized basis either for prestige purposes or because of a confusion between cause and effect. Because most wealthy nations have a steel industry, the leaders of many underdeveloped nations regard their countries as primitive until they develop a domestic steel industry. Because several LDCs have succeeded in producing consumer durables, many others assume that they should try to do so. However, if a country has a serious comparative disadvantage in steel or in making consumer durables, fostering such industries will make that country poor.

COMMODITY PRICE STABILIZATION AGREEMENTS

When all or most producers of a commodity can agree on price and output levels, they can achieve monopoly profits not available in competitive markets. Many LDCs are heavily committed to the production and export of one or more basic commodities such as bananas, bauxite, cocoa, coffee, copper, cotton, iron ore, jute, manganese, meat, oil, phosphates, rubber, sugar, tea, tropical timber, and tin. Why not get together and create an effective cartel that gives producers the enormous profits that are potentially available? This has been tried many times in history; until OPEC, it has always failed. Yet everyone knows that OPEC's success transformed a handful of formerly poor LDCs into the wealthiest of nations.[3]

[3] This has added to the terminological confusion. It was once fashionable to speak of a nonaligned *third world* as another term for LDCs, the first two "worlds" being the developed capitalist and developed socialist countries. Now some commentators divide the LDCs into a richer (oil-producing) *third world* and a still poor *fourth world*.

OPEC's success has not been easy to copy because the special conditions of demand and supply that apply to oil do not apply equally to most other primary commodities. In the case of oil there are few large producing countries, supply is quite inelastic outside those countries, demand is relatively inelastic in the short and middle run, and the largest producers are Arab nations that find discipline in political and religious unity and in a common hatred of Israel. Perhaps equally important, the largest producer —Saudi Arabia—has been prepared to put up with a good deal of cheating by its partners.

Wheat, coffee, cocoa, tin, rubber, and copper have all been suggested as potential targets for similar joint marketing strategies, but none has the right combination of attributes, and only copper has supply and demand situations that are remotely similar to those of oil. The inability to utilize "commodity power" more widely through cartelization has not led to its total abandonment, as we will see in the final section of this chapter.

A NEW INTERNATIONAL ECONOMIC ORDER (NIEO)?

In May 1974 the General Assembly of the United Nations adopted (over the objections of the developed countries) a Declaration on the Establishment of a New International Economic Order. This represented an attempt on the part of LDCs to utilize collective *political* power to achieve a larger share of the world's goods.[4]

NIEO had its origin in the emergence within the United Nations of a political bloc of LDCs that goes back at least to 1964. These nations, economically weak but numerous, were targets of the struggle between the United States and the USSR for allegiance. They agreed to remain "nonaligned" with either of the two major power groups. At an Algiers summit conference of more than 100 nonaligned nations in September 1973, the importance of *economic* goals was

[4] An excellent introduction to this development is Rachel McCulloch's *Economic and Political Issues in the NIEO* (International Institute for Economic Research, 1979). Professor McCulloch's analysis is heavily relied on here.

expressed by the slogan, "Poor of the world, unite!"[5]

The NIEO proposals are aimed basically at wealth transfers instead of wealth creations; they are concerned with a more equal distribution of existing wealth rather than economic development.

Principal Economic Proposals of NIEO

In the many international meetings since 1974, the LDCs have offered dozens of specific demands and proposals covering trade, unilateral and multinational aid, investment, and technology transfers from developed to underdeveloped countries. Three proposals are important.

Primary commodities, buffer stocks, and the common fund. Because many LDCs depend on exports of primary commodities (i.e., raw materials) as their source of foreign exchange, their share of the world's wealth depends crucially on the prices of those commodities. The NIEO Integrated Programs for Commodities was designed to "raise and stabilize" the prices of 18 products by creating a "common fund" to which both producers and consumers would contribute. The fund was to be used to buy up surplus supplies and thus create "buffer stocks" of the commodities.

Even if stabilization were the only goal, this kind of buffer stock policy would have grave difficulties, such as those associated with national agricultural stabilization programs. (See Chapter 7.) However, *increasing* prices (not mere stabilization) was a major part of the proposal. This would involve accumulating ever larger inventories of the commodities in order to keep prices above the free-market levels. The wasteful accumulation of inventories would be one of the real resource costs of this proposal, and the need for continuing contributions to the common fund would be considerable.

To expect consuming countries to contribute

to a fund whose purpose is to permit producers to restrict sales and raise prices sounds like a triumph of hope over reason. Nevertheless, in the context of the OPEC embargo, many developed countries indicated a willingness to discuss the proposal, presumably to prevent the formation of similar cartels in other commodities. As of 1980, nothing more substantial than talk has resulted.

Preferential treatment of LDC manufactures. Newly industrializing LDCs sought preferential tariff and quota treatment for commodities subject to tariff and nontariff barriers. It is all right, the argument said, for the United States to limit textile imports, but the LDCs should be given preference over developed countries in fighting for shares of the full quota.

One of the demands of the NIEO was for a Generalized System of Preferences. After more than a decade of opposition, followed by detailed negotiation, most major industrialized nations, including the United States, have granted some such treatment. The effects have been relatively smaller than the LDCs expected, owing to the exclusion from preferential treatment of commodities that are highly labor intensive and that thus create unemployment problems in the developed countries. Unfortunately, these commodities — such as textiles — are precisely those in which the LDCs have the greatest comparative advantage.

Debt renegotiation and forgiveness. LDCs were major borrowers in international markets well before the OPEC price increases. Total LDC debt grew from less than $40 billion in 1965 to $100 billion in 1973. Five years later the debt was $250 billion, largely because of oil price increases. Combined with current account deficits due to oil imports, both LDCs and their creditors feared the inability of LDCs to repay on schedule the loans that had been made.

Demands of the LDCs at various United Nations conferences on trade and development (known, like super bowl games, by Roman nu-

---

[5] Despite the similarity to the Communist slogan, "Workers of the world, unite!" this movement has been directed with equal vigor against both socialist and capitalist developed countries.

merals—e.g., UNCTAD IV) ranged from debt cancellation and a moratorium on payments for a few years to milder suggestions for case-by-case renegotiation of scheduling and interest payments. Not surprisingly, the general proposals were rejected by developed nations—and were even opposed by some borrowers who feared that if debts were canceled, their future ability to borrow would be diminished.

The so-called debt problem has two aspects. The first, faced by resource-rich LDCs such as Zaire, is a crisis of meeting current payments of interest and principal. Here an adjustment of terms has proven feasible and has been undertaken. The second aspect is one of reduced real income due to rising costs of the LDCs' imports. Here it is an increase in contributed aid to those who have large debts that has been sought. But if aid of, say, $50 billion is appropriate, should it be given in the form of debt forgiveness? Why, critics ask, should those LDCs who have paid their debts be discriminated against?

An Evaluation of NIEO

NIEO succeeded in stimulating discussion for at least three reasons. First, an effective political bloc gradually emerged within the United Nations that was capable of standing firm against divide-and-conquer strategies. Both capitalist and socialist countries wanted the political allegiance of the LDCs, so they were prepared to talk and to listen. Second, the commodity boom of the early 1970s and the remarkable success of OPEC made threats of cartel action frightening (at least temporarily) and made proposals for a common fund for buffer stocks seem moderate in contrast. Third, many developed countries were genuinely willing to consider wealth transfers from rich to poor as morally and politically desirable.

Thus far the major accomplishments of NIEO demands have been small. The issues and proposals have been discussed extensively, but little major redistribution of wealth has resulted.

Why has the talk proven unpersuasive? The main answer is that the political and economic threats made by the LDCs against the developed countries are no longer regarded as substantial. NIEO's future rests on persuasion rather than coercion of the developed countries. Here the very stridency that unified the "South" in their demands has brought forth a unified resistance on the part of the "North."

From an economic point of view NIEO has two major flaws. First, it focuses too much on redistribution and too little on seeking real growth in world output. Second, it puts its faith in bureaucratic allocations of wealth, trade, and natural resources rather than in market mechanisms. Nothing in the world's experience to date suggests that this will increase total world output. Many modern development economists would share the view of Professor McCulloch that the developed countries should be adopting policies to expand rather than contract world wealth. If that is so, the major proposals of NIEO will not prove attractive.

Some Controversial Unresolved Issues

The economics of development, like most fields of economics, is in a state of change. The view presented in this chapter is perhaps the mainline view of economists in developed economies such as our own. Problems look different when viewed from the inside out, and they look different from the perspective of socialist nations than they do from our sort of market-oriented economy.

Yet even within the group of Western economists studying development there are important current controversies.

The Pace of Development

Reformers in underdeveloped countries often think in terms of transforming their economies within a generation or two. The sense of urgency is quite understandable, but unless it is tempered by some sense of historical perspective, totally unreasonable aspirations may develop — only to be dashed all too predictably.

Many underdeveloped countries are probably in a stage of development analogous to that of medieval England, having not yet achieved anything like the commercial sophistication of the Elizabethan era. It took 600 years for England to develop from the medieval stage to its present one. Such a change would be easier now, for much of the needed technology can be imported rather than invented. But what is the proper pace? To effect a similar growth within 50 or 100 years would require a tremendous achievement of the kind accomplished by America, Japan, and a handful of other countries; to aspire to do it in 20 or 30 years may be to court disaster — or to invite an extraordinarily repressive political regime. But to urge patience may be to keep the downtrodden poor, and perhaps exploited, and it may be a cover for failing to do what is required for growth.

The View of Population Policy

The view (presented in this chapter) of population growth as a formidable barrier to development is neo-Malthusian and constitutes what is probably the current conventional wisdom on underdevelopment. However, there are opposing views.

This view allows no place for the value of children in parents' utility functions. Critics point out that the psychic value of children should be included as a part of the living standards of their parents. They also point out that in rural societies even quite young children are a productive resource because of the work they can do; and fully grown children provide old-age security for their parents in societies where state help for the aged is negligible.

The neo-Malthusian theory is also criticized for assuming that people breed blindly, as animals do. Critics point out that traditional methods of limiting family size have been known and practiced since the dawn of history. Thus they argue that large families in rural societies are a matter of choice. The population explosion came not through any change in "breeding habits" but as a result of medical advances that greatly extended life expectancy (which surely must be counted as a direct welfare gain for those affected). Critics argue that once an urban society has developed, family size will be reduced voluntarily. This was certainly the experience of Western industrial countries; why, critics ask, should it not be the experience of the developing countries?

The Cost of Creating Capital

Is it true that LDCs must suffer if they wish to grow? A recent criticism of the conventional wisdom questions the alleged heavy opportunity cost of creating domestic capital. Production of consumption and capital goods are substitutes only when factor supplies are constant. But, critics say, the development of a market economy will lead people to substitute work for leisure.

For example, the arrival of Europeans with new goods to trade led the North American Indians to collect furs and other commodities needed for exchange. Until they were decimated by later generations of land-hungry settlers, the Indians' standard of living rose steadily with no immediate sacrifice. They created the capital needed for their production — weapons and means of transport — in their abundant leisure time. Thus their consumption began to rise immediately.

This too, the argument says, could happen in underdeveloped countries if market transactions were allowed to evolve naturally. The spread of a market economy would lead people to give up leisure in order to produce the goods needed to buy the goods that private traders are introducing from the outside world. In this view it is the pattern of development chosen, rather than development itself, that imposes the need for heavy sacrifices.

Summary

1. Sustained economic development is relatively recent in history and has been highly uneven. About one-fourth of the world's population still exists at a level of bare subsistence, and nearly three-fourths are poor by American standards. The gap between rich and poor is very large and is keenly felt.

2. The pressure for economic development comes in part from the LDCs. The transformation in less than half a century of Soviet Russia from a backward peasant economy to a major industrial power has had a powerful demonstration effect on the quest for economic development. Moreover, as the LDCs have become a cohesive political bloc within the United Nations, they have come to demand economic assistance in their development efforts.

3. Much of the effective push toward more rapid development of the third world has come from the efforts of the World Bank and the development agencies of the developed countries.

4. There are many impediments to economic development; merely to want economic growth and development is not enough to assure it. Population growth, resource limitations, and the inefficient use of resources are among the formidable barriers to economic development in particular underdeveloped countries. So too are a series of institutional and cultural barriers that make economic growth more difficult.

5. A series of basic (and controversial) choices face LDCs as they contemplate development. How much should they intervene in the economy, and how much should they rely on the free market? History has demonstrated that growth is possible with almost any conceivable mixture of free market and central control. Centralized planning can change both the pace of economic development and its direction; it can also prove highly wasteful and destroy individual initiative.

6. Educational policy, while vitally important to the long-run rate of economic development, yields its benefits only in the future. As a result, the improvement of basic education is sometimes bypassed in the search for more immediate results.

7. A population policy is an important and volatile issue in most LDCs. The race between output and population is a critical aspect of development efforts in many countries. Different countries have chosen very different attitudes toward limiting population growth.

8. Acquiring capital for development is invariably a major concern in development. One source is domestic savings, but here the vicious circle of poverty may arise: a country that is poor because it has little capital cannot readily forgo consumption to accumulate capital because it is poor. Importing capital rather than using domestic savings permits heavy investment during the early years of development, with much smaller sacrifices of current living standards. But imported capital is available only when the underdeveloped country has opportunities that are attractive to foreign investors. Much foreign capital for underdeveloped countries in the last three decades has been in the form of contributions by foreign governments and international institutions.

9. Selecting a development strategy involves a number of difficult choices. A country need not simply accept its current comparative advantages; there are reasons for not pushing specialization according to current comparative advantage too far, including the risks of fluctuations or declines in the demand for one's principal product and the overdependence on foreign trade. There may also be noneconomic reasons for preferring a different pattern of development. All considerations must be tempered by knowledge of what will in the end be likely to work.

10. Much current debate about development concerns a choice among (a) agricultural development, (b) exploitation of natural resources, (c) development of import substitution industries, and (d) development of an industrial capacity that will create new export industries. None of the strategies is without problems and risks.

11. Collective rather than individual development efforts became more common in the 1970s. OPEC's success renewed interest in commodity price stabilization cartels, but without notable success. A political initiative calling for a New International Economic Order seems to have achieved little more than discussion over this period.

12. The major thrust of NIEO has been for wealth transfers from developed to less-developed countries (as opposed to wealth creation). Of its major proposals, only the granting of some preference to LDC manufactures has occurred.

13. The view of economic development presented in this chapter is subject to criticism for neglecting to discuss — or misconceiving — important problems. One is the perhaps unrealistic haste that underlies most development efforts. A second is the overemphasis on population growth as a barrier to development. A third is an exaggeration of the opportunity cost of creating capital. Economic development is today a field in ferment.

Topics for Review

The gap between LDCs and developed economies
Barriers to development
Infrastructure
The role of planning in development
Alternative development strategies
Wealth creation versus wealth transfers

Discussion Questions

1. Each of the following is a headline from a recent story in the *New York Times*. Relate them to the problem of economic development.
   a. Africa: Ferment for a Better Life
   b. Black Africa: Economies on the Brink of Collapse because of OPEC
   c. Hungary Reforming Economy to Attract Tourists
   d. Goodyear to Build Plant in Congo for $16 Million
   e. Algeria's 4-Year Plan Stresses Industrial Growth
   f. India: Giant Hobbled by Erratic Rainfall
   g. Foreign Banks to Finance New Guinea Copper Mine
   h. Not All Benefit by Green Revolution
   i. OPEC Nations Provide Loans to Undeveloped Nations to Pay for Oil Imports

2. If you were a member of a U.S. foreign aid team assigned to study needed development projects for a poor recipient country, to which of the following would you be likely to give relatively high priority, and why?
   a. birth control clinics
   b. a national airlines
   c. taxes on imported luxuries
   d. better roads
   e. modernization of farming techniques
   f. training in engineering and business management
   g. primary education
   h. scholarships to students to receive medical and legal training abroad

3. China requires 5 million tons more grain each year just to keep up with its annual population growth of 17 million people. This is about five times Canada's wheat supply at present. What policy choices do these facts pose for the Chinese government? How should it resolve those choices?

4. "This natural inequality of the two powers of population and of production in the earth . . . form the great difficulty that to me appears insurmountable in the way to perfectability of society. All other arguments are of slight and subordinate consideration in comparison of this. I see no way by which man can escape from the weight of this law which pervades all animated nature. No fancied equality, no agrarian regulations in their utmost extent, could remove the pressure of it even for a single century" (T. R. Malthus, *Population: The First Essay*, Chapter 1, page 6).

   Discuss Malthus's "insurmountable difficulty" in view of the history of the past 100 years.

5. To what extent does the vicious circle of poverty apply to poor families living in developed countries? Consider carefully, for example, the similarities and differences facing a poor black family living in Arkansas and one living in Ghana, where per capita income is less than $400 per year.

6. How might each of the following affect a country's economic development?

a. a tradition that a man's land be divided equally among all his children
b. a very unequal distribution of national income
c. specialization in a commodity in which it has a virtual world monopoly
d. a decision to be entirely self-sufficient

7. The president of Venezuela said recently: "The decision of OPEC members to raise petroleum prices should be applauded by all third world countries. It represents the irrevocable decision to dignify the terms of trade, to revalue raw materials and other basic products of the third world." Which underdeveloped countries might be expected to have agreed? Which to have disagreed?

8. "High Coffee Prices Bring Hope to Impoverished Latin American Peasants" reads the headline. Mexico, Kenya, and Burundi, among other underdeveloped countries, have the right combination of soil and climate to increase greatly their coffee production. Discuss the benefits and risks to them if they pursue coffee production as a major avenue of their development efforts.

Comparative Economic Systems

45

Economics is concerned with the basic questions, What is produced? How is it produced? How is the product distributed? These and related questions have been examined in the context of a free-market economy in which private firms and households interact in markets with some assistance and interference from the government. This kind of economy fits the pattern of the United States, Britain, Western Europe, and other areas of the world that together are inhabited by less than a quarter of the world's population. We have studied this kind of economy for several reasons. First, this is the kind of economy *we* live in. Second, it is the economic environment in which the serious study of economics was born and has grown.

Today, however, more than a billion people, a third of the world's population, live in the Soviet Union and China, countries that explicitly reject our kind of economic system. At least another third of the world's population live in countries whose economies have not yet developed to the point where the model of either the free-market or the managed economy fits them closely; many are "uncommitted" economically as well as politically.

Can the same theories and measurements be applied to economies quite different from the free-market economy? So far as economics describes the ways in which people respond to incentives and mobilize scarce means to given ends, the same economic principles are applicable under a variety of different sets of assumptions about ends, means, or incentive systems.

All economies face scarcity, and all must decide how to allocate scarce goods; all may face problems of inflation, unemployment, balance-of-payments deficits, and unsatisfactory rates of growth.

So far as economic analysis concerns these topics, it can contribute valuable insights even where familiar institutions are modified or absent. Furthermore, the study of different economic systems may provide clues to the strengths and weaknesses of different forms of economic organization.

Different Economic Systems

It is common to speak of the economic systems of "capitalism," "socialism," and "communism" as if they were the only three paths to basic economic decisions. But this is at best a simplification and at worst a confusion. There are dozens of economic systems in existence today, not three. Just as there are many differences among the United States, the United Kingdom, Germany, Sweden, Japan, France, Greece, and Brazil, so are there differences among the institutions of the Soviet Union, China, Poland, Bulgaria, Cuba, Czechoslovakia, and Yugoslavia. Countries are dissimilar in many respects: in who owns resources, in who makes decisions, in the role of governmental planning, in the nature of the incentives offered to people, and in the way that the economy performs.

Which dissimilarities are important? Differences of opinion about the answer to this question may lead to important disparities in evaluation. Americans may view their economy as being the reason for their high standard of living and see in their well-stocked stores proof of the superiority of free enterprise capitalism. Russians may look at their economy and see, in its rapid and purposeful growth and the absence of urban unemployment, proof of its superiority to the American economy. Sweden's slum-free public housing, nationalized medicine, and high productivity in privately owned industry may lead Swedes to regard their "mixed" economy as very satisfying.

OWNERSHIP OF RESOURCES

Who owns a nation's farms and factories, its coal mines and forests? Who owns its railroads and airways? Who owns its streams and golf courses? Who owns its houses and hotels?

The answers differ in different countries. One characteristic of the system called capitalism is that the basic raw materials, the productive assets of the society, and the final goods are predominantly privately owned by individuals singly or in groups. By this standard, the United States is predominantly a capitalistic economy, although many of its resources are in fact publicly rather than privately held. In the United States there is some public ownership of power, housing, and utilities as well as of many local transit systems and the postal system. Although a few observers see evidence of creeping or galloping socialism in such projects as the Tennessee Valley Authority (TVA), most agree that in the United States the pattern of ownership is predominantly private.

In contrast, socialism envisions a society in which the ownership of productive assets is public. Communism theoretically is opposed to any form of private property. Today there are no completely communistic or socialistic societies. In the Soviet Union, virtually all factories are state-owned and an attempt has been made to collectivize all farms, but though the Soviets officially designate their economy as socialistic, there are three sectors of that economy—agriculture, retail trade, and housing—where some private ownership exists. If the USSR is not a pure socialist economy, it is sufficiently near the public ownership end of the spectrum to distinguish it from the United States near the private ownership end.

Other countries fall between them on the spec-

FIGURE 45-1
Estimated Differences in Ownership Patterns for Selected Countries

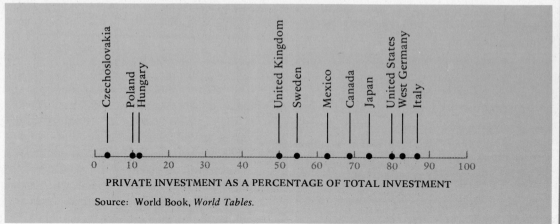

PRIVATE INVESTMENT AS A PERCENTAGE OF TOTAL INVESTMENT

Source: World Book, *World Tables.*

Actual economies never rely solely on private or solely on public investment. These estimates are based on the percentage of gross fixed investment accounted for by the private sector. Such investment provides additions to the stock of productive capital. Private capital investment plays a role even in Communist countries; public capital is a significant part of investment in all countries.

trum. Great Britain has six times in this century elected Labor governments that have been officially committed to socialism to the point of nationalizing key industries: railroads, steel, coal, gas, electricity, atomic power, postal services, telephones, telegraphs, airlines, and some trucking. Although many key industries are publicly owned, the bulk of industries that produce goods and services for household consumption and capital goods for firms are privately owned and controlled. Ownership patterns are genuinely variable rather than of an either/or variety. Figure 45-1 shows the division of fixed investment between public and private sectors in 11 countries.

With respect to the ownership of resources— and virtually every other dimension of an economy—three basic points are worth remembering.

1. **Every real economy is "mixed" rather than pure.**
2. **Among countries the mixture differs in ways that are appreciable and significant.**
3. **Over time, the mixture changes.**

THE DECISION PROCESS (COORDINATING PRINCIPLES)

A distinction is sometimes made between two kinds of systems: a *market system,* in which decisions are made impersonally and in a decentralized way by the interaction of individuals in markets, and a *command system,* in which centralized decision makers decide what is to be done and issue appropriate commands to achieve the desired results.

Again, no country offers an example of either system working alone, but it is true that some economies—those of the United States, France, and Yugoslavia, for example—rely much more heavily on market decisions than do the economies of East Germany, the Soviet Union, and Cuba. Yet even in the United States the command principle has some sway: minimum wages, quotas on some agricultural outputs, and wartime priorities are obvious examples. More subtle examples concern public expenditures and taxes that in effect transfer command of some resources from private individuals to public officials. (The extent of government interference with market forces was discussed in Chapters 24 and 25.)

In the planned economies of the Soviet bloc, where plans and targets, quotas and directives are important aspects of the decision-making system, there is substantial command at work. But markets are used too. At the retail level, for example, people can spend their incomes with substantial discretion on a wide variety of goods.

Table 45-1, though it suppresses many subtle distinctions, focuses on important tendencies in certain twentieth century economies by a simple classification according to ownership and decision patterns. Later in this chapter we shall examine more closely the economic systems of the USSR and Yugoslavia, both of which are considered communist societies. The table suggests at once that they differ significantly from each other as well as from the United States.

Much economic behavior depends more on the decision pattern than on the ownership pattern. Thus in the United Kingdom, while a large number of key industries are publicly owned, their control is vested in semi-autonomous boards over which Parliament exerts very little control. By and large, the boards try to make their enterprises profitable, and to the extent that they succeed, their behavior will be similar to that of profit-seeking privately owned firms. In predicting their market behavior, economic theorists need not concern themselves with the legal distinction between public and private ownership any more than they need concern themselves with the distinction between corporations and partnerships.

In contrast, firms in Hitler's Germany were under a high degree of state control, even though technically they were privately owned. An attempt to predict their behavior using the profit-maximizing model would not have been successful because the central decision makers guiding their actions were concerned with goals quite different from profit maximization.

WHOSE VALUES?

In the market and command systems different groups make the relevant decisions. It follows that different people's judgments will determine those decisions.

In a capitalistic market economy, dollars "vote." The demands of consumers for goods exert a major influence on the nature of the goods produced. Traditionally this is called consumer sovereignty, but it should be noted both that the rich consumer has more say than the poor one and that firms have a great deal of control over what is and is not produced. In an unfettered market economy, the initial distribution of income and wealth influences the nature of economic decisions because it determines who has the dollars that exercise the effective demands.

TABLE 45-1
Comparative Economic Systems: Ownership and Decision Patterns

	Ownership pattern	
Decision pattern	Predominantly private	Predominantly public
Predominantly decentralized with use of market	United States	Yugoslavia
Predominantly centralized with use of command principle	Nazi Germany	USSR

Each of these combinations of private and public ownership and centralized and decentralized control has occurred in practice. This table is a simplification that highlights differences among economic systems. Ownership and decision patterns are *variables;* it would be an interesting exercise to use a grid that gives several, rather than just two, gradations for each variable and then attempt to place current and past economies in the appropriate cells.

Mixed economies often use public policies to modify the decisions that would emerge from the uses of private purchasing power, but they are best regarded as supplementing rather than challenging the principle of consumer and producer sovereignty.

Early Marxists attacked the notion of a market-oriented value system. One of the great slogans of the utopian Marxists was "From each according to his ability, to each according to his need." Such a slogan does not solve the allocational problem: in a world in which desires for goods and services exceed the capacity to produce them, someone has to judge who needs what and then take steps to provide it.

In general, in command systems some group must decide what is to be produced and who is to get it. Because no one has yet devised a scheme by which everyone would automatically give according to his or her ability and in which everyone's needs would be clear to all, decisions have to be made. Whoever makes the decisions might do so on the basis of majority preferences, with each person having one vote, regardless of his or her share of the income. (Cooperatives operate on this principle, each *member* having one vote; the contrast with a corporation, where each *share* has one vote, is marked.) Alternatively, each decision maker might decide on the basis of his or her own preferences (autocracy) or those of a particular group. Or the decision maker might decide on the basis of what he or she thinks is "good for the people."

Different systems are likely to reflect the values of different groups. Planned systems reflect the values of the central authorities somewhat more strongly than do market systems.

INCENTIVE SYSTEMS

Psychologists know that people (and most other living creatures) respond to reward and punishment. Incentives may be of two main kinds—the carrot or the stick—and of almost infinite varieties. Direct monetary rewards, in the form of wages or profits or bribes, are well understood. Indirect monetary rewards, such as special housing, vacations, or subsidized education, are not always as readily identified, but they can be effective. Nonmonetary "carrots" include praise, medals, certificates, and applause. Fines, prison terms, and other penalties are used to punish aberrant behavior in all societies; in some societies coercion and fear provide even stronger motivation.

Capitalistic market economies place major reliance on monetary incentives. Monetary incentives to the individual in a socialistic society are not very different from those in a capitalistic economy. Differential earnings for different occupations are used in socialist economies, and piece rates are common. Gifts and bonuses of housing, cars, and other sought-after goods or privileges are used and valued. Large accumulations of assets are not permitted, but the importance of this is in dispute. There are no millionaires in the Soviet Union, but the desire for power is perhaps as important as the desire for wealth in both capitalistic and socialistic societies.

The big difference in incentive systems lies in whether those responsible for production respond to what it is *profitable* to produce or whether they respond to what they are directed to produce. In the first case, profits can provide their own reward in terms of bonuses, salaries, dividends, and perhaps the funds to permit growth and the accumulation of power. In the second case, it is necessary to provide incentives to managers and workers to achieve the assigned quotas.

ENDS AND MEANS

Many, perhaps most people in Western societies value the *means* of the free market and democratic processes even more highly than they value the *ends* of high and rising living standards. Most Americans distrust the agglomeration of central power and the loss of democratic institutions that accompany communism or any other form of centrally administered command economy. Many believe that there is no need to choose between means and ends because they feel that the free market and democracy produce better results than do alternative systems in terms of both means and ends.

How many Americans would decide to go over to the Soviet system, even *if* it could be *proved* that the Soviet system was certain to produce a higher growth rate than the American free-market system? In the 1930s it was believed that fascist dictatorships were more efficient than democracies. Mussolini, it was said, "made the Italian trains run on time." It is debatable that the belief was correct, but most people accepted it. Yet only a handful of Americans advocated that America become a fascist dictatorship.

In many less-developed countries, ordinary people often put more importance on the ends, higher living standards, than on the means of achieving them. They may regard a change of means per se as unimportant. The choice between a centralized and a decentralized economy may seem to be simply one of which group will exploit them—government officials or powerful monopoly interests. If a highly planned communistic economy offers them a good chance of a 4 percent growth rate, while a democratically oriented market society offers 2 percent, they may well choose the planned society. To warn them that in so choosing they may throw away their freedom is likely to evoke the reply, What has freedom meant to us in the past but the freedom to be hungry and exploited?

THE CHARACTERIZATION OF PARTICULAR ECONOMIES

Although no real economy is simple, it can nevertheless prove helpful to talk about and analyze economies in terms of simple models. For example, it is sometimes helpful to characterize the American economy as one of private ownership, of market decision making, of consumer sovereignty, and of monetary incentives—with, in addition, a relatively large government sector that

modifies the nature of economic decisions to some extent. This kind of capsule summary is useful in focusing on certain patterns that differentiate the United States from other real economies, two of which we shall discuss briefly: the Soviet Union and Yugoslavia.

The Economy of the Soviet Union

The modern *economic* history of the Soviet Union is usually taken to have begun in 1928, 11 years after the Bolshevik revolution had wrested power for a small and militant minority from a small and decaying aristocracy. Russia at the time of World War I was a large and in most ways a backward country with an enormous, poor, largely ignorant and illiterate peasantry, who were to prove as sullenly hostile to their new Bolshevik rulers as they had been to the czars. Backward and poor though Russia was, by 1917 industrialization had been under way for three decades; the nucleus of heavy industry and of an industrial labor force already existed.

During its first decade of existence the new regime hung on by its teeth, contending with recurring famines, internal power struggles, and invasion by the Western powers. By the late 1920s Joseph Stalin had emerged as an effective strong man. Stalin had ruthlessly consolidated the Revolution and his personal power. He was ready to undertake the economic task of lifting Russia from an underdeveloped giant to a major industrial power. Whatever the costs—and they have been enormous—the economic rise of the Soviet Union in five decades is a major achievement.

Basically, Stalin's economic policy had three strategies.

1. To consolidate management over all economic resources in such a way that they would respond surely and quickly to the needs of the regime.
2. To constrict consumption to an absolute minimum so that the maximum possible rate of

capital accumulation, and thus growth, could be achieved.

3. To channel growth into the areas of heavy industrial development required for a major military power.

Neither the current sacrifices that were imposed on the people as consumers nor the Herculean efforts that were asked of them as producers were borne without complaint or opposition. Stalin is perhaps best remembered for his "terrors," dramatized in the ruthless purges in which thousands met death or exile. Terror was pervasive in the omnipresent army, the police, and above all the notorious secret police. Whatever its primary purposes, this regime of terror had the twin economic effects of enforcing centralized power and providing a powerful if unpleasant set of incentives to carry out the orders of the regime.

The famous five-year plans, the first adopted in 1928, began the rapid industrial development that was to transform the Soviet Union into a major military power by World War II and a major world power in the postwar period. The tenth five-year plan, covering the period 1976–1980, was only the second to put major emphasis on production of consumer goods. Whatever the sacrifices were, both in privation and in terror, the Soviet Union today has a stable and relatively prosperous economy with butter as well as guns. It operates with a set of institutions that deals with the basic economic problems very differently from the way the American economy deals with them.

OWNERSHIP

With certain limited exceptions, the central government—the state—owns all land, all natural resources, all capital goods, all business enterprises, and most urban housing.

In the industrial sector, state ownership is virtually complete; in the retail fields, state stores make up about two-thirds of the total sales, with the bulk of the rest accounted for by rural cooperatives. A small amount of farm produce is sold in free "farmers' markets." Most rural housing, and perhaps a third of urban housing, is privately owned (and officially restricted to personal use). The rest is publicly owned.

About a third of all agricultural production comes from farms (called sovkhos) that are owned, run, and managed by the state. Another half of all production comes from collective farms that, while nominally cooperatives into which peasants were once forced, are in fact so closely controlled by the state that their differences from the sovkhos are minor. The remainder of the total agricultural output is produced on privately owned farms and by members of collective farms on garden plots they are allowed to cultivate in their spare time.

Private enterprise is profitable where it is permitted—in agriculture and in personal services of various kinds from psychiatric counseling to carpentry. The official figures probably underestimate the private sector by ignoring the illegal black market in privately produced goods and services.

The black market is a response by households (who are permitted to own savings deposits and personal possessions) to the restricted supply of officially available goods. They are glad to buy goods and services from others, who in turn are glad to earn extra money by producing them.

THE ORGANIZATION OF PRODUCTION

In the industrial sector of the Soviet economy, production is predominantly organized around individual plants that are managed by a "director" (appointed by the central authorities with the approval of the local Communist party group). Directors may appear omnipotent to the workers, but their orders with respect to how and what to produce and how and when to replace equipment or expand operations are handed down from higher up in the planning hierarchy. Directors are in fact more bureaucrat than entrepreneur.

Production decisions are made in a highly

organized pyramidal bureaucracy. The overall planning agency, the USSR GOSPLAN, develops broad plans that are translated into orders for regional GOSPLANs, which in turn hand down directives to particular ministries. Ministries may be either at the industry level or in control of a particular resource. Ministries' instructions ultimately take the form of orders to individual plant managers, who then do their best to carry them out.

The industrial firm's targets include quotas with respect to total output and output of individual commodities. A firm is often given maximum levels of inputs (such as number of employees, tons of coal). The wages a firm can offer are fixed by the government, and there is no open market on which the firm's manager can acquire scarce commodities. Within limits, workers are free to choose any job they are offered, and labor mobility is not really restricted — except that workers on collective farms have not been allowed to leave them at will. Despite rather large occupational wage differences, labor mobility has tended to be low.

Managers are exhorted to fulfill their quotas, and success is rewarded with bonuses, medals, and promotions. If managers are in danger of failing because, for example, they cannot acquire the labor they need, they can persuade their employees (by threat or promise) to work harder and longer, they can appeal to the appropriate ministry for an increase in permitted wages, or they can persuade someone to lower their quota. If they fail for what their superiors refuse to accept as good reasons, they may face demotion — or worse. While these firms are called enterprises, the manager is limited in the kind of enterprise he or she can show. Only since 1969 have managers had the right to decrease their labor force by firing surplus labor and to use the resulting savings to increase the pay of remaining employees.

Clearly, industry is governed by the rules of a command economy. Directives cover many aspects of a firm's operations, though of course they cannot cover all contingencies. *Within* the guidelines of the plan as it is sent down to the given firm, the firm is instructed and encouraged to be efficient and, where possible, to make "above-plan profits."[1] Planned profits go to the state; part of above-plan profits may be retained in the firm and used for the benefit of the employees. Thus there is some scope for maneuver, but the constraints are much tighter than those for a typical American firm. A Soviet enterprise cannot usually experiment with new products or new methods of production without first securing permission. Indeed, because there is such emphasis on meeting or exceeding plan quotas, *quantity* of output becomes more compelling than cost savings or quality.

Western observers — and Soviet observers, too — have often noted that many microeconomic inefficiencies result from the command principle. Among them are excessive stockpiles of some commodities, shortages of others, and poor quality of many goods. Similar inefficiencies are alleged to exist in some American activities, such as military procurement, where centralized command systems are in use. This suggests that inefficiencies of these kinds inhere in highly centralized systems in which incentives are given in terms of fulfilling output quotas rather than earning profits.

Despite inefficiencies, the Soviet system clearly works. They have produced a growing flow of armaments, goods, machines, and space vehicles. Soviet industry has proved adequate to the major demands placed on it; its inefficiencies have been serious but not crippling.

One of the sharpest critics of the inefficiencies of overcentralization and rigid control structure is a Soviet professor, E. Liberman. As will be seen, Yugoslavia has responded to these criticisms more than the USSR, but there is currently within the Soviet Union a great debate on this very issue, and since 1965 there have been a

---

[1] Because prices are specified by the state and are spelled out in the directive, the firm can earn above-plan profits only by exceeding output quotas. Many critics both outside and inside the system have noticed an overconcentration on physical output — on technological rather than economic efficiency.

growing number of decentralizing reforms. Governments, too, respond to incentives. If it is demonstrated that some practice is costing the Soviet Union too heavily in its economic growth, one can be sure that its leaders will attempt to change the offending practice. As in all bureaucracies, this is not always easy to carry out.

A major problem of planned economies concerns innovation. Soviet managers have little incentive to innovate by experimenting with new products or new ways of producing old products. As long as the Soviet Union is catching up to the capitalist countries, it can copy capitalist products and techniques. It is not so clear that a planned economy left on its own could produce as rapid a rate of innovation as is generated by a profit-oriented free enterprise economy where decision making is effectively decentralized. One of the severest critics of the stultifying effects on invention and innovation exerted by a highly centralized economy has been the distinguished Soviet physicist and Nobel Prize winner A. K. Sakharov.

Agricultural production (which in 1928 absorbed 80 percent of the Soviet labor force and today absorbs about 25 percent) is almost as centralized as manufacturing. The results have been much less successful than those in the industrial sector. The collective farms were designed to overcome the inability of Russian agriculture to provide cheap and adequate food supplies. But the compulsion required to bring unwilling individual peasants into the collective farms did not generate cooperative responses. Many observers believe that the lack of incentives and rewards is responsible. Meeting quotas of steel wins bonuses, medals, praise—and pay raises—for the steelworkers; meeting grain quotas is likely to lead to even higher quotas for the next period.

Collective farmers do not receive wages; rather, they share in the income of the farm. But the government's policy, designed to keep food prices down by keeping farm prices low, has kept farm income low, too. In any case, low morale and the inability of farm labor to find other jobs have not led to high productivity, and agricultural production has been a chronic trouble spot in the Soviet economy.

THE DISTRIBUTION OF GOODS AND HOUSEHOLD INCENTIVES

Both the nature and quantity of the goods to be produced are specified by the central planners. Those for consumers are placed in the state-owned shops or in cooperatives, to be sold at government-specified prices that include an important "turnover tax" (see page 857).

Households are free to spend their incomes on these goods. Here individual choice rather than "command" is at work, but even here the function of a market is restricted. If too many consumers want a particular item, for instance, it runs out; no price rise signals producers that there is a higher demand. The shortage is not an effective signal because producers are not motivated to respond to it. As a result there is no assurance that production will be increased. There is no automatic feedback of what consumers *want* and would buy that has an effect on the goods and services actually produced.

The use of the market, rather than direct allocation, in the distribution of consumer goods is explained by the need to avoid the impossible administrative burden of deciding who gets what, rather than by a philosophic desire to let consumers be sovereign. There is a difference between consumer sovereignty, which allows consumer choices to help determine *what is produced,* and consumer freedom to choose from among goods of *predetermined* quantity, quality, and price.

Until recent years Soviet planners were reluctant to respond to such clear consumer signals as shortages of particular goods. The consumer riots in Poland in December 1970 seem to have changed this. After that Soviet planners began to take account of shortages and surpluses of particular consumer goods at existing prices in setting new production targets. To the extent that this occurs, consumer sovereignty has been introduced into the system.

These changes reflect Soviet growth. When the economy was very poor and very high investment levels were needed to stimulate growth, consumers had to be content with whatever crude goods were available. Now that a higher material living standard is being achieved, the variety of consumer goods is increasing, and at the same time consumers are becoming more selective. They no longer buy shoddy or unpopular goods automatically, and the consequent large inventories of unsold products are an embarrassment to the planners. As a result, there is much pressure for, and some experimentation with, a two-phase system. This would allow planners to decide what proportion of the nation's resources to devote to the production of consumer goods. It would also allow consumers, through a decentralized market-type decision mechanism, to exert an influence on how those resources are allocated among various lines of production.

Household incomes come from the state principally in the form of wages and salaries. "To each according to his need" was the Marxian ideal, but in the Soviet Union scientists and engineers, ballet dancers, and athletes apparently need more than do laborers and teachers. Wage *differentials* are in fact very much larger than in the United States; skilled workers characteristically earn three or four times the amount earned by unskilled workers (in contrast to 50 percent more in the United States).

But wages are not the only determinant of the distribution of income. Many goods and services such as medical care, higher education, and old-age pensions are provided free to those who qualify. State housing is provided at low cost. Large families receive special money allowances and special housing. Thus standards of living in the Soviet Union are somewhat less unequal than wage differentials suggest. In contrast to the United States, there are fewer extreme incomes at either end but a somewhat greater spread in the incomes of the middle and upper middle income groups.

Income distribution in the USSR is very much a matter of conscious policy decisions. Through wages, allowances, free and subsidized goods, and the turnover tax (which is like a sales tax but varies from product to product), the central authorities—the party hierarchy—can effectively impress on the economy *their* views as to the appropriate pattern of goods and distribution of income.

PLANNING IN THE SOVIET UNION

The Soviet economic system relies on public ownership, on the command principle, on private choices (within such limits as the central authorities allow), and on complex incentive systems that include differential wages, bonuses, and some compulsion and fear. Planners and the centralized decision makers play a leading role in the Soviet economy.

Two levels of planning warrant particular attention: the short-run (one-year) plans and the medium-range (usually five-year) plans. The medium-range plan is influenced by a yet longer-run "vision" of the society that motivates the leadership—a vision of what the economy promises its citizens 25 years hence. Stalin's vision was of a Russia becoming a full industrial and military power, and he lived to see it realized. Khrushchev began the transition to a vision that embraced more of the "good life," and the present Soviet leadership under Brezhnev accelerated this change. Western living standards, once denounced as bourgeois decadence, are an increasingly visible goal.

Five-year Plans

Five-year plans are, roughly, blueprints for later detailed implementation. They contain no orders to individual plants and no detailed quotas of goods to be produced, but they do prescribe both the level of aggregate income that is to be achieved and the *structure* of the economy by major sectors and industries.

Every five-year plan has included decisions about how drastically to curtail consumption in order to release resources for investment. Each has also decided how much effort is to be devoted to developing educational and technical resources that will be needed in the future in order to have the technical labor force required to staff the new plants spawned by the plan. Less global decisions are also required about such matters as the form capital investment should take. How much should be invested in steel capacity, how much in cement, and how much in roads and railroads?

Once the structural goals are specified, it is necessary to spell out the year-by-year implications for particular industries and regions of the economy. For example, production of the Kiev steel industry may have to grow by X percent next year if other planned activities are not to encounter steel shortages. This kind of derived implication of a five-year plan becomes a control for next year's one-year plan.

One-year Plans

Planning details are spelled out in the one-year plans. They are extremely complex and laborious exercises that work out the myriad microeconomic implications of certain broad objectives. By and large, the one-year plans translate the objectives of the five-year plans into detail sufficient to enable individual plants (or farms) to meet them and to ensure that the supplies of needed resources can be made available in the quantities required at the times needed.

There is obviously an enormous coordinating job here. The planners do not manage it perfectly, though they are saved from making an inordinate number of mistakes by a trial-and-error procedure in which tentative plans are sent to lower bureaucratic levels for comments and suggestions before being issued as final orders. Actual quotas are to some degree negotiated between the directors at the operating levels, who have a strong desire to hold down the quotas expected of them, and the higher-level planners, who must achieve apparent miracles to satisfy overall growth objectives. Over the years, an enormous amount of experience has been ac-

cumulated about the real limits of what is possible. Research by Professor Michael Manove suggests that because of this experience, the planning operation has proven quite successful in defining consistent and attainable plan quotas.

PRICES IN THE PLANNING PROCESS

Not all decisions can be made centrally by the planning agencies. Soviet planners are increasingly using prices to assist in some kinds of allocational decision making. Two different sets of prices are now assigned as part of the planning process, one for production accounting, the other for sales to consumers and payments to factors.

Factor Pricing

For internal productive use, "prices" of commodities or resources are designed to measure the scarcity value of the resources, compared to alternative uses. If efficient use of resources is to occur, a tractor firm that uses steel should pay a price for steel that reflects its scarcity value if used in other products. Similarly, the charge for using the services of a carpenter anywhere should reflect the value of his or her marginal product elsewhere.

But the state may wish to pay carpenters a higher wage than this, either because it has embarked on a program of income redistribution in which carpenters are to be favored or because the state wishes to denote carpentry as a "prestige" occupation. The particular pattern of wage differentials built into the Soviet system may thus reflect the preferences of the central authorities as well as the system's current demands for labor. To avoid productive inefficiency, the planners assign *two* wage rates for carpenters. One is charged as a cost of production; the other (which may be higher or lower) is actually paid out to carpenters and becomes the source of their income.

With one important exception, this dual treatment of factor prices has long been part of the

Soviet planning procedure. The exception concerns the cost of capital. Mustering resources for capital investment has been hard, and brutal sacrifices in terms of curtailed consumption were imposed on Soviet citizens of the 1930s and 1940s. How should this scarce capital, whose opportunity cost is so high, be allocated efficiently among industries and regions?

The obvious answer was to assign a high interest rate that reflected the high opportunity cost of capital. But for many years an interesting doctrinal barrier prevented using this solution. Because "interest" is traditionally a payment to private owners of capital in capitalist societies, interest rates were odious to Marx and to early Marxist planners. Yet if those who use capital, a scarce resource, do not have to pay a price for using it that reflects its scarcity value, they will not be motivated to conserve it. This is just what happened. Soviet planners were reluctant to assign a real scarcity-value interest rate to funds allocated for investment until a series of studies showed that investment allocation was among the least efficient aspects of Soviet planning.

Dogma has yielded to the fact that acquiring the real resources to construct capital goods continues to be the greatest obstacle to further growth in the Soviet Union. Today, a number very much like an interest rate is used to measure the cost of capital.

Consumer Prices and the Turnover Tax

Consumer prices are made up of two parts: the full cost of the good produced, using the correct internal accounting prices for factors, plus the **turnover tax.** The tax is in form an excise tax, and today the *average* turnover tax is about one-third the price of the good. But the tax varies tremendously from commodity to commodity.

The size of the turnover tax is determined by the planners' idea of what goods people should be encouraged or discouraged to consume. In part this is a means for redistributing income. Goods consumed by low-income groups may have very low turnover taxes, for example.

Revenue from the turnover tax is used by the state for new investment. By changing the average rate of the turnover tax, the planners can affect the relative size of consumption and investment. By varying the tax rate on different kinds of commodities, the state affects the relative sacrifice in consumption among different kinds of consumers. For example, if the turnover tax were raised on basic necessities and lowered on luxuries, it would increase the sacrifice of the lower income groups. The pattern of the tax can be made regressive or progressive as the needs and desires of the planners dictate.

Allocation of the turnover tax receipts is at the discretion of the planners. Investment funds produced by the turnover tax on steel might be reinvested in increasing steel output; or they might be diverted to capital investment in electric power, railroads, or the production of luxury goods.

Other Sources of Investment Funds

The tax revenues of the Soviet state do not limit the amount it can spend for investment – or for anything else. The central bank (GOSBANK) can expand the money supply and absorb any government deficit it is asked to absorb. If it prints too much money, it will, of course, create an inflationary gap. With such a gap, there will be longer lines, more shortages, and more grumbling. These results can be avoided only by raising prices – by letting the inflation occur. Another aspect of the money supply is the ability of firms to borrow in order to expand. GOSBANK lends only to those enterprises whose expansion the planners want to encourage. It thus becomes a further device for implementing planners' objectives.

Unlike most Western central banks, GOSBANK is a monopoly commercial bank with thousands of branches. As can be imagined, the central bank controls the commercial banking system completely; it does not use any of the indirect tools of control such as open market operations by which Western central banks seek to control independent commercial banks and the money supply.

COMPARATIVE PERFORMANCE: THE UNITED STATES VERSUS THE SOVIET UNION

In judging the performance of an economy, there are many different criteria and many different ways of viewing it. Moreover, comparing the actual performances of only two economies can be misleading. For example, during the last 40 years the Soviet Union has experienced twice as great a growth rate as the United States. But before concluding that this demonstrates a growth advantage of communism over capitalism, the even higher growth rates achieved in West Germany and Japan—capitalistic countries—should be noted. With this warning in mind, we shall compare elements of the economic performances of the United States and the Soviet Union.

The Standard of Living in the 1970s

Most national income accountants and students of the Soviet economy judge the level of real purchasing power per capita in the Soviet Union to be about 40 percent of that in the United States. This kind of statistic is difficult to interpret. Clearly, most Americans would feel very poor if their present incomes were cut in half. But American real incomes a generation ago were half what they are today, and at that time the United States was the richest nation in history. The adequacy of one's income depends on what everyone else's income is, and on past and future expectations. The Soviet citizens' standard of living is so much higher than it was even a decade ago, and is rising so rapidly, that it probably seems comfortable to them.

Nevertheless it is clear that Soviet citizens are poorer than their American counterparts. Not only is housing poorer and clothing in shorter supply and less elegant, but the average citizen has to work more hours to earn the cost of a pair of shoes or an evening dinner. A small sedan in 1979 cost about twice the annual salary of the average Muscovite, and even at that price there was a three-year wait for delivery. Not surprisingly, the Soviet worker buys less, works longer hours and has shorter vacations.

Notice, however, that these comparisons reflect in good part *our* social values. An observer might note that the Soviet citizen can see better chess, better gymnastics, and better soccer than an American counterpart—and can see them more cheaply. Yet another observer might note that Soviet citizens need not worry about their ability to provide medical and dental care for their families, the possibility of unemployment due to a severe economic slump, or providing for their retirement or the support of their dependents after their own death. A comprehensive set of welfare programs covers all these contingencies for all Soviet citizens.

Growth

From 1928 to 1970 the Soviet Union achieved an overall rate of growth of more than 4.5 percent per year notwithstanding some unbelievable disasters, particularly the famines of the 1930s and the devastating impact of World War II. During the 1960s the Soviet rate of growth was twice the U.S. rate. In more recent times, however, the growth rate has declined (although it is still higher than the U.S. rate). Recent growth experience is shown in Table 45-2.

As we noted, this remarkable growth record has not been costless. It was achieved by hard and conscious choice—by sacrificing current consumption for investment that led to greater production in the future. The relative prosperity of today's Soviet citizens is owed to their parents' forced forbearance. To sustain this growth rate for another generation, present-day citizens may well have to continue to forgo many of the comforts available to Americans. There is little general enthusiasm for such policies, and the regime has eased the restrictions on the consumer sector even at the cost of its growth rate. But the Soviet economy has provided a most compelling demonstration of how an under-developed country can develop in one lifetime, if it will pay the price and if it has the unexploited resources on which to base an expansion.

Economic Stability

If growth has been the great triumph of the Soviet experience, employment stability has been a small one. A highly planned economy, if it is insulated from the outside world, need have no deficient-demand unemployment, no unintended inflation or deflation, and no cyclical phenomena. If it must engage heavily in foreign trade, it is not so easily insulated. In this regard the Soviet Union during its period of rapid growth has been fortunate. It is a large country with ample and varied natural resources (like the United States), and it has not had to rely heavily on foreign trade. Moreover, much of what it does need has been provided from within the Soviet system by the satellite countries of eastern Europe. Purchases from the West require foreign exchange, but here pressures have not been serious, in part because the Soviet Union has been a major gold producer.

Years of crop failure have provided a significant exception to this generalization. Large purchases of grain have been made from the United States and Canada and the Soviet authorities have had to worry about earning sufficient foreign exchange to pay for those purchases.

Although unemployment due to deficient aggregate demand need not and does not occur in the Soviet system, frictional and structural unemployment can occur. The state's ability to control the movement of people away from the farms (through a system of work permits and internal passports) has led to much disguised unemployment in the agricultural sector. There is little doubt that if people had been free to move from the farms, they would have moved in great numbers to the cities in search of the excitement and higher living standards there, and they would have moved at a faster rate than industry could have absorbed them. In a market economy, this would have led to substantial urban overcrowding and unemployment and would have served to depress the wages of those who were successful in finding work. The Soviet tendency has been to hold these people on the farms where they are underemployed and to allow them to move to the cities only as fast as they could be absorbed into jobs there.

Again, a potential clash of values can be seen. Western observers are inclined to stress what to them is the severe loss of personal freedom, while Soviet observers tend to emphasize the gains to the economy of an orderly relocation of labor. In particular, they see the advantage to urban workers of not having their wages depressed by the unemployed migrants from the farm and the advantage to the farm dwellers in being detained on the farm, where they can be fed and housed at lower cost and in greater comfort until jobs are available in the city.

The Soviets have had less success in controlling inflation than in controlling unemployment. Like the princes discussed in Chapter 32, they found increasing the money supply too easy a way to finance public expenditures, particularly

TABLE 45-2

Estimates of Growth of GNP in the USSR, by Sector of Origin

	Average annual rate of growth (percent)		
	1966–1970	1971–1975	1976–1978
Agriculture	4.2	2.1	4.4
Industry	6.3	5.9	3.8
Construction	5.5	5.3	2.6
Transportation	7.5	6.6	4.3
Communications	8.9	7.2	6.1
Trade	6.4	4.8	3.7
Services	4.2	3.4	3.0
Total GNP	5.3	3.7	3.7

Source: CIA, Research Aid, *Soviet Economy: Performance of 1976–1977 and Outlook for 1978.*

The rate of growth in virtually all major sectors of the Soviet economy slowed in the 1970s. Growth rates vary significantly from sector to sector, with agriculture showing the poorest growth performance. Although growth rates have fallen, they are still above those of the United States.

during the war. The high wartime expenditures resulted in a dangerously inflationary piling up of private money balances. But the response of a command economy can be quick and sure, if harsh. When monetary reform came, the state confiscated the bulk of private monetary balances and repudiated some of the public debt that workers had accepted in lieu of part of their wages. Thus workers who thought they had been saving found they really had been taxed.

This was the Soviet response to a problem that existed in all belligerent countries at the end of World War II. Wartime savings and deferred consumption created an enormous backlog of demand. After the war, this demand for goods was far in excess of the supply. The problem was complicated by the fact that any postwar production to meet this pent-up demand for consumer goods would create additional purchasing power.

The Soviet response was to destroy the backlog of purchasing power by monetary reform; the Western answer was to allow people to try to exercise it and accept the inevitable inflation. This reduced the real value of accumulated purchasing power to a level commensurate with the goods actually available for purchase. Both systems achieved the same end of reducing the real value of purchasing power to what was available. To Western eyes, the Soviet solution (confiscation) seems harsh and autocratic; to Soviet eyes, the Western solution (inflation) seems arbitrary and highly inequitable.

Shortcomings of the Soviet Economic Experience

In at least three major ways, a Soviet type of economy compares unfavorably to a Western market economy. First, it is accompanied by numerous microeconomic inefficiencies. Many small interdependent decisions have to be made that it is difficult or impossible to make quickly, consistently, and efficiently, given a centralized decision hierarchy. The shortages, gluts, misshipments, and shortfalls of key quotas that have

annoyed Soviet industry and plagued Soviet agriculture are neither surprising nor wholly avoidable. They are periodically denounced as "planning errors" of a previous regime. Such errors, however, are apparently a cost of choosing to replace an automatic mechanism (whose implicit values the planners have rejected) by a deliberate mechanism that permits the planners to introduce their own values. In recent years, some pressure has developed within Soviet-type economies to retreat from complete planning and to allow market or marketlike mechanisms to do more of the allocating.

A second deficiency has been in the detailed planning process itself, which makes enormous demands on time and energy. When labor was abundant, and when alternative uses of those with the planners' skills were not numerous, this "transactions cost" of planning was perhaps not serious. Increasingly, however, the Soviet bureaucracy has been absorbing a large quantity of the energies of valuable, highly trained men and women in plan formation and implementation. The Soviets have come to recognize this as a real cost. The major surge of interest in techniques of mathematical programming, input-output analysis, and simulation reflects an official effort to substitute capital for high-priced labor in the "production function of planning." They hope both to save resources and to avoid some microeconomic inefficiencies and mistakes.

A third deficiency is that the goods and services produced reflect planners' preferences rather than those of citizens. This is true not only where a deliberate decision is made to reject consumer sovereignty for national purposes, but also generally, for there is no effective market mechanism by which consumers can signal their preferences. Not every family wants the same size apartment, but when the decision as to what proportion of its income it will spend on housing is taken away from the family and it is allocated space according to family size and occupation, there is no way that family *preferences* will play a role.

Source and Costs of the Achievements

A planned command economy has certain advantages over a market-oriented economy: the leaders can set up whatever priorities they wish, and they can then use the full power of the state to give effect to them. In such economies, the power of the state has been used to achieve forced saving to permit capital formation and rapid growth. It has also been used to prevent widespread unemployment. It may well be that the Soviet growth record could not have been achieved had it depended on popular or majority support, for it is by no means clear that the growth benefited the Soviet population of the 1930s and 1940s.

This rapid growth has had costs—costs not only in current consumption forgone, but also the costs of coercing individuals, of their loss of freedom, and of substituting centralized for individual judgments. Because these costs cannot readily be measured, the question of whether the benefits justify the costs is normative, and the answer is a value judgment that each person must reach individually. Most citizens of Western countries are content to have forgone both the benefits and the costs; contemporary Russians may feel they have been justified. Not surprisingly, different people and different governments in the rest of the world come down on different sides.

Politically the present government is in many ways a monstrous and terrible tyranny—as Aleksandr Solzhenitsyn has emphasized. It is not necessary to assume, however, that this degree of tyranny *must* accompany any command economy. After all, the tradition of political tyranny in Russia stretches well back into the time of the czars. Other command economies have had regimes less repressive than that of the USSR. However, command economies must by their very nature be more authoritarian than free-market economies. An important and unsettled question concerns the minimum repression of individual freedom that is consistent with a highly centralized planned economy of the Soviet type.

The Economy of Yugoslavia

Yugoslavia emerged from World War II having fought a double war: first, a long, highly organized, and increasingly successful guerrilla war against the Germans from the time of their original conquest of Yugoslavia in 1941 until their withdrawal in late 1944, and second, a desperate civil war. The victorious leader and military hero, Marshal Tito (Josip Broz), was to serve as its president and dominant figure until his death in 1980. Tito was a professed Communist, but he was not willing to be dominated by Stalin. The political break—the first within the Communist world—occurred in June 1948 and played a significant role in the postwar political situation. Our concern here is with its *economic* by-product: the emergence of a socialist market-type economy.

The economic theory of an economy in which the state owns the means of production but uses markets to allocate resources had been suggested a decade earlier by Oskar Lange and developed by Abba Lerner.[2] To put the Lange-Lerner theory in its simplest form, the business firm (owned by the state) would have a manager who was instructed to follow such rules as: "Take price as given to you and produce output up to the point at which price equals marginal cost" and "Taking wage rates as given, hire labor as long as the additional worker adds more to the

---

[2] The saying "truth is stranger than fiction" is illustrated in the story of Lange, a Polish economist, who was a professor at the University of Chicago when he wrote his celebrated essay "On the Economic Theory of Socialism" (1938). After the war, Lange returned to Communist Poland as a high official of the regime and remained there until his death in 1963. The Soviet-style economy of Poland never moved toward a Lange-type economy. Meanwhile, Yugoslavia, probably in ignorance of Lange's work, emulated the kind of economy Lange had described—and was criticized by Poland for doing so.

value of output than his wages." Whether the prices and wages that were given to the firm came from the central planners (as in Lange's theory) or from markets where households buy goods and sell factor services (as in Lerner's theory) made no difference at the *firm* level. Marketlike forces determined what resources were used and where and how they were used.

When Yugoslavia turned away from the command economy and moved toward what was called the New Economic System, it did so not because it accepted this theory but because in its break with the Soviet Union it needed all the economic success it could achieve, and it found some aspects of a controlled economy more expensive than it could afford.

The modern Yugoslav economic system evolved in two stages. The first (1952–1960) put major emphasis on decentralization and the development of a market system for the allocation of resources. The second, beginning with a series of political, economic, and constitutional reforms in 1961, put major emphasis on the self-government of industrial enterprises.

In particular, Yugoslavs sought to avoid three features of the Soviet experience: (1) the inefficiencies and resulting disasters in agricultural production; (2) micro inefficiencies in industrial production; and (3) the burden of a large planning and administrative operation for which it lacked properly trained and motivated personnel.

By 1948 the Soviet Union was already an industrial power with a well-developed educational system. Yugoslavia was not. It emerged from World War II ravaged by years of struggle, a primitive agricultural society with little industry, few trained personnel, and a low level of general education. Under these circumstances it could ill afford to waste limited resources. Its choice was either to accept Soviet technicians, planners, and economic aid (and, realistically, political domination) or to go its own way. When after 1948 it chose the latter course, it could not afford the luxury of avoidable inefficiencies.

What has emerged, often after substantial trial and error, is a reasonable approximation to a so-cialist market economy, with public ownership of most means of production, with substantially decentralized decision making through markets, but with a large role for planning and the public sector.

THE DECOLLECTIVIZATION OF AGRICULTURE

In the early postwar period, Yugoslavia attempted to follow the Soviet pattern and create state farms or collective farms that would operate efficiently for the greater glory of the state. By the early 1950s, the program had gathered more than a quarter of the arable land under centralized control. The program met increasing hostility and resistance, however, and many who had been placed on collectives were unhappy and eager to leave. The Soviets had used force and fear to create their collectives and the police power of the state to maintain them. Faced with a similar bitter prospect, Yugoslavia in 1953 abruptly reversed its stand. Not only did it stop collectivizing, it allowed farmers to leave the collectives and to resume personal ownership and operation of small farms. Today farmers can produce what they like and sell it where and when they wish. Since 1953, roughly half of the state acreage has returned to private operation, and the remaining state farms are run more nearly as cooperatives than as collectives.

The performance of Yugoslavian agriculture since the reversal in policy compares favorably with the Russian performance. It has increased its output at a rate of 3 percent per year in the last decade, and it has not been plagued by any serious crisis. Moreover, it has not had to absorb scarce planning manpower in its management, which represents a gain compared to the Soviet experience.

LABOR-MANAGED ENTERPRISES

In most nonagricultural sectors of the economy, public (state) ownership is retained, but management of the individual enterprises has been turned over to the workers, blue-collar and white-collar alike, who have virtually full authority over operations and whose pay (above guaranteed minimum wages) is determined by the net income of the enterprise.

A characteristic arrangement might be for the workers in a plant to elect a workers' council, which in turn elects a management board. This board appoints a manager who is responsible to it, but who also has a good deal of discretion. The local political party is consulted in the selection of the manager, and the manager is charged with upholding the state laws as they impinge on the operations of the firm. Any difference from a command system would be mere formality if the managers now received detailed orders from higher up, but they do not. Factors of production and goods are purchased on more or less free markets, and the firm can prosper or suffer. If it prospers, it may, at its discretion, reinvest part of its profits, and it may borrow funds from banks and other firms for expansion.

The firm is subject to various taxes on its income, but beyond that its earnings are distributed to the workers. Nominally, workers received only "profit sharing" and no wages, but the effect of a guaranteed minimum amount to each worker means that profit sharing comes into play only after minimal levels of income have been achieved.

Workers' managements appear to have several advantages for the Yugoslavian state. First, an enormous and demanding administrative burden is transferred from central planning to decentralized markets. Second, workers' morale, and their productivity, seems to have risen in response to their having a real and personal stake in their firm. Third, all sorts of incentives for efficient operation are created.

Along with these familiar advantages of a market-motivated system have come some of the familiar problems of market economies. Once the workers of a firm recognize that their income reflects the firm's profits, they may be tempted to increase those profits in any way they can. Indeed, because of the relatively small scale of most Yugoslavian industry, a potentially severe monopoly problem has arisen.

The earlier theoretical literature about the workings of a socialist market economy assumed that the firm would act as a price taker and thus approximate competitive conditions. In Yugoslavia many firms have discovered that they need not be price takers and have (where allowed) increased prices and restricted output in textbook profit maximizing fashion. In a fully market-oriented society, these monopoly profits would motivate new firms to enter the industry, and entry would continue until monopoly profits had been removed. In Yugoslavia there is a more serious problem. Profits accrue to the workers in a firm, but who is motivated to organize the firm in the first place? Sometimes the local community will do so if it has unemployed workers; more often it waits for some central official to decide that prices are rising too high and further firms should be encouraged or created.

As the last sentence suggests, unemployment has not been avoided in the Yugoslavian system. If one depends on the market mechanism to motivate resource movements, and if such movements are subject to immobilities and supply lags, pockets of unemployment may appear and persist in certain regions, industries, or occupations. Structural unemployment is discussed in Zagreb as well as in Detroit. The Yugoslavs have been no more successful in preventing regional unemployment than have others who rely on market economies.

THE SCOPE AND ROLE OF PLANNING

The Yugoslav economy is somewhat less decentralized than the foregoing description may suggest. It retains many of the major planning functions of a command economy in the form of comprehensive five-year plans.

In some ways, these plans are not very different from those developed in nonsocialist countries such as Italy, France, and (more recently) Greece. A major part of any planning operation must identify general targets for development and work out the disaggregated implications of aggregate targets in terms of requirements for different products, services, factors of production, and raw materials.

The reason these plans are more influential in the Yugoslav economy, where state ownership is common, is that more than two-thirds of all new investment is made by the state with money raised (largely) by taxation.[3] Because a rapid rate of growth and a consequent high level of investment have loomed large in Yugoslavian planning, the decisions with respect to whom to tax and where to invest have played a major role in the economy. These decisions have been made in a highly centralized way. For one example, a clear decision to give urban housing a very low priority relative to heavy industry and to tourist accommodations results in a situation of noticeably poor and dilapidated housing that not only distresses the Yugoslav people but is visible to the eye of even the casual tourist.

The postwar success of the Yugoslavian experiment is shown by its growth rates: During the period of central planning, 1947–1952, before the later reforms went into effect, GNP increased at 2.3 percent per year. During 1952–1960, growth occurred at 9.8 percent per year, and well into the 1970s it occurred at approximately 6 percent per year. Recent data have shown a slowing of Yugoslavian growth rates, particularly in manufacturing, that set in during the late 1960s and extended into the 1970s. Some economists have associated this with the adoption of capital intensive methods of production that are inappropriate to the country's overall factor supplies of plentiful labor and scarce capital. The recent growth performance and its causes are still subject to research and debate. It seems clear, however, that even allowing for some slowdown, Yugoslavia's growth rates have remained well above those of the major western industrialized countries.

Although some of this growth represents the

utilization of previously unemployed resources, and although some represents the first, easy moves toward industrialization, it is nevertheless impressive. Yugoslavia has taken a significant step from the backward, Balkan peasant world into the world of developing countries. It has done so with distinctive economic institutions that have developed pragmatically rather than in response to ideological considerations of either communism or capitalism.

Comparative Systems: A Final Word

Perhaps the most important empirical observation about different economies is that a wide variety of economic systems seem able to coexist and are successful.

No economic system seems to do everything better than any major competing system; indeed, each has its strengths and weaknesses relative to alternative systems. To talk of "better" and "worse" in this context may itself be misleading: different economic systems imply different choices between current and future consumption, between individual or collective choices, between degrees of freedom or coercion, between stability and growth.

The economic institutions of a society reflect in part its values, but they also reflect habits and traditions, experiments and inertia. These institutions change with time in given countries and vary at a given time among countries. In the variety of experience economists hope to find many clues as to which instruments best achieve which ends.

In the contemporary experience, it looks as if the command principle makes the management of certain macro policies much easier than it is in a market system, but it also appears that it is less well suited than the market to handling micro allocations. While a command system can achieve great sacrifices in the short run, the growth evidence suggests no simple conclusion,

[3] The other one-third comes from reinvested enterprise earnings.

for many countries with very different economic systems have achieved rapid growth. It is clear that markets are less personal than bureaucrats, and this makes them more acceptable to many people because they are less arbitrary and less subject to autocratic abuse.

Summary

1. Actual economies can differ from one another in a great variety of ways, and such capsule characterizations as "capitalism," "socialism," and "communism" represent simplifications of complex matters.

2. Among the important dimensions in which economies can differ from one another are (a) the pattern of ownership of goods and resources; (b) the nature of the decision process used, with a particularly important distinction concerning "command" versus "market" decision mechanisms; (c) whose values control the economy and how these values are articulated; (d) the nature of the incentive systems used; and (e) the relative concern about ends and means.

3. Central planning plays a major role in the Soviet economy. Long-term goals are given structure by a series of five-year plans, which in turn are implemented by highly detailed one-year plans. Most of the key decisions are made centrally by the various GOSPLANs, but prices are used both for internal accounting and to affect the distribution of goods and incomes.

4. The turnover tax is important in Soviet pricing. First, it is used as a weapon of distributive policy: as the size of the tax varies from commodity to commodity, the consumers of those commodities are differentially taxed. Second, in its average size the turnover tax determines the fraction of current production withdrawn from current consumption and returned to the state for reinvestment. Third, it takes reinvestment decisions out of the hands of individual industries and sectors and places them with the central authorities. The amount and pattern of investment

is set by the planners directly through GOS-BANK.

5. A comparison of relative performance between the United States and the Soviet Union reveals that the United States has higher levels of real output per capita but a much less impressive recent growth record. The Soviet Union has suffered less than the United States from unemployment but has not avoided inflationary pressures. Microeconomic inefficiencies have been numerous in the Soviet experience, and agriculture has proved to be a serious, chronic problem.

6. A major difference has been the use of force and coercion by the state. This has permitted the Soviet economy to achieve certain objectives, including extremely rapid capital formation, monetary reform, and the orderly mobility of labor from farm to city. To most Westerners, the costs in the form of coercion, loss of freedom, and the substitution of centralized for individual judgments seem to have been high. Most Russians today probably believe them to have been justified.

7. Yugoslavia is an example of a socialist market-type economy in which state ownership is combined with extensive use of markets for decision-making purposes. The Yugoslav system arose as a consequence of the political break with the Soviet Union in 1948.

8. The Yugoslavs have sought to avoid three features of the Soviet experience: (a) the inefficiencies and resulting disasters in agricultural production, (b) micro inefficiencies in industrial production, and (c) the burden of a large planning and administrative operation for which they lacked properly trained and motivated personnel.

9. The Yugoslavian economy exhibits three major differences from a Soviet-type economy: (a) the decollectivization of agriculture, (b) the decentralized management of industrial firms, and (c) the substantial managerial control given to workers. A very significant planning function remains to the Yugoslav central authorities because of the importance of the investment decisions that the state must make.

10. A wide variety of different economic systems seems able to coexist and to show successes. No economic system seems to do all things better than any major competing system; indeed, each has its strengths and weaknesses relative to alternative systems.

Topics for Review

Free-market and command economies
Alternative ownership and decision patterns
Central planning
Decentralized socialist economies

Discussion Questions

1. In an economic report to the 25th Communist Party Congress in 1976, Soviet Prime Minister Aleksei Kosygin said that the crisis of capitalism was marked by inflation and unemployment, in contrast with the Soviet Union's full employment and stable retail prices. How does the Soviet Union avoid the problems of inflation and unemployment? In doing so, does it encounter problems not faced by capitalist countries?

2. According to the mayor of Moscow, that city could never have a crisis of the kind that plagues New York and other American cities. "In my country the city government owns and operates not only schools, hospitals, and other nonprofit enterprises but also such profitable enterprises as all the restaurants, stores, movie theaters, bakeries, food-processing factories, manufacturers of consumer goods, construction companies, and trucks in the city." These activities generate 80 percent of the revenues needed to run the city. The rest of the revenue is raised by taxes collected by the central government and paid to the city. Is a socialist country uniquely able to avoid or solve the problems of its biggest cities? Compare the things the U.S. government might do to help New York meet its deficit with those done for Moscow.

3. Capital is used in the heavy industries of both the United States and the Soviet Union, and in roughly equal amounts. In what sense is the United States capitalistic and Russia socialistic? Who supplies the capital in a communist economy?

4. Russian consumers, believing they will get an inferior product for their money, tend to avoid purchasing television sets and other products produced at the end of the planning period, when factories are rushing to fulfill their output targets. By the same token, American consumers are more reluctant to purchase a car produced either at the beginning or at the end of the model year. Thus it seems that concerns about quality exist in both economies. Are these concerns generated by similar or by different factors? Discuss.

5. During World War II, the U.S. government (a) rationed steel, aluminum, and copper; (b) put price controls on most goods and services but rationed only meat, sugar, and gasoline; (c) used the draft to raise armed forces of 11 million but deferred workers in key industries; (d) purchased about half of the goods and services comprising the GNP; and (e) increased income taxes and introduced an excess profits tax.

   Would you classify the United States as a command economy at that time? Explain. Can you see reasons for each of the five measures outlined above, given the economic goals of the time?

6. How might the economies of the United States, the Soviet Union, and Yugoslavia attempt to achieve each of the following results? Which system would be likely to do it most easily?
   a. achieve full employment
   b. redistribute income from rich to poor
   c. choose the appropriate mix between tractor production and residential construction
   d. determine the relative pay of carpenters and school teachers
   e. avoid a shortage or surplus of men's shirts
   f. increase the rate of saving

7. "What the world of economics needs is an end to ideology and *isms*. If there is a best system of economic organization, it will prove its superiority in its superior ability to solve economic problems." Do you agree with this statement? Would you expect that if the world survives for another 100 years, a single form of economic system would be found superior to all others? Why or why not?

Appendixes

More on Functional Relations

Appendix to Chapter 2

The idea of relations among variables is one of the basic notions behind all science. Such relations can be expressed as functional relations.

FUNCTIONAL RELATIONS: THE GENERAL EXPRESSION OF RELATIONS AMONG VARIABLES

Consider two examples, one from a natural science and one from economics. The gravitational attraction of two bodies depends on their mass and on the distance separating them, attraction increasing with size and diminishing with distance; the amount of a commodity that people would like to buy depends on (among other things) the price of the commodity, purchases increasing as price falls. When mathematicians wish to say that one variable depends on another, they say that one variable is a function of the other. [44][1]

Thus gravitational attraction is a function of the mass of the two bodies concerned and the distance between them, and the quantity of a product demanded is a function of the price of the product.

One of the virtues of mathematics is that it permits the concise expression of ideas that would otherwise require long, drawn-out verbal statements. There are two steps in giving compact symbolic expression to functional relations. First, each variable is given a symbol. Second, a symbol is designated to express the idea of one variable's dependence on another. Thus, if G equals gravitational attraction, M equals the mass of two bodies, and d equals the distance between two bodies, we may write

$$G = f(M, d)$$

where f is read "is a function of" and means "depends

---

[1] Reference numbers in color refer to Mathematical Notes, which begin on page 930.

on." The whole equation defines a hypothesis and is read "gravitational attraction is a function of the mass of the two bodies concerned and the distance between them." The same hypothesis can be written as

$$G = G(M, d)$$

This is read in exactly the same way and means the same thing as the previous expression. Instead of using f to represent "a function of," the left-hand symbol, G, is repeated.[2]

The hypothesis about the variables desired purchases and price can be written

$$q = f(p)$$

or

$$q = q(p)$$

where q stands for the quantity people wish to purchase of some commodity and p is the price of the commodity. The expression says that the quantity of some commodity that people desire to purchase is a function of its price. The alternative way of writing this merely uses different letters to stand for the same functional relation between p and q.

FUNCTIONAL FORMS: PRECISE RELATIONS AMONG VARIABLES

The expression $Y = Y(X)$ merely states that the variables Y and X are related; it says nothing about the form that this relation takes. Usually the hypothesis to be expressed says more than that. Does Y increase as X increases? Does Y decrease as X increases? Or is the relation more complicated? Take a very simple example, where Y is the length of a board in feet, and X is the length of the same board in yards. Quite clearly, $Y = Y(X)$. Further, in this case the exact form of the function is known, for length in feet (Y) is merely three times the length in yards (X), so we may write $Y = 3X$.

This relation is a definitional one, for the length of something measured in feet is defined to be three times its length measured in yards. It is nonetheless useful to have a way of writing relationships that are definitionally true. The expression $Y = 3X$ specifies the

exact form of the relation between Y and X and provides a rule whereby, if we have the value of one, we can calculate the value of the other.

Now consider a second example: Let C stand for consumption expenditure, the total amount spent on purchasing goods and services by all American households during a year. Let Y_d stand for the total amount of income that these households had available to spend during the year. We might state the hypothesis that

$$C = f(Y_d)$$

and, even more specifically,

$$C = 0.8Y_d$$

The first expression gives the hypothesis that the total consumption expenditure of households depends on their income. The second expression says, more specifically, that total consumption expenditure is 80 percent of the total available for spending. The second equation expresses a very specific hypothesis about the relation between two observable magnitudes. There is no reason why it *must* be true; it may be consistent or inconsistent with the facts. This is a matter for testing. However, the equation is a concise statement of a particular hypothesis.

Thus the general view that there is a relation between Y and X is denoted by $Y = f(X)$, whereas any precise relation may be expressed by a particular equation such as $Y = 2X$, $Y = 4X^2$, or $Y = X + 2X^2 + 0.5X^3$.

If Y increases as X increases (e.g., $Y = 10 + 2X$), we say that Y is an *increasing function* of X, or that Y and X *vary directly* with each other. If Y decreases as X increases (e.g., $Y = 10 - 2X$), we say that Y is a *decreasing function of X* or that Y and X *vary inversely* with each other.

Y varying inversely with X merely means that Y changes in the opposite direction from X. This should not be confused with the mathematical special case called "the inverse function" where $Y = 1/X$.

ERROR TERMS IN ECONOMIC HYPOTHESES

Expressing hypotheses in the form of functions is misleading in one respect. When we say that the world behaves so that $Y = f(X)$, we do not expect that knowing X will tell us *exactly* what Y will be, but only that it will tell us what Y will be *within some margin of error*.

---

[2] Any convenient symbol may be used on the right-hand side before the parenthesis to mean "a function of." The repetition of the left-hand symbol may be convenient in reminding us of what is a function of what.

This error in predicting Y from a knowledge of X arises for two quite distinct reasons. First, there may be other variables that also affect Y. When, for example, we say that the demand for butter is a function of the price of butter, $D_b = f(p_b)$, we know that other factors will also influence this demand. A change in the price of margarine will certainly affect the demand for butter, even though the price of butter does not change. Thus we do not expect to find a perfect relation between D_b and p_b that will allow us to predict D_b exactly from a knowledge of p_b. Second, variables can never be measured exactly. Even if X is the only cause of Y, measurements will give various Ys corresponding to the same X. In the case of the demand for butter, errors of measurement might not be large. In other cases, errors might be substantial — as, for example, in the case of a relation between the total consumption expenditure of all American households and their total income. The measurements of consumption and income may be subject to quite wide margins of error, and various values of consumption associated with the same measured value of income may be observed, not because consumption is varying independently of income but because the error of measurement is varying from period to period.

When we say Y is a function of X, we appear to say Y is completely determined by X. Instead of the deter-ministic formulation

$$Y = f(X)$$

it would be more accurate to write

$$Y = f(X) + \epsilon$$

or

$$Y = f(X, \epsilon)$$

where ϵ, the Greek letter epsilon, represents an **error term.** Such a term indicates that the observed value of Y will differ from the value predicted by the functional relation between Y and X. Divergences will occur both because of observational errors and because of neglected variables. While economists always mean this, they usually do not say so.

The deterministic formulation is a simplification; an error term is really present in all assumed and observed functional relations.

This is true, by the way, not only of economics and other subjects dealing with human behavior, but of physics, chemistry, geology, and all other sciences. The old-time dichotomy between "exact" and "inexact" sciences is now abandoned; all theories and all measurements are subject to error.

Graphing Economic Magnitudes

Appendix to Chapter 3

The popular saying "The facts speak for themselves" is almost always wrong when there is a large number of facts. Theories are needed to explain how facts are linked together, and summary measures are needed to assist in sorting out what it is that facts show in relation to theories. The simplest means of providing compact summaries of a large number of observations is through the use of tables and graphs. Graphs play important roles in economics by representing geometrically both observed data and economic theories. Here both uses will be discussed.

GRAPHING ECONOMIC OBSERVATIONS

Because the surface of a piece of paper is two-dimensional, a graph may readily be used to represent pictorially the interrelation between two variables. Flip through this book and you will see dozens of examples. Figure 3A-1 shows more generally how a coordinate grid can permit the representation of any two measurable variables.

Economics is very often concerned only with the positive values of variables, and in such cases the graph is confined to the upper right-hand (or "positive") quadrant. Whenever either or both variables take on a negative value, one or more of the other quadrants must be included.

The Scatter Diagram

The scatter diagram provides a method of graphing any number of observations made on two variables. In Chapter 3 data for income and meat purchases for a large number of American households were studied. To show these data on a scatter diagram, income was measured on the horizontal axis and meat purchases on the vertical axis. Any point in the diagram represents a particular income combined with a particular

FIGURE 3A–1
A Coordinate Graph

FIGURE 3A–1
A Coordinate Graph

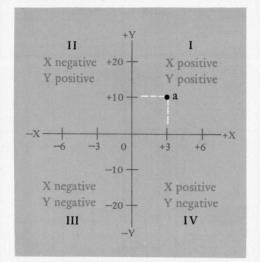

The axes divide the total space into four quadrants according to the signs of the variables. The upper right-hand quadrant is one in which both X and Y are greater than zero; it is usually called the *positive quadrant*. Point a in the figure has *coordinates* $Y = 10$ and $X = 3$ in the coordinate graph. These coordinates *define* point a.

quantity of meat purchased. Thus each household for which there are observations can be represented on the diagram by a dot, the coordinates of which indicate the household's income and the amount of beef it purchases.

The scatter diagram is useful because if there is a simple relation between the two variables, it will be apparent to the eye once the data are plotted.

The scatter diagram in Chapter 3, for example, made it apparent that more meat tends to be bought as income rises (see page 36). It also made it apparent that this relation is only approximately linear. As income rises above $10,000 a year, beef purchases seem to rise less and less with further equal increases in income. The diagram also gives some idea of the strength of the relation: If income were the only determinant of beef purchases, all of the dots would lie on a line; as it is, the points are all somewhat scattered and particular incomes are often represented by several households, each with different quantities of beef purchased. The data used in this example are **cross-sec-**

tional data. The incomes and beef purchases of different households are compared over a single period of time.

Scatter diagrams may also be drawn of a number of observations taken on two variables at successive periods of time. Thus, if one wanted to know whether there was any simple relation between personal income and personal consumption in the United States between 1950 and 1979, data would be collected for the levels of personal income and expenditure per capita in each year from 1950 to 1979, as is done in Table 3A-1. This information could be plotted on a

TABLE 3A–1
Income and Consumption, 1950–1979 (1972 dollars)

Year	Disposable personal income per capita	Personal consumption expenditures per capita
1950	$2,386	$2,229
1951	2,408	2,219
1952	2,434	2,236
1953	2,491	2,283
1954	2,476	2,284
1955	2,577	2,391
1956	2,645	2,415
1957	2,650	2,421
1958	2,636	2,406
1959	2,696	2,493
1960	2,697	2,507
1961	2,725	2,516
1962	2,796	2,589
1963	2,849	2,649
1964	3,009	2,755
1965	3,152	2,872
1966	3,274	2,982
1967	3,371	3,035
1968	3,464	3,156
1969	3,515	3,234
1970	3,619	3,265
1971	3,714	3,342
1972	3,837	3,510
1973	4,068	3,642
1974	3,981	3,586
1975	4,012	3,588
1976	4,144	3,813
1977	4,285	3,973
1978	4,449	4,121
1979	4,509	4,193

Source: Economic Report of the President, 1980

FIGURE 3A–2

A Scatter Diagram Relating Consumption and Disposable Income

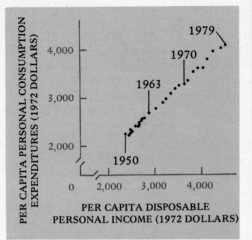

A scatter diagram shows paired values of two variables. The data of Table 3A–1 are plotted here. Each dot shows, for a particular year, the values of per capita personal consumption and per capita disposable personal income. They show a close, positive, linear relationship between the two variables.

scatter diagram with income on the X axis and consumption on the Y axis to discover any systematic relation between the two variables. The data are plotted in Figure 3A-2, and they do indeed suggest a systematic linear relation. In this exercise a scatter diagram of observations taken over successive periods of time has been used. Such data are called **time-series data,** and plotting them on a scatter diagram involves no new technique. When cross-sectional data are plotted, each point gives the values of two variables for a particular unit (say a household); when time-series data are plotted, each point tells the values of two variables for a particular year.

Time-series Graphs

Instead of studying the relation between income and consumption suggested in the previous paragraph, a study of the pattern of the changes in either one of these variables over time could be made. In Figure 3A-3 this information is shown for consumption. In the figure, time is one variable, consumption expendi-

ture the other. But time is a very special variable: the order in which successive events happen is important. The year 1965 followed 1964; they were not two independent and unrelated years. (In contrast, two randomly selected households are independent and unrelated.) For this reason it is customary to draw in the line segments connecting the successive points, as has been done in Figure 3A-3.

A chart such as this figure is called a time-series graph or, more simply, a time series. This kind of graph makes it easy to see if the variable being considered has varied in a systematic way over the years or if its behavior has been more or less erratic.

Ratio (Logarithmic) Scales

If *proportionate* rather than absolute changes in variables are important, it is more revealing to use a ratio scale rather than a natural scale. On a **natural scale** the distance between numbers is proportionate to the absolute difference between those numbers. Thus 200

FIGURE 3A–3

A Time Series of Consumption Expenditures, 1950–1979

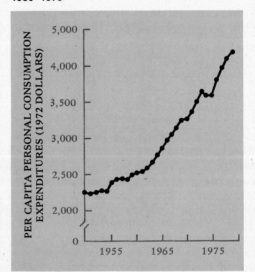

A time series plots values of a single variable in chronological order. The graph shows that, with only minor interruptions, consumption measured in 1972 dollars rose from 1950 to 1979. The data are shown in the last column of Table 3A–1.

TABLE 3A–2
Two Series

Time period	Series A	Series B
0	$10	$ 10
1	18	20
2	26	40
3	34	80
4	42	160

Series A shows constant absolute growth ($8 per period) but declining percentage growth. Series B shows constant percentage growth (100 percent per period) but rising absolute growth.

is placed halfway between 100 and 300. On a **ratio scale** the distance between numbers is proportionate to the absolute difference between their logarithms. Equal distances anywhere on a ratio scale represent equal percentage changes rather than equal absolute changes. On a ratio scale the distance between 100 and 200 is the same as the distance between 200 and 400, between 1,000 and 2,000, and between any two numbers that stand in the ratio 1:2 to each other. For obvious reasons a ratio scale is also called a **logarithmic scale.**

Table 3A-2 shows two series, one growing at a constant absolute amount of 8 units per period and the other growing at a constant rate of 100 percent per period. In Figure 3A-4 the series are plotted first on a natural scale, then on a ratio scale. The natural scale makes it easy for the eye to judge absolute variations, and the logarithmic scale makes it easy for the eye to judge proportionate variations.[1]

GRAPHING FUNCTIONS

Functions were discussed in the Appendix to Chapter 2. Simple functions can be represented in the same two-dimensional space in which data can be graphed. When this is done, we obtain a geometrical expression of the functions. Since economic theory is often expressed in terms of functions, graphing these functions

[1] Graphs with a ratio scale on one axis and a natural scale on the other are frequently encountered in economics. In the cases just illustrated there is a ratio scale on the vertical axis and a natural scale on the horizontal (or time) axis. Such graphs are often called *semi-log* graphs. In scientific work graphs with ratio scales on both axes are frequently encountered. Such graphs are often referred to as *double-log* graphs.

FIGURE 3A–4

The Difference Between Natural and Ratio Scales

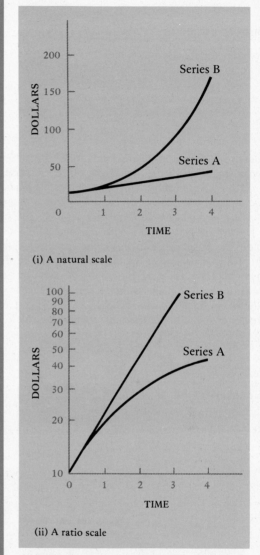

(i) A natural scale

(ii) A ratio scale

On a natural scale, equal distances represent equal amounts; on a ratio scale, equal vertical distances represent equal percentage changes. The two series in Table 3A–2 are plotted in each chart. Series A, which grows at a constant absolute amount, is a straight line on a natural scale but a downward-bending curve on a ratio scale because the same absolute growth is decreasing percentage growth. Series B, which grows at a rising absolute but a constant percentage rate, is upward bending on a natural scale but is a straight line on a ratio scale.

is a way of providing a graphical representation of the theory.

Linear Functions

Consider the functions

$$Y = 0.5X$$

$$Y = X$$

$$Y = 2X$$

These are graphed in Figure 3A-5. All of the Y functions are straight lines through the origin, because if $X = 0$ in each of the above relations, Y also becomes 0. The straight lines differ only because of their slopes; each is a special case of $Y = bX$.

The symbol Δ is used to indicate a change in a variable. Thus ΔX means the value of the change in X, and ΔY means the value of the change in Y. In the first equation, if $X = 10$, then Y is 5, and if X goes up to 16, Y goes to 8. Thus, in this exercise, $\Delta X = 6$ and $\Delta Y = 3$.

Now consider the ratio $\Delta Y / \Delta X$. In the above example it is equal to 0.5. For any change made in X in

FIGURE 3A-6
Straight Lines with Slope of + 2

Parallel straight lines have the same slope but different intercepts. These straight lines differ only in their intercepts. Each is a special case of $Y = a + 2X$.

the first equation, $\Delta Y / \Delta X$ is always 0.5. In the second it is unity, and in the third the ratio is always 2. In general, if we write $Y = bX$, then the ratio $\Delta Y / \Delta X$ is always equal to b.

This ratio defines the slope of a straight line. The greater the slope, the steeper the line. For example, the slopes of the three functions in Figure 3A-5 are 2, 1, and 0.5.

Now consider the equations

$$Y = 2X$$

$$Y = 10 + 2X$$

$$Y = -5 + 2X$$

These are graphed in Figure 3A-6. All three lines are parallel, that is, they have the same slope; they differ only in their intercepts. Each of these is a special case of $Y = a + 2X$. Apparently the addition of a (positive or negative) constant does not affect the slope of the line.

In general, the equation of a straight line may be written

$$Y = a + bX$$

where X and Y are variables while a and b are parameters that determine respectively the intercept and the slope of the line. (The intercept is the value of Y when

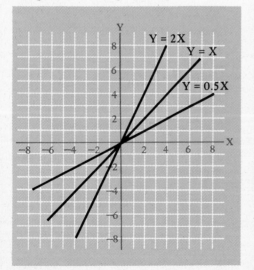

FIGURE 3A-5
Straight Lines Through the Origin

These straight lines differ only in their slopes. Each is a special case of $Y = bX$.

X is zero.) Changing a shifts the curve upward or downward parallel to itself while leaving its slope unchanged.

Each of the straight lines that has been drawn is upward sloping—it has a positive slope. A function such as $Y = 10 - 2X$, or, more generally, $Y = a - bX$, will slope downward.

Figures 3A-5 and 3A-6 provide both the numerical grids which were used to plot the functions and the equations of the lines. Functions are often represented graphically, however, primarily in order to compare their general shapes. In such a situation both the numerical grid and the precise equation are often suppressed.

Nonlinear Functions

Many of the relations encountered in economics are nonlinear. A nonlinear relation is expressed graphically by a curved line and algebraically by some expression more complex than that for a straight line.

FIGURE 3A–7
Three Rectangular Hyperbolas

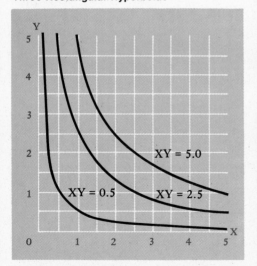

A rectangular hyperbola is an example of a nonlinear relation between two variables. Each of these hyperbolas is one member of the family $XY = a$. If a is also taken as a variable, the family of curves shows the interrelations among the three variables X, Y, and a.

FIGURE 3A–8
A Parabola

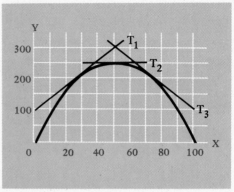

A parabola is an example of a nonlinear relation between two variables. The slope of a parabola, as with any nonlinear function, is not constant. The slope—how Y is tending to change as X changes—can be measured at any point on the function as the slope of a line that is tangent to the function at that point.

Two common examples of nonlinear relations are expressed by the equations

$$Y = \frac{a}{X}$$

$$Y = a + bX + cX^2$$

The first equation describes what is called a rectangular hyperbola. Three examples are plotted in Figure 3A-7. The second equation describes a parabola that takes on various positions and shapes depending on the signs and magnitudes of a, b, and c. One example of such a parabola is given in Figure 3A-8.

Unlike a straight line, which has a constant slope, a variable slope is the essence of a nonlinear function. The slope changes from point to point, but it may be evaluated at any point. The slope of a curve at a point is defined to be the slope of the tangent to the curve at that point. For example, in Figure 3A-8 the slope of the function at $X = 30$ is the slope of the line T_1 that *is tangent to* (just touches) the function at that point. Line T_2 gives the slope of the same function at $X = 50$ and line T_3 at $X = 70$. When the curve is rising, the slope is positive; when the curve is falling, the slope is negative. When the slope is zero (as at $X = 50$), the function is neither rising nor falling.

Functions of Three Variables

Often in economics it is desirable to represent three variables on a two-dimensional graph. Consider the function $XY = a$, where X, Y, and a are all variables. Now look at Figure 3A-7, which plots this function for three different values of a. The variables X and Y are represented on the axes. The variable a is represented by the labels on the curves. A more familiar example of this sort of representation is the contour map of a mountain, where the vertical axis represents latitude, the horizontal axis longitude, and the contour lines are labeled to represent points of equal altitude. The important characteristic of such a map is that a *three-dimensional* mountain can be shown in a two-dimensional graph. Several examples of this kind of procedure occur throughout the book. (See, for example, indifference curves in Chapter 9 and isoquants in the appendix to Chapter 13.)

Elasticity: A Formal Analysis

Appendix to Chapter 6

In Chapter 6 we defined elasticity as

$$\eta = \frac{\Delta p}{\Delta q} \times \frac{\text{average } q}{\text{average } p}$$

where the averages are over the arc of the demand curve being considered. This is called **arc elasticity**, and it measures the average responsiveness of quantity to price over an interval of the demand curve.

Most theoretical treatments use a different but related concept called **point elasticity.** This is the responsiveness of quantity to price at a particular point on the demand curve. The precise definition of point elasticity uses the concept of a derivative, which is drawn from differential calculus.

In this appendix we first study an approximation to point elasticity that uses high school algebra. Then we will replace this approximate definition with the exact definition.

Before proceeding, we should notice one further change. In the chapter text we multiplied all our calculations of demand elasticities by -1, thereby defining elasticity of demand as a positive number. In theoretical work it is more convenient to retain the concept's natural sign. Thus normal demand curves will have negative signs, and statements about "more" or "less" elastic must be understood to refer to the absolute, not the algebraic value of demand elasticity.

The following symbols will be used throughout.

$\eta \equiv$ elasticity of demand
$\eta_s \equiv$ elasticity of supply
$q \equiv$ the original quantity
$\Delta q \equiv$ the change in quantity
$p \equiv$ the original price
$\Delta p \equiv$ the change in price

POINT ELASTICITY ACCORDING TO THE APPROXIMATE DEFINITION

Point elasticity measures elasticity at some point (p,q). In the approximate definition, however, the respon-

FIGURE 6A–1
A Straight-line Demand Curve

Because *p/q* varies with Δ*q*/Δ*p* constant, the elasticity varies along this demand curve, being high at the left and low at the right.

siveness is measured over a small range starting from that point. For example, in Figure 6A-1 the elasticity at point 1 can be measured by the responsiveness of quantity demanded to a change in price that takes price and quantity from point 1 to point 2. The algebraic formula for this elasticity concept is

$$\eta = \frac{\Delta q/q}{\Delta p/p}$$

This is similar to the definition of arc elasticity used in the text except that, since elasticity is being measured at a point, the *p* and *q* corresponding to that point are used (rather than the average *p* and *q* over an arc of the curve).

Let us first try a little manipulation of the above expression. Inverting the denominator and multiplying will result in

$$\eta = \frac{\Delta q}{q} \times \frac{p}{\Delta p}$$

Since it does not matter in which order multiplication is done (i.e., $q \times \Delta p = \Delta p \times q$), the order of the two terms in the denominator may be reversed and written

$$\eta = \frac{\Delta q}{\Delta p} \times \frac{p}{q} \qquad [1]$$

Equation [1] splits elasticity into two parts: $\Delta q/\Delta p$,

the ratio of the change in price, which is related to the *slope* of the demand curve, and *p/q*, which is related to the *point* on the curve at which the measurement is made.

Figure 6A-1 shows a straight-line demand curve. To measure the elasticity at point 1, take *p* and *q* at that point and then consider a price change, say, to point 2, and measure Δ*p* and Δ*q* as indicated. The slope of the straight line joining points 1 and 2 is $\Delta p/\Delta q$. The term in equation [1] is $\Delta q/\Delta p$, which is the reciprocal of $\Delta p/\Delta q$. Therefore the first term in the elasticity formula is the reciprocal of the slope of the straight line joining the two price-quantity positions under consideration.

Although point elasticity of demand refers to a point (*p*,*q*) on the demand curve, the first term in [1] still refers to changes over an arc of the curve. This is the part of the formula that involves approximation and, as we shall see, it has some unsatisfactory results. Nonetheless some interesting results can be derived using this formula as long as we confine ourselves to straight-line demand and supply curves.

1. The elasticity of a downward-sloping straight-line demand curve varies from zero at the quantity axis to infinity (∞) at the price axis. First notice that a straight line has a constant slope, so the ratio $\Delta p/\Delta q$ is the same everywhere on the line. Therefore its reciprocal, $\Delta q/\Delta p$, must also be constant. The changes in η can now be inferred by inspecting the ratio *p/q*. Where the line cuts the quantity axis, price is zero, so the ratio *p/q* is zero; thus $\eta = 0$. Moving up the line, *p* rises and *q* falls, so the ratio *p/q* rises; thus elasticity rises. Approaching the top of the line, *q* approaches zero, so the ratio becomes very large. Thus elasticity increases without limit as the price axis is approached.

2. Where there are two straight-line demand curves of the same slope, the one farther from the origin is less elastic at each price than the one closer to the origin. Figure 6A-2 shows two parallel straight-line demand curves. Pick any price, say, *p*, and compare the elasticities of the two curves at that price. Since the curves are parallel, the ratio $\Delta q/\Delta p$ is the same on both curves. Since elasticities at the same price are being compared on both curves, *p* is the same, and the only factor left to vary is *q*. On the curve farther from the origin, quantity is larger (i.e., $q_1 > q$), and hence p/q_1 is smaller than *p/q*; thus η is smaller.

It follows from theorem 2 that parallel shifts of a straight-line demand curve lower elasticity (at each price) when the line shifts outward and raise elasticity when the line shifts inward.

FIGURE 6A–2
Two Parallel Straight-line Demand Curves

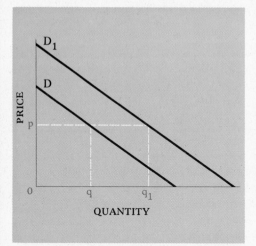

**For any given price the quantities are different
on the two curves; thus the elasticities are different
on the two parallel curves, being higher
on *D* than on *D*₁.**

FIGURE 6A–3
Two Intersecting Straight-line Demand Curves

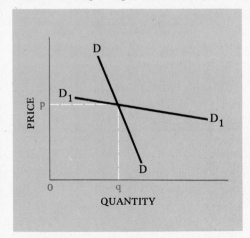

**Elasticities are different at the point of intersection
because the slopes are different,
being higher on *D* than on *D*₁.**

3. *The elasticities of two intersecting straight-line
demand curves can be compared at the point of intersection
merely by comparing slopes, the steeper
curve being the less elastic.* In Figure 6A-3 there are
two intersecting curves. At the point of intersection, p
and q are common to both curves and hence the ratio
p/q is the same. Therefore η varies only with $\Delta q/\Delta p$.
On the steeper curve, $\Delta q/\Delta p$ is smaller than on the flatter
curve, so elasticity is lower.

4. *If the slope of a straight-line demand curve
changes while the price intercept remains constant,
elasticity at any given price is unchanged.*
This is an interesting case for at least two reasons.
First, when more customers having similar tastes to
those already in the market enter the market, the
demand curve pivots outward in this way. Second,
when more firms enter a market that is shared proportionally
among all firms, each firm's demand curve
shifts inward in this way.

Many different approaches are possible. (A geometric
proof could easily be given.) The algebraic proof is
as follows. Consider two straight-line demand curves
with the same price intercept $\bar{p}$ but different slopes b^*
and b^{**}:

$$p = \bar{p} + b^*q$$
$$p = \bar{p} + b^{**}q$$

Take any common price $\hat{p}$ on both curves and solve for
the associated (different) quantities, q_1 on the first
curve and q_2 on the second:

$$\hat{p} = \bar{p} + b^*q_1 = \bar{p} + b^{**}q_2$$

$$q_2 = \frac{b^*}{b^{**}}q_1$$

The elasticity on the second curve at the common
price $\hat{p}$ is

$$\frac{\Delta q_2}{\Delta p} \times \frac{\hat{p}}{q_2}$$

Substituting $\Delta q_2/\Delta p = 1/b^{**}$ and $q_2 = (b^*/b^{**})q_1$
yields

$$\frac{1}{b^{**}} \times \frac{\hat{p}}{\left(\dfrac{b^*}{b^{**}}\right)q_1}$$

which reduces to

$$\frac{1}{b^*} \times \frac{\hat{p}}{q_1}$$

which is the elasticity of the first demand curve at $\hat{p}$.

FIGURE 6A–4

A Straight-line Supply Curve Through the Origin

At every point on the curve, p/q equals $\Delta p/\Delta q$; thus elasticity equals unity at every point.

FIGURE 6A–5

Point Elasticity of Demand Measured by the Approximate Formula

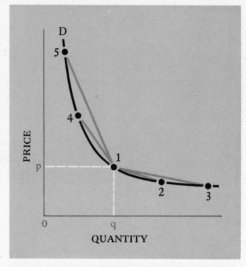

When the approximation of equation [1] is used, there are many elasticities measured from point 1. This is because the slope of the chord between 1 and every other point on the curve varies.

5. *Any straight-line supply curve through the origin has an elasticity of one.* Such a supply curve is shown in Figure 6A-4. Consider the two triangles with the sides p, q, and the S curve, and Δp, Δq, and the S curve. Clearly these are similar triangles. Therefore the ratios of their sides are equal; that is,

$$\frac{p}{q} = \frac{\Delta p}{\Delta q} \qquad [2]$$

Elasticity of supply is defined as

$$\eta_s = \frac{\Delta q}{\Delta p} \times \frac{p}{q} \qquad [3]$$

which, by substitution from [2], gives

$$\eta_s = \frac{q}{p} \times \frac{p}{q} \equiv 1 \qquad [4]$$

6. *The elasticity measured from any point* p, q, *according to equation [1] above, is in general dependent on the direction and magnitude of the change in price and quantity.* Except for a straight line (for which the slope does not change), the ratio $\Delta q/\Delta p$ will not be the same at different points on a curve. Figure 6A-5 shows a demand curve that is not a straight line. To measure the elasticity from point 1, the ratio $\Delta q/\Delta p$

—and thus η—will vary according to the size and the direction of the price change.

Theorem 6 yields a result that is very inconvenient and is avoided by use of a different definition of point elasticity.

POINT ELASTICITY ACCORDING TO THE PRECISE DEFINITION

To measure the elasticity at a point exactly, it is necessary to know the reaction of quantity to a change in price *at that point*, not over a range of the curve.

The reaction of quantity to price change at a point is called dq/dp, and this is defined to be the reciprocal of the slope of the straight line tangent to the demand curve at the point in question. In Figure 6A-6 the elasticity of demand at point 1 is the ratio p/q (as it has been in all previous measures), now multiplied by the ratio of $\Delta q/\Delta p$ measured along the straight line, T, tangent to the curve at 1, that is, by dq/dp.

Thus the exact definition of point elasticity is

Point Elasticity of Demand Measured by the Exact Formula

When the exact definition $\eta = \dfrac{dq}{dp} \times \dfrac{p}{q}$ is used, there is only one elasticity measured from point 1. This is because there is only one tangent to the demand curve at point 1.

$$\eta = \frac{dq}{dp} \times \frac{p}{q} \qquad [5]$$

The ratio dq/dp, as defined, is in fact the differential calculus concept of the *derivative* of quantity with respect to price.

This definition of point elasticity is the one normally used in economic theory. Equation [1] is mathematically only an approximation to this expression. It is obvious from Figure 6A-6 that arc elasticity will come closer to the point elasticity the smaller the price change used to calculate the arc elasticity. The $\Delta q/\Delta p$ in equation [1] is the reciprocal of the slope of the chord connecting the two points being compared. As the chord becomes shorter, its slope gets closer to that of the tangent T. (Compare the chords connecting point 1 to b' and b'' in Figure 6A-6). Thus the error in using [1] as an approximation to [5] diminishes as the size of Δp diminishes.[1]

---

[1] That the statement in the text is true over every range of price change is an accident of the way the curve in Figure 6A-6 is drawn. The fundamental theorem of differential calculus shows, however, that if the demand curve is differentiable, the text statement must be true in the neighborhood of the point in question.

The Derivation of the Demand Curve from Indifference Curves

Appendix to Chapter 9

In this appendix we use indifference theory to study the slope of the demand curve. Taking up the discussion of demand curves from where we left it at the end of Chapter 9, we derive a result that has been important in the history of economics: some demand curves may slope upward rather than downward. The conditions that could give rise to this perverse result are also studied.

DERIVATION OF DEMAND CURVES

To use indifference theory to derive the household demand curve introduced in Chapter 5, it is necessary to depart from the world of two commodities that we used for purposes of illustration in Chapter 9.

What happens to the household's demand for some commodity, say carrots, as the price of that commodity changes, *all other prices being held constant?* In Figure 9A-1 a new type of indifference map is plotted in which the quantity of carrots is represented on the horizontal axis and the value of all other goods consumed is represented on the vertical axis. The indifference curves give the rate at which the household is prepared to swap carrots for money (which allows it to buy all other goods) at each level of consumption of carrots and of other goods. Given the money price of carrots and the household's income, a budget line can be obtained showing all those combinations of carrots and other goods that the household can consume for its given level of money income and the given price of carrots. Now assume a change in the money price of carrots. By joining the points of equilibrium, we can trace a price-consumption line between carrots and all other commodities in the same way that such a line was traced for food and clothing in Figure 9-13.

Note that Figure 9A-1 is similar to Figure 9-13. The axes are labeled differently and the price-consumption line in Figure 9A-1 is crowded into the upper part of the diagram, indicating that whatever the price of carrots, the household does not spend a large part of its income on them. Every point on the price-consump-

FIGURE 9A–1
The Derivation of a Demand Curve

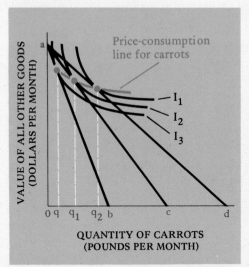

Every point on the price-consumption line corresponds to both a price of the commodity and a quantity of the commodity demanded; this is the information required for a demand curve. The household has $a of income; if it buys no carrots, it can consume $a worth of all other goods. For each price of carrots there is a single budget line. As the price of carrots falls, the budget line pivots from ab to ac to ad, and the quantity of carrots demanded rises from q to q_1 to q_2. This leads to a downward-sloping demand curve for carrots.

tion line corresponds to one price and one quantity of carrots demanded. In the figure the quantity of carrots consumed increases as their price falls. These pairs of price-quantity values can be transferred to a new figure and used to plot a conventional downward-sloping demand curve.

THE SLOPE OF THE DEMAND CURVE

We have derived from the indifference curve analysis of household behavior the information needed to plot a demand curve for a commodity—carrots in the example just considered. If plotted on a conventional price-quantity diagram, the demand curve would be downward-sloping: the lower the price of carrots, the larger the quantity purchased. We now ask if that was an accidental or a necessary result.

The possibility that a commodity might have an

upward-sloping demand curve has been discussed at length in demand theory. A good with such a demand curve is called a **Giffen good,** after the Victorian economist who is thought to have observed such a case.

We must make a careful distinction between two concepts: the so-called **income** and **substitution effects.** A fall in the price of one commodity has something of the effect of a rise in income because it makes it possible for the household to have more of all goods. In indifference theory, the income effect is removed by reducing the household's income *until it can just attain its original level of satisfaction at the new set of prices.*

This is illustrated in Figure 9A-2. The original budget line is at ab and a fall in the price of carrots takes it to aj. The original equilibrium is at E with q of carrots consumed and the final equilibrium is at E_2 with q_2 of carrots consumed. To remove the income effect, imagine reducing the household's income until it is just able to attain its original indifference curve. In other words, shift the line aj inward toward the origin, parallel to itself, until it just touches the indifference curve that passes through E. In the figure, the new budget line is a_1j_1 and the household would be in equilibrium on it at E_1, consuming q_1 of carrots and attaining the same level of satisfaction that it did at E.

It follows immediately from the convex shape of the indifference curves that more carrots are consumed at E_1 than at E. Thus the substitution effect is necessarily negative: price and quantity move in opposite directions, so a fall in the price of carrots increases the quantity consumed.

We have said that the fall in the price of carrots would cause the household to move from E to E_1 on the *same* indifference curve. But this, of course, is not what happens when the price of carrots falls in the real world. No economic dictator reduces everyone's money income to ensure that they get no increase in utility from the price change. Instead, the budget line in Figure 9A-2 pivots from ab to aj and the equilibrium goes directly from E to E_2. To get from the intermediate position E_1 to the final position E_2, we restore the household's income, keeping prices constant. This shifts the budget line outward parallel to itself from a_1j_1 to aj. As long as carrots are a normal good this increases their consumption—in the figure, the increase is from q_1 to q_2. This increase is an *income effect* since real income rises with relative prices constant.

In the actual world, when the price of carrots falls, the budget line moves directly from ab to aj and the consumption of carrots goes from q to q_2. It was seen,

FIGURE 9A–2

The Income Effect and the Substitution Effect in Indifference Theory

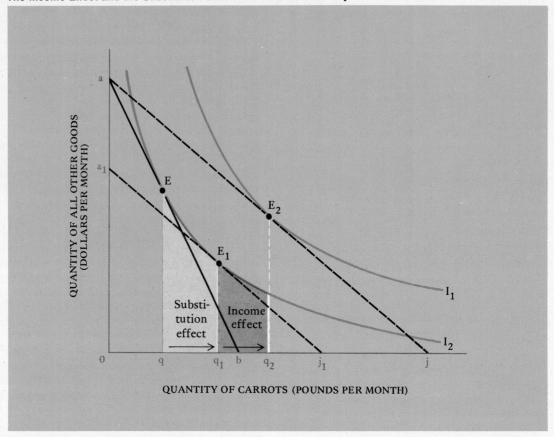

The substitution effect is defined by sliding the budget line around a fixed indifference curve; the income effect is defined by a parallel shift of the budget line. The original budget line is ab with equilibrium at E. A fall in the price of carrots takes the budget line to aj and equilibrium to E_2. The intermediate point E_1 divides the quantity change into a substitution effect qq_1 and an income effect q_1q_2. The intermediate budget line a_1j_1 just allows the household to attain its original level of satisfaction at the new prices.

however, that this movement can be broken up into a substitution effect that takes consumption from q to q_1 and an income effect that takes it from q_1 to q_2.

The change in quantity demanded for one commodity in response to a change in its price can be thought of as a composite of the income and the substitution effects. The theory predicts that the substitution effect is negative; thus a fall in the relative price of a commodity, with the level of satisfaction held constant, leads to a rise in the demand for the commodity. Unless an increase in income is expected to lead to a reduction in consumption of the commodity, because it is an inferior good, the theory gives the unambiguous prediction

that more of the commodity will be demanded when its price falls.

A normal income effect (the good is not inferior) is sufficient to ensure that the demand curve slopes downward. A decrease in price will then lead to an increase in quantity demanded because of both the substitution effect and the increase in real income.

In the case of an inferior good, however, a definite prediction about what will happen cannot be made. Quantity demanded is increased by the substitution effect but decreased by the income effect. Thus the final result depends on the relative strengths of the two op-

FIGURE 9A–3
Negative Income Effects of a Fall in Prices in Indifference Theory

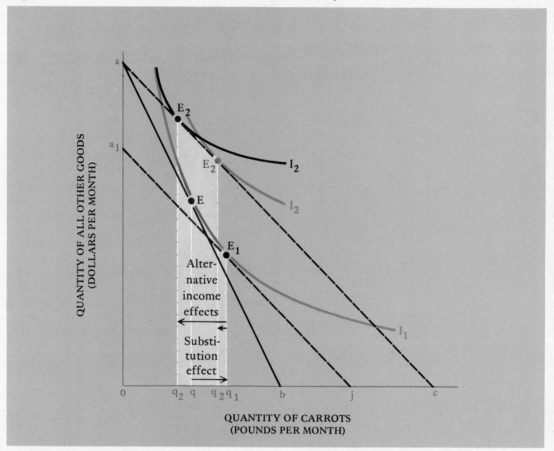

A large enough negative income effect can outweigh the substitution effect and lead to a decrease in consumption in response to a fall in price. Suppose the consumer is in equilibrium at E and the price of carrots decreases. The budget line shifts to ac. With inferior goods, the income effect is in the opposite direction from the substitution effect. Thus it is possible that the new equilibrium at E_2 will involve a smaller quantity of carrots than it did before the price decrease. Two cases are shown. The colored indifference curve I_2 leads to an increase in carrot consumption and thus a downward-sloping demand curve. The black I_2 leads to the black E_2 and an upward-sloping demand curve in which the quantity purchased decreases despite the price decrease. This is the so-called Giffen good case. Note that the two curves labeled I_2 are *alternatives;* they cannot exist simultaneously.

posing effects. Two cases of a negative income effect are shown in Figure 9A-3. The Giffen good case (which leads to an upward-sloping demand curve) occurs only when the negative income effect is large enough to outweigh the substitution effect.

We conclude from this analysis that the Giffen case of an upward-sloping demand curve for a commodity is a theoretical possibility. For this to happen the good must be inferior. But that is not enough; the change in price must have a negative income effect *strong enough* to offset the substitution effect. A combination of circumstances that makes this possible is not often expected, and therefore an upward-sloping market demand curve must be expected to be an infrequent exception to the general prediction that demand curves will slope downward.

Balance Sheets, Income Statements, and Costs of Production: Two Views

Appendix to Chapter 11

Accounting is a major branch of study in and of itself. Many students of economics will want to study accounting at some stage in their careers. It is not our intention to give a short course in accounting in this appendix, but rather to acquaint you with the kinds of summary statements that are used by both economists and accountants. **Balance sheets** report the picture of a firm *at a moment in time*. They balance in the sense that they show the assets (or valuable things) owned by the firm on one side and the claims against those assets on the other side. **Income statements** refer to a *period of time* (e.g., a year) and report in summary fashion the flows of resources through the firm in the course of its operations. Balance sheets thus measure a stock; income statements measure a flow.

In order to illustrate what balance sheets and income statements are, the same example will be treated from two points of view: that of the accountant and that of the economist.

AN EXAMPLE

Late in 1980, James Maykby, the second vice-president of the Acme Artificial Flower Corporation (at a salary of $50,000 per year), decided he would go into business for himself. He quit his job and organized the Maykby Leaf Company. He purchased suitable plant and equipment for $160,000 and acquired some raw materials and supplies. By December 31, 1980, he was in a position to start manufacturing. The funds for his enterprise were $80,000 raised as a bank loan on the factory (on which he is obligated to pay interest of $10,000 per year) and $110,000 of his own funds, which had previously been invested in common stocks. He also owed $10,000 to certain firms that had provided him with supplies.

Maykby, who is a trained accountant, drew up a statement of his company's position as of December 31, 1980 (see Table 11A-1).

Maykby showed this balance sheet to his brother-in-

TABLE 11A-1
Maykby Leaf Company, Balance Sheet, December 31, 1980

Assets		Liabilities and equity	
Cash in bank	$ 10,000	Owed to suppliers	$ 10,000
Plant and equipment	160,000	Bank loan	80,000
Raw materials and supplies	30,000	Equity	110,000
Total assets	$200,000	Total liabilities and equity	$200,000

law, an economist, and was very pleased and surprised[1] to find that he agreed that this was a fair and accurate statement of the position of the company as it prepared to start operation.

During 1981, the company had a busy year hiring factors, producing and selling goods, and so on. The following points summarize these activities of the 12-month period.

1. The firm hired labor and purchased additional raw materials in the amount of $115,000, of which it still owed $20,000 at the end of the year.[2]
2. The firm manufactured artificial leaves and flowers whose sale value was $200,000. At year's end it had sold all of these, and still had on hand $30,000 worth of raw materials.
3. The firm paid off the $10,000 owed to suppliers at the beginning of the year.
4. At the very end of 1981 the company purchased a new machine for $10,000 and paid cash for it.
5. The company paid the bank $10,000 interest on the loan.
6. Maykby paid himself $20,000 "instead of salary."

AN ACCOUNTANT'S BALANCE SHEET AND INCOME STATEMENT

Taking account of all these things and also recognizing that he had depreciation on his plant and equipment,[3] Maykby spent New Year's Day 1982 preparing three

[1] He usually finds that he and his brother-in-law disagree about everything.

[2] In this example all purchased and hired factors are treated in a single category.

[3] The tax people told him he could charge 15 percent of the cost of his equipment as depreciation during 1981, and he decided to use this amount in his own books as well. No depreciation was charged on the new machine.

financial reports (see Tables 11A-2, 11A-3, and 11A-4).

These accounts reflect the operations of the firm as described above. The bookkeeping procedure by which these various activities are made to yield both the year-end balance sheet and the income statement need not concern you at this time, but you should notice several things.

First, note that some transactions affect the balance sheet but do not enter into the current income statement. Examples of these are the purchase of a machine, which is an exchange of assets—cash for plant and equipment—and which will be entered as a cost in the income statements of some future periods as depreciation is charged; and the payment of past debts, which entered the income statements in the period in which the things purchased were used in production.[4]

Second, note that the net profit from operations increased the owner's equity, since it was not "paid out" to him. A loss would have decreased his equity.

Third, note that the income statement, covering a year's operation, provides a link between the opening balance sheet (the assets and the claims against assets at the beginning of the year) and the closing balance sheet.

Fourth, note that every change in a balance sheet between two dates can be accounted for by events that occurred during the year. (See the exhibits to the balance sheet, Table 11A–3.)

After studying these records, Maykby feels that it has been a good year. The company has money in the bank, it has shown a profit, and it was able to sell the goods it produced. He is bothered, however, by the fact that he and his wife have felt poorer than in past years. Probably the cost of living has gone up!

[4] Beginning students often have difficulty with the distinction between *cash* flows and *income* flows. If you do, analyze item by item the entries in Exhibit 1 in Table 11A–3 and in Table 11A–4, the income statement.

TABLE 11A-2

Maykby Leaf Company, Accountant's Balance Sheet, December 31, 1981

Assets		Liabilities and equity	
Cash in bank	$ 65,000	Owed to suppliers of factors	$ 20,000
(See Exhibit 1)		(See Exhibit 4)	
Plant and equipment	146,000	Bank loan	80,000
(See Exhibit 2)		Equity	141,000
Raw materials and supplies	30,000	(See Exhibit 5)	
(See Exhibit 3)		Total liabilities and equity	$241,000
Total assets	$241,000		

TABLE 11A-3

Maykby Leaf Company, Exhibits to Balance Sheet of December 31, 1981

Exhibit 1. Cash

Balance, January 1, 1981	$ 10,000	
+Deposits		
Proceeds of sales of goods	200,000	$210,000
−Payments		
Payments to suppliers (1981 bills)	10,000	
Payments for labor and additional raw materials	95,000	
Salary of Mr. Maykby	20,000	
Purchase of new machine	10,000	
Interest payment to bank	10,000	−145,000
Balance, December 31, 1981		65,000

Exhibit 2. Plant and Equipment

Balance, January 1, 1981	$160,000	
+New machine purchased	10,000	170,000
−Depreciation charged		− 24,000
Balance, December 31, 1981		146,000

Exhibit 3. Raw Materials and Supplies

On hand January 1, 1981	$ 30,000	
Purchases in 1981	115,000	145,000
Used for production during 1981		−115,000
On hand December 31, 1981		30,000

Exhibit 4. Owed to Suppliers

Balance, January 1, 1981	$ 10,000	
New purchases, 1981	115,000	125,000
Paid on old accounts	10,000	
Paid on new accounts	95,000	−105,000
Balance, December 31, 1981		$ 20,000

Exhibit 5. Equity

Original investment	$110,000
+Income earned during year	31,000
(See income statement)	
Balance, December 31, 1981	$141,000

AN ECONOMIST'S BALANCE SHEET AND INCOME STATEMENT

When Maykby's brother-in-law reviews the December 31, 1981, balance sheet and the 1981 income statement, he criticizes them in three respects. He says:

1. Maykby should have charged the company $50,000 for his services, since that is what he could have earned outside.
2. Maykby should have charged the company for the use of the $110,000 of his funds. He computes that had Maykby left these funds in the stock market he would have earned $11,000 in dividends and capital gains.
3. Maykby's depreciation figure is arbitrary. The plant and equipment purchased for $160,000 a year ago now has a *market value* of only $124,000. (Assume he is correct about this fact.)

The brother-in-law prepared three *revised* statements. (See Tables 11A–5, 11A–6, and the exhibit, Table 11A–7.)

It is not hard for Maykby to understand the difference between the accounting profit of $31,000 and the reported economist's loss of $22,000. The difference of $53,000 is made up as follows:

Extra salary	$30,000
Imputed cost of capital	11,000
Extra depreciation	12,000
	$53,000

What Maykby does *not* understand is in what sense he *lost* $22,000 during the year. In order to explain this his brother-in-law prepared the report shown in Table 11A–8.

Although Maykby spent the afternoon muttering to himself and telling his wife that his brother-in-law was not only totally lacking in any business sense but un-pleasant as well, he was observed that evening at the public library asking the librarian whether there was a good "teach-yourself" book on economics. (We do not know her answer.)

The next day, Maykby suggested to the economist that they work out together the expected economic

TABLE 11A-4
Maykby Leaf Company, Accountant's Income Statement for the Year 1981

Sales		$200,000
Costs of operation		
Hired services and		
raw materials used	$115,000	
Depreciation	24,000	
Mr. Maykby	20,000	
Interest	10,000	−169,000
Profit		$ 31,000

TABLE 11A-5
Maykby Leaf Company, Economist's Income Statement for the Year 1981.

Sales		$200,000
Cost of operations		
Hired services and		
raw materials	$115,000	
Depreciation[a]	36,000	
Interest to bank[b]	10,000	
Imputed cost of		
capital	11,000	
Services of Maykby	50,000	−222,000
Loss		$(22,000)

[a] Market value on January 1 less market value on December 31.
[b] Because the bank loan is secured by the factory, its opportunity cost seems to the economist as properly measured by the interest payment.

TABLE 11A-6
Maykby Leaf Company, Economist's Balance Sheet, December 31, 1981

Assets		Liabilities and equity	
Cash	$ 65,000	Owed to suppliers	$ 20,000
Plant and equipment	134,000	Bank loan	80,000
Raw materials, etc.	30,000	Equity (see Exhibit)	129,000
	$229,000		$229,000

profits for next year. "After all," he said, "dwelling on what might have been doesn't really help decide whether I should continue the Leaf Company next year." The economist agreed. Because of expected sales increases, they concluded, the prospects were good enough to continue for at least another year. They dipped deep in the bowl of New Year's cheer to toast those stalwart pillars of society, the independent business person and the economist.

TABLE 11A-7

Exhibit to Balance Sheet, December 31,1981: Equity of Mr. Maykby

Original investment		$110,000
New investment by Mr. Maykby		
Salary not collected	$30,000	
Return on capital not		
collected	11,000	41,000
		151,000
Less loss from operations		22,000
Equity		$129,000

TABLE 11A-8

Maykby's Situation Before and After

	(1) As second vice-president of Acme Flower Company	(2) As owner-manager of Maykby Leaf Company	Difference (2) − (1)
Salary paid	$ 50,000	$ 20,000	− $30,000
Earnings on capital, invested in stocks	11,000	0	− 11,000
Assets owned	110,000 (stocks)	129,000 (equity in Maykby	+ 19,000
Net change		Leaf Co.)	−$22,000

Summary

1. The balance sheet reports the assets and the claims against those assets at a moment in time. Balance sheets always balance because the equity of the owners is *by definition* the amount of the assets less the claims of the creditors of the company.

2. How large the "total assets" figure is depends on the valuations placed on them, and these can differ. The valuation problem arises over and over again — in the matter of inventories, patents, properties, and so forth, owned.

3. In order to avoid arbitrary, misleading, and even deliberately deceptive manipulation of accounts, accountants have developed certain normal and usual procedures of valuation. These may not in all cases reflect the economist's definition of the value of the resources.

4. The income statement reports the revenues and the costs that arise from the firm's use of inputs to produce outputs. It always covers a specified period of time. It also crucially involves the valuation problem: What is the value of the inputs used and outputs produced? Here again there are conventional accounting princi-

ples that may or may not be satisfactory for purposes of economic analysis.

5. The income statement of a firm may be important for several different purposes, and different principles of valuation may be required. For determining its income tax liability, the firm must use the valuations specified as permissible by the tax authorities. For determining its comparative performance compared to other companies, or to itself in other periods, it must use a consistent set of procedures, whatever the principle that governs them. For determining whether it has made the best use of the resources under its control, it must use valuations based on the alternative use of these resources. The economist's concept of opportunity cost is designed to do this job.

6. In general, it is the principles of valuation used and not the form of these statements that are important and decisive in interpreting the operations of the firm. Students of the firm who use reported financial data as an aid to their analysis must be prepared to examine in detail whether the principles of valuation used are appropriate for their purpose and to adjust, correct, or recompute in cases where they are not appropriate.

Isoquants: An Alternative Analysis of the Long-run Production Decision

Appendix to Chapter 13

The production function gives the relation between the factor inputs that the firm uses and the output that it obtains. In the long run the firm can choose among many different combinations of inputs that will yield it the same output. The production function and the choices open to the firm can be given a graphical representation using the concept of an isoquant.

A Single Isoquant

Table 13A-1 illustrates by hypothetical example those combinations of two inputs (labor and capital) that will each serve to produce a given quantity of output. The data from Table 13A-1 are plotted in Figure 13A-1. A smooth curve is drawn through the points to indicate that there are additional ways, not listed in the table, of producing 6 units.

This curve is called an **isoquant.** It shows the whole set of technologically efficient possibilities for producing a given level of output—6 units in this example.[1] It is analogous to the contour line on a map that shows all points of equal altitude and to an indifference curve that shows all combinations of commodities that yield an equal utility.

As we move from one point on an isoquant to another we are *substituting one factor for another* while holding output constant. If we move from point *b* to point *c*, we are substituting 1 unit of labor for 3 units of capital. The **marginal rate of substitution** measures the rate at which one factor is substituted for another with output held constant. Graphically the marginal rate of substitution is measured by the slope of the isoquant at a particular point. Table 13A-1 shows the calculation of some rates of substitution between various points of the isoquant. [45]

[1] This is an example of graphing a three-variable function in two dimensions.

TABLE 13A-1

Alternative Methods of Producing 6 Units of Output: Points on an Isoquant

Method	K	L	ΔK	ΔL	Rate of substitution ΔK/ΔL
a.	18	2			
			−6	1	−6.0
b.	12	3			
			−3	1	−3.0
c.	9	4			
			−3	2	−1.5
d.	6	6			
			−2	3	−0.67
e.	4	9			
			−1	3	−0.33
f.	3	12			
			−1	6	−0.17
g.	2	18			

An isoquant describes the firm's alternative methods for producing a given output. The table lists some of the methods indicated by a production function as being available to produce 6 units of output. The first combination uses a great deal of capital (*K*) and very little labor (*L*). Moving down the table, labor is substituted for capital in such a way as to keep output constant. Finally, at the bottom, most of the capital has been replaced by labor. The rate of substitution between the two factors is calculated in the last three columns of the table. Note that as we move down the table, the absolute value of the rate of substitution declines.

The marginal rate of substitution is related to the marginal products of the factors of production. To see how, consider an example. Assume that at the present level of inputs of labor and capital the marginal product of a unit of labor is 2 units of output while the marginal product of capital is 1 unit of output. If the firm reduces its use of capital and increases its use of labor to keep output constant, it needs to add only one-half unit of labor for one unit of capital given up. If, at another point on the isoquant with more labor and less capital, the marginal products are 2 for capital and 1 for labor, then the firm will have to add two units of labor for every unit of capital it gives up. The general proposition is:

The marginal rate of substitution is equal to the ratios of the marginal products of the two factors of production.

Isoquants satisfy two important conditions: they are downward-sloping and they are convex viewed from the origin.[2] What is the economic meaning of each of these conditions?

---

[2] The same two basic conditions are satisfied by the indifference curves of consumer theory.

FIGURE 13A–1

An Isoquant for Output of Six Units*

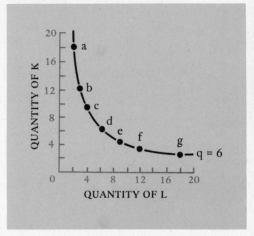

Isoquants are downward-sloping and convex. The downward slope reflects the requirement of technological efficiency. A method that uses more of one factor must use less of the other factor if it is to be technologically efficient. The convex shape of the isoquant reflects a diminishing marginal rate of substitution. Starting from point *a*, which uses relatively little labor and much capital, and moving to point *b*, 1 additional unit of labor can substitute for 6 units of capital (while holding production constant). But from *b* to *c*, 1 unit of labor substitutes for only 3 units of capital. The geometrical expression of this is that moving along the isoquant to the right, the slope of the isoquant becomes flatter.

* The lettered points are plotted from the data in Table 13A-1.

The downward slope indicates that each factor input has a positive marginal product. If the input of one factor is reduced and that of the other is held constant, output will be reduced. Thus, if one input is decreased, production can only be held constant if the other factor input is increased. The marginal rate of substitution has a negative value: Increases in one factor must be balanced by decreases in the other factor if output is to be held constant.

To understand convexity, consider what happens as the firm moves along the isoquant of Figure 13A-1 downward and to the right. Labor is being added and capital reduced so as to keep output constant. If labor is added in increments of exactly one unit, how much capital may be dispensed with each time? The key to the answer is that both factors are assumed to be subject to the law of diminishing returns. Thus the gain in output associated with each additional unit of labor added is *diminishing* while the loss of output associated with each additional unit of capital forgone is *increasing*. It therefore takes ever-smaller reductions in capital to compensate for equal increases in labor. This implies that the isoquant is convex viewed from the origin.

An Isoquant Map

The isoquant of Figure 13A-1 referred to 6 units of output. There is another isoquant for 7 units, another for 7,000 units, and a different one for every rate of output. Each isoquant refers to a specific output and connects alternative combinations of factors that are technologically efficient methods of achieving that output. If we plot a representative set of these isoquants on a single graph, we get an **isoquant map** like that in Figure 13A-2. The higher the level of output along a particular isoquant, the further away from the origin it will be.

FIGURE 13A-2
An Isoquant Map

An isoquant map shows a set of isoquants, one for each level of output. The figure shows four isoquants drawn from the production function and corresponding to 4, 6, 8, and 10 units of production.

FIGURE 13A-3
Isocost Lines

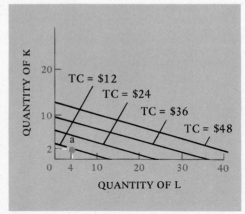

Each isocost line shows alternative factor combinations that can be purchased for a given outlay. The graph shows the four isocost lines that result when labor costs $1 a unit and capital $4 a unit and expenditure is held constant at $12, $24, $36, and $48 respectively. The line labeled *TC* = $12 represents all combinations of the two factors that the firm could buy for $12. Point *a* represents 2 units of *K* and 4 units of *L*.

Isoquants and the Conditions for Cost Minimization

Finding the efficient way of producing any output requires finding the least-cost factor combination. To find this combination when both factors are variable, factor prices need to be known. Suppose, to continue the example, that capital is priced at $4 per unit and labor at $1. In Chapter 9 a budget line was used to show the alternative combinations of goods a household could buy; here an **isocost line** is used to show alternative combinations of factors a firm can buy for a given outlay. Four different isocost lines appear in Figure 13A-3. The slope of each reflects *relative* factor prices, just as the slope of the budget line in Chapter 9 represented relative product prices. For given factor prices a series of parallel isocost lines will reflect the alternative levels of expenditure on factor purchases that are open to the firm. The higher the level of expenditure, the farther the isocost line is from the origin.

In Figure 13A-4 the isoquant and isocost maps are brought together. The economically most efficient

The Determination of the Least-cost Method of Output

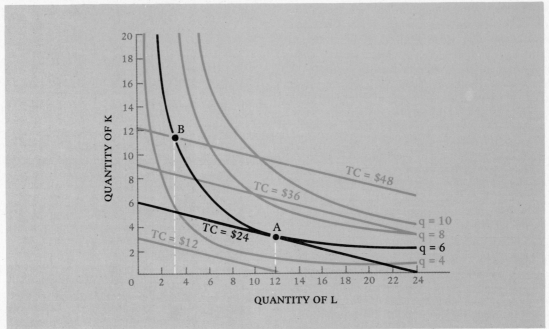

Least-cost methods are represented by points of tangency, such as A, between isoquant and isocost lines. The isoquant map of Figure 13A–2 and the isocost map of Figure 13A–3 are brought together. Consider point A. It is on the 6-unit isoquant and the $24 isocost line. Thus it is possible to achieve the output q = 6 for a total cost of $24. There are other ways to achieve this output, for example at point B, where TC = $48. Moving along the isoquant from point A in either direction increases cost. Similarly, moving along the isocost line from point A in either direction lowers output. Thus either move would raise cost per unit.

method of production must be a point on an isoquant that just touches (i.e., is tangent to) an isocost line. If the isoquant cuts the isocost line, it is possible to move along the isoquant and reach a lower level of cost. Only at a point of tangency is a movement in either direction along the isoquant a movement to a higher cost level. The lowest attainable cost of producing 6 units is $24. This cost level can be achieved only by operating at A, the point where the $24 isocost line is tangent to the 6 unit isoquant. The lowest average cost of producing 6 units is thus $24/6 = $4 per unit of output.

The least-cost position is given graphically by the tangency point between the isoquant and the isocost lines.

Notice that point A in Figure 13A-4 indicates not only the lowest level of cost for 6 units of output but also

the highest level of output for $24 of cost. Thus we find the same solution if we set out either to minimize the cost of producing 6 units of output or to maximize the output that can be obtained for $24. One problem is said to be the "dual" of the other.

The slope of the isocost line is given by the ratio of the prices of the two factors of production. The slope of the isoquant is given by the ratio of their marginal products. When the firm reaches its least-cost position, it has equated the price ratio (which is given to it by the market prices) with the ratio of the marginal products (which it can adjust by varying the proportions in which it hires the factors). In symbols,

$$\frac{MP_K}{MP_L} = \frac{p_K}{p_L}$$

This is equation [2] on page 199. We have now

derived this result by use of the isoquant analysis of the firm's decisions. **[46]**

Isoquants and the Principle of Substitution

Suppose that with technology unchanged — that is, with the isoquant map fixed — the price of one factor changes. Suppose that with the price of capital unchanged at $4 per unit, the price of labor rises from $1 to $4 per unit. Originally, the efficient factor combination of producing 6 units was 12 units of labor and 3 units of capital. It cost $24. To produce that same output in the same way would now cost $60 at the new factor prices. Figure 13A-5 shows why that is not efficient: The slope of the isocost line has changed, which makes it efficient to substitute the now relatively cheaper capital for the relatively more expensive labor.

This illustrates the principle of substitution:

Changes in relative factor prices will cause a partial replacement of factors that have become relatively more expensive by factors that have become relatively cheaper.

Of course, substitution of capital for labor cannot fully offset the effects of a rise in cost of labor, as Figure 13 A-5 (i) shows. Consider the output attainable for $24. In the figure there are two isocost lines representing $24 of outlay — at the old and new price of labor. The new isocost line for $24 lies everywhere inside the old one (except where no labor is used). The isocost line must therefore be tangent to a lower isoquant. This means that if production is to be held constant, higher costs must be accepted — but because of substitution it is not necessary to accept costs as high as would accompany an unchanged factor proportion. In the example 6 units can be produced for $48 rather than the $60 that would have been required if no change in factor proportions had been made.

This leads to the predictions that:

FIGURE 13A–5

The Effects of a Change in Factor Prices on Costs and Factor Proportions

(i) The effect on the isocost line of an increase in the price of labor

(ii) Substitution of capital for labor resulting from an increase in the price of labor

An increase in the price of labor pivots the isocost line inward and thus increases the cost of producing any output. It also changes the slope of the isocost line and thus changes the least-cost method of producing. (i) The rise in price of *L* from $1 to $4 a unit (price of *K* constant at $4) pivots the *TC* line inward. Any output previously produced for $24 will cost more at the new prices if it used any amount of labor. The new cost of producing *A* rises from $24 to $60. (ii) The steeper isocost line is tangent to the isoquant at *C*, not *A*. Costs at *C* are higher than they were before the price increase but not as high as if the factor substitution had not occurred.

A rise in the price of one factor with all other factor prices constant will (1) shift upward the cost curves of commodities that use that factor and (2) lead to a substitution of factors that are now relatively cheaper for the factor whose price has risen.

Both these predictions were stated in Chapter 13; now they have been derived formally using the isoquant technique.

Summary

1. An isoquant is a "contour line" that shows all the combinations of factors that can be used to produce a given amount of output. The slope of the isoquant is the marginal rate of substitution between the two factors of production and is equal to the ratio of their marginal products.

2. An isoquant is downward-sloping because both factors have positive marginal products. If one is diminished, the other must be increased if output is to be held constant. The isoquant is convex viewed from the origin because both factors have diminishing marginal productivity as a result of which equal reductions in one factor (rising marginal productivity) must be compensated for by larger and larger increases in the other factor (falling marginal productivity).

3. An isoquant map is a series of isoquants, each one of which gives the combinations of two factors that will produce a given level of output.

4. The firm will be minimizing its costs of producing a given level of output if it produces where an isoquant is tangent to an isocost line. This implies that the ratio of the marginal products of the factors is equal to the ratio of their prices.

5. A change in factor prices will lead all firms to substitute the factor whose relative price falls for the factor whose relative price rises. Thus the cheaper any one factor is relative to other factors, the larger is the quantity of that factor firms will desire to use.

Topics for Review

A single isoquant and an isoquant map
The marginal rate of substitution
The tangency of an isoquant and an isocost line at the least-cost position
Substitution along an isoquant as a result of a change in relative factor prices

More on Long-run Competitive Equilibrium

Appendix to Chapter 14

In Chapter 14 we showed how the forces of entry and exit in a competitive industry forced firms to an equilibrium position with zero profits. Here we consider further implications of this process and some complications of long-run equilibrium.

LONG-RUN EQUILIBRIUM IMPLIES MINIMUM ATTAINABLE COSTS

A competitive industry will not be in long-run equilibrium as long as any firm can increase its profits by changing its output or its method of production. A firm might change its profits by (a) increasing or decreasing output from an existing plant, (b) opening or closing additional identical plants, or (c) changing the size of the plants it operates.

We saw in Chapter 14 that if a firm is to be in long-run equilibrium, condition (a) implies that price, p, equals short-run marginal cost ($SRMC$) and that (b) implies that price equals short-run ATC. These two conditions were met by firms in the position of Figure 14-6(ii), page 230.

The additional condition (c) means that each existing firm must be producing at the lowest point on its long-run average cost curve. Taken together, these conditions mean that all firms in the industry should be in the position illustrated in Figure 14A-1.[1]

---

[1] We assume that all existing firms and all new entrants face identical $LRATC$ curves. This merely means that all firms face the same set of factor prices and have the same technology available to them. There are some apparent complications when different units of the same factor have different efficiencies; these complications are necessarily left to an intermediate level course. Here we may assert simply that the assumption that total costs are the same for all producing firms in a competitive industry is a consequence of the opportunity cost principle. It does not deny the fact that there are differences among firms; it says only that these differences will be included in the total costs of production because a superior factor owned by one firm could be leased or sold to another firm.

FIGURE 14A-1

The Equilibrium of a Firm When the Industry Is in Long-run Equilibrium

In long-run competitive equilibrium the firm is operating at the minimum point on its *LRATC* curve. In long-run equilibrium each firm must be: (i) maximizing short-run profits, $SRMC = p$; (ii) earning profits of zero on its existing plant, $SRATC = $ price; and (iii) unable to increase its profits by altering the size of plant. These three conditions can only be met when the firm is at the minimum point on its *LRATC* curve, E.

To see why this is so, we shall assume that it is not the case and show how firms may increase their profits. (If they can do so, they were not originally in long-run equilibrium.) Figure 14A-2 shows two firms that have $SRMC = SRATC = $ price. Each of these firms can, however, increase its profits by discarding its present plant when it wears out and building a plant of different size. The smaller firm should increase its plant size, thereby lowering its average total costs. The larger firm should build a smaller plant, thereby lowering its *ATC*. Since each firm is a price taker, each of these changes will increase the firm's profits.

The only way in which a price-taking firm can be in long-run equilibrium with respect to its size is by producing at the minimum point on its *LRATC* curve.

Each firm must be producing at minimum *LRATC* (at a point such as q^* in Figure 14A-2). Since for an in-

dustry to be in long-run equilibrium each firm must be in long-run equilibrium, it follows that in long-run competitive equilibrium all firms in the industry will be selling at a price equal to minimum *LRATC*.

In long-run equilibrium, the firm's cost is the lowest attainable cost, given the limits of known technology and factor prices.

LONG-RUN RESPONSES TO CHANGES IN DEMAND

Suppose a competitive industry is in long-run equilibrium as shown in Figure 14A-1. Now suppose that the demand for the product increases. Price will rise to equate demand with the industry's short-run supply. Each firm will expand output until its short-run marginal cost once again equals price. Each firm will earn profits as a result of the rise in price, and the profits will induce new firms to enter the industry. This shifts the short-run supply curve to the right and forces down the price. Entry continues until all firms are once again just covering average total costs. To recapitulate: The short-run effects of the rise in demand are a rise in price and output; the long-run effects are a further rise in output and a fall in price.

Now consider a fall in demand. The industry starts with firms in long-run equilibrium as shown in Figure 14A-1, and the market demand curve shifts left and price falls. There are two possible consequences.

First, the decline in demand forces price below *ATC* but leaves it above *AVC*. Firms are then in the position shown in Figure 14-6(i), page 230. The firms can cover their variable costs and earn some return on their capital, so they remain in production for as long as their existing plant and equipment lasts. But it is not worth replacing capital as it wears out. Exit will occur as old capital wears out and is not replaced. As firms exit the short-run supply curve shifts left and market price rises. This continues until the remaining firms in the industry can cover their total costs. At this point it will pay to replace capital as it wears out, and the decline in the size of the industry will be brought to a halt. In this case the adjustment may take a very long time, for the industry shrinks in size only as existing plant and equipment wears out.

The second possibility occurs when the decline in demand is so large that price is forced below the level

FIGURE 14A-2
Short-run Versus Long-run Equilibrium of a Competitive Firm

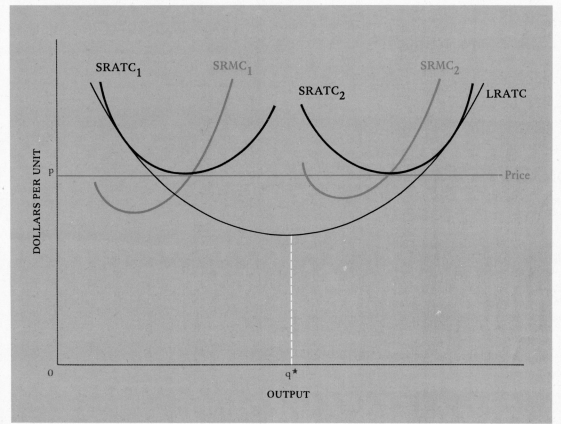

A competitive firm that is not at the minimum point on its _LRATC_ curve cannot be in long-run equilibrium. Suppose two firms have identical _LRATC_ curves but one firm has too small a plant, with costs $SRATC_1$, while the other firm has too large a plant, with costs of $SRATC_2$. Both firms are in short-run equilibrium at price $p = MC = ATC$, but neither is in long-run equilibrium. Firm 1 can increase its profits by building a larger plant (thereby moving downward to the right along its _LRATC_ curve). Firm 2 can increase its profits by building a smaller plant (thereby moving downward to the left along its _LRATC_ curve).

of AVC. In this case firms cannot even cover their variable costs, and some will shut down immediately. Thus the reduction in capital devoted to production in the industry occurs rapidly because some existing capacity is scrapped or sold for other uses. Once sufficient capital has been withdrawn so that price rises to a level that allows the remaining firms to cover their AVC, the rapid withdrawal of capital will cease. Further exit occurs more slowly, as described above.

THE LONG-RUN INDUSTRY SUPPLY CURVE

Adjustments to long-run changes in demand do not necessarily leave the _level_ of long-run costs unchanged. The response of costs to such long-run changes in required equilibrium output is shown by the **long-run industry supply curve** _(LRS)_. This curve shows the relation between equilibrium price and the output firms will be willing to supply after all desired entry or exit has occurred.

The long-run supply curve connects positions of long-run equilibrium after all demand-induced changes have occurred.

When induced changes in factor prices are considered, it is possible for *LRS* to rise, to fall, or to remain constant. Figures 14A-3, 14A-4 and 14A-5 illustrate the three possibilities.

Constant Costs (Constant *LRS*)

The long-run supply curve in Figure 14A-3 is horizontal. This indicates that the industry, given time, will adjust its size to provide whatever quantity may be demanded at a constant price. Such conditions obtain if factor prices do not change as the output of the whole industry expands or contracts. An industry with a horizontal long-run supply curve is said to be a **constant-cost industry.** While conditions of constant *LRS* may exist, such conditions are not necessary.

Increasing Long-run Costs (Increasing *LRS*)

Short-run cost curves rise because of the existence of fixed factors and the law of diminishing returns to variable factors. A different explanation must apply in the long run, since there are no fixed factors.

When an industry expands its output, it needs more inputs. The increase in demand for these inputs may bid up their prices. Such growth-induced changes in prices may be expected whenever rapid growth occurs. The reason for this is that a large industry demands large quantities of certain key materials and certain kinds of skilled labor. As the industry grows larger and larger these become increasingly scarce. Thus growth of the steel industry increases the demand of steel producers for iron ore, for coking coal, and for blast furnace operators, none of which is in perfectly elastic supply. Increasing scarcity of these inputs will tend to raise their price, and this in turn will raise the cost of producing steel.

If costs rise with increasing levels of industry output, so too must the price at which the producers are willing to supply the market. The common sense of this result is that if firms were just covering their costs

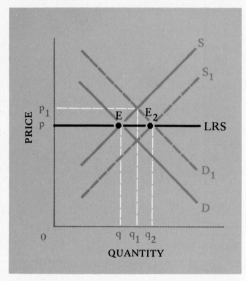

FIGURE 14A-3

A Long-run Supply Curve Under Conditions of Constant Cost

The long-run supply curve connects equilibrium points after the demand-induced shifts in the supply curve. The shift in demand from D to D_1 first raises the price to p_1 as industry output expands along the short-run supply curve. Firms will be earning profits and entry will thus occur. This induces a shift in the short-run supply curve from S to S_1. The long-run supply curve is *LRS*. In the case illustrated the increase in supply is just sufficient to keep the price at p. Thus output has been "at constant cost" in the long run.

before the increase in demand, the price they receive will have to rise enough to cover any increases in factor prices they must pay.

To see more specifically why this result occurs, remember that an increase in the price of inputs will shift the marginal cost (and average cost) curves of all firms upward. This shift in the marginal cost curves of all firms shifts the industry short-run supply curve to the left.

The effect on *LRS* of growth in industry output may be thought of for analytic purposes as occurring in two stages: an increase in the number of firms with no increase in factor prices and an induced increase in factor prices. Figure 14A-4 shows how these two stages lead to an upward-sloping *LRS* curve.

In reality the two stages occur simultaneously. In recent years the very rapid increase in the demand for electric power in the United States has led to a large increase in the number of electric generating plants. This in turn has led to sharp increases in the demand for inputs—and hence to increases in their price. This development has been particularly marked with the prices of coal and oil, the key fuels in electricity generation. Indeed, one of the aspects of what is today called the "energy crisis" is that greatly increased demands for energy have bid up the prices of basic fuels. As one commentator said, "talk of the energy crisis is mood music for higher fuel prices." Higher fuel prices in turn lead to higher prices of the things the fuel is used to make.

Rising *LRS*—**rising supply price** as it is sometimes called—is often a characteristic of sharp and rapid

growth. A competitive industry with rising long-run supply prices is often called a **rising-cost industry.**

Decreasing Long-run Costs (Decreasing *LRS*)?

So far we have suggested that the long-run supply curve may be constant or rising. Could it ever decline, thereby indicating that higher outputs were associated with lower prices in long-run equilibrium?

It is tempting to answer yes because of the opportunities of more efficient scales of operation using greater mechanization and more effective specialization of labor. But this answer would not be correct for perfectly competitive industries because each firm in long-run equilibrium must already be at the lowest point on its *LRATC* curve. If a firm could lower its costs by building a larger, more mechanized plant, it would be profitable to do so without waiting for an increase in demand. Since any single firm can sell all it wishes at the going market price, it will be profitable to expand the scale of its operations as long as its *LRATC* is falling.

There is a reason, however, why the long-run supply curve might slope downward: the expansion of an industry might lead to a fall in the prices of some of its inputs. If this occurs, the firms will find their cost curves shifting downward as they expand their outputs.

As an illustration of how the expansion of one industry could cause the prices of some of its inputs to fall, consider the early stages of the growth of the automobile industry. As the output of automobiles increased, the industry's demand for tires grew greatly. This, as suggested earlier, would have increased the demand for rubber and tended to raise its price, but it also provided the opportunity for Goodyear, Firestone, and other tire manufacturers to build large modern plants and reap the benefits of increasing returns in tire production. At first these economies were large enough to offset any factor price increases, and tire prices charged to manufacturers of automobiles fell. Thus automobile costs fell because of lower prices of an important input.

To see the effect of a fall in input prices caused by the expansion of an industry, suppose that the demand for the industry's product increases. Price and profits will rise and new entry will occur as a result. But when expansion of the industry has gone far enough to bring price back to its initial level, cost curves will be lower

FIGURE 14A-4

A Rising Long-run Supply Curve

If growth in industry size increases factor prices, the *LRS* will be upward-sloping. Suppose an industry is in equilibrium at *E*. Then demand increases from *D* to D_1. In the short run price will rise to p_1. In the long run this increases the number of firms, thereby shifting the supply curve from *S* to S_1 (as shown by the black arrow). This is the supply curve that would pertain with an expanded number of firms if input prices did not change. But the increase in industry production bids up the prices of factors used, thereby shifting the supply curve leftward from S_1 to S_2 (as shown by the colored arrow). Equilibrium E_2 is at price p_2. Price has risen from p to p_2 because firms must recover the costs imposed by the higher input prices.

than they were initially because of the fall in input prices. Firms will thus still be earning profits. A further expansion will then occur until price falls to the level of the minimum points on each firm's new, lower *LRATC* curve. (This case is illustrated in Figure 14A-5.) An industry that has a declining long-run supply curve is often called a **falling-cost industry.**

THE EXISTENCE OF LONG-RUN COMPETITIVE EQUILIBRIUM

The greatest limitation on the usefulness of the model of perfect competition is that it may not be a suitable yardstick for evaluating real-world markets because it may be that perfect competition cannot exist in some circumstances that commonly occur in the real world.

The Problem Caused by Declining Costs

A necessary condition for a long-run competitive equilibrium to exist is that any economies of scale that are available to a firm should be exhausted at a level of output that is small relative to the whole industry's output. We have seen that a competitive firm will never be in equilibrium on the falling part of its *LRATC* — if price is given and costs can be reduced by expanding scale, profits can also be increased by doing so. Thus firms will grow in size at least until all scale economies are exhausted. Provided the output that yields the minimum *LRATC* for each firm is small relative to the industry's total output, there will be a larger number of firms in the industry and the industry will remain competitive. If, however, reaching the minimum *LRATC* makes firms so large that they have significant market power, they will cease to be price takers and perfect competition will cease to exist.

In an industry with declining costs, the market may be too small relative to technology to be compatible with perfect competition. Indeed, if scale economies exist over such a large range that one firm's *LRATC* would still be falling if it served the entire market, a single firm may come to monopolize the market. This is what the classical economists called the case of *natural* monopoly; it is considered in Chapter 18.

The Problem of Constant Costs

Constant long-run costs also create problems for the competitive theory. Only if the firm's *LRATC* curve is U-shaped will there be a determinate size of the firm in a competitive industry. To see why, assume instead that *LRATC* falls to a minimum at some level of output and then remains constant for all larger outputs. All firms would have to be at least the minimum size, but they could be just that size or much larger since price would equal *LRATC* for any output above the minimum efficient size. In other words, there would then be no unique size for the firm. Are there reasons to believe the curve may not be U-shaped?

U-shaped plant curves. There are very good reasons why the *LRATC* curve for a single-plant firm may be expected to be U-shaped. There is a great deal in modern technology that results in lower average costs for large, automated factories compared with smaller factories in which a few workers use relatively unsophisticated capital equipment. As a single plant becomes too large, however, costs may rise because of the sheer difficulty of planning for, and controlling the behavior of, a vast integrated operation. Thus we have no problem accounting for a U-shaped cost curve for the *plant.*

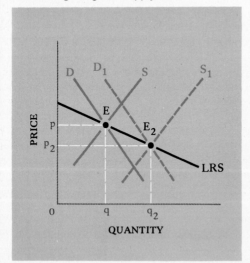

FIGURE 14A-5

A Declining Long-run Supply Curve

If growth in industry size reduces factor prices, the *LRS* will be downward-sloping. From an original equilibrium at *E*, an increase in demand to D_1 leads to an increase in supply to S_1 and a new equilibrium at E_2. Price p_2 is below the original price *p* because lower factor prices allow firms to cover their total costs at the lower price.

U-shaped firm cost curve. What of the U-shaped cost curve for the *firm?* A declining portion will occur for the same reason that the *LRATC* for one plant declines when the firm is so small that it operates only one plant. Now, however, let the firm be operating one plant at the output where its *LRATC* is a minimum. Call that output q^*. What if the firm decides to double its output to $2q^*$? If it tries to build a vast plant with twice the output of the optimal size plant, the firm's average total cost of production may rise (because the vast plant has higher costs than a plant of the optimal size). But the firm has the option of *replicating* its first plant in a physically separate location. If the firm obtains a second parcel of land, builds an identical second plant, staffs it identically, and allows its production to be managed independently, there seems no reason why the second plant's minimum *LRATC* should be different from that of the first plant. *Because the firm can replicate plants and have them managed independently, there seems no reason why any firm faced with constant factor prices should not face constant LRATCs at least for multiples of the output for which one plant achieves the lowest plant LRATC.*

In the modern theory of perfect competition a U-shaped *firm* cost curve is merely *assumed*. Without it —although a competitive equilibrium may exist for an arbitrary number of firms—there is nothing to determine the equilibrium size of the firm and hence the number of firms in the industry. The basic point is that for perfect competition to persist, there must be something that stops firms, not just plants, from increasing in size indefinitely.

Development of the Theory of Monopolistic Competition

Appendix to Chapter 16

At the beginning of this century economists used mainly the two polar models of perfect competition and monopoly. During the period between the two world wars, however, economists became increasingly dissatisfied with them. As is so often the case when there is a scientific crisis, the same breakthrough was made by more than one person. In this case, basically the same theory was developed by the American economist Edward Chamberlin and the English economist Joan Robinson.

The theory of monopolistic competition recognized that manufacturing firms typically sell differentiated products. Indeed, an impressive array of differentiated products, no one precisely the same as another, greets the shopper on any shelf of the supermarket or in any department of a large department store. Product differentiation is a fact of life. It means that every firm has some control over its price and that the firm cannot sell an unlimited amount at the going price. The firm faces a downward-sloping demand curve, not a perfectly elastic one. This is the monopolistic part of monopolistic competition.

Both Chamberlin and Robinson chose mainly to analyze a market that had freedom of entry and that contained a large group of sellers rather than a small group. This is the competition part of monopolistic competition. Indeed, they maintained all the assumptions of perfect competition except the one that all firms sell a homogeneous product. In other words, they let otherwise perfectly competitive firms sell a slightly differentiated product. And this little change had big consequences; it produced what came to be called the monopolistic competition revolution.[1]

---

[1] Chamberlin devoted some space to product differentiation in markets with a few firms and to both free and blockaded entry. Yet the main thrust of the monopolistic competition revolution was in the direction of the large-group case. In the words of Marc Blaug, the historian of economic thought from the University of London, "the 12 pages in *The Theory of Monopolistic Competition* on 'mutual interdependence recognized' constituted a then original contribution to the theory of oligopoly, but this was not the core of Chamberlin's book."

THE THEORY

Assumptions

Consider an industry in which there is a large number of producers and freedom of entry and exit but in which each producer sells a product that is somewhat differentiated from that sold by its competitors. There might, for example, be a large number of competing firms selling soft drinks. Each drink differs in physical composition, has different packaging, and (as advertisers say) has a different "brand image" from that of its competitors.

Product differentiation means that each firm does not face a perfectly elastic demand curve for its product because some people will prefer it to other products even though it is somewhat more expensive. If the firm raises its price slightly, it will lose some but not all of its business to its competitors. As its price is raised more and more above the prices of similar products, the firm can expect fewer and fewer customers to persist in buying its brand. However, if its price is lowered below that charged by competitors, the firm can expect to attract customers — but not everyone will be attracted by a small price differential. Thus the firm will be faced with a downward-sloping but quite elastic demand curve for its product. Generally, the less differentiated the product is from its competitors, the more elastic this curve will be. (If there is no differentiation, the demand curve will be perfectly elastic because the smallest increase in price above those of competitors will lose *all* of the firm's customers, while the smallest decrease in price below those of competitors will attract *all* of the competitors' customers. We are then back at perfect competition.)

Equilibrium of the Firm

The demand and cost curves for a firm in monopolistic competition are shown in Figure 16A-1. The demand curve is downward-sloping but relatively flat for reasons discussed above. The short-run equilibrium is like that of a monopolist. The firm is not a passive price taker; it will juggle price and quantity until profits are maximized where $MR = MC$.

Equilibrium of the Industry

What about the long-run equilibrium of the industry? The firm shown in Figure 16A-1 is earning profits above opportunity costs. Therefore there will be an in-

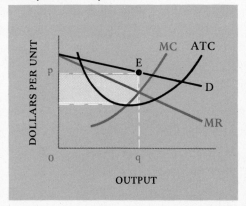

FIGURE 16A-1

The Short-run Equilibrium of a Firm in Monopolistic Competition

Short-run equilibrium of a monopolistically competitive firm is the same as for a monopolist. Short-run equilibrium occurs at output q where $MR = MC$. Profits may exist; in this example they are shown by the shaded area.

centive for new firms to enter the industry. As more firms enter, the total demand for the product must be shared among the larger number of firms, so each can expect to have a smaller share of the market. At any given price, each firm can expect to sell less than it could before the influx of new firms. Here Chamberlin uses a critical "symmetry" assumption, that the entry of one new firm will shift the demand curve for each of the firms already in the industry by the same (small) amount to the left. This movement will continue as long as there are profits; profits provide an attraction for new firms to enter, and the industry will continue to expand.

As the firm's demand curve shifts leftward, the profits diminish and finally a position of equilibrium is reached where $MR = MC$ but profits are zero. This is shown in Figure 16A-2.

A zero-profit equilibrium is possible under conditions of monopolistic competition, in spite of the fact that the individual firm is faced with a downward-sloping demand curve. Each firm is forced into a position in which it has *excess capacity*. That is, it is producing a lower quantity than the capacity level. The firm in Figure 16A-2 could expand its output and reduce average costs, but it does not make use of this productive capacity because to do so would be to reduce average revenue even more than average costs. The

FIGURE 16A-2

The Long-run Equilibrium of a Monopolistically Competitive Firm

In the long run a monopolistically competitive industry has zero profits and excess capacity. Starting from the equilibrium shown in Figure 16A-1, entry of new firms shifts the firm's demand curve to the left and eliminates profits. Point E, where demand is tangent to ATC, represents long-run equilibrium. Price is p and quantity is q. Price is greater and quantity is less than the purely competitive equilibrium price and quantity (p_1 and q_1). At equilibrium, the monopolistically competitive firm has excess capacity of qq_1.

reason for this is that it would have to lower its price to sell the extra output, and the resulting loss of revenue would more than offset the lower cost of production.

PREDICTIONS

The theory of monopolistic competition leads to several major predictions that differ from those of the theory of perfect competition. The first of these predictions has already been developed.

The zero-profit equilibrium of a monopolistically competitive firm occurs at an output less than the one at which average total cost is a minimum.

This prediction is known as the *excess capacity theorem*. It is an implication of the assumptions of downward-sloping demand curves and free entry. To recapitulate: Free entry pushes firms to the point at which the demand curve is tangent to the average total

cost curve. The demand curve slopes downward because buyers are supposed to think in such terms as, "I *prefer* Del Monte peaches"; "I *trust* Mr. Green, even if he is a little more expensive"; and "Isn't that the brand Joe DiMaggio uses?" But if the demand curve slopes downward, it must be tangent to the average total cost in its declining portion.

Two further predictions about prices are closely related to the excess capacity theorem and are also illustrated in Figure 16A-2.

Under monopolistic competition equilibrium price will be greater than marginal cost and greater than the level of minimum ATC. [47]

If the cost curves are the same under monopolistic and perfect competition, equilibrium price will be greater than under perfect competition. Monopolistic competition violates an optimality condition of perfect competition because price exceeds marginal cost. Firms also have unused capacity and do not produce at the lowest point on their *ATC* curves. We have noted in the text, however, that this is not necessarily a waste since producing less of each product, which raises costs, allows more products to be produced, which raises consumers' satisfactions.

A further prediction is that firms in monopolistically competitive industries will offer consumers a wider variety of brands, styles, and perhaps qualities to choose from than will firms in perfect competition. This is the other side of the coin of product differentiation, and it is one whose importance is easily overlooked, for wider choice is itself a benefit.

Monopolistic competition produces a wider range of products but less cheaply than perfect competition.

Economists have often assumed that product differentiation is not worth it, that consumers would be better off with single brands and somewhat lower prices. But this is a decision for individuals to make for themselves, not for economists to make for them.

Another prediction of the theory is this:

It will usually pay the monopolistically competitive firm to engage in nonprice competition of a kind that it would not pay to use in perfect competition.

To see that this is an implication of the theory, recall that a firm in perfect competition can sell as much as it wants at the going price and that it regards itself as a price taker. Therefore there is no need for the firm to spend money in order to increase the amount it can sell. But, in monopolistic competition, expenditures on product differentiation, product quality, and advertising *can* alter the firm's demand curve. Expenditures on advertising and other forms of nonprice competition may thus increase short-run profits.

MODERN DEVELOPMENTS

A major theoretical criticism of the large-group case began with Nicholas Kaldor but was fully articulated only with the work by Kelvin Lancaster on the new theory of demand.

Differentiated products have several characteristics, and each product can be thought of as being located in "characteristic space." This can be represented by a graph in which amounts of one characteristic are measured on each axis. A new product must occupy some point in characteristic space—that is, the product must have quantities of each characteristic. Thus it will have some closely competing products (those whose characteristics are very similar), more less close competitors, and even more further distant competitors. Consequently the new entrant will not affect the demand curves for all the industry's products to the same degree. Closely similar products will be affected a lot, less similar products less so, and so on.

A similar argument applies to geographic differentiation. A city may have 200 drugstores that are only slightly differentiated from each other in all nongeographic characteristics. But each has a specific location and thus a different level of convenience to each buyer. When a new store enters the drugstore industry at Fifth and Main, its arrival will have a major impact on the demand curves facing stores at the corners of Fourth and Main and Sixth and Main. It will have a smaller effect on stores six blocks away and virtually no effect on drugstores on the other side of town.

For these reasons the Chamberlin large-group case, where each product or store is equally in competition with every other product or store, seems hard to justify empirically. A model in which the many firms in an industry are in intense competition with only a rela-

tively few close neighbors seems easier to justify in practice.

The above arguments would hold if each store or product were owned by a separate firm. Empirically, a further shortcoming of the large group case (as observed in Chapter 16) is that a large number of differentiated *products* is much more common than a large number of differentiated *firms*.

Consequently, the main thrust of the development of the modern theory of monopolistically competitive product differentiation has been in the small-group case: a small number of oligopolistic firms compete, each selling its own range of differentiated products.

The modern theory even begins to suggest its own form of the excess capacity theorem: that firms may sometimes create more capital than they need for their own production—as a barrier to entry of new firms. There is a difference, however. In the older theory firms were forced into excess capacity by the impersonal market forces of entry; in the new theory existing firms may consciously create excess capacity as a barrier to entry. This proposition, still a subject of controversy, takes us to the very frontier of current research.

Looking back, we see that the original theory of monopolistic competition contributed at least two important things to the development of economics. At the time that it was first developed, perfect competition was under attack for the lack of realism of its assumptions. The theory of monopolistic competition recognized the facts of product differentiation—the ability of firms to influence prices, and the presence of advertising. The incorporation of these factors into a new theory encouraged economists to consider the question of their effects on the operation of the price system.

A second major contribution of the theory is that many economists have been profoundly influenced by it. It rekindled economists' interest in such important things as how and when firms took each other's reactions into account, what made for easy or restricted entry, and the significance to competition of different products that were roughly similar to one another.

The Derivation of the Demand for Factors

Appendix to Chapter 20

We have said that factor demand is a derived demand. Precisely how is the demand for the factor derived from the demand for the product?

In Chapter 20 we saw that all profit-maximizing firms will hire units of the variable factor up to the point at which the marginal cost of the factor equals the marginal revenue produced by the factor. For a firm that is a price taker in factor markets, this means that it hires a factor up to the point at which the factor's price equals its marginal revenue product.

The Demand Curve for a Profit-maximizing Firm

Consider a single firm with only one variable factor, labor, and one fixed factor, capital. Assume that the average and marginal revenue products of the labor are those shown in Figure 20A-1. The firm wishes to hire the quantity of labor that will maximize its profits.

The demand curve for a factor is the downward-sloping portion of the marginal revenue product curve where it is below the average revenue product curve.

To see why this statement is correct, let us ask a number of questions.

Why do points on the downward-sloping portion of MRP belong on the demand curve? Let us first see why points such as a and b in the figure are on the demand curve. If the wage rate (the price of the variable factor) is w_2, the profit-maximizing firm will hire the factor up to the point where $w = MRP$, that is, up to q_3. This is point a. If the wage rate is w_1, the firm will hire up to q_4. This is point b. Points a and b are thus on the firm's demand curve for the factor.

What is the maximum wage rate the firm will pay? What is the *maximum* wage rate at which the firm will still hire workers? We saw in Chapter 14

FIGURE 20A-1
The Relation of the Demand for a Factor and *MRP*

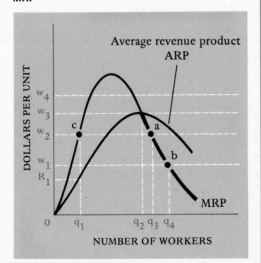

The derived demand curve for a factor is the downward-sloping portion of *MRP* below *ARP*. The heavy black portion of *MRP* is the firm's demand curve for the factor.

that it will never pay to produce a product when its price is below the level of average variable cost. We also saw (see page 194) that where average product is a maximum, average variable cost is a minimum. For any wage rate above w_3 — such as w_4 — the average revenue generated by a unit of labor (shown by *ARP*) would be less than the variable cost of the unit of labor (its wage rate). For such a wage rate it does not pay the firm to hire any workers. In other words w_3, where average revenue product is a maximum, is the highest factor price a firm could pay and still cover variable costs.

Why is the downward-sloping, not the upward-sloping, portion of MRP the demand curve? Consider the wage rate w_2. Here $w = MRP$ at both q_1 (point c) and q_3 (point a). We have already seen that point a is on the demand curve; what about point c? For every unit of labor hired up to q_1, *MRP* is less than the wage rate. In other words, each unit of labor is contributing

less to revenue than to cost. Thus a profit-maximizing firm would be better off hiring zero units than q_1 units. For every unit of labor from q_1 to q_3, *MRP* exceeds the wage rate. Thus, if a firm were hiring q_1 units, it would find each additional unit beyond q_1 (up to q_3) worth hiring. Point c (where *MRP* is rising when it equals the wage rate) is a point of *minimum* profit, not maximum profit. **[48]** A firm at point c would improve its profitability by moving in either direction, to hiring zero workers or to hiring q_3 workers. (We already know that q_3 is better than zero because at that quantity *ARP* is greater than the wage rate.)

Only points where *MRP* cuts the wage rate from above, that is, where *MRP* is downward-sloping, are possible profit-maximizing quantities.

Will There Be a Downward-sloping Portion of *MRP*?

Having shown that only downward-sloping portions of *MRP* are relevant to the demand curve for the factor, we may ask whether we have any reason to believe *MRP* will slope downward. The presence of diminishing returns is sufficient to assure this result, as can be easily shown. Marginal revenue product depends on two things: (1) the physical increase in output that an additional unit of the variable factor makes possible, multiplied by (2) the increase in revenue derived from that extra output. The first of these is called the **marginal physical product** (*MPP*); the second is the by now familiar concept of marginal revenue:

$$MRP = MPP \times MR$$

The hypothesis of diminishing marginal returns was introduced in Chapter 12. This hypothesis says that *MPP* has a declining section over some range of output. If marginal revenue is constant (as it is in perfect competition), *MRP* will have the same shape as *MPP* and must also decline.

Marginal revenue, however, may not be constant. If *MR* declines as output increases (as it does in monopoly and in any other situation in which the firm's demand curve declines), *MRP* must decline even more sharply. The hypothesis of diminishing marginal productivity thus implies diminishing *MRP* and a downward-sloping demand curve for the factor.

The Permanent-income Hypothesis and the Life-cycle Hypothesis

Appendix A to Chapter 31

In the Keynesian theory of the consumption function, current consumption expenditure is related to current income—either current disposable income or current national income. Recent attempts to reconcile the apparently conflicting empirical data on short-term and long-term consumption behavior have produced a series of theories that relate consumption to some longer-term concept of income than the income that the household is currently earning.

The two most influential theories of this type are the **permanent-income hypothesis (PIH)**, developed by Professor Friedman, and the **life-cycle hypothesis (LCH)**, developed by Professors Modigliani and Ando and the late Professor Brumberg. Although there are many significant differences between these theories, their similarities are more important than their differences, and they may be looked at together when studying their major characteristics. In doing this it is important to ask: What variables do these theories seek to explain? What assumptions do the theories make? What are the major implications of these assumptions? How do the theories reconcile the apparently conflicting empirical evidence? And what implications do they have for the overall behavior of the economy?

VARIABLES

Three important variables need to be considered: consumption, saving, and income. Keynesian-type theories seek to explain the amounts that households spend on purchasing goods and services for consumption. This concept is called *consumption expenditure*. Permanent-income theories seek to explain the actual flows of consumption of the services that are provided by the commodities that households buy. This concept is called *actual consumption*.[1] With services and non-durable goods, expenditure and actual consumption occur more or less at the same time and the distinction between the two concepts is not important. The consumption of a haircut, for example, occurs at the time it is purchased, and an orange or a package of corn flakes is consumed very soon after it is purchased. Thus, if we knew purchases of such goods and services at some time, say last year, we would also know last year's consumption of those goods and services. But this is not the case with durable consumer goods. A screwdriver is purchased at one point in time, but it yields up its services over a long time, possibly as long as the purchaser's lifetime. The same is true of a house and a watch and, over a shorter period of time, of a car and a dress. For such products, if we know purchases last year, we do not necessarily know last year's consumption of the services that the products yielded.

Thus one important characteristic of durable goods is that *expenditure* to purchase them is not necessarily synchronized with consumption of the stream of services that the goods provide. If in 1970 Mr. Smith buys a car for $4,000, runs it for six years, and then discards it as worn out, his expenditure on automobiles is $4,000 in 1970 and zero for the next five years. His consumption of the services of automobiles, however, is spread out at an average annual rate of $666 for six years. If everyone followed Mr. Smith's example by buying a new car in 1970 and replacing it in 1976, the automobile industry would undergo wild booms in 1970 and 1976 with five intervening years of slump even though the actual consumption of automobiles would be spread more or less evenly over time. This example is extreme, but it illustrates the possibilities, where consumers' durables are concerned, of quite different time paths of *consumption expenditure,* which is the subject of Keynesian theories of the consumption function, and *actual consumption,* which is the subject of permanent-income type theories.

Now consider saving. The change in emphasis from consumption expenditure to actual consumption implies a change in the definition of saving. Saving is no longer income minus consumption expenditure; it is now income minus the value of actual consumption. When Mr. Smith spent $4,000 on his car in 1970 but used only $666 worth of its services in that year, he was actually consuming $666 and saving $3,334. The purchase of a consumers' durable is thus counted as saving and only the value of its services actually consumed is counted as consumption.

So much for consumption and saving. The third important variable in this type of theory is the income variable. Instead of using current income, the theories use a concept of long-term income. The precise definition varies from one theory to another, but basically it is related to the household's expected income stream over a fairly long planning period. In the LCH it is the income that the household expects to earn over its lifetime.[2]

Every household is assumed to have a view of its expected lifetime earnings. This is not as unreasonable as it might seem. Students training to be doctors have a very different view of expected lifetime income than those training to become high school teachers. Both expected income streams—for a doctor and for a high school teacher—will be very different from that expected by an assembly-line worker or a professional athlete. One possible lifetime income stream is illustrated in Figure 31A-1.

The household's expected lifetime income is then converted into a single figure for *annual* **permanent income.** In the life-cycle hypothesis this permanent income is the maximum amount the household could spend on consumption each year without accumulating debts *that are passed on to future generations.* If a household were to consume a constant amount equal to its permanent income each year, it would add to its debts in years when current income was less than permanent income and reduce its debt or increase its assets in years when its current income exceeded its permanent income; however, over its lifetime it would just break even, leaving neither accumulated assets nor debts to its heirs. If the interest rate were zero, permanent income would be just the sum of all expected incomes divided by the number of expected

---

[1] Because Keynes' followers did not always distinguish carefully between the concepts of consumption expenditure and actual consumption, the word "consumption" is often used in both contexts. We follow this normal practice, but where there is any possible ambiguity in the term we will refer to "consumption expenditure" and "actual consumption."

[2] In the PIH the household has an infinite time horizon and the relevant permanent-income concept is the amount the household could consume forever without increasing or decreasing its present stock of wealth.

FIGURE 31A-1
Current Income and Permanent Income

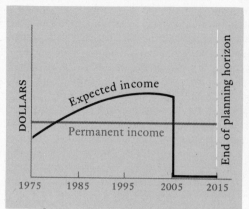

Expected current income may vary greatly over a lifetime, but expected permanent income is defined to be the constant annual equivalent. The graph shows a hypothetical expected income stream from work for a household whose planning horizon was 40 years from 1975. The current income rises to a peak, then falls slowly for a while, and finally falls sharply on retirement. The corresponding permanent income is the amount the household could consume at a steady rate over its lifetime by borrowing early against future earnings (as do most newly married couples), then repaying past debts, and finally saving for retirement when income is at its peak without either incurring debt or accumulating new wealth to be passed on to future generations.

years of life. With a positive interest rate, permanent income will diverge somewhat from this amount because of the costs of borrowing and the extra income that can be earned by investing savings.

ASSUMPTIONS

The basic assumption of this type of theory, whether PIH or LCH, is that the household's actual consumption is related to its permanent rather than to its current income. Two households that have the same permanent income (and are similar in other relevant characteristics) will have the same consumption patterns even though their current incomes behave very differently.

IMPLICATIONS

The major implication of these theories is that changes in a household's current income will affect its actual consumption only so far as they affect its permanent income. Consider two income changes that could occur to a household with a permanent income of $10,000 per year and an expected lifetime of 30 more years. In the first, suppose the household receives an unexpected extra income of $2,000 *for this year only.* The increase in the household's permanent income is thus very small. If the rate of interest were zero, the household could consume an extra $66.66 per year for the rest of its expected lifespan; with a positive rate of interest, the extra annual consumption would be more because money not spent this year could be invested and would earn interest.[3] In the second case, the household gets a totally unforeseen increase of $2,000 a year for the rest of its life. In this event the household's permanent income has risen by $2,000 because the household can actually consume $2,000 more every year without accumulating new debts. Although in both cases current income rises $2,000, the effect on permanent income is very different in the two cases.

Keynesian theory assumes that *consumption expenditure* is related to current income and therefore predicts the same change in this year's consumption expenditure in each of the above cases. Permanent-income theories relate *actual consumption* to permanent income and therefore predict very different changes in actual consumption in each case. In the first case there would be only a small increase in actual annual consumption; in the second there would be a large increase.

In permanent-income theories, any change in current income that is thought to be temporary will have only a small effect on permanent income and hence on actual consumption.

Implications for the Behavior of the Economy

According to the permanent-income and the life-cycle hypotheses, actual consumption is not much affected by temporary changes in income. Does this mean that

---

[3] If the rate of interest were 7 percent, the household could invest the $2,000, consume an extra $161 a year, and just have nothing left at the end of 30 years.

aggregate expenditure, $C + I + G + (X - M)$, is not much affected? *Not necessarily.* Consider what happens when households get a temporary increase in their incomes. If actual consumption is not greatly affected by this, then households must be saving most of the temporary increase in their incomes. But from the point of view of these theories, households save when they buy a durable good just as much as when they buy a financial asset such as a stock or a bond. In both cases actual current consumption is not changed.

Thus spending a temporary increase in income on bonds or on new cars is consistent with both the PIH and the LCH. But it makes a great deal of difference to the short-run behavior of the economy which is done. If households buy stocks and bonds, aggregate expenditure on currently produced final goods will not rise when income rises temporarily;[4] if households buy automobiles or any other durable consumer good, aggregate expenditure on currently produced final goods will rise when income rises temporarily. Thus the PIH and the LCH leave unsettled the question that is critical in determining the size of the multiplier: What is the reaction of household *expenditures* on currently produced goods and services, particularly durables, to short-term, temporary changes in income?

The PIH and LCH theories leave unanswered the critical question of the ability of short-term changes in fiscal policy to remove inflationary and deflationary gaps.

Assume, for example, that a serious deflationary gap emerges and that the government attempts to stimulate a recovery by giving tax rebates and by cutting tax rates—both on an announced temporary basis. This will raise households' current disposable incomes by the amount of the tax cuts, but it will raise their permanent incomes by only a small amount. According to the PIH, the flow of actual current consumption should not rise much. Yet it is quite consistent with the PIH that households should spend their tax savings on durable consumer goods, the consumption of which can be spread over many years. In this case, even though actual consumption this year would not respond much to the tax cuts, expenditure would respond a great deal. Since current output and employment depends on expenditure rather than on real

consumption, the tax cut would be effective in stimulating the economy. However, it is also consistent with the PIH that households spend only a small part of their tax savings on consumption goods and seek to invest the rest in bonds and other financial assets. In this case the tax cuts may have only a small stimulating effect on the economy. It is important to note that the PIH and the LCH do *not* predict unambiguously that changes in taxes that are announced to be only short-lived will be ineffective in removing inflationary or deflationary gaps.

A Reconciliation of the Data

The PIH and the LCH are able to reconcile the observation that the *MPC* appears to be equal to the *APC* in long-period data while it is less than the *APC* in short-period and cross-sectional data.[5] They do this by relating changes in observed income to changes in permanent income.

Long-term time-series data using decade-by-decade averages remove the effects of temporary fluctuations in income. The observed changes in Y mainly represent permanent increases in real income because of economic growth. Long-term time-series studies will thus tend to measure accurately the propensity to consume out of permanent income.

Now consider short-term data. A study covering 10 or 15 years at the most and using annual observations of C and Y will use an income series dominated by temporary changes caused by cyclical fluctuations. When a household loses employment because of a business recession, it does not expect to remain unemployed forever; neither does it expect the extra income that it earns from heavy overtime work during a period of peak demand to persist. It may therefore be assumed that households expect these cyclical changes in current income to be temporary and that they will thus have little effect on permanent income. Since consumption is assumed to depend on permanent income, it follows that the observed relation between consumption and cyclical changes in income will tend to be

---

[4] Except for any indirect effect through changes in interest rates.

[5] The short-run and long-run time-series data are described in Chapter 28 (see especially page 518). Cross-section data are for a number of households at one point in time, and they show for that point in time how household consumption varies with household income. The data yield a consumption function similar to that obtained from short-term time-series data but with an even lower *MPC*.

smaller than the relation shown by the long-term time-series data. What this shows, then, is the lack of relation between changes in consumption and temporary changes in income, not a lack of relation between changes in consumption and changes in permanent income.

A similar analysis shows that cross-section studies are strongly influenced by the behavior of households whose incomes have temporarily departed from their permanent levels. Thus cross-section studies should be expected to yield a much lower observed marginal propensity to consume than that yielded by long-term time-series studies.

CONCLUSION

While permanent-income type theories succeed in reconciling various empirical observations of consumption functions, they leave ambiguous the multiplier effects of temporary increases in income. They are consistent with a constancy in both the *MPC* and the *APC* when *permanent income* changes. They also suggest a high degree of stability of the actual flow of consumption in the face of temporary fluctuations in current income. This is consistent with an *APC* out of *current income* that varies inversely with current income, falling as income rises and rising as income falls.

The Opportunity Cost of Government Activity

In Chapter 1 we saw that the cost of doing something can be measured in terms of the things that might have been done instead. The opportunity cost of government activity is measured in terms of forgone alternatives. The opportunity cost of a particular government expenditure depends on what factors of production the government project will use and from whence they are drawn. In times of heavy unemployment, most of the factors of production might otherwise have remained unemployed. In this case there is no opportunity cost in employing them in the government activity because there is no alternative current production sacrificed by so doing. In contrast, if, in a fully employed economy, the government builds dams, roads, schools, and nuclear submarines, the opportunity cost of these goods are the consumer goods and the capital goods that would have been produced instead.

The opportunity cost of government activity depends on the source of the factors of production used by the government. If the factors would have been unemployed, there is no opportunity cost; if they would have been employed, the opportunity cost is what they would have produced otherwise.

Supposing there is an opportunity cost, who bears it? If the factors of production used by the government are drawn away from the production of consumer goods and services, the opportunity cost will be borne by the present generation; if they are drawn away from the production of capital goods, the opportunity cost will be spread over the future because the current generation is giving up capital rather than consumption goods.

In the case in which factors are drawn away from private investment, government spending reduces investment and thus leads to a smaller stock of private capital; this lowers the economy's capacity to produce consumption goods in the future. If, to take the extreme case, the resources used by the government are drawn entirely from the production of capital goods, once the government activity ceases, the production of capital goods can be resumed. In the interim, however, a large supply of capital goods will have gone unproduced, and the consequences of this will be felt in the future. The stock of capital will for a long time be smaller than it would have been had the government activity not occurred. Because it is the stock of capital that provides the means of producing consumption goods, it follows that the output of such goods will be less than it otherwise would have been for as long as the stock of capital (*not* the current output of capital goods) is smaller than it would have been. Thus the opportunity cost in terms of a reduced output of goods for current consumption will be spread over a long period of time after the government activity ceases.

EFFECTS OF ALTERNATIVE MEANS OF FINANCING GOVERNMENT ACTIVITIES

There are three main ways in which a government can finance an expenditure.

1. It can raise the money by increasing taxes, thereby transferring purchasing power from taxpayers to itself.
2. It can borrow the money from willing lenders, thereby transferring current purchasing power from them to itself in return for the promise of future purchasing power.
3. It can create enough new money to permit itself to bid away the resources it needs.

The major effect of the method of financing government expenditures is on *who* bears the costs, not on how much they are.

The Distribution of the Costs

Consider an economy that is at full-employment national income, so that the government will necessarily incur real opportunity costs when it has goods and services produced.

Costs while the program is in operation. First, assume that the necessary revenue is raised by taxation. If the cost of a new government program is met by increases in taxes, then the current taxpayers will bear the cost by having their purchasing power reduced by taxes. Their purchases of goods and services will be

decreased, and the resources will be transferred to the production of the government's goods. In this case the costs are distributed among the public by the government's decision on whom to tax.[1]

Second, assume that the revenue is raised by borrowing. If the government expenditure is financed by borrowing from households and firms, the reduction in purchasing power for current consumption will be suffered by those who lend their money to the government instead of spending it on currently produced goods and services. People who do not buy government bonds do not postpone current consumption and thus do not bear any of the real current cost of the government activity. In this case the costs are accepted voluntarily by those who decide to save and buy government bonds.

Third, assume that the activity is financed by creating new money. (How this can be done will be studied in Chapter 33; here we are concerned with the consequences.) Because the economy is already in a state of full employment, this method of finance will cause inflation. Aggregate demand, already high enough to purchase all the output the economy is producing, becomes excessive as the government enters the market with its own new demand. The rise in prices will mean that households and firms with fixed budgets will be able to buy less than they would otherwise have bought, and the government will be able to obtain resources for its own activities. Thus fewer resources will be available for private consumption and private capital formation.

In the aggregate, the result of inflationary finance is the same as if the government had reduced private expenditure by taxation. The costs, however, are borne by those who are least able to protect themselves against the government-induced inflation rather than by those selected to pay increased taxes. Inflationary finance is usually regarded as a less just method of taxation than income and corporate taxes because it places much of the burden on the economically weak, the unfortunate, and the uneducated and places the least burden on those best able to adjust to rising prices—often the richest and most powerful groups.

The government, in choosing whether to finance its expenditures by current taxation, by borrowing, or by

---

[1] This is so at least in the first instance. As is seen in Chapter 25, however, the burden of taxes can be shifted and with it the opportunity cost of the government's activity.

creating new money, can exert a considerable influence on the distribution of the burden of the loss of real consumption opportunities that its purchases make necessary.

Costs after the program is completed. Now consider what happens when the government project is finished. To the extent that it was financed by current taxes (or by the inflationary creation of new money) the matter is finished once the government expenditure has been made. Resources can then be transferred back to the production of goods and services, and households' disposable income can be allowed to rise by reducing taxes. But to the extent that the government activity was financed by borrowing from the private sector, the debt remains after the activity has been completed. It is necessary to pay interest each year to the bondholders and eventually to repay the bonds as they reach maturity. To the extent that interest payments and eventual redemption of the bonds are made from tax revenue, taxpayers now suffer a reduction in their consumption below what it would otherwise have been. The transfer is thus reversed. In return for bearing the original reduction in consumption, bondholders (or their heirs) now enjoy a rise in consumption, and taxpayers who are not bondholders suffer a reduction. For a community, the cost in terms of forgone output was borne during the original activity. Once the activity is finished, total production of goods and services for the private sector of the economy returns to normal. The opportunity cost could not be postponed, but individuals who did not buy bonds must now pay for their share of the cost of the activity by transferring some claims on current production to individuals who did buy bonds.

Do Real Burdens Result from the Method of Finance?

We have seen that the current cost of government expenditure is the current production forgone and that the method of finance can influence the distribution of the cost within the society.

The method of finance can also affect the extent to which current generations can shift the real opportunity cost of government activity to future generations.

If, for example, new taxes are placed on consumption

goods, most of the cutbacks in private production may be expected to fall on consumer goods. If, however, funds for the government activity are raised by a special tax on all business investment, it is likely that the production of capital goods rather than of consumption goods will be reduced.

Is there a systematic difference between taxing and borrowing with respect to the possible transfer of the burden to future generations? This is a matter of substantial debate. Some economists believe that the existence of government bonds, by making households feel wealthier than they otherwise would, may make them consume more and save less. This in turn may reduce private capital formation and thus transfer much of the cost of government activity to the future via the reduction in capital stock.

It is possible that the method of finance can impose burdens on the community in addition to the opportunity costs already discussed. The additional burdens are those associated with the existence of a large national debt held within the private sector of the economy. The bonds will continue to exist after the activity is finished, and interest will have to be paid to those households, firms, and financial institutions that hold them. Extra money must be raised in taxes and paid out to bondholders. This is a transfer payment that does not of itself represent a net burden to the society; all we are doing is taxing Peter to pay Paul. There is a burden involved, however, because resources, in terms of tax collectors and inspectors and accountants and clerks to look after bond issues, will be used to raise taxes and pay bondholders. These resources could otherwise have been employed to make goods and services for current consumption. Such real costs are but a tiny fraction of the interest payments on the national debt. Because such interest payments are themselves just over 1 percent of GNP, the real collection and disbursement costs are minute.[2]

Foreign borrowing: a special case. There is one way in which, from the narrow point of view of a single country, the entire cost of the activity can be transferred to future generations. If the government activity

[2] Another real effect occurs if the taxes required to raise the money to pay interest on the debt change market prices and thereby influence the allocation of resources. Since taxes required to service the national debt are a very small part of total taxes raised, these effects of the tax system will occur whether or not it is necessary to raise money to pay interest on the national debt. This cost too is minute.

is financed totally by foreign borrowing, there will be no need to cut down on current consumption at home. In this event the sacrifice in current consumption is borne by the citizens of the lending country.

When the project has been completed, however, interest must be paid on the foreign debt, and usually the debt will have to be repaid. The paying of interest on the debt (and the repaying of the principal) gives foreigners a claim on the country's current production, and when they exercise this claim, there will be less current production available for the citizens of the debtor country. In this way the burden of a current ac-

tivity can be avoided by the current generation and can be passed on to a future one. But notice that this can be done only if the people of some other country can be persuaded to accept the current opportunity cost.

From the *world's* point of view, the sacrifice of alternative outputs is necessarily incurred during the time of the activity. For one country, as for any one group, however, the current cost can be avoided by borrowing, provided some other group can be found that is willing to lend the money to finance the activity. The lending group then shoulders the burden in terms of a current reduction in its consumption.

The Classical Quantity Theory of Money

Appendix to Chapter 34

The classical quantity theory of money arrived at results very similar to those outlined in Chapter 34 for the modern theory. The classical theory, however, used a simpler transmission mechanism that went straight from an excess demand for or supply of money to the aggregate expenditure function. As a result the classical theory could use a simpler theory of the demand for money balances. Although simpler, the theory did not turn out to fit the facts so that the more complex theory of the demand for money presented in Chapter 34 is needed.

The Demand for the Supply of Money

In the classical theory the demand for money depends solely on the transactions motive. This demand, expressed in *nominal* money units, may be written

$$M_d = kPY \qquad (1)$$

where P is the price level and Y is real national income. The value of k is the fraction of the annual value of national income that firms and households wish to hold as transactions balances—which is the only reason for holding money.

Next we express the assumption that the supply of money is a constant determined by the central authorities:

$$M_s = M \qquad (2)$$

where M_s is the supply of money and M is some constant amount (measured in dollars). Equation (2) merely says that the supply of money does not depend on any other factors in the economy; it is simply what the Fed wants it to be.

Finally, we write a condition for equilibrium between the demand for money and the supply of it:

$$M_d = M_s \qquad (3)$$

When (3) holds, households and firms will have, in the

aggregate, just the amount of money balances they require. When (3) does not hold, they will have too much or too little money. The effect that this monetary disequilibrium will have on the economy depends on the transmission mechanism.

The Classical Transmission Mechanism

The transmission mechanism in the classical theory was a very direct one. When, on the one hand, firms and households hold more money than they wish to hold, there is excess supply of money. According to the classical theory, excess money balances will be spent to purchase currently produced goods and services. When, on the other hand, firms and households hold smaller money balances than they would like to hold, there is excess demand for money and they will cut their expenditures below their incomes in an effort to build up their balances.

In the classical and modern theories, the transmission mechanism differs but the final result is the same: excess demand for money reduces aggregate expenditure, and excess supply increases it.

THE QUANTITY THEORY WITH FULL EMPLOYMENT

To see how the quantity theory works, let us assume first that real national income is constant at its full-employment level, so that excess aggregate demand must cause the price level to rise. The substitution of (1) and (2) into the equilibrium condition (3) gives the basic relation between P and M:

$$kPY = M \qquad (4)$$

or

$$PY = M \frac{1}{k} \qquad (5)$$

This merely states that the demand for money (kPY) should equal its supply (M).

If we are dealing with inflationary-gap situations so that income is constant at its full-employment level, and if k is constant, then the price level must rise in proportion to any increase in the quantity of money.

To see how this result comes about, we must consider disequilibrium behavior. Assume that the economy begins in a situation of full-employment equilibrium with the demand for money equal to its supply. Then the central bank increases the supply of money in the hands of households and firms by 10 percent. According to the behavioral hypothesis of the quantity theory, firms and households will try to convert the extra cash into goods and services but, since the economy is already at full employment, their efforts can only open up an inflationary gap. Indeed, the price level must rise until the demand for money is again equal to its supply.

Since the demand for money is kPY, and since k is fixed by assumption, and since Y cannot change because the economy remains at the same level of full-employment output, the demand for money will increase by exactly 10 percent when P increases by 10 percent. Until that time the demand for money will be less than its supply, and the attempt to convert the excess money into currently produced goods and services will generate excess demand that will cause further inflation. Thus equilibrium will be restored only when the price level rises by the same percentage as did the supply of money.

Often the quantity theory is presented and discussed using V (*velocity of circulation*) instead of k. V stands for the average number of times a unit of money turns over in the transactions that create GNP. It is defined as the reciprocal of k. Substituting V for $1/k$ in equation (5) gives

$$PY = MV \qquad (6)$$

Of course it makes no difference whether we work with k or V, as long as we are careful about the way we interpret the two variables.

The stock of money people wish to hold might, for example, be one-tenth of the annual value of national income. If k is .1, then V must be 10. This indicates that if the money supply is to be one-tenth of the value of national income, the average unit of money must change hands ten times in order to bring about an aggregate value of income ten times as large as the stock of money.

THE QUANTITY THEORY WITH UNEMPLOYMENT

The quantity theory became a part of the classical model in which the *equilibrium* level of national income was always at full employment. Thus Y

remained fixed at its full-employment value, and not only did P rise in proportion to a rise in the money supply, but P also *fell* in proportion to a *reduction* in the money supply. Thus Y was determined by its full-employment level and P was determined by the quantity of money. To adapt the classical quantity theory to situations in which actual income is less than potential income, we merely use the assumptions of the Keynesian portion of the aggregate supply curve: the price level is constant while national income varies with aggregate demand. This makes P a constant and Y a variable but preserves the link provided by the quantity theory between the excess demand for money and changes in aggregate demand.

To see what is implied, we take the theory in the form

$$kPY = M$$

which is equation (4), and divide by kP to obtain

$$Y = \frac{1}{kP}M \tag{7}$$

This tells us that:

If P is constant during periods of unemployment, national income (and hence output and employment) will vary in proportion to the money supply.

The reason for this is analogous to the reasons given in the discussion of disequilibrium under inflationary conditions. If firms and households have too much money, they will spend it, and the resulting increase in aggregate demand will raise output and employment. If firms and households have too little money, they will lower their expenditures in an attempt to increase their money balances, and the resulting fall in aggregate demand will lower the equilibrium level of output.

The basic prediction of the quantity theory is that national income valued in current dollars will change in proportion to any change in the quantity of money. In some cases the change will be mainly a price change (a change in P); in others it will be a change in output and employment (a change in Y). In either case, control over the money supply becomes a potent method of controlling either P or Y.

The Phelps-Friedman Theory: Accelerating Inflation and an Unstable Phillips Curve

Appendix to Chapter 36

In the late 1960s Professors Milton Friedman of the University of Chicago and Edmund Phelps of Columbia University began to mount an attack on the theoretical underpinnings of the theory of a stable Phillips curve. They argued that the curve describes a transitory relationship that cannot exist over the long term.

According to their theory, the economy could not remain in a position to the right of Y_F on the Phillips curve shown in Figure 36A–1. Any position with income in excess of Y_F implies substantial continued inflation. But sooner or later people would come to realize that the inflation was permanent. Unions would then demand even larger wage increases, and others would revise their own expectations of continued inflation. This new behavior would accelerate the inflation. When people came to accept the new higher rate as permanent, they would again revise their behavior, and this would accelerate the inflation still further. Extensive empirical research over the first half of the 1970s has given support to the view that the Phillips curve would not remain stable if the economy were to operate a low level of unemployment and a high rate of inflation for a sustained period.

This theory is a mixture of demand-pull and expectational inflation, and it has a number of important aspects that we will study in detail.

The Short-term Phillips Curve for Zero Expected Inflation

In the Phelps-Friedman theory a critical role is played by inflationary expectations. We shall use the symbol P_e to refer to the rate of inflation that decision makers *expect* will rule over their planning period—say, the next year.

The pure demand-pull element of the Phelps-Friedman theory is illustrated in Figure 36A-1 by the Phillips curve labeled $PP(P_e = 0)$. *This particular Phillips curve is drawn on the assumption that people expect a zero rate of inflation.* (This is indicated by the notation $P_e = 0$.) The curve shows that the higher is the level of national income (i.e., the higher is the level of aggregate demand), the higher will be the associated rate of inflation. The point where the *PP* curve for zero expected inflation cuts the axis, labeled Y_F, indicates the level of national income at which there is no significant demand-pull inflation. The percentage of the labor force unemployed at Y_F is the natural rate of unem-

ployment. Because of frictional unemployment, the natural rate of unemployment will certainly be positive; it may well be as high as 4 or 5 percent in the United States today.

Why does the Phillips curve for zero expected inflation cut the axis at Y_F? When national income is at its full-employment level, the Phelps-Friedman theory envisages all markets in the economy being in equilib-

FIGURE 36A-1

The Phelps-Friedman Theory of the Phillips Curve

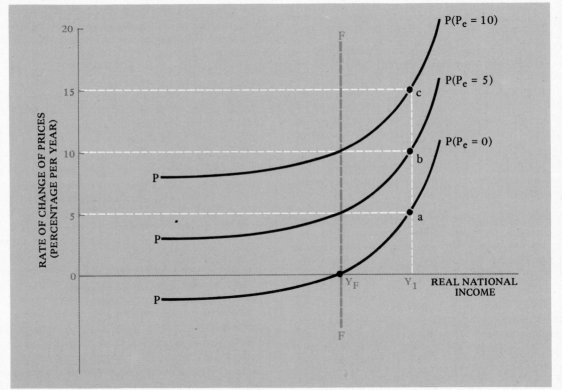

There is a separate Phillips curve for each expected rate of inflation. The Phillips curve of Figure 36-8, shown here as $PP(P_e = 0)$, relates national income to inflation on the assumption that the price level is expected to remain stable. The actual rate of inflation depends on national income and the expected rate of inflation. Thus for each expected rate of inflation the associated short-run Phillips curve lies above the $P_e = 0$ curve by the amount of the expected rate of inflation. Consider, for example, an inflationary gap with national income at Y_1. The actual rate of inflation will be 5 percent when the expected rate is zero (point *a*), 10 percent when the expected rate is 5 percent

(point *b*), and 15 percent when the expected rate is 10 percent (point *c*).

In long-term equilibrium the actual rate of inflation must remain equal to the expected rate (otherwise expectations would be revised). This can only occur at the full-employment level of income Y_F, that is, along *FF*. At Y_F there is no demand pressure on the price level; hence the only influence on actual inflation is expected inflation. Any stable rate of inflation (provided it is validated by the appropriate rate of monetary expansion) is compatible with Y_F and its associated natural rate of unemployment.

rium, with demands equal to supplies. Thus there is no market pressure on any price either to rise or to fall. In these circumstances all prices, and hence the price level, will remain stable.

Why does the Phillips curve for zero expected inflation show prices rising when national income exceeds its full-employment level and falling when national income is less than its full-employment level? Let the economy begin at full-employment income. Consider, first, the effects of a rise in aggregate demand. All individual demand curves shift outward, creating excess demands in all markets. Decision makers will respond in two ways: (1) they will increase their outputs (working overtime, extra shifts, etc.), and (2) they will raise their money prices, seeking thereby to raise their relative prices. Since this happens in all markets, the first response leads to an increase in national income while the second response causes a rise in the price level. Now consider what happens when there is a fall in aggregate demand with national income initially at its full-employment level. Decision makers respond by reducing output and by cutting money prices, seeking thereby to lower their relative prices. Since this happens in all markets, there is a fall in national income combined with some downward movement in the price level.

Why does the price level continue to change as long as national income remains unequal to its full-employment level? We have seen that when there is excess demand in all markets, all decision makers raise their money prices, seeking thereby to raise their relative prices. But by definition *all* relative prices cannot rise. (It is impossible, for example, for rye whiskey to become more expensive relative to Scotch while at the same time Scotch becomes more expensive relative to rye.) Thus at least some decision makers will be frustrated in their attempts to raise their *relative* prices. Take a simple example: if all raise their money prices by 5 percent, seeking thereby to raise their relative prices by 5 percent, a 5 percent inflation will be generated; but no one will have succeeded in raising his or her own prices relative to other prices. As long as the excess demand persists, people will go on raising their money prices, trying unsuccessfully to raise their relative prices. (Some may succeed, but everyone cannot.) Thus general excess demand will be associated with a level of national income above its full-employment level and a *continuing* rise in prices.

An exactly parallel argument shows that when there is general excess supply, decreases in money prices by all decision makers, in an attempt to cut relative prices, will lead to a fall in the general price level, but many *relative* prices will not be decreased. Decision makers, therefore, will cut prices further. Because of these vain attempts to cut relative prices, national income below its full-employment level will be associated with a *continuing* downward pressure on prices.

In summary, the Phelps-Friedman theory holds, first, that general excess demand in the economy will be associated with national income above its full-employment level and with continuing inflation; and second, that general excess supply will be associated with national income below its full-employment level and with a continuing downward pressure on prices. In other words, the Phillips curve for zero expected inflation is upward sloping, and it cuts the axis at Y_F.

The Actual Inflation Rate

The foregoing discussion of upward and downward pressure on the price level relied on the desire to raise relative prices when national income exceeded Y_F and to lower them when national income fell short of Y_F. Since each decision maker's relative price is the relation between their own price and the general price level,[1] it follows that any decision to change relative prices means changing one's money price *relative* to what one *expects* the price level to be (over the time for which one's own price is being set). If a decision maker wishes to raise his or her relative price by 5 percent, this requires a 5 percent increase in the money price when no inflation is expected, a 10 percent increase in the money price when a 5 percent inflation is expected, and so on. If, on the other hand, the decision maker wishes to reduce his or her relative price by 2 percent, this requires a 2 percent reduction in the money price when no inflation is expected, a 3 percent *increase* in the money price when a 5 percent inflation is expected, and so on. In general, a decision to change a relative price by x percent requires a change in the money price by an amount equal to x percent *plus* the expected rate of inflation.

The above discussion explains what determines the actual rate of inflation in this theory.

According to the Phelps-Friedman theory, the actual

---

[1] That is, a relative price is p/P where p is the individual price in question and P is the general price level (which is an average of the economy's prices).

rate of inflation is given by the demand-pull element *plus* the expected rate of inflation.[2]

Thus, for example, if everyone expects a 5 percent inflation, prices and wages will be raised by 5 percent *plus* the amount due to the pull of excess demand, which is shown by the Phillips curve for $P_e = 0$.

Another way of making the same point is to say that there is a separate Phillips curve relating actual inflation to national income for each expected rate of inflation. Each curve is defined for a particular expected rate of inflation, and each is called a short-run Phillips curve. (Each curve is short-run in the sense that the Phillips curve on which the economy is located will be given at any moment of time but will change whenever P_e changes.) This point is illustrated for three levels of expected rates of inflation in Figure 36A-1.

The Relation Between Actual and Expected Inflation

Since actual inflation is equal to expected inflation *plus* an allowance for demand pressure, it follows that actual inflation exceeds expected inflation when national income exceeds Y_F because demand pressures are then positive.[3] When national income equals Y_F, demand pressures are zero, and actual inflation will equal expected inflation. When actual national income is less than Y_F, demand pressures are negative, and actual inflation will be less than the expected rate.[4]

People are assumed to base their expectations about the inflation rate in the immediate future on the actual rates that have occurred over the previous two or three years. Thus whenever actual rates of inflation exceed expected rates, expectations will catch up—but with a lag. For example, if people expect a 5 percent inflation but continue to experience a 7 percent inflation, sooner or later they will revise their expectations upward and come to expect a 7 percent inflation. Conversely, if people expect a 7 percent inflation but experience only a 5 percent inflation,

sooner or later they will revise their expectations downward and come to expect only a 5 percent inflation.

IMPLICATIONS OF THE PHELPS-FRIEDMAN THEORY

Accelerating Inflation

A first important implication of the Phelps-Friedman theory is that if national income is *kept* above Y_F, the rate of inflation will accelerate continuously. Say the economy starts in full-employment equilibrium at stable prices—that is, at the point where the Phillips curve for $P_e = 0$ cuts the axis. Now let aggregate demand increase. Excess demand is created; national income increases; and the economy moves up its short-run Phillips curve to a higher level of national income and, say, a 5 percent inflation. This is shown by point *a* in Figure 36A-1. The inflation occurs because people are trying to adjust their *relative* wages and prices upward in response to excess demand. No one expects an inflation. If the inflation persists, however, it will eventually come to be expected. People will then add a catch-up factor of 5 percent to any wage and price change they plan to make. When they do this, the rate of inflation will accelerate to 10 percent (point *b*). Sooner or later this will come to be expected, and the rate of inflation will then accelerate to 15 percent (point *c*), of which 10 percent is to keep ahead of expected inflation and 5 percent is a response to excess demand.

According to the Phelps-Friedman theory, whenever the economy has a level of national income above full-employment income (or, the same thing, a level of unemployment below the natural rate of unemployment), the actual rate of inflation will eventually accelerate. How fast it accelerates depends on how fast current inflationary expectations adjust to past actual rates.

It follows that if the government tries to maintain excess aggregate demand in the mistaken view that it can increase real national income above Y_F (i.e., lower unemployment below its natural rate) at the cost of a stable rate of inflation, it will be in for a nasty shock. For a while people may not expect the inflation to continue; as a result inflation will proceed at a stable pace. Sooner or later, however, people will come to expect the inflation to continue; they will revise their infla-

---

[2] In symbols: $P_a = PD + P_e$ where P_a is the actual rate of inflation, PD is the inflation rate caused by demand pressure, and P_e is the expected rate of inflation.

[3] The allowance is positive when Y exceeds Y_F and negative when Y falls short of Y_F.

[4] This is easily seen when we look at the relation $P_a = PD + P_e$ given in footnote 2 above. It immediately follows that when $PD > 0$, $P_a > P_e$; when $PD = 0$, $P_a = P_e$; and when $PD < 0$, $P_a < P_e$.

tionary expectations upward, and this will cause the inflation rate to accelerate. Later the new higher rate will come to be accepted; expectations of future inflation will be revised upward, and the actual rate of inflation will once again accelerate.[5]

The Long-run Phillips Curve Is Vertical

When national income equals Y_F in the Phelps-Friedman theory, there is no excess demand pressure on inflation. *Thus the only inflation that can occur when $Y = Y_F$ is expectational inflation.* If everyone expects 5 percent inflation, all prices will be raised by 5 percent and an actual inflation rate of 5 percent will occur. If the money supply is increased by 5 percent to validate this inflation, then full-employment income and the natural rate of unemployment can be maintained indefinitely with a 5 percent expected and a 5 percent actual inflation. But the same argument could be repeated for 10 percent or for any other rate of inflation (or deflation).

In general, since at the natural rate of unemployment there is neither upward nor downward pressure on prices due to excess demand, the only cause of inflation arises from attempts to try to keep up with whatever rate of inflation is expected.[6] Thus full-employment national income and its associated natural rate of unemployment are compatible with *any* actual rate of inflation, provided that, first, the inflation is expected and, second, it is accompanied by the appropriate rate of monetary expansion.

The long-run Phillips curve that relates national income to a stable rate of inflation is vertical at full-employment income.

Policy Implications

The Phelps-Friedman theory has a number of implications for economic policy. If the theory turns out to be

substantially correct, these policy implications will be extremely important. A first implication has already been discussed.

Attempts to reduce unemployment below its natural rate will eventually cause the rate of inflation to accelerate.

A second implication concerns the natural rate of unemployment.

It is essential to discover the natural rate of unemployment because it is the only acceptable target for long-run stabilization policy.

To see why knowing the natural rate of unemployment is so important, assume that the economy has functioned satisfactorily for some time at an average unemployment rate of 5 percent and that the inflation rate has shown no tendency to accelerate. Policymakers will conclude that 5 percent is the natural rate of unemployment. Now assume that unbeknown to the policymakers the natural rate of unemployment rises to 7 percent. If they go on trying to stabilize the economy around a 5 percent unemployment rate, the first indication they will have that something has gone wrong is that the inflation rate will begin to accelerate. It may take some time before policymakers conclude that the acceleration is not due to some transient cause but represents a genuine tendency for continual acceleration. By the time they reach that conclusion and decide to stabilize the economy around a higher level of unemployment, a very rapid inflation may already exist and may have been built into people's expectations. Thus, if the Phelps-Friedman theory is correct, quick and accurate determination of the natural rate of unemployment must be an important part of any effective anti-inflationary policy.

Once an expectational inflation is under way, policymakers may have to take account of a third important policy implication.

A period of excess demand and accelerating inflation will lead to accelerating inflationary expectations. A prolonged period with unemployment above the natural rate may be required before inflationary expectations are revised downward sufficiently to permit the actual inflation rate to fall.

This implication is illustrated in Figure 36A-2. An increase in inflationary expectations moves the econ-

---

[5] As we saw in Chapter 36, the government will have to induce ever more rapid rates of monetary expansion to validate an ever-accelerating inflation rate. But if the government does try to hold national income above Y_F, it will induce, according to this theory, an ever-accelerating rate of inflation that will *have to be validated* by ever-increasing rates of monetary expansion.

[6] The basic Phelps-Friedman relation is $P_a = PD + P_e$. When $Y = Y_F$, there is no excess demand inflation, so $PD = 0$. It follows immediately that we must have $P_a = P_e$ when $Y = Y_F$.

FIGURE 36A-2

Falling Real National Income and Rising Inflation (Stagflation)

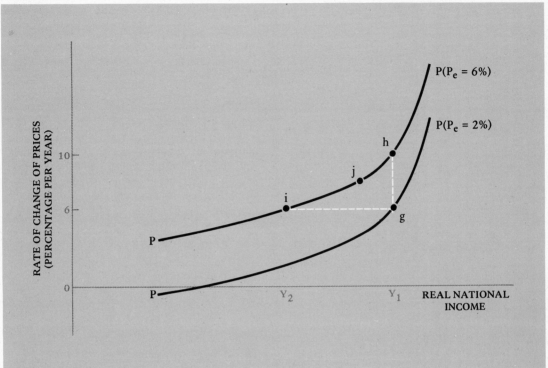

When the expected rate of inflation is rising, a fall in national income can easily be associated with a rise in the actual rate of inflation. The economy is at point *g* with a level of national income of Y_1, an expected rate of inflation of 2 percent, and an actual rate of 6 percent. Since the actual rate exceeds the expected rate, expectations will be revised upward. Suppose people come to expect a 6 percent inflation in the next period. If national income is held constant at Y_1, the economy will move to point *h* and the actual rate of inflation will accelerate to 10 percent. In order to offset this increase in inflationary expectations and hold inflation to 6 percent, national income must be reduced all the way to Y_2 (point *i*). If national income *falls* to any amount less than Y_1 but greater than Y_2 the economy will move to some point such as *j* where *falling* real national income is associated with *rising* inflation.

omy to a higher short-term Phillips curve. This increases inflationary pressures. To offset this a decline in national income is required, which moves the economy downward and to the left along any given short-term Phillips curve. This decreases inflationary pressure. In the early stages of a contraction in national income that is designed to bring an *accelerating* inflation under control, the effect of accelerating expectations may dominate the effect of declining demand and output. As a result, falling national income and rising unemployment may be associated with constant or even rising rates of inflation. When this occurs, the economy is suffering a stagflation—the coexistence of high rates of inflation and high rates of unemployment.

Mathematical Notes

1. It may not be immediately obvious that calculating the ratio of the cost of purchasing a fixed bundle of commodities in two periods is the same thing as calculating the percentage change in each price and then averaging these by weighting each price by the proportion of total expenditure devoted to the commodity. The following expression, however, illustrates the equivalence of these two procedures for the two-commodity case:

$$\frac{q^A p_1^A + q^B p_1^B}{q^A p_0^A + q^B p_0^B} = \frac{p_1^A}{p_0^A}\left(\frac{q^A p_0^A}{q^A p_0^A + q^B p_0^B}\right)$$
$$+ \frac{p_1^B}{p_0^B}\left(\frac{q^B p_0^B}{q^A p_0^A + q^B p_0^B}\right)$$

The qs are fixed quantity weights while the ps are prices; A and B refer to two commodities; 0 and 1 refer respectively to the base period and some subsequent time period. The expression on the left is the fixed bundle q^A and q^B valued at given year prices divided by its value in base year prices. The first term in the expression on the right gives the ratio of the price of good A in the given and the base year multiplied by the proportion of total expenditure in the base year devoted to good A. The second term does the same for good B. Simple multiplication and division reduces the right-hand expression to the left-hand one.

2. Many variables affect the quantity demanded. Using functional notation, the argument of the next several pages can be anticipated. Let Q^D represent the quantity of a commodity demanded and

$$T, \overline{Y}, N, Y^*, p, p_j$$

represent, respectively, tastes, average household income, population, income distribution, its price, and the price of the jth other commodity.

The demand function is

$$Q^D = D(T, \overline{Y}, N, Y^*, p, p_j), j = 1, 2, \ldots, \text{n}$$

The demand schedule or curve looks at

$$Q^D = q(p) \Big|_{T, \bar{Y}, N, Y^*, p_j}$$

where the notation means that the variables to the right of the vertical line are held constant.

This function is correctly described as the demand function with respect to price, all other variables held constant. This function, often written concisely $q = q(p)$, shifts in response to changes in other variables. Consider average income. If, as is usually hypothesized, $\frac{\partial Q^D}{\partial Y} > 0$, then increases in average income shift $q = q(p)$ rightward and decreases in average income shift $q = q(p)$ leftward. Changes in other variables likewise shift this function in the direction implied by the relationship of that variable to the quantity demanded.

3. Quantity demanded is a simple, straightforward, but frequently misunderstood concept in everyday use, but it has a clear mathematical meaning. It refers to the dependent variable in the demand function from note 2 above:

$$Q^D = D(T, \bar{Y}, N, Y^*, p, p_j)$$

It takes on a specific value, therefore, whenever a specific value is assigned to each of the independent variables. A change in Q^D occurs whenever the specific value of any independent variable is changed. Q^D could change, for example, from 10,000 tons per month to 20,000 tons per month as a result of a *ceteris paribus* change in any one price, in average income, in the distribution of income, in tastes, or in population. Also it could change as a result of the net effect of changes in all of the independent variables occurring at once. Thus a change in the price of a commodity is a sufficient reason for a change in Q^D but not a necessary reason.

Some textbooks reserve the term *change in quantity demanded* for a movement along a demand curve, that is, a change in Q^D as a result of a change in p. They then use other words for a change in Q^D caused by a change in the other variables in the demand function. This usage gives the single variable Q^D more than one name, and this is potentially confusing.

Our usage, which corresponds to that in all intermediate and advanced treatments, avoids this practice. We call Q^D quantity demanded and refer to *any* change in Q^D as a *change in quantity demanded*. In this usage it is correct to say that a movement along a demand curve is a change in quantity demanded. But it is incorrect to say that a change in quantity demanded can occur only because of a movement along a demand curve (since Q^D can change for other reasons, e.g., a *ceteris paribus* change in average household income).

4. Continuing the development of note 2, let Q^S represent the quantity of a commodity supplied and

$$G, X, p, p_j, w_i$$

represent, respectively, producers' goals, technology, price, price of the jth other commodity, and costs of the ith factor of production.

The supply function is

$$Q^S = S(G, X, p, p_j, w_i), \begin{aligned} j &= 1, 2, \ldots, n \\ i &= 1, 2, \ldots, m \end{aligned}$$

The supply schedule and supply curve looks at

$$Q^S = s(p) \Big|_{G, X, p_j, w_i}$$

This is the supply function with respect to price, all other variables held constant. This function, often written concisely $q = s(p)$, shifts in response to changes in other variables.

5. Continuing the development of notes 2 and 4, equilibrium occurs where

$$Q^D = Q^S$$

which *for specified values of all other variables* requires $q(p) = s(p)$. This condition is met only at the point where demand and supply curves intersect. Thus supply and demand curves are said to determine equilibrium price. A shift in any of the variables held constant in the q and s functions will shift the demand or supply curve and lead to a different equilibrium.

6. The definition in the text uses finite changes and is called *arc elasticity*. The parallel definition using derivatives is

$$\eta = \frac{dq}{dp} \cdot \frac{p}{q}$$

and is called *point elasticity*. Further discussion appears in the Appendix to Chapter 6.

7. The propositions in the text are proven as follows. Letting TR stand for total revenue we can write:

$$TR = pq$$

$$dTR/dp = q + p\frac{dq}{dp} \qquad [1]$$

But from the equation in note 6

$$q\eta = p\frac{dq}{dp} \qquad [2]$$

which we can substitute in [1] to obtain

$$\frac{dTR}{dp} = q + q\eta = q(1 + \eta) \qquad [3]$$

Because η is a negative number, the sign of [3] is negative if the absolute value of η exceeds unity (demand elastic) and positive if it is less than unity (demand inelastic).

8. The "axis-reversal" arose in the following way. Marshall theorized in terms of "demand price" and "supply price" as the prices that would lead to a given quantity being demanded or supplied. Thus he wrote

$$p^d = D(q) \qquad [1]$$

$$p^s = S(q) \qquad [2]$$

and the condition of equilibrium as

$$D(q) = S(q) \qquad [3]$$

When graphing the behavioral relations [1] and [2], Marshall naturally put the independent variable, q, on the horizontal axis.

Leon Walras, whose formulation of the working of a competitive market has become the accepted one, focused on quantities demanded and supplied *at a given price*. That is

$$q^d = q(p) \qquad [4]$$

$$q^s = s(p) \qquad [5]$$

and for equilibrium

$$q(p) = s(p) \qquad [6]$$

Walras did not go in for graphic representation. Had he done so he would surely have placed p (his independent variable) on the horizontal axis.

Marshall, among his other influences on later generations of economists, was the great popularizer of graphic analysis in economics. Today we use his graphs, even for Walras' analysis. The "axis-reversal" is thus one of those accidents of history that seem odd to people who did not live through the "perfectly natural" sequence of steps that produced it.

9. The distinction made between an incremental change and a marginal change is the distinction for the function $Y = Y(X)$ between $\frac{\Delta Y}{\Delta X}$ and the derivative $\frac{dY}{dX}$.

The latter is the limit of the former as ΔX approaches zero. Precisely this sort of difference underlies the distinction between arc and point elasticity, and we shall meet it repeatedly—in this chapter in reference to marginal and incremental *utility* and in later chapters with respect to such concepts as marginal and incremental *product, cost,* and *revenue*. Where Y is a function of more than one variable—for example, $Y = f(X, Z)$—the marginal relationship between Y and X is the partial derivative $\frac{\partial Y}{\partial X}$ rather than the total derivative.

10. The hypothesis of diminishing marginal utility requires that we be able to measure utility of consumption by a function $U = U(X_1, X_2, \ldots, X_n)$, where $X_1, \ldots, X_n$ are quantities of the n goods consumed by a household. There are now two utility hypotheses. First, $\frac{\partial u}{\partial X_i} > 0$ which says that the consumer can get more utility by increasing consumption of the typical, i^{th}, commodity. Second, $\frac{\partial^2 u}{\partial X_i^2} < 0$ which says that the marginal utility of additional consumption is declining.

11. The relationship of the slope of the budget line to relative prices can be seen as follows. In the two-commodity example a change in expenditure (ΔE) is given by the equation

$$\Delta E = \Delta Cp_C + \Delta Fp_F \qquad [1]$$

Along a budget line, expenditure is constant, that is, $\Delta E = 0$. Thus, along such a line,

$$\Delta Cp_C + \Delta Fp_F = 0 \qquad [2]$$

whence

$$-\frac{\Delta C}{\Delta F} = \frac{p_F}{p_C} \qquad [3]$$

The ratio $-\Delta C/\Delta F$ is the slope of the budget line. It is negative because, with a fixed budget, to consume more F one must consume less C. In words, equation [3] says that the negative of the slope of the budget line is the ratio of the absolute prices (i.e., the relative price). While prices do not show directly in Figure 9-8, they are implicit in the budget line: its slope depends solely on the relative price, while its position, given a fixed money income, depends on the absolute prices of the two goods.

12. Because the slope of the indifference curve is negative, it is the absolute value of the slope that declines as one moves downward to the right along the curve. The algebraic value of course increases. The phrase diminishing marginal rate of substitution thus refers to the absolute, not the algebraic, value of the slope.

13. Assume that changes in tastes are not related to changes in price. Now if tastes change, there is an even chance that they will offset the effect of a rise in p causing a fall in q. Thus there is a .5 chance in any one week that taste changes will cause Δp and Δq to move together. Twenty-six weeks gives 25 changes in p and q and thus $(\frac{1}{2})^{25} =$ one chance in 33,554,432 that taste changes accounted for the observations. Clearly an upward-sloping demand curve is the odds-on favorite compared to the explanation that a coincidence of chance *shifts* in demand and supply produced the observations.

14. Marginal product as defined in the text is really "incremental product." A mathematician would distinguish between this notion and its limit as ΔL approaches zero. Technically, MP measures the rate at which total product is changing as one factor is varied. The marginal product is the partial derivative of the total product with respect to the variable factor. In symbols,

$$MP = \frac{\partial TP}{\partial L}$$

Economists often use the term marginal product interchangeably with incremental product.

15. We have referred specifically both to diminishing *marginal* product and to diminishing *average* product. In most cases, eventually diminishing marginal product implies eventually diminishing average product. This is, however, not necessary, as the following figure shows.

UNITS OF THE VARIABLE FACTOR

In this case, marginal product diminishes after v units of the variable factor are employed. Because marginal product falls toward, but never quite reaches, a value of m, average product rises continually toward, but never quite reaches, the same value.

16. Let q be the quantity of output and X the quantity of the variable factor. In the short run,

$$TP = q = f(X) \tag{1}$$

We now define

$$AP = \frac{q}{X} = \frac{f(X)}{X} \tag{2}$$

$$MP = \frac{dq}{dX} \tag{3}$$

We are concerned about the relation between these two. Whether average product is rising, at a maximum, or falling is determined by its derivative with respect to X.

$$\frac{d\frac{q}{X}}{dX} = \frac{X\frac{dq}{dX} - q}{X^2} \tag{4}$$

This may be rewritten:

$$\frac{1}{X}\left(\frac{dq}{dX} - \frac{q}{X}\right) = \frac{1}{X}(MP - AP) \tag{5}$$

Clearly, when MP is greater than AP, the expression in [5] is positive and thus AP is rising. When MP is less than AP, AP is falling. When they are equal, AP is at a stationary value.

17. The mathematically correct definition of marginal costs is the rate of change of total cost, with respect to output, q. Thus $MC = dTC/dq$. From the definitions, $TC = TFC + TVC$. Fixed costs are not a function of output. Thus we may write $TC = K + f(q)$, where $f(q)$ is total variable costs and K is a constant. From this, we see that $MC = df(q)/dq$. MC is thus independent of the size of the fixed costs.

18. This point is easily seen if a little algebra is used:

$$AVC = \frac{TVC}{q}$$

but

$$TVC = L \times w$$

and

$$q = AP \times L$$

where L is the quantity of the variable factor used and where w is its cost per unit. Therefore

$$AVC = \frac{L \times w}{AP \times L} = \frac{w}{AP}$$

Since w is a constant, it follows that AVC and AP vary inversely with each other, and when AP is at its maximum value, AVC must be at its minimum value.

19. For this note and the next two it is helpful first to define some terms. Let

$$\pi_n = TR_n - TC_n$$

where π_n is the profit when n units are sold.

If the firm is maximizing its profits by producing n units, it is necessary that the profits at output q_n are at least as large as the profits at output zero. If the firm is maximizing its profits at output n, then

$$\pi_n \geq \pi_0 \qquad [1]$$

The condition says that profits from producing must be greater than profits from not producing. Condition [1] can be rewritten

$$TR_n - TVC_n - TFC_n \\ \geq TR_0 - TVC_0 - TFC_0 \qquad [2]$$

But note that by definition

$$TR_0 = 0 \qquad [3]$$
$$TVC_0 = 0 \qquad [4]$$
$$TFC_n = TFC_0 = K \qquad [5]$$

where K is a constant. By substituting [3], [4], and [5] into [2], we get

$$TR_n - TVC_n \geq 0$$

from which we obtain

$$TR_n \geq TVC_n$$

On a per unit basis, it becomes

$$\frac{TR_n}{q_n} \geq \frac{TVC_n}{q_n} \qquad [6]$$

where q_n is the number of units.

Since $TR_n = q_n p_n$ where p_n is the price when n units are sold, [6] may be rewritten

$$p_n \geq AVC_n$$

This proves rule 1.

20. Using elementary calculus, rule 2 may be proved

$$\pi_n = TR_n - TC_n$$

each of which is a function of output q. To maximize π it is necessary that

$$\frac{d\pi}{dq} = 0 \qquad [1]$$

and that

$$\frac{d^2\pi}{dq^2} < 0 \qquad [2]$$

From the definitions

$$\frac{d\pi}{dq} = \frac{dTR}{dq} - \frac{dTC}{dq} = MR - MC \qquad [3]$$

From [1] and [3], a necessary condition of maximum π is $MR - MC = 0$, or $MR = MC$, as is required by rule 2.

21. Not every point where $MR = MC$ is a point of profit maximization. Continuing the equations of the previous footnote,

$$\frac{d^2\pi}{dq^2} = \frac{dMR}{dq} - \frac{dMC}{dq} \qquad [4]$$

From [2] and [4], a necessary condition of maximum π is

$$\frac{dMR}{dq} - \frac{dMC}{dq} < 0$$

which says that the slope of MC must be greater than the slope of MR. Taken with the previous result, it implies that, for q_n to maximize π, $MR_n = MC_n$ at a point where MC cuts MR from below.

22. Marginal revenue is mathematically the rate of change of total revenue with output dTR/dq. Incremental revenue is $\Delta TR/\Delta q$. But the term marginal revenue is loosely used to refer to both concepts.

23. To prove that, for a downward-sloping demand curve, marginal revenue is less than price, let $p = p(q)$. Then

$$TR = p \times q = p(q) \times q$$

$$MR = \frac{dTR}{dq} = q\,\frac{dp}{dq} + p$$

For a downward-sloping demand curve, dp/dq is negative by definition, and thus MR is less than price for positive values of q.

24. These propositions are easily proved using calculus. Let $p = a - bq$, which is the general equation for a downward-sloping straight line ($b > 0$)

$$TR = pq = aq - bq^2$$

and

$$MR = \frac{dTR}{dq} = a - 2bq$$

Comparison with the demand equation shows that the proof is complete.

25. The monopolist that produces in a single plant but sells in two or more markets will equate the marginal revenue in each market with its marginal cost. Thus $MC = MR_1 = MR_2$ is an equilibrium condition for a monopolist selling in two markets. But the ratio of price to marginal revenue is a function of elasticity of demand: the higher the elasticity, the lower the ratio. Thus equal marginal revenues imply a higher price in the market with the less elastic demand curve.

26. Using the expression for MR given in note 23, it can be seen that, at the kink in the demand curve, q and p are unambiguously determined. But dp/dq, the slope of the demand curve, is very different in the upward and downward directions. Thus the level of MR must be different for increases and decreases in price at the same quantity.

27. The proposition that the marginal labor cost is above the average labor cost when the average is rising is essentially the same proposition proved in math note 16. But let us do it again, using elementary calculus. The quantity of labor depends on the wage rate: $L = f(w)$. The marginal cost of labor is $d(wL)/dL = w + L(dw/dL)$. But w is the average cost of labor, and as long as the supply curve slopes upward, $dw/dL > 0$, and thus $MC > AC$.

28. The condition defined for profit-maximizing behavior by a monopsonist is to hire the factor up to the point where demand equals marginal cost. This condition ($MC = MRP$) is defined by equation [1] on page 336. To see why, note that a firm's demand curve for a factor reflects the factor's contribution to the firm's revenue. Let Q be output, R revenue, and L the number of units of labor hired. The contribution to rev-

enue of additional labor is $\frac{\partial R}{\partial L}$. This in turn depends on the contribution of the extra labor to output $\frac{\partial Q}{\partial L}$ (the marginal product of the factor) and $\partial R/\partial Q$, the firm's marginal revenue from the extra output. Thus

$$\frac{\partial R}{\partial L} = \frac{\partial Q}{\partial L} \times \frac{\partial R}{\partial Q}$$

or, $MRP = MP \cdot MR$

29. Let t be the tax rate applied to the profits, π, of the firm. The profits after tax will be $(1 - t)\pi$. If profits are maximized at output q^*, then by definition

$$\pi(q^*) > \pi(q_i)$$

where q_i is any other output.

Now multiply each side by $(1 - t)$. Since $(1 - t)$ is positive for any tax rate less than 100 percent, the direction of the inequality does not change. Thus

$$(1 - t)\pi(q^*) > (1 - t) \times (q_i)$$

This shows that q^* is the profit maximizing output no matter what the tax rate.

30. In the text we define MPC as an incremental ratio. For mathematical treatments it is more convenient to define all marginal concepts as derivatives: $MPC = dC/dY_d$, $MPS = dS/dY_d$, and so on.

31. The graph shows a linear consumption function, $C = a + bY_d$, where $a > 0$ and $0 < b < 1$. The $MPC = dC/dY_d = b$. The $APC = C/Y_d = (a + bY_d)/Y_d = a/Y_d + b$. This declines as Y_d rises, and clearly $APC \to b$ as $Y_d \to \infty$. The break-even level of income is $C = Y_d$ or $a + bY_d = Y_d$, which solves as $Y_d = a/(1 - b)$.

32. Since $S = Y_d - C$, there is a simple relation between the propensities to consume and to save:

$$APC = \frac{C}{Y_d} = \frac{Y - S}{Y_d} = 1 - \frac{S}{Y_d} = 1 - APS$$

and

$$MPC = \frac{\Delta C}{\Delta Y_d} = \frac{\Delta Y - \Delta S}{\Delta Y_d} = 1 - \frac{\Delta S}{\Delta Y_d}$$
$$= 1 - MPS$$

Therefore, $APC + APS = 1$ and $MPC + MPS = 1$, where the propensities are measured out of disposable income.

33. A constant *APC* necessarily implies the equality of *APC* and *MPC*:

$$APC = \frac{C}{Y}$$

If $\frac{C}{Y} = k$

then $C = kY$

and $\frac{\Delta C}{\Delta Y} = k = MPC$

34. All we are doing is using functions of functions. We have $C = c(Y_d)$ and $Y_d = f[Y]$. So by substitution $C = c(f[Y])$.

35. The total expenditure over all rounds is the sum of an infinite series. Letting *J* stand for the initiating expenditure and *r* for the marginal propensity to spend. the total expenditure for *n* rounds can be written

$$\Delta J \, (1 + r + r^2 + r^3 + \cdots + r^n)$$

If *r* is less than 1, the series in brackets converges to $1/(1 - r)$ as *n* approaches infinity. Total expenditure is thus $\Delta J/(1 - r)$. In the example in the box, $r = .5$; therefore total expenditure is 2 times ΔJ.

36. National income, *Y*, is divided into autonomous expenditure, *A*, and induced expenditure, *N*:

$$Y = A + N$$

Any change in *Y* must be accounted for by changes in these components.

$$\Delta Y = \Delta A + \Delta N \qquad [1]$$

Changes in induced expenditure depend on changes in *Y*.

$$\Delta N = n\Delta Y \qquad [2]$$

where $0 < n < 1$ is the marginal propensity to spend out of national income.

Substituting (2) into (1), manipulating it, and letting $w = 1 - n$ yields

$$\Delta Y = A + n\Delta Y$$
$$\Delta Y - n\Delta Y = A$$
$$\Delta Y (1 - n) = A$$

$$\frac{\Delta Y}{\Delta A} = \frac{1}{1 - n} = \frac{1}{w} = K$$

which are the expressions in the text.

37. The accelerator may be stated as a general macroeconomic theory. Define I_n as the volume of net investment this year and ΔY as the increase in national income from last year to this year. The accelerator theory is the relationship between I_n and ΔY.

Assume that the capital-output ratio is a constant.

$$\frac{K}{Y} = \alpha$$

or

$$K = \alpha Y$$

If *Y* is to change, *K* must be changed accordingly:

$$\Delta K = \alpha \Delta Y$$

But the change in the capital stock (ΔK) *is* net investment, so

$$\Delta K \equiv I_n = \alpha \Delta Y$$

38. This is easily proved. In equilibrium, the banking system wants sufficient deposits (*D*) to establish the legal ratio (*r*) of deposits to reserves (*R*). This gives $R/D = r$. Any change in *D* of ΔD has to be accompanied by a change in *R* of ΔR of sufficient size to restore *r*. Thus $\Delta R/\Delta D = r$, so that $\Delta D = \Delta R/r$, and $\Delta D/\Delta R = 1/r$.

39. Proof: Let *r* be the reserve ratio. Let $z = 1 - r$ be the excess reserves per dollar of new deposit. If *X* dollars are deposited in the system assumed in the text, the successive rounds of new deposits will be *X*, zX, z^2X, z^3X. . . . The series
$X + zX + z^2X + z^3X \cdots$
$$= X[1 + z + z^2 + z^3 + \cdots]$$

has a limit

$$X \frac{1}{1 - z} = X \left[\frac{1}{1 - (1 - r)} \right] = \frac{X}{r}$$

40. Suppose the public desire to hold a fraction, *v*, for any new deposits in cash. Now let the banking system receive an initial increase in its reserves of ΔR. It can expand deposits by an amount ΔD. As it does so, the banking system suffers a cash drain to the public of $v\Delta D$. The banking system can only increase deposits to the extent the required reserve ratio, *r*, makes possible. The maximum is:

$$r\Delta D = \Delta R - v\Delta D$$

The left-hand side gives the required reserves, the right-hand side the actual reserves after the cash drain. From this,

$$r = \frac{\Delta R}{\Delta D} - v$$

or

$$\frac{\Delta D}{\Delta R} = \frac{1}{r + v}$$

41. The "rule of 72" is an approximation derived from the mathematics of compound interest. Any measure X_t will have the value $X_t = X_0 e^{rt}$ after t years at a continuous growth rate of r percent per year. Because $X_1/X_0 = 2$ requires $r \times t = 0.69$, a "rule of 69" would be correct for continuous growth. But 69 is an awkward number that is easily divisible only by 3 and 23. The number 72 is very close to 69 and is divisible by the integers 2, 3, 4, 6, 8, 9, 12, 18, 24, and 36. Thus it is convenient to use a "rule of 72" instead of 69. Probably the original reason for the use of 72 is that the rule was developed in the context of compound interest, and if interest is compounded only once a year the product of $r \times t$ for X to double is .72.

42. The time taken to break even is a function of the *difference* in growth rates, not their level. Thus, in the example, had 4 percent and 5 percent or 5 percent and 6 percent been used, it still would have taken the same number of years. To see this quickly, recognize that we are interested in the ratio of two growth paths: $e^{r1t}/e^{r2t} = e^{(r1 - r2)t}$.

43. The derivation of this result is as follows. Let X be your level and Y your competitor's.

$$X_0 = \frac{2}{3} Y_0 \tag{1}$$

$$Y_{10} = Y_0 e^{10r} \tag{2}$$

$$X_{10} = X_0 e^{10(r + a)} \tag{3}$$

If $X_{10} = Y_{10}$ then

$$Y_0 e^{10r} = X_0 e^{10(r + a)} \tag{4}$$

and

$$\frac{Y_0}{X_0} = \frac{3}{2} = e^{10a} \tag{5}$$

for which $a = 0.04$.

44. Modern mathematicians distinguish between a correspondence and a function. There is a *correspondence* between Y and X if each value of X is associated with one or more values of Y. Y is a *function* of X if there is one and only one value of Y associated with each value of X. Mathematicians of an older generation described both relations as functional relations and then distinguished between single-valued functions (in modern language, functional relations) and multi-valued functions (in modern language, relations of correspondence). In the text we adopt the older, more embracing usage of the term functional relation.

45. Strictly speaking, the marginal rate of substitution refers to the slope of the tangent to the isoquant at a particular point while the calculations in Table 13A-1 refer to the average rate of substitution between two distinct points on the isoquant. Assume a production function

$$Q = Q(K, L) \tag{1}$$

Isoquants are given by the function

$$K = I(L, \bar{Q}) \tag{2}$$

derived from [1] by expressing K as an explicit function of L and Q. A single isoquant relates to a particular value at which Q is held constant. Define Q_K, and Q_L as an alternative, more compact notation for $\partial Q/\partial K$ and $\partial Q/\partial L$, the marginal products of capital and labor. Also let Q_{KK} and Q_{LL} stand for $\partial^2 Q/\partial L^2$ and $\partial^2 Q/\partial K^2$ respectively. To obtain the slope of the isoquant, totally differentiate [1] to obtain

$$dQ = Q_K dK + Q_L dL$$

Then, since we are moving along a single isoquant, set $dQ = 0$ to obtain

$$\frac{dK}{dL} = -\frac{Q_L}{Q_K} = MRS$$

Diminishing marginal productivity implies Q_{LL}, $Q_{KK} < 0$ and hence, as we move down the isoquant of Figure 13A-1, Q_K is rising and Q_L is falling, so the absolute value of MRS is diminishing. This is called the hypothesis of a diminishing marginal rate of substitution.

46. Formally the problem is to maximize $Q = Q(K, L)$ subject to the budget constraint

$$p_K K + p_L L = C$$

To do this, form the Lagrangean

$$Q(K, L) - \lambda(p_K K + p_L L - C)$$

The first-order conditions for finding the saddle point on this function are

$$Q_K - \lambda p_K = 0; \quad Q_K = \lambda p_K \qquad [1]$$

$$Q_L - \lambda p_L = 0; \quad Q_L = \lambda p_L \qquad [2]$$

$$-p_K K - p_L L + C = 0 \qquad [3]$$

Dividing [1] by [2] yields

$$\frac{Q_K}{Q_L} = \frac{p_K}{p_L}$$

that is, the ratio of the marginal products, which is (-1) times the MRS, is equal to the ratio of the prices, which is (-1) times the slope of the isocost line.

47. That $p > MC$ follows at once from the two propositions that $MR = MC$ and $p > MR$ for a downward-sloping demand curve, proved in math note 23. That p is greater than minimum ATC follows from the fact that it is equal to ATC where ATC is not a minimum.

48. The condition that for profit maximization MRP be downward-sloping at the point where $w = MRP$ is just an application of the proposition (proved in math notes 20 and 21) that for profit maximization MC must cut MR from below. Consider the output added by the last unit of the variable factor. Its marginal cost is w, and its marginal revenue is MRP. Thus w must cut MRP from below. Since w is a horizontal line, MRP must be falling.

Putting the matter in standard mathematical terms,

$$w = MRP \qquad [1]$$

is a first order condition of *either* maximizing or minimizing. The second order condition for maximization is

$$\frac{dw}{dq} > \frac{dMRP}{dq} \qquad [2]$$

Since

$$\frac{dw}{dq} = 0 \qquad [3]$$

the slope of MRP must be negative to satisfy [2], that is, it must be declining.

Glossary

absolute advantage One nation has an absolute advantage over another nation in the production of a commodity when the same amount of resources will produce more of the commodity in the one nation than in the other.

absolute cost advantages Existing firms have absolute cost advantages when their average cost curves are significantly lower over their entire range than those of firms that are potential entrants into the industry.

absolute price A price expressed in money terms.

accelerator The theory that relates the level of investment to the rate of change of national income.

actual GNP The gross national product that the economy in fact produces.

adaptive expectations The theory that people form expectations about the future behavior of some variable on the basis of its behavior in the recent past. With respect to inflation the *expected* future inflation rate depends on past *actual* inflation rates.

adjustable peg system A system in which monetary authorities peg (i.e., fix) the price of their domestic currency on the foreign exchange market but in which the price at which the currency is pegged can be adjusted (i.e., changed) from time to time.

administered price A price set by conscious decision of the seller rather than by the impersonal forces of demand and supply.

ad valorem tax See *excise tax*.

AE In boldface, the term represents actual aggregate expenditure; in lightface, desired aggregate expenditure.

AE = C + I + G Indicates the three main components of aggregate expenditure in a closed economy: consumption expenditure, investment expenditure, and government expenditure.

AE = C + I + G + (X − M) Indicates the four main components of aggregate expenditure in an open economy: consumption expenditure, investment expenditure, government expenditure, and net exports (exports *minus* imports).

aggregate demand (AD) curve A relation between the total amount of all output that will be demanded by purchasers and the price level of that output. It shows the combination of real national income and the price level that makes aggregate desired expenditure equal to national income and the demand for money equal to the supply of money.

aggregate expenditure (AE) function The function that relates aggregate desired expenditure to national income.

aggregate supply (AS) curve A relation between the total amount of output that will be produced and the price level of that output.

allocation of resources The distribution of the available factors of production among the various uses to which they might be put.

allocative efficiency An allocation of resources in which price equals marginal cost in all industries and which is thus Pareto-optimal; it is often treated as a goal of economic organization.

allocative inefficiency The absence of allocative efficiency. Some consumers could be made better off by producing a different bundle of goods, without any consumers being made worse off.

annuity A specific sum of money, paid at stated intervals, that continues to be paid indefinitely.

antitrust laws Laws designed to control monopolistic practices and monopoly power, including the Sherman Act (1890), the Clayton Act (1914), and the Federal Trade Commission Act (1914).

appreciation of the exchange rate A rise in the free-market value of domestic currency in terms of foreign currencies.

a priori Literally, "at a prior time" or "in advance"; knowledge that is prior to actual experience.

arbitrage The purchase of any commodity in markets where it is cheap in order to sell it in markets where it is dear, with the consequent effect of eliminating intermarket differentials.

arc elasticity Elasticity of demand, for discrete changes in price and quantity. For analytical purposes, it is usually defined by the formula

$$\eta = \frac{\Delta q / q}{\Delta p / p}$$

An alternative formula often used where computations are involved is

$$\eta = -\frac{(q_2 - q_1)/(q_2 + q_1)}{(p_2 - p_1)/(p_2 + p_1)}$$

automatic transfer service (ATS) A savings deposit from which funds are transferred automatically to the depositor's demand deposit to cover checks as they are drawn.

autonomous expenditure In macroeconomics, elements of expenditure that do not vary systematically with other variables such as national income and the interest rate, but which are determined by forces outside of the theory. Also called *exogenous expenditure*.

autonomous variables See *exogenous variables*.

average cost (AC) Some measure of cost divided by the number of units of output.

average fixed costs (AFC) Total fixed costs divided by number of units of output.

average product (AP) Total product divided by the number of units of the variable factor used in its production.

average propensity to consume (APC) The proportion of income devoted to consumption: total consumption expenditure divided by income. The income variable may be disposable income, in which case $APC = C/Y_d$, or it may be national income, in which case $APC = C/Y$.

average propensity to save (APS) The proportion of income devoted to saving: total saving divided by income. The income variable may be disposable income, in which case $APS = S/Y_d$, or it may be national income, in which case $APS = S/Y$.

average revenue (AR) Total revenue divided by quantity. Where a single price prevails, $AR = p$.

average tax rate The ratio of total tax paid to total income earned.

average total cost (ATC) Total cost divided by the number of units of output; the sum of average fixed costs and average variable costs. Also called *cost per unit, unit cost, average cost (AC)*.

average variable costs (AVC) Total variable costs divided by the number of units of output. Also called *direct unit costs, avoidable unit costs*.

balanced budget A situation in which current revenue is exactly equal to current expenditures.

balanced budget multiplier The change in income divided by the tax-financed change in government expenditure that brought it about.

balanced growth policy Simultaneous growth in all sectors of the economy; a growth experience suitable to a closed economy.

balance-of-payments accounts A summary record of a

country's transactions that typically involve payments or receipts of foreign exchange.

balance-of-payments deficit A situation in which a country's receipts on current and capital account fall short of its payments (ignoring transactions by monetary authorities).

balance-of-payments surplus A situation in which a country's receipts on current and capital account exceed its payments (ignoring transactions by monetary authorities).

balance of trade The difference between the value of exports and the value of imports of visible items (goods).

balance sheet A report showing a firm's assets and the claims against those assets at a moment in time. Balance sheets always balance because the owners' equity is defined as the amount of the assets less the claims of the creditors.

bank notes Paper money issued by commercial banks.

barriers to entry Legal or other impediments to entry into an industry. Patents, franchises, economies of scale, and established brand preferences may each lead to such barriers.

barter A system in which goods and services are traded directly for other goods and services.

base period A year or other point in time chosen for comparison purposes in connection with expressing or computing *index numbers* or *constant dollars*.

beggar-my-neighbor policies Policies designed to increase a country's prosperity (especially by reducing its unemployment) at the expense of reducing prosperity in other countries (especially by increasing their unemployment).

blacklist An employer's list of workers who have been fired for union activity.

black market A situation in which goods are sold illegally at prices above a legal maximum price.

bond An evidence of debt carrying a specified amount and schedule of interest payments as well as a date for redemption of the face value of the bond.

bondholders Creditors of the firm, whose evidence of debt is a bond issued by the firm.

boycott A concerted refusal to buy (buyers' boycott) or to sell (producers' or sellers' boycott) a commodity.

bread-and-butter unionism A union movement whose major objectives are wages, hours, and conditions of employment rather than political or social ends.

budget balance The difference between total government revenue and total government expenditure.

budget deficit The shortfall of current revenue below current expenditure.

budget line (isocost line) A line on a diagram showing all combinations of commodities that a household may obtain if it spends a given amount of money at fixed prices of the commodities.

budget surplus The excess of current revenue over current expenditure.

budget surplus function A function relating the size of the government's budget surplus (revenue minus expenditure) to the level of national income. (Deficits are shown as negative surpluses.)

built-in stabilizer Anything that tends to adjust government revenues and expenditures automatically (i.e., without an explicit policy decision) so as to reduce inflationary and deflationary gaps whenever they develop.

business cycles More or less regular patterns of fluctuations in the level of economic activity.

C In boldface, the term represents actual consumption expenditure; in lightface, desired consumption expenditure.

C + I + G − M Indicates the main components of domestic expenditure on domestically produced commodities.

capacity The level of output that corresponds to the minimum level of short-run average total costs. Also called *plant capacity*.

capital A factor of production defined to include all man-made aids to further production.

capital consumption allowance An estimate of the amount by which the capital stock is depleted through its contribution to current production. Often called *depreciation*.

capital deepening Adding capital to the production process in such a way as to increase the ratio of capital to labor and other factors of production.

capitalized value The value of an asset measured by the present value of the income stream it is expected to produce.

capital-output ratio The ratio of the value of capital to the annual value of output produced by it.

capital stock The aggregate quantity of a society's capital goods.

capital widening Adding capital to the production process in such a way as to leave factor proportions unchanged.

cartel An organization of producers designed to limit

or eliminate competition among its members, usually by agreeing to restrict output in an effort to achieve noncompetitive prices.

categorical grants-in-aid Federal grants to state or local governments for specified categories of expenditures such as highways or welfare payments.

ceiling price A maximum permitted price.

central authorities All public agencies, government bodies, and other organizations belonging to or under the control of government.

central bank A bank that acts as banker to the commercial banking system and often to the government as well. In the modern world the central bank is usually the sole money-issuing authority.

certificate of deposit (CD) A negotiable time deposit carrying a higher interest rate than that paid on ordinary time deposits.

ceteris paribus Literally, "other things being equal"; usually used in economics to indicate that all variables except the ones specified are assumed not to change.

change in demand An increase or decrease in the quantity demanded at each possible price of the commodity, represented by a shift of the whole demand curve.

change in supply An increase or decrease in the quantity supplied at each possible price of the commodity, represented by a shift of the whole supply curve.

civilian labor force The total number of employed, other than persons serving in the armed forces, plus the number of unemployed.

cleared market A market in which buyers have been able to buy all they wish and sellers have been able to sell all they wish at the going price; a competitive market in equilibrium.

clearing house An institution where interbank indebtednesses arising from transfer of checks between banks are computed, offset against each other, and net amounts owing are calculated.

closed economy An economy that does not engage in foreign trade.

closed shop A bargaining arrangement in which only union members can be employed. Union membership precedes employment.

coefficient of determination (r^2 or R^2) The coefficient showing the fraction of the total variance of the dependent variable that can be associated with the independent variables in the regression equation; r^2 is used for two variables and R^2 for three or more variables.

collective bargaining The whole process by which

unions and employers arrive at and enforce agreements.

collective consumption goods Goods or services that, if they provide benefits to anyone, necessarily provide benefits to a large group of people or a community.

collusion An agreement among sellers to set a common price and/or to share a market. Collusion may be overt or secret. It may be explicit or tacit.

command economy An economy in which the decisions of the central authorities exert the major influence over the allocation of resources.

commercial banks Privately owned, profit-seeking institutions that provide a variety of financial services. They accept deposits from customers, which they agree to transfer when ordered by a check, and they make loans and other investments.

commodities Marketable items produced to satisfy wants. Commodities may be either *goods*, which are tangible, or *services*, which are intangible.

common-property resource A natural resource that is owned by no one and may be used by anyone.

common stock A form of equity capital usually carrying voting rights and a residual claim to the assets and profits of the firm.

comparative advantage (1) Country A has a comparative advantage over country B in producing a commodity, X, when it can do so at a lesser opportunity cost in terms of other products forgone. (2) As distinguished from absolute advantage: Comparing two countries, A and B, and two commodities, X and Y, country A has a comparative advantage in X when its margin of absolute advantage is greater in X than in Y.

comparative statics Comparative static equilibrium analysis; the derivation of predictions by analyzing the effect of a change in some exogenous variable or parameter on the equilibrium position.

competitive devaluations A round of devaluations of exchange rates by a number of countries, each trying to gain a competitive advantage over the other and each failing to the extent that other countries also devalue.

complement A commodity that tends to be used jointly with the original commodity. Technically, a complement to a commodity is another commodity for which the cross elasticity of demand is non-negligible and negative.

comprehensive income taxation (CIT) A proposal to expand the tax base from the presently defined concept of taxable income, to include income from most sources and to eliminate most exemptions and deductions. CIT can be defined in many different ways, depending on what is added to taxable income.

concentration ratio The fraction of total market sales (or some other measure of market occupancy) made by a specified number of the industry's largest firms. Four-firm and eight-firm concentrations ratios are the most frequently used.

conglomerate merger See *merger*.

conscious parallel action See *tacit collusion*.

constant-cost industry An industry in which costs of the most efficient size firm remain constant as the entire industry expands or contracts in the long run.

constant dollar GNP Gross national product valued in prices prevailing in some base year; year-to-year changes in constant dollar GNP reflect changes only in quantities produced. Also called *real GNP*.

constant dollars A series expressed in terms of the level of prices prevailing in a specified *base period*. Constant dollars are thus free of inflationary or deflationary trends. Used in contrast to *current dollars*.

constant returns A situation in which output increases proportionately with the quantity of inputs as the scale of production is increased.

consumerism A movement that asserts a conflict between the interests of firms and the public interest.

Consumer Price Index (CPI) A measure of the average percentage change in the prices of commodities commonly bought by households; compiled monthly by the Bureau of Labor Statistics.

consumers' durables See *durable good*.

consumers' surplus The difference between the total value consumers place on all units consumed of a commodity and the payment they must make to purchase the same amount of the commodity.

consumption The act of using commodities to satisfy wants.

consumption function The relationship between consumption expenditure and all of the factors that determine it. In the simplest consumption function, consumption depends only on current income.

corporation A form of business organization with a legal existence separate from that of the owners, in which ownership and financial responsibility are divided, limited, and shared among any number of individual and institutional shareholders.

cost (of output) To a producing firm, the value of factors of production used up in producing output.

cost minimization Achieving the lowest attainable cost of producing a specified output. It is an implication

of profit maximization that the firm will choose the least costly method available of producing any specific output.

CPI See *Consumer Price Index*.

craft union A union organized according to a specified set of skills or occupations.

credit rationing Rationing of available funds among borrowers in a situation in which there is excess demand for loans at prevailing interest rates.

cross elasticity of demand A measure of the extent to which quantity of a commodity demanded responds to changes in price of a related commodity. Formula:

$$\frac{\text{percentage change in quantity of } x}{\text{percentage change in price of } y}$$

cross-sectional data Data referring to a number of different observations at the same point in time.

current dollar GNP Gross national product valued in prices prevailing at the time of measurement; year-to-year changes in current dollar GNP reflect changes both in quantities produced and in market prices. Also called *nominal GNP*.

current dollars A measurement expressed in terms of the prices prevailing at the time of measurement.

debt Amounts owed to one's creditors, including banks and other financial institutions.

decision lag A lapse of time between obtaining relevant information about some problem and reaching a decision on what to do about it.

decreasing returns A situation in which output increases less than in proportion to inputs as the scale of production increases. A firm in this situation, with fixed factor prices, is an *increasing cost* firm.

deficient-demand unemployment Unemployment that is due to insufficient aggregate demand and that can be reduced by measures that raise aggregate demand.

deflationary gap The amount by which the aggregate demand schedule must be increased to achieve full-employment income.

demand There are several distinct but closely related concepts: (1) *quantity demanded;* (2) the whole relationship of the quantity demanded to variables that determine it, such as tastes, household income, distribution of income, population, price of the commodity, and prices of other commodities; (3) the *demand schedule;* (4) the *demand curve*. The phrase increase (decrease) in demand means a shift of the demand curve to the right (left), indicating an increase (decrease) in the quantity demanded at each possible price.

demand curve The graphic representation of the *demand schedule*.

demand deposit A bank deposit that is withdrawable on demand and transferable by means of a check.

demand for money The total amount of money balances that the public wishes to hold for all purposes.

demand-pull inflation Inflation arising from excess aggregate demand.

demand schedule The relationship between the quantity demanded of a commodity and its price, *ceteris paribus*.

deposit money Money held by the public in the form of demand deposits with commercial banks.

depreciation (1) The loss in value of an asset over a period of time; includes both physical wear and tear and obsolescence. (2) The amount by which the capital stock is depleted through its contribution to current production.

depreciation of the exchange rate A fall in the free-market value of domestic currency in terms of foreign currencies.

depression A period of very low economic activity with very high unemployment and high excess capacity.

derived demand The demand for a factor of production that results from the demand for products it is used to make.

devaluation of the exchange rate A downward revision in the value at which a country's currency is pegged in terms of foreign currencies.

differentiated products Products sufficiently distinguishable within an industry that the producer of each has some power over its own price; the products of firms in monopolistically competitive industry.

diminishing marginal rate of substitution The hypothesis that the marginal rate of substitution changes systematically as the amounts of two commodities being consumed vary.

dirty float Although foreign exchange rates are left to be determined on the free market, monetary authorities intervene in this market so as to influence exchange rates, but they are *not* publicly committed to holding their country's exchange rate at any announced "par value." Also called *managed float*.

discount rate (1) In banking, the rate at which the cen-

tral bank is prepared to lend reserves to commercial banks. (2) More generally, the rate of interest used to discount a stream of future payments to arrive at their *present value*.

discretionary fiscal policy Fiscal policy that is a conscious response (not according to any predetermined rule) to each particular state of the economy as it arises.

disembodied technical change Technical change that raises output without the necessity of building new capital to embody the new knowledge.

disequilibrium The state or condition of a market that exhibits excess demand or excess supply.

disequilibrium price A price at which quantity demanded does not equal quantity supplied.

disposable income The income that households have available for spending and saving.

dissaving Negative saving; a situation in which household consumption expenditure exceeds disposable income.

distributed profits Earnings of a firm distributed as dividends to the owners of the firm.

dividends That part of profits paid out to shareholders of a corporation.

division of labor The breaking up of a task (e.g., making pins) into a number of repetitive operations, each one done by a different worker.

dollar standard (for international payments) International indebtedness between monetary authorities is settled in terms of dollars, which are not necessarily backed by gold or any other ultimate monetary base.

draft Compulsory recruitment for military service.

dumping In international trade, the practice of selling a commodity at a lower price in the export market than in the domestic market.

duopoly An industry that contains only two firms.

durable good A good which yields its services only gradually over an extended period of time; often divided into the subcategories *producers' durables* (e.g., machines and equipment) and *consumers' durables* (e.g., cars, appliances).

dynamic (or **disequilibrium**) **differential** A difference in factor prices caused by disequilibrium that will tend to lead to corrective movements of resources. In equilibrium these differentials will be eliminated. Observed because it often takes considerable time for equilibrium to be reached.

economic efficiency (in production) A method of producing some quantity of output is economically efficient when it is the least costly method of producing that output.

economic profits or losses (often simply **profits**) The difference in the revenues received from the sale of output and the opportunity cost of the inputs used to make the output. Negative profits are losses.

economic rent That part of the payment to a factor in excess of its *transfer earnings*.

economies of scope Economies achieved by a large firm through multiproduct production, large-scale distribution, advertising, etc. They are an advantage of such firms in addition to economies of scale in production.

economy A set of interrelated production and consumption activities.

efficiency of capital See *productivity of capital*.

effluent charge A fee, fine, or tax on a producer for polluting activity, usually on a per unit basis.

elastic demand The situation existing when for a given percentage change in price there is a greater percentage change in quantity demanded; elasticity greater than 1.

elasticity of demand A measure of the responsiveness of quantity of a commodity demanded to a change in market price. Formula:

$$\frac{\text{percentage change in quantity demanded}}{\text{percentage change in price}}$$

Conventionally expressed as a positive number, it is a pure number ranging from zero to infinity.

embodied technical change A technical change that can be utilized only when new capital, embodying the new techniques, is built.

employment The number of workers 16 years of age and older who hold full-time civilian jobs.

endogenous expenditure See *induced expenditure*.

endogenous variables Variables explained within a theory. Also called *induced variables*.

envelope curve Any curve that encloses, by just being tangent to, a series of other curves. In particular, the *envelope cost curve* is the *LRAC* curve; it encloses the *SRAC* curves by being tangent to them but not cutting them.

equilibrium condition A condition that must be fulfilled for some economic variable, such as price or national income, to be in equilibrium.

equilibrium differentials Differences in factor prices that would persist in equilibrium, without any tendency for them to be removed. These differences may be associated with differences in the factors themselves or with the nonmonetary advantages of different employments.

equilibrium price The price at which quantity demanded equals quantity supplied.

equity capital Capital provided by the owners of a firm.

error term An expressed or implied variable in a functional relationship to allow for (1) omitted variables and (2) errors in measurement.

excess capacity (1) Production at levels below the output at which *ATC* is a minimum. (2) The difference between such actual output and capacity output.

excess capacity theorem The proposition that equilibrium in a monopolistically competitive industry will occur where each firm has excess capacity.

excess demand A situation in which, at the given price, quantity demanded exceeds quantity supplied. Also called *shortage*.

excess reserves Reserves held by a commercial bank in excess of the legally required amount.

excess supply A situation in which, at the given price, quantity supplied exceeds quantity demanded. Also called *surplus*.

exchange rate The price in terms of one currency at which another currency, or claims on it, can be bought and sold.

excise tax A tax on the sale of a particular commodity. A *specific tax* is a fixed tax per unit of the taxed commodity. An *ad valorem tax* is a fixed percentage of the value of the commodity.

execution lag A lapse of time between the decision to do something and its actually being done.

exemption draft A draft in which specified criteria such as age, occupation, the family status determine who is drafted from among the pool of those who meet the basic requirements (of health, etc.) for military service.

exogenous expenditure See *autonomous expenditure*.

exogenous variables Variables that influence other variables within a theory but that themselves are determined by factors outside the theory. Also called *autonomous variables*.

expectational inflation Inflation that occurs because decision makers raise prices (so as to keep their relative prices constant) in the expectation that the price level is going to rise.

externalities (also called **third-party effects**) Effects, either good or bad, on parties not directly involved in the production or use of a commodity.

factor markets Markets in which households sell the services of the factors of production that they control.

factor mobility The ease with which factors can be transferred between uses.

factors of production Resources used to produce goods and services to satisfy wants. Land, labor, and capital are three frequently used basic categories of factors of production.

falling-cost industry An industry in which the lowest costs attainable by a firm fall as the whole scale of the industry expands.

federation In respect to labor unions, a federation is any loose organization of national unions.

fiat money Paper money or coinage that is neither backed by nor convertible into anything else yet is legal tender.

final products The economy's output of goods and services after all double counting has been eliminated.

fine tuning The attempt to maintain national income closely at its full-employment level by means of frequent changes in fiscal or monetary policy.

firm The unit that makes decisions regarding the employment of factors of production and the production of goods and services.

fiscal drag The tendency for a deflationary gap to open up at full-employment income because tax revenues rise faster than government expenditure as full-employment income rises due to economic growth.

fiscal policy The deliberate use of the government's revenue-raising and spending activities in an effort to influence the behavior of such macro variables as the GNP and total employment.

fixed costs Costs that do not change with output. Also sometimes called *overhead cost*.

fixed exchange rate An exchange rate that is fixed or pegged within very narrow bands by the action of monetary authorities.

fixed factors Factors that cannot be increased in the short run.

floating exchange rate An exchange rate that is left to be determined on the free market without any attempt by monetary authorities to determine its value.

foreign exchange (foreign media of exchange) Actual foreign currency or various claims on it such as bank balances or promises to pay.

45° line In macroeconomic graphs, the line that joins all those points at which expenditure equals income.

fractional reserve system In contrast to a 100 percent reserve system, a banking system in which commercial banks are required to keep only a fraction of their deposits in cash or on deposit with the central bank.

freedom of entry and exit The absence of legal or other artificial barriers to entering into production or withdrawing assets from production.

free good A commodity for which no price needs to be paid because the quantity supplied exceeds the quantity demanded at a price of zero.

free-market economy An economy in which the decisions of individual households and firms (as distinct from the central authorities) exert the major influence over the allocation of resources.

free trade A situation in which all commodities can be freely imported and exported without special taxes or restrictions being levied merely because of their status as "imports" or "exports."

frictional unemployment Unemployment caused by the time taken for labor to move from one job to another.

fringe benefits Payments (other than wages) for the benefit of labor. They may include company contributions to pension and welfare funds, sick leave, paid holidays.

full-cost pricing Pricing according to average total cost plus a fixed markup. Usually the costs are standard costs as defined by good accounting practice.

full-employment GNP See *potential GNP*.

full-employment national income (Y_F) See *potential GNP*.

full-employment surplus (FES) An estimate of government tax revenues less government expenditures as they would be at full-employment national income.

function Loosely, an expression of a relation between two or more variables. Precisely, Y is a function of the variables $X_1, \ldots, X_n$ if for every set of values of the variables $X_1, \ldots, X_n$ there is associated a unique value of the variable Y.

functional distribution of income The distribution of income by major factors of production.

G In boldface, the term represents actual government expenditure; in lightface, desired government expenditure.

gains from trade The increased production that results from specialization and trade as opposed to a situation of self-sufficiency. It can be applied to persons, regions, or nations.

Giffen good An inferior good for which the negative income effect outweighs the substitution effect and leads to an upward-sloping demand curve.

given period A year or other point in time for which an *index number* measures a change in some variable that has occurred since some earlier point in time (*base period*).

GNP deflator See *gross national product deflator*.

GNP gap Output that could have been produced if the economy were fully employed but that instead goes unproduced; *potential GNP* minus *actual GNP*.

gold exchange standard A monetary system in which some countries' currencies are directly convertible into gold while other countries' currencies are indirectly convertible by being convertible into the gold-backed currencies at a fixed rate. Under the Bretton Woods version only the U.S. dollar was directly convertible into gold.

goods Tangible commodities such as cars or shoes.

Gresham's law The theory that "bad," or debased, money drives "good," or undebased, money out of circulation because people will keep the good money and spend the bad money.

gross investment The total value of all investment goods produced in the economy during a stated period of time.

gross national product (GNP) The sum of all values added in the economy. It is the sum of the values of all final goods produced and, which is the same thing, the sum of all factor incomes earned.

gross national product deflator An index number derived by dividing GNP measured in current dollars by GNP measured in constant dollars and multiplying by 100. It is in effect a price index with current-year quantity weights measuring the average change in price of all the items in the GNP. Also called the *implicit GNP deflator*.

gross return to capital The receipts from the sale of goods produced by a firm less the cost of purchased goods and materials, labor, land, the manager's talents, and taxes.

homogeneous product (1) identical products; (2) a product similar enough across an industry that no one firm has any power over price; (3) the product of a firm in perfect competition.

horizontal merger See *merger*.

household All the people who live under one roof and who make, or are subject to others making for them, joint financial decisions.

human capital The capitalized value of productive investments in persons. Usually refers to investments resulting from expenditures on education, training, and health improvements.

hypothesis of equal net advantage The hypothesis that owners of factors will choose the use of their factors that produces the greatest net advantage to themselves and therefore will move their factors among uses until net advantages are equalized.

hypothesis of diminishing returns The hypothesis that if increasing quantities of a variable factor are applied to a given quantity of fixed factors, the marginal product and average product of the variable factor will eventually decrease. Also called *hypothesis of diminishing returns, law of diminishing returns, law of variable proportions*.

I In boldface, the term represents actual investment expenditure; in lightface, desired investment expenditure.

identification problem The ambiguity introduced by attempting to use observations of prices and quantities actually exchanged to draw inferences about either supply curves or demand curves when shifts in both curves have occurred.

implicit GNP deflator See *gross national product deflator*.

import cost-push inflation Inflation caused by increases in the prices of a country's major imports.

import substitution industry (ISI) Domestic production for sale in the home market of goods previously imported; usually involves some form of protection or subsidy.

imputed costs The costs of using in production factors already owned by the firm, measured by the earnings they could have received in their best alternative employment.

income-consumption line A line connecting the points of tangency of a set of indifference curves with a series of parallel budget lines, showing how consumption of a good changes as income changes, with relative prices held constant.

income effect The effect on quantity demanded of a change in real income.

income elasticity of demand A measure of the responsiveness of quantity demanded to a change in income. Formula:

$$\frac{\text{percentage change in quantity demanded}}{\text{percentage change in income}}$$

income statement A financial report showing the revenues and costs that arise from the firm's use of inputs to produce outputs, over a specified period of time.

incomes policy Any attempt by the central authorities to influence wage and price formation. The instruments vary from voluntary guidelines at one extreme to legally enforced wage and price controls at the other.

increasing returns A situation in which output increases more than in proportion to inputs as the scale of a firm's production increases. A firm in this situation, with fixed factor prices, is a *decreasing cost* firm.

incremental cost See *marginal cost*.

incremental product See *marginal product*.

incremental revenue See *marginal revenue*.

indexing The automatic increasing of money values as the average level of all prices rises during an inflation.

index numbers Averages that measure changes over time of variables such as the price level and industrial production. They are conventionally expressed as percentages relative to a base period assigned the value 100.

indifference curve A curve showing all combinations of two commodities that give the household equal amounts of satisfaction and among which the household is thus indifferent.

indifference map A set of indifference curves, each indicating a constant level of satisfaction derived by the household concerned, and based on a given set of household preferences.

induced expenditure In macroeconomics, elements of expenditure that are explained by variables within the theory, such as national income and interest rates. Also called *endogenous expenditure*.

industrial union A union organized to include all workers in an industry, regardless of skills.

industry A group of firms producing similar products.

inelastic demand The situation in which for a given percentage change in price there is a smaller percentage change in quantity demanded; elasticity less than unity.

inertial inflation Inflation that persists only because decision makers raise prices (so as to maintain their desired relative prices) when they see that closely related prices have risen.

infant industry argument for tariffs The argument that new domestic industries with potential economies of scale need to be protected from competition from established low-cost foreign producers so that they can grow large enough to reap their own economies of scale and achieve costs as low as those of foreign producers.

inferior goods Goods for which income elasticity is negative.

inflation A rise in the average level of all prices. Sometimes restricted to only prolonged or sustained rises.

inflationary gap The extent to which aggregate desired expenditure exceeds national income at full-employment national income.

infrastructure The basic installations and facilities (especially transportation and communications systems) on which the growth of a community depends.

injections Income earned by domestic firms that does not arise out of the spending of domestic households and income earned by domestic households that does not arise out of the spending of domestic firms.

innovation The introduction of inventions into methods of production.

inputs Materials and factor services used in the process of production. It includes the services of factors of production plus intermediate products.

instrumental variables The variables that the central authorities can control directly: thus their instruments of policy.

interest (i) In microeconomics, the payment for borrowed money, (ii) in macroeconomics, the total income paid for the use of borrowed capital.

interest rate The price paid per dollar borrowed per year. Expressed either as a fraction (e.g., .06) or as a percentage (e.g., 6 percent).

intermediate products All goods and services that are used as inputs into a further stage of production.

internalization A process that results in a producer's taking account of a previously external effect.

invention The discovery of something new, such as a new production technique or a new product.

inventories Stocks of raw materials, or of finished goods, held by firms to mitigate the effect of short-term fluctuations in production or sales.

investment Expenditures on the production of goods not for present consumption.

investment goods Capital goods such as plant and equipment plus inventories; production that is not sold for consumption purposes.

invisibles All those items of foreign trade that are intangible; services as opposed to goods.

isocost line The graphic representation of alternative combinations of factors that a firm can buy for a given outlay.

isoquant A curve showing all technologically efficient factor combinations for producing a specified output; an iso-product curve.

isoquant map A series of isoquants from the same production function, each isoquant relating to a specific level of output.

jurisdictional dispute Dispute between unions over which has the right to organize a group of workers.

kinked demand curve A demand curve with a corner, or "kink," at the prevailing price. The curve is more elastic in response to price increases than to price decreases.

labor A factor of production usually defined to include all physical and mental contributions to economic activity provided by people.

labor boycott An organized boycott to persuade customers to refrain from purchasing the products of a firm or industry whose employees are on strike.

labor force The number of people either employed or actively seeking work. See also *civilian labor force*.

labor union See *union*.

Laffer curve A graph relating the revenue yield of a tax system to the marginal or average tax rate imposed.

laissez faire Literally, "let do"; a policy implying the absence of government intervention in a market economy.

land A factor of production usually defined to include all gifts of nature, including raw materials as well as "land" conventionally defined.

law of diminishing returns See *hypothesis of diminishing returns*.

law of variable proportions See *hypothesis of diminishing returns*.

legal tender Anything that by law must be accepted for the purchase of goods and services or in discharge of a debt, and thus money.

less-developed countries (LDCs) The underdeveloped countries of the world, most of which are in Asia, Africa, and South and Central America. They are also called "undeveloped," "developing," and the "South."

life-cycle hypothesis (LCH) The hypothesis that relates the household's actual consumption to its expected lifetime income rather than, as in early Keynesian theory, to its current income.

limited liability The limitation of the financial responsibility of an owner (shareholder) of a corporation to the amount of money he or she has actually made available to the firm by purchasing its shares.

limited partnership Partnership with limited liability for partners not participating in management.

limit price The minimum price at which a new firm can enter a market without incurring a loss; equal to its minimum average cost. Existing lower-cost firms may be able to discourage new entrants by setting the price below this limit.

liquidity The degree of ease and certainty with which an asset can be turned into a given amount of the economy's medium of exchange.

liquidity preference (LP) function The function that relates the demand for money to the rate of interest.

lockout The employer's equivalent of a strike, in which he temporarily closes his plant.

logarithmic scale A scale in which equal proportional changes are shown as equal distances. Thus 1 inch may always represent doubling of a variable, whether from 3 to 6 or 50 to 100. Contrasted with *natural scale*. (Also called *log scale* or *ratio scale*.)

long run The period of time long enough for all inputs to be varied, but in which the basic technology of production is unchanged.

long-run average cost curve (LRAC) The curve relating the least-cost method of producing any output to the level of output. Sometimes called *long-run average total cost (LRATC)*.

long-run industry supply (LRS) curve The curve showing the relation of the quantity supplied to prices with quantities of all factors freely variable, and allowing time for firms to achieve long-run equilibrium.

Lorenz curve A graph showing the extent of departure from equality of income distribution.

lottery draft A draft in which chance selects from an eligible pool those who will be drafted.

M In boldface, the term represents actual imports; in lightface, desired imports.

M-1A A narrow definition of the money supply: currency in circulation plus demand deposits.

M-1B A less narrow definition of the money supply: M-1A plus NOW, ATS, and other checkable deposits.

M-2 A broader definition of the money supply: M-1B plus savings deposits and small time deposits (under $100,000).

M-3 The broadest definition of the money supply in wide use: M-2 plus large time deposits (over $100,000).

macroeconomics The study of the determination of economic aggregates, such as total output, total employment, and the price level.

managed float See *dirty float*.

marginal cost (MC) The increase in total cost resulting from raising the rate of production by 1 unit; mathematically, the rate of change of cost with respect to output. Also called *incremental cost*.

marginal efficiency of capital (MEC) The marginal rate of return on a nation's capital stock. It is the rate of return on one additional dollar of net investment, i.e., an addition of $1 to capital stock.

marginal efficiency of capital schedule A schedule relating *MEC* to the size of the capital stock.

marginal efficiency of investment (MEI) function The function that relates the quantity of investment to the rate of interest.

marginal physical product (MPP) See *marginal product*.

marginal product (MP) The increase in quantity of total output that results from using 1 unit more of a variable factor; mathematically, the rate of change of output with respect to the quantity of the variable factor. Also called *incremental product* or *marginal physical product (MPP)*.

marginal productivity theory of distribution The implication from profit maximization that the use of a factor should be expanded until its marginal revenue product equals its price.

marginal propensity The ratio of the change of any flow to the change in income that brought it about.

marginal propensity to consume (MPC) The change in consumption divided by the change in income that brought it about (mathematically, the rate of change of consumption with respect to income). The income variable may be disposable income, in which case $MPC = \Delta C/\Delta Y_d$, or it may be national income, in which case $MPC = \Delta C/\Delta Y$.

marginal propensity to save (MPS) The change in saving divided by the change in income that brought it about (mathematically, the rate of change of saving with respect to income). The income variable may either be disposable income, in which case $MPS = \Delta S/\Delta Y_d$, or it may be national income, in which case $MPS = \Delta S/\Delta Y$.

marginal rate of substitution (MRS) (1) In consumption the slope of an indifference curve, showing how much more of one commodity must be provided to compensate for the giving up of one unit of another commodity if the level of satisfaction is to be held

constant. (2) In production, the slope of an isoquant, showing how much more of one factor of production must be used to compensate for the use of one less unit of another factor of production if production is to be held constant.

marginal revenue (MR) (incremental revenue) The change in a firm's total revenue arising from the sale of 1 unit more; mathematically, the rate of change of revenue with respect to output.

marginal revenue product (MRP) The addition of revenue attributable to the last unit of a variable factor. $MRP = MPP \times MR$; mathematically, the rate of change of revenue with respect to quantity of the variable factor.

marginal tax rate The fraction of an additional dollar of income that is paid in taxes.

marginal utility The additional satisfaction obtained by a buyer from consuming 1 unit more of a good; mathematically, the rate of change of utility with respect to consumption.

margin requirement The fraction of the price of a stock that must be paid in cash, while putting up the stock as security against a loan for the balance.

market A concept with many possible definitions. (1) An area over which buyers and sellers negotiate the exchange of a well-defined commodity. (2) From the point of view of a household, the firms from which it can buy a well-defined product. (3) From the point of view of a firm, the buyers to whom it can sell a well-defined product.

market-clearing prices Prices at which quantity demanded equals quantity supplied so that there are neither unsatisfied buyers nor unsatisfied sellers. The equilibrium price in a perfectly competitive market.

market economy A society in which people specialize in productive activities and meet most of their material wants through exchanges voluntarily agreed upon.

market failure Failure of the unregulated market system to achieve socially optimal results. Its sources include externalities, market impediments and imperfections, and nonmarket goals.

market rate of interest The actual interest rate in effect at a given moment.

market sector That portion of an economy in which commodities are bought and sold and producers must cover their costs from the proceeds of their sales.

market structure Characteristics of market organization likely to affect behavior and performance of firms, such as the number and size of sellers, the extent of knowledge about each other's actions, the degree of freedom of entry, and the degree of product differentiation.

markup The amount added to cost to determine price.

medium of exchange Anything that is generally acceptable in return for goods and services sold.

merger The purchase of either the physical assets or the controlling share ownership of one company by another. In a *horizontal* merger both companies produce the same product; in a *vertical* merger one company is a supplier of the other; if the two are in unrelated industries, it is a *conglomerate* merger.

microeconomic policy Activities of the central authorities that alter resource allocation and/or income distribution.

microeconomics The study of the allocation of resources and the distribution of income as they are affected by the workings of the price system and by some government policies.

minimum efficient scale (MES) The smallest size of firm required to achieve the economies of scale in production and/or distribution. Also called *minimum optimal scale (MOS).*

mixed economy Economy in which some decisions are made by firms and households and some by central authorities.

monetarists A group of economists who stress monetary causes of cyclical fluctuations and inflations, who believe that an active stabilization policy is not normally required, and who stress the relative efficacy of monetary over fiscal policy.

monetary disequilibrium A situation in which the demand for money does not equal the supply of money.

monetary equilibrium A situation in which the demand for money equals the supply of money.

monetary policy An attempt to influence the economy by operating on such monetary variables as the quantity of money and the rate of interest.

money Any generally accepted medium of exchange.

money capital The funds used to finance a firm. Money capital includes both equity capital and debt.

money flow The flow of money payments from buyers to sellers in return for goods and services received.

money income A household or firm's income in the form of some monetary unit.

money rate of interest A rate of interest expressed in current dollars.

money substitute Anything such as a credit card or a charge account that permits the holder to purchase goods and services whether or not he or she possesses legal tender at the time.

money supply The total quantity of money existing at a point in time.

monopolistic competition A market structure of an industry in which there are many sellers and freedom of entry, but in which each firm has a product somewhat differentiated from the others, giving it some control over its price.

monopoly A market structure in which the output of an industry is controlled by a single seller or a group of sellers making joint decisions.

monopsony A market situation in which there is a single buyer or a group of buyers making joint decisions. Monopsony and monopsony power are the equivalent on the buying side of monopoly and monopoly power on the selling side.

multiple regression analysis See *regression analysis.*

multiplier The ratio of the change in national income to the change in autonomous expenditure that brought it about.

national debt The current volume of outstanding federal government debt.

national income accounting The set of rules and techniques for measuring the total flows of outputs produced and inputs used by the economy.

natural monopoly An industry characterized by economies of scale sufficiently large that one firm can most efficiently supply the entire market demand.

natural rate of unemployment The rate of unemployment (due to frictional and structural causes) consistent with full-employment national income, Y_F. In the Phelps-Friedman theory this is the rate of unemployment at which there is neither upward nor downward pressure on the price level.

natural scale A scale in which equal absolute amounts are represented by equal distances.

near money Liquid assets easily convertible into money without risk of significant loss of value. They can be used as short-term stores of purchasing power but are not themselves media of exchange.

negative income tax (NIT) A tax system in which households with incomes below taxable levels receive payments from the government based on a percentage of the amount by which their income is below the minimum taxable level.

negotiable order of withdrawal (NOW) A checklike

device for paying funds in one person's time deposit to another person.

neo-Keynesians Sometimes called Keynesians; a group of economists who stress changes in both aggregate expenditure and the money supply as causes of cyclical fluctuations and inflations, who believe that an active government stabilization policy is called for, and who stress the relative efficacy of fiscal policy over monetary policy.

net exports Total exports *minus* total imports $(X - M)$.

net investment Gross investment *minus* replacement investment.

net national product (NNP) Gross national product *minus* a capital consumption allowance.

net private benefit (NPB) The difference between private benefits and private costs.

net social benefit (NSB) The difference between social benefits and social costs. Where private production produces externalities, it is net private benefit plus external benefits and minus external costs.

neutrality of money The doctrine that the money supply affects only the absolute level of prices and has no effect on relative prices and hence no effect on the allocation of resources or the distribution of income.

nominal GNP See *current dollar GNP*.

nonmarket sector That portion of an economy in which commodities are given away and producers must cover their costs from some source other than the proceeds of sales.

nonprice competition Competition by sellers for sales by means other than price cutting. Advertising, product differentiation, trading stamps, and other promotional devices are examples.

nontariff barriers to trade Restrictions, other than tariffs, that may reduce the flow of international trade.

normal goods Goods for which income elasticity is positive.

normal profits A term used by some economists for the imputed returns to capital and risk taking just necessary to keep the owners in the industry. They are included in what the economist, but not the businessman, sees as *total costs*.

normative statement A statement about what ought to be.

NOW See *negotiable order of withdrawal*.

oligopoly A market structure in which a small number of rival firms dominate the industry. The leading firms are aware that they are interdependent.

open economy An economy that engages in foreign trade.

open market operations The purchase and sale on the open market by the central bank of securities (usually short-term government securities).

open shop A bargaining arrangement whereby a union represents its members but does not have exclusive jurisdiction. Membership in the union is not a condition of getting or keeping a job.

opportunity cost The cost of using resources for a certain purpose, measured by the benefit or revenues given up by not using them in their best alternative use.

organization theory In economics, a set of hypotheses in which the decisions of an organization are a function of its size and form of organization.

outputs The quantities of goods and services produced.

paradox of value The apparent contradiction in the observed fact that some absolute necessities to life are cheap in price while some relatively unimportant luxuries are very expensive.

Pareto-efficiency See *Pareto-optimality*.

Pareto-optimality An allocation of resources in which it is impossible by reallocation to make some consumers better off without simultaneously making others worse off. Also called *Pareto-efficiency*.

partnership A form of business organization with two or more joint owners, each of whom is personally responsible for all of the firm's actions and debts.

paternalism Protection of individuals against themselves.

per capita GNP GNP divided by total population. Also called *GNP per person*.

perfect competition A market form in which all firms are price takers and in which there is freedom of entry into and exit from the industry.

permanent income The maximum amount that a household can consume per year into the indefinite future without reducing its wealth. (A number of similar but not identical definitions are in common use.)

permanent-income hypothesis (PIH) The hypothesis that relates actual consumption to permanent income rather than (as in the original Keynesian theory) to current income.

personal income Income earned by individuals before allowance for personal income taxes paid or payable.

petrodollars The excess purchasing power held by the oil-producing countries.

Phillips curve Originally a relation between the percentage of the labor force unemployed and the rate of change of money wages. It can also be expressed as a relation between the percentage of the labor force employed and the rate of price inflation, or between actual national income as a proportion of potential national income and the rate of price inflation.

picket lines Striking workers parading at the entrances to a plant or firm on strike. A picket line is a symbolic blockade of the entrance.

point elasticity Elasticity calculated at a point, i.e., over an interval where changes in the variables approach zero. The formula for point elasticity of demand is

$$\eta = \frac{dq}{dp} \times \frac{p}{q}$$

The minus sign is often dropped.

point of diminishing average productivity The level of output at which average product reaches a maximum.

point of diminishing marginal productivity The level of output at which marginal product reaches a maximum.

policy variables The variables that the government ultimately seeks to control; the variables in whose behavior it is ultimately interested.

political business cycle Cyclical swings in the economy generated by fiscal and monetary policy for the purpose of winning elections.

positive statement A statement about what is, was, or will be, as opposed to a statement about what ought to be.

potential GNP The gross national product the economy could produce if its productive resources were fully employed at their normal intensity of use. Also called *full-employment GNP* or *full-employment national income* (Y_F).

poverty gap (or **income gap**) The number of dollars required to raise everyone whose income is below the poverty level to that level.

poverty level A measure of the minimum amount of annual income required to avoid poverty; approximately $6,700 in the United States for a family of four in 1978.

precautionary motive The desire to hold money bal-

ances for protection against the uncertainty of the timing of cash flows.

preferred stock A form of equity capital with a preference over common stock to receipt of dividends up to a stated maximum amount; may be voting or nonvoting.

present value (PV) The value *now* of a sum payable at a later date or of a stream of income receivable at future dates. *PV* is the discounted value of future payments.

price ceiling A maximum permitted price.

price-consumption line A line connecting the points of tangency between a set of indifference curves and a set of budget lines where one absolute price is fixed and the other varies, money income being held constant.

price discrimination The sale by a single firm of the same commodity to different buyers at two or more different prices for reasons not associated with differences in cost. It may be systematic or unsystematic.

price floor A minimum permitted price.

price index A number that shows the average percentage change that has occurred in some group of prices over some period of time.

price parity The ratio of prices farmers receive for products they sell to the prices they pay for products they buy, compared with some base period; a basic concept in U.S. farm policy.

price-push inflation Inflation caused by increases in prices brought about by the monopoly power of sellers and not associated with excess aggregate demand.

price taker A firm that acts as if it could alter its rate of production and sales without affecting the market price of its product.

price theory The theory of how prices are determined; competitive price theory concerns the determination of prices in competitive markets by the interaction of demand and supply.

principle of substitution The proposition that the proportions in which various inputs are used will vary as the relative prices of these inputs vary.

private cost The value of the best alternative use of resources used in production as valued by the producer.

private sector That portion of an economy in which principal decisions are made by private units such as households and firms.

producers' cooperative (producers' co-op) An organization of producers of a commodity usually formed to serve as a joint selling organization for the producers and often operated as a cartel.

producers' durables See *durable good*.

product differentiation The existence of similar but not identical products sold by a single industry such as the breakfast food and the automobile industries.

production The act of making commodities.

production function A functional relation showing the maximum output that can be produced by each and every combination of inputs.

production possibility boundary A curve on a graph that shows which alternative combination of commodities can just be obtained if all available productive resources are used. It is the boundary between attainable and unobtainable output combinations.

productive efficiency Production at the lowest attainable level of long-run average total cost.

productivity Output produced per unit of input; frequently used to refer to *labor productivity*, measured by output per hour worked.

productivity of capital (efficiency of capital) The increase in production resulting from the use of capital, after allowance for the maintenance and replacement of the capital.

product markets Markets in which firms sell their outputs of goods and services.

profit (1) In ordinary usage, the difference between the value of outputs and the value of inputs. (2) In microeconomics, the value of inputs, which includes the opportunity cost of capital, so that profits are *economic profits*. (3) In macroeconomics, profits exclude interest on borrowed capital but do not exclude the return to owner's (or equity) capital. Profits in macroeconomics are thus the return available to owner's capital—that is, the sum of the microeconomic concepts of the opportunity cost of owner's capital plus economic profits.

progressive tax A tax that takes a larger percentage of income the higher the level of income.

progressivity of taxation The ratio of taxes to income as income increases. If the ratio decreases, the tax is *regressive;* if it remains constant, *proportional;* if it increases, *progressive*.

proportional tax A tax that takes a constant percentage of income at all levels of income and is thus neither progressive nor regressive.

protectionism The partial or complete protection of domestic industries from foreign competition in domestic markets by use of tariffs or such nontariff barriers to trade as import quotas.

proxy A document authorizing the holder to vote one's stock in a corporation.

proxy fight A struggle between competing factions in a corporation to obtain the proxies for a majority of the outstanding shares.

public sector That portion of an economy where production is under control of the central authorities or bodies appointed by them, including all production by governments and nationalized industries.

public utility regulation Regulation of prices and services of industries that have been deemed to be natural monopolies.

pure rate of interest The rate of interest that would rule in equilibrium in a riskless economy where all lending and borrowing is for investment in productive capital.

pure return on capital The amount capital can earn in a riskless investment; hence the transfer earnings of capital in a riskless investment.

quantity actually bought The amount of a commodity that households succeed in purchasing in some time period.

quantity actually sold The amount of a commodity that producers succeed in selling in some time period.

quantity demanded The amount of a commodity that households wish to purchase in some time period. An increase (decrease) in quantity demanded refers to a movement down (up) the demand curve in response to a fall (rise) in price.

quantity exchanged The identical amount of a commodity that households actually purchase and producers actually sell in some time period.

quantity supplied The amount of a commodity producers wish to sell in some time period. An increase (decrease) in quantity supplied refers to a movement up (down) the supply curve in response to a rise (fall) in price.

random sample A sample chosen from a group or population in such a way that every member of the group has an equal chance of being selected.

rate base The total allowable investment to which the rate of return allowed by a regulatory commission is applied. The public utility may build into its prices the amount of profits so determined.

rate of return The ratio of profits earned by a firm to total investment capital.

rate of return on capital (Sometimes used synonymously with *rate of return*.) Frequently used to refer to a specific capital good; the annual net income produced by a capital good, expressed as a percentage of the price of the good.

rational expectations The theory that people learn quickly from their mistakes, that while random errors may be made, systematic and persistent errors are not made.

ratio scale See *logarithmic scale*.

real capital (or **physical capital**) Physical assets, including plant, equipment, and inventories.

real flow The flow of goods and services from sellers to buyers.

real GNP See *constant dollar GNP*.

real income A household's income expressed in terms of the command over commodities that the money income confers; money income corrected for changes in price levels, thus the purchasing power of money income.

real rate of interest A rate of interest expressed in constant dollars. It is the money rate of interest corrected for the change in the purchasing power of money.

recession In general, a downswing in the level of economic activity. The Department of Commerce defines a recession as occurring when real GNP falls for two successive quarters.

regression analysis (sometimes called *correlation analysis*) A quantitative analysis of the systematic interrelationships between two or more variables. *Simple regression* concerns the relation between Y and a single independent variable, X_1; *multiple* regression concerns the relation between Y and more than one indendent variables, $X_1, \ldots, X_n$.

regression equation The mathematical equation describing the statistically determined equation of best fit between variables in regression analysis.

regressive tax A tax that takes a larger percentage of income at lower levels of income.

relative price The ratio of the price of one good to the price of another good; a ratio of two absolute prices.

rent (1) In macroeconomics, the proportion of national income going to the owners of the factor of production, land. (2) In microeconomics, a shorthand for *economic rent*. (3) In everyday usage, the payment for rental housing.

required reserves In banking, the amount of reserves a bank must, by law, keep either in currency or in deposits with the central bank.

reserve ratio In banking, the fraction of deposits of the public that a bank holds in reserves.

resource allocation The allocation of an economy's scarce resources among alternative uses.

return to capital The total amount available for payments to owners of capital; the sum of pure returns to capital, risk premiums, and economic profits.

revaluation of the exchange rate An increase in the value at which a country's currency is pegged in terms of foreign currencies; the opposite of *devaluation*.

revenue sharing A noncategorical grant-in-aid, in which some of the revenue collected by the federal government is returned to state and local governments for unrestricted expenditure.

right-to-work laws State laws that give an individual the right to work in an organized plant without belonging to the union that is the collective bargaining agent of the workers. They are thus legislative prohibitions against closed or union shops.

rising-cost industry An industry in which the minimum cost attainable by a firm rises as the scale of the industry expands.

rising supply price A rising long-run supply curve, caused by increases in factor prices as output is increased, or by diseconomies of scale.

risk premium The return to capital necessary to compensate owners of capital for the risk of loss of their capital.

sample A small number of items, chosen from a larger group or population, that is intended to be representative of the larger entity.

satisficing A hypothesized objective of firms, in contrast to maximizing behavior, whereby firms set target levels of satisfactory performance (e.g., profits) rather than seek to maximize some objective (e.g., profits).

saving Household saving is disposable income not spent on domestically produced or imported consumption goods and services. Firm saving is profits not distributed to owners.

scarce good A commodity for which the quantity demanded would exceed the quantity supplied if its price were zero.

scatter diagram A graph of statistical observations of paired values of two variables, one measured on the horizontal and the other on the vertical axis. Each point on the coordinate grid represents the values of the variables for a particular unit of observation.

search unemployment Unemployment caused by people continuing to search for a good job rather than accepting the first job they come across when unemployed.

sectors Parts of an economy.

securities market See *stock market*.

selective credit controls Controls on credit imposed through such means as margin requirements, installment buying, and minimum down payments on mortgages.

sellers' preferences Allocation of scarce commodities by decision of those who sell them.

services Intangible commodities such as haircuts or medical care.

shop steward The representative of a local union in the shop or plant.

short run The period of time over which the quantity of some inputs cannot, as a practical matter, be varied.

short-run equilibrium Generally, equilibrium subject to fixed factors; for a competitive firm, the output at which market price equals marginal cost; for a competitive industry, the price and output at which industry demand equals short-run industry supply and all firms are in short-run equilibrium. Either profits or losses are possible.

short-run supply curve The curve showing the relation of quantity supplied to prices, with one or more fixed factors; the horizontal sum of marginal cost curves (above the level of average variable costs) of all firms in an industry.

single proprietorship A firm consisting of one owner, where the single owner is solely responsible for the firm's actions and debts.

size distribution of income The distribution of income by size class, without regard to source of income.

snake The agreement among several Western European countries to fix exchange rates among their own currencies and then to let them fluctuate in common against the U.S. dollar. Also called the *joint float*.

social benefit The contribution an activity makes to the society's welfare.

social cost (social opportunity cost) The value of the best alternative use of resources available to society, as valued by society.

special drawing rights (SDRs) Established in 1968, the Special Drawing Account of the International Monetary Fund provides additional international reserves for member countries. Subject to certain repayment provisions, members are able to treat SDRs in the same way as their own holdings of international currencies for financing balance-of-payments surpluses or deficits.

specialization of labor An organization of production in which individual workers specialize in the production of particular goods or services (and satisfy their wants by trading) rather than produce for themselves everything they consume (and thus be self-sufficient).

specific tax See *excise tax*.

speculative motive The desire to hold money balances as a hedge against the uncertainty of the prices of other financial assets.

stabilization policy Any policy designed to reduce the economy's cyclical fluctuations. Attempts by the central authorities to remove inflationary and deflationary gaps when they appear.

stagflation The coexistence of high rates of unemployment with high, and sometimes rising, rates of inflation.

stockholders The owners of a corporation.

stock market (securities market) An organized market where stocks and bonds are bought and sold.

strike The concerted refusal of the members of a union to work.

strikebreakers Nonunion workers brought in by management to operate the plant while a union is on strike. (Derisively called "scabs" by union members.)

structural rigidity inflation The theory that downward inflexibility of money prices means that the adjustment of *relative* prices necessary in any changing economy will cause a rise in the average level of all prices (i.e., an inflation).

structural unemployment Unemployment due to a mismatching between characteristics required by available jobs and characteristics possessed by the unemployed labor. (The sum of frictional plus structural unemployment may be measured by the number of unemployed when the total number of jobs available is equal to the total number of persons looking for acceptable jobs.)

substitute A commodity that satisfies similar needs or desires as the original commodity; technically, a substitute for a commodity is another commodity for which the cross elasticity of demand is nonnegligible and positive.

substitution effect The change in quantity of a good demanded resulting from a change in its relative price, eliminating the effect on real income of the change in price.

supply There are several distinct but closely related concepts: (1) *quantity supplied;* (2) the whole relationship of the quantity supplied to variables that determine it, such as producers' goals, technology, price of the commodity, prices of other commodities, and prices of factors of production; (3) the *supply schedule;* (4) the *supply curve.* The phrase increase (decrease) in supply means a shift of the supply curve to the right (left), indicating an increase (decrease) in the quantity supplied at each possible price.

supply curve The graphic representation of the *supply schedule.*

supply of effort (or **total supply of labor**) The total number of hours of work that the population is willing to supply.

supply of money See *money supply.*

supply schedule The relationship between the quantity supplied of a commodity and its price, *ceteris paribus.*

surplus function See *budget surplus function.*

tacit collusion See also *collusion.* The adoption, without explicit agreement, of a common policy by sellers in an industry. Sometimes also called *conscious parallel action.*

takeover bid See *tender offer.*

tariff A tax applied on imports.

tax base The aggregate amount of taxable income.

tax-based incomes policies (TIPs) Tax incentives for labor and management to encourage them to conform to wage and price guidelines.

tax expenditures The name the Treasury Department gives to exemptions and deductions from taxable income and to tax credits, which amount to subsidies or preferences to taxpayers.

tax incidence The location of the ultimate burden of a tax; the identity of the ultimate bearer or bearers of the tax.

technological efficiency (sometimes called *technical efficiency*) A method of production is technologically efficient if the same output cannot be produced with fewer real resources.

tender offer (takeover bid) An offer to buy directly some or all of the outstanding common stock of a corporation from its stockholders at a specified price per share, in an attempt to gain control of the corporation.

term See *term to maturity.*

terms of trade The relation between the average price of a country's exports and the average price of its imports.

term to maturity The period of time from the present to the redemption date of a bond. Often simply the *term* of the bond.

third-party effects See *externalities.*

time deposit An interest-earning bank deposit, legally subject to notice before withdrawal (in practice the notice requirement is not normally enforced) and not transferable by check.

time series A series of observations on the values of a variable at different points in time.

time-series data Data on variables where measurements are made for successive periods (or moments) of time. Contrasted with cross-sectional data.

total cost (TC) Fixed costs plus variable costs at a given level of output; the sum of the opportunity costs of the factors used to produce that output.

total product (TP) The total amount produced during some period of time by all the factors of production employed over that time period.

total revenue (TR) The total receipts from the sale of a product; price times quantity.

total utility The total satisfaction resulting from the consumption of a given commodity by a buyer in a period of time.

trade union See *union.*

transactions costs Costs that must be incurred in effecting market transactions (such as negotiation costs, billing costs, bad debts).

transactions motive The desire to hold money balances in order to finance purchases and sales.

transfer earnings That part of the payment to a factor in its present use that is just enough to keep it from transferring to another use.

transfer payment A payment to a private person or institution that does not arise out of current productive activity; typically made by governments, as in welfare payments, but also made by businesses and private individuals in the form of charitable contributions.

treasury bill The characteristic form of short-term government debt. A bill is a promise to pay a certain sum of money at some time in the early future (often one, three, or six months). It carries no interest payment; the lender earns interest because the price at which he or she buys the bill is less than its future redemption value.

trigger prices In U.S. trade policy, prices for imported commodities set by the U.S. government on the basis of average total cost of the low-cost producing nation. A foreign country that sells below a trigger price is subject to proceedings under antidumping laws.

turnover tax An excise tax levied on commodities, commonly used in socialist countries.

unbalanced growth policy Growth in only a few sectors of the economy with remaining needs met by international trade.

undistributed profits Earnings of a firm not distributed as dividends but retained by the firm.

unemployment The number of persons who are not employed and are actively searching for a job.

unemployment rate Unemployment expressed as a percentage of the labor force.

union An association of workers authorized to represent them in bargaining with employers. Also called *trade union* or *labor union.*

union shop A bargaining arrangement in which the employer may hire anyone, but every employee must join the union within a specified period of time (often 60 days).

utility The satisfaction that results from the consumption of a commodity.

value added The value of a firm's output *minus* the value of the inputs that it purchases from other firms.

variable A magnitude (such as the price of wheat) that can take on a specific value but whose value will vary among times and places.

variable costs Costs whose total varies directly with changes in output. Also called *direct costs.*

variable factors Factors whose quantity used in production can be varied in the short run.

vertical merger See *merger.*

very long run The period in which even the technological possibilities open to a firm are subject to change.

visibles All those items of foreign trade that are tangible; goods as opposed to services.

wage and price controls Direct government intervention into wage and price formation with legal power to enforce the government's decisions on wages and prices.

wage cost-push inflation Inflation caused by increases in labor costs that are not themselves associated with excess aggregate demand.

wages and salaries Payments made for the use of labor services. Also called *wages.*

windfall profits Profits that bear no relation to current or historical costs, arising usually from a sudden increase in demand or reduction in supply.

withdrawals Income earned by households and not passed on to firms in return for goods and services purchased, and income earned by firms and not passed on to households in return for factor services purchased.

X In boldface, the term represents actual exports; in lightface, desired exports.

X − M In boldface, the term represents actual net exports (which is the difference between total exports and total imports); in lightface, the term represents desired net exports.

X-inefficiency When resources are used less productively than is possible so that society is at a point *inside* its production possibility boundary.

Index

Index

(Continued from front endpapers)

not as controls of theory, but as illustrations. I shall be told that in the Social Sciences verification can never be clean enough to be decisive. I may be told that, in these sciences, observation has been tried and has failed, has led to shapeless accumulations of facts which themselves lead nowhere. I do not believe for a moment that this charge of barrenness of past enquiries can be sustained; to make it is to ignore many achievements of the past and to decry much solid work that is being done at this School and elsewhere. But if the charge of barrenness of realistic economics in the past were justified completely, that would not be a reason for giving up observation and verification. It would only be a reason for making our observations more exact and more numerous. If, in the Social Sciences, we cannot yet run or fly, we ought to be content to walk, or to creep on all fours as infants. . . . For economic and political theorising not based on facts and not controlled by facts assuredly does lead nowhere. . . .

There can be no science of society till the facts about society are available. Till 130 years ago we had no census, no knowledge even of the numbers and growth of the people; till fifteen years ago we had no comprehensive records about unemployment even in this country, and other countries are still where we were a generation or more ago; social statistics of every kind—about trade, wages, consumption—are everywhere in their infancy. . . .

From Copernicus to Newton is 150 years. To-day, 150 years from the *Wealth of Nations,* we have not found, and should not expect to find, the Newton of economics. If we have traveled as far as Tycho Brahe we may be content. Tycho was both a theorist and an observer. As a theorist, he believed to his last day in the year 1601 that the planets went round the sun and that the sun and the stars went round the earth as the fixed centre of the universe. As an observer, he made with infinite patience and integrity thousands of records of the stars and planets; upon these records Kepler, in due course, based his laws and brought the truth to light. If we will take Tycho Brahe for our example, we may find encouragement also. It matters little how wrong we are with our theories, if we are honest and careful with our observations.

Extracts from Lord William Beveridge's farewell address as Director of the London School of Economics, June 24, 1937. Published in POLITICA, September, 1937.